# SMITH & KEENAN'S
# ADVANCED BUSINESS LAW

Eleventh Edition

## Denis Keenan

LLB(Hons), FCIS, CertEd

Of the Middle Temple, Barrister
Formerly Head of Department of Business Studies and Law,
at what is now Anglia Polytechnic University

 LONGMAN

*An imprint of* **PEARSON EDUCATION**

Harlow, England • London • New York • Reading, Massachusetts • San Francisco • Toronto • Don Mills, Ontario • Sydney
Tokyo • Singapore • Hong Kong • Seoul • Taipei • Cape Town • Madrid • Mexico City • Amsterdam • Munich • Paris • Milan

**PEARSON EDUCATION LIMITED**

Edinburgh Gate
Harlow
Essex CM20 2JE
England

and Associated Companies around the World.

*Visit us on the World Wide Web at*
*www.pearsoneduc.com*

---

First published in Great Britain in 1965
Second edition published in 1969
Third edition published in 1974
Fourth edition published in 1977
Fifth edition published in 1982
Sixth edition published in 1985
Seventh edition published in 1988
Eighth edition published in 1991
Ninth edition published in 1994
Tenth edition published in 1997
**Eleventh edition published in 2000**

Copyright © Denis Keenan 2000

ISBN 0 273 64601 X

*British Library Cataloguing-in-Publication Data*
A catalogue record for this book is available from the British Library.

10 9 8 7 6 5 4 3 2 1

Typeset by 30
Printed by Ashford Colour Press Ltd., Gosport

# CONTENTS

Where the goods are unascertained · Transfer of property and risk · Transfer of title by non-owners · Graded questions

# PREFACE
## TO ELEVENTH EDITION

This edition has been subject to considerable updating in terms of case law and statute law. As regards statute law, the Contracts (Rights of Third Parties) Act 1999 is included, which makes major changes to the rule of privity of contract. Also included is the Competition Act 1998, which overtakes much of the previous law on restrictive practices. The effect on confidentiality of the whistleblowing protections of the Public Interest Disclosure Act 1998 are dealt with, as are the Late Payment of Commercial Debts (Interest) Act 1998 provisions.

Many changes have emanated from the Employment Relations Act 1999, in terms particularly of maternity provision, parental leave and time off for family emergencies, as well as trade union recognition. The Working Time Regulations and the Minimum Wage provisions are also now included. The focus in company law has been on the inclusion of the extensive amount of new case law, together with the latest rules on audit exemption and the effect of the euro on share capital.

As regards new features these are:

- the inclusion in the contract chapters from time to time as appropriate of *The business application*. Why? Because the law of contract is still sometimes expressed in the context of Victorian case law, with little or no attempt to show the reader how the principles of those cases apply in business today, or to examine whether business finds them inconvenient, as is quite often the case, or can turn them to advantage and avoid expensive litigation. The other topics in the text, e.g. employment and company law, are more obviously set in a commercial context and do not require this approach;
- the inclusion in the contract chapters of material on e-commerce and electronic signatures, in the context of on-line trading;
- the inclusion of a new chapter on commercial litigation, which contains material to meet the requirements of an advanced student in terms of legal system and services. This chapter contains the Woolf reforms of civil procedure and the courts involved, including the judiciary, the rights of appeal and the appellate judiciary. It concludes with a discussion of the methods of enforcing judgments for debt and damages for business claimants. The text is set in the new Woolf terminology 'Woolfspeak', so far as is required. The expression 'Woolfspeak' seems to have entered the language of the law as a result of a number of articles by circuit and district judges which appeared in the *New Law Journal*.

Apart from these changes, the contents remain the same, since they seem to give the right selection of topics for a student intending a career in business and following a relevant course at a university or college.

With this is mind, I have tried to enhance the usefulness of the book as a teaching vehicle which can be integrated with, and used in, lectures. The essay questions selected from relevant university and professional examinations are intended to validate the content of the text and demonstrate that questions of examination standard can be tackled successfully once the chapter contents have been studied. The objective tests provide a quicker check on learning and can be attempted as students complete each chapter.

Although the book is primarily a teaching vehicle, it provides more than sufficient academic content. The main case summaries are often quite extensive and the case comment frequently contains additional material to provoke thought and interest in those who wish to look at the case more critically.

I would like to thank my publisher, Pat Bond, and Elizabeth Tarrant and other members of staff at Pearson Education who have in one way or another been involved in this edition. My thanks are also due to those who set, printed and bound the book. If the book has any errors and/or omissions, they are down to me.

A *Lecturer's Guide* is available free of charge to lecturers adopting this book. It contains aids which may be useful, such as tutorial material and photocopiable masters of diagrams.

*Maenan*                                                                                     *Denis Keenan*

# WOOLFSPEAK – THE END OF LEGAL LATIN

The above expression, 'Woolfspeak', is now widely used to connote the changes made in the nomenclature of certain legal concepts and practices as a result of the changes to civil procedure set in train by the reforms introduced by the Woolf Report. These were translated into new civil procedure rules with effect from 26 April 1999.

Basically, the legal language that has been a feature of our civil courts for centuries has been swept away by the new rules. Not all of these changes are relevant to this book since some of them affect aspects of law not covered in the book. However, a representative collection of changes which will assist those studying business law during a transitional period of change appears below.

| Civil justice and the modern approach | |
| --- | --- |
| **Old term** | **New term** |
| Writ (to commence a case) | Claim form |
| Pleading (the reason for complaint) | Statement of case |
| Plaintiff (party with complaint) | Claimant |
| Minor/infant (person under 18) | Child |
| *In camera* (public excluded from proceedings) | In private |
| *Ex parte* (application to court without notice to other party) | Without notice |
| Next friend/guardian *ad litem* (adult supporter required when child makes a claim or defends one) | Litigation friend |
| Mareva injunction (to keep assets within jurisdiction) | Freezing injunction |
| Anton Piller order (to compel search of defendant's premises) | Search order |

We thought it best to introduce some of these new expressions in this edition. It is, of course, true that when we refer to a case in, say, 1890 and refer to the 'plaintiff' that remains and will remain historically true. However, if the word 'plaintiff' has gone, and it has, there is little point in the reader being burdened with learning or comprehending two expressions for the same thing. A greater difficulty arises where in the text there is a quotation from a judgment as where in a case dated, say, 1998 we have: 'Lord Snooks said, "The plaintiff cannot I am afraid succeed in this case".' Here we have also decided to make the change so that we get 'The claimant cannot I am afraid succeed in this case.'

We have also retained the expression *'ex parte'* rather than refer to 'application without notice' because the expression appears in the actual name of the case in which such an application was made as in *Bloggs* v *Snooks ex parte Brown* [1967] 1 All ER 20. These citations will remain in the citators as they are and, therefore, must remain unaltered to assist identification of the earlier cases.

We have not seen fit to change references to 'minor' for persons under 18 years of age where this appears in the text. The expression 'child' for a person under 18 is used *only* in connection with the appointment of a 'litigation friend', which a person under the age of 18 requires in order to bring or defend a claim. Apart from that the term 'minor' can be used, if only because it is used in Acts of Parliament, e.g. the Minors' Contracts Act 1987 (*see* Chapter 3). The civil procedure rules can have no effect upon an Act of Parliament or the terminology used in it, thus it survives.

# TABLE OF CASES

# TABLE OF STATUTES

# LAW REPORT ABBREVIATIONS

The following table sets out the abbreviations used when citing the various series of certain law reports which are in common use, together with the periods over which they extend.

| | |
|---|---|
| AC | Law Reports, Appeal Cases 1891–(current) |
| ATC | Annotated Tax Cases 1922–75 |
| All ER | All England Law Reports 1936–(current) |
| All ER Rep | All England Law Reports Reprint, 36 vols 1558–1935 |
| App Cas | Law Reports, Appeal Cases, 15 vols 1875–90 |
| BCC | |
| BCLC | Butterworths Company Law Cases 1983–(current) |
| B & CR | Reports of Bankruptcy and Companies Winding-up Cases 1918–(current) |
| CLY | Current Law Yearbook 1947–(current) |
| CMLR | Common Market Law Reports 1962–(current) |
| Ch | Law Reports Chancery Division 1891–(current) |
| Com Cas | Commercial Cases 1895–1941 |
| Fam | Law Reports Family Division 1972–(current) |
| ICR | Industrial Court Reports 1972–74; Industrial Cases Reports 1974–(current) |
| IRLB | Industrial Relations Law Bulletin 1993–(current) |
| IRLR | Industrial Relations Law Reports 1971–(current) |
| ITR | Reports of decisions of the Industrial Tribunals 1966–(current) |
| KB | Law Reports, King's Bench Division 1901–52 |
| LGR | Local Government Reports 1902–(current) |
| LRRP | Law Reports Restrictive Practices 1957–(current) |
| Lloyd LR or (from 1951) Lloyd's Rep | Lloyd's List Law Reports 1919–(current) |
| NLJ | New Law Journal |
| P | Law Reports, Probate, Divorce and Admiralty Division 1891–1971 |
| P & CR | Planning and Compensation Reports 1949–(current) |
| PIQR | Personal Injuries and Quantum Reports |
| QB | Law Reports Queen's Bench Division 1891–1901; 1953–(current) |
| STC | Simon's Tax Cases 1973–(current) |
| Sol Jo | Solicitors' Journal 1856–(current) |
| Tax Cas (or TC) | Tax Cases 1875–(current) |
| WLR | Weekly Law Reports 1953–(current) |

# THE LAW OF CONTRACT – MAKING THE CONTRACT 1

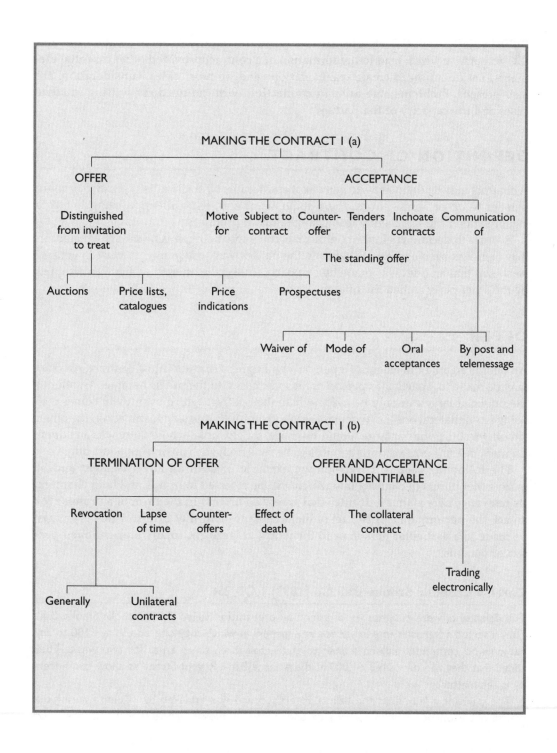

MAKING THE CONTRACT 1 (a)

OFFER

ACCEPTANCE

Distinguished
from invitation
to treat

Motive
for

Subject to
contract

Counter-
offer

Tenders

Inchoate
contracts

Communication
of

The standing offer

Auctions

Price lists,
catalogues

Price
indications

Prospectuses

Waiver of

Mode of

Oral
acceptances

By post and
telemessage

MAKING THE CONTRACT 1 (b)

TERMINATION OF OFFER

OFFER AND ACCEPTANCE
UNIDENTIFIABLE

Revocation

Lapse
of time

Counter-
offers

Effect of
death

The collateral
contract

Trading
electronically

Generally

Unilateral
contracts

The objectives of this chapter are to explain the requirements of a valid offer and acceptance which lead to the formation of a contract provided other essential elements, i.e. intention to create legal relations and, in most cases, consideration, are also present. Problems also arise in connection with the need for writing in some cases and the capacity of the parties.

## DEFINITION OF CONTRACT

A contract may be defined as an *agreement* enforceable by the law between two or more persons to do or abstain from doing some act or acts, their intention being to create legal relations and not merely to exchange mutual promises.

In order to decide whether a contract has come into being, it is necessary to establish that there has been agreement between the parties. In consequence, it must in general be shown that an offer was made by one party (called the offeror) which was accepted by the other party (called the offeree).

## OFFER

An offer is an announcement of a person's willingness to enter into a contract. An offer may be made to a particular person or, in some cases, to the public at large. An offer to the public at large can only be made where the contract which eventually comes into being is a unilateral one, i.e. where there is a promise on one side for an act on the other. An offer to the public at large would be made, for example, where there was an advertisement offering a reward for services to be rendered, such as finding a lost dog.

**The following case is a well-known example of such an advertisement and of many other points in contract law which will be referred to in this and later chapters. Its relevance here is that it decides that where an offer is in the form of a promise for an act, the performance of the act is the acceptance and that offers of this type may be made to a particular person or to the world at large, i.e. to any unmentioned person or persons.**

### Carlill v Carbolic Smoke Ball Co [1893] 1 QB 256

The defendants were proprietors of a medical preparation called 'The Carbolic Smoke Ball'. They inserted advertisements in various newspapers in which they offered to pay £100 to any person who contracted influenza after using the ball three times a day for two weeks. They added that they had deposited £1,000 at the Alliance Bank, Regent Street 'to show our sincerity in the matter'.

The claimant, a lady, used the ball as advertised, and was attacked by influenza during the course of treatment, which in her case extended from 20 November 1891 to 17 January 1892.

She now sued for £100 and the following matters arose out of the various defences raised by the company.

(a) It was suggested that the offer was too vague since no time limit was stipulated in which the user was to contract influenza. The court said that it must surely have been the intention that the ball would protect its user during the period of its use, and since this covered the present case it was not necessary to go further.

(b) The suggestion was made that the matter was an advertising 'puff' and that there was no intention to create legal relations. Here the court took the view that the deposit of £1,000 at the bank was clear evidence of an intention to pay claims.

(c) It was further suggested that this was an attempt to contract with the whole world and that this was impossible in English law. The court took the view that the advertisement was an *offer* to the whole world, not an attempt to *contract* with the whole world but only with that limited portion of the public who came forward and performed the condition on the faith of the advertisement, and that, by analogy with the reward cases, it was possible to make an *offer* of this kind.

(d) The company also claimed that the claimant had not supplied any consideration, but the court took the view that the inconvenience of using this inhalant three times a day for two weeks or more was sufficient consideration. It was not necessary to consider its adequacy. In addition, Bowen LJ clearly realising why companies advertise said, 'But I think also that the defendants received a benefit from this user, for the use of the smoke ball was contemplated by the defendants as being indirectly a benefit to them, because the use of the smoke balls would promote their sale.'

(e) Finally, the defendants suggested that there had been no communication of acceptance, but here the court, looking at the reward cases, stated that in contracts of this kind acceptance may be by conduct.

**Comment:** (i) Motive was also irrelevant in this case because Mrs Carlill presumably did not use the ball with the motive of obtaining the reward, but with the motive of protection against influenza. However, this did not prevent her claim from succeeding.

(ii) Most business contracts are bilateral. They are made by an exchange of promises and not, as here, by the exchange of a promise for an act. Nevertheless, *Carlill's* case has occasionally provided a useful legal principle in the field of business law. (See, for example, *The New Zealand Shipping Co Ltd v A M Satterthwaite and Co Ltd* (1974) in Chapter 2.)

(iii) A deposit of money from which to pay claims is not essential. In *Wood v Lectrik Ltd, The Times*, 13 January 1932 the defendants who were makers of an electric comb had advertised: 'What is your trouble? Is it grey hair? In ten days not a grey hair left. £500 Guarantee.' Mr Wood used the comb as directed but his hair remained grey at the end of ten days of use. All the comb had done was to scratch his scalp. There was no bank deposit by the company, but Rowlatt J held that there was a contract and awarded Mr Wood the £500.

(iv) Where the offer is made to a particular person, it may only be accepted by that person. Thus in *Boulton v Jones* (1857) 2 H & N 564 the defendant ordered (offered to buy) 50 feet of leather hose from Brocklehurst (a business). Boulton had earlier on the same day bought the Brocklehurst business of which he had been the manager. Boulton 'accepted' the order and supplied the hose. It was held that there was no contract since the offer was made to Brocklehurst personally. It was important to Jones that he was dealing with Brocklehurst because he was owed money by him and was intending to deduct that sum from the price of the goods (called a set-off). Since Jones had used the hose before he received Boulton's invoice, he could not be required to return it and Boulton failed in his claim for the purchase price.

# OFFER DISTINGUISHED FROM INVITATION TO TREAT

### General

To be an offer there must be more than an indication of an *interest* in making a contract. If Fred says to Freda 'Would you like to get a reward if you find my lost dog?' we have a mere request for information and not an offer to be bound in contract.

An offer capable of being converted into an agreement by acceptance must consist of a definite promise to be bound provided that certain specified terms are accepted, and not a mere offer to *negotiate*. The distinction is sometimes expressed in judicial language by the contrast of an 'offer' with that of an 'invitation to treat' or invitation to make an offer. The distinction may be considered under the following headings.

### *Auctions*

An advertisement stating that an auction will be held is not an offer to actually hold it. When the auction actually commences bids from those attending are the offers to buy (*Payne* v *Cave* (1789) 3 TR 148). The sale is complete when the hammer falls and until that time any bid may be withdrawn (Sale of Goods Act 1979, s 57).

Where an auction is expressly advertised as subject to a 'reserve price', the rules stated above are not applied and there is no contract unless and until the reserve price is met, and this is so even if the auctioneer knocks the goods down below the reserve price by mistake (*McManus* v *Fortescue* [1907] 2 KB 1). The auctioneer is not liable either for an apparent breach of his warranty of authority to sell because the advertising of the sale as being subject to a reserve price indicates to those attending the sale that the auctioneer's authority is limited.

However, if *dicta* in *Warlow* v *Harrison* (1859) 1 E & E 309 are correct, the addition to the advertisement of an auction sale of the two words 'without reserve' converts it into an offer, presumably to the public at large, that the sale will in fact be subject to no reserve price. If in these circumstances the sale is actually held and a prospective purchaser makes a bid, however low, he accepts the offer of a sale 'without reserve'. The auctioneer, if he then puts a reserve price on any of the lots, is liable to an action for breach of his undertaking that the sale would be without reserve, though it should be noted that the goods in question will not have been sold unless the auctioneer's hammer has fallen.

### *Price lists, catalogues*

The issue of a tradesman's circular or catalogue advertising goods for sale is usually regarded as a mere attempt to induce offers, not an offer itself. The same is true of advertisements to sell goods inserted in newspapers or periodicals.

### *Price indications*

The display of an article with a price on it in a shop window, or on the shelves of a self-service store, is merely an invitation to treat. It is not an offer for sale, the acceptance of which makes a contract. These are not the only examples. The court may find in a variety of circumstances that an alleged offer is a mere price indication. (*See Harvey* v *Facey* (1893) *below.*)

### Company prospectuses/advertisements in connection with sale of securities

A prospectus/advertisement issued by a company in order to invite the public to sub-scribe for its shares (or debentures) is an invitation to treat so that members of the investing public offer to buy the securities when they apply for them and the compa-ny, being the acceptor, will only accept that proportion of public offers which matches the shares or debentures which the company wishes to issue. If there are more offers than shares, the issue is said to be over-subscribed. Some applicants then get no shares at all or only a proportion of what they applied for. The conditions of the issue also allow the company to make a binding contract by a *partial* acceptance in this way. Normally acceptance must be absolute and unconditional.

**The cases which follow illustrate the point that an invitation to treat is not an offer but is in general part of the process of negotiation which may lead to an offer.**

### Harris v Nickerson (1873) LR 8 QB 286

The defendant, an auctioneer, advertised in London newspapers that a sale of office furniture would be held at Bury St Edmunds. A broker with a commission to buy furniture came from London to attend the sale. Several conditions were set out in the advertisement, one being: 'The highest bidder to be the buyer'. The lots described as office furniture were not put up for sale but were withdrawn, though the auction itself was held. The broker sued for loss of time in attending the sale. *Held* – He could not recover from the auctioneer. There was no offer since the lots were never put up for sale, and the advertisement was simply an invitation to treat.

**Comment:** (i) A sensible decision, really. The statement 'I *intend* to auction some office furni-ture' is not the same as an offer for sale, and in any case there seems to be no way of accept-ing the 'offer' in advance of the event.

(ii) In *British Car Auctions* v *Wright* [1972] 3 All ER 462 the auctioneers sold an unroad-worthy vehicle. An attempt to charge them with the offence of 'offering' the car for sale con-trary to road traffic legislation failed. The bidder made the offer and not the auctioneer. *See also Partridge* v *Crittenden* (1968) *below.*)

### Partridge v Crittenden [1968] 2 All ER 421

Mr Partridge inserted an advertisement in a publication called *Cage and Aviary Birds* containing the words 'Bramblefinch cocks, bramblefinch hens. £1.25p each'. The advertisement appeared under the general heading 'Classified Advertisements' and in no place was there any direct use of the words 'offer for sale'. A Mr Thompson answered the advertisement enclosing a cheque for £1.25 and asking that a 'bramblefinch hen' be sent to him. Mr Partridge sent one in a box, the bird wearing a closed ring. Mr Thompson opened the box in the presence of an RSPCA inspector, Mr Crittenden, and removed the ring without injury to the bird. Mr Crittenden brought a prosecution against Mr Partridge before the Chester magistrates alleging that Mr Partridge had offered for sale a brambling contrary to s 6(1) of the Protection of Birds Act 1954 (*see now* Wildlife and Countryside Act 1981, s 6(1)), the bird being other than a close-ringed specimen bred in captivity and being of a species which was resident in or visited the British Isles in a wild state.

The justices were satisfied that the bird had not been bred in captivity but had been caught and ringed. A close-ring meant a ring that was completely closed and incapable of being forced or broken except with the intention of damaging it: such a ring was forced over the claws of a bird when it was between three and ten days old, and at that time it was not possible to determine what the eventual girth of the leg would be so that the close-ring soon became difficult to remove. The ease with which the ring was removed in this case indicated that it had been put on at a much later stage and this, together with the fact that the bird had no perching sense, led the justices to convict Mr Partridge.

He appealed to the Divisional Court of the Queen's Bench Division where the conviction was quashed. The court accepted that the bird was a wild bird, but since Mr Partridge had been charged with 'offering for sale', the conviction could not stand. The advertisement constituted in law an invitation to treat, not an offer for sale, and the offence was not, therefore, established. There was, of course, a completed sale for which Mr Partridge could have been successfully prosecuted, but the prosecution in this case had relied on the offence of 'offering for sale' and failed to establish such an offer.

*Comment:* The case shows how concepts of the civil law are sometimes at the root of criminal cases. (*See also British Car Auctions v Wright* (1972).)

### Pharmaceutical Society of Great Britain v Boots Cash Chemists (Southern) Ltd [1953] 1 QB 401

The defendants' branch at Edgware was adapted to the self-service system. Customers selected their purchases from shelves on which the goods were displayed and put them into a wire basket supplied by the defendants. They then took them to the cash desk where they paid the price. One section of shelves was set out with drugs which were included in the Poisons List referred to in s 17 of the Pharmacy and Poisons Act 1933, though they were not dangerous drugs and did not require a doctor's prescription.

Section 18 of the Act requires that the sale of such drugs shall take place in the presence of a qualified pharmacist. Every sale of the drugs on the Poisons List was supervised at the cash desk by a qualified pharmacist, who had authority to prevent customers from taking goods out of the shop if he thought fit. One of the duties of the society was to enforce the provisions of the Act, and the action was brought because the claimants alleged that the defendants were infringing s 18. *Held* – The display of goods in this way did not constitute an offer. The contract of sale was not made when a customer selected goods from the shelves, but when the company's employee at the cash desk accepted the customer's offer to buy what had been chosen. There was, therefore, supervision in the sense required by the Act at the appropriate moment in time.

*Comment:* (i) It was held in *Esso Petroleum Ltd v Customs and Excise Commissioners* [1976] 1 All ER 117 by the House of Lords that an indication of the price at which petrol is to be sold at a filling station is also only an invitation to treat; (ii) the relevant provisions of the Pharmacy and Poisons Act 1933 are now enacted in ss 2 and 3 of the Poisons Act 1972; (iii) although a trader can *refuse* to *sell* at his wrongly advertised price, he may find himself facing prosecution under ss 20 and 21 of the Consumer Protection Act 1987 where the price ticket shows a lower price than that at which he is prepared to sell; (iv) the concept of invitation to treat also applies to goods displayed in a shop window (*Fisher v Bell* [1960] 3 All ER 731).

## Harvey v Facey [1893] AC 552

The claimants sent the following telegram to the defendant: 'Will you sell us Bumper Hall Pen? Telegraph lowest cash price.' The defendant telegraphed in reply: 'Lowest price for Bumper Hall Pen £900.' The claimants then telegraphed: 'We agree to buy Bumper Hall Pen for £900 asked by you. Please send us your title deeds in order that we may get early possession.' The defendant made no reply. The Supreme Court of Jamaica granted the claimants a decree of specific performance of the contract. On appeal the Judicial Committee of the Privy Council held that there was no contract. The second telegram was not an offer, but was a mere price indication and in the nature of an invitation to treat at a minimum price of £900. The third telegram could not, therefore, be an acceptance resulting in a contract.

**Comment:** (i) The matter of invitation to treat and offer in the context of the sale of land produced the most interesting case of *Gibson v Manchester City Council* [1979] 1 All ER 972. The City Treasurer wrote to Mr Gibson saying that the Council 'may be prepared' to sell the freehold of his council house to him at £2,725 less 20 per cent, i.e. £2,180. The letter said that Mr G should make a formal application which he did. Following local government elections three months later the policy of selling council houses was reversed. The Council did not proceed with the sale to Mr Gibson. He claimed a binding contract existed. The House of Lords said that it did not. The Treasurer's letter was only an invitation to treat. Mr G's application was the offer, but the Council had not accepted it. In the Court of Appeal Lord Denning had said that there was an 'agreement in fact' which was enforceable. It was not always necessary to stick to the strict rules of offer and acceptance in order to produce a binding agreement. The House of Lords would not accept this and Lord Denning's view has not as yet found a place in the law.

(ii) The above cases are unlikely to occur, on their own facts at least, in modern law. Under s 2 of the Law of Property (Miscellaneous Provisions) Act 1989 a contract for the sale of land has to be in writing and must contain all the terms expressly agreed by the parties and each of those terms must be set out in the written agreement, though the Act does allow terms of the agreement to be incorporated in the document where it refers to some other document or documents containing the term. So if people now have to go through that procedure to get a valid contract for a sale of land, they are surely not going to be able to say that they did not intend an offer (and acceptance) and plead invitation to treat. Nevertheless, the cases do provide examples of invitations to treat in other areas, as where A says to B 'Lowest price for my BMW is £10,000' and B tries to 'accept', or where A says to B 'I may be prepared to sell you my BMW for £10,000' and B tries to 'accept'. Examination questions may well be set involving these principles in regard to sales other than land.

*The business application:* A business will not wish to let the court decide whether it has made an offer in a particular case. It is, therefore, common to indicate in documents and statements made and issued by the business that the contents do not constitute an offer as by a phrase such as 'The contents of this document (letter) (form) etc. do not constitute an offer, or part of an offer or a contract (for sale) (of service) etc.'. Obviously, if a contractual offer is intended, the above phrase would not be used.

## ACCEPTANCE GENERALLY

Once the existence of an offer has been proved the court must be satisfied that the offeree has accepted, otherwise there is no contract. The problems arising are considered under the following headings.

### Acceptor ignorant of offer and motive

If B has found A's lost dog and, not having seen an advertisement by A offering a reward for its return, returns it out of goodness of heart, B will not be able to claim the reward. However, as long as the acceptor is aware of the making of the offer his motive in accepting it is immaterial.

The following case is an illustration of this point which is that so long as the acceptor knows the offer exists the reasons for accepting it are of no importance in deciding whether a contract has come into being.

### Williams v Carwardine (1833) 5 C & P 566

The defendant published a handbill by the terms of which he promised to pay the sum of £20 to any person who should give information leading to the discovery of the murderer of Walter Carwardine. Two persons were tried for the murder at Hereford Assizes and were acquitted. Shortly afterwards the claimant, who was living with Williams, was severely beaten by him and, believing that she was going to die and to ease her conscience, she gave information leading to the conviction of Williams for the murder. In an action to recover the reward, the jury found that the claimant was not induced to give the information by the reward offered, but by motives of spite and revenge. *Held* – She was nevertheless entitled to the reward, for she had seen the handbill and had given information. Patteson J said: 'We cannot go into the claimant's motives.'

*Comment:* The point about motive is also made in *Carlill's* case.

### Effect of acceptance 'subject to contract'

Acceptance must be absolute and unconditional. One important form of conditional assent is an acceptance 'subject to contract'. The law has placed special significance on these words and they are always construed as meaning that the parties do not intend to be bound until a formal contract is prepared and signed.

In the past, the main practical use of this phrase was in correspondence relating to sales of land and agreements for leases of land to indicate that the correspondence between the parties was part of a process of negotiation and not in itself contractual. Since, under the Law of Property (Miscellaneous Provisions) Act 1989, a contract for the sale or other disposition of land must be made in writing in a document incorporating all the terms which the parties have expressly agreed and must be signed by each party, solicitors and conveyancers are no longer at risk that pre-contract correspondence signed by one party only might amount to a contract itself, which was a possibility before. The practice of heading correspondence 'subject to contract' in the above context has lost its former importance. However, the form of words is well established in the law as indicating mere negotiation and there is no reason why it should not be used in pre-contractual correspondence in other fields where the parties wish to indicate that they will not be bound by statements in such correspondence unless they appear in a later formal contract. In addition, there are those who feel that it is desirable to continue with the 'subject to contract' formula, even in negotiations concerning land, in case litigation on the 1989 Act reveals an unsuspected trap because of its omission.

Incidentally, it is worth noting that the House of Lords decided in *Walford v Miles* [1992] 2 WLR 174 that an agreement to continue to negotiate until agreement was reached was not enforceable as having no legal content. So if A and B agree that they will continue to negotiate with each other in regard to the sale of property belonging to A until they reach a binding agreement, the agreement to negotiate will have no legal effect and B will have no successful claim if in the course of negotiations between himself and A the latter decides to sell the property to C.

However, a negative undertaking by the vendor that he will not for a given period deal with anyone else once the purchaser has agreed to buy and is getting on with the exchange of contracts is enforceable even if oral. Section 2 of the 1989 Act does not apply. The agreement is not a sale or disposition of land but a mere 'lock-out' agreement not to deal with another for a stated period after which if contracts are not signed the vendor can deal with another. If he does so within the stated period, he is liable in damages. (*See Pitt v PHH Asset Management, The Times*, 30 July 1993.)

## Counter-offer

A counter-offer is a rejection of the original offer and has the effect of cancelling the original offer. However, the communication must amount to a counter-offer. Thus where it appears that the offeree is merely asking something which is more in the nature of a question seeking further information before making up his mind, his request for information will not destroy the offer.

**The cases which follow provide an illustration of these rules, i.e. that as regards rejection of an offer, a distinction must be made between a counter-offer and a request for information.**

### Hyde v Wrench (1840) 3 Beav 334

The defendant offered to sell his farm for £1,000. The claimant's agent made an offer of £950 and the defendant asked for a few days to think about it after which the defendant wrote saying he could not accept it, whereupon the claimant wrote purporting to accept the offer of £1,000. The defendant did not consider himself bound, and the claimant sued for specific performance. *Held* – The claimant could not enforce this 'acceptance' because his counter-offer of £950 was an implied rejection of the original offer to sell at £1,000.

### Stevenson v McLean (1880) 5 QBD 346

The defendant offered to sell to the claimants a quantity of iron 'at £2.00 net cash per ton till Monday'. On Monday the claimants telegraphed asking whether the defendant would accept £2.00 for delivery over two months, or if not what was the longest limit the defendant would give. The defendant received the telegram at 10.01 am but did not reply, so the claimants, by telegram sent at 1.34 pm, accepted the defendant's original offer. The defendant had already sold the iron to a third party, and informed the claimants of this by a telegram despatched at 1.25 pm arriving at 1.46 pm. The claimants had, therefore, accepted the offer before the defendant's

revocation had been communicated to them. If, however, the claimants' first telegram constituted a counter-offer, then it would amount to a rejection of the defendant's original offer. *Held* –
The claimants' first telegram was not a counter-offer, but a mere inquiry for information as to
the availability of credit which did not amount to a rejection of the defendant's original offer, so
that the offer was still open when the claimants accepted it.

*It should be noted, however, that the counter-offer may be accepted by the original offeror.*
The above principles of contract law are of increasing importance because of the modern commercial practice of making quotations and placing orders with conditions
attached, so that the terms and conditions of the contract which may eventually be
made may not be those which the original offeror put forward, since these may have
been changed as a result of a 'battle of forms' between the parties.

**That a process involving exchange of terms may continue for some time until an
act by one of the parties can be regarded as an acceptance of the other's terms is illustrated by the following case.**

### Butler Machine Tool Co Ltd v Ex-Cell-O Corporation (England) Ltd [1979] 1 All ER 965

In this case it appeared that on 23 May 1969 Butler quoted a price for a machine tool of £75,535,
delivery to be within 10 months of order. The quotation gave terms and conditions which were
stated expressly to prevail over any terms and conditions contained in the buyer's order.

One of the terms was a price variation clause which operated if costs increased before delivery. Ex-Cell-O ordered the machine on 27 May 1969, their order stating that the contract was
to be on the basis of Ex-Cell-O's terms and conditions as set out in the order. These terms and
conditions did not include a price variation clause but did contain additional items to the Butler
quotation, including the fact that Ex-Cell-O wanted installation of the machine for £3,100 and
the date of delivery of 10 months was changed to 10–11 months.

Ex-Cell-O's order form contained a tear-off slip which said: 'Acknowledgement: please sign
and return to Ex-Cell-O. We accept your order on the terms and conditions stated therein –
and undertake to deliver by ... date ... signed.' This slip was completed and signed on behalf of
Butler and returned with a covering letter to Ex-Cell-O on 5 June 1969.

The machine was ready by September 1970, but Ex-Cell-O could not take delivery until
November 1970 because they had to rearrange their production schedule. By the time Ex-Cell-
O took delivery, costs had increased and Butler claimed £2,892 as due under the price varia-
tion clause. Ex-Cell-O refused to regard the variation clause as a term of the contract.

The Court of Appeal, following a traditional analysis, decided that Butler's quotation of 23
May 1969 was an offer and that Ex-Cell-O's order of 27 May 1969 was a counter-offer introducing new terms and that Butler's communication of 5 June 1969 returning the slip was an
acceptance of the counter-offer: so that the contract was on Ex-Cell-O's terms and not Butler's,
in spite of the statement in Butler's original quotation.

Thus there was no price variation clause in the contract and Ex-Cell-O did not need to pay
the £2,892.

**Comment:** (i) Most commonly the parties will exchange terms relating to delivery dates, rights
of cancellation, the liability of the supplier for defects, fluctuations in price (as here), and arbitration clauses to settle differences. (ii) Title retention clauses (see Chapter 11) may also be

exchanged in this way. For example, in *Sauter Automation* v *Goodman (HC) (Mechanical Services)* (1987) CLY, para 451, Sauter tendered to supply the control panel of a boiler. The tender contained a title retention clause. Goodman accepted on the basis of their standard contract which did not contain retention arrangements. Sauter did not formally accept what was in effect a counter-offer by Goodman but they did deliver the panel which was deemed acceptance. Goodman went into liquidation but the court held that Sauter could not recover the panel or the proceeds of its sale. The contract was on Goodman's terms. Goodman's terms did not contain a retention arrangement. Sauter were left to prove in the liquidation of Goodman with little, if any, prospect of getting paid.

*The business application:* It is not uncommon to find price variation and fluctuation clauses in longer-term contracts as where the contract involves the manufacture or delivery of goods over, say, a period in excess of one year. These allow for changes e.g. in wages and/or the cost of materials. The alternative would be to try to get a variation in the original contract, but this may be difficult since a business may not be willing to pay more. This way the variation is in the original contract, following acceptance of a qualified offer.

## Acceptance in the case of tenders

It is essential to understand what is precisely meant by 'accepting' a tender since different legal results are obtained according to the wording of the invitation to tender. If the invitation by its wording implies that the potential buyer *will* require the goods, acceptance of a tender sent in response to such an invitation results in a binding contract under which the buyer undertakes to buy all the goods specified in the tender from the person who has submitted it. On the other hand, if the invitation by its wording suggests that the potential buyer *may* require the goods, acceptance of a tender results in a standing offer by the supplier to supply the goods set out in the tender as and when required by the person accepting it. The use of the word 'may' or a phrase such as 'if and when required or demanded' indicates a vagueness in the requirements of the purchaser which prevents a contract for the whole of the goods coming into being. Under the standing offer, each time the buyer orders a quantity there is a contract confined to that quantity, but if the buyer does not order any of the goods set out in the tender, or a smaller number than the supplier quoted for, there is no breach of contract. If the person submitting the tender wishes to revoke his standing offer, he may do so except in so far as the buyer has already ordered the goods under the tender. These must be supplied or the tenderer is in breach of contract.

Take the two examples which follow:

(a) Tenders are invited for the supply of 10,000 tonnes of coal to Boxo plc, delivery to take place as demanded between January and December 200– .
(b) Tenders are invited for the supply of coal not exceeding 10,000 tonnes to Boxo plc if and when demanded between January and December 200– .

Acceptance in the case of (a) above will produce a binding contract. Acceptance in (b) above will lead to a standing offer.

**The following case shows the practical effect of a standing offer.**

### Great Northern Railway v Witham (1873) LR 9 CP 16

The company advertised for tenders for the supply for one year of such stores as it might think fit to order. The defendant submitted a tender in these words: 'I undertake to supply the company for twelve months with such quantities of (certain specified goods) as the company may order from time to time.' The company accepted the tender, and gave orders under it which the defendant carried out. Eventually the defendant refused to carry out an order made by the company under the tender, and this action was brought. *Held* – The defendant was in breach of contract. A tender of this type was a standing offer which was converted into a series of contracts as the company made an order. The defendant might revoke his offer for the remainder of the period covered by the tender, but must supply the goods already ordered by the company.

*Comment:* (i) Tendering by referential bid is invalid. In *Harvela Investments Ltd* v *Royal Trust Co of Canada Ltd* [1985] 2 All ER 966 the claimants submitted a tender for the purchase of shares in the following form: '2,100,000 dollars or 100,000 dollars in excess of any other offer'. The House of Lords held that such a bid was invalid. The decision is obviously a sensible one since if all tenderers had bid in this way there would not have been an ascertainable offer to accept.

(ii) If a person submits a tender which conforms in all respects with the rules laid down for the submission of tenders, e.g. as to date, time, form and so on, then this may give rise to an obligation in those asking for the tenders to at least consider them all if properly submitted. It was held in *Blackpool and Fylde Aero Club Ltd* v *Blackpool BC* [1990] 3 All ER 25 that failure to do so could lead to a successful action in damages for what is in effect a breach of a contract to consider all tenders, at least if properly submitted.

## Inchoate contracts

An alleged contract will not be enforced unless the parties have expressed themselves with reasonable clarity on the matter of essential terms. To make a person liable it must be clear not only that he has *made* a promise but also *what* it is he has promised. A situation may, therefore, exist in which there is sufficient assent to satisfy the basic requirements of offer and acceptance and yet the contract is incomplete (or inchoate) as to certain of its terms. The court will not make up a contract for the parties and enforce it so that the contract will remain unenforceable unless:

(a) the vague term is meaningless and can be ignored; or
(b) the contract itself provides a method of clarifying the contract; or
(c) the court can complete the contract by reference to a trade practice or course of dealing between the parties.

The context in which the problem often arises is that one of the parties to an agreement fails to carry it out and when sued for breach of the agreement defends himself by saying that he would have liked to perform it but because of the vagueness of an essential term he cannot do so.

**The following cases give practical examples of the approach of the courts to this problem.**

## Scammell (G) and Nephew Ltd v Ouston [1941] AC 251

Ouston wished to acquire a new motor van for use in his furniture business. Discussions took place with the company's sales manager as a result of which the company sent a quotation for the supply of a suitable van. Eventually Ouston sent an official order making the following stipulation. 'This order is given on the understanding that the balance of the purchase price can be had on hire-purchase terms over a period of two years.' This was in accordance with the discussions between the sales manager and Ouston, which had taken place on the understanding that hire purchase would be available. The company seemed to be content with the arrangement and completed the van. Arrangements were made with the finance company to give hire-purchase facilities, but the actual terms were not agreed at that stage. The appellants also agreed to take Ouston's present van in part exchange, but later stated that they were not satisfied with its condition and asked him to sell it locally. He refused and after much correspondence he issued a writ against the appellants for damages for non-delivery of the van. The appellants' defence was that there was no contract until the hire-purchase terms had been ascertained. *Held* – The defence succeeded: it was not possible to construe a contract from the vague language used by the parties.

*Comment:* If there is a trade custom, business procedure or previous dealings between parties, which assist the court in construing the vague parts of an agreement, then the agreement may be enforced. Here there was no such evidence.

> *The business application:* In this connection it is worth noting the quite common use in business contracts of the expressions 'best endeavours' and 'reasonable endeavours'. It would be too easy to fall into the *Scammell* trap and assume that these expressions made the contract in which they were used inchoate or uncertain, but this is not the case. The courts have in a number of cases held that the use of these expressions does not have that effect. These are useful rulings because it is not possible in many business situations to necessarily achieve performance. For example, suppose an agent makes a contract to find a publisher to publish an author's book. The agent cannot say that he will find such a publisher but he can and often will use the best endeavours or reasonable endeavours formula. If the agent has on the facts used best or reasonable endeavours and not obtained a publisher, then he is entitled to the fee. If the agent has not on the facts done so, any claim by him will fail. Clearly best endeavours require more effort than reasonable endeavours. (*See Lambert* v *HTV Cymru (Wales) Ltd, The Times,* 17 March 1998, where an all reasonable endeavours contract in connection with book publishing was held to be enforceable.)

## Nicolene Ltd v Simmonds [1953] 1 All ER 822

The claimants alleged that there was a contract for the sale by them of 3,000 tons of steel reinforcing bars and that the defendant seller had broken his contract. When the claimants sought damages, the seller set up the defence that, owing to one of the sentences in the letters which constituted the contract, there was no contract at all. The material words were 'We are in agreement that the usual conditions of acceptance apply.' In fact there were no usual conditions of acceptance so that the words were meaningless, but the seller nevertheless suggested that the contract was unenforceable since it was not complete. *Held* – by the Court of Appeal – that the contract was enforceable and that the meaningless clause could be ignored. Lord Denning said: 'In my opinion a distinction must be drawn between a clause which is meaningless and a clause which is yet to be agreed. A clause which is meaningless can often be ignored, whilst still leaving the contract good: whereas a clause which has yet to be agreed may mean that there is no contract at all, because the parties have not agreed on all the essential terms . . . In the present case there was nothing yet to be agreed. There was nothing left to further negotiation. All that happened was that the parties agreed that 'the normal conditions of acceptance apply'. The clause was so vague and uncertain as to be incapable of any precise meaning. It is clearly severable from the rest of the contract. It can be rejected without impairing the sense or reasonableness of the contract as a whole, and it should be so rejected. The contract should be held good and the clause ignored. The parties themselves treated the contract as subsisting. They regarded it as creating binding obligations between them; and it would be most unfortunate if the law should say otherwise. You would find defaulters all scanning their contracts to find some meaningless clause on which to ride free.'

*Comment:* In this case there was no evidence of any usual conditions either in the trade or between the parties as the result of previous dealings. Thus the expression 'the usual conditions of acceptance apply' had to be regarded as meaningless. It should also be noted that it was possible to enforce the contract without the meaningless term, which was not the situation in *Scammel* (above).

## Foley v Classique Coaches Ltd [1934] 2 KB 1

F owned certain land, part of which he used for the business of supplying petrol. He also owned the adjoining land. The company wished to purchase the adjoining land for use as the headquarters of their charabanc business. F agreed to sell the land to the company on condition that the company would buy all their petrol from him. An agreement was made under which the company agreed to buy its petrol from F 'at a price to be agreed by the parties in writing and from time to time'. It was further agreed that any dispute arising under the agreement should be submitted 'to arbitration in the usual way'. The agreement was acted upon for three years. At this time the company felt it could get petrol at a better price, and the company's solicitor wrote to F repudiating the contract. *Held* – Although the parties had not agreed upon a price, there was a contract to supply petrol at a reasonable price and of reasonable quality, and although the agreement did not stipulate the future price, but left this to the further agreement of the parties, a method was provided by which the price could be ascertained without such agreement, i.e. by arbitration. An injunction was therefore granted requiring the company to take petrol from F as agreed.

*Comment:* If the contract is completely silent on a term, the court may fill in a gap by implying a reasonable term. Thus in a contract for the sale of goods where no price at all is agreed, a reasonable price must be paid (*see now* Sale of Goods Act 1979, s 8(2)). However, where, as in Foley, there is an agreement for the sale of goods 'at a price to be agreed', the contract is not silent on the matter of price and the court cannot use what is now s 8(2) of the 1979 Act. In this connection the High Court decided in *Rafsanjan Pistachio Producers Co-operative* v *Kauffmanns Ltd, The Independent*, 12 January 1998 that a contract which specified that the price was to be 'agreed before each delivery' was an agreement to agree and unenforceable. There was no provision for arbitration.

*The business application:* A price fluctuation or variation clause in the original contract can be used in this situation. The parties may agree in the original contract that the price from time to time of the goods as the contract proceeds shall be increased (or exceptionally decreased) on the basis of relevant indices of labour and materials costs. This is less costly than reference to arbitration.

### Hillas & Co Ltd v Arcos Ltd [1932] 1 All ER Rep 494

The claimants had entered into a contract with the defendants under which the defendants were to supply the claimants with '22,000 standards of soft wood (Russian) of fair specification over the season 1930'. The contract also contained an option allowing the claimants to take up 100,000 standards as above during the season 1931. The parties managed to perform the contract throughout the 1930 season without any argument or serious difficulty in spite of the vague words used in connection with the specification of the wood. However, when the claimants exercised their option for 100,000 standards during the season 1931, the defendants refused to supply the wood, saying that the specification was too vague to bind the parties, and the agreement was therefore inchoate as requiring a further agreement as to the precise specification. *Held* – by the House of Lords – that the option to supply 100,000 standards during the 1931 season was valid. There was a certain vagueness about the specification, but there was also a course of dealing between the parties which operated as a guide to the court regarding the difficulties which this vagueness might produce. Since the parties had not experienced serious difficulty in carrying out the 1930 agreement, there was no reason to suppose that the option could not have been carried out without difficulty had the defendants been prepared to go on with it. Judgment was given for the claimants.

*Comment:* As we have seen in these cases, the defendant is trying to avoid damages for failing to perform the contract by saying 'I would like to perform the contract but I don't know what to do'. If there are, for example, previous dealings, then he does know what to do and the defence fails.

## THE COMMUNICATION OF ACCEPTANCE

An acceptance is not effective to produce a contract merely because the offeree decides that he will accept it. His decision must in most cases be accompanied by some external sign of assent. This takes place by the communication of the acceptance to the offeror, either by the offeree or someone authorised by the offeree to do it.

An acceptance may be made in various ways. It may be made in writing or orally but it must in general be communicated. This provides some protection against inertia selling as where a firm sends a book to a person, A, at his home stating that if no reply is received within seven days it will be assumed that A has accepted the offer to sell the book and is bound in contract. Silence cannot amount to acceptance in this way.

However, the matter is also covered by the Unsolicited Goods and Services Act 1971 (as amended by the Unsolicited Goods and Services (Amendment) Act 1975). Under this legislation a private, but not a business, recipient who receives, for example, unsolicited goods is entitled to treat them as if they had been given to him unless the sender takes them back within six months, or, if the recipient gives notice to the sender that he wants them taken back, within 30 days of the notice being given.

The following case provides an illustration of the rule that silence cannot normally amount to acceptance.

### Felthouse v Bindley (1862) 11 CB (NS) 869

The claimant had been engaged in negotiations with his nephew John regarding the purchase of John's horse, and there had been some misunderstanding as to the price. Eventually the claimant wrote to his nephew as follows: 'If I hear no more about him I consider the horse is mine at £30.75p.' The nephew did not reply but, wishing to sell the horse to his uncle, he told the defendant, an auctioneer who was selling farm stock for him, not to sell the horse as it had already been sold. The auctioneer inadvertently put the horse up with the rest of the stock and sold it. The claimant now sued the auctioneer in conversion, the basis of the claim being that he had made a contract with his nephew and the property in the animal was vested in him (the uncle) at the time of the sale. *Held* – The claimant's action failed. Although the nephew intended to sell the horse to his uncle, he had not communicated that intention. There was, therefore, no contract between the parties, and the property in the horse was not vested in the claimant at the time of the auction sale.

*Comment:* (i) The general principle laid down in this case, i.e. that an offeree who does not wish to accept an offer should not be put to the trouble of refusing it is quite acceptable. However, it is difficult to support the decision on its own facts. John wanted to accept the offer and intended to accept it and since the uncle by his letter waived any right to receive an acceptance, there appears on the facts to be no reason why there should not have been a contract. However, this approach runs fairly consistently through English law in regard to positive obligations involving the payment of money for goods and services. Thus if A employs B to clean his (A's) car but B by mistake cleans A's neighbour's car, the neighbour cannot be required to pay B, even though the neighbour is not prejudiced because, as it happens, he did want his car cleaned.

(ii) It should also be noted that the communication of acceptance must be authorised. In *Powell* v *Lee* (1908) 99 LT 284 Powell offered his services to the managers of a school as headmaster. The secretary to the managers told P that he had been selected, which was true. The secretary had no authority, actual or otherwise, to do this. The managers later selected another candidate as headmaster. P's action for breach of contract failed.

(iii) In a not dissimilar case a deputy headteacher's verbal assurance that a member of staff's temporary promotion would be made permanent had no contractual effect because, among other things, the deputy head had no authority to make a contract which would bind the school governors (see *Pantis* v *Governing Body of Isambard Brunel Junior School* [1997] 573 IRLB 15).

## Waiver of communication

There are some cases in which the offeror is regarded as having waived communication of the acceptance. This occurs, for example, in the case of unilateral contracts, such as a promise to pay money in return for some act to be carried out by the offeree. Performance of the act operates as an acceptance and no communication is required (*see Carlill* v *Carbolic Smoke Ball Co* (1893)). In addition, acceptance need not necessarily be communicated if the post is used (*see below*).

## Mode of communication prescribed by offeror

The offeror may stipulate the mode of acceptance, e.g. to be by letter so that there will be written evidence of it. In such a case, however, the offeror could still waive his right to have the acceptance communicated in a given way and agree to the substituted method.

In addition, an acceptance made in a different way may be effective if there is no prejudice to the offeror, as where the method used is as quick and as suitable as the method prescribed.

**Thus, although the method of communication of acceptance may be prescribed by the offeror, very clear words are required to make the court treat that method as essential, as the following case shows.**

### Yates Building Co v R J Pulleyn & Sons (York) (1975) 119 SJ 370

An option to purchase a certain plot of land was expressed to be exercisable by notice in writing by or on behalf of the intending purchaser to the intending vendor 'such notice to be sent by registered or recorded delivery post'. *Held* – by the Court of Appeal – that the form of posting described was directory rather than mandatory, or, alternatively, permissive rather than obligatory, and in consequence the option was validly exercised by a letter from the intending purchaser's solicitors to the intending vendor's solicitors sent by ordinary post and arriving well within the option period.

*Comment:* The fact that the letter arrived within the option period shows that there was no prejudice to the offeror.

### Oral acceptances

If the offeror has not stipulated a method of acceptance the offeree may choose his own method, though where acceptance is by word of mouth it is not enough that it be spoken; it must actually be heard by the offeror. The reason for this is that, rather obviously, parties cannot be regarded as having made an agreement unless they *know* they have, though unilateral contracts provide an exception as does the post rule (*see below*). As regards the use of the telephone and teleprinter, these are methods of instantaneous communication and it has been held that the contract is not complete unless the offeror hears or sees the acceptance.

Thus where instantaneous methods of communication over long distances are used, actual communication is necessary as the following case illustrates.

### Entores Ltd v Miles Far East Corporation [1955] 2 QB 327

The claimants, who conducted a business in London, made an offer to the defendants' agent in Amsterdam by means of a teleprinter service. The offer was accepted by a message received on the claimants' teleprinter in London. Later the defendants were in breach of contract and the claimants wished to sue them. The defendants had their place of business in New York and in order to commence an action the claimants had to serve notice of writ on the defendants in New York. The Rules of Supreme Court allow service out of the jurisdiction when the contract was made within the jurisdiction. On this point the defendants argued that the contract was made in Holland when it was typed into the teleprinter there, stressing the rule relating to posting. *Held* – Where communication is instantaneous, as where the parties are face to face or speaking on the telephone, acceptance must be received by the offeror. The same rule applied to communications of this kind. Therefore, the contract was made in London where the acceptance was received.

*Comment:* (i) The suggestion was made that the doctrine of estoppel may operate in this sort of case so as to bind the offeror, e.g. suppose X telephones his acceptance to Y, and Y does not hear X's voice at the moment of acceptance, then Y should ask X to repeat the message, otherwise Y may be estopped from denying that he heard X's acceptance and will be bound in contract, presumably because the failure of communication is to some extent the fault of Y, the offeror.

If this is so, the estoppel provides another example of a situation in which acceptance need not actually be communicated.

(ii) The House of Lords approved the *Entores* decision in *Brinkibon* v *Stahag Stahl* [1982] 1 All ER 293. The claimant wanted leave to serve a writ out of the jurisdiction, as in *Entores*. The message accepting an offer had been sent by telex from London to Vienna. The House of Lords held that the writ could not be served because the contract was made in Vienna and not London. The *Entores* decision presumably applies to acceptances by fax.

## Use of the post and telemessages

If the post is a proper and reasonable method of communication between the parties, then acceptance is deemed complete immediately the letter of acceptance is posted, even if it is delayed or is lost or destroyed in the post so that it never reaches the offeror.

The better view is that in English law an acceptance cannot be recalled once it has been posted, even though it has not reached the offeror at the time of recall.

A telemessage is presumably effective as an acceptance when it is given to the Telecom operator. *Cowan* v *O'Connor* (1888) 20 QBD 640 decided that this was so with the old telegram.

**The following case confirms the legal position in regard to letters.**

### Household Fire Insurance Company v Grant (1879) 4 Ex D 216

The defendant handed a written application for shares in the company to the company's agent in Glamorgan. The application stated that the defendant had paid to the company's bankers the sum of £5, being a deposit of 5p per share on an application for one hundred shares, and also agreed to pay 95p per share within 12 months of the allotment. The agent sent the application to the company in London. The company secretary made out a letter of allotment in favour of the defendant and posted it to him in Swansea. The letter never arrived. Nevertheless, the company entered the defendant's name on the share register and credited him with dividends amounting to 25p. Three years later the company went into liquidation and the liquidator sued for £94.75, the balance due on the shares allotted. *Held* – by the Court of Appeal – that the defendant was liable. Acceptance was complete when the letter of allotment was posted, the Post Office being regarded as the agent of the parties to receive the acceptance. The flaw in this reasoning is that the Post Office and its agents do not know what is in the letter but the rule is now so well established that it is beyond challenge.

*Comment:* (i) The rule is clearly one based on convenience rather than principle and, indeed, Bramwell LJ, in a dissenting judgment, regarded actual communication as essential. If the letter of acceptance does not arrive, he said, an unknown liability is imposed on the offeror. If actual communication is required the status quo is preserved, i.e. the parties have not made a contract.

The case also has some unusual features. First the initial deposit on application for the shares was not in fact paid. Instead the defendant was credited with an equivalent sum due to him from the company. Second the dividends declared by the company were not actually paid to the defendant but merely credited to his account with the company. But for the above circumstances the defendant would have been aware long before the end of three years that he was being regarded by the company as a shareholder.

(ii) If the statements of the parties appear to exclude the rule then the court will not apply it and there will be no contract unless the letter is received. Thus in *Holwell Securities Ltd* v *Hughes* [1974] I All ER 161 Dr Hughes gave the claimants an option to purchase his premises, the agreement providing that the option was to be exercised 'by notice in writing'. The claimants exercised the option by a letter which was not received by Dr Hughes and it was held that there was no contract because 'notice' meant that the letter must be received. The case illustrates that the courts regard the post rule as somewhat peculiar in the sense that they will, as here, readily infer an intention that it shall not apply.

(iii) It should also be noted that the letter of acceptance must be properly stamped and addressed. If not there is no communication until the letter arrives.

(iv) It was held in *Miss Sam (Sales) Ltd* v *River Island Clothing Co Ltd* [1994] NLJR 419 that a cheque sent through the post is not payment unless it arrives and there can be no extension of the post rule to this situation unless by express agreement between the parties.

### Communication of cross-offers

There is some controversy as to whether agreement can result from cross-offers. Suppose after discussions between X and Y regarding the sale of X's watch, X by letter offers to sell his watch to Y for £50 and Y by means of a second letter which crosses X's letter in the post offers to buy X's watch for £50. Can there be a contract? The matter was discussed by an English court in *Tinn* v *Hoffman* (1873) 29 LT 271 and the court's decision was that no contract could arise. However, the matter is still undecided and it is possible to hold the view that a contract could come into being where it appears that the parties have intended to create a legally binding agreement on the same basis.

## TERMINATION OF OFFER

It is now necessary to consider the ways in which an offer may be terminated or negatived.

### Revocation – generally

The general rule is that an offer may be revoked, i.e. withdrawn, at any time before acceptance. If there is an option attached to the offer as where the offeror agrees to give seven days for acceptance, the offeror need not keep the offer open for seven days but can revoke it without incurring legal liability unless the offeree has given some consideration for the option. Where consideration, e.g. a payment of, or a promise to pay, money, has been given by the offeree the offeror may still revoke his offer and sell the property which was the subject-matter of the offer to someone else. He will, however, be liable to an action for damages for breach of option. It was thought at one time that where the option to buy property was not supported by consideration, the offer could be revoked merely by its sale to another. However, in modern law it is necessary for the offeror to communicate the revocation to the offeree himself or by means of some other person. (*See Stevenson* v *McLean* (1880) *above* and *Dickinson* v *Dodds* (1876) *below*, the facts of which make this point.)

To be effective revocation must be communicated to the offeree before he has accepted the offer. When revocation is by letter the question arises as to whether it is effective when delivered or when the offeree has read it. The latter solution seems unreasonable because the offeree may delay reading the letter until he has accepted the offer. A better solution would be to regard revocation as effective when the offeree has had a reasonable time or opportunity to read the letter after delivery. Indeed, in *Eaglehill Ltd* v *J Needham (Builders) Ltd* [1972] 3 All ER 895, the House of Lords, when discussing notice of dishonour of a bill of exchange, said that an offer would be revoked when the letter of revocation 'was opened in the ordinary course of business or would have been so opened if the ordinary course of business was followed'.

Communication may be made directly by the offeror or may reach the offeree by some other reliable source. It is not enough in, for example, a sale of goods merely to sell the goods to someone else.

**The following cases provide a useful illustration of the operation of the rules of communication of acceptance and the communication of revocation of offer.**

### Byrne *v* Van Tienhoven (1880) 5 CPD 344

On 1 October the defendants in Cardiff posted a letter to the claimants in New York offering to sell them tin plate. On 8 October the defendants wrote revoking their offer. On 11 October the claimants received the defendants' offer and immediately telegraphed their acceptance. On 15 October the claimants confirmed their acceptance by letter. On 20 October the defendants' letter of revocation reached the claimants who had by this time entered into a contract to resell the tin plate. *Held* – (i) that revocation of an offer is not effective until it is communicated to the offeree; (ii) that the mere posting of a letter of revocation is not communication to the person to whom it is sent. The rule is not, therefore, the same as that for acceptance of an offer. Therefore, the defendants were bound by a contract which came into being on 11 October.

### Dickinson *v* Dodds (1876) 2 Ch D 463

The defendant offered to sell certain houses by letter stating, 'This offer to be left over until Friday, 9 am.' On Thursday afternoon the claimant was informed by a Mr Berry that the defendant had been negotiating a sale of the property with one Allan. On Thursday evening the claimant left a letter of acceptance at the house where the defendant was staying. This letter was never delivered to the defendant. On Friday morning at 7 am Berry, acting as the claimant's agent, handed the defendant a duplicate letter of acceptance explaining it to him. However, on the Thursday the defendant had entered into a contract to sell the property to Allan. *Held* – Since there was no consideration for the promise to keep the offer open, the defendant was

free to revoke his offer at any time. Further, Berry's communication of the dealings with Allan indicated that Dodds was no longer minded to sell the property to the claimant and was in effect a communication of Dodds' revocation. There was, therefore, no binding contract between the parties.

*Comment:* This decision could cause hardship because it may mean that the offeree will have to accept as revocation all kinds of rumour from people who may not necessarily appear to be reliable and well informed. It would be nice to think that in modern law the third party would have to be apparently reliable and likely to know the true state of affairs as where he is the offeror's agent, but there is no actual clear statement in this case that this is so.

## Revocation – unilateral contracts

Where the offer consists of a promise in return for an act, as where a reward is offered in a newspaper for the return of lost property, the offer, although made to the whole world, can be revoked as any other offer can. It is thought to be enough that the same publicity be given to the revocation in the same newspaper as was given to the offer, even though the revocation may not be seen by all the persons who saw the offer. A more difficult problem arises when an offer which requires a certain act to be carried out is revoked after some person has begun to perform the act but before he has completed it. For example, X offers £1,000 to anyone who can successfully swim the Channel and Y, deciding he will try to obtain the money, starts his swim from Dover. Can X revoke his offer, e.g. from a helicopter, when Y is halfway across the Channel? The better view is that he cannot on the grounds that an offer of the kind made by X is two offers in one, namely:

(a)  to pay £1,000 to a successful swimmer; and
(b)  something in the nature of an implied offer not to revoke for a reasonable time once performance has been embarked upon so that a person trying to complete the task has a reasonable chance of doing so.

A similarly fair result can be achieved by regarding Y as accepting the offer when he enters the water, making effective revocation impossible thereafter. However, Y would not qualify for the prize of £1,000 unless and until he had provided the consideration by actually swimming the Channel. It would have been necessary to consider the application of one or other of these solutions in *Carlill*'s case if the company had revoked the offer *after* Mrs Carlill had started to use the ball.

The matter also came before the Court of Appeal in *Errington* v *Errington* [1952] 1 All ER 149. In that case a father bought a house for his son and daughter-in-law to live in. He paid the deposit but the son and daughter-in-law made the mortgage payments after the father gave the building society book to the daughter-in-law, saying, 'Don't part with this book. The house will be your property when the mortgage is paid.' The son left his wife who continued to live in the house. It was held by the Court of Appeal that neither the father nor the claimant, his widow, to whom the house was left by will, could eject the daughter-in-law from the property. As Lord Denning said: 'The father's promise was a unilateral contract – a promise of the house in return for their act of paying the instalments. It could not be revoked by him once the couple entered on the performance of the act . . .'. The Court went on to decide that the son and daughter-in-law would be fully entitled to the house once they had made all the mortgage repayments.

## Lapse of time

If a time for acceptance has been stipulated then the offer lapses when the time has expired. If no time has been stipulated then acceptance must be within a reasonable time, and this is a *matter of fact* for the judge to decide on the circumstances of the case.

**The following case provides an example.**

### Ramsgate Victoria Hotel Co *v* Montefiore (1866) LR 1 Exch 109

The defendant offered by letter dated 8 June 1864 to take shares in the company. No reply was made by the company, but on 23 November 1864 it allotted shares to the defendant. The defendant refused to take up the shares. *Held* – His refusal was justified because his offer had lapsed by reason of the company's delay in notifying its acceptance. He also recovered a part-payment of 1/– (5p) a share.

*Comment:* Much depends upon the subject-matter of the contract and the conditions of the market in which the offer is made. Offers to take shares in companies are normally accepted quickly because prices fluctuate day by day on investment exchanges, and the same would be true of an offer to sell perishable goods. An offer to sell a farm might well not lapse so soon. The form in which the offer is made is also relevant so that an offer by cable could well lapse quickly.

## Conditional offers

An offer may terminate on the happening of a given event if it is made subject to a condition that it will do so. Thus, an offer to buy goods may terminate if the goods offered for sale are seriously damaged before acceptance. Such a condition may be made expressly in the contract but may also be implied from the circumstances.

**Thus, as the following case illustrates, there is an implied condition in an offer to buy goods that the offer is not capable of acceptance after the goods are damaged in a serious way.**

### Financings Ltd *v* Stimson [1962] 3 All ER 386

On 16 March 1961, the defendant saw a motor car on the premises of a dealer and signed a hire-purchase form provided by the claimants (a finance company), this form being supplied by the dealer. The form was to the effect that the agreement was to become binding only when the finance company signed the form. It also carried a statement to the effect that the hirer (the defendant) acknowledged that before he signed the agreement he had examined the goods and had satisfied himself that they were in good order and condition, and that the goods were at the risk of the hirer from the time of purchase by the owner. On 18 March the defendant paid the first instalment and took possession of the car. However, on 20 March the defendant, being dissatisfied with the car, returned it to the dealer though the finance company were not informed of this. On the night of 24–25 March the car was stolen from the dealer's premises and was recovered badly damaged. On 25 March the finance company signed the agreement accepting the defendant's offer to hire the car. The defendant did not regard himself as bound and refused to pay the instalments. The finance company sold the car, and now sued for damages for the defendant's breach of the hire-purchase agreement. *Held* – The hire-purchase agreement was not binding on the defendant because:

(a) he had revoked his offer by returning the car, and the dealer was the agent of the finance company to receive notice;

(b) there was an implied condition in the offer that the goods were in substantially the same condition when the offer was accepted as when it was made.

## Effect of death

The effect of the death of a party or potential party would appear to vary according to the type of contract in question, whether the death is that of the offeror or offeree and whether death takes place before or after acceptance.

### Death of offeror before acceptance

If the contract envisaged by the offer involves a personal relationship, such as an offer to act as an agent, then the death of the offeror prevents acceptance. If the contract envisaged by the offer is not one involving the personality of the offeror, there are two points of view. In *Dickinson* v *Dodds* (1876) Mellish LJ in an *obiter dictum* expressed the opinion: 'that if a man who makes an offer dies the offer cannot be accepted after he is dead'. However, the decision in *Bradbury* v *Morgan* (1862) (*see below*) suggests that the offer can be accepted until the offeree is notified of the offeror's death. The matter is, therefore, unresolved pending a further decision.

### Bradbury v Morgan (1862) 1 H & C 249

The defendants were the executors of J M Leigh who had entered into a guarantee of his brother's account with the claimants for credit up to £100. The claimants, not knowing of the death of J M Leigh, continued to supply goods on credit to the brother, H J Leigh. The defendants now refused to pay the claimants in respect of such credit after the death of J M Leigh. *Held* – The claimants succeeded, the offer remaining open until the claimants had knowledge of the death of J M Leigh.

*Comment:* This was a continuing guarantee which is in the nature of a standing offer accepted piecemeal whenever further goods are advanced on credit. Where the guarantee is not of this nature, it may be irrevocable. Thus in *Lloyd's* v *Harper* (1880) 16 Ch D 290, the defendant, while living, guaranteed his son's dealings as a Lloyd's underwriter in consideration of Lloyd's admitting the son. It was held that, as Lloyd's had admitted the son on the strength of the guarantee, the defendant's estate was still liable under it, because it was irrevocable in the defendant's lifetime and was not affected by the defendant's death. It continued to apply to defaults committed by the son after the father's death.

### Death of offeree before acceptance

Once the offeree is dead, there is no offer which can be accepted and his executors cannot, therefore, accept the offer in his stead. The offer being made to a living person can only be accepted by that person and assumes his continued existence. The rule applies whether the proposed contract involves a personal relationship or not. (*Re Cheshire Banking Co, Duff's Executors' Case* (1886) 32 Ch D 301.)

### Death of parties after acceptance

Death after acceptance has normally no effect unless the contract is for personal services when it is discharged. Thus if X sells his car to Y and before the car is delivered X dies, it would be possible for Y to sue X's personal representatives for breach of contract if they were to refuse to deliver the car. But if X agrees to play the piano at a concert and dies two days before the performance, the contract is discharged and his personal representatives are not expected to play the piano in his stead.

## OFFER AND ACCEPTANCE NOT IDENTIFIABLE

Before leaving the topic of formation of contract it should be noted that the court may from time to time infer the existence of a contract from the words and acts of the parties in a situation where there has been *no offer and acceptance*. An example is provided by a collateral contract, so called because it is associated with another contract from which it derives and is subordinate to.

**The following case is a good practical illustration of the operation of this rule in company law.**

### Rayfield v Hands [1958] 2 All ER 194

The articles of a private company provided by Art 11 that 'Every member who intends to transfer his shares shall inform the directors who will take the said shares . . . at a fair price.' The claimant held 725 fully-paid shares of £1 each, and he asked the directors to buy them but they refused. *Held* – The directors were bound to take the shares. Having regard to what is now s 14(1) of the Companies Act 1985, the provisions of Art 11 constituted a binding contract between the directors, as members, and the claimant, as a member, in respect of his rights as a member. The word 'will' in the article did not import an option in the directors. Vaisey J did say that the conclusion he had reached in this case may not apply to all companies, but it did apply to a private company, because such a company was an intimate concern closely analogous with a partnership.

*Comment:* (i) Although the articles placed the obligation to take shares of members on the directors, Vaisey J construed this as an obligation falling upon the directors in their capacity as members. Otherwise the contractual aspect of the provision in the articles would not have applied.

(ii) The leading case is *Clarke* v *Dunraven* [1897] AC 59 where it was held that competitors in a regatta had made a contract not only with the club which organised the race but also with each other, so that one competitor was able to sue another for damages when his boat was fouled and sank under a rule which said that each competitor was liable 'to pay all damages' that he might cause.

(iii) Section 14(1) of the Companies Act 1985 provides that the provisions of a registered company's articles and memorandum form a contract between the company and its members which both parties are bound to observe. It should be noted that the Contracts (Rights of Third Parties) Act 1999 which is further considered in Chapter 2 clearly excludes the operation of the s 14(1) contract from its provisions so that third parties cannot acquire rights under the contract. Thus the appointment of a person as a solicitor in the articles would not operate as a contract enforceable against the company. The effect of the articles as a contract is dealt with in Chapter 18.

## TRADING ELECTRONICALLY

While the legal rules relating to trading on the Internet are largely a matter of informed surmise and untested in the courts, the following matters should be borne in mind.

### If demands exceeds supply

The seller will wish to avoid actions for breach of contract by reason of his inability to meet orders from customers responding to the seller's website. In these circumstances every website should make clear that the seller is not making an offer to sell or supply the goods but is inviting offers from potential customers (i.e. an invitation to treat). If this is done, the website should be regarded in law as a mere shop-window.

### Customers' orders

Since we are dealing with instantaneous communication customers' orders must be received by the seller. This may not happen given the vagaries of e-mail which may lead to the loss of or the scrambling of an order. The website should carry a cut-off date for receipt of orders. If the acceptance is via a website, the position is likely to be clearer since the seller and the customer can immediately identify whether or not communication has broken down.

### Whose terms apply?

Sellers will not normally be using standard terms for each customer and, to ensure that the seller's terms apply, the potential customer should be asked to scroll through the terms to indicate his agreement to them. This should be done before the contract is made.

### Conflict of laws

In terms of international trading, the seller should state the law which applies to the contract, e.g. English law. Sometimes, however, the law of the customer's state may override the adoption of foreign law for international agreements, and a careful check should be made and legal advice taken before embarking on international sales. If there is uncertainty as to foreign law or the seller does not wish to become involved, orders from a particular country or countries which might raise problems of applicable law should be declined.

## GRADED QUESTIONS

### Essay mode

1 (a) Explain, giving illustrations, the postal rules as they affect offer and acceptance where contracts are concluded through using the post as the method of communication.

(b) On Friday 27 November Buyer sends a telex to Seller offering to buy 1,000 tonnes of sugar at the current market price. The telex is received in Seller's offices after a short delay at 5.00 pm. Since the telex operator has gone home for the weekend, Seller posts a letter in the last post on Friday, accepting the offer. This reaches Buyer at 2.30 pm on Monday 30 November. Meanwhile, at 9.30 am on 30 November, Buyer sends a further telex to Seller withdrawing his offer. This reaches Seller and is read by him immediately at 9.45 am on 30 November. Seller now seeks your advice.
Advise Seller.

*(Institute of Chartered Secretaries and Administrators)*

2 On 1 December Noel advertised his motor-car for sale in the magazine *Car Mart*. The advertisement read as follows:

FOR SALE
1992 Morgan Countryman. Offers around £10,000.
Write to PO Box 100, Car Mart Magazine.

On 2 December Guy posts a letter to the address in the advertisement in which he states the following:

'I've always wanted a Morgan and I will be happy to give you £10,000 for the car. Please telephone me on 8 December between 8 pm and 9 pm to let me know whether this is enough, failing which, I will assume that you've agreed to sell the vehicle to me.'

Noel receives the letter on 6 December and writes the following entry in his diary:

'8 December – Ring Guy at 8 pm to agree sale of car.'

Noel forgets to make the telephone call. On 9 December Guy meets an acquaintance of Noel's who says that Noel has decided to sell the car to Guy. In the meantime Noel has received a higher offer of £12,000 from Donald and writes a letter to Guy advising him that he has had a better offer for the car.
Advise Guy.

*(The Institute of Legal Executives)*

3 (a) In the law of contract explain what is meant by:
(i) an offer;
(ii) an invitation to treat;
(iii) a statement of intention.

(b) A advertised his car for sale in a newspaper for £5,000. B wrote offering to buy the car for £4,500. A replied by return of post stating that he would accept £4,750. Having received no reply from B, A wrote again saying he would accept his offer of £4,500.
Advise A.

*(Association of Chartered Certified Accountants)*

## Objective mode

Four alternative answers are given. Select ONE only. Circle the answer which you consider to be correct. Check your answers by referring back to the information given in the chapter and against the answers at the back of the book.

1   John decides that he will sell his antique desk at auction and so he sends it to the auctioneers with a reserve price of £2,000. Martin the auctioneer notes this in the catalogue and informs those attending that there is a reserve. Michael puts in a bid for £1,800 and the desk is knocked down to him. Martin then informs Michael that a mistake has been made and he cannot have the desk because John refuses to sell it for £1,800.

   A   Michael is not entitled to the desk because the sale was made on the basis of a mistake and the contract is void.
   B   Michael is entitled to the desk because the amount of the reserve price was not communicated to him and he is not therefore bound by the reserve.
   C   Michael knew that there was a reserve and as the auctioneer mistakenly sold the desk for less, Michael is not entitled to it.
   D   Michael is entitled to the desk. His offer of £1,800 has been accepted and, as an agent, Martin is able to bind his principal John.

2   Eric wants to sell his car and advertises it in the local newspaper at £8,000 giving his telephone number. Fred sees the advertisement and, being interested in buying a car at about that price, rings Eric and makes an appointment to see the car. Fred likes the car but not the price. He makes Eric an offer of £7,500. Eric nevertheless insists on £8,000.

   On the following Monday Fred gets a telephone call from Eric during which Eric offers his car for sale to Fred at £7,800 saying that Fred can have until noon on Friday to think about it.

   On Wednesday evening Fred meets his brother Tom in the local. Tom tells him that Eric's son-in-law bought the car on Wednesday morning for £8,000. Fred gulps down his pint and goes over to the public telephone. He rings Eric and says: 'I accept your offer of £7,800 for the car. I will be along in a minute with a cheque.' Eric replies: 'You are too late, it is sold.'

   Fred thinks Eric is in breach of contract and proposes to sue him for damages.

   As regards the legal position of Eric and Fred:

   A   There is no contract between them because Eric's offer was revoked before Fred accepted it.
   B   There is a contract between them because Eric did not revoke the offer himself.
   C   There is a contract between them because Eric promised to keep the offer open until Friday and Fred accepted before then.
   D   There is no contract between them because Eric's offer had lapsed when Fred accepted it.

3   In contract the rules relating to the use of the telephone state that:

   A   An acceptance is always effective when it is spoken into the telephone by the offeree.
   B   An acceptance is effective only if it is heard by the offeror.
   C   An acceptance can be effective when spoken into the telephone even though the offeror does not hear it.
   D   An acceptance is effective only if it is heard by the offeror and he acknowledges to the offeree that he has heard it.

4   Smart, a young sales representative employed by Speedy Ltd, a company manufacturing computers, visits Wiley, a partner in Wiley and Fox, solicitors, with a view to selling a new computer to the firm.

In the course of conversation Smart, being desperate to make his first sale for several days, offers the machine at £300 less than the normal selling price. Wiley says that he will consult Miss Dragon, the head of the computer department, and let Smart have an answer by letter in a few days.

On returning to the area sales office Smart realises that although he has authority to give special prices he might have been unduly generous in his offer to Wiley. Accordingly he consults Allick, the area sales manager, who is not prepared to sell the computer at the price at which Smart has offered it. Smart rings Wiley immediately but is unable to speak to him or any of the other partners in the firm – even Miss Dragon is not available. Smart therefore writes a letter to Wiley revoking the offer and posts it immediately by first-class mail.

When Wiley arrives at his office on the following day he notices that among the incoming mail is a franked envelope bearing the slogan 'Speedy Ltd for your Computers'. It occurs to him that the envelope might contain a retraction of the offer made by Smart and decides not to open it immediately. Instead he dictates a letter to his secretary accepting the offer and tells her to post it before lunch. After lunch Wiley, having ascertained that his secretary has posted his letter, opens the letter from Smart and discovers that it is indeed a revocation of the offer made the previous day. Nevertheless Wiley rings Allick, the area sales manager of Speedy Ltd, and asks for delivery of the computer. Allick replies: 'We cannot possibly sell at that price. Surely you received our letter this morning?' 'Yes', says Wiley, 'it came first delivery but I had already posted my acceptance before I had a chance to open all my mail.' Wiley intends to sue Speedy for breach of contract. Will he succeed?

Which one of the following decisions is the court likely to make?

A   That Wiley accepted Smart's offer when his secretary posted the letter of acceptance and Speedy is bound to sell the machine at Smart's price.

B   That Smart's letter of revocation took effect after Wiley had had a reasonable time in which to read it after delivery. Since such an opportunity occurred before Wiley accepted, Speedy is not bound.

C   That Smart's offer was withdrawn when the letter of revocation was delivered so that Wiley's acceptance was not effective and Speedy is not bound.

D   That Smart's offer was withdrawn when the letter of revocation was posted so that Wiley's acceptance is ineffective and Speedy is not bound.

5   On 1 November Adder, an accountant, receives through the post at his office a large volume entitled *Tax Made Easy*. Accompanying the volume is a note from the publishers, Messrs Galley & Co, stating that the volume will greatly assist Adder in his work and that if he does not reply within seven days Messrs Galley & Co will assume that he wishes to purchase the volume and they will expect to receive a remittance of £12.

Adder does not wish to purchase the book but forgets to reply to Galley & Co. At the end of the month he receives an invoice for £12 from the publishers.

Is Adder obliged to pay for the book?

Which one of the following statements is correct?

A   Adder must pay for the book since he did not tell Galley & Co within seven days that he did not want it.

B   Adder cannot be made to pay for the book but must return it to Galley & Co.

    C   Adder must pay for the book because it is a business not a private transaction.

    D   Adder cannot be made to pay for the book and need only make it available for Galley & Co to repossess.

6    Laura, a keen amateur photographer, wrote to Rex, who had just given up photography because of an eye injury, asking: 'Would you be prepared to sell me your Olympus camera?' Rex replied by letter saying: 'Would you be prepared to pay a fair price, say £350?'

    Laura thought £350 was a reasonable price but she had to sell her own camera in order to raise the money. She wrote to Rex saying: 'I accept your offer to let me have the Olympus at £350 but could you give me until the end of the month to pay?'

    In fact before Laura posted her letter Rex has sold the camera to Dan who had offered him £400.

    As regards the legal position of Laura and Rex:

    A   Rex is in breach of contract because Laura accepted his offer when she posted her letter of acceptance.

    B   Rex is not in breach of contract but he would have been if Laura's acceptance had not been a conditional counter-offer.

    C   Rex is not bound because he never made Laura an offer.

    D   Rex is not bound because when Laura accepted his offer it had been revoked by the sale of the camera to Dan.

7    The Midshires Hospital placed a newspaper advertisement inviting tenders to supply the hospital with fruit and vegetables. Miss Avan Apple, a local greengrocer, applied for a form on which to tender.

    Under the tender she agreed to supply 'such quantities of fruit and vegetables as may be required from 1 January to 31 December'. Miss Apple offered to supply such produce at 10 per cent below the current market price at the time orders were made. Her tender was accepted.

    The hospital ordered a quantity of produce in February and Miss Apple supplied it according to the terms agreed. No further order was received until September. Since Miss Apple had received only one previous order during the period of the tender she refused to deliver the second order.

    Which one of the following statements represents the legal position?

    A   Miss Apple is in breach of contract. A contract to supply fruit and vegetables throughout the year came into being when Midshires accepted her tender.

    B   Miss Apple is not in breach of contract. The Midshires' acceptance did not give rise to any contractual relationship.

    C   Miss Apple is in breach of contract in respect of her failure to supply the produce ordered in September but she can tell Midshires that she will not fulfil any further orders.

    D   Miss Apple is in breach of contract in respect of her failure to supply the produce ordered in September and her tender, being a standing offer, can be accepted by Midshires' orders until the end of the year since a standing offer cannot be revoked.

8    Dora lost her dog and advertised a reward of £50 to the finder. This appeared in the local paper and Clarence saw it. He later found the dog and returned it to Dora who thanked him profusely. She then said: 'There's a reward, you know,' and Clarence replied: 'Yes I know, but I would have brought it home anyway. I could see from its collar where it

lived and I am a great lover of dogs and hate to see them lost.' Dora who was a bit short of cash said to Clarence: 'Oh well, you will not want the reward then,' and slammed the door. Clarence who was also short of cash would like the reward.

Which one of the following statements represents the legal position?

A  Clarence is not entitled to the reward because the main reason for bringing the dog back was his love of dogs and not the reward.

B  Clarence is not entitled to the reward because all newspaper advertisements are invitations to treat and not offers.

C  Clarence is not entitled to the reward because he did not tell Dora he was looking for the dog and so never accepted her offer of a reward.

D  Clarence is entitled to the reward. He saw the offer and accepted by conduct, motive being irrelevant.

*Answers to questions set in objective mode appear on p 707.*

# 2 THE LAW OF CONTRACT – MAKING THE CONTRACT II

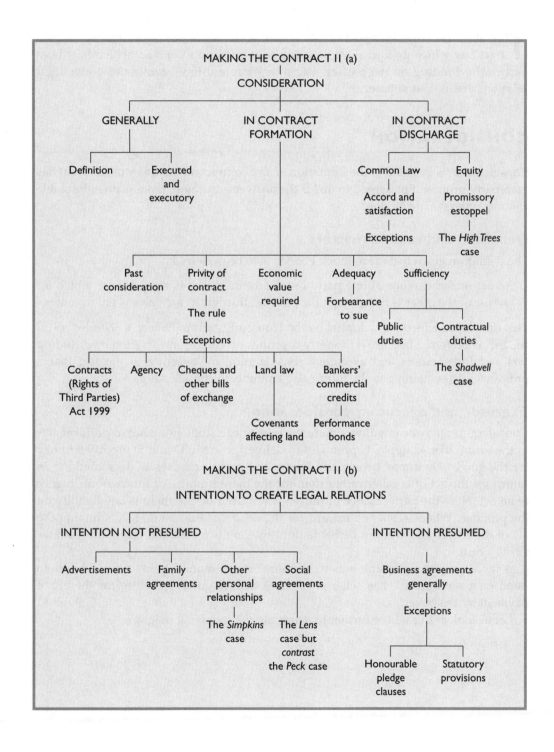

MAKING THE CONTRACT II (a)

CONSIDERATION

GENERALLY

IN CONTRACT FORMATION

IN CONTRACT DISCHARGE

Definition

Executed and executory

Common Law

Equity

Accord and satisfaction

Promissory estoppel

Exceptions

The *High Trees* case

Past consideration

Privity of contract

Economic value required

Adequacy

Sufficiency

The rule

Forbearance to sue

Exceptions

Public duties

Contractual duties

Contracts (Rights of Third Parties) Act 1999

Agency

Cheques and other bills of exchange

Land law

Bankers' commercial credits

The *Shadwell* case

Covenants affecting land

Performance bonds

MAKING THE CONTRACT II (b)

INTENTION TO CREATE LEGAL RELATIONS

INTENTION NOT PRESUMED

INTENTION PRESUMED

Advertisements

Family agreements

Other personal relationships

Social agreements

Business agreements generally

Exceptions

The *Simpkins* case

The *Lens* case but *contrast* the *Peck* case

Honourable pledge clauses

Statutory provisions

The objectives of this chapter are to continue the study of those elements of contract law which go to making *a mere agreement* into a *contract* which is at least *potentially* binding on the parties. Consideration and the intention to create legal relations are looked at here.

# CONSIDERATION

Consideration is essential to the formation of any contract not made by deed. What has each party promised or agreed to do? If the answer is nothing, there is no enforceable contract unless made by deed.

## Definition and related matters

The definition given by Sir Frederick Pollock is to be preferred:

> An act or forbearance of one party *or the promise thereof* is the price for which *the promise* of the other is bought and the promise thus given for value is enforceable.

This definition, which was adopted by the House of Lords in *Dunlop* v *Selfridge* [1915] AC 847, is preferred because it properly describes executed consideration by including acts and forbearances and executory consideration by referring to the fact that a promise to do something in the future also amounts to consideration.

## Executed and executory consideration

Consideration may be *executory* where the parties exchange promises to perform acts in the future. For example, C promises to deliver goods to D and D promises to pay for the goods. Or it may be *executed* where one party promises to do something in return for the act of another rather than for the mere promise of future performance of an act. Here the performance of the act is required before there is any liability on the promise. Where X offers a reward for the return of his lost dog, X is buying the act of the finder and will not be liable until the dog is found and returned. (And *see* *Carlill*'s case.)

A more commercial example is to be found in the request by a seller of goods to 'send cash with order'. The seller *promises* to deliver goods in return for the act of payment by the buyer.

Let us look at this a little further by studying the following diagram.

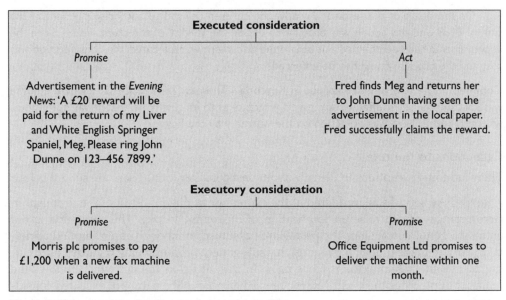

**Executed consideration**

*Promise*

Advertisement in the *Evening News*: 'A £20 reward will be paid for the return of my Liver and White English Springer Spaniel, Meg. Please ring John Dunne on 123–456 7899.'

*Act*

Fred finds Meg and returns her to John Dunne having seen the advertisement in the local paper. Fred successfully claims the reward.

**Executory consideration**

*Promise*

Morris plc promises to pay £1,200 when a new fax machine is delivered.

*Promise*

Office Equipment Ltd promises to deliver the machine within one month.

**Fig. 2.1  Executed and executory considerations**

## CONSIDERATION IN RELATION TO FORMATION OF CONTRACT

The main rules governing consideration in formation of contract are set out below.

### Past consideration

Sometimes the act which one party to a contract puts forward as consideration was performed before any promise of reward was made by the other. Where this is so, the act in question is regarded as past consideration and will not support a contractual claim. This somewhat technical rule seems to be based on the idea that the act of one party to an alleged contract can only be regarded as consideration if it was carried out in respect of some promise of the other. Where this is not so, the act is regarded as gratuitous, being carried out before any promise of reward was made.

**The following case provides a practical example of the operation of this rule.**

### Re McArdle [1951] 1 All ER 905

Certain children were entitled under their father's will to a house. However, their mother had a life interest in the property and during her lifetime one of the children and his wife came to live in the house with the mother. The wife carried out certain improvements to the property and, after she had done so, the children signed a document addressed to her saying: 'In consideration of your carrying out certain alterations and improvements to the property . . . at present occupied by you, the beneficiaries under the Will of William Edward McArdle hereby agree that the executors, the National Provincial Bank Ltd . . . shall repay to you from the said estate when so distributed the sum of £488 in settlement of the amount spent on such improvements

. . . '. On the death of the testator's widow the children refused to authorise payment of the sum of £488, and this action was brought to decide the validity of the claim. *Held* – Since the improvements had been carried out before the document was executed, the consideration was past and the promise could not be enforced.

**Comment:** The rule was also applied in Roscorla v Thomas (1842) 3 QB 234 where a horse was sold and the seller *after the sale* gave a warranty as to its quality, i.e. that it was not vicious, whereas it was. There was no action on the warranty by the buyer.

### Exceptions to the rule

There are some exceptions to the rule about past consideration. These are set out below.

(a) Where services are rendered at the express or implied request of the promisor in circumstances which raise an implication of a promise to pay. This exception is not entirely a genuine one since the promisor is assumed to have given an implied undertaking to pay at the time of the request, his subsequent promise being regarded as deciding merely the actual amount to be paid. In this situation the act which follows the request but precedes the settling of the reward is more in the nature of executed consideration which, as we have seen, will support a contract. Anyway, it is presumably true to say that if Mrs McArdle had been requested by her relatives to do the work, the consideration would not have been regarded as past and her claim would have succeeded.

**The following case provides an example of the position where the service is performed at the defendant's request in circumstances where the parties understand that payment will follow.**

### Re Casey's Patents, Stewart v Casey [1892] 1 Ch 104

Patents were granted to Stewart and another in respect of an invention concerning appliances and vessels for transporting and storing inflammable liquids. Stewart entered into an arrangement with Casey whereby Casey was to introduce the patents. Casey spent two years 'pushing' the invention and then the joint owners of the patent rights wrote to him as follows: 'In consideration of your service as the practical manager in working both patents we hereby agree to give you one-third share of the patents.' Casey also received the letters patent. Some time later Stewart died and his executors claimed the letters patent from Casey, suggesting that he had no interest in them because the consideration for the promise to give him a one-third share was past. *Held* – The previous request to render the services raised an implied promise to pay. The subsequent promise could be regarded as fixing the value of the services so that Casey was entitled to one-third share of the patent rights.

(b) Under s 27 of the Bills of Exchange Act 1882 an antecedent (or previous) debt or liability which is a form of past consideration will support a bill of exchange or cheque. This is essential particularly in the case of cheques, many of which are based upon this form of past consideration. Thus if S sells goods to B a debt comes into being payable in legal tender (i.e. bank notes or coins – *see further* Chapter 8) when the contract is made, so when B decides to pay S by cheque the cheque is based upon a previous or antecedent debt or liability and is for past consideration. However, this idea would not have helped Mrs McArdle if she had been paid by a cheque which was not paid. She could not have sued upon the cheque because what she had done did not create a previous or antecedent debt or liability.

(c)  Under s 29 of the Limitation Act 1980 a person who owes another a debt, or that person's agent if properly authorised, can make a written acknowledgment of the existence of the debt to the creditor or his agent. This extends the time for which the creditor can sue for his debt though once the debt is statute barred, e.g. because it was incurred more than six years previously, it cannot be revived in this way (*see further* Chapter 9). It appears at first sight as if this is an exception to the rule about past consideration because the acknowledgment is supported by a past debt. However, the exception is not wholly genuine because the 1980 Act simply states that *no consideration of any kind* need be looked for.

It should be noted that the Contracts (Rights of Third Parties) Act 1999 has no effect on the rule that consideration must not be past. The 1999 Act has an effect where A contracts with B to give a benefit to C. In these circumstances C may have rights under the 1999 Act to sue A for a failure to perform the contract. However, if the consideration moving between A and B is past, the contract is not enforceable by B or C and the 1999 Act does not apply to change that situation.

## Consideration must move from the promisee and the doctrine of privity of contract

If A wishes to sue successfully upon a promise made by B, it is essential for A (as the recipient of the promise – the promisee) to show that he gave consideration to B (the promisor). The concept is based upon a fundamental assumption of English law that a contract is a bargain. If a person furnishes no consideration, he takes no part in a bargain: if he takes no part in a bargain, he takes no part in a contract.

This general requirement that consideration must be given to support a contractual promise – unless made by deed – remains valid and is not changed by the Contracts (Rights of Third Parties) Act 1999.

There was much discussion as to whether the doctrine was based on consideration or whether it was a matter of privity, i.e. not being a party to the contract. It became settled that consideration was the crucial matter in English law. Thus, at common law if A and B contract to benefit C, C cannot sue because he has not supplied consideration and also because he is not a party. However, it is also clear that if A contracts with B and C to benefit C, C still cannot sue at common law unless he has supplied consideration or unless the contract is by deed where consideration is not required. In all cases B, or his executors, can sue on behalf of C.

Thus for all practical purposes the concepts are similar but not quite identical. The rule about privity of contract states that a person cannot sue unless he is a party to the contract. The rule about consideration moving from the promisee takes matters a step further as regards contracts not made by deed by stating that even if a person is a party to a contract he cannot sue upon it unless he has provided consideration.

This rule will continue to apply, e.g. in a case where the term of a contract purports to confer a benefit on a third party but excludes his right to sue on it as the 1999 Act allows (*see* s 1(2) of the 1999 Act). For example, a holding company may enter into a contract with A to supply goods to one of its subsidiaries but exclude the subsidiary's right to sue upon it because the holding company wishes to retain to itself relevant contractual remedies should A fail in his obligation. This might be particularly so where the subsidiary was not wholly owned by the holding company. Conversely, it will now be possible for a holding company to make contracts for the benefit of its subsidiaries and give them the right to sue for breach of the contract also. This was not possible before because of the requirement of consideration

**The following cases provide an illustration of the old common law rules and enable us to set the cases in the context of the new law.**

### Dunlop v Selfridge [1915] AC 847

The appellants were motor tyre manufacturers and sold tyres to Messrs Dew & Co who were motor accessory dealers. Under the terms of the contract Dew & Co agreed not to sell the tyres below Dunlop's list price, i.e. £4.05 per tyre, and as Dunlop's agents, to obtain from other traders a similar undertaking. In return for this undertaking Dew & Co were to receive discounts, some of which they could pass on to retailers who bought tyres. Selfridge & Co accepted two orders from customers for Dunlop covers at a lower price. They obtained the covers through Dew & Co and signed an agreement not to sell or offer the tyres below list price. It was further agreed that £5.00 per tyre so sold should be paid to Dunlop by way of liquidated damages. Selfridge supplied one of the two tyres ordered below list price, i.e. at £3.65 per tyre. They did not actually supply the other, but informed the customer that they could only supply it at list price. The appellants claimed an injunction and damages against the respondents for breach of the agreement made with Dew & Co, claiming that Dew & Co were their agents in the matter. *Held* – There was no contract between the parties. Dunlop could not enforce the contract made between the respondents and Dew & Co because they had not supplied consideration. Even if Dunlop were undisclosed principals, there was no consideration moving between them and the respondents. The discount received by Selfridge was part of that given by Dunlop to Dew & Co. Since Dew & Co were not bound to give any part of their discount to retailers, the discount received by Selfridge operated only as consideration between themselves and Dew & Co and could not be claimed by Dunlop as consideration to support a promise not to sell below list price.

### *Present legal position*

Apart from the valuable definition of consideration which was given in the case and which has already been referred to, the case would now be dealt with under the Competition Act 1998. A resale price agreement is outlawed by s 2(2)(a) of the Competition Act 1998 as an agreement preventing, restricting or distorting competition. Part I Chapter III of the 1998 Act deals with enforcement which is in the hands of the Director-General of Fair Trading by means of the imposition of cash penalties. The 1998 Act is further considered in Chapter 7 of this book.

If a company operated today as Dunlop did then, it would be investigated by the Director-General and appropriate penalties imposed.

So far as the contract itself is concerned, the automatic result of breaching the 1998 Act is to make the offending provisions of the agreement null and void so that they are unenforceable by organisations such as Dunlop in this case. If it is possible to sever other provisions in the contract, these may be enforced so it may well be that the court would allow an action by a buyer who has taken goods under the contract for breach of condition or warranty in regard to the quality of the goods. The resale price aspect of the agreement would obviously be unenforceable.

*The possibility of claims by individuals where the 1998 Act is infringed are considered in Chapter 7.*

## Beswick v Beswick [1967] 2 All ER 1197

A coal merchant agreed to sell the business to his nephew in return for a weekly consultancy fee of £6.50 payable during his lifetime, and after his death an annuity of £5 per week was to be payable to his widow for her lifetime. After the agreement was signed the nephew took over the business and paid his uncle the sum of £6.50 as agreed. The uncle died on 3 November 1963, and the nephew paid the widow one sum of £5 and then refused to pay her any more. On 30 June 1964, the widow became the administratrix of her husband's estate, and on 15 July 1964 she brought an action against the nephew for arrears of the weekly sums and for specific performance of the agreement for the future. She sued in her capacity as administratrix of the estate and also in her personal capacity. Her action failed at first instance and on appeal to the Court of Appeal, it was decided amongst other things that:

(a) specific performance could in a proper case be ordered of a contract to pay money;
(b) 'property' in s 56(1) of the Law of Property Act 1925 included a contractual claim not concerned with realty and that therefore a third party could sue on a contract to which he was a stranger. The widow's claim in her personal capacity was therefore good (*per* Denning MR and Danckwerts LJ);
(c) the widow's claim as administratrix was good because she was not suing in her personal capacity but on behalf of her deceased husband who had been a party to the agreement;
(d) no trust in her favour could be inferred.

There was further appeal to the House of Lords, though not on the creation of a trust, and there it was held that the widow's claim as administratrix succeeded, and that specific performance of a contract to pay money could be granted in a proper case. However, having decided the appeal on these grounds, their Lordships went on to say that the widow's personal claim would have failed because s 56 of the Law of Property Act 1925 was limited to cases involving realty. The 1925 Act was a consolidating not a codifying measure so that, if it contained words which were capable of more than one construction, effect should be given to the construction which did not alter the law. It was accepted that when the present provision was contained in the Real Property Act 1845, it had applied only to realty. Although s 205(1) of the 1925 Act appeared to have extended the provision to personal property, including things in action, it was expressly qualified by the words: 'unless the context otherwise requires', and it was felt that Parliament had not intended to sweep away the rule of privity by what was in effect a sidewind.

*Comment:* It is unlikely that s 56 does have a very wide application. The sub-section says that a person may take the benefit of an agreement although he is not 'named as a party'. The legislation does not say that he need not be a party. There are those who take the view, therefore, that s 56(1) is designed to cover the situation where there is a covenant over land in favour of, say, 'the owner of Whiteacre', so that the owner of Whiteacre could benefit from the covenant, provided he could be ascertained, even though he was not named in the instrument creating the covenant. If this interpretation is correct then s 56(1) of the 1925 Act has little effect on the law of contract generally.

### Present legal position

The circumstances of this case are ideal for the use of the Contracts (Rights of Third Parties) Act 1999. If the contract between the coal merchant and his nephew had expressly provided that the widow could sue, she would have succeeded in her personal capacity and the case would probably never have come to court. In any case, s 1 (1)(b) of the Act applies in that the contract conferred a benefit on her which in itself would have allowed her to claim under the 1999 Act, on the assumption that her rights had not been excluded as the 1999 Act allows. This allows the rather more straightforward rules of the 1999 Act to apply. Before, the only way to confer benefits on a third party who could sue for failure to give them was to enter into a deed or set up a trust where the law is much more complicated and to an extent uncertain.

## The remedies of the promisee

If A makes a contract with B for the benefit of C then, if the contract is not made by deed and C has not given or promised any consideration, and his rights under the Contracts (Rights of Third Parties) Act 1999 are excluded as the Act allows, C cannot sue A for breach. B can, of course, but what are his remedies?

**The following case and comment are illustrative of the legal position.**

### Jackson v Horizon Holidays [1975] 3 All ER 92

Mr Jackson sued successfully on a contract *he made* with the defendants to provide a holiday which, in the event, was not of the high standard described in the brochure. He received damages for his own loss and disappointment, and for that of his family since the contract was *also made for their benefit.*

*Comment:* (i) This judgment by Lord Denning has been much criticised since it infringes a very old rule of English contract law which states that if A contracts with B in return for B's promise to do something for C, then if B repudiates the contract, C has no enforceable claim, and A is restricted to an action for nominal damages by reason of his having suffered no loss. The judgment was criticised by the House of Lords in *Beswick (see above)* and again in *Woodar Investment Development* v *Wimpey Construction (UK)* [1980] 1 All ER 571 and must, therefore, be regarded with caution. The problem was rather neatly overcome in *Beswick* because the House of Lords, unusually, granted specific performance. However, four Law Lords said that if damages had been awarded they would have been nominal only, though Lord Pearce would have awarded substantial damages. It was suggested in *Woodar* that if *Jackson* could be justified it might be on the basis that the booking of a holiday for a family and/or the ordering of meals for oneself and others in restaurants may be a special case so that the person who makes the booking or gives the order can obtain damages in respect of loss suffered by other persons in the party. If damages are so recovered then, according to Lord Denning in *Jackson*, the recipient must hand the relevant shares over to the other members of the party, and if he does not they could sue him in quasi-contract (*see further* Chapter 9).

(ii) The court may allow a party to the contract to recover the full loss suffered by a third party who was to benefit if the case can be regarded as an *exception to the general rule* that a claimant can only recover damages for his own loss and that a claimant who sues on behalf of the loss of others will only recover nominal damages. Such a situation came before the House of Lords in *Linden Gardens Trust Ltd* v *Lenesta Sludge Disposals Ltd* [1993] 3 All ER 417 where the owner of a site made a building contract with a contractor to erect offices shops and flats. The developed site was transferred to a third party who suffered loss because of bad workmanship by the contractor. The site owner sued for damages and was awarded full damages even though he had parted with the site, but only because their Lordships found that *on the facts* the parties to the contract had envisaged that the site would be transferred to a third party and the contractor had impliedly taken on liability to him. This was merely an exception to the general rule. *The solution is now clear:* make sure that your third-party beneficiaries are named in the contract and then they will be able to sue in their own right under the Contracts (Rights of Third Parties) Act 1999. It may well be that the 1999 Act would have applied here without naming the third party specifically since the 1999 Act allows identification to be by description, e.g. 'the purchaser of the Greenacres development'. This would be the correct approach by a business where the purchaser was not identified at the time of the contract. In addition, the third party need not, under the Act, be in existence at the time of the contract so that if a company is to be formed to purchase the development and is identified, e.g. as the 'company which is to be formed to purchase the Greenacre development', then the company on formation and purchase could sue under the contract for any loss. These are some of the business applications of the 1999 Act.

## Exceptions to the rule of privity

There are, however, some exceptions to the rule, the most important of which in examination terms are as follows.

### The Contracts (Rights of Third Parties) Act 1999

This Act provides for a major and far-reaching method of preventing the application of the privity rule. The Act brings English law into line with the position in Scotland, in most member states of the European Union and in many of the common law countries of the world, including the USA. The harmonisation of business law in this way is of benefit to the business community.

The Act implements the recommendations of the Law Commission in Report No 242, 'Privity of Contract: Contracts for the Benefit of Third Parties', published in July 1996. Before looking at its provisions, it should be noted that there is no change to the rule of law which states that a burden cannot be imposed on a third party without his consent. Thus, in general terms, a person can assign the right to receive money owed to him but cannot without the consent of all parties assign the burden of paying his debts. The Act deals only with the conferring of benefits on third parties.

The provisions of the Act section by section are set out below:

### Section 1

This section is at the heart of the Act. It deals with the circumstances in which a third party may have the right to enforce a term of a contract. He will have that right:

- where the contract contains an express term saying so;
- where a term of the contract purports to confer a benefit on him.

Thus in *Beswick* v *Beswick* (1967) the contract did not actually say that the aunt could sue, but it clearly purported to confer a benefit on her. This part of s 1 will not apply if it appears on a true construction of the contract that the contracting parties did not intend the third party to have a right to enforce it. Thus, if a contract confers a benefit on a child, it may also provide specifically that any claim in respect of it should be brought by either of its parents and in such a case the child could not bring a claim under the Act. The parents would have the third-party rights. In order to acquire the third-party right, the party concerned must be expressly identified in the contract but need not be identified by name. It is enough if the third party is identified as a member of a class, e.g. 'both of my children', or answers to a particular description, as in the *Beswick* case of a 'widow' of a party to a contract which was made during that party's lifetime.

In addition, so long as the third party is adequately described, that party need not be in existence when the contract is made. It might, therefore, be, in the business context, that a company as yet not incorporated but to be incorporated may take benefits under a contract made by its promoter.

Remedies available to the third party will be the same as those available to a party to a contract bringing an action for its breach and the rules relating to damages, injunctions, specific performance and other relief will apply, as will mitgation of loss. Section 1 also defines 'promisor' and 'promisee' as used in the Act. The *promisor* is the person against whom the contractual term is enforceable by the third party. The *promisee* is the contracting party by whom the term is enforceable against the promisor. Thus in a contract by A with B for the benefit of C, A is the promisor and B is the promisee. C sues under third-party rights. Section 1 also makes it clear that the third party may take *advantage* of any exclusion or limitation clause in the contract.

### Section 2

This restricts the way in which the contracting parties can alter the third party's entitlement under the contract without his consent once the third party has the right to enforce the term. There may be no variation or cancellation of the contract after the third party has accepted the term as by written notice to the promisor or relied on it when the promisor knows of or can reasonably be expected to have foreseen that reliance. Suppose A, a wealthy businesswoman, sells one of the many businesses that she owns to B in return for the payment of an annuity of £15,000 a year to her favourite nephew Sam, by B. So long as Sam has not accepted the payment term, A and B could alter it to, say, £12,000 a year, but once Sam has accepted it or, say, B has made a payment under it and can be assumed to expect that Sam will rely on getting future payments, the term cannot be altered without Sam's consent. If he never accepts or if there is no evidence of reliance, Sam is still entitled to the payment, but it could be altered without his consent. Acceptance by post is not effective until received by the promisor. This is contrary to the general rules of contractual acceptance by post. In keeping with the Act's preservation of the freedom of the parties to make their own contract, the above rules relating to third-party consent may be displaced by an express term of the contract providing that the contract can be cancelled or varied without the third party's consent. Where the consent of the third party is required, the court may on the application of both parties to the contract dispense with that consent where:

- it cannot be obtained because his or her whereabouts are unknown; or
- he or she is mentally incapable of giving consent.

This will enable the parties to the contract to change the third-party beneficiary or to remove the contract term so that there are not third-party rights in it.

The courts having power to make the variation are the High Court and the county court.

### Section 3

This deals with the defences, set-offs and counter-claims available to the promisor in proceedings by a third party to enforce a term of the contract. Illustrations are as follows:

- The third party cannot enforce the contract if it is void as where it is affected by agreement, mistake (*see* Chapter 4) or illegality (*see* Chapter 7) or has been discharged as where the promisor has performed the contract, e.g. by making a payment or supplying goods under it, or is unenforceable as where the third party is given rights on a contract of guarantee which is not evidenced in writing (*see* Chapter 3 – Formalities). This provision follows from the fact that in the circumstances the promisee could not enforce it either (s 3(2)).
- A (the promisor) contracts with B (the promisee) that B will sell goods to A who will pay the price of the goods to C (the third party). If B delivers sub-standard goods to A in breach of contract and A is sued by C for the price, then A is entitled to counter-claim to reduce or extinguish the price by reason of B's breach of contract. B could also be faced by this counter-claim if he or she were to sue A (s 3(2)).
- A and B make a contract under which A will pay C if B transfers his car to A. B already owes money to A under a different and unrelated contract, say, in connection with the previous sale of a van. A and B agree to an express term (as the Act requires) in the contract which states that A can raise against a claim by C any matter which would have given A a defence or set-off to a claim by B. Thus, in a claim by C for the money, A can set off what he is owed by B (s 3(3)).

Section 3 also makes clear that the promisor also has available any defence or set off and any counter-claim not arising from the contract with B but which is specific to the third party.

Illustrations are as follows:

- A contracts with B to pay C £2,000. C already owes A £600. A may set off against any claim by C the £600 and need only pay C £1,400.
- C induces a contract between A and B for the benefit of C by misrepresentation, of which B is unaware. A has a defence or a counter-claim for damages when sued by C which he or she would not have had against B (s 3(4)).

The agreement may specifically provide e.g. that A will not raise set-off or counter-claim in an action by C (s 3(5)).

### Section 4

This states that the Act does not affect the rights of the promisee A to enforce any term of the contract, including the term which benefits the third party. Thus B can sue on behalf of C.

## Section 5

This states that if the promisee B has already recovered a sum by way of damages for the promisor's breach, then in a claim by the third party C this sum will be taken into account in terms of any sum recovered by C. This is to prevent A from suffering a double liability.

## Section 6

This excludes certain types of contract from the operation of the Act. Main examples are:

- A third party is prevented from suing an employee for a breach of his contract of employment. Without this exception there could be a risk that workers taking lawful industrial action might be sued and restricted from doing so in unexpected ways. It is worth noting here that the Trade Union and Labour Relations (Consolidation) Act 1992 gives individuals the right to bring proceedings to halt *unlawful* industrial action which deprives them of goods and services.
- The s 6 provisions also prevent third-party rights arising from the 'deemed' contracts under s 14(1) of the Companies Act 1985 under which the memorandum and articles of a registered company constitute a contract between the company and its members in respect of their rights as such. The special nature of these deemed contracts makes them unsuitable for enforcement by a third party under the 1999 Act, which is a general reform. These contracts are considered in more detail in Chapter 18.

Also excluded are contracts for the carriage of goods by sea, as are contracts for the international carriage of goods by road, rail or air, which are covered by international conventions. Nevertheless the Act allows third parties to enforce exclusion or limitation of liability clauses in the above contracts. For example, the person who charters a ship may make a contract with the owner of the goods being carried that the shipowner is not liable for damage resulting from negligent stowage. The Act enables the shipowner as a third party to rely on that exclusion clause should the owner of the goods sue him. The business application is that the price of the carriage will be cheaper if the shipowner knows he can rely on the clause. In a similar way, exclusions and defences available to the carrier of goods can be extended to employees' agents and independent contractors such as stevedores engaged in loading and unloading, and will be effective without the legal gymnastics seen in *New Zealand Shipping Co Ltd* v *A M Satterthwaite & Co Ltd* (1974). This case is considered on p 51. Contracts contained in a bill of exchange promissory note or other negotiable instrument are also excluded (*see below*).

## Section 7

This preserves any rights or remedies which may be available to a party at common law or by statute apart from the Act, for example, by making ineffective a contractual provision which tries to exclude liability for personal injury or death. However, the section ensures that a third party cannot use the 'reasonableness' test under s 2(2) of the Unfair Contract Terms Act 1977 to try to defeat a clause excluding liability for other damage caused by negligence on the ground that the exclusion is unreasonable. (*See further* Chapter 6.) The policy of the Act is to let the parties decide to what extent they should by sued by the third party. The opposing view that the policy of the law should be against unreasonable terms in contracts whoever relies on them and in whatever situation did not prevail.

### Agency

A principal may sue on a contract made by an agent. This exception is perhaps more apparent than real because in fact the principal is the contracting party who has merely acted through the instrumentality of the agent.

### Cheques and bills of exchange

The holder for value of a cheque or bill of exchange can sue prior parties. Thus if A buys goods from B and pays by cheque or other bill of exchange which B then endorses over to C, his son, as a birthday present, then C can sue A although no consideration moved from him to A. C cannot sue B because as between immediate parties absence of consideration makes a claim impossible.

The example has been made a bit impractical so far as cheques are concerned by the passing of the Cheques Act 1992. This makes clear that a cheque crossed 'account payee' or 'a/c payee' with or without the word 'only' is not transferable. The banks are now printing 'account payee' on cheques issued to customers and reinforcing the non-transferability rule by removing the words 'or order' after the payee's name and inserting 'only'. However, the example is quite valid as regards bills of exchange which are not cheques since these remain transferable unless crossed 'account payee' but this is a matter for the parties and bills of exchange which are not so crossed remain transferable. So it is now better to use the bill of exchange proper as an example and not a cheque.

As we have seen, the Contracts (Rights of Third Parties) Act 1999 does not apply to these instruments.

### Land law

The position in land law is that benefits and liabilities attached to or imposed on land may in some circumstances follow the land into the hands of other owners.

**The following cases provide an illustration of this exception.**

### Smith and Snipes Hall Farm Ltd v River Douglas Catchment Board
[1949] 2 All ER 179

In 1938 the defendants entered into an agreement with 11 persons owning land adjoining a certain stream that, on the landowners paying some part of the cost, the defendants would improve the banks of the stream and maintain the said banks for all time. In 1940 one landowner sold her land to Smith, and in 1944 Smith leased the land to Snipes Hall Farm Ltd. In 1946, because of the defendants' negligence, the banks burst and the adjoining land was flooded. *Held* – The claimants could enforce the covenant in the agreement of 1938 even though they were not parties to it. The covenants were for the benefit of the land and affected its use and value and could, therefore, be transferred with it.

### Tulk v Moxhay (1848) 2 Ph 774

The claimant was the owner of several plots of land in Leicester Square and in 1808 he sold one of them to a person called Elms. Elms agreed, for himself, his heirs and assigns, 'to keep the Square Gardens open as a pleasure ground and uncovered with buildings'. After a number of conveyances, the land was sold to the defendant who claimed a right to build on it. The claimant sued for an injunction preventing the development of the land. The defendant, while admitting that he purchased the land with notice of the covenant, claimed that he was not bound by it because he had not himself entered into it. *Held* – An injunction to restrain building would be granted because there was a jurisdiction in equity to prevent, by way of injunction, acts inconsistent with a restrictive covenant on land, so long as the land was acquired with notice of that covenant, and the defendant retains land which can benefit from the covenant.

*Comment:* (i) Such notice may now be constructive where the covenant is registered under land charges legislation. It is assumed everybody knows about the covenant whether they have seen the register or not.

(ii) It was held in *Roake* v *Chadha* [1983] 3 All ER 503 that whether a covenant runs with the land depends upon its wording. If the words used in it prevent the benefit of the covenant, in this case that the plot holder of land would not build more than one house on it, passing to a subsequent owner of the land unless *specifically assigned* to him by the present owner, then the covenant would not run with the land as such but would pass to subsequent owners only if assigned to them. Since this had not been done the claimant, a subsequent owner, could not prevent the defendant from building two houses on his adjoining plot.

These rules of land law remain valid and are unaffected by the Contracts (Rights of Third Parties) Act 1999.

### Leases

The rule of privity of contract had an unfortunate effect on leases of land in the sense that if the original tenant under the lease assigned his tenancy to another tenant with the landlord's consent the original tenant, being in privity with the landlord, could not get rid of the duties under the lease. If, therefore, the person to whom the lease was assigned did not, for example, pay the rent the original assignee could be required to do so and this remained the case where there were further assignments to other assignees. The Landlord and Tenant (Covenants) Act 1996 abolished this liability in the original tenant so that the landlord will only be able to sue the tenant for the time being unless there is an authorised guarantee agreement in force. Under the Act a landlord may require an assigning tenant to enter into a guarantee with the landlord as a condition of the landlord giving his assent to the lease being assigned. Under such an agreement the outgoing tenant would guarantee the performance of the terms of the lease, e.g. payment of rent by his *immediate* (but not subsequent) assignee.

The rules relating to leases are contained in the Landlord and Tenant (Covenants) Act 1996 which applies to the exclusion of the Contracts (Rights of Third Parties) Act 1999.

### Bankers' commercial credits and performance bonds

Bankers' commercial credits also present problems in the field of privity. It is common practice for an exporter, E, to ask the buyer of the goods, B, to open with his banker a credit in favour of E, the credit to remain irrevocable for a specified time. B agrees with his banker that the credit should be opened and in return promises to pay the banker and usually gives him a lien over the shipping documents. The banker will also require a commission for his services. B's banker then notifies E that a credit has been opened in his favour and E can draw upon it on presentation of the shipping documents.

It will be seen that E and B's banker are not in privity of contract. It might be thought that this could give rise to problems in the unlikely event that the banker did not pay. However, this is not so. In fact the buyer/customer of the bank cannot stop payment. In *Malas (Hamzeh)* v *British Imex* [1958] 1 All ER 262 the claimants, who were buyers of goods, applied to the court for an injunction restraining the sellers, who were the defendants in the case, from drawing under a credit established by the buyers' bankers. The Court of Appeal refused to grant this injunction and Jenkins LJ said: 'The opening of a confirmed letter of credit constitutes a bargain between the banker and the vendor of the goods which imposes on the banker an absolute obligation to pay . . . '. Sellers LJ said that there could well be exceptions where the court would exercise a jurisdiction to grant an injunction, as where there was a fraudulent transaction. However, in other situations the binding nature of the bankers' commercial credit is an exception to privity of contract.

There are similar developments rendering performance bonds enforceable by commercial custom, so that where a bank guarantees performance of an export contract by the supplier the bank must pay the buyer if the contract is not performed.

There is no reason why the rights of exporters to sue the relevant bank should not be contained in the contract between B and his banker to provide the credit. However, the rule that the bank always pays (fraud apart) is so much part of international commerce that the case law rules may well be felt sufficient in themselves.

## Economic value

Consideration must be real, which means capable of estimation in terms of economic value.

**This matter has not received much attention in the courts but the following case is an example of its application.**

### White v Bluett (1853) 23 LJ Ex 36

This action was brought by White who was the executor of Bluett's father's estate. The claimant, White, alleged that Bluett had not paid a promissory note given to his father during his lifetime. Bluett admitted that he had given the note to his father, but said that his father had released him from it in return for a promise not to keep on complaining about the fact that he had been disinherited. *Held* – The defence failed and the defendant was liable on the note. The promise not to complain was not real consideration to support his release from the note.

*Comment:* This case illustrates the general point that on formation of contract consideration must be capable of expression in terms of value. On its facts, of course, the case is concerned with consideration on discharge of a contract, in this case the alleged discharge of the promissory note, where the rule is the same. It is the only major illustration of the need for economic value and serves to illustrate the formation rule as well. In addition, the decision seems to be based upon the fact that the son had no right to complain of his disinheritance so that he was not giving up anything which he had a right to. As the judge, Chief Baron Pollock, said: 'the son had no right to complain, for the father might make what distribution of his property he liked; and the son's abstaining from doing what he had no right to do can be of no consideration'.

## Adequacy of consideration

Provided that the consideration satisfies the test of economic value, the court will not normally concern itself with its adequacy. Thus the amount of the consideration offered need not be what the average person would think to be satisfactory. A person who is making a contract is usually able to offer as little as he thinks the other party will accept in return for the promise of that party.

Why is this? Basically because the courts do not exist to repair bad bargains and though consideration must be present, the parties themselves must attend to its value. Under this principle it would be possible to enforce a contract to purchase a Rolls-Royce for a penny; both a Rolls-Royce and a penny are consideration. Obviously inadequate consideration gives rise to suspicion of fraud, duress or undue influence, and possibly unsoundness of mind, but if these are not proved the contract is good. Thus in *Thomas v Thomas* (1842) 2 QB 851 the claimant's husband had expressed the wish that the claimant, if she survived him, should have the use of his house. He left a will of which his brothers were executors. The will made no mention of the testator's wish that his wife should be given the house. The executors knew of the testator's wish and agreed to allow the widow to occupy the house on payment of £1 per year for as long as she remained a widow. The claimant remained in possession of the house until the death of one of the executors, Samuel Thomas. The other executor then turned her out. She sued him for breach of contract. It was held that the claimant's promise to pay £1 a year was consideration and need not be adequate. The action for breach of contract succeeded.

**The following case is also an illustration of the rule of nominal consideration though set in a somewhat complicated commercial situation.**

### Chappell & Co Ltd v Nestlé Co Ltd [1959] 2 All ER 701

The claimants owned the copyright in a dance tune called 'Rockin' Shoes', and the defendants were using records of this tune as part of an advertising scheme. A record company made the records for Nestlé who advertised them to the public for 7½p each but required in addition three wrappers from their 2½p bars of chocolate. When they received the wrappers they threw them away. The claimants sued the defendants for infringement of copyright. It appeared that under the Copyright Act of 1956 a person recording musical works for retail sale need not get the permission of the holder of the copyright, but had merely to serve him with notice and pay 6¼ per cent of the retail selling price as royalty. The claimants asserted that the defendants were not retailing the goods in the sense of the Act and must therefore get permission to use the musical work. The basis of the claimants' case was that retailing meant selling entirely for money, and that as the defendants were selling for money plus wrappers, they needed the claimants' consent. The defence was that the sale was for cash because the wrappers were not part of the consideration. *Held* – The claimants succeeded because the wrappers were part of the consideration and the question of their adequacy did not arise.

*Comment:* (i) Presumably the wrappers could have formed the whole consideration.

(ii) The statutory licence to copy records sold by retail was granted by s 8 of the Copyright Act 1956. This was repealed by the Copyright, Designs and Patents Act 1988, Sch 1, para 21, and permission to reproduce is now required even by those retailing the records. However, the fact was that the wrappers were part of the consideration and the House of Lords ruling as to adequacy survives as a relevant example.

## Forbearance to sue

Although there were once arguments to the contrary, it is now accepted that forbearance to sue may be adequate consideration. It is not necessary to show that the action would have succeeded but merely that if it had been brought to trial it might have done. Thus the court would be unlikely to accept that a bookmaker could supply consideration by forgoing a claim against a client for stake money. Such an action, being based upon an illegal transaction, could have no hope of success.

The person who forbears to sue may actually promise not to do so or merely forbear in fact. A promise is not essential provided the evidence is that there was some causal connection between the forbearance and the acts of the parties.

**The following case is an illustration of implied forbearance.**

### Horton v Horton [1960] 3 All ER 649

The parties were husband and wife. In March 1954, by a separation agreement under seal, the husband agreed to pay the wife £30 a month. On the true construction of the deed the husband should have deducted income tax before payment but for nine months he paid the money without deductions. In January 1955 he signed a document, not under seal, agreeing that instead of 'the monthly sum of £30' he would pay a monthly sum as 'after deduction of income tax should amount to the clear sum of £30'. For over three years he paid this clear sum but then stopped payment. To an action by his wife he pleaded that the later agreement was unsupported by consideration and that the wife could sue only on the earlier deed. *Held* – by the Court of Appeal – that there was consideration to support the later agreement. It was clear that the original deed did not implement the intention of the parties. The wife, therefore, might have sued to rectify the deed and the later agreement represented a compromise of this possible action. Whether such an action would have succeeded was irrelevant; it sufficed that it had some prospect of success and that the wife believed in it.

## Existing duties and consideration – the rule of sufficiency

Whether the performance of an existing duty can amount to consideration is a matter which is often considered under the heading of 'sufficiency of consideration'. To many people the difference between the words 'adequacy' and 'sufficiency' is either small or non-existent. However, to lawyers the two words encompass very different ideas. Adequacy is concerned with the amount of economic value to be supplied or promised. Sufficiency is concerned with the question whether there is any consideration at all. Three main situations should be noted. They are set out below.

### Discharge of a public duty

The discharge of a public duty imposed by law is not consideration. However, where the contractual duty is not precisely coincident with the public duty but is in excess of it, performance of the contractual duty may provide consideration.

**The cases which follow provide illustrations of these rules.**

### Collins v Godefroy (1831) 1 B & Ad 950

The claimant was subpoenaed to give evidence for the defendant in an action to which the defendant was a party. The claimant now sued for the sum of six guineas which he said the defendant had promised him for his attendance. *Held* – The claimant's action failed because there was no consideration for the promise. Lord Tenterden said: 'If it be a duty imposed by law upon a party regularly subpoenaed to attend from time to time to give evidence, then a promise to give him any remuneration for loss of time incurred in such attendance is a promise without consideration.'

### Glasbrook Bros v Glamorgan County Council [1925] AC 270

The question had arisen as to how best to protect a coal mine during a strike. The police authorities thought it enough to provide a mobile force but the colliery manager wanted a stationary guard. It was ultimately agreed to provide the latter at a rate of payment which involved the sum of £2,200. The company refused to pay and when sued pleaded the absence of consideration. The House of Lords gave judgment for the claimants. The police were bound to afford protection but they had a discretion as to the form it should take, and an undertaking to provide more protection than in their discretion they deemed necessary was consideration for the promise of reward.

*Comment:* This case was applied in *Harris v Sheffield United Football Club* [1987] 2 All ER 838 where Boreham J held that the provision of policemen at a football ground to keep law and order was the provision of special services by the police. The police authority is under a duty to protect persons and property against crime or threatened crime for which no payment is due. However, the police have no public duty to protect persons and property against the mere fear of possible future crime. The claim of the police authority for some £70,000 for police services provided at the defendants' football ground over 15 months was allowed. The judge's decision was affirmed by the Court of Appeal.

### Ward v Byham [1956] 2 All ER 318

An unmarried mother sued to recover a maintenance allowance by the father of the child. The defence was that, under s 42 of the National Assistance Act 1948, the mother of an illegitimate child was bound to maintain it. However, it appeared that in return for the promise of an allowance the mother had promised:

(a) to look after the child well and ensure that it was happy; and
(b) to allow it to decide whether it should live with her or the father.

*Held* – There was sufficient consideration to support the promise of an allowance because the promises given in (a) and (b) above were in excess of the statutory duty, which was merely to care for the child.

*Comment:* 'Is a promise to make a child happy real consideration?' (*see White v Bluett* (1853) *above*). This point is not taken in the above case and shows the considerable power which judges have to find or not to find contractual obligations and, in a sense, to manufacture an element of consideration to get round the public duty rule in what appears to have been a deserving case.

*The business application:* While students should have a knowledge of the rules relating to adequacy and sufficiency of consideration, it has to be said that the concepts are unlikely to be met with in business, at least not very often. The reason is simple: those in business seldom if ever (perhaps never) enter into commercial transactions for nothing or for inadequate prices or fees. The problem in business (and for the consumer) is to prevent oneself from being charged too much!

### Discharge of contractual duties under a contract with the same party

The performance of a contractual duty already owed to the defendant is not consideration. However, the carrying out of some additional act beyond what has already been contracted for does provide consideration.

**The following cases make the point.**

### Stilk *v* Myrick (1809) 2 Camp 317

A sea-captain, being unable to find any substitutes for two sailors who had deserted, promised to divide the wages of the deserters among the rest of the crew if they would work the ship home shorthanded. *Held* – The promise was not enforceable because of absence of consideration. In sailing the ship home the crew had done no more than they were already bound to do. Their original contract obliged them to meet the normal emergencies of the voyage of which minor desertions were one.

*Comment:* (i) It must be said that the decision in *Stilk* took a nasty knock in *Williams* v *Roffey Bros and Nicholls (Contractors) Ltd* [1990] 1 All ER 512. The defendants in that case were building contractors. They made a contract to refurbish a block of 27 flats and engaged Mr Williams to carry out carpentry work for £20,000. This turned out to be too low to enable Mr Williams to operate at a profit and after completing some of the flats and receiving interim payments of £16,000 he got into financial difficulties. The defendants, concerned that the job might not be finished on time and that they would in that event have to pay money under a penalty clause in the main contract, made an oral promise to pay Mr Williams a further sum of £10,300 to be paid at the rate of £575 for each flat on which work was completed. Mr Williams was not paid in full for this work and later brought this claim for the additional sum promised. The Court of Appeal *held* that he was entitled to it because where a party to a contract agrees to make an additional payment to secure its performance on time this may provide sufficient consideration contractually to support the extra payment if the agreement to pay is obtained without economic duress or fraud (*see further* Chapter 5) and where it ensures the completion of the contract to the paying party's satisfaction and benefit as by avoiding a penalty which was the position here. Apparently *Stilk* survives only where the person making the promise receives no benefit for it. It would seem to have been possible to find benefit in *Stilk* so that it may well be overruled on its own facts though the Court of Appeal would only say that the principle had been 'refined'.

(ii) The Court of Appeal took a more traditional approach and did not apply the decision in *Williams* in a case entitled *Re Selectmove, The Times*, 13 January 1994 where a company was having difficulty paying its taxes and agreed with the Revenue, through one of its officers, to pay by instalments. Some instalments were paid but then, while sums were still owing, the Revenue demanded the balance at once and on failing to get it started proceedings to wind the company up. The Court of Appeal held that the agreement as to instalments was not binding because it was not supported by consideration. The *Williams* case was distinguished because it related to the supply of goods and services whereas in *Selectmove* the obligation was to pay money. It was well established by the House of Lords in *Foakes* v *Beer* (1884) (*see below*), that an agreement to pay an existing debt by instalments was not enforceable in the absence of consideration or a deed. The facts of *Selectmove* were virtually the same as those in *Foakes* so that the Court of Appeal could hardly have found differently, though of course the Revenue was in no way forced to renege on the instalment arrangement. The company in *Selectmove* could, of course, have protected itself by agreeing to pay the Revenue a slightly higher rate of interest on the money owed by way of diminishing balance which would have amounted to good consideration for the agreement to pay by instalments.

### Hartley v Ponsonby (1857) 7 E & B 872

A greater remuneration was promised to a seaman to work the ship home when the number of deserters was so great as to render the ship unseaworthy. *Held* – This was a binding promise because the sailor had gone beyond his duty in agreeing to sail an unseaworthy ship. In fact the number of desertions was so great as to discharge the remaining seamen from their original contract, leaving them free to enter into a new bargain.

### Discharge of an obligation under a contract with a third party

The actual performance of an outstanding contractual obligation may be sufficient to support a promise of a further payment by a third party.

**The following cases are a selection from a number which illustrate the point.**

### Shadwell v Shadwell (1860) 9 CB (NS) 159

The claimant was engaged to marry a girl named Ellen Nicholl. In 1838 he received a letter from his uncle, Charles Shadwell, in the following terms: 'I am glad to hear of your intended marriage with Ellen Nicholl and, as I promised to assist you at starting, I am happy to tell you that I will pay you one hundred and fifty pounds yearly during my life and until your income derived from your profession of Chancery barrister shall amount to six hundred guineas, of which your own admission will be the only evidence that I shall receive or require.' The claimant duly married Ellen Nicholl and his income never exceeded 600 guineas during the 18 years his uncle lived after the marriage. The uncle paid 12 annual sums and part of the thirteenth but no more. On his death the claimant sued his uncle's executors for the balance of the 18 instalments to which he suggested he was entitled. *Held* – The claimant succeeded even though he was already engaged to Ellen Nicholl when the promise was made. His marriage was sufficient consideration to support his uncle's promise, for, by marrying, the claimant had incurred responsibilities and changed his position in life. Further the uncle probably derived some benefit in that his desire to see his nephew settled had been satisfied.

*Comment:* An engagement to marry is no longer binding as a contract – Law Reform (Miscellaneous Provisions) Act 1970, s1 – but the rule can still be applied in other situations (*see The New Zealand Shipping* case *below*).

## The New Zealand Shipping Co Ltd *v* A M Satterthwaite & Co Ltd [1974] 1 All ER 1015

In this case the makers of an expensive drilling machine entered into a contract for the carriage of the machine by sea to New Zealand. The contract of carriage (the bill of lading) exempted the carriers from full liability for any loss or damage to the machine during carriage and also purported to exempt any servant or agent of the carrier, including independent contractors employed from time to time by the carrier. The machine was damaged by the defendants, who were stevedores, in the course of unloading, and the question to be decided was whether the defendant stevedores, who had been employed by the carrier to unload the machine, could take advantage of the exemption clause in the bill of lading since they were not parties to the contract. It was decided by the Privy Council that they could. The stevedores provided consideration and so became parties to the contract when they unloaded the machine. (*Carlill* v *Carbolic Smoke Ball Co* (1893) (see Chapter 1) applied.) The performance of services by the stevedores in discharging the cargo was sufficient consideration to constitute a contract, even though they were already under an obligation to the carrier to perform those services because the actual performance of an outstanding contractual obligation was sufficient to support the promise of an exemption from liability given by the makers of the drill to the shippers, who were in effect third parties to the contract between the carrier and the stevedores. (*Shadwell* v *Shadwell* (1860) (*see above*) applied.)

*Comment:* (i) It is not easy to see when and where the relevant offers and acceptances were made in this case, but as we have already noted, a court can construe a contract from the circumstances without a precise application of the offer and acceptance formula (see *Rayfield* v *Hands* (1958), Chapter 1).

(ii) The case is and will remain an example of the ingenuity of the legal system to reach conclusions which are thought to be fair in the circumstances of the case. The Contracts (Rights of Third Parties) Act 1999 now provides the answer by allowing the contracting parties to confer third-party rights as required in terms at least of exclusion clauses in these contracts.

> *The business application:* Third parties in these contracts will normally insist that they be given third-party rights and negotiation of contracts will no doubt include discussions as to the extent of these exclusion rights in terms of those involved. The question is could the *Satterthwaite* decision be of help to third parties who had not been granted rights under the 1999 Act. Well possibly, but it must be borne in mind that failure to give third-party rights may be construed, as the 1999 Act allows, as showing an intention by the contracting parties that they should not apply.

## CONSIDERATION IN RELATION TO THE DISCHARGE OF A CONTRACT

All that has so far been said in regard to consideration relates to the *formation* of a contract. As we have seen, there must be offer, acceptance, consideration and intention to create legal relations in order to bring a contract into existence. The rules are rather different where a contract is to be *discharged*. There are a number of ways in which a contract may be discharged, all of which will be dealt with later. However, the one with which we are now concerned is *discharge by agreement* under which contract A is to be discharged by a new contract, B, the question being to what extent does contract B require consideration? The attitude of the common law is different from that of equity, as we shall see.

## COMMON LAW: THE RULE OF ACCORD AND SATISFACTION

At common law if A owes B £10 and wishes to discharge (bring to an end) that obligation by paying B £9 he must:

(a) obtain the agreement (accord) of B; and
(b) provide B with some consideration (satisfaction) for giving up his right to £10 unless the release is by deed.

This is the common law doctrine of accord and satisfaction. The doctrine is an ancient one and an early example of it is to be found in the judgment of Brian CJ in *Pinnel's* case (1602) 5 Co Rep 117a. Pinnel sued Cole in debt for what would now be £8.50 which was due on a bond on 11 November 1600. Cole's defence was that at Pinnel's request he had paid him £5.12 on 1 October and that Pinnel had accepted this payment in full satisfaction of the original debt. Although the court found for Pinnel on a technical point of pleading, it was said that:

(a) payment of a lesser sum on the day due in satisfaction of a greater sum cannot be any satisfaction for the whole; but
(b) payment of a smaller sum at the creditor's request before the due day is good consideration for a promise to forgo the balance for it is a benefit to the creditor to be paid before he was entitled to payment and a corresponding detriment to the debtor to pay early.

**The first branch of the rule in *Pinnel's* case was much criticised but was approved by the House of Lords in *Foakes* v *Beer* (1884) (*see below*) and the doctrine then hardened because of the system of binding precedent.**

### Foakes v Beer (1884) 9 App Cas 605

Mrs Beer had obtained a judgment against Dr Foakes for debt and costs. Dr Foakes agreed to settle the judgment debt by paying £500 down and £150 per half-year until the whole was paid, and Mrs Beer agreed not to take further action on the judgment. Foakes duly paid the amount of the judgment plus costs. However, judgment debts carry interest by statute, and while Dr Foakes had been paying off the debt, interest amounting to £360 had been accruing on the diminishing balance. In this action Mrs Beer claimed the £360. *Held* – she could do so. Her promise not to take further action on the judgment was not supported by any consideration moving from Dr Foakes.

*Comment:* (i) Since the development of equitable estoppel in the *High Trees* case (*see below*), there is no reason why a part-payment should not be enough to discharge the contract. Perhaps *Foakes* should in future be confined to cases where the acceptance of the part-payment results from threats as in *D & C Builders* v *Rees* (1965) (*see below*). This would modify the present rather harsh rule of the common law that only an agreement which is the equivalent of a *contract* can effectively change existing obligations.

(ii) However, it will have been noted that in *Re Selectmove* the Court of Appeal followed *Foakes* even though the promise to allow payment by instalments had in no way been extorted.

## Some qualifications to the rule

The practical effect of the rule that payment of a smaller sum will not do is reduced under the common law by the following, each of which seems to include an element of consideration, however small.

(a) *Where there is a dispute as to the sum owed.* If the creditor accepts less than he thinks is owed to him the debt will be discharged. Thus A says that B owes him £11. B says it is only £9. A agrees to compromise by taking £10. Even if it can be proved that A is really owed £11 he cannot recover the £1. He has compromised his claim.
(b) *Where the creditor agrees to take something different in kind*, e.g. goods, the debt is discharged by substituted performance. Thus, if A gives B a watch worth £5 and B is agreeable to taking it, then the debt of £10 will be discharged.

**In this connection it should be noted that a cheque for a smaller sum no longer constitutes substituted performance as the following case illustrates.**

### D & C Builders Ltd v Rees [1965] 3 All ER 837

D & C Builders, a small company, did work for Rees for which he owed £482 13s 1d. There was at first no dispute as to the work done but Rees did not pay. In August and October 1964, the claimants wrote for the money and received no reply. On 13 November 1964, the wife of Rees (who was then ill) telephoned the claimants, complained about the work, and said, 'My husband will offer you £300 in settlement. That is all you will get. It is to be in satisfaction.' D & C Builders, being in desperate straits and faced with bankruptcy without the money, offered to take the £300 and allow a year to Rees to find the balance. Mrs Rees replied: 'No, we will never have enough money to pay the balance, £300 is better than nothing.' The claimants then said: 'We have no choice but to accept.' Mrs Rees gave the defendants a cheque and insisted on a receipt 'in completion of the account'. The claimants, being worried about their financial position, took legal advice and later brought an action for the balance. The defence was bad workmanship and also that there was a binding settlement. The question of settlement was tried as a preliminary issue and the judge, following *Goddard* v *O'Brien* (1882) 9 QBD 37, decided that a cheque for a smaller amount was a good discharge of the debt, this being the generally accepted view of the law since that date. On appeal it was *held* (*per* the Master of the Rolls, Lord Denning) that *Goddard* v *O'Brien* was wrongly decided. A smaller sum in cash could be no settlement of a larger sum and 'no sensible distinction could be drawn between the payment of a lesser sum by cash and the payment of it by cheque'.

In the course of his judgment Lord Denning said of *High Trees* (*see below*):

It is worth noting that the principle may be applied, not only so as to suspend strict legal rights but also so as to preclude the enforcement of them. This principle has been applied to cases where a creditor agrees to accept a lesser sum in discharge of a greater. So much so that we can now say that, when a creditor and debtor enter on a course of negotiation, which leads the debtor to suppose that on payment of the lesser sum, the creditor will not enforce payment of the balance, and on the faith thereof the debtor pays the lesser sum and the creditor accepts it as satisfaction: then the creditor will not be allowed to enforce payment of the balance when it would be inequitable to do so ... But he is not bound unless there has been truly an accord between them.

In the present case there was no true accord. The debtor's wife had held the creditors to ransom and there was no reason in law or equity why the claimants should not enforce the full amount of the debt.

*Comment:* (i) The case also illustrates the need for equality of bargaining power (*see Lloyd's Bank* v *Bundy* (1974) Chapter 5) and the absence of economic duress in the negotiation (or as here renegotiation) of a contract.

(ii) It was held in *Stour Valley Builders (a Firm)* v *Stuart, The Times*, 22 February 1993, that the fact that a cheque for a lesser sum said to be given in full satisfaction but without consideration was cashed by the recipient did not prevent him from suing for the balance even though the cashing of the cheque might indicate agreement to take a lesser sum. The decision serves to confirm the position at common law that an *agreement*, express or implied, to change existing obligations is ineffective unless it is a *contract*.

(c) *The payment of a smaller sum before the larger is due* gives the debtor a good discharge. This is the second branch of the rule in *Pinnel's* case and makes valid the giving of a discount for early payment.

(d) *Payment at a different place* gives the debtor a good discharge. A creditor may accept the payment of a smaller sum provided the debtor hands over the money at a different place from the one originally agreed. The question of adequacy of consideration does not arise and the court will assume some benefit to the creditor.

## The exceptions to the rule – arrangements and compromises generally

(a) *If a debtor makes an arrangement with his creditors* to compound his debts, e.g. by paying them 85p in the £1, he is satisfying a debt for a larger sum by the payment of a smaller sum. Nevertheless, it is a good discharge, the consideration being the agreement by the creditors with each other and with the debtor not to insist on their full rights. These arrangements would more usually be made today under the Insolvency Act 1986. Section 260 of that Act states that such an arrangement binds every creditor if it is approved by a meeting of creditors at which more than three-quarters in value vote in favour of the arrangement. Therefore, s 260 really provides an exception to the rule of accord and satisfaction.

(b) *Payment of a smaller sum by a third party* operates as a good discharge.

**The following case illustrates this.**

### Welby v Drake (1825) 1 C & P 557

The claimant sued the defendant for the sum of £9 on a debt which had originally been £18. The defendant's father had paid the claimant £9 and the claimant had agreed to take that sum in full discharge of the debt. *Held* – The payment of £9 by the defendant's father operated to discharge the debt of £18.

*Comment:* (i) The basis of the decision may be found both in the law of contract and in the tort of deceit, since it would be a fraud on the third party to sue the original debtor. 'If the father did pay the smaller sum in satisfaction of this debt, it is a bar to the claimant's now recovering against the son: because by suing the son, he commits fraud on the father, whom he induced to advance his money on the faith of such advance being a discharge of his son from further liability' (*per* Lord Tenterden CJ). Also, of course, the creditor breaks his contract with the third party.

(ii) Where there is a payment by a third party the acceptance of, say, a cheque by the creditor will be regarded as an acceptance of the payment in discharge of the debtor's liability. This is not the case where the creditor accepts a smaller payment by cheque from the debtor as distinct from a third party (see *Stour Valley Builders (a Firm)* v *Stuart* (1993) *above*).

## Compromises with joint debtors

Where as in the case of a partnership a creditor of the firm enters into a compromise of a debt owed to him, e.g. by taking less than he is owed from one or more but not all of the partners, the compromise is effective to discharge the liability of the other partners (co-debtors) unless the right to claim the balance from the other partners as co-debtors is specifically reserved, even though in the case of partnership debts the partners are jointly and severally (together and separately) liable to pay the debts of the firm. Thus, in the absence of such reservation of liability, a compromise of a joint debt with one of the joint debtors discharges the others. The rule is not confined to the partnership situation but applies to other situations of joint debt. (*See Morris* v *Wentworth-Stanley, The Times*, 2 October 1998.)

# EQUITY: THE RULE OF PROMISSORY ESTOPPEL

There has always been some dissatisfaction with the common law rule of accord and satisfaction. After all, if A owes B £10 and B agrees to take £9, as he must before there can be any question of discharging the obligation on A to pay £10, why should B be allowed afterwards to break his promise to take £9 and succeed in an action against A simply because A gave him no consideration?

It was to deal with this sort of situation that the equitable rule of promissory estoppel was propounded, first by Lord Cairns in *Hughes* v *Metropolitan Railway* (1877) and later by Denning J (as he then was), in the *High Trees* case (1947) (*see below*). It was affirmed by the House of Lords in *Tool Metal Manufacturing Co Ltd* v *Tungsten Electric Co Ltd* (1955) (*see below*).

The rule of estoppel is basically a rule of evidence under which the court, surprisingly enough, is not prepared to listen to the truth. It occurs at common law out of physical conduct. Suppose A and B go into a wholesaler's premises and A asks for goods on credit. The wholesaler, who knows that B is creditworthy, but has no knowledge of A, is not prepared to give credit until A says, 'Do not worry, you will be paid, B is my partner.' If B says nothing and A receives the goods on credit and does not pay, then B could be sued for the price, even though he can produce evidence that he was not in fact A's partner. This evidence will not be admitted because the wholesaler relied on a situation of partnership created by B's *conduct, and* the statement is concerned with *existing fact* which is essential at common law (see *Jorden* v *Money* (1854) 5 HL Cas 185).

Promissory estoppel in equity is very little different except that the estoppel arises from a *promise*, not *conduct*. The common law does not recognise an estoppel arising out of a promise, or a statement about *future conduct* but equity does.

### Ingredients of promissory estoppel

As a result of the above decisions and others (as indicated), the rule of promissory estoppel has the following ingredients:

(a) It arises from a promise made with the intention that it should be acted upon. The promise must be clear and unambiguous to the effect that strict legal rights will not be enforced. It must also be unconscionable to allow the promise to be disregarded. It is difficult to say when this might be the case. However, the courts may very well, in practice, decide (i) that it is unconscionable, in equity, to revoke any agreement modifying an obligation unless it is done quickly and before any action has been taken on it so that if a tenant actually pays a lower rent under a promise that he may do so it will not be possible to recover the rent forgiven though the payment of the full rent can be required for the future if the landlord gives reasonable notice (*see* the *High Trees* case *below*) or (ii) unless the promise to modify was extorted under duress as in *D & C Builders* v *Rees* (1965) *above*.

(b) It was once thought that the person who had received the promise must do something to show that he had relied on it. If A, a landlord, said B could pay only half his usual rent while he was unemployed, it was thought that B would have to show, for example, that he had spent what should have been the rent money on travelling expenses to find work in the district. Reliance upon the promise in this way is not, it would appear, a necessary requirement (*Alan* v *El Nasr* (1972) – *see below*).

(c) It relates only to variation or discharge of contract by agreement and does not affect the requirement of consideration on formation of contract (*Combe* v *Combe* (1951) – *see below*).

(d) So far as the rule has been developed in cases, it merely suspends rights but does not totally preclude enforcement of the original contract after reasonable notice has been given (*Tool Metal Manufacturing Co Ltd* v *Tungsten Electric Co Ltd* (1955) – *see below*).

(e) The promise must be freely given and not extorted by threats, for if it is then it is not inequitable to allow the promisor to go back on his promise (*D & C Builders Ltd* v *Rees* (1965) – *see above*).

(f) Of considerable importance is a *dictum* by Lord Denning in *D & C Builders* v *Rees* (1965) that the rule could be developed to the point at which it operated, not merely to suspend rights, but to prevent enforcement of them. If this point is reached, then if A owes B £10 and B agrees to take £9, A will be discharged from his obligation to pay £10 without the need for consideration.

Such a situation would involve a virtual overruling of *Foakes* v *Beer* (1884) (*see above*) and would put an end to the first branch of the rule in *Pinnel's* case which is that payment of a lesser sum on the day due in satisfaction of a greater sum cannot be any satisfaction for the whole. Although in the past a number of *dicta* by Lord Denning have been incorporated into the *ratio* of subsequent decisions, the position outlined here has not yet been reached.

## Promissory estoppel – the case law

The following cases which have already been referred to are illustrative of the various aspects of the rule.

### Hughes v Metropolitan Railway (1877) 2 App Cas 439

A landlord gave six months' notice to his tenant to carry out certain repairs and said that if the tenant failed to do the repairs the lease would be forfeited. During the period of six months the landlord started negotiations with the tenant with a view to selling the lease to the tenant. The tenant did not do any repairs while the negotiations were in progress. However, the negotiations broke down during the six-month period and before the end of it the landlord claimed to forfeit the lease for failure to repair. The House of Lords *held* that he could not do so. The landlord had by his conduct led the tenant into thinking that he would not enforce forfeiture at the end of the six-month period. The tenant had relied on this by not doing the repairs. However, the six-month period began to run again from the breakdown in negotiations.

### Central London Property Trust Ltd v High Trees House Ltd [1947] KB 130

In 1937 the claimants granted to the defendants a lease of 99 years of a new block of flats at a rent of £2,500 per annum. The lease was made by deed. During the period of the Second World War the flats were by no means fully let owing to the absence of people from the London area. The defendant company, which was a subsidiary of the claimant company, realised that it could not meet the rent out of the profits then being made on the flats, and in 1940 the parties entered into an agreement which reduced the rent to £1,250 per annum, this agreement being put into writing but not sealed. The defendants continued to pay the reduced rent from 1941 to the beginning of 1945, by which time the flats were fully let, and they continued to pay the reduced rents thereafter. In September 1945, the receiver of the claimant company investigated the matter and asked for arrears of £7,916, suggesting that the liability created by the lease still existed, and that the agreement of 1940 was not supported by any consideration. The receiver then brought this action to establish the legal position. He claimed £625, being the difference in rent for the two quarters ending 29 September and 29 December 1945. *Held* – (a) A simple contract can in equity vary a deed (i.e. the lease), though it had not done so here because the simple contract was not supported by consideration. (b) As the agreement for the reduction of rent had been acted upon by the defendants, the claimants were estopped in equity from claiming the full rent from 1941 until early 1945 when the flats were fully let. After that time they were entitled to do so because the second agreement was only operative during the continuance of the conditions which gave rise to it. To this extent the limited claim of the receiver succeeded. If the receiver had sued for the balance of the rent from 1941 he would have failed.

*Comment:* The rule established by the case, in its developed state, seems to be that where a person has indicated by a promise that he is not going to insist upon his strict rights, as a result of which the other party acts on the belief induced by the other's promise, which may mean no more than making the reduced payments as in this case, then the law, although it does not give a cause of action in damages if the promise is broken, will require it to be honoured to the extent of refusing to allow the promisor the right to act inconsistently with it, even though the promise is not supported by consideration. The doctrine has been called 'equitable estoppel', 'quasi-estoppel' and 'promissory estoppel', in order to distinguish it from estoppel at common law. At common law estoppel arises when the defendant by his conduct suggests that certain existing facts are true. Here the estoppel was based on a promise, not conduct, and the promise related to future conduct, not to existing facts.

## Tool Metal Manufacturing Co Ltd v Tungsten Electric Co Ltd [1955] 2 All ER 657

The appellants were the registered proprietors of British letters patent. In April 1938 they made a contract with the respondents whereby they gave the latter a licence to manufacture 'hard metal alloys' in accordance with the inventions which were the subject of patent. By the contract the respondents agreed to pay 'compensation' to the appellants if in any one month they sold more than a stated quantity of metal alloys.

Compensation was duly paid by the respondents until the outbreak of war in 1939, but thereafter none was paid. It was found as a fact that in 1942 the appellants agreed to suspend the enforcement of compensation payments pending the making of a new contract. In 1944 negotiations for such new contracts were begun but broke down. In 1945 the respondents sued the appellants for breach of contract and the appellants counter-claimed for payment of compensation as from 1 June 1945. As regards the arguments on the counter-claim, it was eventually *held* by the Court of Appeal that the agreement of 1942 operated in equity to prevent the appellants demanding compensation until they had given reasonable notice to the respondents of their intention to resume their strict legal rights and that such notice had not been given.

In September 1950 the appellants themselves issued a writ against the respondents claiming compensation as from 1 January 1947. The respondents pleaded the equity raised by the agreement of 1942 and argued that reasonable notice of its termination had not been given. When this action reached the House of Lords it was *held* – affirming *Hughes* v *Metropolitan Railway Co* and the *High Trees* case – that the agreement of 1942 operated in equity to suspend the appellants' legal rights to compensation until reasonable notice to resume them had been given. However, the counter-claim in the first action in 1945 amounted to such notice, and since the appellants were not now claiming any compensation as due to them before 1 January 1947, the appellants succeeded in this second action and were awarded £84,000 under the compensation claim.

## W J Alan & Co v El Nasr Export and Import Co [1972] 2 All ER 127

A contract for the sale of coffee provided for the price expressed in Kenyan shillings to be paid by irrevocable letter of credit. The buyers procured a confirmed letter expressed in sterling and the sellers obtained part-payment thereunder. While shipment was in progress sterling was devalued and the sellers claimed such additional sum as would bring the price up to the sterling equivalent of Kenyan shillings at the current rate. Orr J held that the buyers were liable to pay the additional sum as the currency of account was Kenyan shillings. On appeal by the buyers it was *held* – allowing the appeal – that the sellers by accepting payment in sterling had irrevocably waived their right to be paid in Kenyan currency or had accepted a variation of the sale contract, and that a party who has waived his rights cannot afterwards insist on them if the other party has acted on that belief differently from the way in which he would otherwise have acted: and the other party need not show that he has acted to his detriment. In the course of his judgment Lord Denning MR said:

... if one party, by his conduct, leads another to believe that the strict rights arising under the contract will not be insisted on, intending that the other should act on that belief, and he does act on it, then the first party will not afterwards be allowed to insist on the strict legal rights when it would be inequitable for him to do so ... There may be no consideration moving from him who benefits by the waiver. There may be no detriment to him acting on it. There may be nothing in writing. Nevertheless, the one who waives his strict rights cannot afterwards insist on them. His strict rights are at any rate suspended so long as the waiver lasts. He may on occasion be able to revert to his strict legal rights for the future by giving reasonable notice in that behalf, or otherwise making it plain by his conduct that he will thereafter insist on them ... I know that it has been suggested in some quarters that there must be a detriment. But I can find no support for it in the authorities cited by the judge. The nearest approach to it is the statement by Viscount Simonds in the *Tool Metal* case that the other must have been led 'to alter his position' which was adopted by Lord Hodson in *Emmanuel Ayodeji Ajayi* v *R T Briscoe (Nigeria) Ltd* [1964] 3 All ER 556. But that only means that he must have been led to act differently from what he otherwise would have done. And, if you study the cases in which the doctrine has been applied, you will see that all that is required is that one should have 'acted on the belief induced by the other party'. That is how Lord Cohen put it in the *Tool Metal* case and it is how I would put it myself.

**Comment:** Since, as in *High Trees*, a tenant who only pays one-half of his rent can hardly be said to have 'acted to his detriment', the better view is that acting to one's detriment is not a requirement of equitable estoppel. It is a requirement of common law estoppel.

## Combe v Combe [1951] 1 All ER 767

The parties were married in 1915 and separated in 1939. In February 1943, the wife obtained a decree nisi of divorce, and a few days later the husband entered into an agreement under which he was to pay his wife £100 per annum, free of income tax. The decree was made absolute in August 1943. The husband did not make the agreed payments and the wife did not apply to the court for maintenance but chose to rely on the alleged contract. She brought this action for arrears under that contract. Evidence showed that her income was between £700 and £800 per annum and the defendant's was £650 per annum. Byrne J, at first instance, *held* that, although the wife had not supplied consideration, the agreement was nevertheless enforceable, following the decision in the *High Trees* case, as a promise made to be acted upon and in fact acted upon. *Held* – by the Court of Appeal – (a) that the *High Trees* decision was not intended to create new actions where none existed before, and that it had not abolished the requirement of consideration to support simple contracts. In such cases consideration was a cardinal necessity. (b) In the words of Birkett LJ the doctrine was 'a shield not a sword', i.e. a defence to an action, not a cause of action. (c) The doctrine applied to the modification of existing agreements by subsequent promises and had no relevance to the formation of a contract. (d) It was not possible to find consideration in the fact that the wife forbore to claim maintenance from the court, since no such contractual undertaking by her could have been binding even if she had given it. Therefore, this action by the wife must fail because the agreement was not supported by consideration.

## DISCHARGE OF CONTRACT BY PERFORMANCE: RELEVANCE OF *HIGH TREES* CASE

The rule of equitable estoppel has relevance in discharge of a contract by performance (*see* Chapter 8). Although the agreed date of delivery must usually be complied with in a contract of sale, the buyer may waive the condition relating to the date of delivery and accept a later date. Such a waiver may be binding on him whether made with or without consideration. It was held by Lord Denning in *Charles Rickards Ltd* v *Oppenhaim* (1950) (*see* Chapter 8) that the binding nature of a waiver without consideration might be based on the *High Trees* case (*see above*) (i.e. a promissory estoppel to accept a later delivery date). Alternatively, the seller may rely on s 11(2) of the Sale of Goods Act 1979 which states: 'Where a contract of sale is subject to any condition to be fulfilled by the seller, the buyer may waive that condition.'

## INTENTION TO CREATE LEGAL RELATIONS

The law will not necessarily recognise the existence of a contract enforceable in a court of law simply because of the presence of mutual promises. It is necessary to establish also that both parties made the agreement with the intention of creating legal relations so that if the agreement was broken the party offended would be able to exercise legally enforceable remedies. In other words, the agreement must be, or at least seem to be, *seriously intended*. The subject can be considered under two headings as follows.

### Case where the parties have not expressly denied their intention to create legal relations

#### *Advertisements*

Most advertisements are statements of opinion and as such are not actionable. Thus unless the advertisement makes false statements of specific verifiable facts, which is rare, the court will not enforce the claims made for the product on a contractual basis. However, where a company deposits money in the bank against possible claims, then the court is likely to hold that legal relations were contemplated (*Carlill* v *Carbolic Smoke Ball Co* (1893)), though a deposit is not essential (*Wood* v *Lectrik Ltd* (1932) – *see* Chapter 1).

#### *Family agreements*

Many of these cannot be imagined to be the subject of litigation but some may be. The question is basically one of construction and the court looks at the words and the surrounding circumstances. The two basic divisions of family agreements are set out below.

(a) *Husband and wife.* With regard to agreements between husband and wife, it is difficult to draw precise conclusions. However, it seems that there is a presumption of no intention to create legal relations, though this can be rebutted (avoided) in appropriate cases if the court thinks on the evidence that there was a serious intent. The following situations have appeared in decided cases.

    (i) Where husband and wife were living together in amity when the agreement was made, then the agreement is not enforceable as a contract because legal proceedings are an inappropriate method of settling purely domestic disputes.

**The following case illustrates this.**

## Balfour v Balfour [1919] 2 KB 571

The defendant was a civil servant stationed in what was then called Ceylon (now Sri Lanka). In November 1915, he came to England on leave with his wife, the claimant in the present action. In August 1916, the defendant returned alone to Ceylon because his wife's doctor had advised her that her health would not stand up to a further period of service abroad. Later the husband wrote to his wife suggesting that they should remain apart, and in 1918 the claimant obtained a decree nisi. In this case the claimant alleged that before her husband sailed for Ceylon he had agreed, in consultation with her, that he would give her £30 per month as maintenance, and she now sued because of his failure to abide by the said agreement. The Court of Appeal held that there was no enforceable contract because the parties did not intend to create legal relations. The provision for a flat payment of £30 per month for an indefinite period with no attempt to take into account changes in the circumstances of the parties did not suggest a binding agreement. Duke LJ seems to have based his decision on the fact that the wife had not supplied any consideration.

(ii) Where husband and wife were living together but not in amity or were separated altogether when the agreement was made, the court may enforce it.

**The following illustration from case law shows this.**

## Merritt v Merritt [1970] 2 All ER 760

After a husband had formed an attachment for another woman and had left his wife, a meeting was held between the parties on 25 May 1966, in the husband's car. The husband agreed to pay the wife £40 per month maintenance and also wrote out and signed a document stating that in consideration of the wife paying all charges in connection with the matrimonial home until the mortgage repayments had been completed, he would agree to transfer the property to her sole ownership. The wife took the document away with her and in the following months paid off the mortgage. The husband did not subsequently transfer the property to his wife and she claimed a declaration that she was the sole beneficial owner and asked for an order that her husband should transfer the property to her forthwith. The husband's defence was that the agreement was a family arrangement not intended to create legal relations. *Held* – by the Court of Appeal – (a) that the agreement, having been made when the parties were not living together in amity, was enforceable (*Balfour* v *Balfour* (1919) *above* distinguished); and (b) that the contention that there was no consideration to support the husband's promise could not be sustained. The payment of the balance of the mortgage was a detriment to the wife and the husband had received the benefit of being relieved of liability to the building society; (c) therefore, the wife was entitled to the relief claimed.

(iii) If the words used by the parties are uncertain, then the agreement will not be enforced, the uncertainty leading to the conclusion that there was no intention to create legal relations. Thus in *Gould* v *Gould* [1969] 3 All ER 728 a contractual intention was negatived where a husband on leaving his wife undertook to pay her £15 per week 'so long as I can manage it'. The uncertainty of this term ruled out a legally binding agreement.

Agreements of a non-domestic nature made between husband and wife are enforceable: e.g. in *Pearce* v *Merriman* [1904] 1 KB 80 it was held that a husband may be his wife's tenant and as such could be made to pay the rent.

(b) *Other family and personal relationships.* The question of intention to create legal relations arises for consideration here as well but it seems that the less close the relationship between the parties the more likely it is that the court *will presume* that legal relations were intended.

**The following case is an illustration of this point.**

### Simpkins v Pays [1955] 3 All ER 10

The defendant and the defendant's granddaughter made an agreement with the claimant, who was a paying boarder, that they should submit in the defendant's name a weekly coupon, containing a forecast by each of them, to a Sunday newspaper fashion competition. On one occasion a forecast by the granddaughter was correct and the defendant received a prize of £750. The claimant sued for her share of that sum. The defence was that there was no intention to create legal relations but that the transaction was a friendly arrangement binding in honour only. *Held* – There was an intention to create legal relations. Far from being a friendly domestic arrangement, the evidence showed that it was a joint enterprise and that the parties expected to share any prize that was won.

*Comment:* A family agreement which went the other way was *Julian* v *Furby* (1982) 132 NLJ 64. J was an experienced plasterer who helped F, his son-in-law, and his wife (J's favourite daughter) to buy, alter and finish a house for them. They later quarrelled and J sued for £4,440. This included materials supplied and F was prepared to pay for these but not for J's labour which, it was understood, would be free. It was *held* by the Court of Appeal that there was never an intention to create a legal relationship between the parties in regard to labour which J and F jointly provided in refurbishing the house.

However, in these cases also *uncertainty* as to the terms of the agreement normally leads to the conclusion that there was no contractual intention.

**The following case shows this.**

### Jones v Padavatton [1969] 2 All ER 616

In 1962 the claimant, Mrs Jones, who lived in Trinidad, made an offer to the defendant, Mrs Padavatton, her daughter, to provide maintenance for her at the rate of £42 a month if she would leave her job in Washington in the United States and go to England and read for the Bar. Mrs Padavatton was at that time divorced from her husband, having the custody of the child of that marriage. The agreement was an informal one and there was uncertainty as to its exact terms. Nevertheless, the daughter came to England in November 1962, bringing the child with her, and began to read for the Bar, her fees and maintenance being paid for by Mrs Jones. In 1964 it appeared that the daughter was experiencing some discomfort in England, occupying one room in Acton for which she had to pay £6 17s 6d per week. At this stage Mrs Jones offered to buy a large house in London to be occupied by the daughter and partly by tenants, the income from rents to go to the daughter in lieu of maintenance. Again, there was no written agreement, but the house was purchased for £6,000 and conveyed to Mrs Jones. The daughter moved into the house in January 1965, and tenants arrived, it still being uncertain what precisely was to happen to the surplus rent income (if any) and what rooms the daughter was to occupy. No money from the rents was received by Mrs Jones and no accounts were submitted to her. In 1967 Mrs Jones claimed possession of the house from her daughter, who had by that time married again, and the daughter counter-claimed for £1,655 18s 9d, said to have been paid in connection with running the house. At the hearing the daughter still had, as the examinations were then structured, one subject to pass in Part I and also the whole of Part II remained to be taken. *Held* – by the Court of Appeal:

(a) that the arrangements were throughout family agreements depending upon the good faith of the parties in keeping promises made and not intended to be rigid binding agreements. Furthermore, the arrangements were far too vague and uncertain to be enforceable as contracts (*per* Danckwerts and Fenton Atkinson LJJ);
(b) that although the agreement to maintain while reading for the Bar might have been regarded as creating a legal obligation in the mother to pay (the terms being sufficiently stated and duration for a reasonable time being implied), the daughter could not claim anything in respect of that agreement which must be regarded as having terminated in 1967, five years being a reasonable time in which to complete studies for the Bar. The arrangements in relation to the home were very vague and must be regarded as made without contractual intent (*per* Salmon LJ).

The mother was, therefore, entitled to possession of the house and had no liability under the maintenance agreement. The counter-claim by the daughter was left to be settled by the parties.

*Comment:* In this case there was an inference of contractual intent in the mother's promise because it caused Mrs Padavatton to leave one job to study for another, but the vagueness of the arrangement negatived that intent as in *Gould* v *Gould* (1969) (*above*).

### Other cases

There may well be other areas where intention to create legal relations is doubtful but which have not been the subject of cases in court. Again, the matter is one of fact for the court. However, in the case of clubs and societies many of the relationships which exist and promises which are made are enforceable only as moral obligations. They are merely *social agreements*. For example, the decision in *Lens* v *Devonshire Club*, *The Times*, 4 December 1914, would suggest that if a person competes for a prize at a local golf club and is the winner, he or she may not be able to sue for the prize which has been won if it is not otherwise forthcoming.

However, in *Peck* v *Lateu*, *The Times*, 18 January 1973, two ladies attended bingo sessions together and had an arrangement to pool their winnings. One of them won an additional 'Bonanza' prize of £1,107 and claimed it was not covered by the sharing arrangements. Pennycuick VC *held* – that there was an intention to create legal relations and to share all prizes won. The claimant was entitled to a share in the prize.

It should also be borne in mind that quotations and estimates may be passed from one person to another without any intention that they should be legally binding *at that stage*.

## Cases where the parties expressly deny any intention to create legal relations

By contrast with family arrangements, agreements of a commercial nature are *presumed* to be made with contractual intent. Furthermore, the test applied by the court is an *objective* one so that a person cannot escape liability simply because *he did not* have a contractual intention. The presumption is a strong one and it was *held* in *Edwards* v *Skyways Ltd* [1964] 1 All ER 494 that the use of the words *ex gratia* in regard to an airline pilot's contractual redundancy payment did not displace the presumption, so that the airline had to make the payments and did not have a discretion whether to make them or not.

However, the Court of Appeal has *held* more recently that a court need not necessarily presume intention to create legal relations just because the parties are in business.

### Kleinwort Benson Ltd v Malaysia Mining Corporation, Berhad [1989] 1 All ER 785

In this case the High Court had decided that a letter of comfort (as they are called) stating that it was the policy of Malaysian Mining to ensure that its subsidiary MMC Metals Ltd was 'at all times in a position to meet its liabilities' in regard to a loan made by Kleinwort to MMC had contractual effect. This meant that Kleinwort was entitled to recover from Malaysian the amount owed to it by the insolvent MMC, which went into liquidation after the tin market collapsed in 1985. Malaysian appealed to the Court of Appeal which reversed the High Court ruling. The problem has always been to decide whether a letter of comfort of the usual kind contains a legal obligation or only a moral one. In the High Court Mr Justice Hirst decided that there was a legal obligation: the Court of Appeal decided that it was only a moral one. The letter, said the Court of Appeal, stated the policy of Malaysian. It gave no contractual warranty as to the company's future conduct. In these circumstances there was no need to apply the presumption of an intention to create legal relations just because the transaction was in the course of business as laid down in *Edwards* v *Skyways* [1964] (*above*).

*Comment:* The wording of the letter of comfort must be looked at and if it appears to create a moral obligation only, then it has no contractual force. It is, of course, no bad thing for those in business to honour moral obligations, but as Lord Justice Ralph Gibson said, moral responsibilities are not a matter for the courts.

Some agreements where the court would normally assume an intention to create legal relations may be expressly taken outside the scope of the law by the parties agreeing to rely on each other's honour. This is a practice which appears to be allowable to pools companies who are especially subject to fraudulent entries but should not be allowed to spread into other areas of *standardised* contracts, i.e. contracts where the consumer has no choice of supplier, as where he requires electrical services laid on which can only be provided by a monopoly corporation.

There is no such objection where businessmen reach agreements at arm's length, and if the parties expressly declare, or clearly indicate, that they do not wish to assume contractual obligations, then the law accepts and implements their decision.

**The following cases illustrate these points.**

## Jones v Vernon's Pools Ltd [1938] 2 All ER 626

The claimant said that he had sent to the defendants a football coupon on which the penny points pool was all correct. The defendants denied having received it and relied on a clause printed on every coupon. The clause provided that the transaction should not 'give rise to any legal relationship ... or be legally enforceable ... but ... binding in honour only'. *Held* – that this clause was a bar to any action in a court of law.

*Comment:* This case was followed by the Court of Appeal in *Appleson* v *Littlewood Ltd* [1939] 1 All ER 464 where the contract contained a similar clause.

## Rose and Frank Co v Crompton (J R) & Brothers Ltd [1925] AC 445

In 1913 the claimants, an American company, entered into an agreement with the defendants, an English company, whereby the claimants were appointed sole agents for the sale in the USA of paper tissues supplied by the defendants. The contract was for a period of three years with an option to extend that time. The agreement was extended to March 1920, but in 1919 the defendants terminated it without notice. The defendants had received a number of orders for tissues before the termination of the contract, and they refused to execute them. The claimants sued for breach of contract and for non-delivery of the goods actually ordered. The agreement of 1913 contained an 'Honourable Pledge Clause' drafted as follows: 'This arrangement is not entered into nor is this memorandum written as a formal or legal agreement and shall not be subject to legal jurisdiction in the courts of the United States of America or England ...'. *Held* – by the House of Lords – that the 1913 agreement was not binding on the parties, but that in so far as the agreement had been acted upon by the defendants' acceptance of orders, those orders were binding contracts of sale. Nevertheless, the agreement was not binding for the future.

> *The business application:* Syllabuses usually require a knowledge of the concept of intention to create legal relations and a student should not neglect a study of it. However, it is worth pointing out that those in business have only rarely to address themselves to the concept and this is why the law as dispensed in the courts has created a presumption that business agreements are to be regarded as binding in the absence of something such as an 'Honourable Pledge Clause,' as in the *Rose and Frank* case. Such clauses are also comparatively rare in the business world.

## Statutory provisions

Sometimes an Act of Parliament renders an agreement unenforceable. Thus under s 1 of the Law Reform (Miscellaneous Provisions) Act 1970, a contract of engagement, which is, in effect, an agreement to marry, is not enforceable at law since there is a statutory presumption that there was no intention to create legal relations. Thus actions for breach of promise are no longer possible.

In addition, under s 29 of the Post Office Act 1969, the acceptance of ordinary letters and packets for transmission does not give rise to a contract between the post office and the sender.

Finally, under s 179 of the Trade Union and Labour Relations (Consolidation) Act 1992, collective agreements between trade unions and employers (or employers' associations) concerning industrial conditions such as hours, wages, holidays, procedures in disputes and so on, are presumed *not* to be intended to be legally enforceable unless they are in writing and contain a provision to that effect.

However under s 70A of the 1992 Act, as inserted by the Employment Relations Act 1999, arrangements made between an employer and a trade union in regard to collective bargaining rights being given to that union have effect as a legally binding contract, specific performance being the only remedy for breach.

## GRADED QUESTIONS

*Essay mode*

1  (a)  It is often said that although consideration need not be 'adequate' it must be 'legally sufficient'. Explain and illustrate this statement.

   (b)  The employees of Machine Tools Ltd have been called out on an unofficial strike during a period in which the firm has a major export order to fulfil. Their contracts contain a 'no-strike' clause under which they have undertaken to submit disputes to arbitration. Cecil, who is in no way connected with Machine Tools Ltd and who is a member of the 'Break the Unions' campaign, offers to pay the employees an additional £20 per week if they return to work immediately. The employees do so and complete the order on time. Cecil later refuses to pay.

   Advise the employees as to whether they are entitled to the promised sum.

   (*Institute of Chartered Secretaries and Administrators*)

2  The many exceptions to the doctrine of privity of contract suggest that the doctrine is unpopular, inconvenient and should be abolished. To what extent has this been achieved?

   (*Author's question*)

3  Three sisters, Mary, Jane and Susan, agree to form a syndicate for the purpose of making a weekly entry in a football pools competition. Mary and Jane know nothing about football, and they give Susan £1 each weekly, letting her fill in and send off the coupon. Susan always fills it in in her own name. After two months, Susan wins £21,000, which she now refuses to share.

   Advise Mary and Jane.

   (*Staffordshire University. BA(Hons) Business Studies*)

*Objective mode*

Four alternative answers are given. Select ONE only. Circle the answer which you consider to be correct. Check your answers by referring back to the information given in the chapter and against the answers at the back of the book.

1  In which of the following situations will the consideration most probably be regarded as being past?

   A  An offer of a reward is made by John, and Dinah, having satisfied the conditions of the offer, claims the reward.

   B  Norman asks Jack to help him negotiate a partnership agreement. Jack does so successfully. Norman then agrees to pay Jack £1,000 for his assistance.

**C** Jim helps his neighbour and friend Julie to lay a lawn. Three days later Julie promises Jim £50 for his work.

**D** Hank agrees to deliver some goods which Jake asked for. No price was agreed for the work at the time but afterwards Hank sent an invoice to Jake for £50.

2 Archie is the author of a number of best-selling novels. Bertie is Archie's publisher. Archie is a supporter of a charity called Redpeace which has as its objects the protection of the environment. Archie wanted to add to the funds of Redpeace so he wrote a novel and Bertie published it.

It was agreed between Archie and Bertie that Redpeace would receive the total royalty of 20p a copy for every book sold. The novel has sold one million copies but Bertie refuses to pay anything to Redpeace.

Which of the following statements is correct?

**A** Redpeace can bring a claim against Bertie and so can Archie.

**B** Only Redpeace can bring a claim against Bertie.

**C** Only Archie can bring a claim against Bertie.

**D** Neither Archie nor Redpeace has any claim against Bertie.

3 In December Mr Smith, who owned a number of unfurnished houses, decided to give his son John a start in his married life by granting him a lease of one of the houses which had recently been vacated by a previous tenant. Under the agreement John received a lease for two years at a rent of £1 per annum and he and his wife took possession.

Mr Smith died in March of the following year leaving all his houses to his wife Vera and appointing two of the partners in a firm of accountants as his executors. Unfortunately Vera had never approved of her son's marriage and she and John were not on speaking terms. Vera now refuses to honour the agreement made by her husband with John and threatens to bring a court action in order to have John and his wife evicted from the house. She claims that the agreement to pay a rent of only £1 annually was manifestly inadequate and no real consideration at all.

Ignoring matters relating to security of tenure under legislation relating to landlord and tenant, which one of the following decisions is the court likely to make if Vera proceeds with her action?

**A** That John and his wife may continue in possession of the house provided they are prepared to agree an economic rent with Vera.

**B** That John and his wife must vacate the house immediately.

**C** That John and his wife must find other accommodation as soon as they can.

**D** That John and his wife are entitled to remain in the house for the rest of the two-year period at the rent agreed with Mr Smith.

4 Lucre, the managing director of a manufacturing company, arranges for a party of overseas buyers to spend the weekend at his country estate in the hope of obtaining export orders for the company. As part of the entertainment Lucre makes a personal agreement with Rodger under which Rodger is to give the guests a two-hour trip in his private plane on the Saturday afternoon. A fee of £500 is agreed by Rodger and the arrangement regarding the air trip is mentioned by Lucre in all the letters of invitation.

On the preceding Thursday Rodger tells Lucre that the fee which has been agreed is not enough and that he will not turn up on the Saturday. Lucre discusses the matter with his sales manager, Sellars, and both agree that it is too late to make other arrangements and that Rodger must somehow be persuaded to carry out the contract.

Later that day Sellars rings Rodger saying, 'I will give you £100 of my own money if you agree to show up on Saturday.' Rodger agrees to do so, and Sellars leaves immediately for a weekend business trip to the continent without discussing the matter with Lucre.

On Friday morning Lucre rings Rodger saying, 'I think I can afford to pay you a little more. Would an extra £100 be all right?' Rodger replies, 'Yes that's enough. See you Saturday.' Rodger turns up on Saturday and carries out a two-hour flight as agreed.

Lucre returns to the office on Monday and in the course of conversation with Sellars learns of the extra payment which Sellars has promised to Rodger. Lucre and Sellars are furious at being treated in this way and Lucre sends Rodger a cheque for £500 with a note saying, 'Sellars and I are disgusted by your behaviour in this matter. The enclosed cheque is in final settlement. You will get no more from either of us.'

Two weeks later Lucre and Sellars each receive a letter from Rodger saying that unless he receives £100 from them both he will sue for the money.

Which one of the following statements correctly represents the legal position?

A  Only Lucre is liable to pay the extra £100 to Rodger.
B  Only Sellars is liable to pay the extra £100 to Rodger.
C  Sellars is not bound to pay the extra £100 to Rodger nor is Lucre.
D  Lucre and Sellars must both pay £100 to Rodger.

5  Kate had run up a debt on her Sparks and Mencers credit card to the extent of £800, including interest. Sparks and Mencers were threatening Kate with a civil action to recover the amount due. Kate's father Peter wrote to Sparks informing them that Kate was only 19 and out of work and was not likely to be able to pay. He said that he did not like credit being offered to young people but in order to protect Kate's future credit he was enclosing a cheque for £650 in full settlement and if this was not acceptable Sparks could return the cheque. The cheque was duly cleared and Sparks have now sent Kate an account for £150 informing her that interest is accruing at 2.5 per cent per month.

Which of the following statements represents the legal position?

A  This is a case of promissory estoppel: by accepting part-payment Sparks are estopped from insisting on their right to the balance owing.
B  Part-payment of a debt does not discharge the debt. Payment by Peter is no different from payment by Kate.
C  Peter's offer to pay £650 is made by a third party; by cashing his cheque Sparks accepted his offer and cannot sue for the balance.
D  Silence cannot be imposed as a condition of acceptance. Sparks have not accepted Peter's offer and can sue for the balance of £150.

6  On 1 October Mr Golightly, the office manager of Twitchett Ltd, was authorised to purchase a calculating machine for the accounts department. On 5 October he saw Sharp, a sales representative of Addom Ltd, which manufactured what Mr Golightly regarded as a suitable machine. After some discussion Mr Golightly selected an Addom Mark I and delivery was arranged for 1 November.

On 12 October Sharp rang Mr Golightly and said, 'We have just received an export order of 100 Addom Mark II machines. This is an important order for us and I wondered whether you would be prepared to accept delivery of your machine on 1 December. I am asking a number of people who have placed small orders to help our production side out in this way.' Mr Golightly agreed to delivery on 1 December 1978.

On 12 November Mr Golightly attended a sale of office machinery and bought a second-hand Addom Mark I for his company. On the same day he rang Sharp saying, 'I have bought a good second-hand machine and shall not require the new one. I am very sorry about this but it is your fault in a way because you could not deliver on time.' Sharp replied: 'But you agreed to take delivery later. I am afraid that we altered our production arrangements on the strength of promises from customers like yourself and we shall sue you for damages if you do not accept the machine.' Mr Golightly replied: 'But you gave us nothing for that promise so we are not bound to accept.'

The machine was delivered on 1 December, but was returned by Mr Golightly. Which of the following statements correctly represents the legal position?

**A** Twitchett Ltd is entitled to reject the machine because Addom Ltd was in breach of contract and Twitchett's waiver requires consideration.

**B** Twitchett is entitled to reject the machine: time of delivery is of the essence of the contract and cannot be waived.

**C** Twitchett is not entitled to reject the machine. It has waived Addom's breach and the waiver does not require consideration.

**D** Twitchett is not entitled to reject the machine because it was in breach itself by buying a second-hand machine.

7 In domestic agreements there is:

**A** A rebuttable presumption that there is an intention to create legal relations.

**B** An irrebuttable presumption that there is no intention to create legal relations.

**C** A rebuttable presumption that there is no intention to create legal relations.

**D** No presumption either way.

8 Harold has promised to pay his wife Jane £100 a month. In which one of the following cases will the promise not be enforceable by Jane?

**A** It was intended as extra housekeeping money.

**B** Jane and Harold's marriage having broken down, it was part of a separation agreement between them.

**C** It was intended as payment for the typing by Jane of a series of articles by Harold for a magazine.

**D** It was the rent for an office which Harold leases from Jane.

*Answers to questions set in objective mode appear on p 707.*

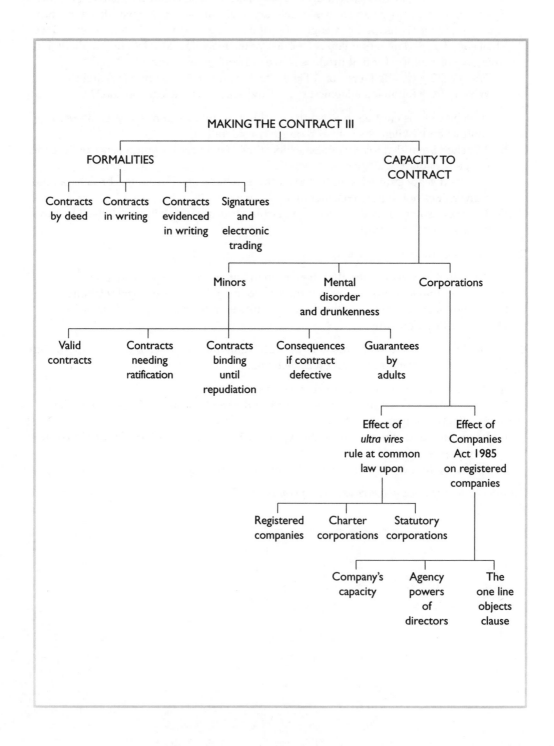

MAKING THE CONTRACT III

FORMALITIES

CAPACITY TO CONTRACT

Contracts by deed

Contracts in writing

Contracts evidenced in writing

Signatures and electronic trading

Minors

Mental disorder and drunkenness

Corporations

Valid contracts

Contracts needing ratification

Contracts binding until repudiation

Consequences if contract defective

Guarantees by adults

Effect of *ultra vires* rule at common law upon

Effect of Companies Act 1985 on registered companies

Registered companies

Charter corporations

Statutory corporations

Company's capacity

Agency powers of directors

The one line objects clause

The objectives of this chapter are to conclude the study of those elements of contract law which go to making a *mere agreement* into a *binding contract*. *Formalities (or the need for writing)* and the requirement that the parties should have *capacity in law* to make the contract are considered here.

## FORMALITIES

In most cases a contract made orally (or by parol, which is an alternative expression) is usually just as effective as a written one. Exceptionally, however, written formalities are required as follows.

### Contracts which must be made by deed

A lease of *more* than three years should be made by deed otherwise no legal estate is created (*see* Law of Property Act 1925, ss 52 and 54). If there is no deed then there is in equity a contract for a lease. This is an estate contract under s 2(3) of the Law of Property Act 1925. It is enforceable against third parties who acquire the freehold from the landlord only if it has been registered at the Land Registry. Registration gives notice to the whole world. Failure to register makes the contract void against a later purchaser of the freehold from the landlord for a consideration, even though in fact the purchaser *knows* the lease exists (Law of Property Act 1925, s 199(1)). The purchaser could turn out the tenant if the lease was not registered. However, where it is registered the tenant is protected. It should be noted, however, that the Court of Appeal decided in *Julian* v *Crago, The Times*, 4 December 1991, that if a tenant A wishes, say, to sell the lease to another person B, the assignment of the lease from A to B must be by deed even where the original lease given to A was oral and for three years *or less*.

As regards the form of a deed, the Law of Property (Miscellaneous Provisions) Act 1989 is now relevant. Section 1 requires, as before, that a deed must be in writing but gets rid of the requirement for sealing where a deed is entered into by an individual. Instead the signature of the individual making the deed must be witnessed and attested. There is no longer any need for the little red wafer! Attestation consists of a statement that the deed has been signed in the presence of the witness.

The section also provides that it must be made clear on the face of the document that it is intended to be a deed. How can this be done? The usual form to satisfy this requirement and attestation is: 'signed as a deed by *XY* in the presence of *AB*'.

As far as companies are concerned, s 36A of the Companies Act 1985 provides that while a company may continue to execute documents by affixing its common seal it need not have such a seal. Any document signed by a director and the secretary of the company or by two directors and said to be executed by the company will be regarded as if the seal had been affixed. If the document is intended to be a deed then this must be made clear on the face of the document and it will then be a deed on delivery, which is presumed, in the case of deeds by individuals and companies, in the absence of a contrary intention, to occur when it is signed. A suitable form for the company deed would be: 'signed as a deed: *AB* director and *CD* secretary (or other director) – for and on behalf of Boxo Ltd'.

## Contracts which must be in writing

The following simple contracts are required by statute to be in writing otherwise they are affected in various ways:

(a) Regulated consumer credit agreements, including hire-purchase agreements, under which the amount of credit does not exceed £25,000 and the customer is not a company (Consumer Credit Act 1974, s 61). If these agreements are not in appropriate written form they cannot be enforced by the dealer, unless the court thinks it is fair in the circumstances to allow him to enforce the contract (*see further* Chapter 14).

(b) Contracts of marine insurance, which must be embodied in a written policy otherwise the contract is not effective, being inadmissible in evidence unless embodied in a written policy signed on behalf of the insurer (Marine Insurance Act 1906, s 22).

(c) Contracts for the sale or other disposition of land are required by statute to be in writing otherwise they are invalid, i.e. there is no contract. Section 2(1) of the Law of Property (Miscellaneous Provisions) Act 1989 provides that a contract for the sale or other disposition of an interest in land can only be made in writing and only by incorporating all the terms which the parties have expressly agreed in one document or, where contracts are exchanged, in each contract. The document must be signed by each party. As regards the requirement that the parties must sign a copy of the agreement, it was held by the Court of Appeal in *Firstpost Homes* v *Johnson* [1995] 4 All ER 355 that the word 'signed' in the 1989 Act meant that the parties must sign their names in their own hand. A typed signature was not enough even though earlier cases on the requirements of writing under the previously applicable legislation had decided that a typed signature was acceptable.

There are some exceptions to the above requirements as follows:

(a) leases for three years or less where the tenant takes possession can be granted orally;

(b) sales at public auctions are excluded and the contract is regarded as made when the auctioneer's hammer falls. There is thus no requirement of writing at all at auction sales.

Since the document must now contain all the terms agreed by the parties and be signed by both parties, solicitors and conveyancers are no longer at risk that pre-contract correspondence signed by only one party might amount to a contract itself as was a possibility before. The practice of heading correspondence 'subject to contract' can now be brought to an end, but some lawyers may advise its retention in case a judicial interpretation reveals an unexpected trap in its omission. Also there should not be a problem as to whether the parties to a sale or other disposition of land intended legal relations since there will be a formal written contract.

## Contracts which must be evidenced in writing

Here we are concerned with contracts of guarantee where s 4 of the Statute of Frauds 1677 requires writing which, though not essential to the formation of the contract, is needed as evidence if a dispute about it comes before a court. The court will not enforce the guarantee in the absence of written evidence.

However, the absence of writing makes a contract of guarantee unenforceable and not void. This is because s 4 of the 1677 Act provides that 'no *action* shall be brought . . .' unless the guarantee is in writing. So if a person is sued upon a guarantee it can be proved *orally* as part of the defence and the judge will not require a written memorandum.

**The following case provides an illustration of this rule.**

### Deutsche Bank AG v Ibrahim and Others, *Financial Times* Law Reports, 15 January 1992

Mr Ibrahim's two daughters were the tenants of two leases. The leases were deposited with the bank to secure Mr Ibrahim's overdraft. The daughters later regretted having done this and tried to get the leases back from the bank. If this was done the bank would lose a good security since it would not then be able to sell the leases to a third party in order to re-pay Mr Ibrahim's overdraft. The bank brought this action to establish that it had a right to the leases. The daughters counter-claimed against the bank for the return of the leases. They were thus in effect *bringing an action* against the bank which *the bank was defending* by trying to establish its right to the leases. Part of the counter-claim was that by depositing the leases the daughters had guaranteed their father's overdraft and yet there was no memorandum in writing signed by the daughters. The court accepted that they had given a guarantee but allowed the bank to prove the contract, i.e. overdraft for the leases, orally because the bank was defending its right to retain the leases as security. The bank succeeded and was allowed to retain the leases.

The provision in the Statute of Frauds applies to guarantees and not to indemnities. It is, therefore, necessary to distinguish between these two. In a contract of indemnity the person giving the indemnity makes himself primarily liable by using such words as: 'I will see that you are paid'.

In a contract of guarantee the guarantor expects the person he has guaranteed to carry out his obligations and the substance of the wording would be: 'If he does not pay you, I will'. An indemnity does not require writing because it does not come within the Statute of Frauds: a guarantee requires a memorandum.

An additional distinction is that it is an essential feature of a guarantee that the person giving it is totally unconnected with the contract except by reason of his promise to pay the debt. Thus a *del credere* agent who, for an extra commission, promises to make good losses incurred by his principal in respect of the unpaid debts of third parties introduced by the agent, may use the guarantee form: 'if they do not pay you, I will' but no writing is required. Such a promise is enforceable even if made orally because even where a person does promise to be liable for the debt of another that promise is not within the Statute of Frauds where it is, as here, an incident of a wider transaction, i.e. agency.

**The following case illustrates the distinction between guarantees and indemnities.**

### Mountstephen v Lakeman (1871) LR 7 QB 196

The defendant was chairman of the Brixham Local Board of Health. The claimant, who was a builder and contractor, was employed in 1866 by the Board to construct certain main sewage works in the town. On 19 March 1866, notice was given by the Board to owners of certain homes to connect their house drains with the main sewer within 21 days. Before the expiration of the 21 days Robert Adams, the surveyor of the Board, suggested to the claimant that he should make the connection. The claimant said he was willing to do the work if he would see him paid. On 5 April 1866, i.e. before the expiration of the 21 days, the claimant commenced work on the connections. However, before work commenced it appeared that the claimant had had an interview with the defendant at which the following conversation took place:

Defendant: 'What objection have you to making the connections?'

Claimant: 'I have none, if you or the Board will order the work or become responsible for the payment.'

Defendant: 'Go on, Mountstephen, and do the work and I will see you paid.'

The claimant completed the connections in April and May 1866, and sent an account to the Board on 5 December 1866. The Board disclaimed responsibility on the ground that it never entered into any agreement with the claimant nor authorised any officer of the Board to agree with him for the performance of the work in question. *Held* – that Lakeman had undertaken a personal liability to pay the claimant and had not given a guarantee of the liability to pay the claimant and had not given a guarantee of the liability of a third party, i.e. the Board. In consequence, Lakeman had given an indemnity which did not need to be in writing under s 4 of the Statute of Frauds. The claimant was, therefore, entitled to enforce the oral undertaking given by the defendant.

*Comment:* Section 4 of the Statute of Frauds 1677 provides that: 'No action shall be brought . . . whereby to charge the defendant upon any special promise to answer for the debt default or miscarriage of another person . . . unless the agreement upon which such action shall be brought or some memorandum or note thereof shall be in writing and signed by the party to be charged therewith or some other person thereunto by him lawfully authorised.' It was held in *Birkmyr v Darnell* (1805) 1 Salk 27 that the words 'debt default or miscarriage of *another person*' meant that the section applied only where there was some person other than the surety who was primarily liable.

The memorandum in writing to satisfy the court need not exist when the contract is made but must be in existence when an action, if any, is brought for breach of the guarantee. A guarantee cannot be proved orally – writing is required as evidence. The memorandum must identify the parties, normally by containing their names. The material terms must be included, e.g. that it is a guarantee of a bank overdraft facility limited to £50,000. The memorandum must also contain the signature of the party to be charged or his agent properly authorised to sign. However, the law is not strict on this point and initials or a printed or typed signature will do (contrast the position under the Law of Property (Miscellaneous Provisions) Act 1989 (*above*)). The 'party to be charged' is the proposed defendant and there may be cases where one party has a sufficient memorandum to commence an action whereas the other may not since the memorandum does not contain the other party's signature. This could happen where the memorandum was in a letter written by Bloggs to Snooks. The letter would presumably be signed by Bloggs but not by Snooks. It would, therefore, be a good memorandum for an action by Snooks but not by Bloggs. Section 3 of the Mercantile Law Amendment Act 1856 dispenses with the need to set out the consideration in the memorandum but it must exist. It is normally the extension of credit by A to B in consideration of C's guarantee of B's liability if B fails to pay.

### Signatures and electronic trading

A problem which faces those who wish to engage in electronic commerce is the fact that the law at present does not recognise the validity of electronic signatures so that e.g. there is no way in which a deed could be made by electronic means. However, the Department of Trade and Industry has published its proposals for an Electronic Communications Bill. Among the main proposals is one to introduce measures to promote the legal recognition of electronic signatures. In this connection the Law of Property (Miscellaneous Provisions) Act 1989 has abolished the previous rule that a deed must be written on paper, thus clearing the way for the making of deeds by electronic means. The Bill proposes that digital signatures be given legal force and will set up a voluntary licensing system for trusted third parties that offer signature and encryption services. The DTI says that existing laws (as set out in this chapter) which require the use of paper will be swept away. Digital signatures are forgery-resistant computer codes which are used to prove someone's identity.

## CAPACITY TO CONTRACT

Adult citizens have full capacity to enter into any kind of contract but certain groups of persons and corporations have certain disabilities in this connection. The most important groups for our purposes are dealt with below.

## MINORS

The Family Law Reform Act 1969, s 1, reduced the age of majority from 21 to 18 years. Contracts made by minors were governed by the common law (including parts of sale of goods legislation) as amended by the Infants Relief Act 1874 and the Betting and Loans (Infants) Act 1892. The Minors' Contracts Act 1987 repealed the relevant parts of the 1874 and 1892 Acts so that minors' contracts are now governed by the rules of common law (including the Sale of Goods Act 1979) as amended by the Minors' Contracts Act 1987.

### Valid contracts

These are as follows:

(a) *Executed contracts for necessaries*. These are defined in s 3(3) of the Sale of Goods Act 1979 as: 'Goods suitable to the condition in life of the minor and to his actual requirements at the time of sale and delivery'. If the goods are deemed necessaries the minor may be compelled to pay a reasonable price which will usually, but not necessarily, be the contract price. The Sale of Goods Act does not, of course, cover necessary *services* such as, for example, a series of treatments by an osteopath. However, the common law applies and follows the Sale of Goods Act by requiring the minor to pay a reasonable price. The minor is not liable if the goods, though necessaries, have not been delivered or the service has not yet been rendered, i.e. there is no claim for breach of contract. This, together with the fact that he is only required to pay a reasonable price, illustrates that a minor's liability for necessaries is only quasi-contractual.

If the goods (or services) have a utility value, such as clothing, and are not merely things of luxury, e.g. a diamond tiara, then they are basically necessaries. Whether the minor will have to pay a reasonable price for them then depends upon:

(i) the minor's income which goes with his condition in life. If he is wealthy then quite expensive goods and services may be necessaries for him, provided they are useful;

(ii) the supply of goods which the minor already has. If the minor is well supplied with the particular articles, then they will not be necessaries even though they are useful and are well within his income.

**All of these points are neatly illustrated by the following case.**

### Nash *v* Inman [1908] 2 KB 1

The claimant was a Savile Row tailor and the defendant was a minor undergraduate at Trinity College, Cambridge. The claimant sent his agent to Cambridge because he had heard that the defendant was spending money freely, and might be the sort of person who would be interested in high-class clothing. As a result of the agent's visit, the claimant supplied the defendant with various articles of clothing to the value of £145 0s 3d during the period October 1902 to June 1903. The clothes included 11 fancy waistcoats. The claimant now sued the minor for the price of the clothes. Evidence showed that the defendant's father was in a good position, being an architect with a town and country house, and it could be said that the clothes supplied were suitable to the defendant's position in life. However, his father proved that the defendant was amply supplied with such clothes when the claimant delivered the clothing now in question. *Held* – The claimant's claim failed because he had not established that the goods supplied were necessaries.

(b) *Contracts for the minor's benefit.* These include contracts of service, apprenticeship and education.

**The following case illustrates this.**

### Roberts *v* Gray [1913] 1 KB 520

The defendant wished to become a professional billiards player and entered into an agreement with the claimant, a leading professional, to go on a joint tour. The claimant went to some trouble in order to organise the tour, but a dispute arose between the parties and the defendant refused to go. The claimant now sued for damages of £6,000. *Held* – The contract was for the minor's benefit, being in effect for his instruction as a billiards player. Therefore the claimant could sustain an action for damages for breach of contract, and damages of £1,500 were awarded.

However, trading contracts of minors are not enforceable, no matter how beneficial they may be to the minor's trade or business. The theory behind this rule is that when a minor is in trade his capital is at risk and he might lose it, whereas in a contract of service there is no likelihood of capital loss.

**The following case provides an example of this rule.**

### Mercantile Union Guarantee Corporation Ltd v Ball [1937] 2 KB 498

The purchase on hire-purchase terms of a motor lorry by a minor carrying on business as a haulage contractor was *held* not to be a contract for necessaries or for the minor's benefit, but a trading contract by which the minor could not be bound.

*Comment:* It would be possible for the owner to recover the lorry, without the assistance of s 3 of the Minors' Contracts Act 1987 (*see below*), because a hire-purchase contract is a contract of bailment not a sale. Thus ownership does not pass when the goods are delivered.

## Contracts not binding unless ratified

These are as follows:

(a) *Loans*. These are not binding on the minor unless he ratifies the contract of loan after reaching 18 which he may now legally do. No fresh consideration is now required on ratification.

(b) *Contracts for non-necessary goods*. Again, these are not binding on the minor unless he ratifies the contract after reaching 18 as he may now legally do. Once again, no fresh consideration is required on ratification.

It should be noted that in spite of the fact that the contracts in (a) and (b) above are not enforceable against the minor, he gets a title to any property which passes to him under the arrangement and can give a good title to a third party as where, for example, he sells non-necessary goods on to someone else (who takes in good faith and for value). This was decided in *Stocks* v *Wilson* [1913] 2 KB 235. Furthermore, any money or property transferred by the minor under the contract can only be recovered by him if there has been a total failure of consideration (*see below*).

## Contracts binding unless repudiated

These are usually contracts by which the minor acquires an interest of a permanent nature in the subject-matter of the contract. Such contracts bind the minor unless he takes active steps to avoid them, either during his minority or within a reasonable time thereafter. Examples of voidable contracts are shares in companies, leases of property and partnerships.

**The following case material illustrates these points.**

### Steinberg v Scala (Leeds) Ltd [1923] 2 Ch 452

The claimant, Miss Steinberg, purchased shares in the defendant company and paid certain sums of money on application, on allotment and on one call. Being unable to meet future calls, she repudiated the contract while still a minor and claimed:

(a) rectification of the Register of Members to remove her name therefrom, thus relieving her from liability on future calls; and

(b) the recovery of the money already paid.

The company agreed to rectify the register but was not prepared to return the money paid. *Held* – The claim under (b) above failed because there had not been total failure of consideration. The shares had some value and gave some rights, even though the claimant had not received any dividends and the shares had always stood at a discount on the market.

*Comment:* In *Davies* v *Beynon-Harris* (1931) 47 TLR 424 a minor was allowed to avoid a lease of a flat without liability for future rent or damages but was not allowed to recover rent paid. However, in *Goode* v *Harrison* (1821) 5 B & Ald 147 a partner who was a minor took no steps to avoid the partnership contract while a minor or afterwards. He was held liable for the debts of the firm incurred after he came of age.

# CONSEQUENCES OF THE DEFECTIVE CONTRACTS OF MINORS

We must now have a look at what happens where there has been some performance of a contract with a minor which is either not binding unless ratified or binding unless repudiated.

## Recovery by minor of money paid

Where a minor has paid money under these defective contracts he cannot recover it unless total failure of consideration can be proved, i.e. that the minor has not received any benefit at all under the contract. The court is reluctant to say that no benefit has been received. This can be seen in the context of a contract not binding unless ratified in *Pearce* v *Brain* (*see below*) and in the context of a contract binding unless repudiated in *Steinberg* v *Scala* (*see above*).

### Pearce v Brain [1929] 2 KB 310

Pearce, a minor, exchanged his motor cycle for a motor car belonging to Brain. The minor had little use out of the car, and had in fact driven it only a short distance when it broke down because of serious defects in the back axle. Pearce now sued to recover his motor cycle, claiming that the consideration had wholly failed. *Held* – (a) That a contract for the exchange of goods, while not a sale of goods, is a contract for the supply of goods, and that if the goods are not necessaries, the contract was void if with a minor (now not binding unless ratified). (b) The car was not a necessary good; but the court considered that the minor had received a benefit under the contract, albeit small, and that he could not recover the motor cycle, i.e. the consideration had not wholly failed.

*Comment:* In *Corpe* v *Overton* (1833) 10 Bing 252 a minor agreed to enter into a partnership and deposited £100 with the defendant as security for the due performance of the contract. The minor rescinded the contract before the partnership came into being. *Held* – He could recover the £100 because he had received no benefit, never having been a partner. There had been total failure of consideration.

### Effect of purchase by minor of non-necessary goods

As we have seen, the minor acquires a title to the goods and can give a good title to a third party who takes them bona fide and for value (*Stocks* v *Wilson* [1913] 2 KB 235). The tradesman who sold the goods to the minor cannot recover them from the third party.

However, as regards recovery from the minor, if he still has the property, s 3 of the Minors' Contracts Act 1987 provides that the court can order restitution, for example, of non-necessary goods to the tradesman, where the minor is refusing to pay for them. As we know, he cannot be sued for the price.

The question of recovery in any particular case is left to the court which must regard it as just and equitable to allow recovery, though a restitution order can be made whether the minor is fraudulent, as where he obtained the goods by overstating his age, *or not*. Fraud is no longer a requirement for restitution. Money will be virtually impossible to recover because it will normally be mixed with other funds and not identifiable. However, the minor could be made, under s 3, to offer up any goods acquired in exchange for the non-necessary goods. The tradesman recovers the goods in the state he finds them and cannot ask for compensation from the minor if they are, for example, damaged.

Thus if Ann, a minor, buys a gold necklace and does not pay for it, the seller can recover the necklace from Ann. If Ann exchanges the necklace for a gold bangle the seller can recover the gold bangle from Ann. If Ann sells the necklace for £500, it is not clear whether the seller can get restitution of the money unless it has been kept separate from Ann's other funds or can be identified in a fund containing other money of Ann's, for example, a bank account into which she has paid her salary. Section 3 says that the seller can recover the article passing under the contract 'or any property representing it'. It is at least arguable that Ann's general funds do not solely represent the necklace in the way that the bangle does. Judicial interpretation is required.

### Guarantees

Section 2 of the Minors' Contracts Act 1987 provides that a guarantee by an adult of a minor's transaction shall be enforceable against the guarantor even though the main contractual obligation is not enforceable against the minor. Thus if a bank makes a loan to a minor or allows a minor an overdraft and an adult gives a guarantee of that transaction, then although the loan or overdraft cannot be enforced against the minor, the adult guarantor can be required to pay.

## MENTAL DISORDER AND DRUNKENNESS

Where the property and affairs of a mental patient are placed under the management of the court by order under Part VII of the Mental Health Act 1983, the mental patient has no capacity to contract as regards that property. However, the other party is bound should the patient's representatives wish to regard him as bound.

Apart from the above, the position is governed by the common law as follows:

(a) A contract made by a person who by reason of mental disease or drunkenness is incapable of understanding what he is doing is valid unless he can prove:
    (i) that he did not understand the nature of the contract; and
    (ii) that the other party knew this to be the case.

(b) A contract made by such a person is binding on him if he afterwards ratifies it at any time when the state of his mind is such that he can understand what he is doing.

(c) Where necessary goods are sold and delivered to a person who by reason of mental incapacity or drunkenness is incompetent to contract, he is bound to pay a reasonable price (Sale of Goods Act 1979, s 3(2)). This is also true of services, but by reason of the common law.

(d) Necessaries are 'goods suitable to the condition in life of such person and to his actual requirements at the time of the sale and delivery' (1979 Act, s 3(3)). The common law defines necessary services in the same way. Therefore, the principle of 'necessaries' is applied to persons with mental incapacity and drunkards in the same way as it is to minors.

**The following cases illustrate the rules set out above.**

### Imperial Loan Co v Stone [1892] QB 599

This was an action on a promissory note. The defendant pleaded that at the time of making the note he was insane and that the claimant knew he was. The jury found that he was in fact insane but could not agree on the question of whether the claimant knew it. The judge entered judgment for the defendant. *Held* – that he was wrong. The defendant in order to succeed must convince the court on both issues.

*Comment:* In *Hart* v *O'Connor* [1985] 2 All ER 880 the Privy Council refused to set aside an agreement to sell farmland in New Zealand because although the seller was of unsound mind, his affliction was not apparent. The price paid was not unreasonable. If it had been the Privy Council said that the contract could have been set aside for equitable fraud as an unconscionable bargain.

### Matthews v Baxter (1873) LR 8 Exch 132

Matthews agreed to buy houses from Baxter. He was so drunk as not to know what he was doing. Afterwards, when sober, he ratified and confirmed the contract. It was held that both parties were bound by it.

*Comment:* A contract with a drunken person must in effect always be voidable by him because presumably the fact that he is drunk will be known to the other party. This is not so in regard to unsoundness of mind which might not be known to the other party.

*The business application:* Lawyers and accountants in practice may have clients who are of advancing years whose sanity may come into doubt at a future time and where there is a desire to avoid the cost and delay of receiver proceedings through the court. In this connection the Enduring Powers of Attorney Act 1985 makes it possible to enter into an agency agreement with, say, a younger member of the family or the practitioner being the agent. Such an agreement does not terminate on the client's loss of mental capacity as other forms of agency do. Thus an application for a receiver is avoided as are the uncertainties that may arise from not knowing precisely when or if the client/principal has become mentally incapable. The instrument creating the power must be in the form prescribed by the 1985 Act. In 1998 the Lord Chancellor issued a Green Paper called 'Who Decides?' that proposes to extend the agent's powers under an enduring power to cover healthcare and the general welfare of the principal, in addition to decisions on property and finance permitted under existing law.

## CORPORATIONS

Regardless of the method by which it is formed, a company on incorporation becomes a *legal person*, acquires an identity quite separate and distinct from its members, and carries on its activities through agents.

The following case is a classic example of what is known as the corporate entity theory.

### Salomon v Salomon & Co [1897] AC 22

Salomon carried on business as a leather merchant and boot manufacturer. In 1892 he formed a limited company to take over the business. The memorandum of association was signed by Salomon, his wife, daughter and four sons. Each subscribed for one share. The company paid £39,000 to Salomon for the business and the mode of payment was to give Salomon £10,000 in debentures, secured by a floating charge, 20,000 shares of £1 each and £9,000 in cash. The company fell on hard times and a liquidator was appointed. The debts of the unsecured creditors amounted to nearly £8,000, and the company's assets were approximately £6,000. The unsecured creditors claimed all the remaining assets on the ground that the company was a mere alias or agent for Salomon. *Held* – The company was a separate and distinct person. The debentures were perfectly valid and, therefore, Salomon was entitled to the remaining assets in part-payment of the secured debentures held by him.

### The *ultra vires* rule – generally

As regards powers, charter corporations have the same powers as ordinary persons and may act legally even though the transaction concerned is not provided for in the charter. However, if a charter corporation does act beyond its powers the Crown may forfeit the charter or a member of the corporation may ask the court to restrain it by injunction from doing acts which are *ultra vires* (i.e. beyond its powers).

The following case is an illustration of a member's injunction to prevent a charter corporation from acting *ultra vires*. A member of a registered company has the same right. However, if a statutory corporation were to act *ultra vires* the Attorney-General would have to ask the court for an injunction on behalf of the public, since these statutory corporations are public corporations and no individual member of the public is able to complain to the court about them. The Attorney-General must do it on behalf of us all. Although there may be a revival of the public corporation structure in the field of business, with which this text is concerned, there is little point at the present time in looking at their legal position further since the undertakings of most of them have been returned to the private sector as registered public limited companies.

### Jenkin v Pharmaceutical Society [1921] I Ch 392

The defendant society was incorporated by Royal Charter in 1843 for the purpose of advancing chemistry and pharmacy and promoting a uniform system of education of those who should practise the same, and also for the protection of those who carried on the business of chemists and druggists. *Held* – The expenditure of the funds of the society in the formation of an industrial committee, to attempt to regulate hours of work and wages and conditions of work between employer and employee members of the society, was *ultra vires* the charter, because it was a trade union activity which was not contemplated by the Charter of 1843. Further, the expenditure of money on an insurance scheme for members was also not within the powers given in the charter, for it amounted to converting the defendant society into an insurance company. The claimant, a member of the society, was entitled to an injunction to restrain the society from implementing the above schemes.

## *Ultra vires* rule – registered companies

The powers of registered companies are determined by the objects clause of the memorandum of association and an act in excess of the powers given in this clause is *ultra vires* and *void*, i.e. of no effect.

The following case provides a classic illustration of the operation of the *ultra vires* rule at common law and before the intervention of Parliament (see *below*).

### Ashbury Railway Carriage & Iron Co v Riche (1875) LR 7 HL 653

The company was formed for the purposes (stated in the memorandum of association) of making and selling railway wagons and other railway plant and carrying on the business of mechanical engineers and general contractors. The company bought a concession for the construction of a railway system in Belgium from Antwerp to Tournai and entered into an agreement whereby Messrs Riche were to construct the railway line. Messrs Riche commenced the work and the company paid over certain sums of money in connection with the contract. The Ashbury company later ran into difficulties, and the shareholders wished the directors to take over the contract in a personal capacity and indemnify the shareholders. The directors thereupon repudiated the contract on behalf of the company and Messrs Riche sued for breach of contract. *Held* – The directors were able to repudiate because the contract to construct a railway system was *ultra vires* and void. On a proper construction of the objects, the company had power to supply materials for the construction of railways but had no power to engage in the actual construction of them. Further, the subsequent assent of all the shareholders could not, in those days, make the contract binding, for a principal cannot ratify the *ultra vires* contracts of his agent.

*Comment:* Such a contract could now be ratified by special resolution of the members (*see below*).

By way of explanation of the decision in the above case it should be said that the *ultra vires* rule was brought in by the courts in earlier times to protect shareholders. It was thought that if a shareholder X bought shares in a company which had as its main object publishing and allied activities then X would not want the directors of that company to start up a different kind of business because he wanted his money in publishing.

In more recent times it has been noted that shareholders are not so fussy about the kind of business the directors take the company into so long as it makes money to pay dividends and raises the price of the company's shares on the stock market thus giving a capital gain. In these days of the conglomerates it is doubtful whether any investor invests in a company because of only one facet of its trading.

The people most affected by the *ultra vires* rule in more recent times were those who had supplied goods or services to a company for a purpose not covered by its objects clause. If the company was solvent no doubt such creditors would be paid, but if it went into insolvent liquidation they would not even be able to put in a claim. Other creditors might get some part of their debts paid, say, 20p in the £1 if the company had any funds, but the *ultra vires* suppliers would get nothing. For this reason it became usual to put in the objects clause of the memorandum a large number of objects and powers, and to include a special clause stating that each clause of the objects clause contained a separate and independent object which could be carried on separately from any of the others. The House of Lords decided in *Cotman* v *Brougham* [1918] AC 514 that this type of clause was legal, and this greatly relieved the problem of *ultra vires* by giving the directors legitimate access to many kinds of business listed in the objects clause.

Also the decision of the Court of Appeal in *Bell Houses Ltd* v *City Wall Properties Ltd* [1966] 2 All ER 674 states that the objects clause can be drafted in such a way as to include a *subjective* objects clause as it is called. This allows the company to carry on any additional business which the members or directors choose.

In this way the limitations which are placed by the common law on a company's business activities by the *ultra vires* rule have been much reduced, though of course the control over the activities of the directors by the members has also been lessened. In fact with a large number of clauses in the objects clause as one finds in the typical memorandum, and with sub-clauses such as those approved in *Cotman* and *Bell Houses*, the modern company's contractual capacity approaches that of a natural person. The *ultra vires* rule as a method of controlling the activities of the boards of companies has been largely abandoned as the twentieth century has progressed. In addition, there has been massive statutory intervention by Parliament to make the *ultra vires* rule ineffective (*see below*).

## The Companies Act 1985

Sections 35 and 35A of the 1985 Act, as inserted by the Companies Act 1989, now represent the United Kingdom's response to Article 9 of the First Directive (No 68/151) issued by the European Community for the harmonisation of company law in the member states of the EC. It is intended largely to eliminate the effect of the *ultra vires* rule on the claims of creditors, though it has perhaps less impact today since, as we have seen, fewer transactions are likely to be *ultra vires* at common law.

However, on the assumption that the narrow scope of a particular company's objects clause may lead to a transaction being *ultra vires* at common law a review of the provisions is worthwhile.

Section 35 deals with the *ultra vires* rule as it relates to the company's capacity to enter into the transaction. The authority and power of its directors to make contracts on the company's behalf as its agents is dealt with by s 35A.

These sections do not abolish the rule but reform it. However, so far as trade creditors are concerned little should now be heard of it. There is a continuing relevance of the rule in other areas which are considered below.

### The company's capacity

Section 35(1) of the Companies Act 1985 states: 'The validity of an act done by a company shall not be called into question on the ground of lack of capacity by reason of anything in the company's memorandum.' The immediate effect of this would be to put right the sort of problem which was raised in *Ashbury*. Something in its memorandum, i.e. its objects clause, confined it to making things for railways but not a whole railway system. Mr Riche's action would now have been successful and he would have got a remedy from the court, i.e. damages for breach of contract. In addition, the drafting techniques approved in *Cotman* and *Bell Houses* will continue to be useful in converting long objects clauses into a series of independent objects and allowing the members or directors to choose new businesses for the company. These clauses will undoubtedly continue in use for many years to come, except where the company is formed with, or changes its objects to, the 'one-line' form permitted by the 1985 Act (*see below*).

### Exceptions to s 35(1)

(a) A shareholder may ask for an injunction to prevent the directors entering into an *ultra vires* contract, but if the contract has been made the court cannot grant an injunction to stop it proceeding, nor can it do so if the members have ratified the contract by a special resolution.

(b) Directors are as before placed under a specific duty to observe the limitations on their powers in the memorandum and the articles and can be sued by the company for any loss caused by a transaction which is outside the company's constitution (s 35A(5)). However, the *ultra vires* act can be ratified by a special resolution of the members, and if it is desired to exempt the directors from liability for damage then *another* special resolution is required. It was not possible for the members to ratify in this way before the present legislation (*see* the *Ashbury* decision).

(c) Where the transaction is with a director of the company or its holding company or a person connected with him, e.g. a spouse, then it is voidable (i.e. the company can have it set aside). However, the members may ratify it by special resolution where the problem is that the transaction is beyond the company's capacity.

These exceptions indicate that the *ultra vires* rule has only been reformed and not abolished. For example, if a member asks for an injunction the question of whether the sort of transaction to be stopped is or is not *ultra vires* will depend upon the contents of the memorandum and the effect of *Cotman* and subjective objects clauses (if any), just as it did in the past since s 35 does not apply to defeat a claim for an injunction by a shareholder, nor does it apply to prevent a claim against the directors if they cause the company loss by acting *ultra vires* or to transactions involving directors and their connected persons.

### Power of the directors to bind the company

Section 35A(1) of the Companies Act 1985 states: 'In favour of a person dealing with a company in good faith, the power of the board of directors to bind the company, or authorize others to do so shall be deemed to be free of any limitation under the company's constitution'.

Actual knowledge of the contents of the memorandum or articles is not in itself bad faith and, under s 35B, the outsider has no duty to inquire as to the directors' powers. Those who have read these documents but have misinterpreted them will be all right. If we look at the *Ashbury* situation it would have been possible for businessmen to misinterpret the objects clause which actually allowed the company to enter into 'general contracting' but the court took a restrictive view and said that this covered only general contracting in the field of making things for railways. Those who have actual knowledge of the company's or directors' lack of authority and act in bad faith will not be all right, as in *International Sales and Agencies Ltd* v *Marcus* [1982] 3 All ER 551 where a sole effective director used the company's power to draw cheques to issue cheques to pay the private loan of a director who had died insolvent. He was aided and abetted by the lender who knew all about the circumstances and who along with the sole effective director was acting contrary to the company's interests. The cheques were held to be invalid and could not be enforced against the company.

In addition, the section deals with a situation where the directors authorise other persons to make contracts on behalf of the company. This is to overcome the common law rule that a company can only act through 'organs' of the company. At common law the board of directors is an organ of the company, but only if acting collectively as a board. Section 35A overcomes this by making it clear that an act done by a person authorised by the board is in effect an act of the board and therefore an act by an organ of the company. Thus if the board authorises the company's purchasing officer to buy materials from outsiders for use in the company's manufacturing process, each purchase will in effect be a transaction decided by the directors. There is no longer an assumption, as in previous law, that all commercial decisions are made at board-room level. If, therefore, the board collectively makes a decision to enter into a transaction which is beyond its powers, the outsider can rely on s 35A to make the transaction enforceable against the company. The same is true if an individual director or other person authorised by the board to act exceeds the powers of the board in respect of a transaction on behalf of the company which he as an authorised person has made, as where for example he is authorised to borrow money but in doing so exceeds any limit put by the board's powers. The loan is enforceable in spite of this.

### Exceptions to s 35A(1)

The section does not apply:

(a) If the act of the directors is illegal. Thus it would not authorise the issue of shares at a discount because this is forbidden by the Companies Act 1985.

(b) It would not help in a situation in which the directors had used their powers for an improper purpose provided this is known to the other party. Thus in *Rolled Steel Products (Holdings) Ltd* v *British Steel Corporation* [1985] 3 All ER 401 a managing director and major shareholder of a company called Scottish Sheet Steel gave a guarantee of that company's debts to British Steel. British Steel wanted additional security and the managing director gave one on behalf of Rolled Steel, which was another company of which he was managing director and major shareholder. The companies were not connected in any way and British Steel knew that the managing director was not acting for the benefit of Rolled Steel and that, therefore, he was using his legitimate power to give guarantees on behalf of Rolled Steel for an improper purpose. The guarantee by Rolled Steel was not enforceable against it. If British Steel had not been aware of the improper purpose, it would have been enforceable.

(c) The company cannot sue on the transaction but only the third party. The section says: 'In favour of a person dealing with a company . . . '. However, the members can ratify the transaction by special resolution if the company's lack of capacity is the problem or by an ordinary resolution if only the directors' powers are in issue.

(d) As before, if the party dealing with the company is a director of the company or its holding company or connected person, e.g. a spouse, the director concerned cannot rely on s 35A. The transaction is voidable by the company, but as already mentioned the company can ratify it by special or ordinary resolution as the case may be.

### The single line clause

Section 3A of the Companies Act 1985 states that a company may alter its objects (or be registered with objects) which merely state that the company is to 'carry on business as a general commercial company'. This means that it can carry on any trade or business whatsoever. All necessary powers will be implied.

If a company does register with or change its objects clause to this new formula it will have effectively opted out of the *ultra vires* rule even for internal purposes of shareholder injunctions, director liability and transactions with directors and their connected persons.

### The rule of constructive notice

At one time knowledge of the contents of a company's constitution was assumed by the courts to be in the minds of all of us even if we had not seen or read it. This was because the memorandum and articles are registered with the Registrar of Companies and the register can be inspected.

Under more recent provisions added by the Companies Act 1989 to the Companies Act 1985, the rule of constructive notice of the contents of the company's memorandum and articles and also company documents kept by the Registrar is abolished.

### Charities

There is a special regime for charities which obviously need special treatment because people give, not so much to the charity as to its objects which should therefore be kept to. Under the Charities Act 1993, in the case of the incorporated charity, s 35 is not available to protect a transaction by a person dealing with a charity unless:

(a) he has given full consideration to the charity in money or money's worth which simply means that it is a deal in which the charity has received the proper value in terms, say, of goods it has received under the contract; *and*

(b) he is not aware that the transaction was beyond the company's objects; *or*

(c) he was not aware that the company was a charity.

The various forms of ratification referred to above do not apply.

## GRADED QUESTIONS

### Essay mode

1  (a)  What do you understand by the expression 'contractual capacity'? Illustrate your answer with examples.

(b)  G, aged 17, entered into the following agreements:

(i)   a contract with a tailor to supply him with a new suit of clothes for £150;

(ii)  a partnership agreement;

(iii) a loan of £2,000 at 10 per cent interest, to be repaid in two years.

Advise G which of the agreements are binding upon him.

*(Association of Chartered Certified Accountants)*

### Objective mode

Four alternative answers are given. Select ONE only. Circle the answer which you consider to be correct. Check your answers by referring back to the information given in the chapter and against the answers at the back of the book.

1  Which of the following contracts is required to be made by deed?

A   A lease of more than three years.

B   A lease of less than three years.

C   A contract of guarantee.

D   Rental property subject to a mortgage.

2  Fred decided that he must move to Canada and Alan enters into a verbal contract to buy his house in Derbyshire for £150,000. Fred and Alan agree all the terms of the contract, including a completion date. Before anything is put into writing, Alan changes his mind. Is the contract:

A  Invalid.     B  Voidable.     C  Illegal.     D  Unenforceable?

3  Compost Ltd, manufacturer of various kinds of health foods, is anxious to expand the export side of the business. Some years ago the company initiated a similar sales drive abroad but unfortunately incurred a number of bad debts which were not recovered because of the difficulties experienced by the company in bringing actions in foreign courts.

Vend, the sales manager of Compost, decides to enter into negotiations with Schloss, who is a general agent with branches in England and Boravia. Schloss agrees for an extra commission to introduce Compost's products in Boravia on terms that he will reimburse Compost if any of the customers he introduces fails to pay for goods received. This agreement is made on the telephone and Schloss agrees to send written confirmation as soon as possible. Shortly afterwards Braunbrot, who is the buyer for Gesundheit, a chain of health food shops in Boravia, rings up Vend and says: 'Schloss tells me that you are prepared to supply us with some items at a very competitive price. You will be receiving our order this week.' A large order from Gesundheit arrives and the goods are despatched by Compost. Unfortunately Braunbrot does not regard the packaging as sufficiently attractive and complains to Schloss. As a result of this complaint, Schloss rings Vend and says: 'Braunbrot does not think much of your packaging and for that matter neither do I. You will get no more orders from him and what is more I will no longer act as your agent here. There is no point now in writing to you regarding our agreement.'

Three months later, Vend learns that Gesundheit have become insolvent and cannot pay for the goods which they received. Vend rings Schloss immediately and asks him to pay Gesundheit's debt as agreed. Schloss refuses to make any payment and Compost is intending to sue him and claim against his assets in England.

The contract between Schloss and Compost is:

**A** A guarantee and enforceable.
**B** An indemnity and unenforceable.
**C** A guarantee and unenforceable.
**D** An indemnity and enforceable.

*With reference to the following information answer questions 4 and 5.*

Dabbler, who was training to be a commercial artist, left art school on his seventeenth birthday without having completed the course and decided to go into business as a dealer in antiques and bric-à-brac. For this purpose he entered into an agreement with Jasper to rent for one year a small shop and obtained £1,000 worth of stock on credit from another dealer, Peddler, with whom he was friendly.

After trading for two months Dabbler found that because of inexperience he was unable to buy articles at a price which would give a reasonable margin of profit, and he therefore decided to give up business and informed Jasper that he would no longer require the shop. Dabbler has not paid any rent to Jasper and still owes Peddler £1,000; he also refuses to hand over the remainder of the original stock on the ground that he might start another business.

**4** As regards the agreement to rent the shop:

**A** Dabbler is liable to occupy the shop for one year and pay the rent.
**B** Dabbler is not bound to occupy the shop for one year but must pay the rent.
**C** Dabbler need not stay in occupation of the shop but must pay two months' rent.
**D** Dabbler need not stay in occupation of the shop and cannot be made to pay any rent.

**5** As regards the stock supplied by Peddler:

**A** Dabbler is liable to pay Peddler in full and may then retain the stock.
**B** Dabbler is only bound to pay Peddler for the goods he has sold and can retain the rest without payment.
**C** The debt cannot be enforced against Dabbler who may also retain the remainder of the stock.
**D** The debt cannot be enforced against Dabbler but he is required by law to return the remainder of the stock to Peddler.

6  The Chartered Institute of Hod Carriers was incorporated by Royal Charter for the purpose of advancing the science of hod carrying and promoting a uniform system of education of those who should practise the same. The Institute has announced a scheme under which it intends to set up a chain of launderettes in the hope that the profits will render an increase in subscriptions unnecessary.

Peregrine, who is a member of the Institute, is outraged by the Council's scheme which he regards as seriously affecting the image of the profession. He asks your advice as to the legal position of the Institute.

Peregrine should be advised:

A  That the scheme is valid and can be implemented without risk to the Institute.
B  That the scheme is *ultra vires* and cannot effectively be implemented because all relevant contracts will be void.
C  That the scheme is *ultra vires* and can be implemented effectively and without risk because all relevant contracts are enforceable.
D  That the scheme although *ultra vires* can be effectively implemented so far as contract law is concerned but the Institute may forfeit its Charter.

7  Under s 35A of the Companies Act 1985, what is the position of a person who innocently enters into an *ultra vires* contract with the company and decided on by the sales director as part of a corporate project which the board had authorised him to carry out?

A  The contract is void and no action can be taken on it.
B  The contract is deemed to be within the contractual capacity of the company and the third party can sue upon it.
C  The third party can only sue the director in person for exceeding his powers.
D  The contract is unenforceable but the third party can retain any property received under it.

8  Lord Seaworthy is 95 years of age and a wealthy retired Rear-Admiral. He suffers from periods of mental incapacity and his family has been advised to place his property and affairs under the management of the court or of his accountant but no steps have been taken to achieve this.

Lord Seaworthy recently visited London with his grandson but during the visit managed to slip away on his own for three hours. He was subsequently found standing under one of the fountains in Trafalgar Square re-enacting a naval battle with a number of paper boats. It now appears that he had visited the Boat Show and purchased a cabin cruiser worth £125,000 after telling the salesman it would look well on his mantelpiece.

The manufacturers of the cabin cruiser, having delivered Lord Seaworthy's purchase, are now pressing for payment. Lady Seaworthy is resisting the claim on the grounds of her husband's mental incapacity. What advice should she receive?

A  That Lord Seaworthy must pay in full.
B  That Lord Seaworthy must pay a reasonable price.
C  That the contract is voidable by Lord Seaworthy.
D  That the contract is void and not binding on Lord Seaworthy.

*Answers to questions set in objective mode appear on p 707.*

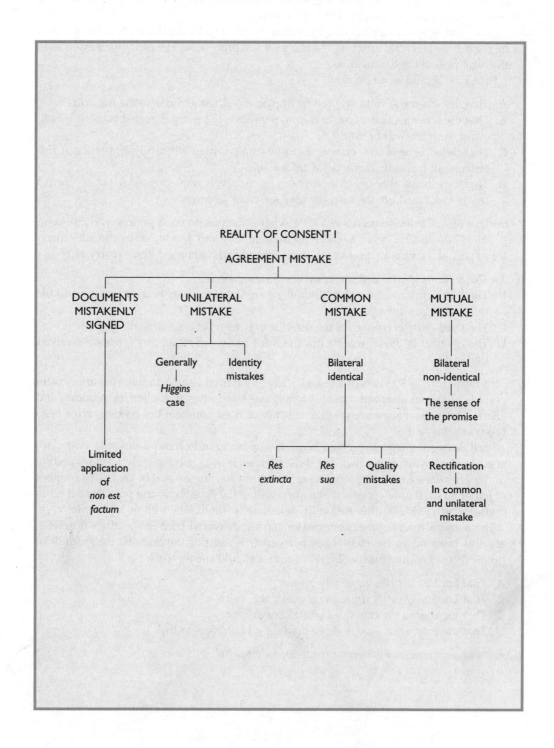

The objective of this chapter is to begin a study of the various factors which can affect an agreement once it has been formed. We begin by dealing with the law relating to mistake which affects the true consent of one or both of the parties so that one or both of them may ask to be released from contractual obligations.

## INTRODUCTION

A contract which is regular in all respects may still fail because there is no real consent to it by one or both of the parties. There is no *consensus ad idem* or meeting of the minds. Consent may be rendered unreal by mistake, misrepresentation, duress and undue influence. There are also instances of inequality of bargaining power where it would be inequitable to enforce the resulting agreement.

It is particularly important to distinguish between mistake and misrepresentation because a contract affected by mistake is void, whereas a contract affected by misrepresentations is only voidable. As between the parties themselves, this makes little difference since in both cases goods sold and money paid can be recovered. However, the distinction can be vital so far as third parties are concerned. If A sells goods to B under circumstances of mistake and B resells them to C, then C gets no title and A can recover the goods from him or sue him for damages in conversion. If, on the other hand, the contract between A and B was voidable for misrepresentation, then if B sold the goods to C who took them bona fide and for value before A had rescinded his contract with B, then C would get a good title and A would have a remedy only against B. For the position where A has rescinded *see Car & Universal Finance Co v Caldwell* (1964) and *Newtons of Wembley Ltd v Williams* (1964) at Chapter 11.

## AGREEMENT MISTAKE IN GENERAL

Mistake, to be operative, must be of *fact* and not of *law*. Furthermore, the concept has a technical meaning and does not cover, for example, errors of judgment as to value. Thus, if A buys an article thinking it is worth £100 when in fact it is worth only £50, the contract is good and A must bear the loss if there has been no misrepresentation by the seller. This is what is meant by the maxim *caveat emptor* (let the buyer beware). An interesting example of how the judiciary can interpret what some might think to be mistakes of law as mistakes of fact is provided by *Solle v Butcher* (*see below*).

The various categories of mistake will now be considered, beginning with the rather special case where a document is signed by mistake.

## DOCUMENTS MISTAKENLY SIGNED

If a person signs a contract in the mistaken belief that he is signing a document of a different nature, there may be a mistake which avoids the contract. He may be able to plead *non est factum* ('it is not my deed'). This is a defence open to a person who has signed a document by mistake. Originally it was a special defence to protect those who could not read who had signed deeds which had been incorrectly read over to them. At one time the defence was available only where the mistake referred to the *kind* of document it was and not merely its contents. Now the defence is available to a person who has signed a document having made a *fundamental* mistake as to the kind of document it is or as to its contents. However, the defendant must prove that he made the mistake despite having taken all reasonable care. If he is negligent he will not usually be able to plead the defence. This means that the plea is rarely successful and in practice not very significant, the more so since Lord Wilberforce said in the *Saunders* case (*below*) that merely to sign a document without actually knowing its contents was in itself negligent even where its contents had been misrepresented. This statement may not, however, cover the signing of commonly confidential documents.

**The following case provides an illustration of the above rules.**

### Saunders v Anglia Building Society [1970] 3 All ER 961

Mrs Gallie, a widow aged 78 years, signed a document which Lee, her nephew's friend, told her was a deed of gift of her house to her nephew. She did not read the document but believed what Lee had told her. In fact the document was an assignment of her leasehold interest in the house to Lee, and Lee later mortgaged that interest to a building society. In an action by Mrs Gallie against Lee and the building society it was *held* at first instance – (a) that the assignment was void and did not confer a title on Lee; (b) although Mrs Gallie had been negligent, she was not estopped from denying the validity of the deed against the building society for she owed it no duty. The Court of Appeal, in allowing an appeal by the building society, held that the plea of *non est factum* was not available to Mrs Gallie. The transaction intended and carried out was the same, i.e. an assignment.

The appeal to the House of Lords was brought by Saunders, the executrix of Mrs Gallie's estate. The House of Lords affirmed the decision of the Court of Appeal but took the opportunity to restate the law relating to the avoidance of documents on the ground of mistake as follows:

(a) The plea of *non est factum* will rarely be available to a person of full capacity who signs a document apparently having legal effect without troubling to read it, i.e. negligently.

(b) A mistake as to the identity of the person in whose favour the document is executed will not normally support a plea of *non est factum* though it may do if the court regards the mistake as fundamental (Lord Reid and Lord Hodson). Neither judge felt that the personality error made by Mrs Gallie was sufficient to support the plea.

(c) The distinction taken in *Howatson v Webb* [1908] 1 Ch 1 that the mistake must be as to the class or character of the document and not merely as to its contents was regarded as illogical. Under the *Howatson* test, if X signed a guarantee for £1,000 believing it to be an insurance policy he escaped all liability on the guarantee, but if he signed a guarantee for

£10,000 believing it to be a guarantee for £100 he was fully liable for £10,000. Under *Saunders* the document which was in fact signed must be 'fundamentally different', 'radically different', or 'totally different'. The test is more flexible than the character/contents one and yet still restricts the operation of the plea of *non est factum*.

*Comment:* (i) The charge of negligence might be avoided where a person was told he was witnessing a confidential document and had no reason to doubt that he was. Many such documents are witnessed each day and the witnesses would never dream of asking to read them nor would they think themselves negligent because they had not done so. Surely the *Saunders* decision is not intended to turn witnesses into snoopers. Thus the decision in the old case of *Lewis v Clay* (1898) 77 LT 653 would probably be the same under modern law. In that case Clay was asked by Lord William Neville to witness a confidential document and signed in holes in blotting paper placed over the document by Neville. In fact he was signing two promissory notes and two letters authorising Lewis to pay the amount of the notes to Lord William Neville. The court *held* that the signature of Clay in the circumstances had no more effect than if it had been written for an autograph collector or in an album and he was not bound by the notes. In fact the survival of the plea of *non est factum* in cases such as Lewis is recognised in certain of the judgments in the House of Lords in *Saunders*. For example, Lord Pearson said that because of the cunning deception in that case and because of the supposedly confidential nature of the documents, he would have allowed the plea in the *Lewis* case to succeed, as indeed it did.

(ii) As between the immediate parties to what is always in effect a fraud, there is, of course, no difficulty in avoiding the contract or transaction mistakenly entered into. The rules set out above are relevant only where the contract or transaction mistakenly entered into has affected a third party, as where he has taken a bill of exchange bona fide and for value on which the defendant's signature was obtained under circumstances of mistake (*Foster v Mackinnon* (1869) LR 4 CP 704) or has lent money on an interest in land obtained by a fraudulent assignment under circumstances of mistake (*Saunders v Anglia Building Society* (1970), *see above*). The principles set out in *Saunders'* case apply also to those who sign blank forms as well as to those who sign completed documents without reading them (*United Dominions Trust Ltd v Western* [1975] 3 All ER 1017).

## UNILATERAL MISTAKE

Unilateral mistake occurs when one of the parties, X, is mistaken as to some fundamental fact concerning the contract and the other party, Y, knows, or ought to know, this. The latter requirement is important because if Y does not know that X is mistaken the contract is good.

**The following case provides an example of this rule.**

### Higgins (W) Ltd *v* Northampton Corporation [1927] 1 Ch 128

The claimant entered into a contract with the corporation for the erection of dwelling houses. The claimant made an arithmetical error in arriving at his price, having deducted a certain rather small sum twice over. The corporation sealed the contract, assuming that the price arrived at by the claimant was correct. *Held* – The contract was binding on the parties.

Rectification of such a contract was not possible because the power of the court to rectify agreements made under mistake is confined to common not unilateral mistake. Here, rectification would only have been granted if fraud or misrepresentation had been present.

*Comment:* (i) Since this case was decided the courts have moved away from the idea that rectification of a contract for unilateral mistake is permissible only if there is some form of sharp practice (*see Thomas Bates & Sons Ltd v Wyndham's (Lingerie) Ltd* (1981) *below*). Even so, rectification would not have been granted in this case because Northampton Corporation was not aware of the claimant's error, which is still a requirement for rectification.

(ii) The rule of unilateral mistake does not seem to apply to mistakes as to the value of the contract. If you go into a junk shop and recognise a genuine Georgian silver teapot marked at £10, then your contract of purchase, if made, would be good in law, although it would be obvious that the seller had made a mistake and that the buyer was aware of it. This is the rule of *caveat venditor* (let the seller beware) and applies provided the seller intends to offer the goods at his marked price.

The cases are mainly concerned with mistake by one party as to the *identity* of the other party. Thus a contract may be void for mistake if X contracts with Y thinking that Y is another person, Z, and if Y knows that X is under that misapprehension. Proof of Y's knowledge is essential but since in most cases Y is a fraudulent person, the point does not present great difficulties.

**The following case and comment shows how the rules are applied.**

### Cundy *v* Lindsay (1878) 3 App Cas 459

The respondents were linen manufacturers with a business in Belfast. A fraudulent person named Blenkarn wrote to the respondents from 37 Wood Street, Cheapside, ordering a quantity of handkerchiefs but signed his letter in such a way that it appeared to come from Messrs Blenkiron, who were a well-known and solvent house doing business at 123 Wood Street. The respondents knew of the existence of Blenkiron but did not know the address. Accordingly the handkerchiefs were sent to 37 Wood Street. Blenkarn then sold them to the appellants, and was later convicted and sentenced for the fraud. The respondents sued the appellants in conversion claiming that the contract they had made with Blenkarn was void for mistake, and that the property had not passed to Blenkarn or to the appellants. *Held* – The respondents succeeded; there was an operative mistake as to the party with whom they were contracting.

*Comment:* (i) It is, however, essential that at the time of making the apparent contract the mistaken party regarded the identity of the other party as vital and that he intended to deal with some person other than the actual person to whom in fact he addressed the offer, as in *Cundy v Lindsay* (1878) (*see above*). The mistake must be as to *identity*, not *attributes*, e.g. creditworthiness. As between the parties the result is much the same since a mistake as to attributes may make the contract *voidable*, but the difference may vitally affect the interests of third parties. Thus in *King's Norton Metal Co Ltd v Edridge, Merrett and Co Ltd* (1897) 14 TLR 98 where the facts were similar to *Cundy*, a fraudulent person called Wallis ordered goods from the claimants using notepaper headed Hallam & Co. The notepaper said that Hallam & Co had agencies abroad and generally represented the company as creditworthy. The claimants sold Hallam & Co some brass rivet wire on credit. The goods were never paid for but Wallis sold the goods on to Edridge Merrett who paid for them and were innocent of the way in which Wallis had obtained them. The claimants sued Edridge Merrett in conversion saying that the contract between them and Hallam/Wallis was void for mistake so that Edridge Merrett did not become owners of the wire because Hallam/Wallis had not. The Court of Appeal *held* that the contract between King's Norton and Edridge was voidable for fraud but not void for mistake. The claimants could not show a confusion of entities. There was no other Hallam or Wallis in their business lives with whom they could have been confused.

(ii) The difference between *Cundy* and *King's Norton* is that in *Cundy* there was another entity to get mixed up with. In *King's Norton* there was no one else to be confused with.

There were formerly difficulties where the parties contracted face to face because in such a case the suggestion could always be made that whatever the fraudulent party was saying about his identity, the mistaken party must be regarded as intending to contract with the person in front of him, whoever he was. Thus in this situation, the court might find on the facts of the case that the contract was voidable for fraud or sometimes void for mistake.

However, the position is now a little clearer as a result of the decision in *Lewis* v *Averay* (1971) (*see below*) where it was said that if the parties contracted face to face the contract will normally be voidable for fraud but rarely void for mistake. However, much depends upon the facts of the case and if the court is convinced on the evidence that identity was vital then even a 'face to face' contract will be regarded as void for mistake, as *Ingram* v *Little* (1961) (*see below*) shows.

### Lewis *v* Averay [1971] 3 All ER 907

Mr Lewis agreed to sell his car to a rogue who called on him after seeing an advertisement. Before the sale took place the rogue talked knowledgeably about the film world giving the impression that he was the actor Richard Green in the 'Robin Hood' serial which was running on TV at the time. He signed a dud cheque for £450 in the name of 'R. A. Green' and was allowed to have the log book and drive the car away late the same night when he produced a film studio pass in the name of 'Green'. *Held* – by the Court of Appeal – that Mr Lewis had effectively contracted to sell the car to the rogue and could not recover it or damages from Mr Averay, a student, who had bought it from the rogue for £200. The contract between Mr Lewis and the rogue was voidable for fraud but not void for unilateral mistake.

*Comment:* It is thought that the contract would be void for mistake in a case such as this if the dishonest person assumed a disguise so that he appeared physically to be the person he said he was.

### Ingram and others *v* Little [1961] 1 QB 31

The claimants, three ladies, were the joint owners of a car. They wished to sell the car and advertised it for sale. A fraudulent person, introducing himself as Hutchinson, offered to buy it. He was taken for a drive in it and during conversation said that his home was at Caterham. Later the rogue offered £700 for the car but this was refused, though a subsequent offer of £717 was one which the claimants were prepared to accept. At this point the rogue produced a cheque book and one of the claimants, who was conducting the negotiations, said that the deal was off and that they would not accept a cheque. The rogue then said that he was P. G. M. Hutchinson, that he had business interests in Guildford, and that he lived at Stanstead House, Stanstead Road, Caterham. One of the claimants checked this information in a telephone directory and, on finding it to be accurate, allowed him to take the car in return for a cheque. The cheque was dishonoured, and in the meantime the rogue had sold the car to the defendants and had disappeared without trace. The claimants sued for the return of the car, or for its value as damages in conversion, claiming that the contract between themselves and the rogue was void for mistake, and that the property (or ownership) had not passed. At the trial judgment was given for the claimants, Slade J finding the contract void. His judgment was *affirmed* by the Court of Appeal, though Devlin LJ dissented, saying that the mistake made was as to the creditworthiness of the rogue, not as to his identity, since he was before the claimants when the contract was made. A mistake as to the substance of the rogue would be a mistake as to quality and would not avoid the contract. Devlin LJ also suggested that legislation should provide for an apportionment of the loss incurred by two innocent parties who suffer as a result of the fraud of a third.

*Comment:* The distinctions drawn in some of these cases are fine ones. It is difficult to distinguish *Ingram* from *Lewis*. As we have seen, the question for the court to answer in these cases is whether or not the offeror at the time of making the offer regarded the identity of the offeree as a matter of vital importance. The general rule seems to be that where the parties are face to face when the contract is made, identity will not be vital and the contract is voidable only. *Ingram* would appear to be the exceptional case.

## Effect of unilateral mistake in equity

If the claimant is asking for an equitable remedy, such as rescission of the contract or specific performance of it, then equitable principles will apply. As far as unilateral mistake is concerned, equity follows the principles of the common law and regards a contract affected by unilateral mistake as void and will, therefore, rescind it or refuse specific performance of it. Rectification of the contract is also available.

**The following case is an example of the refusal of an equitable remedy in circumstances of unilateral mistake.**

### Webster v Cecil (1861) 30 Beav 62

The parties had been negotiating for the sale of certain property. Later Cecil offered by letter to sell the property for £1,250. Webster was aware that his offer was probably a slip because he knew that Cecil had already refused an offer of £2,000, and in fact Cecil wished to offer the property at £2,250. Webster accepted the offer and sued for specific performance of the contract. The court refused to grant the decree.

*Comment:* This is not merely a case of mistake as to the value of the contract because here Webster knew that Cecil did not intend to offer the property at £1,250. The rule of let the seller beware applies where the seller is mistaken as to value but at least intends to offer the goods at his marked price.

# BILATERAL IDENTICAL (OR COMMON) MISTAKE

This occurs where both parties are mistaken and each makes the same mistake. Thus we are dealing here with what may be described as a *shared mistake*. In mutual mistake, which is considered later in this chapter, we are dealing with situations in which both parties are mistaken but each makes a different mistake. These parties do not share the mistake but are in a situation of *mutual misunderstanding*. There is no general rule that common mistake affects a contract and in practice only common mistakes as to the existence of the subject-matter of the contract or where the subject-matter of the contract already belongs to the buyer will make the contract void at common law. The principles applied are considered below.

(a) *Cases of* res extincta. Here there is a common mistake as to the existence of the subject-matter of the contract. Thus, if S agrees to sell his car to B and unknown to both the car had at the time of the sale been destroyed by fire, then the contract will be void because A has innocently undertaken an obligation which he cannot possibly fulfil.

**The following case is an illustration of the application of *res extincta* which shows as well that the goods may actually exist but if they are not in the condition envisaged by the parties the rule will be applied.**

## Couturier v Hastie (1856) 5 HLC 673

Messrs Hastie dispatched a cargo of corn from Salonica and sent the charterparty and bill of lading to their London agents so that the corn might be sold. The London agents employed Couturier to sell the corn and a person named Callander bought it. Unknown to the parties the cargo had become overheated, and had been landed at the nearest port and sold, so that when the contract was made the corn was not really in existence. Callander repudiated the contract and Couturier was sued because he was a *del credere* agent, i.e. an agent who, for an extra commission, undertakes to indemnify his principal against losses arising out of the repudiation of the contract by any third party introduced by him. *Held* – The claim against Couturier failed because the contract presupposed that the goods were in existence when they were sold to Callander.

(b) *Cases of* res sua. These occur where a person makes a contract about something which already belongs to him. Such a contract is void at common law.

**The application of the rule is illustrated by the following case.**

## Cochrane v Willis (1865) LR 1 Ch App 58

Cochrane was the trustee in bankruptcy of Joseph Willis who was the tenant for life of certain estates in Lancaster. Joseph Willis had been adjudicated bankrupt in Calcutta where he resided. The remainder of the estate was to go to Daniel Willis, the brother of Joseph, on the latter's death, with eventual remainder to Henry Willis, the son of Daniel. Joseph Willis had the right to cut the timber on the estates during his life interest, and the representative of Cochrane in England threatened to cut and sell it for the benefit of Joseph's creditors. Daniel and Henry wished to preserve the timber and so they agreed with Cochrane through his representatives to pay the value of the timber to Cochrane if he would refrain from cutting it. News then reached England that when the above agreement was made Joseph was dead, and, therefore, the life interest had vested in (i.e. become owned by) Daniel. In this action by the trustee to enforce the agreement it was *held* that Daniel was making a contract to preserve something which was already his and the court found, applying the doctrine of *res sua*, that the agreement was void for an identical or common mistake.

(c) *Other cases – mistakes as to quality*. These occur when the two parties have reached agreement but have made an identical mistake as to some fact concerning the quality of the subject-matter of the contract. Suppose, for example, that X sells a particular drawing to Y for £5,000 and all the usual elements of agreement are present, including offer and acceptance and consideration, and the agreement concerns an identified article. Nevertheless, if both X and Y think that the drawing is by a well-known Victorian artist when it is in fact only a copy worth £25, then the agreement is made in circumstances of common mistake.

At common law a mistake of the kind outlined above has no effect on the contract and the parties would be bound in the absence of fraud or misrepresentation.

**The following cases illustrate how reluctant the courts have been to recognise a general rule of common mistake.**

### Bell v Lever Bros Ltd [1932] AC 161

Lever Bros had a controlling interest in the Niger Company. Bell was the chairman, and a person called Snelling was the vice-chairman of the Niger Company's Board. Both directors had service contracts which had some time to run. They became redundant as a result of amalgamations and Lever Bros contracted to pay Bell £30,000 and Snelling £20,000 as compensation. These sums were paid over and then it was discovered that Bell and Snelling had committed breaches of duty against the Niger Company during their term of office by making secret profits of £1,360 on a cocoa pooling scheme. As directors of the Niger Company, Bell and Snelling attended meetings at which the selling price of cocoa was fixed in advance. Both of them bought and sold on their own account before the prices were made public. They could, therefore, have been dismissed without compensation. Lever Bros sought to set aside the payments on the ground of mistake. *Held* – The contract was not void because Lever Bros had got what they bargained for, i.e. the cancellation of two service contracts which, though they might have been terminated, were actually in existence when the cancellation agreement was made. The mistake was as to the quality of the two directors and such mistakes do not avoid the contracts. The case is one of common mistake because although Bell and Snelling admitted that they were liable to account to the company for the profit made from office, they convinced the court that they had forgotten their misdemeanour of insider dealing when they made the contract for compensation. They thought they were good directors who were entitled to that compensation.

*Comment:* The case also decided that an employee was not under a duty to disclose to his employer his own misconduct or breaches of duty towards his employer. However, employee/directors do have a duty to disclose their *own* breaches of contract to their companies. This is because their fiduciary position as directors overrides the ordinary employer/employee relationship. However, in the *Bell* case the directors concerned kept the compensation and were not required to disclose their wrongdoing to Lever Bros because they were not directors of Lever Bros but only of Niger. However, a director of, say, company A is under a duty to disclose his wrongdoing, if any, towards company A where he receives his compensation from company A itself. Failure so to disclose will allow the company to claim back a golden handshake of the kind given to Bell and Snelling.

It is worth mentioning that an employee is under a duty to disclose breaches of duty/misconduct of subordinate employees, even though he is not under a duty to disclose to his employer his own misconduct or breaches of duty. This follows from the decision of the Court of Appeal in *Sybron Corporation v Rochem Ltd* [1983] 2 All ER 707.

### Leaf v International Galleries [1950] I All ER 693

In 1944 the claimant bought from the defendants a drawing of Salisbury Cathedral for £85. The defendants said that the drawing was by Constable. Five years later the claimant tried to sell the drawing at Christies and was told that this was not so. He now sued for rescission of the contract, no claim for damages being made. The following points of interest emerged from the decision of the Court of Appeal. (a) It was possible to restore the *status quo* by the mere exchange of the drawing and the purchase money so that rescission was not prevented by inability to restore the previous position. (b) The mistake made by the parties in assuming the drawing to be a Constable was a mistake as to quality and did not avoid the contract. (c) The statement that the drawing was by Constable could have been treated as a warranty giving rise to a claim for damages, but it was not possible to award damages because the appeal was based on the claimant's right to rescind. (d) The court, therefore, treated the statement as a representation and, finding it to be innocent, refused to rescind the contract because of the passage of time since the purchase.

*Comment:* (i) Although this case was decided after *Solle v Butcher* (see below), there was presumably no need for the equitable relief of rescission in regard to the common mistake. After all, Leaf had paid only £85 for the drawing and the court may have regarded the contract as a speculation, each party taking a risk as to the authenticity of the drawing.

(ii) Mr Leaf might well have recovered damages if he had sued for these under what is now s 13 of the Sale of Goods Act 1979 (sale by description – goods described as by Constable) (see *further* Chapter 10).

## Effect of identical bilateral (or common) mistake in equity

The position in equity is as follows.

(a) *Cases of* res extincta *and* res sua. Equity treats these in the same way as the common law, regarding the agreement as void. The equitable remedy of specific performance is not available for such an agreement which may also be rescinded.

**The following case is an example of the equitable approach.**

### Cooper v Phibbs (1867) LR 2 HL 149

Cooper agreed to take a lease of a fishery from Phibbs, his uncle's daughter who became apparent owner of it on her father's death. Unknown to either party, the fishery already belonged to Cooper. This arose from a mistake by Cooper's uncle as to how the family land was held. The uncle innocently thought he owned the fishery and before he died told Cooper so, but in fact it was owned by Cooper himself. Cooper now brought this action to set aside the lease and for delivery up of the lease. *Held* – The lease must be set aside on the grounds of common or identical bilateral mistake; however, since equity has the power to give ancillary relief, Phibbs was given a lien on the fishery for the improvements she had made to it during the time she believed it to be hers. This lien could be discharged by Cooper giving Phibbs the value of the improvements.

(b) *Other cases*. Equity will apparently regard an agreement affected by common mistake as voidable even though the case is not one of *res extincta* or *res sua*.

**The following case is at the root of the equitable approach. The court may order that the contract be set aside on terms, i.e. the court may require the parties to consider, or actually carry out, conditions imposed by the court to achieve a fairer (or more reasonable) solution to the problem.**

### Solle v Butcher [1950] 1 KB 671

Butcher had agreed to lease a flat in Beckenham to Solle at a yearly rental of £250, the lease to run for seven years. Both parties had acted on the assumption that the flat, which had been substantially reconstructed so as to be virtually a new flat, was no longer controlled by the rent restriction legislation then in force. If it were so controlled the maximum rent payable would be £140 per annum. Nevertheless, Butcher would have been entitled to increase that rent by charging 8 per cent of the cost of repairs and improvements which would bring the figure up to about £250 per annum, the rent actually charged, if he had served a statutory notice on Solle before the new lease was executed. No such notice was in fact served. Actually they both for a time mistakenly thought that the flat was decontrolled when this was not the case. Solle realised the mistake after some two years, and sought to recover the rent he had overpaid and to continue for the balance of the seven years as a statutory tenant at £140 per annum. Butcher counter-claimed for rescission of the lease in equity. It was *held* by a majority of the Court of Appeal that the mistake was one of fact and not of law, i.e. the fact that the flat was not within the provisions of the Rent Acts, and this was a bilateral mistake as to quality which would not invalidate the contract at common law. However, on the counter-claim for rescission, it was held that the lease could be rescinded. In order not to dispossess Solle, the court offered him the following alternatives:

(a) to surrender the lease entirely: or
(b) to remain in possession as a mere licensee until a new lease could be drawn up after Butcher had had time to serve the statutory notice which would allow him to add a sum for repairs to the £140 which would bring the lawful rent up to £250 per annum.

*Comment:* (i) It is impossible to say at the present time what are the limits of this case. Equitable remedies are discretionary and it is not certain whether it applies to a contract for the sale of goods, nor whether it requires some form of sharp practice before it is implemented.

(ii) In *Grist v Bailey* [1966] 2 All ER 875 a house was sold cheaply because the parties thought that vacant possession could not be obtained as there was a tenant in it who was protected by the Rent Acts and could not be got out. This was not the case and the tenant gave up possession. Even so, the claimant asked for specific performance, while the defendant asked the court to rescind the contract. The contract was set aside on the terms that the defendant would give the claimant the opportunity to purchase the property 'at a proper price for vacant possession'. Naturally, perhaps, specific performance was not granted.

(iii) In *Solle* Lord Denning followed *Cooper* v *Phibbs* (*see above*), saying that a contract can be set aside in equity for common mistake even if the agreement has been partly performed. This distinguishes rescission in mistake from rescission for misrepresentation where part-performance prevents rescission (*see Long* v *Lloyd* [1958] in Chapter 5).

(iv) It will be noted by way of an explanation of the equitable approach that equitable remedies (or relief) will not be granted as of right but only if it is *reasonable* to do so. In order to satisfy this requirement of reasonableness the court can and does impose terms as a condition of giving a remedy as in *Solle* and *Grist* and also in *Cooper* where the court set aside the lease *provided* Cooper paid over money to Phibbs which she had innocently spent in improving the fishery.

(c) *Rectification*. If the parties are agreed on the terms of their contract but because, for example, of drafting or typing errors certain terms are set out incorrectly, the court may order equitable rectification of the contract so that it properly represents what the parties agreed. Thus if A orally agrees to give B a lease of premises for 99 years and in the subsequent written contract the term is expressed as 90 years by mistake, then if A will not co-operate to change the lease, B may ask the court to rectify it by substituting a term of 99 years for 90 years. In order to obtain rectification it must be proved:

(i)   that there was complete agreement on all the terms of the contract or at least a continuing intention to include certain terms in it which in the event were not included. It is not necessary to show that the term was intended to be legally binding prior to being written down;

(ii)  that the agreement continued unchanged until it was reduced into writing. If the parties disputed the terms of the agreement then the written contract may be taken to represent their final position;

(iii) that the writing does not express what the parties had agreed. If it does then there can be no rectification.

The following cases illustrate the application of the above principles. Of particular importance is the *Thomas Bates* case because it shows that rectification is available also for unilateral mistake.

### Joscelyne v Nissen [1970] I All ER 1213

The claimant, Mr Joscelyne, sought rectification of a written contract made on 18 June 1964, under which he had made over his car-hire business to his daughter, Mrs Margaret Nissen. It had been expressly agreed during negotiations that in return for the car-hire business Mrs Nissen would pay certain expenses including gas, electricity and coal bills but the agreement on these matters was not expressly incorporated in the written contract. Furthermore, the parties had agreed that no concluded contract was to be regarded as having been made until the signing of a formal written document.

Mrs Nissen failed to pay the bills and the claimant brought an action in the Edmonton County Court claiming among other things a declaration that Mrs Nissen should pay the gas, electricity and coal bills and alternatively that the written agreement of 18 June 1964 should be rectified to include a provision to that effect. The County Court judge allowed the claim for rectification although there was no binding antecedent contract between the parties on the issue of payment of the expenses. The Court of Appeal, after considering different expressions of judicial views upon what was required before a contractual instrument might be rectified by the court, *held* that the law did not require a binding antecedent contract, provided there was some outward expression of agreement between the contracting parties. Rectification could be made even though there was no binding contract until the written agreement which was to be rectified was entered into.

### Frederick Rose (London) Ltd v William Pim & Co Ltd [1953] 2 All ER 739

The claimants received an order from an Egyptian firm for feveroles (a type of horsebean). The claimants did not know what was meant by feveroles and asked the defendants what they were and whether they could supply them. The defendants said that feveroles were horsebeans and that they could supply them, so the claimants entered into a written agreement to buy horse-beans from the defendants which were then supplied to the Egyptian firm under the order. In fact there were three types of horsebeans: feves, feveroles and fevettes, and the claimants had been supplied with feves, which were less valuable than feveroles. The claimants were sued by the Egyptian firm and now wished to recover the damages they had had to pay from the defendants. In order to do so they had to obtain rectification of the written contract with the defendants in which the goods were described as 'horsebeans'. The word 'horsebeans' had to be rectified to 'feveroles', otherwise the defendants were not in breach. *Held* –

(a) Rectification was not possible because the contract expressed what the parties had agreed to, i.e. to buy and sell horsebeans. Thus the supply of any of the three varieties would have amounted to fulfilment of the contract.
(b) The claimants might have rescinded for misrepresentation but they could not restore the *status quo*, having sold the beans.
(c) The claimants might have recovered damages for breach of warranty, but the statement that 'feveroles are horsebeans and we can supply them' was oral, and warranties in a contract for the sale of goods of £10 and upwards had in 1953 to be evidenced in writing. This is not the case today.
(d) The defence of mistake was also raised, i.e. both buyer and seller thought that all horse-beans were feveroles. This was an identical bilateral or common mistake, but since it was not a case of *res extincta* or *res sua* it had no effect on the contract.

*Comment:* This case is quite complex on its facts but to put the rule in a simpler context, if A and B orally agreed on the sale of A's drawing of Salisbury Cathedral, thought by A and B to be by John Constable, but in fact by Fred Constable an unknown Victorian artist, and then put that into a written contract, that contract could not be rectified simply because A and B thought that the drawing was by John Constable, because the written contract would be the same as the oral one, as in the above case. The approach is after all logical enough. You cannot sensibly ask the court to make the written agreement conform with the one actually made when it already does!

### Thomas Bates & Sons Ltd v Wyndham's (Lingerie) Ltd [1981] I All ER 1077

The claimant granted in 1956 a lease to the defendants with an option for renewal. This lease had a clause under which the rent on renewal was to be agreed by the parties or by arbitration. The option was exercised in 1963 for a seven-year lease, and again in 1970 for a 14-year lease at a rent of £2,350 per annum for the first five years and thereafter subject to rent review every five years. This lease, which was drafted by the claimants' managing director, did not contain an arbitration clause. The defendants knew that it did not. At the end of the first five-year period the claimants suggested that a new rent should be agreed. The defendants would not agree and took the view that the rent of £2,350 should continue for the whole 14 years unless there was an agreement between the parties to the contrary. Deputy Judge Michael Wheeler QC, sitting in the High Court, ordered rectification and the Court of Appeal affirmed that decision. The clause inserted by the court allowed the rent to be settled by arbitration if the parties did not agree.

*Comment:* At one time it was thought that rectification was available only for a common mistake by both parties. However, as appears from this case, rectification can be given for unilateral mistake. The principles on which it is granted appear in the judgment of Buckley LJ, who said: 'First, that one party, A, erroneously believed that the document sought to be rectified contained a particular term or provision, or possibly did not contain a particular term or provision, which, mistakenly, it did contain; second that the other party, B, was aware of the omission or the inclusion and that it was due to a mistake on the part of A; third that B has omitted to draw the mistake to the notice of A. And I think there must be a fourth element involved, namely that the mistake must be calculated to benefit B.' The general principle upon which the judgment is based would appear to be one of equitable estoppel.

## NON-IDENTICAL BILATERAL (OR MUTUAL) MISTAKE

In a situation where A intends to buy real pearls but the seller intends to sell imitation pearls, and in the absence of misrepresentation by the seller, there is a bilateral mistake which is non-identical. It will be remembered that in the previous category the mistake was bilateral but both parties had made an identical mistake. Here we have what may be described as a *mutual misunderstanding*. Confusion of this non-identical bilateral kind generally exists in the mind of one party only, as in the above example where the seller does not stock real pearls, and may, therefore, have no effect on the contract (*see below*).

### Effect of non-identical bilateral (or mutual) mistake at common law

The contract is not necessarily void because the court will try to find the 'sense of promise'. This usually occurs where, although the parties are at cross purposes, the contract actually *identifies* a credible (or believable) agreement.

If the parties are at cross purposes and the contract does *not identify* a credible (or believable) agreement, it is void.

The basis of the 'sense of the promise' rule is that the court does not ascertain contractual intent from what is in the minds of the parties, i.e. *a subjective intent*, because the parties are confused. Instead the court decides contractual intent in an *objective way* by looking at the parties' dealings to see if these identify a contract. If they do, the court will enforce it: if not, the transaction is void.

## Effect of non-identical bilateral (or mutual) mistake in equity

Equity also tries to find the sense of the promise as identified by the contract, thus following the law. However, equitable remedies are discretionary and even where the sense of the promise as identified by the contract can be ascertained equity will not necessarily grant specific performance if it would cause hardship to the defendant.

**The following cases illustrate the 'sense of the promise' approach.**

### Wood v Scarth (1858) 1 F & F 293

The claimant was suing for damages for breach of contract alleging that the defendant had entered into an agreement to grant the claimant a lease of a public house, but had refused to convey the property. It was shown in evidence that the defendant intended to offer the lease at a rent, and also to include a premium on taking up the lease of £500. The defendant had told his agent to make this clear to the claimant, but the agent had not mentioned it. After discussions with the agent the claimant wrote to the defendant proposing to take the lease 'on the terms already agreed upon' to which the defendant replied accepting the proposal. There was a mutual or non-identical bilateral mistake. The defendant thought that he was agreeing to lease the premises for a rent plus a premium, and the claimant thought he was taking a lease for rental only because he did not know of the premium. The claimant had sued for specific performance in 1855, and the court in the exercise of its equitable jurisdiction had decided that specific performance could not be granted in view of the mistake, as to grant it would be unduly hard on the defendant. However, in this action the claimant sued at common law for damages, and damages were granted to him on the ground that in mutual or non-identical mistake the court may find the sense of the promise and regard a contract as having been made on these terms. Here it was quite reasonable for the claimant to suppose that there was no premium to be paid. Thus a contract came into being on the terms as understood by the claimant, and he was entitled to damages for breach of it. The contract clearly identified the agreement made.

*Comment:* This case shows that equitable remedies are discretionary and not available as of right as damages at common law are. Also note the benefits of the Judicature Acts 1873–75. In this case, which pre-dates those Acts, the action for specific performance was brought in Chancery in 1855 and the action at common law for damages in 1858. Common law and equitable remedies could not be granted in one and the same action until the Judicature Acts were passed.

### Raffles v Wichelhaus (1864) 2 HC 906

The defendants agreed to buy from the claimants 125 bales of cotton to arrive 'ex *Peerless* from Bombay'. There were two ships called *Peerless* sailing from Bombay, one in October and one in December. The defendants thought they were buying the cotton on the ship sailing in October, and the claimants meant to sell the cotton on the ship sailing in December. In fact the claimants had no cotton on the ship sailing in October. The defendants refused to take delivery of the cotton when the second ship arrived and were now sued for breach of contract. *Held* – Since there was a mistake as to the subject-matter of the contract there was in effect no contract between the parties, or at least no contract which clearly identified the agreement made. The claimants' action failed.

## GRADED QUESTIONS

### Essay mode

1  (a)  Certain types of mistake in the formation of a contract affect its validity. Examine those types of mistake which do not affect the validity of a contract.

   (b)  Anthony, a collector, buys a porcelain dish from Charles, believing it to be an eighteenth-century Chinese work. Charles has in no way represented the piece as having any particular age. If Anthony subsequently discovers the porcelain dish to be a modern copy, will he be able to avoid the contract if –
   
   (i)  Charles did not know of Anthony's mistake?
   
   (ii)  Charles did know, but took no steps to enlighten him?

   *(The Institute of Company Accountants)*

2  'In general, contracts entered into under a common mistake or mutual mistake are still binding upon the parties.' To what extent does this statement represent the law?

   *(The Institute of Legal Executives)*

3  Brian agrees to buy a computer from Stella. Explain how the mistakes in each of the following circumstances would affect the contract.

   (a)  Brian believes that he is obtaining credit over six months whereas Stella believes that it is a cash sale.

   (b)  Brian believes that he is buying from David and not from Stella.

   (c)  Both Brian and Stella believe that the contract price of £4,000 represents the true value of the computer but, because of a latent defect in its manufacture, the computer is only worth £2,000.

   (d)  Stella offered to sell the computer for £400. Brian believed that a mistake had been made and that £4,000 was intended but, nevertheless, accepted the offer.

   *(The Chartered Institute of Management Accountants)*

### Objective mode

Four alternative answers are given. Select ONE only. Circle the answer which you consider to be correct. Check your answers by referring back to the information given in the chapter and against the answers at the back of the book.

1  John agreed to buy Geoffrey's vintage 3-litre Lagonda motor car for £20,000. Unknown to John and Geoffrey a fire in David's garage, where the car was stored, the day before the contract had been made had destroyed the car. What is the legal position?

   A  John must pay the contract price since the risk of loss passes to the buyer when the contract is made.

   B  John must pay but can sue David for negligence as a bailee.

   C  John need not pay for the goods as the contract is void since the goods had perished when the agreement was made.

   D  John need not pay for the goods as the contract is voidable because the goods had perished when the agreement was made.

2 Which of the following is a mutual mistake which renders the contract void?

A  A mistake whereby both parties to the contract believe that the subject-matter is a genuine Picasso drawing whereas in fact it is a fake.

B  A mistake whereby X believes he is buying a 1930 Picasso drawing entitled 'Le vierge' whereas Y believes he is selling a 1932 drawing by Picasso entitled 'Le vierge'.

C  A mistake whereby X believes he is contracting by post with Y Ltd with whom he has done business before whereas in fact X is contracting with a fraudulent person W.

D  A contract for the sale of a dog called Meg whereby both parties believe mistakenly that the dog is alive at the time of the contract.

3  John Smith bought a Rolex watch from Golds the jewellers. When asked to pay he told the manager that he was James Smith, a well-known American businessman whose takeover exploits were often reported in the British press. The manager took a cheque from John Smith and the latter departed with the watch. The cheque was dishonoured and Golds are trying to recover the watch from Dennis who bought it from John Smith in good faith and for value. What is the legal position?

A  The contract is void for common mistake. The watch belongs to Golds.

B  The contract is void for unilateral mistake of identity. The watch belongs to Golds.

C  The contract is voidable for mutual mistake. Golds may claim the watch.

D  The contract is voidable for fraud but John Smith has passed on a good title to Dennis.

4  Fusty, an antique dealer, discovered that he was a beneficiary under the will of his deceased maiden aunt, Virginia. She left him the contents of her house including an oil painting of a dog signed 'J. Hargreaves' which he knew she had received as a gift from the Hargreaves family in the 1930s. John Hargreaves was a minor Victorian artist specialising in animal studies whose paintings began to increase in value during the 1960s. Knowing this, Fusty put the painting up for sale in his shop at £600. Garner saw the painting and offered £500 for it. Fusty refused stating that the painting was by John Hargreaves and had belonged to his aunt Virginia who had received it as a gift from the Hargreaves family in the 1930s. On the basis of this assurance Garner paid £600 for the painting and took delivery of it.

Last month Garner held a party at his house at which Dabster, who was an expert on Victorian paintings employed by Christby's, was a guest. Dabster told Garner that the painting was a copy valued at £100 and executed in the 1920s probably by the painter's son Joseph Hargreaves, who was a good amateur artist.

What is the legal position?

A  The contract between Garner and Fusty is void for common mistake.

B  The contract between Garner and Fusty is void for mutual mistake.

C  The contract between Garner and Fusty is void for misrepresentation and Garner can ask for rescission of the contract.

D  Garner's only remedy is to sue Fusty for damages under the Sale of Goods Act 1979.

5 Jake, the son of a restaurant owner, Purvey, was in financial difficulties. Knowing that his father had consistently refused to help him pay his debts, Jake asked Dibbs plc, a finance company, for a loan of £1,000 without security. Dibbs plc were prepared to lend Jake the money provided that Purvey gave an indemnity in respect of the loan and Jake agreed that a form of indemnity should be sent to Purvey for his signature.

Jake managed to intercept all the mail received by Purvey during the following week and extracted the form of indemnity from an envelope franked in the name of Dibbs plc. Jake placed the form on Purvey's desk along with a number of other business documents, marking the place for signature with a cross. Later that day Purvey, who was running late for a luncheon appointment, signed all the documents without bothering to read any of them. Jake then extracted the indemnity and posted it to Dibbs plc, and later Purvey's secretary posted the rest of the mail. In due course Jake received the loan from Dibbs plc and used it to take a holiday to France.

Jake and his father have now been adjudicated bankrupt and Dibbs plc approach you in your capacity as Purvey's trustee in bankruptcy asking your advice as to the liability of his estate with regard to the indemnity. What advice would you give?

A That Purvey is not liable on the indemnity because he did not intend to sign it.
B That Purvey is liable on the indemnity because he was negligent in not checking what he was signing.
C That Purvey is liable on the indemnity because those who sign documents cannot deny liability on them.
D That Purvey is not liable on the indemnity because the bank should have ensured that he received independent advice.

6 The equitable contribution to the existence of a mistake in a contract is to:

A Treat all forms of mistake in the same way as the common law.
B Ignore the concept of mistake altogether.
C Treat all forms of mistake differently from the common law.
D Treat all forms of mistake in the same way as the common law except for common mistake.

7 Bloggs and Snooks orally agreed that Snooks would purchase from Bloggs a painting which both of them thought to be by John Constable. The contract was drawn up in writing the same day. Two weeks later Snooks discovered that the painting was by James Constable, a minor artist. Snooks is proposing to ask the court to rectify the written agreement. What is the legal position?

A Snooks will obtain rectification for common mistake.
B Snooks will not obtain rectification because he has left it too late.
C Snooks will obtain rectification for mutual mistake.
D Snooks will not obtain rectification because there is no literal difference between the oral and written contract.

8 John's house 'The Grange' was advertised as being for sale by auction and on the basis of the auction particulars which were available to all wishing to attend the auction. Joe was interested in the property because he had seen John using an adjacent field to graze half a dozen sheep and Joe thought he would do the same with a few rare breeds. Joe got a copy of the auction particulars which made it quite clear that the field in question was not part of the sale since it did not belong to John: he had only rented it from the

adjacent owner. Joe did not read the particulars, having convinced himself the field would be included in the sale. 'The Grange' was sold to Joe who made the highest bid but at a bit less than 'The Grange' might have fetched at a private sale. The relevant formalities were completed and then Joe discovered that the field was not included in the sale. John intends to ask the court for specific performance but Joe is resisting this. What is the legal position?

**A** Specific performance will be granted on the assumption of a contract only to buy 'The Grange'.

**B** Specific performance will not be granted because there is a common mistake.

**C** Specific performance will be granted on the assumption of a contract to buy 'The Grange' and the adjacent field.

**D** Specific performance will not be granted because the parties are at cross purposes and there is an irreconcilable mutual mistake.

*Answers to questions set in objective mode appear on p 707.*

# THE LAW OF CONTRACT – REALITY OF CONSENT II

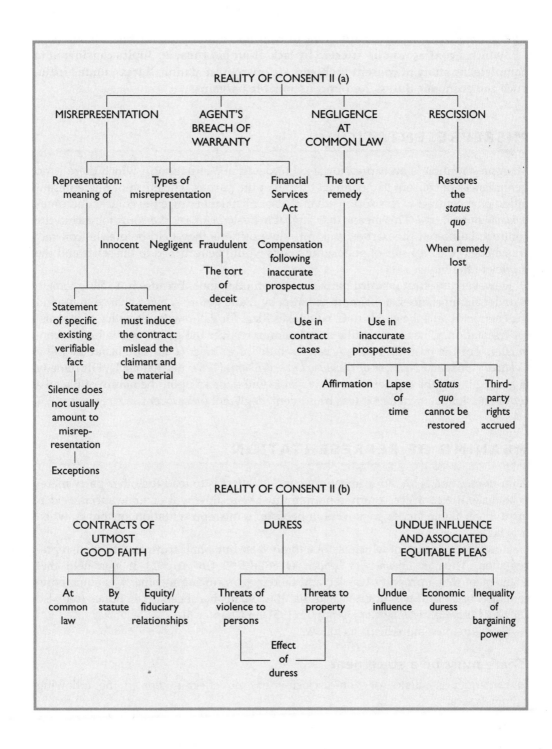

REALITY OF CONSENT II (a)

MISREPRESENTATION    AGENT'S BREACH OF WARRANTY    NEGLIGENCE AT COMMON LAW    RESCISSION

Representation: meaning of    Types of misrepresentation    Financial Services Act    The tort remedy    Restores the *status quo*

Innocent    Negligent    Fraudulent    Compensation following inaccurate prospectus    When remedy lost

The tort of deceit

Statement of specific existing verifiable fact    Statement must induce the contract: mislead the claimant and be material    Use in contract cases    Use in inaccurate prospectuses

Silence does not usually amount to misrep-resentation

Affirmation    Lapse of time    *Status quo* cannot be restored    Third-party rights accrued

Exceptions

REALITY OF CONSENT II (b)

CONTRACTS OF UTMOST GOOD FAITH    DURESS    UNDUE INFLUENCE AND ASSOCIATED EQUITABLE PLEAS

At common law    By statute    Equity/ fiduciary relationships    Threats of violence to persons    Threats to property    Undue influence    Economic duress    Inequality of bargaining power

Effect of duress

The objectives of this chapter are to continue a study of further situations in which a contract can be affected by lack of proper consent. Topics considered to complete the study of consent problems are misrepresentation, duress, undue influence and economic duress, and unconscionable bargains.

## MISREPRESENTATION

Misrepresentation is an expression used to describe a situation in which there is no genuineness of consent to a contract by one of the parties. The effect of misrepresentation on a contract is less serious than that of mistake because the contract becomes *voidable and not void*. This means that the party misled can ask the court to rescind the contract, i.e. to put the parties back into the positions they held before the contract was made. Thus in a sale of goods, the goods would be returned to the seller and the money to the buyer.

However, the effect on third parties is more fundamental because if A sells goods to B under circumstances of misrepresentation by B and before A has a chance to rescind the contract B sells the goods to C, who takes them for value without notice of the misrepresentation, C has a good title and A cannot recover the goods or sue him in conversion. For the position where A has rescinded, *see Car & Universal Finance Co Ltd v Caldwell* (1964) and *Newtons of Wembley Ltd v Williams* (1964) in Chapter 11. His remedy is against B and the type of remedy available will depend upon the nature of B's misrepresentation, i.e. whether it was fraudulent, negligent or innocent.

## MEANING OF REPRESENTATION

A representation is an inducement only and its effect is to lead the other party merely to make the contract. A representation must be a statement of some specific existing and verifiable fact or past event. It becomes a misrepresentation, of course, when it is false.

However, a statement which is not entirely false but a half-truth may be a misrepresentation. Thus in *Dimmock v Hallett* (1886) LR 2 Ch App 21 it was held that a statement that a property was let, and therefore producing income, was a misrepresentation because it was not revealed that the tenants had been given notice (see also *Curtis v Chemical Cleaning and Dyeing Co* (1951) in Chapter 6).

There are three ingredients as follows.

### There must be a statement

In consequence, silence or non-disclosure has no effect except in the following circumstances.

(a) *Failure to disclose a change in circumstances.* Where the statement was true when made but became false before the contract was made, there is a duty on the party making the statement to disclose the change, and if he does not do so, his silence can amount to an actionable misrepresentation.

**An illustration is provided by the following case.**

### With v O'Flanagan [1936] I All ER 727

The defendant was a medical practitioner who wished to sell his practice. The claimant was interested and in January 1934 the defendant represented to the claimant that the income from the practice was £2,000 a year. The contract was not signed until May 1934, and in the meantime the defendant had been ill and the practice had been run by various other doctors who substituted for the defendant while he was ill. In consequence, the receipts fell to £5 per week, and no mention of this fact was made when the contract was entered into. The claimant now claimed rescission of the contract. *Held* – He could do so. The representation made in January was of a continuing nature and induced the contract made in May. The claimant had a right to be informed of a change of circumstances, and the defendant's silence amounted to a misrepresentation.

(b) *Where the contract is uberrimae fidei* (of utmost good faith), such as a contract of insurance (see later in this chapter).
(c) *Where there is a confidential or fiduciary relationship between the parties,* as where they are solicitor and client. Here the equitable doctrine of constructive fraud may apply to render the contract voidable.

Although this branch of the law is closely akin to undue influence, which will be considered later, there is a difference in the sense that in undue influence the person with special influence, such as a solicitor over his client, is often the prime mover in seeking the contract. Constructive fraud, however, could apply where the client was the prime mover in seeking a contract with his solicitor. In such a case if the solicitor remains silent as regards facts within his knowledge material, say, to the contract price, then the client could rescind the contract for constructive fraud.

(d) *Where statute requires disclosure,* as does the Financial Services Act 1986 under which a number of specified particulars must be disclosed in an advertisement/prospectus issued by a company to invite the public to subscribe for shares or debentures. The particulars must give all such information as investors and their professional advisers would reasonably require and reasonably expect to find in the advertisement/prospectus for the purpose of making an informed assessment as to whether to buy the securities.
(e) *In cases of concealed fraud,* following the case of *Gordon* v *Selico Co Ltd, The Times,* 26 February 1986. In that case a flat in a block of flats which had recently been converted by a developer was taken by the claimant on a 99-year lease. Soon after he moved in dry rot was discovered. Goulding J, who was later upheld by the Court of Appeal, decided that deliberate concealment of the dry rot by the developer could amount to fraudulent misrepresentation whereupon damages were awarded to the claimant. Silence can, therefore, amount to misrepresentation in the case of concealed fraud.

## Specific existing and verifiable fact or past event

The representation must be a statement of some specific, existing and verifiable fact or past event, and in consequence the following are excluded.

(a) *Statements of law.* Everyone is presumed to know the law which is equally accessible to both parties and on which they should seek advice and not rely on the statements of the other party. Thus, if A has allowed B, a tradesman, to have goods on credit and C has agreed orally to indemnify A in respect of the transaction, then if A enters into a second contract with B under which A is to receive two-thirds of the price of the goods from B in full settlement on B's representation that C's indemnity is unenforceable at law because it is not in writing, then the second contract would be good because A cannot deny that he knows the law because of the maxim 'ignorance of the law is no excuse'.

(b) *Statements as to future conduct or intention.* These are not actionable, though if the person who makes the statement has no intention of carrying it out, it may be regarded as a representation of fact, i.e. a misrepresentation of what is really in the mind of the maker of the statement.

**The following is an illustration from case law.**

### Edgington *v* Fitzmaurice (1885) 29 Ch D 459

The claimant was induced to lend money to a company by a representation made by its directors that the money would be used to improve the company's buildings and generally expand the business. In fact the directors intended to use the money to pay off the company's existing debts as the creditors were pressing hard for payment. When the claimant discovered that he had been misled, he sued the directors for damages for fraud. The defence was that the statement that they had made was not a statement of a past or present fact but a mere statement of intention which could not be the basis of an action of fraud. *Held* – The directors were liable in deceit. Bowen LJ said: 'There must be a misstatement of an existing fact: but the state of a man's mind is as much a fact as the state of his digestion. It is true that it is very difficult to prove what the state of a man's mind at a particular time is, but if it can be ascertained, it is as much a fact as anything else. A misrepresentation as to the state of a man's mind is, therefore, a misstatement of fact.'

(c) *Statements of opinion.* Again, these are not normally actionable unless it can be shown that the person making the statement held no such opinion, whereupon the statement may be considered in law to be a misstatement of an existing fact as to what was in the mind of the maker of the statement at the time. However, in *Bisset v Wilkinson* [1927] AC 177 it was held that a vendor of land was not liable for stating that it could support 2,000 sheep, because he had no personal knowledge of the facts, the land having never been used for sheep farming. The buyer knew this so it was understood by him that the seller could only be stating his opinion.

Nevertheless, the expression of an opinion may involve a statement of fact. Suppose A writes a reference for B to help B get a house to rent and A says to C the prospective landlord: 'B is a very desirable tenant'. A is doing two things: first he is giving his opinion of B, but also he is making a statement of fact by saying that he believes B to be a very desirable tenant. If in fact, therefore, A actually *believes* B to be a bad tenant, he is lying as to what is in his mind.

**This can be an actionable misrepresentation as the following case illustrates.**

### Smith v Land and House Property Corporation (1884) 28 Ch D 7

The claimants put up for sale on 4 August 1882 the Marine Hotel, Walton-on-the-Naze, stating in the particulars that it was let to 'Mr Frederick Fleck (a most desirable tenant) at a rental of £400 for an unexpired term of 27½ years'. The directors of the defendant company sent the Secretary, Mr Lewin, to inspect the property and he reported that Fleck was not doing much business and that the town seemed to be in the last stages of decay. The directors, on receiving this report, directed Mr Lewin to bid up to £5,000, and in fact he bought the hotel for £4,700. Before completion Fleck became bankrupt and the defendant company refused to complete the purchase, whereupon the claimants sued for specific performance. It was proved that on 1 May 1882 the March quarter's rent was wholly unpaid, that a distress was then threatened, i.e. the landlord was threatening to remove property from the hotel for sale to pay the rent, and that Fleck paid £30 on 6 May, £40 on 13 June, and the remaining £30 shortly before the sale. No part of the June quarter's rent had been paid. The chairman of the defendant company said that the hotel would not have been purchased but for the statement in the particulars that Fleck was a most desirable tenant. *Held* – Specific performance would not be granted. The description of Fleck as a most desirable tenant was not a mere expression of opinion, but contained an implied assertion that the vendors knew of no facts leading to the conclusion that he was not. The circumstances relating to the unpaid rent showed that Fleck was not a desirable tenant and there was a misrepresentation. Bowen LJ said:

> It is material to observe that it is often fallaciously assumed that a statement of opinion cannot involve the statement of a fact. In a case where the facts are equally well known to both parties, what one of them says to the other is frequently nothing but an expression of opinion. The statement of such opinion is in a sense a statement of a fact about the condition of the man's own mind, but only of an irrelevant fact, for it is of no consequence what the opinion is. But if the facts are not equally known to both sides, then a statement of opinion by the one who knows the facts best involves very often a statement of a material fact, for he impliedly states that he knows facts which justify his opinion.

(d) *Sales talk, advertising, 'puffing' (or what is called these days 'hype').* Not all statements in this area amount to representations. The law has always accepted that it is essential in business that a seller of goods or services should be allowed to make statements about them in the course of dealing without necessarily being bound by everything he says. Thus, if a salesman confines himself to statements of opinion such as: 'This is the finest floor polish in the world' or 'This is the best polish on the market', there is no misrepresentation. However, the nearer a salesman gets to a statement of specific verifiable fact, the greater the possibility that there may be an action for misrepresentation. Thus a statement such as: 'This polish has as much wax in it as Snooks' wax polish' may well amount to a misrepresentation if the statement is not in fact true.

### The statement must induce the contract

It must therefore:

(a) have been relied upon by the person claiming to have been misled who must not have relied on his own skill and judgment or some other statement.

Thus in *Attwood v Small* (1838) 6 Cl & Fin 232 the purchaser of a mine elected to verify exaggerated (but not fraudulent) statements of its earnings by commissioning a report from his agents. This failed to reveal the defects in the original statement and the purchaser bought the mine. It was *held* later that he could not rescind the contract because he had relied on the report not the statement. It should be noted that relief is not barred simply because there has been an unsuccessful attempt by the person misled to discover the truth where the misrepresentation is fraudulent. (*Pearson v Dublin Corpn* [1907] AC 217.)

(b) have been material in the sense that it affected the claimant's judgment;

(c) have been known to the claimant. The claimant must always be prepared to prove that an alleged misrepresentation had an effect on his mind, a task which he certainly cannot fulfil if he was never aware that it had been made.

Thus in *Re Northumberland and Durham District Banking Co, ex parte Bigg* (1858) 28 LJ Ch 50 a person who bought shares in a company asked to have the purchase rescinded because the company had published false reports as to its solvency. Although these reports were false, the claimant failed because, among other things, he was unable to show he had read any of the reports or that anyone had told him what they contained;

(d) have been addressed to the person claiming to have been misled.

**The following case is an illustration of the common law approach.**

### Peek v Gurney (1873) LR 6 HL 377

Peek purchased shares in a company on the faith of statements appearing in a prospectus issued by the respondents who were directors of the company. Certain statements were false and Peek sued the directors. It appeared that Peek was not an original allottee, but had purchased the shares on the market, though he had relied on the prospectus. *Held* – Peek's action failed because the statements in the prospectus were only intended to mislead the original allottees. Once the statements had induced the public to be original subscribers, their force was spent.

*Comment:* (i) The decision has a somewhat unfortunate effect because at those times when public issues are over-subscribed it is most likely that persons who did not receive an allotment or an adequate allotment as subscribers will try to purchase further shares within a short time on the Stock Exchange. These people will clearly be relying on the prospectus, but under this decision would have no claim in respect of false statements in it.

(ii) This decision and the one in *Re Northumberland* (*above*) would appear to be affected, at least on their own facts, by the Financial Services Act 1986. As regards who can sue under an inaccurate prospectus s 150(1) states: '... any person who has acquired any of the securities in question and suffered loss in respect of them ...'. This would seem to include all subscribers whether they have relied on the prospectus (or listing particulars) or not. It seems therefore that a subscriber need not be aware of the error or even have seen the listing particulars. The subsection would also seem to cover subsequent purchasers after the first issue thus affecting *Peek* v *Gurney* (*above*), at least on its own facts. However, the 1986 Act applies only to shares issued on the main Stock Exchange with a full listing (*see* (iv) *below*).

(iii) It should be noted also that s 150(1) is a *statutory* remedy in *company law*. So far as the *law of contract* is concerned, the purpose of the statements in the listing particulars (or prospectus) is to invite persons to apply for shares in the company, i.e. to induce the contract with the company, and in contract law the statement must have been seen and relied upon and be material. So far as remedies for contractual misrepresentation, including remedies under the Misrepresentation Act 1967, are concerned, the particulars cannot be relied upon by those who purchase shares from some source other than the company or by persons who have not seen them. In contract law, therefore, *Peek* and *Re Northumberland* survive. However, most claimants will successfully sue under the statutory remedy of s 150(1). There are, however, a number of special defences to a claim under s 150 (1) (*see below*) and where a particular defendant, e.g. a director of the company, can claim one or more of these the claimant may have to revert to a remedy under the Misrepresentation Act 1967 where these special defences, apart from reasonable grounds for believing the statement to be true, do not apply. Such a claimant would be faced with the rulings in *Peek* and *Re Northumberland*, though he would seem to be able to sue under the *Hedley Byrne* case (*see below*) where, once again, the statutory defences do not apply. The claim there is in *tort* (negligence) and not contract. Section 150(4) of the 1986 Act expressly reserves the right of claimants to sue under the Misrepresentation Act 1967 and/or in tort under *Hedley Byrne*.

(iv) A claim in tort for damages for negligent misstatement should also be available under *Hedley Byrne* (*see below*) in that those who publicly advertise a prospectus must surely in the modern context foresee that it will be relied upon by subscribers and by those who purchase from subscribers on the stock market for a reasonable time after the issue of the prospectus. In fact in the most recent decision, *Possfund Custodian Trustee Ltd* v *Victor Derek Diamond, Financial Times*, 13 April 1996, Mr Justice Lightman in the High Court stated that it is in these days at least arguable that those who are responsible for issuing prospectuses owe a duty of care to those who purchase shares in what can be described as the After Market in reliance on the prospectus. This could place liability on the company's directors, the company itself and its financial advisers if they are negligent. The matter did not come to full trial, Lightman J's statement being made in preliminary proceedings. It should be noted that purchasers on the After Market following an issue with a full listing are already protected by the Financial Services Act 1986. Where the issue is on, for example, the Alternative Investment Market, the 1986 Act does not apply. However, the Public Offers of Securities Regulations 1999 (Sls 1999/734 and 1146) do apply to markets such as the AIM and those Regulations state that compensation is payable 'to any person who has acquired the securities . . . and suffered loss'. Therefore, even on the AIM there is a statutory remedy subject to the same director/expert defences as appear in the Financial Services Act 1986. The only advantage of suing under *Possfund* is that not all of these defences are available at common law. The 1999 Regulations did not apply in *Possfund* because the facts of *Possfund* pre-date the Regulations. The Regulations expressly reserve the right of claimants to sue for common law remedies, e.g. negligence under *Hedley Byrne*.

## Knowledge that statement is untrue

If the person to whom the false statement was made knew that it was untrue, then he cannot sue in respect of it because he has not been misled. However, this means actual knowledge and so it is not an acceptable defence to an action for misrepresentation that the representee was given the means of discovering that the statement was untrue, as the following case illustrates.

### Redgrave v Hurd (1881) 20 Ch D 1

The claimant was a solicitor who wished to take a partner into the business. During negotiations between the claimant and Hurd the claimant stated that the income of the business was £300 a year. The papers which the claimant produced showed that the income was not quite £200 a year, and Hurd asked about the balance. Redgrave then produced further papers which he said showed how the balance was made up, but which only showed a very small amount of income making the total income up to about £200. Hurd did not examine these papers in any detail, but agreed to become a partner. Later Hurd discovered the true position and refused to complete the contract. The claimant sued for breach and Hurd raised the misrepresentation as a defence, and also counter-claimed for rescission of the contract. *Held* – Hurd had relied on Redgrave's statements regarding the income and the contracts could be rescinded. It did not matter that Hurd had the means of discovering their untruth; he was entitled to rely on Redgrave's statement.

*Comment:* The case also illustrates an interesting point which is often missed. We say that misrepresentation makes a contract voidable, i.e. valid unless and until avoided by the party misled. We have seen that the ownership of goods will pass, even though the contract was induced by misrepresentation, until the person misled avoids the contract as in *Lewis v Averay* (1971) (see Chapter 4). However, where as in the *Redgrave* case misrepresentation is raised as a defence the defendant will succeed without having any need to show that he has taken steps to avoid the contract.

## Did the statement influence the representee's decision?

The law requires that a misrepresentation must have operated on the mind of the representee. **If it has not, as where the representee was not influenced by it, there is no claim as the following case illustrates.**

### Smith v Chadwick (1884) 9 App Cas 187

This action was brought by the claimant, who was a steel manufacturer, against Messrs Chadwick, Adamson and Collier, who were accountants and promoters of a company called the Blochairn Iron Co Ltd. The claimant sought £5,750 as damages sustained through taking shares in the company which were not worth the price he had paid for them because of certain misrepresentations in the prospectus issued by the defendants. The action was for fraud. Among the misrepresentations alleged by Smith was that the prospectus stated that a Mr J J Grieves MP was a director of the company, whereas he had withdrawn his consent the day before the prospectus was issued. *Held* – That the statement regarding Mr Grieves was untrue but was not material to the claimant, because the evidence showed that he had never heard of Mr Grieves. His action for damages failed.

# TYPES OF ACTIONABLE MISREPRESENTATION AND REMEDIES IN GENERAL

## Innocent misrepresentation

A purely innocent misrepresentation is a false statement made by a person who had reasonable grounds to believe that the statement was true, not only when he made it but also at the time the contract was entered into. As regards reasonable grounds, the representer's best hope of proving this will be to show that he himself had been induced to buy the goods by the same statement, particularly where he is not technically qualified to verify it further (*see Humming Bird Motors Ltd* v *Hobbs* (1986) (*below*) and *Oscar Chess Ltd* v *Williams* (1957) (Chapter 6)). The party misled can ask the court to rescind the contract but has no right to ask for damages. However, the court may at its discretion award damages instead of rescission (Misrepresentation Act 1967, s 2(2)). Rescission in effect cancels the contract and the court may in some cases regard this as a drastic remedy, particularly where there has been misrepresentation on a trivial matter, such as the quality of the tyres on a car. Suppose the seller of a car in a private sale says: 'the previous owner fitted new tyres at 26,000 miles'. If that statement is false but the seller was told this by the previous owner, then the court could award damages instead of rescission, thus leaving the contract intact but giving the party misled monetary compensation. Statements by dealers are often taken to be terms of the contract (*see* Chapter 6).

There has been uncertainty as to whether damages could be awarded under s 2(2) of the Misrepresentation Act 1967 if the remedy of rescission was no longer available as where a third party had acquired rights in the subject-matter of the contract. However, in *Thomas Witter* v *TBP Industries Ltd* [1996] 2 All ER 573 the High Court decided that damages could be awarded under s 2(2), provided that the right to rescind had existed *at some time*. It was not necessary for the right to exist at the time the judgment was given, said the High Court. This seems a reasonable interpretation of the sub-section because the remedy of rescission is so quickly lost anyway that it is unlikely to exist at the time of trial because of, among other things, the passage of time. (*See* later in the chapter.)

## Negligent misrepresentation

A negligent misrepresentation is a false statement made by a person who had no reasonable grounds for believing the statement to be true. The party misled may sue for rescission (*see below*) and/or damages and the requirement to prove that the statement was not made negligently but that there were reasonable grounds for believing it to be true is on the maker of the statement (or representer) (Misrepresentation Act 1967, s 2(1)).

The sub-section recognises only a claim for damages and says nothing about rescission. However, in *Mapes* v *Jones* (1974) 232 EG 717 a property dealer contracted to lease a grocer's shop to the claimant for 21 years but in fact did not have sufficient interest in the property himself to grant such a lease, the maximum period available to him being 18 years. Despite constant requests, no lease was supplied as originally promised and the claimant shut the shop and elected to treat the contract as repudiated. Willis J *held* that the claimant was entitled to rescission for misrepresentation under s 2(1) of the 1967 Act. He also found that the defendant's delay in completion was a breach of condition allowing the claimant to repudiate the contract.

**The following case provides a practical example of the application of s 2(1).**

### Gosling *v* Anderson, *The Times*, 8 February 1972

Miss Gosling, a retired schoolmistress, entered into negotiations for the purchase of one of three flats in a house at Minehead owned by Mrs Anderson. Mr Tidbury, who was Mrs Anderson's agent in the negotiations, represented to Miss Gosling by letter that planning permission for a garage to go with the flat had been given. Mrs Anderson knew that this was not so. The purchase of the flat went through on the basis of a contract and a conveyance showing a parking area but not referring to planning permission which was later refused. Miss Gosling now sought damages for misrepresentation under s 2(1) of the Misrepresentation Act 1967. *Held* – The facts revealed a negligent misrepresentation by Mr Tidbury made without reasonable grounds for believing it to be true. Mrs Anderson was liable for the acts of her agent and must pay damages under the Act of 1967.

*Comment:* (i) This action was against Mrs Anderson who was the other party to the contract. It was decided in *Resolute Maritime Inc and Another* v *Nippon Kaiji Kyokai and Others* [1983] 2 All ER 1 that no action is available against an agent such as Mr Tidbury under s 2(1) of the Misrepresentation Act 1967. Section 2(1) of the 1967 Act begins: 'Where a person has entered into a contract after a misrepresentation has been made to him by another party thereto . . .'. Thus the sub-section only applies when the representee has entered into a contract after a misrepresentation has been made to him by another party to the contract. Where an agent acting within the scope of his authority makes a representation under s 2(1), the principal is liable to the third party misled, but not the agent. The agent will be liable to the third party only if he is guilty of fraud, or, under the rule in *Hedley Byrne* v *Heller* (1963) (*see below*) for negligence at common law. Here the principal will be liable vicariously *along with the agent* for the latter's fraud or negligence if the agent is acting within the scope of his authority.

(ii) As regards proving reasonable grounds, an expert will be expected to verify his statements in a professional way. However, those without relevant technical knowledge will often find that the court will accept a statement as made innocently if the maker of the statement had been induced to purchase the goods himself by the same statement.

Thus in *Humming Bird Motors* v *Hobbs* [1986] RTR 276 H was a young man whom the judge found to be an amateur doing a bit of 'wheeling and dealing' in the motor trade. He bought a car from a dealer who told him that the mileage recorded, 34,900 miles, was correct. H sold the car on to the claimants making the same statement, i.e. that the recorded mileage was, to the best of his knowledge and belief, correct. The claimants discovered that the vehicle had done 80,000 miles and tried to claim damages for negligent misrepresentation. The Court of Appeal decided that H was not negligent; he was an amateur and was merely repeating what he himself believed.

### Fraudulent misrepresentation

A fraudulent misrepresentation is a false representation of a material fact made knowing it to be false, or believing it to be false, or recklessly not caring whether it be true or false. Mere negligence is not enough. An element of dishonesty is required. For example, if Mr Tidbury in the *Gosling* case had *known* that there was no planning permission for the garage but had nevertheless gone on to state that there was, then the element of dishonesty would have been present and he would have been guilty of fraud. The party misled may sue for rescission and/or damages. As regards the action for damages, the claimant sues not on the contract but on the tort of deceit.

**The following is the main case dealing with the definition of fraud.**

### Derry v Peek (1889) 14 App Cas 337

The Plymouth, Devonport and District Tramways Company had power under a special Act of Parliament to run trams by animal power, and with the consent of the Board of Trade (now the Department of Trade and Industry) by mechanical or steam power. Derry and the other appellants were directors of the company and issued a prospectus, inviting the public to apply for shares in it, stating that they had power to run trams by steam power, and claiming that considerable economies would result. The directors had assumed that the permission of the Board of Trade would be granted as a matter of course, but in the event the Board of Trade refused permission except for certain parts of the tramway. As a result the company was wound up and the directors were sued for fraud. The court decided that the directors were not fraudulent but honestly believed the statement in the prospectus to be true. As Lord Herschell said: 'Fraud is proved when it is shown that a false representation has been made (a) knowingly, or (b) without belief in its truth, or (c) recklessly, careless whether it be true or false.'

*Comment:* (i) This case gave rise to the Directors' Liability Act 1890 which made directors of companies liable to pay compensation for negligent misrepresentation in a prospectus, subject to a number of defences. The latest provisions are in the Financial Services Act 1986 (*see below*).

(ii) It will be noticed from this case that the mere fact that no grounds exist for believing a false statement does not of itself constitute fraud. There must also be an element of dishonesty which was not present in this case.

(iii) There is something of a problem with the word 'recklessly' but it seems that the defendant must either *know* that the statement is false or be *almost sure that it is* but is nevertheless reckless and goes on to make it anyway.

## COMPENSATION UNDER THE FINANCIAL SERVICES ACT 1986

Under this Act, where the directors of a company publish an advertisement or prospectus containing false statements made innocently they may have to pay a form of damages called compensation.

There are a number of special defences available under the Act. For example, a director may deny responsibility for the prospectus, as where he ceased to be a director before it was issued. Assuming, however, that he does admit responsibility for the prospectus, the defences are that:

(a) he had reasonable grounds for believing the statement to be true;
(b) the statements were made on the authority of an expert who was thought to be competent;

(c) the statements were a copy of an official document; or

(d) he published a correction or took reasonable steps to see that one was published and he reasonably believed it had been.

Experts, such as accountants, are also liable under the Act for false statements in their reports which are included in the prospectus. Again, the defence of lack of responsibility is available, as where the expert has not consented to the inclusion of his report in the prospectus. However, given that he accepts responsibility for the inclusion of his report, he has a defence if he can show that he had reasonable grounds for believing the statement to be true. Presumably, he could sustain this defence by showing, among other things, that the false statement came from an official document. Furthermore, whether or not a professional person has reasonable grounds will almost always depend upon the steps taken to *verify* the statement. If these are reasonable the professional person will not be liable even if the statement is wrong.

## AGENT'S BREACH OF WARRANTY OF AUTHORITY

Under the law of agency where an agent misrepresents himself as having authority he does not possess, the third party will not obtain a contract with the principal and if he suffers loss as a consequence he may sue the agent for breach of warranty of authority, the action being for damages and brought in *quasi-contract*. Quasi-contract is based on the idea that a person should not obtain a benefit or unjust enrichment or cause injury to another with impunity merely because there is no obligation in contract or another established branch of law which will operate to make him account. The law may in these circumstances provide a remedy by implying a *fictitious promise* to account for the benefit of the enrichment or to compensate for damage caused.

## NEGLIGENCE AT COMMON LAW

### The tort remedy in general

Where the parties concerned were not in a *pre-contractual relationship*, followed by the actual making of a contract, when the statement was made, s 2(1) of the Misrepresentation Act 1967 will not apply. However, an action for damages for negligence will lie in tort, provided the false statement was made negligently.

**The following case in the House of Lords finally affirmed this rule.**

### Hedley Byrne & Co Ltd v Heller & Partners Ltd [1963] 2 All ER 575

The appellants were advertising agents and the respondents were merchant bankers. The appellants had a client called Easipower Ltd who was a customer of the respondents. The appellants had contracted to place orders for advertising Easipower's products on television and in newspapers, and since this involved giving Easipower credit, they asked the respondents, who were Easipower's bankers, for a reference as to the creditworthiness of Easipower. The respondents said that Easipower Ltd was respectably constituted and considered good, although they said in regard to the credit: 'These are bigger figures than we have seen' and also that the reference was given 'in confidence and without responsibility on our part'. Relying on this reply, the appellants placed orders for advertising time and space for Easipower Ltd, and the appellants assumed personal responsibility for payment to the television and newspaper companies concerned. Easipower Ltd went into liquidation and the appellants lost over £17,000 on the advertising contracts. The appellants sued the respondents for the amount of the loss, alleging that the respondents had not informed themselves sufficiently about Easipower Ltd before writing the statement, and were therefore liable in negligence. *Held* – In the present case the respondents' disclaimer was adequate to exclude the assumption by them of the legal duty of care, but, in the absence of the disclaimer, the circumstances would have given rise to a duty of care in spite of the absence of a contract or fiduciary relationship.

*Comment:* (i) The House of Lords stated that the duty of care arose where there was 'a special relationship' requiring care. The boundaries of the *Hedley* case are still not clear but the requirement of a 'special relationship' between the maker of the statement and the recipient is an attempt to get some. Can one complain, for example, if casual advice given on a train-journey by a solicitor turns out to be erroneous? An extract from the judgment of Lord Devlin in the *Hedley* case is helpful. He said '. . . Payment for information or advice is very good evidence that it is being relied upon and that the informer or adviser knows that it is. Where there is no consideration, it will be necessary to exercise greater care in distinguishing between social and professional relationships and between those which are of a contractual character and those which are not. It may often be material to consider whether the adviser is acting purely out of good nature or whether he is getting his reward in some indirect form. The service that a bank performs in giving a reference is not done simply out of a desire to assist commerce. It would discourage the customers of the bank if their deals fell through because the bank had refused to testify to their credit when it was good . . .'. Thus the solicitor's advice should not be actionable because there was no consideration to found contract liability and equally no 'special relationship' to found the tort claim. Of course, the absence of consideration and a contract prevents s 2(1) of the Misrepresentation Act 1967 from applying. However, the requirement of a 'special relationship' as a substitute for consideration brings the *Hedley* tort of negligence much closer to contract than the general law of negligence – a casual statement is not actionable, but there is obviously a claim by persons knocked over by a casual bad driver who is, of course, the worst kind! (For further developments in professional liability *see* Chapter 22.)

(ii) The ease with which the duty to take care placed upon the bank was excluded in this case by the disclaimer was disappointing. However, such a disclaimer of negligence liability would, these days, have to satisfy the test of 'reasonableness' under the Unfair Contract Terms Act 1977 (see Chapter 6). It would seem that such a disclaimer could fall short of the reasonable expectations of those in business who naturally and reasonably expect that a bank will have taken proper care before giving a reference of this kind.

(iii) In this connection it was held in *Smith* v *Eric S Bush* [1987] 3 All ER 179 that it was unreasonable to allow a surveyor to rely on a general disclaimer of negligence where he had been asked by a building society to carry out a reasonably careful visual inspection of the property for valuation purposes (paid for by the would-be purchaser) when the valuer knew that the purchaser would be likely to rely on his report and not get another one. The house was purchased but, because of defects, turned out to be unfit for habitation. The surveyors when sued could not escape liability for damages on the basis of disclaimer (see *further* Chapter 22).

(iv) The case suggests that in so far as such disclaimers are still used by professional persons they may not be effective, at least as regards ordinary consumers of professional services.

(v) However, much would seem to depend on the sophistication of the person misled. In *McCullagh* v *Lane Fox and Partners Ltd, The Times*, 22 December 1995 the Court of Appeal faced a claim against an estate agent for negligently misrepresenting the size of a plot of land to a purchaser. The purchaser's claim failed because the agents had included a disclaimer in the sales particulars which negated the element of proximity and assumption of responsibility required if negligence was to be established. In addition, it was not unfair under s 11 of the Unfair Contract Terms Act 1977 to allow the agents to rely on the disclaimer. The distinction between this case and *Bush* would appear to be the cost of the property (some £800,000) compared with the property in *Bush* (some £17,000) and the normal wordly wise nature of people who buy such expensive properties. Lord Justice Hobhouse said: 'Here the transaction involved a sophisticated member of the public who had had ample opportunity to regulate his conduct having regard to the disclaimer and who would have been assumed by all concerned to have had the benefit of legal advice before exchanging contracts'. The judge went on to say that since disclaimers are usually inserted by estate agents into their contracts it would have been unfair not to allow the defendants to rely on theirs.

## Use of the tort remedy in contract cases

In *Esso Petroleum* v *Mardon* [1976] 2 All ER 5 the court *held* that the principle in *Hedley Byrne* could apply even where the parties concerned were in a pre-contractual relationship and in addition that the person who had made the statement need not necessarily be in business to give advice, provided it is reasonable for one party to rely on the other's skill and judgment in making the statement. Mr Mardon was awarded damages for a negligent misstatement by a senior sales representative of Esso in regard to the amount of petrol he could expect to sell per year from a petrol station which he was leasing from Esso. The facts of *Mardon* pre-dated the 1967 Act and the court could not use it. The decision is obviously important but where the facts have occurred since 1967 the Misrepresentation Act is likely to prove more popular to claimants who have been misled *into making contracts*, since they can ask the representer to show he was not negligent. In *Hedley Byrne* claims, the burden of proof is on the claimant to prove negligence.

There is a very obvious use, however, for the tort of negligence claim even where the careless misstatement has induced a contract. The tort claim allows an action for a misleading *opinion or falsely stated intention*, whereas misrepresentation in all its forms requires a misstatement of *fact*, not opinion or intention. The use of *Hedley Byrne* would today make the legal gymnastics seen in *Edgington* v *Fitzmaurice* (1885) and *Smith* v *Land and House Property Co* (1884) (*see* Chapter 5) unnecessary.

## Use of the tort remedy for inaccurate company securities advertisements

As regards actions against directors and experts in respect of statements in an advertisement for the sale of securities or in a prospectus, there is as we have seen a statutory claim under the Financial Services Act 1986 and under *Hedley Byrne* at common law. The claim against directors under *Hedley Byrne* is specifically preserved by the Financial

Services Act 1986 in s 150(4). A claim under the Misrepresentation Act 1967 is against 'the other party to the contract', i.e. the company or issuing house, and not against directors or agents.

It will be recalled in *Esso Petroleum Co Ltd* v *Mardon* (1976) (*see above*) that the court *held* that it was too restrictive to limit the duty in *Hedley Byrne* to persons who carried on or who held themselves out as carrying on the *business* of giving information or advice. The acceptance of these views means that the duty can apply more widely and brings in company directors in terms that they could be liable on a personal basis for negligence.

In any case, it is a requirement as part of admission of the shares to a full Stock Exchange or AIM (Alternative Investment Market) listing, that the advertisement or prospectus shall state that the directors have taken reasonable care to ensure that the facts stated in it are true and accurate, that there are no misleading omissions and that, accordingly, all the directors take responsibility for the prospectus.

In view of this statement, it is likely that a duty of care is owed only by the individuals involved in the making of the statements and not by the company as such. If this is so, no claim can be made against the company. This would accord with the general principle of capital maintenance inherent in the prospectus remedies, i.e. it is difficult to get one's money back from the company and easier to get compensation from directors or experts, leaving capital contributed with the company.

In view of this it would seem that an action for rescission of the contract (*see below*) against the company will not in the company law context be a likely remedy. In any case, it is very quickly lost, as we shall see.

## REMEDY OF RESCISSION

As we have seen, this remedy is available to a party misled by innocent, negligent or fraudulent misrepresentation. It restores the *status quo*, i.e. it puts the parties back to the position they were in before the contract was made. However, the remedy may be lost:

(a) *By affirmation*. If the injured party affirms the contract he cannot rescind. He will affirm if with full knowledge of the misrepresentation he expressly affirms the contract by stating that he intends to go on with it or if he does some act from which an implied intention may properly be deduced. In the company situation this could, for example, be attending a company meeting to complain about an inaccurate prospectus.

**The following case is a general commercial example of the application of the affirmation rule.**

### Long v Lloyd [1958] 2 All ER 402

The claimant and the defendant were haulage contractors. The claimant was induced to buy the defendant's lorry by the defendant's misrepresentation as to condition and performance. The defendant advertised a lorry for sale at £850, the advertisement describing the vehicle as being in 'exceptional condition'. The claimant telephoned the defendant the same evening when the defendant agreed that his advertisement was a little ambiguous and said that the lorry was 'in first class condition'. The claimant saw the lorry at the defendant's premises at Hampton Court on a Saturday. During a trial run on the following Monday the claimant found that the speedometer was not working, a spring was missing from the accelerator pedal, and it was difficult to engage top gear. The defendant said there was nothing wrong with the vehicle except what the claimant had found. He also said at this stage that the lorry would do 11 miles to the gallon.

The claimant purchased the lorry for £750, paying £375 down and agreeing to pay the balance at a later date. He then drove the lorry from Hampton Court to his place of business at Sevenoaks. On the following Wednesday, the claimant drove from Sevenoaks to Rochester to pick up a load, and during that journey the dynamo ceased to function, an oil seal was leaking badly, there was a crack in one of the road wheels, and he used eight gallons of petrol on a journey of 40 miles. That evening the claimant told the defendant of the defects, and the defendant offered to pay half the cost of a reconstructed dynamo, but denied any knowledge of the other defects. The claimant accepted the offer and the dynamo was fitted straightaway. On Thursday the lorry was driven by the claimant's brother to Middlesbrough, and it broke down on the Friday night. The claimant, on learning of this, asked the defendant for his money back, but the defendant would not give it to him. The lorry was subsequently examined and an expert said that it was not roadworthy. The claimant sued for rescission. *Held* – at first instance, by Glyn-Jones J – that the defendant's statements about the lorry were innocent and not fraudulent because the evidence showed that the lorry had been laid up for a month and it might have deteriorated without the defendant's precise knowledge. The Court of Appeal affirmed this finding of fact and made the following additional points:

(a)  The journey to Rochester was not affirmation because the claimant was merely testing the vehicle in a working capacity.

(b)  However, the acceptance by the claimant of the defendant's offer to pay half the cost of the reconstructed dynamo, and the subsequent journey to Middlesbrough, did amount to affirmation, and rescission could not be granted to the claimant.

*Comment:* (i) Damages could now be obtained for negligent misrepresentation under the Misrepresentation Act 1967, s 2(1), for how could the seller say he had reasonable grounds for believing that the lorry was in exceptional condition or first class condition?

(ii) It seems remarkable that Glyn-Jones J did not find fraud. However, fraud must be proved according to the criminal standard, i.e. beyond a reasonable doubt, and not according to the civil standard which is on balance of probabilities. Fraud is therefore difficult to prove and in this case there was presumably a reasonable doubt in the mind of the judge on the issue of fraud.

(iii) The Court of Appeal would not accept that the statement that the lorry was in first class condition was a term of the contract (see *further* Chapter 6) but decided that it was only a misrepresentation.

(b)  *By lapse of time*. This is a form of implied affirmation and applies as follows:

(i)  In innocent and negligent misrepresentation the position is governed by equity and the passage of a reasonable time, even without knowledge of the misrepresentation, may prevent the court from granting rescission: *Leaf* v *International Galleries* (1950) – *see* Chapter 4.

(ii)  In fraudulent misrepresentation the position is governed by s 32 of the Limitation Act 1980 and lapse of time has no effect on rescission where fraud is alleged as long as the action is brought within six years of the time when the fraud was, or with reasonable diligence could have been, discovered.

(c) *Where the* status quo *cannot be restored.* Rescission is impossible if the parties cannot be restored to their original positions as where goods sold under a contract of sale have been consumed.

**The following case provides a further example.**

## Clarke v Dickson (1858) 27 LJQB 223

In 1853 the claimant was induced by the misrepresentation of the three defendants, Dickson, Williams and Gibbs, to invest money in what was in effect a partnership to work lead mines in Wales. In 1857 the partnership was in financial difficulty and with the claimant's assent it was converted into a limited company and the partnership capital was converted into shares. Shortly afterwards the company commenced winding-up proceedings and the claimant, on discovery of the falsity of the representations, asked for rescission of the contract. *Held* – Rescission could not be granted because capital in a partnership is not the same as shares in a company. The firm was no longer in existence, having been replaced by the company, and it was not possible to restore the parties to their original positions.

*Comment:* (i) It should be noted that in addition to the problem of restoration, third-party rights, i.e. creditors, had accrued on the winding-up of the company and this is a further bar to rescission (*see below*).

(ii) However, the court still retains its power to rescind 'on terms' where the problem is only one of deterioration of the subject-matter. In *Erlanger* v *New Sombrero Phosphate Co* (1878) 3 App Cas 1218 rescission was granted of a contract to purchase a phosphate mine even though some phosphate had been extracted from it since the sale. The House of Lords gave rescission on terms that the purchaser must account to the seller for profits made from the sale of the phosphate extracted since purchase.

(d) *Where a third party has acquired rights in the subject-matter of the contract.* Thus if X obtains goods from Y by misrepresentation and pawns them with Z, Y cannot rescind the contract on learning of the misrepresentation in order to recover the goods from Z. Nor can he sue Z in conversion (*Lewis* v *Averay* (1971) – *see* Chapter 4).

It should be noted that the third party must have supplied consideration as in *Lewis.* If the third party has received the property as a gift it can be recovered from him.

## Rescission and contractual debt

The fact that a party to a contract rescinds it because e.g. of non-performance by the other party does not mean that the party rescinding has thereby abandoned an action for debts owed under the contract. Thus in *Stocznia Gdanska SA* v *Latvian Shipping* [1998] 1 All ER 883 S rescinded a contract with L to build two ships because of L's failure to pay the first instalment of the price when due. The House of Lords later decided that a claim by S for the unpaid instalment, which represented the cost of the design and laying of the keel of a ship, was recoverable.

# CONTRACTS *UBERRIMAE FIDEI* (UTMOST GOOD FAITH)

Silence does not normally amount to misrepresentation. However, an important exception to the rule occurs in the case of certain contracts where from the circumstances of the case one party alone possesses full knowledge of all the material facts and in which therefore the law requires him to show utmost good faith. He must make full disclosure of all the material facts known to him otherwise the contract may be avoided by the other party. The contracts concerned are as follows.

## At common law

Contracts of insurance provide the only true example of a contract *uberrimae fidei*. There is a duty on the person taking up the insurance to disclose to the insurance company all facts of which he is aware which might affect the premium or acceptance of the risk. Failure to do so renders the contract voidable at the option of the insurance company and the insurance company can refuse to continue to cover the risk or refuse to pay a claim though it must return the premiums. This could happen, for example, where a person seeking insurance did not disclose that he had been refused insurance by another company.

In addition, most proposals for insurance require the proposer to sign a declaration in which he warrants that the statements he has made are true and agrees that they be incorporated into the contract as terms. Where this is so any false statement which the proposer makes will be a ground for avoidance of the contract by the insurance company, even though the statement was not material in terms of the premium.

**Thus the duty of disclosure in insurance contracts may be widened by the terms of the contract itself as the following case illustrates.**

### Dawsons Ltd v Bonnin [1922] 2 AC 413

Dawsons Ltd insured their motor lorry against loss by fire with Bonnin and others, and signed a proposal form which contained the following as Condition 4: 'Material misstatement or concealment of any circumstances by the insured material to assessing the premium herein, or in connection with any claim, shall render the policy void.' The policy also contained a clause saying that the 'proposal shall be the basis of the contract and shall be held as incorporated therein'. Actually the proposal form was filled up by an insurance agent, and although he stated the proposer's address correctly as 46 Cadogan Street, Glasgow, he also stated that the vehicle would usually be garaged there, although there was no garage accommodation at the Cadogan Street address and the lorry was garaged elsewhere. Dawsons' secretary, who signed the proposal, overlooked this slip made by the agent. The lorry was destroyed by fire and Dawsons claimed under the policy. *Held* – on appeal, by the House of Lords – the statement was not material within the meaning of Condition 4. However, the basis clause was an independent provision, and since the statement, though not material, was untrue, the policy was void for breach of condition. Viscount Cave said: 'The meaning and effect of the basis clause, taken by itself, is that any untrue statement in the proposal, or any breach of its promissory clauses, shall avoid the policy, and if that be the contract of the parties, the question of materiality has not to be considered.'

*Comment:* (i) The Unfair Contract Terms Act 1977 does not apply to contracts of insurance. This resulted from a deal between the insurance companies and the government under which the insurance companies agreed to abide by voluntary statements of practice. These have no legal effect but some moral force. If the insurance company follows these statements of practice then certainly in consumer, i.e. non-business, insurance the worst effect of the basis clause should be eliminated.

(ii) However, even if we get rid of the basis clause problem, the rules of disclosure of material matters by the person seeking insurance remains a difficulty. It is based upon s 18(2) of the Marine Insurance Act 1906. This should not have been used as a basis for *all* insurances. Those seeking marine insurance are well aware of the risks they seek to insure. Those seeking, for example, domestic fire insurance are not. The Law Commission Report entitled *Non-Disclosure and Breach of Warranty* places a heavy burden on insurance companies to phrase their questions so as to elicit the kind and amount of information they want and not to leave it, as at present, to the person seeking insurance to make uninformed guesses as to what might be material to the insurers. The common law has already taken steps in this direction in *Hair* v *Prudential Assurance* [1983] 2 Lloyd's Rep 667, the court deciding in that case that if a person seeking insurance answered honestly all the questions put to him by the proposal for insurance he should not be required to disclose any other matters. The questions should reveal all material issues.

(iii) The courts continue to try to assist the insured in terms of the utmost good faith rule which has for so long been the insurer's best friend. In *Pan Atlantic Insurance Co Ltd* v *Pine Top Insurance Co Ltd* [1994] 3 All ER 581 the House of Lords decided that whereas in the past a mere innocent non-disclosure had enabled insurers to avoid the contract it was now necessary to show that the insurer had actually been *induced* by the non-disclosure to enter into the policy on its terms. Their Lordships did decide, however, that there was a presumption that an insurer would have been influenced by a non-disclosure of a material fact. This means that the person insured will have the burden of proving that the insurer was not influenced by the non-disclosure. This rather weakens the decision so far as the insured is concerned.

(iv) Further progress by the courts in defending the rights of the consumer against the harsher application of the utmost good faith rule is to be seen in *Economides* v *Commercial Union Insurance Co plc* [1997] 3 All ER 636 where the Court of Appeal decided, at least in so far as the private consumer buying insurance cover is concerned, that the insured's duty to the insurance company is primarily one one of honesty, and he need only disclose those material facts which are known to him. Mr E's flat was burgled and £31,000 worth of valuables were stolen, mainly those belonging to his parents. His contents insurance had been valued by Mr E at £16,000 and maximum cover for valuables was £5,333. The defendants repudiated liability on the grounds of misrepresentation as to value and failure to disclose material facts. Mr E was, of course, under-insured and could only recover part of his loss, but the defendants did not want to pay at all. The Court of Appeal decided in favour of Mr E's recovery of the reduced sum.

*The business application:* The importance to those in business of the decisions in *Pan Atlantic* and *Economides* are as follows:

- those in the insurance business will to some extent have relied in the past on the fact that the duty of utmost good faith has been applied equally strictly to both businesses and to private consumers. The *Economides* case is important in that the Court of Appeal adopted a less rigorous approach in favour of the private consumer – basically a test of honesty.

> Mr E honestly believed the valuation to be correct, in fact his father had told him so. If insurers wish to place on the assured an obligation to take steps to get professional valuations, they must specify this as a requirement on the proposal form.
> - those who are not in the insurance business should be heartened by the inducement rule of *Pan Atlantic* and note also that the ruling in *Economides* may well come to apply to small businesses where the owners are often little better informed about insurance than the ordinary consumer.

## By statute

As regards contracts to take shares in a company, there is a duty on the directors or its promoters, under the Financial Services Act 1986, to disclose various matters essential to an informed assessment as to whether an investor should purchase the securities. These provisions, and those in earlier statutes which preceded them, had to be put into the law by Parliament because the judiciary had always refused to regard the sale of securities by a company as a contract *uberrimae fidei*. They did not, therefore, require the advertisement or prospectus under which the shares were issued necessarily to disclose all the material facts.

## In equity–fiduciary relationships

In contracts between members of a family, partners, principal and agent, solicitor and client, guardian and ward, and trustee and beneficiary, the relationship of the parties requires that the most ample disclosure be made. The duties of disclosure arising from the above fiduciary relations recognised by equity are not situations of *uberrimae fidei*. In contracts *uberrimae fidei* it is the nature of the contract, i.e. insurance, which requires disclosure regardless of the relationship of the parties. In the fiduciary situation, it is the relationship of parties and not the particular contract which gives rise to the need to disclose.

**The following case is an illustration in a family situation.**

### Gordon v Gordon (1819) 3 Swan 400

Two brothers made an agreement for division of the family estates. The elder supposed he was born before the marriage of his parents and was, therefore, illegitimate. The younger knew that their parents had been married before the birth of the elder brother and the elder brother was, therefore, legitimate and his father's heir. He did not communicate this information to his elder brother. Nineteen years afterwards the elder brother discovered that he was legitimate and the agreement was set aside following this action brought by him. He would have had no case if at the time of the agreement both brothers had been in honest error as to the date of their parents' marriage.

## DURESS

Duress will affect all contracts and gifts procured by its use. Duress, which is a common law concept, means actual violence or threats of violence to the person of the contracting party or those near and dear to him. The threats must be calculated to produce fear of loss of life or bodily harm.

## Threats of violence

A contract will seldom be procured by actual violence but threats of violence are more probable. The threat must be illegal in that it must be a threat to commit a crime or tort. Thus to threaten an imprisonment, which would be unlawful if enforced, constitutes duress, but not, it is said, if the imprisonment would be lawful. However, the courts are unlikely to look with favour on a contract obtained by threatening to prosecute a criminal. A contract procured by a threat to sue for an act which was not a crime, e.g. trespass, would not be affected by duress.

The following case provides an example of the avoidance of a contract made under duress by threats of violence.

### Welch v Cheesman (1973) 229 EG 99

Mrs Welch lived with the defendant, C, for many years in a house which she owned. C was a man given to violence, and after he threatened her Mrs Welch sold the house to him for £300. C died and his widow claimed the house which was worth about £3,000. Mrs Welch brought this action to set aside the sale of the house to C on the grounds of duress and she succeeded.

## Threats to property

In *Skeate* v *Beale* (1840) 11 Ad & EL 983 a tenant owed £19 10s in old money and agreed to pay £3 7s 6d immediately and the remaining £16 2s 6d within a month if his landlord would withdraw a writ of distress under which he was threatening to sell the tenant's goods. The tenant later disputed what he owed and the landlord tried to set up the agreement and sued for the remaining £16 2s 6d. It was *held* that the landlord was entitled to £16 2s 6d under the agreement which was not affected by duress since the threat was to sell the tenant's goods. However, more recently the courts have been moving away from the view that threats to property cannot invalidate contracts. In *The Siboen and The Sibotre* [1976] Lloyd's Rep 293 it was said that duress could be a defence if a person was forced to make a contract by the threat of having a valuable picture slashed or his house burnt down.

## Duress probably renders a contract *voidable*

This, at least, is the view expressed in Cheshire & Fifoot's *Law of Contract* (a leading text on contract law), though other writers have argued that the effect of duress is to render a contract void. However, the judgments of the Privy Council in *Barton* v *Armstrong* [1975] 2 All ER 465 and *Pao On* v *Lau Yiu Long* [1979] 3 All ER 65 suggest that duress has the same effect as fraud, i.e. it renders a contract voidable. The issue is an important one for third parties, since if B procures goods from A by duress and sells the goods to C, who has no knowledge of the duress, A will be able to recover the goods from C if the contract is void, but will not be able to do so if it is voidable. On the authorities to date, therefore, A would have no claim against C.

## UNDUE INFLUENCE AND ASSOCIATED EQUITABLE PLEAS

The doctrine of undue influence was developed by equity. The concept of undue influence is designed to deal with contracts *or gifts* obtained without free consent by the influence of one mind over another.

If there is no special relationship between the parties, undue influence may exist, but must be proved by the person seeking to avoid the contract.

Where a confidential or fiduciary relationship exists between the parties, the party in whom the confidence was reposed must show that undue influence was not used, i.e. that the contract was the act of a free and independent mind. It is desirable, though not essential, that independent advice should have been given.

There are several confidential relationships which are well established in the law, namely parent and child, solicitor and client, trustee and beneficiary, guardian and ward and religious adviser and the person subject to the religious advice. In these cases there is a presumption of undue influence by the parent, the solicitor, the trustee and so on. There is no presumption of such a relationship between husband and wife, nor, according to the Court of Appeal in *Mathew* v *Bobbins* (1980) 256 EG 603 between employer and employee. However, a presumption of undue influence may be made between husband and wife where there are special circumstances such as the lack of sufficient mental capacity in either party to resist the influence of the other leading to gifts of property which are quite out of character with the donor's normal inquiring disposition when disposing of property (*Simpson* v *Simpson*, *The Times*, 11 June 1988). The fiduciary relationship between parent and child ends usually, but not necessarily, on the child's reaching 18 or on his or her getting married.

**The following case illustrates this.**

### Lancashire Loans Ltd v Black [1934] 1 KB 380

A daughter married at 18 and went to live with her husband. Her mother was an extravagant woman and was in debt to a firm of moneylenders. When the daughter became of age, her mother persuaded her to raise £2,000 on property in which the daughter had an interest, and this was used to pay off the mother's debts. Twelve months later the mother and daughter signed a joint and several promissory note of £775 at 85 per cent interest in favour of the moneylenders, and the daughter created a further charge on her property in order that the mother might borrow more money. The daughter did not understand the nature of the transaction, and the only advice she received was from a solicitor acting for the mother and the moneylenders. This was in no sense independent advice. The moneylenders brought this action against the mother and daughter on the note. *Held* – The daughter's defence that she was under the undue influence of her mother succeeded, in spite of the fact that she was of full age and married with her own home.

**A further illustration of a situation of presumed undue influence in the case of religious influence appears opposite. The situation is one of gift rather than contract but the principles are the same.**

## Allcard v Skinner (1887) 36 Ch D 145

In 1868 the claimant joined a Protestant institution called the sisterhood of St Mary at the Cross, promising to devote her property to the service of the poor. The defendant Miss Skinner was the Lady Superior of the Sisterhood. In 1871 the claimant ceased to be a novice and became a sister in the order, taking her vows of poverty, chastity and obedience. By this time she had left her home and was residing with the sisterhood. The claimant remained a sister until 1878 and, in compliance with the vow of poverty, she had by then given property to the value of £7,000 to the defendant. The claimant left the order in 1879 and became a Roman Catholic. Of the property she had transferred, £1,671 remained in 1885 and the claimant sought to recover this sum, claiming that it had been transferred in circumstances of undue influence. Held – The gifts had been made under pressure of an unusually persuasive nature, particularly since the claimant was prevented from seeking outside advice under a rule of the sisterhood which said, 'Let no sister seek the advice of any extern without the superior's leave'. However, the claimant's claim was barred by her delay because, although the influence was removed in 1879, she did not bring her action until 1885.

However, there may be a presumption of undue influence even though the relationship between the parties is not in the established categories outlined above. In *Re Craig Dec'd* [1970] 2 All ER 390 Ungoed-Thomas J ruled that presumption of undue influence arose on proof:

(a) of a gift so substantial or of such a nature that it could not on the face of it be accounted for on the grounds of the ordinary motives on which ordinary men acted, and

(b) of a relationship of trust and confidence such that the recipient of the gift was in a position to exercise undue influence over the person making it.

**This principle was applied in the following case.**

## Hodgson v Marks [1970] 3 All ER 513

Mrs Hodgson, who was a widow of 83, owned a freehold house in which she lived. In 1959 she took in a Mr Evans as a lodger. She soon came to trust Evans and allowed him to manage her financial affairs. In June 1960, she transferred the house to Evans, her sole reason for so doing being to prevent her nephew from turning Evans out of the house. It was orally agreed between Mrs Hodgson and Evans that the house was to remain hers although held in the name of Evans. Evans later made arrangements to sell the house without the knowledge or consent of Mrs Hodgson. The house was bought by Mr Marks and Mrs Hodgson now asked for a declaration that he was bound to transfer the property back to her. The following questions arose:

(a) whether Evans held the house in trust for Mrs Hodgson. It was *held* – by Ungoed-Thomas J – that he did. The absence of written evidence of trust as required by s 53 of the Law of Property Act 1925 was not a bar to Mrs Hodgson's claim. The section does not apply to implied trusts of this kind;

(b) whether Evans had exercised undue influence. It was held that he had and that a presumption of undue influence was raised. Although the parties were not in the established categories, Evans had a relationship of trust and confidence with Mrs Hodgson of a kind which raised a presumption of undue influence.

However, Mrs Hodgson lost the case because Mr Marks was protected by s 70 of the Land Registration Act 1925, which gives rights to a purchaser of property for value in respect of interests in that property of which the purchaser is not aware. In this case Mr Marks bought the house from Mr Evans, the house being in the name of Evans and he had no reason to suppose that Mrs Hodgson had any interest in it.

*Comment:* (i) Mrs Hodgson's appeal to the Court of Appeal in 1971 succeeded and she got her house back, the court holding that in spite of s 70 a purchaser must pay heed to the possibility of rights in all *occupiers*. Mrs Hodgson was obviously in occupation with Mr Evans and inquiries should have been made by the purchaser as to her rights in the property.

(ii) The application of the presumption in a relationship which was not one of the established ones is also illustrated by *Goldsworthy v Brickell* [1987] 1 All ER 853, where a contract to grant a tenancy of a farm advantageous to the defendant in that, for example, it did not allow the landlord, G, to make any rent increases, was set aside. The defendant, B, who had become the tenant, was a neighbour of G's. G was 85 and had come to rely implicitly on the advice of B. Undue influence was presumed although neighbours are not within the established categories where undue influence is generally presumed.

### Effect of undue influence on third parties

A contract between A and B procured by undue influence cannot be avoided by rescission against third parties who acquire rights for value without notice of the facts. Where this has happened the party suffering the undue influence, say, A, will have to rely on tracing the proceeds of sale into the original purchaser's, i.e. B's, assets. The contract may be avoided and the property recovered from third parties for value with notice of the facts and also against volunteers (i.e. persons who have given no consideration) even though they were unaware of the facts.

### Effect of undue influence on the parties to the contract

Undue influence renders the contract voidable so that it may be rescinded. However, since rescission is an equitable remedy, there must be no delay in claiming relief after the influence has ceased to have effect. Delay in claiming relief in these circumstances may bar the claim since delay is evidence of affirmation. This is illustrated by the case of *Allcard v Skinner* (*above*).

## ECONOMIC DURESS

Apart from the old concepts of duress and undue influence, the courts are developing in modern times wider rules to protect persons against improper pressure and inequality of bargaining power as it affects contracts. This development was perhaps best described by Lord Denning in *Lloyds Bank v Bundy* [1974] 3 All ER 757 where he said, having discussed duress and various forms of undue pressure in contract:

Gathering all together, I would suggest that through all these instances there runs a single thread. They rest on 'inequality of bargaining power'. By virtue of it, the English law gives relief to one who, without independent advice, enters into a contract on terms

which are very unfair or transfers property for consideration which is grossly inadequate, where his bargaining power is grievously impaired by reason of his own needs or
desires, or by his own ignorance or infirmity coupled with undue influence or pressures
brought to bear on him by or for the benefit of the other.

Economic duress is within this concept. Suppose A agrees to build a tanker for B by an
agreed date at an agreed price and B enters into a contract with C under which the
tanker is to be chartered to C from the agreed completion date or shortly afterwards. If
A then threatens not to complete the contract by the agreed date unless B pays more
and B makes an extra payment because he does not want to be liable in breach of contract to C, then the agreement to pay more is affected by economic duress. (See the
judgment of Mocatta J in *North Ocean Shipping Co Ltd* v *Hyundai Construction Co Ltd. The
Atlantic Baron* [1978] 3 All ER 1170.)

The decision of the House of Lords in *Universe Tankships Inc of Monrovia* v
*International Transport Workers' Federation* [1982] 2 All ER 67 is instructive in that it
affirms the existence of the doctrine of economic duress. In that case a ship called the
*Universe Sentinel*, which was owned by Universe Tankships, was 'blacked' by the
respondent trade union, the ITF, which regarded the ship as sailing under a flag of convenience. ITF was against flag-of-convenience ships and refused to make tugs available
when the ship arrived at Milford Haven to discharge her cargo. The blacking was lift-
ed after Universe Tankships had made an agreement with ITF regarding improvements
in pay and conditions of the crew and had paid money to ITF which included a contribution of $6,480 to an ITF fund known as The Seafarers' International Welfare
Protection and Assistance Fund. Universe Tankships sued for the return of the $6,480
on the basis of economic duress, and the House of Lords *held* that they were entitled to
recover it. It appears from the judgments that the effect of economic duress is to make
the contract voidable and to provide a ground for recovery of money paid as money
had and received to the claimant's use – a form of quasi-contractual claim.

The decision in *Universe Tankships* was applied by the Court of Appeal in *B & S
Contracts & Design* v *Victor Green Publications* [1984] IGR 419 where A agreed to erect
stands for B who was doing a presentation at Olympia. A's employees threatened to
strike unless they received extra money which they had demanded and to which
they were not entitled. A said the contract could not proceed unless these extra sums
were paid by B as an increase in the contract price. B paid the extra sums to get the
work done and then recovered them in this action. The money was paid under economic duress.

It should also be noted that where extra contractual payments have been arranged
under circumstances of economic duress they cannot be recovered in a claim before a
court. Thus in *Atlas Express* v *Kafco* [1989] 1 All ER 641 Atlas, a national road carrier,
made a contract to deliver cartons of basketware to Woolworths stores for Kafco who
were a small company importing and distributing the basketware. A price of £1.10 per
carton was agreed but the first load had fewer cartons than had been anticipated and
Atlas told Kafco that they would not carry any more without a minimum payment per
trip regardless of the number of cartons carried. Kafco could not find another carrier
quickly and, being worried about their contract with Woolworths if the latter did not
get their supplies, Kafco agreed to the new terms but later refused to pay the new rate,

only the per carton rate. The High Court *held* that the claim of Atlas for the minimum rate must be dismissed. The circumstances amounted to economic duress and there was no proper consent by Kafco.

## UNCONSCIONABLE BARGAINS

The court will, in what it regards as an appropriate case, set aside a contract which is affected by improper pressure by one party or where there is inequality of bargaining power. The major distinction between unconscionable bargains and undue influence is that the former extends to contracts with consideration whereas undue influence can be used also to set aside gifts where there is no consideration as in the *Allcard* case. The judiciary do not always make the distinction clear. However, mere inequality is not in itself enough: the court will look at all the circumstances of the case.

**The following case and comment illustrates the legal position.**

### Lloyds Bank v Bundy [1974] 3 All ER 757

The defendant and his son's company both banked with the claimants, the defendant having been a customer for many years. The company's affairs deteriorated over a period of years and at the son's suggestion the bank's assistant manager visited the defendant and said that the bank could not continue to support an overdraft for the company unless the defendant entered into a guarantee of the account. The defendant received no independent advice, nor did the bank's assistant manager suggest that he should do so. The defendant charged his house as security for the overdraft and shortly afterwards the company went into receivership. The bank obtained possession of the house from the defendant in the county court, where the assistant branch manager in evidence said that he thought that the defendant had relied upon him implicitly to advise him about the charge.

The defendant appealed to the Court of Appeal in an attempt to set aside the guarantee and the security and it was *held* – allowing the defendant's appeal – that in the particular circumstances a special relationship existed between the defendant and the bank's assistant manager, as agent for the bank, and the bank was in breach of its duty of fiduciary care in procuring the charge which would be set aside for undue influence. The defendant, without any benefit to himself, had signed away his sole remaining asset without taking independent advice.

*Comment:* (i) While the majority of the Court of Appeal (Cairns LJ and Sir Eric Sachs) were content to decide the appeal on the conventional ground that a fiduciary relationship existed between the bank and its customer, which is to suggest that a new fiduciary relationship has come into being, Lord Denning took the opportunity to break new ground by deciding that in addition to avoiding the contract on the grounds of fiduciary relationship, Mr Bundy could also have done so on the basis of 'inequality of bargaining power'. Although inequality of bargaining power obviously includes undue influence, Lord Denning made it clear that the principle does not depend on the will of one party being dominated or overcome by the other. This is clear from that part of the judgment where he says: 'One who is in extreme need may knowingly consent to a most improvident bargain, solely to relieve the straits in which he finds himself.' This approach is, of course, at variance with the traditional view of undue influence which was that it was based on dominance resulting in an inferior party being unable to exercise independent judgment or on a relationship of trust and confidence.

(ii) It should be noted that cases such as this which introduce into the law a requirement that a contract must be fair may eventually develop to the point where adequacy of consideration is required in contract. This is not the case at the present time.

(iii) In *National Westminster Bank plc v Morgan* [1983] 3 All ER 85 the Court of Appeal set aside a charge over a wife's share in the matrimonial home after she executed it without legal advice in order to secure a loan from the bank to clear a building society mortgage, and after the bank manager had assured her that the charge would not be used to secure her husband's business advances, whereas it did in fact extend to such advances. However, the bank had no intention of using the charge other than to secure the advance to clear the building society mortgage; nor did it.

The above decision, which moved in the direction of saying that banks would have to ensure that all their customers had independent legal advice before taking out a bank mortgage was reversed by the House of Lords in *National Westminster Bank plc v Morgan* [1985] 1 All ER 821. Undue influence, the House of Lords said, was the use by one person of a power over another person to take a certain course of action generally to his or her disadvantage. A bank manager need not advise independent legal advice in a situation such as this. The manager in this case had stuck to explaining the legal effect of the charge which, though erroneous as to the terms of the charge, correctly represented his intention and that of the bank. The security represented no disadvantage to Mrs Morgan. It was exactly what she wanted to clear the building society loan on her home. The House of Lords also rejected the view that a court would grant relief where there was merely an inequality of bargaining power. Their Lordships rejected that view which was expressed by Lord Denning in *Bundy*. The courts will not, said the House of Lords, protect persons against what they regard as a mistake merely because of inequality of bargaining power. This is a much harder line.

(iv) In *Bundy*, therefore, the Court of Appeal *held* that the bank in not advising the person giving the security to get independent advice exercised undue influence and for this reason set the security aside. In *Morgan* the House of Lords *held* that no presumption of undue influence existed. In *Cornish v Midland Bank* [1985] 3 All ER 513 the Court of Appeal decided that the proper way to deal with these cases was not through undue influence but by using the law of negligence, though only where the bank had given wrong advice.

In *Cornish* the claimant had signed a second mortgage on a farmhouse jointly owned with her husband in order to secure £2,000 which her husband had borrowed from the bank. She did so because the bank clerk involved said that the mortgage was like a building society mortgage. But it was not because, unlike a building society mortgage, it covered all future borrowing by the husband. The bank later tried to enforce the security. Eventually the Court of Appeal *held* that the bank was liable in negligence for the wrong advice of its clerk who made a negligent misstatement causing damage, i.e. that £2,000 was the borrowing limit when it was not. The mortgage was not set aside for undue influence so that the bank was entitled to the proceeds of the sale of the farmhouse but had to pay the claimant £11,231 damages plus interest for negligence. Thus, although it would be good practice for a bank to advise independent advice, it is not necessary for it to do so. The security will be good and there is no presumption of undue influence. However, if an employee of the bank *actually* gives negligent advice or fails to explain the consequences of the charge and/or fails to advise the taking of independent advice (see *Midland Bank plc v Perry*, *The Times*, 28 May 1987), the bank will be able to enforce the security but will be liable in damages under the ruling in *Hedley Byrne v Heller & Partners* (1963) (*see above*).

(v) This may, in some cases, make the security of little use to the bank because it will have to set off the damages it is required to pay against the money it receives from the sale of the security. Much depends of course on the amount of damages awarded. Nevertheless the above cases, i.e. *Morgan, Cornish* and *Perry* do seek to remove these security situations from the realm of undue influence and it seems that the courts which decided these cases were diverging from the older rules previously provided by equity for married women who provided security for their husbands' debts. A security is a business transaction and those giving securities must look after themselves as mostly they have had to in business law. However, the older rules seem to survive since in *Barclays Bank plc v O'Brien* [1992] 4 All ER 983 the Court of Appeal held that wives must be treated more tenderly and needed extra protection. This may offend some but it is a social reality where many women are not trained in the ways of business. The court decided that a married woman (or co-habitee) who provides security for her husband's or partner's debts must be treated as a special protected class of guarantor because of the emotional involvement of which the bank is on constructive notice because of the relationship. Unless the transaction is fully explained and understood, the protected guarantor will be able to treat the guarantee as void.

(vi) What then is new about *O'Brien?* First and most importantly is the fact that the bank was fixed with *constructive notice* of the possibility that the wife may not have fully understood the transaction either because she had been misled by the husband or had not been fully informed. It was not necessary for the bank manager to have *actual knowledge* of this. What this means in effect is that when taking a security on property which is jointly owned, as in the *O'Brien* case, by persons with an emotional involvement the person taking the security must *assume* that there may be deceit or undue influence upon the wife or partner though the security will be good if the bank official ensures that the wife or partner fully understands the transaction and its risks either by means of his own explanations or as a result of independent advice. If following explanation or advice the wife or partner signs a document to the effect that the transaction and its risks are understood the Court is likely to accept this as evidence of the wife's or partner's liability on the guarantee.

(vii) It is worth noting that in a similar case entitled *CIBC Mortgages plc v Pitt* [1994] 4 All ER 433 the House of Lords held that a wife who had been pressurised into giving security over the jointly-owned family home was bound by it. The distinction was made in *Pitt* that the loan was made *jointly* to the husband and wife and not to the husband alone so that the wife derived some benefit from it. In such cases, said the House of Lords, the rule of constructive notice does not arise and in the absence of actual knowledge of pressure which was not the case in *Pitt* the bank has not the same need to follow what is in effect a 'counselling' approach.

(viii) More recently the Court of Appeal gave guidance including the extent of the *O'Brien* advice to be given by solicitors (*see Royal Bank of Scotland plc v Etridge* (No 2) [1998] 4 All ER 705). The court made the assumption that the claimant is the wife and the person using the influence is the husband (or partner), although similar principles would apply to a situation where the wife used the undue influence. The guidance is as follows:

● the client must be told that she is not under any obligation to enter into the transaction;
● the solicitor must be satisfied that the client is not subject to any improper influence, and then consider whether the transaction is one which she ought the be allowed to make even if she was not subject to influence. If it is not, she should be advised not to enter into it;

- if the lender is asking for an 'all monies' guarantee or charge, the solicitor should make clear to the client that she is being asked to undertake liability for any existing indebtedness, new debts and future debts and not merely the amount contemplated in the current arrangements, and that the client may be unable to control the amount of future indebtedness;
- if a wife is being asked to give an unlimited guarantee, she should be told of the option of giving a limited guarantee or charge and the solicitor should offer to negotiate for her. It is not acceptable practice to assume that the arrangements are not negotiable.

Further examples of inequality of bargaining power may be found in *Clifford Davis Management* v *WEA Records* [1975] 1 All ER 237 where A, an experienced manager, obtained a contract with a pop star, B, who had little or no business experience, under which B gave A the copyright in all his compositions for a period of years. It was held that B could avoid the contract because A had exploited his superior bargaining power.

## NO GENERAL RULE THAT ALL CONTRACTS MUST BE FAIR

There is no rule of law which states that a fair price must be paid in *all* transactions and some unfair contracts will be held binding provided the parties were of equal bargaining strength. In *Burmah Oil Co Ltd* v *The Governor of the Bank of England, The Times*, 4 July 1981, Burmah was in financial difficulties and sold a large holding of shares which it had in British Petroleum to the government at a price below the Stock Exchange price. Burmah then brought an action to set the contract aside. The court refused to do so. Although there was authority to set aside a transaction where one party had acted without independent advice, or where the bargaining strength of one party was grievously impaired, neither of those situations existed in this case. The relationship was purely commercial and the contract for the sale of shares must stand.

Cases such as *Burmah Oil* indicate that the broad principle of 'inequality of bargaining power' can be misleading. A further example is provided by *Alec Lobb (Garages) Ltd* v *Total Oil GB Ltd* (1985) (*see* Chapter 7) where the directors of a company which was desperate to raise money negotiated a disadvantageous mortgage over its property which was nevertheless upheld as valid. Lawful business pressure seems to be justified no matter how much inequality of bargaining power may exist. The more recent case of *Leyland Daf Ltd* v *Automotive Products plc, The Times*, 9 April 1993, is also of interest. The Court of Appeal decided that Automotive was entitled to withhold supplies of brake and clutch systems to Leyland which owed them £758,955 and was in administrative receivership. The receivers urgently needed the supplies to carry on the company's trade in the hope of finding a buyer for it. The Court of Appeal also decided that Automotive was not in breach of Art 86 of the Treaty of Rome (abuse of a dominant position) (*see further* Chapter 7).

## GRADED QUESTIONS

*Essay mode*

1  (a)  Adam, when negotiating for the sale of his business as a school outfitter, told Barry, a prospective purchaser, that his customers included all the schools within five miles. He also made exaggerated statements regarding annual turnover and profits.

Adam urged Barry to check the accounts. He did not. If he had, he would have discovered the truth.

Two days before Barry bought the business the largest school in the area informed Adam that they had decided that from next term uniforms would no longer be compulsory. Only after the contract for the sale of the business was signed did Barry become aware of the true position.

Advise Barry.

(b)  What circumstances may lead to the loss of the right of rescission?

*(Staffordshire University BA Business Studies. Business Law)*

2  Frank is an antique dealer and a world-famous authority on eighteenth-century French furniture. Clive, who has just bought an old house and wishes to buy antique furniture for it, admires a set of dining chairs in Frank's antique shop. Frank tells him that the chairs are 'undoubtedly eighteenth century' and 'might well have come from Versailles itself'. Clive pays £8,000 for the chairs and takes them home. Two days later Clive is polishing one of the chairs and sees a label underneath the seat which says: 'Made by Arnold Sidebotham, Leeds, 1927'. Clive finds this label on all the chairs and establishes very quickly that the label is correct. Arnold Sidebotham did make the chairs in 1927. The chairs are worth about £425.

Frank's error is honest. He had bought the chairs in a sale at an old country house and did not bother to examine them closely.

What remedies does Clive have against Frank?

*(The Institute of Company Accountants. Law Relating to Business)*

3  To what extent have the courts been prepared to recognise that a contract can be vitiated by economic duress?

*(The Institute of Legal Executives. Part II: Law of Contract)*

*Objective mode*

Four alternative answers are given. Select ONE only. Circle the answer which you consider to be correct. Check your answers by referring back to the information given in the chapter and against the answers at the back of the book.

1  A representation:

A  Always consists of a statement inducing a contract.
B  Is a term of a contract.
C  Can never consist in a false opinion.
D  May be a statement inducing a contract or in some cases non-disclosure or a false opinion.

**2** A person may sue upon a misrepresentation at common law:

   **A** If he knew it was untrue.
   **B** If he was given information which showed it to be untrue which he did not read.
   **C** If it was not material to his decision to make the contract.
   **D** If it was not addressed to him.

**3** A negligent misstatement is a false statement made:

   **A** Dishonestly.
   **B** Without reasonable grounds for believing it to be true.
   **C** Knowing it to be false.
   **D** Without caring whether it is true or false.

**4** Rescission is an equitable remedy which:

   **A** Is available only for innocent misrepresentation.
   **B** Puts the parties in the position they would have been in if the contract had been performed.
   **C** Is available only for fraudulent misrepresentation.
   **D** Puts the parties in the position they would have been in if the contract had not been made.

**5** A presumption of undue influence does not exist between:

   **A** Solicitor and client.
   **B** Trustee and beneficiary.
   **C** Religious adviser and the person subject to the religious advice.
   **D** Employer and employee.

*With reference to the following information answer questions 6, 7 and 8.*

Mrs Pelfer, a wealthy widow and property owner aged 72, became interested in the beliefs of a religious sect called the Brothers and Sisters of Charity. She went to see Brother Reynard, who was the leader of the sect and asked what she might do to assist in the work. Brother Reynard suggested that she should first join the sect and decide over a period of time where she might best make her contribution. Mrs Pelfer became a member of the sect and attended regular prayer meetings which were held at Brother Reynard's home. On one such occasion Brother Reynard suggested to Mrs Pelfer that the sect ought to have its own premises and asked her if she would sell one of her properties, Warren Manor, to the sect at less than market price.

   Mrs Pelfer at first refused but six months later she sold the property to Brother Reynard for half its market value having been told repeatedly by him that in doing so she would be assured of a place in Heaven on her death. The conveyance and other legal formalities were carried out for her by Proctor who was also solicitor to the sect.

   Two months after conveying Warren Manor to Brother Reynard Mrs Pelfer who has not received any money in respect of the sale either from Brother Reynard or from Proctor, was received into the Church of England and now wishes to recover the property.

6  The contract for the sale of Warren Manor is:

    **A**  Valid.
    **B**  Voidable.
    **C**  Void.
    **D**  Unenforceable.

7  Mrs Pelfer will be able to recover her property because the contract of sale of Warren Manor is affected by:

    **A**  Mistake.
    **B**  Duress.
    **C**  Misrepresentation.
    **D**  Undue influence.

8  Which of the following cases has been relevant to you in reaching your decisions?

    **A**  *Hodgson* v *Marks* (1970).
    **B**  *Peek* v *Gurney* (1873).
    **C**  *Smith* v *Chadwick* (1884).
    **D**  *Allcard* v *Skinner* (1887).

*Answers to questions set in objective mode appear on p 707.*

# 6 THE LAW OF CONTRACT – CONTRACTUAL TERMS

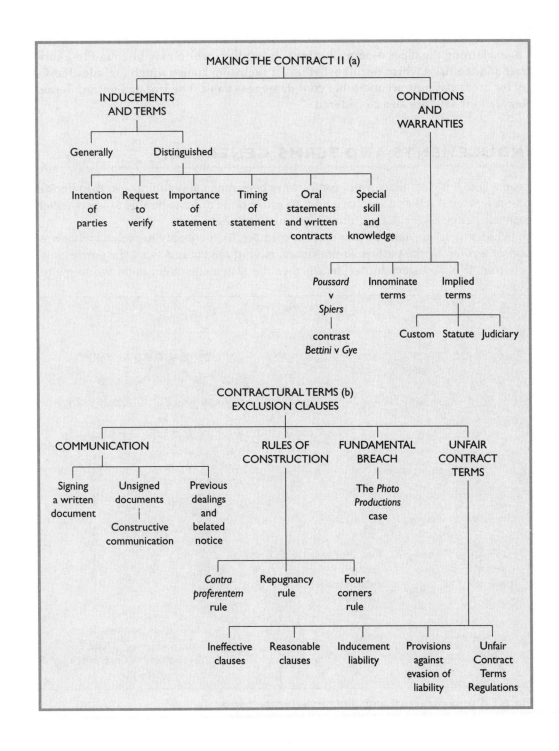

MAKING THE CONTRACT II (a)

INDUCEMENTS AND TERMS

CONDITIONS AND WARRANTIES

Generally    Distinguished

Intention of parties | Request to verify | Importance of statement | Timing of statement | Oral statements and written contracts | Special skill and knowledge

*Poussard* v *Spiers* | contrast *Bettini* v *Gye*

Innominate terms

Implied terms

Custom    Statute    Judiciary

CONTRACTURAL TERMS (b)
EXCLUSION CLAUSES

COMMUNICATION

RULES OF CONSTRUCTION

FUNDAMENTAL BREACH

UNFAIR CONTRACT TERMS

Signing a written document | Unsigned documents | Previous dealings and belated notice

Constructive communication

The *Photo Productions* case

*Contra proferentem* rule | Repugnancy rule | Four corners rule

Ineffective clauses | Reasonable clauses | Inducement liability | Provisions against evasion of liability | Unfair Contract Terms Regulations

The objectives of this chapter are to consider the contents of the contract by explaining the types of terms, express or implied, which may be found in a contract and the rules which decide whether an exclusion clause which excludes liability for breach of contract and other civil damage is valid. The Unfair Contract Terms Regulations 1994 are also considered.

## INDUCEMENTS AND TERMS GENERALLY

Even where it is clear that a valid contract has been made, it is still necessary to decide precisely what it is the parties have undertaken to do in order to be able to say whether each has performed or not performed his part of the agreement.

In order to decide upon the terms of the contract, it is necessary to find out what was said or written by the parties. Furthermore, having ascertained what the parties said or wrote, it is necessary to decide whether the statements were mere inducements

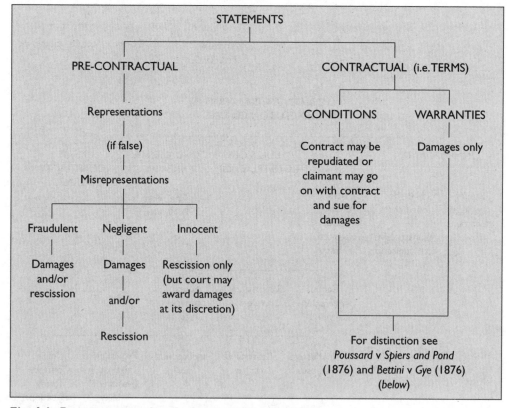

**Fig. 6.1  Pre-contractual and contractual statements**

(or representations) or terms of the contract, i.e. part of its actual contents. The distinction in diagrammatic form together with an indication of remedies appears in Fig 6.1.

The distinction is less important than it was since the passing of the Misrepresentation Act 1967. Before the Act became law there was often no remedy for a misrepresentation which was not fraudulent, and in such a case the claimant's only hope of obtaining a remedy was to convince the court that the defendant's statement was not a mere inducement but a term of the contract of which the defendant was in breach and for which damages might be obtained. As we have seen, under the Misrepresentation Act 1967 the new form of negligent misrepresentation which did not exist before will now give rise in many cases to an action for damages even in respect of a mere misrepresentation or inducement.

### Written contracts and outside evidence

It is a general rule of the common law that outside (or extrinsic) evidence cannot be brought to vary a written contract (*Goss* v *Nugent* (1833) 5 B & Ad 58). This is known as the parol evidence rule. However, the courts have been prepared to admit outside evidence if it can be shown that the written contract was not intended to express the whole agreement of the parties. Thus in *Walker Property Investments* (*Brighton*) *Ltd* v *Walker* (1947) 177 LT 204 a prospective tenant under a written tenancy agreement was allowed to add an oral agreement to the agreement under which, as he satisfied the court, he was entitled to the use of two basement rooms and the garden. Reference to this was omitted from the tenancy agreement.

> *The business application:* To ensure that a written agreement governs the legal relationship of the parties, the written contract should contain an *entire agreement clause*. This states that the contract covers the entire agreement together with a specific acknowledgement that the parties have no remedy in respect of prior representations other than representations that are repeated as terms in the written contract. It should also be stated that the only remedy for breach of the terms shall be damages for breach of contract and confirmation that the entire agreement clause does not exclude liability for fraud. An entire agreement clause should be effective in a contract between those in business. If included in a contract between a business and a consumer, it may very well be regarded as unreasonable and void.

## INDUCEMENTS AND TERMS DISTINGUISHED

Nevertheless, it is still necessary to consider the main tests applied by the courts in order to distinguish between a mere misrepresentation and a term of the contract, bearing in mind always that the question whether a statement is an inducement or a term and, if a term, whether a condition or warranty *is a matter of fact for the judge*. Fact decisions of this sort vary widely according to the circumstances of each case, so that it is virtually impossible to predict with absolute accuracy what the outcome of a particular case will be. However, by way of illustration the following headings contain the major guidelines which are applied.

## The statements and intentions of the parties

The court will always be concerned to implement the intentions of the parties as they appear from statements made by them. Thus in *Gill & Duffus SA* v *Société pour l'Exportation des Sucres SA* [1985] 1 Lloyd's Rep 621 the defendants agreed to sell sugar to Gill. A term of the contract (not specified as a condition or warranty) said that the defendants were to name a port at which the sugar was to be loaded by November 14 'at latest'. The defendants did not nominate a port by that time and so Gill refused to take any sugar from the defendants and regarded the contract as cancelled. The defendants then tried to make a nomination of a port, but Gill refused to accept it saying that they had repudiated the contract because of the defendants' breach of condition (or repudiatory breach). Following a decision unfavourable to them at arbitration, Gill appealed. Leggatt J said that there were no words in the English language by which a deadline could be appointed more concisely, more precisely, or with more finality than 'at latest'. They meant what they said and the judge had no doubt that the intention of the parties as gathered from the contract itself would be best carried out by treating the promise not as a mere warranty but as a condition precedent by the failure to perform which the other party was relieved of liability. Gill's contention was accepted. There was a repudiatory breach of condition. Where in a contract the parties have indicated that a particular undertaking is to be a term of the contract, the courts will in general abide by the wishes of the parties. However, the court will not slavishly follow the parties' statements and where, for example, the parties appear to have regarded a trivial matter as a vital term of the agreement, the court may still take the view that it is not.

Thus, so far as a written contract is concerned, the court may disregard a statement by the parties that a particular undertaking is a condition and say instead that it is a warranty. So far as wholly oral contracts are concerned, the court may ignore the statements of the parties and decide that a particular undertaking is a condition, a warranty, or a mere inducement.

Thus in *L Schuler AG* v *Wickham Machine Tool Sales* [1973] 2 All ER 39 the claimants entered into a contract for four years with the defendants giving them the sole right to sell panel presses in England. A clause of the contract provided that it should be a condition of the agreement that the defendants' representative should visit six named firms each week to solicit orders. The defendants' representatives failed on a few occasions to do so and the claimants alleged that they were entitled to repudiate the agreement on the basis that a single failure was a breach of condition giving them an absolute right to treat the contract as at an end. The House of Lords said that such minor breaches by the defendants did not entitle the claimants to repudiate. The House of Lords construed the clause on the basis that it was so unreasonable that the parties could not have intended it as a condition, giving Schuler a right of repudiation but rather as a warranty. Thus Schuler were themselves in breach of contract leaving Wickham with a claim for damages against Schuler.

This case is also an example of the court trying to give redress in regard to an unconscionable bargain and to correct unscrupulous commercial conduct.

## The nature of the statement

A statement is likely to be an inducement rather than a term if the person making the statement asks the other party to check or verify it, e.g. 'The car is sound but I should get an engineer's report on it'.

By contrast, a statement is likely to be a term rather than a mere inducement if it is made with the intention of preventing the other party from looking for defects and succeeds in doing this, e.g. 'The car is sound, you need not look it over'.

## The importance of the statement

If the statement is such that the claimant would not have made the contract without it, then the statement will be a term of the contract and not a mere inducement.

**The following case illustrates this point.**

### Bannerman v White (1861) 10 CB (NS) 844

The defendant was intending to buy hops from the claimant and he asked the claimant whether sulphur had been used in the cultivation of the hops, adding that if it had he would not even bother to ask the price, by which he meant that he would not make the contract. The claimant said that no sulphur had been used, though in fact it had. It was *held* that the claimant's assurance that sulphur had not been used was a term of the contract and the defendant was justified in raising the matter as a successful defence to an action for the price.

## The timing of the statement

A statement made during preliminary negotiations tends to be an inducement. Where the interval between the making of the statement and the making of the contract is distinct then the statement is almost certain to be an inducement. Thus in *Routledge* v *McKay* [1954] 1 All ER 855 the claimant and defendant were discussing the possible purchase and sale of the defendant's motor cycle. Both parties were private persons. The defendant, taking the information from the registration book, said, on 23 October, that the cycle was a 1942 model. On 30 October a written contract of sale was made. The actual date of the cycle was later found to be 1930. The buyer's claim for damages for breach of warranty failed in the Court of Appeal. In this case the interval between the negotiations and the contract was well marked and the statement was not a term. However, the interval is not always so well marked and in such cases there is a difficulty in deciding whether the statement is an inducement or term.

## Oral statements later put into writing

If the statement was oral and the contract was afterwards reduced to writing, then the terms of the contract tend to be contained in the written document and all oral statements tend to be pre-contractual inducements. Even so, the court may still consider the apparent intentions of the parties and decide that they had made a contract which was part oral and part written (*see Evans* v *Merzario* (1976) *below*). As we have seen, those in business may avoid uncertainty and costly litigation by inserting in the contract an entire agreement clause.

## Special skill and knowledge or lack of same

Where one of the parties has special knowledge or skill with regard to the subject-matter of the contract, then the statements of such a party will normally be regarded as terms of the contract. In addition, it will be difficult for an expert to convince the court that a person with no particular knowledge or skill in regard to the subject-matter has made statements which constitute terms of the contract.

**The following cases and comment illustrate this.**

### Oscar Chess Ltd v Williams [1957] I All ER 325

In May 1955, Williams bought a car from the claimants on hire-purchase terms. The claimants took Williams' Morris car in part-exchange. Williams described the car as a 1948 model and produced the registration book, which showed that the car was first registered in April 1948, and that there had been several owners since that time. Williams was allowed £290 on the Morris. Eight months later the claimants discovered that the Morris car was a 1939 model there being no change in appearance in the model between 1939 and 1948. The allowance for a 1939 model was £175 and the claimants sued for £115 damages for breach of warranty that the car was a 1948 model. Evidence showed that some fraudulent person had altered the registration book but he could not be traced, and that Williams honestly believed that the car was a 1948 model. *Held* – The contract might have been set aside in equity for misrepresentation but the delay of eight months defeated this remedy. This mistake was a mistake of quality which did not avoid the contract at common law and in order to obtain damages the claimants must prove a breach of warranty. The Court was unable to find that Williams was in a position to give such a warranty, and suggested that the claimants should have taken the engine and chassis number and written to the manufacturers, so using their superior knowledge to protect themselves in the matter. The claimants were not entitled to any redress. Morris LJ dissented, holding that the statement that the car was a 1948 model was a fundamental condition.

*Comment:* (i) No doubt Mr Williams would have been liable for innocent and not negligent misrepresentation under the Misrepresentation Act 1967 for he had reasonable grounds to believe that the car was a 1948 Morris. He was merely repeating an earlier deception made when he bought the vehicle.

(ii) Since the remedy of rescission had been lost by reason of delay, the court would not even now grant that remedy or damages at the court's discretion, which the court can do but only if the remedy of rescission is still available. The reluctance of the court to say that statements by non-dealers are contractual terms for breach of which damages can be recovered leads to an unfair result as in this case. After all, Mr Williams obtained £115 more for his Morris than it was worth. The decision seems to be based on the fault of the agents of Oscar Chess in not discovering the date of the vehicle. In most cases the courts do not concern themselves with fault when dealing with the terms of a contract. If, as in the *Oscar Chess* case, A warrants to B that goods have certain characteristics, it is no defence, if they have not, that the giver of the warranty honestly and reasonably believed they had. (Compare the law relating to misrepresentation.) However, a term will more often be inferred where the person making the relevant statement is in a position to know whether it is true or not as in the case of a dealer and such a person will be regarded as at fault if he does not. Equally, as this case shows, it is much harder for a private individual to give a warranty to a dealer who may be regarded as at fault for not knowing better.

(iii) A contrast is provided by *Dick Bentley Productions Ltd v Harold Smith (Motors) Ltd* [1965] 2 All ER 65 where a dealer sold a Bentley to a customer, the instruments showing that it had done only 30,000 miles since a replacement engine was fitted when in fact it had done 100,000 miles since that time. The seller was held liable for breach of condition whereas in *Oscar Chess* the seller who was not a dealer was not.

## CONDITIONS AND WARRANTIES

Having decided that a particular statement is a term of the contract and not a mere inducement, the court must then consider the importance of that statement in the context of the contract as a whole. Not all terms are of equal importance. Failure to perform some may have a more serious effect on the contract than failure to perform others. The law has applied special terminology to contractual terms in order to distinguish the vital or fundamental obligations from the less vital, the expression *condition* being applied to the former and the expression *warranty* to the latter. A condition is a fundamental obligation which goes to the root of the contract. A warranty, on the other hand, is a subsidiary obligation which is not so vital that a failure to perform it goes to the root of the contract.

*This distinction is important in terms of remedies.* A breach of condition is called a repudiatory breach and the injured party may elect either to repudiate the contract or claim damages and go on with the contract.

It should be noted that the claimant must go on with the contract and sue for damages if he has affirmed the contract after knowledge of a breach of condition. He may do this expressly as where he uses the goods, or by lapse of time as where he simply fails to take any steps to complain about the breach for what in the court's view is an unreasonable period of time. A breach of warranty is not repudiatory and the claimant must go on with the contract and sue for damages.

Whether a term is a condition or warranty is basically a matter for the court which will be decided on the basis of the commercial importance of the term. As we have seen, the words used by the parties are, of course, relevant, but are not followed slavishly by the court which may still decide differently from the parties on the basis of the commercial importance of the term.

It should be noted that the word *warranty* is sometimes used in a different way, e.g. by a manufacturer of goods who gives a *warranty* against faulty workmanship offering to replace parts free. The term *warranty* is used by the manufacturer as equivalent to a guarantee. We are concerned here with its use as a term of a contract.

**A useful illustration of the distinction between a condition and a warranty is provided by the following two cases.**

### Poussard v Spiers and Pond (1876) 1 QBD 410

Madame Poussard had entered into an agreement to play a part in an opera, the first performance to take place on 28 November 1874. On 23 November Madame Poussard was taken ill and was unable to appear until 4 December. The defendants had hired a substitute, and discovered that the only way in which they could secure a substitute to take Madame Poussard's place was to offer that person the complete engagement. This they had done, and they refused the services of Madame Poussard when she presented herself on 4 December. The claimant now sued for breach of contract. *Held* – The failure of Madame Poussard to perform the contract as from the first night was a breach of condition, and the defendants were within their rights in regarding the contract as discharged.

*Comment:* This case merely illustrates the availability of repudiation, for serious breach of contract and of course repudiation discharges the contract. Madame Poussard was not liable to pay damages for breach because unlike the defendants in *Gill & Duffus SA* (*see above*) she could not help the breach, the contract being also frustrated (*see* Chapter 8).

### Bettini v Gye (1876) 1 QBD 183

The claimant was an opera singer. The defendant was the director of the Royal Italian Opera in London. The claimant had agreed to sing in Great Britain in theatres, halls and drawing rooms for a period of time commencing on 30 March 1875, and to be in London for rehearsals six days before the engagement began. The claimant was taken ill and arrived on 28 March 1875, but the defendant would not accept the claimant's services, treating the contract as discharged. *Held* – The rehearsal clause was subsidiary to the main purposes of the contract, and its breach constituted a breach of warranty only. The defendant had no right to treat the contract as discharged and must compensate the claimant, but he had a counter-claim for any damage he had suffered by the claimant's late arrival.

*Comment:* This case is also concerned with the availability of repudiation, and the court decided that the breach was not sufficiently serious. The court suggested that if Gye wanted redress he should cross-claim for damages against Bettini. If and when he did and there is no report suggesting that he did, the matter of Bettini's illness excusing his breach would have had to be raised. Presumably it would have been a defence even though in this case the contract was not discharged by frustration.

## INNOMINATE TERMS

In modern law there are also terms which the parties call conditions and where the breach has *in fact* had a serious result on the contract. The court will then agree that the breach should be treated as a breach of condition and the contract can be repudiated. There are also terms which the parties call warranties and where the breach has *in fact* not been serious. The court will then agree that the breach shall be treated as a breach of warranty and the contract cannot be repudiated. The parties must go on with it though the person injured by the breach has an action for damages.

There also what are called *innominate terms* which the parties may have called conditions or warranties. The effect of these on the contract will depend upon how serious the breach has turned out to be *in fact*. If the breach has turned out to be serious, the court will then treat the term as a condition, even if called a warranty by the parties, so that the contract can be repudiated. If *in fact* the breach has not had a serious effect on the contract the court will treat it as a breach of warranty, even if called a condition by the parties, so that the parties must proceed with the contract, though the injured party will have an action for damages.

Thus if Dodgy Motors advertises a car for sale as having done 32,000 miles, this statement is likely to be a warranty giving an action for damages only if in fact the car has done, say, 34,000 miles. If, however, the car had done 60,000 miles, the court would be likely to regard the statement as a condition allowing repudiation of the contract (and *see Cehave NV* v *Bremer Handelsgesellschaft mbH* (1975) at Chapter 10).

## IMPLIED TERMS

Before leaving the topic of the contents of the contract, it must be appreciated that in addition to the express terms inserted by the parties, the contract may contain and be subject to implied terms. Such terms are derived from custom or statute, and in addition a term may be implied by the court where it is necessary in order to achieve the result which in the court's view the parties obviously intended the contract to have.

### Customary implied terms

A contract may be regarded as containing customary terms not specifically mentioned by the parties.

**The following case provides an illustration.**

### Hutton v Warren (1836) 150 ER 517

The claimant was the tenant of a farm and the defendant the landlord. At Michaelmas 1833, the defendant gave the claimant notice to quit on the Lady Day following. The defendant insisted that the claimant should cultivate the land during the period of notice, which he did. The claimant now asked for a fair allowance for seeds and labour of which he had had no benefit, having left the farm before harvest. It was proved that by custom a tenant was bound to farm for the whole of his tenancy and on quitting was entitled to a fair allowance for seeds and labour. *Held* – The claimant succeeded. 'We are of opinion that this custom was, by implication, imported into the lease. It has long been settled that, in commercial transactions, extrinsic evidence of custom and usage is admissible to annex incidents to written contracts in matters with respect to which they are silent. The same rule has also been applied to contracts in other transactions of life, in which known usages have been established and prevailed; and this has been done upon the principle of presumption that, in such transactions, the parties did not mean to express in writing the whole of the contract by which they intended to be bound, but to contract with reference to those known usages' (*per* Parke B).

*Comment:* (i) Michaelmas Day is 29 September and is a quarter day for payment of rent as well as a Christian feast. Lady Day is 25 March. It is also a quarter day for the payment of rent and is so called because it is a Christian feast.

(ii) The case also provides an example of an exception to the parol evidence rule which has already been considered. Outside evidence was admitted although there was a written contract, as Parke B explains. An entire agreement clause in the contract should have prevented the judge from implying a customary term if it had impliedly excluded the allowance by stating that the terms of the written contract covered the entire agreement. However, it should be borne in mind that the courts have a long history of implying terms from business practice, and an entire agreement clause may not always work where the terms of the contract, as here, do not follow business conduct and normal business relationships. However, if the contract by its terms covers conditions in common use in the trade or business, as relevant, then an entire agreement clause will normally prevent the implication of other terms.

## Statutory implied terms

In a contract for the sale of goods or hire purchase, the Sale of Goods Act 1979 and the Supply of Goods (Implied Terms) Act 1973, ss 8–11 (as amended by Sch 4, Part 1, para 35 to the Consumer Credit Act 1974, s 17 of the Supply of Goods and Services Act 1982 and the Sale and Supply of Goods Act 1994) deal with the matter of implied terms. These are considered in Chapter 10.

## Judicial implied terms

### Implication according to parties' intentions

A contract may sometimes leave a particular event unprovided for. However, the court may imply a term into a contract whenever it is necessary to do so in order that the express terms decided upon by the parties shall have the effect which was presumably intended by them. This is often expressed as the giving of 'business efficacy' to the contract, the judge regarding himself as doing merely what the parties themselves would *in fact* have done in order to cover the situation if they had addressed themselves to it. The court is not easily convinced that a term should be implied. It is more likely to do so to avoid a grossly unfair result if it does not. This would have been the situation in *The Moorcock* (*below*) because without the implied term the owners of the ship would have had no claim for the considerable damage caused to their ship.

### The Moorcock (1889) 14 PD 64

The appellants in this case were in possession of a wharf and a jetty extending into the River Thames, and the respondent was the owner of the steamship *Moorcock*. In November 1887, the appellants and the respondents agreed that the ship should be discharged and loaded at the wharf and for that purpose should be moored alongside the jetty. Both parties realised that when the tide was out the ship would rest on the river bed. In the event the *Moorcock* sustained damage when she ceased to be waterborne owing to the centre of the vessel settling on a ridge of hard ground beneath the mud. There was no evidence that the appellants had given any warranty that the place was safe for the ship to lie in, but it was *held* – by the Court of Appeal – that there was an implied warranty by the appellants to this effect, for breach of which they were liable in damages. *Per* Bowen LJ:

> Now, an implied warranty, or as it is called, a covenant in law, as distinguished from an express contract or express warranty, really is in all cases founded on the presumed intention of the parties, and upon reason. The implication which the law draws from what must obviously have been the intention of the parties, the law draws with the object of giving efficacy to the transaction and preventing such a failure of consideration as cannot have been within the

contemplation of either side; and I believe if one were to take all cases, and they are many, of implied warranties or covenants in law, it will be found that in all of them the law is raising an implication from the presumed intention of the parties with the object of giving to the transaction such efficacy as both parties must have intended that at all events it should have. In business transactions such as this, what the law desires to effect by the implication is to give such business efficacy to the transaction as must have been intended at all events by both parties who are businessmen; not to impose on one side all the perils of the transaction, or to emancipate one side from all chances of failure, but to make each party promise in law as much, at all events, as it must have been in the contemplation of both parties that he should be responsible for in respect of those perils or chances.

**Comment:** (i) This statement of the law is to the effect that the court cannot imply a term because it is desirable or reasonable to do so but only when it is commercially necessary to do so. Lord Denning, particularly, in *Liverpool City Council v Irwin* (1977) (*see below*) put forward the view that the court could imply a term whenever it was reasonable to do so even if it was not necessary to do so to make the contract work in a commercial sense. This view is still not entirely accepted by the judiciary in general.

(ii) Although the court most often implies covenants or terms which are *positive*, i.e. the party concerned *has to do something, negative* covenants can be implied. Thus in *Fraser v Thames Television Ltd* [1983] 2 All ER 101 the members of a group called Rock Bottom brought an action alleging that Thames had broken an agreement with them about a TV series, an implied term of which was that Thames would not use the idea for the series, which was based on the history of the group and its subsequent struggles, unless the members of the group were employed as actresses in the series. Hirst J implied this negative term on the grounds that it was necessary to give business efficacy to the agreement between the parties.

### Implication as a matter of law

Sometimes, however, the courts imply a term which is quite complex so that the parties would not, *in fact*, have addressed themselves to it. Here the judge is saying *as a matter of law* how the contract should be performed. This is illustrated by *Liverpool City Council v Irwin* [1977] AC 239 where the House of Lords *held* that it was an implied term of a lease of a maisonnette in a block of properties owned by the Council that the landlord should take reasonable care to keep the common parts of the block in a reasonable state of repair, although the obligation to do so would *not* have been accepted by the landlord.

When *Irwin's* case was in the Court of Appeal, Lord Denning, in deciding that there should be an implied term regarding maintenance, rejected the business efficacy test as the only test, saying that the court could imply a term whenever it was *just and reasonable* to do so, whether or not the term was strictly *necessary* to the performance of the contract or not. Although the House of Lords implied a term relating to maintenance, it did not go along with the view of Lord Denning that the test should be reasonableness regardless of necessity. The Court of Appeal returned to the 'necessary' approach in *Mears v Safecar Security* [1982] 2 All ER 865 and refused to imply a term into a contract of service that payment should be made to an employee during sickness. Stephenson LJ was of opinion that the term could not be implied because, although it might be *reasonable* to imply a term relating to sick-pay, it was not *necessary* in a contract of employment. The term relating to maintenance in *Irwin* was in a sense not absolutely vital to performance of the contract in that the tenants could have walked up the stairs, even in the dark, to their flats if lift and light maintenance had not been carried out, but it was much closer to being necessary to performance of the contract than was the sick-pay term in *Mears*.

The Court of Appeal also decided in *Morley* v *Heritage plc* (1993) 470 Industrial Relations Law Bulletin II that a contract of employment does not contain an implied term that an employee will receive pay in lieu of unused holiday entitlement on termination of the employment. Mr Morley was the group financial director of Heritage. His written service agreement gave him 20 working days holiday a year, but said nothing about entitlement to accrued holiday pay. When he left his employment he had 13 days of unused holiday and claimed £2,000 plus interest in lieu of this. The Court of Appeal would not imply a term to make the payment because, although it might be reasonable to do so, it was not necessary to the performance of an employment contract. A claim that the term should have been implied on the basis of custom and practice failed because there was no such custom or practice in the company. The claim might well have succeeded if there had been.

The decision in *Morley* was distiguised in *Janes Solicitors* v *Lamb-Simpson* (1996) 541 IRLB 15. In that case the Employment Appeal Tribunal decided that there was an implied contractual term to pay accrued holiday pay. Ms Lamb-Simpson had not been given written particulars of her employment and the EAT felt able to imply the term. In *Morley* there was a detailed written contract between the parties which dealt with holiday entitlement and holiday pay but said nothing about accrued holiday pay. It seemed, therefore, that the parties had addressed themselves to the relevant area and if something was not covered it was because it was not intended.

## EXCLUSION CLAUSES

A contract may contain express terms under which one or both of the parties excludes or limits liability for breach of contract or negligence. Although such express terms are permissible, both the courts and Parliament have been reluctant to allow exclusion clauses to operate successfully where they have been imposed on a weaker party, such as an ordinary consumer, by a stronger party, such as a person or corporation in business to supply goods or services.

The judges have protected consumers of goods and services against the effect of exclusion clauses in two main ways, i.e. by deciding that the exclusion clause never became part of the contract, and by construing (or interpreting) the contract in such a way as to prevent the application of the clause.

It is still important to look at the judicial contribution because even though an exclusion clause can now, under the Unfair Contract Terms Act 1977 (*see below*), be regarded as not applying if it is unreasonable there is no need to consider the issue of reasonableness if the clause has not been communicated or does not apply under the rules of the construction (*see below*). Perhaps more important, a reasonable clause will not apply if it has not been communicated and it must also survive the rules of construction.

## Was the clause part of the contract?

The court will require the person wishing to rely on an exclusion clause to show that the other party agreed to it at or before the time when the contract was made, otherwise it will not form part of the agreement. In this connection:

(a) *Where a contract is made by signing a written document*, the signer will in general be bound by everything which the document contains, even if he has not read it, unless the signature was induced by misrepresentation as to the effect of the document. An exception is the rule of *non est factum*, provided the signer is not negligent.

**The effect of signing a document containing an exclusion clause is illustrated by the following case.**

### L'Estrange v Graucob (F) [1934] 2 KB 394

The defendant sold to the claimant, Miss L'Estrange, who owned a café in Llandudno, a cigarette slot machine, inserting in the sales agreement the following clause: 'Any express or implied condition, statement or warranty, statutory or otherwise, is hereby excluded'. The claimant signed the agreement but did not read the relevant clause, apparently because she thought it was merely an order form, and she sued for breach of what is now s 14(3) of the Sale of Goods Act 1979 (goods not fit for purpose) (see *further* Chapter 10), in respect of the unsatisfactory nature of the machine supplied which often jammed and soon became unusable. *Held* – The clause was binding on her, and her claim failed, although the defendants made no attempt to read the document to her nor call her attention to the clause. 'Where a document containing contractual terms is signed, then in the absence of fraud, or I will add, misrepresentation, the party signing it is bound, and it is wholly immaterial whether he has read the document or not' (*per* Scrutton LJ).

*Comment:* (i) The ruling in this case would appear to apply even where the party signing cannot understand the document, as where a signer cannot read or does not understand the language in which the document is written (*The Luna* [1920] P 22). This would not, of course, apply if the person relying on the clause knew that the other party could not read (*Geir v Kujawa* [1971] Lloyd's Rep 364). It will, of course, be realised that s 6(3) of the Unfair Contract Terms Act 1977 would now apply. Section 6(3) prevents exclusion of the Sale of Goods Act implied terms in a non-consumer case such as this only if the clause is reasonable. In addition, s 3 of the 1977 Act would require reasonableness because the contract was on the supplier's standard terms which were applicable to everyone and could not be varied (*see below*). It is also interesting to note that the judiciary did not develop their doctrine of fundamental breach (*see below*) until the mid-1950s otherwise they would surely have applied it to make invalid an exclusion clause as wide-ranging and unfair as this one.

(ii) The ruling in the *Geir* case has assumed more importance now that business within Europe has expanded and indeed because of the increase in international trade generally. Where such trade is with a country in which English is not the first language exclusion clauses and other terms should be translated as appropriate. In a case involving Allianz, a German company, the court decided that an exclusion clause in an insurance policy issued by Allianz in France but without a translation into French did not apply. However, illiteracy or failure to understand English in the UK business scene is still no defence and an English clause will apply (see *Thompson v LMS Railway* (1930) *below*).

The following case illustrates the result of misrepresenting the effect of an exclusion clause in a signed document.

### Curtis v Chemical Cleaning and Dyeing Co [1951] 1 All ER 631

The claimant took a wedding dress, with beads and sequins, to the defendant's shop for cleaning. She was asked to sign a receipt which contained the following clause: 'This article is accepted on condition that the company is not liable for any damage howsoever arising'. The claimant said in evidence: 'When I was asked to sign the document I asked why? The assistant said I was to accept any responsibility for damage to beads and sequins. I did not read it all before I signed it.' The dress was returned stained, and the claimant sued for damages. The company relied on the clause. *Held* – The company could not rely on the clause because the assistant had misrepresented the effect of the document so that the claimant was merely running the risk of damage to the beads and sequins.

*Comment:* It will be appreciated that the assistant's statement was true as far as it went. As we have seen, half-truths such as this can amount to misrepresentation (see Chapter 5).

(b) *Where the terms are contained in an unsigned document*, the person seeking to rely on an exclusion clause must show that the document was an integral part of the contract which could be expected to contain terms. However, if the document is contractual in the sense outlined above, the clause will apply even though the claimant did not actually know about the exclusion clause in the sense that he had not read it. Communication may be constructive so long as the document adequately draws the attention of a reasonable person to the existence of terms and conditions.

An example of constructive communication appears in the following case.

### Thompson v LMS Railway [1930] 1 KB 41

Thompson, who could not read, asked her niece to buy her an excursion ticket to Manchester from Darwin and back, on the front of which were printed the words, 'Excursion. For conditions see back'. On the back was a notice that the ticket was issued subject to the conditions in the company's timetables, which excluded liability for injury however caused. Thompson was injured and claimed damages. *Held* – Her action failed. She had constructive notice of the conditions which had, in the court's view, been properly communicated to the ordinary passenger.

*Comment:* (i) The railway ticket was regarded as a contractual document. (Contrast *Chapelton below.*)

(ii) The injuries, which were caused when the train on returning to Darwin at 10 pm did not draw all the way into the station so that the claimant fell down a ramp, would have been the subject of an action at law today because the Unfair Contract Terms Act 1977 outlaws exclusion clauses relating to death and personal injury. Thus, on its own facts, this case is of historical interest only, though still relevant on the question of constructive notice.

The following case provides a contrast on the issue of constructive communication.

## Chapelton v Barry Urban District Council [1940] 1 All ER 356

The claimant Chapelton wished to hire deck chairs and went to a pile owned by the defendants, behind which was a notice stating:'Hire of chairs 2d per session of three hours.' The claimant took two chairs, paid for them, and received two tickets which he put into his pocket after merely glancing at them. One of the chairs collapsed and he was injured. A notice on the back of the ticket provided that:'The council will not be liable for any accident or damage arising from hire of chairs'. The claimant sued for damages and the council sought to rely on the clause in the ticket. *Held* – The clause was not binding on Chapelton. The board by the chairs made no attempt to limit the liability, and it was unreasonable to communicate conditions by means of a mere receipt.

*Comment:* The defendants would now have had to face an additional problem, i.e. was the clause reasonable?

This rule of constructive communication will not necessarily be applied if the term in the contract is particularly burdensome for the other party. In such a case the law may require that the burdensome clause is actually brought to the attention of the other party. This results from the decision of the Court of Appeal in *Interfoto Picture Library Ltd* v *Stiletto Visual Programmes Ltd* [1988] 1 All ER 348. In that case Interfoto sent some transparencies to Stiletto for it to make a selection. The delivery note, which is a contractual document, contained a clause that if the transparencies were not returned within 14 days Stiletto would pay £5 per day for each transparency retained after that. Stiletto delayed returning the transparencies for some three weeks and ran up a bill of some £3,783. When Stiletto was sued for this sum the court said that it could not be recovered by Interfoto because the clause was not specifically drawn to the attention of Stiletto. The court awarded damages of £3.50 per transparency per week but would not apply the clause.

(c) *As regards previous dealings,* where the defendant has not actually given the claimant a copy of conditions or drawn his attention to them when making a particular contract, the doctrine of constructive notice will not apply, at least in consumer transactions, in order to enable the defendant to rely on previous communications in previous dealings, unless, perhaps, the dealings have been frequent. Thus in *Hollier* v *Rambler Motors* [1972] 1 All ER 399 it appeared that the claimant had had his car repaired five times in five years (i.e. infrequently) by the defendants and had signed a form containing a clause stating, 'the company is not responsible for damage caused by fire to customers' cars on the premises'. On the occasion in question the claimant was not required to sign a form when leaving his car for repair. In the event the car was damaged by fire caused by the defendants' negligence. In an action by the claimant the defendants pleaded the clause. It was *held* by the Court of Appeal that the claimant succeeded and that the clause did not apply. Previous dealings were not incorporated and in any case as a matter of construction the wording was not sufficiently plain to exclude negligence. However, where the parties are, for example, large corporations, terms used in previous dealings between the parties themselves *or in the trade generally* may be incorporated.

Thus in *British Crane Hire Corporation Ltd* v *Ipswich Plant Hire Ltd* [1974] 1 All ER 1059 the defendants hired a crane from the claimants who were the owners. The agreement was an oral one, though after the contract was made the defendants received a printed form from the claimants containing conditions. One of these was that the hirer of the crane was liable to indemnify the owner against all expenses in connection with its use. Before the defendants signed the form the crane sank into marshy ground, though this was not the fault of the defendants. The claimants were put to some cost in repairing the crane and now sued the defendants for an indemnity under the contract. The defendants argued that the indemnity had not been incorporated into the oral contract of hire. It was held that the bargaining power of the defendants was equal to that of the claimants and the defendants knew that printed conditions in similar terms to those of the claimants were *in common use in the business*. The conditions had, therefore, been incorporated into the oral contract on the basis of the common understanding of the parties and the claimants' claim for an indemnity succeeded.

(d) *Any attempt to introduce an exclusion clause after the contract has been made is ineffective* because the consideration for the clause is then past. **An illustrative case and comment appears below**.

### Olley v Marlborough Court Ltd [1949] 1 All ER 127

A husband and wife arrived at a hotel as guests and paid for a room in advance. They went up to the room allotted to them; on one of the walls was the following notice: 'The proprietors will not hold themselves responsible for articles lost or stolen unless handed to the manageress for safe custody.' The wife closed the self-locking door of the bedroom and took the key downstairs to the reception desk. There was inadequate and, therefore, negligent staff supervision of the keyboard. A third party took the key and stole certain of the wife's furs. In the ensuing action the defendants sought to rely on the notice as a term of the contract. *Held* – The contract was completed at the reception desk and no subsequent notice could affect the claimant's rights.

*Comment:* (i) It was said in *Spurling* v *Bradshaw* [1956] 1 WLR 461 that if the husband and wife had seen the notice on a previous visit to the hotel it would have been binding on them, though this is by no means certain in view of cases such as *Hollier* (*see above*) which suggest that in consumer transactions previous dealings are not necessarily incorporated unless perhaps the dealings have been frequent.

(ii) A further illustration is provided by *Thornton* v *Shoe Lane Parking Ltd* [1971] 1 All ER 686 where the Court of Appeal decided that the conditions exempting the company from certain liabilities on a ticket issued by an automatic barrier at the entrance to a car park were communicated too late. The contract was made when the claimant put his car on the place which activated the barrier. This was before the ticket was issued.

(e) *An exclusion clause may be made ineffective by an inconsistent oral promise*. **The following case illustrates this point**.

### J Evans & Son (Portsmouth) Ltd v Andrea Merzario Ltd [1976] 2 All ER 930

The claimants imported machines from Italy. They had contracted with the defendants since about 1959 for the transport of these machines. Before the defendants went over to the use of containers the claimants' machines had always been crated and carried under deck. When the defendants went over to containers, they orally agreed with the claimants that the claimants' goods would still be carried under deck. However, on a particular occasion a machine being transported for the claimants was carried in a container on deck. At the start of the voyage the ship met a swell which caused the container to fall off the deck and the machine was lost. The contract was expressed to be subject to the printed standard conditions of the forwarding trade which contained an exemption clause excusing the defendants from liability for loss or damage to the goods unless the damage occurred while the goods were in their actual custody and by reason of their wilful neglect or default, and even in those circumstances, the clause limited the defendants' liability for loss or damage to a fixed amount. The claimants sought damages against the defendants for loss of the machine alleging that the exemption clause did not apply. It was *held* by the Court of Appeal that it did not apply. The printed conditions were repugnant to the oral promise for, if they were applicable, they would render that promise illusory. Accordingly, the oral promise was to be treated as overriding the printed conditions and the claimants succeeded, the exemption clause being inapplicable.

*Comment:* (i) The court may also regard these oral promises as collateral contracts (*see also* Chapter 1), i.e. in this case a collateral contract to carry the machine under deck, that collateral contract not having an exclusion clause in it.

(ii) It is hard to see how an entire agreement clause could have changed the decision in this case. The claimants were given a firm oral assurance that their machines would be carried below deck and this amounted to a separate contract apart altogether from the basic arrangement in which an entire agreement clause would have been included, though there is no mention of one in the report.

(f) *At common law the doctrine of privity of contract may also prevent the application of an exclusion clause.* Thus, if A, the owner of a road haulage company, excludes his own and his employees' liability for damage to the goods of his business customers by a properly communicated clause, an employee who causes damage to the goods will be liable, although his employer will not be, provided the clause is reasonable under the Unfair Contract Terms Act 1977, because the employee has not supplied consideration for the contract which is between his employer and the customers.

Reference should, however, be made to the case of *NZ Shipping* v *A M Satterthwaite* (*see* Chapter 2) where by application of the rules relating to acceptance in unilateral contracts and the performance of existing contractual duties owed to a third party the court was able to hold that a stevedore could take the benefit of an exclusion clause in the shipping company's contract of carriage.

The Contracts (Rights of Third Parties) Act 1999 may now apply. A may enter into a contract with a builder to build a house for his daughter Jane to live in. A may name Jane as having third-party rights under the contract. Let us suppose that the contract contains an exclusion clause exempting the builder from liability caused by his negligent building. There is a provision in s 7(2) of the 1999 Act which can best be understood by an example. The builder's negligence results in death or personal injury to A or to his daughter Jane. Any exclusion clause inserted by the builder in his contract with A is void and of no effect in so far as it tries to exclude liability for death or personal injury, and the 1999 Act leaves this untouched. The 1977 Act outlaws such clauses. However, if by reason of negligence by the builder a wall collapses and A's car is damaged, he can sue the builder unless the builder can show that this clause is reasonable. However because of s 7(2) of the 1999 Act, if it is Jane's car which is damaged, the clause, even if unreasonable, will be effective to excuse the builder's liability to her. There are those who think that unreasonable exclusion clauses should be void whoever relies on them, but the 1999 Act does not reflect this view.

# CONSTRUCTION OF EXCLUSION CLAUSES

Rules of construction (i.e. interpretation) of contract may, when applied, prevent the application of an exclusion clause. The major rules of construction are as follows.

## The *contra proferentem* rule

Under this rule, if there is any ambiguity or room for doubt as to the meaning of an exclusion clause, the courts will construe it in a way unfavourable to the person who put it into the contract. An example of the application of this rule is to be seen in *Hollier v Rambler Motors* (*see above*) because the Court of Appeal, having decided that previous dealings were not incorporated, went on to use the rule by saying that the wording in the form was not sufficiently plain to exclude negligence. That ambiguity had, therefore, to be construed against the defendants who put it into the contract. Those who wish to exclude liability for negligence must use clear words, said the House of Lords in *Smith* v *South Wales Switchgear* [1978] 1 All ER 18.

**A further illustration of the application of the rule appears below.**

## Alexander v Railway Executive [1951] 2 All ER 442

Alexander was a magician who had been on a tour together with an assistant. He left three trunks at the parcels office at Launceston station, the trunks containing various properties which were used in an 'escape illusion'. The claimant paid 5d for each trunk deposited and received a ticket for each one. He then left saying that he would send instructions for their dispatch. Some weeks after the deposit and before the claimant had sent instructions for the dispatch of the trunks, the claimant's assistant persuaded the clerk in the parcels office to give him access to the trunks, though he was not in possession of the ticket. The assistant took away several of the properties and was later convicted of larceny. The claimant sued the defendants for damages for breach of contract, and the defendants pleaded the following term which was contained in the ticket and which stated that the Railway Executive was 'not liable for loss mis-delivery or damage to any articles where the value was in excess of £5 unless at the time of the deposit the true value and nature of the goods was declared by the depositor and an extra charge paid'. No such declaration or payment had been made. *Held* – The claimant succeeded because, although sufficient notice had been given constructively to the claimant of the term, the term did not protect the defendants because they were guilty of a breach of a fundamental obligation in allowing the trunks to be opened and things to be removed from them by an unauthorised person.

*Comment:* (i) Devlin J said that a deliberate delivery to the wrong person did not fall within the meaning of 'mis-delivery', and this may be regarded as the real reason for the decision, as it involved the application of the *contra proferentem* rule.

(ii) Note also that the receipt or ticket for the goods deposited was held to be a contractual document. (Contrast *Chapelton above.*)

## The repugnancy rule

This rule says in effect that the exemption clause is in direct contradiction to the main purpose of the contract and is, therefore, repugnant to it. Where such repugnancy exists, the exemption clause can be struck out. Thus, if A makes a contract to supply oranges to B but includes a clause which allows him to supply any sort of fruit, the clause is repugnant to the main purpose of the contract and could be struck out. Thus, A would be liable in breach of contract if he supplied B with apples and could not rely on the clause to excuse his breach of contract.

**An illustration from case law appears below.**

### Pollock v Macrae 1922 SC (HL) 192

The defendants entered into a contract to build and supply marine engines. The contract had an exclusion clause which was designed to protect them from liability for defective materials and workmanship. The engines supplied under the contract had so many defects that they could not be used. The House of Lords struck out the exclusion clause as repugnant to the main purpose of the contract which was to build and supply workable engines. The claimant's suit for damages was allowed to proceed.

## The four corners rule

Under this rule exemption clauses only protect a party when he is acting within the four corners of the contract. Thus he is liable for damage which occurs while he is deviating from the contract and he would not be protected by the exclusion clause.

**An illustration from case law appears below.**

### Thomas National Transport (Melbourne) Pty Ltd and Pay v May and Baker (Australia) Pty Ltd [1966] 2 Lloyd's Rep 347

The owners of certain packages containing drugs and chemicals made a contract with carriers under which the packages were to be carried from Melbourne to various places in Australia. The carriers employed a subcontractor to collect the parcels and take them to the carriers' depot in Melbourne. When the subcontractor arrived late at the Melbourne depot it was locked and so he drove the lorry full of packages to his own house and left it in a garage there. This was in accordance with the carriers' instructions to their subcontractors in the event of late arrival at the depot. There was a fire and some of the packages were destroyed. The cause of the fire was unknown. However, the alleged negligence of the carriers consisted in their instruction to the subcontractors to take the goods home. The court said it was unthinkable that valuable goods worth many thousands of pounds should be kept overnight at a driver's house, regardless of any provision for their safety. The owners sued the carriers who pleaded an exemption clause in the contract of carriage. *Held* – by the High Court of Australia – that the claimants succeeded. There had been a fundamental breach of contract. The intention of the parties was that goods would be taken to the carriers' depot and not to the subcontractor's house, in which case the carriers could not rely on the clause.

*Comment:* (i) The decision, which was partly based on fundamental breach of contract (*see below*), is perhaps better founded on the four corners rule, i.e. the exclusion clause is available only so long as the contract is being performed in accordance with its terms.

(ii) For the avoidance of doubt, Australian courts' decisions are of persuasive authority in UK courts.

## THE DOCTRINE OF FUNDAMENTAL BREACH

This doctrine was usually invoked where a claimant sought a remedy on a contract containing exemption clauses which had been adequately communicated. The doctrine said, in effect, that where one party had fundamentally broken his contract, that is done something fundamentally different from what he had contracted to do, an exclusion clause could not protect him, and that this was a *rule of law* and not a *rule of construction*, so that the court had no discretion in the matter.

After some years of differing judicial opinion regarding this, the House of Lords eventually affirmed that there was no rule by which exclusion clauses were *automatically* inapplicable to exclude liability for a fundamental breach of contract. It was in each case a question of construction whether in fact the clause covered the breach which had taken place. Fundamental breach, which survives as a rule of construction, is only a simple presumption that exclusion clauses are not intended to apply where there is a very serious breach of contract. This presumption can be rebutted (as in *Photo Production, below*) and is not *automatically* applied.

**The case which affirmed that this was the legal position appears below.**

### Photo Production Ltd v Securicor Transport Ltd [1980] 1 All ER 556

The claimant company had contracted with the defendant security company for the defendant to provide security services at the claimant's factory. A person employed by the defendant lit a fire in the claimant's premises while he was carrying out a night patrol. The fire got out of control and burned down the factory. The trial judge was unable to establish from the evidence precisely what the motive was for lighting the fire – it may have been deliberate or merely careless. The defendant relied on an exclusion clause in the contract which read:

> Under no circumstances shall the company (Securicor) be responsible for any injurious act or default by any employee of the company unless such act or default could have been foreseen and avoided by the exercise of due diligence on the part of the company as his employer . . .

It was accepted that Securicor was not negligent in employing the person who lit the fire. He came with good references and there was no reason for Securicor to suppose that he would act as he did. It was *held* by the House of Lords that the exclusion clause applied so that Securicor was not liable. All the judges in the House of Lords were unanimous in the view that there was no rule of law by which exclusion clauses automatically became inapplicable to a fundamental breach of contract, which this admittedly was. Although the Unfair Contract Terms Act 1977 was not in force at the time this action was initially brought and, therefore, could not be applied to the facts of this case, the existence of the Act and its relevance was referred to by Lord Wilberforce who said that the doctrine of fundamental breach had been useful in its time as a device for avoiding injustice. He then went on to say:

But ... Parliament has taken a hand; it has passed the Unfair Contract Terms Act 1977. This Act applies to consumer contracts and those based on standard terms and enables exception clauses to be applied with regard to what is just and reasonable. It is significant that Parliament refrained from legislating over the whole field of contract. After this Act, in commercial matters generally, when the parties are not of unequal bargaining power, and when risks are normally borne by insurance ... there is everything to be said ... for leaving the parties free to apportion the risks as they think fit ...

**Comment:** (i) In *Harbutt's Plasticine Ltd* v *Wayne Tank & Pump Co Ltd* [1970] 1 All ER 225 Lord Denning accepted that the principle which said that no exclusion clause could excuse a fundamental breach was not a rule of law when the injured party carried on with (or affirmed) the contract. Where this was so, rules of construction must be used and the exclusion clause might have to be applied. However, if the injured party elected to repudiate the contract for fundamental breach and, as it were, pushed the contract away, the exclusion clause went with it and could never apply to prevent the injured party from suing for the breach. The same, he said, was true where the consequences were so disastrous (as they were in *Photo Production*) that one could assume that the injured party had elected to repudiate. The *Photo Production* case overrules *Harbutt*, as does s 9(1) of the Unfair Contract Terms Act 1977. This provides that if a clause, as a matter of construction, is found to cover the breach and if it satisfies the reasonableness test, it can apply and be relied on by the party in breach, even though the contract has been terminated by express election or assumed election following the disastrous results of the breach.

(ii) The House of Lords also allowed a Securicor exemption clause to apply in circumstances of fundamental breach in *Ailsa Craig Fishing Co Ltd* v *Malvern Fishing Co Ltd* [1983] 1 All ER 101. In that case the appellant's ship sank while berthed in Aberdeen harbour. It fouled the vessel next to it which was owned by Malvern. The appellant sued Malvern. Securicor was the second defendant. Securicor had a contract with the appellant to protect the ship. The accident happened as a result of a rising tide. At the time, the Securicor patrolman had left his post to become involved in New Year celebrations. Although there were arguments by counsel to the contrary, the House of Lords *held* that the exclusion clause covered the circumstances of the case, provided the words were given their natural and plain meaning. It, therefore, applied to limit the liability of Securicor and the appellant failed to recover all its loss.

(iii) The Unfair Contract Terms Act 1977 gives its strongest protection to those who deal as consumers. The contracts in *Photo Production* and *Ailsa Craig* were non-consumer contracts where both parties were in business. It by no means follows that in a consumer transaction (*see below*) the court would have allowed a defendant to rely on a 'Securicor' type of clause. It might well be regarded as unreasonable in that context.

*The business application:* It is worth noting that the apportionment of loss referred to by Lord Wilberforce and as applied in the *Photo Production* case and the *Ailsa Craig* case will result in the claimant's insurance company bearing the loss. Many cases in the field of business law are, in effect, battles between insurance companies in regard to liability. They always sue or defend through their clients, since the loss is not directly that of the insurance company, but if the loss is the fault of the insured, the insurance contract requires the the insurance company to indemnify the client, and that is the nature of the insurer's interest in the case. An insurance policy will commonly contain an express condition that the insured can be required by the insurer to bring a claim before or after the insurer has paid the insured.

## THE APPROACH OF PARLIAMENT TO EXCLUSION CLAUSES

Parliament has tried to prevent the widespread use of exclusion clauses by the passing of various statutes, the main one being the Unfair Contract Terms Act 1977.

The strongest protection is given by the Act to persons who deal as consumers (C), though those dealing otherwise than as consumers, e.g. where the goods are bought for use in a business, are covered. To be a consumer, one must be dealing as a *private buyer* with a *person in business* (B). Thus a contract between a *private buyer* and a *private seller* is not a consumer deal.

However, in *R & B Customs Brokers Co Ltd* v *United Dominions Trust Ltd* [1988] 1 All ER 847 the Court of Appeal decided that when a business buys goods it may still take advantage of consumer law applying to an ordinary member of the public if the transaction concerned is not a regular one. The facts of the case were that R & B Customs bought a car for the use of a director. The contract excluded an implied term under s 14(3) of the Sale of Goods Act 1979 that the goods were fit for the purpose. Such an exclusion does not operate if the sale is between a person in business and a consumer. It was *held* that R & B Customs must be treated as a consumer. The purchase of the car was not a frequent transaction and unless regularity could be established the transaction could not be regarded as an integral part of the business and was not, therefore, in the course of business.

### Clauses rendered ineffective by the Unfair Contract Terms Act

These clauses, which are ineffective against a party to the contract, and are also ineffective against a claim by a person with third-party rights under the Contracts (Rights of Third Parties) Act 1999, are as follows:

(a) Any exclusion clause contained in a contract or notice by which B tries to exclude or restrict his liability for death or personal injury resulting from negligence is wholly ineffective (ss 2 and 5). However, in *Thompson* v *Lohan* [1987] 2 All ER 631 A hired plant together with operatives to B. The contract contained a clause stating that B was liable for the negligence of the operatives who were A's employees. This clause was held by the Court of Appeal not to be contrary to s 2 of the Unfair Contract Terms Act. It was not designed to restrict or exclude liability to those who might be injured by the negligence of the operatives but merely decided whether A or B was to bear the liability.

(b) A manufacturer's guarantee cannot exclude or restrict the manufacturer's liability for loss or damage arising from defects in goods if used by a consumer which results from negligence in manufacture or distribution (s 5). The section is concerned with actions either in negligence or on the collateral contract (*see further* Chapter 1) which the guarantee can create against the manufacturer who is not the seller of the goods to the customer. The section is not concerned with a contractual relationship between the seller and the customer which is covered by ss 6 and 7. Thus a manufacturer's 12-month guarantee for a vacuum cleaner which said that the goods would, if defective, be replaced or repaired free of charge but ended with a phrase such as: 'This guarantee is in lieu of, and expressly excludes, all liability to compensate for loss or damage howsoever caused' would not prevent a claim by the purchaser against the manufacturer if he/she was injured by receiving an electric shock because of the cleaner's defective wiring (*see Donoghue* v *Stevenson* (1932), Chapter 11).

(c) A clause under which B tries to exclude his liability, whether by guarantee or otherwise, to C for breach of the implied terms in the Sale of Goods Act 1979 (on a sale) or the Supply of Goods (Implied Terms) Act 1973 (as amended) (on a hire-purchase transaction), e.g. that the goods are fit for the purpose or of satisfactory quality, is wholly ineffective, as is a clause which tries to exclude against the consumer the implied terms in the Supply of Goods and Services Act 1982 in a contract of pure hiring, e.g. of a car, or a contract for work and materials, as in the repair of a car (ss 6(2) and 7(2), Unfair Contract Terms Act 1977).

Section 6 also applies to non-business liability. However, since the implied terms requiring satisfactory quality and fitness for the purpose do not apply to non-business transactions, only s 13 of the Sale of Goods Act 1979 (sale by description) can be implied. However, s 13 cannot be excluded in a non-business transaction with a consumer.

## EXCLUSION CLAUSES APPLICABLE IF REASONABLE

### General

These are as follows:

(a) Any clause by which B tries to exclude or restrict his liability for loss arising from negligence other than death or personal injury (s 2(2)).

Such a clause may be raised successfully to defeat a claim by a third party who has acquired rights under the Contracts (Rights of Third Parties) Act 1999 whether the clause is reasonable or not. An unreasonable clause could be effective. The reasonableness test would be applied in an action between the promisor and promisee.

(b) Any clause by which B tries to exclude or restrict his liability to a non-consumer for breach of the implied terms in the Sale of Goods Act 1979, the Supply of Goods (Implied Terms) Act 1973, and the Supply of Goods and Services Act 1982 relating, for example, to contracts of hiring and work and materials (s 6(3) and 7(3)).

(c) Any clause by which B tries to exclude his liability for breach of contract if the contract is with a consumer or, in the case of a non-consumer contract, the agreement is on B's written standard terms (s 3(1) and (2)(a)). There is no definition of 'written standard terms' in the 1977 Act, but it obviously covers cases in which the seller requires that all (or nearly all) of his customers purchase goods on the same terms with no variation from one contract to another. An example is provided by *L'Estrange* v *Graucob* (1934) (*above*). This section applies also to cases where the clause purports to allow B to render a substantially different performance, as where a tour operator tries to reserve the right to vary the accommodation or itinerary or reserves the right to render no performance at all (s 3(2)(b)).

(d) As regards *indemnity clauses in consumer transactions*, B may agree to do work for C only if C will indemnify B against any liability which B may incur during performance of the contract, e.g. an injury to X caused by B's work (s 4). B may, for example, be a builder who takes an indemnity from C, the owner of a property on which B is to do work in regard to any injuries which B's work might cause to third parties. Such an indemnity will be unenforceable by B unless reasonable. Such clauses are unlikely to be found reasonable and B will have to cover himself by insurance. The section does not cover non-consumer situations and the indemnity found in *British Crane Hire* (*see above*) would still be enforceable (and *see Thompson* v *Lohan* (1987) *above*).

## Inducement liability

Any clause purporting to exclude liability for misrepresentation applies only if reasonable, whether the transaction is with a consumer or a non-consumer (Misrepresentation Act 1967, s 3, as substituted by s 8(1) of the Unfair Contract Terms Act 1977). Thus an estate agent may not be able to exclude his liability for falsely representing the state of a house unless the court feels that it was reasonable for the agent to exclude his liability, as it might do if the property is very old and there has been no survey. However, the matter of reasonableness is a matter for the court in each case, and much depends upon the circumstances. (Contrast *Smith* v *Eric S Bush* with the decision in *McCullagh* v *Lane Fox* (*see* Chapter 5)). It is also worth noting that the Property Misdescription Act 1991 makes it a criminal offence to make a false or misleading statement about property matters in the course of an estate agency or property development business.

Section 3 also applies to non-business liability. A private seller cannot exclude his liability for misrepresentation unless he can show that the exclusion clause concerned satisfied the test of reasonableness.

**An example of the application of the inducement liability rules is provided by the following case.**

### Walker v Boyle [1982] 1 All ER 634

The vendor of a house was asked in a pre-contract enquiry whether the boundaries of the land were the subject of any dispute. The vendor asked her husband to deal with the enquiries. He said that there were no disputes. There were, in fact, disputes but the husband did not regard them as valid because he believed that he was in the right and his view could not be contradicted. His answers were nevertheless wrong and misleading. Contracts were later exchanged. These contracts were on the National Conditions of Sale (19th Edition) produced under the aegis of the Law Society. Condition 17(1) excluded liability for misleading replies to preliminary enquiries. The purchaser later heard of the boundary disputes and claimed in the High Court for rescission of the contract and the return of his deposit. Dillon J held that condition 17(1) did not satisfy the requirements of reasonableness as set out in s 3 of the Misrepresentation Act 1967 (as substituted by s 8(1) of the Unfair Contract Terms Act 1977). The claimant, therefore, succeeded.

*Comment:* (i) The National Conditions of Sale have been revised and, as regards misrepresentation, the contract now only attempts a total exclusion of the purchaser's remedies if the misrepresentation is not material or substantial in terms of its effect and is not made recklessly or fraudulently.

(ii)  The provisions relating to inducement liability were also applied in *South Western General Property Co Ltd* v *Marton, The Times,* 11 May 1982; the court *held* that conditions of sale in an auction catalogue which tried to exclude liability for any representations made, if these were incorrect, were not fair and reasonable. The defendant had relied upon a false statement that some building would be allowed on land which he bought at an auction, even though the facts were that the local authority would be most unlikely to allow any building on the land. The clauses excluding liability for misrepresentation did not apply and the contract could be rescinded.

# REASONABLENESS

## The burden of proof

The burden of proving the clause is reasonable lies upon the party claiming that it is – usually B, the person in business (s 11(5)).

## Meaning of reasonableness

Although the matter is basically one for the judge, the following guidelines appear in the 1977 Act.

(a)  The matter of reasonableness must be decided on the circumstances as they were when the contract was made (s 11(1)).
(b)  Where a clause limits the amount payable, regard must be had to the resources of the person who included the clause and the extent to which it was possible for him to cover himself by insurance (s 11(4)). The object of this rule is to encourage companies to insure against liability in the sense that failure to do so will go against them if any exclusion clause which they have is before the court. However, in some cases it may be right to allow limitation of liability, e.g. in the case of professional persons such as accountants where monetary loss may be caused to a horrendous amount following negligence and be beyond their power to insure against.
(c)  Where the contract is for the supply of goods, i.e. under a contract of sale, hire purchase, hiring, or work and materials, the criteria of reasonableness are laid down by s 11(2) of and Sch 2 to the 1977 Act. They are:
    (i)    strength of the bargaining position of the parties. Thus if one party is in a strong position and the other in a weaker in terms of bargaining power, the stronger party may not be allowed to retain an exclusion clause in the contract;
    (ii)   availability of other supplies. Again, if a seller is in a monopolistic position so that it is not possible for the buyer to find the goods readily elsewhere, the court may decide that an exclusion clause in the contract of a monopolistic seller shall not apply;
    (iii)  inducements to agree to the clause. If the goods have been offered for sale at £10 without an exemption clause but at £8 with the inclusion of the clause, the court may see fit to allow the clause to apply at the lower price because there has been a concession by the seller in terms of the price;
    (iv)   buyer's knowledge of the extent of the clause. If the clause had been pointed out to the buyer and he is fully aware that it reduces the liability of the seller, then this will be relevant in deciding whether the seller should be allowed to

rely on the clause. If a buyer is reasonably fully informed and aware of the seller's intentions as regards exclusion of liability, then the buyer may have to accept the clause;

(v) customs of trade and previous dealings. If, for example, exclusion clauses are usual in the trade or have been used by the parties in previous dealings, then the court may decide that an exclusion clause should apply. It should be noted that previous dealings do not seem relevant in consumer transactions, unless quite regular, but they are in this area where one is considering a non-consumer situation;

(vi) whether the goods have been made, processed or adapted to the order of the buyer. Obviously if the seller has been required by the buyer to produce goods in a certain way, then it may well be fair and reasonable for the seller to exclude his liability in respect of faults arising out of, for example, the buyer's design which he insisted was used. It would probably be reasonable to exclude the implied term under the Sale of Goods Act 1979 that the goods were fit for the purpose (*see further* Chapter 10).

Although the above criteria are strictly speaking confined to the exclusion of statutory implied terms in, for example, the Sale of Goods Act 1979, they are being applied in other situations. For example, Judge Clarke in the *Woodman* case (*see below*) felt it was right to use them where what was at issue was a negligent service. The Supply of Goods and Services Act 1982 has not changed the law regarding the exclusion of liability of a supplier of services. Services are not specifically mentioned in the 1977 Act but they fall within the ambit of ss 2 and 3 which deal with negligence and breach of contract respectively.

### The test of reasonableness: the case law

**The following is a selection of case law on the 1977 Act to illustrate its application.**

### Mitchell (George) (Chesterhall) Ltd v Finney Lock Seeds Ltd [1983] 1 All ER 108

This case is a landmark. It was the last case heard by Lord Denning, one of the foremost opponents of exclusion clauses which could operate unfairly, in the Court of Appeal. In it he gave a review of the development of the law relating to exclusion clauses in his usual clear and concise way. The report is well worth reading in full. Only a summary of the main points can be given here.

George Mitchell ordered 30lb of cabbage seed and Finney supplied it. The seed was defective. The cabbages had no heart; their leaves turned in. The seed cost £192 but Mitchell's loss was some £61,000, i.e. a year's production from the 63 acres planted. Mitchell carried no insurance. When sued, Finney defended the claim on the basis of an exclusion clause limiting their liability to the cost of the seed or its replacement. In the High Court Parker J found for Mitchell. Finney appealed to the Court of Appeal. The major steps in Lord Denning's judgment appear below.

(a) *The issue of communication – was the clause part of the contract?* Lord Denning said that it was. The conditions were usual in the trade. They were in the back of Finney's catalogue. They were on the back of the invoice. 'The inference from the course of dealing would be that the farmers had accepted the conditions as printed – even though they had never read them and did not realise that they contained a limitation on liability . . .'.

(b) *The wording of the clause.* The relevant part of the clause read as follows: 'In the event of any seeds or plants sold or agreed to be sold by us not complying with the express terms of the contract of sale or with any representation made by us or by any duly authorised agent or representative on our behalf prior to, at the time of, or in any such contract, or any seeds or plants proving defective in varietal purity we will, at our option, replace the defective seeds or plants, free of charge to the buyer or will refund all payments made to us by the buyer in respect of the defective seeds or plants and this shall be the limit of our obligation. We hereby exclude all liability for any loss or damage arising from the use of any seeds or plants supplied by us and for any consequential loss or damage arising out of such use or any failure in the performance of or any defect in any seeds or plants supplied by us for any other loss or damage whatsoever save for, at our option, liability for any such replacement or refund as aforesaid.'

Lord Denning said that the words of the clause did effectively limit Finney's liability. Since the Securicor cases (*see Photo Production* and *Ailsa Craig, above*), words were to be given their natural meaning and not strained. A judge must not proceed in a hostile way towards the wording of exclusion clauses as was, for example, the case with the word 'misdelivery' in *Alexander v Railway Executive* (1951) (*see above*).

(c) *The test of reasonableness.* Lord Denning then turned to the new test of reasonableness which could be used to strike down an exclusion clause, even though it had been communicated, and in spite of the fact that its wording was appropriate to cover the circumstances. On this he said: 'What is the result of all this? To my mind it heralds a revolution in our approach to exemption clauses; not only where they exclude liability altogether and also where they limit liability; not only in the specific categories in the Unfair Contract Terms Act 1977, but in other contracts too ... We should do away with the multitude of cases on exemption clauses. We should no longer have to go through all kinds of gymnastic contortions to get round them. We should no longer have to harass our students with the study of them. We should set about meeting a new challenge. It is presented by the test of reasonableness.'

(d) *Was the particular clause fair and reasonable?* On this Lord Denning said: 'Our present case is very much on the borderline. There is this to be said in favour of the seed merchant. The price of this cabbage seed was small: £192. The damages claimed are high: £61,000. But there is this to be said on the other side. The clause was not negotiated between persons of equal bargaining power. It was inserted by the seed merchants in their invoices without any negotiation with the farmers. To this I would add that the seed merchants rarely, if ever, invoked the clause ... Next, I would point out that the buyers had no opportunity at all of knowing or discovering that the seed was not cabbage seed: whereas the sellers could and should have known that it was the wrong seed altogether. The buyers were not covered by insurance against the risk. Nor could they insure. But as to the seed merchants the judge said [Lord Denning here refers to Parker J at first instance]: "I am entirely satisfied that it is possible for seedsmen to insure against this risk ... ". To that I would add this further point. Such a mistake as this could not have happened without serious negligence on the part of the seed merchants themselves or their Dutch suppliers. So serious that it would not be fair to enable them to escape responsibility for it. In all the circumstances I am of the opinion that it would not be fair or reasonable to allow the seed merchants to rely on the clause to limit their liability.'

Oliver and Kerr LJJ also dismissed the appeal.

The suppliers asked for leave to appeal to the House of Lords but the Court of Appeal refused. However, the House of Lords granted leave and affirmed the decision of the Court of Appeal in 1983 (see [1983] 2 All ER 737).

**Comment:** This is in effect an application of s 6(3) of the Unfair Contract Terms Act 1977. It was actually brought under the Sale of Goods Act 1979 which contained transitional provisions and s 55(3) of the 1979 Act plus para 11 of Sch 1 applied to this contract. For contracts made after 31 January 1978, the Unfair Contract Terms Act 1977, s 6(3) would apply.

Section 2(2) came up for consideration in two County Court cases which were brought under the Act. In *Woodman* v *Photo Trade Processing Ltd*, heard in the Exeter County Court in May 1981, Mr Woodman took to the Exeter branch of Dixons Photographic for processing a film which carried pictures of a friend's wedding. The film was of special value because Mr Woodman had been the only photographer at the wedding, and he had said he would give the pictures as a wedding present. Unfortunately, the film was lost and when Dixons were sued they relied on an exclusion clause which, it appeared, was standard practice throughout the trade and had been communicated. The clause read as follows: 'All photographic materials are accepted on the basis that their value does not exceed the loss of the material itself. Responsibility is limited to the replacement of film. No liability will be accepted consequential or otherwise, however caused.' His Honour Judge Clarke found in the County Court that the customer had no real alternative but to entrust his film to a company that would use such an exclusion clause and that, furthermore, Dixons could have foreseen that the film might be irreplaceable and, although they could argue that the exclusion clause enabled them to operate a cheap mass-production technique, it could not be regarded as reasonable that all persons, regardless of the value of their film, should be required to take their chance of the system losing them. The judge, therefore, granted compensation of £75 to Mr Woodman and held that the exclusion clause was unreasonable.

In *Waldron-Kelly* v *British Railways Board*, which was heard in the Stockport County Court in 1981, the claimant delivered a suitcase to Stockport railway station so that it could be taken to Haverfordwest station. The contract of carriage was subject to the British Railways Board general conditions 'at owner's risk' for a price of £6.00. A clause exempted the Board from any loss, except that if a case disappeared then the Board's liability was to be assessed by reference to the weight of the goods, which in this case was £27.00 and not to their value, which in this case was £320.00. The suitcase was lost while it was in the control of British Rail. In the County Court Judge Brown *held* that the claimant succeeded in his contention that the exclusion clause was unreasonable and, therefore, of no effect. The judge held that in the case of non-delivery of goods the burden of proof to show what had happened to the goods was on the bailee. British Rail had failed to show that the loss was not its fault, and in any case the fault and loss were not covered by the exclusion clause because it did not satisfy the test of reasonableness.

Further, in *Stag Line Ltd* v *Tyne Ship Repair Group Ltd* [1984] 2 Lloyd's Rep 211 Staughton J, in finding that exclusion clauses inserted into the contract by the defendants were not fair and reasonable, said:

The courts would be slow to find clauses in commercial contracts made between parties of equal bargaining power to be unfair or unreasonable, but a provision in a contract, which deprived a ship owner of any remedy for breach of contract or contractual negligence unless the vessel were returned to the repairer's yard for the defect to be remedied would be unfair and unreasonable because it would be capricious; the effectiveness of the remedy would depend upon where the ship was when the casualty occurred and whether it would be practical or economic to return the vessel to the defendants' yard.

Also in *Rees-Hough Ltd* v *Redland Reinforced Plastics Ltd* [1984] *Construction Industry Law Letters*, His Honour Judge Newey QC decided that it was not fair and reasonable for the defendants to rely on an exclusion clause in their standard terms and conditions of sale. They had sold pipes to the claimants which were not fit for the purpose for which the defendants knew they were required, nor were they of merchantable (now satisfactory) quality under the Sale of Goods Act 1979 (*see further* Chapter 10) and the clause excluded liability for this. Clearly, then, it is difficult to apply exclusion clauses which try to prevent liability for supplying defective goods.

Where there is no contract, as in the *Hedley Byrne* situation where a bank used a 'without responsibility' disclaimer, s 2(2) of the Act applies the reasonable test to the disclaimer (*see further* Chapter 22).

## PROVISIONS AGAINST EVASION OF LIABILITY

### General

If an attempt is made to exclude or restrict liability in contract X by a clause in a secondary contract Y, then the clause in Y is ineffective (s 10). For example, C buys a television set from B. There is an associated maintenance contract. The sale of a television would be within s 6 of the 1977 Act and so there could be no exclusion of B's implied obligations. Any attempt to exclude or restrict these obligations in the maintenance contract would also fail. If the transaction was a non-consumer one, the 'reasonable' test would have to be applied.

Nor can the Act be excluded by a clause which states that the contract is to be governed by the law of another country which does not outlaw exclusion clauses, at least if it is part of an evasion scheme, or if the contract is with a United Kingdom consumer and the main steps in the making of the contract took place in the UK (s 27).

The Act does not apply to insurance contracts, nor to contracts for the transfer of an interest in land (s 1(2) and Sch 1, para 1(a) and (b)). House purchase is, therefore, excluded, though inducement liability cannot be excluded unless reasonable (*see above*). Nor does it apply to certain contracts involving the supply of goods on an international basis because these are covered by conventions. Furthermore, it should be noted that a written arbitration agreement will not be treated as excluding or restricting liability for the purposes of the 1977 Act and such an agreement is valid (s 13(2)).

### Fair Trading Act 1973

Under s 13 of this Act the Director-General of Fair Trading can in the course of investigating consumer trade practices deal in particular with 'terms and conditions on which or subject to which goods or services are supplied'. This, of course, concerns exemption clauses being used in consumer transactions. If after investigation the Director-General feels that a particular practice in terms of exemption clauses should cease, he will make a report to the Minister who may introduce a statutory instrument to stop the practice. For example, the Consumer Transactions (Restrictions on Statements) Order 1976 (No 1813) as amended by SI 1978/127 makes it a criminal offence to sell or supply goods and purport that the implied terms in sale of goods and hire-purchase legislation can be excluded in a consumer sale since this might suggest to the customer that he has no rights so that he will not bother to try to enforce them.

# UNFAIR CONTRACT TERMS REGULATIONS

The Unfair Terms in Consumer Contracts Regulations 1999 (SI 1999/2083) implement the EC Directive on Unfair Terms in Consumer Contracts (93/13/EEC).

### Terms covered (reg 3)

The Regulations apply to any term in a contract between a seller or supplier who is acting for purposes relating to his business and a consumer, i.e. a natural person (not a company) who is acting for purposes outside of business where the term has not been individually negotiated. Although the Regulations apply to oral contracts, it is businesses which use pre-printed contract terms, the substance of which cannot be influenced by the consumer, which are most affected by the changes introduced by the Regulations.

No assessment is to be made of the fairness of terms which identify the goods or services to be supplied or the price or remuneration involved provided such terms are in plain intelligible language. The fact that some terms of a contract have been negotiated will not prevent the contract being unfair if on an overall assessment it is found to be a pre-formulated standard contract. The seller or supplier must prove that a term in dispute was individually negotiated.

Under Sch 1 certain contracts and their terms are excluded from the scope of the Regulations, e.g. employment contracts and contracts relating to the incorporation and organisation of companies and partnerships. In addition, a contract which complies with other relevant UK legislation, e.g. the Package Travel Regulations, will not be further tested under the Unfair Terms Regulations. Sales by auction are not excluded.

### Unfair terms (reg 4)

An unfair term is any term which contrary to the requirement of good faith causes a significant imbalance in the rights and obligations of the parties under the contract to the detriment of the consumer. The concept of good faith is thus introduced more widely into English law having really only applied before to the disclosure requirement in a contract of insurance which is a contract of utmost good faith.

Schedule 2 sets out matters which go to deciding whether the contract meets the requirement of good faith. These are:

- the strength of the bargaining positions of the parties;
- whether the consumer had an inducement to agree to the term, e.g. where the goods were cheaper if the term was included, it might survive;
- whether the goods or services were sold or supplied to the special order of the con-

sumer – e.g. where goods were made to a consumer's design or adapted to the consumer's requirements it might be fair to include a term relating to the possible unfitness of the goods for the intended purpose;
- the extent to which the seller or supplier has dealt fairly and equitably with the consumer.

Schedule 3 gives an indicative and non-exhaustive list of terms which may be regarded as unfair. This does not mean that they are automatically unfair. There are 17 examples including clauses:

- excluding or limiting the liability of a seller or supplier in the event of the death or personal injury of or to a consumer resulting from an act or omission of that seller or supplier;
- requiring any consumer who fails to meet his obligations to pay a disproportionately high sum in compensation. This could include, e.g. a non-refundable deposit;
- enabling the seller or supplier to alter the contract unilaterally;
- limiting the consumer's rights in the event of total or partial non-performance by the seller or supplier;

and so on.

It is worth noting here the somewhat unfortunate overlap between the 1994 Regulations and the Unfair Contract Terms Act 1977. The first example in the above list which is 'unfair' under the Regulations is actually totally barred by the 1977 Act in s 2(1). The other examples given here or in Sch 3 would probably be regarded as inapplicable because they do not satisfy the 'reasonableness' test of the 1977 Act. The Government did not feel able to align the 'reasonableness' test and the 'fairness' test but did announce in the Final Consultation Document in September 1994 that the Regulations would not limit the 1977 Act, so we can take it that our first example is totally outlawed so that there is no need to apply the 'fairness' test.

There are differences between the two pieces of legislation. The Act applies to exclusion clauses in consumer contracts but can extend to business contracts, negotiated contracts and exclusion notices. The Regulations apply only to consumer contracts where the terms were not individually negotiated and, in that sense, are narrower but since they are not limited to exclusion clauses their effect may be much wider. Regulation 4 also states that an assessment of the unfair nature of a term should take into account – (a) the nature of the goods or services for which the contract was concluded; (b) the circumstances attending the conclusion of the contract; and (c) the other terms of the contract or of another contract on which it is dependent.

## Consequences of inclusion of unfair terms (reg 5)

An unfair term is not binding on the consumer, but the contract will continue to bind the parties if it is viable without the unfair term.

## Construction of written contracts (reg 6)

Standard form contracts offered to consumers must be expressed in plain intelligible language. If there is any doubt about the meaning of a term, the interpretation most favourable to the consumer shall prevail.

## Enforcement by the Director-General of Fair Trading

The Regulations conclude by imposing on the Director-General of Fair Trading (DGFT) a duty to consider complaints that contracts which have been drawn up for general use are unfair unless the complaint appears to be vexatious or frivolous. The DGFT may apply to the court for an injunction against persons who appear to be recommending or using unfair terms in contracts with consumers. The DGFT may also arrange for the dissemination of information and advice concerning the operation of the Regulations.

## Terms possibly affected

It may well be argued that an overdraft that is payable on demand is unfair because it operates in effect as a contract which can be terminated without notice. This gives further support to a recent trend under which borrowers are suing banks who have withdrawn overdraft facilities so that the borrower is forced into insolvency procedures. It is also likely that many guarantees given by company directors and other business persons as a security for a business overdraft are too complex and not expressed in plain intelligible language. It may also be unfair to provide, as bank guarantees often do, that all sums payable under the guarantee must be paid without set-off. There may also be problems with building society residential mortgages, particularly in terms of the heavy penalties incurred by borrowers for early redemption of mortgage contracts to discourage them taking up a more favourable mortgage elsewhere.

Of interest in this connection is the case of *Falco Finance Ltd* v *Michael Gough* (1998) 149 NLJ 7. The case was heard by His Honour Judge Elystan Morgan at Warrington County Court. Under earlier legislation, a number of terms in Mr Gough's mortgage were held to be unenforceable because they were contrary to the Regulations as follows:

- the advertised rate of 8.99 per cent interest rose by a further 5 per cent for the whole of the term remaining if even part of an instalment was paid a day late;
- the instalments were calculated on a flat-rate basis not a reducing balance, i.e. on the assumption that the debt remained outstanding in full throughout the term even though it was gradually being paid off;
- if after having paid off a few instalments Mr Gough had wanted to move to another lender, he would have had to borrow £5,000 more than the entire debt to pay off the finance company.

The mortgage was also declared an extortionate credit bargain (*see further* Chapter 14), which was unusual because the payments themselves were not found to be grossly exorbitant, but they had 'grossly contravened ordinary principles of fair dealing'.

## Reform

The Department of Trade and Industry has issued a consultation paper entitled 'Widening the Scope of Action under the Unfair Terms in Consumer Contracts Regulations 1994'. At the present time only the Director-General of Fair Trading is allowed, in a representative role, to seek sanctions to prevent the continued use of unfair terms. Under the proposed changes, consumer groups such as the Consumers' Association will, for the first time, have power to act on behalf of consumers in court against traders who:

- issue contracts which are baffling, illegible or designed to deceive;
- change agreed prices, e.g. increasing the monthly subscription for a service without giving the consumer the right to withdraw from the contract;
- deny consumers their legal rights, e.g. by limiting or excluding suppliers' liability for unsatisfactory work.

These provisions are now in force (*see* SI 1999/2083).

## GRADED QUESTIONS

### Essay mode

1 (a) The Unfair Contract Terms Act 1977 has placed considerable restrictions on the ability of a business to exclude or restrict its liability through the use of contract terms or notices.
   Explain and illustrate this statement.

   (b) Microbyte manufactures personal computers which are sold through dealers to the general public. Its managing director knows that there is a risk that some of the components which are bought in from outside suppliers for use in the computers will be faulty. He seeks your advice on how Microbyte should attempt to ensure through its conditions of purchase that any liability which is associated with such faults is passed on to the component suppliers.
   Advise the managing director.

   *(The Institute of Chartered Secretaries and Administrators)*

2 When parties enter into a contract it is virtually impossible for them to include express terms to cover every eventuality. If a dispute later arises, it may then be necessary for terms to be implied into the contract.
   Explain:
   (a) when these implied terms will be introduced:
      (i) by the courts, and
      (ii) by statute;
   (b) the extent to which it is possible to exclude or vary these terms at the time of contracting.

   *(The Chartered Institute of Management Accountants)*

3 (a) In the law of contract what is the effect of:
      (i) A mutual mistake?
      (ii) A common mistake?
   (b) Albert advertised his car for sale in a local newspaper. He was visited by Brian who expressed an interest in buying the vehicle. The sale price of the car was £2,000 and Brian offered to pay for it by cheque. Albert was reluctant to accept a cheque, upon which Brian produced a driving licence which indicated, falsely, that Brian was the well-known footballer, Dan.
   Albert decided to let Brian have the car, but the cheque has now been dishonoured. Meanwhile Brian has sold the car to Cedric and has subsequently disappeared with the proceeds of the sale.
   Advise Albert.

   *(Association of Chartered Certified Accountants)*

4  'If there is one thing more than another which public policy requires, it is that men of full age and competent understanding shall have the utmost liberty of contracting and that their contracts when entered into freely and voluntarily shall be held sacred and shall be enforced by courts of justice' (*per* Sir George Jessel in *Printing and Numerical Registering Co v Sampson* (1875)).

Discuss the extent to which state and judicial intervention in the use of exclusion clauses has rendered the above statement obsolete.

(*University of Huddersfield. BA and BA(Hons) Business Studies*)

## Objective mode

Four alternative answers are given. Select ONE only. Circle the answer which you consider to be correct. Check your answers by referring back to the information given in the chapter and against the answers at the back of the book.

1  On Monday Tom and Jerry, who are workmates, were discussing the sale to Jerry of Tom's car. Tom said that he had fitted new tyres at 30,000 miles but this was not true, Tom having forgotten that they were fitted at 25,000 miles. On Friday afternoon Jerry agreed to buy Tom's car. In the above circumstances Tom's statement about the tyres will be regarded as:

A  A condition of the contract.
B  A warranty.
C  A misrepresentation.
D  A non-actionable hyping of the car.

2  Fred offered his car for sale to Joe saying that it had done 30,000 miles. Joe bought it. In fact it had done 31,000 miles.

Fred's statement in the offer about the mileage was a:

A  Warranty.
B  Condition.
C  Non-actionable hyping of the car.
D  Misrepresentation.

3  A judge will imply a term into a contract:

A  Only if the parties intended it.
B  If the parties intended it and as a matter of law even if they did not.
C  Only as a matter of law and regardless of the intentions of the parties.
D  If the parties intended it or as a matter of law but only if it is commercially necessary to do so.

4  Jane took a dress into a dry cleaning company for cleaning. She signed a document without reading it. It said the company exempted itself from damage accidental or negligent. The dress was returned torn on the hem. What is the legal position?

A  Such an exclusion clause can never be binding because of the Unfair Contract Terms Act 1977.
B  The clause is not binding because it was not actually communicated to Jane.
C  The clause was constructively communicated to Jane but will not be binding unless reasonable.
D  The clause is binding merely because it was constructively communicated to Jane.

5 Jack, a plumber, took his video into Electrics Ltd for repair. Jack had taken his video into Electrics only once in the past six years. On that occasion he had been given a document stating that the company was not liable for damage caused to customers' equipment while on the premises of the company. The video was damaged beyond repair when it was knocked off a shelf by a football during a lunch-time game between three employees of Electrics in the warehouse. Jack has been told that he cannot claim because of the previous communication of the exclusion clause.

The legal position is that:

A Jack is bound by the previous notice and cannot claim.

B Jack is not bound by the previous notice because the Unfair Contract Terms Act 1977 outlaws clauses of this kind.

C Jack is not bound by the clause but only because the previous notice does not specifically exclude negligent damage.

D Jack is not bound by the notice because his previous dealing with Electrics is not regular and also because the clause, even if reasonable, does not exclude negligent damage.

6 Mary parked her car in the customers' car park of Garrod's store, at the cost of £2. At the entrance to the car park there were two notices. One, placed on the right of the entrance, read: 'No liability is accepted for death of, or injury to, a customer'. The other, placed on the left of the entrance but not visible because two Garrod's vans were parked in front of it, read: 'Cars parked at owner's risk'.

While she was parking the car in one of the spaces provided, two employees of Garrod's, who were cleaning the upper windows of the store, negligently dropped a bucket of water through the windscreen of Mary's car causing facial injury to Mary and completely ruining some other goods which Mary had just bought from another store.

Advise Mary.

A Mary has no claim because the two notices taken together are effective to exclude Garrod's liability.

B Mary can claim for her facial injury only because the notice she has seen is outlawed by the Unfair Contract Terms Act 1977. The other clause relating to property damage is constructively communicated and effective.

C Mary can claim for all the damage because the notice she saw contains a clause outlawed by the Unfair Contract Terms Act 1977 and the other notice was not communicated.

D Mary can claim for her facial injuries because the notice she saw is outlawed by the Unfair Contract Terms Act 1977. She may be able to claim for the property damage, but only if the court decides that the clause on the second notice was unreasonable.

7 Booker, the accountant of Bloggs Ltd, a small manufacturing company, wished to appoint a successor to Scribe, a clerk in charge of wages and salaries who was leaving to take up another appointment. After interviewing a number of applicants, Booker decided to appoint Dodger, who had some ten years' previous experience in a similar post.

Dodger agreed to accept the appointment with effect from 1 February and gave his employer two months' notice. He also undertook as part of the agreement to spend up to four Saturday mornings during the period of notice at the offices of Bloggs Ltd so that Scribe, who was leaving on 31 January, could introduce him to the company's procedures. Two dates in December and two in January were agreed between Scribe and Dodger, but by the end of December Dodger had presented himself on only one occasion.

On 4 January Booker rang Dodger and asked him why he had not attended at the company's offices as agreed. Dodger replied that Saturday was inconvenient because he played for a local football team which always trained for one hour on Saturday morning prior to an afternoon match. Dodger did, however, agree to attend on the first date in January but said that he could not make the second, adding, 'I have been doing similar work for ten years and I already understand most of your procedures from my visit in December.' Booker replied that this arrangement was not suitable and concluded, 'You need not bother to turn up on 1 February. I would not dream of taking an unreliable person such as yourself into employment here.'

Dodger's employer refused to accept the withdrawal of his resignation and he was out of work for two months.

What is the legal position?

(*Note*: Statute law relating to unfair dismissal is not relevant here and should be ignored.)

A  Booker was legally entitled to repudiate the contract and Dodger has no remedy against Booker.
B  Booker should have honoured the contract and taken Dodger into employment. Each party may sue the other for loss.
C  Dodger may make Booker take him into employment.
D  Neither party has a claim against the other because the employment never began.

8  Rudy, a former employee of the Russian government, who sought and obtained political asylum in England, has set up in business as a bookseller. Rudy speaks English quite well but cannot read the language as yet. His pride compels Rudy to conceal this from everyone. Rudy ordered a number of textbooks for sale to students at a local college from Hawker, who was a representative of Booker Ltd, the publishers, with whom he had not previously done business. Hawker gave Rudy a sold note containing the following clause: 'All goods are sold subject to their being in stock when the order reaches head office'.

The books which Rudy ordered have not been delivered and since the first college term has now commenced, it is likely that the students will purchase their textbooks from another retailer in a neighbouring town who has stocks on his shelves.

Rudy proposes to sue Booker Ltd for breach of contract, but he has been told by Hawker that he will have no claim in view of the clause set out in the sold note. Hawker says the clause is part of the contract and that the books will be despatched shortly when they come into Booker Ltd's stock.

Given that the exclusion clause appears to be reasonable, what is the legal position?

A  Booker will be liable because Rudy cannot read English.
B  Booker will be liable because the sold note is not a contractual document.
C  Booker will not be liable because the sold note is a contractual document and its contents were constructively communicated to Rudy.
D  Booker will be liable because it did not get Rudy to sign the sold note.

*Answers to questions set in objective mode appear on p 707.*

# 7 CONTRACTS IN RESTRAINT OF TRADE AND RESTRICTIVE PRACTICES

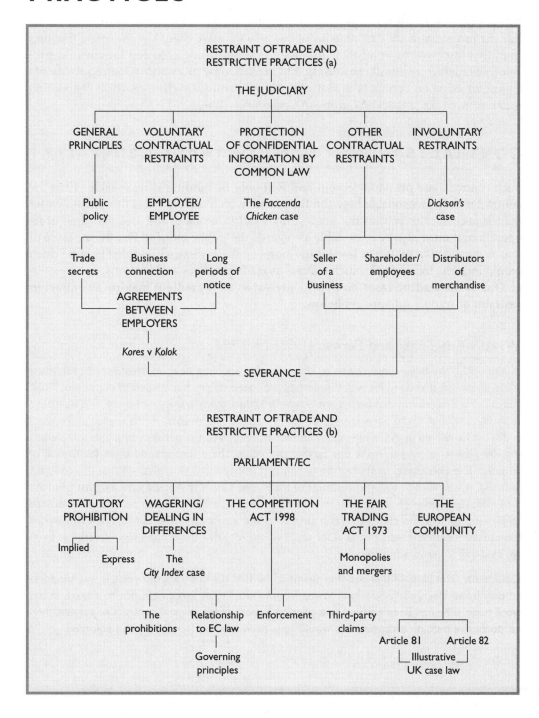

The objectives of this chapter are to consider transactions which are made void by the judiciary or by Parliament not because they are illegal in the sense that any morally blameworthy conduct is involved but because if enforced they would produce unsatisfactory results in society. There is in view of examination requirements a concentration on contracts in restraint of trade and restrictive practices legislation together with the impact of European Community law.

## CONTRACTS IN RESTRAINT OF TRADE GENERALLY

Such contracts are prima facie void and will only be binding if reasonable. Thus the contract must be reasonable between the parties which means that it must be no wider than is necessary to protect the interest involved in terms of the area and time of its operation. It must also be reasonable as regards the public interest. Finally, the issue of reasonableness is a matter of law for the judge on the evidence presented to him which would include, for example, such matters as trade practices and customs.

**One of the leading cases on public interest as an ingredient making a contract in restraint of trade void appears below.**

### Wyatt v Kreglinger and Fernau [1933] 1 KB 793

In June 1923, the defendants wrote to the claimant, who had been in their service for many years, intimating that upon his retirement they proposed to give him an annual pension of £200, subject to the condition that he did not compete against them in the wool trade. The claimant's reply was lost and he did not appear ever to have agreed for his part not to engage in the wool trade, but he retired in the following September and received the pension until June 1932 when the defendants refused to make any further payments. The claimant sued them for breach of contract. The defendants denied that any contract existed and also pleaded that if a contract did exist, it was void as being in restraint of trade. The Court of Appeal gave judgment for the defendants and although there was no unanimity with regard to the *ratio decidendi*, it appeared to two judges that the contract was injurious to the interests of the public, since to restrain the claimant from engaging in the wool trade was to deprive the community of services from which it might derive advantage.

*Comment:* The basis of this decision seems to be that if a contract did exist, it was supported only by an illegal consideration moving from Wyatt, i.e. an agreement not to engage in the wool trade. If he had been entitled to a pension as part of his original contract of service, then no doubt the pension arrangements would have been severed (*see below*) and enforced.

# VOLUNTARY CONTRACTUAL RESTRAINTS OF TRADE ON EMPLOYEES GENERALLY

Here the contract is entered into voluntarily by the parties and as regards employees it should be noted that there are only two things an employer can protect:

(a) *Trade secrets.* A restraint against competition is justifiable if its object is to prevent the exploitation of trade secrets learned by the employee in the course of his employment. In this connection it should be noted that the area of the restraint must not be excessive. Furthermore, a restraint under this heading may be invalid because its duration is excessive.

**An example of the application of the above principles is set out below.**

## Forster & Sons Ltd v Suggett (1918) 35 TLR 87

The works manager of the claimants, who were mainly engaged in making glass and glass bottles, was instructed in certain confidential methods concerning, among other things, the correct mixture of gas and air in the furnaces. He agreed that during the five years following the termination of his employment he would not carry on in the United Kingdom, or be interested in, glass-bottle manufacture or any other business connected with glass-making as conducted by the claimants. It was *held* that the claimants were entitled to protection in this respect and that the restraint was reasonable.

*Comment:* The Court of Appeal decided in *PSM International and McKechnie* v *Whitehouse and Willenhall Automation* [1992] IRLR 279 that the court has power to prevent a contract made following abuse of trade secrets from being carried out. Thus if A is employed by B and goes to work for C and, by using trade secrets obtained while working with B, helps C to obtain a contract with D, then the court can grant B an injunction to restrain C from fulfilling its contract with D, where there is evidence that B has lost the contract with D because of the misuse of its trade secrets, even though the effect on D appears unfair. C is not liable to D for breach of contract because it is frustrated (*see further* Chapter 8) since it could not be carried out without C being in contempt of court.

(b) *Business connection.* Sometimes an employer may use a covenant against *solicitation* of persons with whom the employer does business. The problem of area is less important in this type of covenant, though its duration must be reasonable. The burden on the employer increases as the duration of the restraint is extended, though in rare situations a restraint for life may be valid.

**Illustrative case law is set out below.**

## Home Counties Dairies v Skilton [1970] 1 All ER 1227

Skilton, a milk roundsman employed by the claimants, agreed, among other things, not for one year after leaving his job 'to serve or sell milk or dairy produce' to persons who within six months before leaving his employment were customers of his employers. Skilton left his employment with the claimants in order to work as a roundsman for Westcott Dairies. He then took the same milk round as he had worked when he was with the claimants. *Held* – by the Court of Appeal – that this was a flagrant breach of agreement. The words 'dairy produce' were not too wide. On a proper construction they must be restricted to things normally dealt in by a milkman on his round. 'A further point was taken that the customer restriction would apply to anyone who had been a customer within the last six months of the employment and had during that period ceased so to be, and it was said that the employer could have no legitimate interest in such persons. I think this point is met in the judgment in *G W Plowman & Sons Ltd* v *Ash* [1964] 2 All ER 10 where it was said that a customer might have left temporarily and that his return was not beyond hope and was therefore a matter of legitimate interest to the employer' (*per* Harman LJ).

**Comment:** (i) It was *held* by the Court of Appeal in *John Michael Design* v *Cooke* [1987] 2 All ER 332 after referring to *Plowman* v *Ash* that a restraint in a contract of employment preventing an employee (A) from competing with his former employer (B) could be enforced by an injunction even to prevent the former employee from doing business with a customer (C) of his former employer who had made it clear that he would not do business with B again. There was always the possibility that C would change his mind.

(ii) It is better in these customer/client restraints to restrict the restraint to not soliciting. If the restraint prevents, in addition, the employee from working in a given area it may fail. Thus in *Office Angels Ltd* v *Rainer-Thomas and O'Connor* [1991] IRLR 214 the defendants were employed as manager and temporaries consultant respectively by the claimants who ran an employment agency in Bow Lane in the City of London. They agreed in their contracts that they would not for a period of six months after leaving their employment with the claimants solicit those of the claimants' customers who had been customers while they were employed by the claimants, and in addition would not set up in business or engage in trade or business as an employment agency within a radius of 3,000 metres of those branches of the company in which they had been employed for not less than four weeks during the six months prior to the termination of their employment or in the case of a branch or branches in the Greater London area then within a radius of 1,000 metres. They left their employment and joined another employment agency operating within the forbidden area. The Court of Appeal found the restriction as to area unreasonable so that the whole clause was void and the claimants could not stop solicitation of their customers under the terms of the clause. The case represents the modern approach to non-solicitation restraints, and seems to be the correct one. If the employees agree not to poach customers/clients then it surely does not matter whether they set up in business next door or not so long as they do not poach the customers/clients. If they do that can be stopped. To add an area does little to protect a customer/client restraint and can lead to the unenforceability of the whole restraint clause as in this case.

(iii) Other cases of interest in this area are *Morris Angel and Son Ltd* v *Hollande and Lee* [1993] IRLR 169, where the Court of Appeal held that a covenant restraining an employee from dealing with his employer's business contacts for a year after his employment ceased could be enforced by the company to which the business was transferred but only in regard to the contracts of the original employer who took the covenant and not to those of the transferee who had no such covenant with the employee. *Briggs* v *Oates* [1991] 1 All ER 411 is also of interest in that it decided that if a contract containing an employee restraint is repudiated by the employer all contractual obligations are discharged with the contract and the restraint cannot be enforced. Thus, if an employer were unilaterally to reduce the restrained employee's pay so that he left under a constructive dismissal (*see further* Chapter 17), the employer could not subsequently legally enforce the restraint in the former employee's contract.

(iv) Of particular interest because it relates to a restraint placed upon an employee/partner of a professional firm is *Taylor Stuart v Croft* [1998] 606 IRLB 15. The High Court had to deal with a contractual restraint of trade on an accountant/salaried partner which placed a three-year restraint on him in terms of working for clients of the firm after his employment terminated. This restraint was regarded by the High Court as unreasonable and unenforceable. Other restraints, namely soliciting, canvassing and enticing away clients, were enforceable. A liquidated damages clause in the contract payable by the salaried partner for breach of the restraints was regarded as penal and unenforceable being two-and-a-half times the salaried partner's gross annual income (see *further* Chapter 9). However, since the salaried partner had after leaving the firm taken some steps to canvass his former clients, e.g. by telephoning them, and some had taken their work to him, a claim for unliquidated damages would seemingly have succeeded. The claimants had, however, relied on enforcing the penal liquidated damages clause and, therefore, their action failed.

## Fitch v Dewes [1921] 2 AC 158

A solicitor at Tamworth employed a person who was successively his articled clerk and managing clerk. In his contract of service, the clerk agreed, if he left the solicitor's employment, never to practise as a solicitor within seven miles of Tamworth Town Hall. *Held* – The agreement was good because during his service the clerk had become acquainted with the details of his employer's clients, and could be restrained even for life from using that knowledge to the detriment of his employer.

**Comment:** (i) Although the restraint was for life, it did cover a rather small area in which at the time there were comparatively few people so that Fitch was a very influential employee. It is unlikely that such a restraint would be regarded as valid today, particularly in a more densely populated area.

(ii) The Privy Council stated quite clearly in *Deacons v Bridge* [1984] 2 All ER 19 that a restraint such as this would only be applied in unusual circumstances. The decision seems confined to its own facts though the statements of principle in the case by the House of Lords are more enduring.

**The business application:** Ignoring *Fitch v Dewes* (1921) which is a 'one off' decision, restraints of trade have not always found favour with the smaller business such as a small to medium professional firm of accountants or lawyers, or with small traders such as the owners of hair-styling salons. The canvassing of clients after leaving service can be damaging and does go on. However, the advice generally received by such business organisations is that a six-month restraint is all that a court is likely to accept under the 'reasonableness' principles and since injunctive relief would be the best remedy to stop canvassing on pain of contempt of court and possible fine or imprisonment (the latter being rather unlikely) in this context by the time the lawyers have got a case in motion and to the court the acceptable period of six months is likely to be up anyway, though a claim for damages is available if clients and customers have been lost, the question being, of course, can the ex-employee pay them? The three-year period allowed in *Taylor Stuart* is, therefore, of value. It is longer than what has in general been allowed and would give time to seek injunctive relief for a large part of the time.

In large concerns and in respect of higher management, restraint clauses may well be worthwhile to protect the business and retain skilled employees (see *below* Restraint in the City).

### Restraint in the City of London

The problems involved in holding on to key staff in City financial institutions has been a matter of much publicity in recent times.

An important Court of Appeal decision gives some protection against poaching. It held that a provision in a company manager's service contract prohibiting him during employment, and for one year after leaving, from offering a partnership or employment to any person who had at any time during the manager's employment also been employed by the company as a director or senior employee of the company, was a reasonable restraint and enforceable. A clause which prohibited the poaching of any employee, regardless of status, was struck down as too wide. (*See Dawnay Day & Co Ltd v D'Alphen* [1997] IRLR 422.)

The managers concerned were acting as inter-dealer brokers with Dawnay Day, an investment bank. The managers had also entered into a joint venture with Dawnay Day but non-solicitation of staff clauses in the shareholder's agreement were held to be in unreasonable restraint of trade because they were too wide, since they applied to all staff from top to bottom of the company.

The importance of the case lies in the fact that there were conflicting decisions in previous case law as to whether an employer had a legitimate interest in maintaining a stable, trained workforce.

This case takes the line that there is a legitimate interest which can be protected. It is of great importance to the City since, if there was no legitimate interest in retaining the senior workforce, a competitor could take senior staff into his own organisation, in effect taking over the former employer's business without actually paying for it. It is important to note that the case does not cover the situation where an employee leaves because a job is advertised in the other organisation, for which he applies. The basis of the case is *solicitation* of employees.

## CONTRACTUAL RESTRAINTS ON EMPLOYEES THROUGH THE PERIOD OF NOTICE

In recent times the court has had to consider the validity of contracts of service with restrictively long periods of notice which have sometimes been given to able and ambitious executives. Typically such contracts provide that if the employee leaves he must give notice of, say, one year and during that time the employer can suspend him from work but agree to give him full pay and other benefits. The contract should also provide that the employer may exclude the employee from the workplace so that he cannot after serving his notice obtain any further information which might be of benefit to the new employer nor can he work for the new employer during the period of notice without being in breach of contract. He can either do nothing or pursue his hobbies. This is why the period of notice has been called 'garden leave'.

A specific provision in the contract is essential if the employee is to be excluded from work. *William Hill Organisation* v *Tucker* [1998] IRLR 313 decides that otherwise the employee has a right to work. A 'garden leave' contract typically does not contain a restraint clause, but the employee can be restrained from competing during the long period of leave because he is still employed during the leave period and *owes a duty of fidelity to his employer at common law not to compete*. The 'garden leave' contract is an alternative to a restraint clause and is in some ways more flexible in that the court may grant the employer an injunction to prevent competition during the period of notice if *on the facts* it is reasonable to do so since the competition is serious. This happened in *GFI Group Inc* v *Eaglestone* (1994) 490 IRLB 2 where the High Court held that an injunction could be granted to prohibit a highly-paid foreign exchange options broker from working for a rival firm during his notice period of 20 weeks so that for that period of time he could not assist a competing organisation to deal with the business connections of his employer. If the competition is not so serious, then a claim for damages can be brought as the Court of Appeal decided in *Provident Financial Group plc* v *Whitegates Estate Agency* [1989] IRLR 84. If, however, a restraint clause is put into a severance package when the employee leaves, it must satisfy the test of reasonableness. The duty of fidelity at common law does not exist since the former employee is no longer employed. Thus, if the clause is too wide, the court cannot give any protection even if *on the facts* the competition is severe, as the Court of Appeal decided in *JA Mont (UK) Ltd* v *Mills* [1993] IRLR 172.

For example:

(a) A, a surveyor with a firm of estate agents, is on 'garden leave' and takes a job with a major competing estate agency in the same town. The court may well grant an injunction on the grounds of A's breach of the duty of fidelity at common law. However, if the court feels that injunctive relief is unreasonable, a claim for damages could be brought. If A went to work for a firm of estate agents in the next town, the court may decide *on the facts* that no relief of any kind should be given.

(b) If A had left his job and as part of a severance package he was restrained from working for a firm of estate agents anywhere in the UK for five years, the restraint would obviously be too wide and wholly void. That being so the court could not give the employer *any relief*, even if A went to work for a rival firm of estate agents next door to his former employer!

## NON-CONTRACTUAL RESTRAINTS ON EMPLOYEES: CONFIDENTIAL INFORMATION

The position is different where the employee has no restraint of trade clause in his contract and is not on 'garden leave'. Thus in *Faccenda Chicken Ltd* v *Fowler* [1986] 1 All ER 617, Mr Fowler was sales manager for Faccenda Chicken Ltd for seven years and set up a van sales operation whereby refrigerated vans travelled around certain districts offering fresh chicken to retailers and caterers. He left the company and set up his own business selling chickens from refrigerated vans in the same area. Eight of the company's employees went to work for him. Each of the salesmen in the company knew the names and addresses of the customers, the route and timing of deliveries, and the different prices quoted to different customers.

The company unsuccessfully brought an action for damages in the High Court, alleging wrongful use of confidential sales information and were also unsuccessful in a counter-claim for damages for breach of contract by abuse of confidential information in Mr Fowler's action against them for outstanding commission.

It is generally the case that rather more protection in terms of preventing an employee from approaching customers can be obtained by an express term which is reasonable in terms of its duration. In the absence of an express term, it is clear from this decision of the Court of Appeal that confidential information of an employer's business obtained by an employee in the course of his service may be used by that employee when he leaves the job unless, as the Court of Appeal decided, it can be classed as a trade secret or is of such a confidential nature that it merits the same protection as a trade secret. For example, there would have been no need for a term in the contract of service in *Forster* (*see above*). The court could have prevented use of the secret process for a period without this. It should, however, be noted that in *Faccenda* the Court of Appeal did say that if the employees had written down lists of customers, routes, etc, as distinct from having the necessary information in their memories, and presumably being unable to erase it, short of amnesia, they might have been restrained for a period from using the lists. This follows the case of *Robb* v *Green* [1895] 2 QB 315 where the manager of a firm dealing in live game and eggs copied down the names of customers before leaving and then solicited these for the purposes of his own business after leaving the employment of the firm. He was restrained from soliciting the customers.

The Court of Appeal has held that an ex-employee who made negative remarks about the financial situation and management of the company from which he had resigned as managing director did not owe an implied duty of confidentiality with regard to the information disclosed about the ex-employer.

The information, it said, did not come within the category of a 'trade secret' (see *Brooks* v *Olyslager OMS (UK) Ltd* [1998] 601 IRLB 6).

When Mr Brooks resigned from the company, it was under a compromise agreement giving him three months' salary in three monthly instalments. Immediately following his resignation, he telephoned an investment banker who had an interest in the company. During the conversation, he intimated that the company's management was autocratic, the company was insolvent and would only last a month, its budgets were over-optimistic and that it would be taken over by its holding company.

When it heard about these remarks, the company refused to pay the salary instalments and claimed that Mr Brooks was in breach on an implied duty of confidentiality. He claimed damages in the lower court and was awarded them.

The issue in the Court of Appeal related mainly to the duty of confidentiality. The court did not agree that there was such a duty in this case and in respect of the information disclosed. There was no evidence that knowledge of the company's financial affairs was not already in the public domain. Also, Olyslager had not sought to show that what Mr Brooks had said was untrue or malicious, nor that his statements had caused any financial loss. The company's case was based on its desire to prevent Mr Brooks from disclosing the reasons why he had resigned and from making statements that were in any way detrimental to its interest.

There was no such broad right in law. Accordingly, Mr Brooks was entitled to his damages for breach of the compromise agreement and the company was not entitled to an injunction to prevent further disclosures of the kind put forward in this case. They were not trade secrets.

## Whistle-blowing

When discussing an employee's duty of confidentiality, mention should be made of the provisions of the Public Interest Disclosure Act 1998. The Act protects workers from being dismissed or penalised for disclosing information about the organisation in which they work that they reasonably believe exposes financial malpractice, miscarriages of justice, dangers to health and safety, and dangers to the environment. Disclosure may be made to an employer, but where the disclosure relates to the employer or there is danger of victimisation, it may be made e.g. to a regulator such as the Financial Services Authority for City frauds. Whistle-blowers who are dismissed or otherwise victimised may complain to an employment tribunal.

# EMPLOYEE RESTRAINTS ARISING FROM AGREEMENTS BETWEEN MANUFACTURERS AND TRADERS

The courts are concerned to prevent an employer from obtaining by indirect means restraint protection which he could not have obtained in an express contract with the employee.

**The following case is an illustration of the operation of this principle.**

## Kores Manufacturing Co Ltd v Kolok Manufacturing Co Ltd [1958] 2 All ER 65

The two companies occupied adjoining premises in Tottenham and both manufactured carbon papers, typewriter ribbons and the like. They made an agreement in which each company agreed that it would not, without the written consent of the other, 'at any time employ any person who during the past five years shall have been a servant of yours'. The claimants' chief chemist sought employment with the defendants, and the claimants were not prepared to consent to this and asked for an injunction to enforce the agreement. *Held* – by the Court of Appeal –

(a) a contract in restraint of trade cannot be enforced unless:
    (i)   it is reasonable as between the parties; and
    (ii)  it is consistent with the interests of the public;
(b) the mere fact that the parties are dealing on equal terms does not prevent the court from holding that the restraint is unreasonable in the interests of those parties;
(c) the restraint in this case was grossly in excess of what was required to protect the parties and accordingly was unreasonable in the interests of the parties;
(d) the agreement therefore failed to satisfy the first of the two conditions set out in (a) above and was void and unenforceable.

*Comment:* The restrictive agreement which was at the root of *Kores Manufacturing Co Ltd* v *Kolok Manufacturing Co Ltd* was not covered by the Restrictive Trade Practices Act 1976 which was not concerned with agreements between traders in regard to their employees and was decided on common law principles. These principles are that the agreement must be reasonable between the parties and reasonable in the public interest. Both of these points arose in

*Kores*, the Court of Appeal holding that the agreement was unreasonable as between the parties and also that it was contrary to the public interest, though the *ratio* is based on the fact that the agreement was unreasonable as between the parties.

## RESTRAINTS IMPOSED ON THE VENDOR OF A BUSINESS

In allowing restraints to protect the goodwill of the business sold, the law is only responding to commercial necessity. Unless the vendor was legally able to undertake not to compete, no one would buy the business. Nevertheless, such a restraint will be void unless it is required to protect the business sold and not to stifle competition.

It should be noted, however, that the protection of the business sold may in rare situations involve a world-wide restraint.

**Illustrative case law appears below.**

### British Reinforced Concrete Co *v* Schelff [1921] 2 Ch 563

The claimants carried on a large business for the manufacture and sale of BRC Road Reinforcements. The defendant carried on a small business for the sale of 'Loop Road Reinforcements'. The defendant sold his business to the claimants and agreed not to compete with them in the manufacture or sale of road reinforcements. It was *held* that the covenant was void. All that the defendant transferred was the business of selling the reinforcements called 'Loop'. It was, therefore, only with regard to that particular variety that it was justifiable to curb his future activities.

*Comment:* It would have been possible to sever the restraint by deleting the part relating to manufacture, but the court said that even if this were done it would still be too wide. Not to 'sell any road reinforcements in any part of the UK' was much too wide for what was a very small business, so the court decided.

### Nordenfelt *v* Maxim Nordenfelt Guns and Ammunition Co [1894] AC 535

Nordenfelt was a manufacturer of machine guns and other military weapons. He sold the business to a company, giving certain undertakings which restricted his business activities. This company was amalgamated with another company and Nordenfelt was employed by the new concern as managing director. In his contract Nordenfelt agreed that for 25 years he would not manufacture guns or ammunition in any part of the world, and would not compete with the company in any way. *Held* – The covenant regarding the business sold was valid and enforceable, even though it was world-wide, because the business connection was world-wide and it was possible in the circumstances to sever this undertaking from the rest of the agreement (*see below*). However, the further undertaking not to compete in any way with the company was unreasonable and void.

# RESTRICTIONS ON SHAREHOLDER-EMPLOYEES

The courts will generally allow wider restraints in the case of vendors of businesses than in the case of employees. However, what is the position where the employee is also a shareholder and, therefore, also a proprietor of the business?

**The following case is the first of its kind to come before the courts.**

## Systems Reliability Holdings plc v Smith [1990] IRLR 377

In 1986 Mr Smith commenced work with a company called Enterprise Computer Systems (ECS). He was a computer engineer engaged upon the reconfiguration of IBM mainframe computers. He became highly skilled in the modification and rebuilding of the latest generation of IBM's 3090 computer. His skill was instrumental in making ECS a leading company providing computer services. He was dismissed on 1 February 1990.

While he was employed by ECS, Mr Smith had purchased shares totalling 1.6 per cent of the holding in the company. After his dismissal, Systems Reliability Holdings plc acquired all the shares in ECS and Mr Smith received £247,000 for his 1.6 per cent holding. The share sale agreement had a restrictive covenant. Mr Smith had seen and initialled the agreement in final draft form. The covenant said: 'None of the specifically restricted vendors will during the restricted period directly or indirectly carry on or be engaged or interested ... in any business which competes with any business carried on at the date of this agreement ... by the company or any of its subsidiaries.'

Mr Smith was one of the specifically restricted vendors and the restricted period was in effect one of 17 months from the date of the sale. There was a further covenant which provided that: 'None of the vendors will at any time after the date of this agreement disclose or use for his own benefit or that of any other person any confidential information which he now possesses concerning the business or affairs or products of or services supplied by the company or any of the subsidiaries or of any person having dealings with the company or any of its subsidiaries.'

Soon after his dismissal and the share sale, Mr Smith set up in business supplying computer services. Systems Reliability asked for an injunction to enforce the restrictive covenant in the share sale agreement.

The High Court *held* that a restrictive covenant imposed upon the defendant as part of the claimants' acquisition of the shares in the company in which he was formerly employed was entirely reasonable and would be enforced against him notwithstanding that his shareholding in the company had amounted to only 1.6 per cent of the total. The present case was a true vendor and purchaser situation in which the defendant had received £247,000 for his 1.6 per cent share holding. There was no public policy to prevent the defendant from taking himself out of competition for what was a comparatively short period of 17 months, as required under the agreement, which on the evidence was entirely reasonable, or to prevent the imposition of world-wide restriction, which was also reasonable given that the business was completely international. The covenant would, therefore, be enforced.

*Comment:* As we have seen, the courts have traditionally allowed wider restraints on competition to be placed on the vendors of businesses than on employees. In Mr Smith we have a mix of the two and the court applied the wider vendor/purchaser approach.

It must, of course, be significant that Mr Smith got £247,000 for a comparatively small shareholding and it must remain doubtful whether the court would apply the vendor/purchaser test to an employee whose shareholding was merely nominal. Presumably, here the tighter employer/employee test of reasonableness would apply.

The matter is one of some importance because the number of employee/shareholders has increased rapidly over the past few years.

## RESTRICTIONS ACCEPTED BY DISTRIBUTORS OF MERCHANDISE

In order to increase the efficiency of distribution, a manufacturer or wholesaler may refuse to make merchandise available for distribution to the public unless the distributor accepts certain conditions restricting his liberty of trading. This is the main purpose of the solus agreement used by petrol companies. Such agreements are void unless reasonable.

There is an important distinction here between a garage proprietor who borrows money on mortgage of his own property from a petrol company and agrees to sell only that company's products for a period of time. The rule relating to unreasonable restraints of trade applies to the mortgage. However, if the petrol company is the owner of the land and garage premises and grants a lease to a tenant who will run the garage, then the rule relating to unreasonable restraints of trade does not apply to an agreement in the lease to take the petrol company's products.

**The following cases provide an illustration.**

### Esso Petroleum Co Ltd v Harper's Garage (Stourport) Ltd [1967] 1 All ER 699

The defendant company owned two garages with attached filling stations, the Mustow Green Garage, Mustow Green, near Kidderminster, and the Corner Garage at Stourport-on-Severn. Each garage was tied to the claimant oil company, the one at Mustow Green by a solus supply agreement only with a tie clause binding the dealer to take the products of the claimant company at its scheduled prices from time to time. There was also a price-maintenance clause which was no longer enforceable and a 'continuity clause' under which the defendants, if they sold the garage, had to persuade the buyer to enter into another solus agreement with Esso. The defendants also agreed to keep the garage open at all reasonable hours and to give preference to the claimant company's oils. The agreement was to remain in force for four years and five months from 1 July 1963, being the unexpired residue of the ten-year tie of a previous owner. At the Corner Garage there was a similar solus agreement for 21 years and a mortgage under which the claimants lent Harper's £7,000 to assist them in buying the garage and improving it. The mortgage contained a tie covenant and forbade redemption for 21 years. In August 1964, Harper's offered to pay off the loan but Esso refused to accept it. Harper's then turned over all four pumps at the Corner Garage to VIP, and later sold VIP at Mustow Green. The claimant company now asked for an injunction to restrain the defendants from buying or selling fuels other than Esso at the two garages during the subsistence of the agreements. Held – by the House of Lords – that the rule of public policy against unreasonable restraints of trade applied to the solus agreements and the mortgage. The shorter period of four years and five months was reasonable so that the tie was valid but the other tie for 21 years in the solus agreement and the mortgage was invalid, so that the injunction asked for by the claimants could not be granted.

*Comment:* The House of Lords appears to have been influenced by the report of the Monopolies Commission on the Supply of Petrol to Retailers in the United Kingdom (Cmnd 1965, No 264) which recommended the period of five years.

## Cleveland Petroleum Co Ltd v Dartstone Ltd [1969] 1 All ER 201

The owner of a garage and filling station at Crawley in Sussex leased the property to Cleveland and it in turn granted an underlease to the County Oak Service Station Ltd. The underlease contained a covenant under which all motor fuels sold were to be those of Cleveland. There was power to assign in the underlease and a number of assignments took place so that eventually Dartstone Ltd became the lessee, having agreed to observe the covenants in the underlease. Dartstone then challenged the covenant regarding motor fuels and Cleveland asked for an injunction to enforce it. The injunction was granted. Dealing in the Court of Appeal with *Harper's* case Lord Denning MR said:

> It seems plain to me that in three at least of the speeches of their Lordships a distinction is taken between a man who is already in possession of the land before he ties himself to an oil company and a man who is out of possession and is let into it by an oil company. If an owner in possession ties himself for more than five years to take all his supplies from one company, that is an unreasonable restraint of trade and is invalid. But if a man, who is out of possession, is let into possession by the oil company on the terms that he is to tie himself to that company, such a tie is good.

*Comment:* (i) The essential distinction is, as we have seen, that where the restraint on the use of the land is contained in a conveyance or lease the common law rules of restraint of trade do not apply. The person who takes over the property under a conveyance or lease has given nothing up. In fact he has acquired rights which he never had before even though subject to some limitations.

(ii) In *Alec Lobb (Garages) Ltd v Total Oil GB Ltd* [1985] 1 All ER 303 the claimant company borrowed from the defendant to develop a site. As part of the loan arrangements, the claimant agreed to buy the defendant's petrol for 21 years. Since the company was already in occupation of the garage and filling station when the agreement was made, it was subject to the doctrine of restraint of trade being a *contract* and not a *lease*. The High Court said that 21 years was too long and that the restraint was unenforceable. The Court of Appeal rejected that view and with it the opinion of the Monopolies Commission that it was not in the public interest that a petrol company should tie a petrol filling station for more than five years in the circumstances of this case.

Therefore, the *Lobb* case seems to show that the courts may not be prepared to help the so-called weaker party, i.e. the garage owner, as they were in the past. In the *Lobb* case the Court of Appeal said that each case must depend on its own facts. In fact the longer restriction seems on the facts of the case to have been justified. The loan by Total was a rescue operation greatly benefiting Lobb and enabling it to continue in business. There were also break clauses in the arrangement at the end of seven and 14 years if Lobb wished to use them. In view of the ample consideration offered by Total, the restraint of 21 years was not, according to the Court of Appeal, unreasonable and was, therefore, valid and enforceable.

(iii) These agreements would in any case appear to be contrary to the prohibition contained in the Competition Act 1998. Section 2 (2)(e) of the Act prohibits agreements which require the acceptance of supplementary trading conditions which have no connection with the subject-matter of the contract. This would cover cases in which a manufacturer or a supplier insisted that a retailer did not stock the products of a rival manufacturer, which is at the root of solus agreements, and yet has nothing essentially to do with the supply and sale of petrol and other products, such as oil, normally sold by a garage.

## INVOLUNTARY RESTRAINTS OF TRADE

We have so far considered, subject to an exception in the case of confidential information, restrictions against trading contained in contracts. However, the doctrine is not confined to these voluntary restraints. It extends to involuntary restraints imposed by trade associations or professional bodies upon their members. Such restraints are void unless reasonable.

**The following case provides an example.**

### Pharmaceutical Society of Great Britain v Dickson [1968] 2 All ER 686

The Society passed a resolution to the effect that the opening of new pharmacies should be restricted and be limited to certain specified services, and that the range of services in existing pharmacies should not be extended except as approved by the Society's council. The purpose of the resolution was clearly to stop the development of new fields of trading in conjunction with pharmacy. Mr Dickson, who was a member of the Society and retail director of Boots Pure Drug Company Ltd, brought this action on the grounds that the proposed new rule was *ultra vires* as an unreasonable restraint of trade. A declaration that the resolution was *ultra vires* was made and the Society appealed to the House of Lords where the appeal was dismissed, the following points emerging from the judgment:

(a) where a professional association passes a resolution regulating the conduct of its members, the validity of the resolution is a matter for the courts even if binding in honour only, since failure to observe it is likely to be construed as misconduct and thus become a ground for disciplinary action;

(b) a resolution by a professional association regulating the conduct of its members is *ultra vires* if not sufficiently related to the main objects of the association. The objects of the society in this case did not cover the resolution, being 'to maintain the honour and safeguard and promote the interests of the members in the exercise of the profession of pharmacy';

(c) a resolution by a professional association regulating the conduct of its members will be void if it is an unreasonable restraint of trade.

*Comment:* (i) Once again, the court is concerned with business efficiency and an arrangement under which retail chemists are prevented from selling general merchandise is not likely to lead to greater efficiency and competition. It was, therefore, struck down as too restrictive.

(ii) Agreements which involve the rules relating to the regulation of professional bodies are excluded from the operation of the Competition Act 1998 (*see* s 3 and Sch 4) but their activities are subject to common law principles of restraint of trade.

## CONSEQUENCES WHERE THE CONTRACT IS CONTRARY TO PUBLIC POLICY: SEVERANCE

Where a contract is rendered void by the judiciary, it is enforceable only in so far as it contravenes public policy. Thus lawful promises may be severed and enforced. A contract of service which contains a void restraint is not wholly invalid and the court will sever and enforce those aspects of it which do not offend against public policy. Thus an employee who has entered into a contract of service which contains a restraint which is too wide can recover his wages or salary.

The court will not add to a contract or in any way redraft it but will merely strike out the offending words. What is left must make sense without further additions, otherwise the court will not sever the void part in order to enforce what is good. For example, A agrees 'not to set up a competing business within ten miles' in a covenant when he sells his business. If we suppose that five miles would be reasonable, the court will not in fact substitute 'five' and then enforce the covenant because this would mean making a contract for the parties.

It is important also to note that the court will not delete the invalid part of a restraint clause if it is the major part of the restraints imposed.

Thus in *Attwood* v *Lamont* [1920] 3 KB 571 the heads of each department in a business of a general outfitter were required to sign a contract agreeing, among other things, after leaving the business not to be engaged in 'the trade or business of a tailor, dressmaker, general draper, milliner, hatter, haberdasher, gentlemen's, ladies' or children's outfitters, at any place within a radius of ten miles of the employers' place of business at Regent House, Kidderminster . . . '. Lamont, who was employed as cutter and head of the tailoring department, left and began to compete, doing business with some of his former employer's customers. The employer then tried to enforce the above restraint which was drawn too wide in terms of the various departments covered, since Lamont had never been concerned with departments other than the tailoring department. The court refused to sever the tailoring covenant from the rest because that would have meant severing almost the whole of the restraint in order to leave the restraint regarding tailoring.

A contrast is provided by *Goldsoll* v *Goldman* [1915] 1 Ch 292. In that case the defendant sold imitation jewellery and when he sold his business he agreed 'not for two years to deal in real or imitation jewellery in any part of the United Kingdom'. The court was prepared to sever the words 'real or' in order to make the restraint valid and restrict the defendant from competing in imitation jewellery. Only two words needed to be deleted and this was a very small part of the restraint as a whole.

*The business application:* Those in business may well insert a clause into their contracts which seeks to ensure that severance will take place even in circumstances where the courts would not be prepared to exercise their own powers of severance which are described above. Such a clause is often in three parts as follows:

- *so that it operates to remove any illegal provision altogether.* For example, the clause may provide that if any provision of the agreement is found by the court to be invalid or unenforceable, that invalidity or unenforceability shall not affect the other provisions of the agreement which shall remain in full force and effect;

- *so that it cuts down any illegal provision in extent but does not cut it out altogether.* For example, the clause may state that if any provision of the agreement is found to be invalid or unenforceable but would be valid or enforceable if some part of it were deleted the provision is to apply with such modifications as may be necessary to make it valid. In an anti-competition clause, for instance, there might be a number of sub-clauses restricting competition for one year, two years or three years, so that although the claimant under the contract is trying for three years, the court, if it finds this too long, may delete sub-clauses for two and three years and enforce the contract for one year as the courts are assisted to do by the severance clause.
- *so that it states that the parties will agree a substitute clause.* This is more difficult because an agreement to agree is not, in general, enforceable in English law (*see Walford v Miles* [1992] 2 WLR 174 in Chapter 1). However, the court has been prepared to imply a term to negotiate in good faith additional terms to be inserted into a written agreement (*see Donwin Productions Ltd v EMI Films Ltd* [1984] CLY para 365). If at worst this clause is not enforced by the courts, it carries some moral persuasion to a party wishing to renegotiate against one who does not, since the contract says that the parties will attempt renegotiation.

## PUBLIC POLICY: THE CONTRIBUTION OF PARLIAMENT

Some contracts are prohibited by statute in terms that they are illegal, the word 'unlawful' being used in the statute concerned. In this context 'statute' includes the orders, rules and regulations that ministers of the Crown and other persons are authorised by Parliament to issue.

The statutory prohibitions with which we are concerned may be express or implied.

### Implied statutory prohibition

In these cases the statute itself does not say expressly that contracts contravening its provisions are necessarily illegal. The statute may affect the formation of a particular contract as where a trader does business without taking out a licence. In some cases the statute may affect the manner of performance of the contract as where a trader is required to deliver to a purchaser a written statement such as an invoice containing, for example, details of the chemical composition of the goods.

In either case, whether failure to comply with a statutory provision renders the contract illegal is a matter of construction of the statute and is for the judge to decide.

If, in the opinion of the judge, the Act was designed to protect the public, then the contract will be illegal. Thus in *Cope v Rowlands* (1836) 2 M & W 149 an unlicensed broker in the City of London was held not to be entitled to sue for his fees because the purpose of the licensing requirements was to protect the public against possibly shady dealers. Furthermore, in *Anderson Ltd v Daniel* [1924] 1 KB 138 a seller of artificial fertilisers was *held* unable to recover the price of goods which he had delivered because he had failed to state in an invoice the chemical composition of the fertilisers as was required by Act of Parliament.

On the other hand, if in the opinion of the judge the purpose of the legislation was mainly to raise revenue or to help in the administration of trade, contracts will not be affected. Thus in *Smith v Mawhood* (1845) 14 M & W 452 it was held that a tobacconist could recover the price of tobacco sold by him even though he did not have a licence to sell it and had not painted his name on his place of business. The purpose of the statute involved was not to affect the contract of sale but to impose a fine on offenders for the purpose of revenue. In addition, in *Archbolds (Freightage) Ltd v Spanglett Ltd* [1961] 1 QB 374 a contract by an unlicensed carrier to carry goods by road was held valid because the legislation involved was only designed to help in the administration of road transport.

### Express statutory prohibition

Sometimes an Act of Parliament may expressly prohibit certain types of agreement. For example, the Competition Act 1998 in s 2 (2)(a) prohibits agreements, decisions or practices which directly or indirectly fix purchase or selling prices, and this would include resale price maintenance agreements. As regards enforcement, this is dealt with in Chapter III of the 1998 Act, and where the Director-General of Fair Trading is satisfied that a breach of the prohibition has occurred, he may give a direction to the parties concerned to modify or terminate the agreement and to refrain from entering into similar agreements.

Failure to comply with such a direction leaves the parties exposed to damages by those adversely affected by the agreement and the Director-General may ask for a court order to enforce his direction. Breach of that order would be considered as a basis for contempt of court proceedings.

## WAGERING CONTRACTS: INSURANCE AND DEALING IN DIFFERENCES

In essence, for a wager to exist it must be possible for one party to win and one party to lose and there must be two persons or two groups opposed to each other in their views as to a future event. Thus, where X, Y and Z each puts £5 into a fund to be given to the party whose selected horse wins a given race, there is no wager. The only commercial importance of the concept of wagering and the only reason why it is introduced in a book of this nature relates to insurance and dealing in differences (*see below*). A contract is not a wager if the person to whom the money is promised on the occurrence of the event has an interest in the non-occurrence of that event, e.g. where a person has paid a premium to insure his house against destruction by fire. Such an interest is called an *insurable interest* and is not a wager. However, to insure someone else's property would be a wager and not a valid contract of insurance.

The Gaming Act 1845 renders wagering contracts void so that there is no action for the bet or for the winnings. However, it should be noted that if the bet or the winnings have actually been paid over they cannot be recovered. Payment operates as waiver of the Act and the payment over of the money confers a good title to that money upon the person to whom it is paid.

It has become more common in recent times for persons to deal in differences, i.e. to bet on the future rises or falls in selected stock exchange indexes. No securities are bought or sold, the only transaction being the payment by one party to the other of the eventual difference in the indexes according to the accuracy or otherwise of the gambler's predictions.

It was decided in *City Index Ltd* v *Leslie* [1991] 3 All ER 180 that such a contract was validated by s 63 of the Financial Services Act 1986 so long as it was made 'by way of business'. The claimants offered clients a differences service and recovered £34,580 plus interest from the defendant whose predictions of rise and fall had not been successful.

## THE COMPETITION ACT 1998

The Competition Act 1998 (the 1998 Act) received the Royal Assent on 9 November 1998. It replaces a number of statutes which have up to now governed the competitive conduct of businesses in the UK. Most important are:

- the Restrictive Trade Practices Acts 1976 and 1977;
- the Restrictive Trade Practices Court Act 1976;
- the Resale Prices Act 1976;
- the anti-competitive practices provisions of the Competition Act 1980.

The scale and complex monopoly provisions of the Fair Trading Act 1973 are retained. This is despite the introduction in the 1998 Act of prohibitions based on Arts 85 (now 81) and 86 (now 82) of the EC Treaty of Rome.

The 1998 Act will operate in parallel with EC competition rules. Section 60 contains a 'governing principles' clause which seeks to ensure that questions arising under the 1998 Act in regard to competition within the UK are dealt with in a manner which is consistent with the treatment of corresponding questions arising in Community law in relation to competition within the Community.

### Anti-competitive agreements and practices: Chapter I prohibitions

Chapter I of the 1998 Act contains prohibitions that are closely modelled on Art 81 of the EC Treaty. It prohibits:

- agreements between two or more undertakings, decisions by associations of undertakings or concerted practices,
- that have as their object or effect the prevention, restriction or distortion of competition and which may affect trade within the UK or part of it, and where
- the agreement decision or practice is, or is intended to be, implemented in the UK.

All of the above elements must be satisfied if the prohibition is to apply and, in addition, the effect on competition must be 'appreciable'. The European Court of Justice in *Volk* v *Vervaeke* [1969] ECR 295 applies and rules that the prohibition in Art 81 and, therefore, in Chapter 1 does not cover insignificant effects. For examination purposes, it is sufficient to give the Director-General of Fair Trading's statement that he will take the view in administering the 1998 Act that agreements will *not* have an appreciable effect on competition if the market share of the parties to it does not exceed 10 per cent, nor will *most* agreements where market shares are below 25 per cent. As regards the requirement that there must be an effect on trade within the UK, ECJ rulings will apply.

It is not necessary for examination purposes to know this case law. However, it is necessary to know that, by reason of the principles they establish, it is likely that any economic activity carried out in the UK will be capable of affecting trade within the UK. So, provided that the parties to an agreement have more than 10 per cent of the UK, market, the agreement will be subject to scrutiny under the 1998 Act.

## Practices and provisions which infringe the Chapter I prohibition

The 1998 Act sets out a non-exhaustive list of a number of practices and provisions which will infringe the prohibition (there is a similarity with Art 81) as follows:

- directly or indirectly fixing purchase or selling prices or other trading conditions. This would include attempts to fix resale prices;
- limiting or controlling production markets, technical development or investment;
- agreements to share markets or sources of supply or doing so in practice;
- discrimination by applying different conditions to equivalent transactions with other trading parties so that they are at a competitive disadvantage;
- making the conclusion of contracts subject to the acceptance by the other parties of supplementary obligations which are unconnected with the subject of those contracts either by their nature or according to their commercial use.

## Chapter I exclusions

These include:

- mergers which have been cleared by the Secretary of State under existing legislation, i.e. the Fair Trading Act 1973 which will continue. Acquisition of a controlling interest in a company is also excluded as where A acquires more than 50 per cent of the voting shares in B;
- agreements controlled by other legislation, such as the general control of contracts between a company and its directors under the Companies Act 1985 (*see further* Chapter 20);
- agreements involving the rules regulating the conduct of a professional service, such as accounting, legal, and medical services where there is control by a professional body under its rules, e.g. the Law Society, provided the professional body is designated by the Secretary of State;
- agreements which under previous law were not sent for investigation by the Restrictive Practices Court by the Secretary of State because they were not considered significant. There is, however, a 'claw-back' provision under which the Director-General of Fair Trading can reconsider them if they appear to infringe the Chapter I prohibition which is unlikely.

The Secretary of State can make other exclusions as required:

- vertical agreements are excluded so long as they are not price-fixing agreements. A vertical agreement is one entered into by organisations operating at different levels of the market, as in the case of an agreement between a manufacturer and a distributor. A horizontal agreement is normally one made between organisations operating at the same level in the market, as in the case of an agreement between manufacturers or between distributors;

- agreements concerning land, i.e. agreements that create or transfer estates. Thus the law of landlord and tenant is undisturbed as are agreements relating to land use, e.g. restrictive covenants over land restricting the use of the land.

However, the Secretary of State has order-making powers where there may be adverse effects on competition in terms of e.g. access to facilities, such as marinas and taxi ranks.

## Chapter I exemptions

There are three exemptions as follows:

(a) an individual exemption granted by the Director-General of Fair Trading where it can be shown that the agreement will contribute to improving production or distribution or promote technical or economic progress and allows consumers a fair share of the resulting benefit. Furthermore, any restrictions must be indispensable and there must be no elimination of competition. Potentially exempt agreements should be notified to the DGFT and the DGFT may also give guidance without formal notice as to whether the agreement might or might not be exempted.
(b) a block exemption given by the Secretary of State on the recommendation of the DGFT covering particular classes of agreement which satisfy the criteria for individual exemption;
(c) agreements which are the subject of individual or block exemption under Art 81 are automatically exempt under the 1998 Act.

## Abuse of a dominant position – the Chapter II prohibitions

The prohibition on the abuse of a dominant position appears in Chapter II of the 1998 Act and is closely modelled on Art 82 of the EC Treaty of Rome.

Chapter II prohibits:

- any conduct on the part of one or more undertakings
- which amounts to an abuse
- of a dominant position in the market, and
- which may affect trade within the UK or *any* part of it.

In the same way as Art 82, the 1998 Act sets out a non-exhaustive list of the types of conduct which can amount to an abuse. The list includes:

- the imposition of unfair purchase or sale prices, e.g. unfairly high selling prices or unfairly low purchase prices and predatory pricing;
- the limitation of production, markets or technical developments to the prejudice of consumers, such as restricting output with a resulting rise in prices or refusal to supply;
- the imposition of unfair trading conditions over and above pricing, e.g. quality of products and service;
- applying dissimilar conditions to equivalent transactions thereby placing some organisations at a competitive disadvantage;
- tying, i.e. making the conclusion of a contract depend on the acceptance by other parties of obligations which have no connection with the subject-matter of the contracts, e.g. A, a manufacturer, requires a retailer not to stock the products of a rival manufacturer, B. Conversely, a retailer might prevent a manufacturer from supplying rival outlets.

Article 82 is not followed entirely since the Art 82 provision refers to a *substantial* part of the Community, whereas Chapter II refers to *any part* of the UK, so that localised markets are covered, e.g. the provision of bus services in local areas.

### What is dominance?

The 1998 Act does not set out thresholds for defining dominance but EC law cases will apply and these show that dominance has been found to exist where market shares have been in excess of 40 per cent in some cases and 45 per cent in others. This is also the Commission's view. The OFT Guidance note, however, quotes a lower market share: i.e. 20–40 per cent.

## Exemptions and exclusions

As with Art 82, there are no exemptions from Chapter II. There are exclusions which are similar to the exclusions provided in regard to the Chapter I prohibition.

It is possible to notify the DGFT in regard to conduct that may amount to a Chapter II prohibition for guidance or decision as to whether the prohibition does or does not apply.

## SCALE AND COMPLEX MONOPOLIES

The provisions of the Fair Trading Act 1973 have been retained in regard to scale and complex monopolies.

### Scale monopolies

A scale monopoly exists when at least one quarter of particular goods or services supplied in the UK are supplied by or to one and the same person.

The scale monopoly provisions of the 1973 Act allow the investigation of a particular market by the Competition Commission. Investigation was formally by the Monopolies and Mergers Commission. Investigation usually follows a reference by the DGFT where the behaviour of one business organisation supplying at least 25 per cent of particular goods or services in the UK could operate against the public interest. The remedies, should the Competition Commission find that the situation is against the public interest, are wide but importantly include the acceptance of behavioural undertakings not to pursue policies against the public interest and/or undertakings to sell off certain parts of the monopolistic organisation called divestment. This is a main reason for retaining the FTA 1973 provisions. Although in most cases the monopoly will be covered by the Chapter II prohibition, it may be that individual cases would be better dealt with by behavioural undertakings or divestment rather than relying on prohibition alone. In practice, it is likely that the FTA 1973 provisions will be used to regulate utilities which have natural monopolies, as was the case when British Gas plc demerged the transportation of gas from the general business of supply.

### Complex monopolies

A complex monopoly situation exists where at least one-quarter of particular goods or services are supplied in the UK by two or more business organisations which, whether by agreement or not or voluntarily or not, conduct their business in such a way as to prevent, restrict or distort competition. The DGFT can report these situations to the Competition Commission for investigation and report if he believes the public interest is adversely affected.

If the Commission does find that the monopoly is operating against the public interest, the Secretary of State has the power to impose divestment and behavioural undertakings. It is expected that the FTA 1973 powers will be used where businesses are not acting in collusion or concert and yet there is an anti-competitive situation. If there is evidence of collusion, the Chapter I prohibition will be applied.

Basically the UK has retained certain of its FTA 1973 powers because the new prohibitions in following the lines of Arts 81 and 82 also contain some of the defects in enforcement which have arisen from the blunt approach of prohibition.

## ENFORCEMENT

The DGFT may institute any of the following procedures where there are reasonable grounds for suspecting infringement of the 1998 Act.

### An order for production of documents

This will follow notice to the undertaking concerned such as the DGFT feels is reasonable in the circumstances of the case. The notice may require the production of documents or specific information. Copies of documents may be taken and explanations of them may be required.

### Dawn raid – without a warrant

Two working days' notice to the undertaking is required unless, e.g. the undertaking is already under investigation. The investigating officer(s) may enter premises and carry out an investigation; require the production of documents and information held on computer; take copies of documents and information and require explanations of those materials.

### Dawn raid with a warrant

No notice is required and, again, the investigating officer(s) may enter and search premises, take copies of documents and require explanations of documents or information on where they can be found.

### Sanctions for failure to comply

If a person does not co-operate with an investigation, a criminal offence may have been committed, punishable by a fine or imprisonment. In more specific terms, the offences might be:

● intentional obstruction of an officer;
● destruction, disposal, falsification or concealment of documents:
● providing false or misleading information.

Further sanctions are fines on the undertaking of up to 10 per cent of turnover; directions to modify or cease the abusive conduct, or to modify or terminate any agreement or to refrain from entering into similar agreements in the future; or a court order to enforce compliance with a direction. In this connection, decisions of the DGFT may be appealed to the Competition Commission.

## RELATIONSHIP WITH EC COMPETITION LAW

### Dual notifications

Where the agreement affects trade in the EU beyond merely the UK, dual notification to the DGFT and the European Commission will normally be made. After all, only the European Commission can give exemption from the Treaty of Rome, and since the 1998 Act gives an automatic parallel exemption, the dual application would appear to be the best course.

### Governing principles

UK law will now move along the same lines as EC law on this subject by reason of a clear direction that the 1998 Act requires those applying the Chapters I and II prohibitions – in practice, the courts, appeal tribunals and the Office of Fair Trading – to ensure, as far as possible, that there is no inconsistency with the way in which Arts 81 and 82 have been interpreted by the European Court of Justice or the European Court of First Instance. There is also a duty to have regard to relevant statements or decisions of the European Commission.

This 'governing principle' appears in s 60 of the 1998 Act and is quite new to English law.

## THIRD-PARTY ACTIONS

The 1998 Act does not give any express right for third parties, such as competitors or customers, to seek damages or other remedies for infringement of the Chapters I and II prohibitions. For an injured third party, complaint to the OFT under Chapters I and II is likely to be the best route for obtaining redress, though the OFT cannot award damages, but can set about remedying the position. Nevertheless, there is strong but not binding authority in English courts that third parties may recover damages for breaches of what were Arts 85 and 86 of the Treaty of Rome. Damages have, however, never been awarded. For a short discussion of the position, *see Garden Cottage Foods Ltd* v *Milk Marketing Board* [1983] 2 All ER 770 later in this chapter. Section 60 of the 1998 Act (the governing principles) also refers to the need for consistency between UK and Community law and refers to decisions of the ECJ and the Commission on civil liability for breaches of Community law.

# THE EUROPEAN COMMUNITY APPROACH TO RESTRICTIVE PRACTICES

Under Arts 81 and 82 of the Treaty of Rome all agreements between business organisations which operate to prevent or restrict competition in the Market are void.

## Restrictive trading agreements and the Treaty of Rome generally

We have already considered the position under English domestic law with regard to restrictive trading agreements and the relationship with the European Court and the Commission. Some brief consideration must now be given to the position under Community law.

### Policy and source of law

The provisions of the Treaty, which have been part of our law since January 1973, are based, as UK law is, on the protection of the public interest. The basis of the competition policy is to be found in Arts 81 and 82 of the Treaty. These ban practices which distort competition between members of the Community (Art 81), and prohibit the abuse of a monopolistic position by an organisation within the Market (Art 82). There is an additional aim of raising living standards.

## Application of Articles 81 and 82, Treaty of Rome

It is perhaps inappropriate in a non-specialist book of this nature to go through the many illustrative cases on the above articles of the Treaty of Rome which have been heard by the European Court of Justice. However, by way of illustration and to show the application of the Articles in English cases before English courts, we can consider the following. When doing so, it is worth noting that following the judgment of the European Court in *BRT v SABAM* [1974] ECR 51 that Arts 85 (now 81) and 86 (now 82) have direct effect in the UK, our courts have shared responsibility for the enforcement of Community competition law as the cases illustrate. They also provide examples of situations which might come before UK courts under Prohibitions I and II of the 1998 Act.

Now under the Competition Act 1998 UK courts are dealing with the prohibitions set out in Chapter I and Chapter II and so are applying English law, which is substantially the same as the Treaty of Rome provisions. In addition, the interpretation of the prohibitions will follow the line taken by European courts, so that there will be a fusion of rulings (*see* the Governing Principles provision (*above*) of s 60 of the 1998 Act).

## Article 81

Of interest here is the case of *Cutsforth v Mansfield Inns* [1986] 1 All ER 577. C supplied coin-operated machines to 57 Humberside public houses owned by Northern County Breweries. M acquired Northern and requested all the tenants of the old Northern public houses to operate equipment supplied by M's list of nominated suppliers. M refused to put C on that list. This was *held* to be an infringement of Art 85 (now 81), and an injunction was granted preventing M from interfering with C's agreements with the tenants of the 57 public houses and from taking any action to limit the freedom of those tenants to order machines from C. M was not infringing Art 86 (now 82) because they were not in a dominant position in the market.

## Article 82

An illustration of the use of Art 86 in an English court of law is provided by *Garden Cottage Foods Ltd* v *Milk Marketing Board* [1983] 2 All ER 770. Garden Cottage (the company) was a middle-man transferring butter from the Board to traders in the bulk market in Europe and the UK, and taking a cut of the price. In March 1982, following some packaging problems which the company appeared to have overcome, the Board refused to supply direct. It said that supplies must be obtained from one of four independent distributors nominated by the Board.

These distributors were the company's competitors. The company would have to pay more to them for its supplies than if it bought direct from the Board. Therefore, it could not compete on price, and would be forced out of business.

The company alleged that the Board was in breach of Art 86 (now 82) of the Treaty of Rome. This provides: 'Any abuse by one or more undertakings of a dominant position when in the Common Market or in a substantial part of it, shall be prohibited as incompatible with the Common Market in so far as it may affect trade between Member States . . .'.

The Court of Appeal, and later the House of Lords (*see Garden Cottage Foods Ltd* v *Milk Marketing Board* [1983] 2 All ER 770), decided that there had been a breach of Art 86 (now 82).

As regards remedies the Court was asked to grant an injunction restraining the Board from refusing to maintain normal business relations contrary to Art 86 (now 82). The case was dealt with on that basis. However, the House of Lords was of the opinion that the remedy of damages was available for breach of the Treaty but there is still some uncertainty about this. UK courts have not as yet clarified precisely what remedies are available in this area. It will be recalled that more recently the Court of Appeal decided in *Leyland Daf Ltd* v *Automotive Products* (1993) (*see* Chapter 5) that Automotive was not in breach of Art 86 (now 82) when they refused to supply goods to Leyland unless Leyland paid £758,955 which they owed to Automotive.

## Enforcement by European Commission

The responsibility for enforcement of the Articles lies with the European Commission. The Commission is able to levy fines of up to 10 per cent of worldwide turnover as a penalty for infringement. The classic decision of the Commission was in the *Tetra Pak II* (1992 OJL 72/1) case where the Commission levied a fine of 75m ECU (£52m) on an organisation for abuses of Art 86 (now 82).

## EC Merger Regulation

Mergers which potentially set up monopolistic undertakings are dealt with under the Fair Trading Act 1973 where the merger has only a UK dimension. Where there is an impact on other European states, the rules of the EC must be taken into account.

Under the EC Merger Regulation, which came into force on 21 September 1990, 'concentrations' (mergers) involving a combined worldwide turnover of more than 5 billion ECU (£3.9bn), and in which at least two of the parties also have a European turnover exceeding 250 million ECU (around £200m), and not more than two-thirds of the aggregate Community-wide turnover of the undertakings concerned are in one and the same member state, fall to the European Commission for assessment as the *exclusive* competition authority. Such mergers must be formally notified to the EC Commission not more than one week after the conclusion of the agreement or the announcement of the public bid or the acquisition of a controlling interest (whichever of these is the earliest). Article 223 of the EC Treaty allows member states to take measures to protect essential security interests and remove such mergers from the Commission's jurisdiction. In recent times a proposed acquisition of British Aerospace was removed from the Commission's jurisdiction by the UK government.

Changes were made to the above regulations by Council Regulation No 1310/97, which came into force on 1 March 1998. The old system, as outlined above, remains in place but the notification requirements have been extended to a wider category of trans-actions and, in addition to the above thresholds, mergers must also be filed in Brussels if:

- the aggregate combined worldwide turnover of the undertakings concerned is more than 2.5 billion ECU;
- in each of at least three member states the combined aggregate turnover of all the undertakings involved is more than 100 million ECU;
- in each of at least three member states identified above, aggregate turnover of each of at least two of the undertakings involved is more than 25 million ECU; or
- the aggregate Community-wide turnover of each of at least two of the undertakings concerned is more than 100 million ECU. However, if each of the undertakings involved in the transaction achieves more than two-thirds of its aggregate Community-wide turnover in one and the same member state, the EC merger regu-lation will not apply and the parties will have to make any required filings under national law.

## GRADED QUESTIONS

### Essay mode

1  Explain the controls over anti-competitive practices which were introduced by the Competition Act 1998. How are these controls related to the competition rules of the European Community?

*(The Institute of Chartered Secretaries and Administrators)*

2  International Instruments Ltd employ Ronald as a sales manager and Geoffrey as a computer software designer.

   (a) In Ronald's contract of employment there is a provision that should he wish to leave the company he will give one year's notice; and that he will not for a period of one year after leaving their employment solicit or approach any former customer of theirs nor will he work in the very specialised industry in which International Instruments Ltd are market leaders anywhere in the European Community.

   (b) In Geoffrey's contract of employment there is a provision that he will give one year's notice of intention to leave the company should he wish to do so.

   Both Ronald and Geoffrey leave the company suddenly and without giving notice. Ronald goes to work for another company, Amalgamated Instruments Ltd, who are engaged in approximately the same area of business as International Instruments Ltd although at the moment they have no products which are in direct competition; however, International Instruments suspect that Ronald is about to approach former customers and may well have been recruited with a view to leading an assault on International Instruments Ltd's market share with new products which Amalgamated Instruments are preparing to bring out.

Geoffrey has decided to leave computing to set up his own Woodland Craft Centre. His sudden departure has caused major disruption and it will be some months before a suitable replacement can be obtained.

Advise International Instruments Ltd on their rights and remedies against Ronald and Geoffrey.

*(The Institute of Legal Executives)*

3 Four years ago Victor joined the firm of Sparks, an electrical retail business, as a TV and radio repair man. Sparks agreed to train Victor, including sending him on a day-release course at a local college to gain a diploma in TV engineering. When entering into his contract of employment, Victor agreed to abide by a term stating that if he were to leave Sparks he would not engage in any activity related to the manufacture, sale, service or repair of any radio, TV, or other domestic electrical appliances for a period of three years within a radius of five miles of Sparks' shop.

Victor has now had a disagreement with Sparks, and wishes to leave. He has been offered a job as a technical sales assistant at a local electrical discount warehouse.

Advise Victor on the legal principles involved in determining whether Sparks may prevent him from taking this job, with reference to appropriate case law.

*(Staffordshire University, BA Business Studies. Business Law)*

### Objective mode

Four alternative answers are given. Select ONE only. Circle the answer which you consider to be correct. Check your answers by referring back to the information given in the chapter and against the answers at the back of the book.

*With reference to the following information answer questions 1 to 5.*

Upon entering the service of Pans plc (who manufacture kitchenware) as sales manager, Egon undertook by his contract that if, for any reason, he should leave that service he would never:

by clause (a) solicit any of the company's customers;
by clause (b) divulge to anyone details of certain secret processes;
by clause (c) set up in competition with the company.

Egon, who is now considering leaving Pans' employment, shows you a copy of the contract and wishes to know to what extent if he does leave he will be bound by the terms set out in (a) to (c) above.

1   Which one of the following areas of law is relevant?

    **A**  Treaty of Rome.
    **B**  Restrictive trade practices.
    **C**  Restraint of trade.
    **D**  Failure of consideration.

2   Which of the following statements is a correct application of the relevant law to clauses (a), (b) and (c)?

    **A**  Clauses (a), (b) and (c) are unenforceable.
    **B**  Clauses (a) and (c) are enforceable; clause (b) is unenforceable.
    **C**  Clauses (a) and (b) are enforceable; clause (c) is unenforceable.
    **D**  Clauses (a) and (b) are unenforceable; clause (c) is enforceable.

3   Which one of the following cases is relevant in reaching a correct conclusion in regard to clause (a)?

    **A**  *Forster v Suggett* (1918).
    **B**  *Home Counties Dairies v Skilton* (1970).
    **C**  *Robb v Green* (1895).
    **D**  *Kores Manufacturing Co Ltd v Kolok Manufacturing Co Ltd* (1958).

4   Which one of the following cases is relevant in reaching a correct conclusion in regard to clause (b)?

    **A**  *Robb v Green* (1895).
    **B**  *Home Counties Dairies v Skilton* (1970).
    **C**  *Forster v Suggett* (1918).
    **D**  *Kores Manufacturing Co Ltd v Kolok Manufacturing Co Ltd* (1958).

5   Which one of the following cases is relevant in reaching a correct conclusion in regard to clause (c)?

    **A**  *Faccenda Chicken Ltd v Fowler* (1986).
    **B**  *Nordenfelt v Maxim Nordenfelt Guns and Ammunition Co* (1894).
    **C**  *Esso Petroleum Co Ltd v Harper's Garage (Stourport) Ltd* (1967).
    **D**  *Wyatt v Kreglinger and Fernau* (1933).

*With reference to the following information answer questions 6 and 7.*

In order to ensure that its petrol and allied products are sold exclusively by certain garages and filling stations, Chronic Petroleum Ltd includes 'ties' to that effect for a period of five years in the supply agreements with those retail outlets. A competing oil company, Wizz Petroleum Ltd, offers Green, the owner of a garage which is a Chronic outlet, an interest-free loan of £40,000 if Green will breach his 'tie' with Chronic and sell exclusively the products of Wizz.

Green needs the cash urgently to develop the site and is keen to accept the offer made by Wizz.

Advise Green as to the legal implications involved.

6 Which of the following statements is a correct application of the law?

A Chronic Petroleum will be able to enforce its tie against Green and prevent the arrangement with Wizz.

B Green can go ahead with the arrangement with Wizz since the tie with Chronic is unenforceable.

C Chronic's tie is unenforceable without the approval of the Monopolies and Mergers Commission.

D Both the ties of Chronic and Wizz are illegal. Green would not be bound by either of them.

7 Which one of the following cases is relevant in reaching the correct conclusion in question 6 above?

A *Cleveland Petroleum* v *Dartstone* (1969).

B *Attwood* v *Lamont* (1920).

C *Goldsoll* v *Goldman* (1915).

D *Esso Petroleum* v *Harper's Garage (Stourport) Ltd* (1967).

8 Roach Ltd is a company whose business is the importing of fish through the port of Grimstoft. Tranter (Transport) Ltd is an associated company operating refrigerated vans to distribute fish to various parts of the country including the city of Midchester. This arrangement has enabled Roach Ltd to quote keener prices and provide a better delivery service than could be done by using other transport contractors.

Some months ago the members of the Midchester Fish Merchants Association, representing wholesalers in the Midchester Wholesale Fish Market, passed the following resolution: 'That all fish consigned to the Midchester Wholesale Fish Market be transported only in vehicles officially nominated by the Chairman of the Association and members of the Association shall not accept fish from any vehicle not so nominated.'

Shortly afterwards the Chairman of the Association nominated Carters Ltd as sole transporters and a letter outlining the new arrangement was sent to all importers sending fish to the Midchester Market.

In consequence, Roach Ltd cannot now send fish to Midchester Fish Market except by using transport provided by Carters Ltd. This involves additional costs which will necessitate an increase in the price for which the fish can be sold. Roach Ltd threatened to sue the Midchester Fish Merchants Association and the Association thereupon notified the agreement to the Department of Fair Trading.

As regards the agreement it is likely:

A That it is unenforceable under prohibition II of the Competition Act 1998.

B That it is enforceable and not contrary to law.

C That it is unenforceable under prohibition I of the Competition Act 1998.

D That it is unenforceable under the Fair Trading Act 1973.

*Answers to questions set in objective mode appear on p 707.*

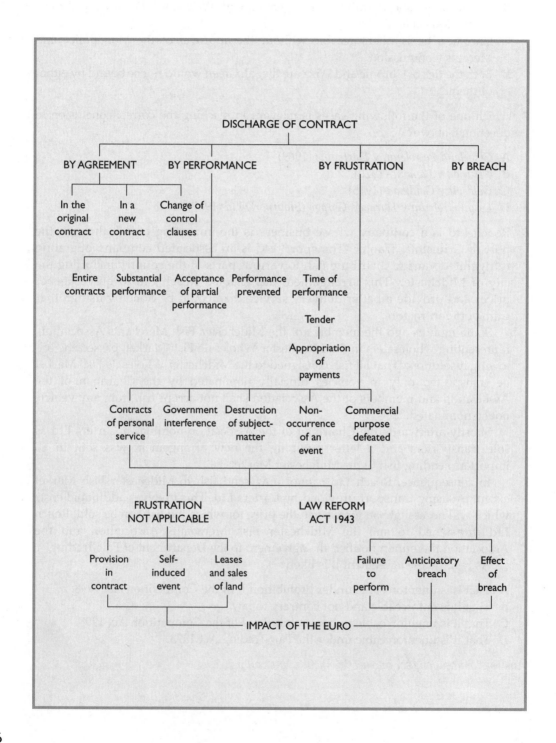

The objectives of this chapter are to consider the four methods by which a contract can be discharged or terminated and to provide an initial explanation of the rules relating to the limitation of actions which, while they do not properly speaking discharge a contract, may prevent an action being brought upon it.

The discharge of a contract means in general that the parties are freed from their mutual obligations. A contract may be discharged in four ways: *lawfully* by agreement, by performance or by frustration, and *unlawfully* by breach.

## DISCHARGE BY AGREEMENT

Obviously, what has been created by agreement may be ended by agreement. Discharge by agreement may arise in the following ways.

### Out of the original agreement

Thus the parties may have agreed at the outset that the contract should end automatically on the expiration of a fixed time. This would be the case, for example, with a lease of premises for a fixed term. Alternatively, the contract may contain a provision entitling one or both parties to terminate it if they wish. Thus a contract of employment can normally be brought to an end by giving reasonable notice. This area of the law is, of course, subject to statutory minimum periods of notice laid down by s 86 of the Employment Rights Act 1996. They are one week after one month's service, two weeks after two years' service and an additional week for each year of service up to 12 weeks after 12 years' service. Section 86 provides that the employee must, once he has been continuously employed for one month, give at least one week's notice to his employer to terminate his contract of employment. This is regardless of the number of years of service. Individual contracts may provide for longer periods of notice both by employer and employee.

### Out of a new contract

If the contract is *executory*, i.e. a promise for a promise, and there has been no performance, the mutual release of the parties provides the consideration and is called bilateral discharge. The only difficulty here is in relation to the form of the release. The position is as follows:

(a) written contracts may be rescinded or varied by oral agreement;
(b) deeds may be rescinded or varied orally;
(c) contracts required to be evidenced in writing, i.e. guarantees (*see* Chapter 3), may be totally discharged by oral agreement but variations must be in writing;
(d) contracts which are required to be in writing under the Law of Property (Miscellaneous Provisions) Act 1989, i.e. contracts involving a sale or other

disposition of land, are a special case so far as written contracts are concerned. They can be wholly discharged by an oral agreement but variation requires a written document containing the variation and signed by both parties. Thus a written contract for the sale of land, if varied by a change in the completion date, will require the variation to be in writing and must comply with the provisions of the 1989 Act (*see McCausland and Another* v *Duncan Lawrie and Another, The Times*, 18 June 1996).

If the contract is executed, as where it has been performed or partly performed by one party, then the other party who wishes to be released must provide consideration for that release unless it is effected by deed. This is referred to as unilateral discharge. In other words, the doctrine of accord and satisfaction applies. This matter has already been dealt with and is really an aspect of the law relating to consideration (*see* Chapter 2).

### Change of control clauses

Before entering into a contractual arrangement, many companies will have carried out some research into the stability of the other proposed party. These matters can, of course, be adversely affected by a change in the shareholder control of the proposed party and, therefore, the contract when made may be drafted to allow one party to terminate the agreement where a controlling shareholder in the other party is changed by a transfer of shares. Such clauses do not normally operate to end the agreement automatically, but at least the parties have agreed to give a party the right to terminate if he so desires. Such a clause can be most helpful, for example, where the new controlling shareholder is a competitor.

## DISCHARGE BY PERFORMANCE GENERALLY

A contract may be discharged by performance, the discharge taking place when both parties have performed the obligations which the contract placed upon them. Whether performance must comply exactly with the terms of the contract depends on the following.

## CONSTRUCTION OF THE CONTRACT AS ENTIRE

**According to the manner in which the court construes the meaning, the contract maybe an entire contract. Here the manner of performance must be complete and exact. An illustration is provided by the following case.**

### Bolton v Mahadeva [1972] 2 All ER 1322

Bolton installed a central heating system in the defendant's house. The price agreed was a lump sum of £560. The work was not done properly and it was estimated that it would cost £179 to put the system right. The Court of Appeal decided that the lump sum payment suggested that the contract was entire and since Bolton had not performed his part of it properly and in full he could not recover anything for what he had done.

*Comment:* The case of *Cutter* v *Powell* (1795) 6 Term Rep 320 is sometimes used to illustrate the point about entire contracts. The facts of the case were that a seaman agreed to serve on a ship from Jamaica to Liverpool for the sum of 30 guineas (£31.50 today) to be paid on completion of the voyage. He died when the ship was 19 days short of Liverpool. The court *held* that the contract was entire and his widow was not entitled to anything on behalf of his estate. While the case is valid as an illustration it has been overtaken on its own facts by more recent law. The Merchant Shipping Act 1995 now provides for the payment of wages for partial performance in such cases and the Law Reform (Frustrated Contracts) Act 1943 would also have assisted the widow to recover because the seaman had conferred a benefit on the master of the ship prior to his death (which would now frustrate the contract) giving the widow the right to sue the master of the ship for the benefit of the seaman's work up to the time of his death.

There is obviously some hardship when the entire contract rule is applied because some work is done by A for B which B does not pay for and certain other approaches have been worked out by the judiciary as follows.

## SUBSTANTIAL PERFORMANCE

If the court construes the contract in such a way that precise performance of every term by one party is not required in order to make the other party liable to some extent on it, then the claimant may recover for work done, though the defendant may, of course, counter-claim for any defects in performance. In this connection it should be noted that in construing a contract to see whether a particular term must be fully performed or whether substantial performance is enough, the court will refer to the difference between conditions and warranties. A condition must be wholly performed whereas substantial performance of a warranty is often enough. (*Poussard* v *Spiers and Pond* (1876) and *Bettini* v *Gye* (1876) – *see* Chapter 6.)

**An example of construction in favour of substantial performance appears below.**

### Hoenig v Isaacs [1952] 2 All ER 176

The defendant employed the claimant who was an interior decorator and furniture designer to decorate a one-room flat owned by the defendant. The claimant was also to provide furniture, including a fitted bookcase, a wardrobe and a bedstead, for the total sum of £750. The terms of the contract regarding payment were as follows: 'Net cash as the work proceeds and the balance on completion.' The defendant made two payments to the claimant of £150 each, one payment on 12 April and the other on 19 April. The claimant said that he had completed the work on 28 August, and asked for the balance, i.e. £450. The defendant asserted that the work done was bad and faulty, but sent the claimant a sum of £100 and moved into the flat and used the furniture. The claimant now sued for the balance of £350, the defence being that the claimant had not performed his contract, or alternatively that he had done so negligently, unskilfully and in an unworkable manner.

The Official Referee assessed the work that had been done, and found that generally it was properly done except that the wardrobe door required replacing and that a bookshelf was too short and this meant that the bookcase would have to be remade. The defendant claimed that the contract was entire and that it must be completely performed before the claimant could recover. The Official Referee was of opinion that there had been substantial performance, and that the defendant was liable for £750 less the cost of putting right the above mentioned defects, the cost of this being assessed at £55 18s 2d. The court accordingly gave the claimant judgment for the sum of £294 1s 10d.

*Comment:* (i) The Official Referee is a judge designated to consider cases referred to him by a court because they involve consideration of documents and accounts to assess what damages should be payable.

(ii) The case also illustrates that while full performance is essential to the right to be paid perfect performance is not required. This contract had been performed, but badly. Nevertheless, a claim could be made for the price of the work less a deduction, like damages, for the defendant's breach of the contract by bad work.

## ACCEPTANCE OF PARTIAL PERFORMANCE

If, for example, S agrees to deliver three dozen bottles of brandy to B and delivers two dozen bottles only, then B may exercise his right to reject the whole consignment. But if he has accepted delivery of two dozen bottles he must pay for them at the contract rate (Sale of Goods Act 1979, s 30(1)). It is worth noting here that s 30(2A) of the Sale of Goods Act 1979 (inserted by the Sale and Supply of Goods Act 1994) provides that a commercial buyer (as distinct from a consumer) may not reject goods for delivery of the wrong quantity where the seller can show that the excess or shortfall is so slight that it would be unreasonable to do so. In the above example the shortfall is not slight and a commercial buyer could reject the goods.

However, the mere conferring of a benefit on one party by another is not enough; there must be evidence of acceptance of that benefit by the party upon whom it was conferred. The acceptance must arise following a genuine choice.

**The following case provides an example of a situation in which there was no genuine choice.**

### Sumpter *v* Hedges [1898] 1 QB 673

The claimant entered into a contract with the defendant under the terms of which the claimant was to erect some buildings for the defendant on the defendant's land for a price of £565. The claimant did partially erect the buildings up to the value of £333, and the defendant paid him for that figure. The claimant then told the defendant that he could not finish the job because he had run out of funds. The defendant then completed the work by using materials belonging to the claimant which had been left on the site. The claimant now sued for work done and materials supplied, and the court gave him judgment for materials supplied, but would not grant him a sum of money by way of a *quantum meruit* (an action for reasonable payment for work done), for the value of the work done prior to his abandonment of the job. The reason given was that, before the claimant could sue successfully on a *quantum meruit*, he would have to show that the defendant had voluntarily accepted the work done, and this implied that the defendant must be in a position to refuse the benefit of the work as where a buyer of goods refuses to take delivery. This was not the case here; the defendant had no option but to accept the work done, so his acceptance could not be presumed from conduct. There being no other evidence of the defendant's acceptance of the work, the claimant's action for the work failed.

*Comment:* In practice, this form of injustice to the builder is avoided because a building contract normally provides for progress payments as various stages of construction are completed, thus making it a divisible agreement.

## FULL PERFORMANCE PREVENTED BY THE PROMISEE

Here the party who cannot further perform his part of the contract may bring an action on a *quantum meruit* against the party in default for the value of work done up to the time when further performance was prevented.

**The following case provides an illustration.**

### De Barnardy v Harding (1853) 8 Exch 822

The claimant agreed to act as the defendant's agent for the purpose of preparing and issuing certain advertisements and notices designed to encourage the sale of tickets to see the funeral procession of the Duke of Wellington. The claimant was to be paid a commission of 10 per cent upon the proceeds of the tickets actually sold. The claimant duly issued the advertisements and notices, but before he began to sell the tickets the defendant withdrew the claimant's authority to sell them and in consequence the claimant did not sell any tickets and was prevented from earning his commission. The claimant now sued upon a *quantum meruit* and his action succeeded.

## TIME OF PERFORMANCE

Section 41 of the Law of Property Act 1925 provides that stipulations as to the time of performance in a contract are not construed to be of the essence of the contract and, therefore, need not be strictly complied with, unless equity would have regarded them as such. There are the following exceptional situations in which time was of the essence even in equity.

(a) The contract fixes a date and makes performance on that date a condition.
(b) The circumstances indicate that the contract should be performed at the agreed time. These cases are:
   - *contracts for the sale of land or a business* because uncertainties as to the ownership of land have traditionally been regarded as undesirable and uncertainties as to the ownership of a business can affect its goodwill;
   - *commercial contracts*, such as the sale of goods;
   - *contracts for the purchase of shares* because share values are often volatile, which could affect the price at which it was agreed to sell them.

**The following case shows that in a commercial business contract the time fixed for delivery is of the essence. This includes early delivery!**

### Bowes v Shand (1877) 2 App Cas 455

The action was brought for damages for non-acceptance of 600 tons (or 8,200 bags) of Madras rice. The sold note stated that the rice was to be shipped during 'the months of March and/or April 1874'. A total of 8,150 bags was put on board ship on or before 28 February 1874, and the remaining 50 bags on 2 March 1874. The defendants refused to take delivery because the rice was not shipped in accordance with the terms of the contract. *Held* – The bulk of the cargo was shipped in February and, therefore, the rice did not answer the description in the contract and the defendants were not bound to accept it.

*Comment:* A buyer can reject in these circumstances even though there is nothing wrong with the goods and he merely wants to reject because the market price has fallen, as was the case here.

(c)  Where the time of performance was not originally of the essence of the contract or has been waived but one party has been guilty of undue delay, the other party may give notice requiring that the contract be performed within a reasonable time.

**An illustration from case law appears below.**

### Chas Rickards Ltd v Oppenhaim [1950] 1 KB 616

The defendant ordered a Rolls-Royce chassis from the claimants, the chassis being delivered in July 1947. The claimants found a coachbuilder prepared to make a body within six or at the most seven months. The specification for the body was agreed in August 1947, so that the work should have been completed in March 1948. The work was not completed by then but the defendant still pressed for delivery. On 29 June 1948, the defendant wrote to the coachbuilders saying that he would not accept delivery after 25 July 1948. The body was not ready by then and the defendant bought another car. The body was completed in October 1948, but the defendant refused to accept delivery and counter-claimed for the value of the chassis which he had purchased. *Held* – Time was of the essence of the original contract, but the defendant had waived the question of time by continuing to press for delivery after the due date. However, by his letter of 29 June he had again made time of the essence and had given reasonable notice in the matter. Judgment was given for the defendant on the claim and counter-claim.

*Comment:* That a waiver of a date of delivery without consideration is binding can be based on promissory estoppel (as in *High Trees* – see Chapter 2) said Denning LJ in *Rickards*, or on s 11(2) of the Sale of Goods Act 1979, which states: 'Where a contract of sale is subject to any condition to be fulfilled by the seller, the buyer may waive that condition'. This section was used to justify a waiver without consideration by McCardie J in *Hartley* v *Hymans* [1920] 3 KB 475.

This is an example of the doctrine of promissory estoppel being used by a claimant, i.e. as a sword not a shield, because a seller may tender delivery after the originally agreed date relying on the buyer's promise to accept such delivery by reason of his waiver. If the buyer then refuses to accept the delivery, the seller can claim damages and is in essence suing upon the waiver which is unsupported by consideration.

*The business application – clause making time the essence:* In spite of what is said above, it is not possible to rely in every case on the willingness of the court to imply that time is of the essence of the contract. Thus it is better to have an express term in the contract to this effect. Such a clause would have overcome the problems of a buyer of shares where the seller did not produce the share certificates in time, so that transfer was delayed and, yet, the court refused to regard this as a breach of condition and would not let the buyer call off the contract. Instead, the seller was awarded specific performance of it. This decision of the High Court in *Grant v Cigman* [1996] 2 BCLC 24 emphasises the need for a specific clause in the contract relating to time of performance which will be enforced by the court, which then has no need to imply a provision relating to time being of the essence.

The following is an example:

Time shall be of the essence of this agreement both as regards times, dates or periods specified in the agreement and as to times, dates or periods that may by agreement between the parties be substituted for them.

## TENDER

With regard to the manner of performance, the question of what is good tender arises. Tender is an offer of performance which complies with the terms of the contract. If goods are tendered by the seller and refused by the buyer, the seller is freed from liability, given that the goods are in accordance with the contract as to quantity and quality. As regards the payment of money, this must comply with the following rules.

(a) It must be in accordance with the rules relating to legal tender. By s 1(2) and (6) of the Currency and Bank Notes Act 1954 a tender of a note or notes of the Bank of England expressed to be payable to bearer on demand is legal tender for the payment of any amount. A tender of notes of a bank other than the Bank of England is not legal tender, though the creditor may waive his objection to the tender if he wishes. As regards coins, s 2 of the Coinage Act 1971, as amended by the Currency Act 1983, provides that coins made by the Mint shall be legal tender as follows:

(i) certain gold coins for payment of any amount. We are referring here to the gold sovereign. These are legal tender if struck after 1837. Even though the sovereign contains just under ¼ ounce of gold, it is valid only for £1, although it is worth much more as a collector's item;

(ii) coins of cupro-nickel or silver of denominations of more than 10 pence, i.e. 20p, 50p, £1 and £2 coins are legal tender for payment of any amount not exceeding £10;

(iii) coins of cupro-nickel or silver of denominations of not more than 10 pence (in practice, the 5p and 10p coins) are legal tender for payment of any amount not exceeding £5;

(iv) coins of bronze, i.e. the 2p and 1p coins are legal tender for payment of any amount not exceeding 20 pence.

There is power of proclamation to call in coins which then cease to be legal tender or to make other coins legal tender.

(b) There must be no request for change.
(c) Tender by cheque or other negotiable instrument or by charge card or credit card or Switch card is not good tender unless the creditor does not object. It should be noted that if a proper tender of money is refused the debt is not discharged, but if the money is paid into court the debtor has a good defence to an action by his creditor and the debt does not bear interest.

In connection with payment by credit card or charge card, the consumer normally discharges his obligation to the seller by payment in this way. If the card company cannot pay the seller as where that company is insolvent, the seller has no redress against the consumer, subject always to the terms of the contract (*Re Charge Card Services* [1988] 3 All ER 702).

## APPROPRIATION OF PAYMENTS

In connection with performance, it is important to consider the rules governing appropriation of payments. Certain debts are barred by the Limitation Act 1980 and money which has been owed for six years under a simple contract or 12 years under a specialty contract without acknowledgment may not be recoverable by an action in the courts. Where a debtor owes several debts to the same creditor and makes a payment which does not cover them all, there are rules governing how the money should be appropriated. These are as follows.

(a) The debtor can appropriate either expressly by saying which debt he is paying or by implication as where he owes £50 and £20 and sends £20.
(b) If the debtor does not appropriate, the creditor can appropriate to any debt, *even to one which is statute-barred* (*see further* Chapter 9). However, if the statute-barred debt is £50 and the creditor appropriates a payment of £25 to it, the balance of the debt is not revived and cannot be sued for (*Mills* v *Fowkes* (1839) 5 Bing NC 455).
(c) Where there is a current account, there is a presumption that the creditor has not appropriated payments to him to any particular item. The major example is a bank current account. Appropriation here is on a chronological basis, i.e. the first item on the debit side of the account is reduced by the first item on the credit side: a first in first out principle. This follows from the rule in *Clayton's Case* (1816) 1 Mer 572.

**The following case provides an illustration.**

### Deeley v Lloyds Bank Ltd [1912] AC 756

A customer of the bank had mortgaged his property to the bank to secure an overdraft limited to £2,500. He then mortgaged the same property to the appellant for £3,500, subject to the bank's mortgage. It is the normal practice of bankers, on receiving notice of a second mortgage, to rule off the customer's account, and not to allow any further withdrawals since these will rank after the second mortgage. In this case the bank did not open a new account but continued the old current account. The customer thereafter paid in sums of money which at a particular date, if they had been appropriated in accordance with the rule in *Clayton's Case*, would have extinguished the bank's mortgage. Even so the customer still owed the bank money, and they sold the property for a price which was enough to satisfy the bank's debt but not that of the appellant. *Held* – The evidence did not exclude the rule in *Clayton's Case*, which applied, so that the bank's mortgage had been paid off and the appellant, as second mortgagee, was entitled to the proceeds of the sale.

*Comment:* The operation of *Clayton's Case* is normally prevented by the bank stating in the mortgage that it is a continuing security given on a running account varying from day to day and excluding the repayment of the borrower's liability which would otherwise take place as credits are paid in.

## DISCHARGE BY FRUSTRATION GENERALLY

If an agreement is impossible of performance from the outset, it is void at common law (*Couturier* v *Hastie* (1856) – *see* Chapter 4). This is also at the root of s 6 of the Sale of Goods Act 1979 which provides that where there is a contract for the sale of specific goods and the goods, without the knowledge of the seller, have perished at the time when the contract is made, it is void (*see further* Chapter 11). However, some contracts are possible of performance when they are made but it subsequently becomes impossible to carry them out in whole or in part, and they are then referred to as frustrated.

The judges developed the doctrine of discharge by frustration, which applies, as the House of Lords decided in *Davis Contractors Ltd* v *Fareham* UDC [1956] 2 All ER 145, in the restricted set of circumstances where, without the fault of either party, there has been such a change in the significance of the obligation that the thing undertaken would, if performed, be a different thing than that contracted for. The subject is considered under the following heads.

## CONTRACTS FOR PERSONAL SERVICE

Such a contract is discharged by the death of the person who was to perform it; thus if A agrees to play the piano at a concert and dies before the date on which the performance is due, his personal representatives will not be expected to go along and play in his stead.

Incapacity of a person who has to perform a contract may discharge it. However, temporary incapacity is not enough unless it affects the contract in a fundamental manner (*Poussard* v *Spiers and Pond* (1876) – *see* Chapter 6).

The doctrine of frustration will usually only apply where there is no fault by either party. Where performance of the contract is prevented by the fault of one party, that party is in breach of contract and that is the proper approach to the problem.

**The following cases provide examples.**

### Storey v Fulham Steel Works (1907) 24 TLR 89

The claimant was employed by the defendant as manager for a period of five years. After he had been working for two years he became ill, and had to have special treatment and a period of convalescence. Six months later he was recovered, but in the meantime the defendants had terminated his employment. The claimant now sued for breach of contract, and the defendants pleaded that the claimant's period of ill-health operated to discharge the contract. *Held* – The claimant's illness and absence from duty did not go to the root of the contract, and was not so serious as to allow the termination of the agreement.

### Norris v Southampton City Council [1982] IRCR 141

Mr Norris was employed as a cleaner. He was convicted of assault and reckless driving and was sentenced to a term of imprisonment. His employers wrote dismissing him and Mr Norris complained to an industrial tribunal that his dismissal was unfair. The tribunal held that the contract of employment was frustrated and that the employee was not dismissed and, therefore, not entitled to compensation. The Employment Appeal Tribunal, to which Mr Norris appealed, laid down that frustration could only arise where there was no fault by either party. Where there was a fault, such as deliberate conduct leading to an inability to perform the contract, there was no frustration but a repudiatory breach of contract. The employer had the option of whether or not to treat the contract as repudiated and if he chose to dismiss the employee he could do so, regarding the breach as repudiatory. The question then to be decided was whether the dismissal was fair. The case was remitted to the industrial tribunal for further consideration of whether there was unfair dismissal on the facts of the case.

## GOVERNMENT INTERFERENCE

In times of national emergency, the government may often requisition property or goods in the national interest. This will have the effect of frustrating relevant contracts.
   **The following case illustrates this point.**

### Re Shipton, Anderson & Co and Harrison Bros' Arbitration [1915] 3 KB 676

A contract was made for the sale of wheat lying in a warehouse in Liverpool. Before the seller could deliver the wheat, and before the property in it had passed to the buyer, the government requisitioned the wheat under certain emergency powers available in time of war. *Held* – Delivery being impossible by reason of lawful requisition by the government, the seller was excused from performance of the contract.

## DESTRUCTION OF THE SUBJECT-MATTER OF THE CONTRACT

Physical destruction of the subject-matter of the contract operates to frustrate it.
   **The following case illustrates this point.**

### Taylor v Caldwell (1863) 3 B & S 826

The defendant agreed to let the claimant have the use of a music hall for the purpose of holding four concerts. Before the first concert was due to be held the hall was destroyed by fire without negligence by any party, and the claimant now sued for damages for wasted advertising expenses. *Held* – The contract was impossible of performance and the defendant was not liable.

*Comment:* A modern example of the rule is to be found in *Vitol SA v Esso Australia*, *The Times*, 1 February 1988, where the buyers of petroleum were discharged from the contract by frustration when the vessel and cargo were destroyed by a missile attack in the Gulf.

## NON-OCCURRENCE OF AN EVENT

Where the taking place of an event is vital to the contract, its cancellation or postponement will, in the absence of a contrary provision, frustrate it. However, if the main purpose of the contract can still be achieved there will be no frustration.

**The following cases provide examples of these rules.**

### Krell v Henry [1903] 2 KB 740

The claimant owned a room overlooking the proposed route of the Coronation procession of Edward VII, and had let it to the defendant for the purpose of viewing the procession. The procession did not take place because of the King's illness and the claimant now sued for the agreed fee. *Held* – The fact that the procession had been cancelled discharged the parties from their obligations, since it was no longer possible to achieve the real purpose of the agreement.

*Comment:* This type of decision is rare since the court will in general assume that the parties to a contract are not concerned with the motive for which it was made (*see Herne Bay Steamboat Co v Hutton* (1903) *below*). However, this seems to be an exceptional situation where the motive and contract were fused and could not be separated. '. . . it is the coronation procession and the relative position of the rooms which is the basis for the contract as much for the lessor as the hirer . . .', said Vaughan Williams LJ.

Also a contract will remain binding even if it turns out to be more expensive or difficult to perform than was thought. Thus a contract to ship ground nuts from the Mediterranean to India was not frustrated by the closure of the Suez Canal so that the goods would have to go around the Cape of Good Hope, which was twice as far. (*See Tsakiroglou & Co Ltd v Noblee Thorl GmbH* [1961] 2 All ER 179.)

### Herne Bay Steamboat Co v Hutton [1903] 2 KB 683

The claimants agreed to hire a steamboat to the defendant for two days, in order that the defendant might take paying passengers to see the naval review at Spithead on the occasion of Edward VII's coronation. An official announcement was made cancelling the review, but the fleet was assembled and the boat might have been used for the intended cruise. The defendant did not use the boat, and the claimants employed her on ordinary business. The action was brought to recover the fee of £200 which the defendant had promised to pay for the hire of the boat. *Held* – The contract was not discharged, as the review of the fleet by the Sovereign was not the foundation of the contract. The claimants were awarded the difference between £200 and the profits derived from the use of the ship for ordinary business on the two days in question.

*Comment:* (i) It may be thought that it is difficult to reconcile this case with *Krell* (see *above*). However, whatever the legal niceties may or may not be, there is clearly a difference in fact. To cruise round the fleet assembled at Spithead, even though the figure of the Sovereign (minuscule to the viewer, anyway) would not be present, is clearly more satisfying as the subject-matter of a contract than looking through the window at ordinary London traffic.

(ii) In addition, Vaughan Williams LJ and the Court of Appeal felt that motive was less relevant here. The judge said, 'I see nothing that makes this case differ from a case where, for instance, a person has engaged a brake (a form of carriage) to take himself and a party to Epsom to see the races there, but for some reason or other, such as the spread of an infectious disease, the races are postponed. In such a case it could not be said that he could be relieved of his bargain.' Romer LJ added, 'The ship (as a ship) had nothing particular to do with the review of the fleet except as a convenient carrier of passengers to see it; and other ships suitable for carrying passengers would have done equally as well.'

## COMMERCIAL PURPOSE DEFEATED

Physical destruction of the subject-matter is not essential to frustration. It extends to situations where although there is no physical destruction the essential commercial purpose of the contract cannot be achieved – a rule referred to as 'frustration of the common venture'.

**The following case provides an illustration.**

### Jackson v Union Marine Insurance Co Ltd (1874) LR 10 CP 125

The claimant was the owner of a ship called *Spirit of the Dawn* which had been chartered to go with all possible dispatch from Liverpool to Newport, and there load a cargo of iron rails for San Francisco. The claimant had entered into a contract of insurance with the defendants, in order that he might protect himself against the failure of the ship to carry out the charter. The vessel was stranded in Caernarfon Bay while on its way to Newport. It was not refloated for over a month, and could not be fully repaired for some time. The charterers hired another ship and the claimant now claimed on the policy of insurance. The insurance company suggested that since the claimant might claim against the charterer for breach of contract, there was no loss, and the court had to decide whether such a claim was possible. *Held* – The delay consequent upon the stranding of the vessel put an end, in the commercial sense, to the venture, so that the charterer was released from his obligations and was free to hire another ship. Therefore, the claimant had no claim against the charterer and could claim the loss of the charter from the defendants.

## SITUATIONS IN WHICH THE DOCTRINE DOES NOT APPLY

It is now necessary to consider the three situations where the application of the rules relating to frustration are limited.

## Express provision in the contract

In such a case the provisions inserted into the contract by the parties will apply. Thus in some of the coronation seat cases, e.g. *Clark* v *Lindsay* (1903) 19 TLR 202, the contracts provided that if the procession was postponed the tickets would be valid for the day on which it did take place or that the parties should get their money back with a deduction for the room owner's expenses. These took effect to the exclusion of the principles of frustration.

## Self-induced events

The rules relating to frustration do not apply where the event making the contract impossible to perform was the voluntary act of one of the parties.

**The following case provides an example.**

### Maritime National Fish Ltd *v* Ocean Trawlers Ltd [1935] AC 524

The respondents were the owners and the appellants the charterers of a steam trawler, the *St Cuthbert*. The *St Cuthbert* was fitted with, and could only operate with, an otter trawl. When the charterparty was renewed on 25 October 1932, both parties knew it was illegal to operate with an otter trawl without a licence from the minister. The appellants operated five trawlers and applied for five licences. The minister granted only three and said that the appellants could choose the names of three trawlers for the licences. The appellants chose three but deliberately excluded the *St Cuthbert* though they could have included it. They were now sued by the owners for the charter fee, and their defence was that the charterparty was frustrated because it would have been illegal to fish with the *St Cuthbert*. It was *held* that the contract was not frustrated, in the sense that the frustrating event was self-induced by the appellants and that therefore they were liable for the hire.

*Comment:* An otter trawl is a type of net which can, because of its narrow mesh, pick up small immature fish. Its use is restricted for environmental reasons.

## Leases and contracts for the sale of land

Judicial opinion has been divided as to whether leases and contracts for the sale of land can be frustrated since these create an interest in land which survives any frustrating event.

**The following cases and comment set out the present position.**

### Cricklewood Property and Investment Trust Ltd *v* Leighton's Investment Trust Ltd [1945] AC 221

In May 1936, a building lease was granted between the parties for 99 years, but before any building had been erected war broke out in 1939 and government restrictions on building materials and labour meant that the lessees could not erect the buildings as they intended, these buildings being in fact shops. Leighton's sued originally for rent due under the lease and Cricklewood, the builders, said the lease was frustrated. The House of Lords *held* that the doctrine of frustration did not apply because the interruption from 1939 to 1945 was not sufficient in duration to frustrate the lease, and so they did not deal specifically with the general position regarding frustration of leases, basing their judgment on the question of the degree of interruption. In so far as they did deal with the general position, this was *obiter*, but Lord Simon thought that there could be cases in which a lease would be frustrated, and the example that he quoted was a building lease where the land was declared a permanent open space before building took place; here he thought that the fundamental purpose of the transaction would be defeated. Lord Wright took much the same view on the same example. Lord Russell thought frustration could not apply to a lease of real property, and Lord Goddard CJ took the same view. Lord Porter expressed no opinion with regard to leases generally and so this case does not finally solve the problem.

*Comment:* (i) Even if the courts were prepared to apply the doctrine of frustration, it would not often apply to leases, particularly long leases. In a lease for 99 years a tenant temporarily deprived of possession as by requisition of the property would hardly ever be put out of possession long enough to satisfy the test of frustration (*see below*).

(ii) In *National Carriers v Panalpina (Northern) Ltd* [1981] 1 All ER 161 the House of Lords was of the opinion that a lease could be frustrated. The claimants leased a warehouse to the defendants for 10 years. The Hull City Council closed the only access to it because a listed building nearby was in a dangerous condition. The access road was closed for 20 months. The defendants refused to pay the rent for this period. The House of Lords said that they must. A lease could be frustrated, they said, but 20 months out of 10 years was not enough to frustrate it in the particular circumstances of this case. Once again, therefore, the decision of the House of Lords on the matter of frustration of leases was *obiter*.

(iii) In *Amalgamated Investment and Property Co Ltd* v *John Walker & Sons Ltd* [1976] 3 All ER 509 Buckley LJ was prepared to presume that the doctrine of frustration could be applied to contracts for the sale of land, though once again this decision was *obiter* because he did not have to apply the doctrine in this case. Walker sold a warehouse to Amalgamated, both parties believing that the property was suitable and capable of being redeveloped. After the contract was made, the Department of the Environment included it in a list of buildings of architectural and historic interest so that development became more difficult. The Court of Appeal *held* that the contract was not frustrated. The listing merely affected the value of the property and the purchaser always took the risk of this in terms of a listing order or, indeed, compulsory purchase. The contract could be completed according to its terms and specific performance was granted to Walker. Nor was the contract voidable under *Solle* v *Butcher* (1950) (*see* Chapter 4) because the mistake did not exist at the date of the contract.

## THE LAW REFORM (FRUSTRATED CONTRACTS) ACT 1943

This important statute has laid down the conditions which will govern the rights and duties of the parties when certain contracts are frustrated.

### Before 1943

The common law doctrine of frustration did not make the contract void *ab initio* (from the beginning) but only from the time when the frustrating event occurred. Thus money due and not paid could be claimed and money paid before the frustrating event was not recoverable.

**A somewhat startling application of these rules appears below.**

### Chandler v Webster [1904] 1 KB 493

The defendant agreed to let the claimant have a room for the purpose of viewing the Coronation procession on 26 June 1902 for £141 15s. The contract provided that the money be payable immediately. The procession did not take place because of the illness of the King and the claimant, who had paid £100 on account, left the balance unpaid. The claimant sued to recover the £100 and the defendant counter-claimed for £41 15s. It was *held* by the Court of Appeal that the claimant's action failed and the defendant's counter-claim succeeded because the obligation to pay the rent had fallen due before the frustrating event.

*Comment:* This case is included only to show how important the Law Reform (Frustrated Contracts) Act 1943 really is!

## After 1943

The position under the Act is as follows:

(a) money paid is recoverable;
(b) money payable ceases to be payable;
(c) the parties may at the discretion of the court recover expenses in connection with the contract or retain the relevant sum from money received, if any;
(d) it is also possible to recover on a *quantum meruit* (a reasonable sum of money as compensation) where one of the parties has carried out acts of part performance before frustration, provided the other party has received what the Act calls 'a valuable benefit' under the contract other than a money payment 'before the time of discharge', i.e. to the time of the frustrating event. There are difficulties in regard to the expression 'valuable benefit', particularly where the work is destroyed, since the Act is not clear as to whether a sum can be recovered by the person conferring the benefit where there has been destruction of his work. In *Parsons Bros* v *Shea* (1965) 53 DLR (2d) 86 a Newfoundland court, in dealing with an identical provision under the Newfoundland Frustrated Contracts Act 1956, *held* that the carrying out of modifications to a heating system in a hotel subsequently destroyed by fire could not be regarded as conferring any 'benefits' upon the owner. However, in *BP Exploration* v *Hunt* (*No 2*) [1982] 1 All ER 125 the claimants were engaged to develop an oilfield on the defendant's land and were to be paid by oil from the wells. After the wells came on stream but before BP had received all the oil which the development contract provided they should have, the wells were nationalised by the Libyan government which gave the defendant some compensation. The contract was obviously frustrated but Goff J, who was later affirmed by the Court of Appeal and the House of Lords, gave BP a sum of 35 million dollars as representing the 'benefit' received by the defendant prior to the frustrating event.

Clearly, here there was a surviving benefit conferred before the frustrating event and at the time of it, e.g. the value of the oil already removed by Mr Hunt before nationalisation and, of course, his claim for compensation against the Libyan government. None of these things would have been available to him before BP's discovery and extraction of oil on his land. Since the benefit conferred up to the time of frustration clearly survived the frustrating event, i.e. the nationalisation, the case does not resolve the problems posed by *Parsons Bros* v *Shea* (*above*) where the benefit did not survive the frustrating event.

However, it is the better view that there is no need for the benefit conferred to survive the frustrating event. The court can make an award provided benefit was once conferred. The fact that it did not survive the frustrating event can be taken into account by the court when assessing (and probably reducing) how much it gives to the claimant.

> *The business application – a force majeure clause:* It may be unwise in business to rely on the court declaring a contract to be frustrated and, of course, if the court takes the view that there is no frustration, the defendant may be required to pay damages for breach to the other party. It is common, therefore, to include in business contracts what are known as *force majeure* clauses. The expression means 'irresistible compulsion or coercion' and a typical clause will contain events likely to impede performance such as strikes, accidents to machinery, government restrictions in terms of licences, wars and epidemics and so on. The contract will go on to allow the parties to suspend or cancel the contract if one of the events has happened, and there will be no frustration. As Lord Denning said in *The Eugenia* [1964] 1 All ER 161, 'The contract must govern.'

## DISCHARGE BY BREACH

This occurs where a party to a contract fails to discharge it lawfully but instead breaches one or more of the terms of the contract. There are several forms of breach of contract as follows:

(a) failure to perform the contract is the most usual form as where a seller fails to deliver goods by the appointed time or where, although delivered, they are not up to standard as to quality or quantity;

(b) express repudiation which arises where one party states that he will not perform his part of the contract;

(c) some action by one party which makes performance impossible.

Any breach which takes place before the time for performance has arrived is called an *anticipatory breach*. Thus the situations described in (b) and (c) above are anticipatory breaches.

Where the breach is anticipatory the aggrieved party may sue at once for damages. Alternatively, he can wait for the time for performance to arrive and see whether the other party is prepared at that time to carry out the contract.

**The following cases provide illustrations of these points.**

### Hochster v De la Tour (1853) 2 E & B 678

The defendant agreed in April 1852 to engage the claimant as a courier for European travel, his duties to commence on 1 June 1852. On 11 May 1852, the defendant wrote to the claimant saying that he no longer required his services. The claimant commenced an action for breach of contract on 22 May 1852, and the defence was that there was no cause of action until the date due for performance, i.e. 1 June 1852. *Held* – The defendant's express repudiation constituted an actionable breach of contract.

*Comment:* (i) This decision should not be accepted as entirely logical. It is odd in a way to say that a person who has stated that he will not perform a contract when the time comes to perform it is for that reason in *breach of contract* and can be sued. This is particularly so where, as in this case, the defendant might still at the commencement of the proceedings have performed the contract when the time came. Of course, by the time the case came to court, it was obvious that the defendant had not performed his part of the contract and the device of anticipatory breach at least prevented the claimant's action from being defeated on the technicality that when he served his writ there was in fact no breach of contract as such. A case in which A was obliged to commence performance of a contract in December and said in the previous January that he would not do so and which came before the court in September of the same year might be decided differently because A would still have time to change his mind.

A more modern example of the application of the rule in *Hochster* is to be found in *Sarker* v *South Tees Acute Hospitals NHS Trust* [1997] ICR 673. The Trust sent a letter of appointment to a post within the Trust to S. It stated that her employment was to begin on 1 October, but on 6 September the offer was withdrawn. The Employment Appeal Tribunal held that S was an employee and could bring a claim for wrongful dismissal based on breach of contract. A claim for unfair dismissal could be brought in similar circumstances, but it would have to be a case not requiring one year's service, as where dismissal was connected with pregnancy (see *further* Chapter 15).

## Omnium D'Enterprises and Others v Sutherland [1919] 1 KB 618

The defendant was the owner of a steamship and agreed to let her under a charter to the claimant for a period of time and to pay the second claimants a commission on the hire payable under the agreement. The defendant later sold the ship to a purchaser, free of all liability under his agreement with the claimants. *Held* – The sale by the defendant was a repudiation of the agreement and the claimants were entitled to damages for breach of the contract.

*Comment:* (i) The charterer would have no claim against the purchaser of the vessel because restrictive covenants do not pass with chattels (which a ship is) but only with land. Compare *Dunlop* v *Selfridge* (1915) and *Tulk* v *Moxhay* (1848) (see Chapter 2).

(ii) This decision is more logical because by selling the ship the defendant had clearly put it beyond his power to perform the charter.

## White and Carter (Councils) Ltd v McGregor [1961] 3 All ER 1178

The respondent was a garage proprietor on Clydebank and on 26 June 1957, his sales manager, without specific authority, entered into a contract with the appellants whereby the appellants agreed to advertise the respondent's business on litter bins which they supplied to local authorities. The contract was to last for three years from the date of the first advertisement display. Payment was to be by instalments annually in advance, the first instalment being due seven days after the first display. The contract contained a clause that, on failure to pay an instalment or other breach of contract, the whole sum of £196 4s became due. The respondent was quick to repudiate the contract, for on 26 June 1957 he wrote to the appellants asking them to cancel the agreement, and at this stage the appellants had not taken any steps towards carrying it out. The appellants refused to cancel the agreement and prepared the advertisement plates which they exhibited on litter bins in November 1957, and continued to display them during the following three years. Eventually the appellants demanded payment, the respondent refused to pay, and the appellants brought an action against him for the sum due under the contract. *Held* – The appellants were entitled to recover the contract price since, although the respondents had repudiated the contract, the appellants were not obliged to accept the repudiation. The contract survived and the appellants had now completed it. The House of Lords said that there was no duty to mitigate loss until there was a breach which the appellants had accepted and they had not accepted this one.

*Comment:* (i) Although the respondent's agent had no actual authority, he had made a similar contract with the appellants in 1954, and it was not disputed that he had apparent authority to bind his principal.

(ii) It is worth pointing out that there was in this case no evidence that the appellants could have mitigated their loss. No evidence was produced to show that the demand for advertising space exceeded the supply so it may be that the appellants could not have obtained a new customer for the space on the litter bins intended for the respondent. Thus White & Carter may have had a 'legitimate interest' in continuing with the contract. Perhaps if evidence that mitigation was possible had been produced the House of Lords would have applied the principles of mitigation to the case, or held that White & Carter had no 'legitimate interest' in continuing the agreement. The judgments in the House of Lords indicate that a 'legitimate interest' is required in a contractor who wishes to claim for the price of unwanted services and Mr McGregor did not set out to prove that White & Carter did not have one. This view is supported by a decision of the Court of Appeal in *Attica Sea Carriers Corporation* v *Ferrostaal Poseidon Bulk Reederei GmbH* [1976] 1 Lloyd's Rep 250 where the charterer of a ship agreed to execute certain repairs before he redelivered it to the owner and to pay the agreed hire until that time. He did not carry out the repairs but the owner would not take redelivery of the ship until they had been done and later sued for the agreed hire. It was *held* that the owner was not entitled to refuse to accept redelivery and to sue for the agreed hire. The cost of the repairs far exceeded the value which the ship would have if they were done and the owner had therefore no legal interest in insisting on their execution and the payment of the hire. The court held that he should have mitigated his loss by accepting redelivery of the unrepaired ship so that his only remedy was damages and not for the agreed hire.

This line was followed also in the case of *Clea Shipping Corporation* v *Bulk Oil International, The Alaskan Trader* [1984] 1 All ER 129. A vessel had been chartered by the claimant owners to the defendants, the hire charge having been paid in advance. However, the ship broke down and required extensive repairs. The charterers thereupon gave notice that they intended to end the contract. However, the claimants decided to keep the agreement open and undertook the repairs and then informed the defendants that the vessel was at their disposal. The claimants said they were exercising their right of election conferred upon the innocent party in such circumstances to keep the contract open, thus entitling them to keep the hire money instead of suing for damages. Lloyd J denied the existence of an unfettered right of election for an innocent party to keep the contract running in such circumstances. He found that, in the absence of a 'legitimate interest' in the contract's perpetuation by the party faced with repudiation, the party concerned could, though innocent, be forced to accept damages in lieu of sums falling due under the contract subsequent to the actionable event. This restraint is founded on general equitable principles, to be based on what is reasonable on the facts of each case.

## ANTICIPATORY BREACH AND SUPERVENING EVENTS

It may be dangerous to wait for the time of performance to arrive since the contract may, for example, have become illegal thus providing the party who was in anticipatory breach with a good defence to an action.

**The following case provides an example of this risk.**

### Avery v Bowden (1855) 5 E & B 714

The defendant chartered the claimant's ship *Lebanon* and agreed to load her with a cargo at Odessa within 45 days. The ship went to Odessa and remained there for most of the 45-day period. The defendant told the captain of the ship that he did not propose to load a cargo and that he would do well to leave, but the captain stayed on at Odessa, hoping that the defendant would change his mind. Before the end of the 45-day period the Crimean War broke out so that performance of contract would have been illegal as a trading with the enemy. *Held* – The claimant might have treated the defendant's refusal to load a cargo as an anticipatory breach of contract but his agent, the captain, had waived that right by staying on at Odessa, and now the contract had been discharged by something which was beyond the control of either party.

*Comment:* A modern application of the above rule can be seen in *Fercometal Sarl* v *Mediterranean Shipping Co Ltd* [1988] 2 All ER 742. The claimants chartered a ship to the defendants. The charterparty (i.e. the contract) provided that if the ship was not ready to load during the period 3–9 July the defendants could cancel the contract. On 2 July the defendants said that they were not going on with the contract anyway but the claimant did not accept that breach and provided the ship, but this was not ready to load until 12 July and the defendants said again that they would not go on with the contract. The claimants sued for damages and failed. They could have based an action on the first breach but had not done so. Their action on the second 'breach' failed because the ship was not ready to load.

## EFFECT OF BREACH ON CONTRACT

Not every breach entitles the innocent party to treat the contract as discharged. It must be shown that the breach affects a vital part of the contract, i.e. that it is a breach of condition rather than a breach of warranty (contrast *Poussard* v *Spiers* with *Bettini* v *Gye* (*see* Chapter 6)), or that the other party has no intention of performing his contract as in *Hochster* v *De la Tour* (*see above*) or has put himself in a position where it is impossible to perform it as in *Omnium D'Enterprises and Others* v *Sutherland* (*see above*).

## OTHER MATTERS RELEVANT TO BREACH

Two further points arise in connection with breach of contract. The first is that the concept of contributory negligence does not apply. In *Basildon District Council* v *JE Lesser (Properties) Ltd* [1985] 1 All ER 20 the claimant sued for breach of contract in regard to the building of dwellings which had become unfit for habitation without repair. There was a defence that the damages payable should be reduced on the basis that the council's officers were guilty of contributory negligence. It was said that they should have noticed the lack of appropriate depth in foundations on seeing the building contractors' original drawings. It was decided by the High Court that the defence of contributory negligence did not apply in contract but only in tort.

It should be noted, however, that the obligation in the above case was entirely contractual. If the claimant could have sued, either in contract or in tort, as where the damage arises from a breach of contract and a tort, then even if the injured party decides to sue for breach of contract only the damages can be reduced if he is contributorily negligent (*see Forsikrings Vesta* v *Butcher* [1988] 2 All ER 43).

Secondly, the Drug Trafficking Offences Act 1986 in s 24 brings in what is called a 'laundering' offence under which anyone knowingly assisting with the retention, control or investment of drug trafficking proceeds could be liable to a maximum of 14 years' imprisonment. Banks, building societies, accountants, solicitors and other advisers are given protection by the Act if they disclose their suspicions about their client's finances if these seem to be connected with drug trafficking. However, the Act ensures that they cannot be sued for breach of contract if they pass on to the appropriate authorities their suspicions that any funds or investments may be connected with drug trafficking.

## IMPACT OF THE INTRODUCTION OF THE EURO

The immediate problem to be looked at is that of ensuring that commercial contracts affected by the arrival of the euro on 1 January 1999 do not operate where required beyond that date. The main reason for this will be that, as we have seen, a wide variety of contracts governed by English law provide that where a party is unable to perform his contractual obligations through factors beyond his control (such as in this case the abolition (eventually) of the currency in which he is required to tender payment), the contract is automatically discharged by frustration – a concept which has no direct equivalent in the rest of the EU, where law is based on Roman Law – or under a *force majeure* clause. The Maastricht Treaty deals with this by providing that, in the absence of an express contrary intention by the parties, the introduction of the euro will not:

- alter any term of the contract;
- discharge or excuse performance under any contract; or
- on its own give any party the right unilaterally to alter or terminate any contract.

The parties can, by expressing a contrary intention, agree that the introduction of the euro will end the original contractual intention.

Nevertheless, for contracts continuing beyond 1 January 1999, there will have to be some renegotiation to establish the equivalence of value between the originally contracted currency and the euro.

# GRADED QUESTIONS

## Essay mode

1 (a) How true is it to say that for a contract to be discharged by performance, that performance must be precise and exact?

   (b) Geoff agreed to paint Terry's house at an agreed price. When Geoff had finished the work Terry discovered that, although most of the painting was satisfactory, Geoff had forgotten to put a coat of gloss paint on one of the doors. Geoff was now ill and could not complete the work. Terry refused to pay him the contract price, claiming that the contract had not been completely executed and that therefore Geoff was entitled to be paid only a reasonable sum for the work he had actually undertaken. This, Terry claimed, was much less than the contract price.
     Advise Geoff.

*(The Institute of Company Accountants)*

2 Miller decides to stage a big band concert and engages a number of eminent musicians, paying each of them 10 per cent of the agreed fee at the time the separate contracts are made. Four days before the concert he is informed that four of the musicians will not be appearing. Shaw cannot get a visa to enter the country and Armstrong claims that his fee is not large enough. Dorsey has injured his fingers chopping firewood, while James says that he is incapacitated with a heavy cold. Miller believes that the concert will be a failure and decides to cancel it.
   Advise Miller as to:

(a) the effect of each incident on the contracts, whether he may recover the advance payment from any of these four musicians, and whether he has any further claim for compensation against any of them;

(b) his legal position with respect to the other members of the band who are willing to appear, and to the public who have bought tickets for the concert.

*(The Chartered Institute of Management Accountants)*

3 In what ways may a contract be discharged?

*(Association of Chartered Certified Accountants)*

4 Distinguish between the various types of misrepresentation, and show what remedies are available to the injured party. Are there any limitations on these remedies?

*(Staffordshire University. BA(Hons) Business Studies. Business Law)*

## Objective mode

Four alternative answers are given. Select ONE only. Circle the answer which you consider to be correct. Check your answers by referring back to the information given in the chapter and against the answers at the back of the book.

*With reference to the following information answer questions 1 and 2.*

Hatcher, an interior designer specialising in offices, was employed by Tally Ltd to design the interior of a small branch accounts office at Grantchester. The terms of payment were contained in a letter from Hatcher to Tally Ltd which set out the work to be done and concluded:

'The foregoing, complete, for the sum of £5,000 net. Terms of payment are net cash as the work proceeds and balance on completion.'

Hatcher commenced work in January and received £1,250 from Tally Ltd in February and a similar sum in April. The work was completed on 30 June and Tally Ltd moved staff and equipment into the new office on 1 July and full use was made of all the facilities provided by Hatcher. On 10 July Hatcher asked for payment of the balance of £2,500 but Tally Ltd replied complaining of bad workmanship but sent a further £500 saying that no more would be paid until the work had been completed to their satisfaction. In fact two doors were badly warped and will have to be replaced and a row of bookshelves which are shorter than specified will have to be remade. These defects can be put right for about £100 but Hatcher cannot do the work since he has now gone to America to carry out another contract. Nevertheless, he is demanding payment of £2,000.

1  Which one of the following legal concepts is relevant?

    **A**  The doctrine of frustration.
    **B**  Anticipatory breach.
    **C**  Entire contracts.
    **D**  Accord and satisfaction.

2  Which one of the following statements is correct?

    **A**  Hatcher is entitled to £2,000.
    **B**  Hatcher is entitled to £2,000 less a deduction for defects.
    **C**  Hatcher is entitled to a reasonable price.
    **D**  Hatcher is not entitled to anything.

*With reference to the following information answer questions 3 and 4.*

For some years past it has been the practice of Pathfinders Ltd, travel agents, to advertise their package tours on the screens of certain cinemas in London and the Midlands during January and February. The necessary contracts have been made annually by local branch managers on receipt of a letter from head office describing the particular tours to be advertised in their areas. Having considered its advertising policy for 2000, Pathfinders Ltd decided to abandon cinema advertising in favour of an increased television campaign, and during September 1999, letters were sent to branch managers outlining the new policy and instructing them not to make advertising contracts with local cinemas for 2000.

However, in July 1999 Earlybird, the manager of Pathfinders' Midchester branch, had entered into contracts on behalf of his company with the managers of certain cinemas belonging to a large chain and also with Luxor Cinemas, a small but successful chain operating only in the Midlands. The contracts were to run a series of advertisements on package holidays in France, Italy and Germany which Earlybird understood to be his company's policy for 2000, his information having been received unofficially from Clara, his girlfriend, who worked at head office.

As soon as he received the official letter from head office, Earlybird rang Stoney, the manager of the local Luxor cinema, and told him to cancel the contract. Stoney refused saying that he had no way of replacing the business and had already prepared the necessary frames of film in accordance with Earlybird's specification and that these would be run as agreed in January and February 2000. Earlybird wrote to head office informing them of the situation and they wrote to Luxor Cinemas saying that they did not regard themselves as bound by the unauthorised arrangements made by Earlybird, and would not pay for the advertising which they did not now require. Luxor Cinemas refused to accept this arrangement and ran the advertisements as agreed. They have now submitted an invoice for the agreed charge and Pathfinders Ltd are refusing to pay. What is the legal position?

3  One of the following legal concepts is relevant. Select:

    **A**  Remoteness of damage.
    **B**  Novation.
    **C**  Frustration of contract.
    **D**  Anticipatory breach of contract.

4  As regards the advertising arrangements made by Earlybird:

    **A**  Pathfinders can be made to pay the full cost of the advertising.
    **B**  Pathfinders can be required to pay only a reasonable price.
    **C**  Pathfinders are liable to pay Luxor the cost of preparation of the frames of films and no more.
    **D**  Pathfinders need pay nothing.

5  Frustration arises where:

    **A**  An event occurs after a contract has been made rendering its performance difficult to perform.
    **B**  A party expressly undertakes to do something which he then finds he cannot achieve.
    **C**  A contract is impossible to perform when it is made.
    **D**  A contract becomes impossible to perform after it has been entered into.

6  Which of the following statements about an active misrepresentation is true?

    **A**  It always involves the making of an express false statement whether made innocently, negligently or fraudulently.
    **B**  It is a type of breach of contract.
    **C**  It usually involves a misstatement of fact but may sometimes involve a false opinion.
    **D**  It cannot occur in contracts of utmost good faith.

*Answers to questions set in objective mode appear on p 708.*

# 9 REMEDIES AND LIMITATION OF ACTIONS

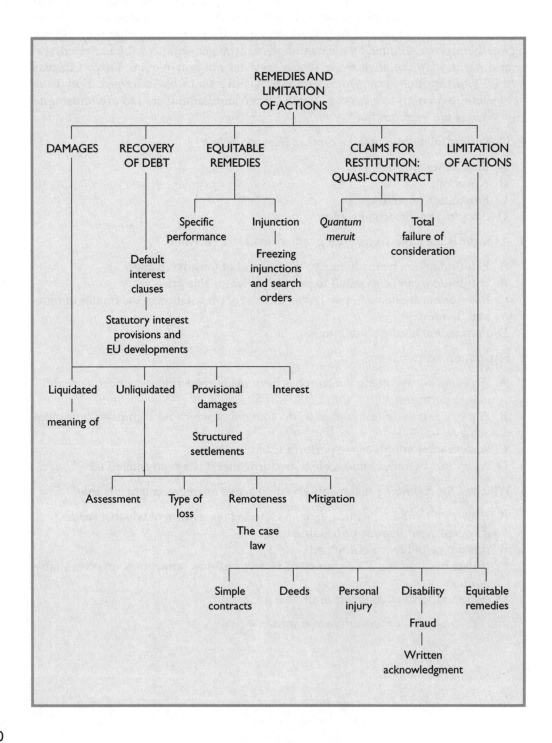

The objectives of this chapter are to consider the various remedies which exist both in common law and equity to redress losses arising from contractual relationships and the rules which cover the recovery of monetary compensation through damages together with the time limits which are placed on the bringing of claims and the recovery of debt.

## DAMAGES GENERALLY

This is the main remedy for breach of contract and the rules of law relating to an award of damages are considered below.

## LIQUIDATED DAMAGES

In some cases the parties foreseeing the possibility of breach may attempt in the contract to assess in advance the damages payable. Such a provision for *liquidated* damages will be valid if it is a genuine pre-estimate of loss and not a *penalty* inserted to make it a bad bargain for the defendant not to carry out his part of the contract. The court will not enforce a *penalty* but will award damages on normal principles used in the assessment of unliquidated damages (*see below*).

Certain tests are applied in order to decide whether or not the provision is a penalty. Obviously, extravagant sums are generally in the nature of penalties. Where the contractual obligation lying on the defendant is to pay money, then any provision in the contract which requires the payment of a larger sum on default of payment is a penalty because the damage can be accurately assessed. Where the sum provided for in the contract is payable on the occurrence of any one of several events, it is probably a penalty, for it is unlikely that each event can produce the same loss. If the sum agreed by the parties is regarded as liquidated damages, it will be enforced even though the actual loss is greater or smaller.

**The following cases provide illustrations of the above rules.**

### Ford Motor Co (England) Ltd v Armstrong (1915) 31 TLR 267

The defendant was a retailer who received supplies from the claimants. As part of his agreement with the claimants the defendant had undertaken:

(a)  not to sell any of the claimants' cars or spares below list price;
(b)  not to sell Ford cars to other dealers in the motor trade;
(c)  not to exhibit any car supplied by the company without their permission.

The defendant also agreed to pay £250 for every breach of the agreement as being the agreed damage which the manufacturer will 'sustain'. The defendant was in breach of the agreement and the claimants sued. It was *held* by the Court of Appeal that the sum of £250 was in the nature of a penalty and not liquidated damages. The same sum was payable for different kinds of breach which were not likely to produce the same loss. Furthermore, its size suggested that it was not a genuine pre-estimate of loss.

*Comment:* A contrast is provided by *Dunlop* v *New Garage & Motor Co Ltd* [1915] AC 79 where the contract provided that the defendants would have to pay £5 for every tyre sold below the list price. The House of Lords *held* that this was an honest attempt to provide for a breach and was recoverable as liquidated damages. Privity problems did not arise here, even though the Contracts (Rights of Third Parties) Act 1999 was not then in force, because the wholesalers were Dunlop's agents (*see further* Chapter 2).

### Cellulose Acetate Silk Co Ltd v Widnes Foundry Ltd [1933] AC 20

The Widnes Foundry entered into a contract to erect a plant for the Silk Co by a certain date. It was also agreed that the Widnes Foundry would pay the Silk Co £20 per week for every week it took in erecting the plant beyond the agreed date. In the event the plant was completed 30 weeks late, and the Silk Co claimed for its actual loss, which was £5,850. *Held* – The Widnes Foundry was only liable to pay £20 per week as agreed.

## UNLIQUIDATED DAMAGES

### Assessment

Unliquidated damages are intended as compensation for the claimant's loss and not as punishment for the defendant. Thus where no loss has been suffered, as where a seller fails to deliver the goods but the buyer is able to purchase elsewhere at no extra cost, the court will award *nominal* damages, i.e. an award of a small sum, e.g. £2, to reflect the view that any loss or damage is purely technical. An additional example arises in actions for loss of earnings arising from a breach of contract where damages are reduced after taking into account the claimant's liability to taxation.

Exemplary or punitive damages which exceed the actual loss suffered by an amount intended to punish the offending party are not awarded for breach of contract. The intention is that the claimant should be placed in the same situation as if the contract had been performed.

Thus, in an action by an employee for wrongful dismissal, the court will base its award on 'net' wages, i.e. after deduction of income tax and national insurance contributions. An award based on 'gross' wages or salary would make the employee better off than if the contract had continued.

**The following cases and comment illustrate the judicial approach.**

### Beach v Reed Corrugated Cases Ltd [1956] 2 All ER 652

This was an action brought by the claimant for wrongful dismissal by the defendants. The claimant was the managing director of the company and he had a 15-year contract from

21 December 1950 at a salary of £5,000 per annum. His contract was terminated in August 1954 when he was 54 years old and the sum of money that he might have earned would have been £55,000, but the general damages awarded to him were £18,000 after the court had taken into account income tax, including tax on his private investments.

*Comment:* (i) In a later case and on similar reasoning it was held that what the claimant would have paid by way of national insurance contributions must also be deducted (*see Cooper v Firth Brown Ltd* [1963] 2 All ER 31).

(ii) It must be said that some of the 'tax must be deducted' cases are far from clear in terms of how the court reaches its final conclusion. The clearest of all is *Shove v Downs Surgical plc* [1984] 1 All ER 7 where the claimant had been wrongfully dismissed 30 months before the end of a fixed-term contract of employment as managing director. The figures involved are set out in the judgment as follows:

|  | £ |
|---|---|
| Gross pay for the 30 months | 90,000 |
| Court's estimate of net pay | 53,000 |
|  |  |
| *Initial award* | 53,000 |
|  |  |
| Of this £30,000 is tax free. (See now s 188 of the Income and Corporation Taxes Act 1988.) | 30,000 |
|  | 23,000 |
| This is taxable in Mr Shove's hands. (*See now* s 148 of the Income and Corporation Tax Act 1988.) The tax will be, say, £6,000 on the £23,000, depending on personal circumstances. |  |
|  |  |
| Therefore, the court's final award to Mr Shove is | 59,000 |
|  |  |
| To give | 53,000 net |

(iii) In *C & P Haulage v Middleton* [1983] 3 All ER 94 C & P let Mr Middleton have a licence for six months renewable of premises from which he conducted a business as a self-employed engineer. He lived in a council house and would have used his own garage there, but the council objected. There was a quarrel between the parties and M was evicted from the premises before the licence term expired. This was a breach of contract by C & P. M stopped a cheque which was payable to C & P because of his grievance. They sued him on it. He counter-claimed for damages because of his eviction. In fact the council had let him use his own garage for the remainder of the six months' term. *Held* – by the Court of Appeal – that since he had paid no rent for the premises in which he had worked following his eviction, he was no worse off than if the contract had been properly carried out. It was not the function of the court to put a claimant in a better position than he would have been if the contract had not been broken. Only nominal damages were awarded.

(iv) Damages have been awarded for the loss of a chance. This is not prevented by the rule that the claimant must not be better off. Thus in *Chaplin v Hicks* [1911] 2 KB 786 the claimant who had won earlier stages of a beauty contest was, by error of the defendant organiser, not invited to the final. Although it was by no means certain that she would have won, the claimant was awarded £100 damages. In a similar case, the Court of Appeal affirmed an award of a sum of money for loss of a chance where, because of personal injuries suffered in a road accident caused by the negligence of the defendant, the claimant was unable to qualify and obtain employment as a drama teacher. Once again, a percentage of the damages was awarded for loss of a chance (see *Doyle* v *Wallace* [1998] *Current Law* para 125).

## Type of loss recoverable

Damages can include compensation for financial loss, personal injury and damage to property. Also there may be included a sum by way of compensation for disappointment, vexation and mental distress.

The following case provides an illustration of the mental distress awards.

### Jarvis v Swans Tours Ltd [1973] 1 All ER 71

Swans promised the claimant a 'Houseparty' holiday in Switzerland. Some of the more important things promised were a welcome party on arrival: afternoon tea and cake, Swiss dinner by candlelight, fondue party, yodeller evening and farewell party. Also the hotel owner was said to speak English.

Among the matters which the claimant complained about was the fact that the hotel owner could not speak English. This meant he had no one to talk to since, although there were 13 people present during the first week, he was on his own for the second week. The cake for tea was potato crisps and dry nutcake. The yodeller evening consisted of a local man who came in his overalls and sang a few songs very quickly. The Court of Appeal *held* that the claimant was entitled to an award of £125 damages. (Incidentally the holiday had cost £63.)

*Comment:* Damages for disappointment, inconvenience or loss of enjoyment are not awarded except in contracts which are for the provision of pleasure. Such damage may be foreseeable in other contracts but is not awarded as a matter of public policy. Thus in *Alexander v Rolls-Royce Motor Cars, The Times*, 4 May 1996 the Court of Appeal held that the owner of a Rolls Royce car could not claim an extra measure of damages for disappointment, loss of enjoyment or distress as part of an award of damages for breach of a contract to repair. It was accepted by the court that the car had been bought for pleasure, prestige and enjoyment, but that was not enough to bring the case outside the general rule that disappointment damages were not awarded for breach of a commercial contract.

## Remoteness

Apart from the question of *assessment*, the matter of *remoteness of damage* arises. The consequence of a breach of contract may be far-reaching and the law must draw a line somewhere and say that damages incurred beyond a certain limit are too remote to be recovered. Damages in contract must, therefore, be proximate.

The modern law regarding remoteness of damage in contract is based upon the case of *Hadley* v *Baxendale* (*see below*), as further explained in *The Heron II* (*see below*). These cases are authority for the statement that damages in contract will be too remote to be recovered unless they arise naturally, i.e. in the usual course of things, or if they do not arise naturally they are such that the defendant, as a reasonable man, *ought* to have had them in contemplation as likely to result. Damage which does not arise naturally and which would not have been in the contemplation of the reasonable man can only be recovered if the defendant was made aware of it *and* agreed to accept the risk of the loss.

**The following cases illustrate the above rules.**

### Hadley v Baxendale (1854) 9 Exch 341

The claimant was a miller at Gloucester. The driving shaft of the mill being broken, the claimant engaged the defendant, a carrier, to take it to the makers at Greenwich so that they might use it in making a new one. The defendant delayed delivery of the shaft beyond a reasonable time, so that the mill was idle for much longer than should have been necessary. The claimant now sued in respect of loss of profits during the period of additional delay. The court decided that there were only two possible grounds on which the claimant could succeed. (a) That in the usual course of things, the work of the mill would cease altogether for want of the shaft. This the court rejected because, to take only one reasonable possibility, the claimant might have had a spare. (b) That the special circumstances were fully explained, so that the defendant was made aware of the possible loss. The evidence showed that there had been no such explanation. In fact the only information given to the defendant was that the article to be carried was the broken shaft of a mill, and that the claimant was the miller of that mill. *Held* – The claimant's action failed, the damage being too remote.

*Comment:* (i) The loss here did not arise *naturally* from the breach because there might have been a spare. The fact that there was no spare was not within the contemplation of the defendant and he had not even been told about it, much less accepted the risk. The defendant did not know that there was no spare nor as a reasonable man ought he to have known there was not.

(ii) Damage caused by a supervening event may also be too remote. In *Beoco v Alfa Laval Co, The Times*, 12 January 1994 Alfa installed a heat exchanger at Beoco's works. It developed a crack and a third party, S, was brought in to repair it. The work was done negligently and shortly afterwards the exchanger exploded causing damage to property and economic loss of profit until it was put right. It was held that Alfa was liable in damages for the costs of replacing the heat exchanger and for loss of profit up to the time of repair but not subsequently. Although the matter is not raised in the report, presumably S would be liable for the subsequent loss.

### The Heron II (Koufos v Czarnikow) [1967] 3 All ER 686

Shipowners carrying sugar from Constanza to Basra delayed delivery at Basra for nine days during which time the market in sugar there fell and the charterers lost money. It was *held* that they could recover damages from the shipowners because the very existence of a 'market' for goods implied that prices might fluctuate and a fall in sugar prices was likely or in contemplation.

*Comment:* (i) The existence of a major sugar market at Basra made it within the *contemplation* of the defendants that the claimant might sell the sugar and not merely use it in a business.

(ii) As Lord Hodson said in his judgment: 'Goods may be intended for the purpose of stocking or consumption at the port of destination and that the contemplation of the parties that the goods may be resold is not necessarily to be inferred.' He went on to decide, however, that resale must be inferred as in contemplation because Basra was a well-known sugar market. Damages of £4,183 were awarded, this being the fall in the price of sugar between the date when the ship did arrive and the date when she should have arrived.

(iii) The contemplation test was, of course, set out in *Hadley* as the above Comment to the summary of the case shows. So what is new about the ruling of the House of Lords in *Heron II*? Well, *Heron II* deals with a problem that had arisen following the interpretation by subsequent courts in subsequent cases that the test in *Hadley* was foreseeability of damage. *Heron II* merely restores, in an authoritative way, the *Hadley* rule of contemplation. This is a tighter test for loss. A person may *foresee* all sorts of damage but not actually *contemplate* it. This makes the contract damage ruling different from the tort damage ruling in, say, personal injury following on a negligent act, where the test is foreseeability.

### Horne v Midland Railway Co (1873) LR 8 CP 131

The claimant had entered into a contract to sell 4,595 pairs of boots to the French Army at a price above the market price. The defendants were responsible for a delay in the delivery of boots, and the purchasers refused to accept delivery, regarding time as the essence of the contract. The claimant's action for damages was based on the contract price, namely 4s per pair, but it was held that he could only recover the market price of 2s 9d per pair unless he could show that the defendants were aware of the exceptional profit involved, and that they had undertaken to be liable for its loss.

*Comment:* In *Simpson v London & North Western Rail Co* (1876) 1 QBD 274 the claimant entrusted samples of his products to the defendants so that they could deliver them to Newcastle for an agricultural exhibition. The goods were marked: 'Must be at Newcastle on Monday certain'. The defendants did not get them to Newcastle on time and were held liable for the claimant's prospective loss of profit arising because he could not exhibit at Newcastle. They had agreed to carry the goods knowing of the special instructions of the customer.

### Victoria Laundry Ltd v Newman Industries Ltd [1949] 2 KB 528

The defendants agreed to deliver a new boiler to the claimants by a certain date but failed to do so, being 22 weeks late, with the result that the claimants lost: (a) normal business profits during the period of delay, and (b) profits from dyeing contracts which were offered to them during the period. It was *held* that (a) but not (b) were recoverable as damages.

*Comment:* The general loss of profit in this case arises naturally from the breach and no further 'contemplation' or 'notice' test need be applied. The loss of profit on the dyeing contracts was not *known* to the defendants nor as reasonable men *ought* they to have had it in *contemplation*.

## MITIGATION OF LOSS

The injured party has a duty to *mitigate* or minimise his loss, i.e. he must take all reasonable steps to reduce it. Thus a seller whose goods are rejected must attempt to get the best price for them elsewhere, and the buyer of goods which are not delivered must attempt to buy as cheaply as possible elsewhere. Loss arising from failure to take such steps cannot be recovered.

**The following case also provides an illustration.**

### Brace v Calder [1895] 2 QB 253

The defendants, a partnership consisting of four members, agreed to employ the claimant as manager of a branch of the business for two years. Five months later the partnership was dissolved by the retirement of two of the members and the business was transferred to the other two, who offered to employ the claimant on the same terms as before, but he refused the offer. The dissolution of the partnership constituted a wrongful dismissal of the claimant and he brought an action for breach of contract seeking to recover the salary that he would have received had he served the whole period of two years. It was *held* that he was entitled only to nominal damages since it was unreasonable to have rejected the offer of continued employment.

However, the claimant is not under a duty to mitigate his loss before there has been a breach of contract which the claimant has accepted as a breach. No doubt this is logical but it can produce startling results (*see White and Carter (Councils) Ltd v McGregor* (1961) in Chapter 8). However, the requirement of a 'legitimate interest' in keeping the contract going makes the position more equitable (*see*, for example, *Clea Shipping* in Chapter 8).

## PROVISIONAL DAMAGES FOR PERSONAL INJURIES

The Administration of Justice Act 1982, s 6 makes provision for a court to award provisional damages for contractual claims for personal injuries. Thus, in an action for a fracture to the hip caused to a passenger in an accident involving a negligently driven bus, the court can make an order for damages payable at once for the fracture and an award of provisional damages in case in the future chronic arthritis affects the injured passenger. If it does, but not otherwise, the provisional damages may also be recovered without another visit to the court to prove the damage.

Section 3 of the Damages Act 1996 provides that where a claimant dies of his injuries after receiving a provisional award, his dependants will not be prevented from claiming *as dependants* for loss of dependency. This is a separate claim made by the executors of the deceased on behalf of all those who were dependent on him, e.g. a wife. The claim will extend only to losses not covered by the original award. Since there is also a potential claim by the deceased's estate, in such a case the Act makes clear that dependants' claims will be preferred, if there are are any, thus preventing double recovery by the dependants and then by the estate.

## STRUCTURED SETTLEMENTS

In more recent times, the courts have set up a system of structured settlements. The settlement of a damages claim is by means of a permanent income instead of a single lump sum. They are more likely to be found in personal injury cases arising from a negligent act than in contract cases, but they are worth a mention in an examination. The defendant in these cases is normally indemnified by an insurance company which actually pays the damages, and the court may direct the insurer to pay the claimant monthly payments guaranteed, e.g. for life, and inflation proofed. The payments are not subject to income tax. The claimant is thus not concerned with investment problems and is also protected against personal extravagance and payment of tax.

## INTEREST ON DEBT AND DAMAGES

Under the provisions of s 15 of and Sch 1 to the Administration of Justice Act 1982, which inserted s 35A of the Supreme Court Act 1981, the court has power to award interest on debt or damages at the end of the trial or where judgment is obtained in default, i.e. where there is no defence and no trial. Interest may also be awarded where the defendant settles after service of writ but before judgment. Interest is not available where a person settles *before* service of writ no matter how long he has kept the other party waiting. The interest payable is at such rate as the court thinks fit or as rules of court may provide. The rate currently payable on judgment debts under s 17 of the Judgments Act 1838, which is likely to be a guideline, is 8 per cent per annum (SI 1993/564 (L2)). The interest is tax free (Administration of Justice Act 1982, s 74).

## RECOVERY OF DEBT

Where one party has performed his part of the contract but the other has failed to pay, e.g. following a supply of goods complying with the contract requirements, the claim of the supplier is for *debt* rather than *damages*. The main point to be considered here is the possibility of recovering interest on unpaid debts. The topic may be considered by looking at the business procedure which involves the use of a default interest clause in the contract and then by looking at statutory provisions.

### Default interest clauses

A default interest clause can be included in support of any obligation to pay a sum of money by a given date. A rate of 3 or 4 per cent over the Bank of England base rate is common and this is payable from the stated due date until payment. The court would enforce such a clause, but any attempt to make an interest charge except during the period for which the debt was due may very will be unenforceable as a penalty.

### Statutory provisions

The Late Payment of Commercial Debts (Interest) Act 1998, which received the Royal Assent on 11 June 1998, should be noted. It provides specific help to small companies and other businesses which commonly do not use default interest clauses, by giving them the right to claim interest on late payment of their bills. This will be phased in in three stages. First, small businesses will receive the right for use against all large enterprises, including public-sector organisations; the right will then be extended after a period of probably two years for use by small businesses against all enterprises including other small businesses and the public sector; then, finally, after a period of probably two years, the right would be extended to allow all businesses of whatever size to claim statutory interest against each other and public bodies. Where no credit period is specified in a contract or there is no written contract, the Act sets a default credit period of 30 days from delivery either of the invoice for payment or of the goods or service, whichever is the later.

The relevant statutory instruments implementing and supporting the 1998 Act appear below:

- SI 1998/2479 (C56) The Late Payment of Commercial Debts (Interest) Act 1998 (Commencement No 1) Order 1998 brought the 1998 Act into force on 1 November 1998 for the purposes of the first phase, i.e. in relation to commercial contracts for the supply of goods or services where the supplier is a small business and the purchaser is a large business or a UK public authority. A business is a small business if the number of full-time employees is 50 or fewer. A large business is a business in which the number of full-time employees employed in the business is more than 50. There are provisions for aggregation in the case of associated businesses. An employee is defined to include those who work in the business under a contract of employment and other than under such a contract, such as partners and sole owners. Provision is made for counting part-time employees as fractions of full-timers and averaging provisions under which the number of employees over a period is taken to produce an average for the relevant 50 figure are included;
- SI 1998/2765 The Late Payment of Commercial Debts (Rate of Interest) Order 1998 sets the rate of interest under s 6 of the 1998 Act, and came into force on 1 November 1998. The variable rate is set at the Official Dealing Rate of the Bank of England plus 8 per cent. The Official Dealing Rate is announced from time to time by the Bank's Monetary Policy Committee and is published daily in the *Financial Times* under London Money Rates, where it is referred to as the 'UK clearing bank base lending rate';
- SI 1998/2481 The Late Payment of Commercial Debts (Interest) Act 1998 (Transitional Provisions) Regulations 1998 provide, with effect from 1 November 1998, that while the 1998 Act is not fully in force it shall be presumed in any proceedings unless the contrary is proved that the business of the purchaser is a large business. To displace this presumption, the purchaser would have to prove on the balance of probabilities that it was a small business. Where on a claim for interest any dispute arises about the size of the supplier, it will be for the supplier to prove that it is a small business.

The size of a public authority does not affect its rights or liabilities under the Act.

The Lord Chancellor's Department published a consultation paper on the proposal to allow interest to accrue on County Court judgment debts under £5,000 where the creditor has claimed interest under the late payment legislation. Currently, interest accrues on County Court judgments of £5,000 or more and the rate is 8 per cent. These provisions are now enacted by the County Courts (Interest on Judgment Debts) (Amendment) Order 1998 (SI 1998/2400), which came into force on 1 November 1998.

## EU DEVELOPMENTS

EU industry ministers have reached agreement on a European-wide Directive to combat late payment of debt. Progress is now being made towards the adoption of the Directive. The Directive entitled *Combating the Late Payment of Commercial Debt* is to provide interest at 6 per cent above the Bank of England or European Central Bank base rate in the event of late payment. The parties will retain freedom of contract to decide when debts should be paid, but interest would start to accrue 30 days after the date for payment. Member states may introduce provisions more favourable to creditors. The advantage of the Directive will be that small and medium entities can be sure of rights similar to those in the UK wherever they do business in the EU.

## EQUITABLE REMEDIES

Damages are the common law remedy for breach of contract. However, in some situations equity will provide more suitable remedies and these will now be considered.

### A decree for specific performance

This is an equitable remedy which is sometimes granted for breach of contract, where damages are not an adequate remedy or where specific performance is regarded by the court as a more appropriate remedy (*see Beswick* v *Beswick* (1967), Chapter 2). It is an order of the court and constitutes an express instruction to a party to a contract to perform the actual obligations which he undertook in a contract. For all practical purposes, the remedy is now largely confined to contracts for the sale of land, though it may be an appropriate remedy in the case of a contract to pay an annuity because the exact value of the annuity will depend on how long the annuitant lives and this cannot be known at the time of the breach (*see Beswick* v *Beswick* (1967), Chapter 2). It is not normally granted in the case of contracts for the sale of goods because other goods of a similar kind can be purchased and the difference assessed in money damages. In addition, it should be noted that specific performance will not be granted if the court cannot adequately supervise its enforcement. Thus contracts of a personal nature, such as employment, which rely on a continuing relationship between the parties will not generally be specifically enforced because the court cannot supervise performance on the day-to-day basis which would be necessary. However, if constant supervision by the court is not required, a decree of specific performance may be made of a personal service undertaking. Thus in *Posner* v *Scott-Lewis* [1986] 3 All ER 51 Mervyn-Davies J decided that the tenants of a block of flats could enforce by specific performance an undertaking in their leases that the defendant landlords would employ a resident porter to keep the communal areas clear. The court had only to ensure that the appointment was made. The claimants were not asking the court to supervise the porter's day-to-day work. Furthermore, specific performance will not be awarded either to or against a minor because a minor's contracts cannot in general be enforced against him and those which can, i.e. beneficial contracts (see Chapter 3), are in the nature of contracts of personal service. Equity requires equality or mutuality as regards its remedies and this does not exist in the case of minors' contracts.

## An injunction

This is an order of the court used in this context to direct a person not to break his contract. The remedy has a somewhat restricted application in the law of contract and will be granted to enforce a negative stipulation in a contract where damages would not be an adequate remedy. Being an equitable remedy, it is only ordered on the same principles as specific performance, so that it will not normally be awarded where damages are an adequate remedy (*see Garden Cottage Foods Ltd v Milk Marketing Board* (1983), Chapter 7). Its main use in the contractual situation has been as an indirect means of enforcing a contract for personal services but a clear negative stipulation is required. The court will not imply one.

**The following cases illustrate the application of these rules.**

### Warner Brothers Pictures Incorporated *v* Nelson [1937] 1 KB 209

The defendant, the film actress Bette Davis, had entered into a contract in which she agreed to act exclusively for the claimants for 12 months. She was anxious to obtain more money and so she left America, and entered into a contract with a person in England. The claimants now asked for an injunction restraining the defendant from carrying out the English contract. *Held* – An injunction would be granted. The contract contained a negative stipulation not to work for anyone else, and this could be enforced. However, since the contract was an American one, the court limited the operation of the injunction to the area of the court's jurisdiction, and although the contract stipulated that the defendant would not work in any other occupation, the injunction was confined to work on stage or screen.

*Comment:* (i) Even where, as here, there is a negative stipulation, the court will not grant an injunction if the pressure to work for the claimants is so severe as to be for all practical purposes irresistible. In this case it was said that Bette Davis could still earn her living by doing other work.

(ii) The idea that persons such as Bette Davis or others subjected to injunctions of negative stipulations would take other work was challenged by the Court of Appeal in *Warren v Mendy* [1989] 3 All ER 103 on the grounds of 'realism and practicality'. The Court of Appeal said that it was unrealistic to suppose that such persons would take up other work, i.e. that boxers would become clerks, and actresses secretaries. Thus the making of an injunction of a negative stipulation in this sort of case was in general terms likely to operate as a decree of specific performance. This means that it is in modern law less likely that such injunctions will be granted or that the *Warner Brothers* case will be followed though it is not overruled.

### Whitwood Chemical Co *v* Hardman [1891] 2 Ch 416

The defendant entered into a contract of service with the claimants and agreed to give the whole of his time to them. In fact he occasionally worked for others, and the claimants tried to enforce the undertaking in the service contract by injunction. *Held* – An injunction could not be granted because there was no express negative stipulation. The defendant had merely stated what he would do, and not what he would not do, and to read into the undertaking an agreement not to work for anyone else required the court to imply a negative stipulation from a positive one. No such implication could be made.

*Comment:* It is because of the fact that the granting of an injunction of a negative stipulation is so close to specific performance that it is restricted to cases where the negative stipulation is express.

## Freezing injunction

This remedy, which can be of assistance to a party suing for breach of contract, has developed considerably over recent times. It was formerly known as Mareva injunction, but is now called a freezing injunction under the Civil Procedure Rules which followed the Woolf reforms in 1999. In general terms, a court will not grant an injunction to prevent a person disposing of his property merely to assist a person suing, for example, for a debt, to recover his money. However, the freezing injunction is an exception to that general rule and is granted to restrict removal of assets outside the jurisdiction, often by a foreign defendant, where this is a real and serious possibility. The injunction took its original name from the second case in which it was awarded, i.e. *Mareva Compania Naviera SA* v *International Bulk Carriers SA* [1975] 2 Lloyd's Rep 509. The power of the High Court to issue a freezing injunction is now recognised by s 37 of the Supreme Court Act 1981 and the Civil Procedure Rules which make it clear that the power applies to domestic as well as foreign defendants, whether the latter are resident in this country or not (*The Siskina* [1977] 3 All ER 803). However, the power is only to freeze assets within the jurisdiction of the English court. It cannot be used to freeze assets abroad. An order of a local court must be obtained (*Babanaft International Co SA* v *Bassante* [1988] 138 NLJ 203). It is, however, a valuable addition to existing contractual remedies, particularly when business is now so often conducted on an international scale.

## A search order

This is an order which may be issued under the Civil Procedure Rules, which permits the representatives of a claimant to enter the defendant's premises to inspect and remove vital material or evidence where it is contemplated that there is a risk that the defendant might destroy or dispose of them. It was previously referred to as an Anton Piller order.

## Rescission

This is a further equitable remedy for breach of contract. The rule is the same when the remedy is used for breach as it is when it is used for misrepresentation. If the contract cannot be completely rescinded it cannot be rescinded at all; it must be possible to restore the *status quo*. All part payments must be returned. In this connection, the fact that a claimant has rescinded the contract does not prevent that claimant from bringing an action for debts owed under the contract prior to rescission. These are not regarded as abandoned by the order of rescission (*see Stocznia Gdanska SA* v *Latvian Shipping Co* [1998] 1 All ER 883).

## Refusal of further performance: a self-help remedy

If the person suffering from the breach desires merely to get rid of his obligations under the contract, he may refuse any further performance on his part and set up the breach as a defence if the party who has committed the breach attempts to enforce the contract against him.

# CLAIMS FOR RESTITUTION: QUASI-CONTRACT

Quasi-contract is based on the idea that a person should not obtain a benefit or an unjust enrichment as against another merely because there is no obligation in contract or another established branch of the law which will operate to make him account for it. The law may in these circumstances provide a remedy by implying a fictitious promise to account for the benefit or enrichment. This promise then forms the basis of an action in quasi-contract.

In practice the following two areas are important.

## Claims on a *quantum meruit*

This remedy means that the claimant will be awarded as much as he has earned or deserved. The remedy can be used contractually or quasi-contractually as follows.

(a) *Contractually.* Here it may be used to recover a reasonable price or remuneration where there is a contract for the supply of goods or services but the parties have not fixed any precise sum to be paid. This area is also covered by statute law in the case of a sale of goods by s 8 of the Sale of Goods Act 1979, and in the case of a supply of goods, e.g. a new oil filter in a car repair contract, or the mere supply of a service by s 15 of the Supply of Goods and Services Act 1982.

(b) *Quasi-contractually.* A claim on this basis may be made where, for example, work has been done under a void contract. The claimant cannot recover damages for breach because no valid contract exists, but he may in some circumstances recover on a *quantum meruit*. The following case illustrates this point.

### Craven-Ellis v Canons Ltd [1936] 2 All ER 1066

The claimant was employed as managing director by the company under a deed which provided for remuneration. The articles provided that directors must have qualification shares, and must obtain these within two months of appointment. The claimant and other directors who appointed him never obtained the required number of shares so that the deed was invalid. However, the claimant had rendered services, and he now sued on a *quantum meruit* for a reasonable sum by way of remuneration. *Held* – he succeeded on a *quantum meruit*, there being no valid contract.

## Total failure of consideration: actions for money had and received

Of particular importance here is the action for total failure of consideration. A total failure will result in the recovery of all that was paid. A common reason for total failure of consideration arises where A, who has no title, sells goods to B and B has to give up the goods to the true owner. B can then recover the whole of the consideration from A, his action being based upon the quasi-contractual claim of money had and received.

It should be noted that the action is based on failure of consideration and not its absence. Thus money paid by way of a gift cannot be recovered in quasi-contract.

**The following case is an illustration of an action for total failure of consideration.**

### Rowland v Divall [1923] 2 KB 500

In April 1922, the defendant bought an 'Albert' motor car from a man who had stolen it from the true owner. One month later the claimant, a dealer, purchased the car from the defendant for £334, repainted it, and sold it for £400 to Colonel Railsdon. In September 1922, the police seized the car from Colonel Railsdon and the claimant repaid him the £400. The claimant now sued the defendant for £334 on the grounds that there had been a total failure of consideration since the claimant had not obtained a title to the car. *Held* – The defendant was in breach of s 12 of the Sale of Goods Act, which implies conditions and warranties into a sale of goods relating to the seller's right to sell, and there had been a total failure of consideration in spite of the fact that the car had been used by the claimant and his purchaser. The claimant contracted for the property in the car and not the mere right to possess it. Since he had not obtained the property, he was entitled to recover the sum of £334 and no deductions should be made for the period of use.

*Comment:* (i) Although the court purported to deal with this case as a breach of s 12(1) of the Act, it would appear that in fact they operated on common law principles and gave complete restitution of the purchase price because of total failure of consideration arising out of the seller's lack of title. The condition under s 12(1) had by reason of the claimant's use of the car and the passage of time become a warranty when the action was brought, and if the court had been awarding damages for breach of warranty it would have had to reduce the sum of £334 by a sum representing the value to the claimant of the use of the vehicle which he had had.

(ii) The drawback to making an allowance to the seller for use is that he gets an allowance for a car which is not his and the owner might sue the buyer in damages for conversion so that he would have to pay an allowance and damages to the true owner in conversion. In other words, he would pay for use twice.

(iii) It is also relevant to say that the court felt an allowance for use should not be made because the claimant had paid the price for the car to become its *owner*, and not merely to have use of it. So why should he be subject to an allowance for use when that is not what he wanted or bargained for? As Bankes LJ said:' he did not get what he paid for – namely a car to which he would have title'.

## Payments made under a mistake

This is a further aspect of restitution by use of an implied promise in the recipient to repay the sum(s) involved.

### Payment under a mistake of fact

A claim lies (derived from the old action for money had and received) where money has been paid under a mistake of fact. The error may arise from an error in calculation as where defective arithmetic causes a debtor to pay more than he owes the creditor or where there is duplication of an item again in the debtor's accounts so that he pays it twice.

### Payment under mistake of law

Until recent times, there was no claim for money paid under mistake of law. However, the House of Lords overturned this old rule in *Kleinwort Benson Ltd* v *Lincoln City*

*Council* [1998] 4 All ER 513 where their Lordships ruled that money paid under a contract which was *ultra vires* or beyond the legal powers of the Council was nevertheless recoverable by the claimant who had made the payment.

## LIMITATION OF ACTIONS

Contractual obligations are not enforceable for all time. After a certain period the law bars any remedy in the main because evidence becomes less reliable with the passage of time. Time is the greatest enemy of the truth! The Limitation Act 1980 lays down the general periods within which an action may be brought. They are as follows.

(a) an action on a simple contract may be brought within six years from the date when the cause of action accrued;
(b) an action upon a contract made by deed may be brought within 12 years from the date when the cause of action accrued.

However, where what the claimant is asking for includes a claim for damages in respect of personal injury, the period is three years.

However, a person may suffer personal injury the extent of which only comes to light more than three years after the breach of contract which caused it. For example, A is a passenger on B's coach and B's careless driving causes an accident as a result of which A suffers injury consisting of bruising of the face. Four years later A goes blind as a result of the accident. Under the Limitation Act 1980, A has three years from his knowledge of the blindness to sue B and the court's permission is not required. The court may extend this period at its discretion, though in this case application must be made to the court for the extension.

A right of action 'accrues' from the moment when breach occurs, not from the date when the contract was made. Thus, if money is lent today for four years, the creditor's right to recover it will not expire until 10 years from today.

If when the cause of action accrues the claimant is under a disability by reason of minority or unsoundness of mind, the period will not run until the disability is ended or until his death, whichever comes first. Once the period has started to run subsequent insanity has no effect.

If the claimant is the victim of fraud or acts under a mistake, the limitation period will not begin to run until the true state of affairs is discovered or should with reasonable diligence have been discovered.

**The following case was decided on the above rules of the common law which are now in the Limitation Act 1980.**

### Lynn v Bamber [1930] 2 KB 72

In 1921 the claimant purchased some plum trees from the defendant and was given a warranty that the trees were 'Purple Pershores'. In 1928 the claimant discovered that the trees were not 'Purple Pershores' and sued for damages. The defendant pleaded that the claim was barred by the current Limitation Act. *Held* – The defendant's fraudulent misrepresentation and fraudulent concealment of the breach of warranty provided a good answer to this plea, so that the claimant could recover.

*Comment:* (i) The present jurisdiction is s 32 of the Limitation Act 1980.

(ii) In *Peco Arts Inc v Hazlitt Gallery Ltd* [1983] 3 All ER 193 the claimants bought from the defendants in November 1970 what purported to be an original drawing in black chalk on paper *Etude pour le Bain Turc* by J A D Ingres for the price of $18,000. In 1976 it was revalued by an expert for insurance purposes. No doubts were cast upon its authenticity. However, on a valuation in 1981 it was discovered that the drawing was a reproduction. The claimants sought rescission and recovery of the purchase price plus interest on the grounds of mutual, common or unilateral mistake of fact. The trial was adjourned on the first day because the parties wished to simplify the issues. After this the only defence was the Limitation Act 1980, i.e. that the claimants' claim was statute-barred. It was held that it was not and judgment was given for the claimants. Webster J decided that a prudent buyer in the position of the claimants would not normally have obtained an independent authentication but would have relied on the defendants' reputation, as the claimants had done. Further, the claimants were entitled to conclude that the drawing was an original as the valuers who had examined it in 1976 had not questioned its authenticity. There was no lack of diligence on the part of the claimants. Accordingly, the action was not time barred and there would be judgment for the claimants.

(iii) The *Peco* case does not decide what the effect of the mistake was, and to that extent does not go contrary to *Leaf* and *Bell* (Chapter 4). These matters were not contested by the defendants. In *Leaf* the court was deciding how soon an action must be brought for rescission for *innocent misrepresentation*. The issue here was how soon must an action be brought where the claimant sought relief for the consequences of an operative mistake.

The Limitation Act does not truly discharge a contract, which is why it has been dealt with separately here. The Act merely makes the contract unenforceable in a court of law and if the defendant does not plead the statutes of limitation, the judge will enforce the contract. In addition, where the contractual claim is not for damages but for a debt or other liquidated (i.e. ascertained) demand, time for making a claim can be extended by a subsequent payment of money not appropriated by the debtor, because, as we have seen, the creditor can appropriate it, or by the debtor or his duly authorised agent making a written acknowledgment of the debt to the creditor or his agent. Time begins to run again from the date of the acknowledgment. However, once a debt is statute-barred it cannot be revived by acknowledgment, and creditor appropriation to a statute-barred debt does not revive the balance (if any) (Limitation Act 1980, s 29).

Equitable remedies, i.e. specific performance or an injunction, are not covered by the ordinary limitation periods but will usually be barred much earlier under general equitable rules. An equitable remedy must be sought promptly and, according to the nature of the contract, a short delay of weeks or even days may bar the remedy.

Finally, the enforcement of a judgment debt does not become barred by lapse of time under s 24 of the Limitation Act 1980 so that a judgment once obtained can be enforced, e.g. by a sale of the defendant's goods even though the relevant statutory period has elapsed. The amount of interest recoverable from judgment until payment is similarly not limited to the relevant period but is limited to six years before the judgment is executed. Thus, if A obtains a judgment against B in 1998, he can still execute it to take the defendant's property for sale even though he leaves it until, say, 2005 to execute it. However, he can only recover interest on the judgment for six years prior to 2005 (*Lowsley* v *Forbes*, *The Times*, 5 April 1996).

## GRADED QUESTIONS

### Essay mode

1  (a) Explain the difference between liquidated damages and penalties in the law of contract. What criteria do the courts use to determine whether a provision stipulating for the payment of a particular sum is a penalty? Why is the distinction between liquidated damages and penalties important?

(b) Digger agrees to hire a crane to Contractor for a period of 12 months at a rate of £2,000 per month. The terms of the contract provide that: 'Contractor may terminate this agreement on giving one month's notice in writing. If this option is exercised, Contractor will pay £16,000 to Digger by way of agreed compensation.' After eight months, Contractor gives Digger one month's notice in writing terminating the agreement. He now wishes to know whether he is bound to pay Digger £16,000.

Advise Contractor.

*(Institute of Chartered Secretaries and Administrators)*

2  R is an accountant. He agrees with S, a garage proprietor, that he will assist S with his annual tax return if S will service his car for him. He also agrees with T, a landscape gardener, that he will advise T on the installation of a computerised financial management system if T, in return, will carry out some landscaping work at the house of R's daughter, U.

R assists S and advises T, but both refuse to carry out their side of the agreements. Because his car has not been serviced R is late for an important meeting with a client after the car breaks down on the way to the meeting. As a result of this the client switches his work, worth some £5,000 per annum, to another accountant. U is very anxious to have the landscaping work done on her garden and because T has a reputation for doing good quality work she is keen that it is done by T.

Advise R and U as to the nature of the contractual remedies, if any, which may be available to them.

*(Association of Chartered Certified Accountants)*

3  (a) What principles of law are applied by the courts in determining what damages should be awarded to a claimant who has successfully established that the defendant was in breach of his contractual obligations?

(b) Fred is a commercial traveller who regularly uses George's garage for servicing his company vehicle. On one occasion he is told that his car will be ready for 11 am the next day and he therefore arranges to visit his most important client Bert at noon. He arrives at the garage at 11 am to be told by George that the service is not yet finished because a mechanic has not turned up. The car is not therefore usable. Fred abandons his plan to visit Bert because of the non-availability of his vehicle. Bert is annoyed and transfers his custom to another supplier. Fred, having lost his most lucrative account, is dismissed by his employer. Fred's family suffer the trauma of the drastic reduction in income. Is George liable for all these consequences of his breach of contract?

*(The University of Huddersfield. BA and BA (Hons) Business Studies: Business Law)*

## Objective mode

Four alternative answers are given. Select ONE only. Circle the answer which you consider to be correct. Check your answers by referring back to the information given in the relevant chapter and against the answers at the back of the book.

*With reference to the following information answer questions 1, 2 and 3.*

Kitchener Ltd agree to supply and fit an electric cooking range in a new restaurant belonging to Cook and situated near a major junction on the M99. The contract provided that the range should be delivered and fitted during the period 29 to 30 May so that the restaurant could open on 3 June. Cook has provided restaurant facilities from older premises on the site, serving on average 750 meals a week. These premises were, to the knowledge of Kitchener Ltd, to be demolished during the week ending 27 May.

Unknown to Kitchener Ltd, Cook had organised as part of the opening ceremony of the new restaurant a beauty contest which was to take place on the forecourt of the restaurant, and had also entered into a contract to supply meals to the canteen of a local factory from 5 June.

Kitchener Ltd, which had taken orders in excess of production capacity, was unable to supply and fit the range until 27 June. Cook opened the restaurant on 1 July and the beauty contest which was held on that date was won by Gloria who received a prize of £200. Unfortunately Freda, who was one of the eight girls entered for the contest, did not attend, Cook having failed to notify her of the revised date. The supply of meals to the factory commenced on 3 July.

Cook intends to sue Kitchener Ltd for damages for loss of profit and Freda is suing Cook for damages for his breach of contract in failing to notify her of the revised date of the contest.

1    As regards Cook's claim for loss of profit:

    **A** He will only recover damages for the estimated loss of profit on ordinary customers between 3 June and 1 July.

    **B** He will recover damages for loss of profit on ordinary customers and the meals he was unable to supply to the factory.

    **C** He will recover only for the loss of profit on factory meals.

    **D** He will not recover anything because Kitchener Ltd did not accept the risk of any loss.

2    One of the following cases is relevant to Cook's claim. Select:

    **A** *Hochster* v *De la Tour* (1853).

    **B** *Brace* v *Calder* (1895).

    **C** *Warren* v *Mendy* (1989).

    **D** *Victoria Laundry* v *Newman Industries* (1949).

3 As regards Freda's claim:

    **A** She will recover something by way of damages from Cook even though she might not have won the contest.

    **B** She will not recover any damages from Cook.

    **C** She can try to get restitution of part of the prize from Gloria.

    **D** She can ask for specific performance to make Cook hold the beauty contest again.

*With reference to the following information answer questions 4 and 5.*

Layouts Ltd agree to design and install new equipment at a factory belonging to Bloggo Ltd within 20 weeks from the receipt of the final approval of drawings. A clause in the contract provided that, if this period was exceeded, Layouts Ltd would pay Bloggo Ltd the sum of £200 per week for every week in excess of the 20 weeks. This is a fair estimate of the likely loss.

In the event Layouts Ltd, which had made a number of similar contracts with other companies, found that it was unable to carry out the work in time and the installation of the equipment designed for Bloggo Ltd was eventually completed 30 weeks after final approval of drawings.

The ten-week delay has in fact resulted in a loss of profit to Bloggo Ltd of £4,000 and Bloggo Ltd is now claiming this sum by way of damages. Layouts Ltd is standing by the contractual arrangements under which it sees its liability as limited to £2,000.

4 Which one of the following legal concepts will apply to the case?

    **A** *Quantum meruit.*

    **B** Quasi-contract.

    **C** Frustration of contract.

    **D** Liquidated damages and penalties.

5 Which of the following decisions is the court likely to make?

    **A** That Bloggo Ltd is entitled to recover the sum of £4,000.

    **B** That Bloggo Ltd is entitled to recover £2,000 as agreed.

    **C** That Bloggo Ltd is not entitled to recover anything since the clause is a penalty.

    **D** That Bloggo Ltd cannot recover anything because the contract is frustrated since Layouts Ltd could not find it possible to perform it.

6 Under the Unfair Contract Terms Act 1977 what is the effect of a notice disclaiming liability for death or personal injury?

    **A** Void.

    **B** Voidable.

    **C** Valid.

    **D** Unenforceable.

*Answers to questions set in objective mode appear on p 708.*

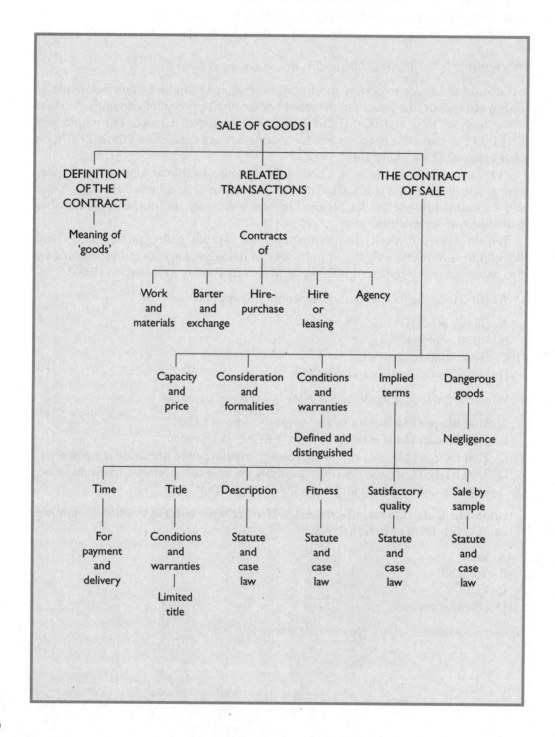

The objectives of this chapter are to consider the principles and rules laid down by case law and statute – mainly the Sale of Goods Act 1979 (as amended) – in regard to this highly important type of business transaction in terms of the definition of goods, contracts of sale and related transactions, and conditions and warranties both express and implied. The remaining principles and rules will be dealt with in subsequent chapters.

The law relating to the sale of goods is to be found in the Sale of Goods Act 1979 (as amended). This is a consolidating measure bringing together a number of previous Acts, but in particular the Sale of Goods Act 1893. Certain provisions of the Factors Act 1889 are also relevant, as are rules of the common law not dealt with by legislation. All section references are to the Sale of Goods Act 1979 (as amended) unless otherwise stated.

## DEFINITION: CONTRACT OF SALE OF GOODS

A contract of sale of goods is a contract whereby the seller transfers or agrees to transfer the property in goods to the buyer for a money consideration called the price (s 2(1)). The definition covers:

(a) *a contract of sale* in which the property in goods is transferred from seller to buyer;
(b) *an agreement to sell* in which the transfer of property takes place at a future time or on fulfilment of certain conditions (s 2(5)). A contract for the sale of goods yet to be manufactured is an agreement to sell because the property in the goods cannot pass until they are manufactured and ascertained.

Unless the contract otherwise provides, the property in goods which are the subject of a contract of sale passes to the buyer when the contract is made. English law does not require actual delivery of the goods, and the contract of sale operates as the conveyance.

Property is defined as the general property in goods and not merely a special property (s 61), and therefore to say that the property passes to the buyer normally means that he gets ownership and not mere possession. A contract which does not pass ownership at all, e.g. a contract to rent a TV set, is outside the definition (but see Supply of Goods and Services Act 1982, Chapter 13).

However, under s 12(3) A may transfer goods to B on the basis of whatever title he or a third person may have. This may turn out to be a right of possession only. Nevertheless, such a contract is a contract of sale of goods. A common example of the use of s 12(3) occurs where the sale is of goods taken in execution by the bailiffs to satisfy a judgment debt. Some of these goods, which are sold very cheaply, may not be owned by the debtor, as where he has them on hire-purchase, although the bailiffs try to avoid this. If a finance company takes the goods away from the buyer, he has no claim for breach of condition under s 12, but the warranties of quiet possession in s 12 apply (*see* later in this chapter). Thus a purchaser has no claim unless the true owner repossesses the goods which he may not in the event do.

Delivery is the voluntary transfer of possession from one person to another, and whether the property in the goods passes on delivery is a question to be decided from the contract or, where the contract is silent, from the circumstances.

## MEANING OF GOODS

Section 61 provides that goods includes all personal chattels but excludes all choses in action (e.g. cheques and share certificates) and money, although a coin which is a curio piece is goods for the purposes of a contract of sale (*Moss* v *Hancock* [1899] 2 QB 211). The term also includes *emblements*, i.e. crops to be severed before sale or under the contract of sale. Products of the soil are generally sold with a view to severance and though they may sometimes be of the nature of land for the purposes of the Law of Property (Miscellaneous Provisions) Act 1989 (*see* Chapter 3), they are usually goods within the meaning of the Act of 1979. The Act does not apply to the sale of an interest in the land itself. The sale of gravel *in situ* under land would not be covered by the Act. Nor would crops sold with the land on which they are growing because they are not in such a case to be 'severed before sale or under the contract of sale' as s 61 requires.

Goods may be:

(a) *existing goods*, i.e. goods actually in existence when the contract is made. They may be either specific or unascertained in the sense that they have yet to be appropriated to the contract (s 5(1));
(b) *future goods*, i.e. goods yet to be acquired or manufactured or grown by the seller (s 5(1)) as in *Sainsbury* v *Street* [1972] 3 All ER 1127 where the seller agreed to sell to the buyers a crop of some 275 tons of barley to be grown by him on his farm;
(c) *specific goods*, i.e. goods identified and agreed upon at the time the contract of sale is made (s 61(1)), e.g. the sale of a raincoat at a market stall;
(d) *unascertained goods*, as where A agrees to sell to B 200 bags of flour from a stock of 2,000 lying in A's warehouse. The main problem in examination terms arises in questions which are concerned with when ownership in such goods passes from seller to buyer. These problems will be considered later.

## CONTRACTS OF SALE AND RELATED TRANSACTIONS

Students are sometimes asked to illustrate their knowledge of what goes to make a contract of sale of goods by making a comparison with business transactions which are broadly within the 'supply of goods' environment but to which the Sale of Goods Act does not apply. These are considered below.

### Contracts for sale and contracts for work and materials

If the contract is for the sale of goods it is governed by the Sale of Goods Act 1979; a contract for work and materials is not. Hence the need to distinguish between the two.

A contract for work and materials results in the transfer of goods, but also involves the supply of skill and labour over and above what is required to produce the goods as an essential and significant part of the contract. Thus in *Cammell Laird & Co Ltd* v *Manganese Bronze & Brass Co Ltd* [1934] AC 402 the construction of two ship's propellers was held to be a contract of sale of goods; so, too, was a contract for the making of a fur coat from selected skins (*see Marcel (Furriers) Ltd* v *Tapper* [1953] 1 All ER 15).

Before 1983 contracts for work and materials were governed by common law only. The court would normally imply into those contracts terms which were similar to those implied into contracts of sale by the sale of goods legislation, e.g. that the goods were fit for the purpose and of merchantable (now satisfactory) quality. Now the Supply of Goods and Services Act 1982 applies (*see* Chapter 13). However, as a matter of contrast between the two types of contract, some examples of work and materials must be given. In *Robinson* v *Graves* [1935] 1 KB 579 it was held that a contract to paint a portrait was a contract for work and materials and not a sale of goods, even though the property in a chattel, i.e. the portrait, was eventually to be transferred. In general terms, all forms of repair and maintenance contracts fall into the category of work and materials, e.g. repair of cars, the servicing of computers and X-ray and photocopying machines, roof repairs, painting and decorating, and the installation of double-glazing and air-conditioning and so on.

## Contracts for sale and barter or exchange

Section 2(1) requires that the consideration in a sale of goods be money, and contracts of pure exchange are not within the Sale of Goods Act. Difficulties arose where a seller took goods in part-exchange, as where a car dealer took in part-exchange the car of the purchaser in reduction of the purchase price of another car. Certainly the contract was a sale of goods so long as money was a substantial part of the consideration, and even if it was not the court might regard the transaction as a sale if the parties appeared to have done so. Thus where the difference in price between the car which was 'traded in' and the one which was purchased is marginal, there would most probably be a sale since that is what the parties envisaged.

Since the 1982 Act was passed, the problem of sale or barter is of no real practical importance. Whether the contract is a contract of sale or an exchange of goods for goods, or goods for money and goods, almost identical terms will be implied in the contract under the 1979 Act (if a sale) or under the 1982 Act (barter and exchange).

## Sale and hire-purchase

A sale of goods differs from a hire-purchase transaction because a hire-purchase contract gives the hirer a mere bailment of the goods, with an option to purchase them, an option which the hirer may or may not exercise after payment of the agreed instalments. There is a contract of sale when the hirer exercises his option to purchase, which he will normally do, since the purchase price is then nominal and the eventual sale of the goods is the object of the contract. However, because under a contract of hire-purchase a person does not *legally* commit himself to purchase the goods, there is no contract of sale.

A further distinction is that, while a contract of sale normally involves two parties only, a hire-purchase contract generally involves three. The owner of the goods selected by the hirer sells them to a finance company which in turn hires them to the hirer.

The Sale of Goods Act does not apply to the hiring contract, but certain terms are implied into that contract by ss 8–11 of the Supply of Goods (Implied Terms) Act 1973 (as substituted by the Consumer Credit Act 1974, Sch 4, para 35, which made some changes in terminology in the original provisions of the 1973 Act), and are available against the finance company.

The distinction between a contract of sale and hire-purchase is also important in the matter of title. If the contract is one of hire-purchase it does not come within the provisions of s 25(1) of the Sale of Goods Act, under which a buyer in possession can give a good title to a purchaser if he sells the goods, because the hirer is not a person who has bought or agreed to buy the goods. He is hiring with an option to purchase and is under no obligation to buy. The hirer, therefore, cannot give a good title to a third party and, on the insolvency of the hirer, the owner of the goods can recover them.

Where the contract is one of sale, but payment is to be made by instalments, the contract may pass the property, in which case there is an unconditional contract of sale and the buyer, having ownership, can give a good title to a third party. On the insolvency of the buyer, an insolvency practitioner takes the goods, and the seller must prove in the insolvency for the instalments.

If, although the goods have been delivered, the passing of the property is postponed until all instalments are paid, then there is a conditional contract of sale; such a contract is within s 25(1) and the buyer can give a good title to a third party if the total purchase price exceeds £25,000. If the total purchase price is £25,000 or under, the contract is governed by the Consumer Credit Act 1974, and the conditions and warranties implied will be those under the Supply of Goods (Implied Terms) Act 1973 and not those under the Sale of Goods Act, and the buyer cannot give a good title to third parties, though there are exceptions in the case of motor cars (*see* Chapter 14). In both cases, however, the seller can claim the goods on the insolvency of the buyer. (Hire-purchase contracts are considered further in Chapter 14.)

### Sale and hire (or leasing)

Hire-purchase and hire have a lot in common. However, the distinction between them is that a contract of hire is only a contract of bailment which gives the hirer only the right to possess the goods. Hire-purchase is, as its name suggests, hire *plus* purchase. The hirer in hire-purchase has a right to possess plus an option to buy the goods when the instalments have been paid. Contracts of hiring were governed by the common law; now the Supply of Goods and Services Act 1982 applies. Examples of hiring agreements abound; office equipment, photocopying machines, typewriters and cars are commonly hired. More modern expressions include 'leasing', 'contract hire' and 'rental agreements', but whatever called they are all contracts of hire and the rights and obligations of the parties are in the 1982 Act (*see* Chapter 13).

### Sale and agency

Brief mention should be made of certain problems arising in agency. If the person who is selling the goods is an agent, there will be privity of contract between the buyer and the manufacturer or other supplier, e.g. wholesaler. If the seller is not an agent but, for example, a distributor who has purchased the goods himself, no action can be brought against the supplier in respect of the condition and quality of the goods (*Dunlop* v *Selfridge* (1915) in Chapter 2, but *see* now *Junior Books Ltd* v *Veitchi Co Ltd* (1982) in Chapter 11, bearing in mind that this case has not received much support from the judiciary in recent times, and the Contracts (Rights of Third Parties) Act 1999 in Chapter 2).

Problems may arise in relation to title. If the seller is an agent, he cannot pass a title in the goods to a buyer unless the sale is within the agent's actual or apparent authority (*see* Chapter 21) or he has the goods on 'sale or return' terms. (*See further* Chapter 11.)

Thus a contract under which F (a finder) transfers goods to a purchaser is not a contract of sale to which the Act applies. F is not the owner, nor is he the agent of the owner.

## Sale and loans on security

If A, who is the owner of goods, borrows money by using the goods as security and gives a charge or mortgage over them but retains possession, the transaction resembles a sale in the sense that the lender has a right to take the goods if A does not repay the loan or interest. This is not, however, a sale, but in view of the fact that A retains the goods so that third parties might give him credit on the strength of his apparent absolute ownership of them, the transaction must be committed to writing as a bill of sale which must be registered under the Bills of Sale Acts 1878 and 1882. If the transaction is unregistered (which is often the case), the contract is void and the lender will not be able to seize the goods or even recover the agreed interest, although the actual loan itself is recoverable in quasi-contract as money had and received (*North Central Wagon Finance Co Ltd* v *Brailsford* [1962] 1 All ER 502).

## THE CONTRACT OF SALE

We are now in a position to consider certain of the general principles of the law of contract as they apply to a sale of goods.

### Capacity of the parties

Capacity to buy and sell is regulated by the general law concerning capacity to contract and to transfer and acquire property. The problems relating to capacity have already been dealt with in Chapter 3 on the law of contract and no further comment is necessary, other than to refer again to the capacity problems which may arise in business from dealing with minors and to a lesser extent these days to companies.

### The price

Section 8 provides that the price may be:

(a) fixed by the contract; or
(b) left to be fixed in a manner provided by the contract, e.g. by a valuation or an arbitration; or
(c) determined by the course of dealing between the parties, e.g. previous transactions between them or any relevant custom of the trade or profession.

If the price is not fixed, there is a presumption that the buyer will pay a reasonable price. What is a reasonable price is a question of fact dependent upon the circumstances of each case. Thus a contract of sale of goods should not be regarded as *inchoate* simply because the parties have not agreed a price. (For inchoate agreements *see* Chapter 1.)

Section 9 provides that where the price is to be determined by the valuation of a third party, and no such valuation is made, then the contract is avoided, but:

(a) if the goods or part thereof have been delivered to the buyer and he has appropriated them to his use, the buyer must pay a reasonable price for them;

(b) if the valuation is prevented by *either party* to the contract, the non-defaulting party may sue for damages against the party in default.

It is difficult to see how the buyer would be able to prevent valuation, but presumably the Act is concerned to cover all possibilities. Section 9 applies only if the agreement names a valuer. Thus a sale of 'stock at valuation' is an agreement to sell at a reasonable price, and s 8 will apply if the parties do not appoint a valuer or otherwise agree a price.

If the buyer pays part of the price when he makes the contract, it may be a *deposit* or a *part-payment*. If it is a deposit, it will be forfeited if the buyer does not go on with the contract. A part-payment must be returned. Whether a payment is one or the other is a matter for the parties to decide in their contract. If they do not do so the court will have to discover as best it can what their intention was. In this connection the use of the word 'deposit' without more is a strong indication of a guarantee that the purchaser will complete and that the payment will be forfeit if he does not.

## The consideration

It has already been mentioned that the consideration for a sale must consist wholly or in part of money; otherwise the transaction is an exchange or barter. Where goods are to be conveyed without consideration, there is a gift, and any agreement to be enforceable must be made by deed, though actual delivery of the goods together with an intention to make a gift and not merely to lend will give the recipient or donee a good title.

## Formalities of the contract

Under s 4 contracts for the sale of goods can be made in writing (either with or without a deed), or by word of mouth or partly in writing and partly by word of mouth, or may be implied from the conduct of the parties. By reason of what is now s 36 of the Companies Act 1985, registered companies need not now contract by a deed, except where an ordinary person would have to do so. For example, a company must use a deed to convey land. The Corporate Bodies Contracts Act 1960 extends this privilege to all companies no matter how formed.

Nevertheless, provisions in other statutes may affect a sale. For example, s 24 of the Merchant Shipping Act 1894 provides that the sale of a ship or a share in a ship must be in writing. Furthermore, since s 61 defines goods as including emblements, e.g. growing crops which are agreed to be severed before sale or under the contract of sale (which covers most cases), it may be that crops which are not to be severed are land under the Law of Property Act 1925, in which case the contract if made before severance may have to be made in writing under the Law of Property (Miscellaneous Provisions) Act 1989 (*see* Chapter 3). Singleton LJ seemed to think writing was required in such a case in *Saunders* v *Pilcher* [1949] 2 All ER 1097 where a person bought a cherry orchard 'inclusive of this year's fruit crop'. The crop was not severed before sale or under the contract of sale and Singleton was of the view that s 61 had no application and that the contract including the fruit crop was a sale of land.

In addition, certain formalities are prescribed for credit sale agreements covered by the Consumer Credit Act 1974 (see Chapter 14).

The provisions of the Bills of Sale Acts may also affect the position regarding formalities. It is necessary to distinguish two situations.

(a) *A straight sale – the seller retaining possession*
   (i) If the sale is and remains oral, the Acts do not apply and the buyer takes the risk (subject to an action for breach of contract or non-delivery) that the seller may dispose of the goods either voluntarily (by subsequent sale) or involuntarily (by, for example, execution of a judgment or on insolvency).
   (ii) If, as usual, the buyer takes written evidence by means of a bill of sale this must be registered, though it need not be in any special form. If this is not done, the contract of sale is void in respect of involuntary dispositions, e.g. to an insolvency practitioner or a sheriff levying execution; but if the seller, while still in possession of the goods already sold, voluntarily transfers the property by way of sale to a third party, the latter may obtain a good title under s 24 of the Sale of Goods Act or under s 8 of the Factors Act 1889.
(b) *A sale operating as a security – the seller retaining possession*
   (i) The Sale of Goods Act does not apply (*see* s 62(4) of that Act).
   (ii) The Bills of Sale Act 1882 covers the transaction and unless there is a registered bill of sale made out in the form required by ss 8–10 of the Act of 1882 the transaction is void altogether, even as between the parties, though money advanced on an unregistered bill may be recovered in quasi-contract (*see* Chapter 9) as money had and received (*North Central Wagon Finance Co Ltd* v *Brailsford* [1962] 1 All ER 502). Thus involuntary and voluntary dispositions by the seller are effective to give title.

The position where a seller of goods delivers them but provides in the contract that ownership is not to pass until the goods are paid for is considered in Chapter 11.

## CONDITIONS AND WARRANTIES

In Chapters 5 and 6 on the law of contract we have discussed the problems relating to statements made in the course of negotiating an agreement, and we have seen that such statements may be:

(a) pre-contractual, i.e. representations; or
(b) contractual, i.e. terms of the contract which may be either conditions or warranties.

The importance of the distinction lies in the remedies which are available.

## Conditions and warranties defined and distinguished

In the chapter on the law of contract we were concerned in the main with *express* statements made by the parties; here we are concerned with the conditions and warranties *implied* into contracts for the sale of goods by the Sale of Goods Act 1979 (as amended) and with how those conditions and warranties are defined by the Act.

The Act does not define a condition, but a condition may be said to be a material term or provision which, while going to the root of the contract, falls short of non-performance. A condition is a contractual term of a major description.

A warranty is defined by s 61 as an agreement with reference to goods which are the subject of a contract of sale, but collateral to the main purpose of the contract, the breach of which gives rise to a claim for damages, but not the right to reject the goods and treat the contract as repudiated. Although s 61 uses the word 'collateral' which gives the impression that a warranty is a term outside the contract, a warranty in the intention of s 61 is a term inside the contract but of a minor description which does not go to the root of the contract.

The Act does not say how we are to distinguish between conditions and warranties, and, although the words used by the parties are relevant, a stipulation may nevertheless be a condition though called a warranty in the contract (s 11(3)). When in doubt as to the nature of a stipulation, the court will look at the contract and the surrounding circumstances, and decide what the intentions of the parties were by looking at the effects of the breach and whether those intentions can best be carried out by treating the statement as a condition or as a warranty. **This as we have seen is the concept of the intermediate or innominate term and the following case provides an illustration of its application.**

### Cehave NV v Bremer Handelsgesellschaft mbH (The Hansa Nord) [1975] 3 All ER 739

The defendants sold citrus pulp pellets to the claimants. A term of the contract was 'shipment to be made in good condition'. The goods were not delivered all at once but in consignments, and when a particular consignment arrived at Rotterdam the market price of the goods had fallen and it was found that 1,260 tons of the goods out of a total consignment of 3,293 tons was damaged. The claimants rejected the whole cargo on the grounds that the shipment was not made in good condition. They then claimed the recovery of the price which amounted to £100,000. In the event, a middleman bought the goods at the price of £33,720 and resold them to the claimants at the same price. The claimants then used the pellets for making cattle food as was the original intention. The total result of the transaction, if it had been left that way, was that the claimants had received goods which they had bought for £100,000 for the reduced price of £33,720. The Court of Appeal decided in favour of the sellers. The court held that the contractual term 'shipment to be made in good condition' was not a condition within the meaning of the Sale of Goods Act, but was an intermediate or innominate term. As Lord Denning MR said: 'If a small portion of the whole cargo was not in good condition and arrived a little unsound, it should be met by a price allowance. The buyers should not have the right to reject the whole cargo unless it was serious or substantial.'

Lord Denning also rejected the view that the goods were not of merchantable (now satisfactory) quality simply because they were not perfect in every way. He said that the definition now contained in s 14(2) of the Sale of Goods Act 1979 (as amended) was to be preferred because it was more flexible than some of the earlier judicial decisions on previous legislation. In fact the definition delegates to the court the task of deciding what is merchantable (now satisfactory) quality in the circumstances of each particular case.

*Comment:* (i) This intermediate or innominate term approach was endorsed by the House of Lords in *Reardon Smith Line* v *Hansen-Tangen* [1976] 3 All ER 570.

(ii) This breach did not seem to have affected the use of the goods and looks like a business ploy to get them more cheaply. The views of Lord Denning in this case are now contained in s 15A of the Sale of Goods Act 1979 (inserted by the Sale and Supply of Goods Act 1994) under which the right to reject the goods for slight breaches is retained in consumer contracts but in non-consumer contracts a business buyer will, where the breach is slight, have to take delivery and sue for any loss.

## IMPLIED TERMS AND NEGLIGENT MISSTATEMENT – THE RELATIONSHIP

With regard to the relationship of the Misrepresentation Act 1967 and the implied terms of the Sale of Goods Act 1979 the following matters should be noted:

(a) claims based on negligent misrepresentation under s 2(1) of the 1967 Act will usually be joined with claims for damages for breach of condition or warranty. This is especially likely where the action is based on a misdescription going to the *identity* of the goods under s 13 of the 1979 Act (see later in this chapter),

(b) under the 1967 Act, the burden of disproving that the misrepresentation was negligent is on the representor, which is helpful to the claimant. Nevertheless, the best remedy for a misdescription going to the *identity* of the goods is still one based on the Act of 1979 because liability under that Act is strict and cannot be avoided by the seller showing he was not negligent.

It should also be noted that, in addition to the various remedies for loss arising out of false pre-contractual representations and breaches of contractual terms, an action for negligence may lie in tort provided the false statement is made negligently and a special relationship of proximity exists between the parties (*Hedley Byrne & Co Ltd* v *Heller and Partners Ltd* (1963) – *see* Chapter 5). This action is probably of less importance in the context of contract since s 2(1) of the Act of 1967 provides a statutory cause of action in negligence specifically designed for the contractual situation.

However, the 1967 Act is available *only* in regard to negligent misrepresentation *by the other party to the contract*. Where the contract is induced by the negligent misstatement of an outsider, *Hedley Byrne* and not the Misrepresentation Act 1967 must be used in order to get a remedy.

Thus a seller who makes a false statement about his goods may be liable at civil law in misrepresentation or for breach of an express or implied term. He may also be convicted of an offence under trade description legislation.

## TERMS IMPLIED BY THE SALE OF GOODS ACT

Some contracts of sale are very detailed; the parties have dealt with all or most eventualities. Many contracts of sale are not so detailed. The only thing the parties have dealt with is the goods to be sold and the price to be paid. The provisions of the Sale of Goods Act are designed in large measure to fill in the gaps by implied terms and other rules, e.g. as to the passing of the property and damages. We must now consider the question of implied terms.

## TIME

Where this has not been dealt with expressly the following rules apply.

### Payment

The Act provides that, unless a different intention appears from the contract, stipulations as to the time of payment are not deemed to be of the essence of a contract of sale. Whether any other stipulation as to time is of the essence of the contract or not depends upon the terms of the contract (ss 10(1) and(2)).

Thus failure to pay on time is a breach of warranty rather than a breach of condition. Consequently where under the contract payment is to be made before delivery of the goods but is not so made, at least for a short time, the seller cannot repudiate the contract and resell the goods, but may sue the buyer for damages for loss, if any, because of late payment and the court is able to add interest (*see* Chapter 9). This seems to give the buyer a compulsive credit but would appear to be the correct interpretation of the law (*see Payzu Ltd* v *Saunders* [1919] 2 KB 581). However, where payment is delayed for an excessive time, the seller may treat the contract as abandoned and resell the goods. The seller can, of course, provide expressly for a right of resale in the absence of prompt payment, and this right is implied where the goods are perishable (s 48(3)). Even where the goods are not perishable an unpaid seller may make time of the essence by giving notice to the buyer of his intention to resell, in which case the buyer must tender the price within a reasonable time or the seller can resell (*R V Ward* v *Bignall* [1967] 2 All ER 449).

### Delivery

The Act does not lay down any rules regarding the time of delivery of the goods, but the decided cases show that, where the time of delivery is fixed by the contract, failure to deliver or allow collection on time is a breach of condition and the buyer can reject the goods even though they are not damaged or in any way affected by the delay (*Bowes* v *Shand* (1877) – *see* Chapter 8). Where the goods are unaffected the buyer will normally only reject if external circumstances such as a fall in the market price lead him to do so. Nevertheless his right to reject has in the past remained. However, in view of the decision in *Cehave NV* v *Bremer Handelsgesellschaft mbH* (1975) (*see* Chapter 10) it may be that the courts are not so fully committed to the principle that any breach of condition by the seller entitles the buyer to take advantage of a fall in the market to reject the goods. Where the seller is bound to send the goods to the buyer but no time of delivery is fixed by the contract the seller is bound to deliver the goods within a reasonable time (s 29(3)). Failure to deliver within a reasonable time may amount to breach of condition (*Borthwick (Thomas) (Glasgow) Ltd* v *Bunge & Co Ltd* [1969] 1 Lloyd's Rep 17). It is assumed that this rule applies also where the seller's duty is to have the goods ready for collection.

The time of delivery may be waived by the buyer even after the delivery date and such a waiver is binding even though the seller has given no consideration for it. The basis of this rule according to Denning LJ in *Charles Rickards Ltd* v *Oppenhaim* (1950) was equitable estoppel (*see further* Chapter 8).

Other rules relating to delivery will be considered when dealing with performance of the contract (*see* Chapter 12).

## TITLE

The rules governing title are as follows.

### Implied condition as to title

Section 12(1) provides that, unless the circumstances show a different intention, there is an implied condition on the part of the seller that in the case of a sale he has the right to sell the goods, and that in the case of an agreement to sell, he will have the right to sell the goods at the time when the property is to pass (*Rowland* v *Divall* (1923), Chapter 9).

The decision in *Rowland*, which has been applied in subsequent cases (*see Karflex Ltd* v *Poole* [1933] 2 KB 251), produces, as we have seen, an unfortunate result in that a person who buys goods to which the seller has no title is allowed to recover the whole of the purchase price even though he has had some use and enjoyment from the goods before he is dispossessed by the true owner. It is thus difficult to suggest that there has been total failure of consideration. The Law Reform Committee (*see* 1966 Cmnd 2958, para 36) has recommended that, subject to further study of the law relating to restitution, an allowance in respect of use and enjoyment should be deducted from the purchase price and the balance returned to the claimant (*see also* comment to the *Rowland* case). It should be noted that the 1979 Act does not deal with this matter.

Section 12(1) might be construed as meaning that the seller must have the power to give ownership of the goods to the buyer, but if the goods can only be sold by infringing a trade mark, the seller has no right to sell for the purposes of s 12(1). **The following case illustrates this point.**

### Niblett Ltd *v* Confectioners' Materials Co Ltd [1921] 3 KB 387

The defendants agreed to sell to the claimants 3,000 cases of condensed milk to be shipped from New York to London. Of these cases, 1,000 bore labels with the word 'Nissly' on them. This came to the notice of the Nestlé Company and they suggested that this was an infringement of their registered trade mark. The claimants admitted this and gave an undertaking not to sell the milk under the title of 'Nissly'. They tried to dispose of the goods in various ways but eventually discovered that the only way to deal with the goods was to take off the labels and sell the milk without mark or label, thus incurring loss. *Held* – by the Court of Appeal – that the sellers were in breach of the implied condition set out in s 12(1) of the Sale of Goods Act. A person who can sell goods only by infringing a trade mark has no right to sell, even though he may be the owner of the goods. Atkin LJ also found the sellers to be in breach of the warranty under s 12(2) because the buyer had not enjoyed quiet possession of the goods.

### Implied warranties as to title

Section 12(2) provides that there is:

> An implied warranty that the goods are free, and will remain free until the time when the property is to pass, from any charge or encumbrance not disclosed or known to the buyer before the contract is made, and that the buyer will enjoy quiet possession of the goods except so far as it may be disturbed by the owner or other person entitled to the benefit of any charge or encumbrance so disclosed or known.

This does not apply where a limited interest is sold, but ss 12(4) and (5) do and contain similar provisions (*see below*).

It is not easy to see what rights this sub-section gives over those in s 12(1). The law does not recognise encumbrances over chattels unless the person trying to enforce them is in possession of the goods or in privity of contract with the person who is in possession (*Dunlop* v *Selfridge* (1915) – *see* Chapter 2). Thus if A uses his car as security for a loan from B then:

(a) if B takes the car into his possession, the charge will be enforceable if necessary by a sale of the vehicle;
(b) the charge is equally enforceable against the car while it is still in A's possession, though if A sells it to C, B will be prevented by lack of privity of contract from enforcing any remedies against the vehicle once it is in the possession of C.

Thus if situation (a) above applied, the sub-section is unnecessary since A could not deliver the vehicle even if he sold it and would, therefore, be liable in damages for non-delivery to C. If situation (b) above applied, the encumbrances would not attach to the vehicle once C had taken possession. C would not, therefore, require a remedy.

However, the usefulness of s 12(2) is illustrated by the decision of the Court of Appeal in *Microbeads AC* v *Vinhurst Road Markings Ltd* [1975] 1 All ER 529. In this case A sold road-marking machines to B. After the sale, C obtained a patent on the machines so that their continued use by B was in breach of that patent, and C was bringing an action against B in respect of this. In a claim by A against B for the purchase price, B wished to include in their defence breach of ss 12(1) and (2). It was held by the Court of Appeal that they could include breach of s 12(2) but not breach of s 12(1). There had been no breach of s 12(1) at the time of the sale so that A had not infringed that sub–section but since B's quiet possession had been disturbed after sale, A was in breach of s 12(2).

### Sales under a limited title

Under s 12(3), the sale of a limited interest is now possible. Where the parties intend only to transfer such a title as the seller may have, there is an implied warranty that all charges or encumbrances known to the seller and not known to the buyer have been disclosed to the buyer before the contract is made (s 12(4)), and an implied warranty that the buyer's quiet possession will not be disturbed (s 12(5)). There is an action by the buyer for breach of these warranties if, for example, he is dispossessed by the true owner. Furthermore, the seller is not able to contract out of this liability.

Sales under a limited title are common where the sale is of goods taken in execution by the bailiffs to satisfy a judgment debt.

## SALE BY DESCRIPTION

Section 13(1) provides that, where there is a contract for the sale of goods by description, there is an implied condition that the goods shall correspond with the description.

(a) A sale is by description where the purchaser is buying on a mere description, having never seen the goods. A classic example occurs in the case of mail-order transactions.
(b) A sale may still be by description even though the goods are seen or examined or even selected from the seller's stock by the purchaser, as in a sale over the counter, because most goods are described if only by the package in which they are contained. Therefore, a sale in a self-service store would be covered by s 13 though no words were spoken by the seller.

**The following case provides an example of the rule that inspection or sight of the goods will not necessarily prevent the sale from being by description.**

### Beale v Taylor [1967] 3 All ER 253

The defendant advertised a car for sale as being a 1961 Triumph Herald 1200 and he believed this description to be correct. The claimant answered the advertisement and later visited the defendant to inspect the car. During his inspection he noticed, on the rear of the car, a metal disc with the figure 1200 on it. The claimant purchased the car, paying the agreed price. However, he later discovered that the car was made up of the rear of a 1961 Triumph Herald 1200 welded to the front of an earlier Triumph Herald 948. The welding was unsatisfactory and the car was unroadworthy. *Held* – by the Court of Appeal – that the claimant's claim for damages for breach of the condition implied in the contract by s 13 of the Sale of Goods Act succeeded. The claimant had relied on the advertisement and on the metal disc on the rear and the sale was one by description even though the claimant had seen and inspected the vehicle.

*Comment:* It is, however, necessary for the buyer to show that it was the intention of the parties that the description should be relied upon by the buyer. In *Harlingdon Ltd v Hull Fine Art Ltd* [1990] 1 All ER 737 Hull was a company of art dealers controlled by Mr Christopher Hull. It was asked to sell two oil paintings described as being by Münter, a German artist of the Impressionist School. Mr Hull had no knowledge of the German Impressionist School. He contacted Harlingdon who were art dealers specialising in that field. Mr Hull told them that the paintings were by Münter. Harlingdon sent an expert to examine the paintings and at this stage Mr Hull made it clear that he was not an expert in the field. Following the inspection, Harlingdon bought one of the paintings which turned out to be a forgery. Harlingdon sued for breach of s 13. It was *held* by the Court of Appeal that the claim failed. Harlingdon had not relied on the description of the painting, but bought it after a proper and expert examination. The 'description' had not, therefore, become an essential term or condition of the contract.

It should be noted that this matter was not raised in *Leaf* v *International Galleries* (1950) (*see* Chapter 4) because Mr Leaf did not claim a breach of s 13. Presumably if he had done so he would have been required to show that it was the intention of the parties that he should rely on the description that the painting was by John Constable. This will normally be fairly easy to prove where the purchaser is an inexpert consumer. However, it was held in *Cavendish-Woodhouse* v *Manley* (1984) 82 LGR 376 that a seller could show that the sale was not by description by using such phrases as 'Sold as seen' or 'Bought as seen'. Such phrases do not, however, avoid the conditions of fitness and merchantable (now satisfactory) quality because the phrases were not regarded as general exclusion clauses.

If s 13 applies, it is enforced strictly, and every statement which forms part of that description is treated as a condition giving the buyer the right to reject the goods, even though the misdescription is of a minor nature. There is no such thing as a 'slight breach' of condition.

Buyers have been allowed to reject goods on seemingly trivial grounds, e.g. misdescriptions of how the goods are packed, and for any reason or even for no reason, and regardless of the fact that no damage has been suffered.

**The following case illustrates this point.**

### Moore & Co v Landauer & Co [1921] 2 KB 519

The claimants entered into a contract to sell the defendants a certain quantity of Australian canned fruit, the goods to be packed in cases containing 30 tins each. The goods were to be shipped 'per *SS Toromeo*'. The ship was delayed by strikes at Melbourne and in South Africa, and was very late in arriving at London. When the goods were discharged about one half of the consignment was packed in cases containing 24 tins only, instead of 30, and the buyers refused to accept them. *Held* – Although the method of packing made no difference to the market value of the goods, the sale was by description under s 13 of the Sale of Goods Act, and the description had not been complied with. Consequently, the buyers were entitled to reject the whole consignment by virtue of the provisions of what is now s 30(4) of the Sale of Goods Act (*see further* Chapter 12).

*Comment:* (i) The court seems to have adopted a somewhat purist approach to s 13 and had no real regard to the effect which the breach of description had on the contract, i.e. substantially none. Decisions such as this were described by Lord Wilberforce in the *Reardon-Smith* case as 'excessively technical'.

(ii) Under s 15A of the Sale of Goods Act 1979 (as inserted by the Sale and Supply of Goods Act 1994) the right of rejection is retained in consumer contracts but a business buyer will, where as here the breach is of slight or no effect, have to take delivery and sue for loss, if any.

However, if the defect is a matter of quality and/or condition of the goods rather than an identifying description, s 14 (*see below*) rather than s 13 applies. Although the Sale of Goods Act applies in the main to sales by dealers, s 13 applies even where the seller is not a dealer in the goods sold (*Varley* v *Whipp* [1900] 1 QB 513).

There can be no contracting out of s 13 at all where a business sells to a consumer or the contract is between persons in a private capacity. In a non-consumer sale contracting out is allowed to the extent that it is 'fair or reasonable' (*see further* Chapter 6).

Where the sale is by sample as well as by description, s 13(2) provides that the bulk must correspond with both the sample and the description. Thus in *Nichol* v *Godts* (1854) 10 Ex 191 a purchaser bought by sample 'foreign refined rape oil'. It was *held* that the goods must not only correspond with the sample, which they did, but also be in fact 'foreign refined rape oil' and not a mixture of rape and hemp oil which was inferior.

## Sale by description and misrepresentation distinguished

It should be noted that the description must be an identifying description to come under s 13. Statements regarding the state of a car's tyres, e.g. 'they were fitted 5,000 miles ago', are concerned more with quality and/or condition of the goods and s 13 probably does not apply, the claim being for misrepresentation. If s 13 did apply, then every trivial statement about the goods would be a breach of condition and the law relating to misrepresentation would have no place – a rather unlikely situation.

Statements such as the one above do not identify the goods. Suppose I were to say to a student: 'The notes you require are in the boot of my car. Here are the keys. My car is the one which had new tyres fitted 5,000 miles ago.' How could the student find the car? Not easily: the statement does not identify the vehicle!

## Sales in the course of a business

Although ss 12 and 13 of the 1979 Act apply to private sales as well as business sales, the s 14 implied terms of fitness and satisfactory quality apply only to sales *in the course of a business*. A problem may, therefore, arise where a milkman sells his old float in order to buy a new one. If the float is not fit for the purpose and/or of satisfactory quality, to what extent will the implied terms of s 14 be available to the person who has bought the float? Is it a private sale or a sale in the course of a business? It was decided by the Court of Appeal that it could be in the course of a business and that s 14 should be interpreted widely (*see Stevenson* v *Rogers* [1999] 1 All ER 613). Earlier statute law on sale of goods had confined s 14 to situations where the seller *dealt* in the goods, but the 1979 Act, following recommendations of the Law Commission, required only that the goods be sold *in the course of a business*, so that even an irregular sale of business property could be included and carry the implied conditions of fitness and satisfactory quality. If the sale is integral to the business, that is enough, even though the goods are not routinely sold by the business. Thus in *Stevenson* the sale by a person in business as a fisherman of one of his boats was within the 1979 Act and the condition of satisfactory quality applied. The decision in *Stevenson* runs contrary to the decision of the Court of Appeal in the *R & B Customs Brokers* case (1988) (*see* Chapter 6) where, because the purchase of a car by a business was irregular and not an integral part of the business, the company was treated as a consumer for the purpose of exclusions clauses. The Court of Appeal considered this case in *Stevenson*, but said that since it was an interpretation of the Unfair Contract Terms Act 1977, it could stand in that field, but the reasoning was not to be applied to the Sale of Goods Act 1979.

## IMPLIED CONDITIONS AS TO FITNESS

Section 14(3) lays down the following conditions.

Where the seller sells goods in the course of a business and the buyer (or debtor in a credit sale), expressly, or by implication, makes known: (a) to the seller, or (b) to the dealer in a credit sale any particular purpose for which the goods are being bought, there is an implied condition that the goods supplied under the contract are reasonably fit for that purpose whether or not that is a purpose for which such goods are commonly supplied, except where the circumstances show that the buyer (or debtor) does not rely, or that it is unreasonable for him to rely, on the skill or judgment of that seller or dealer.

There is no need for the buyer to specify the particular purpose for which the goods are required when they have in the ordinary way only one purpose, e.g. a hot-water bottle. If ordinary goods in everyday use are required for a particular purpose, this must be made known to the seller.

**The following cases illustrate these rules.**

### Priest v Last [1903] 2 KB 148

The claimant, a draper who had no special knowledge of hot-water bottles, bought such a bottle from the defendant who was a chemist. It was in the ordinary course of the defendant's business to sell hot-water bottles and the claimant asked him whether the indiarubber bottle he was shown would stand boiling water. He was told that it would not, but that it would stand hot water. The claimant did not state the purpose for which the bottle was required. In the event the bottle was filled with hot water and used by the claimant's wife for bodily application to relieve cramp. On the fifth time of using, the bottle burst and the wife was severely scalded. Evidence showed that the bottle was not fit for use as a hot-water bottle. *Held* – The claimant was entitled to recover the expenses he had incurred in the treatment of his wife's injuries for the defendant's breach of s 14(3) of the Sale of Goods Act. The circumstances showed that the claimant had relied on the defendant's skill and judgment, and although he had not mentioned the purpose for which he required the bottle, he had in fact used it for the usual and obvious purpose.

*Comment:* There was no question of the wife suing the chemist under Sale of Goods legislation because she was not a party to the contract. She could today have sued the manufacturer or the chemist in *negligence* (*see Donoghue v Stevenson* (1932), Chapter 11) if she could have proved negligence in either of them.

### Griffiths v Peter Conway Ltd [1939] 1 All ER 685

The defendants, who were retail tailors, supplied the claimant with a Harris tweed coat which was made to order for her. The claimant wore the coat for a short time and then developed dermatitis. She brought this action for damages alleging that the defendants were in breach of s 14(3) of the Sale of Goods Act because the coat was not fit for the purpose for which it was bought. Evidence showed that the claimant had an abnormally sensitive skin and that the coat would not have affected the skin of a normal person. *Held* – The claimant failed because s 14(3) did not apply. The defendants did not know of the claimant's abnormality and could not be expected to assume that it existed.

## Fitness for the purpose: meaning of reliance

In these days of national advertising under brand names it is somewhat unrealistic to assume that the buyer very often relies on the seller's skill and judgment. However, in order to make the law work, reliance on the seller's skill and judgment will be readily implied even to the extent of saying that, at least in sales to the general public as consumers, the buyer has gone to the seller because he relies on the seller having selected his stock with skill and judgment. The buyer must show that he has made known the purpose for which the goods are being bought. Reliance will then be presumed, unless it can be disproved, or if the seller can show that reliance was unreasonable.

The court has to decide what amounts to 'unreasonable reliance'. However, presumably the seller can disclaim responsibility. For example, suppose B goes into S's general stores and sees some tubes of glue. If he then asks whether the glue will stick metal to plastic and S says: 'I am not expert enough to say', then if B buys the glue and it does not stick metal to plastic, it would surely be unreasonable for B to suggest that he relied on S's skill and judgment.

There will in general be no implication of reliance where the buyer knows that the seller deals in only one brand of goods, e.g. where a public house sells only one brand of beer.

**The following cases provide illustrations of these rules.**

### Grant v Australian Knitting Mills Ltd [1936] AC 85

This was an appeal from the High Court of Australia to the Privy Council in England by a Dr Grant of Adelaide, South Australia. Dr Grant bought a pair of long woollen underpants from a retailer, the respondents being the manufacturers. The underpants contained an excess of sulphite which was a chemical used in their manufacture. This chemical should have been eliminated before the product was finished, but a quantity was left in the underpants purchased by Dr Grant. After wearing the pants for a day or two, a rash, which turned out to be dermatitis, appeared on the appellant's ankles and soon became generalised, compelling the appellant to spend many months in hospital. He sued the retailers and the manufacturers for damages. *Held* – (a) The retailers were in breach of the South Australian Sale of Goods Act 1895 (which is in the same terms as the English Act of 1979). They were liable under s 14(3) because the article was not fit for the purpose. They were liable under s 14(2) because the article was not of merchantable (now satisfactory) quality. (b) The manufacturers were liable in negligence, following *Donoghue* v *Stevenson* (see Chapter 11). This was a latent defect which could not have been discovered by a reasonable examination. It should also be noted that the appellant had a perfectly normal skin. (Compare *Griffiths* v *Peter Conway Ltd* (1939) above.)

*Comment:* Section 13 (sale by description) also applied even though this was a sale of a specific object which was seen by the purchaser. On this point Lord Wright said: 'a thing is sold by description though it is specific, so long as it is sold . . . as a thing corresponding to a description, e.g. woollen under-garments, a hot-water bottle, a secondhand reaping machine, to select a few obvious illustrations'. On the issue of reliance Lord Wright said: 'the reliance will be in general inferred from the fact that a buyer goes to the shop in confidence that the tradesman has selected his stock with skill and judgment'.

(ii) This case provides an interesting contrast between the liability of the supplier who was liable although not negligent, Sale of Goods Act liability being strict, and the liability of the manufacturer where the claimant was put to the extra burden of proving the manufacturer negligent. (*See* now Consumer Protection Act 1987 at Chapter 11.)

### Wren v Holt [1903] 1 KB 610

The claimant was a builder's labourer at Blackburn, and the defendant was the tenant of a beerhouse in the same town. The beerhouse was a tied house so that the defendant was obliged to sell beer brewed by a concern called Richard Holden Limited. The claimant was a regular customer and knew that the beerhouse was a tied house, and that only one type of beer was supplied. The claimant became ill and it was established that his illness was caused by arsenical poisoning due to the beer supplied to him. He now sued the tenant. *Held* – There was no claim under s 14(3) because the claimant could not have relied on the defendant's skill and judgment in selecting his stock, because he was bound to supply Holden's beer. However, s 14(2) applied, and since the beer was not of merchantable (now satisfactory) quality, the claimant was entitled to recover damages.

## Fitness: application to non-manufactured goods

The rules relating to fitness for the purpose under s 14(3) apply also to non-manufactured goods.

The following case illustrates this point.

### Frost v Aylesbury Dairy Co Ltd [1905] 1 KB 608

The defendants, whose business was the selling of milk, supplied milk to the claimant's household. The account book supplied to him contained several statements regarding the precautions taken by the defendants to keep their milk free from germs. This action was brought by the claimant for damage sustained by him on the death of his wife by typhoid fever contracted from the milk supplied by the defendants. *Held* – The claimant succeeded because the circumstances showed that he had relied on the defendant's skill and judgment to select and supply milk free from germs. He was, therefore, entitled to the benefit of s 14(3) of the Sale of Goods Act because the milk was not fit for human consumption. It was not a defence that no skill or judgment would have enabled the sellers to find out the defect. This emphasises that the liability of the supplier under the Sale of Goods Act is strict.

## Fitness: second-hand goods

In deciding the matter of fitness for the purpose in the case of second-hand goods, the buyer must expect that defects are likely to emerge sooner or later. However, if defects occur fairly quickly after sale, this is strong evidence that the goods were not reasonably fit at the time of sale.

The following case shows this point.

### Crowther v Shannon Motor Company [1975] 1 All ER 139

The claimant, relying on the skill and judgment of the defendants, bought a second-hand car from them. After being driven for over 2,000 miles in the three weeks after the sale the engine seized and had to be replaced. In his evidence the previous owner said that the engine was not fit for use on the road when he sold it to the defendants and on that basis the Court of Appeal held that there was a breach of s 14(3) at the time of resale. The fact that a car does not go for a reasonable time after sale is evidence that the car was not fit for the purpose at the time of sale.

*Comment:* This case makes clear that there is an obligation of reasonable durability on the seller of the goods.

### Fitness and satisfactory quality distinguished

Before proceeding to consider satisfactory quality, we must distinguish the two heads of liability, i.e. fitness and satisfactory quality. Under s 14(2) an article is regarded as not satisfactory where there is a manufacturing defect but a perfect article would have served the purpose; in other words, it is the right article but it is faulty. Under s 14(3) an article is regarded as not fit for the purpose because of its design or construction. It may be perfect in terms of its manufacture but its construction or design does not allow it to fit the purpose and consequently no amount of adjustment or repair will ever make it right. In other words, it is a perfect article but the wrong article for the purpose.

**The following case provides a useful illustration.**

### Baldry v Marshall [1925] 1 KB 260

The claimant was the owner of a Talbot racing car and was anxious to change it for a touring car because his wife refused to ride in the Talbot. The claimant wrote to the defendants asking for details of the Bugatti car for which they were agents. The claimant knew nothing of the Bugatti range, but asked for a car that would be comfortable and suitable for touring purposes. The defendants' manager said that a Bugatti would be suitable. The claimant later inspected a Bugatti chassis and agreed to buy it when a body had been put on it. When the car was delivered it was to all intents and purposes a racing car and not suitable for touring. The claimant returned the car, but he had paid £1,000 under the contract and now sued for its return on the grounds that the defendants were in breach of s 14(3) of the Sale of Goods Act, the car not being fit for the purpose. *Held* – The claimant had relied on the skill and judgment of the defendants and it was in the course of their business to supply cars. Therefore, there was a breach of s 14(3).

*Comment:* It will be appreciated that the Bugatti was of merchantable (now satisfactory) quality.

## SATISFACTORY QUALITY

By s 14(2) (as amended by the Sale and Supply of Goods Act 1994) *where the seller sells goods in the course of a business* there is an implied condition that the goods supplied under the contract are of satisfactory quality, except that there is no such condition:

(a) as regards defects specifically drawn to the buyer's attention before the contract is made; or

(b) if the buyer examines the goods before the contract is made, as regards defects which that examination ought to reveal.

If the seller does not normally deal in goods of the type in question, there is no condition as to fitness (nor as to satisfactory quality unless the sale is by sample which is dealt with below). The *only* condition in such a case is that the goods correspond with the description. This arises because s 14(1) provides that except as provided by s 14 and s 15 (sale by sample), and subject to any other enactment, there is no implied condition or warranty about the quality or fitness for any particular purpose of goods supplied under a contract of sale. If, therefore, S (who is not a dealer) sells a car to B with no express terms as to quality and fitness, the court is prevented by s 14 from implying conditions or warranties, even though S seems, from the circumstances, to have been warranting the car in good order.

The s 14 provision regarding satisfactory quality applies where the sale is by a dealer who does not ordinarily sell goods of precisely the same description. Thus if B ordered an 'X' brand motor bike from S who has not formerly sold that make, s 14 applies if the motor bike is unfit or not of satisfactory quality.

There is no need under s 14(2) for the buyer to show that he relied on the seller's skill and judgment, and the seller is liable for latent defects even though he is not the manufacturer and is merely marketing the goods as a wholesaler or retailer. Such a seller can, however, obtain an indemnity from the manufacturer if the buyer successfully sues him for defects in the goods.

### Sales through an agent

Section 14(5) is concerned with the problem of a private seller who sells through an agent. The sub-section provides that the implied conditions of fitness and satisfactory quality operate if the agent is selling in the ordinary course of business unless the principal is not acting in the course of business and the buyer is aware of this, or reasonable steps have been taken to bring it to his notice. Thus, for example, an auctioneer acting for a private seller could exclude these sections by making it clear that the principal was a private seller.

### Examination of the goods

The buyer is not obliged to examine the goods but if he does do so he will lose the protection of s 14(2) if he fails to notice obvious defects, at least in respect of such defects as where a new washing machine is examined and the buyer misses a rather obvious scratch on the front of the machine. The buyer can also lose his right to complain where the seller actually points out the defects.

### The price paid

Under s 14 the price paid by the buyer is a factor to be taken into account. Goods (provided they are not defective) are not unsatisfactory simply because their resale price is slightly less than that which the buyer paid, though they may be if the difference in purchase and resale price is substantial.

**The following case provides an example.**

### B S Brown & Son Ltd v Craiks Ltd [1970] I All ER 823

Brown and Son ordered a quantity of cloth from Craiks who were manufacturers. Brown's wanted it for making dresses but did not make this purpose known to Craiks who thought the cloth was wanted for industrial use. The price paid by Brown's was 36.25p per yard which was higher than the normal price for industrial cloth but not substantially so. The cloth was not suitable for making dresses and Brown's cancelled the contract and claimed damages. Both parties were left with substantial quantities of cloth but Craiks had managed to sell some of their stock for 30p per yard. Having failed in the lower court to establish a claim under s 14(3) since they had not made the purpose known to Craiks, Brown's now sued for damages under s 14(2). *Held* – by the House of Lords – that the claim failed. The cloth was still commercially saleable for industrial purposes though at a slightly lower price. It was not a necessary requirement of merchantability (now satisfactory quality) that there should be no difference between purchase and resale price. If the difference was substantial, however, it might indicate that the goods were not of merchantable (now satisfactory) quality. The difference in this case was not so material as to justify any such inference.

*Comment:* (i) Even where the goods are not purchased for resale the purchase price may be relevant. Thus the sale of a car with a defective clutch would be a sale of unsatisfactory goods, but if the seller makes an allowance in the price to cover the defect, it may not be (*Bartlett* v *Sydney Marcus Ltd* [1965] 2 All ER 753).

(ii) The case also decides that goods may be satisfactory if they are fit for one of the purposes for which they might be used even though they are unfit when used for another purpose.

## How were the goods described?

As regards the description applied to the goods, old cars or other mechanical items which are sold and described as scrap need not be of satisfactory quality. Furthermore, 'shop-soiled', 'fire-damaged', 'flood-salvage' and so on might imply non-satisfactory lines. In addition, old items, such as antiques and curios would not presumably be required to be in perfect working order. However, as we have seen it was *held* in *Cavendish-Woodhouse* v *Manley* (1984) 82 LGR 376 that the phrase on an invoice 'bought as seen' merely confirms that the purchaser has seen the goods. It does not exclude any implied terms as to quality or fitness.

## Duration of satisfactory quality

As regards the time during which the goods must be satisfactory, the law is not clear. So far as perishable goods are concerned, the decision in *Mash and Murrell* v *Joseph I Emmanuel* [1961] 1 All ER 485 is relevant. In that case potatoes, though sound when loaded in Cyprus, were rotten by the time the ship arrived in Liverpool, though there was no undue delay. It was held by Diplock J that the sellers were liable under s 14(2) because the goods should have been loaded in such a state that they could survive the normal journey and be in satisfactory condition when they arrived. In addition, the seller is liable for defects inherent in the goods when they are sold and will not escape merely because the defects do not become apparent until a later time. Circumstances such as those seen in *Crowther* v *Shannon Motor Co* (1975) (*see above*) provide an illustration of this situation.

## Goods partially defective

Where part only of the goods is unsatisfactory it seems to depend on how much of the consignment is defective. In *Jackson* v *Rotax Motor and Cycle Co Ltd* [1910] 2 KB 937 the claimants supplied motor horns to the defendants and one consignment was rejected by the defendants who alleged they were unmerchantable (now unsatisfactory). Half the goods were dented and scratched because of bad packing and the Court of Appeal *held* that the buyers were entitled to reject the consignment.

In this connection we have already considered s 15A of the Sale of Goods Act 1979 (as inserted by the Sale and Supply of Goods Act 1994) under which a consumer can reject goods where the breach is slight but a business buyer will, where the breach is slight, have to take delivery and sue for any loss. Clearly in the *Jackson* case s 15A would have allowed rejection. The breach was hardly slight.

## Merchantable quality: an unsatisfactory test

The test of merchantable quality in the Sale of Goods Act 1979 before amendment was regarded as somewhat unsatisfactory. A buyer of goods had no rights at all where there were a number of minor defects, such as small scratches and dents in a new car. The car was not necessarily unmerchantable because of these defects, nor was it unfit for the purpose. The Law Commission in Working Paper 85 suggested a new test as follows: 'The goods should be of such quality as would in all circumstances of the case be fully acceptable to a reasonable buyer who had full knowledge of their condition, quality and characteristics.'

However, case law began to show a more helpful interpretation even of existing law by the judiciary. In *Shine* v *General Guarantee Corporation* [1988] 1 All ER 911 the Court of Appeal held that a second-hand car was not of merchantable quality where the manufacturers' rust warranty had been terminated because, unknown to the buyer, the car had been involved in an accident and had been submerged in water. The claimant brought his action on learning this, though he had only minor problems with the car. Bush J said: 'Irrespective of its condition, it was a car which no member of the public knowing the facts would touch with a barge pole unless they could get it at a substantially reduced price to reflect the risk they were taking.' He went on to add that a car was not just a form of transport, it was also an investment and those who bought cars must have in mind their eventual saleability and in the case of Mr Shine, and no doubt others, pride in what was a specialist car (a Fiat X19 Bertoni-bodied sports car) for the enthusiast.

Again, in *Rogers* v *Parish (Scarborough) Ltd* [1987] 2 All ER 232 the Court of Appeal decided that a new Range Rover was not of merchantable quality or fit for the purpose, although it was capable of being driven and the defects repaired. Mustill LJ made clear that it was not enough to consider whether a car was roadworthy and driveable. There were other relevant factors. These were: 'The appropriate degree of comfort, ease of handling and reliability and, one may add, a pride in the vehicle's outward and interior appearance ... The buyer was entitled to value for his money.' These cases did begin to extend the concept of merchantability more into line with what most customers would think it should be. Legislation has now intervened (*see below*).

### Satisfactory quality: the current test

Section 1 of the Sale and Supply of Goods Act 1994 inserts in s 14 of the Sale of Goods Act 1979 a reformed definition of the concept of quality and merchantable quality has gone. As we have seen, there was always doubt about its scope and minor defects were not necessarily covered. Thus in *Millars of Falkirk Ltd* v *Turpie*, 1976 SLT 66 it was decided that a new car with a slight leak of oil in the power-assisted steering was, even so, of merchantable quality. Similarly a scratch on a new car's dashboard would not prevent it from being merchantable.

Now a sale in the course of a business carries an implied condition that the goods are of 'satisfactory quality'. To be of such quality the goods must meet the standard that a reasonable person would regard as satisfactory taking into account any description, price and other relevant circumstances. This is a general test but the section then explains that the quality of goods includes their state and condition and gives specific and non-exhaustive aspects of quality:

- fitness for all the purposes for which the goods are commonly supplied;
- appearance and finish;
- freedom from minor defects;
- safety;
- durability.

As before, defects specifically brought to the buyer's attention before contract or, if the buyer has examined the goods, those he ought to have noticed are not covered. Nevertheless many more defects will now be covered and the Law Commission (*see above*) took the view that in the *Millars* case the car would have failed the new test they proposed.

The above rules also apply to goods supplied under a contract for work and materials, e.g. an oil filter supplied when servicing a car (*see further* Chapter 13).

## FITNESS AND SATISFACTORY QUALITY

### Private sales

The rules as to fitness for purpose and satisfactory quality do not apply to private sales of second-hand goods and there is still a fairly wide application of the maxim *caveat emptor* (let the buyer beware). In practice only manufacturers, wholesalers, retailers and dealers in new or second-hand goods will be caught by the implied conditions. The courts cannot imply conditions and warranties into private contracts similar to those implied by the Act into sales by dealers, because, as we have seen, s 14(1) forbids it.

### Extension to items supplied with goods

The implied terms relating to fitness and satisfactory quality extend also to other items supplied under the contract of sale of goods, e.g. containers, foreign matter and instructions for use.

**The following cases cover these areas.**

### Geddling v Marsh [1920] I KB 668

The defendants were manufacturers of mineral waters and they supplied the same to the claimant who kept a small general store. The bottles were returnable when empty. One of the bottles was defective, and while the claimant was putting it back into a crate, it burst and injured her. *Held* – Even though the bottles were returnable, they were supplied under a contract of sale within s 14 of the Sale of Goods Act. The fact that the bottles were only bailed to the claimant was immaterial. There was an implied warranty of fitness for the purpose for which they were supplied, and the defendant was liable in damages.

*Comment:* Bray J was careful to point out that his decision was an interpretation of s 14 of the Sale of Goods Act only. It does not decide that the liability of a bailor is the same as that of a vendor.

### Wilson v Rickett, Cockerell & Co Ltd [1954] I QB 598

The claimant, a housewife, ordered from the defendants, who were coal merchants, a ton of 'Coalite'. The Coalite was delivered and when part of it was put on a fire in an open grate, it exploded causing damage to the claimant's house. In this action the claimant sought damages for breach of s 14 of the Sale of Goods Act. The County Court judge found that the explosion was not due to the Coalite but to something else, possibly a piece of coal with explosive embedded in it, which had got mixed with the Coalite in transit and had not come from the manufacturers of the Coalite. Therefore, he held that s 14(3) applied only to the Coalite and dismissed the action since the Coalite itself was fit for the purpose. The Court of Appeal, however, in allowing the appeal, pointed out that fuel of this kind is not sold by the lump but by the bag, and a bag containing explosive materials is, as a unit, not fit for burning. The explosive matter was 'goods supplied under the contract' for the purposes of s 14 and clearly s 14(2) applied, because the goods supplied were not of merchantable (now satisfactory) quality. Damages were awarded to the claimant. Regarding the applicability of what is now s 14(3), the Court of Appeal did not think this applied since the sale was under a trade name, and the claimant had not relied on the defendants' skill and judgment in selecting a fuel.

*Comment:* The assumption of no reliance where goods are purchased under a trade name no longer applies under the 1979 Act.

### Wormell v RHM Agriculture (East) Ltd [1986] I All ER 769

Mr Wormell, who was an experienced arable farmer, was unable by reason of cold, wet weather to spray his winter wheat crop to kill wild oats until much later than usual in the spring of 1983. He asked the defendants to recommend the best wild-oat killer which could be used later than normal. The agricultural chemical manager recommended a particular herbicide and Mr Wormell bought £6,438 worth of it.

The instructions on the cans stated that it ought not to be applied beyond the recommended stage of crop growth. It was said that damage could occur to crops sprayed after that stage and the herbicide would give the best level of wild-oat control at the latest stage of application consistent with the growth of the crop.

Mr Wormell felt that the need to kill the wild oats was so important that he would risk some damage to the crops by applying the herbicide quite late. From his understanding of the instructions, the risk was not that the herbicide would not be effective on the wild oats, but if the spray was used after the recommended time, then the crop might be damaged. The herbicide was applied but proved to be largely ineffective.

Mr Wormell claimed damages for breach of contract in respect of the sale of the herbicide. He alleged that it was not of merchantable (now satisfactory) quality, contrary to s 14(2) of the Sale of Goods Act, nor was it fit for the purpose for which it was supplied, namely to control weeds, and in particular, wild oats, contrary to s 14(3) of the same Act.

RHM argued that since the herbicide would kill the wild oats, the fact that the instructions caused it to be applied at a time when it was not effective did not make the herbicide itself unmerchantable (now unsatisfactory) or unfit for the purpose.

Piers Ashworth QC, sitting as a Deputy Judge of the High Court, said that one had to look at how Mr Wormell understood the instructions and how a reasonable user would understand them. Mr Wormell understood the instructions to mean that the herbicide would be effective if it was sprayed at any time, but if sprayed late there was a risk of crop damage. The judge concluded that a reasonable farmer would have understood the instructions in the same way. He thought that the instructions were consequently misleading.

For the purposes of the Sale of Goods Act 'goods' included the container and packaging for the goods and any instructions supplied with them. If the instructions were wrong or misleading the goods would not be of merchantable (now satisfactory) quality or fit for the purpose for which they were supplied under s 14(2) and (3). This statement was approved in a 1987 appeal to the Court of Appeal though on the facts the Court found the instructions adequate.

*Comment:* The decision was reversed by the Court of Appeal because the instructions were misunderstood. However, the Court of Appeal agreed that there is a legal obligation to give adequate guidance as to how the product is to be used.

## Injury to third party, purchaser's indemnity

It should be noted that if a retailer sells goods which are faulty and in breach of s 14, he is obliged to indemnify the purchaser if the faulty goods injure a third party to whom the purchaser is found liable. However, no such indemnity is payable if the purchaser has continued to use the goods having become aware that they are faulty and dangerous.

**The following case makes this point.**

### Lambert v Lewis [1981] 1 All ER 1185

Mr Lewis owned a Land Rover and a trailer. His employee, Mr Larkin, was driving it when the trailer broke away. It collided with a car coming from the opposite direction. Mr Lambert, who was driving that car, was killed and so was his son. His wife and daughter, who were also passengers, survived and then sued Mr Lewis for damages in negligence. He joined the retailer who sold him the towing hitch which had become detached from the trailer and was basically the cause of the collision. The retailer was sued under s 14 (goods not fit for the purpose nor of merchantable (now satisfactory) quality). The court found that the towing hitch was badly designed and a securing brass spindle and handle had come off it so that only dirt was keeping the towing pin in position. It had been like that for some months and Mr Lewis had coupled and uncoupled the trailer once or twice a week during that time and knew of the problem.

The claimants succeeded in their action against Mr Lewis. He failed in his claim against the retailer. The House of Lords decided that when a person first buys goods he can rely on s 14.

However, once he discovers that they are defective but continues to use them and so causes injury, he is personally liable for the loss caused. He cannot claim an indemnity under s 14 from the retailer. The chain of causation is broken by the buyer's continued use of the goods while knowing that they are faulty and may cause injury.

*Comment:* The above summary does not concern itself with the possible liability of the manufacturers in terms of the design problem. However, a point of interest arises in connection with it. The issue of the manufacturers' liability was taken by an action in negligence. The court refused to construe a collateral contract between Mr Lewis and the manufacturers although he bought the hitch on the strength of the manufacturers' advertising. (Compare *Carlill*, Chapter 1, where such a contract was rather exceptionally construed.)

### Usage of trade

Section 14(4) provides that an implied warranty or condition as to quality or fitness for a particular purpose may be attached to a contract of sale by usage. Where the transaction is connected with a particular trade, the customs and usages of that trade give the context in which the parties made their contract and may give a guide as to their intentions. Thus in a sale of canary seed in accordance with the customs of the trade it was *held* that the buyer could not reject the seed delivered on the grounds that there were impurities in it. A custom of the trade prevented this but allowed instead a rebate on the price paid (*Peter Darlington Partners Ltd* v *Gosho Co Ltd* [1964] 1 Lloyd's Rep 149).

## SALE BY SAMPLE

Section 15(1) states that a contract of sale is a contract of sale by sample where there is a term in the contract, express or implied, to that effect. The mere fact that the seller provides a sample for the buyer's inspection is not enough: to be such a sale there must be either an express provision in the contract to that effect, or there must be evidence that the parties intended the sale to be by sample.

There are three implied conditions in sale by sample:

(a) *the bulk must correspond with the sample in quality* (s 15(2)(a));
(b) *the buyer shall have a reasonable opportunity of comparing the bulk with the sample* (s 15(2)(b)). The buyer will not be deemed to have accepted the goods until he has had an opportunity to compare the bulk with the sample, and will be able, therefore, to reject the goods, even though they have been delivered, if the bulk does not correspond with the sample. He is not left with the remedy of damages for the breach of warranty (see s 34, in Chapter 11);
(c) *the goods shall be free from any defect, making their quality unsatisfactory, which would not be apparent on reasonable examination of the sample* (s 15(2)(c)).

The effect of s 15(2)(c) is to exclude the implied condition of satisfactory quality if the defect could have been discovered by reasonable examination of the sample whether or not there has in fact been any examination of the sample. This is presumably based upon the premise that the seller is entitled to assume that the buyer will examine the sample. The provision is in contrast with s 14(2) where the implied condition of satisfactory quality is not excluded unless an examination has actually taken place.

A reasonable examination for the purpose of a sale by sample is such an examination as is usually carried out in the trade concerned.

**The following case shows how s 15 applies.**

### Godley v Perry [1960] 1 All ER 36

The first defendant, Perry, was a newsagent who also sold toys, and in particular displayed plastic toy catapults in his window. The claimant, who was a boy aged six, bought one for 6d. While using it to fire a stone, the catapult broke, and the claimant was struck in the eye, either by a piece of the catapult or the stone, and as a result he lost his left eye. The chemist's report given in evidence was that the catapults were made from cheap material unsuitable for the purpose and likely to fracture, and that the moulding of the plastic was poor, the catapults containing internal voids. Perry had purchased the catapults from a wholesaler with whom he had dealt for some time, and this sale was by sample, the defendant's wife examining the sample catapult by pulling the elastic. The wholesaler's supplier was another wholesaler who had imported the catapults from Hong Kong. This sale was also by sample and the sample catapult was again tested by pulling the elastic. In this action the claimant alleged that the first defendant was in breach of the conditions implied by s 14(2) and (3) of the Sale of Goods Act.

The first defendant brought in his supplier as third party, alleging against him a breach of the conditions implied by s 15(2)(c), and the third party brought in his supplier as fourth party, alleging breach of s 15(2)(c) against him. *Held* –

(a)  The first defendant was in breach of s 14(2) and (3) because:
   (i)  the catapult was not reasonably fit for the purpose for which it was required. The claimant relied on the seller's skill or judgment, this being readily inferred where the customer was of tender years (s 14(3));
   (ii)  the catapult was not merchantable (now not of satisfactory quality) (s 14(2)).
(b)  The third and fourth parties were both in breach of s 15(2)(c) because the catapult had a defect which rendered it unmerchantable (now 'unsatisfactory') and this defect was not apparent on reasonable examination of the sample. The test applied, i.e. the pulling of the elastic, was all that could be expected of a potential purchaser. The third and fourth parties had done business before, and the third party was entitled to regard without suspicion any sample shown to him and to rely on the fourth party's skill in selecting his goods.

## LIABILITY OF SELLER WHERE GOODS ARE IN A DANGEROUS CONDITION

The Sale of Goods Act 1979 deals only with contractual rights and duties. However, a seller of goods may be liable in the tort of negligence or under the Consumer Protection Act 1987 to the buyer or third parties because the goods sold are dangerous and might cause injury.

**The following case provides an illustration.**

### Fisher v Harrods (1966) 110 SJ 133

The defendants bought a jewellery cleaner from a manufacturer without making enquiries as to its safety in use. It contained substances which were injurious to the eyes but no indication or warning of this was given either on the bottle or in any other way. A bottle of the cleaner sold by the defendants injured the claimant who was not the buyer. The contents would not come out of the container. The claimant applied gentle pressure. The bung flew out and some of the contents damaged her eyes. She now claimed damages from the defendants and it was held that they had been negligent in the circumstances of the case by failing to make enquiries of the manufacturer, failing to have the cleaner analysed, and selling it without a warning. Damages of £1,995 were awarded.

*Comment:* (i) The action against Harrods was particularly important to the claimant because the manufacturers of the cleaner had few assets and were not insured.

(ii) An action would also have been available today under the Consumer Protection Act 1987 against the supplier if he had refused to give the name of the manufacturer and of course against the manufacturer himself. However, since an action against the manufacturer would have been uneconomic and Harrods would have been likely to have given his name, the action against Harrods in negligence at common law would have had to be pursued as it was in this case. There was no claim in contract because the claimant was not the purchaser.

## GRADED QUESTIONS

### Essay mode

1  (a)  What liability is imposed on the seller of goods as regards their satisfactory quality and their fitness for the purpose of those goods?
   (b)  To what extent, if any, is the seller able to exclude his liability in respect of such obligations?

*(The Institute of Company Accountants)*

2  (a)  Explain the legal protection given in the Sale of Goods Act to a buyer with respect to the quality of the goods bought.
   (b)  Henry bought some meat from Bernard, a butcher, but the meat, unknown to Bernard, was contaminated. Wilma, Henry's wife, cooked the meat but, after eating it, both Henry and Wilma became seriously ill. Advise Bernard as to his possible liability.

*(The Chartered Institute of Management Accountants)*

3  P approached Q Garages Ltd and informed a car salesman that he wished to buy a second-hand car. One of the cars for sale at the garage was advertised as '1996 model Volvo estate, one previous owner, excellent condition, good for thousands of trouble-free miles. Exceptional value at only £5,000'. P expressed an interest in the vehicle. Following a test drive, P purchased the vehicle.

After four months, during which time the car covered 10,000 miles, the car broke down and required expensive engine repairs. In addition, P has recently discovered that the car is, in fact, a 1995 model.

Advise P as to his rights, if any, under the Sale of Goods Act 1979.

*(Association of Chartered Certified Accountants)*

## Objective mode

Four alternative answers are given. Select ONE only. Circle the answer which you consider to be correct. Check your answers by referring back to the information given in the relevant chapter and against the answers in the back of the book.

1  Is an agreement by Rose in 1999 to buy, from Premier Garages Ltd, a year 2000 factory-built BMW 323 in a certain colour with extras as specified by her (the car to be obtained from the manufacturers by Premier):

   A  A contract for the sale of future goods?
   B  A contract for the supply of work and materials?
   C  A contract for the sale of unascertained goods?
   D  A contract for the sale of goods by sample?

2  Jane enters into a hire-purchase agreement with Merchant Credit Ltd for the purchase of a second-hand car for a deposit of £1,000 followed by 12 monthly instalments of £150 with an option to purchase on completion of these payments. Jane is not protected by the Sale of Goods Act 1979:

   A  Because the Act does not apply to second-hand goods.
   B  Because the Act does not apply to motor vehicle sales.
   C  Because the contract is not for sale of goods but for hire of goods and governed by a different statute.
   D  Because the whole price should be paid at once to be a sale of goods.

3  Carol wishes to buy a new carpet for her bedroom. She goes to Barry's showroom and sees a carpet of the colour and design she requires. The carpet is described as 'best quality Axminster' and costs £20.00 per square yard. Carol orders the carpet but on delivery discovers that it is not 'Axminster' but an inferior mixture of wool and nylon. What is the legal position?

   A  Carol must accept the carpet since she saw and inspected it. The maxim is *caveat emptor*.
   B  Carol may reject the carpet. Since she has made known the purpose for which the carpet was required, it must be of satisfactory quality.
   C  Carol must accept the carpet, since the condition that goods must correspond to the description cannot apply if the buyer has inspected and selected the goods in question.
   D  Carol may reject the carpet for breach of condition that the goods must correspond with the description.

4  Porter, a gentleman of means, advertised one of his private motor cars for sale at £1,000. Alice, an impecunious student, bought the car intending to use it to get to work. The car was a 1981 Gasper and was unreliable and temperamental. Alice sued for the return of the price paid.

   A  Porter is liable since the goods were not fit for the purpose required impliedly made known to him by Alice.
   B  Porter is not liable since there is no implied condition of fitness for use in a private sale.

    **C** Porter is not liable since Alice should have known that as the price was low the conditions of satisfactory quality or fitness for use would be excluded.

    **D** Porter is liable. Since Alice was going to use the car for business, the condition of satisfactory quality will apply.

**5** In a contract for the sale of goods there is an implied warranty under the Sale of Goods Act 1979 that:

    **A** The seller has the right to sell the goods.

    **B** In goods sold by description, the goods correspond with the description.

    **C** In goods sold by sample, the bulk corresponds with the sample.

    **D** The goods are free from any charge or encumbrance not known to the buyer.

**6** In the law of contract the so-called 'postal rules' state that:

    **A** Both acceptance and revocation will take effect from the time the letter conveying the acceptance or revocation is properly posted.

    **B** Where any written offer is made, acceptance is effective as soon as the letter of acceptance is posted.

    **C** Where the post has been signified as an acceptable means of communication, the acceptance is effective as soon as the letter of acceptance is posted.

    **D** Where the post has been signified as an acceptable means of communication, the acceptance is effective when the letter of acceptance is delivered.

*Answers to questions set in objective mode appear on p 708.*

# ⬛⬛ THE SALE OF GOODS II

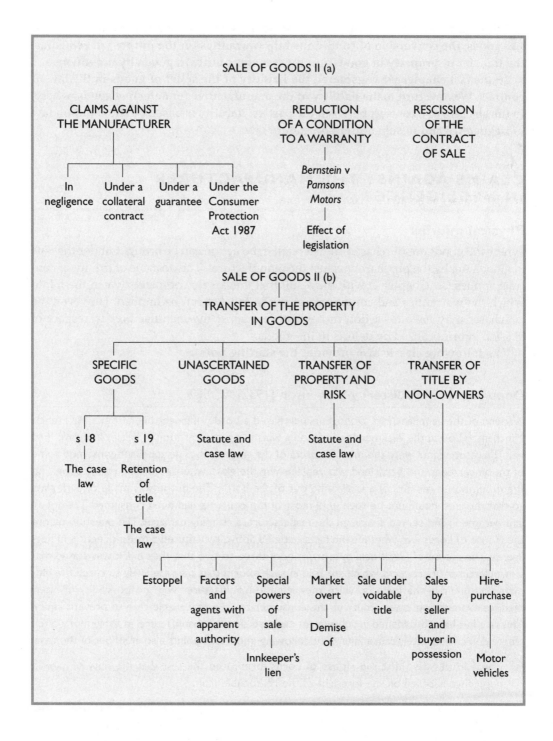

SALE OF GOODS II (a)

CLAIMS AGAINST THE MANUFACTURER
- In negligence
- Under a collateral contract
- Under a guarantee
- Under the Consumer Protection Act 1987

REDUCTION OF A CONDITION TO A WARRANTY
- *Bernstein v Pamsons Motors*
- Effect of legislation

RESCISSION OF THE CONTRACT OF SALE

SALE OF GOODS II (b)

TRANSFER OF THE PROPERTY IN GOODS

SPECIFIC GOODS
- s 18
  - The case law
- s 19
  - Retention of title
    - The case law

UNASCERTAINED GOODS
- Statute and case law

TRANSFER OF PROPERTY AND RISK
- Statute and case law

TRANSFER OF TITLE BY NON-OWNERS
- Estoppel
- Factors and agents with apparent authority
- Special powers of sale
  - Innkeeper's lien
- Market overt
  - Demise of
- Sale under voidable title
- Sales by seller and buyer in possession
- Hire-purchase
  - Motor vehicles

The objectives of this chapter are to consider civil claims against manufacturers of goods, the conversion of conditions into warranties for the purpose of remedies, the transfer of property in goods and the transfer of title in goods by non-owners.

In the last chapter we considered the liability of the seller of goods in the law of contract. We now turn to the liability of the manufacturer for defective goods, where, in the absence of a contract between the parties, liability is based on the common law of negligence and to some extent on statute law.

## CLAIMS AGAINST THE MANUFACTURER IN NEGLIGENCE

### Physical injuries

Where the goods are purchased from a retailer, no action can be brought under the Sale of Goods Act by the purchaser against the manufacturer. The doctrine of privity of contract applies (*see* Chapter 2) with the result that there is no contract between them into which the warranties and conditions set out in the Act can be implied. However, the purchaser may have an action in negligence against the manufacturer in respect of *physical* injuries caused by defects in the goods.

**The following classic case provides the starting point.**

### Donoghue (or M'Alister) v Stevenson [1932] AC 562

A friend of the appellant, Mrs Donoghue, purchased a bottle of ginger beer from a Mr Francis Minchella, who ran the Wellmeadow café, on a warm August afternoon in Paisley and gave it to her. The respondents were the manufacturers of the ginger beer. The appellant consumed some of the ginger beer and her friend was replenishing the glass, when, according to the appellant, the decomposed remains of a snail came out of the bottle. The bottle was made of dark glass so that the snail could not be seen until most of the contents had been consumed. The appellant became ill and served a writ on the manufacturers claiming damages. The question before the House of Lords was whether the facts outlined above constituted a cause of action in negligence. The House of Lords *held* by a majority of three to two that they did. It was stated that a manufacturer of products, which are sold in such a form that they are likely to reach the ultimate consumer in the form in which they left the manufacturer with no possibility of intermediate examination, owes a duty to the consumer to take reasonable care to prevent injury. This rule has been broadened in subsequent cases so that the manufacturer is liable more often where defective chattels cause injury. The following important points also arise out of the case:

(a) it was in this case that the House of Lords formulated the test that the duty of care in negligence is based on the foresight of the reasonable man;

(b) Lord Macmillan's remark that the categories of negligence are never closed suggests that the tort of negligence is capable of further expansion, though as yet there is difficulty in cases involving economic (money) loss as distinct from physical injury;

(c) the duty of care with regard to chattels as laid down in the case relates to chattels not dangerous in themselves. The duty of care in respect of chattels dangerous in themselves, e.g. explosives, is much higher;

(d) the appellant had no cause of action against the retailer in contract because her friend bought the bottle, so there was no privity of contract between the retailer and the appellant. Therefore, terms relating to fitness for purpose and merchantable (now satisfactory) quality, implied into such contracts by the Sale of Goods Act, did not apply here.

*Comment:* A remedy under the Sale of Goods Act could have been given to the appellant if the reasoning of Tucker J in *Lockett* v *A & M Charles Ltd* [1938] 4 All ER 170 had been applied in *Donoghue*. In *Lockett* husband and wife went into a hotel for lunch. The wife ordered whitebait, which was not fit for human consumption. She only ate a small amount of the whitebait and was then taken ill. In the subsequent action against the hotel, Tucker J held that, although the husband ordered the meal, there was an assumption in these cases that each party would be, if necessary, personally liable for what he or she consumed. There was, therefore, a contract between the hotel and the wife into which Sale of Goods Act terms could be implied and she was awarded damages because the whitebait was not fit for the purpose or of merchantable (now satisfactory) quality. This approach is surprisingly modern in spite of the fact that the case was decided in 1938.

The rule arrived at in *Donoghue* v *Stevenson* has been widened since 1932, and now applies to defective chattels generally which cause injuries to purchasers (*see Grant* v *Australian Knitting Mills Ltd* (1936), in Chapter 10). However, although the above case shows that the manufacturer has a duty to take care, evidence may show that he was not in breach of that duty because he took proper precautions.

In addition, liability in negligence is not strict as it is under the Sale of Goods Act. The claimant must prove negligence in the process of manufacture. However, assistance is given by the plea of *res ipsa loquitur* (the thing speaks for itself). If this plea is accepted by the court, the defendant must show he was not negligent or explain how the matter could have come about without his negligence. If he fails to do this, the claimant wins the case.

**The following case provides an illustration.**

## Daniels *v* R White and Sons [1938] 4 All ER 258

The claimants, who were husband and wife, sued the first defendants, who were manufacturers of mineral waters, in negligence. The claimants had been injured because a bottle of the first defendants' lemonade, which they had purchased from a public house in Battersea, contained carbolic acid. The claimants pleaded *res ipsa loquitur*. This plea was accepted by the court and the defendant was, therefore, required to produce evidence of a safe system and proper supervision. Evidence showed that the manufacturers took all possible care to see that no injurious matter got into the lemonade, and that the husband when he bought the lemonade from the public house asked for it by mentioning the manufacturers' name. It was *held* that the manufacturers were not liable in negligence because the duty was not to ensure that the goods were in perfect condition but only to take reasonable care to see that no injury was caused to the eventual consumer. This duty had been fulfilled. The second defendant, who was the landlady of the Battersea public house from which the goods were purchased, was held liable under s 14(2) of the Sale of Goods Act, because the goods were not of merchantable (now satisfactory) quality. This liability does not depend on proof that the seller has not exercised reasonable care. Liability under the Sale of Goods Act is strict.

*Comment:* (i) The court in this case does not seem to have taken the point that if the system was a good one then the alien matter must have got into the lemonade because of the negligence of an employee, and since an employer is liable for the negligence of his employees, White's ought to have been liable in this case. The decision has been much criticised and MacKenna J in *Hill* v *James Crowe (Cases)* [1978] I All ER 812 refused to follow it saying that a manufacturer can be vicariously liable for the negligence of his workman, notwithstanding the fact that he has a good system of work and adequate supervision.

(ii) A more successful case was *Steer* v *Durable Rubber Manufacturing Co Ltd, The Times,* 20 November 1958, where the claimant was a six-year-old girl. She was scalded when her hotwater bottle burst. The bottle was only three months old. She had no evidence to show exactly how the bottle was defective. However, the Court of Appeal accepted a plea of *res ipsa loquitur* after it was established that a bottle of this kind would normally last for at least three years. The manufacturers could not show that they had not been negligent and were held liable.

(iii) The decision of the Court of Appeal in *Carroll* v *Fearon* [1998] *Current Law* para 3995 is also of interest. In that case one of the tyres on a car suffered a sudden and complete tread strip while on a motorway causing a collision, one fatality and a number of serious injuries when there was a head-on accident. The manufacturers of the tyre defended a claim for negligence by saying that the claimants must prove what act(s) of theirs made the tyre defective. However, the court ruled that the manufacturers were negligent and liable and that it was not necessary for the claimants to identify *specific* acts of negligence in the process of manufacture of the tyre.

In certain of the cases mentioned above, the question of inspection of the goods was raised. It was an important fact in the decision in *Donoghue* v *Stevenson* (1932) that the bottle was made of dark glass, so that the snail could not be seen on external inspection of the bottle, and that normally no inspection of goods would take place until they reached the consumer. It is not thought that in the developing law of negligence a manufacturer can rely on an inspection revealing the defects in his product, except perhaps in a special case where it is known that an expert inspection normally takes place. If such an inspection does not take place, or fails to find the defect which it should have found, the manufacturer may regard this as a *novus actus interveniens* (a new act intervening) breaking the chain of causation between his negligence and the injury so that the claimant's action will fail.

## Economic loss

Product liability in negligence has, up to recent times, been confined to defective chattels which cause *physical* injury to purchasers as in *Donoghue* and *Grant*.

The law seemed to have taken a step forward in the following case by extending product liability in negligence to complaints relating to defects in goods which had caused economic loss rather than physical injury. This seems unlikely to develop at the present time for the reasons given in the comment to the case.

## Junior Books Ltd v Veitchi Co Ltd [1982] 3 All ER 201

Junior Books (J) owned a building. Veitchi (V) were flooring contractors working under a contract for the main contractor who was doing work on the building. There was no privity of contract between J and V. It was alleged by J that faulty work by V left J with an unserviceable building and high maintenance costs so that J's business became unprofitable. The House of Lords decided in favour of J on the basis that there was a duty of care. V were in breach of a duty owed to J to take reasonable care to avoid acts or omissions including laying an allegedly defective floor which they ought to have known would be likely to cause the owners econom-ic loss, including loss of profits caused by the high cost of maintaining the allegedly defective floor, and in so far as J were required to mitigate the loss by replacing the floor itself, the cost of replacement was the appropriate measure of V's liability. The standard of care required is apparently the contractual duty and so long as the work is up to contract standard, then the defendant in a case such as this will not be in breach of his duty. Lord Fraser of Tullybelton said:

> Where a building is erected under a contract with a purchaser, then provided the building, or part of it, is not dangerous to persons or to other property and subject to the law against misrepresentation, I can see no reason why the builder should not be free to make with the purchaser whatever contractual arrangements about the quality of the product the purchaser wishes. However jerry-built the product, the purchaser would not be entitled to damages from the builder if it came up to the contractual standards.

*Comment:* (i) The decision in this case has been doubted in a number of more recent deci-sions. In *Simaan General Contracting Co* v *Pilkington Glass* [1988] 1 All ER 791 the claimants S Ltd were the main contractors to construct a building in Abu Dhabi for a sheikh. The erection of glass walling together with supplying the glass was subcontracted to an Italian company (Feal). Feal bought the glass from the defendants Pilkingtons (P Ltd). The glass units should have been a uniform shade of green but some were various shades of green and some were red. The sheikh did not pay S Ltd. They chose to sue P Ltd in tort rather than Feal in contract for their loss, i.e. the money which the sheikh was withholding. *Held* – by the Court of Appeal – that since there was no physical damage, this was purely a claim for economic loss and P Ltd had no duty of care. S Ltd's claim failed. Feal would have been liable under the Supply of Goods and Services Act 1982 (see Chapter 13) but for some reason were not sued. Economic loss can be recovered in contract. Dillon LJ said of *Junior Books* that it had 'been the subject of so much analysis and discussion that it cannot now be regarded as a useful pointer to any development of the law. It is difficult to see that future citation from *Junior Books* can ever serve any useful purpose.'

(ii) The decision in *Junior Books* came at the end of a long line of cases which had moved away from the old rule in negligence liability that damages were not recoverable unless it was shown that a duty of care existed to a situation in which the opposite view was taken, i.e. given that there was fault damages were recoverable and there was no need for an over-concentration on the duty of care. The *Simaan* case, along with others, represents a move back to the earlier and less liberal approach of duty of care and the older case law. Liability was being considerably extended by the more liberal approach and insurance indemnity harder to get and more costly, hence the less liberal line.

## Contributory negligence

Even though the claimant has managed to prove negligence in the manufacturer, the latter may still be able to obtain a reduction in the damages or even defeat the claim by proving that the claimant was guilty of contributory negligence as where he contributed to the damage or was even entirely responsible for it by, for example, failing to observe operating instructions or using the product after knowledge that it was defective. The Law Reform (Contributory Negligence) Act 1945 applies. Under it the court may, for example, assess damages at £20,000 but decide that the claimant was 50 per cent to blame and reduce the damages to £10,000. In an extreme case the court may decide that the claimant was 100 per cent to blame so that he recovers nothing.

## Third-party proceedings

Strict liability under the Act of 1979 can, in effect, be imposed on a manufacturer by means of third- (or fourth-) party proceedings. Thus, if the seller is sued by the buyer for breach of an implied condition under the Act, the seller may claim an indemnity from his own supplier, which may be the manufacturer. If the retailer has purchased from a wholesaler, the retailer may claim an indemnity from the wholesaler, who may in turn claim an indemnity from the manufacturer who supplied the goods. In this way the manufacturer can be made to pay for defects affecting the quality or fitness of the goods. *Godley* v *Perry* (1960) provides an example of joinder of parties (*see* Chapter 10). In connection with third-party proceedings, it should be borne in mind that the retailer may be unable to make a successful claim because of a 'reasonable' exclusion clause in the contract between him and his previous suppliers. In addition, the retailer's claim will be ineffective if one or more of the previous suppliers is insolvent.

# COLLATERAL CONTRACTS WITH THE MANUFACTURER

The manufacturer may also be liable for defects in quality or fitness under a collateral contract. Thus in *Shanklin Pier Ltd* v *Detel Products Ltd* [1951] 2 All ER 471 Shanklin entered into a contract with A to paint the Pier and asked A to use paint made by Detel, the suitability of which had been communicated to Shanklin by Detel's agent. The paint was not suitable and Shanklin recovered damages against Detel for breach of a contract which the court *held* was collateral to the main contract with A. This applies, however, only where a specific and express undertaking has been given by the manufacturer to the seller, and it is doubtful whether such a claim could be based on statements made in a manufacturer's public advertisements. There are no firm illustrations of this in English law, though *Carlill* v *Carbolic Smoke Ball Co* (1893) (*see* Chapter 1) could perhaps be developed. The court did not in fact go for the collateral contract solution in *Lambert* v *Lewis* (1981) (*see* Chapter 10). The action against the manufacturer in that case was framed in negligence.

The Law Commission has recognised the need to provide some general form of action against the manufacturer but has felt that this cannot be done by a simple amendment to the Sale of Goods Act 1979. The Commission, therefore, recommends that a wider study of the problem be made before embarking upon legislative measures (Exemption Clauses, First Report, para 63).

## MANUFACTURERS' GUARANTEES

A manufacturer's guarantee (or warranty, as it is sometimes called) normally amounts to a warranty to repair or replace during a specified time with the addition in the case of vehicles of a mileage limit. Such guarantees are presumably enforceable by the buyer as a collateral contract as in *Carlill* v *Carbolic Smoke Ball Co* (1893) (*see* Chapter 1).

They cannot affect the purchaser's right to sue upon the implied conditions and warranties set out in the Sale of Goods Act 1979 or at common law for negligence because under s 5 of the Unfair Contract Terms Act 1977 a clause in a manufacturer's or distributor's guarantee cannot operate to exclude or restrict the manufacturer's or distributor's liability to the customer provided the goods are of a type ordinarily supplied for private use or consumption and prove defective while in consumer use, i.e. not used exclusively for the purposes of a business.

## STATUTORY PRODUCT LIABILITY: CLAIMS AGAINST THE MANUFACTURER

### Part I of the Consumer Protection Act 1987

This brings into law strict product liability so that the consumer will no longer have to prove negligence when claiming compensation for damage or injury caused by products which are defective or unsafe. Civil liability will arise if damage is caused by a defective product. The Act is by no means a 'cure-all' because the claimant will still have to prove that the product *caused* the injury – not always an easy matter.

Damage is described as death, personal injury, or loss of or damage to *private* property. Thus damage to business property is not included. Furthermore, damage to property cannot be recovered unless it exceeds £275. If it does, then the whole amount is recoverable, including the first £275. This is to prevent trivial claims for damage to property.

In assessing whether the product is unsafe, the court must have regard to any warnings as to its use in advertising and marketing in general, instructions for use, how long ago the goods were supplied, and whether the product was put to what might be described as a reasonable use.

The following may be liable under the Act: the manufacturer of the product; a person who puts his name on the product thus holding himself out to be the manufacturer, i.e. a supermarket 'own brand' which is made for it by another manufacturer; an importer and a supplier if that supplier will not respond to a request to identify the person who supplied the product to him.

It is a defence to show that: (a) the product was not supplied in the course of a business; (b) the defect did not exist when the product was supplied; (c) technical knowledge was such that the defect could not have been known (called the 'development risk defence'). Thus the manufacturers of the drug Thalidomide might well have had a defence under the Act. However, manufacturers pressed for the retention of the development risk defence so as not to inhibit the development of new products.

The Act provides that any attempt to exclude liability by a term of a contract or notice will be ineffective. An injured party has three years in which to commence an action after the injury and discovery of the producer. There is a time bar on claims in any event, this being ten years from when the product was supplied.

The Act does not impose liability on the producer of game or agricultural produce provided it has not undergone an industrial process.

## Part II of the Consumer Protection Act 1987

This repeals the Consumer Safety Act 1978 and the Consumer Safety (Amendment) Act 1986 and provides a better legal framework to give the public protection from unsafe goods. The main provisions are as follows:

(a) a person is guilty of an offence if he supplies any *consumer* goods which fail to comply with the general safety requirement. Section 10 of the 1987 Act which contained the general safety requirements is disapplied by the General Product Safety Regulations 1994 (SI 1994/2328). The Regulations now contain the general safety requirements for goods and these are expanded so that producers of *consumer* goods and those involved in the supply chain, e.g. distributors, will have to ensure, among other things, that their internal systems are equipped to supply the consumer with information required by the Regulations, e.g. warnings of any risks in use and precautions to be taken, and that product recall procedures are adequate. The goods must be ordinarily intended for private use or consumption;

(b) the government may make safety regulations for the purpose of defining the general safety requirement set out in (a) above;

(c) the Department of Trade and Industry may serve upon a supplier a 'prohibition notice' prohibiting him from supplying goods which are considered unsafe or a 'notice to warn' requiring him to publish a warning about the goods at his own expense;

(d) a suspension notice may also be served by enforcement authorities, e.g. weights and measures authorities, prohibiting a supplier from supplying specified goods where the authority has reasonable grounds for suspecting that there has been a contravention of the general safety requirement, any safety regulations or any prohibition notice.

Part II is primarily enforced by criminal sanctions, with which examination syllabuses are not normally concerned. However, the duties laid down in Part II can assist a claimant in a civil claim which is why reference has been made to them. A claimant injured by goods which infringe the safety requirements of the Act will be able to bring a claim for damages in negligence on the basis that the manufacturer or others, e.g. a distributor, is in breach of his statutory duty under the Act. This will make the claimant's action much easier since he or she will not have to show a duty of care at common law. In this respect the Act is available to those who have no contractual claim against the seller as where they have received the goods as a gift.

Part III of the Act is concerned with misleading price indications but here again the sanctions are criminal and not civil.

# TREATING A BREACH OF CONDITION AS A BREACH OF WARRANTY

Section 11(2) provides that the buyer can waive a breach of condition altogether or may treat it as a breach of warranty. If he chooses to treat the breach of condition as a breach of warranty, then he may sue for damages but cannot reject the goods.

However, unless there is a contrary provision in the contract, a breach of a condition implied under the Sale of Goods Act must be treated as a breach of warranty *where the contract is not severable and the buyer has accepted the goods or part thereof* (s 11(4)).

Problems of severability arise where the goods are delivered by instalments. Where the price is paid for the whole consignment and delivery is by instalments, the contract is probably not severable, and acceptance by the buyer of early instalments will prevent him from rejecting later instalments which are not in accordance with the contract.

However, if, under the terms of the contract, each instalment is to be paid for separately the contract is probably severable (s 31(2)), and acceptance of earlier instalments will not prevent the buyer from rejecting later deliveries which are not in accordance with the contract.

A contract may, however, be regarded as severable in a number of other situations. Thus in *Longbottom & Co Ltd* v *Bass Walker & Co Ltd* [1922] WN 245 a contract for the sale of cloth was regarded as severable where delivery was by instalments but the price was paid as part of a monthly account and not separately for each delivery of cloth.

In this context it should be noted that if the buyer has got the right to reject an instalment he may reject part of it and not all of it where only part of the instalment fails to conform with the contract. This right of partial rejection is contained in s 35A of the Sale of Goods Act 1979 (as inserted by the Sale and Supply of Goods Act 1994).

Section 11(4) does not come into force when the goods are merely delivered; there must be some act by the buyer indicating his acceptance of the goods. A buyer is deemed to have accepted the goods:

(a) when he informs the seller that he has accepted them; or
(b) where, after delivery, and provided he has had a reasonable opportunity to examine the goods to see if they comply with the contract, he acts in a manner inconsistent with the continued ownership of the seller, as where he consumes the goods or uses them to secure a bank loan; or
(c) where, after the lapse of a reasonable time, he still retains the goods, without giving notice of rejection (ss 34 and 35(1)).

A combination of s 11(4) and s 35(1) could produce injustice for the consumer. For example, it was *held* by Rougier J in *Bernstein* v *Pamsons Motors (Golders Green) Ltd* [1987] 2 All ER 220 that a purchaser of a new car could not repudiate the contract and return the car for breach of condition under s 14 (fitness and quality) when the engine seized up at 142 miles. The judge said that because he had owned the car for three weeks he had had a reasonable time to try the car out under s 35(1). He was only entitled to damages of £232 for general inconvenience. The judge said he must in law accept the car as repaired under his warranty. The case was unfortunate for the consumer who could lose his right to return seriously defective goods even before a latent defect had emerged. The problem was really the law's reliance on *time* as the yardstick for discovering defects. In the case of many consumer goods a period of *use* would be better.

Thus the right to return goods appeared to be lost quite rapidly after purchase – three weeks in the above case. Those who wished to return unsatisfactory goods had to get back to the shop quickly and complain. It was a pity in a way that Mr Bernstein's appeal to the Court of Appeal was never heard because the Appeal Court might have taken a different view. However, when Pamsons heard he was going to appeal they settled by giving him all his money back! (*See Which?*, December 1987.)

The matter is now governed by a revised s 35 (inserted by the Sale and Supply of Goods Act 1994). The amendments state that a consumer does not lose the right to reject without a reasonable chance to examine the goods. Also, a material factor in deciding acceptance after a reasonable time without intimation of rejection will be the buyer's opportunity for examination. The Parliamentary Committee on the 1994 Act thought that periods of non-use would not count towards 'a reasonable opportunity for examination' but case law is required to establish this and currently none is available. A further change is that the fact that the buyer has sold or given the goods to a third party or asked for or agreed to a repair by the seller is not an act inconsistent with the seller's ownership. Thus the contract can be avoided for the benefit of the original buyer or a third party if the goods are defective.

## RESCISSION OF A CONTRACT OF SALE

It is useful at this point to compare the rules set out in s 11 of the Act of 1979 with the right to rescind a contract of sale for misrepresentation arising from a misstatement of fact. The rules relating to rescission are governed by separate principles (*see* Chapter 5). Since the Misrepresentation Act 1967, rescission of a contract of sale is barred only where there is affirmation, lapse of time, inability to make restitution or acquisition of rights by innocent third parties for value. It seems that a buyer's right to rescind for misrepresentation and his right to reject for breach of condition are now much the same in principle, since an act which amounts to acceptance under s 35(1) of the 1979 Act will almost always amount to affirmation so as to bar rescission. There may, however, be exceptional cases where rescission is available when rejection is not. For example, under s 35(1) if a buyer does not intimate his rejection of the goods within a reasonable time after an opportunity to examine, he is deemed to have accepted them and cannot reject. In equity lapse of time is not in itself sufficient to prevent rescission unless it amounts to affirmation, or the person making the representation (i.e. the seller) is prejudiced. Thus, if in spite of lapse of time there is no prejudice to the seller, equity may allow rescission, although the right to reject has been lost under s 35(1).

However, given the amendments made to s 35 by the Sale and Supply of Goods Act 1994, acceptance will depend more on the period of use of the goods and not be based purely on lapse of a short time. It is, therefore, likely that by the time acceptance is deemed to have taken place after a reasonable period of user, the right to rescind will also have been lost.

# TRANSFER OF THE PROPERTY IN GOODS

The provisions of the Act regarding the transfer of the property in the goods are important because the parties to contracts of sale do not usually express their intentions as to the passing of the property. In addition, the risk normally passes when the property passes and the seller can in general terms only sue for the *price* as distinct from *damages* if the property has passed.

The relevant statutory provisions are outlined in the following sections.

# WHERE THE GOODS ARE SPECIFIC

### General

We will consider six cases.

### Section 17

Section 17 provides that, where there is a contract for a sale of specific or ascertained goods, the property in them is transferred to the buyer at such time as the parties intend it to be transferred and, for the purpose of ascertaining the intention of the parties, regard shall be had to the terms of the contract, the conduct of the parties, and the circumstances of the case. Thus, an obligation on one party to insure is an indication that he has the risk and, by inference, and in the absence of an express provision to the contrary, the property (*Allison* v *Bristol Marine Insurance Co Ltd* (1876) 1 App Cas 209).

Section 17 is the overriding one, i.e. the intentions of the parties must be taken into account first. The following rules apply only if no different intention appears.

### Section 18, rule 1

Section 18, rule 1, provides that, where there is an unconditional contract for the sale of specific goods, in a deliverable state, the property in the goods passes to the buyer when the contract is made, and it is immaterial whether the time of payment or the time of delivery, or both, are postponed.

However, since s 18 provides that the statutory rules do not apply if a contrary intention appears, it may be that *an agreement to the postponement of payment or delivery* would indicate that the parties do not want the property to pass. The mere fact that the buyer has not paid and the seller has not delivered does not prevent ownership passing.

Other factors may indicate that there is no intention to pass the property. Thus in *Ingram* v *Little* (1961) (*see* Chapter 4) it seems to have been assumed that no property was to pass until the method of payment, i.e. cash or cheque, had been agreed by the parties, and in *Lacis* v *Cashmarts* [1969] 2 QB 400 it was *held* that in a supermarket the property did not pass until the price was actually paid on the basis, said the court, of 'commercial practice'.

**The following case is relevant to these rules.**

### Underwood Ltd v Burgh Castle Brick & Cement Syndicate [1922] 1 KB 343

The claimants agreed to sell a condensing engine to the defendants. At the time the contract was made the engine was at the claimants' premises in Millwall and was fixed to a bed of concrete by bolts. It was necessary to detach the engine before it could be delivered. The engine was damaged in the course of preparing it for dispatch, and when it was delivered the defendants refused to accept it. The claimants argued that the property had passed when the contract was made, so that the defendants must accept their own goods. *Held* – The property had not passed to the defendants because the goods were not in a deliverable state when the contract was made. The engine was at that time a fixture and not in the true sense of the word a moveable chattel.

*Comment:* If the goods are identified and agreed upon and ready for delivery, the buyer becomes owner immediately the contract is made unless there is a contrary intention under s 17. Thus in *Dennant* v *Skinner and Collom* [1948] 2 All ER 29, a van in a deliverable state was knocked down at auction to a purchaser. He paid by cheque and when he paid he signed a statement that the ownership was not to pass to him until the cheque had cleared. The court *held* that the ownership had passed to him on the fall of the hammer. The condition in the statement was made too late and after the purchaser became owner. Section 18, rule 1 applied.

### Section 18, rule 2

In the case of specific goods not in a deliverable state, s 18, rule 2, provides that the property does not pass until the seller puts them into a deliverable state, and the buyer is notified thereof. For example, if a person buys a suit from a tailor's shop but the trousers need shortening, the property or ownership will not pass until the alterations are done and the buyer has been informed of this. It is assumed that 'notice' to the buyer means what it says and that if a letter of notification is posted to the buyer, it is not effective on posting but only when it reaches him and would have been read in the ordinary course of business (*see Holwell Securities* v *Hughes* (1974), Chapter 1).

### Section 18, rule 3

In the case of conditional sales of specific goods, s 18, rule 3, provides that, where there is a contract for the sale of specific goods in a deliverable state, but the seller is bound to weigh, measure, test or do some other act or thing with reference to the goods for the purpose of ascertaining the price, the property does not pass until such act or thing is done, and the buyer has notice thereof. So if you buy a sack of potatoes for 12p per lb, the property will not pass until the seller has weighed the sack and told you how much it will cost. Rule 3 applies only to acts which must be done by the seller. Thus where X sold a consignment of cocoa to Y at an agreed price per 60 lb, the arrangement being that Y would resell the cocoa and weigh it in order to ascertain the amount owed to X, it was *held* that the fact that Y had to weigh the cocoa did not make the contract conditional. The property passed to Y before the price was arrived at (*Nanka Bruce* v *Commonwealth Trust Ltd* [1926] AC 77).

### Section 18, rule 4

In the case of sales on approval, or on sale or return, or other similar terms, s 18, rule 4, provides as follows.

(a) The property passes to the buyer when he signifies his approval or acceptance to the seller, or does any other act adopting the transaction, such as pledging the goods with a third party (rule 4(a)).

**The following case illustrates this point.**

### London Jewellers Ltd v Attenborough [1934] 2 KB 206

A fraudulent person named Waller told the claimants that he could sell jewellery to a well-known actress and the claimants gave him certain items of jewellery for that purpose. Waller signed a note in respect of each article and the note described the goods as being 'on appro' or on approval. Waller was also entitled to the difference between the selling price and the price marked on the note. Waller pledged the goods using women agents, and the defendants, who were pawnbrokers, received the goods bona fide. Waller was later arrested and charged with theft while a bailee, and the claimants sued the defendants in detinue and conversion. *Held* – The defendants had a good title and were not liable. When Waller pledged the goods he signified that he adopted the transaction and had approved them. The property, therefore, passed to him at that moment and he was able to give the defendants a good title.

(b) If the buyer does not signify his approval or acceptance to the seller but *retains the goods without giving notice of rejection*, then the property passes on the expiration of the time, if any, fixed for the return of the goods, or on the expiration of a reasonable time (rule 4(b)). What is a reasonable time is a question of fact. This part of the rule applies only if it is the buyer who retains the goods. Thus, if goods on sale or return are seized and retained by the buyer's unpaid creditors, the property will not pass under 4(b) (*Re Ferrier* [1944] Ch 295).

It is worth noting that a letter giving notice of rejection is adequate and sufficient to trigger the buyer's right to return the goods. The seller is not entitled to have the goods returned immediately, so long as they are made available to the seller within a reasonable time of the notice of rejection (*see Atari Corp (UK) Ltd* v *Electronics Boutique Stores (UK) Ltd* [1998] 1 All ER 1010).

**The following case provides an example of the application of rule 4(b).**

### Poole v Smith's Car Sales (Balham) Ltd [1962] 2 All ER 482

In August 1960, the claimant, a car dealer, supplied two second-hand cars to the defendants who were also car dealers. The cars were supplied on 'sale or return' terms while the claimant went on holiday, the agreement being that the defendants would return the cars if they were not sold in that time. One car was sold and paid for on 21 September 1960, but the other car, a 1956 Vauxhall Wyvern, had not been sold or returned by the end of October 1960. The claimant tried to get it returned by making telephone calls but finally he wrote a letter to the defendants, dated 7 November, in which he said that, if the car was not returned by 10 November 1960, it would be deemed sold to the defendants. The car was not returned until about 24 November and was then in a bad condition, having been used by the defendants' employees for their own purposes. The claimant rejected the car and sued for its price, i.e. £325, which was the sale or return value agreed in August 1960. *Held* – The contract was one of delivery 'on a sale or return' and, therefore, fell within s 18, rule 4. The property had passed to the defendants because it had not been returned within a reasonable amount of time, and the court was particularly concerned with the depreciation of a 1956 car between September and October when the market was declining. The defendants must pay the contract price as agreed.

Where the goods are on approval and the seller has expressly provided in the contract that the property is not to pass until they are paid for, then rule 4 will not operate because the express provision indicates a contrary intention. But if the buyer sells or disposes of the goods, a third party may still get a good title under the doctrine of estoppel, or under s 2 of the Factors Act 1889.

**The following case demonstrates this point.**

### Weiner v Harris [1910] 1 KB 285

The claimant was a jeweller and he entrusted certain goods to a person called Fisher who was a traveller in the jewellery trade. The terms of the agreement were that Fisher had the goods on 'sale or return' and that they were to remain the property of the claimant until sold or paid for. The defendant was a moneylender and he advanced money to Fisher on the security of the goods. The claimant now sued to recover the goods from the moneylender. *Held* – The defendant had a good title in spite of the terms of the contract between the claimant and Fisher. Fisher was a mercantile agent for the purposes of s 1 of the Factors Act 1889, and, therefore, had power to pledge the goods under s 2 of the Factors Act 1889 (see later in this chapter).

### Section 19

Section 19(1) provides that, where there is a contract for the sale of specific goods or where goods are subsequently appropriated to the contract, the seller may, by the terms of the appropriation or contract, reserve the right of disposal of the goods until certain conditions are fulfilled. In such a case, even if the goods are delivered to the buyer, or to a carrier or other bailee for the purpose of transmission to the buyer, the property in the goods does not pass until the conditions imposed by the seller are fulfilled.

The section does not safeguard the seller as much as might appear because the buyer, being a person who has bought or agreed to buy the goods, can give a good title to a third party under s 25(1) of the Act.

Section 19(3) provides that where the seller of goods draws a bill of exchange (*see* Chapter 2) on the buyer for the price, and transmits the bill of exchange and bill of lading to the buyer together to secure acceptance or payment of the bill of exchange, the buyer is bound to return the bill of lading if he does not honour the bill of exchange, and if he wrongfully retains the bill of lading, the property in the goods does not pass to him.

Here again, there is no complete safeguard for the seller. It is true that the passing of the property is conditional upon the bill of exchange being accepted and honoured, but a transfer of the bill of lading to a third party who takes bona fide and for value gives the third party a good title under s 25(1) of the Sale of Goods Act, and prevents the seller from exercising his right of lien or stoppage *in transitu* (*see* Chapter 12) against the third party under s 47(2) of the Sale of Goods Act and s 10 of the Factors Act 1889.

## Reservation of title by seller

It is now common for sellers of goods to try to protect themselves against the worst effects of a company receivership or liquidation by inserting retention clauses of one form or another into their contracts of sale. These are allowed by s 19(1) of the Sale of Goods Act 1979 (*see opposite*). These clauses, sometimes called 'Romalpa' clauses after the name of the case in which they first gained prominence in the UK, have as their purpose the retention of the seller's ownership in the goods until the buyer has paid for them, even though the buyer is given possession of the goods.

If the clause works and the purchasing company goes into receivership or liquidation because of insolvency, then the seller is able to recover the goods which the purchasing company still has in stock. The seller will normally find such a procedure more advantageous than:

(a) proving in a liquidation for whatever he can get by way of dividend leaving his goods to be sold for the benefit of creditors generally, or

(b) in a receivership leaving his goods with the receiver who may in law continue the company's business without paying its existing debts, including that of the seller.

Retention clauses have been used on the Continent for much longer than they have in the UK. They are an understandable reaction by unsecured trade creditors to the increasing number of insolvencies in which a bank is found to hold a debenture giving a floating charge over the insolvent company's assets to secure an overdraft. The bank, being a secured creditor, takes the company's assets first, subject to certain preferential payments, through the medium of a receivership leaving trade creditors unprovided for.

**There have been a number of legal decisions on the use of retention clauses. The following are among the most instructive.**

## The Romalpa case (Aluminium Industrie Vaassen BV v Romalpa Aluminium) [1976] 2 All ER 552

This was the first case which alerted the legal and accountancy professions to the problems which retention clauses might cause in insolvency practice.

The facts of the case were that AIV sold aluminium foil to Romalpa, the contractual conditions of sale being:

(a) that the ownership of the material to be delivered by AIV would only be transferred to the purchaser when he had met all that was owing to AIV, no matter on what grounds;

(b) that Romalpa should store the foil separately;

(c) that if the foil was used to make new objects, those objects should be stored separately and be owned by AIV as *security* for payment;

(d) that Romalpa could sell the new objects, but so long as they had not discharged their debt, they should hand over to AIV, if requested, the claims they had against purchasers from Romalpa – in effect, the proceeds of sale.

Romalpa got into financial difficulties and was in debt to its bankers in the sum of £200,000. The bank had a debenture secured over Romalpa's assets and appointed a receiver under that debenture. At the time of the receiver's appointment, Romalpa owed AIV £122,000, and in order to recover some of that money at the expense of the bank, AIV sought, under their conditions of sale, to recover from Romalpa foil valued in round terms at £50,000 and the cash proceeds of resold foil of some £35,000. The proceeds had been received from third-party purchasers from Romalpa after the receiver was appointed and he had kept the fund of £35,000 separate so that it was not mixed with Romalpa's other funds and was, therefore, identifiable. It is important to note that the receiver conceded the right of the seller to trace the proceeds of sale in terms that the proceeds part of the clause was registrable under the Companies Act 1985. Thus the court did not have to reach an argued decision as to whether the retention clause could apply to proceeds of sale.

The Court of Appeal *held* that the foil was recoverable since there was a fiduciary relationship between AIV and Romalpa. This arose because ownership in the goods had not passed to Romalpa, so that Romalpa was a bailee of AIV's goods and AIV was the bailor. This relationship is fiduciary and allows the bailor to recover the goods from his bailee. These rules derive from *Re Hallett's Estate* (1880) 13 Ch D 696.

Therefore, Romalpa was accountable to AIV for the foil and the receiver conceded that AIV could trace the proceeds of sale.

As regards a claim by counsel for Romalpa that the retention clause created a charge which should have been registered under s 396 of the Companies Act 1985, and that the retention clause was inoperative because there had been no such registration, the court decided that since ownership had not passed to Romalpa, the charge was not over the property of Romalpa and so s 396 did not apply, that section being confined to charges over the property of a company. In addition, the Romalpa clause included a contractual charge over mixed objects. The court did not give a decision as to the position in regard to this charge since there was no need in the case to use it. The claim was merely for foil remaining in the buyer's possession and this could be recovered on the basis of the bailor/bailee relationship. The proceeds of sale were also recovered but not as a result of any argued decision of the court on the matter. Recovery was conceded by the receiver. It seems extremely unlikely that proceeds will be recovered in future unless the clause is registered as a charge.

### Borden (UK) Ltd v Scottish Timber Products Ltd [1979] 3 All ER 961)

In this case Borden (B) supplied resin to Scottish Timber (S) which S used in making chipboard. B inserted the following retention clause in the contract under which the resin was supplied:

> Goods supplied by the company shall be at the purchaser's risk immediately on delivery to the purchaser or into custody on the purchaser's behalf (whichever is the sooner) and the purchaser should therefore be insured accordingly. Property and goods supplied hereunder will pass to the customer when: (a) the goods the subject of this contract, and (b) all other goods the subject of any other contract between the company and the customer which, at the time of payment of the full price of the goods sold under this contract, have been delivered to the customer but not paid for in full, have been paid for in full.

S went into receivership and B sought to trace their resin into chipboard made from the resin.

The Court of Appeal decided that S was not a bailee in spite of the clause. Bailment implied the right to redelivery of the resin and B must have known that there would be no true bailment because resin was supplied only in sufficient quantities for two days' production because that is all the resin which S had room to store. B must, therefore, have been taken to know that the resin would be mixed with goods belonging to S almost immediately. The resin had ceased to exist except as chipboard over which there was *no contractual charge*. Thus there was no fiduciary relationship; tracing was not available. If the clause had created a contractual charge over the board, it would, apparently, have been registerable, being created by S at least in part over its own property. The decision in *Romalpa* was not overruled but distinguished.

*Comment:* (i) The *Borden* case, and a rather large number of subsequent cases, suggest that in the company situation retention clauses over mixed goods will not be effective unless they are registered under s 396 of the Companies Act 1985 as a charge over the assets of the purchasing company.

(ii) Furthermore, where the goods are to be used in manufacture, the court is reluctant to find that a bailment exists. In a bailment – as, for example, where you leave a suitcase in a left luggage office – it is normally the intention that the goods should be returned to the owner in their existing state. A person who delivers goods to another knowing that they will be used in manufacture must give that other some sort of ownership of them. This prevents a bailment so that any goods in stock which have yet to be used in manufacture cannot be traced. There is no fiduciary relationship.

## A summary of the present position

The number of cases on retention clauses is large and to some extent each has depended on its own facts. However, where goods are delivered other than for use in a manufacturing process, involving mixture with the buyer's goods, a retention clause may well succeed provided the seller's goods can be identified in the buyer's stock. There is no indication in the law report of what the buyer intended to do with the foil in *Romalpa*, but certainly it was unmixed and retained by the buyer as an item of stock and was recovered under a decision of the court.

Up to now no attempt to extend retention of title to manufactured goods and/or the proceeds of sale has succeeded in the courts. Clauses which attempt to do this create a charge which is void as against an insolvency practitioner, such as a liquidator or receiver, unless registered at Companies House. *Borden* decides the manufactured goods point and more recently *Re Weldtech Equipment* [1991] BCLC 393 decided that a retention over proceeds of sale is a charge over the buyer company's book debts and is void if not registered. We have noted that in *Romalpa* the receiver did not contest the right to recover proceeds of sale in terms that it created a registrable charge.

## Reservation of title: an extension of rights

In the past, retention clauses in contracts of sale have worked only in relation to monies owed in respect of the goods actually made the subject of a retention clause. However, the House of Lords decided in an appeal from the Scottish Court of Session (in which English law would also apply in the same way) that a retention of title provision can cover not only the price of the very goods which are the subject of a particular contract of sale containing a retention clause, but also the debts due to the seller under other contracts.

### Armour and Carron Co Ltd v Thyssen Edelstahlwerke AG, *The Times*, 25 October 1990

Thyssen were the owners of steel strip. They transferred possession in it to Carron under what was undoubtedly a contract of sale. Carron agreed that it should receive possession of the steel strip on delivery but should not acquire the property (ownership) until *all* debts due to Thyssen had been paid. It was also agreed that debts due to companies in the Thyssen group were deemed to be such debts. Armour & Co were the receivers of the assets of Carron, which had not paid the £71,769 purchase price of the steel strip.

When the matter came before the Second Division of the Inner House of the Court of Session, the argument put forward by the receivers of Carron that the clause was really an attempt to create a security over moveable property was accepted. However, this was rejected by the House of Lords on the grounds that it was not possible to create a security over goods which you did not own.

The judgment of the House of Lords was based upon an application of ss 17 and 19 of the Sale of Goods Act 1979. Here, said the House of Lords, Thyssen, by the terms of the contract of sale, had in effect reserved the right of disposal of the steel strip until fulfilment of the conditions that *all* debts due to them by Carron had been paid. By reason of the 1979 Act, that had the effect that the property in the goods did not pass to Carron until that condition had been fulfilled.

The same was true where the provision covered not only the price of the very goods which were the subject of a particular contract of sale, but also debts due to the seller under other contracts.

Therefore, the steel strip belonged to Thyssen and not to the receivers on behalf of Carron.

*Comment:* Presumably, also, since the goods were not the property of the company, the retention clause was not in the nature of a registerable charge over the company's property because the property was not that of the company. If, however, the goods are mixed with those of the company, as in *Borden (UK) Ltd* v *Scottish Timber Products Ltd* [1979] 3 All ER 961 (seller's resin mixed with the company's goods to make chipboard), then the retention clause would have been in the nature of a floating charge over part, at least, of the company's property and void in insolvency proceedings unless registered. This decision would seem to make no change in the position in *Borden*.

However, where the goods are identifiable in stock at the time of the insolvency proceedings, the seller can recover them, not only if the price of the goods themselves are not paid, *but also if other debts due to the seller have not been met.*

## Reservation of title: appointment of an administrator

Once a petition has been presented to the court for the appointment of an administrator to the purchasing company, the owner of goods delivered under a retention clause cannot take steps to recover them. This is designed to assist the administrator in his function of corporate rescue. He can take steps to recover against a receiver or liquidator, and indeed if a receiver or liquidator sells goods subject to a valid retention clause he is personally liable in damages to the owner for conversion of the goods (*Schott Sohne* v *Radford* [1987] CLY 3585). The administration procedure which is contained in the Insolvency Act 1986 is designed and intended to promote the survival of companies as a going concern and to secure the preservation of jobs. An administrator is appointed by the court on the petition of the company or on the petition of the directors or on the petition of any creditor. The debt need not be of any minimum value and unsecured creditors can petition. This is a major contrast with the appointment of a receiver, now called an administrative receiver, who can only be appointed by secured creditors. The Insolvency Act 1986 gives an administrator full powers to manage the company, hopefully to the point at which he can make it viable again and vacate office in favour of a permanent management.

## WHERE THE GOODS ARE UNASCERTAINED

Section 16 provides that, where there is a contract for the sale of unascertained goods, no property in the goods is transferred to the buyer unless and until the goods are ascertained. This is a common-sense rule because until the goods have been identified it is not possible to say in which goods the property is passing. Where an unidentified part of a bulk is sold, there is no appropriation until there is severance of the goods sold from the rest.

The following case provides an illustration.

### Laurie and Morewood *v* John Dudin & Sons [1926] I KB 223

On 2 February 1925, Messrs Alcock and Sons sold to John Wilkes & Sons 200 quarters of maize from 618 quarters belonging to Alcock and Sons and lying in the defendants' warehouse. Wilkes & Sons were given a delivery note which they sent to the defendants who were, therefore, on notice of the sale. On 18 February, Wilkes & Sons sold the 200 quarters of maize to the claimants and gave them a delivery note which the claimants sent to the defendants on 19 February. On both occasions, when they received delivery notes the defendants merely made entries in their books and no attempt was made to appropriate the goods to the contract. Wilkes & Sons failed to pay Alcock and Sons for the maize and Alcock and Sons instructed the defendants to withhold delivery. The claimants now sued the defendants in detinue, claiming that the property in the maize had passed to them. *Held* – The claimants' action failed. The maize did not belong to them because there had been no appropriation of the goods and, therefore, the property in the maize had not passed either to Wilkes & Sons or to the claimants.

There are many contracts for the sale of unascertained goods where the parties do not deal in their contract with the passing of the property. Where this is so s 18, rule 5, applies. Rule 5(1) provides that where there is a contract for the sale of unascertained or future goods by description, and goods of that description and in a deliverable state are unconditionally appropriated to the contract either by the seller with the assent of the buyer, or by the buyer with the assent of the seller, the property in the goods thereupon passes to the buyer.

The relationship between s 16 and s 18, rule 5(1), is a difficult one. It seems that the court may take the view that the property has passed where part of a larger quantity is sold leaving what is left belonging to the buyer, even though there is no unconditional appropriation of that balance within the terms of s 18, rule 5(1), if the court thinks that it was the intention of the parties that ascertainment should also be appropriation.

The following case and comment makes this point.

### Wait and James v Midland Bank (1926) 31 Com Cas 172

The sellers sold 1,250 quarters of wheat on credit from a larger cargo lying in a warehouse. The buyers were given delivery orders which were acceptable to the warehouseman for purposes of delivery when required. The buyers did not ask for delivery but pledged the delivery orders to a bank as security. At this time no severance of the buyers' wheat had taken place. Later the sellers sold and delivered the remainder of the wheat leaving the buyers' share of the cargo in the warehouse. It was *held* by Roche J that the second sale had the effect of passing the property in the remaining wheat to the first buyers and the bank's security was good against the 1,250 quarters left.

*Comment:* (i) Roche J appears to have assumed that ascertainment was enough to pass the property. There had been no unconditional appropriation as required by s 18, rule 5.

(ii) This case was applied in *Karlshamns Oljefabriker* v *Eastport Navigation* [1982] 1 All ER 208. The buyer entered into four contracts under which he purchased a total of 6,000 tons of copra. This formed part of 22,000 tons of copra that was loaded on to the vessel *Elafi*, which belonged to the defendants. It was to be shipped from the Philippines to Sweden. 16,000 tons were offloaded at Hamburg and Rotterdam. The remaining 6,000 tons went on to Sweden. On arrival in Sweden, it was discovered that the copra had been damaged by water. The *Elafi* was allegedly not seaworthy. The buyers said the goods were not theirs because the property had not passed. It was *held* in the High Court that it had. Mr Justice Mustill, in applying the *Wait* case, referred to the judgment of Roche J and noted that it omitted any mention of s 18, rule 5. He then went on to say:

> In my judgment, this objection adds nothing to the argument in relation to ascertainment. It is true that in some cases the ascertainment of goods may not be the same as the unconditional appropriation of them, although the distinction would usually be difficult, if not impossible to draw. But here I cannot see any difference . . . Before leaving the question of appropriation I should draw attention to one other factor, namely that the want of an unconditional appropriation is not an absolute bar to the passing of the property but merely one of the factors to be taken into account when ascertaining the presumed intentions of the parties.

The Sale of Goods (Amendment) Act 1995 amends s 18, rule 5 to give statutory recognition to ascertainment by exhaustion. Thus, if A buys 200 bottles of wine from a bulk of 1,000 bottles and the seller disposes of 800 of them, the remaining 200 belong to A. It is not necessary for A to have made a prepayment.

The case law which appears above continues to be useful as a practical illustration of ascertainment by exhaustion.

Assent to appropriation may be express or implied and be given before or after appropriation is made. Under s 20(1) risk passes with the property. The person who has the risk is not necessarily in possession of the goods.

**This is illustrated by the following case.**

### Pignataro v Gilroy & Son [1919] 1 KB 459

By a contract made on 12 February 1918, the defendants sold to the claimant 140 bags of rice, the claimant to take delivery within 14 days. The rice was unascertained when the contract was made. On 27 February, the claimant sent a cheque for the rice and asked for a delivery order. On 28 February the defendants sent a delivery order for 125 bags which were lying at a place called Chambers' Wharf. A letter accompanying the delivery order said that the remaining 15 bags were at the defendants' place of business at 50 Long Acre, and requested the claimant to collect them there. The claimant did not send for the 15 bags until 25 March when it was found that they had been stolen without negligence on the part of the defendants. *Held* – the goods were at the claimant's risk. He had not dissented from the appropriation made by the defendants, and his assent to it must, therefore, be implied.

The necessity for the buyer's assent to appropriation gives rise to difficulties where a consumer orders goods by post. Where under a commercial contract the seller is required to ship the goods to the buyer, the shipping is regarded as an unconditional appropriation and the assent of the buyer is *assumed* (*James v Commonwealth* [1939] 62 CLR 339). This rule seems inappropriate in the case of consumer sales by post. Though the law is not clear, it is suggested that the posting of consumer goods should not pass the property, otherwise the goods are, unknown to the buyer, at his risk during transit. There is no need to assume the consumer's consent to appropriation since in that sort of case he has agreed merely to dispatch of the goods and not to a particular appropriation.

An example of an unconditional appropriation, i.e. delivery to a carrier, is given in s 18, rule 5(2), which provides that where, in pursuance of the contract, the seller delivers goods to the buyer or to a carrier or other bailee (whether named by the buyer or not) for the purpose of transmission to the buyer, and does not reserve the right of disposal, he is deemed to have unconditionally appropriated the goods to the contract. However, delivery to a carrier does not pass the property if identical goods destined for different owners are mixed nor if the seller is bound to weigh, measure or test the goods in order to ascertain the price.

**The following two cases provide illustrations of these rules.**

### Healey v Howlett & Sons [1917] 1 KB 337

Howlett & Sons were fish dealers in Ireland and they supplied fish to English customers. They had an agent at Holyhead, all fish being sent to the agent who selected parcels of fish for dispatch to customers in England. The appellant was a fish salesman in London and he ordered 20 boxes of mackerel from the respondents. The respondents dispatched 122 boxes of mackerel to their agent in Holyhead to fulfil the appellant's order and others. The agent selected 20 boxes for dispatch to the appellant, but because of delays in getting the fish to Holyhead, the fish was found to be bad on arrival in London. The delay in getting the fish to Holyhead was not the respondents' fault. The appellant refused to pay the respondents and the respondents sued for the full price on the ground that the dispatch of 122 boxes of fish to their agent was sufficient appropriation to pass the property to Healey in respect of his 20 boxes. Howlett succeeded at first instance and Healey now appealed from that decision. *Held* – There was no appropriation until the agent at Holyhead earmarked the 20 boxes for the appellant. The fish had deteriorated before arrival at Holyhead and was at the respondents' risk under s 16 when it did deteriorate. The appellant was, therefore, not liable to pay for the fish.

*Comment:* A puts 100 boxes of fish on a train from Holyhead to London. No appropriation is made but 25 boxes are for B at Colwyn Bay, 25 for C at Crewe, 25 for D at Rugby, and 25 for E at London. Appropriation is made at each station. The goods are damaged in an accident at Watford. Do the goods belong to E? *Wait* and *Karlshamns* (*see above*) would suggest that they do, and that position is reinforced by amendments made to the Sale of Goods Act 1979 by the Sale of Goods (Amendment) Act 1995, which now provides for ascertainment by exhaustion.

### National Coal Board v Gamble [1958] 3 All ER 203

The Coal Board supplied coal to a buyer at a colliery by loading from a hopper into the buyer's lorry. The lorry was then driven to a weighbridge so that the weight of the coal could be ascertained and a weight-ticket, as required by statute, issued. The court *held* that the property did not pass until the coal had been weighed and the ticket given to and accepted by the buyer. The court was also of opinion that under the system in operation at the colliery any coal in excess of the buyer's requirement could have been unloaded before the weight-ticket was issued and accepted. It would seem, therefore, that the court was assuming that although appropriation took place when the coal was loaded on to the lorry, it was not unconditional until it was weighed and the weight-ticket accepted by the buyer.

## Unascertained goods and prepayment

The Sale of Goods (Amendment) Act 1995 amends the Sale of Goods Act 1979 to deal with a situation in which A agrees to buy '1,000 tonnes of grain out of a cargo of grain in the holds of the ship *Cloudy Dawn*'. A has made a prepayment to the seller. Previously if there was no appropriation of a particular 1,000 tonnes to A the ownership remained with the seller and if he was insolvent the goods were available for sale by an insolvency practitioner, and A could only claim for the return of his prepayment in the insolvency proceedings and might get little or nothing. Under the amendments referred to above A now becomes a co-owner with other such buyers having a claim on the bulk and it does not become available for sale by the insolvency practitioner. Whole or partial prepayment is, however, essential. The new rule is not limited to goods in a deliverable state. Those who have only made part payments will only be able to claim that part of the consignment which relates to the amount paid. Co-owners can deal with their share of the goods without the consent of the others and persons, such as insolvency practitioners, who release the goods to co-owners are protected against claims by others who may receive short delivery if in fact there is insufficient bulk to meet all claims. The provisions are not restricted to insolvency situations, but obviously they are at their most useful in that context. The above provisions can be excluded or amended by a term of the particular contract.

## TRANSFER OF PROPERTY AND RISK

The question of the transfer of property in goods is important, because risk generally passes with the property. The maxim is *res perit domino* (a thing perishes to the disadvantage of its owner).

Section 20 provides that, unless otherwise agreed, the goods remain at the seller's risk until the property therein is transferred to the buyer, but when the property in them is transferred to the buyer, the goods are at the buyer's risk whether delivery has been made or not – i.e. the rule applies, irrespective of who had possession of the goods at the time the property passed (*see Pignataro* v *Gilroy & Son* (1919) above). It seems that there may sometimes be a transfer of risk without transfer of the property and a transfer of the property without risk.

**The following cases provide an illustration of this.**

### Sterns Ltd *v* Vickers Ltd [1923] 1 KB 78

On 3 January 1920, the Admiralty sold to Vickers Ltd 120,000 gallons of white spirit out of a larger quantity of 200,000 gallons then lying at Thames Haven in Tank No 78. The tank belonged to a storage company called London and Thames Haven Oil Wharves Company. Vickers Ltd sold the spirit to Sterns Ltd, who did not take delivery for some months. When they did take delivery, the specific gravity of the spirit had changed by deterioration over time. Sterns Ltd claimed damages for breach of warranty against the sellers. *Held* – The spirit was at the claimants' risk from the time of sale and the defendants were not liable for breach of warranty.

*Comment:* This seems to be a wholly exceptional case. The property had clearly not passed to Sterns because there had been no appropriation.

### Head *v* Tattersall (1870) LR 7 Ex 7

Tattersall sold a horse to Head, warranting that it had hunted with the Bicester Hounds, and giving Head the right to return the horse by a certain date if it did not comply with the warranty. Head discovered that the horse had not hunted with the Bicester Hounds and returned it to Tattersall within the time stipulated. However, while the horse was in Head's possession, it was injured though without negligence on his part. *Held* – in the circumstances it was possible to take the view that the property had passed but not the risk, and Tattersall was obliged to accept the injured horse.

*Comment:* The general rule is that where goods are delivered on approval or on sale or return the property in them remains with the seller until the buyer adopts the transaction. However, this case shows that it is possible to enter into a transaction which has a similar purpose but under which the property passes immediately to the buyer, but not the risk. The legal principle would seem to be that the risk remains with the seller where, under the contract, the buyer has a right of rejection.

Of course, the goods may be dispatched at the seller's risk, in which case s 33 provides that, where the seller of goods agrees to deliver them at his own risk at a place other than that where they are then sold, the buyer must, nevertheless, unless otherwise agreed, take any risk of deterioration in the goods necessarily incident to the course of transit.

In connection with this it is necessary to note two further provisions of s 20:

(a) Where delivery has been delayed through the fault of either buyer or seller, the goods are at the risk of the party at fault as regards any loss which might not have occurred but for such fault.

**The following case demonstrates this.**

### Demby, Hamilton & Co Ltd v Barden [1949] I All ER 435

The claimants were sellers of apple juice, and on 8 November 1945 they entered into a contract with the defendants who were wine merchants. Under the contract the claimants were to supply and the defendants were to buy 30 tons of apple juice to be delivered by lorry in weekly instalments, the contract to be completed by the end of February 1946. The claimants crushed a quantity of apples and put the juice into casks, but the property did not pass at that stage since the casks were not specifically appropriated to the contract. 20½ tons of apple juice were delivered and at that stage the buyers said that they could not take the other instalments until further notice. The last delivery was made on 4 April 1946. The claimants repeatedly asked for delivery instructions, and on 7 November 1946 they informed the defendants that the contents of the remaining casks had gone putrid and had been thrown away. The claimants now sued for the price of the goods sold and delivered, and for damages in respect of the apple juice which had been thrown away. *Held* – Under the proviso to s 20, the goods were at the buyer's risk because he was responsible for the delay. If the sellers could have sold the remainder of the apple juice elsewhere, the loss might have fallen on them, but their contract with the defendants obliged the claimants to hold the goods available for delivery as and when required by the defendants. The claimants' action for the price of the goods sold and for damages succeeded.

(b) Nothing in s 20 affects the duties and liabilities of either seller or buyer as a bailee of the goods of the other party (s 20(3)). A seller must still take proper care of the goods even though the buyer is late in taking delivery of them. Thus the risk which passes with the property does not include damage due to the other party's negligence.

## TRANSFER OF TITLE BY NON-OWNERS

### General

The sections in the Sale of Goods Act which will be discussed here are concerned with the circumstances in which a person who is not the owner of goods can give a good title to those goods to a third party.

The general rule of common law is expressed in the maxim *nemo dat quod non habet* (no one can give what he has not got). It follows that, if the seller's title is defective, so is the buyer's. This rule of the common law is confirmed by s 21(1) which provides that, subject to certain other sections of the Act, where goods are sold by a person who is not the owner thereof, and who does not sell them under the authority or with the consent of the owner, the buyer acquires no better title to the goods than the seller had, unless the owner of the goods is by his conduct precluded from denying the seller's authority to sell.

There are, however, the following main exceptions to the rule.

### Estoppel

Where the owner of goods, by his words or conduct, represents to the buyer that the seller is the true owner, the owner is precluded from denying the title of the buyer. The doctrine of estoppel is preserved in the final words of s 21(1) of the Act, i.e. 'unless the owner of the goods is by his conduct precluded from denying the seller's authority to sell'.

**The following case provides an example.**

### Henderson & Co v Williams [1895] 1 QB 521

The claimants were sugar merchants at Hull. The defendant was a warehouseman at Hull and Goole. On 3 June 1894, a fraudulent person named Fletcher, posing as the agent of Robinson, negotiated a purchase of sugar from Messrs Grey & Co, who were Liverpool merchants. The sugar was lying in the defendant's warehouse at Goole, and Messrs Grey & Co sent a telegram and later a letter advising the defendant that the sugar was to be held to the order of Fletcher, and the defendant entered the order in his books. Robinson was a reputable dealer and a customer of Messrs Grey & Co, and of course Fletcher had no right to act on Robinson's behalf. Fletcher sold the goods to the claimants who, before paying the price, got a statement from the defendant that the goods were held to the order of Fletcher. The defendant later discovered Fletcher's fraud and refused to release the sugar to the claimants who now sued in conversion. *Held* – The defendant was stopped from denying Fletcher's title and was liable in damages based on the market price of the goods at the date of refusal to deliver. Further, the true owners, Messrs Grey & Co, could not set up their title to the sugar against that of the claimants, since they had allowed Fletcher to hold himself out as the true owner.

Estoppel does not arise merely because the owner of goods allows another to have possession of them (*Mercantile Bank of India Ltd v Central Bank of India Ltd* [1938] AC 287) and attempts have been made to set up a doctrine of estoppel by negligence, the third party alleging that it is the negligence of the true owner which has given the non-owner the apparent authority to sell. However, in order to establish negligence, it is necessary to show the existence of a duty of care in the owner, and such a duty, which is a matter of law, does not seem to exist where the owner has even by negligence lost his property or facilitated its theft or other form of fraudulent disposition. (*See*, for example, *Cundy v Lindsay* (1878) and *Ingram v Little* (1961), Chapter 4.)

However, where the owner is face-to-face with the person who defrauds him when the contract is made, it would seem that an element of negligence in the owner will prevent him from recovering the property from a third party (*see Lewis v Averay* (1971), Chapter 4).

So if X loses his watch and Y finds it and sells it to Z, then X can still claim his property, and it does not matter that X's negligence enabled Y to sell the watch to Z. In order for s 21(1) to apply to estop the true owner from denying the authority of the seller to sell, there must be a representation by statement or conduct by the true owner that the seller was entitled to sell the goods.

**The following case illustrates this point.**

### Eastern Distributors Ltd v Goldring [1957] 2 QB 600

A person named Murphy was the owner of a Bedford van and wished to buy a Chrysler car from Coker who was a car dealer. Murphy could not find the money to pay the hire-purchase deposit on the Chrysler. Coker suggested that Murphy authorise him to sell the van to a finance company and get an agreement from the finance company under which they agreed to sell the van to Murphy on hire-purchase terms and then Murphy could apply the proceeds of the sale of his van in putting down deposits on the van and the Chrysler.

Murphy gave Coker authority, but limited it to selling the van and arranging the hire-purchase of the van and the Chrysler. Under the authority given to him, Coker was bound to effect both transactions and not one only. Murphy then signed the necessary documents leaving Coker to fill them in. In the proposal form for the hire-purchase of the van, Coker described himself as owner of the vehicle, and without authority from Murphy sold the van to the claimants, who were the finance company, as if it were his own. The claimants then hired it out to Murphy and sent him a copy of the agreement. The hire-purchase of the Chrysler was not carried out and later Coker told Murphy that the whole deal had fallen through, and was cancelled. Murphy then sold the van which he believed to be his own to Goldring, who bought in good faith and without knowledge of Murphy's previous dealings. Murphy made no payments under the hire-purchase agreement, and the claimants terminated it and claimed the van or its value from the defendant. *Held* – by the Court of Appeal –

(a) Coker had no actual authority to sell the van separately to the claimants but only as part of a double transaction. However, Murphy, by providing Coker with documents which enabled him to represent himself to the claimants as entitled to the van, had clothed Coker with apparent authority to sell and was prevented by s 21(1) of the Sale of Goods Act from denying that authority. The claimants had obtained a good title and Murphy had no title to give Goldring.

(b) Section 25(1) of the Sale of Goods Act did not make the sale to Goldring valid, because Murphy was, after the hire-purchase agreement, not in possession as a seller but as a bailee by virtue of the agreement.

*Comment:* (i) If Goldring was a private purchaser, he would now obtain a good title under the Hire Purchase Act 1964, Part III, as substituted by s 192 of and Sch 4, para 22 to the Consumer Credit Act 1974.

(ii) Section 21(1) does not apply to an agreement to sell. In *Shaw* v *Commissioner of Police of the Metropolis* [1987] 3 All ER 405 A advertised his car for sale. B said he was interested in buying it. A let B have possession and signed a letter certifying that he had sold the car to B. A also signed the transfer slip attached to the car registration document to the same effect. B agreed to sell the car to C, the property to pass when B had been paid. B left the car with C and was not paid. B was not seen again. A claimed the car from C. The Court of Appeal said A was entitled to it. Lloyd LJ did not doubt that the signing of the letter and the transfer slip by A was 'the clearest possible representation intended to be relied on by the ultimate purchaser that the claimant had transferred the ownership to B'. Therefore, if C had bought the car he would have acquired a good title under s 21, but it was accepted that the property in the car was not to pass until B was paid which he never was. Therefore, C had only 'agreed to buy'. Since s 21 applied 'where goods are sold', the Court of Appeal decided that the section could not apply to an agreement to sell and therefore A was still entitled to his car.

(iii) Section 25 of the 1979 Act did not apply because B had not apparently 'bought or agreed to buy' on the evidence but had merely taken possession. Section 2 of the Factors Act 1889 did not help either because there was no evidence that B was a mercantile agent.

## Sales by factors and sales by other agents under apparent or usual authority

Section 21(2) provides that nothing in the Sale of Goods Act shall affect the provisions of the Factors Act 1889 or any enactment enabling the apparent owner of goods to dispose of them as if he were the true owner thereof. The Sale of Goods Act thus preserves the power of disposition in such cases.

Section 62(2) provides that the rules relating to the law of principal and agent are to be preserved, and so a sale by an agent without actual authority will give the purchaser a good title if the sale is within the agent's ostensible or usual authority. (*See further* Chapter 21.)

## Special powers of sale

Section 21(2)(b) provides that nothing in the Act shall affect the validity of any contract of sale under any special common law or statutory power of sale, or under the order of a court of competent jurisdiction. Thus a pawnbroker has the right to sell goods which have been pledged with him if the loan is not repaid. The person who buys from the pawnbroker will get a good title to the goods.

A *sheriff* has power by statute to sell goods taken by the bailiffs from the premises of a person who has not paid a judgment debt, and under s 1 of the Innkeepers Act 1878, an *innkeeper's lien* over the goods of his guests for his charges may be converted into a power of sale. A sale giving a good title by a *bailee* who has carried out work on goods, e.g. a watch repairer, is possible under the provisions of the Torts (Interference with Goods) Act 1977, s 12.

The Rules of the Supreme Court give the court a jurisdiction to order the sale of goods which for any just and sufficient reason it may be desirable to have sold at once, as where they are perishable goods. The purchaser of the goods sold will obtain a good title in spite of the owner's lack of consent.

## The demise of market overt

The rule of market overt provided that a buyer who bought goods according to the usages of the market could get a good title to the goods even though the seller had none, e.g. if they were stolen. This aided the sale of stolen property in a time of rising crime, and the rule that applied to all shops in the City of London and to public markets legally constituted by Royal Charter, statute or custom was abolished by the Sale of Goods (Amendment) Act 1994.

## Sales under a voidable title

Section 23 provides that, when the seller of goods has a voidable title, but his title has not been avoided at the time of the sale, the buyer acquires a good title to the goods, provided he buys them in good faith and without notice of the seller's defect of title. Thus, if B obtains goods from S by giving S a cheque which he knows will not be met, and B sells the goods to T, who takes them bona fide and for value, T obtains a good title, provided that S has not avoided the contract with B before B sells to T. The section only applies to sales, but pledges are subject to the same rule by virtue of the common law. Where the fraud is such as to render the original contract of sale void for mistake, the fraudulent buyer cannot give a good title to a third party (*see Cundy* v *Lindsay* (1878), Chapter 4).

If the original owner of the goods sold in circumstances of fraud or misrepresentation wishes to avoid the contract, he should inform the buyer who misled him. If he cannot find him, the contract is avoided when the original owner has done everything he can in the circumstances to avoid the contract.

**This is illustrated in the following case.**

### Car & Universal Finance Co Ltd v Caldwell [1964] 2 All ER 547

On 12 January 1960, Mr Caldwell sold a motor car to a firm called Dunn's Transport, receiving a cheque signed 'for and on behalf of Dunn's Transport, W. Foster, F. Norris'. Caldwell presented the cheque to the bank but it was dishonoured, and so he went to see the police and asked them to recover the car. He also saw officials of the Automobile Association and asked them to trace the car by their patrols. The car was found on 20 January 1960, in the possession of a director of a company of car dealers called Motobella & Co Ltd. The company claimed to have bought it on 15 January from Norris and to have a good title, though the director concerned was on notice of the defect in Norris's title. On 29 January, the defendant's solicitors demanded the car from Motobella and at the same time Norris was arrested and pleaded guilty to obtaining the car by false pretences. The defendant sued Motobella & Co Ltd for the return of the car and obtained judgment, but when he tried to repossess the car, a finance house, Car & Universal Finance Co Ltd, claimed that it belonged to them. It appeared that Motobella had transferred the ownership to a finance house called G & C Finance on 15 January 1960, and they had transferred it to the claimants on 3 August 1960, the latter company taking the vehicle in good faith. In this action the claimants claimed the car. It was *held* that Caldwell was entitled to it because, among other things, he had avoided the contract of sale to Norris when he asked the police to get the car back for him, so that later sales of the car to Motobella and to G & C Finance did not pass the property.

*Comment:* (i) Although this case decides that a contract of sale induced by fraud can be rescinded without actually communicating with the fraudulent person, the third party will in many cases keep the property by relying on s 25(1) of the Sale of Goods Act 1979. This happened in *Newtons of Wembley Ltd* v *Williams* [1964] 3 All ER 532. In that case the seller had rescinded a contract under which the buyer obtained goods by fraud but it was *held* that as the buyer had bought the goods and was in possession with the seller's consent, he could still pass a good title under what is now s 25(1) of the Sale of Goods Act 1979 to a third-party buyer who acted in good faith. The *Car & Universal Finance* case was distinguished on the grounds that there the person who bought from the seller with a voidable title had notice of the defect in his title and so could not be protected by s 25(1).

(ii) The distinction is really between a *direct* and an *indirect* sale. In *Caldwell* the fraudsman did not sell direct to the purchaser. The first sale was to Motobella which had notice of the defect in title and so s 25(1) did not apply, said the court, to give a good title to the finance house. In the *Newtons* case the sale was direct by the fraudsman to the innocent third party and the latter got a good title under s 25(1). The distinction between a direct and an indirect sale is somewhat illogical and the Law Commission recommended in its 12th Report, Cmnd 2958 1966, that until the person deceived actually got in touch with the fraudsman, all sales direct or indirect should give a good title to innocent purchasers.

## Sale by a seller in possession of the goods after sale

Section 24, which is similar to s 8 of the Factors Act 1889, provides that, where a person, having sold goods, continues in possession of the goods, or of the documents of title to the goods, the delivery or transfer by that person or by a mercantile agent acting for him, of the goods or documents of title under any sale, pledge, or other disposition thereof, to any person receiving the same in good faith and without notice of the previous sale, shall have the same effect as if the person making the delivery or transfer were expressly authorised by the owner of the goods to make the same.

The section applies where the property in the goods has passed but the seller still retains possession. If the property in the goods has not passed, the seller gives a good title by virtue of his ownership and not by virtue of the section.

There are a number of decisions which suggest that it is not enough to prove that the seller was still in possession but that the third party must show that the seller was in possession as a seller and that he had not changed his legal position by some subsequent transaction, e.g. as where he had become a bailee under a hire-purchase agreement (*see*, for example, *Eastern Distributors* v *Goldring* (1957), *above*). These decisions were put in doubt by the ruling of the Privy Council in *Pacific Motor Auctions* v *Motor Credits Ltd* [1965] 2 All ER 105. In that case dealers sold cars to the claimants, but remained in possession of them for display purposes. They were authorised to sell as agents for the claimants. This authority was later revoked by the claimants, but the dealers sold to the defendants who were bona fide purchasers. It was *held* that the defendants had obtained a good title by reason of the provision in the New South Wales Sale of Goods Act, which was identical to s 24 of the 1979 Act. The Privy Council decided that the words 'continues . . . in possession' in s 24 must be regarded as referring to the continuity of physical possession regardless of any private transaction between seller and buyer which might alter the legal title under which possession was held. This decision was followed later by the Court of Appeal in *Worcester Works Finance Ltd* v *Cooden Engineering Co Ltd* [1971] 3 All ER 708 and it would seem that there is now no need to show that the seller was in possession as a seller.

The section only protects the title of third parties, and the original buyer can sue the seller either in conversion, or for breach of contract when he fails to deliver the goods, or he may protect himself by means of a Bill of Sale.

## Sale by a buyer in possession

Section 25(1) of the Sale of Goods Act, which is similar to s 9 of the Factors Act 1889, provides that, where a person, having bought or agreed to buy goods, obtains, with the consent of the seller, possession of the goods or the documents of title thereto, the delivery or transfer by that person, or by a mercantile agent acting for him, of the goods or documents of title, under any sale, pledge, or other disposition thereof, to any person receiving the same in good faith and without notice of any lien or other right of the original seller in respect of the goods, shall have the same effect as if the person making the delivery or transfer were a mercantile agent in possession of the goods or documents of title with the consent of the owner.

The section applies where the buyer has possession, but the property has not passed to him. If the buyer has the property in the goods, he can give a good title without the aid of the section.

The section does not apply to persons in possession under hire-purchase contracts, because a person who is hiring the goods is not a person who has agreed to buy them. A hire-purchase contract is a contract of bailment only, with an option to purchase. However, Part III of the Hire Purchase Act 1964 (as substituted by s 192 of and Sch 4, para 22 to the Consumer Credit Act 1974) protects a bona fide private (not a trade) purchaser of a motor vehicle who has bought it from a person in possession under a hire-purchase or conditional sale agreement (*see* Chapter 14).

A person who has goods on *approval* cannot pass a good title under this section because he has not bought or agreed to buy the goods; he has a mere option. However, he may pass a good title by virtue of his ownership if, by selling the goods, he indicates his approval (*see London Jewellers Ltd* v *Attenborough* (1934)).

It appears that the 'consent' of the seller may be sufficient to protect the title of a purchaser from the original buyer even if the latter obtained the goods by criminal fraud, as where he paid for them by a cheque which he knew would not be met (*Du Jardin* v *Beadman Bros* [1952] 2 All ER 160). Furthermore, the fact that the seller withdraws his consent after he has given the buyer possession does not prevent s 9 of the Factors Act 1889 from operating to protect the title of a purchaser from the buyer, since s 2(2) of the 1889 Act specifically provides for this situation.

It should be noted that where the buyer has possession of the documents of title, but not of the goods, complications can arise in respect to the seller's lien and right of stopping the goods in transit (*see* Chapter 12).

It was thought that s 9 could also operate to validate the title of a purchaser from a thief because the purchaser could be regarded as in possession with the consent of the seller (i.e. the thief). This unfortunate result could be avoided if the court decided, as a matter of interpretation, that 'seller' meant 'owner' in this situation. This was the view taken by the trial judge in *National Employers Mutual General Insurance Association* v *Jones* [1987] 3 All ER 385. Thieves stole a car. They sold it to A. He sold it to B who sold it to C (a dealer). C then sold it to D (another dealer), and D sold it to Jones. In all of the transactions the buyers were unaware of the theft. The question before the court was whether Jones had a good title under s 25(1) of the Sale of Goods Act 1979 and s 9 of the Factors Act 1889. The trial judge found that Jones had no title, so did the Court of Appeal but for different reasons. May LJ said that if a person who 'buys' a car from a thief, then himself 'sells' it, he is not a 'seller' and indeed, the contract between him and his purchaser is not a 'contract of sale'. In other words, May LJ was really suggesting that the sale by a thief to an innocent purchaser is not a contract of sale at all. That being the case, the Sale of Goods Act could not apply to it, nor did s 9 of the Factors Act. A person who 'buys' goods from a thief is not 'a person having bought or agreed to buy goods'. A contract of sale presupposes that the seller has or will obtain a good title. This is not true of a thief who is not a seller under relevant law (*see* Sale of Goods Act 1979, s 2(1): 'A contract of sale of goods is a contract by which the seller transfers or agrees to transfer the property in the goods to the buyer . . . '). The House of Lords affirmed the decision (*see* [1988] 2 All ER 425).

As regards retention clauses, the rule in the ordinary case is that if A sells goods to B under a retention clause which states that the property (ownership) of the goods will not pass to B unless and until he pays for them and B sells them on to a sub-purchaser C but does not pay for the goods, then A cannot recover them from C because C will have got a good title from B. This is because B is a buyer in possession and title is conferred on C by the above-mentioned provisions of the Sale of Goods Act 1979 and the Factors Act 1889. This does not seem to work, however, where the sale between B and C is also subject to a retention clause, as was the case in *Re Highway Foods International Ltd (in administrative receivership), The Times*, 1 November 1994. The reason no title passes seems to be that although the sub-purchaser C does not know that there is a retention clause in the original contract and so is unaware that the original buyer has no title, he is at least aware that he has no title on delivery because of the retention clause in the sub-contract.

## Hire-purchase: motor vehicles

As we have seen, Part III of the Hire Purchase Act 1964 protects the title of a bona fide private purchaser of a motor vehicle from a seller in possession under a hire-purchase agreement (*see* Chapter 14).

## GRADED QUESTIONS

*Essay mode*

1 Explain, giving illustrations, the rules of the Sale of Goods Act 1979 which concern the passing of property in unascertained goods. In what circumstances will these rules be of practical importance in commercial transactions?

(*The Institute of Chartered Secretaries and Administrators*)

2 (a) Albert contracts with Zebedee to buy a milling machine which Zebedee has hitherto used in his farmyard business. The machine weighs 20 tons and is embedded in a concrete floor. The contract provides that Zebedee must detach the machine from the floor, dismantle it, deliver it and re-erect it in Albert's mill. Albert pays a deposit of £3,000 out of a total price of £12,000. On the night after the contract is signed the premises of Zebedee are struck by lightning and the milling machine is totally destroyed. Advise Albert.

(b) Explain the importance and use of Romalpa clauses in modern contracts giving illustrations from decided cases.

(*The Institute of Legal Executives*)

3 Brenda visits Sparks, an electrical appliance retailer, to buy a food processor. She sees on display a 'Keninex' model. The accompanying sales literature, which Brenda glances at, proclaims: 'If you can eat it Keninex can beat it' and 'Keninex means simplicity – even a child can use it'. Sparks uses the display model to give a demonstration, using it to shred and mix vegetables. Brenda is extremely impressed and buys a Keninex, which Sparks takes from his storeroom and hands over in a sealed cardboard box. Sparks explains that the processor has a 12-month guarantee, details of which are inside the box.

On unpacking the box at home Brenda discovers that there is no plug fitted. There was a plug on the display model. Fortunately she has a spare plug and uses that. She then is so keen to use the processor that she omits to read either the guarantee or the instructions, which are in leaflets inside the box. The guarantee requires her to fill in a card and post it to Keninex Ltd. The instructions explain that the body of the processor is held on to the base by two spring-loaded screws, which are tightened down for packing, but which must be loosened before use to prevent vibration. Sparks did not mention this.

Brenda first uses the processor to beat up some eggs. Due to the excessive vibration it slides off the table and falls on the floor. This chips the plastic body, which in any event appears very thin and flimsy, but the machine remains operative. Having checked the instructions and loosened the screws, Brenda then attempts to use the shredding part of the processor to shell some walnuts. This causes the metal blades in the shredder to disintegrate. Fortunately no injury or other damage is caused.

Discuss the legal factors involved in considering any claims Brenda might have against either Sparks or Keninex Ltd.

*(Staffordshire University. LLB (Hons) Consumer Law)*

### Objective mode

Four alternative answers are given. Select ONE only. Circle the answer which you consider to be correct. Check your answers by referring back to the information given in the relevant chapter and against the answers at the back of the book.

1  C Gram is the manufacturer of patent medicines and produces a cough mixture called Kicka Cough Linctus. Casper, an opera singer, had caught a severe cold and was concerned to recover from the associated cough before his next engagement that evening. His wife, Marbella, had recently bought a bottle of Kicka Cough from Brian, a chemist, but it remained unopened, since she had recovered. The linctus should have contained 2 per cent alcohol but because of a temporary defect in the bottling plant at C Gram some bottles contained 75 per cent alcohol. Some of these bottles had been supplied to retailers, including Brian. An hour before going on stage Casper drank recommended doses of the linctus and became drunk. He staggered all over the stage, forgot his lines and sang obscene rugby songs. He lost the remainder of the engagement and wishes to bring a claim but is not sure whom to sue. He thinks C Gram would have more money to pay damages than Brian.

The legal position is that:

A  Casper can only claim against Brian.
B  Casper can only claim against C Gram.
C  Casper can claim against either C Gram or Brian.
D  Casper has no claim since he did not purchase the linctus.

2  Rambo orders a new Vectra from Red Garages Ltd for delivery in one month, specifying various extras. His car arrives at Red Garages and before its pre-delivery checks is stolen and taken for a joy ride by Richard and Edwin, local juvenile delinquents, and is damaged.

A  Rambo must accept the loss since property in specific goods passes when the contract is made, and risk passes with the property.
B  Red Garages must make good the damage since the property in the car remained with them until they had put the goods in a deliverable state.

**C** It is up to Red Garages to sue Edwin and Richard and recover the loss from them.

**D** Red Garages will be liable to Rambo as negligent bailees of his motor car. They should have taken proper care of it.

3 When there is a contract for the sale of specific goods and the seller is bound to do something to the goods for the purpose of putting them into a deliverable state, the property does not pass.

**A** Until such thing is done.

**B** Until such thing is done and the buyer assents to it being done.

**C** Until such thing is done and the buyer has notice that it has been done.

**D** Until such thing is done and the buyer has had an opportunity to see that it has been done.

4 Dilwyn agrees to purchase a quantity of Beaujolais Nouveau from Monsieur Scopes, a dealer in Burgundy. Monsieur Scopes agrees to deliver at his own risk to Dilwyn's warehouse in Liverpool, the journey to take one month. In that time the Beaujolais is no longer as 'nouveau' as it should be and Dilwyn reckons its price has gone down 50p per bottle. Is Scopes responsible for this deterioration?

**A** Yes, because the goods were at the seller's risk during transit.

**B** No, because the buyer must take any risk of deterioration in the goods necessarily incidental to the course of transit.

**C** Yes, because the risk and property were not to pass until delivery.

**D** No, because being specific goods in deliverable state the property and risk passed when the contract was made.

5 John agreed to buy Geoffrey's vintage 3-litre Lagonda motor car for £15,000. Unknown to John and Geoffrey a fire had occurred in David's garage, where the car was stored, the day before the contract had been made and had destroyed the car. What is the legal position?

**A** John must pay the contract price since the risk of loss passes to the buyer when the contract is made.

**B** John must pay but can sue David for negligence as a bailee.

**C** John need not pay for the goods as the contract is void since the goods had perished when the agreement was made.

**D** John need not pay for the goods as the contract is voidable since the goods had perished when the agreement was made.

6 Which of the following is a prerequisite for the successful operation of a reservation of title clause in a contract of sale of goods?

**A** The buyer must be insolvent when the clause is enforced.

**B** The goods must be identifiable.

**C** The rights of third parties must not be prejudiced.

**D** The buyer must be solvent when the contract is made.

*Answers to questions set in objective mode appear on p 708.*

# 12 THE SALE OF GOODS III

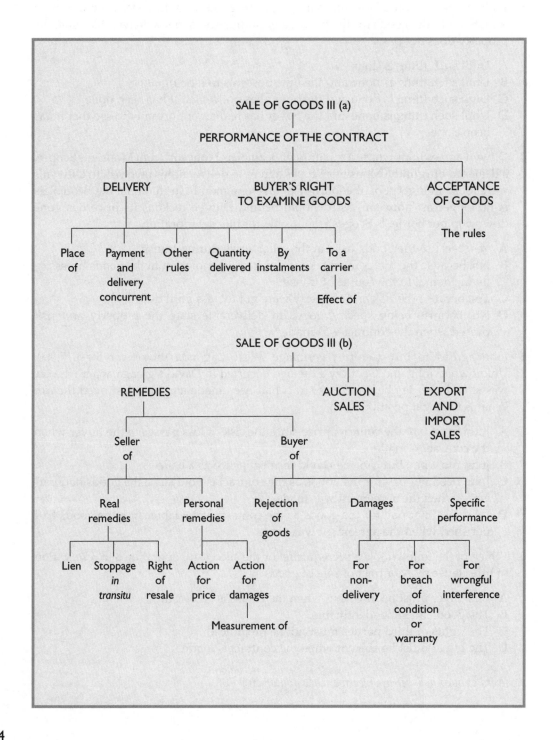

SALE OF GOODS III (a)

PERFORMANCE OF THE CONTRACT

DELIVERY

BUYER'S RIGHT
TO EXAMINE GOODS

ACCEPTANCE
OF GOODS

The rules

Place
of

Payment
and
delivery
concurrent

Other
rules

Quantity
delivered

By
instalments

To a
carrier

Effect of

SALE OF GOODS III (b)

REMEDIES

AUCTION
SALES

EXPORT
AND
IMPORT
SALES

Seller
of

Buyer
of

Real
remedies

Personal
remedies

Rejection
of
goods

Damages

Specific
performance

Lien

Stoppage
*in*
*transitu*

Right
of
resale

Action
for
price

Action
for
damages

Measurement of

For
non-
delivery

For
breach
of
condition
or
warranty

For
wrongful
interference

The objectives of this chapter are to consider the principles of law which are relevant in a contract of sale of goods in terms of the performance of the contract, and the remedies of seller and buyer. The chapter concludes with a consideration of auction and export and import sales.

## PERFORMANCE OF THE CONTRACT GENERALLY

A contract of sale of goods is, like any other contract, discharged or brought to an end by proper performance of it by the parties. The relevant rules are set out below.

## DELIVERY

Section 61(1) defines delivery as the voluntary transfer of possession from one person to another. There are various forms of delivery as follows:

(a) by physical transfer as where the goods are handed to the buyer with the intention of transferring possession;
(b) by delivery of the means of control as where the key of a warehouse or store is handed to the buyer;
(c) by attornment as where the goods are in the possession of a third party, e.g. a warehouseman, who acknowledges to the buyer that he holds the goods on his behalf (s 29(4));
(d) by delivery of documents of title as where a bill of lading representing the goods is delivered (s 29(4)). A vehicle registration document is not a document of title for this purpose, said the Court of Appeal in *Beverley Acceptances* v *Oakley* [1982] RTR 417;
(e) by constructive delivery as where the buyer already has possession of the goods as a bailee. Thus in a hire-purchase contract the character of possession changes when the instalments have been paid and the hirer becomes owner by constructive delivery. This form of delivery also applies where a seller agrees to hold the goods as a bailee or agent of the buyer.

### Place of delivery

Section 27 provides that it is the duty of the seller to deliver the goods, and of the buyer to accept and pay for them, in accordance with the terms of sale. The seller's duty to deliver does not mean he must necessarily take or send them to the buyer.

Section 29(1) provides that whether it is for the buyer to take possession of the goods or for the seller to send them to the buyer is a question depending in each case on the contract, express or implied, between the parties.

The place of delivery, in the absence of express agreement to the contrary, is the place of business of the seller or, if he has no place of business, his residence (s 29(2)). If the contract is for the sale of specific goods which to the knowledge of the parties when the contract is made are in some other place, then that place is the place of delivery (s 29(2)). Thus, in the absence of a contrary intention, the buyer is under a duty to collect the goods.

Where the seller is, under a special contract, bound to deliver the goods, he discharges the duty by delivering them to a person who, being at the buyer's premises, appears respectable and likely to be authorised to take delivery, even if in the event he is not.

**The following case provides an illustration.**

### Galbraith & Grant Ltd v Block [1922] 2 KB 155

The claimants were wine merchants and they sued the defendants for £16 2s 11d being the price of a case of champagne delivered to the defendant who was a licensed victualler. The defendant admitted the contract but said that champagne had never been delivered to him. Evidence showed that the defendant asked the claimants to deliver the goods and they employed a carrier who delivered them to the defendant's premises and obtained a receipt signed in the defendant's name by a person on the defendant's premises who seemed to the carrier to have authority to receive them. In fact the person to whom the goods were delivered had no authority to receive them and did not hand them over to the defendant. It was held that, where a vendor had been told to deliver goods at the buyer's premises, he fulfils his obligation if he delivers them to those premises and without negligence gives them over to a person apparently having authority to receive them. The trial judge had not taken sufficient evidence on the care taken by the carriers, so it was not possible to say whether they were negligent or not, and the case was sent back for a new trial on this point.

Delivery of goods to the wrong address may amount to conversion by the carrier, thus providing the owner with a remedy in tort against him if the goods are not recovered.

## Payment and delivery are concurrent conditions

Section 28 provides that, unless otherwise agreed, e.g. where the seller gives credit to the buyer, delivery and payment of the price are concurrent conditions. The seller must be ready and willing to give possession of the goods to the buyer in exchange for the price, and the buyer must be ready and willing to pay the price in exchange for possession of the goods.

Thus, if the buyer is suing the seller for non-delivery, he need not give evidence that he has paid, but merely that he was ready and willing to pay. In an action for non-acceptance of the goods, the seller need not prove that he has tendered delivery, but merely that he was ready and willing to deliver.

## Other rules as to delivery

Where under the contract of sale the seller is bound to send the goods to the buyer, but no time for sending them is fixed, the seller is bound to send them within a reasonable time (s 29(3)) and at a reasonable hour (s 29(5)). What is reasonable in both cases is a matter of fact.

## Quantity of goods delivered

Where the seller delivers to the buyer a quantity of goods less than he contracted to sell, the buyer may reject them, but if he accepts, he must pay for them at the contract rate (s 30(1)).

Where the seller delivers to the buyer a quantity of goods larger than he contracted to sell, the buyer may accept the goods included in the contract and reject the rest, or he may reject the whole. If the buyer accepts the whole of the goods so delivered, he must pay for them at the contract rate (s 30(3)).

If the goods delivered are mixed with goods of a different description not included in the contract, the buyer may accept the goods which are in accordance with the contract and reject the rest, or he may reject the whole if he is a consumer. In non-consumer cases a business buyer will, where the breach is slight, have to take delivery and sue for any loss (see Sale of Goods Act 1979, s 35A, as amended by the Sale and Supply of Goods Act 1994).

The above provisions are subject to any usage of trade, special agreement, or course of dealing between the parties (s 30(5)). An example is provided from earlier case law now affirmed and made stronger by the statutory changes referred to above. In *Shipton, Anderson & Co Ltd* v *Weil Bros* [1912] 1 KB 574 the sellers were to deliver 4,950 tons of wheat and in fact delivered 4,950 tons and 55 lb. The court held that the buyers were not entitled to reject the whole consignment, which they in fact did, since the excess of 55 lb was so trifling. The sellers were awarded damages for breach of contract by the buyers (and *see also Moore & Co* v *Landauer & Co* [1921] 2 KB 519, Chapter 10).

## Right of partial rejection

Section 35A of the Sale of Goods Act 1979 (as inserted by the Sale and Supply of Goods Act 1994) gives a right of partial rejection. Before this change in the law, as we have seen, a limited right of partial rejection existed where the seller delivered non-conforming goods, e.g. on an order for one dozen bottles of champagne the seller sends 10 champagne and two sparkling wine – all or just the two odd ones could be rejected. Also, the unwanted goods had to be of a different description: the new rules set out below apply to defective goods of the same description. Under s 35A consumer and business buyers may:

- accept all conforming and reject all non-conforming goods; or
- accept all conforming, some non-conforming and reject the rest; or
- reject all the goods; or
- keep all the goods; or
- keep most of the goods rejecting only seriously defective goods.

Suppose, therefore, that A intends to tile his kitchen and orders 200 tiles. On delivery, 30 are cracked. A can retain the 170 good tiles and reject the 30. Alternatively, he can retain the 170 good tiles and some of the 30, e.g. for use if cut tiles are needed on corners or elsewhere, and reject the rest, but he still retains his right to reject the whole 200.

Where delivery is by instalments (*see overleaf*), the above rules apply to rejection of an instalment.

## Delivery by instalments

Unless otherwise agreed, the buyer of goods is not bound to accept delivery by instalments (s 31(1)). Thus the seller cannot excuse short delivery by undertaking to deliver the balance in due course. Where there is a contract of sale of goods to be delivered by stated instalments, which are to be separately paid for, and the seller makes defective deliveries in respect of one or more instalments, or the buyer neglects or refuses to take delivery of or pay for one or more instalments, it is a question in each case depending on the terms of the contract and the circumstances of the case, whether the breach of contract is a repudiation of the whole contract, or whether it is a severable breach giving rise to a claim for compensation but not a right to treat the whole contract as repudiated (s 31(2)).

The main tests to be considered in applying s 31(2) are:

(a) the ratio quantitatively which the breach bears to the contract as a whole; and
(b) the degree of probability or improbability that such a breach will be repeated.

**The following case and comment provides an illustration.**

### Maple Flock Co Ltd v Universal Furniture Products (Wembley) Ltd [1934] 1 KB 148

The claimants agreed to sell to the defendants 100 tons of black linsey flock at £15 2s 6d per ton to be delivered three loads a week, 1½ tons per load, as required. The claimants guaranteed that the flock should not contain more than 30 parts of chlorine to 100,000 parts of flock. The sixteenth delivery contained 250 parts of chlorine to 100,000 parts of flock. The buyers repudiated the contract and refused to take further deliveries. The sellers sued for breach of contract. Evidence showed that the first 15 deliveries were as per contract, and the claimants' plant and equipment was good so that there was little chance of subsequent deliveries being affected. *Held* – The matter was covered by s 31(2) of the Sale of Goods Act and the main tests to be applied in cases falling under that section were: (a) the ratio quantitatively which the breach bears to the contract as a whole, and (b) the degree of probability or improbability that such a breach will be repeated.

In this case a delivery of 1½ tons was defective out of a contract to supply 100 tons and there was little chance of the breach being repeated. The buyers were not, therefore, entitled to repudiate the contract and were liable for breach. They could have recovered damages in respect of the defects in the sixteenth delivery but did not claim any because the delivery had been used in the manufacture of bedding and furniture before the sample was tested and found defective.

*Comment:* (i) In *Munro (Robert A) & Co Ltd v Meyer* [1930] 2 KB 312, where the contract was for the sale of 1,500 tons of bone meal and 611 tons were found to be defective, it was *held* that the buyers were entitled to repudiate the contract.

(ii) In *Regent OHG Aisenstadt und Barig v Francesco of Jermyn Street Ltd* [1981] 3 All ER 327 the claimants were delivering suits to the defendants by instalments. In one consignment there was one suit short. The defendants, who wished to cancel the arrangement, repudiated the contract under s 30(1). Mustill J found that the contract was divisible and s 31 applied. The defendants were liable in damages for non-acceptance of the instalment and repudiation of the contract.

As we have seen, provided the buyer has a right to reject an instalment he can reject only part of it, should he wish, on the lines set out above.

### Delivery to a carrier

Where the seller is authorised or required to send the goods to the buyer, delivery by the seller to a carrier is, in the absence of any evidence to the contrary, deemed delivery to the buyer (s 32(1)). In the absence of a contrary agreement the seller is required to make a contract with a carrier which is reasonable in terms of the goods to be carried. If he does not and the goods are lost or damaged, the buyer may refuse to regard delivery to the carrier as delivery to himself and may sue the seller for damages (s 32(2)). Where the carriage involves a sea voyage where it is usual to insure, the seller must make it possible for the buyer to insure otherwise the goods are at the seller's risk during sea transit (s 32(3)).

Where the seller of goods agrees to deliver them at his own risk at a place other than that where they are when sold, the buyer must, unless otherwise agreed, take the risk of accidental destruction or deterioration, but not the risk of damage caused by the fault of the seller (s 33). Where the goods are perishable, they are not considered satisfactory unless they are sent off by the seller in time to reach their destination in saleable condition (*see Mash & Murrell Ltd* v *Joseph I Emmanuel Ltd* (1961), Chapter 10).

## THE BUYER'S RIGHT TO EXAMINE THE GOODS

A buyer who has not previously examined the goods is not regarded as having accepted goods delivered to him unless and until he has had a reasonable opportunity of examining them for the purpose of ascertaining whether they are in conformity with the contract. Unless otherwise agreed, when the seller tenders delivery of goods to the buyer he is bound, on request, to give the buyer a reasonable opportunity of examining the goods to see whether they are in conformity with the contract (s 34(2)). The seller may attempt to introduce a waiver of the right to inspection. When goods are delivered to a person's home, he may be asked to sign a document saying 'received this item in good condition'. However, even if a consumer signs such a waiver, it is unenforceable against him under s 35(3) of the Sale of Goods Act 1979 (as inserted by the Sale and Supply of Goods Act 1994). In a non-consumer deal, waiver by the buyer may be enforceable.

## ACCEPTANCE OF THE GOODS

The buyer is deemed to have accepted the goods:

(a) when he intimates to the seller that he has accepted them; or
(b) when the goods have been delivered to him and he does any act in relation to them which is inconsistent with the ownership of the seller; or
(c) when after the lapse of a reasonable time, he retains the goods without intimating to the seller that he has rejected them. Under s 35(5) a reasonable time is related to having had a reasonable opportunity to examine the goods so that a reasonable period of user applies rather than the mere passage of time without use or much use.

Section 35 provides that s 34 is always to prevail over s 35 so that a buyer is not prevented from rejecting goods until he has examined them or at least has had a reasonable opportunity of examining them. It should be noted, however, that delay in rejection will not defeat a claim for repudiation for breach of condition unless there has been a reasonable opportunity to examine the goods so that a period of reasonable user rather than mere lapse of time is now relevant. The fact that the buyer has sold or given the goods to a third party or has asked for or agreed to a repair is not an act inconsistent with the seller's ownership. The contract can be cancelled for the benefit of the buyer or third party if the goods are defective.

The effect of this provision is, therefore, that persons who buy goods such as refrigerators, washing machines and radios will be able to examine and test them in their own homes. If the goods are faulty, they will be able to repudiate the contract and return the goods demanding a refund of the purchase price. However, the goods must be returned as soon as a defect appears. If the defect does not appear within what the court regards as a reasonable period of user, the buyer may not be able to repudiate the goods but be left with a claim for damages.

However, much depends upon the circumstances of the case; for example, many stores provide fitting rooms for garments and failure to use these may prevent a claim that a garment is not acceptable because it does not fit, user being irrelevant here. Also, if the buyer accepts part of goods forming a commercial unit, e.g. one volume of a set of encyclopedias, he is deemed to have accepted the rest.

Where the buyer has the right to refuse to accept the goods and does so refuse, he is not actually bound to return them, although commonly a consumer will do so but only to notify the seller of the refusal (s 36). If the seller is able to deliver the goods and requests the buyer to take delivery, the buyer must do so within a reasonable time. If he does not do so, he is liable to the seller for any resulting loss and also for a reasonable charge for the care and custody of the goods. If the buyer's refusal amounts only to a request to postpone delivery for a short time, the seller is still bound to deliver. If, however, the refusal is absolute or involves a long postponement, it may amount to a repudiation of the contract, which discharges the seller from liability to deliver and gives him a right of action in damages against the buyer (s 37(2)).

## REMEDIES OF THE SELLER

We are now in a position to look at the remedies of the seller. These consist of remedies against the goods sold and personal remedies against the buyer.

### Real remedies against the goods: generally

The unpaid seller, in addition to his personal remedies, e.g. an action for damages, has under Part V of the Act, certain real remedies against the goods.

Section 39(1) provides that, even if the property in the goods has passed to the buyer, the unpaid seller of goods, as such, has by implication of law:

(a) a lien on the goods or the right to retain them for the price while he is still in possession of them;

(b) in the case of the insolvency of the buyer, a right of stopping the goods *in transitu* (in transit) after he has parted with possession of them;

(c) a right of resale as limited by the Act.

Section 39(2) provides that, where the property in goods has not passed to the buyer, the unpaid seller has, in addition to his other remedies, a right of withholding delivery similar to and co-extensive with his rights of lien and stoppage *in transitu* where the property has passed to the buyer.

The rights set out in s 39(1) may only be exercised by an unpaid seller, and s 38(1) provides that a seller of goods is deemed to be an unpaid seller:

(a) when the whole of the price has not been paid or tendered;

(b) when a bill of exchange or other negotiable instrument has been received as conditional payment, and the condition on which it was received has not been fulfilled by reason of the dishonour of the instrument or otherwise.

The term seller includes in certain circumstances the agent of the seller (s 38(2)). Thus where the goods are sold through an agent who has either paid the price to his principal, or made himself liable to pay the price under the terms of his contract of agency, the agent can exercise any of the rights of the unpaid seller.

## Lien

A lien is generally speaking the right of a creditor in possession of the goods of his debtor to retain possession of them until the price has been paid or tendered, or his debt has been secured or satisfied. *A lien does not normally carry with it a power of sale*, though the unpaid seller of goods has a statutory power, and will generally exercise his lien as a preliminary to resale.

The lien conferred by the Act is a particular lien, though a general lien may be conferred by an express contractual provision. Under a particular lien the unpaid seller can retain only the goods which are not paid for, and not other goods belonging to the buyer. However, where delivery is being made by instalments and an unpaid seller has made part delivery of the goods, he may exercise his lien on the remainder, unless such part delivery can, in the circumstances, be construed as a waiver of the right of lien by the seller (s 42).

Where the goods have been sold without any stipulation as to credit, the unpaid seller who is in possession of them is entitled to retain possession until payment or tender of the price (s 41(1)(a)). A lien can also be claimed, even though credit has been given:

(a) where the goods have been sold on credit but the term of credit has expired (s 41(1)(b)). This presupposes that although credit was given the buyer did not take delivery of the goods. If he had done so, no lien could be exercised because the seller would not have the goods; and

(b) where the buyer becomes insolvent (s 41(1)(c)).

A person is deemed to be insolvent within the meaning of the Act if he either has ceased to pay his debts in the ordinary course of business, or cannot pay his debts as they become due (s 61(4)).

The effect of the insolvency provision is that the seller cannot be compelled to deliver the goods to an insolvent person and to prove for a dividend in the bankruptcy. However, a trustee in bankruptcy can have the goods if he tenders the whole price.

The seller's lien is a possessory lien. The seller must be in possession of the goods, but he need not be in possession as a seller and may exercise his right of lien even if he is in possession of the goods as agent or bailee for the buyer (s 41(2)). The seller's lien is for the price of the goods, and cannot be exercised in respect of other costs, e.g. storage charges and the like (*Soames* v *British Empire Shipping Co* (1860) 8 HL Cas 338).

## Loss of lien

The right of lien is lost:

(a) if the price is paid or tendered;
(b) if the right of lien has been waived by the seller;
(c) if the buyer or his agent lawfully obtains possession of the goods;
(d) if the unpaid seller delivers the goods to a carrier or bailee for the purpose of transmission to the buyer, without reserving the right of disposal of the goods. A right of *stoppage in transitu* may arise here, but only if the buyer is insolvent.

A *waiver* may be an express waiver under the contract between the parties, or may be implied from the conduct of the seller. For example, suppose B buys furniture on credit from S and; after the sale has taken place, S then asks B to lend him the furniture for a week until he can get more furniture to display in his shop. Here the conduct of S would imply that, although the property was B's, he held the furniture on a new contract of loan, and that his right of lien on the contract of sale was waived.

The exercise of a lien by the seller does not rescind the contract (s 48(1)) and the right of lien is not lost when the seller obtains a judgment from the court for the price of the goods (s 43(2)).

## Stoppage *in transitu*

When the buyer of goods becomes insolvent, the unpaid seller who is not in possession of the goods has the right of stopping them *in transitu*, i.e. he may resume possession of the goods as long as they are in course of transit, and may retain them until payment or tender of the price (s 44). The seller is 'unpaid' where only part of the price has been paid.

The remedy is only available when the buyer is insolvent and, if exercised, means that the seller need not allow the goods to form part of an insolvent estate, leaving himself with a mere right to prove for a dividend for the price. Nevertheless, the exercise of stoppage *in transitu* does not rescind the contract of sale, nor does it vest the property in the goods in the unpaid seller (*Booth SS Co Ltd* v *Cargo Fleet Iron Co Ltd* [1916] 2 KB 570). Thus, if the buyer's trustee in bankruptcy tenders the price, the seller must deliver the goods or be liable for breach of contract. Three conditions must be satisfied before the right can be exercised: (a) the seller must be unpaid; (b) the buyer must be insolvent; and (c) the goods must still be in transit.

Section 45(1) provides that goods are deemed to be in course of transit from the time when they are delivered to a carrier by land or water, or other bailee for the purpose of transmission to the buyer, until the buyer, or his agent in that behalf, takes delivery of them from such carrier or other bailee.

We have seen that delivery to a carrier is prima facie deemed to be a constructive delivery of the goods to the buyer, and where the carrier is the agent of the buyer, this constitutes actual delivery and there can be no stoppage *in transitu*. Where, however, the carrier is an independent contractor, the remedy is available until the goods are actually delivered to the buyer.

If the buyer or his agent obtains delivery of the goods before their arrival at the appointed destination, the transit is at an end (s 45(2)). If, after the arrival of the goods at the appointed destination, the carrier or other bailee acknowledges to the buyer, or his agent, that he holds the goods on his behalf and continues in possession of them as bailee for the buyer or his agent, the transit is at an end, and it is immaterial that a further destination for the goods may have been indicated by the buyer (s 45(3)).

**The following case provides an illustration.**

## Kendall v Marshall, Stevens & Co (1883) 11 QBD 356

This was an action to recover damages for conversion of 55 bales of waste cotton. The claimant was the liquidator of a person called Leoffer, trading as Higginbottom & Co. The defendants were shipping agents and carriers, and the second defendants were Peter Ward & Son of Bolton, who sold the bales of cotton. It appeared that on 9 November 1880, Ward & Son sold the cotton to Leoffer and on 12 November Leoffer asked the vendors to send the goods to Marshall, Stevens & Co at Garston. He also informed Marshall, Stevens & Co that they were to ship the goods as soon as possible to Durend & Co at Rouen, France. The actual transit of the goods was therefore from Bolton to Rouen. On 13 November, the goods were sent by the vendors to Marshall, Stevens & Co and they arrived at Garston on 15 November. The railway company's advice note which accompanied the goods gave Marshall, Stevens & Co notice that unless the goods were collected by a certain time, the company would hold them as warehousemen at owner's risk and not as common carriers. On 18 November, Leoffer filed a petition for the liquidation of his estate, and on 22 November, Ward & Son telegraphed Marshall, Stevens & Co to stop the goods. This was done and they were returned to Bolton on 24 November. The liquidator sued in conversion to recover the value of the goods for the benefit of the estate. *Held* – The right to stop the goods expired when they arrived at Garston and when the railway company's notice had expired, which it had in this case. Once the railway company held the goods as warehousemen, the goods were in the constructive possession of the buyer, Leoffer, and the defendants were liable in conversion.

If, however, the goods are rejected by the buyer, and the carrier or other bailee continues in possession of them, the transit is not deemed to be at an end, even if the seller has refused to take them back (s 45(4)). When goods are delivered to a ship chartered by the buyer, it is a question depending on the circumstances of the particular case, whether they are in the possession of the master as a carrier, or as an agent of the buyer (s 45(5)). The ship's master will not normally be the agent of the buyer where the goods are shipped under a charter for one voyage. The master will be the buyer's agent where the ship belongs to the buyer, and may well be where the ship is chartered by the buyer for several voyages, as under a time charter.

Where the carrier or other bailee wrongfully refuses to deliver the goods to the buyer or his agent, the transit is deemed to be at an end (s 45(6)).

Where part-delivery of the goods has been made to the buyer or his agent, the remainder of the goods may be stopped in transit, unless such part-delivery has been made under such circumstances as to show an agreement to give up possession of the whole of the goods (s 45(7)).

The unpaid seller's right of lien or stoppage *in transitu* is not affected by any sale or other disposition of the goods which the buyer may have made, unless the seller has agreed to it. However, where documents of title, e.g. bills of lading with respect to the goods, have been lawfully transferred to the buyer, and he has transferred them to a third party who takes them in good faith and for value by way of sale, the seller's right of lien or stoppage *in transitu* is defeated (s 47).

Where the transfer of the document of title is not by way of sale but is, for example, by way of a security for a loan, the seller can still exercise his lien or right of stoppage *in transitu* but subject to the rights of the lender.

**The following case provides an illustration.**

### Leask v Scott Bros (1887) 2 QBD 376

Green & Co, who were merchants, were indebted to the claimant, who was a broker, and asked him for a further advance of £2,000. The claimant agreed to make the further advance but wanted some security. Green & Co gave him a bill of lading which they had received from the defendants for goods shipped to Green & Co. Two days later Green & Co became insolvent and the defendants stopped the goods in transit. The jury found that the claimant took the bill of lading honestly and fairly and that he gave valuable consideration on the understanding that he was being given a security. *Held* – The claimant was entitled to the goods as against the defendants up to the amount of the advance.

*Comment:* If the goods which the seller stops or exercises a lien on are worth £3,000 and the lender has lent £2,000, the lender is entitled to £2,000 of the proceeds of sale of the goods and the seller is entitled to £1,000 of the proceeds in preference to the general creditors of the buyer. The seller will have to prove in the bankruptcy of the buyer for the balance.

### Exercise of the right

The unpaid seller may exercise his right of stoppage *in transitu* either by taking actual possession of the goods, or by giving notice of his claim to the carrier or other bailee in whose possession the goods are. Such notice may be given either to the person in actual possession of the goods or to his principal. In the latter case, the notice, to be effectual, must be given at such time and under such circumstances that the principal, by the exercise of reasonable diligence, may communicate it to his servant or agent in time to prevent delivery to the buyer (s 46(1), (2) and (3)).

When notice of stoppage *in transitu* is given by the seller to the carrier, or other bailee in possession of the goods, he must redeliver the goods to or according to the direction of the seller. The expenses of such redelivery must be borne by the seller (s 46(4)). If the carrier delivers the goods after notice to the contrary, the unpaid seller has his remedy, for what it is worth, against the buyer who will by definition be insolvent, *or* may sue the carrier in tort for conversion.

The carrier can refuse to redeliver if his charges have not been paid, and his lien overrides the seller's right of stoppage *in transitu*. However, unless a general lien is conferred by the contract, a carrier's lien is normally a particular lien so that he can only refuse to redeliver the actual goods in respect of which charges are outstanding, and not other goods dispatched by the seller.

## The right of resale

The unpaid seller of goods has a right to resell, without being in breach of contract, in the following circumstances:

(a) where the buyer repudiates the contract either expressly or by conduct, the seller can resell the goods, retain any profit made, returning to the buyer any part payments;

(b) where the contract of sale expressly provides for resale in case the buyer should make default, and the seller resells the goods on default, the original contract of sale is rescinded, but without prejudice to any claim the seller may have for damages (s 48(4));

(c) where the goods are of a perishable nature, or where the unpaid seller gives notice to the buyer of his intention to resell, and the buyer does not within a reasonable time pay or tender the price, the unpaid seller may resell the goods and recover from the original buyer damages for any loss occasioned by the breach of contract (s 48(3)). The contract of sale is not rescinded by the seller's mere exercise of his right of lien or stoppage *in transitu*, but it is when the unpaid seller resells the goods or part of them, either under s 48(4), where the contract expressly provides for resale, or under s 48(3), which gives a right of resale even where there is no express provision in the contract.

In either event resale, whether of the whole or part of the goods, rescinds the contract and the property reverts to the seller, who has then no action for the price against the buyer. Thus, if the unpaid seller resells at a profit, he does not have to account to the original buyer for it. If the original buyer has made a payment for the goods, the seller can keep this if it is a *deposit* to be forfeited if the contract does not proceed. If it is regarded as a *part-payment*, it must be returned to the original buyer. Which of these it is will be dealt with either by the contract or by the court in case of dispute.

If the seller sells at a loss, he has an action for *damages* from which must be deducted any payment received from the buyer.

**The following case illustrates the application of the law.**

### R V Ward Ltd v Bignall [1967] 2 All ER 449

The defendant bought a Ford Zodiac and a Vanguard from the claimants for a total price of £850, paying a deposit of £25 and leaving both cars with the claimants until payment of the balance. The defendant refused to pay the balance, alleging that he had been misled as to the date of manufacture of the Vanguard, although he did offer to take the Zodiac but his offer was refused. Eventually the claimants resold the Vanguard for £350 and brought an action against the defendant, claiming £497 10s, being the balance of the total purchase price less £350 with the addition of £22 10s for expenses incurred in advertising in order to resell the cars. *Held* – by the Court of Appeal – that when an unpaid seller exercised his right to resell the whole or part of the goods under s 48(3) of the Sale of Goods Act, he could no longer perform his contract which must therefore be regarded as rescinded. Accordingly the claimants' proper claim was for damages for non-acceptance. Sellers LJ said:

> ... the [claimants] cannot recover the price of the Zodiac, which is in the circumstances their property. They can, however, recover any loss which they have sustained by the buyer's default. The parties have sensibly agreed that the value of the Zodiac in May 1965 was £450. The total contract price was £850, against which the [claimants] have received £25 in cash and £350 in respect of the Vanguard, and have to give credit for £450 for the Zodiac. To the loss of £25 must be added the sum for advertising, which was admittedly reasonably incurred – £22 10s 0d. The [claimants'] loss was, therefore, £47 10s 0d.
>
> I would allow the appeal and enter judgment for £47 10s 0d in favour of the [claimants] ...

### Power of seller to give a second buyer a title

A seller has power to give a title, whether he has the right to sell or not, in the following circumstances:

(a) where, although the goods are sold, the property is still in the seller;

(b) under s 24 of the Sale of Goods Act 1979, or s 8 of the Factors Act 1889, if he is in possession;

(c) under s 48(2) of the Sale of Goods Act 1979, which provides that where an unpaid seller who has exercised his right of lien or stoppage *in transitu* resells the goods, the buyer acquires a good title thereto as against the original buyer.

Unless the seller resells in accordance with the rules laid down in s 48(3) and (4), he will usually be liable in breach of contract to the original buyer, though in most cases the second buyer will obtain a good title to the goods.

## PERSONAL REMEDIES OF THE SELLER

In addition to the real remedies discussed above, the seller has a personal action against the buyer either:

(a) for the price under s 49(1); or

(b) for damages for non-acceptance under s 50(1).

The passing of the property and the conduct of the buyer will determine the sort of action which the seller will bring, and the property may, of course, have passed before delivery.

If the property has passed and the buyer has accepted the goods, the seller has an action for the price. If the property has not passed and the buyer will not accept the goods, the seller has an action for damages. Finally, if the property has passed and the buyer will not accept the goods, the seller has an action either for the price, or for damages. If the seller sues for the price, he may also include a claim for losses or expenses, e.g. in storing the goods because the buyer would not take them (s 37(1)). If the seller sues for damages, such losses will be taken into account. Where the price is due in foreign currency, it is now possible for an English court to give judgment for the debt in the foreign currency itself (*Miliangos* v *George Frank (Textiles) Ltd* [1975] 3 All ER 801). A claimant may also claim in a foreign currency for damages for breach of contract (*The Folias* [1979] 1 All ER 421) and in tort, e.g. for conversion of goods (*The Despina* [1979] 1 All ER 421). The *Miliangos* rule does not apply to the claims of creditors in the winding-up of a company. Here the claim in foreign currency must be converted into sterling at the date of the winding-up (*see Re Lines Bros Ltd* [1982] 2 All ER 183). This is to prevent the introduction of further complications in the administration of the assets of a company on winding up.

Section 49(2) provides that where, under a contract of sale, the price is payable on a certain day irrespective of delivery, and the buyer wrongfully neglects or refuses to pay such price, the seller may maintain an action for the price, although the property in the goods has not passed, and the goods have not been appropriated to the contract.

## MEASUREMENT OF DAMAGES

### The concept of available market

In an action for damages, the main problem is that of assessment. Section 50(2) provides that the measure of damages is the estimated loss directly and naturally resulting, in the ordinary course of events, from the buyer's breach of contract.

Section 50(3) further expands the concept by providing that, where there is an available market for the goods in question, the measure of damages is prima facie to be ascertained by the difference between the contract price and the market or current price at the time or times when the goods ought to have been accepted, or, if no time was fixed for acceptance, then at the time of refusal to accept.

An available market exists where on the facts of the case the seller is in a position where the goods can be readily disposed of to a number of buyers, *all of whom want the identical article which is for sale*, e.g. as in the case of a new motor car. Given an available market, if the supply exceeds the demand, the seller is entitled to the loss of profit on sale to a defaulting buyer.

If, however, the demand for the goods exceeds the supply so that the seller can readily sell every item he can obtain from the manufacturers, he is not entitled to loss of profit on the first sale where he has made the same profit on a substituted sale following the first buyer's default.

Section 50(3) does not apply where there is no available market, as is the case with second-hand cars, and damages must be assessed on general principles, i.e. what is the estimated loss directly and naturally resulting in the ordinary course of events from the buyer's breach of contract?

**The following three cases clarify the application of these rules.**

### Thompson (W L) Ltd v Robinson (Gunmakers) Ltd [1955] 1 All ER 154

On 4 March 1954, the defendants agreed in writing with the claimants, who were motor car dealers, to purchase from them a Standard Vanguard car. On 5 March 1954, the defendants said they were not prepared to take delivery. The claimants returned the car to their suppliers who did not ask for any compensation. The claimants now sued for damages for breach of contract. The selling price of a Standard Vanguard was fixed by the manufacturers and the claimants' profit would have been £61 1s 9d. When the agreement was made there was not sufficient demand for Vanguards in the locality as would absorb all such cars available for sale in the area, but evidence did not show that there was no available market in the widest sense, i.e. in the sense of the country as a whole. *Held* – The claimants were entitled to compensation for loss of their bargain, i.e. the profit they would have made being £61 1s 9d because they had sold one car less than they would have sold. Even if the 'available market' concept as used in s 50(3) of the Sale of Goods Act meant taking in the whole of the country, it would not be just to apply s 50(3) in this case. It is after all possible to translate 'available' as meaning 'at hand'. Therefore, s 50(3) was no defence to the claimants' action. Section 50(3) need not be applied if the court thinks it would be unjust in the circumstances.

*Comment:* The evidence in this case that the car could not be sold and *would never be sold by the claimants* was compelling since they had returned it to the suppliers. In the *Charter* case (*below*) the claimants had actually sold the car which the defendant had refused to buy to someone else.

### Charter v Sullivan [1957] 1 All ER 809

The claimants who were motor dealers agreed to sell a Hillman Minx car to the defendant for £773 17s 0d which was the retail price fixed by the manufacturer. The defendant refused to complete the purchase and the claimants resold the car a few days later to another purchaser at the same price. The claimants sued for breach of contract, the measure of damages claimed being £97 15s 0d, the profit the claimants would have made on the sale to the defendant if it had gone through. Evidence showed that the claimants could have sold the second purchaser another Hillman Minx which would have been ordered from the manufacturers' stock had the defendant taken the first Hillman Minx as agreed. The claimants' sales manager said in his evidence, 'We can sell all the Hillman Minx cars we can get.' This evidence was accepted by the trial judge. The claimants were really suggesting that, but for the defendant's refusal to complete, they would have sold two cars and not one and in so doing would have made two lots of profit. *Held* – Section 50(3) of the Sale of Goods Act did not apply here because the language of the subsection postulates that in the case to which it applies there will or may be a difference between the contract price and the market or current price which cannot be the case where the goods are, as here, saleable only at a fixed retail price. Having discarded s 50(3), the Court of Appeal applied s 50(2) which provides that damages should be the loss directly and naturally resulting in the ordinary course of events from the buyer's breach of contract. This was in the view of the court nominal damages of £2 only, because, as the claimants' sales manager said, the claimants could always find a purchaser for every Hillman Minx car they could get from the manufacturers and so the claimants must have sold the same number of cars and made the same number of fixed profits as they would have sold and made if the defendant had duly carried out his promise.

### Lazenby Garages v Wright [1976] 2 All ER 770

The claimants were dealers in new and second-hand cars. They bought a second-hand BMW for £1,325. The defendant agreed in writing to buy it for £1,670 but before taking delivery he changed his mind and refused to purchase the car. Six weeks later the claimants sold the same car for £1,770 to someone else but claimed damages from the defendant in the sum of £345, being the loss of profit on the agreed sale to him. The defendant contended that the claimants had suffered no loss. The judge found that there was no 'available market' within s 50(3) of the Sale of Goods Act, but applying s 50(2) awarded the claimants £172.50 on the basis that they would have had a 50/50 chance of selling an additional car had they sold the BMW to the defendant. On appeal it was *held* – by the Court of Appeal – allowing the appeal, that a second-hand car was a unique article, unlike new cars which are much the same and sell at fixed retail prices. Since the claimants had sold the car at a higher price, they had suffered no loss on the transaction, and their action failed.

*Comment:* Since each second-hand car is unique, no two being in the same condition, there is no available market for them. There is no group of people interested in buying the same second-hand car. No group of people would be looking for, for example, a Ford Escort which had done 20,000 miles having two good and two worn tyres. In these circumstances the seller has to find a specific market.

## Sales in an available market

Where there is an available market and the seller has sold the goods at the market price, then:

(a) if that price is less than the contract price, the seller can recover the balance by way of damages;
(b) if the market price is the same as or even higher than the contract price, the seller will only be entitled to nominal damages;
(c) if the seller sells for less than the market price, then he cannot recover the difference between the contract price and the resale price. It is the seller's duty to mitigate or reduce the loss and not to aggravate it;
(d) even if the seller keeps the goods after the buyer's breach of contract, and then later sells them for more than the market price was at the date of the breach, the seller can still recover the difference between the contract price and market price at the date of the breach, if the market price was then lower than the contract price.

Thus in *R Pagnan & Fratelli* v *Corbisa Industrial Agropacuaria* [1970] 1 All ER 165 Salmond LJ said, '. . . The innocent party is not bound to go on the market and buy or sell at the date of the breach. Nor is he bound to gamble on the market changing in his favour. He may wait if he chooses: and if the market turns against him this cannot increase the liability of the party in default; similarly, if the market turns in his favour, the liability of the party in default is not diminished.'

Suppose the contract price was £100 and the market price at the time of the breach was £80, then the seller is entitled to £20 damages. However:

(a) if he sells on the day of the breach for £60, the damages will still only be £20;
(b) if, hoping the market will improve, he delays the sale, he will still have the right to £20 damages and can retain the proceeds of the subsequent sale.

## Anticipatory breach

Where there is an anticipatory breach of contract, e.g. where the goods are to be delivered in May but the buyer tells the seller in February that he will not accept, then if the seller refuses to accept the breach but sues upon the actual breach date, damages are assessed on the market price at the date when the goods were to be delivered and accepted, i.e. the May market price. Where the seller accepts an anticipatory breach and sues upon it immediately, the date for delivery having not yet arrived when the case is tried, the court will have to estimate the market price at the date of delivery as best it can.

As regards the matter of *mitigation*, where there is an anticipatory breach and the market is falling, there are two possible situations.

(a) If the seller does not accept the repudiation, he need not resell the goods at once but is entitled to wait until the delivery date. If the buyer refuses to take delivery, the seller may resell and may recover from the original buyer as damages the difference between contract and market price at that date. It should be noted that the seller cannot be required to accept an anticipatory breach (*see White and Carter (Councils) Ltd* v *McGregor* (1961) at Chapter 8).

(b) If the seller accepts the repudiation, he must do all that he reasonably can to decrease the damages when the market is falling. If he delays in selling the goods, he will only be able to recover as damages the difference between contract and market price at the date of repudiation.

However, he has only to act reasonably and need not get the highest price possible. Thus in *Gebrüder Metelmann GmbH & Co KG* v *NBR (London) Ltd* [1984] 1 Lloyd's Rep 614 the sellers, having accepted the buyers' repudiation, sold sugar immediately to a terminal market which stored sugar for future sales, rather like a marketing board. A higher price could have been obtained by shopping around the physical market. Nevertheless, the court held that the sellers had acted reasonably and their damages against the buyers could not be reduced by the higher price obtainable on the physical market.

### Goods with no market

Where there is no market for the goods, as where the goods were made or procured specially for the purposes of the contract and cannot be sold to another buyer (e.g. because they are highly specialised goods), then there are two possible situations:

(a) where the seller has actually made or procured the goods, he can claim the whole contract price, that is to say the cost to him of procuring or making the goods plus his profit;

(b) where the seller has not made or procured the goods, he can claim his profit only.

## REMEDIES OF THE BUYER

A number of remedies are available to the buyer where the seller is in breach of the contract. They are rejection of the goods, a claim for damages and an action for specific performance.

### Rejection of the goods

The buyer may repudiate the contract and reject the goods where the seller is in breach of a condition. The effect of this is that the buyer may refuse to pay the price, or recover it if paid, or sue for damages, basing the latter claim on the seller's failure to deliver goods in accordance with the contract.

If the buyer rejects the goods, the property revests in the seller, and the buyer has no lien on the goods for the return of money paid by him under the contract. Section 36 provides that, unless otherwise agreed, where goods are delivered to the buyer, and he refuses to accept them, having the right to do so, he is not bound to return them to the seller, but it is sufficient if he intimates to the seller that he refuses to accept them.

Obviously, the right to reject the goods will be lost where the property in them has passed to the buyer, and they have been accepted by him following a reasonable opportunity to examine them. A breach of condition will have to be treated as a breach of warranty and repudiation will not be possible (*see further* Chapter 11).

It is perhaps unfortunate that the law gives no right to a replacement of the goods but only to receive one's money back.

## Damages

### For non-delivery

Where the seller wrongfully neglects or refuses to deliver the goods to the buyer, the buyer may maintain an action against the seller for damages for non-delivery (s 51(1)). The measure of damages is the estimated loss directly and naturally resulting, in the ordinary course of events, from the seller's breach of contract (s 51(2)).

The buyer will, therefore, recover the difference (if any) between the market price and the contract price (s 51(3)), and if he can buy similar goods cheaper in the market, the damages will be nominal. Where there is an anticipatory breach by the seller, the market price for the purpose of damages is that ruling when delivery ought to have been made, though if the buyer accepts the breach, he must buy quickly if the market price is rising for he has a duty to mitigate loss.

In addition, where a buyer has lawfully rejected goods under a contract and makes a new agreement with the seller for the sale and purchase of the same goods at a reduced price, then although the buyer can sue under the original contract, the principle of mitigation of damages allows the court to take account of any profit made by the buyer on the subsequent contract provided that the subsequent contract is a part of a continuous dealing between the parties.

If, therefore, S delivers 100 tonnes of wheat at £30 per tonne to B, and B lawfully rejects the wheat because it is not up to standard then, according to s 51(3), B has an action for damages based on the difference between the contract price and the market price. If we suppose that the market price was £32 per tonne, B should recover damages of £200. If, however, at a later date B agrees to accept the same wheat at £28 per tonne, he has no loss which is claimable, s 51(3) being a mere guide to the assessment of damages which does not preclude other methods of assessment in appropriate cases (*R Pagnan & Fratelli* v *Corbisa Industrial Agropacuaria* [1970] 1 All ER 165).

*Profit or loss on resale contracts made by the buyer is generally ignored in assessing damages for non-delivery* (but *see Heron II* (1967) at Chapter 9). Thus in *Williams* v *Agius* [1914] AC 510 W agreed to buy from A a cargo of coal at a price of 16s 3d per ton. Later he agreed with X, a sub-purchaser, to sell him a similar cargo at 19s per ton. A failed to deliver the coal and W's damages were assessed to the buyer's benefit at the difference between the contract price of 16s 3d and the market price on the date when the delivery should have been made, which in this case was 23s 6d.

This rule was affirmed by the High Court in *Altonpride v Canbright, Lawtel Report,* 12 October 1998. The court ruled that in a case of damages for non-delivery of goods, the calculation of the correct figure is based upon the value of the goods on the open market and is not the value that the individual had agreed to sell the goods to a third party. The correct calculation is, therefore, the difference between the contracted price agreed between the claimant and the defendant and the higher market value at the time of the failure to deliver.

However, in *T H Hall Ltd v W H Pim & Co Ltd* [1928] All ER Rep 763 the House of Lords laid down exceptions to the rule that losses of profit on resale would be ignored. In general terms, a sub-sale will be taken into account where the first contract contemplates the creation of sub-sales so that the seller knows from the beginning that in the event of non-delivery the buyer could suffer loss in connection with such sales. In addition, the subcontract must be for the sale of the same goods as are to be supplied under the first contract and the subcontract must be created before the delivery date under the first contract and must not be an extravagant or unusual bargain. In *Hall v Pim* the buyers agreed to buy a cargo of wheat at 51s 9d per quarter and the contract clearly referred to the fact that goods might be resold. Later the buyers made a sub-sale of the same cargo at 56s 9d per quarter. When the seller refused to deliver the cargo the market price was 53s 9d per quarter and the buyers were awarded damages assessed at 5s per quarter and also damages which the buyers had to pay to their sub-buyer because they could not deliver.

**The following cases illustrate the position where a sub-sale is not of the same goods and also that notice of sub-sales may be constructive as well as actual.**

### Slater v Hoyle and Smith Ltd [1920] 2 KB 11

The claimants, who were manufacturers of cotton cloth, sued for damages for the refusal of the defendants to accept 1,375 pieces of unbleached cotton cloth, being the balance of 3,000 pieces which the defendants agreed to purchase from the claimants. The defence was that the 1,625 pieces delivered and paid for were unmerchantable (now unsatisfactory), and the defendants counterclaimed for damages in respect of this. The defendants had contracted to sell *bleached* cloth to other persons, and had bleached and sold 691 pieces of the cloth bought from the claimants for this purpose. The claimants took the view that the defendants should not recover on their counter-claim damages for 1,625 pieces of cloth as unmerchantable (now 'unsatisfactory') but 1,625 less the 691 pieces actually sold. *Held* – The subcontract should not be taken into account and the defendants should recover on their counter-claim for the reduced value of the 1,625 pieces of cloth delivered to them. The subcontracts were not known to the claimants, and a sub-sale cannot be relied upon in mitigation of damages unless the sub-sale is of the identical article bought. Here what was bought was unbleached cloth and what was sold was bleached.

### Pinnock Brothers v Lewis and Peat Ltd [1923] 1 KB 690

The claimants bought from the defendants some East African copra cake which, to the defendants' knowledge, was to be used for feeding cattle. The cake was adulterated with castor oil and was poisonous. The claimants resold the cake to other dealers, who in turn sold it to farmers, who used it for feeding cattle. Cattle fed on the cake died, and claims were made by the various buyers against their sellers, the whole liability resting eventually on the claimants. In this action the claimants sued for the damages and costs which they had been required to pay. Two major defences were raised, the first being an exemption clause saying that the goods were not warranted free from defects, and the other that the damage was too remote. The court dismissed the exemption clause and *held* that, when a substance is quite different from that contracted for it cannot merely be defective. Further, the damage was not too remote, since it was in the implied contemplation of the defendants that the cake would at some time be fed to cattle.

### For breach of condition or warranty

Where there is a breach of warranty by the seller or where the buyer elects, or is compelled, to treat any breach of condition on the part of the seller as a breach of warranty, the buyer is not by reason only of such breach of warranty entitled to reject the goods. However, he may:

(a) set up against the seller the breach of warranty in diminution or extinction of the price; or
(b) maintain an action against the seller for damages for the breach of warranty (s 53(1)).

When there is late delivery, damages will be assessed on the basis of the actual loss resulting from the breach. Thus, if X should have delivered goods to Y on 1 January when the market price was £3.50 a tonne, and in fact delivers them on 1 February when the market price is £2.50 a tonne, the measure of damages would appear to be £1 a tonne. But if Y in fact resells the goods at £3.25 a tonne, the damages will only be the difference between £3.25 and £3.50, i.e. 25p a tonne.

In the case of breach of warranty of quality, the loss resulting is prima facie the difference between the value of the goods at the time of delivery to the buyer, and the value they would have had if they had answered to the warranty (s 53(3)).

Losses incurred or damages paid by the buyer on subcontracts are, as we have seen, generally ignored in actions for breach of condition or warranty, as they are in actions for non- (or late) delivery unless the buyer can show either:

(a) that the seller had actual notice of the subcontracts; or
(b) that from the circumstances the seller had constructive notice of the subcontracts.

### For wrongful interference

Where the property in the goods has passed to the buyer, he may bring an action for wrongful interference with goods. The action may be to recover possession or for damages.

## Specific performance

Under s 52(1), in any action for breach of contract to deliver specific or ascertained goods, the court may, if it thinks fit, on the claimants' application by its judgment or decree direct that the contract shall be performed specifically, without giving the defendant the option of retaining the goods on payment of damages.

It will be appreciated that the remedy of specific performance is discretionary and will only be granted where damages would be insufficient. Thus in *Behnke* v *Bede Shipping Co* [1927] 1 KB 649 a shipowner agreed to buy a ship called *The City* which he required immediately and which satisfied all relevant shipping regulations in terms of equipment. There was only one other ship available. An order for specific performance was made since damages would not have been an adequate remedy in this case.

The court will not normally grant specific performance of a contract for the sale of unidentified goods, but its power to grant an injunction may have much the same effect.

**The following case illustrates this point.**

### Sky Petroleum *v* VIP Petroleum [1974] 1 All ER 954

In March 1970 the claimants agreed to buy from the defendants all the petrol they required at their filling stations. The agreement was for ten years. In December 1973, when the petrol crisis was at its height, the defendants said they would terminate the agreement on the grounds that the claimants were in breach of contract, having exceeded the credit provisions. This would have meant that the claimants would lose their only source of petrol supplies, and they applied for an injunction to restrain the defendants from withholding the supply. It was *held* – by Goulding J – that the injunction would be granted, even though in this case it had the same effect as specific performance.

## AUCTION SALES

Where goods are put up for sale by auction in lots, each lot is prima facie deemed to be the subject of a separate contract of sale (s 57(1)). A sale by auction is complete when the auctioneer announces its completion by the fall of the hammer, or in other customary manner. Until such announcement is made, any bidder may retract his bid (s 57(2)).

It seems also that, at an auction, each bid lapses when a new one is made. So, if X bids £10 for certain goods, and then Y bids £12, X's bid of £10 lapses. If Y withdraws his bid before the auctioneer has accepted it, the auctioneer cannot return to X's bid and accept that; X must be prepared to bid again.

A sale by auction may be notified to be subject to a reserve or upset price, and a right to bid may also be expressly reserved by or on behalf of the seller (s 57(3)). Where a right to bid is expressly reserved, but not otherwise, the seller, or any person on his behalf, may bid at the auction (s 57(4)).

### Seller's right to bid

If in a sale by auction the seller does not specifically reserve the right to bid, it is not lawful for the seller to bid himself or to employ any person to do so, or for the auctioneer knowingly to take any bid from the seller or any such person. Any sale contravening this rule may be treated as fraudulent by the buyer (s 57(5)).

If there is no express statement as to the seller's right to bid, but he does bid, the buyer may repudiate the contract or sue for damages where he has paid a greater price than he would have had to pay because the seller has been bidding against him.

The seller is not allowed to bid merely because the sale is advertised to be without a reserve price. There must be some express notification of the seller's right to bid. Where the sale is subject to reserve price, and the seller bids without notification, the buyer may repudiate the contract or sue for damages, though, if the reserve was not reached, the would-be buyer will not have suffered loss, since he would not have obtained the *goods* even if the seller had not made bids.

## Significance of reserve price

Where a sale is expressly notified to be subject to a reserve price, the auctioneer has no power to sell below that reserve price. In addition, the auctioneer cannot be made liable for breach of warranty if he will not sell below the reserve, nor is the owner liable for breach of contract since the auctioneer has no apparent authorityto sell except at or above the reserve price.

**The following case provides an illustration.**

### McManus v Fortescue [1907] 2 KB 1

The defendants were auctioneers and offered for sale certain property on the terms of a printed catalogue and conditions of sale. Condition No 2 was as follows:

> Each lot will be offered subject to a reserve price, and the vendors reserve the right of bidding up to such reserve price. The highest bidder for each lot shall be the purchaser. If any dispute arises concerning a bidding, the lot in question shall be put up again and re-sold, or the auctioneer may determine the dispute.

The lot in question was a corrugated iron building for which the claimant made a bid of £85. This was the highest bid and the auctioneer knocked the lot down to the claimant. Before the memorandum of sale was made and signed by the auctioneer, he opened a sealed envelope containing the reserve price and discovered that it was £200. The auctioneer then withdrew the lot and would not sign the memorandum of sale or accept the claimant's deposit. The claimant now sued the auctioneer for breach of his duty to sign the memorandum of sale. *Held* – When the hammer falls on a bid at an auction sale of property subject to a reserve, the auctioneer agrees on behalf of the vendor to sell at the amount of the last bid *provided* that such bid is equal to the reserve that has been made. The claimant's action failed.

Where there is no express statement as to a reserve price, the auctioneer is still entitled to refuse to accept any bid. The bid is an offer which the auctioneer is not forced to accept.

Where an auction is expressly advertised to be without reserve, it is clear that there is no sale of the goods if the auctioneer refuses to accept a bid (s 57(2)). It is, however, possible that the auctioneer may be personally liable for breach of warranty of authority on the ground that he has contracted to sell to the highest bidder (*Warlow v Harrison* (1859) E & E 309).

The Auctions (Bidding Agreements) Act 1927, as amended by the Auctions (Bidding Agreements) Act 1969, provides for certain criminal penalties designed to prevent illegal auction rings which involve the giving of consideration to a person to abstain from bidding. Of interest as regards the civil law is s 3 of the 1969 Act which provides that a sale at auction to any one party to an agreement with a dealer not to bid for the goods may avoid the contract. If the goods have been resold and cannot be handed back to the seller, all the parties to the ring are liable to the seller to make good the loss he has suffered by selling at a lower price as a result of the activities of the ring.

# EXPORT AND IMPORT SALES

Certain special clauses have been used over the years in sales where delivery has involved carriage by sea. These clauses have given rise to certain main types of contract, the major terms of which have become largely standardised, though there are variations as regards detailed provisions. These contracts and their major terms are dealt with briefly below.

## FOB contracts

Under such a contract the seller must put the goods *free on board* a ship for dispatch to the buyer. The buyer is generally responsible for selecting the port of shipment and the date of shipment of the goods. Where the contract provides for a range of ports from which the goods are to be shipped then it is the buyer's right and duty to select one of them and to give the seller sufficient notice of his selection (*David T Boyd & Co Ltd* v *Louis Louca* [1973] 1 Lloyd's Rep 209). The seller pays all charges incurred prior to the goods being put on board, but the buyer is liable to pay the freight and insurance. Once the goods are over the ship's rail, they are normally at the buyer's risk.

It is a matter for the buyer to insure the goods and his risk if they are lost, damaged, delayed or uninsured en route (*Frebold* v *Circle Products Ltd* [1970] 1 Lloyd's Rep 499). The seller may under a particular contract be responsible for shipping the goods and where this is so it is important to know whether the seller ships on his own account as principal or as an agent for the buyer. If he ships as principal the property in the goods will not normally pass on shipment, though it will usually do so if he ships as agent (*President of India* v *Metcalfe Shipping Co* [1969] 3 All ER 1549).

Section 32(3) provides that, unless otherwise agreed, where the goods are sent by the seller to the buyer by a route involving sea transit, under circumstances in which it is usual to insure, the seller must give such notice to the buyer as may enable him to insure them during their sea transit, and, if the seller fails to do so, the goods shall be deemed to be at his risk during such sea transit. Thus delivery to the carrier will not necessarily pass the risk in FOB contracts.

Nowadays the seller often makes the contract of carriage. It must be reasonable in terms of the nature of the goods and other circumstances. If it is not and the goods are lost or damaged in the course of transit, the buyer may decline to treat the delivery to the carrier as a delivery to himself or may hold the seller responsible in damages (s 32(2)).

## CIF contracts

### Generally

A CIF contract is one by which the seller agrees to sell goods at a price which includes the *cost* of the goods, the *insurance* premium required to insure the goods, and the *freight* (or cost) of transporting them to their destination.

## Duties of the seller

These are:

(a) to ship goods of the description contained in the contract under a contract of affreightment which will ensure the delivery of the goods at the destination contemplated in the contract. Undertakings in the contract as to time and place of shipment are nearly always treated as conditions. Thus the buyer may reject the goods if they are shipped too late or too soon (see *Bowes* v *Shand* (1877) at Chapter 8);

(b) to arrange for insurance which will be available to the buyer;

(c) to make out an invoice for the goods;

(d) to tender the documents to the buyer in exchange for the price, so that the buyer will know the amount of the freight he must pay as part of the price, and so that he can obtain delivery of the goods if they arrive, or recover for their loss if they are lost on the voyage.

## Refusal of buyer to accept goods

In a CIF contract the buyer or his agent may repudiate the contract:

(a) by refusing to accept the documents if they do not conform with the contract; and

(b) by rejecting the goods on delivery if following inspection they do not comply with the contract.

## Passing of the risk

The risk passes in a CIF contract when the goods are shipped and the buyer will still have to pay for the goods if they are lost on the voyage, though he will have the insurance cover. The property in the goods does not pass until the seller transfers the documents to the buyer and the latter has paid for them (*Mirabita* v *Imperial Ottoman Bank* (1878) 3 Ex D 164). If the goods have been shipped, but the documents have not been transferred, there is a conditional appropriation of the goods to the contract which will not become unconditional until the buyer takes up the documents and pays for them. It will be seen, therefore, that a CIF contract is in essence a 'sale of documents', the delivery of which transfers the property and the possession of the goods to the transferee. However, a CIF contract is regarded as a sale of goods because it contemplates the transfer of goods in due course, and for this reason the Act of 1979 applies.

Where S sells goods to B under an export contract and the ownership (or property) has not passed because B has not paid S (*see* the *Mirabita* case *above*), then if in transit the goods are lost or damaged by, say, the carrier's negligence, B can claim on the insurance policy but could not sue the carrier for any economic loss which may have arisen because the goods were not available to him. This was decided by the House of Lords in *Leigh & Sillivan Ltd* v *Aliakmon Shipping Co* [1986] 2 All ER 145 where Lord Brandon said: 'there is a long line of authority for a principle of law that, in order to enable a person to claim in negligence for loss caused to him by reason of loss of or damage to property, he must have had either the legal ownership of or a possessory title to the property concerned at the time when the loss or damage occurred and it is not enough for him to have only contractual rights in relation to such property which have been adversely affected by the loss of or damage to it'.

This part of the law is now changed by the Carriage of Goods by Sea Act 1992. Section 2 of that Act provides that the person who is entitled to delivery of the goods 'shall have transferred to and vested in him all rights of suit under the contract of carriage as if he had been a party to that contract'. Thus a claim against the carrier is now sustainable by B in the example above.

## FAS contracts

In a *free alongside ship* contract the seller is required to deliver the goods to the buyer at a named port of discharge and place them alongside the ship which is to carry them. If the ship cannot enter port, the seller must pay for barges or lighters to take the goods alongside the ship. The buyer must concern himself with loading. If the seller does not make delivery, the buyer cannot be made to pay the price, or, if the price has been paid, it can be recovered on the basis of total failure of consideration. The property and the risk in the goods pass when the goods are delivered alongside the ship, and the seller is under no obligation to insure them: if he does so it is entirely for his own benefit.

## FOR contracts

The seller is responsible under a FOR (*free on rail*) contract for all charges incurred in delivering the goods to an appropriate rail depot for transportation to the buyer.

## FOT contracts

The seller is responsible under a FOT (*free on truck*) contract for all charges incurred in delivering the goods to a carrier by road and for the loading of these on to the lorry or truck which is to transport them.

## Ex-works or ex-store contracts

Here it is the duty of the buyer to take delivery of the goods at the works or store of the seller as the case may be. The property and risk usually pass when the buyer takes delivery. These sales are almost always of unascertained goods, the appropriation taking place when the goods are selected or handed over at the works or store. They are perhaps not ideally categorised as export sales because they consist of the mere collection of goods by the buyer who may then deal with them as he wishes. There need not in fact be any export involving carriage by sea.

## GRADED QUESTIONS

### Essay mode

1  (a) In what circumstances does a seller acquire a lien over goods he has sold?
   (b) Michael sold a consignment of diamonds in London to Simon for £10,000. Simon paid £4,000 when the sale was made and agreed to pay the balance of the price on delivery of the stones to his premises in Manchester. Michael instructed Transit Security Services Ltd to deliver the stones to Simon and to collect the balance of the purchase money. On arrival in Manchester, Transit Security Services

Ltd were informed that Simon was insolvent and notified Michael. Michael ordered Transit Security Services Ltd to withhold delivery. Simon claims that he is not insolvent and threatens to sue Michael and Transit Security Services Ltd.

Advise Michael and Transit Security Services Ltd.

*(The Institute of Company Accountants)*

2  How are damages assessed for breach of a contract for the sale of goods?

*(Staffordshire University. BA(Hons) Business Studies)*

3  In what circumstances may a seller of goods resell them to a second buyer, without rendering himself liable to the person who originally agreed to buy those goods.

AND:

Smith, a wholesaler, takes an order on 1 August for the sale of 1,000 boxes of Christmas crackers to Brown, a market trader, at a price of £2,500. Brown agrees to collect the boxes from Smith's warehouse by 1 October. On 15 September Brown telephones Smith to tell him he will have to cancel the order because he is shortly giving up his market stall due to lack of trade. By this time the market value of the crackers has fallen to £2,250, and by 1 October it will be approximately £2,000. It is likely that there will be a continued decline in the value as Christmas approaches, because suppliers reduce prices to clear stock.

The boxes are still stacked in Smith's warehouse, and no money has yet been paid.

Consider what Smith can claim by way of a remedy, raising any additional factors beyond those stated which might affect the position.

*(Staffordshire University. BA(Hons) Business Studies)*

## Objective mode

Four alternative answers are given. Select ONE only. Circle the answer which you consider to be correct. Check your answers by referring back to the information given in the relevant chapter and against the answers at the back of the book.

1  Alf, a car dealer, sold a second-hand car to Bob for £600, which was the agreed market price. Bob left a part-payment of £20, promising to return later in the day and pick it up. Before taking the car away, Bob had another look at it and said he thought it was older than Alf alleged, and refused to accept it. Alf wrote to Bob, giving him one week to pay for the car and take delivery, otherwise he would sell it. Bob did not pay, and Alf sold the vehicle to Charlie for £550 after advertising it again at a cost of £20. Bob has told Alf he can keep the £20 part-payment. Alf is not satisfied.

If Alf brought the matter before a court, which of the following amounts would be received by way of damages against Bob?

A  £50.
B  £70.
C  Nothing.
D  £20.

2 An unpaid seller has a lien on the goods until payment of the whole of the price. This lien is:

   A Equitable.
   B Possessory.
   C Discretionary.
   D Constructive.

3 The right of stoppage *in transitu* can be exercised by an unpaid seller only if:

   A The goods have been sold without stipulation as to credit.
   B The buyer is insolvent.
   C The term of credit has expired.
   D None of the goods have been delivered.

4 Where there is a contract for the sale of unascertained or future goods by description the property in the goods passes to the buyer when goods of that description are unconditionally appropriated to the contract:

   A Either by the buyer with notice to the seller or by the seller with notice to the buyer.
   B Either by the buyer with the assent of the seller or by the seller with the assent of the buyer.
   C Either by the buyer or the seller with an opportunity for examination of the goods by the other party.
   D By delivery to a carrier by the seller.

5 Polly agrees to buy William's vintage Bentley after inspecting and approving it at William's address in Brighton. Polly asks William to arrange for Vintage Traction Ltd to deliver it to Polly's address in North Wales on a trailer, which he does. Vintage Traction Ltd present Polly with a bill for £200 which she pays but then presents to William on the basis that 'delivery is the responsibility of the seller'. What is the legal position?

   A William must pay for the delivery costs since it is the duty of the seller to deliver the goods.
   B Polly must pay for the delivery costs since the place of delivery is the seller's place of business or residence.
   C William must pay for delivery since the place of delivery is the buyer's place of business or residence.
   D William must pay for delivery since this is a case where delivery should have been agreed and William arranged the transport and should pay for it.

6 Fergus, a hotel proprietor, decides to sell the hotel's deep-freeze and advertises it. Robert, a boarding-house proprietor, inspects the deep-freeze and makes an offer of £100 bearing in mind its general condition. Fergus agrees but excludes 'any liability for non-satisfactory condition'. The freezer does not like the move and refuses to work.

   A Robert can claim back the £100 since this is a consumer purchase in which it is not possible to exclude the condition of satisfactory quality.

   **B** Since Robert required the freezer for his own business then this would not be a consumer sale and the exclusion clause would be valid provided it was reasonable.

   **C** Robert cannot claim back the £100 since the price was so low it is not reasonable for the condition of satisfactory quality to be applied. *Caveat emptor.*

   **D** Robert can claim back the £100 since an exclusion clause cannot excuse total non-performance of the contract.

7 The Sale of Goods Act, s 20, states that the risk in goods passes at the same time as the property. Which of the following is an exception to this?

   **A** Under a free on board (FOB) contract.

   **B** Under a cost insurance and freight (CIF) contract.

   **C** Under an 'ex-ship' contract.

   **D** When goods are sent on approval or on sale or return.

*Answers to questions set in objective mode appear on p 708.*

# 13 CONTRACTS FOR THE SUPPLY OF GOODS AND SERVICES

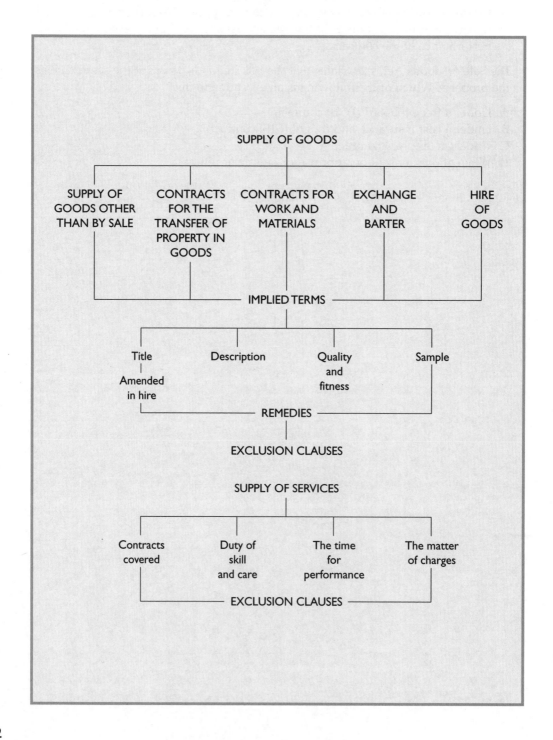

The objectives of this chapter are to consider the law relating to contracts for work and materials, e.g. car repairs, and for the supply of services and the implied terms therein.

## SUPPLY OF GOODS OTHER THAN BY SALE

As regards the rights of those who purchase goods, we have seen that the Sale of Goods Act 1979 (as amended) applies and that ss 12–15 of that Act imply terms to which a buyer may resort if the goods are faulty, defective or unsuitable. Conditional sales and credit sales come within the 1979 Act. Those who take goods on hire-purchase are similarly protected by ss 8–11 of the Supply of Goods (Implied Terms) Act 1973.

As regards contracts for work and materials, the supply of goods (or the materials used) is governed by Part I of the Supply of Goods and Services Act 1982. The services supplied (or the work element) are governed by Part II of the 1982 Act.

Contracts of exchange or barter, hire, rental or leasing are governed by Part I of the 1982 Act, while contracts for services only, e.g. a contract to carry goods or advice from an accountant or solicitor, are governed by Part II of the 1982 Act. The relevant provisions of the Act are dealt with in detail below. Section references are to the 1982 Act unless otherwise indicated.

The 1982 Act was amended by the Sale and Supply of Goods Act 1994. The relevant amendments are included in the material appearing below.

## CONTRACTS FOR THE TRANSFER OF PROPERTY IN GOODS

The contracts concerned are dealt with in s 1(1) which provides that a contract for the transfer of goods means a contract under which one person transfers, or agrees to transfer to another, the property in goods, unless the transfer takes place under an excluded contract. These excluded contracts are set out in s 1(2). They are contracts for the sale of goods, hire-purchase contracts, and those where the property in goods is transferred on a redemption of trading stamps. (These are governed by the Trading Stamps Act 1964.) Transfer of property rights in goods by way of mortgage, pledge, charge or other security are excluded, as are gifts.

There must be a contract between the parties. If not, the statutory implied terms cannot be relied upon if the goods supplied prove to be defective. Thus a chemist supplying harmful drugs under a National Health Service prescription will not come within the Act. This is because the patient does not provide consideration. The chemist collects the prescription charge for the government and not for himself. The payment to the chemist does not come from the patient unless it is a private prescription where the patient has paid the full amount. Otherwise an action against the chemist would have to be framed in the tort of negligence.

As regards promotional free gifts, e.g. the giving away of a radio to a purchaser of a television set, the free gift may not be within the 1982 Act. The matter is not free from doubt, but s 1(2)(d) excludes contracts for the supply of goods which are enforceable only because they are made by deed which would seem to exclude other gifts. Furthermore, the Law Commission Report (No 95 published in 1979) on which the Act is based concludes that gifts are outside the scope of the Act.

## CONTRACTS FOR WORK AND MATERIALS

Reference has already been made to the distinction between these contracts and contracts of sale of goods and some examples have been given (*see* Chapter 10). It is impossible to provide a complete list of contracts for work and materials but they fall under three broad heads as follows.

(a) *Maintenance contracts.* Here the organisation doing the maintenance supplies the labour and spare parts as required. An example would be a maintenance contract for lifts.
(b) *Building and construction contracts.* Here the builder supplies labour and materials. An example would be the alteration of an office or workshop involving the insertion of new windows and extending the central heating system.
(c) *Installation and improvement contracts.* Here the contractor does not have to build or construct anything but, for example, fits equipment into an existing building or applies paint to it. Examples are the fitting of an air-conditioning system, or painting and decorating an office or workshop.

## THE TERMS IMPLIED

### Title

Section 2 implies terms about title. Under s 2(1) there is an implied condition that the supplier has a right to transfer the property in the goods to the customer. Under s 2(2) two warranties are implied:

(a) that the goods are free from any charge or encumbrance which has not been disclosed to the customer; and
(b) that the customer will enjoy quiet possession except when disturbed by the owner or other person whose charge or encumbrance has been disclosed.

The customer would have an action here if he suffered loss as a result of the true owner reclaiming or suing in conversion where the materials fitted had been stolen. Section 2(3), (4) and (5) is concerned with sales under a limited title. If under the contract the supplier is to give only such title as he may possess, s 2(1) does not apply but warranties are implied that the supplier will disclose all charges and encumbrances which he knows about and that the customer's quiet possession of the goods will not be disturbed by, for example, the supplier or the holder of an undisclosed charge or encumbrance.

Cases involving bad title have occurred not infrequently in the sale of goods but the problem seems to have arisen only rarely in contracts for work and materials.

## Description

Under s 3 there is an implied condition that where a seller transfers property in goods by description, the goods will correspond with the description. If the goods are supplied by reference to a sample as well as a description, they must correspond with the sample as well as the description. Section 3 applies even where the customer selects the goods.

Section 3 will operate, for example, where a person is having his house or business premises extended and agrees with the contractor a detailed specification which describes the materials to be installed. It will not operate in some types of maintenance contract where the materials to be replaced are unknown until the maintenance is carried out. The materials fitted in the course of such a contract will not be described *before* the contract is made but probably only in an invoice *after* it has been made, which is too late to apply s 3. It should be noted that ss 2 and 3 apply to supplies in the course of a business *and* to a supply by a person other than in the course of a business, e.g. a milkman 'moonlighting' by doing the odd decorating job, provided there is a contract. They would not apply to a mere friendly transaction without consideration.

## Quality and fitness

The first implied term in this area is in s 4 and it relates to *satisfactory quality* (s 4(2)). Satisfactory quality is defined in s 4 in the same way as it is for a sale of goods (*see* Chapter 10). This condition of satisfactory quality does not apply to defects:

(a) drawn to the customer's attention before the contract is made; or
(b) which any prior examination the customer *has actually made* ought to have revealed.

Thus, if the materials used are dangerous, unsafe, defective or faulty, and will not work properly under normal conditions, the supplier is in breach of s 4(2).

However, if the materials are described as 'seconds' or 'fire-damaged', the customer cannot complain if the materials are of lower quality than goods not so described.

As regards defects which ought to have been revealed where the customer has examined the goods, it is not likely that materials used in a contract for work and materials will be identified before the contract or that the customer will examine them. If they are examined, the customer should ensure that it is done properly so that obvious defects are seen and the goods rejected.

The second implied term in s 4 relates to *fitness for the purpose* (s 4(5)). Where a customer makes known, either expressly or by implication, to the supplier any particular purpose for which the goods are being acquired, there is an implied condition that the goods are reasonably fit for the purpose. This condition does not apply where the customer does not rely on, or it is not reasonable for him to rely on, the skill or judgment of the supplier.

If, for example, a factory process requires a lot of water supplied under high pressure, e.g. to clean special equipment, and the factory owners ask for the installation of a system of pressure hoses and a pump, revealing to the contractor precisely what the requirements are, then the contractor will be in breach of s 4(5) if the pressure is inadequate. This will be so even though the pressure hoses and pump are of satisfactory quality and would have been quite adequate for use in a different type of installation.

Of course, the way out of the fitness problem for the supplier is for him to make it clear to the customer that he has no idea whether the equipment will be suitable for the customer's special requirements. In such a case he will not be liable, though he may put some customers off by his unhelpful attitude.

### Sample

If under the contract there is a transfer of the property in goods by reference to a sample, then under s 5 there is an implied condition that:

(a) the bulk will correspond with the sample in quality;
(b) the customer will have a reasonable opportunity of comparing the bulk with the sample; and
(c) there will not be any defect making the goods unsatisfactory which would not have been apparent on a reasonable examination of the sample.

Except as provided by ss 4 and 5, no conditions or warranties as to quality or fitness are to be implied into contracts for the transfer of goods. Sections 4 and 5 apply only to a supply of goods in the course of a business, and not to a supply by our friend the moonlighting decorator.

## REMEDIES

In so far as the implied terms are conditions and are broken by the supplier, then the customer can treat the contract as repudiated. The customer is discharged from his obligation to pay the agreed price and may recover damages. The breach of implied warranties gives the customer only the right to sue for damages.

## EXCHANGE AND BARTER

The most likely transactions to emerge here are the exchange of goods for vouchers and coupons as part of promotional schemes. Part I of the 1982 Act applies and the retailer who supplies the goods under a contract to the customer is the one who is liable if they are in breach of, for example, the implied terms of fitness and/or satisfactory quality. The manufacturer will be liable to the retailer, of course.

An exchange transaction in which goods are simply exchanged is not a sale but is covered by the 1982 Act. Where part of the consideration is money, as in a part-exchange of an old car for a new one with a cash difference, the contract is presumably a sale of goods because money is at least part of the consideration. It does not really matter now whether it is a sale or a supply, because the implied terms are almost identical.

Often where there has been a sale of faulty goods the seller exchanges them for other goods of the same type, although he is under no legal duty to do so unless a particular contract expressly provides. What happens if the other goods are faulty? The substitute goods must comply with the implied terms as to title, description, quality and fitness, and there is no longer any point in going into legal niceties as to whether the exchange is a sale or supply.

### The terms implied

The implied terms in exchange or barter are the same as those implied in a contract for work and materials, i.e. s 2 (title), s 3 (description), s 4(2) (satisfactory quality), s 4(5) (fitness) and s 5 (sample).

## CONTRACTS FOR THE HIRE OF GOODS

The main areas of hiring (or renting or leasing) are as follows:

(a) *office equipment*, e.g. office furniture and a variety of machines, including telephones;
(b) *building and construction plant and equipment*, e.g. cranes and JCBs;
(c) *consumer hiring*, e.g. cars, televisions and videos.

Under s 6(1) a contract for the hire of goods means a contract under which one person bails, or agrees to bail, goods to another by way of hire. There must be a contract, so that when the next-door neighbour makes a free loan of his lawnmower the Act does not apply. Also excluded are hire-purchase agreements. A contract is a contract of hire whether or not services are also provided. This would be the case where a supplier rented a television to a customer and also undertook to service it.

## THE TERMS IMPLIED

### Title

Section 7 deals with title. It reflects s 2 except that as it is a contract of hire there is provision only for the transfer of possession and not ownership. There is an implied condition on the part of the supplier that he has the right to transfer possession of the goods to the customer by hiring for the appropriate period. There is also a warranty that the customer will enjoy quiet possession of the goods except where it is disturbed by the owner or other person entitled to the benefit of any charge or encumbrance disclosed to the customer before the contract was made.

If, for example, the undisclosed true owner retakes possession so that the supplier is in breach of s 7, then the customer will have an action for damages. These will reflect the value he had had under the contract before the goods were taken from him. Thus if C pays S £120 for the year's rent of a television but the undisclosed true owner takes it back after, say, two months, the damages would, on the face of it, be £100.

Neither of the terms in s 7 prevents the supplier from taking the goods back himself, provided the contract allows this, as where it provides expressly for the repossession of the goods on failure to pay the rental or the court is prepared to imply that it does.

347

## Description

Section 8 is the equivalent of s 3. Where the supplier hires or agrees to hire the goods by description there is an implied condition that the goods will correspond with the description. If the goods are hired by reference to a sample as well as by description, they must correspond with the description as well as the sample. Section 8 applies even where the customer selects the goods. If the goods do not match the description, the customer will be able to reject them and recover damages for any loss.

## Quality and fitness

Section 9 enacts the same provisions for hiring contracts as s 4 does for contracts of work and materials and exchange and barter. Except as provided by ss 9 and 10 (hire by sample), there are no implied terms regarding quality or fitness for any purpose of goods hired.

There are two terms in s 9 as follows.

(a) *An implied condition that the goods hired are of satisfactory quality*. There is no such condition where a particular defect has been drawn to the customer's attention before the contract was made or to defects which he should have noticed if he actually examined the goods.

(b) *An implied condition that the goods hired are reasonably fit for any purpose to which the customer is going to put them*. The purpose must have been made known to the supplier, expressly or by implication. The condition does not apply if the customer does not rely on the skill of the seller or if it is unreasonable for him to have done so.

Once again, where goods are to be hired for a special purpose, the supplier should make it clear that the customer must not rely on him if he wishes to avoid the implied condition of fitness. This has rather special application to those who supply DIY equipment on hire. A supplier in this area should certainly not overestimate the capacity of, for example, power tools, in order to get business. If he does, he certainly faces s 9 liability.

Where the goods are leased by a finance house, it is responsible for breach of the implied terms in the hiring contract. It is in effect the supplier. This is also true of hire-purchase where the implied terms of the Supply of Goods (Implied Terms) Act 1973 apply against the finance company.

As regards fitness for the purpose, it is enough to involve the finance company in liability if the customer has told the distributor of the purpose. Generally, of course, the finance house will have an indemnity against the distributor under which it may recover any damages it has to pay, so it will all get back to the distributor in the end.

The above conditions relate to the state of the goods at the beginning of the hiring and for a reasonable time thereafter. It does not impose upon the supplier a duty to maintain and repair. This must be provided for separately in the contract.

Thus in *UCB Leasing Ltd* v *Holtom* [1987] 137 NLJ 614 the Court of Appeal decided that where a car was the subject of a long leasing agreement, the owner was not under an obligation to provide a vehicle which was fit for the purpose during the whole period of the leasing. Instead, rather like a sale of goods, the obligation is to provide a vehicle which is fit at the outset of the agreement. If it is not, the hirer must rescind quickly (subject to a reasonable period of user) if he wishes to return the car. If he does not do so he cannot return the vehicle but is entitled to damages only.

## Sample

Section 10 applies and is in line with s 5 (*above*). Section 10 states that in a hiring by sample there is an implied condition that the bulk will correspond with the sample in quality; that the customer will have a reasonable opportunity to compare the bulk with the sample; and that there will be no defects in the goods supplied rendering them unsatisfactory which would not have been apparent on a reasonable examination of the sample.

As with ss 4 and 5 (*above*) the terms of ss 9 and 10 are implied only into contracts for hiring entered into in the course of a business. Thus if there is a hiring for value with a private owner, or a mere friendly lending without consideration, s 9 of the Act would not apply. Incorrect and express statements by a private owner would be actionable in the common law of contract provided that there was consideration. In a friendly lending there could be an action for negligent misstatements made by the owner about the goods if they cause damage (*see Hedley Byrne* v *Heller & Partners* (1963), Chapter 5).

## EXCLUSION CLAUSES

Section 11 of the 1982 Act applies the provisions of the Unfair Contract Terms Act 1977 to exclusion clauses in work and materials, barter and exchange, and hiring contracts. The effect of this is set out below.

(a) *Consumer transactions*. In a contract covered by Part I of the Act, the rights given by the implied terms under ss 3–5 and ss 8–10 of the 1982 Act cannot be excluded or restricted. We have already described the circumstances in which a person deals as a consumer (see Chapter 6).

(b) *Business contracts*. In these circumstances the supplier can only rely on an exclusion clause if it is reasonable. However, the obligations relating to title in s 2 of the 1982 Act cannot be excluded in a business dealing relating to work and materials and barter and exchange any more than they can in a consumer dealing (*see* s 7, Unfair Contract Terms Act 1977, as amended by s 17(2) of the 1982 Act).

However, the term in s 7 relating to the right of possession in the case of a hiring can be excluded in a consumer or business contract if reasonable.

## THE SUPPLY OF SERVICES

The main areas of complaint in regard to services have been the *poor quality of service*, e.g. the careless servicing of cars; *slowness in completing work*, where complaints have ranged over a wide area from, for example, building contractors to solicitors; *the cost of the work*, i.e. overcharging. Part II of the Act is concerned to deal with these matters.

## The contracts covered

Under s 12(1) a contract for the supply of a service means a contract under which a person agrees to carry out a service. A contract of service (i.e. an employment contract) or apprenticeship is not included, but apart from this no attempt is made to define the word 'service'. However, the services provided by the professions, e.g. accountants, architects, solicitors and surveyors, are included.

Section 12(4) gives the Secretary of State for Trade and Industry power to exempt certain services from the provisions of Part II. Of importance here is the Supply of Services (Exclusion of Implied Terms) Order 1982 (SI 1982/1771) which retains the common law liability in negligence of lawyers by exempting barristers and solicitors when acting as advocates before various courts and tribunals. It also exempts services rendered by a director to his company, thus retaining existing common law liability in this area, too. This is largely because consultation with the relevant interests is incomplete in terms of what sort of liability there should be in the areas referred to.

Part II applies *only to contracts*. If there is no contract there cannot be implied terms. This will exclude work done free as a friendly gesture by a friend or neighbour. If, however, injury is caused to a person who is not in a contractual relationship with a supplier as a result of the negligence of the supplier, there may be an action in the tort of negligence at common law (*see* Chapter 22).

## Duty of care and skill

This duty applies to contracts which are purely for service, e.g. advice from an accountant or solicitor, and also to the service element of a contract for work and materials. Section 13 provides that where the supplier of a service is acting in the course of a business there is an implied term that the supplier will carry out that service with reasonable skill and care. This means that the service must be performed with the care and skill of a reasonably competent member of the supplier's trade or profession. In other words, the test is objective, not subjective. Thus an incompetent supplier may be liable even though he has done his best. A private supplier of a service, e.g. a moonlighter, will not have this duty.

There is no reference to conditions and warranties in regard to this implied term. Generally, therefore, the action for breach of the term will be damages. In a serious case repudiation of the contract may be possible. This is rather like the intermediate term concept discussed in Chapter 6.

Cases such as *Woodman* v *Photo Trade Processing Ltd* and *Waldron-Kelly* v *British Railways Board*, which were brought on the basis of the common law tort of negligence, would now be brought under the 1982 Act (*see further* Chapter 6) as indeed could *Curtis* v *Chemical Cleaning and Dyeing Co* (*see* Chapter 6).

## Time for performance

Section 14 provides that a supplier who acts in the course of a business will carry out the service within a reasonable time. This term is only implied where the time for performance is not fixed by the contract, but left to be fixed in a manner agreed by the contract, or determined by the dealings of the parties. Section 14 states that what is a reasonable time is a question of fact. A claimant can seek damages for unreasonable delay. Of course, if a time for performance is fixed by the contract, it must be performed at that time and the question of reasonableness does not arise. Time is of the essence in commercial contracts unless the parties expressly provide otherwise or there is a waiver (*see further* Chapter 8).

## The charges made for the service

Under s 15 the customer's obligation is to pay 'a reasonable charge' which is again a matter of fact. This matter is not implied where the charge for the service is determined by the contract, left to be determined in a manner agreed by the contract, or determined by the dealings of the parties. The section in essence enacts the common law rule of *quantum meruit* (*see* Chapter 9); it protects both the supplier and the customer, and applies to a supply in the course of a business and to a supply by a moonlighter.

# EXCLUSION CLAUSES

Section 16 of the 1982 Act applies the provisions of the Unfair Contract Terms Act 1977 to exclusion clauses in regard to services. Section 2 of the 1977 Act is, as we have seen, concerned with liability for negligence. There can be no exclusion of liability if death or personal injury is caused. In other cases an exclusion clause may apply if reasonable.

Section 3 of the 1977 Act is concerned with liability for breach of contract. Broadly speaking, as we have seen, there can be no exclusion of liability for breach of contract, or a different performance or non-performance, unless reasonable. The terms implied by the 1982 Act cannot be excluded in a consumer transaction. They can in a non-consumer deal if reasonable. The criteria relating to bargaining power and so on apply only to the exclusion of implied terms in a non-consumer transaction relating to goods, but they will no doubt be applied by analogy to contracts under the 1982 Act.

# GRADED QUESTIONS

### Essay mode

1  (a) Explain, with illustrations, the distinction between a contract for the sale of goods and a contract for work and materials.
   (b) De Luxe Kitchens has published the following advertisement in the national press: 'Free Double Oven worth £500 when you buy a Luxury Fitted Kitchen from us'. Alec responds to the advertisement and has a fitted kitchen supplied and installed by De Luxe Kitchens. The installation is quite satisfactory but the oven is defective and does not work. Alec seeks your advice.
      Advise Alec as to his remedies, if any, in relation to the oven.
                                    (*Institute of Chartered Secretaries and Administrators*)

2  (a) In what circumstances, if any, may the purchaser of goods acquire a valid title from the vendor where the vendor is not the owner of the goods?
   (b) S owns a personal computer which he uses for word processing. Following a malfunction S took the machine to T Ltd, a firm in business selling and repairing personal computers. T Ltd told S that the repair would be a straight-

forward matter, but it took them over five months to repair the machine and return it to S. When the machine was returned its plastic cover was badly scratched and damaged in several places. An invoice was sent with the machine saying 'Parts – £3.00; two hours labour – £80.00'. S is extremely annoyed at what he considers to be the gross delay in repairing the machine, the damage to its cover and at what he thinks is an exorbitant charge for the repair.

Advise S as to his rights, if any, under the Supply of Goods and Services Act 1982.

(*Association of Chartered Certified Accountants*)

3  Simon agrees to sell goods to Brian, delivery to be made by three instalments. The first instalment has been delivered and the second instalment has just been dispatched when Simon hears that Brian is in financial difficulty. The third instalment is in Simon's warehouse awaiting dispatch.

(a)  What action may Simon take to safeguard his position?

(b)  Explain how a reservation of title clause might give Simon better protection in this situation.

(*The Chartered Institute of Management Accountants*)

### Objective mode

Four alternative answers are given. Select ONE only. Circle the answer which you consider to be correct. Check your answers by referring back to the information given in the relevant chapter and against the answers at the back of the book.

1  Mrs Smith wanted a new fitted kitchen. She eventually agreed with a company called Boxo Ltd to carry out the work. The materials and labour were supplied by Boxo Ltd but Mrs Smith did ask them to fit a 'Whoosh' extractor fan. After being used normally for two months, the motor stopped and could not be put right. Mrs Smith could not contact the company which made the fan because it had been wound up. She, therefore, contacted Boxo Ltd saying that it was their responsibility. Boxo's representative said: 'Oh, no it's not. You told us to get a "Whoosh". Actually, if you had left it to us we would have fitted a "Zoom".'

Advise Mrs Smith.

A  Mrs Smith has no claim since she did not rely on the skill and judgment of Boxo Ltd.

B  Mrs Smith can claim against Boxo Ltd because they should have advised that a 'Zoom' be fitted.

C  Mrs Smith has no claim because the fan ran for two months and she has affirmed the contract.

D  Mrs Smith may only claim against the company which made the fan.

2  Mrs Mopp's electric pop-up toaster would not toast because she could not push the handle down fully. She took it to a small electrical shop owned by Fred Sparks for repair. Fred said: 'Leave it with me. I'll fix it. Call back in a couple of hours.' Mrs Mopp returned some two hours later and Fred said: 'It's fine now, that'll be £20.' Mrs Mopp was a bit shocked and asked what was wrong with the toaster. Fred said: 'Not much; we had to bend the handle straight and oil it, that's all.' Mrs Mopp said:

'But surely you cannot charge me £20 for that.' 'Sorry, Madam,' said Fred, 'it's our minimum charge; labour costs, you know.'

Advise Mrs Mopp.

A Mrs Mopp is obliged by statute to pay £20.

B Mrs Mopp is obliged by statute to pay only a reasonable charge.

C Mrs Mopp is obliged to pay £20 because she did not agree a fee for the work.

D Mrs Mopp is obliged by the common law to pay £20.

3 James has offered to sell his Te Fenage Mutant Ninja Turtle collection to Eddie and has promised to keep the offer open until Thursday. On Tuesday he decides he wants to withdraw the offer and posts a letter of revocation that day. On Wednesday, Eddie posts his letter of acceptance. Both letters reach their destination on Thursday.

Can Eddie sue James?

A Yes, James promised to keep the offer open until Thursday. As Eddie accepted by that day his acceptance is valid.

B No, James posted his letter of revocation before Eddie posted his letter of acceptance, therefore, James' letter takes precedence.

C Yes, as he had not received notice of revocation Eddie's acceptance is binding once the letter has been posted.

D No. Acceptance must reach the offerer before revocation takes place.

4 Alan promises Dave £1,000 if he completes a 20 km run. Dave faints 500 m from the finishing line. Can Dave claim the £1,000?

A Dave can sue Alan for the whole sum under the doctrine of substantial performance.

B Dave can sue Alan for part of the sum as a *quantum meruit*.

C Dave cannot sue Alan as Dave's completion of the run was a condition for recovery under the contract.

D Dave cannot sue Alan as his failure to complete the run will be regarded as self-induced frustration.

5 Tom and Dick enter into face-to-face negotiations. Dick has made out that he is a wealthy film star and, therefore, thoroughly creditworthy. Dick is neither of these things. If Tom makes Dick an offer and Dick accepts, the contract is:

A Void, as Tom has made a mistake as to Dick's attributes.

B Voidable, as Dick has fraudulently misrepresented the true facts.

C Void, as Tom has made a mistake as to Dick's identity.

D Void, as there has been a mutual mistake as to purpose.

6 In which of the following situations would there not be a termination of an offer?

A Where there is a revocation directly communicated by the offeror prior to receipt of acceptance.

B Where there is acceptance subject to conditions laid down by the offeree.

C Where a specific time period for acceptance expires just prior to the acceptance.

D Where the offeror dies and the contract is not for personal services.

*Answers to questions set in objective mode appear on p 708.*

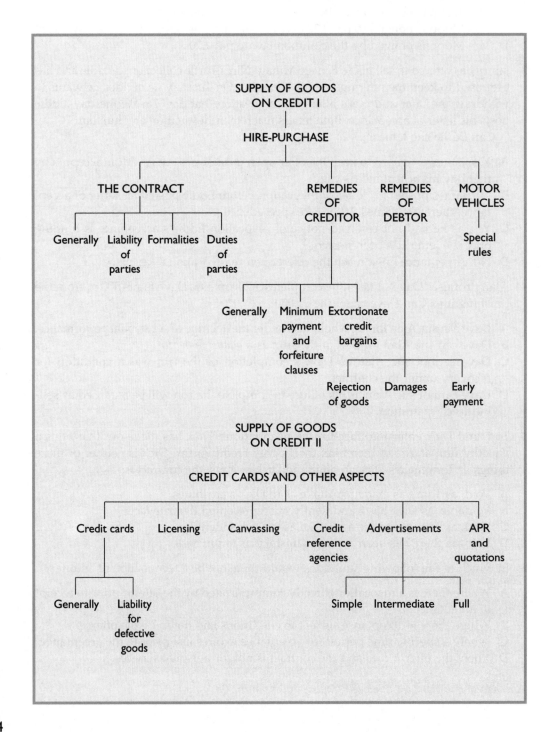

The objectives of this chapter are to set out the principles and rules laid down by statute – in the main by the Consumer Credit Act 1974 – in terms of the liability of the parties to a hire-purchase agreement, the formalities, the duties of creditor and debtor, and their remedies if there is default. The chapter concludes with the provisions of the Hire Purchase Act 1964 relating to motor vehicle hire-purchase and some of the more important business aspects of the Consumer Credit Act, e.g. credit cards.

## HIRE-PURCHASE GENERALLY

A *hire-purchase contract* takes the form of a bailment under which the goods are hired. This contract of bailment is accompanied by an option to purchase the goods, subject to the conditions of the agreement being complied with. The law is derived from two sources as follows:

(a) the common law, where the total credit exceeds £25,000 or the hirer is a corporation; and

(b) the Consumer Credit Act 1974 which applies where the total credit does not exceed £25,000 and the hirer is an individual or a partnership but not a corporation. This is known as a *regulated agreement*.

Under s 189(1) of the 1974 Act, the operation of the above rules is to be calculated by reference to the balance of the price which is financed and not to the total price of the goods. If the cash price of the goods is £27,000 and the hirer (being an individual) pays a deposit of £4,000, the agreement is a consumer credit agreement within the Act. The balance financed, i.e. £23,000, does not exceed £25,000.

Under s 17 of the 1974 Act, 'small agreements', i.e. those where the amount of credit does not exceed £50, are not in principle excluded from the Act, but some provisions of Part V of the Act, e.g. the 'cooling off' period, do not apply to small agreements.

Throughout this chapter section references are to the 1974 Act unless otherwise indicated. The whole of the Consumer Credit Act 1974 was brought into force by SI 1983/1551, with the exception of ss 123–5. These sections, which prevent a creditor from taking bills of exchange and promissory notes in discharge of sums payable by a debtor or hirer under a regulated agreement, were brought into force by SI 1984/436. Cheques can be taken but can only be paid into a bank and not endorsed over to another. The object of this is that holders in due course cannot arise. They would be entitled to payment of the instrument from the debtor or hirer, even though the contract between the debtor or hirer and the dealer was affected, e.g. by fraud as to the quality of the goods hired. A holder in due course can overcome defects of this kind.

## THE LIABILITY OF THE PARTIES

Before reading the following material, revise again the distinction between a hire-purchase contract and a conditional sale agreement set out in Chapter 10.

### Hire-purchase and conditional sale agreements

Financial institutions conducting business in these areas are liable under the contract in their own right and not jointly and severally with the supplier, under ss 8–11 of the Supply of Goods (Implied Terms) Act 1973. Thus the conditions and warranties as to title, description, satisfactory quality, fitness and sample apply. They have an indemnity against the supplier under the Sale of Goods Act 1979 if they are sued by the debtor because there is a contract of sale between them and the supplier.

In addition, they are liable under s 56(4) of the 1974 Act for misrepresentation and breach of terms by the supplier arising from the negotiations leading to the hire-purchase or conditional sale agreement. For this purpose the supplier is the agent of the financial institution. The action is brought directly against the finance house under s 56(4). There is no need to construe a collateral contract as in *Andrews v Hopkinson* [1956] (*see below*). This liability cannot be excluded (s 56(3)) but the finance house has an indemnity against the supplier.

The agreement must be a regulated agreement. That is, an agreement in which the credit is not more than £25,000 or the hirer is a corporation.

### Retailer and hirer

There is no contract between the supplier and the debtor under a hire-purchase transaction financed by a finance house. If there is anything wrong with the goods there is no straightforward contractual claim against the retailer. (This was decided in *Drury v Victor Buckland Ltd* [1941] 1 All ER 269.) The law on this matter has not been changed by the 1974 Act.

The supplier may, of course, become liable to indemnify the finance company if the latter has been held liable for what are, in effect, the supplier's breaches (*Porter v General Guarantee Corporation* (1982) RTR 384).

However, a debtor may have an action against the retailer or supplier in *negligence* where the goods are in a dangerous condition or by establishing a separate contract with the supplier, the consideration for which is the debtor's agreement to enter into a hire-purchase contract with the finance company.

Thus in *Andrews v Hopkinson* [1956] 3 All ER 422 a dealer, during the sale of a car, told the customer: 'It's a good little bus, I would stake my life on it'. Following this remark the customer made a hire-purchase contract with a finance company. However, soon after taking delivery of the car he had an accident in it because of its defective steering mechanism. The court *held* that the dealer was liable in damages to the customer on two grounds: (a) there was a contract between the dealer and the customer. This consisted of the dealer's promising that the car was a 'good little bus' in return for the customer's agreeing to apply to a finance company to acquire the car on hire-purchase terms. The dealer was therefore liable for breach of his warranty as to the car's condition; (b) the defect in the steering mechanism was due to lack of inspection and proper servicing by the dealer who was therefore liable, regardless of contract, to anyone foreseeably injured by his negligence under the neighbour principle in *Donoghue* v *Stevenson* (1932) (*see* Chapter 11).

As we have seen, the action against the finance company is based on s 56. There is no need to construe a collateral contract. However, it is necessary to construe such a contract for a claim against the supplier.

## Finance company and retailer

The relationship is basically that of buyer and seller. However, under ss 56(2) and 69(1) of the 1974 Act, the retailer is also made an agent of the finance company for two purposes, i.e. as regards the making of representations about the goods whether these are terms of the contract or not, and also in regard to receiving notices of cancellation under the 'cooling-off' provisions of the 1974 Act. The above sections apply only where the agreement is a regulated agreement and is protected by the 1974 Act but where they are applicable they cannot be excluded by the agreement (s 173). Finally, under s 75(2) the finance company has a statutory right to an indemnity from the dealer where the finance company has been made liable for a breach of the hire-purchase agreement which is a result of the dealer's acts.

## Finance company and guarantor

The supplier may give a guarantee of payment by the debtor to the finance company. This is, of course, to protect the finance company, but in order to protect the supplier it is usual to ask the debtor to obtain his own guarantor. The contract of guarantee usually allows the finance company, for example, to extend the period of credit without discharging the guarantor. Such a discharge would occur if there was no special provision in the contract. If the debtor terminates the agreement, e.g. under s 99, then if he discharges his liability the guarantor is also discharged. Section 113 makes it clear that the guarantor can in no situation be liable to a greater extent than the debtor is. Section 113 is designed to prevent evasion of the Act by the use of a security which is what a guarantee is.

A guarantor who pays the finance company because the debtor does not do so stands in the finance company's place and may use its remedies against the debtor. The better view is that this includes the right to seize the goods.

There are a number of provisions in the 1974 Act which relate to guarantors. These are as follows:

(a) a guarantor, along with the debtor, is not liable if an agreement controlled by the Act does not comply with the statutory formalities (*see below*);
(b) a guarantor is entitled to a copy of the contract of guarantee and to the agreement together with a statement of account (ss 107–9);
(c) a guarantor and the debtor are discharged from liability if the owner seizes the goods without a court order when a third of the price has been paid (ss 91 and 113);
(d) the statutory provisions relating to guarantees apply also to contracts of indemnity (ss 189(1)).

There is one situation where s 113 allows a security to be enforced, even though the regulated agreement itself is not enforceable. This occurs where the security is an indemnity or guarantee and the only reason that the regulated agreement cannot be enforced is that the debtor or hirer is not of full age or capacity. The reason for this is that tradesmen will often not give credit to a person under 18 unless an indemnity or guarantee is given by an adult. The exception referred to above means that the indemnity or guarantee will not be valueless if the minor debtor or hirer defaults. The exception is contained in s 113(7) (as amended by s 4 of the Minors' Contracts Act 1987). (For the general law on the subject of guarantees and indemnities of a minor's liability *see* Chapter 3.)

## FORMALITIES

The Act gives certain formalities for regulated agreements, i.e. agreements under which a person is given credit not exceeding £25,000.

Under s 55 the pre-contractual requirements are left to be made by regulation. SI 1983/1553 (as amended by SI 1988/2047) applies and, for example, the debtor must be told in writing what the cash price of the goods is, as was the case under hire-purchase legislation.

Regulations set out in SI 1983/1553 also provide in the main for the form and contents of regulated agreements and cover the following:

(a) the names of the parties to the agreement and their addresses;
(b) the amounts of all payments due under the agreement and when and to whom they are payable;
(c) the total charge for the credit, i.e. the cost to the debtor of having the credit;
(d) the true annual rate of the total charge for the credit, expressed as a percentage rate per annum;
(e) the debtor's right to pay off his debt earlier than agreed.

Furthermore, the agreement and every copy of it must:

(f) contain all the terms of the agreement, and
(g) contain details of the debtor's rights to cancel the agreement.

As regards the signing of the agreement, this must, under s 61(1), be by the debtor *personally* who consequently cannot sign through an agent. The creditor may sign personally or through an agent.

The debtor must not be given blank forms to sign, the details in them being filled in at a later date by the creditor or supplier.

Section 61 provides that a regulated agreement is not properly executed unless it is in such a state that all its terms are readily legible when it is sent or given to the debtor or hirer for signature.

If the requirements relating to form are not complied with, the creditor is unable to *enforce* the agreement unless the court so orders (s 65). If it does not so order, the creditor cannot repossess the goods, because that is an enforcement of the agreement (*R v Modupe, The Times*, 27 February 1991), even where the debtor has stopped payment of instalments.

It was *held* in *Lombard Tricity Finance Ltd* v *Paton* [1988] *New Law Journal Practitioner* 332 that it is lawful for a consumer credit agreement to contain a provision that the lender may vary the rate of interest at his absolute discretion subject to proper notice to the borrower.

## THE PARTIES AND THEIR DUTIES

The duties of the parties to a hire-purchase agreement must now be dealt with.

### Duties of owner

Sections 8–11 of the Supply of Goods (Implied Terms) Act 1973 (as substituted by Sch 4, Part 1, para 35 to the Consumer Credit Act 1974) lay upon the owner duties identical to those of a seller of goods. The implied conditions and warranties are the same and exclusion clauses are, under the Unfair Contract Terms Act 1977, forbidden in consumer sales, though allowed if reasonable in non-consumer sales. All of this applies in all the credit agreements under consideration with no financial limit and is applicable also even if a corporation is a party to the contract.

### Duties of debtor

These depend upon the agreement and regulations made under the 1974 Act. However, it can be said that:

(a) the debtor must pay the instalments while the agreement is in force;
(b) if the debtor terminates the agreement then if it is covered by the 1974 Act he is liable to pay:
    (i) instalments in arrear;
    (ii) an additional sum to make up the total payments to 50 per cent of the total price (unless they already reach or exceed that figure). Thus, if the total price is £520 and the debtor terminates after he has paid £180 and owes £20 in unpaid instalments, he must pay the £20 and a further £60 so as to bring his total payments up to one-half of the total price. But if he has paid, or becomes liable to pay, more than one-half of the total price before the termination, he cannot recover or be relieved from the excess. By s 100(3) the court may make an order for the payment of a sum less than one-half of the total price where it is satisfied that a sum less than half would equal the loss sustained by the creditor. Thus the one-half minimum payment is in practice the maximum amount recoverable by the creditor;
    (iii) damages if he has not taken reasonable care of the goods;
(c) the debtor must take reasonable care of the goods and, e.g. in the case of cars, take out a comprehensive insurance policy for the full value.

Finally, the agreement will usually contain prohibitions on the debtor under which he cannot move the goods from the place where they are normally kept or garage a car in other than its usual place. There are also commonly provisions preventing resale, pledge and parting with the possession of the goods. Regulations made under the Act control any additional prohibitions which can be inserted into agreements.

Under s 80(1) the debtor has a duty to inform the owner, if requested, where the goods are kept and breach of this requirement is a criminal offence triable summarily before magistrates.

Section 86 contains provisions designed to prevent or inhibit the creditor or owner under a regulated agreement from, e.g. terminating the agreement or accelerating payment by reason only of the death of the debtor.

# REMEDIES OF THE CREDITOR

These will depend upon whether the agreement is regulated by the 1974 Act, or not.

## Agreements which are not regulated

Here we must consider claims for instalments and general damages and seizure of the goods.

### Claims for instalments and general damages

The agreement may provide that where the debtor has accepted delivery of the goods failure to pay an instalment when due renders the whole amount due and payable immediately. A provision of this kind may be valid in a non-regulated agreement unless it is an extortionate bargain for the purposes of the 1974 Act or a penalty (*see* Chapter 9).

### Claims for instalments – contractual rights to terminate the contract

If a debtor exercises a contractual right to terminate the contract, the money, if any, which the contract requires him to pay in that event is not damages and is not, therefore, subject to the penalties rule. If, however, the debtor terminates his contract by breach any sum mentioned as payable on termination of the contract is then of the nature of liquidated damages and the penalty rules apply.

**The following case provides an illustration.**

### Bridge v Campbell Discount Co Ltd [1962] I All ER 385

A contract of hire-purchase of a Bedford Dormobile required the debtor to pay on termination: (a) arrears of payments due before termination; plus (b) an amount which together with payments made and due before termination amounted to two-thirds of the hire-purchase price. This was in addition to the fact that the creditor was entitled to the return of goods. After paying the deposit and one instalment, the hirer wrote to the owners saying: 'Owing to unforeseen personal circumstances I shall be unable to pay any more payments on the Bedford'. The owner repossessed the vehicle and sued for £206 3s 4d under the clause. The Court of Appeal *held* that the hirer was exercising his option to determine the contract, the 'fee' for which was £206 3s 4d under the clause. Since this sum was never intended as damages, it was not subject to the rules regarding penalties. The House of Lords reversed this decision, *holding* that, from the general tone of the letter, the hirer was in breach of the contract and was not exercising his option. On this view the sum of £206 3s 4d could be regarded as liquidated damages and was subject to the rules regarding penalties. Accordingly the sum was irrecoverable because it was in the nature of a penalty. The £206 3s 4d was not a genuine pre-estimate of the owner's loss, because if one included the value of the returned goods, the clause would in nearly all cases give the creditor more than 100 per cent of the purchase price.

### Claims for instalments – where creditor sues for damages

The amount recoverable will depend upon the following.

(a) Where the debtor is in serious breach which amounts to repudiation of the contract, as, for example, when a debtor has repeatedly refused to pay instalments, the creditor may accept this as repudiation of the contract and sue for general damages. This will be, according to the decision in *Yeoman Credit* v *Waragowski* [1961] 3 All ER 145, the total hire-purchase price, subject to the following deductions:
   (i)   the value of the goods if and when repossessed;
   (ii)  payments already made;
   (iii) arrears of instalments due before termination which the court will award separately to the finance company.

The *Waragowski* formula will in most cases mean that the finance company recovers virtually the whole of the hire-purchase price.

(b) Where the debtor's breach is not sufficiently serious to be regarded as a repudiation, but the creditor exercises his right to terminate the contract, as where there has been an occasional failure to pay instalments by the debtor, the measure of damages is as follows:
   (i)  the instalments in arrears at the date of the commencement of the action or, if the goods have been repossessed, to the date of repossession (*Financings Ltd* v *Baldock* [1963] 1 All ER 443), plus
   (ii) damages for failure to keep the goods in proper repair if, as is commonly the case, the agreement contains a provision to that effect (*Brady* v *St Margaret's Trust Ltd* [1963] 2 All ER 275.

If the debtor refuses to accept delivery of the goods, the creditor may sue for damages for non-acceptance, which appears to be his only remedy, whatever a particular contract may provide (*National Cash Register Co Ltd* v *Stanley* [1921] 3 KB 292).

The amount of the damages will depend upon the market situation as follows:

(a) if the supply of goods is greater than, or matches demand, the loss is:
   (i)  the total amount which would have been paid under the contract if it had run its full term; less
   (ii) deductions, e.g. in regard to depreciation of the goods which will not arise because the goods were not accepted;
(b) if demand exceeds supply the creditor may be regarded, as in the case of a sale, as having no loss (see *Charter* v *Sullivan* (1957) Chapter 12), or at most as having lost rental, less deductions, e.g. for lack of depreciation, between the time of repudiation and the finding of a new debtor.

### Seizure of goods

Under hire-purchase agreements, this normally occurs on breach by the debtor, e.g. failure to pay instalments, or on the death of the debtor, or where another creditor is taking the debtor's goods to pay a judgment debt (execution).

In an unregulated agreement, it is a matter for the contract itself to decide what the rights of seizure are. If the contract so provides, a creditor can, so far as the common law is concerned, seize goods even though, say, nine-tenths of the purchase price has been paid. However, relief may be obtainable under those provisions of the 1974 Act which relate to extortionate bargains.

## Regulated agreements

As regards claims for instalments or damages, s 129 of the 1974 Act gives the court power to make a 'time order' under which the debtor is given more time to pay.

As regards awards of money, s 129 gives the court absolute discretion in the matter, whether the debtor has repudiated the agreement or not and whether the goods have been delivered or not. In short, however he may frame his action, the creditor is at the mercy of the court.

As regards seizure of the goods, where a debtor is not a company and the credit does not exceed £25,000 (i.e. where the agreement is regulated) the right to retake the goods is much modified by the 1974 Act. The restrictions are as follows:

(a) under s 87, the creditor is unable to terminate the agreement or recover possession of the goods, or exercise any other remedy except possibly sue for instalments due, unless he has served a *default notice* on the debtor giving the debtor at least seven days in which to remedy any breach of the agreement. This gives the debtor fair warning that action may be taken against him;

(b) under s 90, if one-third of the total price has been paid by the debtor the creditor has no right to take possession of the goods without a court order unless the debtor has terminated the agreement himself. Should a creditor retake the goods in defiance of this section, s 91 states that the debtor is released from all liability under the agreement and may recover from the creditor all sums paid by him under the agreement. The 1974 Act seems to confirm that there is no breach of these provisions by the creditor taking possession if the hirer abandons the goods, as where he leaves a damaged car at a garage and disappears, so that they are no longer in his possession;

(c) under s 92 the creditor has no right without a court order to enter the debtor's premises to retake possession of any goods let to him under a hire-purchase agreement. This section applies whether or not one-third of the price has been paid, but again, the debtor may consent to the creditor's entry for the purpose of retaking the goods.

If the creditor brings an action to recover possession of the goods, the court has wide discretionary powers under ss 129–36 to make reasonable orders regardless of the terms of the contract. The court may, for example, make an order for delivery but postpone its coming into force so that the debtor may have an opportunity to pay the balance due in such a way as the court thinks fit in terms of the number of instalments and their amount and the times on which they shall be payable. This is the most usual order for the court to make and in practical terms it means that the hirer will obtain additional time to pay and that the instalments will be reduced in amount, based on his ability to pay.

## MINIMUM PAYMENTS AND FORFEITURE CLAUSES

Some agreements may contain express provisions relating to forfeiture of payments made and additional minimum payments by the debtor if the contract is terminated, either voluntarily by the debtor himself, or by the creditor seizing the goods for non-payment of the rental. For example, a particular contract may provide:

(a) that all payments made up to the termination of the contract are to be forfeited (a forfeiture clause); and
(b) that the debtor is to bring his total payments up to a certain percentage (generally ranging between 50 per cent and 75 per cent) of the full price if his payments do not reach that figure (a minimum payments clause).

Forfeiture of payments can produce an inequitable result, as where a contract involving the credit purchase of a car priced at £6,000 is terminated when the hirer has paid £5,500. Even so, forfeiture clauses are permissible, except as regulated by statute, and no form of relief, either in law or equity, is available.

A minimum payments clause may, however, be avoided if it is not regarded by the court as a genuine pre-estimate of loss but in the nature of a penalty (*see* Chapter 9). Avoidance on this ground applies, however, only to a situation in which the debtor has broken the contract as where he is refusing to make the agreed payments. If the debtor voluntarily returns the goods he may be regarded as exercising a right to terminate given by the contract, the 'fee' for this 'privilege' being the minimum payment provided in the contract. The courts are, however, inclined to regard voluntary termination by the debtor as, in effect, a breach of contract except where the debtor was obviously fully aware of his rights and appears to have been exercising them (*see Bridge* v *Campbell Discount Co Ltd* (1962) *above*).

The above provisions are now of less practical importance. The Consumer Credit Act has two sets of rules relating to the enforcement of clauses of this kind, the first being general and applying to all credit agreements, and the second being applicable to regulated agreements only.

### General provisions

Wide powers are given to the court under ss 137–40 to reopen credit agreements so as to do justice between the parties. The power is not confined to regulated consumer credit agreements as 'credit agreements' means any agreement between a debtor and a creditor and there are no maximum financial limits or other exemptions.

The power is available if the credit bargain is extortionate, i.e. the payments are grossly exorbitant, or it otherwise grossly contravenes ordinary principles of fair dealing (s 138). The section gives a number of factors to be taken into account, including prevailing interest rates, the debtor's age, experience, business capacity, state of health and financial pressure upon him, and the degree of risk accepted by the creditor, his relationship to the debtor and whether an inflated cash price was quoted for goods or services.

If the court finds that the agreement is extortionate, it may re-open the transaction and has sweeping powers to adjust the rights and duties of the parties under s 139(2). In particular, the court may set aside or reduce any obligation which has been imposed on the debtor or may require the creditor to repay any sums which the debtor has already paid.

The number of reported cases brought before the courts have been few and it is, therefore, interesting to note the case of *Barcabe Ltd* v *Edwards* (1983) 133 NLJ 713. Here, the borrower, a low-paid working man with four children and little business capacity, answered the lender's advertisement in a newspaper. The lender's credit reference check showed no money judgments against him. He took an unsecured loan of £400 at a flat rate of interest of 100 per cent per annum (APR 319 per cent). Judge Gosling, of the Birmingham County Court, reduced the flat rate of interest to 40 per cent per annum (APR 92 per cent). There was evidence that the money could have been obtained elsewhere at about half this rate. The Office of Fair Trading is of the opinion that the reason there are so few cases is that borrowers may be too scared to come before the courts. However, this case illustrates that the law can be of assistance if only borrowers will invoke it. Nevertheless, the rate which the court substituted is still very high. In *Ketley* v *Scott* [1981] LCR 241 a bridging loan of £20,500 made to enable the defendant to complete immediately on a house purchase at an APR of 57.35 per cent was *held* by Foster J not to be extortionate due to the speed at which the loan was made, the risk involved and the deceit of the defendant, who failed to disclose particulars of another legal charge over the property.

In *Castle Phillips & Co* v *Wilkinson and Another* [1992] CCLR 83 a County Court held that a credit bargain was clearly extortionate because: (a) the rate of interest was $3\frac{1}{3}$ times the rate charged by a building society; (b) the security for the loan of the house was excessive in terms of the amount advanced; and (c) the defendants who had defaulted on the agreement were persons of little financial understanding. The agreement was reopened so that an interest rate of 20 per cent per annum would be charged, i.e. a building society rate on a remortgage plus one-third to reflect the short-term nature of the loan which was a bridging loan.

These provisions will also cover minimum payments and forfeiture clauses. It is difficult to say how the courts will operate such wide powers in varying circumstances, but it is to be expected that the courts will generally regard a minimum payments or forfeiture agreement as extortionate if it contains provisions which would give the creditor significantly more than the repayment of his capital together with interest at the agreed rate on the assumption that the rate of interest itself is not extortionate. Thus minimum payments and forfeiture clauses will normally be unenforceable unless they provide solely for sufficient payments to make good any loss to the creditor caused by the debtor's breach or other act.

## Regulated agreements – additional provisions

So far as regulated agreements are concerned, the 1974 Act provides additional safeguards against minimum payments and forfeiture clauses. As regards forfeiture clauses, the debtor's protection lies in provisions under which the creditor cannot retake possession of the goods without a court order when one-third of the price has been paid. If the court does allow a creditor to retake the goods, it will give the debtor every chance to pay the balance and avoid forfeiture. If the debtor has not paid one-third of the price, the Act does not prevent the creditor from retaking the goods, but he must first serve a notice of default and cannot enter the debtor's premises to recover the goods. In this situation there is nothing to prevent forfeiture of the amounts paid by the debtor other than the provisions relating to extortionate agreements. These are not likely to apply since the amounts paid by the debtor, i.e. less than one-third of the price, will not normally be sufficient to cover the drop in the value of the goods, unless they were second-hand.

In connection with minimum payments clauses, s 99 entitles the debtor to terminate the agreement at any time before the final payment falls due and then the Act provides for its own minimum payments clause. The debtor in this situation is liable to pay enough to bring his total payments up to one-half of the total price, but if the creditor's loss is less than that, then his actual loss is the maximum of the debtor's liability.

## REMEDIES OF THE DEBTOR

### To reject the goods

The debtor may reject the goods for breach of condition by the creditor. The conditions are those set out in the Supply of Goods (Implied Terms) Act 1973 (as substituted by the Consumer Credit Act).

As regards the right to reject, the provisions of s 11(4) and ss 34 and 35 of the Sale of Goods Act 1979, which deal with acceptance and the right of examination of the goods, do not apply to hire-purchase contracts and the courts have to decide the question of the debtor's right to repudiate on the general principles of the law of contract. If, for example, the debtor has affirmed the contract the right to repudiate will have been lost. It should, however, be noted that the right to repudiate is not necessarily lost simply because there has been considerable use of the goods.

Thus in *Farnworth Finance Facilities* v *Attryde* [1970] 2 All ER 774 Mr Attryde bought a motor cycle on hire-purchase. The machine had many faults and although Mr Attryde always complained about them he did drive the machine for some 4,000 miles before deciding to repudiate the contract. He was then sued by the finance company. It was *held* by the Court of Appeal that Mr Attryde had not affirmed the contract by using the machine. He had always complained about the defects and had indicated that he would only finally accept the machine if they were remedied. Mr Attryde repudiated after payment of four monthly instalments. Lord Denning seems to have taken the view that the rules about loss of the right to repudiate were different here because, unlike a sale, the property had not passed. The machine did not belong to the defendant but was at the stage of repudiation only hired.

### Damages

The debtor is not likely to claim damages. If the goods are defective he will normally stop paying the instalments and wait for the creditor to sue him. Consequently, there is little authority on the law relating to damages in this area. However, if an action was brought by the debtor for damages, the position would appear to be as follows:

(a) if the debtor keeps the goods and has them repaired, the cost of repairing the goods is the appropriate measure of damages, together with damages for loss of use while they are being put right (*Charterhouse Credit Co* v *Tolley* [1963] 2 All ER 432);

(b) if the debtor elects to treat the contract as repudiated and rejects the goods, there is some doubt as to the measure of damages which he is entitled to recover. However, it would seem that he can claim the return of all monies paid by him at the time of the termination of the agreement, plus any sum actually spent on repairing the goods bailed to him, less a deduction for the use of the goods during the period they have been in his possession (*Charterhouse Credit Co v Tolley* [1963] 2 All ER 432).

## To terminate the contract

Under s 99 in a regulated credit agreement the debtor can terminate the agreement at any time before the final payment falls due merely by giving notice to the creditor. The debtor is not obliged to return the goods to the creditor but must make them available when the creditor calls to collect them. The same rules apply to a conditional sale agreement in which the price is payable by instalments. The buyer can determine the agreement even after the property has passed to him, but not if he has sold the goods to a third party.

## Cooling-off

The 1974 Act, in ss 67–74, substantially reproduces the cooling-off provisions of the old Hire Purchase Act. Under these provisions the debtor can cancel the agreement *not later than five days after service on him of a second copy of the agreement as required by s 63*, if the agreement has not been signed at the premises of the creditor, or the supplier or some associated party. Thus the exact cooling-off period depends upon how much time elapses between the debtor signing the agreement and his receipt of the second copy. Certainly it will be in most cases more than five days.

The cooling-off period is designed to prevent high-pressure salesmanship being carried out on the debtor's doorstep or in his home and not to affect transactions in shops. The provisions do not apply where the transaction takes place on 'appropriate trade premises'. This means premises at which goods of the description to which the contract relates or goods of a similar description are normally offered or exposed for sale in the course of the business carried on at those premises.

In order to exercise the right to cancel the agreement, the debtor can give 'notice of cancellation' to the creditor or his agent (which includes the supplier of the goods). The notice need not be in any particular form so long as the intention to cancel is clearly indicated. It may be sent by post and to assist service by this method the agreement must give the name and address of the person to whom the notice may be sent.

When the notice is served, it operates to cancel the agreement as to the provision of credit and also any 'linked transaction', e.g. an agreement to maintain the goods which was entered into at the same time as the hire-purchase agreement.

Once the notice has been served, the debtor must take reasonable care of the goods (if they have been delivered to him) for 21 days. He is not under a duty to return the goods but must allow the creditor to collect them, though he may insist on being repaid anything he has paid under the agreement before he allows the owner to retake the goods. Where the debtor has traded in goods in part-exchange to the supplier, these must be returned to him or an amount equal to the part-exchange allowance repaid to him.

It should be noted that under the Consumer Credit Act the cooling-off provisions are no longer restricted to hire-purchase agreements but extend to a wider variety of consumer transactions. Thus a loan of an amount not exceeding £25,000 will be subject to cancellation under the cooling-off provisions if the agreement is signed at the debtor's own house. In the event of cancellation, the money must be repaid. In addition, the Timeshare Act 1992 entitles a consumer who has entered into a timeshare contract to a minimum 14-day cooling-off period for the cancellation of the contract if governed by UK law or if one of the parties to it is in the UK when it is entered into. It is to some extent a weakness of the 1992 Act that it does not apply to timeshare agreements entered into outside the UK, even where there are UK parties, unless the contract is expressed to be governed by UK law.

### Early payment

The Consumer Credit Act, ss 94 and 95 provide that the debtor may pay off the whole amount due under a hire-purchase or other credit agreement, at any time. Regulations made under the Act give the debtor a right to a rebate on the credit charges where he has paid early.

## PROVISIONS RELATING TO MOTOR VEHICLES

Formerly, if the hirer of a motor vehicle sold the vehicle while it was bailed to him under a hire-purchase or conditional sale agreement, the purchaser did not get a good title and the true owner of the vehicle, usually a finance company, could recover the vehicle from the purchaser or sue him in conversion. This was so even though the hirer had all the appearances of ownership, including the registration document. Part III of the Hire Purchase Act 1964, i.e. ss 27–9 (as substituted but not repealed by s 192 of, and Sch 4, para 22, to the Consumer Credit Act 1974), is all that remains of the 1964 Act. It is designed to protect bona fide purchasers for value of motor vehicles where the seller is a mere bailee under a hire-purchase or conditional sale agreement and where he disposes of the vehicle before the property is vested in him. The provisions do not apply unless the vehicle has been let under a hire-purchase agreement or there is an agreement to sell under a conditional sale agreement. Thus they do not apply to an ordinary hiring, nor to situations such as those in *Central Newbury Car Auctions Ltd* v *Unity Finance Ltd* [1956] 3 All ER 905 where a dealer allowed a fraudulent person to take possession of a vehicle after he had signed hire-purchase forms which were then rejected by the finance company. It was *held* that a purchaser from the fraudulent person was not protected because the vehicle was not let under a hire-purchase agreement.

### Private purchasers

A private purchaser is a purchaser who at the time of the disposition is not a motor vehicle dealer or a person engaged in financing motor vehicle deals.

Where the disposition is to a private purchaser who takes the vehicle in good faith and without notice of the hire-purchase or conditional sale agreement, that disposition shall have effect as if the title of the owner or seller of the vehicle had been vested in the hirer or buyer immediately before that disposition. Thus a private purchaser gets a good title and the owner or seller must pursue his remedies against the hirer or buyer.

**The following case provides an illustration.**

### Barker v Bell (Ness, third party) [1971] 2 All ER 867

A man called Hudson had a Morris Mini on hire-purchase from Auto Finances (Hallamshire) Ltd. He sold it to Mr Ness, who was not a dealer in cars, after telling him that the car had formerly been on hire-purchase but that the last instalment had been paid. Hudson produced a receipt for £6 across which was written 'Final Payment'. This receipt was in fact from Bowmakers Ltd and had no connection with the hire arrangements with Auto Finances, though Mr Ness had no way of knowing this. Mr Ness resold the vehicle and eventually the car was purchased by a dealer, Mr Barker. The vehicle was repossessed by Auto Finances from Mr Barker who then sued the dealer from whom he bought the car, Mr Bell. Mr Bell brought in Mr Ness as third party. It was *held* – by the Court of Appeal – that Mr Ness had obtained a good title from Hudson and that in consequence Barker and Bell had good titles even though they were dealers. Mr Ness was a bona fide purchaser without notice of a hire-purchase agreement as required by s 27(2) of the Hire Purchase Act 1964. 'Notice' meant notice of a relevant existing agreement. A hire-purchase agreement which had supposedly been paid off was irrelevant for this purpose.

*Comment:* (i) The case also illustrates that once a private purchaser gets a good title, subsequent purchasers – even dealers – also get one. Therefore, Mr Barker need not have given up the car to Auto Finances. Since Mr Barker got a good title – as indeed did Mr Bell – there was no claim against Mr Ness for breach of condition as to title, and presumably no claim against Mr Bell either, though the appeal to the Court of Appeal was by Mr Ness and concerned only his position.

(ii) Those who regard the private purchaser/good title provisions as a good thing are presumably thinking of a situation in which the private purchaser is intending to keep the vehicle. However, if he wishes to sell it matters may be very different. In *Barber v NWS Bank plc* [1996] 1 All ER 906 Mr Barber bought a car under a conditional sale agreement and it was then discovered that there was a prior finance agreement on the car with money outstanding. Mr Barber's title was protected by the Hire Purchase Act 1964 but he could not sell it – in practice 'no dealer would touch it'. This is hardly surprising when you think about it. 'I bought this car under a conditional sale agreement from a person without a title but never mind – the Hire Purchase Act 1964 applies' is hardly a good sales pitch! Mr Barber sued the seller for the deposit he had made on the car after repudiating the agreement and returning the vehicle. The Court of Appeal supported his claim and ordered the return of the deposit. So a private purchaser is not forced to accept his good title if it does not suit him to do so.

## Trade or finance purchasers

Where the disposition is made to a trade or finance purchaser, i.e. a person who deals in motor vehicles or finances such transactions, then the trade or finance purchaser does not get a good title.

In this connection it should be noted that a person who carries on a part-time business of buying and selling motor cars is a 'trade or finance purchaser' under the Hire Purchase Act 1964 and is not within the protection given to a 'private purchaser' by that Act, even where he acquires a vehicle in his private capacity for personal use.

**The following case shows this point.**

### Stevenson v Beverley Bentinck [1976] 2 All ER 606

The claimant was a tool inspector who dealt in motor cars in his spare time. He bought a Jaguar for his own use without enquiring as to whether or not it was subject to any hire-purchase agreement. The car was subject to a hire-purchase agreement between the defendants and the seller. The latter having defaulted on his monthly instalments, the defendant repossessed the car. The claimant sought the return of the car or damages for conversion. It was *held* – by the Court of Appeal – that the claimant was not protected because his part-time business brought him within the definition of 'trade or finance purchaser' and judgment was given for the defendants.

However, if a private purchaser buys the vehicle from a trade or finance purchaser, either by paying cash for it as a result of paying up all the instalments under a hire-purchase or conditional sale agreement, then the trade or finance purchaser is deemed to have had a good title in order that the private purchaser shall obtain one.

## Factors

The provisions of the Act operate without prejudice to the provisions of the Factors Act or of any other Act enabling the apparent owner of goods to dispose of them as if he were the true owner. Thus a person may still claim a title because the person from whom he bought the goods was a factor. However, the provisions of the 1964 Act are wider than those of the Factors Act in that they protect a purchaser even though the goods have not been *delivered* to him, in the sense that he has bought the vehicle but not taken delivery. Under the Factors Act, delivery is an essential part of the protection of title.

## Liabilities after unlawful disposal

The liability of the hirer (or debtor) who has unlawfully disposed of the vehicle is not affected by the 1964 Act. Thus he may still be guilty of theft at criminal law and liable in conversion at civil law, provided that the creditor has served a default notice under ss 87–9 of the Consumer Credit Act 1974 on the debtor so that the creditor has a right to immediate possession. Where the sale is by auction, the auctioneer may similarly be liable in conversion (*Union Transport Finance* v *British Car Auctions* [1978] 2 All ER 385). The liability of any trade or finance purchaser to whom the hirer disposes of the vehicle is also unchanged, and such a person could be sued in conversion. The first private purchaser is not liable in conversion and as we have seen subsequent purchasers from him are not liable even though they be trade or finance purchasers (*see Barker* v *Bell* (1971) *above*).

## Presumptions of the Act

In order to assist a purchaser to establish his title in any action, the 1974 Act provides that certain presumptions shall be made which will apply unless evidence is brought to the contrary.

(a) If the purchaser who seeks to establish his title can show that the vehicle he has acquired was let to someone under a hire-purchase or conditional sale agreement and that a private purchaser acquired the vehicle in good faith and without notice of the letting agreement, it is presumed that the hirer or buyer made the original disposition and that the Act applies to perfect the purchaser's title.

(b) If it is proved that the hirer or buyer did not in fact make the disposition, but that a purchaser from him did so, then it is presumed that the said purchaser was a private purchaser in good faith and without notice so that the present purchaser's title is again perfected by the Act.

(c) If it is proved that the purchaser from the hirer or buyer was not a private purchaser but a trade or finance purchaser, then it is presumed that the purchaser from the trade or finance purchaser was a private purchaser in good faith and without notice and that the present purchaser's title is again perfected under the Act.

A disposition for the above purposes includes any sale or contract of sale, including a conditional sale agreement, any letting under a hire-purchase agreement, or the transfer of the property to the hirer on payment of agreed instalments.

## CREDIT CARDS AND ASPECTS OF CONSUMER CREDIT

The 1974 Act does not refer to credit cards as such but refers instead to credit tokens. These are defined so as to cover both a store credit card, e.g. a Marks & Spencer Chargecard, issued by a retailer to the holder of an 'option' or 'budget' account facility, and also bank credit cards, such as Visa or Access, where application may be made to any bank for a card. A 'credit token agreement' is defined by the Act as 'a regulated agreement for the provision of credit in connection with a credit token'.

The definition excludes American Express and Diners Club, which are charge cards, because they require accounts to be settled in full monthly. Both cards are credit tokens but the agreement covering the use of them is not a credit token agreement. Both American Express and Diners Club are subject to the prohibition on sending unsolicited credit tokens discussed below, but they are not otherwise governed by the Act.

Cheque guarantee cards are not credit tokens within the Act because they cannot be used by the debtor to obtain cash or services or goods on credit.

The legal position as between suppliers of goods and services, those issuing credit or charge cards and the card holders was looked at by the Court of Appeal in *Re Charge Card Services Ltd* [1988] 3 All ER 702. It was *held* that the use of a card by the card holder operates to discharge his obligation to the supplier, in the absence of special terms in a particular contract, so that the unpaid supplier can only recover what he is owed from the card issuer. It was an unfortunate result in this case for the suppliers because the charge card issuer was insolvent (*see also* Chapter 8).

### Prohibition of unsolicited credit tokens

Section 51(1) of the 1974 Act states: 'It is an offence to give a person a credit token if he has not asked for it'. A credit token is defined in s 14(1) of the Act as follows: 'A credit token is a card, voucher, coupon, stamp, form, booklet or other document or thing given to an individual by a person carrying on a consumer credit business, who *undertakes* – (a) that on the production of it (whether or not some other action is also required) he will supply cash, goods and services . . . on credit'. It is thus an offence to send a credit token to any person without a request in a document signed by him.

**The following case provides an example.**

## Elliott v Director-General of Fair Trading [1980] 1 WLR 977

In an attempt to boost their sales, Elliott & Sons, shoe retailers, mailed to selected members of the public an envelope containing advertising literature relating to the Elliott Credit Account Card and a card which had the appearance of a bank credit card. The front of the card said: 'Elliott Shoe Account', and on the back there was a box for the holder's signature and the words: 'This credit card is valid for immediate use. The sole requirement is your signature and means of identification. Credit is immediately available if you have a bank account.' The Director-General of Fair Trading instituted proceedings against the company alleging that the cards were sent contrary to s 51(1) of the 1974 Act. The central issue in the case was whether the cards were credit tokens within the meaning of the Act. In the Magistrates' Court the company was found guilty of a contravention of s 51(1) and appealed to the Divisional Court. In the Divisional Court counsel for the company argued that the word 'undertakes' in s 14(1) implied that there was a need for a contractual agreement, i.e. making an offer capable of being accepted so as to impose upon the trader a legally binding obligation to supply to the consumer goods on offer. Taking this one step further, counsel argued that since the production of the card did not entitle the customer to a supply of goods on credit, but only to apply for a credit card when he signed an agreement, the card was not a credit card; the card was not valid for immediate use, the sole requirement was not a signature, and credit was not immediately available since, in order to get credit, a customer would have to fill in a direct debiting mandate to his bank.

However, the Divisional Court did not accept these arguments. There was no need, it said, for a contractual agreement to exist. One looked at the card and asked, whether on its face or its back, the company undertook on the production of it that cash or goods would be supplied. The fact that none of the statements on the card was true did not prevent it being a credit token within the Act. The court found that the card in this case did fall within the meaning of s 51(1) and that the company was guilty of a contravention of that sub-section.

Section 66 of the 1974 Act deals with the situation in which a credit token, e.g. a credit card, is intercepted before it reaches the person for whom it was intended and is used to obtain credit. The section, which applies whether the token was unsolicited or requested, provides that the person for whom it was intended shall not be liable for its wrongful use unless he has accepted it. He accepts it, not when it reaches him, but when he signs a receipt for it or uses it.

Section 84 of the 1974 Act deals with a situation in which there is unauthorised use of a token after the debtor has accepted it. The debtor may be made liable for the unauthorised use but his liability cannot exceed £50 (or the limit of credit if lower) in regard to the whole of the period he is not in possession. The section does not apply to misuse by a user who obtained possession with the debtor's consent.

The section further provides that the debtor is not liable for any misuse after he has given notice to the creditor, e.g. Barclaycard. Notice may be oral, e.g. by telephone, but the agreement may provide for confirmation in writing. At least seven days must be allowed. If no confirmation is received in those circumstances the oral notice is invalid and the debtor becomes liable for all misuse. A debtor cannot be made liable for misuse unless the name, address and telephone number of the person to whom notice of loss or theft is to be given is shown clearly and legibly in the agreement. The creditor is required under s 171 to prove that any misuse occurred before notice was given.

### Liability for defective goods

Section 75 of the 1974 Act gives the debtor rights against a creditor where the purchase of goods or services is financed, either by a loan arranged through the supplier or by the use of a credit card, and there has been a misrepresentation or breach of contract by the supplier. Where a consumer has a claim against a creditor under s 75 the creditor has a claim to be indemnified by the supplier for any resulting loss. It should be noted that an action under s 75 is only available where the credit card agreement is a 'regulated agreement' (*see above*), so that while those issuing bank credit cards are liable for the defaults of their franchise holders, cards such as American Express or Diners Club are not.

In addition, the section only applies if the cash price of the item is between £100 and £30,000. Liability does not arise if the goods are purchased with a bank overdraft or with a cash advance under a credit card.

Section 56 is also relevant in that it provides that in the case of regulated agreements the dealer is deemed to be acting as the credit provider's agent so that the latter is responsible, e.g. for misrepresentations during negotiations concluded on his behalf.

## Other important aspects of the 1974 Act

### Licensing

Those who grant credit, or arrange credit, or who offer goods to consumers on hire *as a business*, must have a licence from the Office of Fair Trading or be covered by a group licence (ss 21 and 146). For example, the Law Society has a group licence covering solicitors with a practising certificate. So also has the Institute of Chartered Accountants in England and Wales for its practising members. Debt collectors are also included, as are credit reference agencies and debt adjusters and debt counsellors such as the Citizens Advice Bureaux. Licences are granted for periods of five years but can be withdrawn at any time (ss 31 and 32). Details of licence applications are kept in a public register maintained by the Director-General of Fair Trading (s 35). Under s 39 unlicensed trading is a criminal offence. In addition, agreements made with unlicensed traders will be unenforceable against the debtor or hirer unless the Director-General of Fair Trading has made a validating order.

The above provisions do not apply to private lenders (*Wills* v *Wood* (1984) 128 SJ 222), e.g. a father who lends his son money to buy a house does not need a licence. The lending etc. must be as part of a business but business includes a profession or trade (s 189(1)).

Further, s 189(2) provides that a person is not to be treated as carrying on a particular type of business merely because he *occasionally* enters into transactions belonging to a business of that type.

### Canvassing

Under ss 48 and 49 it is an offence to canvass debtor-creditor agreements other than on trade premises. Thus traders are restricted from offering credit in a person's home. However, if a previous request has come from the potential debtor, which must be in writing and signed, no offence is committed. Convictions under these sections have, in the main, been for canvassing in response to an oral request.

### Fees of credit brokers

A consumer may go through a credit broker for an introduction to a person who will give him credit. This is very often the trader who supplies the goods or services to the consumer. Under s 155 the credit broker may only make a small token charge (such as regulations may from time to time provide) for his services if no credit agreement is made by the consumer within six months of the introduction.

### Credit reference agencies

Before a supplier of goods or services gives credit he may consult a credit reference agency. This is an organisation which collects information relating to the financial standing of people. The agencies collect *facts*, such as details of County Court judgments for debt. They do not give *opinions* as to creditworthiness. The trader can obtain the facts on a particular person's file. Section 158 gives a consumer the right to know what information is held by the agency in regard to him and ask that it be corrected if it is wrong.

The Act also helps the consumer to find the agency. There are national credit agencies and also local ones. If the consumer knows the name of the agency he can write at any time asking for a copy of any file relating to him. He does not have to be seeking credit at the time. A small fee (as regulations may from time to time provide) is payable (s 158). If a trader is asked for credit the consumer has a right under s 157 to be given the name and address of any agency which the trader intends to contact. The consumer's request must be in writing and made within 28 days after the consumer last dealt with the trader on the matter. The trader has seven working days to supply the information.

A consumer who thinks an entry on the file of a credit agency is wrong and may prejudice him may, under s 159, require the agency to remove or correct it. The agency then has 28 days to say whether or not it has done this. If it has not the consumer can require the agency to put on his file a notice of correction of not more than 200 words which the consumer has drawn up. If the agency will not do this, then either the consumer or the agency may apply to the Director-General of Fair Trading who may make such an order as he thinks fit. Failure to obey the Director-General's order is a criminal offence.

There have been few convictions under this head, but they have occurred in the case of an agency which refused to disclose a file and in the case of a trader who refused to say which agency he was consulting.

### Advertising

Section 56 of the 1974 Act forbids advertisements for credit or hire which are misleading. Regulations made under the Act set out the form which advertisements must take. Under the Consumer Credit (Advertisement) Regulations 1989 (SI 1989/1125) there are three kinds of advertisements about credit as follows.

373

1. *Simple advertisements*. Simple advertisements are those designed just to state that the individual is in the credit business. They include boards at sports events and give-away items, such as pens and matches. For this reason, simple advertisements are only allowed to have a very limited amount of information.

(a) Simple advertisements *may* include:
  (i)   the advertiser's name, which must be the name shown on the consumer credit licence;
  (ii)  the address;
  (iii) the telephone number;
  (iv)  a logo of the advertiser's, of his associate and of his trade association;
  (v)   occupation, e.g. credit broker or finance company.
(b) Other information may be included but *not*:
  (i)   any suggestion that the advertiser or anyone else is willing to provide loans;
  (ii)  any reference to a cash price of anything;
  (iii) any interest rate.

If any of these are included, the advertisement must comply with the detailed provisions that apply to intermediate or full credit advertisements.

2. *Intermediate advertisements*. These advertisements allow some choice of what can be included. Some items are compulsory, some may be included and some are forbidden. Intermediate advertisements must offer to provide written quotations so that clients know how to get all the information they need.

(a) Intermediate advertisements *must* include:
  (i)   name;
  (ii)  address;
  (iii) telephone number (except for an advertisement permanently on trade premises, or in an advertisement including a credit broker's or dealer's name and address).
(b) They *must* include all the following items if they apply to the credit facility being advertised:
  (i)   a statement that the loan may be secured on land plus this warning in capital letters: YOUR HOME IS AT RISK IF YOU DO NOT KEEP UP REPAYMENTS ON A MORTGAGE OR OTHER LOAN SECURED ON IT;
  (ii)  if it is a foreign currency mortgage this warning in capital letters: THE STERLING EQUIVALENT OF YOUR LIABILITY UNDER A FOREIGN CURRENCY MORTGAGE MAY BE INCREASED BY EXCHANGE RATE MOVEMENTS;
  (iii) mention of any other security requirement;
  (iv)  mention of any insurance requirement;
  (v)   mention of any deposit requirement;
  (vi)  a statement so that a debtor can calculate the amount of any credit brokerage fee;
  (vii) a statement that written quotations are available on request;
  (viii) cash price of any goods or services featured and the APR plus a statement, if applicable, that the APR can vary;
  (ix)  if the APR is not given, a statement that the total amount payable is no greater than the cash price.

(c) They *may* include the following:
  (i) details of any security requirements not affecting the borrower's home;
  (ii) the types of credit facility and periods of availability;
  (iii) any restrictions of credit availability;
  (iv) a description of any different treatment between cash and credit buyers;
  (v) the amount, maximum or minimum, of credit available;
  (vi) details of any advance payments needed but only if the APR is given;
  (vii) the APR plus, if appropriate, a statement that it can vary;
  (viii) any rate of interest, but only if the APR is also quoted;
  (ix) name, address and telephone number of the creditor.
(d) They must *not* quote the total amount payable. If the advertisement includes any attempt to give a quotation of the cost, it has to comply with the rules governing full credit advertisements.

3. *Full advertisements*. Full credit advertisements give detailed information about the facilities offered. Much of the information is compulsory and extra information is allowed.

(a) A full advertisement *must* include:
  (i) name;
  (ii) address (except for an advertisement permanently on trade premises, or in an advertisement including a credit broker's or dealer's name and address).
(b) It *must* include all the following items if they apply to the credit facility being advertised:
  (i) a statement that the loan may be secured on land plus this warning in capital letters: YOUR HOME IS AT RISK IF YOU DO NOT KEEP UP REPAYMENTS ON A MORTGAGE OR OTHER LOAN SECURED ON IT;
  (ii) if it is a foreign currency mortgage this warning in capital letters: THE STERLING EQUIVALENT OF YOUR LIABILITY UNDER A FOREIGN CURRENCY MORTGAGE MAY BE INCREASED BY EXCHANGE RATE MOVEMENTS;
  (iii) details of any other security requirement;
  (iv) mention of any insurance requirement;
  (v) mention of any deposit requirement;
  (vi) a statement so that a debtor can calculate the amount of any credit brokerage fee;
  (vii) a statement that written quotations are available on request;
  (viii) cash price of any goods or services featured and the APR plus a statement, if applicable, that the APR can vary;
  (ix) any restrictions of credit availability;*
  (x) a description of any different treatment between cash and credit buyers;*
  (xi) if the APR is not given, a statement that the total amount payable is no greater than the cash price;*
  (xii) for cash loans, or where any interest is charged, the APR plus, if applicable, a statement that it can vary;*
  (xiii) the frequency, number and amount of any advance payments;*
  (xiv) the frequency, number and amount of loan repayments, plus if MIRAS (mortgage interest relief at source) applies, whether the figures are before or after tax relief;*

    (xv)  the total amount payable under the loan agreement including the credit itself and any advance payments;*

    (xvi) details of any other charges payable.*

\* Extra items that must be included in a full advertisement compared with an intermediate advertisement.

### Annual percentage rate (APR)

APR includes the interest on the loan itself *plus* any charges which have had to be paid as a condition of getting the loan, e.g. maintenance charges for a TV set on hire-purchase. The reason why APR is necessary is to make it possible to compare the cost of one type of credit with another. The concept removes problems of comparison which arise from, for example, different periods of payment and different levels of deposit. Credit traders must calculate APR according to standard formulae which are laid down in regulations made under the 1974 Act. It should be noted that simply because APR is expressed as a percentage, it should not be confused with rates of interest. For example, APR 30 per cent does not mean that the consumer will be paying a flat rate of 30 per cent, i.e. £30 on £100 over 12 months.

### Calculating APR

In, say, a purchase of goods, the total charge for credit is divided by the price of the goods, and the resulting figure is looked up on the Consumer Credit Tables. This gives the APR. Thus, in the purchase of a music centre for a cash price of £375, the calculation would be as follows:

(a) *Hire-purchase from Barchester Stores*:    Repayment by 24 monthly instalments of £21.39.

(b) *Borrowing from the Barchester Bank*:    Loan of £375 repayment by 24 monthly instalments of £19.17

    *APR for hire-purchase*:

| | | |
|---|---:|---:|
| Cost of credit = | 24 × £21.39 = | £513.36 |
| | *Less* Cash price | £375.00 |
| | Cost of credit | £138.36 |

$$\text{APR} = \frac{\text{Cost of credit}}{\text{Cash price}} \quad \frac{£138.36}{£375.00} = 0.3690$$

0.3690 in the Consumer Credit Tables gives an APR of 37.3%

    *APR for bank loan*:

| | | |
|---|---:|---:|
| Cost of credit = | 24 × £19.17 = | £460.08 |
| | *Less* Value of loan | £375.00 |
| | Cost of credit | £85.08 |

$$\text{APR} = \frac{\text{Cost of credit}}{\text{Loan}} \quad \frac{£85.08}{£375.00} = 0.2269$$

0.2269 in the Consumer Credit Tables gives an APR of 22.4%

Clearly, the bank loan is the better bet. This is obvious enough from the instalments but the *precise* measure of the difference is given by the APR. APR is of greater assistance in comparing e.g. different repayment periods and different sizes of loan and cash prices. Suppose we are trying to compare the following credit with the two above.

A loan of £500 from a finance house repayable at £34.10 per month over 18 months.

Cost of credit =

$$18 \times £34.10 = £613.80$$
$$Less \text{ Value of loan} \quad \underline{500.00}$$
$$\text{Cost of credit} \quad £113.80$$

$$APR = \frac{\text{Cost of credit}}{\text{Loan}} \quad \frac{£113.80}{£500.00} = 0.2276$$

0.2276 in the Consumer Credit Tables gives an APR of 30.7%

Thus the loan from the bank is the best, the loan from the finance house is second, and the hire-purchase from Barchester Stores is the worst.

### Quotations

Under s 52 those offering credit were required to give a written quotation if the consumer asked for one. The Consumer Credit (Quotations) (Revocation) Regulations 1997 revoke the requirement to give hire-purchase and consumer credit quotations.

## GRADED QUESTIONS

### Essay mode

1 Discuss any *two* of the following provisions of the Consumer Credit Act 1974:
   (a) Section 75 of the Act which imposes liability on 'connected lenders';
   (b) Part III of the Act which is concerned with the licensing of persons involved in the provision of credit;
   (c) Sections 67–73 of the Act under which consumer credit agreements may be cancelled by the customer in certain circumstances.
   
   *(The Institute of Chartered Secretaries and Administrators)*

2 (a) How does a hire-purchase contract differ from:
      (i)  a credit sale contract, and
      (ii) a conditional sale contract?
   (b) Henry buys a second-hand car from Ian after reading Ian's advertisement in the local newspaper. Henry pays Ian in cash the £2,500 agreed price and takes delivery of the car. A week later Henry is visited by a representative of the Automobile Finance Company who informs him that the car is the subject of a hire-purchase agreement with Ian who has not paid all the instalments. Henry refuses to surrender the car.
      Discuss the legal position.
      
      *(The Institute of Company Accountants)*

3 *Either*:

(a) The Consumer Credit Act 1974 contains provisions which attempt to protect consumers from being induced by misleading or incomplete information, or by pressure sales techniques, into committing themselves to a credit agreement from which they will then be unable to escape without substantial loss.

Outline these provisions and comment on their effectiveness.

*Or*:

(b) Four months ago Ben entered into a hire-purchase agreement for a dining-room suite, total hire-purchase price £900. The deposit was £300 with 24 monthly instalments of £25. He has paid four of these instalments, but has now lost his job, so will have great difficulty in keeping up the payments. He is considering the idea of selling the suite for cash and hoping that with this money and the hope of getting another job he will be able to pay off the debt. Unfortunately the table has been badly scratched, so the value of the suite has diminished considerably.

Advise Ben of his legal position and suggest possible courses of action.

*(Staffordshire University. LLB (Hons): Consumer Law)*

## Objective mode

Four alternative answers are given. Select ONE only. Circle the answer which you consider to be correct. Check your answers by referring back to the information given in the relevant chapter and against the answers at the back of the book.

*With reference to the following information answer questions 1 to 3.*

Snooks had a 1993 Austin Metro on hire-purchase from Motor Finance Ltd. In January, when returning from a party, he scraped the vehicle on the wall of a hump-backed bridge causing considerable damage to the near-side wing and door.

The following day when Snooks was surveying the damage outside his lodgings he was approached by Sharp, a student, who said it would 'cost a bomb' to repair the car and that he would take it off Snooks' hands for £50. Snooks agreed to sell and Sharp asked him whether the car was on hire-purchase; Snooks said it wasn't.

To prove the point, Snooks went to his room and produced a receipt from Vehicle Finance Ltd for £6 dated some three months earlier. Across the receipt was written 'Final Payment'. This receipt related to an earlier hire-purchase transaction in respect of another vehicle which Snooks had owned.

Later the same day Sharp gave Snooks £50 for the car and was given a receipt in the following terms:

> I, Snooks, hereby confirm the said vehicle, Austin Metro L113 PJC, is not covered by any HP agreement whatsoever, and I accept the sum of £50 from Mr Sharp in absolute payment for the above-named vehicle.

Sharp repaired the car and in February sold it to a dealer, Pedlar, who later in the month sold it to another dealer, Hawker.

On 1 March, while the vehicle was in Hawker's possession, an agent of Motor Finance Ltd saw it and on 4 March the company sent men to claim it from Hawker. They brought with them a letter from the company in the following terms:

You have purported to acquire the above vehicle which is the property of this company under a rental agreement with one J. Snooks of Barchester. The bearer of this letter has instructions to collect our property forthwith, and legal proceedings will be taken against any person attempting to prevent him from carrying out these instructions.

Hawker let the men take the car and intends to sue Pedlar for damages. Pedlar has said that he will bring Sharp into the action and claim damages from him. Snooks has left his lodgings and cannot be found. Examination of the legal position is required.

1 One of the following is relevant to the success or otherwise of the claims by Hawker against Pedlar and Pedlar against Sharp. Select:

A Sale of Goods Act 1979.
B Misrepresentation.
C Hire Purchase Act 1964.
D Mercantile Law Amendment Act 1856.

2 Only one of the following remedies or actions is available to compensate Motor Finance Ltd. Select:

A To repossess the vehicle from Hawker.
B To sue Pedlar.
C To sue Sharp.
D To sue Snooks.

3 Which one of the following is the owner of the vehicle?

A Pedlar.
B Hawker.
C Sharp.
D Motor Finance Ltd.

4 The Consumer Credit Act 1974 applies to all contracts as defined by it if the debtor is not a corporation and if the total credit does not exceed:

A £2,000.
B £300.
C £500.
D £25,000.

5 Protected goods are goods hired out under a regulated agreement under which at least one of the following fractions of the price has been paid or tendered and which has not been terminated by the debtor. Select:

A One-third.
B One-half.
C Two-thirds.
D Three-quarters.

6 Fred had a stereo on hire-purchase from Crafty Finance Ltd. The total credit was £240 and Fred agreed to pay £20 per month. Fred has terminated the agreement and returned the stereo. He had paid two instalments and terminated before the third was due. Unless the court decides otherwise or the agreement provides to the contrary, Fred must pay Crafty Finance Ltd:

**A** Nothing.
**B** £80.
**C** £20.
**D** £200.

*The answers to questions set in objective mode appear on p 708.*

# 15 EMPLOYMENT I

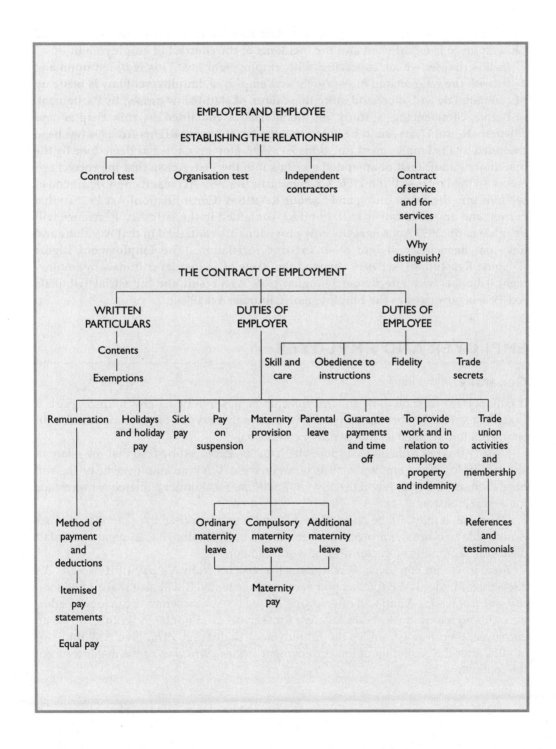

The objectives of this chapter are to explain how the relationship of employer and employee is established and the incidents of the contract of employment.

In this chapter we are concerned with employment law. This is based upon and deals with the relationship of employer and employee. Employment law is made up of common law and, more and more these days, of statute law passed by Parliament.

Before commencing a study of the materials contained in this chapter and Chapters 16 and 17, it should be noted that the Employment Rights Act 1996 has been amended by the Employment Relations Act 1999. However, this has been done by the insertion of additional or amended sections into the 1996 Act so that the correct reference to the law is still the 1996 Act. Similarly, the 1999 Act inserts new or amended sections into the Trade Union and Labour Relations (Consolidation) Act 1992 so that current and amended law is still, in effect, contained in the 1992 Act. Reference will be made to the 1999 Act where the new provisions are contained in that Act alone and have not been inserted into other existing legislation. (The Employment Rights (Dispute Resolution) Act 1998 changed the name of industrial tribunals to employment tribunals with effect from 1 August 1998. As a result, the Industrial Tribunals Act 1996 is now cited as the Employment Tribunals Act 1996.)

## EMPLOYER AND EMPLOYEE

### Generally

It is important to know how this relationship comes into being and to distinguish it from the relationship between a person who buys the services of someone who is self-employed (often called an independent contractor).

Usually it is not difficult to decide whether A is employed by B so that the relationship of employee and employer exists between them. If A is an employee he or she will have been *selected* by B; A will usually work *full-time* for B under a degree of *supervision* for a *wage or salary*.

Of course, A may still be an employee even though working *part time*. A part-timer is now able to claim the protection of employment legislation, e.g. in regard to unfair dismissal, regardless of the number of working hours.

Also, if A is an employee, B will deduct *income tax* from A's pay (if it exceeds A's allowances) under PAYE (pay as you earn) arrangements. B will also make *social security contributions* for A and will often provide a *pension scheme* which A can join. In addition, although a contract of employment (or service) need not be in writing, if A is an employee, then B must, under the Employment Rights Act 1996, give A within two months after the beginning of the employment *written particulars* of the major terms of the contract.

## The control test

In earlier times the above tests would not all have been available, particularly the deduction of income tax which, after some earlier experiments beginning in 1799, was finally brought in for good in 1842. Social security legislation and the modern deductions from pay, together with contributions from the employer, have only come in on the present scale since the Second World War.

In times past, therefore, a person, whether employed or self-employed, would simply receive money from the employer and it was less easy to distinguish one from the other.

There was, even so, a need to do so, because an employer was liable to pay damages to those injured by his employee if those injuries took place during the course of the employee's work. This is called an *employer's vicarious liability*.

A person was not vicariously liable for injury caused to others by a self-employed (or independent) contractor who was doing work for him. Obviously, then, it was necessary to find a test to decide whether A was, or was not, an employee of B.

The earliest test was called 'the control test'. Since it is not normally necessary to use this test today in order to decide whether A is the employee of B because we have much more evidence of the relationship now, why should we bother with it?

The answer is that it is sometimes necessary to decide whether B, who is truly employed by A, has been temporarily transferred to another person, C, so that C (the temporary employer) and not A (the general employer) is liable vicariously for the injuries caused to a person or persons by B.

**The following case provides an illustration.**

## Mersey Docks and Harbour Board v Coggins & Griffiths (Liverpool) Ltd [1947] AC 1

The Board owned and hired out mobile cranes driven by skilled operators who were employees of the Board. Coggins & Griffiths, who were stevedores, hired one of the Board's cranes and an operator, Mr Newell, to unload a ship.

In the course of unloading the ship, a person was injured because of Mr Newell's negligence and the court had to decide whether the Board or Coggins & Griffiths were vicariously liable along with Mr Newell for the latter's negligence. The matter was one of control because the Board was quite clearly the general employer. Actually, the answers given by Mr Newell to questions put to him by counsel in court were highly important. At one point he said: 'I take no orders from anybody'. Since he was not truly employed by Coggins & Griffiths *and* since he did not, so he said, take orders from them, there was no way in which he could be regarded as under their control. Therefore, his true employers, the Board, were vicariously liable for Mr Newell's negligence.

*Comment:* It is *presumed* in these cases that the general employer continues to be liable and it is up to him to satisfy the court that control has passed to a temporary employer. This is a very difficult thing to do and the temporary employer will not be liable very often, though it is a possibility.

## The organisation test

Later on a test called the 'organisation or integration' test was brought in because the control test was not necessarily suitable for employees who were highly skilled.

There was a possibility that even though there was a lot of general evidence of employment, such as PAYE deductions from pay, an employer would not be vicariously liable for the acts of a highly skilled employee, such as a doctor, or, really, anyone qualified and experienced and acting in a professional field, if that employer could convince the court in his defence that he did not have the necessary control of the skilled person.

This has not been possible because of the organisation test put forward by Lord Denning in *Stevenson, Jordan & Harrison Ltd* v *Macdonald & Evans Ltd* [1952] 1 TLR 101. He decided in that case, in effect, that an employee is a person who is integrated with others in the workplace or business, even though the employer does not have a detailed control of what he does.

## Independent contractors – the self-employed

The main feature here is the absence of control or meaningful supervision which can be exercised by those who buy the services of an independent contractor by means of what is called a *contract for services*.

## Particular cases examined

In the majority of cases there is no difficulty in deciding whether a person is employed or self-employed. For example, factory employees, office clerical staff and agricultural workers are clearly employees. Garage proprietors, house-builders and dry cleaners are contractors independent of the members of the public who use them.

A particularly compelling example comes from a comparison between a chauffeur and a person who owns and drives his own taxi. The chauffeur is an employee; the taxi-driver is an independent contractor. Suppose, then, that Fred is employed as my chauffeur: I would have enough control over him to ask him to drive more slowly in a built-up area. In the case of the taxi-driver, I would not have (or even feel I had) the necessary control to insist on a change of speed.

## Contract of service or for services – why distinguish?

First of all, because of the existence of *vicarious liability*, an employer is liable, for example, for damage caused to another by his employee's negligent acts while that employee is acting in the course of his employment, that is, doing his job, but not otherwise.

Secondly, the *rights and remedies provided by employment legislation*, such as the Employment Rights Act 1996, are available to an employee, but not to the self-employed. We shall be looking at these rights and remedies more closely later in this chapter.

# THE CONTRACT OF EMPLOYMENT

## Generally

The ordinary principles of the law of contract apply. So in a contract of employment there must be an offer and an acceptance, which is in effect, the agreement. There must also be an intention to create legal relations, consideration and capacity, together with proper consent by the parties, that is, no mistake, misrepresentation, duress or undue influence. In addition, the contract must not be illegal.

However, since we have already looked at these general principles of the law of contract, it is only necessary to highlight certain matters which are of importance in the context of employment law.

## Written particulars

A contract of employment does not require any written formalities and can be made orally. However, certain written particulars of it are required to be given to the employee by the Employment Rights Act 1996 (ERA) following consolidation of earlier legislation from 1978. Employees have a right to receive a written statement of particulars of employment once they have been employed for two months. A main exception relates to employees whose employment is for less than one month. The statement can be given within the first two months of employment if the employer wishes but need not be given to those who are to be employed for less than one month. The employee may take the employer to an employment tribunal if the statement has not been received by the end of the two-month period (ERA 1996, s 1).

It is also worth noting that there may be no right to a statement where the person concerned works what is called a 'zero-hours' arrangement. Under such an arrangement the worker is on call, if available, as and when required by the employer, and such an arrangement may not give rise to a contract of employment. However, in *Carmichael* v *National Power plc* [1998] ICR 1167 the Court of Appeal decided that a group of women who worked as guides at power stations and were called on to do so as required were employees and entitled to written particulars. The court said that from the *facts of the case* there was a mutual obligation to provide work from time to time and to undertake that work as required. There will be cases that go the other way (*see*, for example, *Clark* v *Oxfordshire Health Authority* [1998] IRLR 125, where the Court of Appeal *on the facts* decided that there was no mutual obligation to provide work and do work in the case of nurses in a 'nurse bank', though in that case the 'zero-hours' arrangement stated that the nurses were 'not regular employees and had no entitlement to guaranteed or continuous work'. Nevertheless, the *Carmichael* case is a bit of a blow to those 'employers' who seek to avoid employment rights by these 'zero-hours' arrangements.

### Contents – generally

The statement must contain the following information.

(a) *The names of the employer and the employee.* A letter of engagement will usually be sent to the employee at his address. This will identify him and the letter-heading will identify the employer.
(b) *The date when the employment began.* This is important if it becomes necessary to decide what period of notice is to be given. The 1996 Act provides for certain minimum periods of notice to be given by employers. For example, they must give one week's notice after four weeks' service, two weeks' after two years' service, and so on up to 12 weeks' notice after 12 years' service (*see further* Chapter 17). The date when the job began obviously settles this point.

In addition, the length of the employment affects the period necessary to make certain claims. For example, redundancy claims require two years' continuous service *since the age of 18.* Unfair dismissal requires one year of continuous service (*see* the Unfair Dismissal and Statement of Reasons for Dismissal (Variation of Qualifying Period) Order 1999), with some exceptions which will be noted, usually with a particular employer (but *see below*), regardless of the age at which the service began, unless the dismissal is automatically unfair, as where it was e.g. because the employee was (or proposed to become) a member of a trade union.

(c) *Whether the employment counts as a period of continuous employment with a previous employment, and the date of commencement of the previous employment where this is so.* This is important because the rights of an employee to complain of unfair dismissal, or to claim a redundancy payment, depend upon whether that employee has served the necessary period of continuous employment. This may be with one employer, but if it is with more than one employer, it must be possible to regard the employments with the various employers as continuous. Situations of continuous employment, despite a change of employer, taken from the Employment Rights Act 1996, are:

(i) *A transfer between associated employers.* For example, if A is employed by B Ltd and is transferred to work for C Ltd, and B Ltd and C Ltd are subsidiaries of X plc, then A's employment with B Ltd and C Ltd is regarded as continuous.

(ii) *A sale of the business in which the employee was employed to another person.* There are other provisions which now relate to this situation and protect employees from a break in continuous employment on a change of employer. The Transfer of Undertakings (Protection of Employment) Regulations 1981 apply. The main provisions of the Regulations in regard to the transfer of a business are that employees who are employed by the old employer 'immediately before' the transfer automatically become the employees of the new employer. The new employer takes over the employment protection liabilities of the old employer, but not, according to *Angus Jowett & Co v NUTWG* [1985] IRLR 326, liability to pay a protective award. A protective award is payable when an employer fails to consult with a recognised trade union or worker representatives when he is intending to make the workforce or some part of it redundant (*see further* Chapter 17). So, if A gives notice of future redundancy to his employees without proper consultation with their union or worker representatives and they are still working for him when he sells the business to B, then A and not B is liable to pay the protective award.

## Employment immediately before transfer

There has been some difficulty with regard to the interpretation of the words 'immediately before'. Administrative receivers who took over insolvent companies on behalf of secured creditors, such as banks, used this when selling off the company. Purchasers would normally insist as a condition of buying the company that all employees be dismissed before the transfer. The administrative receiver concerned would, therefore, see that the employees were dismissed sometimes only one hour before the contract of purchase was signed. In cases brought by the employees for unfair dismissal or a redundancy payment, the court had ruled that they were not transferred and must bring their claims against the insolvent transferor company with little prospect of success since the purchase money would normally be taken by secured creditors, such as banks, to pay off debts owed to them.

However, in *Litster* v *Forth Dry Dock and Engineering Co Ltd* [1989] 1 All ER 1134 the House of Lords *held* that an employee dismissed shortly before the transfer of business for a reason connected with the transfer, e.g. purchaser insistence, was to be regarded as being employed 'immediately before' the transfer so that employment protection liabilities were transferred to the purchaser. This is a fairer interpretation of the Regulations, but it will make it more difficult to sell off insolvent companies.

## Commercial venture

The above Regulations excluded transfer of undertakings not in the nature of a 'commercial venture'. This seemed to exclude the contracting out of services by government, local authorities and the NHS, so that employees' contract rights were not transferred to the new provider of the service. This greatly assisted the privatisation of public services since the attraction and profitability of these privatisation schemes often depends as much on the private contractor's being able to change the terms of employment – sometimes for the worse – as it does upon the alleged efficiency of the new private-sector management. Following amendments made to the Regulations in 1993, the commercial venture requirement was abolished and so public-sector outsourcing of services is covered.

## Transfer of economic entity

The public-sector exclusion was in any case out of line with the EC Transfers Directive which the UK Regulations were supposed to implement. In addition, it was thought that there must be the transfer of an 'economic entity' involving the transfer of property with the workforce. There have since been a number of decisions, particularly those of *Rask and Christensen* v *ISS Kantineservice A/S* [1993] 464 IRLB 12 (European Court of Justice) and *Dines* v *Initial Health Care Services* [1993] IRLR 521 (Court of Appeal), which decided that transfer of property was not necessary and that the 'economic entity' test was too restrictive. The *Rask* case involved the contracting-out of a canteen service. The new provider ran the service for the company 'in-house' as before and the service was provided exclusively for the company as before and for a fixed fee. Nevertheless, the ECJ held that the transaction was covered by the EC Transfers Directive. Since amendments made to the Regulations in 1993, it is no longer necessary for there to be a transfer of 'property'. This is in line with the *Rask* decision.

## Second-generation contractors

The cases referred to above apply to first-generation contractors, i.e. in an outsourcing of services to the first private contractor. If that first-generation contractor is replaced by another (or second-generation) contractor, the position may be different. In the *Süzen* case [1997] IRLR 255 the European Court stated that there will not be a transfer of economic activity merely because the incoming contractor was carrying out a similar economic activity as the outgoing contractor. There has to be a transfer of significant tangible and intangible assets, or by the new employer taking over a major part of the workforce.

The decision had an impact in the UK in *Betts v Brintel Helicopters* [1997] 2 All ER 840 where the Court of Appeal adopted the reasoning in *Süzen* and held that there was no transfer when Shell changed the supplier of its helicopter transport contract from Brintel to KLM. The ramifications of this case are that a first-generation contractor may find himself faced with redundancy costs which he would previously have expected to pass on to the new and second-generation contractor.

The quite dramatic effect of the *Süzen* ruling is also seen in the decision of the EAT in *Superclean Support Services plc v Lansana* [1997] 579 IRLB 11, where there was a change in the contractor providing cleaning services to Imperial College, London. It was held that, in the absence of a transfer of assets or employees to the new contractor, *Süzen* must be applied and no relevant transfer had taken place under the UK Regulations. Superclean was not obliged to take on Mr Lansana, who had been employed by the former contractor, and was not liable to him for not doing so. The question of whether Mr Lansana's dismissal by his former employer was unfair was referred to a fresh tribunal for hearing.

The insistence on the requirement in *Süzen* that employees actually be transferred was downplayed in *ECM (Vehicle Delivery Services) Ltd v Cox* [1998] 596 IRLB 8, where the EAT held that an incoming contractor taking over from the original contractor could not avoid the application of the 1981 Regulations merely by refusing to take on the outgoing contractor's employees. By doing so, the incoming contractor was held to have unfairly dismissed them.

The ERA provides that an employee who does not wish to transfer may tell the old or new employer this and his contract terminates. He is not unfairly dismissed or redundant. If he wants notice, he should transfer and give notice to the new employer, who may make a payment in lieu.

## Summary

The *broad* effect of the Regulations is, therefore, that the transferee of the business is liable for pre-transfer dismissals which cannot be justified (see *Stirling District Council v Allan* [1995] 520 IRLB 16) and in a claim for unfair dismissal the transferee inherits the transferor's reasons for dismissal, good or bad (*BSG Property Services v Tuck* [1996] 542 IRLB 9). Also, sex discrimination claims, even if based on the conduct of the transferor, can be made against the transferee (*DJM International Ltd v Nicholas*, *The Times*, 22 November 1995). These decisions may lead future transferees of a business to try to obtain from the transferors an indemnity regarding such claims as part of the sale and transfer agreement. It should be noted that the European Commission's latest draft of a Directive which will amend the EC Business Transfer Directive will make it mandatory for member states to provide for the transferor and transferee to be jointly liable in respect of employment liabilities which are incurred before the transfer.

## Consultation on transfer

There is also a requirement in the Collective Redundancies and Transfer of Undertakings (Protection of Employment) (Amendment) Regulations 1995 (SI 1995/2587) that the employer must consult with 'appropriate representatives', i.e. union or worker representatives, even if only one person is to be transferred.

Further details of these Regulations appear in Chapter 17 as part of the wider context of consultation on redundancy, though consultation is required on transfer whether there are to be redundancies or not. In particular, the employer must explain what measures the transferee and himself intend to take in regard to the employee(s) to be transferred.

(iii) *A change in the partners where a person is employed by a partnership.* A partnership is not a separate person at law as a company is. Employees of a partnership are employed by the partners as people. So, if A works for a partnership of C and D, and D retires and is replaced by E, then A's employers have changed but his employment with C and D and C and E is regarded as continuous. Therefore, if C and E unfairly dismiss A he can make up his one year's continuous service to be able to claim by adding together his service with C and D and C and E in order to make a claim against C and E.

(iv) *A succession of contracts between the same parties is regarded as continuous.* So, if A works for B as a clerk and is then promoted to a manager under a new contract, the two contract periods can be added together to make a period of continuous employment.

On a general note it is worth mentioning that the Employment Appeal Tribunal decided in *Colley* v *Corkingdale t/a Corker's Lounge Bar* [1996] 542 IRLB 8 that the requirement of continuous service (or employment) necessary to make a claim for unfair dismissal could be established by a contract under which Miss Colley worked only alternate weeks.

### Contents – terms of the employment

The written particulars then go on to set out the terms of the employment. The terms which must be given are:

(a) the scale or rate of pay and the method of calculating pay where the employee is paid by commission or bonus;

(b) when payment is made – that is weekly or monthly – and the day or date of payment;

(c) hours to be worked, e.g. 'The normal working hours are . . . '. Compulsory overtime, if any, should be recorded to avoid disputes with employees who may sometimes not want to work it. It should, of course, be borne in mind that the Working Time Regulations (SI 1998/1833) provide for a maximum 48-hour working week averaged over 17 weeks, except where the individual has specifically opted out;

(d) holiday entitlement and provisions relating to holiday pay if the employee leaves in a particular year without taking a holiday. If holiday entitlement is set out clearly, it can help to avoid disputes regarding a requirement to work in what is a normal holiday period in the area or during the school holidays. It must, of course, be borne in mind that the Working Time Regulations give at least three weeks of paid annual leave, rising to four weeks after 23 November 1999;

(e) sick pay and injury arrangements must be set out;

(f) whether or not there is a pension scheme;

(g) the length of notice which the employee must give and the length of notice the employee is entitled to receive. We have already said that there are minimum periods of notice required to end contracts of employment and full details of these appear in Chapter 17. The contract can, of course, provide for a longer period of notice but not a shorter one;

(h) the job title, which is important in dealing with redundancy cases where to justify that a dismissal is because of redundancy and is not an unfair dismissal, the employer may show that there has been a reduction in 'work of a particular type'. The job title indicates what type of work the employee does. In equal pay claims, also, it may show that a man or woman is employed on 'like work'. Under the ERA 1996 amendments the employer can give a brief job description instead of a job title.

(i) In 1993 (*see* now ERA 1996), new items were added to the required particulars as follows:
  – the duration of temporary contracts;
  – work location or locations;
  – collective agreements affecting the job;
  – where the job requires work outside the UK for more than one month, the period of such work; the currency in which the employee will be paid and any other pay or benefits provided by reason of working outside the UK. Employees who begin work outside the UK within two months of starting must have the statement before leaving the UK.

Particulars can be given in instalments, provided that all are given within two months. However, there must be a 'principal statement' in one document giving the following information:

  – the identities of the parties;
  – the date when the employment began;
  – where the employment counts as a period of continuous employment with a previous one, a statement that this is so and the date when it began;
  – the amount and frequency of pay, e.g. weekly or monthly;
  – the hours of work;
  – holiday entitlement;
  – job title (or description);
  – work location.

Certain particulars can be given by reference to a document, e.g. a collective agreement with a trade union, but any such document must be readily accessible to the employee. These particulars are pension arrangements, sickness provisions, notice entitlement and details of disciplinary matters and grievance procedures.

*Disciplinary procedures* deal, for example, with the number of warnings – oral or written – which will be given before suspension or dismissal. *Grievance procedures* relate to complaints in regard to any aspect of the employment with which the employee is not satisfied. The employee should be told to whom to complain and any right of appeal beyond that, say, to more senior management. This procedure must be available if the employee is not satisfied with the disciplinary decision or for other grievances. Employers who along with associated employers have fewer than 20 employees are exempt from the need to provide disciplinary procedures but must give the name of a person to whom a grievance complaint can be made. This exemption can be found in s 3 of the Employment Rights Act 1996. Presumably if the number of employees grows to 20 or more the employer must set up disciplinary procedures and notify the employees of them, but the matter is not dealt with specifically in the legislation.

### Changes in the particulars

Changes which must be given to the employee in writing as soon as possible and in any case not later than one month after the change may also be given by reference to a document, e.g. a collective agreement which is readily accessible, provided a similar document was used to give the original information.

## Terms of employment – collective agreements

If the terms of the employment can be changed by a collective agreement with a trade union, the particulars should say so because if this is the case, the terms of the job can be changed *without* the employee's consent. The results of the employer's negotiations with the unions are incorporated into the contracts of the employees, and become binding as between employer and employee even though the agreement between the employer and the trade union is 'binding in honour only' (*Marley* v *Forward Trust Group Ltd* [1986)] IRLR 369).

In other cases, the terms of the employment cannot be changed unless the employee has agreed and if the employer introduces a variation in the contract as by, say, lowering pay, then the employer is in breach of the contract.

It was *held* in *Rigby* v *Ferodo Ltd* [1987] IRLR 516 that an employee can sue successfully for damages from his employer where he has suffered a cut in pay to which neither he nor his union has agreed.

## Failure to comply with the obligation to give written particulars

Section 11 of the 1996 Act provides that if an employer fails to give written particulars in the time scale required, or fails to notify changes in the terms of the contract, the employee can go to an employment tribunal. If a statement is given but the employee thinks it is not complete, either the employee or the employer can go to an employment tribunal to see which of them is right.

The tribunal may make a declaration that the employee has a right to a statement and also say what should be in it. The statement as approved by the tribunal is then assumed in law to have been given by the employer to the employee and forms the basis of the contract of employment. Failure to give written particulars does not make the contract of employment unenforceable by the parties.

As regards claims before tribunals regarding written particulars, the Court of Appeal held in *Eagland* v *British Telecom plc* [1992] IRLR 323 that a tribunal could not merely invent terms. Section 2(1) of the Employment Rights Act 1996 (ERA) allows the employer to give no details if none exist, provided that the statement says so, at least under the non-mandatory headings, such as holiday pay, sick pay and pensions. It would, therefore, be wrong of a tribunal to invent terms in these areas and force them as implied terms on an employer who had not agreed to them and where there was no inference of agreement from the conduct of the parties.

However, in the case of mandatory terms which s 1 of the ERA requires to be stated in the written particulars, such as remuneration and hours of work, the Court of Appeal said that it would be exceptional if the evidence did not allow a tribunal to make an inference of agreement or to identify an agreement from the evidence. However, if this were not possible, the tribunal might have to imply one. This seems a fair approach. It must be rare indeed to find a contract of employment in which there is no intention to pay wages!

Written particulars are a right of the employee not a mere entitlement. Therefore, they must be given whether the employee asks for them or not (*Coales* v *John Wood (Solicitors)* [1986] IRLR 129). Even so, an employee has a right to request a statement if he has never had one or it is out of date. Dismissal for asserting this right is unfair, regardless of service and hours worked, under s 104 of the ERA.

### Health and safety

The Health and Safety at Work Act 1974 states that an employer must prepare, and revise when necessary, a statement of his policy in regard to the health and safety at work of his employees. This must be contained in a separate document but it is often given out with the written particulars which are now being considered. Employers with fewer than five employees are not required to give this statement.

### Sample statement of written particulars of terms of employment

Figure 15.1 *below* provides a sample letter setting out terms of employment suitable for a secretary with a firm of publishers having 18 members of staff in all. The employee should be required to sign the employer's copy in the following way:

> *I have received and read a copy of the above particulars which are correct in all respects.*
> *Signed Jane Doe*
> *Date 9 March 2000.*

### Exemptions from the written particulars requirements

There are some situations under the ERA where an employer does not have to give the written particulars. Those which may be found in the average business are as follows:

(a) employees with fully written contracts containing all the necessary items need not be given also the written particulars;
(b) it is not necessary to give an employee written particulars if he or she is employed for a specific job, e.g. to clear a backlog of office work, which is not expected to last more than one month. If it does last for more than one month the worker is entitled to written particulars.

It should be noted that certain of the former exceptions, e.g. that there was no need for particulars where the employee was the husband or wife of the employer, have been repealed.

To:     Ms Jane Doe
        350 Elton Road
        Manchester M62 10AS

The following particulars are given to you pursuant to the Employment Rights Act 1996.

1.  The parties are as follows:
    Name and address of Employer:     Michael Snooks Ltd
                                      520 London Square
                                      Manchester M42 14SA

    Name and address of Employee:     Jane Doe
                                      350 Elton Road
                                      Manchester M62 10AS

2.  The date when your employment began was 2 February 2000.
    Your employment with John Bloggs Ltd from whom Michael Snooks Ltd purchased the business and which began on 3 February 1997 counts as part of your period of continuous employment with Michael Snooks Ltd. No employment with a previous employer counts as part of your period of continuous employment.

3.  The following are the particulars of the terms of your employment as at 9 March 2000.
    (a)  You are employed at 520 London Square, Manchester, M42 14SA, as a secretary in the Educational Publishing Department.
    (b)  The rate of your remuneration is £300 per week.
    (c)  Your remuneration is paid at weekly intervals.
    (d)  Your normal working hours are from 9.30 am to 5 pm, Mondays to Fridays inclusive.
    (e)  (i)    You are entitled to four weeks' holiday with pay after one completed year of service and to five weeks' holiday with pay every year after two completed years of service. These holidays are to be taken at a time convenient to the employer between 1 May and 30 October in each year. If an employee's employment terminates before all holiday accrued due has been taken, the employee is entitled to payment in lieu thereof on leaving the said employment. You are also entitled to the customary holidays with pay, i.e. New Year's Day, Good Friday, Easter Monday, May Day, Spring Bank Holiday, Late Summer Bank Holiday, Christmas Day and Boxing Day.
         (ii)   Regulations as to payment while absent during sickness or injury are available for inspection during normal working hours in the office of the secretary/PA to the Personnel Manager.
         (iii)  There is no pension scheme applicable to you.
    (f)  The length of notice which you are obliged to give to end your contract of employment is one week and the length of notice you are entitled to receive unless your conduct is such that you may be summarily dismissed is as follows:
         (i)    One week if your period of continuous employment is less than two years;
         (ii)   One week for each year of continuous employment if your period of continuous employment is two years or more but less than 12 years; and
         (iii)  Twelve weeks if your period of continuous employment is 12 years or more.
    (g)  There are no collective agreements which affect the terms and conditions of the employment.
    (h)  There is no requirement for work outside the United Kingdom.

NOTE
If you are not satisfied with any disciplinary decision relating to you or seek redress of any grievance relating to your employment, you can apply in the first place to the publisher, Educational Publishing Department. Details of the procedure available and to be followed in connection with your employment are posted in the staff room.

Date ninth day of March 2000.

                            Signed
                            Sarah Snooks
                            Company Secretary

**Fig. 15.1  Sample statement of written particulars of terms of employment**

# RIGHTS AND DUTIES OF THE PARTIES TO THE CONTRACT

The duties of an employer and an employee come from common law Acts of Parliament and delegated legislation, e.g. Regulations and orders. They will be dealt with under the headings which follow.

## DUTIES OF AN EMPLOYER

### To comply with the Working Time Regulations

The Working Time Regulations 1998 (SI 1998/1833) came into force on 1 October 1998. They enact the European Working Time Directive (93/104). From that date there are detailed rules which govern hours of work and entitlement to paid holidays as set out below:

- a maximum 48-hour working week, averaged over 17 weeks;
- at least three weeks of paid annual leave, rising to four weeks from 23 November 1999;
- a daily rest period of at least 11 consecutive hours between each working day;
- a weekly rest period of at least 24 hours in each seven-day period. This may be averaged over a two-week period, i.e. a worker is entitled to 48 hours' rest in 14 days;
- an in-work rest break of 20 minutes for those working more than six hours a day. This should not be taken at either the start or the end of a working day and should not overlap with a worker's daily rest period;
- the normal hours of night workers should not exceed an average of eight hours for each 24 hours over a 17-week period.

### Who is a worker?

Generally speaking, a worker is a person employed under a contract of service, but the majority of agency workers will be included as will trainees who are engaged on work experience. The Regulations also apply in part to domestic employees though the working time limits do not apply but they are entitled to the rest breaks, rest periods and paid annual leave. Those who are genuinely self-employed are not covered.

### What is working time?

*Working time* is defined by the Working Time Regulations (WTR) as when a worker is working at his employer's disposal and carrying out his duty or activities. *Training time* is included but, according to DTI Guidance, time when a worker is 'on call' but is otherwise free to pursue his own activities or is sleeping would not be working time. Lunch breaks spent at leisure would not be working time, but working lunches and working breakfasts would be. Travelling to and from a place of work is unlikely to be working time. The Regulations usefully allow workers or their representatives and employers to make agreements to add to the definition of working time.

### The 48-hour week

The law does not say that employees cannot work more than 48 hours in any one week. The 48-hour limit is averaged over a 'reference period' which will generally be a 17-week rolling period, in the absence of any other agreement. This gives a certain amount of flexibility for businesses to cope with surges in demand, so long as the average over the whole reference per period is not exceeded.

The reference period may be increased to 26 weeks if the worker is a special case, as in hospital work, or where there is a foreseeable surge of activity as in agriculture, tourism and postal services. The reference period can be increased to 52 weeks by a workforce agreement (*see below*) or by individual agreement with the employer (*see below*).

A High Court judge has ruled that all contracts of employment should be read as providing that an employee should not work more than an average of 48 hours in any week during the 17-week working time reference period, unless the relevant employee has opted out in writing. The judge also ruled that if the average hours are equalled or exceeded during the reference period, an employee may refuse to work *at all* during the remainder of the period until the working hours come down to the required level. (*See Barber and Others* v *RJB Mining (UK) Ltd* [1999] 613 IRLB 16.)

Mr Justice Gage gave his ruling in a case brought by five members of the pit deputies' union NACODS against RJB Mining, their employer. They had all been required to carry on working, although they had all worked in excess of 816 hours in the 17-week reference period. The judge also granted them an injunction (breach of which by the employer could lead to sanctions of contempt of court) to the effect that they could refuse to work any more during a 17-week reference period where the 48-hour average had been equalled or exceeded. The decision could present a number of employers with major problems, particularly in terms of staff in key areas. They could face the prospect of a number of workers being able to refuse to do any more work until their hours came down to the required level.

### Paid annual leave

The right to paid annual leave arises after 13 weeks' employment. The entitlement is to three weeks of leave, rising incrementally to four weeks from 23 November 1999. The Regulations should be referred to, but where a worker's leave year starts on 1 January and he or she works five days a week, the leave entitlement under the Regulations would be, given that there are 39 days between 23 November 1999 and the start of a new leave year, $5 \times 39$ divided by 365 (the days in the year) = 0.53. This is rounded up to one day and means that the worker is entitled to 16 days' paid annual leave for the leave year 1999 and four weeks (or 20 days) thereafter. This is not additional to contractual entitlements so that taking contractual paid leave in a particular leave year counts against the worker's entitlement under the Regulations. In the absence of any agreement, the employer can require a worker to take all or any of the leave at specified times, subject to giving the worker notice of at least twice the period of the leave to be taken. The worker is also required to give notice to the employer of the wish to take leave. The notice period must again be at least twice the period of the leave to be taken.

### Length of night work

Night work is presumed to be work between 11 pm and 6 am, unless otherwise defined by agreement.

### Excluded sectors

The Regulations, other than those parts which apply to young workers (*see below*), do not currently apply to workers who are employed in the following sectors:

- air transport;
- rail;
- road transport;
- sea transport;
- inland waterway and lake transport;
- sea fishing;
- other work at sea, e.g. offshore work in the oil and gas industry.

The Regulations, do not apply to the activities of doctors in training but the European Commission is to bring forward proposals in regard to this sector. The Regulations do not apply to the activities of specific services, such as the police or the armed forces.

In this connection, an agreement has been reached between EU employers and employee organisations to extend the Working Time Directive to rail and maritime transport workers. The agreement in each area will now be converted into proposals for legislation to be ratified by the Council of Ministers. This may lead to the amendment of the UK position where these areas of work are currently excluded from the working time provisions.

### Derogations

Employees whose working time is not measured or predetermined are exempt from the provisions relating to the 48-hour week, daily and weekly rest periods, rest breaks and limits on night work but not the holiday provisions. Examples given in the WTR include 'managing executives or other persons with autonomous decision making powers, family workers and ministers of religion'. This seems to be a very limited exception that will only cover individuals who can choose the hours which they work. It is not likely to cover professional staff who have core hours but work additional hours as required. Since the definition is not entirely clear, employers would be advised to make the position clear by agreement.

### Collective and workforce agreements

The Regulations allow employers to modify or exclude the rules relating to night work, daily and weekly rest periods and rest breaks and extend the reference period in relation to the 48-hour week – *but not the 48-week itself* – by way of agreement as follows:

- a collective agreement between an independent trade union and the employer (or an employers' association);
- a workforce agreement with representatives of the relevant workforce *or if there are 20 workers or fewer the agreement may be with a majority of the workforce which obviates the need to elect worker representatives*. As regards worker representatives, these may be representatives elected for other purposes, e.g. health and safety consultation;

- individuals may also choose to agree with their employer to work in excess of the 48-hour weekly time limit. *This is all that an individual agreement can cover*;
- in addition, a workforce agreement may apply to the whole of the workforce or to a group of workers within it.

These agreements can only last for a maximum of five years.

### Records

In outline the position is as follows.

### Weekly working time

An employer must keep adequate records to show that he has complied with the weekly working time limit. The records must be kept for two years. It is up to the employer to determine what records must be kept. Pay records may adequately demonstrate a worker's working hours.

Similar provisions apply in regard to records showing that the limits on night work are being complied with. Records need not be kept in regard to rest periods and in-work rest breaks nor in regard to paid annual leave.

### Compensatory rest

Employers who make use of the derogations or who enter into collective or workforce agreements must provide an equivalent period of rest or, if this is not possible, give appropriate health and safety protection. Thus the Regulations allow, through agreement, flexibility in the way its rights are delivered, but they do not allow those rights to be totally avoided.

### Health and safety assessments

An employer must offer a free health assessment to any worker who is to become a night worker. Employers must also give night workers the opportunity to have further assessments at regular intervals.

### Young (or adolescent) workers

The Regulations also apply rights to persons over the minimum school-leaving age but under 18. These are set out below:

- *weekly working hours*: adult and young workers are treated the same;
- *night work limit*: adult and young workers are treated the same;
- *health assessments for night workers*: adolescent workers are entitled to a health and capacity assessment if they work during the period 10 pm to 6 am. Such an assessment for an adolescent worker differs in that it considers issues like physique, maturity and experience and takes into account the competence to undertake the night work that has been assigned;
- *daily rest*: for young workers this is 12 hours' consecutive rest between each working day;
- *weekly rest*: for young workers the general requirement is two days off per week;
- *in-work rest breaks*: for young workers the general provision is 30 minutes if the working day is longer than 4½ hours;
- *paid annual leave*: adult and young workers are treated the same.

### Enforcement and remedies

The weekly working time limit, the night work limit and health assessments for night workers are enforced by the Health and Safety Executive or local authority environmental health officers. The usual criminal penalties for breach of the health and safety law apply. In addition, workers who are not allowed to exercise their rights under the Regulations or who are dismissed or subjected to a detriment – whether a pay cut, demotion or disciplinary action – for doing so will be entitled to present a complaint to an employment tribunal. In view of the abolition on the ceiling of awards for unfair dismissal, employment tribunal claims could be much more expensive than health and safety fines,

## To provide remuneration

In business organisations the duty of the employer to pay his employees and the rate or amount of pay is decided as follows: (a) by the contract of employment; or (b) by the terms of what is called a collective agreement made between a trade union and the employer. The terms of this agreement, including the part on pay, are then assumed to be part of the individual contracts of employment of the members. The employer must also comply with the National Minimum Wage Act 1998 (*see below*).

The pay which the worker is to get should nearly always be definite because it is included in the written particulars, which we have just dealt with, and also because the ERA requires itemised pay statements.

If there is no provision for payment in the contract – which is highly unlikely – then if the worker sued for payment, the court would fix a fair rate of pay for the job by taking evidence as to what rates of pay were usual in the type of work being done.

Unless the employment contract allows an employer to reduce an employee's pay during short-time working or the employee agrees to a reduction, the employer must continue to pay full wages during a period of enforced short-time working (*Miller* v *Hamworthy Engineering Ltd* [1986] IRLR 461).

However, it was decided by the House of Lords in *Miles* v *Wakefield Metropolitan District Council* [1987] 1 All ER 1089 that when an employee refuses to perform his contractual duties because he is taking industrial action, his employer can understandably lawfully withhold wages for the relevant period of time. The same is true where a worker returns to work after a strike but refuses to work normally. The employer is not obliged to accept the part-performance and could terminate the contract. However, if he does not but decides to accept the part-performance he can withhold wages for hours lost (*see British Telecommunications* v *Ticehurst* [1992] ICR 383).

## The national minimum wage

The National Minimum Wage Act 1998 received the Royal Assent on 31 July 1998. It is in part an enabling Act and its order- and Regulation-making powers came into force on 31 July. Remaining provisions were in force by 1 April 1999 (*see* SI 1998/2574). This section combines the main provisions of the Act with those of Regulations so far issued under it. (*See* National Minimum Wage Regulations 1999.) Section references are to the 1998 Act, unless otherwise indicated.

The Act provides workers with a floor below which their wages will not fall, regardless of the size of the employer's business. Those who work part time will benefit most.

### Entitlement

Those entitled must be 'workers' who work or ordinarily work in the UK under a contract of employment and are over compulsory school leaving age (ss 1(2) and 54(3)). Casual workers are included, as are agency workers (s 34) and home-workers (s 35).

Regulations may exclude any age group below 26 and prescribe different rates for different age groups below 26 (s 3). The self-employed are excluded and there are other exclusions in ss 43–45, e.g. voluntary workers defined in s 44. These include charity workers, who are e.g. either unpaid or receive only reasonable travel and out-of-pocket expenses.

The Regulations also state that those exempt from the provisions are the under-18s, those employed under a contract, and those working and living as part of a family (e.g. au pairs).

### Level

The national minimum wage (NMW) is such single hourly rate as the Secretary of State may prescribe (ss 1(3) and 2). The initial NMW introduced in April 1999 is at the rate of £3.60 an hour before deductions. A minimum 'development rate' will apply to 18–21-year-olds, and for up to six months to those aged 22 or over starting a new job with a new employer under a scheme of accredited training, such as a National Vocational Qualification.

The development rate introduced in April 1999 is – for 18 to 21-year-olds £3.00 an hour (rising to £3.20 an hour in June 2000), and £3.20 an hour for accredited trainees.

### Increases in level

This will depend upon the advice of the Low Pay Commission (LPC) and the economic situation, and will not be automatic. The LPC, which is given a statutory framework by ss 5–8 and Sch 1, advised a basic rate of £3.70 from June 2000.

### Extensions

There is power to apply the Act to those who do not fit the current definition of a 'worker' (s 41). This could be used to deal with changes in working practices and to close loopholes which bad employers may exploit.

### Calculation

The Regulations set out the averaging period to be used in calculating whether a worker has been paid the NMW. It is set at a month (i.e. a 'calendar month') except where workers are currently paid by reference to periods of shorter than one month, e.g. a week, a fortnight or four weeks. In the latter cases, the pay reference period for NMW purposes will be the worker's existing pay period. In addition, the hourly rate for those who are paid annual salary will be calculated on an average basis. Therefore, the lowest salary for a 35-hour week would seem to be £3.60 × 35 × 52 = £6,552.

### What counts as remuneration?

The Regulations deal with a number of instances of what does and does not count towards discharging an employer's obligation to pay the NMW. Examples of things which do not count are advances of wages, pensions, redundancy payments and benefits in kind with the exclusion of living accommodation.

### Enforcement

The Secretary of State appoints enforcement officers (s 13) and the Inland Revenue and Contributions Agency (combined in April 1999) is responsible for enforcement by checking employers' records to ensure compliance. Complaints by employees will be investigated and spot checks will be made on employers.

Organisations that refuse to pay the NMW will face fines of twice the NMW, i.e. £7.20 a day for each employee (s 21). If defiance continues, the fine goes up to a maximum of £5,000 for each offence (s 31). Workers have the right to recover the difference between what they have been paid and the NMW before a tribunal as an unlawful deduction from wages (s 17). There is no limit of time on back claims.

### Records

The record-keeping obligations were eased following consultation and it is now merely provided that an employer has to keep records 'sufficient to establish that he is remunerating the worker at a rate at least equal to the national minimum wage'. The records may be in a format and with a content of the employer's choosing and must be capable of being produced as a single document when requested either by an employee or the Inland Revenue. The DTI publishes guidance on the kinds of records that will be regarded as sufficient.

### Corporate offences

Where a relevant offence is committed by a company, its directors and other officers are jointly responsible with the company where they have consented to or connived at the offence or been neglectful in regard to it (s 32).

### Contracting out

Section 29 makes void any agreement to exclude or limit the Act's provisions or to prevent a complaint from being made to a tribunal, unless there has been conciliation by a conciliation officer or a valid compromise agreement.

### Victimisation and unfair dismissal

Section 23 gives workers the right not to be subject to any detriment e.g. failure to promote because they have asserted rights under the 1998 Act. Under s 25, employees who are dismissed or selected for redundancy for similarly asserting rights will be regarded as automatically unfairly dismissed so that a complaint may be made to a tribunal even by those who do not have one year's service.

### Low Pay Commission

The government has asked the Low Pay Commission which was put on to a statutory footing when ss 5–8 of the National Minimum Wage Act 1998 came into force on

1 November 1998 to report on a number of matters. These include whether or not 21-year-olds should be covered by the NMW's adult rate. The LPC has also been asked to monitor and evaluate the impact of the NMW in terms of pay, employment and competitiveness in low-paying sectors and small businesses, and the effect on pay differentials.

## To give holidays and holiday pay

The rights and duties of the parties here depend upon what the contract of employment says or what the terms of a collective agreement with the union are, though there is no total freedom of contract where the Working Time Regulations apply (*see above*). Again, there should be no doubt about holidays and holiday pay because the ERA states that this information is to be given to the employee in the written particulars.

## To provide sick pay

Entitlement to sick pay must be dealt with by the written particulars. An employer has *no general duty to provide sick pay from his own funds*. As we have already seen (Chapter 6), there is no implied term in a contract of service that an employee is entitled to sick pay (*Mears* v *Safecar Security* [1982] 2 All ER 865). There is a *statutory duty* under the ERA to pay an employee who goes sick during the statutory period of notice and is not able to work out all or part of the notice.

Employers are required to provide what is called *statutory sick pay* (SSP) on behalf of the government. The law is to be found in the main in the Social Security Contributions and Benefits Act 1992. The Social Security Administration Act 1992 (as amended) deals with the administration of the SSP and statutory maternity pay (SMP) (*see below*). It is not necessary for examination purposes to go into all the details of the SSP scheme, a general understanding of it being all that is required. Nor is it necessary to deal with all the rates and thresholds of earnings because these change annually and are not the stuff of which examination questions are made. However, the following matters could be relevant.

(a) As regards reimbursement of SSP, there is now no distinction between small employers, i.e. those whose annual national insurance contributions bill does not exceed £20,000, and other employers. Under the Statutory Sick Pay Percentage Threshold Order 1995 all employers recover SSP on the 'percentage threshold scheme'. This works as follows: the employer takes the figure of NIC (employers and employees) paid in any given tax month. The employer then ascertains the SSP paid in the same month. If this is more than 13 per cent of the NIC figure, he recovers the excess.

(b) In broad terms, SSP is paid by an employer for up to 28 weeks of incapacity for work during a three-year period. The first three days of sickness are waiting days and no SSP is payable. However, as regards the second and subsequent periods of sickness, if the employee has not been back at work following the first period of sickness for eight weeks or more, the periods are linked and there are no waiting days, SSP beginning on the first day of sickness in the second or subsequent period. An illustration appears overleaf.

*John's pattern of sickness*

| 3 waiting days | 10 weeks of incapacity and SSP | 10 weeks at work | 3 waiting days | 18 weeks of incapacity and SSP | |
|---|---|---|---|---|---|

*Norma's pattern of sickness*

| 3 waiting days | 10 weeks of incapacity and SSP | 5 weeks at work | 8 weeks of incapacity and SSP | 4 weeks at work and SSP | 10 weeks of incapacity and SSP |
|---|---|---|---|---|---|

In Norma's case, since she has not returned to work for the requisite period of more than 8 weeks, her periods of incapacity are linked and no waiting days are applied to the second period of incapacity because it is not a new one.

(c) Both John and Norma have now exhausted their entitlement to SSP against their employer. An employer's liability to pay SSP ends when he has paid the employee for 28 weeks during a three-year period commencing with the first incapacity. During the remainder of the three years John and Norma cannot have SSP but will be able to resume that right when a new period of three years begins, three years after the first incapacity.

Employees who are incapacitated after their entitlement has run out are entitled to State benefits. It is not possible to avoid the SSP provisions and any clause in a contract of employment which sets out to do this is void. However, from April 1997, the government, while retaining the underlying liability to pay SSP, will exempt any employer who pays contractual remuneration including occupational sick pay at or above SSP rates for a day of incapacity for work from the need to operate the detailed SSP rules.

## To provide pay during suspension

(a) *On medical grounds.* Under the ERA an employee who has had at least four weeks' continuous service with his employer and who is suspended from work, for example, under the Health and Safety at Work Act 1974, normally on the advice of an Employment Medical Adviser, not because he is ill but because he might become ill if he continues at work, since he is currently engaged on an industrial process which involves a potential hazard to his health, is entitled to be paid his normal wages while he is suspended for up to 26 weeks. This could occur, for example, where there was a leak of radioactivity at the workplace.

An employee may complain to an employment tribunal under the ERA if his employer has not paid him what he is entitled to during a period of suspension and the tribunal may order the employer to pay the employee the money which he should have had.

(b) *On disciplinary grounds.* Suppose an employee takes a day off without permission, in order to go to a football match. His employer decides to suspend him for a further day without pay. Is this legal? Well, there is no implied right to suspend an employee for disciplinary reasons without pay. In practice, if the employer wants a power to suspend it must be made an express term of the contract which is agreed to by the employee and be in the written particulars of the job. If so, it will be justified and the employee will have to accept it.

(c) *On maternity grounds*. The ERA provides for suspension on maternity grounds. Formerly a pregnant woman could be fairly dismissed if because of her condition she could not do her work, e.g. because of health and safety regulations, and either there was no suitable alternative work or she had refused it. The ERA substitutes suspension on grounds of pregnancy, recent childbirth or breastfeeding while the hazard continues. The employee may complain to a tribunal if she is not offered available and suitable alternative work. Suspension continues even if such an offer is refused but pay ceases. For those who have not refused an offer, e.g. because it was not possible for the employer to make one, pay continues during suspension but only to a maximum of 'a week's pay' (currently £220). Those not so paid when entitled can claim compensation before a tribunal within three months of the day for which pay is claimed.

## Maternity provision – ante-natal care

Under the ERA, a pregnant employee who has, on the advice of her doctor or midwife or health visitor, made an appointment to get ante-natal care should have time off to keep it and also be paid. Part-time employees are entitled to this time off and it does not make any difference how many hours they work each week; there is no service requirement. It should be noted that the ante-natal care provision is not really a right, the Act saying merely that an employer shall not unreasonably refuse it. Except for the first appointment, the employer can ask for proof of the appointment in the form, for example, of an appointment card, together with a certificate from a doctor, midwife or health visitor. An employer who, acting unreasonably, does not give the employee these rights can be taken to a tribunal by the employee, but this must normally be during the three months following the employer's refusal. Compensation may be given to the employee, both where the employer has failed to give time off and also where he has given time off but has failed to pay the employee. In either case, the compensation will be the amount of pay to which she would have been entitled if time off with pay had been given as the law requires.

## Maternity provision – leave and pay

### Maternity leave

Part I of Sch 3 to the Employment Relations Act 1999 provides for basic rights and Regulation-making powers relating to maternity leave. They replace the previous provisions of the Employment Rights Act 1996 and achieve this by inserting new clauses into the 1996 Act.

There are three periods of maternity leave:

- ordinary maternity leave;
- compulsory maternity leave;
- additional maternity leave.

### Ordinary maternity leave

This is leave of 18 weeks which coincides with the 18-week period for statutory maternity pay (*see below*) which is dealt with by social security legislation. The right applies to all employees regardless of the length of service and is subject only to two requirements as follows:

- the employee must notify her employer that she is pregnant; and
- when her baby is expected.

The above matters are covered by prescribed conditions as to how and when notification is to be given. (*See below* – The job on return).

### Compulsory maternity leave

A woman who is entitled to maternity leave under the ERA 1996 shall not work nor be permitted by her employer to work for a period of two weeks after the birth. The provisions put the onus on the employer not to allow the woman to work during the compulsory leave period. If the employer fails to comply with the prohibition, he is liable on conviction before magistrates to a fine not exceeding £500.

The purpose of this provision derives from the fact that a woman starting her maternity leave 11 weeks before the baby is due (*see below*) could run out of leave if the baby is born late. In such a case, the compulsory leave ensures that maternity leave continues for two weeks following birth. With an ordinary maternity leave provision of 18 weeks, it is difficult to envisage such a situation occurring, but if it does the Regulations provide that the ordinary maternity leave period lasts until the end of the compulsory leave period. Compulsory leave applies to all women employees regardless of their length of service.

### Additional maternity leave

This leave period is the period which follows immediately after the end of the 18-week period of ordinary maternity leave and, although an employee can choose the date on which the additional period ends, it must end within 29 weeks of the birth. It follows that since a woman can commence her leave 11 weeks before the birth is due, the maximum leave a woman entitled to additional leave could get is 40 weeks. Employees with at least one year's service with the employer will qualify for additional maternity leave.

### Choosing when to start leave

A woman can choose when to start maternity leave at any time from the 11th week before the expected week of the birth. Maternity leave will start automatically if a woman is absent from work with a pregnancy-related illness in the six weeks prior to the birth and at the latest when the baby is born, as where there is an unexpected early birth.

### The job on return

So far as ordinary maternity leave is concerned, the woman is entitled to return from leave to the job in which she was employed before her absence with her employment rights including seniority and pension rights intact, and on terms not less favourable than those which would have applied if she had not been absent. She is, however, subject to and may benefit from any changes which may e.g. have been negotiated in her absence. The same is true of women on additional maternity leave, except that they are not entitled to return to the same job. Here the employer has the flexibility to offer suitable alternative work where it is not reasonably practicable to take the woman back in her old job.

### Loss of right to return

A woman is required to inform her employer before her absence begins that she intends to return and to notify him of the return date towards the end of leave. The employer can postpone the notified right of return up to four weeks but must specify the reason why he is doing so.

In the past, failure by the woman to comply with any of these procedural requirements could lead to the loss of her right to return. This was so, even where the employer was clear that the woman did intend to return and when, e.g., from conversation with the woman concerned, and even if, e.g., the requisite notices were not in writing or within the notice time scales. The job could also be lost where a woman was unable to return, having followed procedural requirements because of sickness, for even a pregnancy-related sickness, such as post-natal depression. Prescribed Regulations under the amended ERA 1996 will end the above somewhat disproportionate penalty and postpone the starting and finishing date for maternity leave until the required notice to return is served. So if a woman wishes to return to work and get back on higher income, she will have to serve a notice to return.

### Redundancy during maternity leave

All employees who become redundant during the maternity leave period must, regardless of service or hours worked, be offered any suitable available vacancy on terms not substantially less favourable than the original contract. The new contract must start immediately. Unfair dismissal can be claimed by those to whom no such offer is made where it was possible to make it. This ensures that the protection of women who are on maternity leave is not reduced. However, if there is no suitable alternative employment, they would have to take redundancy as would any other employee.

### Dismissal during maternity leave

A woman who is dismissed during maternity leave can regard the dismissal as unfair if it is for reasons relating to pregnancy or maternity. However, the right to return may be disapplied where the dismissal during maternity leave is fair, as it might be if, e.g., it related to conduct occurring prior to maternity leave.

### Compensation for redundancy and unfair dismissal

Under provisions introduced by the Employment Relations Act 1999, redundancy payments and compensation are based on an employee's normal pay rather than the pay she received while on maternity leave.

### Employers' schemes

The legal provisions allow a woman to choose whichever is the better of her contractual or statutory rights in a particular respect where the employer has a maternity leave scheme which is altogether, or in some respects, more favourable than the statutory scheme.

## Maternity pay

This is covered by the Social Security Contributions and Benefits Act 1992 (as amended) and the relevant provisions are set out below. However, before continuing, it should be noted that the provisions relating to maternity pay are separate from what is called maternity leave. Maternity leave can be for a longer period, i.e. 40 weeks, whereas maternity pay is only for a maximum of 18 weeks.

Employers are reimbursed 92 per cent of the SMP they have paid out or, under special arrangements for small employers, 105.5 per cent (i.e. more than they have actually paid out) if their total NIC liability in the previous tax year was not more than £20,000 (SI 1999/363). The extra payment to small employers is to assist with costs of administration.

(a) *As regards the amount and time for which it is paid, the entitlement* is as follows:
- a woman who is over 16 and who has been continuously employed in the same employment for 26 weeks by the beginning of the 15th week before the expected week of childbirth is entitled to SMP regardless of hours of work, provided that her average earnings are at least £66 per week;
- the SMP rate for all qualifying women is 90 per cent of the average of two months' earnings for six weeks followed by an enhanced rate of £59.55 (as for Statutory Sick Pay) a week for 12 weeks. If 90 per cent of earnings is less than £59.55 per week then the woman will receive £59.55 for 18 weeks;
- a maternity allowance of £59.55 will be paid for 18 weeks to claimants *in employment* who do not qualify for SMP as where they have not been continuously employed in the same employment for 26 weeks but who have paid Class 1 NI contributions for at least 26 weeks in the 66 weeks before the baby is due. These contributions could have been in different employments and not continuous employment as SMP requires;
- although women who are in employment when they claim will receive a maternity allowance of £59.55 as indicated above, the allowance remains at £51.70 for those who are self-employed or have recently become unemployed;
- a woman who works on beyond the beginning of the sixth week before the expected week of childbirth will not by doing so lose any SMP.

The above provisions are subject to any improved benefits in the employee's contract, which may provide for full pay instead of the 90 per cent of earnings.

However, in *Gillespie and Others* v *Northern Health and Social Services Board and Others* (1996) 541 IRLB 13 the European Court of Justice held that the principle of equal pay under Community law does not require that women should continue to receive full pay as distinct from 90 per cent of earnings during maternity leave, though an individual's contract may provide for this. The court did, however, rule that where a woman's maternity pay is calculated on the basis of pay received before her maternity leave starts, then that calculation must take account of any backdated pay rises subsequently awarded and which take effect in the period used to work out her maternity pay. Where a woman is in receipt of SMP payable at 90 per cent of normal weekly earnings, those weekly earnings are calculated using payments actually made to her in the eight weeks immediately preceding the 14th week before the week in which her baby is expected, and formerly no account was taken of back-dated pay rises awarded after that period. Under the Statutory Maternity Pay (General) Amendment Regulations 1996, employers must revise the earnings-related element of SMP if a pay rise is awarded to take effect in the period used to calculate the amount of SMP due.

(b) *Delays and complaints.* If the employer does not pay SMP to an employee who believes that she is entitled to it or if the employer delays in making a decision, the employee is entitled to and should ask for a written explanation of the employer's position. If the employee does not agree with the explanation or if a decision continues to be delayed, the employee may ask for a formal decision from the Inland Revenue officer at the local National Insurance Claims Office. The Inland Revenue officer will collect evidence from the employer and the employee and make a decision. The Contributions Agency and the Inland Revenue were combined in April 1999.

An employer who refuses to pay after a final decision has been made that he should commits a criminal offence.

If the employee cannot obtain payment from the employer, as where he is insolvent, she may apply to the Department of Employment for payment. If the Department of Employment makes the payment, it may recover from the employer as by proving in the insolvency.

## Parental leave

The Employment Relations Act 1999 inserts provisions in the ERA 1996 under which the Secretary of State *must* make Regulations entitling a parent to a minimum of three months' leave in order to care for a child. The leave is to be available to men and women, in the latter case in addition to maternity leave. The details of the law are to be contained in Regulations which may not be made or implemented with the coming into force of the Act. There has been much criticism from small employers about the costs and practicalities of granting parental leave as a right. The DTI may set up a Family Commission to review the plan and allow it to be implemented more flexibly in concerns employing small numbers of people. The following major matters are left to be decided by Regulations:

- the qualifying service before entitlement which is intended to be one year;
- the length of the leave which is intended to be three months taken during the first five years of the child's life, unless it has special needs.

Regulations will also make appropriate provisions for adoptive parents who may adopt children older than five or need leave before formal adoption takes place.

There are protections for those who take the leave in terms of preservation of seniority and selection for redundancy, and unfair dismissal, as well as victimisation. Complaints against the employer will be made to employment tribunals.

## To make payments during lay-off – guarantee payments
### Lay-off

To avoid difficulty, the right of the employer to lay off employees without pay because of lack of work should be made an express term of the contract of employment.

However, even if the employer has given himself that right in the contract he must still comply with the provisions of the ERA in the matter and cannot have clauses in the contract which are worse for the employee than the basic statutory rights which provide for guarantee payments.

### Guarantee payments

The ERA provides that employees with four weeks or more of continuous service are entitled to a guarantee payment up to a maximum sum, which is currently £15.35 per day, if they are not provided with work on a normal working day, e.g. because of a threatened power cut (*Miller* v *Harry Thornton* (*Lollies*) *Ltd* [1978] IRLR 430). This does not apply if the failure of the employer to provide work is because of industrial action or if the employee has been offered suitable alternative work but has refused it.

An employee can only receive a payment for five workless days during any period of three months. The effect of this is that in order to get payment for a day of lay-off the three months before that day of lay-off must be looked at to see whether the employee has already received the maximum five days' guarantee pay. If the lay-off was, for example, on 20 June and the worker had been paid for lay-offs on 5 June, 27 May, 21 May, 4 April and 2 April, he would not be entitled to a payment but he would for a lay-off on 3 July.

An employee can go to a tribunal if the employer fails to pay all or part of a guarantee payment which the employee should have had. The tribunal can order the employer to pay it. The employee must apply to the tribunal within three months of the workless day or within such longer period as the tribunal thinks reasonable if it is satisfied that it was not reasonable or practicable for the employee to present the claim in three months.

## To pay during statutory time off

The ERA gives employees certain rights to time off work (*see also* p 421). In some cases the employee is also entitled to be paid during the time off. These situations are dealt with here as part of the law relating to the right to be paid. They are as follows.

## Time off for carrying out union duties

Under s 168 of the Trade Union and Labour Relations (Consolidation) Act 1992 an employer must allow an employee, who is an official of an independent trade union (that is, a union which is not dominated or controlled by the employer and is not liable to interference by the employer, as some staff associations may be), which is recognised by the employer, to take time off during working hours to carry out the duties of a trade union official if those duties are concerned with industrial relations between the employer and his employees.

Time off must also be given for union officials to take training in aspects of industrial relations which are relevant to matters for which the union is recognised by the employer. Thus, although trade union officials will be allowed paid time off for core union activities such as collective bargaining with management, they will not be allowed paid time off for, for example, courses to improve general education and training such as courses on the general issues raised by mergers and takeovers of companies and, in particular, the pension rights of employees. However, voluntary arrangements between employers and employees may well ensure that such courses continue in some organisations.

If there is a breach by the employer of this duty, the employee may complain to a tribunal which may declare the employee's rights in its order, so that the employer may carry them out, and may also award money compensation.

In *Hairsine* v *Kingston-upon-Hull City Council* [1992] 446 IRLIB 10 the Employment Appeal Tribunal held that a trade union official's right to paid time off for training was limited to hours when the employee would normally be at work. If a particular course falls outside these hours, the employee is not entitled to paid time off 'in lieu' during his or her contractual hours.

## Redundant employees

An employee who has been continuously employed by his employer for at least two years and who is given notice of dismissal because of redundancy has a right before the period of his notice expires to reasonable time off during working hours so that he can look for another job or make arrangements for training for future employment.

While absent the employee is entitled to be paid, but not more than two-fifths of a week's pay in respect of the whole period of notice. If an employer is in breach of the above provisions, the employee can complain to a tribunal within three months, but the tribunal's compensation is limited to two-fifths of a week's pay.

## Other cases

Pregnant employees are entitled to paid time off for ante-natal care.

The Pensions Act 1995 provides for the election of some employees as trustees of their own occupational pension scheme. These member-nominated trustees, as they are called, are entitled under the ERA to paid time off so that they may perform their duties and undergo relevant training. In addition, the Collective Redundancies and Transfer of Undertakings (Protection of Employment) (Amendment) Regulations 1995 provide that in a redundancy situation an employer may consult elected workers' representatives instead of, or as well as, a recognised trade union. The ERA states that these representatives are entitled to time off with pay during normal working hours to carry out their duties as representatives. The same is true of worker representatives who are to be consulted by the employer on health and safety matters where there is no recognised union that can appoint safety representatives (see the Health and Safety (Consultation with Employees) Regulations 1996: SI 1996/1513). In all cases the right is to 'reasonable' time off taking into account all the circumstances.

The ERA (as amended by the Teaching and Higher Education Act 1998) gives people aged 16 to 18 the right to take reasonable paid time off work in order to study or train for a designated qualification by a specified awarding body. These include a large number of National Vocational Qualifications including, for example, the NVQ awarded by the Association of Accounting Technicians. These rights are enforceable by way of complaint to an employment tribunal (*see below*) and dismissal for asserting these rights is automatically unfair.

If an employer fails to give time off or fails to pay for it, there may be a complaint by the employee to an employment tribunal. The tribunal may make an award of money compensation in such amount as it finds due.

## Itemised pay statements

Under the ERA itemised pay statements must be provided for all employees, including part-timers. Before these provisions (now in the ERA) came into force, an employer could simply state the amount of take-home pay with no details of how it had been arrived at.

Under the ERA the employee must receive a statement at the time of or before receiving his pay, showing gross pay and take-home pay and the variable deductions, e.g. income tax, which make up the difference between the two figures. Details of how it is paid must also be given, e.g. is it contained in the pay packet or has it been credited to a bank account?

As regards fixed deductions, e.g. savings, these need not be itemised every pay day. If the employer gives the employee a separate statement setting out the fixed deductions he may simply show a lump sum representing these in the weekly/monthly pay statement. This fixed-deduction statement must be updated in writing if it is changed and in any case it must be reissued every 12 months.

If the employer does not comply with the pay-statement requirements, the employee can complain to a tribunal which will make a declaration of the law that a statement should have been given and as to what it should have included. The employer must comply with this declaration. In addition, the tribunal may order the employer to give back to the employee any deductions which were made from the employee's pay and which were not notified to him during the 13 weeks before the date of the application by the employee to the tribunal.

Although it was originally envisaged that employers would have to provide workers, when or before they were paid, with a written statement to help them to establish whether or not they had been paid at least the national minimum wage, the idea was dropped and the Regulations as amended following consultation do *not* require employers to provide such a statement.

## Method of payment and deductions from pay

Under Part II of the ERA employees no longer have a right to be paid in cash. The Truck Acts 1831–1940, which used to give this right, were repealed in 1986. Payment may still, of course, be made in cash, but an employer can, if he wishes, pay the employee, for example, by cheque or by crediting the employee's bank account. It should be noted, however, that if a worker was paid in cash before 1986 the method of payment may only be changed if the worker agrees to a variation of the contract of service.

Deductions from pay are unlawful unless they are: (a) authorised by Act of Parliament, such as income tax and national insurance deductions; or (b) contained in a written contract of employment or the worker has previously signified in writing his agreement or consent to the making of them. In *Discount Tobacco and Confectionery Ltd v Williamson* [1993] IRLB 5 the EAT held that deductions from an employee's pay in regard to stock shortages will be legal only if those deductions relate to losses that occurred *after* the employee gave written consent to them, and if not the deductions were invalid and must be repaid to the employee. There is a good reason for this and it is that the power to make deductions should be given before the need to exercise it arises and when the employee is not under pressure because he or she may think there will be no further shortages. Once there are shortages, the employee is under much more pressure to agree to make them good, even if he is not in fact responsible for them, in order to keep his job. As regards (b) deductions from the wages of workers in the retail trade, e.g. petrol station cashiers, for stock and cash shortages are limited to 10 per cent of the gross wages and deductions may only be made within the period of 12 months from the date when the employer knew or ought to have known of the shortage. Outstanding amounts may be recouped from a final pay packet when the employee leaves even though the deduction exceeds 10 per cent. These provisions and claims regarding failure to pay commission (*see Franks Investment Management Ltd* v *Robertson, The Times*, 12 November 1996) are enforceable by the employee against the employer exclusively in employment tribunals.

## Equal pay

The Equal Pay Act 1970 (EPA) (as amended) implies a term called an equality clause into contracts of service. This clause means that a man or a woman must be given contractual terms not less favourable than those given to an employee (the comparator) of the opposite sex when they are each employed: (a) *on like work*, in the same employment; (b) *on work rated as equivalent* in the same employment, e.g. by a job evaluation scheme; or (c) *on work which is in terms of demands made on the worker*, under such headings as effort, skill and decision making, *of equal value* to that of a worker in the same employment.

As regards the relationship between the EPA and the Sex Discrimination Act 1975, the EPA covers not only matters concerning wages and salaries, but also other terms in the contract of service, such as sick pay, holiday pay and unequal working hours. Other forms of sex discrimination in employment, such as discrimination in recruitment techniques, are covered by the SDA (*see further* Chapter 16).

### Application of the Equal Pay Act

The Act applies to all forms of full and part-time work. There are no exemptions for small employers or in respect of people who have only recently taken up the employment, though the Act does not apply, for example, to those who do their work wholly outside Great Britain.

The Act applies to discrimination against men but in practice claims are normally made by women. We shall from now on consider the law on the basis of a claim by a woman.

The main provisions of the Equal Pay Act are set out below.

An employee can bring an equal pay claim against his employer if he can identify a person (or persons) of the opposite sex ('the comparator') who is paid more than the claimant. The relevant rules do not permit claims for equal pay with other people of the same sex.

A claim can also relate to contract terms other than pay, if the comparator's contract is more favourable in that respect than the complainant's contract.

There are three sets of questions to be considered, as follows:

(a) Are the complainant and the comparator 'in the same employment'?
(b) Have their jobs been given the same rating under a job evaluation scheme? If not, are the employed on 'like work'? If not, are they employed on work of equal value?
(c) Is the pay or other differential genuinely due to a material factor other than the difference of sex? Or can the employer make out any other defence to the claim?

The claim will succeed if the answers to (a) and any part of (b) are yes and if the answer to each part of (c) is no. Some of the terms mentioned above and the defences available to the employer will now be considered in more detail.

### In the same employment

The complainant and the comparator will certainly be in the same employment if they are both employed by a company at the same office or other establishment.

They will also be in the same employment if they are employed by the company at different establishments, so long as common terms and conditions are observed at each one. This is a very broad requirement which is easily satisfied.

A case in point is *British Coal Corpn* v *Smith* [1996] 3 All ER 97, where women canteen workers and cleaners employed in the coal industry claimed that their work was of equal value to that of surface mineworkers and, in some cases, clerical workers employed in their own and at separate establishments. The House of Lords decided that the women could use the above categories of persons as comparators. They were not limited to choosing a comparator from their own establishment. It was a matter for a court or tribunal to decide what was a relevant class of employees. In addition, when considering common terms and the conditions it was not necessary to show that these were identical but only that they were broadly similar so as to allow an effective comparison.

What if the complainant and the comparator are employed at the same establishment, or at establishments where common terms and conditions are observed, but they are not both employed by the same company? The two will then be in the same employment only if both employers are 'associated'. This means that one of them must be a company directly or indirectly controlled by the other or that both must be companies directly or indirectly controlled by the same person or company (and *see* Associated employers *below*).

### The two jobs

Two employees are employed on 'like work' if their jobs are the same or broadly similar. Any differences must be differences which would normally be reflected in the rate of pay.

Even if two jobs are wholly dissimilar, a claim can be made if the jobs are of 'equal value'. For example, a female secretary may name a male accounts clerk as a comparator. Or a male driver may specify a female receptionist (and *see British Coal Corpn* v *Smith* (1996) *above*).

If the claim reaches that stage, the evaluation of the two jobs may be referred by a tribunal to an expert, who measures the demands of the jobs under various headings, such as the skill required, the responsibility which is carried and any unpleasant working conditions involved.

Under the Sex Discrimination and Equal Pay (Miscellaneous Amendments) Regulations 1996 (SI 1996/438) the procedure for claims for equal pay for work of equal value is changed so that a tribunal considering such a claim will no longer be obliged to refer the question of equal value to an independent expert. It will have power to do so where it is satisfied that there are no reasonable grounds for determining that the work in question is of equal value.

### Defences

One obvious defence to a 'like work' claim is that the two jobs are not in fact to be regarded as being 'like work'. So far as equal value claims are concerned, the evaluation of the two jobs may be referred to an expert, if the employer argues at the outset that the disparity between the two jobs is so great and so obvious that there can be no reasonable grounds for proceeding with the matter. It may also be able to argue that the comparator and the complainant are not in fact 'in the same employment'. There are also two other possible defences, both of which must be raised at the outset and not after the matter has been referred to the independent expert.

*The material factor defence*: In order to establish the material factor defence, the employer must show that:

(a) the pay or other differential complained of is *genuinely* due to the factor in question;
(b) there is no element of sex discrimination;
(c) the factor is one which it is reasonable for the employer to have regard to when fixing or agreeing the rate of pay or other contract term complained of, otherwise the factor cannot be material.

In many cases, the material factor which is relied on is a personal factor, such as the superior qualifications or longer experience of the comparator. However, the material factor need not be limited in that way. It has been held that an employer may be entitled to pay a new employee more than an existing employee of the opposite sex doing similar work, if the higher rate of pay is necessary in order to fill the vacancy and if it is not a disguised form of sex discrimination. It is possible, although perhaps less likely, that in recessionary times an employer may be entitled to pay a new employee less than an existing comparative employee of the opposite sex. The following cases provide examples.

### Capper Pass v Lawton [1977] 2 All ER 11

A female cook who worked a 40-hour week preparing lunches for the directors of Capper was paid a lower rate than two male assistant chefs who worked a 45-hour week preparing some 350 meals a day in Capper's works canteen. The female cook claimed that by reason of the EPA (as amended) she should be paid at the same rate as the assistant chefs since she was employed on work of a broadly similar nature.

It was held by the EAT that if the work done by a female applicant was of a broadly similar nature to that done by a male colleague, it should be regarded as being like work for the purposes of the EPA unless there were some practical differences of detail between the two types of job. In this case the EAT decided that the work done by the female cook was broadly similar to the work of the assistant chefs and that the differences of detail were not of practical importance in relation to the terms and conditions of employment. Therefore, the female cook was entitled to be paid at the same rate as her male colleagues.

*Comment:* (i) An interesting contrast is provided by *Navy, Army and Air Force Institutes* v *Varley* [1977] 1 All ER 840. Miss Varley worked as a Grade E clerical worker in the accounts office of NAAFI in Nottingham. NAAFI conceded that her work was like that of a Grade E male clerical worker employed in NAAFI's London office. However, the Grade E workers in Nottingham worked a 37-hour week, while the male Grade E clerical workers in the London office worked a 36½-hour week. Miss Varley applied to an industrial tribunal under the EPA for a declaration that she was less favourably treated as regards hours worked than the male clerical workers in London and that her contract term as to hours should be altered so as to reduce it to 36½ hours a week. The industrial tribunal granted that declaration but NAAFI appealed to the EAT which held that the variation in hours was genuinely due to a material difference other than the difference of sex. It was due to a real difference in that the male employees worked in London where there was a custom to work shorter hours. Accordingly, NAAFI's appeal was allowed and Miss Varley was held not to be entitled to the declaration. The judge said that the variation between her contract and the men's contracts was due really to the fact that she worked in Nottingham and they worked in London.

(ii) Another common example of a sensible material difference occurs where, for example, employee A is a new entrant of, say, 21, and employee B is a long-serving employee of, say, 50, and there is a system of service increments, then it is reasonable to pay B more than A though both are employed on like work. Obviously, however, it is not enough to say that because at the present time men are on average paid more than women this is a material difference justifying paying a woman less in a particular job. This was decided in *Clay Cross (Quarry Services) Ltd* v *Fletcher* [1979] 1 All ER 474.

(iii) It was decided in *Rainey* v *Greater Glasgow Health Board* [1987] 1 All ER 65 that it is in order for an employer to pay more to a man if this is necessary to meet skill shortages. In this case a man was brought in from the private sector because of the shortage of prosthetists (persons who fit artificial limbs). He was paid more than a woman prosthetist who went into service with the public sector immediately after training. It would appear, also, that an employer may pay a man more for doing the same job where the man has greater experience. In other words, the employer can reward experience by giving a man higher pay (*McGregor* v *General Municipal Boilermakers and Allied Trades Union* [1987] ICR 505).

(iv) An employer may also pay a man more for doing the same job if the man works nights and the women do not (*Thomas* v *National Coal Board* [1987] IRLR 451).

(v) The fact that there is no sex discrimination is not relevant in turning down an equal pay claim. There must be a 'material difference'. Thus if in a collective agreement made with a trade union, but with no element of sex discrimination, group A (mainly men) receives a higher hourly rate than group B (mainly women), the employer cannot successfully defend an equal pay claim by the women merely because there is no sex discrimination. There must be 'material difference'. This was decided in *Barber* v *NCR (Manufacturing) Ltd* [1993] IRLR 95.

(vi) In *Ratcliffe* v *North Yorkshire County Council* [1995] 526 IRLB 12 the House of Lords decided that a local authority was not justified in cutting women school catering assistants' pay in order to tender for work at a commercially competitive rate. 'Market forces' do not necessarily amount to a genuine material factor other than sex. The result of this case is likely to have ramifications for public-sector competitive tendering exercises by council agencies. If these agencies cannot reduce wages in this way, the chances of a private-sector employer who is paying staff less are greatly enhanced.

*Job evaluation:* The employer will have a complete answer to the claim if the jobs of the complainant and the comparator have been given different ratings under a job evaluation scheme, so long as that scheme has been carried out objectively and analytically. Job evaluation is a sophisticated exercise and a special consultant should be engaged to carry out the study for the employer.

It may even be possible, if an employer is faced with an equal pay claim, to obtain a postponement of the proceedings while a job evaluation study is carried out. The employer may find, however, that the effect of the study is to reinforce the claim rather than to defeat it.

*Equal value:* If the job which a woman does is in terms of the demands made upon her, for instance under such headings as effort, skill and decision-making, of equal value to that of a man in the same employment, then the woman is entitled to the same pay and other contractual terms as the man, as she is if her work has been graded as of higher value (*Murphy* v *Bord Telecom Eireann* [1988] IRLR 267). It might be thought that in such a case she should be paid more but at least the law can ensure equal pay for her. The point about the 'equal value' ground is that it is available even if the jobs are totally dissimilar so that a woman secretary may name a male accounts clerk as a comparator.

A complaint may be made to a tribunal on the grounds of equal value even if the two jobs have been regarded as unequal in a job evaluation study. However, there must be reasonable grounds to show that the study was itself discriminatory on the grounds of sex. It was held in *Bromley* v *H & J Quick Ltd* [1987] IRLR 456 that the job evaluation need not be analytical but can be based on employees' expectations. This seemed a rather odd decision because circumstances over the years have lowered women's expectations in regard to pay in the first place, and if the study is based on expectations, the argument becomes somewhat circular. The decision was out of line with the experience of those working in the field of race and sex discrimination. The decision was reversed by the Court of Appeal in early 1988 (*see* [1988] IRLR 249). A non-analytical scheme would be unlikely to satisfy the requirements of European law according to the decision of the European Court of Justice in *Rummler* v *Dato-Druck GmbH* [1987] IRLR 32.

It was once thought that in claims for equal pay the tribunal must look not merely at pay, but also at fringe benefits. In *Hayward* v *Cammell Laird Shipbuilders Ltd* [1986] ICR 862, a qualified canteen cook, Miss Julie Hayward, who had convinced a tribunal that she was of equal value with male painters, joiners and thermal heating engineers and, therefore, entitled to equal pay, was told by the EAT that she could not isolate the term about pay. The EAT asked the tribunal to look at the case again. Although Miss Hayward's pay was not equal, her employers claimed that she had better sickness benefit than the men and also paid meal breaks and extra holidays which they did not have. So it might be possible to say that she was, looked at overall, treated as well. However, Julie Hayward won her appeal in the House of Lords. It was *held* that her claim to equal pay for work of equal value was justified even though she had better fringe benefits. Her employers were not entitled to compare her total package but should instead consider her basic pay. The decision should ensure that miscellaneous benefits are not seen as 'pay' and will not be used to keep wages down in future.

It is also interesting to note that in *Pickstone* v *Freemans plc* [1986] ICR 886 the EAT decided that a woman could not bring a claim that her work was of equal value to that done by a man employed by the same company in a different job because men were employed in the same job as her own on the same rates of pay and terms.

On the facts of the case this meant that the woman could not claim that her work as a warehouse packer was of equal value to that of a checker warehouse operative merely because she worked on the same terms as other male warehouse packers. The decision was eventually overruled by the House of Lords which decided that a woman is not debarred from making a claim for parity of pay with a male comparator in a different job merely because a man is doing the same job as herself for the same pay. The decision effectively kills off the device of employing a 'token man' with the women employees as a way of defeating equal pay claims.

### Associated employers

As we have seen, comparison of contracts of service for equality purposes is usually made with people who work at the same place. However, comparison can be made with people who work at different places so long as the employer is the same or is an associated employer. As regards an associated employer, this would be the case with a group of companies. Thus, if H plc has two subsidiaries, A Ltd and B Ltd, workers in A Ltd could compare themselves with workers in B Ltd, and workers in B Ltd with those in A Ltd, and workers in A Ltd and B Ltd could compare themselves with workers in H plc. Workers in H plc could, of course, compare themselves with workers in A Ltd and B Ltd.

### Exceptions and extension

An equal pay claim can be made under UK legislation only if both the complainant and the comparator are employed at an establishment or establishments in Great Britain. There is an exception for the armed services, but even that exception would probably not prevent a claim being made under Community law, as mentioned below.

No qualifying service is required for claims to equal pay. A claim can be brought by an employee immediately after he or she has started work.

Rights are also given to persons who are not employees in the conventional sense. The definition of 'employment' in the Equal Pay Act is the same as that contained in the laws relating to sex discrimination and racial discrimination. It includes not only a person who works under a contract of service or of apprenticeship but also one who works under a contract personally to execute any work or labour.

### Community law and ECJ rulings

Before reading this section, it should be noted that the Treaty of Amsterdam came into force on 1 May 1999. It makes amendments to various EU Treaties and also renumbers the provisions of the Treaties of Rome and Maastricht. So far as the Treaty of Rome is concerned, the following often-used articles are renumbered as indicated. Article 119 (equal pay, pensions and equal treatment) becomes Art 141. Article 85 (agreements preventing or restricting or distorting competition) becomes Art 81 and Article 86 (abuse of a dominant position) becomes Art 82.

A claim can be brought under UK legislation only if the complainant and the comparator are or have been employed at the same time. However, any gaps or exceptions in UK legislation can be overridden by Community law. Article 141 of the EC Treaty establishes the principle that men and women are entitled to equal pay for work of equal value.

If, for example, a man who leaves an employment is replaced by a woman who receives a lower rate of pay, the woman will not be entitled to make a claim under UK legislation based on her predecessor's or successor's rate of pay. She can, however, make the claim under Art 141.

An example appears below where the Employment Appeal Tribunal decided that an employment tribunal could hear a claim for equal pay under Art 119 (now 141) of the Treaty of Rome where the applicant relied on a man appointed *after* her resignation as her comparator. (*See Hallam Diocese Trustee* v *Connaughton* [1996] IRLR 505.)

Miss Josephine Connaughton (C) held the first post of Director of Music with the appellants. She gave notice of termination of employment in April 1994. At that time her salary was £11,138 per year. A man was appointed to take her place: his salary was £20,000 per year. C could not invoke the comparison required by the Equal Pay Act 1970 (as amended by the Sex Discrimination Act 1975). This legislation requires the comparator to be a male employee contemporaneously in the same employment and there was none.

However, it was agreed that the legislation must be regarded as supplemented by Art 119 (now 141) of the Treaty of Rome to the extent to which the principle of equal pay for ment and women for equal work was not fully achieved by the UK legislation. The EAT relied on the decision of the European Court of Justice in *Macarthys* v *Smith* [1980] ICR 672 where it was ruled that under Art 119 the principle of equal pay was not restricted to situations of contemporaneous employment. Thus C's successor was an effective comparator and the appellant's appeal was dismissed.

In the *Macarthys* case Mrs Smith relied on a male predecessor as a comparator. This case decides that a successor can also be relied on as a comparator. Article 119 provides: 'Each Member State shall . . . subsequently maintain the application of the principle that men and women should receive equal pay for equal work'. Its provisions take priority over UK legislation even in the private sector by reason of the European Communities Act 1972. The Article has direct effect in the UK.

On the matter of comparators and Art 119 the case of *Lawrence* v *Regent Office Care Ltd*, *The Times*, 24 November 1998, is of interest. The claimants had been employed as dinner ladies and cleaners by North Yorkshire County Council. They became employed by Regent following the contracting out of school meals and cleaning services by the Council to Regent. They then claimed in this case that their employment rights including pay were inferior to *current* employees of the Council, and that under Art 119 it was legitimate in law to cite the *current* Council workers as comparators. The EAT did not agree. The UK legislation and Art 119 required that the claimant and the comparator must be broadly in the same establishment or service.

The effect of a successful claim is twofold. For the future (though not applicable in the *Connaughton* case), the complainant has a contractual entitlement to the higher rate of pay or other contract term enjoyed by the comparator. However, the tribunal can also award compensation in respect of the disparity to date but no back pay can be awarded for a period of more than two years before the date of the employment tribunal application. Other than this, there is no actual financial limit on the amount that can be awarded.

### Procedure and remedies

An employee who wishes to make an equal pay claim does so by making an employment tribunal application. Proceedings may be brought at any time during the employment or within six months after it ends. There is conflicting case law on this but the safe course is to regard the above limits as applying. (*See Etherson* v *Strathclyde Regional Council* [1992] ICR 579.)

As we have seen, the effect of a successful claim is twofold. For the future, the complainant has a contractual entitlement to the higher rate of pay or other contract term enjoyed by the comparator. The tribunal can also award compensation in respect of the disparity to date, but no back pay can be awarded for a period of more than two years before the date of the industrial tribunal application. There is no actual financial limit on the amount which can be awarded, so that if, say, the disparity in net pay were £10,000 per annum at the commencement of proceedings and the case were to be heard one year afterwards, the amount awarded could be as much as £30,000.

A recent challenge to the compensation limit failed in terms of the general period of two years but succeeded in the special circumstances of the case. In *Levez* v *T H Jennings* (*Harlow Pools*) *Ltd* [1999] 608 IRLB 2 the ECJ ruled that the two-year limitation on back-dated compensation under the UK Equal Pay Act 1970 is not *as such* contrary to EC law. However, Community law does preclude its application in some situations, as in this case, where the employer misled the employee as to the pay of her comparators.

### Collective agreements

In a case before the European Court of Justice, *Enderby* v *Frenchay Hospital Authority* (Case C-127/92), Attorney-General Lenz gave an opinion that an employer could not rely on the fact that rates of pay have been set by different collective bargaining arrangements, even though these are not tainted with sex discrimination. The variation must be justified as being due to a 'material factor', which is not the difference of sex. Just because the woman is covered by a different collective agreement from the male comparator is not enough. Employers should even so carry out a pay audit of the workforce. The opinion has been accepted by the European Court (and *see also Barber* v *NCR* (*Manufacturing Ltd* [1993] IRLR 95).

## Pensions and equality

This is dealt with by the Pensions Act 1995. Sections 62–66 require all occupational pensions schemes to provide equal treatment for men and women with regard to:

- the terms on which they become members of the scheme; and
- the terms on which members are treated in relation to any pensionable service from 17 May 1990 (the date of the judgment in *Barber* v *Guardian Royal Exchange Assurance Group* (1990), *see further* Chapter 16). Thus, in regard to service from that date, pension schemes must provide equal benefits for men and women.

## Employer's duty to provide work

There is, in general, no duty at common law for an employer to provide work. If the employer still pays the agreed wages or salary, the employee cannot regard the employer as in breach of contract. The employee has no right to sue for damages for wrongful dismissal but must accept his pay. The main authority for this is *Collier* v *Sunday Referee* [1940] 2 KB 647, where Mr Justice Asquith said: 'If I pay my cook her wages she cannot complain if I take all my meals out.'

There are some exceptions at common law. For example, a salesman who is paid by commission must be allowed to work in order to earn that commission and if he is not his employer is in breach of contract and can be sued for damages. This is also the case with actors and actresses because they need to keep a public image which requires occasional public performances and also with skilled workers who may need to work to preserve and enhance their skills (*see William Hill Organisation* v *Tucker* [1998] IRLR 313 – later in this chapter).

## Employee's property

An employer has in fact no duty to protect his employee's property.

**The following case illustrates this.**

### Deyong v Shenburn [1946] 1 All ER 226

The claimant entered into a contract of employment with the defendant under which the claimant was to act the dame in a pantomime for three weeks. Rehearsals took place at a theatre and on the second day the claimant had stolen from his dressing room his overcoat as well as two shawls and a pair of shoes forming part of his theatrical equipment. In the County Court the judge found that the defendant had been negligent in failing to provide a lock on the dressing room door and having no one at the stage door during the morning of the particular rehearsal day to prevent the entry of unauthorised persons. However, the County Court judge decided that the defendant was under no duty to protect the clothing. The claimant appealed to the Court of Appeal which also decided that the defendant was not liable. The Court of Appeal accepted that if there was an accident at work caused by the employer's negligence, then in an action for personal injury the employee could also include damage to his clothing if there had been any. In addition, if in such an accident the employee's clothes were, say, torn off his back but he suffered no personal injury, then it would seem that he could be entitled to recover damages in respect of the loss of his clothes. However, outside of this an employer has no duty to protect the property of his employee.

*Comment:* This decision was also applied in the later case of *Edwards* v *West Herts Group Hospital Management Committee* [1957] 1 All ER 541 where the claimant, a resident house physician at the defendants' hospital, had some articles of clothing and personal effects stolen from his bedroom at the hostel where he was required to live. He brought an action for breach of an implied duty under his contract of employment to protect his property. His action was dismissed in the County Court and his appeal to the Court of Appeal was also dismissed on the basis that there was no such contractual duty in respect of property.

## Employee's indemnity

An employer is bound to indemnify (that is, make good) any expenses, losses and liabilities incurred by an employee while carrying out his duties.

**The following case illustrates this.**

## Re Famatina Development Corporation Ltd [1914] 2 Ch 271

A company employed a consulting engineer to make a report on its activities. The written report contained matters which the managing director alleged were a libel upon him and he brought an action against the engineer in respect of this on the basis of the publication of the report to the directors of the company, all of whom had received a copy. The managing director's action failed but the engineer incurred costs in defending the claim, not all of which he could recover and he now sought to recover them from the company.

The Court of Appeal decided that the comments made in the report were within the scope of the engineer's employment. His terms of engagement required him to report fully and frankly and in the circumstances he was entitled to the indemnity.

**Comment:** There is no duty to indemnify an employee against liability for his own negligence. Thus, if by negligence an employee injures a third party in the course of employment and the third party sues the employee, the employer is not required to indemnify the employee and indeed, if the employer is sued as vicariously liable (see p 365) he has a right to an indemnity against the employee. This was decided in *Lister v Romford Ice and Cold Storage Ltd* [1957] 1 All ER 125, though the action is unlikely to be brought because it upsets industrial relations.

## Trade union membership and activities

Under the Trade Union and Labour Relations (Consolidation) Act 1992 employers have a duty not to take action against employees just because they are members of, or take part in at an appropriate time, the activities of a trade union which is independent of the employer. According to the decision in *Post Office* v *Union of Post Office Workers* [1974] 1 All ER 229 this includes activities on the employer's premises. As will be seen, the above provisions, while prohibiting discrimination by positive acts, do not cover situations of omission as where an employer gives a benefit to non-union members but fails to give it to union members. The Employment Relations Act 1999 inserts provisions into the Trade Union and Labour Relations (Consolidation) Act 1992 under which discrimination by omission is also prohibited.

Under the provisions of s 152 of the 1992 Act, dismissal for failing to join a trade union is always automatically unfair, i.e. there is no service requirement, even if there is a closed shop situation within the industry concerned. This provision greatly weakens the maintenance by trade unions of closed shops.

If action is taken against employees, they may complain to a tribunal which can award money compensation or make an order saying what the trade union rights of the employee are so that the employer can grant them in the future. If the employee has been dismissed, then the unfair dismissal remedies apply (*see further* Chapter 17).

In addition, s 137 of the 1992 Act gives job seekers a new right not to be refused employment or the services of an employment agency on the grounds that they are or are not trade union members. The Act also protects people who will not agree to become or cease to be union members or to make payments in lieu of membership subscriptions. This means that it is no longer lawful to operate any form of closed shop. Any individual who believes that he or she has been unlawfully refused employment or the service of an employment agency because of union or non-union membership can complain to an employment tribunal within three months of the refusal. If the case is made out, the tribunal can award compensation up to the current maximum of £50,000.

The compensation will generally be paid by the employer or employment agency concerned, but in cases where a trade union is joined as a party and the tribunal decides that the unlawful refusal resulted from pressure applied by the union, it may order the union to pay some or all of the compensation.

The tribunal can also recommend that the prospective employer or employment agency should take action to remedy the adverse effect of their unlawful action on the complainant.

## Time off work without pay

Under the ERA, employees have a right to time off work in certain circumstances. Sometimes they are also entitled to pay. These cases have already been looked at as part of the law relating to pay. However, there are other cases in which employees are entitled to time off but the employer is not under a duty to pay wages or salary for it. These are as follows.

(a) *Trade union activities.* An employee who is a member of an independent trade union which the employer recognises is entitled to reasonable time off for trade union activities. The Advisory, Conciliation and Arbitration Service (ACAS), a statutory body set up in 1975 to promote, e.g. dispute resolution, has published a Code of Practice 3 which gives guidance on the time off which an employer should allow. Paid time off for union *officials* for union duties has already been considered.

(b) *Public duties.* Employers also have a duty to allow employees who hold certain public positions and offices reasonable time off to carry out the duties which go along with them. Details are given in Part VI of the ERA, which covers such offices as magistrate, member of a local authority, member of an employment tribunal, and member of certain health, education, water and river authorities. There has recently been an extension to members of boards of visitors and visiting committees for prisons, remand centres and young offender institutions.

(c) *Family emergency.* The Employment Relations Act 1999 inserts provisions into the ERA 1996 giving employees the right to take a reasonable amount of unpaid time off work to deal with a family emergency, such as a sudden illness (or accident) of a member of the employee's family or someone who relies on the employee. A 'family emergency' is defined further as including child sickness, criminal injury, serious problems with a child's school and the unplanned absence of childminders. The intention is to exclude the right to take time off for matters such as a leaky washing machine at home.

Complaints in regard to failure to give time off under (a), (b) and (c) above may be taken to an employment tribunal. In general, the complaint must be made within three months of the date when the failure to give time off occurred. An employment tribunal may make an order declaring the rights of the employee so that these can be observed by the employer and may also award money compensation to be paid by the employer where there is injury to the employee, e.g. hurt feelings.

## Testimonials and references

There is no law which requires an employer to give a reference or testimonial to an employee or to answer questions or enquiries which a prospective employer may ask him. This was decided in *Carroll* v *Bird* [1800] 3 Esp 201. However, if an employer does give a reference or testimonial, either orally or in writing, which is false, he commits a criminal offence under the Servants' Characters Act 1792. The employer may also be liable in civil law to pay damages to certain persons as follows.

(a) *To a subsequent employer*, who suffers loss because of a false statement *known* to the former employer to be untrue (*Foster* v *Charles* (1830) 7 Bing 105). The action is on the tort of deceit.

The Rehabilitation of Offenders Act 1974 is also relevant here. The provisions of the Act are an attempt to give effect to the principle that when a person convicted of crime has been successfully living it down and has avoided further crime, his efforts at rehabilitation should not be prejudiced by the unwarranted disclosure of the earlier conviction.

The Act, therefore, prevents any liability arising from failure by an employee to disclose what is called a spent conviction to a prospective employer. For example, the Act removes the need to disclose convictions *resulting in a fine* recorded more than five years before the date of the reference or testimonial.

Sentences of imprisonment for life or of imprisonment for a term exceeding 30 months are not capable of rehabilitation. The rehabilitation period for a prison sentence exceeding six months but not exceeding 30 months is ten years, and for a term not exceeding six months it is seven years and, as we have seen, if the sentence was a fine, it is five years.

If an employer does refer to a spent conviction in a testimonial or reference the employee may sue him for *libel* in the case of a written testimonial or reference, or *slander* where the testimonial or reference is spoken. The defence of justification, i.e. that the statement that there was a conviction is true, will be a defence for the employer only if he can show that he acted without malice.

While discussing the 1974 Act it is worth noting that it makes provisions for questions by employers relating to a person's previous convictions to be treated as not applying to spent convictions.

The Act also provides that any failure to disclose a spent conviction shall not be a proper ground for dismissing or excluding a person from any office, profession, occupation, or employment, or for prejudicing him in any way in any occupation or employment.

However, the Rehabilitation of Offenders Act 1974 (Exceptions) (Amendments) Order 1986, SI 1986/1249, allows those who employ persons who will have contact with those under the age of 18 to ask, for example, questions designed to reveal even spent convictions, particularly any with a sexual connotation.

Certain employees are excluded from the 1974 Act and their convictions can be disclosed. Included in the exception are doctors, chartered and chartered certified accountants, insurance company managers and building society officers (*see* Financial Services Act 1986, s 189).

(b) *To the former employee*, for libel or slander if things have been stated in a testimonial or reference which damage the employee's reputation. However, the employer has the defence of qualified privilege, as it is called, so that he can speak his mind about the employee, and so in order to get damages the employee would have to prove that the employer made the statement out of malice, as where there was evidence that the employer had a history of unreasonable bad treatment of the employee.

An action in negligence can also be brought by the former employee because there is a duty of care (*see further* Chapter 22).

**The following case illustrates this.**

### Spring v Guardian Assurance plc [1994] 3 All ER 129

Mr Spring failed to get three jobs for which he applied because of a bad reference given to him by the defendant employer. It stated that while he had been employed by the defendants as an insurance sales manager he had not managed the sales team fairly and among other things he had kept the best leads for himself. The person who prepared the reference did so on the basis of internal memoranda, though she was not malicious in any way. However, the judge found that there was a duty of care and that Mr Spring could base his case in negligence, which does not require the existence of malice. There should have been a more rigorous check on the memoranda and it had been negligent not to do this. It was no defence to an action in negligence that the person preparing the reference may have honestly believed what the memoranda said.

The House of Lords affirmed the judge's ruling by deciding that an employer who gives an employee a reference is under a duty to take reasonable care in its preparation or he will be liable in negligence if the reference is inaccurate and the employee suffers damage. In such a situation it is not necessary to prove malice in the employer as it is if the claim is made in libel.

**In the following case the Court of appeal ruled in a way helpful to employers that an employer's duty of care to an ex-employee when a reference is given does not involve a requirement for the reference to be full and comprehensive.**

### Bartholomew v Hackney LBC, Court of Appeal, 23 October 1998, unreported

Mr B was suspended from his employment following allegations of financial irregularities which, if proved, could have amounted to gross misconduct. A disciplinary investigation was pending. These investigations had not been concluded when Mr B voluntarily left his employment and was paid in lieu of notice. The reference he was given stated that he had left his post voluntarily and at the time of leaving he was suspended from his employment on a charge of gross misconduct and that disciplinary proceedings were pending.

He lost the new position and made a claim for damages against his former employer on the ground of a breach of a duty of care owed to him because, having mentioned the suspension, the former employer was under a duty to give the full details surrounding it.

The Court of Appeal ruled that an employer did not have a duty to give a full and comprehensive reference. The ex-employer would have misled any future employer if the suspension had not been mentioned but having done so there was no duty to give full details.

*Comment:* As we have seen, the employer was not required to give a reference at all, but having done so, he was under a duty to the employee not to make negligent misstatements. (*See Spring* v *Guardian Assurance plc* (1994). Failure to mention the allegations of gross misconduct and the resignation of the employee pending the enquiry could have made the ex-employer liable to a new employer who had employed Mr B.

(c) *Defacing references.* An employee who maliciously defaces his own reference or testimonial commits a criminal offence under the Servants' Characters Act 1792.

(d) *What constitutes a satisfactory reference?* Suppose an employer offers a job to an applicant for employment 'subject to satisfactory references', which are then taken up. Who decides whether or not the references are satisfactory? In *Wishart* v *National Association of Citizens' Advice Bureaux* [1990] IRLR 393, the Court of Appeal dealt with this matter on which there had previously been no direct authority. It was, the court said, a matter for the potential employer. So, if potential employers do not think references are satisfactory, they are not! Presumably, however, the employer must be reasonable and not regard a perfectly good reference as unsatisfactory merely to get out of a contract. Better in any case not to make an offer of any kind until the references are to hand.

## Non-contractual duties of the employer

Before leaving the contractual duties of the employer, it should be noted that he has other duties in regard to the health, safety and welfare of his employees. These are based mainly on the common law of tort of negligence and statutes such as the Health and Safety at Work Act 1974.

## DUTIES OF AN EMPLOYEE

### To use reasonable skill and care in the work

The *common law* provides that an employee who claims to have a particular skill or skills but shows himself to be incompetent may be dismissed without notice. His employer can also raise the matter of the incompetence of the employee if the employer is sued under *statute law*, i.e. the ERA, for unfair dismissal (*see further* Chapter 17).

The common law also requires unskilled employees to take reasonable care in carrying out the job. However, they may be dismissed only if there is a serious breach of this implied term of the contract.

### To carry out lawful and reasonable instructions

The law implies a term into a contract of employment which requires the employee to obey the lawful and reasonable instructions of his employer. However, an employee is not bound to carry out illegal acts. In *Gregory* v *Ford* [1951] 1 All ER 121 one of the decisions of the court was that an employee could not be required to drive a vehicle which was not insured so as to satisfy the law set out in road traffic legislation. If the employee does refuse, he is not in breach of his contract.

### The duty to give faithful service (or the duty of fidelity)

This is an implied term of a contract of employment. Certain activities of employees are regarded by the law as breaches of the duty to give faithful service. Thus, as we have seen, an employee who while employed copies the names and addresses of his employer's customers for use after leaving the employment can be prevented from using the information (*Robb* v *Green* (1895) – *see also* Chapter 7).

However, the implied term relating to fidelity does not apply once the contract of employment has come to an end. Therefore, a former employee cannot be prevented under this implied term from encouraging customers of his former employer to do business with him, though he can be prevented from using actual lists of customers which he made while still employed. If an employer (A) wants to stop an employee (B) from trying to win over his, A's, *customers*, then the contract of employment between A and B must contain an *express* clause in restraint of trade preventing this. Such a clause must, as we have seen, be reasonable in time and area (*see also* Chapter 7).

A former employee can, however, be prevented by the court from using his former employer's *trade secrets* or *confidential information without* a clause in the contract about restraint of trade.

**However, the Court of Appeal ruled in the following case that an ex-employee who made negative remarks about the financial situation and management of the company from which he had resigned as managing director did not owe an implied duty of confidentiality in regard to the information disclosed because the information did not come within the category of a 'trade secret'.**

### Brooks v Olyslager OMS (UK) (1998) 601 IRLB 6

When Mr Brooks resigned from the company it was under a compromise agreement giving him three months' salary in three monthly instalments. Immediately following his resignation, he telephoned an investment banker who had an interest in the company. During the conversation he intimated that the management of the company was autocratic, the company was insolvent and would only last a month, the company's budgets were over-optimistic and that it would be taken over by its holding company. On learning of these remarks, the company refused to pay the salary instalments and claimed that Mr Brooks was in breach of an implied duty of confidentiality. He claimed damages in the lower court and was awarded them. The issue in the Court of Appeal related mainly to the duty of confidentiality. The court did not agree that there was such a duty in this case and in respect of the information disclosed there was no evidence that knowledge of the company's financial affairs was not already in the public domain. Also, Olyslager had not sought to show that what Mr Brooks had said was untrue or malicious nor that his statements had caused any financial loss The company's case was based on its desire to prevent Mr Brooks from disclosing the reasons why he had resigned and from making statements which were in any way detrimental to its interest. There was no such broad right in law. Accordingly, Mr Brooks was entitled to his damages for breach of the compromise agreement and the company was not entitled to an injunction to prevent him from making further disclosures of the kind put forward in this case. They were not trade secrets.

## Confidential information

It is an implied term of a contract of service that the employee must not disclose *trade secrets*, e.g. a special way of making glass as in *Forster & Sons Ltd v Suggett* (1918) (*see* Chapter 7), or *confidential information* acquired during employment. There is no need for an express clause in the contract.

However, the use by an employee of knowledge of trade secrets and information cannot be prevented if it is just part of the total job experience. An employee cannot be prevented from using what he could not help but learn from doing the job.

The following case shows this.

### Printers & Finishers v Holloway (No 2) [1964] 3 All ER 731

The claimants brought an action against Holloway, their former works manager, and others, including Vita-tex Ltd, into whose employment Holloway had subsequently entered. They claimed an injunction against Holloway and the other defendants based, as regards Holloway, on an alleged breach of an implied term in his contract of service with the claimants that he should not disclose or make improper use of confidential information relating to the claimants' trade secrets. Holloway's contract did not contain an express covenant relating to non-disclosure of trade secrets.

The claimants were flock printers and had built up their own fund of 'know-how' in this field. The action against Vita-tex arose because Holloway had, on one occasion, taken a Mr James, who was an employee of Vita-tex Ltd, round the claimants' factory. Mr James' visit took place in the evening and followed a chance meeting between himself and Holloway. However, the plant was working and James did see a number of processes. It also appeared that Holloway had, during his employment, made copies of some of the claimants' documentary material and had taken these copies away with him when he left their employment. The claimants wanted an injunction to prevent the use or disclosure of the material contained in the copies of documents made by Holloway.

The court *held* that the claimants were entitled to an injunction against Holloway so far as the documentary material was concerned, although there was no express term in his contract regarding non-disclosure of secrets.

However, the court would not grant an injunction restraining Holloway from putting at the disposal of Vita-tex Ltd his memory of particular features of the claimants' plant and processes. He was under no express contract not to do so and the court would not extend its jurisdiction to restrain breaches of confidence in this instance. Holloway's knowledge of the claimants' trade secrets was not readily separable from his general knowledge of flock printing.

An injunction was granted restraining Vita-tex Ltd from making use of the information acquired by Mr James on his visit.

Before leaving the topic of confidentiality two further points should be noted, as follows.

### The concept of 'garden leave'

If an employee leaves without giving the employer proper notice in order to set up a competing business or work for a competitor, the employer may be able to get an injunction to prevent the employee from acting in this way. As we have seen in Chapter 7, the action is most useful where the employee has a contract requiring a long period of notice. If, therefore, a senior manager whose contract requires 12 months' notice gives one month's notice in order to set up a rival business taking a number of his employer's main customers with him, then even if there are no post-employment restraints in the contract, the employer may get an injunction to prevent the setting up of the rival business for 12 months. We have already noted that this principle was established in *Evening Standard Co Ltd* v *Henderson* [1987] IRLR 64 (and *see* Chapter 17) though it is, of course, a relevant consideration in granting the injunction that the employer is prepared to pay the employee during the notice period even though he does not return to work but prefers instead to tend his garden!

However, in *William Hill Organisation* v *Tucker* [1998] IRLR 313 the Court of Appeal restricted garden leave claims by employers. Obviously, duties of confidentiality are not owed to an employer once the employee has left his employ, except in the case where there is an express contract in restraint of trade. Garden leave allows injunctions to be made because while the employee is under notice he is still employed and owes the common law of fidelity. However, in *Tucker*'s case the employee claimed that since the employer was intending to pay him but not to allow him to work, the employer was in breach of his obligation to provide Tucker *as a skilled worker* with work. This was a repudiation of the contract by the employer which Tucker had accepted, bringing the employer/employee relationship to an end and with it the fiduciary duties, leaving no basis for granting an injunction. The Court of Appeal ruled that a skilled worker needs practice to preserve and enhance those skills and if the employer wishes to pay and suspend the employee from work, there must be an express term in the contract allowing the employer to cease to provide work. There was no such term in the *Tucker* case.

It was held by the Court of Appeal in *Credit Suisse Asset Management Ltd* v *Armstrong*, *The Times*, 3 June 1996 that in the ordinary case it is not appropriate for the court to order set-off where a long period of notice (or garden leave) has been required before the employee's contract terminates against a covenant in restraint of trade which begins to run from the end of the long period of notice. What was in effect a 12-month restriction on the employee was allowed: six months' garden leave followed by six months' post-employment restraint of trade.

### Confidentiality in reverse

It is also interesting to note that, while it is normal for employers to bring claims against employees to prevent them from using confidential information obtained in the employment, confidentiality works both ways. Thus in *Dalgleish* v *Lothian and Borders Police Board* [1991] IRLR 422 the Board was asked by Lothian Council for details of the names and addresses of its employees so that the Council could identify poll tax defaulters. The court granted the employee an injunction to prevent this. The information was confidential between employer and employee. As more and more people become concerned about data protection, this case shines a welcome light on the employee's right of privacy and the employer's duty not to infringe it by wrongful disclosure.

## THE CONTRACT OF EMPLOYMENT AND SUNDAY TRADING

The Sunday Trading Act 1994 contains provisions repealing previous restrictions on Sunday trading. Recognising the impact of this on shop workers, the ERA 1996 (in Part IV) provides them with important rights. These rights are:

- not to be dismissed or made redundant for refusing to work on Sunday; and
- not to suffer a detriment for the same reason.

These rights extend to all shop workers if they are asked to do shop work on a Sunday. They are not available to Sunday-only workers.

The ERA defines a shop worker as an employee who is required or may be required by contract to work in or about a shop on a day when the shop is open to serve customers. However, the worker need not actually serve customers and the provisions extend beyond sales assistants and check-out operators to clerical workers doing work related to the shop, managers and supervisors, cleaners, storepersons, shelf-fillers, lift attendants and security staff.

A shop is defined as including any premises where any retail trade or business is carried on. This does not include the sale of meals, refreshments or intoxicating liquor for consumption on the premises, e.g. public houses, cafés and restaurants, nor places preparing meals or refreshments to order for immediate consumption off the premises, e.g. take-aways.

The ERA defines two categories of shop workers:

- protected shop workers, i.e. those employed as such when the provisions came into force and those taking up employment afterwards whose contracts do not require Sunday working;
- opted-out shop workers, i.e. those who are employed after commencement of the provisions under contracts which require them to work on Sundays but who opt out of this by giving three months' notice to the employer (*see below*).

Protected workers have the rights immediately, regardless as to whether they have previously agreed to a contract requiring them to work on a Sunday. No procedures are involved. They can simply decide that they no longer wish to work on Sundays. Protected workers are able to give up their right to refuse to work on Sundays but only if:

- the employer is given a written 'opting-in notice', which must be signed and dated and state expressly that they do not object to Sunday working or actually wish to work on Sundays; and
- they then enter into an express agreement with the employer to work on Sunday or on a particular Sunday.

Opted-out workers, i.e. those engaged after the commencement of the provisions or who have opted in to Sunday working have the right to opt out. To do this they must give the employer a signed and dated written notice stating that they object to Sunday work. They then have to serve a three-month notice period. During this time they are still obliged to do Sunday work and if they refuse will lose statutory protection under the ERA. However, they cannot be dismissed or made to suffer some other detriment merely because they have given an opting-out notice. After the period of three months has expired, the worker has a right not to do Sunday work.

The ERA provides that dismissal or redundancy of protected and opted-out workers will be regarded as unfair dismissal if the reason or principal reason was that the worker(s) concerned have refused or proposed to refuse to work on Sundays. Protected and opted-out workers also have the right not to be subjected to any other detriment, e.g. non-payment of seniority bonuses for refusing to work on Sunday. The above rights apply regardless of age, length of service or hours of work.

*Employer's explanatory statement.* The ERA provides that employers are required to give every shop worker who enters into a contractual agreement to work on Sunday a written explanatory statement setting out their right to opt out. If an employer does not issue such a statement within two months of the worker entering into such a contractual agreement, the opt-out period is reduced from three months to one.

The ERA gives a prescribed form of statement which appears in Fig. 15.2.

---

**EMPLOYER'S EXPLANATORY STATEMENT**

**Statutory Rights in Relation to Sunday Shop Work**

You have become employed as a shop worker and are or can be required under your contract of employment to do the Sunday work your contract provides for.

However, if you wish, you can give a notice, as described in the next paragraph, to your employer and you will then have the right not to work in or about a shop which is open once three months have passed from the date on which you gave the notice.

Your notice must be: in writing; be signed and dated by you; say that you object to Sunday working.

For three months after you give the notice, your employer can still require you to do all the Sunday work your contract provides for. After the three-month period has ended, you have the right to complain to an employment tribunal if, because of your refusal to work on Sundays on which the shop is open, your employer dismisses you, or does something else detrimental to you, for example, failing to promote you.

Once you have the rights described, you can surrender them only by giving your employer a further notice, signed and dated by you, saying that you wish to work on a Sunday or that you do not object to Sunday working and then agreeing with your employer to work on Sundays or on a particular Sunday.

---

**Fig. 15.2 ERA 1996: prescribed form of employer's explanatory statement**

Other important provisions are as follows:

- employees who do not do Sunday work have no entitlement to compensation either in terms of extra weekday hours or remuneration;
- an agreement between a shop worker and his or her employer cannot legally contain a general exclusion of the ERA provisions;
- the ERA provides that the dismissal of an employee for a statutory right contained in Part IV of that Act is to be regarded as automatically unfair.

Betting offices and bookmaking establishments are allowed to do business on Sundays and the ERA protects workers against unfair dismissal or victimisation if they object to working on Sunday. The provisions are largely the same as those in the shop-workers' case and appear in Part IV of the ERA. They also apply to workers regardless of age, hours of work or length of service.

## GRADED QUESTIONS

### Essay mode

1 Although a contract of employment need not be in writing, s 1 of the Employment Rights Act 1996 does require that an employer provide his employee with written particulars of his contract of employment within two months of its commencement. What information do these written particulars provide?

*(The Institute of Company Accountants)*

2 (a) Under what circumstances, if any, does an employer who continues to pay wages also have a common law obligation to provide work for his employees?

(b) What are the statutory rights of an employee who is laid off or put on short time because no work is available?

*(The Chartered Institute of Management Accountants)*

3 Explain, with reference to decided cases, how the courts make the distinction between a contract of service (an employer–employee relationship) and a contract for services (a principal–independent contractor relationship). Why is it important to make this distinction?

*(Staffordshire University. BA Business Studies: Business Law)*

### Objective mode

Four alternative answers are given. Select ONE only. Circle the answer which you consider to be correct. Check your answers by referring back to the information given in the relevant chapter and against the answers at the back of the book.

1 Vicarious liability will render an employer liable for:

A Torts which he commits in the course of his business.
B Torts which his employees commit in the course of his business.
C Torts which his independent contractors commit in the course of his business.
D Torts which anyone commits in the course of his business.

2 An employee must be given particulars of his contract of service within one of the following periods. Select:

A Two weeks after the employment begins.
B Two months after the employment begins.
C One month after the employment begins.
D Three months after the employment begins.

3 One of the following statements is correct. Select:

A An employer has a statutory duty to give holidays but not holiday pay.
B An employer has a statutory duty to give holidays and holiday pay.
C An employer is never bound to give holidays and holiday pay.
D An employer may be bound to give holidays and holiday pay.

**4** As regards guarantee payments, an employee can only receive pay for:

    **A** Four workless days in any period of two months.
    **B** Five workless days in any period of five months.
    **C** Six workless days in any period of three months.
    **D** Five workless days in any period of three months.

**5** The permitted length of ordinary maternity leave is:

    **A** 14 weeks.
    **B** 21 weeks.
    **C** 18 weeks.
    **D** 40 weeks.

**6** When deciding questions of equal pay for women, the court must take into account:

    **A** Basic pay only.
    **B** Basic pay and fringe benefits.
    **C** The fact that a man is doing the same job for the same pay.
    **D** The findings of a job evaluation scheme properly conducted.

*The answers to questions set in objective mode appear on p 708.*

# 16 EMPLOYMENT II

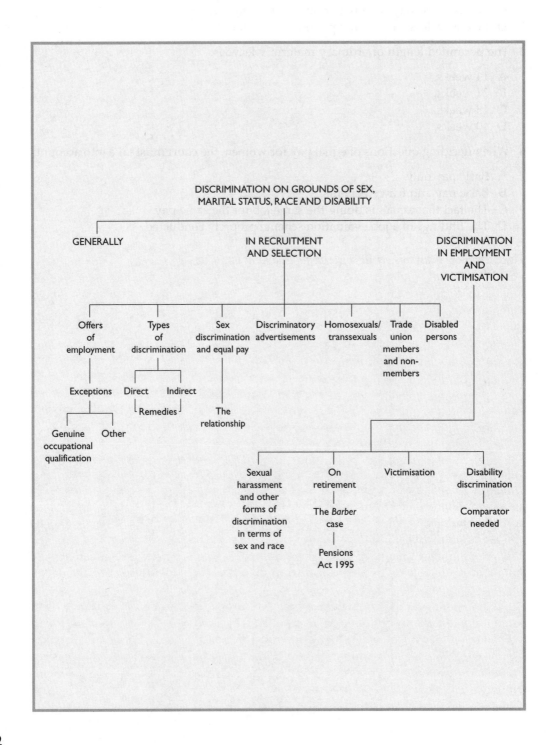

DISCRIMINATION ON GROUNDS OF SEX, MARITAL STATUS, RACE AND DISABILITY

GENERALLY

IN RECRUITMENT AND SELECTION

DISCRIMINATION IN EMPLOYMENT AND VICTIMISATION

Offers of employment

Types of discrimination

Sex discrimination and equal pay

Discriminatory advertisements

Homosexuals/ transsexuals

Trade union members and non-members

Disabled persons

Exceptions

Direct    Indirect

Remedies

The relationship

Genuine occupational qualification    Other

Sexual harassment and other forms of discrimination in terms of sex and race

On retirement

The *Barber* case

Pensions Act 1995

Victimisation

Disability discrimination

Comparator needed

The objectives of this chapter are to explain the law which applies to discrimination when employees are recruited into a job together with discrimination at the workplace.

## DISCRIMINATION ON THE GROUNDS OF SEX, MARITAL STATUS OR RACE: GENERALLY

The law relating to these forms of discrimination is to be found in the Sex Discrimination Acts 1975 and 1986, the Race Relations Act 1976, the Employment Act 1989 and the Employment Rights Act 1996 (ERA). Before looking at the detail of the relevant legislation, we will consider some of the more general provisions of the Employment Act 1989.

Section 1 provides that any legislation dealing with employment and vocational training passed before the Sex Discrimination Act 1975 is overridden by the 1989 Act unless specifically continued in force by that Act. The 1989 Act identifies certain discriminatory provisions and either removes or preserves them (*see below*). However, because there could be some discriminatory provisions in existing legislation which have not been identified, s 1 overrides them.

Section 2 supports s 1, giving the Secretary of State power, by statutory instrument, to remove or amend any discriminatory legislation which may be discovered in the future. Section 1 overrides it unless and until it is discovered, and, for the avoidance of doubt, s 2 and s 6 allow the Secretary of State to repeal, or amend, or retain it, when it is discovered.

Section 3 amends s 51 of the Sex Discrimination Act 1975 which exempts acts of discrimination required by statute before 1975. Section 51 was a blanket provision and s 3 cuts it down so that it is still within the law to discriminate in regard to women if it is done to protect them in matters relating to pregnancy and maternity or to comply with those provisions of the Health and Safety at Work Act 1974 which relate to the protection of women.

The specific areas of protection are enacted by s 4 and are set out in Sch 1 to the 1989 Act. They include industrial processes which involve the use of lead and radiation. It is still within the law to discriminate against women workers in these areas because of the risk of foetal damage.

The provisions preventing women from returning to work in a *factory* within four weeks of childbirth are retained in force.

Section 7 repeals previous law so that women can now work in mines and quarries and clean machinery in factories. The prohibition on women lifting loads 'so heavy as to be likely to cause injury' remain, but discrimination is removed by extending the prohibition to men.

Section 8 repeals previous law which had placed a variety of restrictions on the employment of young persons being persons who are over school leaving age. These matters are now dealt with by the Working Time Regulations, which were considered in Chapter 15. Restrictions on young persons working with dangerous machines, e.g. locomotives, are retained.

## DISCRIMINATION ON GROUNDS OF SEX, MARITAL STATUS OR RACE IN RECRUITMENT AND SELECTION OF EMPLOYEES

The relevant provisions of the Sex Discrimination Acts 1975 and 1986, the Race Relations Act 1976, the Employment Act 1989 and the ERA are set out below.

### Offers of employment

It is unlawful for a person in relation to an employment by him at a place in England, Wales or Scotland to discriminate against men or women on grounds of sex, marital status, colour, race, nationality or ethnic or national origins:

(a) in the arrangements he makes for the purpose of deciding who should be offered the job; or
(b) in the terms on which the job is offered; or
(c) by refusing or deliberately omitting to offer the job.

'Arrangements' is a wide expression covering a range of recruitment techniques, e.g. asking an employment agency to send only white applicants, or male applicants. Discrimination by employment agencies themselves is also covered.

A decision of the European Court is in point here and has implications for UK employers. Elizabeth Dekker was refused a job at a youth centre in The Netherlands. She was pregnant when she applied for the job and told the selection committee this. She claimed damages under a Dutch equal treatment law implementing EC Directive 76/207. The European Court decided (*see Dekker* v *Stichting Vormingscentrum etc* [1991] IRLR 27) that since maternity could never concern anyone but a woman, to take the state of pregnancy into account in justifying the refusal of a job was direct discrimination on the grounds of sex. Mrs Dekker's claim was successful. It should be noted that this case is not concerned with *dismissal because of pregnancy*, which is covered by legislation, but the *refusal of a job because of pregnancy*, which is not. It should no longer be necessary to use sex discrimination law to deal with a pregnancy dismissal because no service requirement is now necessary for a claim for unfair dismissal for a pregnancy-related cause (*see* Chapter 15). *Dekker* covers job refusal because of pregnancy, where service is irrelevant since there is none.

As regards the terms of the contract of employment, it is unlawful to discriminate against an employee on the grounds listed above in terms of the employment which is given to him or the terms of access to opportunities for promotion, transfer or training, or to any other benefit, facilities or services, or subjecting him to any other detriment. Thus it is unlawful to discriminate in regard to matters such as privileged loans and mortgages by banks and building societies and discounts on holidays given to employees of travel firms.

A person who takes on workers supplied by a third party rather than employing them himself is obliged by the Acts not to discriminate in the treatment of them or in the work they are allowed to do. This means that temporary staff supplied by an agency are covered by the anti-discrimination provisions.

The anti-discrimination provisions are also extended to partnerships as regards failure to offer a partnership, or the terms on which it is offered including benefits, facilities and services. The provision regarding race (but not sex discrimination) applies only to firms of six or more partners, although there is a power in the legislation to reduce this number. The provision as it stands will allow race (but not sex) discrimination in the majority of medical practices but not, for example, in the major accounting and law firms.

## Exceptions

There are some circumstances in which it is lawful to discriminate and these will now be considered.

### Genuine occupational qualification

So far as sex discrimination is concerned, an employer may *recruit (or promote)* a man to a job where male sex is a 'genuine occupational qualification' (GOQ) for a particular job. This could arise, for example, for reasons of physiology as in modelling male clothes, or authenticity in entertainment, as where a part calls for an actor and not an actress. Sometimes a man will be required for reasons of decency or privacy, such as an attendant in a men's lavatory. Sometimes, too, where the job involves work outside the United Kingdom in a country whose laws and customs would make it difficult for a woman to carry out the job, being a male may be a GOQ. As regards marital status, it may be reasonable to discriminate in favour of a man or a woman where the job is one of two to be held by a married couple, as where the woman is to be a housekeeper living in with her husband who is to be employed as a gardener, or a married couple is required to manage a club and live in.

There are, of course, a number of situations where female sex would be a GOQ for a certain type of job.

**The following case illustrates this point.**

### Sisley v Britannia Security Systems [1983] IRLR 404

The defendants employed women to work in a security control station. The claimant, a man, applied for a vacant job but was refused employment. It appeared that the women worked 12-hour shifts with rest periods and that beds were provided for their use during such breaks. The women undressed to their underwear during these rest breaks. The claimant complained that by advertising for women the defendants were contravening the Sex Discrimination Act 1975. The defendants pleaded genuine occupational qualification, i.e. that women were required because the removal of uniform during rest periods was incidental to the employment. The Employment Appeal Tribunal accepted that defence. The defence of preservation of decency was, in the circumstances, a good one. It was reasonably incidental to the women's work that they should remove their clothing during rest periods.

However, s 7(4) of the 1975 Act imposes a duty on employers to take reasonable steps to avoid relying on GOQ exceptions.

**The following case and comment illustrates this point.**

### Etam plc v Rowan [1989] IRLR 150

Steven Rowan applied for a vacancy as a sales assistant at Etam's shop in Glasgow which sold only women's and girls' clothing. He was not considered for the post because of his sex and complained to an industrial tribunal.

Etam said that he had not been discriminated against because being a woman was a genuine occupational qualification (GOQ) for the job within the meaning of s 7(2)(b) of the Sex Discrimination Act 1975: it was likely to involve physical contact with women in a state of undress in circumstances where they might reasonably object to the presence of a man.

Mr Rowan's case was based on s 7(4), which imposes a duty on employers to take reasonable steps to avoid relying on the GOQ exception. Section 7(4) in the context of this case provides that the GOQ exceptions do not apply if the employer already has female employees who are capable of carrying out the relevant parts of the job, whom it would be reasonable to employ on such duties and the number of suitable women employees is sufficient to meet the employer's likely requirements without giving rise to undue inconvenience.

The Industrial Tribunal found in favour of Mr Rowan and made a compensatory award of £500. The employers appealed to the Employment Appeal Tribunal. The EAT dismissed the appeal, on the basis that Mr Rowan would have been able quite adequately to carry out the bulk of the job of sales assistant. Such parts as he could not carry out, such as attendance on women in fitting rooms for the purpose of measuring or otherwise assisting them, could easily have been done by other sales assistants without causing any inconvenience or difficulty for the employer.

*Comment:* It is worth noting that in *Wylie v Dee & Co (Menswear) Ltd* [1978] IRLR 103, a woman was refused employment in a men's tailoring establishment in which the remainder of the staff were men because it was inappropriate for her to measure the inside legs of male customers. She complained to an industrial tribunal and succeeded on the basis that this task could have been carried out by male employees.

As regards race, it is lawful to discriminate where there is a GOQ for the job as, for example, in the employment of a West Indian social worker or probation officer to deal with problems relating to young West Indians. Other instances are dramatic performances or other entertainment, artists or photographic models and employment in places serving food or drink to be purchased and *consumed* on the premises by the public. Thus being Chinese is a GOQ for employment in a Chinese restaurant, but not necessarily in a 'take-away'.

### Other major exceptions

These are as follows.

(a) *Private households.* Race discrimination is not unlawful where the employment is in a private household. Sex and marital discrimination is now unlawful even in private households (Sex Discrimination Act 1986). However, the 1986 Act provides that sex discrimination may take place where the job is likely to involve the holder of it doing his work or living in a private house and needs to be held by a man because objection might reasonably be taken to allowing a woman the degree of physical or social contact with a person living in the house or acquiring the knowledge of intimate details of such a person's life. This gives, in effect, a new GOQ for a man.

(b) *Work outside Great Britain*. Discrimination legislation does not apply to work which is done wholly or mainly outside Great Britain. However, it does apply to work on a British ship, aircraft or hovercraft unless the work is wholly outside Great Britain. The Court of Appeal decided in *Haughton* v *Olau Line (UK) Ltd* [1986] 2 All ER 47 that an industrial tribunal had no jurisdiction to hear a claim for unlawful discrimination contrary to the Sex Discrimination Act 1975 where the case was brought by a woman who was employed by an English company on a German registered ship which operated mainly outside British territorial waters. Her employment was not 'at an establishment within Great Britain' as the 1975 Act requires.

(c) *Special cases*. Certain public-sector jobs are not entirely covered by the sex discrimination provisions – e.g. there may be discrimination as regards height in the police and prison service. The armed forces were given protection by SI 1994/3276 except where discrimination is necessary to ensure 'combat effectiveness'. Furthermore, the legal barriers to men becoming midwives have been removed.

Other special cases are set out in s 5 of the Employment Act 1989 under which the appointment of head teachers in schools and colleges may be restricted to members of a religious order where such a restriction is contained in the trust deed or other relevant instrument. Furthermore, a university professorship may be restricted to a man if there is a statutory requirement that the holder of the post should also be a canon. In practice this will apply only to certain professorships of divinity. Finally, academic appointments in university colleges may be restricted to women where this was required when the 1989 Act came into force. In practice the provision applies to two colleges at Oxford – Somerville and St Hilda's – and to two at Cambridge – Lucy Cavendish and Newnham. The Secretary of State has power to remove these exemptions by statutory instrument.

## Types of discrimination

There are two forms of discrimination, as follows.

(a) *Direct discrimination*, which occurs where an employer or prospective employer treats a person less favourably than another on grounds of sex, race, or marital status, as where an employer refuses, on grounds of sex or race, to grant a suitably qualified person an interview for a job. In addition, the segregation of workers once in employment on the grounds of sex or race is also unlawful direct discrimination.

**Examples are provided by the following cases.**

### Coleman v Skyrail Oceanic Ltd, *The Times*, 28 July 1981

The claimant, Coleman, who was a female booking clerk for Skyrail, a travel agency, was dismissed after she married an employee from a rival agency. Skyrail feared that there might be leaks of information about charter flights and had assumed that her dismissal was not unreasonable since the husband was the breadwinner. The Employment Appeal Tribunal decided that the dismissal was reasonable on the basis that the husband was the breadwinner. However, there was an appeal to the Court of Appeal which decided that those provisions of the Sex Discrimination Act which dealt with direct discrimination and dismissal on grounds of sex had been infringed. The assumption that husbands were breadwinners and wives were not was based on sex and was discriminatory. The claimant's injury to her feelings was compensated by an award of £100 damages.

*Comment:* The claimant was also *held* to be unfairly dismissed having received no warning that she would be dismissed on marriage. The additional and discriminatory reason regarding the breadwinner cost the employer a further £100.

### Johnson v Timber Tailors (Midlands) [1978] IRLR 146

When the claimant, a black Jamaican, applied for a job with the defendants as a wood machinist the defendants' works manager told him that he would be contacted in a couple of days to let him know whether or not he had been successful. Mr Johnson was not contacted and after a number of unsuccessful attempts to get in touch with the works manager, was told that the vacancy had been filled. Another advertisement for wood machinists appeared in the paper on the same night as Mr Johnson was told that the vacancy had been filled. Nevertheless, Mr Johnson applied again for the job and was told that the vacancy was filled. About a week later he applied again and was again told that the job had been filled although a further advertisement had appeared for the job on that day. An industrial tribunal decided that the evidence established that Mr Johnson had been discriminated against on the ground of race.

(b) *Indirect discrimination,* as where an employer has applied requirements or conditions to a job but the ability of some persons to comply because of sex, marital status or race is considerably smaller and cannot be justified.

**Examples are provided by the following cases.**

### Price v The Civil Service Commission [1978] 1 All ER 1228

The Civil Service required candidates for the position of executive officer to be between 17½ and 28 years. Belinda Price complained that this age bar constituted indirect sex discrimination against women because women between those ages were more likely than men to be temporarily out of the labour market having children or caring for children at home. The Employment Appeal Tribunal decided that the age bar was indirect discrimination against women. The court *held* that the words 'can comply' in the legislation must not be construed narrowly. It could be said that any female applicant could comply with the condition in the sense that she was not obliged to marry or have children, or to look after them – indeed, she might find someone else to look after them or, as a last resort, put them into care. If the legislation was construed in that way it was no doubt right to say that any female applicant could comply with the condition. However, in the view of the court, to construe the legislation in that way appeared to be wholly out of sympathy with the spirit and intention of the Act. A person should not be deemed to be able to do something merely because it was theoretically possible; it was necessary to decide whether it was possible for a person to do so in practice as distinct from theory.

## Bohon-Mitchell v Council of Legal Education [1978] IRLR 525

The claimant, an overseas student, complained of discrimination in regard to a requirement of the defendants that a student would have to undergo a 21-month course, as opposed to a diploma of one year, to complete the academic stage of the bar where he did not have a UK or Irish Republic university degree. This rule was regarded by an industrial tribunal to be discriminatory because the proportion of persons not from the UK or Irish Republic who could comply was considerably smaller than persons from the UK or Irish Republic who could and the rule was not justifiable on other grounds. The claimant satisfied the tribunal that there had been indirect discrimination.

*Comment:* The other side of the coin is illustrated by *Panesar* v *Nestlé Co Ltd* [1980] IRLR 64 where an orthodox Sikh who naturally wore a beard which was required by his religion, applied for a job in the defendants' chocolate factory. He was refused employment because the defendants applied a strict rule under which no beards or excessively long hair were allowed on the grounds of hygiene. The claimant made a complaint of indirect discrimination but the defendants said that the rule was justified. The Court of Appeal decided that as the defendants had supported their rule with scientific evidence there was in fact no discrimination.

### Remedies

Allegations of discrimination may be the subject of a complaint to an employment tribunal which may, among other things, award monetary compensation under s 65(1)(b) of the Sex Discrimination Act 1975 and s 56(1)(b) of the Race Relations Act 1976 (for direct discrimination) and under the Sex Discrimination and Equal Pay (Miscellaneous Amendments) Regulations 1996 (SI 1996/438) (for indirect sex discrimination only). By reason of the Sex Discrimination and Equal Pay (Remedies) Regulations 1993 (SI 1993/2798) and Race Relations (Remedies) Act 1994, there is no cap on these monetary awards. The Acts of 1975 and 1976 formerly contained caps of £11,000.

In addition, the Equal Opportunities Commission, which is responsible for keeping under review the working of sex discrimination legislation, including equal pay, and the Commission for Racial Equality (CRE), which has a similar function in terms of racial discrimination, may carry out formal investigations into firms where discrimination is alleged and may issue non-discrimination notices requiring the employer to comply with the relevant legislation.

The employer may appeal to an employment tribunal within six weeks of service of the notice. If there is no appeal, or the employment tribunal confirms the notice, then the employer must comply with it, and if he does not the relevant Commission may ask the County Court for an injunction which, if granted, will make an employer who ignores it in contempt of court and he may be fined and/or imprisoned for that offence.

The Commissions are also required to enter non-discrimination notices which have become final in a Register. Copies of the Register are kept in Manchester (Equal Opportunities Commission) and in London (Commission for Racial Equality), and are available for inspection to any person on payment of a fee and copies may also be obtained.

Under s 6 of the Sex Discrimination Act 1986, terms of contracts, collective agreements and organisational rules which are discriminatory on the grounds of sex, e.g. not employing women with children or bonus schemes which exclude part-timers, most of whom are women, are void. However, there was no mechanism for individuals to get a legal ruling on these provisions. As a result of an amendment to s 6 by s 32 of the Trade Union Reform and Employment Rights Act 1993, job-seekers, employees and prospective members of trade or professional organisations can now ask a tribunal to give a declaration that a term is void. The tribunal cannot amend the term. The parties must decide what should fill the gap.

## Time limits

The complainant must make a tribunal application within three months after the act complained of. A tribunal can extend this period on the ground that it is just and equitable to do so, but extensions are not lightly granted.

## Relationship between the Sex Discrimination Act and the Equal Pay Act

The two Acts do not overlap. Complaints of discrimination in regard to pay and other non-monetary matters governed by the contract of employment, such as hours of work, are dealt with under the Equal Pay Act and complaints of discrimination in regard, for example, to access to jobs, are dealt with under the Sex Discrimination Act. A complaint to an employment tribunal need not be based from the beginning on one Act or the other. A tribunal is empowered to make a decision under whichever Act turns out to be relevant when all the facts are before it.

## Discriminatory advertisements for employees

The sex discrimination and racial discrimination legislation make it unlawful to place advertisements for employees which are discriminatory unless they relate to a recognised exceptional case, as where, for example, there is a GOQ. Thus job descriptions such as 'waiter', 'salesgirl', 'stewardess' or 'girl friday' have largely disappeared from our newspapers and one now finds the descriptions 'waiter/waitress' or the expression 'male/female' as indicating that both sexes are eligible for employment. However, one still sees advertisements which are clearly intended to attract female applicants which, nevertheless, remain within the law, e.g. 'publishing director requires sophisticated PA/secretary with style and charm who can remain cool under pressure'.

Before legislation relating to discrimination came into force, advertisements in the UK were discriminatory mainly as regards sex, but obviously an advertisement which said 'Chinese only' would be unlawful unless there was a GOQ as, for example, there would be where the advertisement was for a waiter in a Chinese restaurant.

As regards sanctions, the placing of discriminatory advertisements may lead to the issue of a non-discrimination notice by the appropriate Commission which, if not complied with, may lead to proceedings being taken by the Commission in an employment tribunal. If the employment tribunal accepts the contention of discrimination and yet the advertiser does not comply but continues to advertise in a discriminatory way, the Commission may take proceedings in the County Court for, among other things, an injunction, and if this is not complied with, the advertiser is in contempt of court and may be punished by a fine or imprisonment until he complies.

In addition, it is a criminal offence to place a discriminatory advertisement and those who do so may be tried by magistrates and are subject to a fine. The person who publishes the advertisement, e.g. a newspaper proprietor, also commits a criminal offence. However, he may not know precisely that the advertisement is discriminatory. For example, without a knowledge of the advertiser's business, he cannot really know whether there is a GOQ or not. Accordingly, he is given a defence to any criminal charge if he can show that in publishing the advertisement:

(a) he relied on a statement by the person placing it to the effect that it was not unlawful and on the face of it might come within one of the exceptional cases; and
(b) it was reasonable for him to rely on that statement.

## HOMOSEXUALS AND TRANSSEXUALS

The Queen's Bench Division of the High Court referred the question of whether sex discrimination may include homosexuals under the EC Equal Treatment Directive to the European Court (*see R v Secretary of State for Defence, ex parte Perkins* [1997] IRLR 297).

However, more recently a lesbian railway clerk who was denied free travel concessions for her partner had won the first stage of her claim against South-West Trains. An Advocate-General of the ECJ gave an opinion that the company had broken European sex discrimination rules. Since the case relates to discrimination during employment it is further considered later in this chapter. However, it should be noted at this stage that the Opinion of the Advocate-General was not confirmed by the ECJ and Ms Grant lost her case (*see Grant v South-West Trains Ltd* [1998] ICR 449).

In view of the above ruling, the reference to the ECJ in the *Perkins* case was withdrawn by the court (*see R v Secretary of State for Defence, ex parte Perkins (No 2)*, *The Times*, 16 July 1998).

Although it is established that general complaints of discrimination on the grounds of homosexuality are not within the Sex Discrimination Act 1975, the Court of Appeal has decided that if a gay man complains specifically that a gay woman would have been treated differently in, e.g. a recruitment situation, there may be a claim under the 1975 Act. (*See Smith v Gardner Merchant Ltd*, *The Times*, 23 July 1996.)

As regards transsexuals, *The Sex Discrimination (Gender Reassignment) Regulations 1999* (SI 1999/1102) extend the Sex Discrimination Act 1975 to cover discrimination on grounds of gender reassignment in employment and vocational training following the ruling of the ECJ in *P v S and Cornwall CC* [1996] All ER (EC) 397. In that case the ECJ ruled in favour of a transsexual who was dismissed after a sex change. The decision put the UK government under some pressure to clarify UK law, hence the above Regulations. There are no similar Regulations applying to homosexuals.

## TRADE UNION MEMBERS AND NON-MEMBERS

Discrimination against job applicants on the ground of trade union membership or non-membership is now dealt with in much the same way as racial, sex and disability discrimination. It is unlawful to refuse employment to a person because that person:

(a) is a trade union member or is unwilling to leave a union or agree not to join a union;

(b) is not a trade union member or is unwilling to become or remain a member;

(c) is unwilling to make payments or allow deductions from his pay because he is not a member.

Refusing employment on any of the above grounds is equally unlawful, whether it relates to unions in general or to some particular union or group of unions. A failure to offer a job or offering a job on unreasonable terms is treated as refusal to offer the job.

These provisions apply to applicants for employment under a contract of service or apprenticeship. There is not the extended definition of employment which applies in racial and sex discrimination and equal pay cases.

There are two ways in which an unlawful refusal of employment on any of the above grounds can be conclusively proved, as follows:

(a) if the job is advertised in terms which indicate or might reasonably be understood as indicating an intention to do so;

(b) if employment is refused pursuant to an arrangement or practice under which new employees have to be put forward or approved by a union.

## Time limits

Complaints that a job has been refused on grounds of trade union membership or non-membership are also dealt with by employment tribunals.

There is a time limit of three months from the date of the refusal. This time limit is strictly applied. It can be extended only where it was not reasonably practicable for the proceedings to be commenced in time. This basis for extension, which is the same as that which applies in unfair dismissal cases (*see* Chapter 17), is even stricter than the 'just and equitable' basis which applies in racial and sex discrimination cases.

# THE DISABILITY DISCRIMINATION ACT 1995

This Act received the Royal Assent on 8 November 1995. The employment provisions came into force on 2 December 1996.

## Applicants for employment

From 2 December 1996, it is unlawful under s 4 of the Act to discriminate against a disabled person:

- in the arrangements, including the advertisements, made for deciding who should be offered employment and its terms;
- by refusing to offer or deliberately not offering employment.

In other words, it is unlawful to discriminate against a disabled person in deciding who to interview, who to give the employment to and the offer's terms. Section 5 carries an employer's defence which allows discrimination if, but only if, the reason for it is both material to the circumstances of the case and substantial. Thus, less favourable treatment may be justified if the employer believes on reasonable grounds that the nature of the disability substantially affects the disabled person's ability to perform the required task(s).

It is also against the law for trade associations, trade unions and professional bodies to treat a disabled person less favourably than someone else.

The Act will receive further consideration later in this chapter, but it will suffice to say here that employers are required to make adjustments in the working conditions and workplace to accommodate disabled persons, though cost may be taken into account in deciding what is reasonable (s 6).

### Exceptions

The employment part of the Act did not apply to employers who employed fewer than 20 people but they were (and are) encouraged to follow good practice guidelines. However, from 1 December 1998, the employment provisions of the 1995 Act are extended to organisations employing 15 or more people. The Act does not apply to operational staff employed in the armed forces, the police or prison services, the fire services or to anyone employed on board ships, hovercraft or aeroplanes. Complaints must be made to an employment tribunal within three months of the act complained of. Remedies are considered later in this Chapter.

The government has established a Disability Rights Commission, and may lower the small employer exception further in stages after getting advice from the Commission.

## THE ASYLUM AND IMMIGRATION ACT 1996

This Act is relevant in terms of recruitment and is now in force. It contains provisions designed to prevent illegal working by immigrants, overstayers and those breaching their immigration conditions. Under Regulations made by the Secretary of State (SI 1996/3225), employers must take steps to check the existence (but not the authenticity) of documents, such as birth certificates or certificates of registration or naturalisation, to prevent illegal working. If such checks have been carried out and illegal employment takes place nevertheless, the employer is not liable. Failure to check responsibly can result in a fine on the employer of up to a maximum of £5,000. In the case of a corporate employer, directors and other officers and management of the company may be similarly prosecuted if they have connived at the offence or it has been committed as a result of their neglect. There is no need to check existing employees. The Act does not apply to employees under the age of 16 or to self-employed or agency workers. Furthermore, employers are not required to check the status of employees who come to the organisation following a transfer of undertakings (*see further* Chapter 15). Non-EEA students must get permission from the local Jobcentre for a specific job, and as regards university students permission may be obtained from the Department of Education and Employment.

## AGE DISCRIMINATION

The government has decided to operate by means of a voluntary code of practice. Discriminatory job advertisements are banned, as are situations in which employers fail to promote people or give them pay rises on account of their age. Attempts to introduce clauses against ageism into the Employment Relations Act 1999 failed, as did a number of Private Members' Bills.

As regards terms relating to age in contracts of employment, the following case can conveniently be dealt with here. In it the Employment Appeal Tribunal ruled that an employer was not in fundamental breach of the contract of employment when it required an employee to retire at 55 years of age to further a company policy of achieving a younger workforce.

This was so even though the contract incorporated an equal opportunities policy containing a commitment to give equal opportunities regardless of age. (*See Secretary of State for Scotland* v *Taylor* [1997] 581 IRLB 8.)

The EAT decided that it could not have been the intention of the parties that the age discrimination provision in the equal opportunity arrangements would apply after an employee had reached the contractual age of retirement, which in this case was, under the contract of employment, 55.

Mr Taylor's claim for direct discrimination because of his employer's breach of the contractual equal opportunities arrangements failed.

## CRIMINAL RECORDS

The Home Office plans to give easier access to job applicants' criminal records. A White Paper sets out proposals for a new Criminal Records Agency that would charge job applicants for providing information to them about criminal records as where the employer asked for this. The provisions are in Part V of the Police Act 1997 which has received Royal Assent. The sections relevant to the above matters are not yet in force.

In order to implement Part V of the 1997 Act, the government has announced that the Home Department will set up a self-financing Criminal Records Bureau for England and Wales. It will take some two years to establish the bureau. During this period the government will be consulting widely in terms of the plan to give extended access to criminal records for employment purposes.

## MEDICAL EXAMINATIONS

It was held in *Baker* v *Kaye* [1997] 569 IRLB 13 that a doctor retained by an employer to carry out pre-employment medical assessments of prospective employees owes a duty of care to those examined to take reasonable care in carrying out his examination and assessment of suitability of employment. If he fails to do so, he may be sued in negligence by the prospective employee who is not, for medical reason alleged in the doctor's report, offered the job.

The above decision was reversed in *Kapfunde* v *Abbey National plc*, *The Times*, 6 April 1998 by the Court of Appeal. K applied for a job with the defendant. She filled in a medical questionnaire which was considered by a doctor. He did not see K but concluded from the questionnaire that she would have a higher than usual level of absence. She did not get the job. It was held that Abbey National was not liable even if the doctor's assessment could have been proved to have been negligent because it did not employ him. As regards a claim against the doctor personally, it was held that contrary to *Baker* there was no special relationship leading to a duty of care. Commenting on *Baker*, the Court of Appeal said there was no duty of care in that case either even though the doctor did actually see the claimant in that case before making an assessment.

## DISCRIMINATION ONCE IN EMPLOYMENT

We have already considered the law relating to discrimination in formation of the contract, i.e. in recruitment and selection, and in terms of remuneration, namely equal pay. Discrimination on termination of the contract will be dealt with later when we look at discriminatory dismissal. Here we are concerned with discrimination in the treatment of employees during the course of the contract of employment.

### Discrimination on the grounds of sex or race

Under the sex and race discrimination legislation it is unlawful to discriminate against a person on grounds of sex or race as regards opportunities for promotion, training or transfer to other positions, or in the provision of benefits, facilities, or services, or by dismissal, or by any other disadvantages, or detriment.

Segregation of a person on racial grounds is also form of discrimination, as it would be on sexual grounds, though the latter is much less likely.

The UK legislation also prohibits racial discrimination in relation to pay and other terms of employment. Sex discrimination in relation to contract terms generally leads to a complaint under the Equal Pay Act rather than the Sex Discrimination Acts and indeed a claim relating to the rate of pay and other contract terms for the payment of money can be brought only under the Equal Pay Act. The practical effect of this is that a woman employed by a company cannot complain about her rate of pay simply on the ground that a man in her position would be paid more; she must point to an actual male comparator (who under Community law can be her predecessor or successor in the job) who is paid more than she is.

The definition of employment for the purposes of racial and sex discrimination complaints includes not only employment under a contract of service or apprenticeship but also employment under a contract personally to execute any work or labour. The effect is that even a person who is self-employed in the true sense of the word may be able to bring a complaint of racial or sex discrimination against a company. Rights are also given to contract workers and partners.

An example of the broad nature of discrimination law is provided by the following case where the Employment Appeal Tribunal decided that sales counter workers employed by an independent company were working for the store which gave that independent company a concession within the store and could complain against the store for racial discrimination.

Section 7 of the Race Relations Act 1976 makes it clear that a person is liable for race discrimination in the case of contract workers supplied to him by an agency where those workers do work for him. But it appears that s 7 also covers discrimination by dismissal where the dismissal is by a concessionaire operating within the defendant's business environment. The person who is discriminated against can be regarded as working for the defendant and not solely for the concessionaire.

Section 7(1) of the 1976 Act provides:

This section applies to any work for a person (the principal) which is available for doing by individuals (contract workers) who are employed not by the principal himself but by another person who supplies them under a contract made with the principal.

### Harrods Ltd v Remick: Harrods Ltd v Seely: Elmi v Harrods Ltd [1996] ICR 846

The claims by all three complainants were for racial discrimination. Ms Remick was employed as a pen consultant by Schaeffer pens (UK) Ltd, which had a sales counter in Harrods, and Mrs Seely was a cosmetics consultant employed by Brigade International Ltd which also had a concession in Harrods. Store approval was withdrawn by Harrods following what Harrods regarded as breaches of its dress code, in particular Mrs Seely's case the wearing of a nose stud. Both ladies were dismissed by their respective concessionaires in order to keep the concession. Mrs Elmi applied for a job with florists Moyses Stevens, which also had a concession in the store, but because of refusal of store approval, she could not be employed.

The EAT decided that an employment tribunal had jurisdiction to hear all three complaints of racial discrimination.

The problem for the complainants in this case was whether they could show that they worked for Harrods under the provisions of s 7(1). The EAT said that s 7(1) should be construed widely: the complainants could be regarded as doing work 'for' Harrods for the benefit of Harrods and ultimately under Harrods' control as Harrods could refuse or withdraw store approval for the worker to do the work available.

The decision applies also to sex discrimination since s 9 of the Sex Discrimination Act 1975 is in similar terms, as is s 12 of the Disability Discrimination Act 1995. It is understandable that the case caused some problems since, at first sight, it would not be thought that the complainants did work 'for' Harrods. However, thanks to the willingness of the EAT to widen the provisions, it was held that they did. Other employment rights, such as unfair dismissal, continue to rely rigidly upon the existence of a contract of service between the complainant and the defendant. The decision of the EAT was upheld by the Court of Appeal (see *Elmi* v *Harrods; Harrods* v *Remick; Harrods* v *Seely* [1997] 1 All ER 82).

At first sight, it might be thought that discrimination by an employer is confined to his own discriminatory acts towards employees. However, the Employment Appeal Tribunal has decided that an employer can be regarded as having subjected employees to racial harassment by allowing a third party to inflict racial abuse of them in circumstances in which he could have prevented the harassment or reduced the amount of it.

### Burton v De Vere Hotels Ltd [1997] ICR 1

The appellants were two young Afro-Caribbean women. They were employed as casual waitresses at the Pennine Hotel, Derby. On the relevant occasion some 400 men, members and guests of the City of Derby Round Table, attended a dinner at the hotel, the speaker being Mr Bernard Manning.

The appellants heard Mr Manning making jokes about the sexual organs and sexual abilities of black men. He made racially offensive remarks to them and created an atmosphere which, said the EAT, probably encouraged some guests further to abuse them. The appellants brought complaints against their employer under the Race Relations Act 1976. Section 4 of that Act is relevant and provides that it is unlawful for a person in the case of a person employed by him to discriminate against that employee by subjecting him to detriment.

The employment tribunal found that the two employees had suffered the detriment of racial harassment, but had been subjected to it by Mr Manning and the guests and not by the employers. There was an appeal to the EAT by the appellants. The EAT did not agree with the employment tribunal. The problem was to decide the extent of the duty of an employer to protect the employee from harassment by third parties. This involved an examination of the true meaning of the word 'subjecting' to detriment. In the EAT's view, 'subjecting' connoted 'control'. A person subjected another to something if he caused or allowed that something to happen in circumstances where he could control whether it happened or not. Here the employer, by good employment practice, could have prevented the harassment or reduced the extent of it. Mrs Justice Smith said that the hotel manager ought to have warned his assistant managers to keep a lookout for Mr Manning and to withdraw the young waitresses if things became unpleasant. He did not do so because he did not give the matter a thought. He should have done.

If the assistant managers had been properly instructed, said the judge, the two young women would not have suffered any harassment. They might possibly have heard a few offensive words before they were withdrawn but that would have been all. Therefore, the employer 'subjected' the appellants to the racial harassment which they received from Mr Manning and the guests. The case was remitted to the employment tribunal for the assessment of compensation. It will be borne in mind that there is no cap on such compensation.

Of course, the employer will not always be in control. As the EAT said, the employer of a bus or train conductor might feel that an employee would face a genuine risk of racial harassment at times, and yet the prevention of such harassment would be largely beyond the control of the employer. All he could do would be to make his attitude to such behaviour known to the public and to offer his employee support if harassment occurred. However, where there is control, there is likely to be liability if it is not exercised properly.

## Promotion

**The following case is illustrative of the problems relating to sex discrimination in promotion; it also introduces a major change in discrimination law. In it the Employment Appeal Tribunal decided that for a requirement or condition of employment to be capable of construction as sexual discrimination it need not be an absolute bar to employment. It may be indirectly discriminatory even though it is only 'desirable' for employees to comply with it. If the decision becomes accepted as an authoritative interpretation of the Sex Discrimination Act 1975, it will represent a major change in the law and have important practical consequences.**

**As regards the law, women who complain of indirect sex discrimination must show that the employer applies to them a requirement or condition which is such that the proportion of women who can comply with it is considerably smaller than the proportion of men who can comply with it and which is a detriment to them and cannot be justified on non-sexual grounds. (Sex Discrimination Act 1975 s 1.) The decision in the case turned on the meaning of 'requirement or condition'. Section 1 of the Race Relations Act 1976 is in similar terms.**

### Falkirk Council v Whyte (1997) Equal Opportunities Review, Issue 75 at p 44

Jacqueline Whyte and two of her colleagues applied unsuccessfully for a management post at Cortonvale Prison. They later brought proceedings against the Council which ran the prison to challenge one of the matters applied in the process of selection in terms of the qualifications, i.e. management training and surpervisory experience, on the grounds that it was indirectly discriminatory against women.

An employment tribunal upheld the complaint. Although management training and supervisory experience were expressed to be 'desirable' and not 'absolute', nevertheless it was clear that, in terms of the way the interview panel operated, they were decisive factors in the selection at Cortonvale. They were, said the employment tribunal, applying a liberal interpretation of s 1 of the 1975 Act, in terms of requirements or conditions within that section.

The tribunal then found that the requirement for management training and supervisory experience had a disproportionate effect upon women who were mainly in basic-grade posts. Further, the requirement was not justified on an objective balance between the employer's needs and its discriminatory effect.

The EAT held that the tribunal was entitled to give a liberal interpretation to the meaning of 'requirement or condition', in the 1975 Act.

The tribunals refused to follow the race discrimination case of *Perera v Civil Service Commission* [1983] IRLR 186 where it was decided that a requirement or condition had to be an absolute bar to obtaining the job in question. Nevertheless, a change in the interpretation seems inevitable. The 'absolute bar' test is out of line with the broader provisions of Art 140 of the Treaty of Rome and the Equal Treatment Directive. The decision may mark the end of the restrictive interpretation of indirect discrimination under which employers have hitherto avoided scrutiny of their selection, promotion and pay criteria by phrasing them as preferences and not absolute requirements.

The decision is concerned with sex discrimination, but since the Race Relations Act 1976 contains parallel provisions, it is obviously capable of application also to race discrimination situations.

## Detrimental treatment – generally

An employer must not discriminate when subjecting an employee to a detriment. The meaning of 'detriment' was considered by the Court of Appeal in the case of *Jeremiah* v *Ministry of Defence* [1979] IRLR 436. Female examiners at an ordnance factory who volunteered for overtime were not required to work in a particularly dirty part of the factory; male examiners who volunteered were required to work there but received an extra payment to compensate them. A male examiner brought a successful complaint of sex discrimination, even though he had suffered no financial loss. He had been subjected to a real detriment, or disadvantage, and his employers could not cancel out that disadvantage by making a payment to him.

More recently certain workers were awarded compensation of £1,000 each for racial discrimination after they were banned from taking leave from work to attend a religious festival. They wanted to take a day off for the religious festival of Eid. (*See Hussain* v *JH Walker* [1996] ICR 291.)

## Detrimental treatment – sexual harassment

Many complaints of sex discrimination relate to sexual harassment. Neither sexual harassment nor racial harassment is referred to in terms in the relevant legislation. It is regarded as detrimental treatment, which is included in the relevant legislation. However, a leaflet entitled 'Sexual Harassment in the Workplace: a Guide for Employers' (PL 923) which is available free of charge from offices of the Employment Service gives as examples: unwelcome sexual attention; suggestions that sexual favours may further an employee's career (or refusal may hinder it); insults or ridicule of a sexual nature; lewd, suggestive or over-familiar behaviour and display or circulation of sexually suggestive material. However, the Employment Appeal Tribunal has decided that for a male manager to conduct an annual appraisal interview with a woman subordinate in a small room without a female chaperone is not in itself sexual harassment (*see British Telecommunications plc* v *Williams* [1997] IRLR 668). Apparently only one copy of the appraisal review was available in the room so that Ms W had to sit close to the manager to read it. The interview lasted between one and a half and two hours with no other female present. Ms W stated that she found this physical proximity threatening and distasteful but the EAT rejected the idea that it could in itself be sexually intimidating for a female employee to undergo an appraisal interview in a small room with a male employee.

A person who experiences sexual harassment at work is being subjected to a detriment on the ground of his or her sex; a person who experiences racial discrimination at work is being subjected to a detriment on racial grounds.

Harassment is actionable whether it is physical or verbal, whether it is aggressive or simply unwanted and whether it involves threats or promises (for example, of promotion in return for sexual favours). A complaint can be brought either by a person who is still employed or by a person who has resigned because of the harassment.

The Employment Appeal Tribunal has given guidance on dealing with claims of sexual harassment, stating, in particular, that it is important not to separate a case into a series of specific incidents: the incidents should be looked at as a whole so that in the case before it the EAT decided that a series of events, each of which looked at on its own would not amount to harassment, did so when considered together. (*See Mr P Reed and Bull Information Services Ltd* v *Ms D Stedman*, EAT, 22 January 1999, unreported.)

Ms S complained of many incidents of sexual harassment which occurred when she was alone with her manager and others when she was in a group with other colleagues. She did not confront her manager but she did make a complaint to him about his behaviour. The EAT held that her employer, B Ltd, was liable (as the employer may be in these cases) since the personnel department was aware of S's deteriorating health and she had complained to other members of staff. No investigation as to the cause of her illness or as to her complaints was carried out. Obviously, a very serious incident will amount on its own to harassment, but a series of less serious incidents may have the same long-term effect.

Many acts of racial or sexual harassment are carried out by comparatively junior employees. The question of the employer's responsibility for harassment and other unauthorised acts of discrimination is considered later in this chapter.

It should also be noted that when harassment is intended and studied, the Criminal Justice and Public Order Act 1994 creates a criminal offence of intentional harassment. It appears as the new s 4A inserted into the Public Order Act 1986.

The penalty on conviction by magistrates is imprisonment for up to six months and/or a fine of up to £5,000. It covers harassment on the grounds of race, sex, disability, age and sexual orientation.

It is clear from the wording of s 4A that harassment in the workplace is covered. This means that employees who are harassed by colleagues at work or by their employer are now able to report the matter to the police. Employees should be put on notice of this new offence.

The Protection from Harassment Act 1997 is also relevant. The Act is very wide ranging and covers racial and sexual harassment and bullying at work. These areas can now be the subject of *civil* as well as criminal proceedings under the Act.

## Responsibility for employees and agents

An employer has usually been held responsible for any act of discrimination by an employee in the course of his employment. The question when an act is to be taken as done in the course of a person's employment is considered in general terms in Chapter 15. There have, however, been very few, if any, cases in which an act of racial or sexual harassment or any other act of discrimination by an employee has been held to have been done outside the course of his employment.

However, the Employment Appeal Tribunal decided that acts of racial harassment by employees were outside the scope of their employment so that they alone were liable and the employer was not. The decision was also relevant to cases of sexual harassment. If followed it could have had a serious effect on discrimination legislation (*see Tower Boot Co Ltd* v *Jones* [1995] IRLR 529).

It appears from the facts of the case that Mr Jones, a black man aged 16, was the subject of racial harassment by his fellow employees. He was whipped and branded with a hot screwdriver. Metal bolts were thrown at his head and a racist note was pinned to his back. He was called names such as 'baboon', 'chimp' and 'monkey'. He sought compensation from his employer on the grounds of racial discrimination.

Section 32(1) of the Race Relations Act 1976 was relevant. It states:

Anything done by a person in the course of his employment shall be treated for the purpose of this Act . . . as done by his employer as well as by him, whether or not it was done with the employer's knowledge or approval.

The employment tribunal found that the violent acts and racial taunts occurred during the course of employment and the employer was liable. There was an appeal by the employer to the EAT, which reversed this finding, holding that the employer was not liable because the acts were not carried out by the employees in the course of employment.

The EAT followed the traditional approach to course of employment used for many years to decide whether a negligent act of an employee was within the scope of employment so as to make the employer also liable vicariously for it at common law. The common law rule is that the employer is not liable for entirely unauthorised acts. He is liable where the employee uses an improper method of performing an authorised task, e.g. lighting a cigarette when delivering petrol thus causing damage (*see Century Insurance Co Ltd* v *Northern Ireland Road Transport Board* [1942] AC 509).

However, Mr Justice Buckley said in the EAT: 'We cannot, by any stretch of the imagination, see how the acts complained of by Mr Jones, including deliberate branding with a hot screwdriver and whipping, could be described as an improper mode of performing authorised tasks.'

The effect of this ruling was to make it very easy for an employer to avoid vicarious liability for racial and sexual discrimination by introducing the defence that the employee was not employed to discriminate and so was acting beyond the scope of employment. As regards sex discrimination, the relevant section is s 41(1) of the Sex Discrimination Act 1975 which repeats the wording of s 32(1) of the Race Relations Act 1976. Admittedly, there is a claim against the employees concerned, but the chances of actually recovering any substantial compensation are not good.

However, the Court of Appeal allowed an appeal by Raymondo Virtue Jones against the decision of the EAT and stated that the words 'in the course of his employment' in s 32(1) of the Race Relations Act and (by implication) in s 41(1) of the Sex Discrimination Act 1975, were not to be construed restrictively by reference to case law governing an employer's vicarious liability in tort, so that an employee's racially (and by inference) sexually abusive acts did not have to be connected with acts authorised to be done as part of his work in order to make the employer liable (*see Jones* v *Tower Boot Co Ltd* [1997] NLJR 60).

The Court of Appeal said that a wide purposive interpretation should be given to 'course of employment' for discrimination purposes, otherwise the more heinous the act of discrimination the less likely it would be that the employer would be liable.

Furthermore, an employer had a defence under discrimination legislation where he could show that he had used his best endeavours to prevent employees harassing others. The conscientious employers had, therefore, nothing to fear.

The purposive approach to interpretation of Acts of Parliament is comparatively modern and under it the judge should adopt the construction of legislation which will promote the general aims or purposes underlying the provisions, in this case the elimination or control of discrimination.

The employer can also be held responsible for any act of discrimination by an agent (such as an employment agency), so long as the agent had express or implied authority to do the act in question.

As we have seen, there is one important defence in relation to unauthorised discrimination by an employee, should the employer be regarded as liable for it. This defence is made out if the employer can show that it took such steps as were reasonable practicable to prevent the employee from doing the act in question or acts of that description. If the defence is made out, the employee can be held personally responsible for the act of discrimination, but the employer will be absolved from liability.

The steps which the employer should take, in order to prevent discrimination by employees, include the following:

(a) adopt an equal opportunity policy;
(b) communicate the policy to employees and job applicants;
(c) appoint a partner or director with responsibility for seeing that the policy is carried out;
(d) amend the disciplinary rules, so that the definition of misconduct will include racial and sexual harassment and other deliberate acts of discrimination;

(e)  provide managers with training in their responsibilities;

(f)  establish a procedure for complaining of acts of discrimination; and

(g)  generally try to create a climate in the office in which racial and sex discrimination will be seen as unacceptable.

### The codes of practice

Codes of practice in relation to both sex discrimination and racial discrimination are in force. Failure to comply with any provision of a code of practice is not in itself an offence, but can be taken into account in any employment tribunal proceedings.

Both commissions (the Commission for Racial Equality and the Equal Opportunities Commission) have also issued non-statutory guidance documents on a number of matters. Both have responsibilities for seeing that the law is enforced and the power both to assist individual complainants and to take proceedings in their own names. They also, however, have sections to advise employers on the steps which they should take to comply with the law and become genuine equal opportunity employers.

### Time limits

Any complaint of sex or racial discrimination has to be pursued by way of an employment tribunal application. There is a time limit of three months, which runs from the date of the act of discrimination complained of, and which will not lightly be extended. However, some leeway is allowed to tribunals, which have a discretion in regard to the application of time limits. Thus in *British Coal Corpn* v *Keeble* [1997] IRLR 336 the EAT ruled that a tribunal was allowed to let two women bring claims for sex discrimination after the three-month because they were mistaken over their legal situation following incorrect union advice.

There are, however, special rules where the complaint relates to an act of discrimination which extends over a period. The time limit of three months does not then start to run until the period comes to an end.

### Compensation and other remedies

The usual remedy for a successful complaint of discrimination is an order for payment of compensation. The employment tribunal can also make a recommendation, e.g. that the employer obviates or reduces the adverse effect on the complainant, unreasonable failure to comply with which can lead to a further award of compensation, but recommendations are made comparatively rarely.

The compensation can include compensation for injured feelings and aggravated damages, and there is no overall limit.

### Reform

The Equal Opportunities Commission has published a consultation document entitled 'Equality in the 21st Century: a New Approach'. This document proposes a new statute to amend the Sex Discrimination Act 1975 and the Equal Pay Act 1970. The new statute would also provide a simplified and enhanced framework of maternity rights and benefits.

The EC Directive on the burden of proof in sex discrimination cases has been extended to the UK. Essentially it provides for the reversal of the current position in which the claimant bears the burden of proving sex discrimination to the tribunal. Under the Directive, once prima facie evidence of probable or presumable discrimination has been proved, the employer must disprove it or the claimant will succeed. The Directive must be implemented in the UK by 13 July 2001.

## Pensions – equal treatment

Sections 62 to 66 of the Pensions Act 1995 require all occupational pension schemes to provide equal treatment for men and women with regard to:

- the terms on which they become members of the scheme; and
- the terms on which members are treated in relation to any pensionable service from May 17 1990 (the date of the *Barber* judgment – *see below*).

The government has also decided to equalise state pension age at 65. This is covered by the Pensions Act 1995, Sch 4. The change is to be phased in from 2010 to 2020.

### Barber v Guardian Royal Exchange Assurance Group, *The Times*, 18 May 1990

Douglas Barber was a member of the pension fund set up by the defendants, Guardian Royal Exchange (GRE). The fund applied a non-contributory 'contracted-out' scheme approved under the Social Security Pensions Act 1975.

Under the GRE scheme the normal pensionable age was fixed for the category of employee to which Mr Barber belonged at 62 for men and 57 for women. The difference was equivalent to that which existed under the State Social Security Scheme (65 for men and 60 for women).

There was a *GRE Guide to Severance Terms*. It formed part of Mr Barber's contract of service and provided that, in the event of redundancy, members of the pension fund were entitled to an immediate pension, subject to having attained the age of 55 (men) or 50 (women).

Mr Barber was made redundant on 31 December 1980. He was then aged 52. GRE paid him the cash benefits provided for in the severance terms, a statutory redundancy payment and an *ex gratia* payment. He was, of course, entitled to a deferred retirement pension from the date of his sixty-second birthday.

A woman in the same position as Mr Barber would have received an immediate retirement pension as well as the statutory redundancy payment, the total value of which would have been greater than the amount paid to Mr Barber. Mr Barber commenced proceedings before an industrial tribunal because he took the view that he had been subjected to unlawful sexual discrimination. His claim was dismissed by the tribunal and eventually reached the Court of Appeal which decided to stay the proceedings and ask the European Court at Luxembourg to give a ruling on the following questions.

First, were redundancy benefits, including pension benefits, 'pay' within Art 119 of the Treaty of Rome which deals with equal pay? The European Court said that they did fall within Art 119.

Second, did each element of a redundancy package have to be equal or was it enough if the total package was the same? The European Court said that the principle of equal pay must be applied to each item of a redundancy package. It was not enough that the value of the total package was the same.

Third, did Art 119 have direct effect in the UK without the need for UK legislation implementing it? The answer given by the Court was that Art 119 was of direct effect in national courts of Member States of the EC and no national legislation was required to implement it.

*Comment:* (i) The judgment of the European Court makes clear that pensions are 'pay' within the equal pay provisions of Art 119. They must therefore be equal as between men and women. So all pensions granted on or after 17 May 1990 (the date of the judgment), whether immediate or deferred, are to be equal in terms of amount and payable at the same age where the same circumstances, such as length of service and salary, apply (see *now* the Pensions Act 1995).

(ii) The European Court decided in 1993 that the ruling in this case was not retrospective so that there is no requirement to equalise benefits earned prior to 17 May 1990 (the date of the original decision that equalisation was required). The court also decided that schemes may equalise pension ages upwards so that, for example, women retire at 65 along with men and not at 60 as the scheme might well have provided before (see *now* Pensions Act 1995).

Although the *Barber* decision states that Art 119 has direct effect, pensions equality in the UK is to be found in the Pensions Act 1995, and the UK government which put the 1995 Act through Parliament was satisfied that the Act together with regulations made under it would satisfy EC requirements.

## Discrimination against married persons

The anti-discriminatory provisions outlined in the previous section are applied also to discrimination against married persons. An employer must not treat a married person of either sex, on the ground of his or her marital status, less favourably than he treats or would treat an unmarried person of the same sex, e.g. there must not be a marriage bar attached to a particular employment, unless, of course, there is a GOQ.

## Victimisation in employment

Under the sex and racial discrimination legislation, it is unlawful to treat a person less favourably than another because that person asserted rights under the equal pay or other anti-discriminatory legislation relating to sex or race or has helped another person to assert such rights or has given information to the Equal Opportunities Commission or the Commission for Racial Equality, or it is thought that he or she might do so. Damages can be awarded where victimisation has occurred. An example is to be found in *Cornelius* v *Manpower Services Commission* [SXD 36117/86] where Manpower Services refused to consider C for a permanent post for which she had applied because one of the references which she supplied indicated that she was involved in an unresolved sexual harassment case.

## DISABILITY DISCRIMINATION

In the preceding pages of this chapter we have considered the law relating to race, sexual and disability discrimination in terms of the recruitment of employees, and race and sex discrimination once persons are employed. To these forms of discrimination in employment must now be added discrimination against the disabled. The Disability Discrimination Act 1995 applies and its main employment provisions are set out below.

## What is disability?

Section 1 defines a disabled person as a person who has a physical or mental impairment which has a substantial and long-term adverse effect on his or her ability to carry out normal day to day activities. Schedule 1 expands on this and states, among other things, that 'mental impairment' includes an impairment resulting from or consisting of a mental illness only if the illness is well recognised clinically. It also states that impairments which would have an effect on a person's ability but for medical treatment or some form of aid are included. Section 3 allows the Secretary of State to issue guidance and there are various rule-making powers to carry the definition further.

A variety of conditions can be brought under the general definition of physical and mental impairment. For example, in *Howden* v *Capital Copiers (Edinburgh) Ltd* [1998] 586 IRLB 11 an employee who had frequent absence through sickness caused by abdominal pains was dismissed by reason of disability and a tribunal awarded him £12,659, which included £1,000 for injury to his feelings. The employee was a stock controller and the pains were suggestive of uteric colic, although there was no exact diagnosis. Without pain control he experienced a severe griping pain and had to lie down. He would also lose the use of his hands and suffer, among other things, from spasms, lack of co-ordination, speech impediment and loss of concentration. Following some 35 days' sickness absence during 1996, he was dismissed without warning. The tribunal held that the abdominal pain was a 'physical impairment', notwithstanding the absence of exact diagnosis, which had a substantial adverse effect on the employee's ability to carry out normal day-to-day activities and, given that the condition had lasted for more than two years, it was long term (*see below*).

It is clear from the above decision that employers should be especially cautious before they dismiss an employee on the grounds of ill-health since the condition may be regarded as a 'disability' for the purposes of the 1995 Act. It will, therefore, be prudent to obtain a detailed medical report to see whether this might be so. If the illness does or could fall within the definition of a disability, the employer should consult with the employee to see whether any adjustments can be made to the work situation, such as a transfer to a new position or maybe allowing the employee to work from home or by providing additional training or making modifications to the workplace or equipment. It is the need to take these steps which distinguishes dismissal for an unsatisfactory sickness record from a disability dismissal, though it was said that when comparing the period(s) of absence with other workers it was legitimate to compare disability absence with non-disability absence (*see Clark* v *Novacold Ltd* [1998] 586 IRLB 11). It should also be noted that in *O'Neill* v *Symm & Co Ltd* [1998] ICR 481 the EAT accepted that chronic fatigue syndrome (ME) fell within the definition of disability. The case is further considered at page 457.

There was an appeal by the employee in *Clark* to the Court of Appeal (*see Clark* v *TDG Ltd trading as Novacold, The Times*, 1 April 1999). The court rejected the procedure of comparison with non-disabled persons stating that in this respect the DDA 1995 was different from the legislation on sex and race discrimination. The test was:

- Had the employee been discriminated against on the grounds of his disability? Was he fired because of it? If the answer is yes, then the employee has been discriminated against;
- Having reached that point, the employee has no claim if the employer can *justify* the dismissal, which is the employer's defence under the Act.

Thus, where an employee is unable to attend work because of a disability, it is not correct to make a comparison with a non-disabled employee and see whether the disabled employee has been dismissed were a non-disabled person who was unable to return to work because of sickness would not have been. The tribunal must ask itself whether the claimant was dismissed because of his disability. If he was dismissed while unable to work because of illness resulting from a disability, the employee is discriminated against because he cannot perform the functions of the job because of disability. However, the claimant will not succeed in a claim if the employer can justify the dismissal, as might be the case in *Clark* where a consultant was unable to say when Mr Clark might be able to return to work. This might well justify his dismissal but without the need for the comparisons made under the sex and race legislation. The Court of Appeal referred the case to an employment tribunal to see whether the employer could justify the dismissal.

The EAT has decided that to dismiss a person who can carry out his or her duties is not necessarily unfair if those duties can be carried out with some difficulty to the organisation in which the work is being done. In *Goodwin* v *The Patent Office*, *The Times*, 11 November 1998 the complainant suffered from paranoid schizophrenia and this had a substantial effect on his day-to-day activities. However, an employment tribunal decided that because he was capable of getting to work and communicating with his colleagues, there was no substantial adverse effect and his dismissal was unfair. The EAT did not agree because there had been complaints from female staff about his disturbing behaviour. The EAT said that the fact that a person *can* carry out activities is not decisive if they are only carried out with difficulty as in this situation with the applicant's communication with his colleagues, who were disturbed by his behaviour.

### Impairment of long-term effect

Schedule 1 applies and states that impairment is of long-term effect if it has lasted for 12 months, or is likely so to last, or is likely to last for life. A severe disfigurement is included. The effect on normal day-to-day activities is dealt with by a list in para 4 of Sch 1, which includes mobility, manual dexterity, physical co-ordination and lack of ability to lift or speak, hear, see, remember, concentrate, learn or understand or to perceive the risk of physical danger. Also included are those who have a progressive condition, such as HIV, resulting in impairment of ability, even though the effect is not currently substantial. Persons who are on the register of disabled persons kept under s 6 of the Disabled Persons (Employment) Act 1944 on 12 January 1995, and when relevant provision comes into force, are deemed disabled.

The Act also covers in s 2 'a person who has had a disability' even though he or she may no longer be disabled. This applies in regard to employment, services and discrimination in regard to premises and follows a government pledge that those with a history of disability should be covered.

### Employees who are within the definition

Under s 4 it is unlawful for an employer to discriminate against a disabled employee;

- in the terms of employment and the opportunities for promotion, transfer, training or other benefits or by refusing the same;
- by dismissal or any other disadvantage.

This is firmed up as regards pensions by s 17, which makes clear that trustees and managers of occupational pension schemes are under a general duty not to discriminate against the disabled. This rule will be implied into the rules of occupational pension schemes. However, it is envisaged that pension benefits of disabled people might justifiably be less than those who are not disabled.

As regards insurance benefits, where an employer makes arrangements for employees with an insurance company for matters such as private health insurance, the insurance company will under s 18 act unlawfully if it treats a disabled person in a way which would be an act of discrimination if done by the insurance company to a member of the public generally. This covers refusal to insure, the levying of higher premiums unless justified as it may be if there are reasonable grounds for supposing that the disabled person represents a higher than normal risk.

## Employer's defence

Section 5, which deals with the meaning of discrimination, allows employer discrimination if, but only if, the reason is both material to the circumstances of the case and substantial. Thus less favourable treatment may be justified if the employer believes on reasonable grounds that the nature of the disability substantially affects the disabled person's ability to perform the required task. It should be noted that the 1995 Act gives employers this defence which is not available in sex and race discrimination cases.

Reasonableness is, of course, related to practicability in terms of how useful the adjustments will be and the cost and the ability of the organisation to meet them. The value of the employee, which includes training, skill and service, is also a relevant factor. Thus a high cost adjustment might be required as reasonable for a long-serving managing director but not for a temporary cleaner. It is difficult to predict what is reasonable until relevant cases before employment tribunals are reported.

In this connection, an employment tribunal accepted the defence of justification in *Kelly* v *Hampshire Constabulary* (9 December 1997, unreported). The applicant suffered from cerebral palsy and so needed help in various ways, including eating and using the toilet. The employers offered him employment on the basis that they would try to make the necessary arrangements to accommodate him. The employers were later able to satisfy a tribunal that, although they had made every effort to do this, it was in fact impossible for them to accommodate him and because of this they were held not to have discriminated when the employment did not continue.

It is, of course, essential that the employer is aware of the disability. *See O'Neill* v *Symm & Co Ltd* [1998] ICR 481, where the employers were not liable for the dismissal of an accounts clerk suffering from ME because they had not been aware of the nature of her illness and so could not have treated her less favourably than an employee who did not have the disability. The dismissal was for the amount of sick leave taken and non-production of a doctor's certificate, which the contract of employment required. In addition, the employers had not infringed the requirement of the Act to take all reasonable steps to find out about the disability since, in the circumstances of the case, there was nothing to put the employers on inquiry.

### Duty to make adjustments

Section 6 includes 12 examples of steps, e.g. altering working hours, acquiring or modifying equipment, arranging for training and providing supervision, which an employer may have to take so as to comply with a new duty to make reasonable adjustments to working arrangements or the physical features of premises where these constitute a disadvantage to disabled persons. However, s 6 specifies that regard shall be had to the extent to which it is practical for the employer to take the steps involved, the financial and other costs to be incurred, the extent of any disruption to the employer's activities and his financial and other resources.

It is important to note that ss 5 and 6 apply in a redundancy situation so that in selecting a disabled person for redundancy the employer must observe the rules of adjustment in s 6 or satisfy the 'reasonableness' test in s 5: *Morse* v *Wiltshire County Council* [1998] IRLR 1023.

Section 16 contains provisions relating to adjustments in leasehold premises. The tenant employer must seek the consent of the landlord. The latter must not withhold consent unreasonably.

### Exemption for small businesses

Section 7(1) provides that nothing in Part II of the Act (Employment) shall apply to an employer who has fewer than 20 employees. The Secretary of State may substitute a lower number.

However, the government has announced that from 1 December 1998 the employment provisions of the 1995 Act will be extended to organisations employing 15 or more people. Nevertheless, it appears that some 92.5 per cent of employers will still remain outside the scope of the Act. The government has also confirmed that it will amend the 1995 Act to remove the need for it to conduct a review of the effect of the exemption before lowering the threshold further and to allow it to do that in stages after getting advice from the Disability Rights Commission now this is in place.

### Validity of agreements

Section 9 provides that any term in a contract of employment or other agreement is void if, e.g. it requires a person to do anything which would contravene Part II or prevent a complaint to an employment tribunal, unless in the latter case the exclusion is in writing and follows independent legal advice or the matter has been settled by reference to a conciliation officer.

### Discrimination by other persons

An important provision is contained is s 12, which provides protection for disabled contract workers who work for an employment business. The hirer must not discriminate against them.

### Victimisation

It also amounts to discrimination under the Act if someone is treated less favourably because he has brought, or given, evidence in claims under the Act, or merely made allegations that the Act has been infringed.

## Enforcement

Under s 8, employment complaints are to be presented to an employment tribunal. Regulations have been made to allow a restricted reporting order where 'evidence of a personal nature' is likely to be heard.

The claim must be brought within three months of the act complained of and the tribunal may take any of the following steps as it considers just and equitable:

- make a declaration of the rights of the complainant and as a basis for these to be adopted by the employer;
- order monetary compensation with no limit;
- recommend steps to be taken by the employer within a specified period to obviate or reduce the adverse effects of which the employee complains.

The services of ACAS can also be invoked with a view to a settlement without a tribunal hearing.

There is no cap upon the compensation which may be awarded for disability discrimination. In *Kirk v British Sugar plc*, Nottingham Employment Tribunal, December 1997/January 1998, unreported, a partially sighted employee who was able to prove that his defective eyesight was the dominant factor in his selection for redundancy was awarded £100,000. The scores he achieved in his assessment were influenced by his disability and were not an objective assessment based upon his past work performance. The tribunal accepted that a partially sighted person would have greater difficulties in obtaining employment and based the award on the finding that he would not get alternative employment for the rest of his working life of 15 years, less 20 per cent to take account of the risk that had he stayed on his eyesight might have deteriorated to the point where he could not continue.

## Questionnaires

Disabled persons who think they have been subject to discrimination can serve questionnaires on the employer in the same way as for sex and race claims.

## The Disability Rights Commission

The Disability Rights Commission Act 1999 set up the Disability Rights Commission. The DRC will:

- provide direct assistance to litigants on the lines of the EOC and CRE;
- work towards eliminating discrimination against disabled people;
- promote equal opportunities for disabled people;
- provide information and advice in particular to disabled people, employers and service providers;
- prepare codes of practice and encourage their use;
- review the working of the Disability Discrimination Act 1995;
- investigate discrimination and ensure compliance with the law;
- arrange for a conciliation service between service providers and disabled people to help resolve disputes on access to goods and services.

## Policy statement

As we have seen in the case of sex and race discrimination, it is useful to draft a policy statement to staff regarding disability discrimination and how it should be dealt with.

# GRADED QUESTIONS

### Essay mode

1  Jane applied for a job as a sales assistant in the Macho Man clothing shop. She was refused employment because she would, said the manager, have to take intimate measurements of male customers. There are four other sales assistants all of whom are male.

   Advise Jane.                                                              *(Author's question)*

2  John aged 17 has recently taken up employment in the packing department of Macy's Fashions. He is the only male employee in the packing department, the others being older women. John has complained to you that he is being constantly subjected to remarks by some of the women comparing his physique and likely sexual prowess unfavourably with a variety of male pin-ups which the women have posted conspicuously in various parts of the warehouse.

   Advise John.                                                             *(Author's question)*

### Objective mode

1  An employer may practise sex and racial discrimination where sex or race is a ————. Complete.

2  Mrs Bloggs says: 'I want some part-time help with my housework, but I shall tell the employment agency that I do not want a coloured person.'

   Mrs Bloggs is acting contrary to law.                                    TRUE/FALSE

3  Mr Bloggs is about to place an advertisement for a job in his restaurant. It says: 'Waiter required for upmarket restaurant in Barchester. Apply Box 30.'

   Mr Bloggs is quite within his legal rights to do this.                   TRUE/FALSE

4  Mr Redneck, the owner of a mini-market employing 18 members of staff, advertised for a clerical assistant. John, who is of West Indian origin and well qualified for the post, has applied for it. There were two other applicants who were white. There was a preliminary interview followed by the main interview held one week later. During that week Mr Redneck sent more details of the job requirements to the white applicants but not to John. Consequently, John could not prepare himself so well for the main interview and was not successful.

   What is the legal position?

   A  John appears to be able to claim direct racial discrimination.
   B  John can claim indirect racial discrimination.
   C  John has no claim since Mr Redneck can choose which employees he wishes.
   D  John has no claim because Mr Redneck is a small employer.

5 Jane is a member of a religious sect which does not allow its followers to cover their heads. Jane applied for a job at a bakery, but was turned down because she would not wear the headgear required for purposes of hygiene.

What is the legal position?

A Jane appears to be able to claim indirect racial discrimination.
B Jane can claim direct racial discrimination.
C Jane has no claim.
D Jane has been victimised on the grounds of sex.

6 Mabel applied for a job as a PA/Secretary to the finance director of a car distribution company. She revealed that in her previous employment she had brought a claim of sex discrimination in respect of a promotion which she did not get. The case is proceeding. The company has written to her stating that in view of the claim she will not be invited to the interview.

Advise Mabel.

A Mabel has been victimised and may obtain an injunction requiring the company to interview her.
B This is a case of direct discrimination because Mabel is a woman.
C Mabel has been victimised but can only claim damages.
D Mabel has suffered indirect discrimination because she is a woman.

*The answers to questions set in objective mode appear on p 708.*

# 17 EMPLOYMENT III

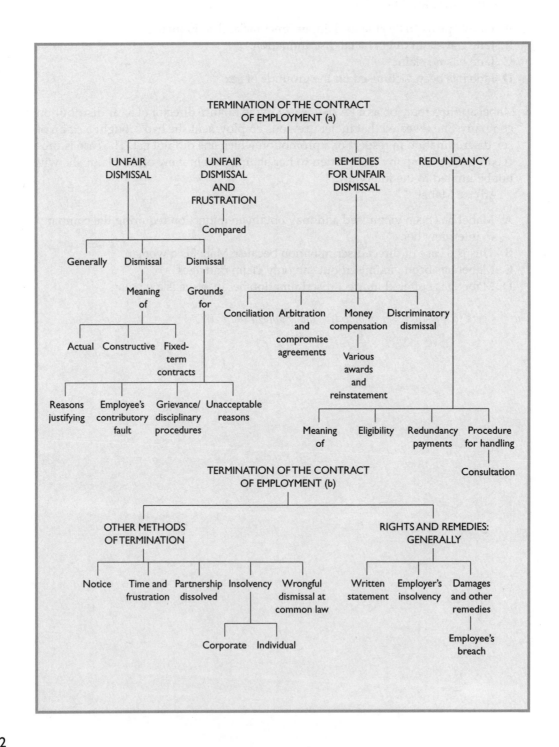

TERMINATION OF THE CONTRACT
OF EMPLOYMENT (a)

UNFAIR DISMISSAL

UNFAIR DISMISSAL AND FRUSTRATION

REMEDIES FOR UNFAIR DISMISSAL

REDUNDANCY

Compared

Generally    Dismissal    Dismissal

Meaning of    Grounds for

Actual    Constructive    Fixed-term contracts

Conciliation    Arbitration and compromise agreements    Money compensation    Discriminatory dismissal

Various awards and reinstatement

Reasons justifying    Employee's contributory fault    Grievance/disciplinary procedures    Unacceptable reasons

Meaning of    Eligibility    Redundancy payments    Procedure for handling

Consultation

TERMINATION OF THE CONTRACT
OF EMPLOYMENT (b)

OTHER METHODS OF TERMINATION

RIGHTS AND REMEDIES: GENERALLY

Notice    Time and frustration    Partnership dissolved    Insolvency    Wrongful dismissal at common law

Written statement    Employer's insolvency    Damages and other remedies

Corporate    Individual

Employee's breach

462

The objectives of this chapter are to complete the study of employment law by considering the termination of the contract of employment, including discriminatory dismissal and redundancy together with rights and remedies on dismissal.

## TERMINATION OF THE CONTRACT OF EMPLOYMENT

### Unfair dismissal — generally

Before a person can ask an employment tribunal to consider a claim that another has unfairly dismissed him or her, it is, once again, essential to establish that the relationship of employer and employee exists between them. In this connection, the Employment Rights Act 1996 (ERA) provides that an employee is a person who works under a contract of service or apprenticeship, written or oral, express or implied.

**An example of a case where a person failed in an unfair dismissal claim because he was unable to show that he was an employee is given below.**

### Massey v Crown Life Insurance Co [1978] 2 All ER 576

Mr Massey was employed by Crown Life as the manager of the Ilford branch from 1971 to 1973, the company paying him wages and deducting tax. In 1973, on the advice of his accountant, Mr Massey registered a business name of J R Massey and Associates and with that new name entered into an agreement with Crown Life under which he carried out the same duties as before but as a self-employed person. The Inland Revenue was content that he should change to be taxed under Schedule D as a self-employed person. His employment was terminated and he claimed to have been unfairly dismissed. The Court of Appeal decided that, being self-employed, he could not be unfairly dismissed.

In addition to showing that he is an employee, the claimant must comply with an age requirement. The unfair dismissal provisions do not apply to the dismissal of an employee from any employment if the employee has on or before the effective date of termination attained the age which, in the undertaking in which he is employed, was the normal retiring age for an employee holding the position which he held, or for both men and women aged 65 (ERA, s 109).

However, such persons are not excluded where the dismissal is automatically unfair, e.g. for taking part in trade union activities.

As regards the period of employment, the general unfair dismissal provisions do not apply to the dismissal of an employee from any employment if the employee, whether full-time or part-time, has not completed one year's continuous employment ending with the effective date of termination of employment unless the dismissal is automatically unfair. Such dismissals are actionable regardless of service or hours worked. There are exceptions in the case of maternity dismissals, health and safety dismissals and dismissals for asserting statutory rights, e.g. asking for written particulars. These dismissals are automatically unfair and are not service-based.

As regards persons ordinarily employed outside Great Britain, the ERA states that an employee has no protection against unfair dismissal if he is engaged in work wholly or mainly outside Great Britain. However, maternity dismissals are covered and the ERA 1996 s 196 applies.

Certain other categories are excluded by the ERA, e.g. members of the police force and those taking unofficial industrial action. The Employment Relations Act 1999 provides that a worker who is dismissed by reason of taking official and legal industrial action will be able to claim unfair dismissal, provided that the dismissal takes place within the period of eight weeks beginning with the day on which the employee took part in industrial action. Thus, in a long period of official industrial action, these rules of dismissal protection would not apply.

Members of the armed forces are now covered by the unfair dismissal provisions of the ERA, provided that they have first availed themselves of services redress procedures (ERA, s 192).

It should also be noted that s 9 of the Employment Tribunals Act 1996 contains provisions to test the strength of the case of each party before a full hearing proceeds. Pre-hearing reviews are introduced at which the chairman of the tribunal may sit alone without the two lay assessors. The chairman may, at his discretion and following an application by one of the parties, or of his own motion, require a deposit of up to £150 from the other party as a condition of proceeding further if it is considered that his or her case has no reasonable prospect of success, or that to pursue it would be frivolous, vexatious or otherwise unreasonable.

## Dismissal – meaning of

An employee cannot claim unfair dismissal unless there has first been a dismissal recognised by law. We may consider the matter under the following headings.

### Actual dismissal

This does not normally give rise to problems since most employees recognise the words of an actual dismissal, whether given orally or in writing.

A typical letter of dismissal appears below.

---

Dear Mr Bloggs

I am sorry that you do not have the necessary aptitude to deal with the work which we have allocated to you. I hope that you will be able to find other work elsewhere which is more in your line. As you will recall from your interview this morning, the company will not require your services after the 31st of this month.

---

### Constructive dismissal

This occurs where it is the employee who leaves the job but is compelled to do so by the conduct of the employer. In general terms, the employer's conduct must be a fundamental breach so that it can be regarded as a repudiation of the contract. Thus, if a male employer were to sexually harass a female employee, then this would be a fundamental breach entitling her to leave and sue for her loss on the basis of constructive dismissal.

It would also occur if the employer unilaterally changed the terms and conditions of the employment contract as by unilaterally reducing wages under the contract (*see Rigby* v *Ferodo* [1987] IRLR 516). Furthermore, the EAT decided in *Whitbread plc (t/a Thresher)* v *Gullyes* [1994] 509 IRLB 14 that an employee who resigned from a management position because her employer did not give her proper support – because, among other things, the most experienced staff were transferred out of her branch without consultation – was constructively dismissed.

### Fixed-term contracts

When a fixed-term contract expires and is not renewed, there is a dismissal. Under the provisions of the Employment Rights Act 1999, the ERA 1996 is amended so that an employee can no longer waive his right to claim unfair dismissal where a contract for one year or more is not renewed. A claim for redundancy payment can still be waived where the contract is for two years or more.

## Dismissal – grounds for

If an employer is going to escape liability for unfair dismissal, he must show that he acted *reasonably* and, indeed, the ERA s 92 requires the employer to give his reasons for dismissal to the employee in writing.

It should be remembered that the question of whether a dismissal is fair or not is a matter of *fact* for the particular tribunal hearing the case, and one cannot predict with absolute accuracy what a particular tribunal will do on the facts of a particular case. Basically, when all is said and done, the ultimate question for a tribunal is – 'was the dismissal fair and reasonable' in fact?

Section 98 of the ERA includes in the test of reasonableness required in determining whether a dismissal was fair, the 'size and administrative resources of the employer's undertaking'. This was included as a result of fear that the unfair dismissal laws were placing undue burdens on small employers and causing them not to engage new workers. Earlier legislation also removed the burden of proof from the employer in showing reasonableness so that there is now no 'presumption of guilt' on the employer and the tribunal is left to decide whether or not the employer acted reasonably.

### Reasons justifying dismissal

These are as follows.

(a) *Lack of capability or qualifications: unsuitability.* This would usually arise at the beginning of employment where it becomes clear at an early stage that the employee cannot do the job in terms of lack of skill or mental or physical health. It may be imagined that claims for unfair dismissal would not often arise in this area: generally incompetence would be discovered and a dismissal made before the employee concerned had completed the necessary one year's service to be entitled to claim. However, there are examples, as seen below. It should be remembered that the longer a person is in employment the more difficult it is to establish lack of capability.

By way of illustration we can consider the case of *Alidair v Taylor* [1978] IRLR 82. The pilot of an aircraft had made a faulty landing which damaged the aircraft. There was a board of inquiry which found that the faulty landing was due to a lack of flying knowledge on the part of the pilot, who was dismissed from his employment. It was decided that the employee had not been unfairly dismissed, the tribunal taking the view that where, as in this case, one failure to reach a high degree of skill could have serious consequences, an instant dismissal could be justified.

However, it was decided in *British Sulphur v Lawrie* [1987] IRLB 338 that the dismissal of an employee who was alleged to be unwilling or incompetent to do a particular job could still be unfair if the employee was not provided with adequate training.

As regards qualifications, this could occur where a new employee does not have the qualifications claimed or fails to get a qualification which was a condition of employment, as in the case of legal and accounting trainees who fail to complete their examinations. It should also be noted that the Court of Appeal decided in *Nottinghamshire County Council v P, The Times*, 18 May 1992, that even though an employee had to be dismissed from an employment for which he had become unsuitable, it could still be unfair dismissal if the employer failed to make a reasonable investigation of possible alternative employment. P was an assistant groundsman at a girls' school and had pleaded guilty to a charge of indecent assault on his daughter. Obviously, he could not be allowed to continue to work at the school, but the Council should have considered alternative employment within the authority. Failure to do so could amount to unfair dismissal. The case was sent back to an industrial tribunal to see what efforts the Council had made if any.

(b) *Conduct*. This is always a difficult matter to deal with and much will depend upon the circumstances of the case. However, incompetence and neglect are relevant, as are disobedience and misconduct, e.g. by assaulting fellow employees. Immorality and habitual drunkenness could also be brought under this heading and, so it seems, can dress where this can be shown to affect adversely the way in which the contract of service is performed.

**The following case provides an illustration.**

### Boychuk v H J Symons (Holdings) Ltd [1977] IRLR 395

Miss B was employed by S Ltd as an accounts clerk, but her duties involved contact with the public from time to time. Miss B insisted on wearing badges which proclaimed the fact that she was a lesbian and from May 1976 she wore one or other of the following: (a) a lesbian symbol consisting of two circles with crosses (indicating women) joined together; (b) badges with the legends: 'Gays against fascism' and 'Gay power'; (c) a badge with the legend: 'Gay switchboard' with a telephone number on it and the words: 'Information service for homosexual men and women'; (d) a badge with the word 'Dyke', indicating to the initiated that she was a lesbian.

These were eventually superseded by a white badge with the words 'Lesbians ignite' written in large letters on it. Nothing much had happened in regard to the wearing of the earlier badges, but when she began wearing the 'Lesbians ignite' badge, there were discussions about it between her and her employer. She was told that she must remove it – which she was not willing to do – and that if she did not she would be dismissed. She would not remove the badge and was dismissed on 16 August 1976 and then made a claim for compensation for unfair dismissal.

No complaint was made regarding the manner of her dismissal in terms, e.g. of proper warning. The straight question was whether her employers were entitled to dismiss her because she insisted on wearing the badge. An industrial tribunal had decided that in all the circumstances the dismissal was fair because it was within an employer's discretion to instruct an employee not to wear a particular badge or symbol which could cause offence to customers and fellow employees. Miss B appealed to the Employment Appeal Tribunal which dismissed her appeal and said that her dismissal was fair. The court said that there was no question of Miss B having been dismissed because she was a lesbian or because of anything to do with her private life or private behaviour. Such a case would be entirely different and raise different questions. This was only a case where she had been dismissed because of her conduct at work. That, the court said, must be clearly understood.

*Comment:* (i) The decision does not mean that an employer by a foolish or unreasonable judgment of what could be expected to be offensive could impose some unreasonable restriction on an employee. However, the decision does mean that a reasonable employer, who is, after all, ultimately responsible for the interests of the business, is allowed to decide what, upon reflection or mature consideration, could be offensive to customers and fellow employees, and he need not wait to see whether the business would in fact be damaged before he takes steps in the matter.

(ii) In *Kowalski* v *The Berkeley Hotel* [1985] IRLR 40 the EAT decided that the dismissal of a pastrycook for fighting at work was fair though it was the first time he had done it. Also, on the issue of conduct, the EAT decided in *Marshall* v *Industrial Systems and Control Ltd* [1992] IRLR 294 that a company acted reasonably in dismissing its managing director after discovering that along with another manager he was planning to set up a business competing with the company and to take on the business of its best customer and that active steps had been taken to achieve this. It should be noted that an employee does not breach the duty of loyalty merely by forming an intention to compete at some future date (*Laughton* v *Bapp Industrial Supplies Ltd* [1986] IRLR 245). As regards smoking at work it was decided in *Dryden* v *Greater Glasgow Health Board* [1992] 447 IRLIB 11 that employees have no implied contractual right to smoke at work. If, as in Ms Dryden's case, the employee leaves because he or she is not allowed to smoke, there is no constructive dismissal. The employer in this case had offered counselling but without success.

An employee's use of drugs or alcohol outside the workplace is unlikely to amount to a fair reason for dismissal, nor will the mere fact that an employee did not reveal that he or she used drugs or alcohol when interviewed for a post. However, use of drugs or excessive drinking may constitute a fair reason for dismissal where the employer believes on reasonable grounds that it makes the employee *unsuitable for the position held.*

(c) *Redundancy.* Genuine redundancy is a defence. Where a person is redundant, his employer cannot be expected to continue the employment, although there are safeguards in the matter of *unfair selection for redundancy.*

(d) *Dismissals which are union-related*. These are known as the *'section 152 reasons'*. They are set out in the Trade Union and Labour Relations (Consolidation) Act 1992, s 152. An employee will be regarded as automatically unfairly dismissed so that no particular period of service or hours worked is required if the principal reason for the dismissal was that he was, or proposed to become, a member of a trade union which was independent of the employer; that he had taken part or proposed to take part in the activities of such a union at an appropriate time, i.e. outside working hours or within working hours with the consent of the employer; that he was not a member of any trade union or of a particular one or had refused or proposed to refuse to become or remain a member. Under the relevant provisions of the Trade Union and Labour Relations (Consolidation) Act 1992 all closed-shop dismissals are now automatically unfair.

Dismissal will also be automatically unfair if the employee is selected for redundancy on any of the above 'trade union' grounds. Furthermore, the Court of Appeal decided in *Fitzpatrick* v *British Railways Board* [1991] IRLR 376 that a dismissal for trade union activities in a previous employment was automatically unfair.

It is also worth noting at this point that under s 146 of the Trade Union and Labour Relations (Consolidation) Act 1992 an employee has a right not to have action taken against him short of dismissal, such as victimisation in terms of not being offered overtime, where this is related to union membership or activities. There is, however, a provision into the 1992 Act under which protection against victimisation continues but does not prevent an employer, acting reasonably, from implementing a decision to negotiate personally with his employees and not through a union and to offer inducements such as increased pay to those who sign personal contracts, while denying these benefits to those who do not sign. The position in regard to job applicants under the Trade Union and Labour Relations (Consolidation) Act 1992 has already been considered (*see* Chapter 15).

(e) *Statutory restriction placed on employer or employee*. If, for example, the employer's business was found to be dangerous and was closed down under Act of Parliament or ministerial order, the employees would not be unfairly dismissed. Furthermore, a lorry driver who was banned from driving for 12 months could be dismissed fairly.

(f) *Some other substantial reason*. An employer may on a wide variety of grounds which are not specified by legislation satisfy an industrial tribunal that a dismissal was fair and reasonable.

Crime and suspicion of crime may be brought under this heading, though if dismissal is based on suspicion of crime, the suspicion must be reasonable and in all cases the employee must be told that dismissal is contemplated and in the light of this information be allowed to give explanations and make representations against dismissal.

Where an employee has been charged with theft from the employer and is awaiting trial, the best course of action is to suspend rather than dismiss him, pending the verdict. Investigations which the employer must make, as part of establishing a fair dismissal, could be regarded as an interference with the course of justice. It is best, therefore, not to make them, but to suspend the employee. The case of *Wadley* v *Eager Electrical* [1986] IRLR 93 should be noted. In that case husband and wife worked for the same company. The wife was convicted for stealing £2,000 from the company while employed as a shop assistant. The husband was a service engineer with the company. Husband and wife were dismissed and it was held that the husband's dismissal was unfair. He was a good employee of 17 years' standing and no misconduct had been made out against him.

The matter of fair or unfair dismissal depends also upon the terms of the contract. If the difficulty is that a particular employee is refusing to do work which involves him, say, spending nights away from home, then his dismissal is likely to be regarded as fair if there is an *express term* in his contract requiring this. Of course, the nature of the job may require it, as in the case of a long-distance lorry driver where such a term would be implied, if not expressed.

Employees who are in breach of contract are likely to be regarded as fairly dismissed. However, this is not an invariable rule. Thus a long-distance lorry driver who refused to take on a particular trip because his wife was ill and he had to look after the children would be unfairly dismissed (if dismissal took place) even though he was, strictly speaking, in breach of his contract.

### Grievance and disciplinary procedures

These are usually part of the contract. The employer must comply with them if he wishes to avoid liability. If a series of oral and written warnings is laid down, the procedure should be observed. However, reasonableness will always prevail.

No matter how good the employer's reason for dismissal may be, there may still be a claim by the employee for unfair dismissal if the dismissal was 'unfair in all the circumstances'.

In *Whitbread & Co plc* v *Mills* [1988] IRLR 43 the President of the Employment Appeal Tribunal, Mr Justice Wood, gave guidance on the issue of whether an employer had acted reasonably as the law requires. In applying the guidance, let us assume that the main reason for dismissal is the acceptable one of incompetence – as in the case of a senior member of a publisher's staff who commissions books without proper market research so that they do not sell and the publisher is caused loss.

Having reached the conclusion that the incompetence is established, the employer must, according to Mr Justice Wood, satisfy a tribunal on four other matters, otherwise the dismissal might still be unfair, though the employee's compensation might be reduced for contributory fault (*see below*). The four matters are:

(a) Can the employer satisfy a tribunal that he complied with the pre-dismissal procedures which a reasonable employer could and should have applied in the circumstances of the case? If the tribunal finds that the employer has not acted reasonably in this regard, at the date of dismissal, then according to the decision in *Polkey* v *A E Dayton Services Ltd* [1988] ICR 564 it is not open to the tribunal to say that the procedures do not matter since it is clear that the employee was incompetent. The unfairness of the dismissal could still give the employee a successful claim.

Thus the decision of the House of Lords in *Polkey* makes clear the importance of consultation in regard to the fairness of a dismissal. There may be grounds for dismissal, but if there is no proper consultation, the dismissal may still be unfair, though the compensation will generally be reduced if there were grounds for dismissal. It should be noted that, although *Polkey* was a case of unfair redundancy dismissal, the principle that procedural unfairness leads to a finding of unfair dismissal applies to other categories of dismissal and not just to redundancy cases. However, it is not always necessary to consult, said the House of Lords in *Polkey*, as where the employer has reasonably taken the view, having thought about it, that the exceptional circumstances of a particular case make it, for example, undesirable. Thus in *Eclipse Blinds v Wright* [1992] 444 IRLIB 12 Mrs Wright was dismissed because of poor health. The employer had received a medical report with her consent. It revealed that she was much more seriously ill than she had thought and, rather than upset her in a consultation process, the personnel officer wrote her a letter in sympathetic terms ending her employment on the grounds of incapability. The court decided that she had not been unfairly dismissed even though there was no proper consultation.

(b) Where there is a contractual appeal process the employer must have carried it out in its essentials. A minor departure may sometimes be ignored but a total or substantial failure entitles a tribunal to find that the dismissal was unfair. Even though no contractual appeal process exists, it may nevertheless be reasonable, as was decided in *West Midland Co-operative Society Ltd v Tipton* [1986] ICR 192, for some sort of appeal to be arranged since this is encouraged by the code of practice issued by the Advisory, Conciliation and Arbitration Service.

(c) Where conduct is the main reason the employer must show, on a balance of probabilities, that at the time of the dismissal he believed the employee was guilty of misconduct and that in all the circumstances of the case it was reasonable for him to do so.

(d) During the disciplinary hearings and the appeal process, the employer must have been fair to the employee. In particular, the employee must have been heard and allowed to put his case properly or, if he was not at a certain stage of the procedures, this must have been corrected before dismissal.

Under reforms made to disciplinary hearings by the Employment Relations Act 1999, an employee has a *right* to be accompanied at such hearings by a trade union representative or a fellow employee. This applies even if an employer does not recognise trade unions. As a result, hearings are likely to become more adversarial and formal, and so lengthier. Legal advice should perhaps now be sought by employers in the hearings, bearing in mind that a combined basic and compensatory award could exceed £60,000.

### Employee's contributory fault

This can reduce the compensation payable to the employee by such percentage as the tribunal thinks fit. Suppose an employee is often late for work and one morning his employer, who can stand it no more, sacks him. The dismissal is likely to be unfair in view of the lack of warning but a tribunal would very probably reduce the worker's compensation to take account of the facts.

Principles of natural justice also apply; it is necessary to let the worker state his case before a decision to dismiss is taken. Furthermore, reasonable enquiry must be made to find the truth of the matter before reaching a decision. Failure to do this will tend to make the dismissal unfair.

### Unacceptable reasons for dismissal

These are as follows.

(a) *Dismissal in connection with trade unions.* This has already been considered.

(b) *Unfair selection for redundancy.* An employee dismissed for redundancy may complain that he has been unfairly dismissed if he is of the opinion that he has been unfairly selected for redundancy, as where the employer has selected him because he is a member of a trade union or takes part in trade union activities, or where the employer has disregarded redundancy selection arrangements based, for example, on 'last in, first out'. Ideally, all employers should have proper redundancy agreements on the lines set out in the Department of Employment booklet, *Dealing with Redundancies.*

However, even though there is in existence an agreed redundancy procedure, the employer may defend himself by showing a 'special reason' for departing from that procedure, e.g. because the person selected for redundancy lacks the skill and versatility of a junior employee who is retained.

There is, since the decision of the Employment Appeal Tribunal in *Williams* v *Compair Maxam* [1982] ICR 156, an overall standard of fairness also in redundancy arrangements. The standards laid down in the case require the giving of maximum notice; consultation with unions, if any; the taking of the views of more than one person as to who should be dismissed; a requirement to follow any laid down procedure, e.g. last in, first out; and finally, an effort to find the employees concerned alternative employment within the organisation. However, the EAT stated in *Meikle* v *McPhail* (*Charleston Arms*) (1983) that these guidelines would be applied less rigidly to the smaller business. The statutory provisions relating to consultation on redundancy are considered later in this chapter.

(c) *Industrial action.* The position in this context has already been considered.

(d) *Dismissals in connection with pregnancy and childbirth.* The relevant law has already been considered in Chapter 15.

(e) *Pressure on employer to dismiss unfairly.* It is no defence for an employer to say that pressure was put upon him to dismiss an employee unfairly. So, if other workers put pressure on an employer to dismiss a non-union member so as, for example, to obtain a closed shop, the employer will have no defence to a claim for compensation for the dismissal if he gives in to that pressure. If an employer alleges that he was pressurised into dismissing an employee and that pressure was brought on him by a trade union or other person by the calling, organising, procuring or financing of industrial action, including a strike, or by the threat of such things, and the reason for the pressure was that the employee was not a member of the trade union, then the employer can join the trade union or other person as a party to the proceedings if he is sued by the dismissed worker for unfair dismissal. If the tribunal awards compensation, it can order that a person joined as a party to the proceedings should pay such amount of it as is just and equitable, and if necessary this can be a complete indemnity so that the employer will recover all the damages awarded against him from the union.

(f) *Transfer of business.* The Transfer of Undertakings (Protection of Employment) Regulations 1981 apply. Under the Regulations if a business or part of it is transferred and an employee is dismissed because of this, the dismissal will be treated as automatically unfair. However, the person concerned is not entitled to the extra compensation given to other cases of automatically unfair dismissal.

If the old employer dismissed before transfer, or the new employer dismissed after the transfer, either will have a defence if he can prove that the dismissal was for 'economic, technical or organisational' reasons requiring a change in the workforce and that the dismissal was reasonable in all the circumstances of the case.

**The following case is relevant.**

### Meikle v McPhail (Charleston Arms) [1983] IRLR 351

After contracting to take over a public house and its employees, the new management decided that economies were essential and dismissed the barmaid. She complained to an industrial tribunal on the grounds of unfair dismissal. Her case was based upon the fact that the 1981 Regulations state that a dismissal is to be treated as unfair if the transfer of a business or a reason connected with it is the reason or principal reason for the dismissal. The pub's new management defended the claim under another provision in the 1981 Regulations which states that a dismissal following a transfer of business is not to be regarded as automatically unfair where there was, as in this case, an economic reason for making changes in the workforce. If there is such a reason, unfairness must be established on grounds other than the mere transfer of the business.

The EAT decided that the reason for dismissal was an economic one under the Regulations and that the management had acted reasonably in the circumstances so that the barmaid's claim failed.

*Comment:* It should be noted that in *Gateway Hotels Ltd* v *Stewart* [1988] IRLR 287 the EAT decided that on a transfer of business dismissal of employees of the business transferred prior to the transfer at the insistence of the purchaser of the business is not an 'economic' reason within the regulations so that the dismissals are unfair.

(g) *Health and safety dismissals and detriments.* Designated or acknowledged health and safety representatives must not be subjected to detriments, for example, loss of overtime, for carrying out health and safety activities in the workplace. Dismissal for these reasons is automatically unfair which means that there is no service requirement. These provisions also apply to ordinary employees, regardless of service, who leave or refuse to return to the workplace because of a health hazard reasonably thought to exist. The same is true under the Health and Safety (Consultation with Employees) Regulations 1996 (SI 1996/1513) where the dismissal is of a worker safety representative elected to take part in the health and safety consultation process where there is no recognised union.

(h) *Dismissal for asserting statutory right.* This protects employees regardless of service against dismissal for trying to enforce employment rights under the EPA that can be brought before a tribunal. Dismissal will be unfair even if the worker does not in fact have the right provided he has acted in good faith.

(i) *Dismissal for performing the duties of a member-nominated trustee of an occupational pension scheme.*

(j) *Dismissal for performing the duties of an employee representative in redundancy consultation or putting up for election to be one.*

## Automatically unfair dismissals

Having noted some of these in various parts of the text, it may be useful to bring them together in a list, remembering that dismissals of this kind do not require any particular period of service with the employer.

The reasons which make a dismissal automatically unfair can briefly be listed as follows:

(a)  trade union membership or activities;

(b)  not belonging to a trade union or particular union;

(c)  pregnancy;

(d)  selection for redundancy on any of the above grounds;

(e)  the transfer of the undertaking or a reason connected with it (unless there is an ETO (economic, technical or organisational reason). It should, however, be noted at this point that the one-year qualifying period does not apply where the complaint is based on dismissal for one of the automatically unfair reasons, though if the dismissal related to the transfer of an undertaking the one-year qualifying period does apply;

(f)  asserting a statutory employment right under ERA 1996, s 104;

(g)  in health and safety cases involving union safety representatives and now including being an employee safety representative or putting up for election to be one;

(h)  performing the duties of a member-nominated trustee under the Pensions Act 1995;

(i)  being an employee representative in redundancy consultation or putting up for election to be one (ERA 1996, s 103);

(j)  refusing (in certain circumstances) to do shop or betting work on a Sunday;

(k)  exercising rights under the Working Time Regulations including rights as an employee representative in connection with the workforce agreements (s 101(A), ERA 1996, as inserted by the regulations);

(l)  asserting rights under the National Minimum Wage Act 1998 (s 104(A), ERA 1996, as inserted by the NMW Act 1998);

(m) asserting rights to time off for study and training under s 63A of the ERA 1996, as inserted by the Teaching and Higher Education Act 1998.

## Unfair dismissal and frustration of contract

In cases appearing before employment tribunals, there is a certain interplay between the common law rules of frustration of contract (*see* Chapter 8) and the statutory provisions relating to unfair dismissal. At common law, a contract of service is frustrated by incapacity, e.g. sickness, if that incapacity makes the contract substantially impossible of performance at a particularly vital time, or by a term of imprisonment. If a contract has been so frustrated, then a complaint of unfair dismissal is not available because the contract has been discharged on other grounds, i.e. by frustration. Thus termination of a contract of service by frustration prevents a claim for unfair dismissal.

It is, of course, necessary now in terms of sickness/incapacity for the employer to be alert to the rules about disability discrimination, particularly where an adjustment to working conditions might enable an employee or recruit to do the job satisfactorily.

## Remedies for unfair dismissal

These are as follows.

### Conciliation

An employment tribunal will not hear a complaint until a conciliation officer has had a chance to see whether he can help, provided that he or she has been *requested* so to do by a party to the potential complaint. A copy of the complaint made to the employment tribunal will in such a situation be sent to a conciliation officer of the Advisory, Conciliation and Arbitration Service (ACAS) and, if he is unable to settle the complaint, nothing said by the employer or employee during the process of conciliation will be admissible in evidence before the tribunal.

The reference of cases to a conciliation officer has led to the settlement of some one-third of them before the tribunal hearing but the parties do not have to become involved in this procedure.

### ACAS arbitration and compromise agreements

The following provisions of the Employment Rights (Dispute Resolution) Act 1998 should be noted.

Part II of the Act contains provisions to allow parties to opt for their dispute to be resolved by independent binding arbitration and gives ACAS powers to pay for and provide an arbitration service for claims of unfair dismissal and unlawful discrimination.

Part II also contains provisions making changes to the law relating to compromise agreements. Currently, the parties to an individual employment rights dispute may conclude that dispute by reaching, for example, a financial settlement. For such an agreement to be binding, the parties must have settled after an ACAS-appointed conciliation officer has taken action, or, alternatively, the terms of the settlement must be contained in a private compromise agreement. Formerly, a compromise agreement that had not involved ACAS had to be made in circumstances where the employee had received independent legal advice from a qualified lawyer. the 1998 Act changes this to advice from any independent adviser, provided that advice is covered by an insurance policy or an indemnity provision for members of a profession or professional body (ss 9 and 10). This will allow trade unions, advice agencies and others – in addition to lawyers – to give relevant advice.

Other provisions of Part II allow ACAS-appointed conciliation officers to conciliate in claims relating to statutory redundancy payments where before they had no duty to conciliate, as they have in almost all other individual employment rights disputes (s 11).

There are also provisions that clarify, streamline and make more flexible current legislation under which employers and employer-recognised trade unions can, by making a dismissal procedures agreement, opt out of the statutory rules on unfair dismissals (s 12).

### Other remedies

An employee who has been dismissed may:

(a) seek reinstatement or re-engagement; or
(b) claim compensation.

The power to order (a) above is discretionary and in practice is rarely exercised. However, reinstatement means taken back by the employer on exactly the same terms and seniority as before; re-engagement is being taken back but on different terms.

### Calculation of compensation

Before proceeding further with a study of the calculations, it should be noted that the basic award is based on *gross* pay, but the compensatory award is based on *net* pay, as the sample calculations show. It should also be noted that the cap of £50,000 on unfair dismissal compensatory awards is removed for staff who are unfairly dismissed for blowing the whistle on illegal practices or over health and safety matters and who are protected against such dismissal by the Public Interest Disclosure Act 1998. There is, therefore, no ceiling on such awards. It was feared that some senior executives might have been deterred from whistle-blowing since they would have the most salary to lose.

The compensation for unfair dismissal is in four parts as follows.

(a) *The basic award* (maximum: £6,600 for those with 20 years' service or more). This award is computed as a redundancy payment (*see* p 482 before reading on) except that there is no maximum age limit. Contributory fault of the employee is taken into account.

*Example*: Fred, a 35-year-old lorry driver employed for 10 years earning £350 per week (take home £300) is unfairly dismissed. He did his best to get a comparable job but did not in fact obtain one until two weeks after the tribunal hearing. Fred had a history of lateness for work and his contributory fault is assessed at 25 per cent.

*Fred's basic award*: Fred is in the category over 22 years of age but under 41 years of age for redundancy which allows one week's pay for every year of service:

$$
\begin{array}{lll}
10 \times £350 & £3,500 & \\
\textit{Less: } 25\% & \underline{£875} & \\
& \underline{£2,625} & = \text{ basic award}
\end{array}
$$

If Fred's dismissal had been automatically unfair, for example for union membership, the minimum award would be £2,900. This may be reduced for contributory fault.

(b) *Compensatory award* (maximum: £50,000). This consists of:
   (i)   estimated loss of wages, net of tax and other deductions to the date of the hearing less any money earned between the date of dismissal and the hearing;
   (ii)  estimated future losses;
   (iii) loss of any benefits such as pension rights and expenses;
   (iv)  loss of statutory rights. It is rare to get an award under this heading but it can be given for loss of minimum notice entitlement. For example, Fred has been continuously employed for 10 years. He was entitled to 10 weeks' notice, which he did not get. He now has a new job but it will take him time to build up that entitlement again. A tribunal can award something for this. Once again, contributory fault is taken into account.

*Fred's compensatory award*:

|  |  | £ |
|---|---|---|
| The loss up to the hearing | 10 × £300 | 3,000 |
| Loss up to time of getting new job | 2 × £300 | 600 |
|  |  | 3,600 |
| *Less*: 25% |  | 900 |
|  |  | 2,700 |

|  | £ |  |
|---|---|---|
| Loss of statutory rights: a nominal figure of | 100 |  |
| *Less*: 25% | 25 | 75 |
|  |  | 2,775 |

*Fred's total award is therefore*:

|  | £ |
|---|---|
| Basic | 2,625 |
| Compensatory | 2,775 |
|  | £5,400 |

If Fred has lost anything else, such as the use of the firm's van at weekends and/or pension rights, these would be added to the compensatory award subject to 25 per cent discount for contributory fault.

Those on higher salaries may very will reach the maximum of £50,000, but this will be likely only in cases of higher-ranking executives.

(c) *Additional award*: This is available in addition to the above where an employer fails to comply with an order for reinstatement or re-engagement unless it was not practicable for him to do so.

    (i) If the original dismissal was unlawful under the Race Relations Act or Sex Discrimination Act or the Disability Discrimination Act, it is not less than 26 weeks' pay nor more than 52 weeks' pay with a maximum of £220 per week, and an overall maximum of £11,440 and a minimum of £5,720.

    (ii) In other cases (not where dismissal is automatically unfair – *see below*), it is not less than 13 weeks' pay nor more than 26 weeks' pay calculated as in (i) above, with a maximum of £5,720 and a minimum of £2,860.

(d) *A special award*. This is payable where the dismissal is on grounds of trade union membership i.e. for one of the 'section 152 reasons' or activities or health and safety duties and the employee has asked for reinstatement or re-engagement but the tribunal has refused to make such an order. It can make a special award instead. The compensation is a week's pay but without limit as to amount, multiplied by 104 weeks with a minimum amount of £14,500 and a maximum of £29,000. However, if a tribunal does make an order for reinstatement or re-engagement and the employer does not comply but cannot show that it was reasonably impracticable for him to do so, the compensation is increased to a week's pay (no limit) multiplied by 156 with a minimum of £21,800 and no maximum. In all cases, a deduction will be made for contributory fault, if any, of the employee.

Any unemployment or supplementary benefits received by the employee are deducted from any award made by a tribunal. However, the employer must pay the amount(s) in question direct to the DSS.

As regards *ex gratia* payments, the general principle is that if the employer has made an *ex gratia* payment to the complainant in connection with the dismissal, credit will be given for this payment in fixing the amount of compensation if and only if the dismissal is in the context of being unfairly chosen for redundancy. This results from the provisions of s 122 of the ERA as interpreted in *Boorman* v *Allmakes Ltd, The Times*, 21 April 1995. If the dismissal is not in that context the employee keeps the *ex gratia* payment in addition to any compensation.

(e) *Time limits*. A claim for compensation against an employer for unfair dismissal must reach the tribunal within three months of the date of termination of employment. A worker can claim while working out his notice, but no award can be made until employment ends.

A tribunal can hear a claim after three months if the employee can prove that:

(i) it was not reasonably practicable for him to claim within three months;

(ii) he did so as soon as he could in the circumstances.

### Internal appeal procedures

Part III of the Employment Rights (Dispute Resolution) Act 1998 contains provisions relating to internal appeal procedures and unfair dismissal awards. They are intended to encourage more use to be made of internal procedures, which will hopefully increase the number of cases settled without recourse to a tribunal hearing.

A new s 127A is added to the ERA 1996. It provides that where a tribunal finds that an applicant was unfairly dismissed and (a) the employer has an internal procedure for appealing against dismissal, and (b) the applicant did not appeal under that procedure, the tribunal is to reduce the compensatory award by such amount, if any, as it thinks is just and equitable.

Conversely, where the employer has an appeals procedure that the employee wishes to use, but the employer prevents the employee from appealing by use of it, the tribunal shall make a supplementary award to the employee of such amount, if any, as it thinks is just and equitable. However, s 127A(4) limits the reduction or the supplementary award to a maximum of two weeks' pay (s 13).

## DISCRIMINATORY DISMISSAL

In addition to legislation relating to unfair dismissal generally, the Sex Discrimination Act 1975, the Race Relations Act 1976 and the Disability Discrimination Act 1995 deal with complaints to industrial tribunals for dismissal on the grounds of sex, marital status, race or disability. The nature and scope of these provisions have already been considered and it is only necessary to add here that there are provisions in the ERA which prevent double compensation being paid, once under sex discrimination legislation, race discrimination legislation or disability discrimination legislation, and once under the general unfair dismissal provisions of the ERA.

## REDUNDANCY

The ERA gives an employee a right to compensation by way of a redundancy payment if he is dismissed because of a redundancy.

## Meaning of redundancy

Under the ERA redundancy is *presumed* to occur where the services of employees are dispensed with because the employer ceases or intends to cease carrying on business, or to carry on business at the place where the employee was employed, or does not require so many employees to do work of a certain kind. Employees who have been laid off or kept on short time without pay for four consecutive weeks (or for six weeks in a period of 13 weeks) are entitled to end their employment and to seek a redundancy payment if there is no reasonable prospect that normal working will be resumed.

## The contract test and the function test

A difficult and somewhat indefinite situation arises where the court or tribunal has to decide whether an employer does not require so many employees to do work of a certain kind. Is it right to decide the question by looking at what the employee's contract requires him to do, or is it right to look at the work that the employee is actually doing, where this is different from the main contract work, as, for instance, where there is a flexible contract clause?

**The following cases illustrate the difficulties that have faced courts and tribunals.**

### Johnson v Peabody Trust [1996] 554 IRLB 6

In 1977 Mr Johnson was employed as a labourer by the Peabody Trust, which is a housing association owning more than 13,000 properties. By 1985 he had developed skills as a roofer and had been paid and promoted accordingly. From 1988 his written contract of employment stated that his employment was that of a roofer, but it contained a clause which said: 'Where possible tradespersons will be expected to carry out multi-trade operations'. In 1990 Peabody made some 30 painters and decorators redundant and in 1993 nine other employees from the works department were dismissed due to operating losses. Of the nine, Peabody decided that a roofer should be made redundant. Mr Johnson was dismissed.

In the three years before his dismissal, Mr Johnson had done some roofing work but had also been engaged on bricklaying, painting, carpentry, tiling and plastering.

Mr Johnson, seeking, presumably, a higher award, claimed that there had not been a redundancy but that his dismissal was unfair. The case eventually reached the EAT.

Mr Johnson referred to what is now s 139(1)(b) of the Employment Rights Act 1996, which provides that a dismissal shall be taken to be by reason of redundancy if it is attributable wholly or mainly to the fact that the requirements of the employer's business 'for employees to carry out work of a particular kind . . . has ceased or diminished'. In this connection, Mr Johnson pointed to the clause in his contract which stated that he would be required to carry out 'multi-trade operations'. He pointed out that Peabody's requirements for all kinds of work, particularly plastering, had not diminished and submitted that no redundancy situation existed in his case.

The EAT said that the 'contract test' rather than the 'function test' should be applied in interpreting s 139. The proper approach was to look at whether there had been a cessation or diminution in the requirements of the business for the specific type of work which the employee could be asked to perform under his or her contract, rather than for the work which the employee was actually doing at the time.

Applying the contract test in this case, the EAT held that Mr Johnson was employed under his contract as a roofer. The fact that he could be required to help on other work when roofing was not available did not alter this fact. Peabody could not require Mr Johnson to work on multi-trade operations if it had roofing work for him to do instead.

The EAT concluded that Mr Johnson had been made redundant rather than unfairly dismissed and his appeal failed.

## Safeway Stores plc v Burrell [1997] IRLB 8

In this case the EAT, which is not bound by its own decisions, rejected both the 'contract' and the 'function' tests. It decided in particular that in reaching conclusions as to whether there had been a diminution or cessation in the requirements of the employer's business for employees (not just the employee) to carry out work of a particular kind, or an expectation of such in the future, and the employee concerned was dismissed wholly or mainly because of this, there is a redundancy situation and it is irrelevant to consider the employee's contract of employment and its terms, or his functions. Mr Burrell was employed by Safeway as the manager of its petrol station at Penzance. A revision of the store's management structure was undertaken and the manager's job disappeared, to be replaced by the new post of petrol station controller at lower pay. Mr Burrell would not apply for this job because of that and was made redundant. A week after he left, a new job description was issued for the post of controller which differed on paper to some extent from Mr Burrell's old job description. Mr Burrell later claimed he had been unfairly dismissed.

The employment tribunal found that he had been dismissed, but not for redundancy, and because of this the dismissal was unfair. Safeway had not shown that it was because of redundancy and, therefore, that defence failed. The employment tribunal held that the job Mr Burrell had been doing still had to be done; it was merely the job title which had been changed. Therefore, applying the function test Mr Burrell was not redundant, though applying the contract test he was, since the post of manager no longer existed. The employment tribunal preferred the function test in this case. Safeway appealed to the EAT asking that the contract test be applied.

The EAT rejected both tests going instead for a 'group' test which could lead to what is known as a 'bumped redundancy' situation.

The example given by the EAT may assist in understanding. An employee is employed to work as a fork-lift truck driver. He delivers materials to six production machines on the shopfloor. Each machine has its own operator. The employer decides that only five machines are required and one machine operator is now in excess of requirements. This is, under the ERA 1996, a redundancy situation. Selection for dismissal is made on the LIFO (last in, first out) rule. The test is made across the group of workers needed to produce the end product of the machines. The driver falls to be dismissed under this rule. His dismissal is for redundancy. Under both the contract and the function tests he was employed as a fork-lift truck driver and there is no diminution in the requirement for this work. However, there was a diminution in the requirement for machine operators and this caused the driver's dismissal.

*Comment:* The decision seems rather more understandable and fair if, using, e.g. the LIFO rule, the most recent employee in a 'group' working towards the production of a particular article or articles is dismissed in a situation of diminution of work within the group.

The case was sent to another employment tribunal to see whether, in particular, Safeway had established redundancy under the above approach and if not, whether the dismissal was 'for some other substantial reason' which would be a defence.

### Church v West Lancashire NHS Trust [1998] 588 IRLB 7

In this case a different EAT affirmed that the test for redundancy is not strictly contractual or functional, but 'a sensible blend of the two' on the facts of the case. However, it found that transferred or 'bumped' redundancies do not fall within the statutory definition of redundancy.

As a matter of causation, the diminution or cessation in an employer's requirement for employees to carry out work of a particular kind must relate to the work carried out by the employee in the contract or functional sense. Thus, the forklift truck driver in the example given above would not be regarded as redundant under the *Church* test, but might according to the facts have been unfairly dismissed.

Mr Church was dismissed from his post in the computer services group of the Trust. However, only one post was truly surplus to requirements and that was not his post. His post remained as before. In these circumstances the EAT was prepared to say that Mr Church was not dismissed for redundancy.

*Comment:* The decision in *Church* appears to better fit the relevant statutory provisions.

## Eligibility

In general terms, all those employed under a contract of service as employees are entitled to redundancy pay, including a person employed by his/her spouse. Furthermore, a volunteer for redundancy is not debarred from claiming. However, certain persons are excluded by statute or circumstances. The main categories are listed below:

(a) a domestic servant in a private household who is a close relative of the employer. The definition of 'close relative' for this purpose is father, mother, grandfather, grandmother, stepfather, stepmother, son, daughter, grandson, granddaughter, stepson, stepdaughter, brother, sister, half-brother, or half-sister;

(b) an employee who has not completed at least two years of continuous service since reaching the age of 18. Alternate week working does not break continuity (*Colley* v *Corkindale t/a Corker's Lounge Bar* [1996] 542 IRLB 8). These provisions remain unchanged under amendments made by the Unfair Dismissal and Statement of Reasons for Dismissal (Variation of Qualifying Period) Order 1999, which apply only to claims for unfair dismissal;

(c) the right to claim a redundancy payment is lost at the age of 65 or, if earlier, the normal retiring age in the business for employees holding the position in question provided it is the same for men and women. No employee who is 65 or more at the relevant date can be entitled to claim a redundancy payment; a person aged 65 or more can, on the other hand, complain of unfair dismissal if he has not yet reached the normal retiring age for employees holding a similar position, a rare but possible situation;

(d) where in the case of a fixed-term contract of two years or more the employee has agreed in writing in the contract or at any stage of the contract to forgo his right to claim redundancy payment. These provisions remain unchanged under amendments made by the Employment Relations Act 1999, which apply only to claims for unfair dismissal;

(e) employees who normally work outside Great Britain under their contract;

(f) an employee who is *dismissed for misconduct* will lose the right to a redundancy payment. Thus, if we look back at the circumstances in the *Boychuk* and *Kowalski* cases, we can note that, although these cases were brought for unfair dismissal, they would also have been situations in which the employees concerned would have lost the right to a redundancy payment because it would be held that the dismissal was not for redundancy. In such cases, therefore, the only issue will be the possibility of unfair dismissal;

(g) where the employee goes on *strike,* this has been regarded *a form of misconduct* (*see Simmons* v *Hoover* [1997] ICR 61), and if the employer dismisses the employee(s) involved, they will lose the right to redundancy payment – a claim for unfair dismissal is not affected. If, however, the redundancy dismissal provokes a strike, the right to a redundancy payment is not lost. It depends which comes first, the strike or the redundancy. If the strike does produce a redundancy dismissal by the employer, there is no redundancy claim. If the redundancy provokes the strike, an employment tribunal may make an award of such redundancy pay as it feels is just and equitable. The section suffers from considerable, and some think unneccesary, complexity.

An employee who accepts an offer of suitable alternative employment with his employer is not entitled to a redundancy payment. Where a new offer is made, there is a trial period of four weeks following the making of the offer, during which the employer or the employee may end the contract while retaining all rights and liabilities under redundancy legislation.

**An employee who unreasonably refuses an offer of alternative employment is not entitled to a redundancy payment, as illustrated in the following case.**

## Fuller *v* Stephanie Bowman [1977] IRLR 7

F was employed as a secretary at SB's premises which were situated in Mayfair. These premises attracted a very high rent and rates so SB moved its offices to Soho. These premises were situated over a sex shop and F refused the offer of renewed employment at the same salary and she later brought a claim before an industrial tribunal for a redundancy payment. The tribunal decided that the question of unreasonableness was a matter of fact for the tribunal and F's refusal to work over the sex shop was unreasonable so that she was not entitled to a redundancy payment.

*Comment:* (i) It should be noted that in *North East Coast Ship Repairers* v *Secretary of State for Employment* [1978] IRLR 149 the Employment Appeal Tribunal decided that an apprentice who, having completed the period of his apprenticeship, finds that the firm cannot provide him with work, is not entitled to redundancy payment. This case has relevance for trainees and others completing contracts in order to obtain relevant practical experience.

(ii) In *Elliot* v *Richard Stump Ltd* [1987] IRLR 215 the EAT decided that a redundant employee who is offered alternative employment by an employer who refuses to accept a trial period is unfairly dismissed. In *Cambridge and District Co-operative Society Ltd* v *Ruse* [1993] IRLR 156 the EAT held that it was reasonable for an employee to refuse alternative work if the new job involved what he reasonably believed to be a loss of status. In that case the manager of a Co-op mobile butcher's shop was offered a post in the butchers' section of a Co-op supermarket, which he refused to accept because he was under another manager, which he felt, quite reasonably, involved a loss of status. He was successful in his claim for a redundancy payment.

As regards time limits, the employee must make a written claim to the employer or to an employment tribunal within six months from the end of the employment. If the employee does not do this, an employment tribunal may extend the time for a further six months, making 12 months in all, but not longer, from the actual date of termination of the employment, provided that it can be shown that it is just and equitable having regard to the reasons put forward by the employee for late application and to all relevant circumstances.

## Amount of redundancy payment

Those aged 41 to 65 (60 for women) receive one-and-a-half weeks' pay (up to a maximum of £220 per week) for each year of service up to a maximum of 20 years. In other age groups the above provisions apply, except that the week's pay changes, i.e. for those aged 22 but under 41, it is one week's pay, and for those 18 but under 22, it is a half-week's pay.

For example, a man of 52 who is made redundant having been continuously employed for 18 years and earning £240 per week as gross salary at the time of his redundancy would be entitled to a redundancy payment as follows:

| | | |
|---|---|---|
| 34 to 41 years = 7 years at one week's pay | = | 7 weeks |
| 41 to 52 years = 11 years at one-and-a-half week's pay | = | 16½ weeks |
| | | 23½ weeks |

It follows, therefore, that the redundancy payment would be 23½ weeks × £220 = £5,170.

Consider also the case of an employee aged 62 dismissed on the ground of redundancy. His normal retiring age would have been 65; he had been continuously employed for 30 years; his gross weekly wage was more than £220. His redundancy payment will be based on his last 20 years of service and will be entitled to the current maximum of £6,600 (20 × 1½ × £220 = £6,600).

Employees over 64 have their redundancy payment reduced progressively so that for each complete month by which the age exceeds 64 on the Saturday of the week on which the contract ends, the normal entitlement is reduced by one-twelfth. Thus a man or woman aged 64 years and three months would have three-twelfths of the award deducted. The rule relating to the reduction in women's redundancy pay is not changed by the retirement provisions referred to in Chapter 16. Complaints by employees in respect of the right to a redundancy payment or questions as to its amount may, as we have seen, be made to an employment tribunal, which will make a declaration as to the employee's rights which form the basis on which payment can be recovered from the employer.

## Procedure for handling redundancies

Any agreed formula must be followed, for example, last in, first out. Selection procedures may also be based on poor work performance or attendance record and there is no requirement on the employer to find out reasons for this (*Dooley* v *Leyland Vehicles Ltd* [1986] IRLR 36). If there is no agreed procedure, the employer must decide after considering the pros and cons in each case. It should be noted that the dismissal may well be unfair if some reasonable system of selection is not followed. In this connection the EAT decided in *Rogers* v *Vosper Thorneycroft (UK) Ltd* [1988] IRLR 22 that 'last in, first out' is a relevant system, but merely asking for volunteers is not. There must be some criteria, though calling for volunteers is acceptable as a preliminary step in the matter of eventual selection. The decision was affirmed by the Court of Appeal (*see The Times*, 27 October 1988).

Everyone should as far as possible be allowed to express their views, for example, through elected representatives, if any. Every attempt should be made to relocate a redundant worker. Failure to do so can result in a finding of unfair dismissal – unless, of course, there was no chance of finding suitable alternative work. Fairness in the search for alternative work involves looking at other companies within a group (EAT decision in *Euroguard Ltd* v *Rycroft* [1993] 477 IRLB 5).

Selecting, say, a white, single, young woman or a West Indian single man to go, rather than a married white man with two children and a mortgage might appear to be humane. However, unless the decision is made on the basis of competence, experience, reliability, and so on, the dismissal is likely to be unfair and also a breach of the Sex Discrimination Act 1975 and/or the Race Relations Act 1976.

## Consultation over collective redundancies

The Collective Redundancies and Transfer of Undertakings (Protection of Employment) (Amendment) Regulations 1995 (SI 1995/2587) apply. The Regulations substantially amend s 188 of the Trade Union and Labour Relations (Consolidation) Act 1992 as follows:

- the obligation to consult about redundancies now arises where the employer is proposing to dismiss as redundant 20 or more employees at one establishment within a period of 90 days or less. This change has removed the need to consult from some 96 per cent of UK businesses;
- where consultation is required, the employer must consult all those who are 'appropriate representatives';
- appropriate representatives of employees are:
  (i) employee representatives elected by them; or
  (ii) if an independent trade union is recognised by the employer, representatives of the union.

Where the employees elect representatives and belong to a recognised union, the employer has a choice of whether to consult the union representatives or the elected representatives. It should be noted that the Regulations extend the requirement to consult to non-union workplaces. They further provide that:

- employee representatives may be elected by the employees for the specific purpose of consultation or may be members of an existing works council or joint consultative committee. In all cases the employee representatives must be employed by the employer and not be outsiders. No method of election is stipulated in the Regulations which means that *ad hoc* procedures as and when a redundancy situation is to arise are acceptable;
- consultation must begin 'in good time' as distinct from the 'earliest opportunity' as was formerly required and, in any case;

- where the employer is proposing to dismiss 100 or more employees at one establishment within 90 days or less, consultation must begin 90 days before the first dismissals take effect. In cases involving less than 100 but at least 20 employees, consultation must begin 30 days before that date;
- appropriate representatives must be given access to employees who are to be or may be made redundant and facilities, e.g. a telephone and office, must be made available to them.

The employer's other obligation is to notify the Department of Trade and Industry of proposed redundancies. The obligation is to give written notice to the Department:

- at least 90 days before the first dismissals take place in the case of 100 or more redundancies;
- at least 30 days before the first dismissal takes effect in the case of 20 or more redundancies.

The employer must give a copy of the notice to the relevant appropriate representatives.

If there are special circumstances which make it not reasonably practicable for the employer to comply with the requirements, he must do everything that is reasonably practicable. If the special circumstances prevent the full required notice being given, the employer must give as much notice as possible. Failure to comply with the above DTI requirements means that the employer can be prosecuted and fined.

Complaints about failure to consult can be made to an employment tribunal by any employee who has been or might be dismissed as redundant or by a recognised trade union or by any employee representative. The tribunal may make a protective award requiring the employer to pay remuneration for up to 90 days where 90 days' minimum notice should have been given, or up to 30 days in any other case in which consultation was required.

Consultation was firmed up by legislation in 1993 which inserted new provisions into the Trade Union and Labour Relations (Consolidation) Act 1992 under which consultation must cover specific areas as follows: (a) the reason for the redundancy proposals; (b) the numbers and description of employees to be dismissed; (c) the method of selection for redundancy; (d) the procedure and timing of dismissals; and (e) the method of calculating any non-statutory redundancy payments, i.e. payments extra to the basic requirement. Consultation must also include a consideration of ways to avoid the redundancies and/or to reduce the number to be dismissed and to mitigate the consequences of the dismissals which do take place.

If a company is in the hands of an insolvency practitioner that practitioner must also follow the above procedures, though there may be special circumstances, such as the immediate collapse of the company, which make this impossible.

General standards of fairness for redundancy were laid down by the EAT in *Williams v Compair Maxam* [1982] ICR 156. These were the giving of maximum notice; consultation with unions, if any; the taking of the views of more than one person as to who should be dismissed; the requirement to follow any laid down procedure, e.g. last in, first out; and, finally, an effort to find the employees concerned alternative employment within the organisation. It should be noted that in *Meikle v McPhail* (*Charleston Arms*) [1983] IRLR 351 the EAT stated that these guidelines would be applied less rigidly to the smaller business.

As we have seen, when a worker is to be made redundant, the ACAS code of practice and the decision in *Williams* v *Compair Maxam* (1982) (*above*) both stress the importance of consultation, and as we have seen the decision of the House of Lords in *Polkey* stresses the need for the employer to consult and follow fair procedures. This applies as much in redundancy as it does in unfair dismissal. An employer who does not act properly will no longer be able to say that, since subsequent events justified redundancy as where the firm was insolvent, there was no point in consultation. An employer who fails to consult may face the more costly claim of unfair dismissal rather than redundancy. However, *Polkey* does not lay down that there must *always* be consultation, as the *Eclipse Blinds* case shows, but in most cases the law will require it.

### The role of ACAS

ACAS has now taken on redundancy pay entitlement as an issue on which it has a duty to conciliate. The Employment Rights (Dispute Resolution) Act 1998 confers a duty on ACAS to conciliate if a person puts in an application to an employment tribunal concerning entitlement to redundancy pay.

### Collective agreements on redundancy

The Secretary of State may, on the application of the employer and the unions involved, make an order modifying the requirements of redundancy pay legislation if he is satisfied that there is a collective agreement which makes satisfactory alternative arrangements for dealing with redundancy. The provisions of the agreement must be 'on the whole at least as favourable' as the statutory provisions, and must include, in particular, arrangements allowing an employee to go to an independent arbitration or to make a complaint to an employment tribunal.

## OTHER METHODS OF TERMINATION OF CONTRACT OF SERVICE

Having considered the termination of the contract by unfair or discriminatory dismissal or redundancy, we must now turn to other ways in which the contract of service may be brought to an end. These are set out below.

### By notice

A contract of service can be brought to an end by either party giving notice to the other, although where the employer gives notice, even in accordance with the contract of service or under the statutory provisions of the ERA, he may still face a claim for unfair dismissal or a redundancy payment.

The most important practical aspect is the length of notice to be given by the parties, in particular the employer. The ERA contains statutory provisions in regard to *minimum* periods of notice and the only relevance of the express provisions of a particular contract of service on the matter is that a contract may provide for longer periods of notice than does the ERA. Under the ERA an employee is entitled to one week's notice after employment for one month or more; after two years' service the minimum entitlement is increased to two weeks, and for each year of service after that it is increased by one week up to a maximum of 12 weeks' notice after 12 years' service.

An employee, once he has been employed for one month or more, must give his employer one week's notice and the period of one week's notice applies for the duration of the contract so far as the employee is concerned, no matter how long he has served the employer. It should be noted that, so far as oral notice is concerned, it does not begin on the day it is given but on the following day. This means, for example, that in the case of oral notice seven days' notice means seven days exclusive of the day on which the notice is given (*see West* v *Kneels Ltd* (1986) *below*). There appears to be no particular ruling on written notice and so it may be that one could give notice starting from the date of the letter if the letter was served on the employee (or employer) on that day. However, it would seem preferable to commence the notice from the day after service of the letter.

### West v Kneels Ltd [1986] IRLR 430

Julie West claimed that her employers had dismissed her unfairly. An industrial tribunal decided that the claim failed because she had not been employed for the necessary qualifying period. This was true if the week's notice commenced on the day it was given. If it started the next day she would qualify. Mr Justice Popplewell decided that it accorded with good industrial practice that in the case of oral notice seven days' notice meant seven days exclusive of the day on which the notice was served. This meant that Julie West had in fact been employed for the necessary qualifying period.

Breach of the provisions relating to minimum periods of notice do not involve an employer in any penalty, but the rights conferred by the ERA will be taken into account in assessing the employer's liability for breach of contract. Thus an employer who has dismissed his employee without due notice is generally liable for the wages due to the employee for the appropriate period of notice at the contract rate.

It should be noted that the ERA provisions regarding minimum periods of notice do not affect the common law rights of an employer to dismiss an employee at once without notice for misconduct, e.g. disobedience, neglect, drunkenness or dishonesty. An example is to be found in *Connor* v *Kwik Fit Insurance Services Ltd* (Scottish Court of Session, 1996) where the managing director of an insurance company, who had falsely declared when signing a professional indemnity insurance form that he had not been involved with any company that had been wound up, was guilty of gross misconduct and could be summarily dismissed.

In practice, a contract of service is often terminated by a payment instead of notice and this is allowed by the ERA.

In these days when there is a great need for skilled personnel, it is tempting for employees to break their contracts by leaving at short notice to go to other jobs. However, in *Evening Standard Co Ltd* v *Henderson* [1987] IRLR 64 the employer, Evening Standard, was granted an injunction to restrain an employee from working for a rival during his contractual notice period of 12 months as long as the employer agreed (which he did) to provide him with remuneration and other contractual benefits until the proper notice period would have run out, or, alternatively, let him stay at work until the proper notice period had expired (and *see also* Chapter 7).

## By agreement

As in any other contract, the parties to a contract of employment may end the contract by agreement. Thus, if employer and employee agree to new terms and conditions on, for example, a promotion of the employee, the old agreement is discharged and a new one takes over.

An employee could agree to be 'bought off' by his employer under an agreement to discharge the existing contract of service. In this connection it should be noted that discharge of a contract of service by agreement is not a 'dismissal' for the purposes, for example, of an unfair dismissal claim, but should a claim for unfair dismissal be brought by an employee who has been 'bought off', the tribunal concerned will want to see evidence of a genuine and fair agreement by employer and employee and may allow a claim of unfair dismissal if the discharging agreement is one-sided and biased in favour of the employer.

## By passage of time

In the case of a fixed-term contract, as where an employee is engaged for, say, three years, the contract will terminate at the end of the three years, though there may be provisions for notice within that period.

## By frustration

A contract of service can, as we have already seen, be discharged by frustration which could be incapacity, such as illness. However, other events can bring about the discharge of a contract of service by frustration, e.g. a term of imprisonment. Thus in *Hare v Murphy Bros* [1974] 3 All ER 940 Hare was a foreman employed by Murphy Bros. He was sentenced to 12 months' imprisonment for unlawful wounding and could not, obviously, carry out his employment. The court held that his contract was frustrated.

Furthermore, death of either employer or employee will discharge the contract by frustration from the date of the death so that, for example, the personal representatives of the employer are not required to continue with the contract. However, the estate has a claim for wages or salary due at the date of death.

Under the ERA claims for unfair dismissal arising before the employer's death survive and may be brought after the death of the employer against his estate. Furthermore, the death of a human employer is usually regarded as a 'dismissal' for redundancy purposes and the employee may make a claim against the employer's estate.

If the employee is re-engaged or the personal representatives renew his contract within eight weeks of the employer's death, the employee is not regarded as having been dismissed. Where an offer of renewal or re-engagement is refused on reasonable grounds by the employee, then he is entitled to a redundancy payment. If he unreasonably refuses to renew his contract or accept a suitable offer of re-engagement he is not entitled to such a payment.

## Partnership dissolution

A person who is employed by a partnership which is dissolved is regarded as dismissed on dissolution of the firm. Under the ERA this is regarded as having occurred because of redundancy.

The dismissal is also regarded as wrongful at common law and there may be a claim by the employee for damages but these will be nominal only if the partnership business continues and the continuing partners offer new employment on the old terms (*Brace* v *Calder* (1895) – *see* Chapter 9).

A partnership is dissolved whenever one partner dies or becomes bankrupt or leaves the firm for any reason, e.g. retirement. However, the business usually continues under a provision in the partnership articles but there is nevertheless a technical dissolution.

Of course, if a firm or sole trader sells the business as a going concern, employees are transferred to the new employer automatically under the Transfer of Undertakings (Protection of Employment) Regulations 1981.

## Appointment of an administrator – corporate rehabilitation

The object of administration orders is to allow a company to be put on a profitable basis if possible, or at least disposed of more profitably than would be the case if other forms of insolvency proceedings, such as liquidation, were used. On the appointment of an administrator the company's executive and other directors are not dismissed but their powers of management are exercisable only if the administrator consents. He also has power to dismiss and appoint directors.

Since an administrator is made an agent of the company by the court under the administration order, employees are not automatically dismissed. In addition, an administrator who wishes to trade with the company and for that purpose to retain employees may adopt their contracts of employment. Such adoption is automatic. This does not mean that he and his firm will become employers in the true sense. However, if when the administrator finishes his work and leaves the company, there are outstanding, e.g. any wages or salaries of retained employees, they must be paid before the administrator is entitled to his fees and expenses. The effect of adoption is not, therefore, to make an administrator or an administrative receiver personally liable for wages or salary, but adoption may affect their fees and expenses. This provision, which is also applied to an administrative receiver (*see below*), is to correct a possible unfairness which existed under the previous law before the coming into force of the present insolvency provisions which are contained in the Insolvency Act 1986. In earlier times an administrator or administrative receiver would have been able to take the services of an employee of the company for a short period of time and then say 'your contract is with the company: the company is insolvent and I do not intend to pay you'. Thus the employee might work without any right to pay. As we have seen under the provisions of the Insolvency Act 1986, if an administrator or an administrative receiver allows an employee of the company to contribute his services, then he is deemed to have adopted the contract and the employee must be paid before the insolvency practitioner is entitled to his fees and expenses.

If, of course, an administrator or administrative receiver dismisses an employee, that employee can make a claim for a redundancy payment.

It is worth noting that the above provisions of the Insolvency Act 1986 relating to adoption of employment contracts gave insolvency practitioners an incentive to opt out of the liability and statements made in the High Court in *Re Withall and Conquest and*

*Specialised Moldings Ltd* (1987) (unreported) to the effect that a form of letter sent to employees during the first 14 days of an administration or administrative receivership disclaiming adoption would work to the extent that during an administration or receivership remuneration including holiday pay and contributions to occupational pension schemes would be paid, as was the practice anyway where the insolvency practitioner traded on, but no more. The major concern of insolvency practitioners was to get rid of the potential liability to make payments in lieu of notice. If trading fails an insolvency practitioner is rarely able to give employees notice and in the case of senior employees the notice period may be three months or more and since such employees are usually on high salaries the potential burden is considerable. However, in *Powdrill* v *Watson*, *The Times*, 1 March 1994 the Court of Appeal held that the letter was of no effect and that after the requisite 14 days employment contracts were adopted including liability to pay in lieu of notice. In order to sustain the administration and receivership procedures which would have otherwise collapsed leaving liquidation as the only insolvency procedure, the government rushed through Parliament the Insolvency Act 1994 which confirms that contracts are adopted but restricts the liability of the insolvency practitioner to certain 'qualifying liabilities'. Only these liabilities will be payable in priority to other claims such as the holder of a floating charge (*see* Chapter 20) and preferential creditors (*see also* Chapter 20) or result in personal liability for the insolvency practitioner. The qualifying liabilities are wages or salaries including sickness and holiday pay and contributions to occupational pension schemes. Payments in lieu of notice are not included. The liabilities concerned must have been incurred after the adoption of the contract. Other employment liabilities will remain but will be treated as unsecured claims against the company and may not be paid in view of the insolvency unless the insolvency practitioner can trade out of trouble.

## Appointment of an administrative receiver

Where a company has borrowed money and given security for the loan by charging its assets under a debenture, the debenture holders may, if, for example, they are not paid interest on the loan, appoint a receiver and manager, now referred to as an administrative receiver. The most common appointment is by a bank in respect of an overdraft or loan facility to a company.

If the administrative receiver is appointed under the terms of the debenture, he is under the Insolvency Act 1986 an agent of the company, and where this is so employees of the company are not dismissed on his appointment and their employment with the company is continuous for the purposes of employment legislation. Employees are, however, dismissed if the administrative receiver sells the undertaking or where continuance of the employees' contracts would be inconsistent with the appointment of a receiver, as could be the case in regard to the contract of a managing director. However, even a managing director may not be regarded as dismissed where the receiver has a part-time appointment, as was the case in *Griffiths* v *Secretary of State for Social Services* [1973] 3 All ER 1184.

If the appointment is made by the court, then the administrative receiver is not the agent of the company but an officer of the court and his appointment terminates the contracts of all employees, and the continuity of their employment with the company ceases and they have a claim for a redundancy payment. The receiver may, of course, continue the employment by offering what are, in effect, new contracts, but where this is so there is a break in the continuity in the employment for the purposes of employment legislation. The employees are now employed by the administrative receiver and not by the company to which he has been appointed.

What is said above relates to the continuation of employment by the *company*. The situation in which an administrator or administrative receiver can adopt contracts of employment *himself* have already been considered.

## Company liquidation

The possibilities are as follows:

(a) *A compulsory winding-up*. Here the court orders the winding-up of the company, usually on the petition of a creditor because it cannot pay his debt. The making of a compulsory winding-up order by the court may have the following effects according to the circumstances of the case:
  (i) where the company's business ceases, the winding-up order will operate as a wrongful dismissal of employees;
  (ii) where the liquidator continues the business, as where he allows employees to continue with work in progress in order to make complete and more saleable products, he may be regarded as an agent of the company so that the employment continues. Alternatively, the court may regard the appointment of the liquidator as a giving of notice to the employee who then works out that notice under the liquidator. It is, however, the better view that employees may, if they so choose, regard themselves as dismissed because the company has ceased to employ them, the new contract being with the liquidator. In practice, if the liquidator continues to use the services of the employees and pays them, the Department of Employment treats the redundancy of the employees as occurring at the time of their eventual dismissal by the liquidator.
(b) *A voluntary winding-up*. This commences on the resolution of the members and if the company's business ceases there is a dismissal of employees. If the company's business continues, the position would appear to be as set out in (a)(ii) above.

## Bankruptcy

The bankruptcy of a human employer, or indeed of the employee, does not automatically discharge the contract of service, though it will, if there is a term to that effect in the agreement. Thus, the employment can continue, though in practical terms it may be impossible to pay employees' wages, and in this case they will be discharged and will be able to make a claim for a redundancy payment, as well as one in the bankruptcy for wages accrued due in regard to which they have a preferential claim in the bankruptcy.

A trustee in bankruptcy cannot insist that an employee continue in service because the contract is one of a personal nature. The bankruptcy of an employee will not normally affect the contract of service unless there is a term to that effect in the contract. Company directors provide a special case since the articles of most companies provide for termination of the office on becoming bankrupt.

## Wrongful and summary dismissal at common law

The claim at common law for wrongful dismissal is based on a general principle of the law of contract, i.e. wrongful repudiation of the contract of service by the employer.

The common law action has, of course, been largely taken over by the statutory provisions relating to unfair dismissal and a common law claim is only likely to be brought by an employee who has a fixed-term contract at a high salary. Thus a company director who has a fixed-term contract for, say, three years at a salary of £50,000 per annum might, if wrongfully dismissed, find it more profitable in terms of damages obtainable to sue at common law for breach of contract, though the employer may be able to resist the claim where the employee was guilty, for example, of misconduct, disobedience or immorality.

This may well change since there is now a raised cap of £50,000 in unfair dismissal cases and no cap at all where dismissal is because the employee has blown the whistle on his employer and reports e.g. a health and safety infringement within the organisation to the Health and Safety Executive or a suspected fraud to a City of London regulator, such as the Financial Services Authority.

In other cases where the contract of service is not for a fixed term, there is no claim for damages at common law, provided that the employer gives proper notice or pays wages instead of notice, though in such a case the employee has, at least potentially, a claim for unfair dismissal which he could pursue. Again, the employer may resist a claim for unfair dismissal on the basis of misconduct, disobedience or immorality. We have already given some consideration to these matters in the context of statutory unfair dismissal.

Under powers given by s 3 of the Employment Tribunals Act 1996, employment tribunals can hear cases of wrongful dismissal, though there is a cap of £25,000 (i.e. *less* than the statutory claim for unfair dismissal) on the damages that can be awarded. Claims for higher sums must be made in the County Court or High Court.

### The wrongful dismissal claim

Some of the main reasons for preferring a wrongful dismissal claim are as follows:

- an employee who is dismissed may not have completed the one year's service required for an unfair dismissal claim or may be over normal retiring age. These bars do not apply to wrongful dismissal claims;
- the time limit – i.e., three months – for bringing claims of unfair dismissal may have expired. The period for wrongful dismissal, which is a common law claim in the County Court or High Court, is six years from dismissal. However, the three-month period applies to wrongful dismissal claims before an employment tribunal, unless the tribunal decides that it was not 'reasonably practicable' for the complaint to be presented during that period;
- awards for unfair dismissal may be reduced substantially by a sum representing the fault of the employees – e.g. late arrival at work. Damages for wrongful dismissal are not subject to a deduction for contributory fault;
- the damages for wrongful dismissal in the case, e.g., of a highly-paid person could still well exceed the maximum amount of compensation available for unfair dismissal – where the compensatory award is currently a maximum of £50,000.

### When does wrongful dismissal occur?

The main situations of wrongful dismissal are as follows:

- where the contract is of indefinite duration but terminable by notice, the termination of the contract without notice or with shorter notice than that to which the employee is entitled, and, of course, summary dismissal without any notice at all;
- in the case of a fixed-term contract, termination before the fixed term expires;
- in the case of a contract to carry out a specific task, termination before the task is completed;
- where the employer dismisses the employee on disciplinary grounds but does not follow a procedure laid down in the contract;
- selection for redundancy in breach of a procedure set out in the contract.

### When dismissal is justified

Various forms of misconduct will justify a dismissal. As we have seen in *Connor* v *Kwik Fit Insurance Services Ltd* (1996) the managing director of an insurance company, who had falsely declared when signing a professional indemnity insurance form that he had not been involved with any company that had been wound up, failed in a claim for wrongful dismissal. Again, in *Blayney* v *Colne Liberal Club* (heard on 24 July 1995) a bar steward's claim for wrongful dismissal failed. He had been summarily dismissed for failure to hand over the bar takings to his employer or to put them in the safe and hand over the safe keys.

## RIGHTS AND REMEDIES ON DISMISSAL

These are as follows.

## Written statement of reasons for dismissal

At common law an employer is not required to give his employee any reasons for dismissal. However, the ERA provides that where an employee is dismissed, with or without notice, or by failure to renew a contract for a fixed term, he must be provided by his employer on request, within 14 days of that request, with a written statement giving particulars of the reasons for his dismissal. This provision applies only to employees who have been continuously employed for a period of one year (ERA, s 92), though there is no service requirement in pregnancy dismissals. All women, regardless of service or hours worked, have a right to written reasons for dismissal if dismissed while pregnant or during the statutory maternity leave period and regardless of whether the woman requests it or not. The written statement is admissible in evidence in any proceedings relating to the dismissal and if an employer refuses to give a written statement the employee may complain to an employment tribunal. If the tribunal upholds the complaint, it may make a declaration as to what it finds the employer's reasons were for dismissing the employee and must make an award of two weeks' pay without limit as to amount to the employee.

## Employer's insolvency

If the employer is bankrupt or dies insolvent, or where the employer is a company and is in liquidation, the unpaid wages of an employee have under Sch 6 to the Insolvency Act 1986 priority as to payment but only to a maximum of £800 (taken by insolvency practitioners to be the *gross* wage) and limited to services rendered during the period of four months before the commencement of the insolvency. Any balance over £800 or four months ranks as an ordinary debt. Also preferential is accrued holiday remuneration payable to an employee on the termination of his employment before or because of the insolvency.

The Schedule adds to the above preferential debts by including in the list sums owed in respect of statutory guarantee payments, payments during statutory time off for trade union duties, ante-natal care and to look for work, remuneration on suspension for medical grounds, or remuneration under a protective award given because of failure to consult properly on redundancy. Statutory sick pay and statutory maternity pay are also preferential.

It should also be noted that under the ERA an employee may, in the case of his employer's insolvency, make a claim on the National Insurance Fund rather than relying on the preferential payments procedure set out above. The relevant insolvency practitioner, e.g. an administrative receiver, will *normally* calculate what is due and obtain authorisation through the Department of Trade and Industry. In so far as any part of this payment is preferential, the rights and remedies of the employees concerned are transferred to the DTI, which becomes preferential in respect of them.

The limits of the employee's claim on the National Insurance Fund are as follows.

(a) arrears of pay for a period not exceeding eight weeks with a maximum of £220 per week;
(b) holiday pay with a limit of six weeks and a financial limit of £220 per week;
(c) payments instead of notice at a rate not exceeding £220 per week;
(d) payments outstanding in regard to an award by an employment tribunal of compensation for unfair dismissal;
(e) reimbursement of any fee or premium paid by an apprentice or articled clerk.

There is no qualifying period before an employee becomes eligible and virtually all people in employment are entitled and the amount of £220 refers to the employee's *gross* wage.

It should be noted that claims on the National Insurance Fund were, in the past, not admitted unless the relevant insolvency practitioner gave the DTI a statement of the amount due, though this could be waived and payments made if there was likely to be an unreasonable delay in providing the statement. Chapter VI of the ERA now provides that the Department may make payments without a statement if it is satisfied that adequate evidence of the amounts due has been made available. Nevertheless, the relevant insolvency practitioner will normally provide a statement.

## Damages for wrongful dismissal

An award of damages is the most usual remedy for wrongful dismissal. The period by reference to which damages will be calculated is either:

- in the case of a contract of indefinite duration, the period between the date of wrongful dismissal and the earliest date on which the employer could lawfully have terminated the contract – generally the date required by the period of notice set out in the contract. If no such period is expressed in the contract, the court will imply a 'reasonable' period or the minimum period laid down in s 86 of the Employment Rights Act 1996, whichever is the longer; or
- if the employee was employed under a fixed-term contract, the damages period will in general be the unexpired remainder of the fixed term, unless the employer could terminate the contract by notice before the fixed term expired, in which case the damages period will be the period of that notice.

Case law has laid down 'reasonable' periods of notice in the absence of specific provision in the contract. These vary from three months for a company director (*James* v *Kent & Co Ltd* [1950] 2 All ER 1099) to one week for a hairdresser's assistant (*Marulsens* v *Leon* [1919] 1 KB 208) – though, according to length of service, the Employment Rights Act 1996 periods, which may be longer in the latter case, could apply.

### Heads of damage

No damages can be recovered for the manner of dismissal – e.g., for hurt feelings – nor for the fact that the dismissal may make it more difficult to get another job.

However, a claim may be made for loss of pension rights, share option rights and other fringe benefits such as a company car, but only to the extent that it was made available for private use.

### Mitigation of loss

The ex-employee must take reasonable steps to find other suitable employment or become self-employed, otherwise damages will be reduced by the sum that could reasonably have been earned from new employment or self-employment during the damages period. The court will take into account the nature of any reference given to the employee and the difficulty a dismissed employee may have in finding other suitable work.

### Damages are compensatory

If the employee had worked during the damages period, he would have received net, not gross, pay. Thus, under the common law rule set out in *BTC* v *Gourley* [1955] 3 All ER 796, the court will deduct from the gross award a notional sum to represent income tax. Under the Income and Corporation Taxes Act 1988, the first £30,000 of the net award is tax-free. If the net award exceeds that sum, the balance will be taxed again in the ex-employee's hands. Therefore, the court will add a sum to the non-exempt balance to ensure that after payment of tax on the sum awarded, the ex-employee is left with an appropriate net sum (*see Shove* v *Downs Surgical plc* [1984] 1 All ER 7).

## The equitable remedy of specific performance and injunction

A decree of specific performance is, as we have seen, an order of the court and constitutes an express instruction to a party to a contract to perform the actual obligations which he undertook under its terms. If the person who is subject to the order fails to comply with it, he is in contempt of court and potentially liable to be fined or imprisoned until he complies with the order and thus purges his contempt. For all practical purposes the remedy is not given to enforce performance of a contract of service, largely because the court cannot supervise that its order is being carried out. A judge would have to attend the place of work on a regular basis to see that the parties were implementing the contract.

An injunction is, as we have seen, an order of the court whereby an individual is required to refrain from the further doing of the act complained of. Again, a person who is subject to such an order and fails to comply with it is in contempt of court and the consequences set out above follow from the contempt. An injunction may be used to prevent many wrongful acts, e.g. the torts of trespass and nuisance, but in the context of contract the remedy has been granted to enforce a negative stipulation in a contract in a situation where it would be unjust to confine the claimant to damages. An injunction has been used as an indirect method of enforcing a contract for personal services, but a clear negative stipulation is required. Reference should be made to *Warner Brothers* v *Nelson* (1937) in Chapter 9 as an illustration of the application of the negative stipulation rule and the developments in it in more recent times.

In this connection it should also be noted that s 236 of the Trade Union and Labour Relations (Consolidation) Act 1992 provides that no court shall by way of specific performance or an injunction compel an *employee* to do any work or attend any place for the doing of any work. Thus although, as the *Warner Bros* case illustrates, an injunction was potentially available to enforce compliance with a contract of employment, the prohibition in s 236 (*above*) prevents a court from issuing a decree of specific performance or an injunction *against an employee*. The section would not affect the use at least of an injunction where the contract was for services and not employment, as would be the case between a boxer and his manager though even there the courts are reluctant to make the order (*see Warren* v *Mendy* (1989) in Chapter 9).

## Employee's breach of contract

An employer may sue his employees for damages for breach of the contract of service by the employee. Such claims are potentially available, for example, for damage to the employer's property, as where machinery is damaged by negligent operation, as was the case in *Baster* v *London and County Printing Works* [1899] 1 QB 901, or for refusal to work resulting in damage by lost production, as was the case in *National Coal Board* v *Galley* [1958] 1 All ER 91. Such claims are rare and impractical because of the fact that the employee will not, in most cases, be able to meet the claim, and also, perhaps more importantly, because they lead to industrial unrest. In these circumstances we do not pursue the matter further here.

## GRADED QUESTIONS

### Essay mode

1 When may an employee claim a redundancy payment?

*(The Institute of Company Accountants)*

2 Alan was recently made redundant and his employer Tom gave him no advance notice nor was there any consultation. His employer has approached you seeking advice. Apparently Alan is claiming unfair dismissal. His employer says: 'I am all for consultation and so on but frankly it would not have made any difference if I had consulted with him. The business would have closed anyway.'
Explain the legal position to Alan's employer Tom.     *(Author's question)*

3 (a) Explain the extent to which the Unfair Contract Terms Act 1977 has restricted the use of exclusion clauses and limitation of liability clauses in contracts.

(b) Wily & Co contract to supply printed circuits to Shadydeals Ltd. The circuits have been made to a detailed specification supplied by Shadydeals Ltd. On the back of the invoice, there is stated in print so tiny as to be almost illegible, a set of standard conditions including the following provision:

'The company accepts no liability under the Sale of Goods Act 1979 or any other legislation in respect of the quality of the goods or their fitness for any purpose whatsoever.'

The printed circuits turn out to be defective, and Shadydeals have raised an action for damages against Wily & Co, who have raised the defence that they are not liable by virtue of their exclusion clause.

Advise Shadydeals of their chances of success in court.

*(Napier University)*

4 (a) Misconduct of the employee is a good defence against both actions for wrongful dismissal and claims for unfair dismissal. What is meant by misconduct in this context?

(b) Mary and Jane, two shop assistants, are short of money and decide to borrow from the till. Mary leaves a note in the till and replaces the money the following morning, Jane neither leaves a note nor does she replace the money. If the employer later discovers what has happened, may he dismiss them?

*(The Chartered Institute of Management Accountants)*

### Objective mode

1 Boxo Ltd engaged Tom to work full-time running a branch office in Preston. After one year he was asked to run a branch in The Netherlands for three months while the manager was on sick leave. During the period of three months Tom was dismissed.

What is the legal position?

A Tom cannot claim unfair dismissal because he does not have two years' service.

B Tom cannot claim unfair dismissal because he was dismissed while in The Netherlands.

C Tom cannot claim unfair dismissal because to do so he requires three years' service.

D Tom can claim unfair dismissal in the circumstances of this case.

2 Three months ago Thames Ltd employed Reggie as a part-time clerical worker. It turned out that Reggie was a keen member of a trade union. He approached other employees after working hours and tried to persuade them to join the union. The management of Thames which had up until then been a non-union company fired Reggie because of his union activities.

What is the legal position?

A Reggie cannot claim unfair dismissal because he does not have the requisite service.
B Reggie can claim unfair dismissal in these circumstances.
C Reggie cannot claim unfair dismissal because Thames is a non-union company.
D Reggie cannot claim unfair dismissal because he is a part-timer.

3 Barney, an accounts clerk, has completed a period of one year's employment. His manager has now concluded that he has no aptitude and the employer, the Derwent Group plc, has dismissed him. Tomos has been employed by Derwent for two years as a cashier/manager. He has recently been convicted of dishonesty in relation to the funds of a charity of which he is the treasurer. He received a suspended prison sentence and was dismissed by Derwent. In neither case did Derwent consider whether a suitable vacancy could be found for Barney or Tomos.

What is the legal position?

A Barney can claim unfair dismissal and so can Tomos.
B Barney can claim unfair dismissal but Tomos cannot because of his dishonesty.
C Barney cannot claim unfair dismissal and nor can Tomos.
D Barney can claim unfair dismissal but Tomos cannot because he does not have the requisite service.

4 Fred aged 45 was dismissed on the ground of redundancy after eight years' continuous service. His gross weekly pay is £200. His redundancy payment is therefore:

A £2,000.
B £1,600.
C £2,400.
D £1,000.

5 Correctly complete the following:

Under the Employment Rights Act an employee is entitled to _____ _____ notice after employment for _____ _____ or more; after _____ _____ service the minimum entitlement is increased to _____ _____ and for each year of service after that is increased by _____ _____ up to a maximum of _____ weeks' notice after _____ years' service.

6 Correctly complete the following:

If the employer is bankrupt or dies insolvent, or where the employer is a company and is in liquidation, the unpaid wages of an employee have priority as to payment, but only to a maximum of _____ and limited to service rendered during the period of _____ before the commencement of the insolvency.

*Answers to questions set in objective mode appear on p 708.*

# 18 COMPANY LAW IN THE STUDY OF BUSINESS I

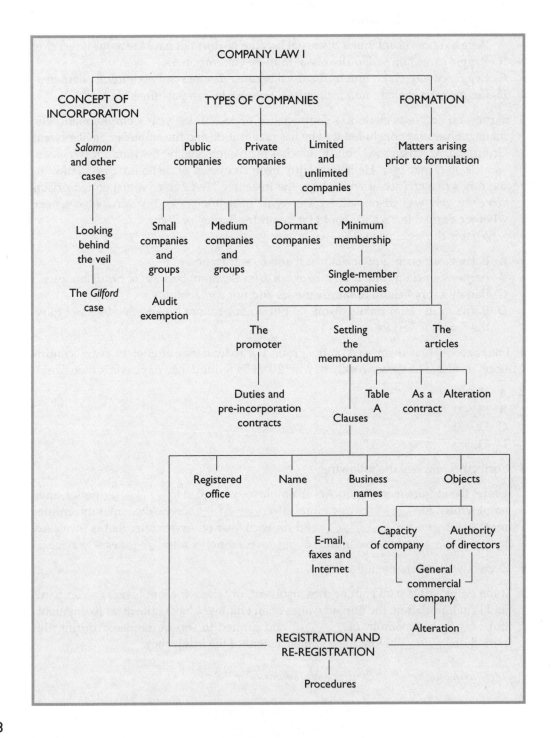

The objectives of this chapter are to consider the incorporation of a registered company as a concept: to define and describe the different types of company together with company promotion and the constitution of the registered company, that is, the memorandum and articles, registration and re-registration. Section references are to the Companies Act 1985 unless otherwise stated.

When Table A is referred to, the relevant Regulations are to be found in Statutory Instrument 1985/805, unless otherwise stated. Private companies may pass unanimous written resolutions without a meeting of members. Thus, when a resolution is referred to, it is followed by '(or written)' to indicate that a private company can adopt this procedure. Further details, including situations where the written resolution procedure cannot be used, appear in Chapter 20.

## CONCEPT OF INCORPORATION

A registered company may consist of one person or a number of persons. On registration the business is personified so that it may be distinguished from its members. It is an entity separate from its member or members as the following cases illustrate.

### Salomon v Salomon & Co Ltd [1897] AC 22

Salomon carried on business as a leather merchant and boot manufacturer. In 1892 he formed a limited company to take over the business. The memorandum of association was signed by Salomon, his wife, his daughter, and four of his sons. Each subscribed for one share. The company paid £39,000 to Salomon for the business, and the mode of payment was to give Salomon £10,000 in debentures, secured by a floating charge on the company's assets, and 20,000 shares of £1 each and the balance in cash. Less than one year later the company fell on hard times and a liquidator was appointed. If Salomon's debenture was valid he was as a secured creditor entitled to be paid before the unsecured trade creditors. The assets were sufficient to pay off the debentures but in that event the trade creditors would receive nothing. The unsecured creditors claimed all the remaining assets on the ground that the company was a mere alias or agent for Salomon. *Held* – The company was a separate and distinct person. The debentures were perfectly valid, and Salomon was entitled to the remaining assets in payment of the secured debentures held by him.

*Comment:* There was no fraud upon creditors or shareholders. The creditors of the old business had been paid off. The unsecured creditors concerned in this case were creditors of the new company. The House of Lords took the view that they must be deemed to know the risk they were taking if the company went into liquidation with insufficient funds. The members who had fully paid shares could not be required to pay more. Any profit which Mr Salomon might have made as a promoter selling his business to the company, and in fact the price of some of the assets was fixed prior to sale at figures exceeding their balance sheet value by some £8,000, was fully disclosed and approved by the shareholders, i.e. his family.

### Macaura v Northern Assurance Co Ltd [1925] AC 619

Macaura was the owner of a timber estate in County Tyrone and he formed an estate company and sold the timber to it for £42,000. The purchase money was paid by the issue to Macaura and his nominees of 42,000 fully paid shares of £1 each. No other shares were issued. He also financed the company and was an unsecured creditor for £19,000, its other debts being trifling. Macaura effected an insurance policy on the timber in his own name, and not in that of the company or as agent for the company, and on 23 February 1922 most of the timber was destroyed by fire. Macaura claimed under his policies, but he was *held* not to have an insurable interest. He could only be insuring either as a creditor or as a shareholder of the company, and neither a simple creditor nor a shareholder has an insurable interest in a particular asset which the company holds, since the company is an independent entity.

*Comment:* Unlike a shareholder a debenture holder can insure the property of the company on which his debenture is secured. (*Westminster Fire Office* v *Glasgow Provident Investment Society* (1888) 13 App Cas 699.) The difference in the debenture holder's position is justifiable since as a secured creditor he has an interest in the company's property which of course the share-holder does not have.

The Court of Appeal has more recently ruled that the long-standing rule in *Salomon* should not be overlooked by those who wish to lay claim to the assets of a group of companies.

### Ord v Belhaven Pubs Ltd [1998] 2 BCLC 447

In 1991 the claimants, Mr and Mrs Ord, brought an action against Belhaven, the legal owner of a public house at Stanford called the Fox Inn. The claim was, among other things, for damages for misrepresentation and breach of warranty arising out of the purchase by the Ords in 1989 of a 20-year lease of the pub from Belhaven. The claim related to alleged misrepresentations by the defendant as to the turnover and profitability of the Fox Inn which, in spite of the invest-ment of money and effort by the Ords, was not, in fact, a going concern. In 1992, after the proceedings began and following a recession in the property market, the group, of which Belhaven was a subsidiary, was restructured and the hotels owned by Belhaven were transferred to the parent company, Ascot Holdings plc. Thereafter Belhaven, which was a wholly-owned subsidiary of Ascot, effectively ceased trading, although it continued to own the Fox Inn. The claimants, being concerned that Belhaven would not have sufficient funds to meet any judgment which they might obtain against it, asked the court for leave to substitute as the defendant in their claim, either Ascot or another wholly-owned subsidiary in the group.

This was allowed initially by the High Court and Ascot was substituted as defendant, but the case came to the Court of Appeal and the decision of the High Court was reversed. The Court of Appeal would not draw aside the corporate veil of the group of companies and, in effect, regarded the companies in the group as one entity represented by the holding company Ascot. There was no impropriety in the restructuring, ruled the Court of Appeal: it was just the ordi-nary trading of a group of companies as a response to a recession. There was no question of transfers at undervalue or any other wrongdoing. In these circumstances the group was enti-tled to organise its affairs in the way that it had and to expect the court to apply the *Salomon* principles in the ordinary way.

### Looking behind the corporate personality

The idea of corporate personality can lead to abuse and where, for example, it has been used to avoid legal obligations the courts have been prepared to ignore the separate personality of the company (or draw aside the corporate veil or curtain) and treat the business as if it was being run by its individual members.

**An illustration of this is provided by the following case.**

### Gilford Motor Co v Horne [1933] Ch 935

Mr Horne had been employed by Gilford. He had agreed to a restraint of trade in his contract under which he would not approach the company's customers to try to get them to transfer their custom to any similar business which Mr Horne might run himself. Mr Horne left his job with Gilford and set up a similar business using a registered company structure. He then began to send out circulars to the customers of Gilford inviting them to do business with his company. Gilford asked the court for an injunction to stop Mr Horne's activities and he said that he was not competing, but his company was, and that the company had not agreed to a restraint of trade. An injunction was granted against both Mr Horne and his company to stop the circularisation of Gilford's customers. The corporate structure could not be used by Mr Horne to evade his legal contractual duties.

## PUBLIC COMPANIES

Section 1 defines a public company as a company limited by shares or limited by guarantee with a share capital whose memorandum states that the company is a public company, normally in clause 2 of the memorandum. Two persons, at least, are required to form a public company and become its first shareholders. A public company must also have two directors. Under s 25 the name of a public company must end with the words 'public limited company' (or the Welsh equivalent if the registered office is to be situated in Wales). The abbreviation 'plc' may be used (or its equivalent in Welsh where the registered office is to be in Wales) (s 27).

If the company is to be a public company, the authorised capital must, under ss 11 and 118, be at least £50,000. The Secretary of State may specify some other sum by Statutory Instrument.

Under s 117 a public company, registered as such on its original incorporation, cannot commence business or exercise any borrowing powers unless the Registrar has issued it with what is known as a s 117 certificate or, alternatively, it has re-registered as a private company. A private company does not require such a certificate. The main requirements when seeking a s 117 certificate are that the Registrar must be satisfied that the nominal value of the company's allotted share capital is not less than the authorised minimum (£50,000) and that not less than one-quarter of the nominal value of each issued share in the company, plus the whole of any premium (if any) on such shares, has been received by the company, whether in cash or otherwise. A share allotted under an employees' share scheme must not be taken into account in determining the nominal value of the company's allotted share capital unless it is paid up as to one-quarter of the nominal value of the share and the whole of any premium on the share.

In order to obtain a s 117 certificate, the company must file with the Registrar a statutory declaration, that is, a statement before a commissioner for oaths, signed by a director or secretary of the company stating: (a) that the nominal value of the company's allotted share capital is not less than the authorised minimum; and (b) the amount paid up at the time of the application on the allotted share capital of the company.

The certificate, when issued, is conclusive evidence that the company is entitled to commence business and borrow. Failure to comply with s 117 may result in a fine on the company and any officer in default. If a company does commence business or borrow without a s 117 certificate any transactions with traders and lenders are nevertheless good and enforceable against the company. However, if the company cannot meet its obligations under a transaction within 21 days of being called upon to do so the directors are jointly and severally liable to indemnify the other party to the transaction in respect of any loss or damage suffered by him as a result of the company's failure to comply with its obligations. Thus the company remains liable and the directors acquire a personal liability if, for example, the company goes into insolvent liquidation without discharging its indebtedness on the transaction.

## PRIVATE COMPANIES

A private company may be formed by two or more persons. However, the Twelfth EC Company Law Directive on single member private limited companies was adopted by the European Communities Council on 21 December 1989. Regulations (SI 1992/1699) were made implementing the Directive from 15 July 1992. From that date, a private company limited by shares or by guarantee may be formed with only one member or may allow its membership to fall to one. There are consequential amendments to other parts of company law. These will be considered as appropriate as the company law chapters of the book proceed, but for now it should be noted that the Regulations *do not apply* to private unlimited companies. The *management requirement* is only one director though more can be appointed if required. A private company is defined in s 1 as a company which is not a public company. There are no statutory restrictions on the right to transfer the shares of the company or on the number of its members, but the articles may contain such restrictions. However s 170 of the Financial Services Act 1986 contains a general prohibition under which a private company may not advertise its shares or debentures in the UK, thus preventing an offer to the public.

### Small and medium-sized companies – generally

Private companies are further subdivided by ss 246–9 which introduce accounting exemptions. They give the benefit of confidentiality of information but involve the preparation of two sets of accounts – one for members and one for the Registrar. The exemptions draw a distinction between the reporting requirements in regard to the accounts which small or medium companies prepare for their members and those which they file with the Registrar. They are allowed to file what are called 'abbreviated' and 'modified' accounts.

Small companies are permitted (but not required) to dispense with the filing of the directors' report and profit and loss account and file only an abbreviated balance sheet.

Full particulars of the exemptions, which are better studied as part of an accounting course, appear in Sch 8A but the major result is that members of the public examining the abbreviated balance sheet through Companies House will have no trading information and will know nothing about directors' emoluments or the company's dividends.

A medium-sized company may modify only its profit and loss account. Apart from this full accounts and reports must be filed. Once again details of this exemption, which are better studied as part of an accounting course, appear in s 246A, but the main effect is that the profit and loss account omits details of turnover, cost of sales, gross profit or loss and other operating income which are combined as one item under the heading of 'Gross Profit or Loss'. A major reason for this was that the details now omitted were sometimes used to the unreasonable disadvantage of medium-sized companies by their larger competitors as indicative of their areas of trade which might be poached.

In the case of medium-sized companies, a full and unmodified set of accounts and directors' and auditors' reports must be laid before the members of the company in a general meeting unless the company has passed what is called an elective resolution dispensing with the need to do this. The full accounts and reports will then be sent to the members though any member or the company's auditor is given the right to require the accounts and reports to be laid before a general meeting of members. Further details appear in Chapter 20.

## Small company shorter form financial statements

A small company does not have to prepare full accounts even for its members. SI's 1992/2452 and 1997/220 are relevant and provide for a new and shortened format for the members' accounts and provide that a small company need not set out in the notes to the accounts a number of items required by Sch 4, for example, particulars of staff employed. The directors' report to which the members are entitled (but which need not be filed) is also shortened by removing the requirement to give information regarding a fair review of the business, the amount to be paid as dividend and the amount to be carried to reserves, asset values, insurance effected for officers or auditors, para 6 of Sch 7 (miscellaneous disclosures), health and safety arrangements, and steps taken to encourage employee involvement in the business.

Although the above matters are better and more profitably studied as part of a financial accounting course, the position after revision by SI 1997/220 is as follows:

● Sch 8 gives the form and content of the accounts of small companies prepared for members;
● Sch 8A gives the form and content of the accounts of small companies delivered to the Registrar of Companies;
● section 246 gives details of exemptions applicable to small companies in respect of other Schedules to the 1985 Act, e.g. Sch 7;
● section 246A gives the exemptions applicable to the accounts of medium-sized companies delivered to the Registrar.

## Small companies and accounting standards

In this connection, it should be noted that the Accounting Standards Board (ASB) has decided to free smaller companies with a turnover of £2.8 million or less from the burden of complying with many of the accounting standards. By conforming to the Financial

Reporting Standard for Smaller Entities (FRSSE), such companies will be able to ignore other accounting standards. However, they may choose not to adopt it in which case they will remain subject to the full range of standards and abstracts. The remaining requirements are condensed into one self-contained volume. The result is to reduce the amount of accounting material by over three-quarters of the previous requirements. The critics of FRSSE would prefer an even greater simplification, even total exemption from all accounting standards, but the ASB is not prepared to go so far.

## Small and medium-sized companies – definitions

### Small companies

A small company is one which has been within the limits of *two* of the following thresholds since incorporation or, if not within the limits at incorporation, then for the current financial year and the one before:

- turnover: £2.8 million or less
- balance sheet total (i.e. total assets): £1.4 million or less
- employees: 50 (average) or less.

### Medium-sized companies

A medium company is one which has been within the limits of *two* of the following thresholds since incorporation or, if not within the limits at incorporation, then for the current financial year and the one before:

- turnover: £11.2 million or less
- balance sheet total (i.e. total assets): £5.6 million or less
- employees: 250 (average) or less.

Under the Companies Act 1985 (Miscellaneous Accounting Amendments) Regulations 1996, in the case of small and medium companies the average number of persons that the company employs can now be calculated on a monthly average basis and not a weekly average as before (Sch 4, para 56(2),(3)(a) and s 247(6) amended).

## Small and medium-sized companies – subsequent failure to qualify

If a company ceases to satisfy the exemption requirements for *two* successive years, it must file full accounts for the second year.

## Small and medium-sized companies – exemptions inapplicable

Under s 246 the exemptions do not apply if the company concerned is or at any time during its financial year was: (a) a public company; (b) a banking or insurance company; (c) an organisation authorised to conduct investment business under the Financial Services Act 1986; or (d) a member of an 'ineligible' group, e.g. a group containing any of the companies in (a) to (c) above.

Section 246 also provides that a parent company does not qualify as a small company or a medium-sized company in regard to a financial year unless the group which it heads qualifies respectively as a small group or a medium-sized group (*see below*).

## Small and medium-sized groups

A parent company need not prepare group accounts for a financial year in relation to which the group headed by that parent company qualifies as a small or medium-sized group and is not an ineligible group.

The qualifying conditions are met by a group which satisfies two or more of the following thresholds: (a) in the parent company's first financial year as a parent company; and (b) in its second or subsequent financial year as a parent company in that year and the preceding year. The current thresholds are as follows:

|  | Small | Medium |
|---|---|---|
| Aggregate turnover | £2.8 million (net) or £3.36 million (gross) (or less) | £11.2 million (net) or £13.44 million (gross) (or less) |
| Aggregate balance sheet total | £1.4 million (net) or £1.68 million (gross) (or less) | £5.6 million (net) or £6.72 million (gross) (or less) |
| Number of employees | 50 (average) (or less) | 250 (average) (or less) |

A group can choose to meet the gross or net formula for any item; thus turnover may be gross and balance sheet total net. The net formula is calculated after adjustments are made in the consolidation of the accounts; for example, the elimination of inter-company balances.

If the group fails to satisfy the exemption requirements for two successive years it must prepare group accounts in the second year.

Under the Companies Act 1985 (Miscellaneous Accounting Amendments) Regulations 1996, in the case of a small or medium group the average number of persons that the company employs can now be calculated on a monthly average basis and not a weekly average as before.

## Small and medium-sized groups – exemptions inapplicable

Under s 248 a group is ineligible if any of the companies in it is a plc, or a banking or insurance company or an authorised person under the Financial Services Act 1986.

## Role of the auditor

Under the Companies Act 1985 (Miscellaneous Accounting Amendments) Regulations 1996, the requirement for auditor confirmation by positive statement that a company is entitled to the exemptions given by s 248 to small and medium companies is removed. In addition, the Regulations insert s 237(4A) which provides that if the company's auditors (if any) are of the opinion that the board is not able to claim on behalf of the company the relevant exemptions they must state that fact in their report on the company's individual financial statements.

## Audit exemption for small companies

To meet the exemption conditions and so remove the requirement to have its annual accounts audited, the company's turnover must not exceed £350,000, or for companies that are charities £90,000. Gross income is substituted for charitable companies (s 249A). In addition, to meet either set of conditions (by reason of s 249B(1), (1A)):

- the company must qualify as a small company for the year, for the purposes of the abbreviated accounts exemptions;
- the company's balance sheet total must not exceed £1.4m;
- the company must not at any time during the year have been:
    - a parent company or a non-dormant subsidiary undertaking;
    - a public company;
    - a banking or insurance company;
    - an authorised person or an appointed representative under the Financial Services Act 1986;
    - an insurance broker;
    - a trade union special registered body under the Trade Union and Labour Relations (Consolidation) Act 1992, s 117(1), which are treated as corporate entities.

It should be noted that a company which is a non-dormant subsidiary of a body corporate or partnership or an unincorporated association carrying on a business with or without a view of profit cannot claim the *above* exemptions. Members holding 10 per cent or more of the issued share capital (or any class therof) may require the company to have an audit for a financial year by depositing a written notice at the company's registered office not later than one month before the year end.

## Audit exemption and small groups

A parent or non-dormant subsidiary company can claim exemption from audit if the group of which it is a member satisfies all of the following conditions throughout the financial year into which the period of group membership falls (*see* s 249B(1B), (1C)):

- the group qualifies as a small group for the purposes of s 249 and is not at the time of preparing accounts or at any time in the financial year an ineligible group;
- the group's aggregate turnover in that year is not more than £350,000 (or £420,000 gross); and
- the group's aggregate balance sheet total for that year is not more than £1.4m net (or £1.68m gross).

### Effect on dormant companies

The 1997 Regulations make clear that exemption from audit is available to dormant companies under the dormant company provisions (*see below*) or the audit exemption procedure. The audit exemption provisions have the advantage that they do not require a special or written resolution of the members.

## Disclosure in annual report and accounts

The balance sheet of a company taking advantage of either of the audit exemptions must include a statement to the effect that:

- the company is eligible to claim the exemption;
- no notice has been deposited at the company's registered office by members holding 10 per cent or more of the issued capital (or any class therof) requiring that the company shall have an audit for the financial year; and
- the directors acknowledge their responsibilities for:
  - ensuring that the company keeps proper accounting records; and
  - preparing accounts which give a true and fair view.

The statement must appear on the face of the balance sheet above the signature required by s 233, i.e. by a director of the company on behalf of the board. The name of the signatory must also be stated.

## Format of accounts

Even if the accounts are not audited, they should nevertheless comply with the provisions of the Companies Act 1985.

## References to audit in articles

Companies with articles based on the current (1985) version of Table A are unlikely to have problems since the 1985 version does not impose an obligation to appoint auditors. Article 130 of the 1948 version does and companies with that or a similar article should take legal advice regarding change to ensure that they are not precluded from implementing the audit exemption. Furthermore, Art 127 of the 1948 version, which requires that the accounts be sent to members accompanied by an auditor's report, will also require amendment.

## Reform

Before concluding the discussion of the distinction between public and private companies in terms e.g. of share capital, commencement of business and issue of securities to the public, together with accounting and auditing exemptions, it should be noted that the government announced in June 1999 that it was considering raising the turnover threshold for companies required to undergo statutory audits from £350,000 to as much as £4.2 million, thus saving audit fees for some 300,000 companies.

## Dormant companies

Under s 250 (as amended), certain private companies may be eligible to be regarded as dormant companies. A dormant company is a 'small' company as defined above. It will be regarded as dormant if it has had no 'significant accounting transaction' since incorporation or since the end of the previous financial year. A holding company required to prepare group accounts cannot be a dormant company, even if it has had no significant accounting transactions itself.

Such companies do not have to appoint an auditor, though accounts must still be prepared and filed. Full accounts and reports as required by law other than the auditors' report must be prepared for the members but dormant companies, being 'small' companies, may file an abbreviated balance sheet with the Registrar. Obviously in both cases the accounts will be unaudited. In all cases the balance sheet must include a statement by the directors that the company was dormant throughout the financial year.

A 'significant accounting transaction' is *any* transaction which is required to be entered in the company's accounting records other than one which arises from the taking of shares in the company by a subscriber to the memorandum because of an undertaking by him to do so in the memorandum. Since dormant companies must file an annual return and pay the current filing fee to the Registrar, they are, in practice, subsidiary companies, the relevant fee(s) being paid by the non-dormant holding company.

Under s 250 (as amended) a company which has:

(a) been dormant since the time of its incorporation can pass a special (or written) resolution excluding s 384 (obligation to appoint auditors) at any time. It is no longer restricted to passing the resolution before the first general meeting at which accounts are laid since it may have passed an elective resolution opting out of this requirement (*see further* Chapter 20). All private companies are entitled to dormant status under this head; or

(b) in the past been active but has now become dormant may pass the special (or written) resolution at any time after copies of the annual accounts have been sent out in compliance with s 238(1) (publication of accounts and reports). There is no requirement that accounts have to be laid before the members at a general meeting at which the resolution is passed since the company may have opted out of the requirement to do this. If the private company has traded in the past, the exemptions are only allowed to 'small' companies entitled to file abbreviated accounts or companies which would have been but for membership of an ineligible group.

As an alternative to filing a resolution, there may be completed Form DEB 8, available on request from the Registrar of Companies to whom it should be returned.

The amendments to s 250 stem from SI 1992/3003.

## Articles of association

The company's articles should be referred to since the resolution must not contravene the articles. Article 130 of Table A to the CA 1948 requires the appointment of auditors unless altered by special (or written) resolution. There is no similar provision in Table A to the CA 1985.

## Provisions of company law applicable to dormant companies

These are as follows:

(a) rights to receive or demand copies of accounts and reports under ss 238 and 239 continue, but there is obviously no need for a non-existent auditors' report;

(b) it is not necessary to lay or circulate a copy of the auditors' report nor deliver a copy to the Registrar;

(c) the copy of the balance sheet delivered to the Registrar must contain a statement by the directors, immediately above the signature, to the effect that the company was dormant throughout the year.

## Loss of exemption

The directors, or failing them the members, must appoint auditors if the company ceases to be dormant, which it would on the occurrence of a significant accounting transaction.

## Exemption inapplicable

A banking or insurance company or a person authorised to give financial advice under the Financial Services Act 1986 cannot validly pass a resolution to acquire dormant status. However, a plc that does not have to prepare consolidated accounts can pass a resolution not to appoint auditors if it is dormant (s 250(2)(a) is deleted by the CA 1985 (Miscellaneous Accounting Amendments) Regulations 1996).

## Dormant companies and the audit exemption

Companies House has confirmed that a dormant company will, subject to the rules relating to excluded categories, be able to take advantage of the audit exemption procedure available to small companies. It can, therefore, choose which procedure to-adopt to claim exemption from audit.

## Dormant companies' accounts – a standard format

Companies House has issued a standard format for the accounts of certain dormant companies. The aim is to assist companies which have been *dormant since incorporation* to prepare their accounts in a format acceptable for registration by Companies House. The Form (DCA) is only suitable for dormant companies *where the company's only transaction is the issue of subscriber shares and the company is not a subsidiary*. Annual return fees are borne by the directors.

# LIMITED AND UNLIMITED COMPANIES

A registered company may be:

(a) *Limited by shares*, i.e. the liability of the members to contribute to the debts and other liabilities of the company is limited by the memorandum to the amount, if any, unpaid on their shares. Little more needs to be said about this well-known form of limitation of liability except that in the case of the smaller private company it tends to be illusory since those, such as banks, who give the company an overdraft or other significant credit facilities will, in practice, require personal guarantees and other security from its directors and/or major shareholders.

(b) *Limited by guarantee*. Formerly companies limited by guarantee could be registered with or without a share capital. Companies limited by guarantee with a share capital may not now be registered though companies which had registered before the law was changed by the CA 1980 remain in existence. Since they cannot now have a share capital they must, of necessity, be formed as private companies since the presence of a share capital is fundamental to the definition of a public company. Consideration is given only to the law applying to companies limited by guarantee.

In a guarantee company the members have no liability in terms of the calling up of the guarantee unless and until the company goes into liquidation. If the company cannot meet its liabilities in full, those who are members at the time are required to contribute towards the company's assets, so that it may try to meet its obligations, including the costs of winding-up, in accordance with the guarantee. The amount guaranteed will be whatever sum is stated in the memorandum and it is frequently a small sum such as £100 (*see* Table C to the CA 1985: SI 1985/805). There is no reason in law, however, why a larger or smaller sum should not appear in the memorandum.

If those who are members at the date of winding-up cannot meet their obligations under the guarantee, or where they can meet their liabilities in full but this does not meet the company's obligations in full, then the liquidator has access to those who were members during the year prior to the commencement of the winding-up but only in respect of debts and liabilities incurred while they were members (Insolvency Act 1986, s 74). The members of a guarantee company are not shareholders, except in some of the earlier companies, and accordingly it is necessary for Table A to be modified, and Table C to the CA 1985 accommodates the necessary changes, for example, that a member may resign from the company following seven days' notice to the company. These are to be clear days, that is, exclusive of the date of service of the notice and the date of the withdrawal from membership. These companies provide a suitable organisation for professional bodies, trade associations and the like where subscription income is more important than share capital, and where a Royal Charter has not been obtained, particularly since in certain circumstances there is no need to include the word 'limited' – which denotes commerciality – as part of the name.

It should be noted that the guarantee is not an asset of the company but merely a contingent liability of its members until winding-up. Consequently, it cannot be charged by the company as a security nor can it be increased or reduced by an alteration of the memorandum or by agreement with the members nor by any procedure equivalent to the increase or reduction of share capital. (*Hennessy* v *National Agricultural and Industrial Development Association* [1947] IR 159.)

Once incorporated as a guarantee company, there is no provision in company legislation for re-registration as a company limited by shares or vice versa.

Unless the company is an earlier one with a share capital, each member has one vote at general meetings (s 370), but is not entitled to appoint a proxy to vote at meetings (*see* s 372(2)). Special articles may make provision for proxies.

## Unlimited companies

The personal liability of members of this type of company is the reason why they are not widely used. However, they are sometimes formed by those who wish to keep the company's accounts away from the public gaze (*see below*). In addition, there are advantages in having separate corporate status with perpetual succession since the death or bankruptcy of a member of the company has no effect upon its continued existence, whereas these events cause at least a technical dissolution in a partnership and the need, subject to the partnership agreement, to provide funds for the estate of the deceased or bankrupt partner by way of return of capital.

Unlimited companies must be private companies since a public company nowadays is by definition a company limited by shares.

Unlimited companies may be formed as such or re-registered as such either with or without a share capital. A share capital, where it exists, will provide a basis for the sharing of profit, though other methods, such as percentages, may be used and contained in the articles.

As regards liability, where there is a share capital the members can be called upon to pay for their shares in full, including any premium, even while the company is a going concern. In addition, if the company goes into liquidation and the company's assets are not sufficient to meet its debts and liabilities including the costs of winding-up, the members must contribute rateably according to the nominal value of their shareholding. Where there is no share capital, the members contribute equally according to the number of them at the time of liquidation until all the company's obligations have been met. In the event of any members defaulting, the others are liable to make good the deficiency. If the company's debts and liabilities cannot be met by the members on winding-up, the liquidator can, under s 74 of the Insolvency Act 1986, call upon past members (or shareholders) to contribute to the assets of the company if they were members (or shareholders) within the 12 months preceding the commencement of the winding-up, and only in respect of debts or liabilities which arose while they were members (or shareholders).

## Special features of unlimited companies

An unlimited company may reduce its share capital by extinguishing liability on partly paid shares, or even repaying capital to the members by passing a special (or written) resolution to that effect, and the permission of the court is not required, as it would be in the case of a limited company. In addition, although an unlimited company cannot issue redeemable shares, it may, if its articles permit, reduce its capital by buying back the shares of its members even from out of its capital.

As regards a reduction of capital by purchase of shares, if the company knew, at the time of purchase, that the members would not be able to meet their liabilities on winding-up, the court would set the purchase aside as a fraud on creditors (*Mitchell* v *City of Glasgow Bank* (1879) 4 App Cas 624). It will be noted in Chapter 19 that limited companies can also purchase their own shares under the provisions of Part V, Chapter VII of the 1985 Act. However, limited company purchases are subject to the not inconsiderable restrictions of that Act. (*See further* Chapter 19.) Unlimited companies are not subject to these restrictions and require only permission in the articles. An unlimited company can enjoy privacy in regard to its financial affairs because it need not deliver copies of its annual accounts and the relevant reports to the Registrar, not even abridged or modified ones, though it must prepare audited accounts for its members, unless it has taken the audit exemption when unaudited accounts will suffice.

The provision in regard to filing the accounts does not apply if at any time during the accounting reference period, the company concerned was a subsidiary or holding company of a limited company or was potentially under the control of two or more limited companies which because of share or voting rights could control the unlimited company if they acted in concert even though they have not as yet done so. Section 254, which contains the exemption, defines a limited company to include a foreign company the liability of whose members is limited. This section also provides that the exemption does not apply if at any time during the accounting period the company carried on business as a promoter of a trading stamp scheme within the Trading Stamps Act 1964.

## Other matters

An unlimited company is required to file an annual return but not a return of allotments under s 88 following an issue of shares. There is no requirement to keep a register of charges over the company's assets at the registered office, but it must register such charges at the Companies Registry.

As regards the memorandum and articles, a model for an unlimited company with a share capital appears in Table E to the CA 1985 (*see* SI 1985/805). There is no model for an unlimited company without a share capital and special drafting is required. This is also the case where there is a share capital since Table E cannot be adopted as the company's constitution; it is only a guide and special articles and memorandum must be submitted on registration and be, as nearly as circumstances permit, in the form set out in Table E. As regards membership, where there is no share capital, the normal form is that the subscribers to the memorandum become the first members on incorporation and thereafter such persons as the directors shall admit to membership. Provisions for retirement by notice are included in the company's articles.

## Minimum membership

In all the types of company which have been considered above, there must, under s 1, and subject to SI 1992/1699 (*see below*), be at least two members. Under s 24 if a company carries on business for more than six months without having at least two members, a person who is a member of the company, and is aware that it is carrying on business with only one member, is jointly and severally liable with the company for the payment of the company's debts contracted after that period while he was a member of the company. In addition, as soon as the membership falls below the statutory minimum, there is a ground on which a petition may be presented for a winding-up by the court. A one-member situation can arise where one member transfers his shares to the only other member and, perhaps less obviously, where a member dies and his personal representatives are not put on the share register in their personal capacity. They are not members unless registered.

## The single-member private limited company

The Companies (Single-Member Private Limited Companies) Regulations 1992 (SI 1992/1699), parts of which have already been referred to, provide for the existence of such companies.

The Regulations implement Council Directive No 89/667/EEC on single-member private limited liability companies. They also amend relevant parts of company legislation to accommodate one-member companies. The Regulations do away with the necessity for the 'artificial' member who exists in many private companies which in fact have a sole proprietor but where a spouse or partner holds a nominee share to fulfil the previous two-member requirement.

The same is true of subsidiaries, whether trading or dormant, where someone, such as a group company secretary or a separate nominee company, has, in the past, had to hold a share or shares in the subsidiary, normally under a declaration of trust, and a blank transfer form in favour of the parent company.

The Regulations apply to private companies limited by shares or guarantee. They do not apply to plcs and unlimited companies, the latter being of necessity private companies.

### Registration of single-member companies

The documents that are sent to Companies Registration Office are the same as those required for multi-member companies. One subscriber to the memorandum is required, who must take at least one share where there is a share capital, so that the minimum share capital of the company is £1 and not £2 as in the case of multi-member companies. Other members can be added in future if so desired.

The necessary amendments to company legislation are considered below, but it should be noted at this stage that there is no amendment to s 283 so that although the sole member can be the sole director under s 282, he cannot act also as the company secretary. (*See further* Chapter 20.) Therefore, the single member company must have two officers, i.e. a director (A) and a secretary (B).

### Conversion to single-member status

There are no re-registration requirements. Conversion is achieved by transferring the nominee holding to the beneficial owner. No resolutions of the company are required and there are no filing requirements at Companies House.

However, the Regulations add a new s 352A to the CA 1985, under which, when the number of members falls to one, a statement that this is the case must be entered on the register of members at the side of the name and address of the sole member. If the membership increases to two or more, then on the occurrence of that event a statement that the company has ceased to have only one member must be entered in the register of members alongside the name and address of the person who was formerly the sole member. A default fine is imposed on the company and officers in default, but since there are no filing requirements, it will be difficult to ascertain when there has been default.

### Meetings of the single-member company

The Regulations add a new s 370A to the CA 1985. This provides that, notwithstanding any provision to the contrary in the articles (so that no changes in the company's constitution are required), one member present in person or by proxy shall be a quorum. A new s 382B is also added, and this provides that if the sole member takes any decision which could have been taken in a general meeting he shall (unless it is a written resolution) provide the company with a written record of it. The Regulations do not deal with the form of this record and although it would seem desirable for the sole member to sign it in case of dispute, there is no requirement of signature in the Regulations.

It will be seen that a new s 370A is not a significant change since all the formalities of calling and holding a meeting would have to be gone through. However, s 382B is significant in that it allows the sole member to conduct member business informally without notice or minutes.

Filing requirements still apply when, say, the articles are altered informally, and an AGM must still be held unless the company has opted out by elective resolution.

Where this has been done and the company has also dispensed by elective resolution with the requirement to lay its accounts and reports before a general meeting, it will mean that in the single-member company no member meetings will be required, though board meetings, along with resolutions and minutes, are still required; though even here, subject to the articles, the written resolution procedure provided for by reg 93 of Table A to the CA 1985 may be used.

Single-member companies may conduct member business by written resolution provided they follow the formalities of s 381A, which involve, for example, sending a copy of the intended written resolution to the auditors for confirmation that the resolution does not concern them as auditors, or if it does, that a general meeting need not be held (but *see* now Chapter 20).

Written resolutions cannot in multi-member companies be used to remove directors and auditors but the s 382B procedure would seem to be available so that removal of a non-member director or the auditor without a meeting or without director or auditor representation could be achieved in that way, though the Regulations are silent on this. However, there is case law which suggests that an informal decision of members will not always suffice where company legislation requires special procedures. (*See Re Barry Artist* [1985] 1 WLR 1305 where the court stated that it would not in future accept an informal decision to reduce share capital.)

### Contracts with a sole member who is also a director

The Regulations add a new s 322B to the CA 1985. This provides that the terms of a contract with a sole member/director must either be set out in a written memorandum, or be made the subject of a report to the next available board meeting and be recorded in the board minutes.

This provision does not apply if the contract is in writing or if it is entered into in the ordinary course of business, as where the company purchases raw materials from the sole member/director.

### Other main changes in company legislation

Section 24 provides, as we have seen, that where the membership of a company falls to one, the sole member may, in certain circumstances, become liable for its debts. It is also a ground for compulsory winding-up under s 122(1)(e) of the Insolvency Act 1986. The Regulations make clear that these sections do not apply to *any* private companies limited by shares or guarantee.

### The articles of single-member companies – generally

Questions have been raised by those in business as to the need for special articles for these companies. Regulation 2 of the single-member company Regulations provides that any enactment shall (in the absence of any express provision to the contrary) apply with such modifications as may be necessary in relation to the single-member company. The word 'enactment' covers subordinate legislation such as Table A. If Table A carries conflicts with the company's structure as a single-member company it will be read to fit single-member status. However, this would not affect any express provision in a company's own special articles, though as we have seen s 370A specifically overrides provisions in special articles by allowing a quorum of one for general meetings. Therefore, any special articles should be reviewed and changed if required to suit single-member status.

### Death of the sole member

If a sole member/director dies, there is no board to approve the transfer of his or her shares under the terms of the will or on intestacy. The company is then, in effect, paralysed being without a board or shareholders. The articles should, therefore, be altered so as to allow, for example, the company secretary to authorise a transfer or allow the personal representatives of the deceased member to appoint a director of the company if the company is without any. That director could then approve the transfer and the business of the company could continue.

There is also a common law rule that the directors must actively refuse a transfer within a reasonable time. Under reg 25 and s 183 any power of veto vested in the directors must be exercised within two months after the lodging of the transfer and after that time the court could compel the registration of the transferee (*see* Chapter 19). Nevertheless, it is better that the articles should address this matter.

## FORMATION OF COMPANIES: PRE-REGISTRATION MATTERS

It is common in business to use a company formation agency to effect the actual registration of a company. However, there are matters to be considered by those who are to run a business through the medium of a company and which arise prior to the commencement of registration procedures. These are considered here.

## PROMOTERS

There is no general definition of a promoter in the Companies Act 1985. Whether a person is or is not a promoter is a matter of fact rather than law. There are some judicial attempts at definition but these are, perhaps naturally, imprecise. However, a promoter will usually be in some sort of controlling position with regard to the company's affairs, both before it is formed and during the early stages of its existence, and will be in a position analogous to a director during that period. Those who merely give advice to those who are promoting companies, such as accountants and solicitors, are not likely for that reason alone to be regarded as promoters.

The purchaser of a ready-made company is a promoter because the term would seem to cover a person who promotes a business project through the medium of a company.

The promotion of companies today is unlikely to involve problems of fraud because the persons involved are usually promoting companies to acquire their own businesses and there is not normally any involvement of outsiders. However, the following matters are worthy of some consideration.

### Fiduciary duties

These may come into play if the promoter intends to sell property to the company when in existence. If he does so, he must take care to sell it through the medium of a board of directors which is capable of, and does, exercise an independent judgment in regard to the transaction in terms of its benefit to the company; otherwise the transaction may be set aside by the court if there are those within the company; who oppose it. An alternative to approval by the board is to obtain the approval of the members by ordinary (or written) resolution.

Where a promoter makes any profit on the transaction, this must be handed over to the company unless its retention is approved, again by a board capable of an independent judgment or the members by ordinary (or written) resolution.

These matters are not of great importance in the case of a small private company where the corporators are working in amity and are likely to continue to do so. Where there might be a breakdown in relationships, as is the case with some family companies, it may be necessary to pay greater attention to the above matters in order to avoid costly litigation in the future.

## Pre-incorporation contracts – generally

Where the company concerned is in process of formation and is not ready-made, the company has no legal existence until a certificate of incorporation is issued by the Registrar. Therefore, it has no capacity to make contracts and the consequence of that is that if a promoter or some other person tries to make a contract for the company before its incorporation then:

(a) the company when formed is not bound by it;
(b) the company cannot ratify the agreement after incorporation;
(c) unless the agreement has been made specifically to the contrary it will take effect as one made personally by the promoter or other person purporting to act for the company, and the third party (*see* s 36C). The promoter or other person is, therefore, personally liable on it. This is the case whether the contract is made orally or in writing or by deed.

## Pre-incorporation contracts – solutions to personal liability

The following methods may be used to ensure that the company becomes, after incorporation, an effective party to a pre-incorporation transaction:

(a) A draft agreement may be settled with the other party so that when the company is formed it enters into the draft agreement thus giving it contractual force when signed also by the other party. In order to ensure that the company does enter into the contract, the memorandum or articles of a new company can be drafted to include a provision binding the directors to adopt it. It will be noted that the promoter is never liable here because there is no contract with him.
(b) The promoter can make the contract himself and be bound by it, provided the other party agrees that the promoter shall be released from his obligations under the contract if and when the company enters into a new, but as regards terms, identical contract with the other party after incorporation. This is really recommended only for those cases – which are many – where the promoter(s) will be in effective control of the company after incorporation and can ensure the making of the new contract. Simply making the contract with the third party and allowing the

promoter to assign the benefit of it to the company when it is formed is not recommended because English law does not allow a person to assign the burden of a contract. Therefore, the promoter remains personally liable for the performance of the agreement even after assignment to the company.

(c) Where the promoter is anxious that the company should acquire property which he does not himself own, he may take an option to purchase for, say, three months. If the company later wishes to take the property, the promoter may assign the benefit of the option to the company or enforce it for the benefit of the company. If the company does not take over the property, the promoter is not liable himself to do so but he may lose any money which he paid for the option.

(d) Section 36C states that the promoter is personally liable 'subject to any agreement to the contrary'. Thus the promoter could agree when making the contract that he should not be personally liable on it, even if the company after incorporation did not make a new contract. This may not satisfy a third party who wants a form of initial binding agreement, but it is sanctioned by the 1985 Act.

Obviously, it is better not to make contracts on behalf of a company while it is in the course of incorporation, but it may be necessary sometimes to do so. In the case of a ready-made or 'shelf' company, there is, of course, no problem. The company exists and contracts can be made which will be binding on it from the beginning.

## THE REGISTERED OFFICE

The memorandum of the company states, merely, the situation of the registered office and not its address. Since this book is not concerned with Scottish companies, it will suffice to say that the situation of the registered office may be stated to be in England and Wales, or in Wales. A company which has its registered office in Wales may alter this clause of its memorandum to provide that its registered office is situated in Wales where originally it said England and Wales. A special (or written) resolution is required and apart from this there can be no alteration of the registered office clause.

In terms of pre-incorporation activity, the actual location (address) of the registered office must be decided upon. The actual address of the registered office must be filed with the other necessary documents when registration of the company is sought.

### Purpose of the registered office

A major purpose of the registered office is to keep the various statutory registers and records for the purposes of inspection. These registers and records are further considered in Chapter 20. In addition, the registered office is the company's address. It provides a place where legal documents, notices and other communications can be served. Under s 725 a document can be served on a company by leaving it at or sending it by post to the registered office or principal place of business, a copy going by post to the registered office. If the company has no registered office or principal place of business, writs, summonses and notices and so on may be served on the directors or the secretary at an office which is not registered or at their private residences. In the case of a writ or summons, leave of the court would be required. As an interesting development, a recent change in the County Court Rules allows service of writs and other legal process for actions in the County Court, as distinct from the High Court, on a company not only at the company's registered office but also at any place of business, such as a branch, which has some connection with the cause or issue. So if business has been conducted through a branch office which has resulted in the supply of defective goods or services, legal process can be served on the branch office. This assists the consumer, in particular, who will be more familiar with the branch through which he has had dealings than with the registered office. When the Registrar receives a communication returned as undeliverable at the registered office, he will eventually set in motion the procedures for striking the company off the register as a defunct company.

In order to assist those who wish to serve legal process or other notices and documents on companies, a company must, under s 351, have in legible characters on all business letters and order forms the place of registration, the number with which it is registered and the address of the registered office.

The address of the registered office must be consistent with the domicil of the company as appearing in its memorandum. Thus a company registered in England and Wales or Wales cannot have a registered office in Scotland.

## Change of address of registered office

The actual address of the registered office may be changed within the domicil. Thus it is possible for a company whose memorandum states that its registered office is to be situated in 'England' or 'England and Wales' to change its registered office to somewhere else in England and Wales since 'England' includes Wales for this purpose. In spite of the fact that the law of England and Wales is the same, a company which has chosen to have its registered office in Wales, either initially or by change, cannot change its registered office to a place in England. In any case, an English or Welsh company cannot change its registered office to a place in Scotland. The law is different there and the move would take the office out of the domicil set out in the company's memorandum.

Regulation 70 of Table A gives the directors wide management powers which, by implication, allow them to resolve to change the address of the registered office. The company must under s 287 notify the Registrar of the change. The Registrar must, under s 711, publish, in the *London Gazette*, notice of the receipt by him of a change in the situation of the registered office. The change takes effect only when the notice is registered by the Registrar but until the end of a period of 14 days, beginning with the day on which it is registered, a person may validly serve a document on the company at its former registered office.

Where the change is made close to the company's annual return date notification may be made on the annual return form.

## Taxation

It should be noted, as a practical point, that a change in the address of the registered office may involve a change in the company's Tax District.

## COMPANY NAMES

Chapter II of Part I of the CA 1985 sets up a system for controlling company names. This operates along with the Business Names Act 1985 where the latter is relevant.

### On registration

Under s 26 a company name will not be registered if:

(a) it includes, otherwise than at the end of the name, any of the following words or their permitted abbreviations: 'limited', 'unlimited' or 'public limited company', or their Welsh equivalents;

(b) it is the same as a name already on the index of names kept by the Registrar of Companies; this can be inspected free of charge;

(c) its use would in the opinion of the Secretary of State constitute a criminal offence or be offensive. These situations will be rare but the Registrar did turn down the names 'Prostitutes Ltd' and 'Hookers Ltd' when a prostitute applied for registration of the business of prostitution (*see Attorney-General* v *Lindi St Claire* (*Personal Services*) *Ltd* [1981] 2 Co Law 69).

Under s 26 certain names will not be registered without approval, as follows:

(a) the consent of the Secretary of State is required for the registration of a name by a company implying national or multinational pre-eminence, e.g. International and European; local or central government connection, patronage or sponsorship, e.g. 'Council' as in 'County Council Supplies Ltd'; business pre-eminence or representative status, e.g. Federation or Institution; certain specific objects or functions, e.g. Insurance or Trust;

(b) there are also sensitive names which will only be registered if the applicant has obtained a letter of non-objection from the relevant government department or other body: e.g. 'Royal' or 'Royalty' requires a letter of non-objection from the Home Office, while 'Charity' or 'Charitable' requires a letter from the Charity Commission.

The above provisions of s 26 apply to a new name where an existing company wishes to change its name.

A company wishing to use the words 'association' or 'society' in its name must be limited by guarantee. Its constitution must provide for one member one vote and it must have non-profit distribution clauses in its memorandum. A company wishing to use the word 'international' in its name must provide the Registrar with a statement that it will be trading in at least two named countries outside the UK.

Where a word requiring the approval of the Secretary of State is to be used, then when sending Form 12 (on incorporation) or the requisite resolution (on a change of name) a letter together with any required evidence must be included, e.g. that in the case of the word 'holdings' the company is a holding company with one or more subsidiaries. Where the approval of another body is required, as in the case of the word 'charity', the company must send on incorporation or change of name a statement confirming that an approach has been made to the relevant body, e.g. the Charity Commission, together with a copy of any response received.

## Trade marks

The name of a company either initially or on change must not include a trade mark unless the consent of the owner is obtained. The Registrar of Companies does not search the Trade Marks Index and the fact that he has accepted a name does not mean that trade mark rights do not exist in it. Possible infringement is a matter for the promoters of the company who should themselves, or through an agent, make a search of the Trade Marks Index at the Trade Marks Registry of the Patent Office.

## Change of name

A company may change its name voluntarily, or the Secretary of State may direct a change, as follows.

### Voluntary change

Under s 28 a company may at any time change its name by special (or written) resolution and a copy must be filed with the Registrar under s 380 within 15 days of its passing, together with the appropriate fee.

### Compulsory change

Three areas are relevant, as follows.

(a) Within 12 months of registration in a particular name, the Secretary of State may, under s 28, direct a change in a name, within such period as he may specify, if the registered name is the same as or 'too like' a name appearing in the Index of names at the time of registration. An example of a too like name would occur where the names had a distinctive element in common, such as Widget Ltd and Widget Holdings Ltd. The addition of the word 'Holdings' does not sufficiently qualify the name since 'Widget' is the distinctive element, and therefore the name 'Widget Holdings Ltd' is too like 'Widget Ltd'. If Widget Holdings was the last to be registered and Widget Ltd draws the attention of the Registrar to the situation, giving reasons for confusion or possible confusion, and asking for a direction to be made, then there is a discretion in the name of the Secretary of State to make a direction.

   After the passing of 12 months (and during the first 12 months) the common law action for passing off would be available where the offending name was the same as or too like an existing one.

(b) Where it appears to the Secretary of State that a company has given misleading information in connection with its registration in a particular name, he may, under s 28, and within five years of registration, direct a change within such period as he may specify. This could cover cases where, the name being sensitive, false information has been given to the approving authority – as where promoters have given false information to the Charity Commission in order to get permission to use 'Charity' or 'Charitable' in the name of a company which is used for personal gain.

(c) The Secretary of State has power to direct a company to change its name if it gives so misleading an indication of its activities as to be likely to cause harm to the public. Section 32 applies and is designed to deal with 'shell' companies as where a company named, for example, 'Prosper Investments Trust' is acquired and used for the purpose of making cheap washing machines. The power is exercisable at any time and is not limited to 12 months or five years as are the directions under s 28 set out above. The company must comply with the direction within six weeks unless it exercises its right to appeal to the court, as it may do within three weeks after the direction is notified to it. The court may set aside the direction or confirm it.

Directions under s 32 are rare, but such a direction was given by the Secretary of State in regard to the Association of Certified Public Accountants of Britain which the Secretary considered to be a registered name which was likely to mislead the public. The direction was based upon the word 'certified' which might be confused with the Association of Chartered Certified Accountants. An application to the court to set aside the direction was dismissed (*see Association of Certified Public Accountants of Britain* v *Secretary of State for Trade and Industry, The Times,* 12 June 1997).

Where a company changes its name either voluntarily or compulsorily under the above provisions, the change will not affect any of its rights and obligations or make defective any legal proceedings commenced in its former name: these may continue.

On a change of name the Registrar will issue a new certificate of incorporation and must publish the fact that he has done so in the *London Gazette*.

## BUSINESS NAMES

### The Business Names Act 1985

This Act deals with the control of business names by sole traders, partnerships and companies. Only the provisions relating to companies will be considered here. The Act applies to companies which carry on business in Great Britain under a name which does not consist of the corporate name without addition. However, an addition indicating that the business is carried on in succession to a former owner does not make the name a business name. Thus 'Boxo Ltd (formerly H & C Brown)' is not a business name.

A business name must not be one which would be likely to give the impression that the business is connected with local or central government, unless the approval of the Secretary of State has been given, nor must the name consist of sensitive words, unless permission has been granted by the appropriate authority.

### Use of a business name

Let us suppose that Boxo Ltd trades through a number of retail outlets under the name 'Paris Fashions'. In such a case the rules relating to business names apply to Boxo Ltd. These rules require the company to state in legible characters on all its business letters, written orders for goods or services to be supplied to the business, invoices, receipts and written demands for payment of debts, the corporate name and an address within Great Britain at which service of any document relating in any way to the business will be effective. This will normally be the address of the registered office.

The corporate name and an address for service must also be disclosed in a prominent position, so that it can be read by customers and suppliers, in any premises where the business is carried on, provided that customers and/or suppliers of any goods or services have access to the premises but not otherwise.

The Act also requires that the corporate name and an address for service be given immediately and in writing to anyone who is doing or negotiating or discussing business with Paris Fashions and asks for them. This would be complied with by the handing over of an appropriately worded business card.

## Breach of provisions

The criminal sanction consists of default fines on the company and its officers such as the directors and the secretary.

At civil law failure to comply with any of the requirements as to the publication of the corporate name may mean that the company will not be able to enforce a transaction with a person who is unaware of the corporate name, and has been unable to pursue a claim against the company, as where goods supplied to him on credit were substandard, or who has otherwise suffered financial loss. The court may allow the company's claim for debt to proceed if it thinks it is just and equitable to do so and the company may counter-claim for the debt if it is sued by the customer.

## Protection of business names

The fact that there is no registration of business names places businesses that use them in a more difficult position in terms of protecting the name than companies which trade in their corporate names.

As we have seen, the Registrar keeps an index of company names and a company cannot be registered in a name that is the 'same' as a name already on the index. In addition, we have noted that the Secretary of State can direct a company to change its name within 12 months of registration if it is 'too like' the name of a company on the index. The above provisions do not apply to business names and a passing off action would have to be brought. This is a difficult and often expensive claim. If the name is in the nature of a trade mark it can be registered and protected more easily. The Trade Marks Act 1994 has extended this possibility particularly in allowing registration of geographical locations, e.g. 'The Barbican Tandoori'.

## Overseas companies

The rules relating to company names and business names apply to overseas companies carrying on business in Great Britain provided they have a place of business here.

# EXEMPTION FROM USING THE WORD 'LIMITED'

Under ss 30–2 certain companies are exempt from the requirement to use the word 'limited', or its Welsh equivalent, or any abbreviation meaning the same thing, in their names.

## Companies eligible

The exemption applies:

(a) to private companies limited by guarantee which are the only companies which may apply;

(b) where the objects of the company are to promote commerce, art, science, education, religion, charity, or any profession and anything incidental or conducive to any of those objects;

(c) where the company's memorandum or articles require that the company's profits or income be applied to the promotion of its objects. They must also prohibit payment of dividends and require all surplus assets on a winding-up to be transferred to another body with similar or charitable objects.

## Formalities to obtain the exemption

These are as follows:

(a) the making of a statutory declaration – in the case of a company about to be formed – by a solicitor engaged in the formation of the company or by a person named as a director or secretary of the company in the statement delivered on incorporation under s 10 (statement of first directors and secretary) or in the case of a company changing its name to omit 'limited' by a director or secretary of the company (Form 30 (5)(c));

(b) the statutory declaration is made to the Registrar and states that the company is one whose memorandum and articles are appropriately limited so that the exemption applies;

(c) where an existing company is changing its name to omit the word 'limited', a special (or written) resolution must be passed and sent to the Registrar with the statutory declaration;

(d) only the normal incorporation fee is payable where the exemption is sought on incorporation and there is no fee where the name is changed, if the change is merely to omit the word 'limited'. If the change is more extensive than that, the usual fee for change of name is payable.

## Provisions applicable after exemption

(a) An exempt company must not alter its memorandum or articles so that they no longer comply with the exemption requirements. If it does so, officers in default are liable to a fine.

(b) The company is exempt from the requirements of the CA 1985 relating to the publication of its name and the sending of lists of members to the Registrar with the annual return, provided it does not in fact continue to use the word 'limited' in its name in spite of the exemption.

(c) If it appears to the Secretary of State that the company is breaking the limitations in its constitution, as where it is carrying on business for profit, he has power to direct the company to change its name by adding 'limited'. A company which has received such a direction can only subsequently omit the word 'limited' if the Secretary of State approves. Initially the omission is as of right.

The exemption is not fully effective because s 351 requires a limited company exempt from the obligation to use 'limited' as part of its name to mention in all business letters and order forms that it is in fact a limited company. However, the company at least avoids the need to use the word 'limited' as part of its name, and because of this may overcome the general public view that it is commercial and profit orientated, as the word 'limited' connotes.

## PUBLICATION OF THE NAME

The CA 1985 provides that the company's full name must appear legibly and conspicuously:

(a) outside the registered office and all places of business (s 348);
(b) on the common seal (if it has one) (s 350);
(c) on all business letters, notices and official publications and all bills of exchange, cheques, promissory notes, orders for money or goods, receipts and invoices signed or issued on its behalf (s 349).

The company's business letters and order forms must also show: the place of registration, the registered number and registered office address and a statement that the company is limited (where it is exempt from using that word in its name) and a statement that the company is an investment company as defined in s 266 (where this is the case).

Fines may be imposed on the company and its officers for failure to comply and the officers of the company may incur personal liability under s 349 in the terms set out in Chapter 20.

The above provisions are in addition to the Business Names Act 1985 requirements. Companies are not obliged to state the names of their directors on their business stationery. If a company decides to do so, except as a signatory to or in the text of a letter, then the names of all directors must be shown (s 305). There is no need to show share capital but if it is shown, it must be the paid-up capital (s 351).

### E-mail, faxes and company details

For the purposes of the Companies Act 1985, it is considered that external e-mails and faxes are to be regarded as letters and that the items required to be shown on business letters and order forms should similarly be shown when e-mail and/or fax are used.

### Abuse of names by Internet users

Persons can select any name for their Internet address, provided it has not already been registered. If an unauthorised individual or business registers an Internet address which includes the business name or trade mark of a company, this may prevent that company from using its own name in its Internet address. Action which could be taken by the company in such a situation is set out below:

- the company could offer to purchase the address from the user;
- complaint could be made to the Internet service provider;
- legal action could be taken if the name is a registered trade mark and the offending Internet address is used in the course of trade in the UK;
- the company may rely on the law of passing off, provided that it can be shown that there is goodwill attached to the name in the UK and that the use of the name by the Internet user is a misrepresentation made in the course of trade in the UK to customers and prospective customers of the company.

The best solution is for the company to register its name first. This can be done through a provider of Internet services.

The High Court has shown itself willing to issue an injunction to prevent the use of an Internet name in a passing off claim. (*See Pitman Training Ltd* v *Nominet UK* [1997] 1 *Current Law* 4875).

An additional problem which has arisen because of the rapid growth of the Internet and its use by business organisations for e-mail and commerce generally, is the parallel growth of a breed of speculators who register domain names which form a crucial part of a particular business website and e-mail address, in the hope, for example, of offering it for sale to the business concerned with the possibility of receiving a high price for exclusivity. In *BT plc* v *One in a Million, The Times*, 2 December 1997, the High Court granted injunctions to restrain defendants who had registered company names and/or trade marks as domain names on the Internet on the basis of passing off and trade mark infringement. The court also said that since the names were now of no use to the defendants, they should be assigned to the claimants. The decision means that, at least in the UK, it should be easier to protect Internet domain names.

## THE COMPANY'S OBJECTS

The memorandum, which is filed with the Registrar on formation, lists the activities in which the company may engage. This clause is normally in standard form. An agency will commonly include the company's main activity as its first object and follow this with many subclauses containing a wide variety of activities which the company may undertake if it wishes. It is also common to insert a paragraph stating that each clause contains a separate and independent object so that, for example, a company whose main object was publishing could use an investment clause for any kind of investment and not just investment in a publishing activity. The House of Lords decided in *Cotman* v *Brougham* [1918] AC 514 that such a clause was legal.

It is also common to include a clause often referred to as a 'subjective objects clause'. This allows the company to carry on any additional business not provided for in the objects clause which the members (or the directors) think can be conveniently pursued by the company. The normal form is to make the decision depend upon an ordinary resolution of the members, but the director formula is quite acceptable in case law (*see Bell Houses Ltd* v *City Wall Properties* [1966] 2 All ER 674). It depends how much power it is thought right to put in the hands of the directors.

Thus the modern company's contractual capacity approaches that of a natural person and the *ultra vires* (beyond the powers of) rule as a method of controlling the activities of the directors has been largely abandoned. This is increasingly the case since company formation agents are, unless told otherwise, using the 'general commercial company' formula described later in this chapter.

### The Companies Act 1985

Section 35 (as inserted by the CA 1989) deals with the *ultra vires* rule as it relates to the company's *capacity* to enter into the transaction. The authority and power of its directors and other officers to make, say, a contract on its behalf is considered later in this chapter. Section 35 does not abolish the rule but reforms it and, as far as trade creditors of a company are concerned, little should now be heard of it. There is a continuing relevance of the rule in other areas which are considered below.

### The company's capacity

Section 35 provides that the validity of an act of a company shall not be called into question by reason of anything in the company's memorandum. Thus in the leading case of *Ashbury Railway Carriage and Iron Co* v *Riche* (1875) LR 7 HL 653 the *contents* of the objects clause only allowed the company to make things for railways. The contract with Mr Riche, which was made by the company as part of a transaction to build a whole railway system from Antwerp to Tournai, was held to be *ultra vires* but would now have been enforceable since, so far as outsiders like Mr Riche are concerned, the contents of (what is in) the memorandum does not affect the validity of the transaction in terms of the company's capacity to enter into it.

### The rights of members

Under s 35 any member can ask the court for an injunction to prevent the directors from *entering into an ultra vires transaction,* but not if the members have ratified it by a special (or written) resolution. If the directors have entered into an *ultra vires* transaction, an injunction is not available, but it is if they are contemplating such a transaction. If the situation is such that an action for an injunction can go ahead, the *ultra vires* rule and the contents of the memorandum and the special clauses referred to above will continue to be relevant in deciding whether or not the intended transaction can be restrained. Thus the rule is reformed not abolished.

### Transactions with directors of the company or its holding company

Under s 322A transactions with the directors of the company or its holding company are voidable (capable of being made legally ineffective) by the company if they are *ultra vires,* and once again the contents of the objects clause and not s 35 will be relevant. Transactions with the directors' connected persons are included as are transactions with directors' associated companies. Connected persons are dealt with more fully in Chapter 20 but, as an example, the spouse of a director is a connected person and an associated company is one in which the director has 20 per cent or more of the issued share capital or controls 20 per cent or more of the votes. It will be appreciated that if there are weighted voting rights in the articles, a person may own less than 20 per cent of the shares but have more than 20 per cent of the votes.

The above transactions are not voidable by the company where the problem is that they are beyond the objects of the company if the members have ratified them by a special (or written) resolution. For the situation where the directors have exceeded their own powers but not those of the company, *see* later in this chapter.

### Liability of directors

Directors have in the past been liable to pay damages to the company if they entered into an *ultra vires* transaction which caused the company loss, which of course it may not do. This is still the position and the objects clause is relevant in deciding the liability of the directors. However, s 35(3) allows the members to relieve the directors of this liability by passing a special (or written) resolution. This must be a separate resolution; a resolution ratifying the transaction is not enough.

### Charities

There is a special regime for charities which obviously need separate treatment because people give, not so much to the charity, but to its objects which should, therefore, be adhered to. Under s 65 of the Charities Act 1993, s 35 is not available to a person dealing with a charity unless:

(a) he has given full consideration to the charity in money or money's worth, i.e. it is a deal in which the charity gets proper value; *and*
(b) he is unaware that the transaction was beyond the company's objects; or
(c) he was unaware that the company was a charity.

The various powers of ratification referred to above do not apply.

### Ordinary creditors

So far as the company's capacity is concerned, there should be no problems and their transactions should be enforceable against the company by reason of s 35. Also of assistance are the following:

(a) there is now no constructive notice of the company's objects as there was before. Section 711A applies and means that there is no deemed knowledge that a particular transaction is not within the objects;
(b) there is no duty to enquire as to the capacity of the company nor, under s 35A, as to the authority of its agents to make a particular transaction;
(c) transactions are enforceable against the company even by those who have actual knowledge that it is not within the company's objects. Section 35A(2)(b) applies so that even if a creditor had read the memorandum and realised that a transaction was not within the objects, he could still enforce it against the company.

## The general commercial company

Under s 3A a company may alter its objects to state (or be registered with an objects clause so stating) that it is to carry on business as a general commercial company. This means that it can carry on any trade or business whatsoever. The section also gives the company power to do all such things as are incidental or conducive to that end without listing them in the objects clause.

If a company does register with, or change its objects to, this formula, it will have effectively opted out of the *ultra vires* rule even for internal purposes in terms of shareholder injunctions, dealings with directors and director liability for loss – which have already been considered.

Additional objects would be required if, for example, the company wished to make charitable and/or political donations since these activities would not come within the ambit of 'trade or business'. It is not known at the time of writing how many companies will adopt the new formula, in particular because of the wide powers it gives to the directors. It seems ideal for the family business, being run through a private company, where the shareholders and the directors are one and the same. But it may not suit all situations, and legal advice should be taken before registration or change to the commercial company formula. Company formation agents will, unless told otherwise, use the 'general commercial company' formula in their ready-made companies.

## ALTERATION OF THE OBJECTS

Under s 4 the objects clause can be altered by a special (or written) resolution for any reason. Once a resolution to alter the objects clause has been passed, it stands and will be effective unless within 21 days of its being passed the holder(s) of 15 per cent of the company's issued share capital, or if the share capital is divided into classes, 15 per cent of the holders of any class, apply to the court to cancel it (s 5). These dissentients must not have voted for the resolution. Obviously, the dissentient rights will not be exercised where the resolution is written because such resolutions must be unanimous. The court may by order confirm or reject the alteration in whole or in part on such conditions as it thinks fit (s 5). It is perhaps unlikely to reject the resolution since it will have been passed by a three-quarters' majority special resolution so that the dissentients may be regarded as out of step. However, the court may intervene if the special resolution was passed at a poorly attended meeting with few proxies, so that a large group of votes were not cast at the meeting. Subject to this, however, the court has power to order the purchase of the dissentients' shares by the other members or, that failing, by the company from its own funds. In the latter case the court will sanction a reduction of capital.

The special (or written) resolution altering the memorandum must be filed with the Registrar within the usual 15 days and if, as would be usual, no application to the court is made the company must, within 15 days from the end of the period for making an application, that is, within 36 days of the resolution, deliver to the Registrar a printed copy of the memorandum as altered (s 6). The Registrar will not normally accept the altered memorandum before this time though he would where there had been a unanimous written resolution and nobody could object.

If an application can and is made the company must forthwith give notice to the Registrar.

## AUTHORITY OF DIRECTORS AS AGENTS

It is convenient to consider here the authority of the directors to bind the company to a transaction as agents. A transaction will not necessarily be enforceable because it is within the company's capacity, in terms of the provisions in its objects clause, or by reason of s 35, if the directors do not have authority as agents to enter into it on behalf of the company.

### Directors' powers

Table A to the CA 1985 in reg 70 and Table A to the CA 1948 in Art 80 give wide powers to the directors by allowing them to exercise 'all the powers of the company' unless, for example, company legislation requires the members to act. Thus the directors are unable to alter the articles. In both Tables A the members may restrict these wide powers – by a special resolution in the case of the 1985 Act and by an ordinary resolution in the case of the 1948 Act. In a private company, unanimous written resolutions would suffice.

If it is thought necessary to restrict the powers of the directors in the articles, as where the articles contain a restriction on borrowing by the directors so that, for example, the company has unlimited power to borrow but they can only borrow up to half the paid-up capital, what is the position as regards a lender whose loan exceeds this amount? There was some protection in case law in the past but for all practical purposes the matter is now covered by s 35A of the CA 1985.

The section provides that in favour of a person dealing with the company in good faith the power of the board of directors to bind the company or authorise others to do so shall be deemed free of any limitation under the company's constitution and this includes any specific limitation imposed by a member resolution on the lines of Table A (above) or arising from an agreement with the members. A person is not to be regarded as acting in bad faith just because he knows that the act is beyond the powers of the directors and, under s 35B, there is no duty to enquire nor is there constructive notice. Provided the above requirements are met, a transaction entered into by the board acting *collectively* will bind the company.

In addition, the section deals with a situation where the directors authorise other persons to make contracts on behalf of the company. This is to overcome the common law rule that a company can only act through 'organs' of the company. At common law the board of directors is an organ of the company but only if acting collectively. Section 35A overcomes this by making it clear that an act done by a person authorised by the board is in effect an act of the board and, therefore, an act by an 'organ' of the company. Thus, if the board authorises the company's purchasing officer to buy materials from outsiders for use in the company's manufacturing process, each purchase will be a transaction decided on by the directors. There is no longer an assumption, as there was in previous and to some extent defective legislation, that all commercial decisions are made at board-room level. If, therefore, the board collectively makes a decision to enter into a transaction which is beyond its powers, s 35A will make the transaction enforceable against the company and the same is true if an individual authorised by the board exceeds the powers of the directors in respect of a transaction on behalf of the company which he, as an authorised individual, has made.

## Good faith

Under s 35A a person is to be regarded as acting in good faith unless the contrary is proved. Thus the burden of proof will be on the company if it wishes to avoid a transaction on the 'bad faith' ground. Section 35A also provides that a person is 'dealing with' a company even though the transaction is gratuitous in that no consideration has been provided to the company. This protects, for example, charitable donations by the directors beyond their powers.

## Members' injunctions

A member of a company is not prevented by s 35A from asking the court for an injunction to stop the directors from acting beyond their powers, but this cannot be done if the transaction has been entered into, or if the members have ratified it by an ordinary (or written) resolution.

## Directors' liability

The directors are liable to compensate the company, as they always have been, if they cause the company loss by acting outside their powers. Relief from this liability can be given by the members by special (or written) resolution.

## Charities

Once again, there are special rules for charities. Section 35A will not protect a person dealing with a charity unless he has given full consideration and he did not know that the transaction was beyond the powers of the directors or he did not know that he was dealing with a charity.

# ARTICLES OF ASSOCIATION

The articles of association regulate the rights of the members of the company and contain provisions for its internal management. The articles deal with such matters as the appointment and powers of directors, general meetings of the company, the voting rights of members and the transfer of shares and dividends. The rights of different classes of shareholders may also be found in the articles but not in Table A which merely provides in reg 2 that shareholders' rights shall be as determined by the members by ordinary resolution. So under Table A the rights are part of the terms of issue.

## Table A

Under s 8, a company may adopt all or any of the regulations contained in Table A as its articles. Table A is contained in the Companies (Tables A to F) Regulations 1985 (SI 1985/805), and is a model set of articles applicable to a company whether public or private which is limited by shares. A company may either:

(a) register its own articles and, if it does, the provisions of Table A will only apply where matters set out in Table A are not omitted from or specifically included in the special articles; *or*

(b) adopt Table A in a modified form; *or*

(c) register a memorandum without articles in which case Table A will apply in its entirety.

As we have seen, guarantee and unlimited companies must register articles and there are models in Tables C to E, but these are not applicable for an unlimited company without a share capital. Such a company requires specially drafted articles.

If a company wishes to register its own articles, then under, s 7(3), they must be printed, divided into paragraphs numbered consecutively, be signed by each subscriber to the memorandum in the presence of a witness and be dated.

Articles which conflict with legislation are of no effect and if any article conflicts with a provision in the memorandum, which is likely only in the case of class rights which can appear in either or both of those documents, the provisions of the memorandum prevail.

It should also be noted that if the company is governed by a Table A earlier than SI 1985/805 without amendment, then certain more modern statutory provisions, such as the issue of redeemable equity shares and the purchase by a company of its own shares, will not be possible until amendment because the articles will not contain a provision allowing these procedures as the legislation requires.

## Special articles

A not uncommon use of special provisions in the articles of private companies is where the holding company seeks to add extra provisions not found in Table A to the articles of a subsidiary as a means of control over the subsidiary. The most usual clauses inserted into the articles of the subsidiary are to the effect that certain transactions of the subsidiary require the approval of the shareholders of the subsidiary company by ordinary resolution (a 'general meeting' provision) (where the majority voting power is in the holding company) or the consent of a nominated director of the subsidiary who is usually a representative of the parent company (a 'special director' provision).

The transactions of the subsidiary which are controlled may include:

- the acquisition by the subsidiary of shares in any other company;
- the execution of or alteration to any terms of the employment contracts of key employees;
- the establishment of pension or bonus schemes;
- the lending of money;
- borrowing over a set limit – though this can be controlled by changing the signing powers on the bank mandate form;
- the appointment and resignation of the company secretary;
- the disposal or acqusition of assets over a set figure;
- the disposal of any assets which are regarded as vital to the business; and
- entering into transactions involving conflicts of interest between the subsidiary and e.g. its directors or connected persons or any other transaction which is not, in the circumstances, at arms's length.

## Articles as a contract

By reason of s 14, the articles (and memorandum) when registered bind the company and its members in contract as if these documents had been signed as a deed by each member and contained undertakings on the part of each member to observe the provisions of the memorandum and articles. The main result of this statutory contract, which is relevant mostly in terms of provisions in the articles, is that:

(a) *The articles constitute a contract between the company and each member.* Furthermore, although s 14 does not specifically say so, the articles bind the company to the members to observe the provisions of the articles since a contract cannot be one-sided. The main advantages of this to the private company are that the articles can be drafted to contain a clause that disputes between the company and its members as to their rights must be referred to arbitration since this may be a quicker and sometimes, but not always, a cheaper solution than reference in the first instance to an ordinary court of law. Also the articles may contain a pre-emption clause under which a member who wishes to sell his shares *must* offer them first to the other members who may purchase them at a fair price as agreed by the company's auditors. This means that outsiders cannot easily break into a family company and makes a private company difficult, if not impossible, to take over without the agreement of all the members. The advantage of the contract to the member is that he can, by legal process, enforce the rights given to him by the articles so that he cannot, for example, be denied his voting rights.

**Illustrative case law appears overleaf.**

### Hickman v Kent or Romney Marsh Sheep Breeders' Association [1915] 1 Ch 881

The articles of the association provided that any dispute between a member and the company must be taken first to arbitration. H, a shareholder, who was complaining that he had been wrongfully expelled from the company, took his case first to the High Court. The court decided that the action could not continue in the High Court. H was contractually bound by the articles to take the dispute to arbitration first.

### Pender v Lushington (1877) 6 Ch D 70

In this case the chairman of a meeting of members of a company refused to accept Pender's votes, which Pender as a member was trying to exercise in a manner contrary to the wishes of the board. The articles gave one vote for every 10 shares to the shareholders. This caused a resolution proposed by Pender to be lost. He asked the court to grant an injunction to stop the directors acting contrary to the resolution. The court *held* that an injunction should be granted. The articles were a contract binding the company to the members.

(b) *The articles constitute a contract between the members and the members.*

**This is illustrated by the following case.**

### Rayfield v Hands [1958] 2 All ER 194

A clause in the articles of a company provided that: 'Every member who intends to transfer shares shall inform the directors who will take the said shares equally between them at a fair value'. R, a member, told the defendant directors that he wanted to sell his shares. They refused to take and pay for them, saying that they had no liability to do so.

The court decided that the word 'will' indicated an obligation to take the shares and the clause imposed a contractual obligation on the directors to take them. This was in the nature of a collateral contract. When a member bought shares he made a contract with the company but also a collateral contract with the other members to observe the provisions of the articles. Thus the members could sue each other and there was no need for the company, with whom the main contract was made, to be made a party to the action.

*Comment:* Although the article placed the obligation to take shares on the directors, the judge generously construed this as an obligation falling upon the directors in their capacity as members. Otherwise, the contractual aspect of the provision in the articles would not have applied. The articles are not a contract between the company and the directors, who, in their capacity as directors, are outsiders for this purpose (*see below*). The pre-emption clause is also exceptional. Such clauses usually say that members wishing to transfer their shares *will* offer them to the other members first but that those members may purchase them. The word 'may' does not produce a contract. It gives a choice whether to purchase or not. The requirement to make the offer is contractual.

(c) *The articles do not constitute a contract with outsiders but only with the members in respect of their rights as members.* It is, therefore, important for an officer/employee such as a company secretary or a finance director to have an express contract and not have the terms of his appointment only in the articles. The leading case illustrating the difficulties which may be encountered is *Eley* v *Positive Government Security Life Assurance Co* (1876) 1 Ex D 88 where the articles said that Mr Eley was to be employed, for his lifetime, as the company's solicitor. The company ceased to employ him but it was held that he was not entitled to damages because the articles did not constitute a contract between him and the company except in terms of his rights as a member but not in his capacity as solicitor. He was incidentally a member, but this made no difference.

## Alteration of the articles

The articles may, under s 9, be altered by a special resolution in general meeting (*see further* Chapter 20), or, in private companies, by a written resolution. The alteration is as valid as if the provision had been in the original articles and can only itself be changed by the special or written resolution procedure, though the court is given power, under s 461, to change the articles, for example, as part of a procedure of assisting minority shareholders to overcome the unfairly prejudicial conduct of the majority (*see* Chapter 20). A future alteration, following a court order, requires the permission of the court, otherwise a relevant resolution is of no effect. All articles can be altered freely by following the relevant resolution procedure. Any attempt to make the articles or a particular article unalterable is contrary to s 9 and of no effect.

A copy of the resolution altering the articles, together with a printed copy of the revised articles, must be filed with the Registrar within 15 days of the resolution. Most forms of printing are acceptable.

## Restrictions on alteration

The most important restrictions upon the alteration of the articles are:

(a) under s 16, there can be no effective alteration to impose further liability on the members, as by, for example, requiring them to take more shares, unless the member concerned agrees in writing. This prevents the company from coercing its members to provide further capital if it cannot raise it from them voluntarily;

(b) where the company has shares of more than one class and the class rights are in the articles, a resolution to alter the articles and change the rights will not be effective unless the consent of the class has been obtained, either in writing or by extraordinary resolution or written resolution. There are provisions under which dissentients to the 75 per cent majority required may apply to the court to have the variation cancelled, but this would obviously not apply where the class consent was by unanimous written resolution (*See further* Chapter 20);

(c) the change must be 'for the benefit of the company', i.e. the members. This boils down to the fact that resolutions introducing articles providing for the expulsion of members without adequate cause are of no effect, though some have been allowed for good cause. An example is provided by *Sidebottom* v *Kershaw, Leese & Co* [1920] 1 Ch 154 where articles were altered to force a sale of shares by a member carrying on a business in direct competition with the company.

## REGISTRATION

### Documents to be sent to the Registrar

If the registered office is to be situated in England and Wales the address of the relevant registry is The Registrar of Companies, at Companies House in Cardiff.

The following documents are required for registration of a company:

(a) the memorandum of association;
(b) articles of association (if any). Private companies will usually adopt 'short form' articles which say that Table A applies, often with exclusions or modifications of certain of the regulations;
(c) Form 10, which gives details of the first directors and of the secretary together with the address of the registered office. The form must be signed by or on behalf of the subscribers of the memorandum and must contain a consent, signed by each of the directors and the secretary (or joint secretaries), to act in the relevant capacity;
(d) Form 12, which is a statutory declaration made by a solicitor engaged in the formation of the company, or by a person named as a director or secretary of the company in Form 10 above. It states that all the requirements in regard to the registration have been complied with, and the Registrar can accept it as sufficient evidence of compliance. The declaration is made before a commissioner for oaths, for example, a solicitor.

Following a Companies House review, Forms 10 and 12 are available for completion in Welsh to those companies eligible to deliver bilingual forms under the Companies Act. They may now be accompanied by a memorandum and articles in Welsh without a certified translation into English.

### Effect of incorporation

If the Registrar is satisfied with the contents of the various documents he will, on payment of the registration fee, issue a certificate of incorporation. This incorporates the members of the company into a legal person and limits their liability if the memorandum requires this. The certificate is conclusive evidence that all the requirements relating to registration have been complied with so that if any irregularity had occurred in the relevant procedures it would not be possible to successfully attack the validity of the company's incorporation. The certificate is not conclusive evidence that the company's objects are legal and if registration with illegal objects has taken place the Attorney-General can take steps on behalf of the Crown to ask the court to cancel the registration.

From the date impressed upon the certificate the company becomes a body corporate with the right to exercise the powers given in its memorandum. The company's life dates from the first moment of the day of its incorporation, and private companies can commence business immediately but, as we have seen, a public company must obtain a s 117 certificate before it can trade or borrow.

Finally, registration effects the appointment of the first directors and the secretary. Since the Registrar will not incorporate a company without Form 10 the first directors and the secretary are always properly appointed. It is worth noting that any appointment in the articles delivered with the registration documents as director or secretary of the company is void unless the person concerned is also named and consents in Form 10.

## Ready-made companies

It will be appreciated that where a ready-made company is used the above procedures will already have been gone through. The promoters may wish to change the ready-made company's name and will have to appoint directors and a secretary, and notify those appointments to the registrar on Form 288. Forms 10 and 12 are unnecessary in this context. Form 288 (notice of change of directors or secretaries or in their particulars) is used because the ready-made (or shelf) company will have had directors and a secretary on its formation. These persons will have resigned on the purchase of the ready-made company and new persons will be appointed. Thus it is a change in these offices which is being notified and not original appointments.

## Publicity

The Registrar is required to publish in the *London Gazette* the issue of any certificate of incorporation, but there is no statutory requirement that the certificate be displayed at the registered office or kept at any particular place.

## Channel Islands and Isle of Man companies

Obviously, these companies can trade in Great Britain without undertaking any registration procedures. However, if they establish a place of business here, they must, within one month of so doing, file with the Registrar:

(a) a copy of the instrument or instruments defining the constitution of the company certified to be a true copy by, for example, an officer of the company on oath taken before an authorised person;

(b) Form 691, which sets out a list of the directors and secretary, the name and address of at least one person resident in Great Britain to accept service of documents and notices, and the date on which the company's place of business in Great Britain was established.

Any alteration in the particulars must be filed within 21 days of the alteration. The company's name and country of incorporation must be stated on every place of business and on all letterheads, notices and official publications of the company in Great Britain, as must the fact – if it applies – that the liability of its members is limited.

These companies, having established a place of business here, must thereafter file documents with the Registrar in the usual way – subject to some minor exceptions in s 699: for example, a resolution altering the objects need not be filed. They must, in particular, file accounts and reports in the usual way (s 702) and notify changes of directors and secretary (s 692) and resolutions altering the constitution (s 692) but not if made by statute or statutory instrument. If these companies cease to have a place of business here they must immediately notify the Registrar of Companies, and from the date on which notice is given there is no obligation to file documents (s 696).

## Branch registration

The above long-standing regime relates to place of business registration. However, more recently a regime of branch registration has been introduced to comply with the EC Eleventh Company Directive (89/666/EEC). The relevant regulations are the Companies and Credit and Financial Institutions (Branch Disclosure) Regulations 1992 (SI 1992/179). The distinction between a place of business and a branch gives rise to difficulties. Companies House Guidance Note CHN 25 lists warehouse facilities, administrative offices, share transfer registration offices and internal data processing facilities as types of activity which fall into the place of business registration requirements. However, in general terms a branch must under the Directive be able to negotiate directly with third parties who may then transact business direct with the branch without having to deal, for example, with a head office.

## Registration of branches

Registration with the Registrar of Companies is required within one month of opening the branch. A certified copy of the constitution of the company whose branch it is together with a copy of the latest accounts and certified translations, if applicable, are required together with the appropriate fee. Company details and branch details are also required to be registered.

## Disclosure requirements for branches

The requirement for a place of business to show its corporate name and the country of incorporation on all places of business and on all billheads, notices and official publications applies also to branches. The branch stationery must give the place of registration of the overseas company of which it is a branch and its registration number. If the liability of the company's members is limited, this must also be stated. If the overseas company is incorporated outside the EC, the place of registration of that company, its legal form and registration number must be stated together with the head office location and if it is being wound up, e.g. in a reconstruction, if this is applicable.

## Accounting requirements for branches

The requirements are dependent on the home state of the company's incorporation. The position is as follows:

- if the accounts are required to be disclosed and delivered in the home state, then copies of the accounts should be delivered to the Registrar within three months of the date for delivery in the home state;
- if accounts are required to be disclosed but not registered in the home state, copies of the relevant accounts must be delivered within six months of the first date of disclosure in the home state; or
- if no disclosure or delivery is required by the home state, accounts must still be delivered within 13 months after the end of the relevant accounting period.

As regards the first two of the above requirements, the accounts must be prepared and disclosed to accord with the requirements of the home state law. If that law permits modified accounts, they may be filed in respect of the branch. In regard to the last of the above requirements, the accounts must be prepared in accordance with the Overseas Companies (Accounts) (Modifications and Exemptions) Order 1990 (SI 1990/440).

The above provisions relating to branch registration do not apply where the overseas company operates in Great Britain through a subsidiary company registered here.

# RE-REGISTRATION

In terms of examination questions, only three types of re-registration need be considered: private to public if the company wishes to go to the public for capital; private limited to private unlimited so that financial secrecy can be maintained because accounts do not have to be filed; and private unlimited to private limited should the members decide at some stage after incorporation that limited liability would be desirable.

## Conversion of companies from private to public

Sections 43–8 apply and a private company may be re-registered as a public company if:

(a) the members pass a special (or written) resolution which alters the company's memorandum to conform with the statutory requirements of a public company. The articles may require amendment; for example, a public company must have a minimum of two directors, though if Table A has applied this requires a minimum of two anyway;

(b) it has not previously been re-registered as unlimited;

(c) the requirements as regards share capital are met. This means that the nominal value of the allotted share capital is not less than £50,000 and in respect of all the shares, or as many as are needed to make up the authorised minimum, the following conditions are satisfied:

(i) no less than one-quarter of the nominal value of each share and the whole of any premium on it is paid up. Employees' shares may be ignored unless paid up as above;

(ii) none of the shares has been fully or partly paid up by means of an undertaking to do work or perform services where this has not already been performed or otherwise discharged; and

(iii) where any share has been allotted as fully or partly paid up for a non-cash consideration which consists solely or partly of an undertaking to do something other than to perform services, e.g. an undertaking to transfer a non-cash asset to the company, either the undertaking has been performed or otherwise discharged or there is a contract between the company and the person involved under which the undertaking must be performed within five years

(d) an application for the change is made to the Registrar on Form 43(3) signed by a director or the secretary of the company;

(e) the application is accompanied by the following documents:

(i) a printed copy of the memorandum and articles as altered;

(ii) a copy of the company's balance sheet prepared as at a date not more than seven months before the date of the application, but not necessarily in respect of an accounting reference period, together with a copy of an unqualified report by the company's auditors in regard to that balance sheet. If there is a qualification, the auditor must be in a position to state in writing that it is not material in determining whether, at the date of the balance sheet, the company's net assets were at least equal to the sum of its called-up capital and non-distributable reserves;

(iii) a copy of a written statement by the company's auditors that in their opinion the balance sheet referred to at (ii) above shows that the amount of the company's net assets at the date of the balance sheet was not less than the aggregate of its called-up share capital and non-distributable reserves;

(iv) Form 43(3)(e), which is a statutory declaration by a director or secretary of the company: (a) that the requirements in regard to the making of the necessary changes in the company's constitution have been complied with; and (b) that between the balance sheet date and the application for re-registration there has been no change in the financial position of the company which has caused the net assets to become less than the aggregate of the called-up share capital plus non-distributable reserves.

It should be noted that audit exemption regulations do not dispense with the requirement of an audit report on the balance sheet. This means that small companies can exempt themselves from the requirement to appoint an auditor unless and until it becomes necessary to do so for a purpose other than the audit of annual financial statements. Other areas where an auditor is still required will be picked up as they occur in the text.

### Additional requirements relating to share capital

If between the date of the balance sheet and the passing of a special or written resolution to convert to a public company, the company has allotted shares which are wholly or partly paid for by a non-cash consideration, then before application to re-register is made:

(a) the consideration must have been valued in accordance with s 103 by a person, or persons, qualified to audit the accounts of a public company (*see further* Chapter 19); and

(b) a report regarding the value has been made to the company by the person or persons referred to in (a) above during the six months preceding the allotment of the shares.

### Registrar's function

If the Registrar is satisfied with the application, and provided that there is not in existence a court order reducing the company's share capital below the authorised minimum, he will on payment of a fee, issue a certificate of incorporation stating that the company is a public company, the change in status taking effect as from the date of issue of the certificate. The certificate is conclusive evidence that the re-registration requirements have been complied with and that the company is a public company.

## Conversion of private limited companies to private unlimited companies

A private company limited by shares or guarantee may be re-registered as an unlimited company, but only if all the members consent. Sections 49 and 50 apply. The following documents must be delivered to the Registrar:

(a) Form 49(1) which is an application for re-registration signed by a director or secretary. It sets out the alterations required in the memorandum and articles and, if the company is to be unlimited with a share capital, the memorandum and articles must be brought into line with Table E of SI 1985/805;

(b) attached to the application are the following:
  (i) Form 49(8)(a), which gives space to set out the signed assents of the members or on their behalf;
  (ii) Form 49(8)(b), which is a statutory declaration by the directors of the company that Form 49(8)(a) does indeed contain the assents of all the members;
  (iii) a printed copy of the memorandum incorporating the alterations set out in Form 49(1); for example, the company's name will no longer end with the word 'Limited';
  (iv) a printed copy of the articles also incorporating the changes set out in Form 49(1); for example, an unlimited company can reduce its share capital and/or share premium without going to the court and the articles must allow this.

The Registrar will, if satisfied with the application documents, issue a certificate that the company is unlimited with or without a share capital as the case may be. The certificate is conclusive evidence of this and when it is issued the alterations required in the company's constitution take effect as if the members had resolved that they should.

There can be no conversion back to a limited company. In addition, a company cannot re-register as unlimited if it has previously re-registered as limited. The reason for this is that, as we have seen, unlimited companies do not in general have to file accounts and re-registration back and forth between limited and unlimited status is not allowed to prevent selective filing of accounts.

## Conversion of private unlimited companies to private limited companies

Under ss 51 and 52 an unlimited company, subject to what is said above, may be re-registered as a limited company by following the procedures set out below:

(a) a special (or written) resolution must be passed:
  (i) stating whether the company is to be limited by shares or guarantee;
  (ii) stating the share capital if applicable;
  (iii) making the necessary alterations in the memorandum and articles;
(b) there is then delivered to the Registrar:
  (i) Form 51, which is the application for re-registration signed by a director or secretary; and
  (ii) printed copies of the memorandum and articles as altered.

The special (or written) resolution must be sent to the Registrar within 15 days of passing. The documents listed at (b) above must be sent to the Registrar but not earlier than the date of lodging the resolution. Normally all would be sent together.

Once again, the Registrar will, if satisfied with the application, issue a certificate of incorporation stating that the company is a limited company. As before, the certificate is conclusive evidence of that fact and on the issue of the certificate any alterations in the company's constitution take effect.

## Effect of conversion

Under s 78 of the Insolvency Act 1986, on conversion from a limited company to an unlimited one, the members at the date of the application have unlimited liability for its debts. Past members who do not continue are liable for debts incurred while they were members if calls on their shares are still unpaid or under the guarantee for up to 12 months after the commencement of the liquidation.

Under s 77 of the Insolvency Act 1986, the effect where an unlimited company becomes limited is that those who become members after conversion are liable only to the extent of capital unpaid on their shares or under the guarantee. Those who were members at the date of conversion and are still members at the date of liquidation are fully liable for debts incurred before conversion. Those who were members at the date of conversion but have ceased to be members after conversion and before winding-up are liable for debts incurred before conversion for up to three years after it took place.

## GRADED QUESTIONS

### Essay mode

1   Philip, who is in the process of forming a company, wishes to avoid personal liability upon any contracts he may enter into on behalf of the proposed company.
    Advise Philip.

*(The Institute of Chartered Accountants in England and Wales)*

2   In what circumstances will an agent bind a company to a contract made with a third party? What effect do the memorandum and articles of association have on the power of agents to bind companies to such contracts?

*(The Institute of Chartered Secretaries and Administrators)*

3   (a) In the celebrated case of *Salomon* v *Salomon & Co Ltd* [1897] AC 22, Lord Halsbury LC observed:

'Either the limited company was a legal entity or it was not. If it was, the business belonged to it and not to Mr. Salomon. If it was not, there was no person and no thing to be an agent at all and it is impossible to say at the same time that there is a company and there is not.'

Comment.

(b) Tiedeman was the owner of a large bulk-carrier called *Ocean-Star*. The ship was valued at £1 million and was insured for that sum with Lloyd's in Tiedeman's name. Subsequently Tiedeman incorporated Tiedeman Ltd in which he held all the shares but one which was held by his wife as his nominee. *Ocean-Star* was then sold to Tiedeman Ltd and the purchase price was secured by a debenture issued in favour of Tiedeman giving as a security a fixed charge on the only asset of the company, *Ocean-Star*. While carrying a valuable cargo on charter to a Kuwait company the *Ocean-Star* was attacked by Iranian gunboats and sunk.

Consider whether Tiedeman or in the alternative Tiedeman Ltd could claim to be indemnified by Lloyd's for the loss of the bulk-carrier.

*(University of Plymouth)*

4  (a) Section 14(1) of Companies Act 1985 provides that the memorandum and articles of association constitute an agreement between the company and its members as if they have signed and sealed a contract to abide by its provisions. Comment.

(b) A, B and C are members of X Ltd. The company has now discovered that C is also a major shareholder in a rival company. It is causing concern that C might be extracting information about X Ltd's business which could confer unfair advantage on its rival. X Ltd wishes to alter its articles of association so as to require any member competing with X Ltd to sell his or her shares as required to any person or persons named by the directors of the company, or to the directors themselves. Advise X Ltd.

*(University of Plymouth)*

## Objective mode

Four alternative answers are given. Select ONE only. Circle the answer which you consider to be correct. Check your answers by referring back to the information given in the chapter and against the answers at the back of the book.

1  The members of a social club wish to form a legal entity. There is no commercial risk but they do not want too much disclosure of their affairs to the public. What type of company should they form?

  **A**  A company limited by guarantee.
  **B**  An unincorporated association.
  **C**  A private company limited by shares.
  **D**  A private unlimited company.

2  Meg used to be employed by Trent Ltd. Her contract contained a clause under which she agreed not to compete with Trent Ltd. The clause was reasonable in terms of its duration and area. Meg has now formed a company called Meg (Corporate Services) Ltd and has started to compete against Trent Ltd through the company. Will Trent Ltd be able to obtain an injunction to prevent Meg (Corporate Services) Ltd from competing against Trent Ltd?

  **A**  No, because Meg (Corporate Services) Ltd is a separate entity.
  **B**  Yes, because the company has been formed as a device to avoid the restraint clause.
  **C**  No, since the company is not liable for the actions of its shareholders.
  **D**  Yes, because Meg (Corporate Services) Ltd is engaged in wrongful trading.

3 Fred is a minority shareholder who did not vote in favour of an alteration to the company's objects. He holds 16 per cent in nominal value of the company's share capital and wishes to challenge the alteration. He must petition the court within how many days of the passing of the resolution?

A 7.
B 14.
C 21.
D 28.

4 Ribble Ltd has a share capital of 1,000,000 ordinary shares. The holders of 800,000 shares vote on a resolution to change the company's name. The minimum number of votes which must be cast in favour of the resolution for it to be effective is:

A 400,001.
B 500,000.
C 600,000.
D 750,000.

5 Fred bought some shares in Tyne Ltd on 1 February 200X. To whom does Fred become bound in contract?

A The company only.
B The members of Tyne on 1 February 199X.
C Tyne and those who are at present members.
D Tyne and those who were members of Tyne on 1 February 200X.

6 Table A will apply automatically except where it is excluded or modified by special articles of association in the case of:

A Private companies limited by shares only.
B Public companies limited by shares only.
C All companies limited by shares.
D All limited companies.

*The answers to questions set in objective mode appear on p 709.*

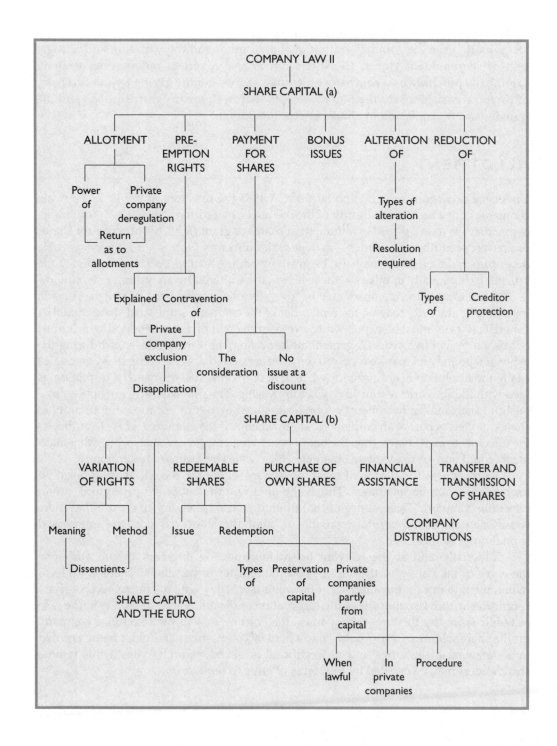

The objectives of this chapter are to consider the basic legal environment surrounding the issue and alteration of share capital and the variation and abrogation of shareholders' rights. Consideration is also given to redemption of share capital, the purchase by a company of its own shares and the giving by the company of financial assistance for the purchase of its shares. Company distributions and the transfer and transmission of shares are also included.

## ALLOTMENT

Under the provisions of ss 80 and 80A of CA 1985 the directors of public and private companies must have the authority of the members, by ordinary (or written) resolution, before they exercise a power of allotment of shares or grant rights to subscribe for shares or convert securities into shares – as where the directors propose to issue convertible debentures. Authorisation may also be given by adding an appropriate provision to the articles. Exceptionally in this case the articles can be altered by an ordinary resolution.

The authority of the members may be given for one specific issue or may be general: for example, authority to issue the remainder of the company's unissued share capital. A general authority must be expressed to expire at the end of a stated period which must not be more than five years. A general authority may be varied or revoked during the expressed period and may be renewed for a further period not exceeding five years. Once again, the resolution is ordinary (or written) and, exceptionally for such a resolution, is filed with the Registrar within 15 days of its passing. The provisions do not apply, obviously, to shares taken by subscribers under the memorandum nor more importantly to shares allotted as part of an employees' share scheme. If the members refuse to authorise the directors to allot shares, then the board could allot employees' shares, but other allotments could only be made by the members themselves by ordinary resolution.

The procedures for allotment must, of course, follow the receipt of an application for a specific number of shares. This is the offer and the allotment procedures are in effect the company's acceptance of that offer. It is also necessary to ensure that there is sufficient unissued capital available to allot the shares. If not, the authorised capital must be increased.

Additionally, and at the relevant board meeting, the directors should authorise the entry of the names of the allottees on the register of members. There is no legal requirement to inform the allottees of the allotment. They will, of course, receive share certificates within two months of the registration of the allotment, unless, as in the case of public issues by the larger companies, the holding is held by a nominee company for the shareholders in terms rather like a bank account, the shareholder being entitled to a statement of holdings and no certificate is issued, though even in this regime shareholders may be entitled by the terms of issue to request one.

### Deregulation

The above provisions need not concern private companies since the members may elect by an elective resolution (*see further* Chapter 20) that the authority given to the directors by resolution or in the articles may be given for an indefinite period or for a fixed period of longer than five years renewable. These authorities may be revoked or varied by ordinary (or written) resolution, and, once again, must state the amount of securities which may be allotted: for example, the remainder of the company's unissued share capital. If the election subsequently ceases to have effect (*see further* Chapter 20), any authority which is then in force expires immediately, if given more than five years previously, otherwise it operates for the remainder of the five-year period.

Allotments made in contravention of any of the authorisation rules are not invalid but the directors are liable to prosecution.

## PRE-EMPTION RIGHTS

Section 89 gives the holders of a company's ordinary (or equity) shares a right of pre-emption. This is designed to ensure that the rights of the existing ordinary share-holders, as, for example, in terms of a voting position within the company, are not affected by the issue of further ordinary shares to others. The section applies to both public and private companies and each ordinary shareholder must receive an offer, in what is in effect a rights issue, unless the relevant provisions have been disapplied (*see below*). The offer is subject to four basic requirements, set out in s 90:

(a)  it must be in writing;
(b)  it must be delivered by post or personally;
(c)  it must state a period of not less than 21 days within which it may be accepted;
(d)  the offer must be proportional to the member's existing holding.

Once the offer period has expired, the shares which have not been accepted by members may be offered, in different proportions, to the other members or to outsiders. Members are not automatically entitled to receive an offer of shares not accepted by other members unless there is a provision in special articles to that effect.

Offers to joint holders may be made to the person whose name appears first on the share register and, in the case of the death or bankruptcy of a member, the offer should be addressed to the relevant personal representatives. Where the member has not supplied an address in the UK or holds a share warrant, the offer requirements are satisfied by publishing the offer, or notice of a place where it can be inspected, in the *London Gazette*.

The pre-emption provisions are triggered by an issue of equity shares for cash and would not apply to an issue of preference shares for cash or an issue of equity shares wholly or partly for a non-cash consideration, as in a merger of companies by a share for share exchange. In addition, pre-emption rights do not apply where shares are allotted under an employees' scheme and in such a case the company is not bound to make an offer to members who are not employees. However, employees in a share scheme are entitled to participate in pre-emption rights where an offer of equity shares is made to shareholders generally.

### Contravention

If the pre-emption provisions are not complied with, the company and any officer knowingly in default is, under s 92, jointly and severally liable to compensate shareholders for their loss. Claims must be brought within two years of the filing of the return of allotments under which the provisions were contravened. The actual allotment is legally valid.

### Private company exclusion

A private, but not a public company, may, under s 91, disapply pre-emption rights by a provision in the articles stating this or by having or including a provision in the articles about pre-emption rights which is inconsistent with the legislation.

## DISAPPLICATION

Both public and private companies may, under s 95, disapply pre-emption rights by a provision in the articles or by a special or written resolution of the members. In either event the maximum period for disapplication is five years or such shorter period as the articles or special or written resolution may state.

Even in a private company which has given the directors a power of allotment for an indefinite period the members must still approve the disapplication of pre-emption rights, though the written resolution procedure can be used to do this. This assumes that the private company concerned has not opted out of the pre-emption provisions altogether.

Under s 95 the directors must recommend the disapplication and no special or written resolution to allow it, or to renew it, may be proposed unless with the notice of the meeting (in the case of a special resolution), the directors have circulated a written statement giving their reasons for making the recommendation and stating the amount which will be paid when the shares which are the subject of disapplication are allotted and giving a justification of the price. There are penalties if misleading information is included in the statement.

If a private company uses the written resolution procedure, the statement by the directors must be supplied to each member at or before the time at which the resolution is given to him to sign.

Under s 711 the Registrar must publish a notice in the *London Gazette* of the receipt by him of any resolution in connection with authority to allot and disapplication of pre-emption rights.

## PAYMENT FOR SHARES

The shares allotted by a company and the premium, if any, on them may be paid for in cash or a non-cash consideration including goodwill and know-how.

### Payment in cash

This is generally, and rather obviously, effected by handing cash or a cheque to the company. However, if a company pays an existing debt by an issue of shares to the creditor this set-off arrangement is regarded as a payment in cash. Section 739 provides, in effect, that the issue of shares to satisfy a liquidated sum, such as an existing quantified debt, is not an issue for a consideration other than cash.

### Considerations other than cash

There are a great many restrictions on the issue by public companies of shares for non-cash considerations. The main object is to prevent the watering-down of the share capital which takes place, for example, when a public company issues fully paid shares to the value of, say, £100,000 for an asset worth, say, £50,000. In such a case the asset must be valued under s 103 by an independent accountant who must state that its value is at least equal to the value of the shares being allotted for it, otherwise the allottee will have to make up the difference.

In private companies non-cash considerations are legal and very often consist of the sale of property to the company or the rendering of services. The consideration offered must be sufficient to support a contract in law, but it need not be adequate since the general law of contract does not require this (*see* Chapter 2). The valuation rules of company legislation do not apply and the directors' valuation is accepted by the courts unless there is fraud. This means, in effect, that a private company can issue its shares at a discount.

### No issue at a discount

Section 100 prohibits the issue by all companies of their shares at a discount though, as we have seen, this may happen in a private company where there is a non-cash consideration for the reason that the directors' valuation is accepted so that there is, *in law* at least, no issue at a discount. The position is different where a private company issues shares for cash at a discount and the allottee is liable to pay the company the full amount of the discount and pay interest there on at the appropriate rate – which under s 107 is currently 5 per cent per annum. Persons who take the shares from the original allottee are jointly and severally liable (*see further* Chapter 21) with him to pay the amount mentioned above if the third party has not given consideration. If he has, he can still be jointly and severally liable, as above, but only if he knew of the issue at a discount.

Debentures may be issued at a discount, but if there is a right to convert the debentures into fully-paid shares, the debentures are legally valid but the right to exchange is void.

## BONUS ISSUES

A company may capitalise its profits and apply them in paying up, wholly or in part, unissued shares in the company to be allotted to existing members. This is known as a bonus issue or, alternatively, as a scrip or capitalisation issue. Normally bonus shares are fully paid. This is a requirement under reg 110 of Table A.

There are no direct statutory provisions so that a bonus issue may be made only if the articles permit. Under reg 110 of Table A the directors may with the authority of an ordinary (or written) resolution of the company:

(a) resolve that certain reserves or profits of the company be capitalised. Under reg 110 these funds are:
    (i) undivided profits not required to pay a dividend on preference shares. An issue of fully or partly paid bonus shares is not a distribution for the purpose of control by the CA 1985 and, therefore, unrealised profits may be utilised;
    (ii) the share premium account;
    (iii) the capital redemption reserve;
(b) appropriate the capitalised sum to the members in the same proportion as they would have been entitled if distributed as a dividend;
(c) apply the sum in paying up in full unissued shares or debentures of the company of a nominal value equal to that sum; and
(d) allot the shares or debentures as fully paid to those members, or as they otherwise direct.

Regulation 110 also provides that the directors may make such provisions, by the issue of fractional certificates or by payment in cash or otherwise, as they may determine, in the case of shares or debentures becoming distributable in fractions.

Where there is an allotment of bonus shares the company must make a return of the allotment under s 88. Since the shares are allotted for a consideration other than cash the contract constituting the title of the allottees must be registered also. Table A, reg 110 allows the directors to authorise any person to enter into an agreement on behalf of the members who are allotted bonus shares and this obviates the need to make a contract with them all. However, since s 80 allows particulars of the contract to be registered instead where it has not been made in writing, the company need not actually file a contract but merely particulars of it and in practice a company will adopt this method.

## RETURN AS TO ALLOTMENTS

Under s 88 whenever a company makes an allotment of its shares it must, within one month of the allotment, deliver to the Registrar Form 88(2), being a return of the allotments stating the number and nominal value of the shares comprised in the allotment, the names and addresses of the allottees, and the amount paid-up and unpaid on each share whether on account of the nominal value of the share or by way of premium.

Where shares have been allotted as fully or partly paid, otherwise than in cash, the consideration must be specified in the return. If the contract under which the consideration is supplied is written, a contract in writing must be sent with Form 88(2). If the contract is not written, a written note of its terms must be made out and sent to the Registrar. Compliance with these requirements is enforced by a fine on every director, manager, secretary, or other officer of the company who is a party to the default. The court may grant relief where the omission to deliver any document within the time prescribed is accidental or due to inadvertence or it is just and equitable to grant relief, and may make an order extending the time for delivery of the document for such period as the court thinks fit.

# ALTERATION OF SHARE CAPITAL

The share capital of a company may be altered under s 121 provided the company follows the appropriate procedures which are set out below.

(a) *Increase of nominal or authorised capital.* A company may, if authorised by its articles, increase its nominal or authorised capital by new shares of such amount as the resolution prescribes. This is done by an ordinary resolution in general meeting or by written resolution as appropriate. Regulation 32 of Table A gives authorisation. Section 121 says that the alteration must be made in general meeting but the written resolution procedure is available since the only exceptions to its use are removal of directors under s 303 and auditors under s 391. (See Sch 15A, para 1.) However, the matter is one for the members and cannot, under reg 70 of Table A, be delegated to the directors (*see further* Chapter 18).

Notice of the increase must be given to the Registrar within 15 days of the passing of the resolution. A copy of the resolution effecting the increase must also be filed.

The new shares may be ordinary or preference unless the memorandum otherwise provides. It is usual to increase the nominal capital only when existing capital has been issued but an increase can be made before this position is reached.

(b) *Consolidation of capital.* A company may, under s 121, if authorised by its articles (*see* reg 32), consolidate its capital by amalgamating shares of smaller amounts into shares of larger amounts, e.g. 20 shares of nominal value 5p each into shares of nominal value £1.

(c) *Conversion into stock.* A company may, if authorised by its articles (*see* reg 32), convert its paid-up shares into stock or re-convert stock into paid-up shares of any denomination. Stock is the holding of a member expressed in pounds instead of a number of shares of a certain value each. Thus, instead of saying that a member has 10 shares of one pound each one would say that the member holds £10 of stock. Stock cannot be issued direct; if shares have been converted into stock and additional capital is subsequently required in the form of stock the new capital must be issued as shares and converted into stock.

(d) *Subdivision.* This would occur where, for example, a company subdivides every £1 share into, say, 10 shares of 10p each. The proportions of amounts paid and unpaid must remain the same where the shares concerned are partly paid, e.g. if before subdivision every £1 share was 50p paid then the new shares of, say, 10p each must be treated as 5p paid. The company cannot regard some of the new shares as fully paid and some as partly paid.

(e) *Cancellation of unissued nominal capital.* A company can reduce the amount of share capital available for issue and this does not operate as a reduction of capital (*see below*). A cancellation is sometimes used to get rid of shares which have been created, but not issued, with rights which the company now finds onerous.

## Resolution required

The resolution required to make the alterations set out in (b), (c), (d) and (e) above is the one laid down in the articles. Regulation 32 requires an ordinary resolution though private companies could use the written resolution procedure. The company must in all four cases notify the Registrar within one month of the alteration.

## REDUCTION OF CAPITAL

A company limited by shares or a company limited by guarantee and having a share capital may, under s 135, and if authorised by its articles, reduce its share capital (or share premium account or capital redemption reserve). The method is by special resolution followed by the confirmation of the court. Private companies can use the unanimous written resolution procedure followed by the confirmation of the court. In addition where the share capital is divided into shares of different classes a reduction cannot proceed unless the consent of three-quarters of each class of shareholders affected is obtained since a reduction is a variation of rights (*see below*).

### Types of reduction

Under s 135 share capital can be reduced 'in any way'. The section, however, envisages three forms of reduction in particular. These enable a company to reduce for the reasons set out below.

(a) *It may have more capital than it needs* and may wish to return some of it to its shareholders. For example, a company may wish to return paid-up capital following a sale of part of its undertaking where it intends in future to confine its activities to the remaining part(s) of the business. The company could achieve its purpose by reducing the nominal value of its shares. A share capital of 50,000 shares of £1 each fully paid could become a share capital of 50,000 shares of 50p, each fully paid, the company returning 50p per share in cash to the members.

(b) *Share capital already issued may not be fully paid* and yet the company may have all the capital it needs. A reduction may be effected here by extinguishing the liability to pay the uncalled capital so that, for example, a share of £1 partly paid would become a share of 50p fully paid. However, liability for unpaid capital cannot be reduced by crediting a partly paid share as paid-up to a greater extent than it has in fact been paid-up. Thus the company cannot leave the nominal value of the shares at £1 and cancel one share from every two held by shareholders, regarding the remaining one of the two as fully paid.

(c) *Where the assets have suffered a realised loss as in Re Jupiter House Investments (Cambridge) Ltd* [1985] 1 WLR 975 where the company had incurred a substantial loss on the sale of some of its property. In such a case a share capital of 50,000 shares of £1 each fully paid could be reduced to 50,000 shares of 50p each fully paid and no capital would be returned to shareholders.

(d) *To comply with the law relating to distributions,* under which a company cannot pay a dividend unless and until any deficit on the profit and loss account is made good. In such a situation a company may wish to cancel a share premium account in order to make good the deficit. Such a procedure is, of course, a reduction of capital requiring the approval of the court. The court in confirming the reduction may also agree to the transfer of any balance remaining in the share premium account to a distributable reserve and allow its use to write off future losses leading to deficits on the P & L account so that a further application to the court is not required. The court may also be prepared to allow funds to be released from the share premium account to be used to redeem preference shares or redeemable equity shares and to purchase the company's own shares thus making it unnecessary to follow the more complex procedures of s 171 of the CA 1985 (power of companies to redeem or purchase own shares from capital) (*see Quayle Munro Ltd, Petitioners* [1994] 1 BCLC 410).

In cases under (a) above, a reduction may be confirmed by the court even if the money to make the payment is borrowed (*Re Nixon's Navigation Co* [1897] 1 Ch 872). It may even be borrowed from the shareholders whose shares are to be reduced. Thus, if a company wishes to simplify its capital structure by replacing all its preference shares by exchanging them for loan stock, it may do so on the authority of *Re Thomas de la Rue Ltd* [1911] 2 Ch 361.

## Protection of creditors

Before the company's petition for confirmation of the resolution for reduction is heard, the court must be asked to settle a list of creditors. Each creditor must be given, by post, details of the reduction and a consent form. The fact of the reduction and details of it must be advertised as the court may direct. The advertisements will give a date by which creditors not on the list must make a claim to be entered on it. The court will not proceed to consider the petition unless it is satisfied, by affidavit of the company's solicitor and one of its officers, that all creditors named in the list or who have notified their claims have been paid or have consented to the reduction. If they have not, the company must give security for the amount claimed to the satisfaction of the court or satisfy the court that the claim is disputed and is invalid. Where the reduction is as set out in (c) above the creditors are not deprived of any funds because the assets have seriously depreciated and no money is returned nor is liability to pay calls cancelled. Nevertheless, the court may still require the company to take the steps outlined above as, for example, where the court does not believe that the reduction is necessary or genuine. It is also the function of the court to see, in a type (c) reduction and in the two other types, that the reduction is operated fairly as between shareholders.

Despite what is said above, the court may be prepared to accept an undertaking by the company that creditors will be asked to consent and if they do not will be paid off. The court may in such a case decide that it is unnecessary to follow the procedures outlined above in terms of creditor protection (*see Quayle Munro Ltd, Petitioners* [1994] 1 BCLC 410).

## Payment of shareholders on reduction

The matter of repayment of shareholders should be treated as if the company was being wound up. Thus, if capital is being repaid for the reasons set out in a type (a) or (b) reduction, as set out above, the preference shares should be reduced first if they have priority in a winding-up for repayment of their capital. If the reduction is because of loss of assets, the ordinary shareholders should be reduced before the preference shareholders.

## Procedure after confirmation by the court

The court may in its discretion make an order confirming the reduction on such terms and conditions as it thinks fit. If the reduction is confirmed, the court will approve a minute giving the new capital structure and that minute must be filed at the Companies Registry. The Registrar will issue a certificate of registration to the company and the minute when registered will be deemed to be substituted for the corresponding capital provision in the memorandum and is valid and alterable as if it had originally been contained in the memorandum. Copies of the memorandum issued after the date of the registration must show the capital as altered. The reduction must be advertised if the court directs this and the company can be required by the court to add the words 'and reduced' after its name for a period of time though this latter power of the court is not normally exercised today.

### Reduction — private companies and unlimited companies

A private company, by following certain procedures, can purchase its own shares, even partly from capital. This provides, in effect, an easier and less expensive way of reducing capital since the court is not involved. However, the shareholders concerned must be willing to sell their shares to the company. With a reduction by special resolution through the court, minority shareholders who dissent will have their capital reduced, whether willing or not.

Unlimited companies may also reduce share capital and any share premium account account without permission of the court: s 135 of the 1985 Act requires court approval only if the company is limited.

## VARIATION AND ABROGATION OF CLASS RIGHTS

If the shares of a company are divided into different classes, such as ordinary and preference, s 125 provides that class rights, for example as to voting, dividend and rights on winding-up, cannot be varied or abrogated, i.e. taken away, unless certain procedures are followed. These are considered below.

### Meaning of variation

In general terms, rights are only regarded as varied if there is a change in the actual rights themselves, as where the company proposes to make its existing cumulative preference shares non-cumulative. The creation of rights in others is not a variation. This somewhat narrow view of the courts has been confirmed in a number of legal decisions (*see White* v *Bristol Aeroplane Co Ltd* [1953] 1 All ER 40). Thus, if the company had A ordinaries and B ordinaries each with one vote per share and the company proposed to give the B ordinaries two votes per share, this would not be a variation of the rights of the A ordinaries because they would still have one vote as before (*see Greenhalgh* v *Arderne Cinemas Ltd* [1946] 1 All ER 512).

### Method of variation or abrogation

Section 125 provides that where class rights are set out in the company's articles (as is usually the case), but the articles contain no provision relating to the variation or abrogation of those rights, the rights may not be varied unless either:

(a)  the holders of three-quarters in nominal value of the issued shares of the class consent in writing; or

(b)  the holders of three-quarters in nominal value of the issued shares of the class pass an extraordinary resolution at a separate meeting of the class.

The articles themselves can be altered by a special (or written) resolution, but such an alteration is ineffective unless the above procedures have been followed.

So far as private companies are concerned, the unanimous written resolution procedure can be followed instead of the holding of a class meeting.

If the articles contain a method of variation, which Table A does not, then the procedure in the articles must be followed and not s 125. The alteration of the articles to include a method of variation or abrogation is in itself a variation of rights.

If the class rights are in the memorandum and neither the memorandum nor the articles contain a method of variation that can be followed, then the rights can be changed only with the unanimous consent of all the members or under a scheme of arrangement under s 425, which involves an application to the court for approval.

## Right to dissent

Under s 127 the holders of not less than 15 per cent of the issued shares of the class, being persons who did not consent to or vote for the resolution to vary, may apply to the court to cancel the variation. Application may be made within 21 days after the date on which the resolution was passed or consent given. It may be made on behalf of all the dissentients by one or more of them appointed by the dissentients in writing. The variation then has no effect unless and until confirmed by the court.

The company must send to the Registrar, within 15 days of the making of the court order, a copy of that order. In default the company and every officer who is in default is liable to a fine.

## Special rights – registration of particulars

In order to ensure that the public has access to the details of a company's class rights, s 128 provides that if a company allots shares with rights which are not recorded in its memorandum or articles nor contained in a resolution required to be sent to the Registrar (*see further* Chapter 20), it must send to the Registrar, within one month of allotment, the particulars of the relevant rights. This does not apply if the shares have rights which are in all respects the same as those previously allotted, save that they do not carry the same rights to dividend during the 12 months immediately following allotment. Newly allotted shares sometimes have restrictions as to payment of dividends in the first year of issue. This does not mean that they must *for that reason alone* be treated as different from shares previously allotted.

The same procedure must be followed where there is a variation of rights of existing shares or a renaming of them by a method which does not require the filing of a resolution because there is no amendment of the memorandum or articles, as where the changes are carried out by ordinary resolution under special terms of issue. Similar provisions apply under s 129 to the rights of members of a company which does not have a share capital.

Further publicity as to classes of shares (or members) is provided by s 352 which states that the different classes of shares (or members), where there are different classes, must be stated for each member in the register of members. This is particularly useful to a minority which, in trying to mount opposition to the board, is seeking to get in touch only with voting shares or members.

The Registrar is required by s 711 to publish in the *London Gazette* the receipt by him of any statement or notice delivered under the above provisions.

## EFFECT OF THE EURO ON SHARE CAPITAL

### A fresh issue

A company can issue shares denominated in other currencies. It was decided in *Re Scandinavian Bank Group* [1987] 2 All ER 70 that a company could reconstruct its capital into four currencies so as better to reflect the composition of its assets. The capital was divided into dollar shares (50%), sterling shares (20%), Dm shares (15%) and Swiss franc shares (15%). However, court approval is required for the reconstruction. Nevertheless, the court decided that the above denomination was consistent with CA 1985 s 2(5)(a). If the company is a public company, there must be at least £50,000 denominated in sterling.

As a result of the above authority, a UK company may, therefore, issue shares denominated in euros from 1 January 1999. Normal issuing procedures will apply, subject to adapting references to the euro.

### Existing capital in foreign currency

Where a UK company already has shares that are denominated in a foreign currency, e.g. deutschmarks, the shares will probably continue to be referred to in that currency during the transitional period. When this ends on 31 December 2001 (under a regulation based on Art 235 of the EC Treaty), euro references will take over. This may result in awkward nominal values requiring rounding up or down with a need to adjust the company's reserves.

### Redenomination

From 1 January 1999, a UK company has had EC authority to convert a portion of its existing capital into euros. However, under CA 1985 this can only be done by a reduction of share capital or a purchase of own shares or a bonus issue, and these methods are not really satisfactory. The government is, therefore, considering reforms and the introduction of a new procedure for redenomination. The most fundamental proposal is to introduce 'no-par' shares (not currently possible in UK law). This would do away with the need to round up and down since the shares would have no nominal value.

### DTI consultation and the euro

The DTI commenced an initial consultation process on the redenomination of share capital. From 1 January 1999, many companies in the UK could start to conduct some or all of their business in euros. As part of that process, some UK companies may wish to redominate their nominal share capital. The consultation process examined possible changes to CA 1985 to facilitate redenomination of the nominal or par value of the shares into the euro and other currencies. In addition, and importantly, the consultation sought views on whether companies should have the option of issuing no-par value shares.

Having completed the consultation referred to above, the government has announced that it is planning to introduce new legislation to provide companies with a simpler legal mechanism for redenominating their share capital. UK company law does not currently provide an easy and specific mechanism for existing shares already denominated in one currency to be converted automatically into another currency. In addition to providing a new mechanism, the legislation will also provide that the minimum share capital of a company may be denominated in any currency and not just sterling. There is no reference at the moment to the issue of no-par shares.

## Proposed mechanism for redenomination

This will permit companies to resolve that references to share capital in one currency e.g. sterling will be to the equivalent amount in any other legal currency by passing:

● an ordinary resolution of the members; or
● a resolution of the directors but in this case only where the UK has commenced a transitional period leading to membership of the single currency. The directors' resolution would be subject to veto by an ordinary resolution of the members.

The legislation will also set out various alternatives that can be used to determine the conversion rate in advance of any freezing of the sterling/euro rate.

EC law already provides that share capital denominated in a national currency will automatically be treated as having been redenominated in euros, but the UK domestic legislation is desirable to firm up the EU provisions and to deal with any domestic technical problems which may arise. There will be no requirement for UK companies to issue new share certificates following redenomination because there will be no new issue of shares.

The amendments to the CA 1985 will be introduced by secondary legislation using the Deregulation and Contracting Out Act 1994, which allows primary legislation to be repealed and amended by statutory instrument passed by a special parliamentary procedure.

# REDEEMABLE SHARES

The Companies Act 1985 allows the issue of redeemable shares whether equity or preference. The relevant sections are ss 159 and 160. Section 159A which was inserted by s 113 of the CA 1989 is not in force at the time of writing and there are no definite plans to bring it into force at all. It awaits a ministerial decision and is only treated lightly in this chapter. The provisions are designed in the main to encourage investment in the equity of small businesses in circumstances where the proprietors, often members of a family, can at an appropriate stage buy back the equity investments without parting with family control on a permanent basis.

## The issue of redeemable shares

A company limited by shares or by guarantee with a share capital may, if authorised by its articles, issue redeemable shares. They may be issued as redeemable at the option of the company or the shareholder. Regulation 3 of Table A authorises the issue of redeemable shares. Earlier Tables A only authorise the issue of redeemable preference shares and must be changed if it is desired to issue redeemable equity shares.

Redeemable shares may be issued only if there are in issue other shares which cannot be redeemed. It is, therefore, not possible for a company to redeem all its share capital and end up under a board of directors with no members.

## The redemption of redeemable shares

Redeemable shares may not be redeemed unless they are fully paid. The issued capital of a company is the creditors' buffer and it is this figure, and not the paid-up capital, which must be replaced.

The terms of the redemption must provide that the company shall pay for the shares on redemption and not, for example, at a later date, as by creating a creditor. Creditors do not, without special contractual provision, receive interest on an outstanding debt so that failure to pay on redemption would give the company the resource of the share capital without cost.

## Financing the redemption

This is largely a matter of accounting practice. Section 160 applies but, in outline, redeemable shares may only be redeemed out of distributable profit or out of the proceeds of a fresh issue of shares (which need not be redeemable), made for the purpose. Any premium payable on redemption will normally be payable out of distributable profits, but if the shares being redeemed were issued at a premium, the premium on their redemption may be paid for out of a fresh issue of shares made for the purposes of redemption up to an amount equal to:

(a) the aggregate of the premiums received by the company when it issued the shares being redeemed; *or*
(b) the current amount of the company's share premium account (including any sum transferred to that account in respect of premiums on the new shares) *whichever* is *less* and in that case the share premium account can be reduced by the amount of any premium paid out of the proceeds of issue of the new shares. This is designed to protect the creditors' buffer – which is the share capital plus non-distributable reserves, e.g. the capital redemption reserve and the share premium account. Thus under the above formula the share premium account can only be written down to the extent of the amount of the new issue of shares which will replace the amount so written down, thus preserving the buffer intact. Share capital replaces what has been written off the share premium account.

Private companies may redeem shares (or purchase their own shares not issued as redeemable) partly out of capital. Shares when redeemed are cancelled, so that the company does not become a member of itself and this will reduce the issued share capital of the company by the nominal value of the shares redeemed. Authorised capital is not reduced. A company which has issued all of its authorised capital need not increase it merely to issue the new shares necessary to redeem existing ones.

## Miscellaneous matters relating to redeemable shares

As regards failure to redeem its shares (or purchase after agreement), a company cannot be liable in damages for such a failure. The shareholder may obtain an order for specific performance but not if the company can show that it cannot meet the cost of redemption out of distributable profits. In addition, following judicial statements in *Re Holders Investment Trust* [1971] 2 All ER 289 a shareholder whose shares are not redeemed on the date agreed may be able to obtain an injunction to prevent the company from paying dividends, either to ordinary shareholders or to any subordinate class of preference shareholders, until the redemption has been carried out. *Re Holders* also confirms that such a shareholder may petition for a winding-up under s 122 of the Insolvency Act 1986 on the just and equitable ground.

If the company goes into liquidation and, at the date of commencement of the winding-up, has failed to meet an obligation to redeem (or purchase) its own shares and this obligation occurred before the commencement of the winding-up, the terms of the redemption (or purchase) can be enforced by the shareholder against the company as a deferred debt in the liquidation, but not if between the due date for redemption (or purchase) and the date of commencement of the winding-up the company could not lawfully have made a distribution equal in value to the price at which the shares were to have been redeemed (or purchased). The expression 'deferred debt' in this context means deferred to the claims of all creditors and preference shareholders having rights to capital which rank before the shares being redeemed (or purchased). However, the shares being redeemed (or purchased) rank in front of the claims of the ordinary shareholders. Shares which are already issued cannot be converted into redeemable shares since this is not considered to be an 'issue' within the terms of s 159 (*see Re St James' Court Estate Ltd* [1944] Ch 6).

## Time of redemption

At the present time there are no requirements requiring the company to fix the time of redemption at the time of issue, though there is no reason why this should not be done by, for example, making the shares redeemable at the option of the company between stated dates. Section 160(3) provides that, subject to the provisions of Chapter VII of the 1985 Act, redemption of shares may be effected on such terms and in such manner as may be provided by the company's articles. The government has announced that the proposal to repeal this provision in s 133 of the CA 1989 will not now go ahead and that s 159A, also introduced by s 133 and containing restrictive provisions regarding the terms and manner of redemption, will not now be implemented. Section 133 will be repealed when the next legislative opportunity arises. The main objection to the provisions of the CA 1989 was that the date of redemption and an indication of the price at which redemption would take place was to appear in the terms of issue *at the time of issue*. These decisions are not easy to make in terms of possible changes in the company's fortunes, even if only temporary, and the fluctuations of share prices on the Stock Exchange.

## PURCHASE OF OWN SHARES

Formerly the rule of capital maintenance, designed to protect creditors, prevented a limited company from using its resources to purchase its own shares from its shareholders. The strictness of that rule has now been relaxed and purchase by a company of its own shares is allowed subject to safeguards. The procedures to be followed are set out in ss 162–81. They must be complied with strictly.

In this connection the decision of the High Court in *Re R W Peak (Kings Lynn) Ltd* [1998] 1 BCLC 193 should be noted. In that case an agreement by a company to purchase its own shares was declared void because the company's articles did not permit such a purchase as s 162(1) requires. In addition, there was no special or unanimous written resolution authorising the purchase contract before it was entered into as s 164(2) requires. Furthermore, even a waiver of the requirements by the two members of the company was not effective dispensation of the statutory requirements because ss 162 and 164 are not merely for the benefit of current members, but also serve to protect creditors in a situation where there is, in effect, a reduction of share capital. The ruling in this case would render void an issue of redeemable equity shares, unless the articles allowed this, which Tables A prior to the current Table A to CA 1985 do not.

### Why purchase own shares?

Among the most important reasons for purchase of own shares are the following:

(a) so far as private companies are concerned, it gives their shares some marketability. Individuals may be more easily persuaded to invest in private companies if they know that the company can buy them out even if the other shareholders do not have sufficient resources to do so;

(b) in family companies, a shareholder may die or want, in effect, to resign or retire. Perhaps the other shareholders cannot agree how many shares each should take or they cannot afford to buy them. In order to avoid an outsider taking them, the company can buy them;

(c) in the case of shareholder disputes, there is now the possibility of reaching a compromise with a member or members, whereby they are bought out by the company – thus avoiding the situation where the price of getting rid of a disenchanted member is the introduction of an outsider;

(d) the provision is useful also in the case of executive directors who have taken shares in the company. Suppose a finance director has taken shares on appointment but leaves at the end of his contract for a better position. The company can buy his shares so that he truly severs his connection with the company following resignation as a director. The shares must be cancelled, but this does not affect the authorised capital and new shares can be issued to the next finance director on appointment.

### Types of purchase – generally

There is a 'market purchase' and an 'off-market' purchase. A market purchase includes only purchases of shares subject to a marketing agreement on a *recognised investment exchange*. Private companies will, therefore, be restricted to the 'off-market' purchase.

An off-market purchase is a purchase of any types of shares.

Any market or off-market purchases must, if they are to be legal, have authorisation in the articles. Regulation 35 of Table A gives such authorisation.

## Market purchase

A company may make a market purchase of its own shares, provided that the purchase has been authorised by an ordinary resolution of the members in general meeting. The resolution must:

(a) specify the maximum number of shares which the company may acquire under the resolution;

(b) state the maximum and minimum prices which the company may pay for those shares. There will normally be a minimum price set out in the resolution, but for the maximum a formula would be used, e.g. an amount equal to 105 per cent of the average of the upper and lower prices shown in the quotations for ordinary shares of the company in the daily list of the Stock Exchange on the three business days immediately preceding the day on which the contract to purchase is made;

(c) specify a date when the authority given by the resolution will expire. *This must not be later than 18 months after the passing of the resolution.*

The authority given may be varied, revoked or renewed by a further ordinary resolution of the members.

A company may complete a purchase after the date of the authority given by the ordinary resolution has expired, in view of the fact that the contract for the purchase was made before the expiry date and the terms of the ordinary resolution cover execution of the contract after the expiry date.

The ordinary resolution giving the authority must be filed with the Registrar within 15 days of being passed and a copy must be embodied in or annexed to every copy of the articles issued thereafter.

## Off-market purchases

A company may make an off-market purchase under a specific contract which has received advanced authorisation by a special (or written) resolution of the company. That authorisation may be varied or revoked by special (or written) resolution before the purchase is made. If the authorisation is subject to a time limit, it may also be renewed by special (or written) resolution. Public companies must give in the resolution a date on which the authorisation expires. This must not be later than 18 months after the date of the resolution. However, private companies are not so restricted and if the authorisation does not have an expiry date (which it need not), then there is no time limit upon it.

The shareholder whose shares are being purchased should not vote, the shares being purchased on a special resolution to confer, vary, revoke or renew an authority. If he does so, the authority will not be effective unless the resolution would have been passed with the requisite majority without his votes. If he holds other shares, then he cannot vote at all on a show of hands but can vote those other shares on a poll. Any member of the company may demand a poll on the special resolution. The position as regards unanimous written resolutions is that the 1985 Act contains provisions which say that the person whose shares are being purchased is not to be regarded as a person who can vote in respect of any of his shares. So the resolution must be agreed unanimously by the other members.

A copy of the contract of purchase or a memorandum in writing of its terms, if it is not in writing, must be available for inspection by any member at the registered office for at least 15 days prior to the date of the meeting at which the special resolution is to be passed and available at the meeting itself, otherwise the resolution is of no effect. The contract or memorandum must include, or have attached to it, a written memorandum giving the names of the shareholders to whom the contract relates if they do not appear in the contract or memorandum. This provision is changed if the written resolution procedure is used and instead the relevant documents must be supplied to each member at or before the time at which the resolution is supplied to him for signature.

Where a written resolution is used, the procedure can be shortened since the documents referred to above can be sent to the members with the resolution, and the 15-day display period does not arise.

The special (or written) resolution must be filed with the Registrar within 15 days of its passing and a copy of it must be embodied in, or attached to, every copy of the articles issued after the resolution has been passed.

## Contingent purchase contracts

A company may enter into a contract to buy its own shares on the future happening of a certain event, for example, a contract to buy the shares of an employee on death or retirement. This is a 'contingent purchase contract' and can only be made if approved by a special (or written) resolution and the following of the procedures set out above.

## Assignment and release

The rights of the company under any contract to buy its own shares by a purchase or contingent purchase contract are not capable of assignment so that the company cannot sell, or buy back, its rights to purchase a member's shares and so create a market in purchase contracts. The company cannot release its right to purchase under any approved contract unless the release has been approved in advance by a special (or written) resolution. This is to prevent the company from providing funds to, say, selected shareholders by buying the right to purchase their shares and then later releasing that right, i.e. in effect buying a sort of option which it is never intended to exercise.

## Disclosure

A company which has purchased its own shares must within 28 days deliver Form 169 to the Registrar. This is a return stating the number and nominal value of each class of shares purchased and the date on which they were delivered to the company and the amount paid for them. In addition, the company must keep at its registered office any contract or contingent contract for the purchase of its shares and any variation thereof or a memorandum of its terms if it is not in writing. These documents must be kept for

10 years after the final purchase of the shares and must be open to inspection in a private company by any member. Outsiders have no right of inspection as they have in public companies.

Stamp duty is payable when a company buys its own shares. Form 169 is the document which is liable to duty, being treated as the instrument of transfer.

## Failure by company to purchase shares

The company is not liable to pay damages in respect of a failure to purchase (or redeem) its shares. However, a shareholder may apply to the court for specific performance of the contract of purchase (or the terms of redemption) but no order is to be made if the company can show that it could not pay the price from distributable profits.

In a liquidation, a shareholder may enforce a contract of purchase (or the terms of redemption) against the company as a deferred debt provided that the due date for purchase (or redemption) was before the date of the commencement of the winding-up, unless it is shown that the company could not at any time between the due date for purchase (or redemption) and the commencement of the winding-up have paid for the shares from distributable profits. Because it is a deferred debt in a winding-up, all other debts and liabilities are paid in priority to the purchase price (or redemption price) as are shareholders with a prior right to return of capital, e.g. preference shareholders. Subject to that the purchase (or redemption) price is paid in priority to amounts due to other members as members, e.g. share capital, in a winding-up.

## Provisions to ensure preservation of capital

All companies may purchase (or redeem) shares from profits, or from a fresh issue of shares, which need not be redeemable. Where the purchase or redemption is from profits an amount equivalent to the nominal value of the shares purchased or redeemed must be transferred to a capital redemption reserve. This reserve can, as we have seen, only be reduced under s 135, though it may be written down in the accounting records for the purpose of paying up unissued shares to be allotted to the members as fully paid bonus shares. Thus the creditors' fund or buffer is protected because the shares purchased (or redeemed) are replaced by a new issue of shares or a non-distributable capital reserve.

The provisions regarding the financing of a premium on purchase are the same as those applying on redemption and have already been considered.

## PURCHASE OR REDEMPTION PARTLY OUT OF CAPITAL

The CA 1985 gives a power to private companies to purchase, or redeem, shares partly (but not wholly) from capital when the company concerned has neither sufficient distributable profits nor the ability in the circumstances to raise all the money required by a new issue of shares. These provisions allow, in effect, a private company to reduce its capital without going to the court for confirmation as the rules relating to capital reduction require. Thus a private family company could purchase the shares of a retiring member and so keep out non-family members even though profits were insufficient to make the purchase in full and the members of the family did not wish to subscribe to a fresh issue which would be enough to pay the full purchase price.

## Conditions

The following conditions must be satisfied before a payment out of capital can be made:

(a) the articles of the company must authorise it. A general power to purchase is not enough. Regulation 35 of Table A to the CA 1985 allows a payment from capital by private companies. Previous Tables A would not allow purchase, or purchase from capital, and would have to be changed;

(b) the payment must not exceed the 'permissible capital payment'. Under this rule the company is required to utilise its available profits and any proceeds arising from a new issue, if any, before making a payment out of capital. Only the deficiency, if any, can be met from capital;

(c) a sole director, or all the directors, and not just a majority of them, must make a statutory declaration specifying the amount of the permissible capital payment and also that they are of the opinion that the company will be able to pay its debts:

    (i) immediately following the purchase (redemption); and

    (ii) for one year immediately following also, so that the directors are saying, in effect, that the company can continue as a going concern throughout the year;

(d) attached to the statutory declaration is a report by the auditors addressed to the directors stating that the auditors have enquired into the company's affairs; that the permissible capital payment (*see below*) has been properly determined; and that they are not aware of anything to indicate that the opinion of the directors as to going concern is unreasonable. The audit exemption Regulations do not dispense with the requirement of an audit report on the permissible capital payment so that a company wishing to make a purchase partly from capital must have an auditor;

(e) the payment must be approved by a special (or written) resolution to safeguard the interests of those members who are not selling. There is a mandatory right for any voting member, or his proxy, to demand a poll on the special resolution. The resolution must be passed on, or within one week after, the date on which the directors make the statutory declaration. The resolution will be effective only if the statutory declaration and auditors' report are available for inspection at the meeting at which it is passed. Once again, the special resolution is invalid if it was passed only because the shares being purchased were voted. However, a member whose shares are being purchased may vote other shares, if he has any, on a poll but not on a show of hands. The position regarding voting and circularisation of documents in the case of a unanimous written resolution has already been described;

(f) the payments out of capital must be made not earlier than five weeks (to allow for objections; *see below*), nor later than seven weeks after the date of the resolution.

## Permissible capital payment

Although permissible capital payment (PCP) is a matter of accounting practice, some basic examples are given to illustrate what is contained in s 171.

(a) *Where the PCP is less than the nominal amount of the shares purchased.* Here the difference must, under s 171, be transferred to the Capital Redemption Reserve (CRR).

Shareholders' funds before purchase

|  | £ |
|---|---|
| Share capital | 100 |
| Share premium | 10 |
| Total capital | 110 |
| Profit & Loss (P & L) balance | 20 |
| Net assets | 130 |

Assume that there is now a purchase of 20 shares of £1 each at a premium of 50p and there is no fresh issue of shares. The PCP is: cost of purchase, £30, less *all* available profits of £20. PCP = £10. The premium is written off to P & L, as s 160 requires, and the £10 difference between the nominal value and the PCP is transferred to CRR, as s 171 requires.

Shareholders' funds after purchase

|  | £ |
|---|---|
| Share capital | 80 |
| Share premium | 10 |
| CRR | 10 |
| Net assets | 100 |

The net assets are obviously reduced because £30 of cash has been used to buy the shares.

(b) *Where the PCP is greater than the nominal amount of the shares purchased.* Here, under s 171, the difference is written off to CRR, or share premium account, or revaluation reserve, if any, or even, in the last analysis, to share capital. Suppose that in the example given in (a) above the company had purchased 30 shares of a nominal value of £1 each at £2 each with no fresh issue. The PCP is: cost of purchase, £60, less all available profits of £20. PCP = £40. The nominal amount of the shares purchased is £30 so £10 must be written off against capital, or a capital account first, if available. In this example we shall take the share premium account because we do not have any other capital reserves, but if that had not been enough, we should have had to proceed to reduce share capital.

Shareholders' funds after purchase

|  | £ |
|---|---|
| Share capital | 70 |
| Share premium | — |
| Total capital | 70 |
| P & L balance | — |
| Net assets | 70 |

The net assets have obviously reduced because £60 of cash has been used to buy the shares.

The above examples apply with the necessary changes in nomenclature to a redemption from capital.

## Publicity

The company must, under s 175, publish in the *London Gazette* and in a notice to each creditor, or that failing, in a national newspaper, within the week following the date of the authorising resolution the fact that the company has authorised a payment out of capital and giving the proposed PCP and stating, in particular, that any creditor may, at any time within the five weeks immediately following the date of the resolution (which is also specified), apply to the court for an order prohibiting payment.

The same publicity must be given to the fact that the directors' statutory declaration and the special auditors' report there on are available for inspection at the registered office of the company, where they must remain for five weeks after the date of the authorising resolution. A copy of the statutory declaration and the auditors' report must be filed with the Registrar before the first date of publicising the proposed payment either in the *London Gazette* or in the notice to creditors or in the national newspaper.

## Dissentient shareholders and/or creditors

A member or a creditor may, within five weeks from the passing of the resolution, apply to the court for an order cancelling the resolution. The right does not, of course, extend to a member who consented to the resolution and is obviously inapplicable, so far as members are concerned, where the unanimous written resolution procedure has been followed.

If an application is made, the company must notify the Registrar forthwith and within 15 days of any court order (or such longer period as the court directs) deliver a copy of the order to the Registrar.

The court has various powers other than cancellation and it may, for example, approve arrangements for the purchase of the shares of dissentient members.

## Civil liability of past shareholders and directors

Under s 76 of the Insolvency Act 1986:

(a) if winding-up takes place within 12 months of a purchase (redemption) from capital and the company's assets are not sufficient to pay its debts and liabilities; then

(b) the person(s) from whom the shares were purchased (or redeemed), and the directors who signed the statutory declaration; are

(c) jointly and severally liable to contribute to the assets of the company to the amount of the payment received by the shareholder(s) when the company purchased (or redeemed) the shares. There is a right of contribution between those liable in such amount as the court thinks just and equitable.

Those in (b) above are given, under s 124 of the Insolvency Act 1986, a right to petition for a winding-up on the grounds: that the company cannot pay its debts; and that it is just and equitable for the company to be wound up.

The purpose of this is to enable them to limit the amount of their liability by initiating a winding-up before the company's assets are further dissipated leading to an increase in the contribution required of them.

Directors who signed the statutory declaration are not liable if they had reasonable grounds for forming the opinion set out in the declaration (s 76(2) of the 1986 Act).

### Transfer of purchased shares

A stock transfer form is not required on completion. The seller merely hands over his share certificate(s) to the company for cancellation, but the company as purchaser is still required to pay transfer stamp duty, unless this is abolished, from a date to be decided, under ss 107–11 of the Finance Act 1990. It is, however, unlikely that this legislation will be introduced.

### Reform

At the present time, shares which are purchased by a company must be cancelled. A company cannot, for this purpose at least, be a member of itself. However, the DTI is consulting on changes to the law. The main proposal is that up to 10 per cent of the issued share capital purchased by the company need not be cancelled but that the company should be allowed to hold the shares in treasury and resell them. This is permitted by the Second EC Company Law Directive. However, the consulation document states that if the proposals are brought into law, the requirements for disclosure and shareholder approval will need to be strengthened. The right to vote treasury shares will be suspended. Other issues are whether dividends should be paid on treasury shares, and whether they should be subject to pre-emption rights in the members of the company.

## FINANCIAL ASSISTANCE FOR PURCHASE OF SHARES

### Previous position

The prohibition on the giving by companies of financial assistance for the purchase of their own shares, or shares in their holding companies, by someone other than the company, was introduced in the Companies Act 1929. The object was largely to defeat the asset stripper who might, for example, acquire the shares in a company by means of a loan from a third party so that he came to control it and once in control could repay the loan from the company's funds and then sell off its assets leaving the company to go into liquidation with no assets to meet the claims of creditors. The company concerned was usually one whose shares were, perhaps because of the poor management policies of the board, undervalued.

Initially the only sanction of the law appeared to be a default fine which could be levied following criminal proceedings for contravening the relevant legislation. However, following cases such as *Heald* v *O'Connor* [1971] 2 All ER 1105, it was shown that there were civil law consequences too since any transaction infringing the rules was *criminal* and it was also *illegal* in civil law. Thus any loans made to achieve financial assistance might be regarded as void and irrecoverable and if the company had given the lender a debenture to secure the loan, or a guarantee to repay it, these securities were void and unenforceable, as was any other security given by anyone else, including the person borrowing the money. Although the above results were not inevitable and depended on the circumstances of the case, they provided a worrying background to those in business.

The same civil law consequences would apply if a person infringed the current law set out below. Breach of the present law is stated to be 'unlawful' and is attended by criminal sanctions as before though the penalties are increased.

## Problems created by earlier legislation

The rule against the giving of financial assistance struck potentially at a range of ordinary transactions of companies. Indeed there were even lawyers prepared to state that the purchase of shares in a company by an innocent recipient of dividends from it might be infringing the financial assistance rule!

The main problem, however, was the threat posed to the management buy-out. If we suppose, as an example, that in a family business senior management has reached the age of retirement and is unable to find any purchaser for the business who knows it and can run it successfully, other than those persons who are coming up within the company as the next generation of management. In such a case those in management, below the owner/directors, may use a buy-out technique to acquire the business with the blessing of the owner/directors. A management buy-out is commonly achieved by a bank's lending the managers the money to buy the shares. Typically the managers can only provide between 10 and 20 per cent of the funds required. The loan is often secured on the assets that the management is acquiring and thus the company is giving financial assistance – an act which would infringe previous legislation. However, the present law allows this and other transactions to be regarded as lawful.

## The present law

This is contained in ss 151–8 of the CA 1985 and the relevant rules are set out below.

### The prohibition

It is unlawful, as before, for a company, including both limited and unlimited companies, to give a person (which includes registered companies and other corporate bodies) financial assistance for the purchase of its own shares, or those of its holding company, directly or indirectly, whether before, or at the same time as, the shares are acquired, or after they are acquired. There is no prohibition on a subsidiary company providing financial assistance for the purchase of shares in its fellow subsidiaries or in a holding company providing assistance for the purchase of shares in one of its subsidiaries.

### The meaning of financial assistance

(a) Financial assistance is given if the company concerned makes a gift of the shares, or a gift of funds to buy them; or guarantees a loan used to buy its shares; or gives an indemnity to the lender; or secures the loan by giving a charge over its assets to the lender. Assistance would also be given if the company waived or released, for example, its right to recover a debt from a person A so that A could use the released funds to buy shares in the company.

(b) The 1985 Act contains a 'sweep-up' provision which forbids any other form of financial assistance if the net assets of the company are thereby reduced to a material extent. The test is not liquidity but net worth based on the actual, not book, value of the assets. Thus a purchase by a company for cash at market value of a fixed asset from a person who later bought its shares would not be financial assistance because the company's net assets would not be reduced and cash would be replaced by the asset purchased.

However, the provisions would catch artificial transactions, as where the company paid twice the market value for an asset in order to assist the seller to buy its shares.

A classic example is provided by *Belmont Finance* v *Williams (No 2)* [1980] 1 All ER 393. Belmont Finance was a member of the Williams group of companies and engaged in property development. The directors of Belmont were keen to get the services of a Mr Grosscurth who had an 'expertise and flair in property development'. They wanted him on the Belmont board but he wanted to be a substantial shareholder in Belmont as well. Mr Grosscurth owned a company called Maximum Finance which was worth £60,000. Belmont agreed to buy Maximum Finance for £500,000 and Mr Grosscurth used the money to buy a substantial stake in Belmont. In later proceedings this transaction was regarded as unlawful financial assistance by Belmont – and it still would be today – because the transaction obviously reduced the net assets of Belmont, although what happened would not otherwise have been forbidden.

### When is financial assistance lawful?

(a) The giving of financial assistance is lawful if the *principal purpose* of the company's action is not merely to give financial assistance, as where the assistance is given as an incidental part of some larger purpose of the company, as in the case of a management buy-out (but *see below*). In addition, the assistance *must* be given in good faith and in the best interests of the company giving the assistance. The company's defence is, therefore, founded upon the purpose in giving the assistance and since this is a matter of fact to be decided on the evidence, should the transaction be challenged, it would be as well for the purpose to be set out clearly in the relevant board minutes.

This book did not initially set out to consider the legal validity of the management buy-out, but since there are some problems, particularly in relation to public companies, on which the Department of Trade and Industry is to propose changes in legislation, a brief mention of the difficulties should be made. As we have seen, it is necessary to find 'a larger purpose of the company' of which the giving of the assistance is merely an incident. The House of Lords in *Brady* v *Brady* [1988] 2 All ER 617 said that it was not enough to show that there were 'other reasons' for the assistance being given. Reasons were not the same as 'a larger purpose of the company'. Although the decision was not directly concerned with a management buy-out but with a company reconstruction, it could be said that a management buy-out is the 'reason' for the assistance and not 'a larger purpose of the company'. Clearly, if A sells an asset to B Ltd at the proper market price and uses the money to buy shares in B Ltd, then the assistance is exempt because B Ltd has 'a larger purpose', i.e. the acquisition of the asset, but in a management buy-out it may be a struggle to convince the court that there is 'a larger purpose of the company'. Plcs are most at risk since, as we shall see, private companies can disapply the larger purpose rule by following the procedures outlined later in this chapter and it is, after all, mainly in such companies that management buy-outs take place. It is likely to be some time before changes to current legislation can be made since an Act of Parliament is required.

However, the DTI has commenced the process of consulation and has issued a consultation document entitled 'Company Law Reform: Financial Assistance by a Company for the Acquisition of its Own Shares'. Of particular importance is a proposal to alter for public companies the 'principal or larger purpose' test to 'whether the predominant reason was to provide financial assistance'. This is to deal with the decision in *Brady*. Clearly, in a management buy-out the predominant reason is the buy-out and not to provide financial assistance.

The consulation document also suggests that lawful commissions and indemnites for underwriting share issues should be added to the list of exemptions in s 153(3) of the CA 1985 and proposes to introduce a defence to the criminal sanctions in current legislation. There is also a proposal that unlimited private companies should be removed from the scope of the provisions and that private limited companies should be allowed to provide financial assistance, so long as it is not 'materially prejudicial' to the company, or alternatively the members have approved the transaction in advance.

(b) The following are also permitted:

    (i)   a distribution of assets in Company A by way of dividend, or in a winding-up, where the distribution is used to buy shares in A or in its holding company or, in the case of winding-up, in A's former holding company;

    (ii)  an allotment of bonus shares;

    (iii) any arrangement or compromise such as a reconstruction under the Insolvency Act 1986 s 245 or s 110 and Part I (company voluntary arrangements) which results, for example, in a liquidator transferring the assets of Company A to Company B so that the shareholders of A receive shares in B, into which A is merged, and which in a sense A's assets have assisted them to acquire;

    (iv) where the funds used to buy shares in the company or its holding company arise from a reduction of its capital, or a redemption or purchase of its shares under the 1985 Act. In the case where the company has reduced its capital the money received by the shareholder in the reduction will, if reinvested, most likely be invested in shares in the reduced company's holding company;

    (v)  the lending of money by a company to a person which he uses to enable him to acquire shares in this company, or its holding company, if lending is part of the ordinary business of the company – as is the case with a bank. The fact that a company has power to lend money by its memorandum does not make lending money part of its ordinary business unless making loans is one of its main businesses. The loan which facilitates the acquisition of the shares must not be made for the purpose of acquiring the shares. It must be merely coincidental that the borrower uses it to buy shares in the company. Thus if a person gets a general overdraft facility from a bank and uses it, or part of it, to buy shares in the bank there is no illegal financial assistance;

    (vi) the provision by the company, in good faith in the interests of the company, of financial assistance for the purposes of an employees' share scheme. This amendment to the 1985 Act introduced by the Companies Act 1989 means that assistance is no longer limited, as before, to the provision of money for the acquisition of shares but applies to all forms of assistance for the purposes of an employees' share scheme, e.g. repaying some or all of the borrowings taken out by the scheme in order to buy the company's shares. The giving of guarantees of loans to acquire the company's shares would also be permissible. A company may also now finance an employees' scheme which benefits employees and their dependants and not merely the employees. Directors of the company may be included in these schemes if they are employed by the company, as is generally the case with executive directors;

(vii) loans by a company to its employees, other than directors, to enable them to subscribe for or purchase fully paid shares in the company or its holding company, to be held by them in their own right.

The lending set out in (v)–(vii) is permissible in public companies only if the company's net assets are not thereby reduced or to the extent that they are reduced the financial assistance is provided from distributable profits (*see* s 154). This is a general restriction on private companies when they give financial assistance and is considered below.

It is also worth noting that s 151 does not prevent a foreign subsidiary from giving financial assistance for the acquisition of shares in its English parent company. There is no need in such a case to follow the CA 1985 procedures (*see Arab Bank plc v Mercantile Holdings Ltd* [1994] 2 All ER 74).

### Relaxation of restrictions in private companies

A private company can give financial assistance in the same circumstances as a public company (*see above*: 'When is financial assistance lawful?'). *But in addition* a private company is not affected by the 'principal purpose' rule and can therefore provide assistance as the sole purpose and object of a particular exercise.

However, a private company cannot give financial assistance for the acquisition of its own shares or those of its holding company if its net assets would thereby be reduced, unless in such a situation the financial assistance is provided from distributable profits to the extent of the reduction in the assets. For this purpose 'net assets' means the aggregate assets less the aggregate liabilities (including provisions) determined according to their *book* value.

It was held by the Court of Appeal in *Hill v Mullis and Peake*, 6 May 1998 (unreported) that, in a case of dispute as to the reduction of assets, the court would hear and normally follow the evidence of an accountant as expert witness.

The net assets must be as stated in the company's accounting records immediately before the financial assistance is given. The board will need to have the relevant accounts drawn up at that date. If the assistance is by way of gift the net assets will be reduced and the assistance will have to be covered by, and made out of, distributable profits. Where the assistance is, as in many management buy-outs, by way of a charge on the company's assets to secure a bank loan granted to the purchasers of the shares, this will not be regarded as a reduction in net assets.

In a further relaxation the Court of Appeal has decided that s 151 of the Companies Act 1985, which prohibits companies from giving financial assistance for the acquisition of their own shares, does not apply in a private company where the assistance consists of the payment by the company concerned of a salary, bonus and pension (given sufficient profits) to a shareholder in return for the transfer of his shares into the joint names of himself and his two sons. The point about assistance relates, of course, to the acquisition of a joint interest by the sons (*see Parlett v Guppys (Bridport) Ltd* [1996] 2 BCLC 34).

This was a transfer of shares from the ownership of A into the ownership of B and C, but this does not seem to have been vital to the decision. Presumably the ruling would support, in a private company, the payment of a salary etc out of future divisible profits to A, provided that A transferred his shares to B, or B and C, and so on, although the Court of Appeal's comments regarding the amount of package is worth noting. However, it would seem that in the above circumstances B (or B and C) would not be regarded as having acquired the shares with financial assistance from the company. This salary etc procedure might prove useful in family company arrangements, and seems to represent a relaxation of the financial assistance rule in private companies, particularly in view of the fact that the Court of Appeal accepted that the services to be rendered by the shareholder in return for the salary package were not worth what the company was, through the package, paying for them, so that on that footing there was a reduction in net assets. However, the court said that the assets were not reduced to 'a material extent' and so the deal did not infringe the relevant law.

A private company cannot give assistance for the purpose of acquiring shares in its holding company unless it complies with the principal purpose rule if the holding company, or any intermediate holding company, is a public company. This is to ensure that public companies cannot avoid the principal purpose rule by a group scheme of some sort.

The practical effect of the above provisions is that a private company can give virtually any kind of financial assistance, provided that the company is solvent and the procedures set out below are followed in all cases.

## Procedure

Whether or not the financial assistance is the principal, or only, purpose or whether it is an incidental purpose, as in a management buy-out, a private company must follow a statutory procedure before the assistance is given.

### Creditor protection

As we have seen, a private company can give financial assistance if the company's net (book value) assets will not be reduced or if the financial assistance is provided from distributable profits. However, since a private company is not required, as we shall see, to take into account unrealised losses in determining distributable profits, a statutory declaration of solvency is required.

The directors of the company (and any holding company and intermediate holding company if the assistance is for the purchase of shares in the holding company) giving the financial assistance must make a statutory declaration which must state:

(a) particulars of the company's business and the assistance to be given and identifying the recipient of the assistance;
(b) that the giving of the assistance will not prevent the company from paying its debts in the immediate future;
(c) that, as regards the prospects of the assisting company for the following year, the company will be able to pay its debts as they fall due throughout the year. If the assisting company is to be put into liquidation within a year but is now, for example, assisting a purchase of shares in its holding company, the period must be

for one year following the start of its winding-up. In forming an opinion on these matters, contingent and prospective liabilities must be taken into account, such as commitments under hire-purchase agreements.

The statutory declaration referred to above must have an auditors' report attached to it. The report, which is addressed to the directors, states that the auditors have enquired into the company's affairs and are not aware of anything indicating that the directors' opinion regarding the company's ability to pay its debts is unreasonable.

The audit exemption regulations do not dispense with the requirement of an audit report on the reasonableness of the directors' opinion so that a private company wishing to give financial assistance must have an auditor.

### Shareholder protection

Within a week of the directors' making the statutory declaration referred to above, a special (or written) resolution must be passed by the company (and if the assistance is for the purchase of shares in its holding company by that holding company and any intermediate holding company) approving the assistance. If a company is a wholly owned subsidiary, it is not necessary to pass a resolution for the reason that there are no shareholders to protect in the sense required by the 1985 Act. However, as we have seen, the directors of any holding company or intermediate holding company must participate in the statutory declaration of solvency procedure even where the relevant company is wholly owned.

Although a 75 per cent majority of those who vote is enough to pass the special resolution, it is important, in practice, that every shareholder vote in favour as would be the case with a written resolution. If they do not, a four-week delay is imposed to enable shareholders not voting for the special resolution to make application to the court to cancel it. The resolution must be filed with the statutory declaration (or the statutory declaration alone for a wholly owned subsidiary which need not pass a resolution) plus the auditors' report within 15 days of passing the resolution or 15 days of making the statutory declaration where there is no resolution.

## When can the assistance be given?

Once the procedure outlined above has been followed, the assistance can be given at any time within eight weeks from the date of the statutory declaration, provided that all shareholders voted in favour of it. Otherwise, the four-week delay for minority objection will have to be taken out of the first half of the eight-week period. Assistance will in such a case have to be given in the second half of the eight-week period. If there is an application to the court, the timetable is then a matter for the court and this may, if there is delay in dealing with the application (which eventually fails), ask for another statutory declaration.

## Dissentient rights

The holders of not less than 10 per cent in aggregate of the nominal value of the company's issued share capital or of any class thereof who did not consent to the special resolution, where that procedure was followed, may apply to the court to cancel it. The court may require the company to buy out the dissentients, if necessary from the company's funds, thus effecting a reduction of capital, or make an order cancelling the resolution – which will then be ineffective. If an application to the court is made by dissentients, the company must forthwith give notice to the Registrar and send to the Registrar a copy of the court order within 15 days of its making.

## Table A

Table A to the CA 1985 does not prevent the giving of financial assistance, but Tables A to previous Companies Acts do and must be changed if procedures leading to financial assistance are to be followed.

## Management buy-outs and fair dealing by directors

Schemes of financial assistance given to directors to achieve a management buy-out may be caught and made illegal by Part X of the 1985 Act – loans etc to directors (*see further* Chapter 20). If a loan is made to a director by a bank for a buy-out and the company gives a security over its assets, this makes the loan, in effect, a loan by the company. The Part X rules also apply to shadow directors (*see* Chapter 20). Thus financial assistance for such a buy-out should be given only to management who are not at the time at board level. If they afterwards become directors, the outstanding loan will not come within the Act, but any further advances will, as will the addition of unpaid interest to the principal sum. Other devices may be used, as where the directors seeking a buy-out form a company to borrow the money so that the bought-out company becomes the wholly owned subsidiary of the newly formed holding company.

## Financial assistance – auditors' duty

In *Coulthard* v *Neville Russell* (*A Firm*), *The Times*, 18 December 1997, the Court of Appeal decided that, as a matter of principle, auditors have a duty of care, not only to the company as a client, but also to its directors to advise them that a transaction which the company and its directors intend to carry out might be a breach of the financial provisions of CA 1985. It will be appreciated that the giving of unlawful financial assistance may affect the contracts concerned with it at civil law and can result in criminal proceedings under which the company may be required to pay an unlimited fine, and its officers, if convicted, may receive a custodial sentence of up to two years and/or an unlimited fine.

Because auditors are often asked to advise, and do advise, directors on the treatment of items in the accounts and because of their likely attitude as auditors to particular future transactions, it may well be that the duty to give advice on the statutory legal position could frequently arise. The decision seems to widen the scope of potential liability for negligence. The allegations accepted as a basis for a duty of care in this case seem to depend on an omission, i.e. the failure to advise that a particular transaction which the directors tell the auditors they intend to do may be illegal.

## COMPANY DISTRIBUTIONS

The matter of company distributions, e.g. dividends, is a specific and rather special aspect of capital maintenance. The basic rules, which appear in Part VIII of the 1985

Act, appear below. They should ideally be supplemented with a study of accounting practice which is important in this area. However, the following material would satisfy the requirements of a law paper.

## WHAT IS A DISTRIBUTION?

It is every description of distribution of a company's assets (not only a dividend) to members of the company, whether in cash or otherwise, except distributions made by way of: (a) a fully or partly paid issue of bonus shares; (b) the redemption or purchase of any of the company's shares under Chapter VII of Part V of the 1985 Act; (c) the reduction of share capital by extinguishing or reducing liability on any partly-paid shares or by paying off share capital; and (d) a distribution of assets to members of a company in a winding-up.

Thus, if Boxo Ltd, a television and video hire company, run by, say, five family shareholders, decided that instead of paying shareholders a cash dividend, it would give each shareholder free equipment, that would be a distribution and subject to the statutory rules considered below.

In essence, these rules state that a distribution can only be made out of profits available in terms of the provisions of ss 263–9 and by reference to accounts which are properly prepared under ss 270–6.

## PROFITS AVAILABLE

The basic rule is that a company's profits available for distribution are:

(a) its accumulated realised profits (both revenue and capital) not previously distributed or capitalised (as by being applied in financing a bonus issue or the purchase or redemption of the company's shares with a transfer to a capital redemption reserve); *less*
(b) its accumulated realised losses (both revenue and capital) not written off in a reduction or reorganisation of capital.

In addition, para 12 of the fourth Schedule to the 1985 Act states that: 'only profits realised at the balance sheet date shall be included in the profit and loss account'.

From the above provisions it follows that:

(a) unrealised profits, either revenue or capital, are no longer distributable;
(b) a realised capital loss following, for example, the sale of an asset at a loss will reduce the profit available for distribution. The 1985 Act requires the making good of unrealised capital losses following such actions as the downward revaluation of an asset still retained by the company, *but only for public companies*. The depreciation of fixed assets is required, and realised losses to be taken into account when calculating the sum available for dividend include amounts written off or retained for depreciation. This ensures that dividends will be restricted to allow for depreciation subject to what is said below;

(c) the use of the word 'accumulated' is important. It means that the position in the current year cannot be regarded in isolation. The profit and loss account is, in that sense therefore, a continuous account. Thus, if Boxo Ltd makes a trading loss of £1,000 in year 1 and £2,000 in year 2, but a trading profit in year 3 of £1,000, it must make a profit in excess of £2,000 in year 4 before any dividend can be paid – unless the company applies to the court for a reduction of capital so cancelling the losses;

(d) undistributed profits of previous years cannot be brought forward and distributed without taking into account a revenue loss on the current year's trading;

(e) an unrealised capital profit cannot be applied in writing off a realised revenue loss.

## ACCOUNTING PRACTICE

Reference should be made to the fourth Schedule to the 1985 Act which states, in effect, that references in the Schedule to realised profits are to such profits as fall to be treated as realised profits in accordance with principles generally accepted with respect to the determination for accounting purposes of realised profits at the time when the relevant accounts are prepared. This implies that it is for the accounting profession to specify, in more detail, as required, the meaning of realised profits and that the term may in this way be amended from time to time so as to encompass changes in accounting practice.

Since the impact and contents of the relevant *Statements of Standard Accounting Practice* and more recently *Financial Reporting Standards* form part of the study of Financial Accounting, nothing further will be said here.

However, the case of *Lloyd Cheyham & Co* v *Littlejohn & Co* [1987] BCLC 303 is important. Here the judge said: 'SSAPs are very strong evidence as to what is the proper standard which should be adopted and unless there is some justification a departure ... will be regarded as constituting a breach of duty.' The statement shows how necessary it is to follow these extra-legal statements of practice when preparing financial accounts.

While the following of appropriate standards will continue to be a vital part of accountancy practice, it will be possible for a court to find liability in negligence even though a relevant standard has been followed, if the implications of the decision of the House of Lords in *Bolitho* v *City and Hackney Health Authority* [1997] 4 All ER 771 are taken to their logical conclusion. The Law Lords qualified the long-established principle that so long as medical practitioners relied on 'a responsible body of professional opinion' they would not be liable in negligence. The court was 'not bound', they said, 'to hold that a defendant doctor escapes liability for negligent treatment or diagnosis just because he leads evidence from a number of medical experts who are generally of the opinion that the defendant's treatment or diagnosis accorded with sound medical practice ... The court has to be satisfied that the exponents of the body of opinion relied on can demonstrate that such an opinion has a logical basis'.

Although the case is a medical one, it is likely to be given general application. It seems now that it will not necessarily be enough to meet an allegation of negligence with the response that the actions complained of are accepted and practised by many others. The courts will wish to be satisfied that the practice in question stands up to logical scrutiny. Canadian courts have already pronounced on the position regarding accountants. The Court of Appeal of British Columbia in *Kripps* v *Touche Ross* (1992) 94 DLR (4th) 284 *held* against Touche Ross on the ground that 'the accountants had known that a simple application of (a Canadian accounting standard) would omit material information'. While *Bolitho* is an important case, it is unlikely that courts will often find that existing accounting standards are illogical, though they have now acquired the right to do so in appropriate circumstances. The decision is perhaps not too surprising. Professional persons cannot really expect to be judges in their own cause.

## RELATED STATUTORY RULES

The relevant statutory rules, running alongside accounting practice, are summarised below.

(a) An unrealised profit cannot be applied in paying up debentures or any amounts outstanding on partly paid shares;
(b) As we have seen, provisions for depreciation (and contingencies) are to be regarded as realised losses when considering profits available for distribution. In addition, a deficit on the revaluation of an asset gives rise to a provision which must be treated as a realised loss except in two cases when the provision may be treated as an unrealised loss:
   (i) where the deficit offsets an unrealised profit previously recorded on the same asset;
   (ii) where the deficit arises on a revaluation of *all* the fixed assets. This applies even though goodwill is not revalued, and notwithstanding that goodwill is treated by the accounting statements formats of the 1985 Act as a fixed asset.

   The revaluation does not necessitate the changing of the amounts of every fixed asset but only that every such asset be considered for revaluation by the directors. They must be satisfied that those assets whose values have not been changed have an aggregate value not less than their aggregate amount as appearing in the financial statements. The above rules will not apply unless the notes to the accounts state:
   (i) that the directors have considered the value at any time of any fixed assets of the company without actually revaluing those assets;
   (ii) that they are satisfied that the aggregate value of those assets at the time in question is, or was, not less than the aggregate amount at which they are, or were, for the time being stated in the company's financial statements;
   (iii) that the relevant items affected are accordingly stated in the relevant accounts on the basis that a revaluation of the company's fixed assets, which included the assets in question, took place at that time.

   The 'aggregate' approach enables losses on certain assets to be compensated for by increases in the value of others;
(c) Where a fixed asset is revalued upwards and subsequently depreciated, only that part of the depreciation applicable to the value of the asset before its revaluation is treated as reducing realised profits. The excess may be added back to distributable profits;
(d) Development costs, e.g. the costs of developing a saleable company product before any revenue is received from its sale or use, must, in general, be treated as a realised loss. If they are shown as an asset, i.e. capitalised, they are to be

treated as a realised loss except in so far as the development costs represent an unrealised profit made on the revaluation of those costs. The basic rule of realised loss does not apply either if the directors justify, in the light of special circumstances, that the amount carried forward shall not be treated as a realised loss. For example, the directors may feel that the future benefits in terms of revenue from the product can be reasonably anticipated in the near future and may wish to set off the expenditure on development against future revenue from its sale, or use, rather than treat it as a realised loss in a particular year.

The grounds of justification must be included in the notes to the accounts on capitalised development costs as required by the fourth Schedule.

## OVERRIDING THE STATUTORY PROVISIONS

The requirement to bring into the profit and loss account only realised profits can be overtaken in two ways as follows:

(a) the fourth Schedule to the 1985 Act allows the directors to depart from the realised profit principles if there are special reasons for doing so, but particulars of the reasons and the effect of the departure must be given in a note to the accounts;

(b) the requirement of a true and fair view overrides other requirements so that an unrealised profit must be included if this is essential to give a true and fair view.

## PUBLIC COMPANIES: A CAPITAL MAINTENANCE RULE

Section 264 imposes a further restriction on plcs. These companies cannot make a distribution in a situation where the amount of net assets is less than the aggregate of share capital and undistributable reserves after making a distribution. This means, in effect, that a plc must deduct any net unrealised losses from net realised profits before making a distribution. The following provides an illustration.

|  |  | Company A £ |  | Company B £ |
|---|---|---|---|---|
| Share capital |  | 50,000 |  | 50,000 |
| Surplus or deficit on revaluation of fixed assets |  | 4,000 |  | (4,000) |
| Realised profits | 7,000 |  | 7,000 |  |
| Realised losses | (2,000) | 5,000 | (2,000) | 5,000 |
| Total share capital and reserves/net assets | = | 59,000 |  | 51,000 |
| *Distributable profit* |  |  |  |  |
| (a) if private company |  | 5,000 |  | 5,000 (no capital maintenance rule) |
| (b) if public company |  | 5,000 |  | 1,000 (capital maintenance rule applies) |

## SPECIAL CASES

Investment and insurance companies are subject to different rules and only a general treatment of the special rules applicable is required for examination purposes. The relevant sections are 265, 266, 267 and 268, and basically they give an investment company, i.e. a public listed company whose business consists of investing its funds mainly in securities with the object of spreading investment risk, and giving its members the benefits of the management of its funds, an option when making a distribution of using either the capital maintenance rule referred to above or an assets/liability ratio test under which it can make a distribution but only out of its accumulated realised revenue profits less accumulated revenue losses – so long as this does not reduce the amount of its assets to less than one-and-a-half times the aggregate of its liabilities immediately after the proposed distribution.

As regards insurance companies, the Act provides that an amount properly transferred to the profit and loss account of an insurance company from a surplus on its long-term business, e.g. life assurance, shall be considered as realised profit and available for distribution provided it is supported by an actuarial investigation showing a surplus, in the sense of assets over liabilities, attributable to the long-term business.

## RELEVANT ACCOUNTS

The 1985 Act requires companies to decide whether a distribution can be made and the amount of it by reference to 'relevant accounts'. The statutory provisions appear in ss 270–6, but the relevant accounts will most usually be the last annual accounts. The accounts must have been laid before the company in a general meeting, though a private company may elect to dispense with that requirement (*see further* Chapter 20). In any case, the accounts must have been prepared in accordance with the CA 1985 and give a true and fair view or have been so prepared subject only to matters which are not material for the purpose of determining the legality of the proposed distribution.

The auditors of the company must have made an unqualified report on the accounts. If the report is qualified, then the auditors must state in writing whether in their opinion the substance of the qualification is material for the purpose of determining the legality of the proposed distribution. A copy of any statement by the auditors relating to the qualification must have been laid before the company in a general meeting or, where the accounts are not laid, a copy of the statement must be circulated to the members. No further details are given here on what is a matter of audit practice but the case of *Re Precision Dippings Ltd* [1985] 3 WLR 812 should be borne in mind because it shows that compliance with the auditors' report requirement is not a mere procedural matter. In that case the company paid a dividend of £60,000 to its holding company. This exhausted the subsidiary's cash resources and some months later it went into liquidation. The liquidator then tried to recover the payment plus interest because he alleged that it contravened the 1985 Act and was invalid. For the year in question the auditors' report contained a qualification as to the basis of valuing work in progress. The auditors had not made the distribution statement and the directors were unaware that it was required.

After the company had gone into liquidation the auditors issued a statement that in their opinion the basis of the valuation was not material for the purpose of the payment of the dividend. This statement was later accepted by a resolution of the shareholders. Nevertheless, the court held that the distribution rules were a major protection for creditors and the audit report was an important part of that protection. It must be available *before* the distribution is made and, since it was not, the payment of the dividend was invalid and the holding company held the £60,000 as a constructive trustee for the subsidiary. The resolution of the shareholders could not ratify, or confirm, the dividend payment. Shareholders cannot dispense with, or waive, legal requirements.

It should be noted, however, that the above provisions requiring the involvement of auditors do not apply to companies that have dispensed with the audit requirement altogether nor to companies that have a reporting accountant. There is no substitution of the reporting accountant for the auditor. For these companies, therefore, there is no audit or reporting accountant requirement for the last accounts on distribution of profits.

## THE EFFECT OF PAYING DIVIDENDS OUT OF CAPITAL

Section 277(1) provides that if a member of a company knows, or has reasonable grounds to believe, at the time a distribution was made to him that it contravened Part VIII of the 1985 Act, he is liable to repay it (or the illegal part) to the company. Section 277 does not deal with the civil liability of the directors who made the improper distribution. However, since they have misapplied the company's property, they are in breach of their fiduciary duty to the company (*see further* Chapter 20) and are, therefore, jointly and severally liable (*see further* Chapter 21) to the company to replace the dividend paid. The authority for this is *Flitcroft's Case* (1882) 21 Ch D 519.

Section 277(2) makes it clear that the liability of the members at common law is preserved and it follows from this, and the decision in *Moxham v Grant* [1900] 1 QB 88, that directors who have repaid the dividend to the company have a right of indemnity against each shareholder who received the dividend to the extent of the dividend received, and at common law it does not matter, for the purposes of this director indemnity, whether the shareholder concerned knew or did not know that it was paid out of capital.

The directors may claim relief from the court if they have acted honestly and reasonably (*see further* Chapter 20) and there may be a claim against negligent auditors.

## DECLARATION AND PAYMENT OF DIVIDENDS

The matter of declaration and payment of dividends is usually dealt with by the articles. The relevant provisions of Table A to the 1985 Act are in regs 102–8. There is no absolute right to a dividend, and where the articles follow the pattern of Table A the members can declare a dividend by ordinary or written resolution but cannot declare a dividend exceeding the amount, if any, recommended by the directors. Thus, if the directors do not recommend payment of dividend, the members cannot declare one either on preference or on ordinary shares. Under Table A the members can, of course, reduce the recommended dividend. As regards the dividend payable in a particular year, the matter is usually already decided because the dividend has often been paid before the general meeting to seek its approval is held. The members could reduce the dividend recommended and paid, and this would involve adjustments in the accounts for the following year. Dividend payments have in the past been put to the members for approval at the annual general meeting, but where a private company has elected not to hold annual general meetings, approval of the payment of dividend can be sought from the members at any time to suit the administrative convenience of the company – in terms of the date on which a dividend payment is to be made – but member approval is required under reg 102.

Table A provides that all dividends shall be declared and paid according to the amount paid up on the shares. Unless the articles otherwise provide, dividends are payable in cash but Table A provides in reg 105 that the company may distribute specific assets in whole or part-satisfaction of what is due. Table A, reg 106 also provides that payment may be by cheque sent through the post to the registered address of the shareholder. In the case of joint holders the cheque is sent to the one whose name appears first on the register of members or, alternatively, as the joint holders may direct in writing. Any one of two or more joint holders may give an effectual receipt. Regulation 107 states that no dividend shall bear interest against the company unless otherwise provided by the rights attached to the shares. Dividends when declared can be sued for if not paid for up to 12 years from the date of declaration.

### Interim dividends

The directors may declare a dividend part way through the accounting reference period; such dividend is in the nature of a part-payment of the dividend for the period as a whole. At the end of the period a final dividend is paid in respect of the balance. Regulation 103 provides that the directors may from time to time pay to the members such interim dividends as appear to the directors to be justified by the distributable profits of the company. Under reg 103 an interim dividend does not require member approval.

When directors propose to pay an interim dividend reference may have to be made, under s 270, to interim accounts or initial accounts. Interim accounts are necessary if, under the last annual accounts, a distribution would be unlawful – as where the amount of distributable reserves calculated by reference to the last annual accounts is insufficient to make the distribution required. The interim accounts must show that a distribution is lawful, otherwise it cannot be made. Initial accounts are required where a company wishes to pay an interim dividend during its first accounting reference period at a time when, clearly, the first annual accounts have not been drawn up.

## PROCEDURE FOR THE PAYMENT OF DIVIDENDS

The company may close its register of members for a short time. Section 358 allows closure for up to 30 days a year (*see further* Chapter 20). This is to ensure that the register remains static while the procedure for payment is carried out. Dividend warrants are prepared in favour of those persons whose names appear on the register and the warrants are posted as soon as possible after the dividend is declared. However, companies encourage the use of a dividend mandate system under which the payment is made direct into the shareholder's bank account. Much depends on the number of members. However, it is current practice not to close the register but to declare a dividend payable to shareholders registered as at close of business on a given date (the striking date). Companies are not concerned with equities when paying dividends. The registered shareholder (or the first-named of joint holders, or as otherwise directed) on the striking day, or the first day when the register is closed, is the person to whom the dividend is payable. If such a person has recently sold his holding but there is as yet no transfer cum (with) dividend, the purchaser, or where shares are listed, his broker, can claim it from the seller. If the sale was ex (without) dividend, the seller keeps the dividend and no claim arises. The purchase price obviously reflects the cum or ex dividend element.

Many companies include a power in their articles to forfeit unclaimed dividends. Table A, reg 108 does so and provides that any dividend which has remained unclaimed for 12 years from the date when it became due for payment shall, if the directors so resolve, be forfeited and cease to remain owing by the company. In the case of listed companies, requirements of the listing agreement as appearing in the Listing Rules issued by the Council of the Stock Exchange would also have to be considered. Knowledge of the Rules is not an examination requirement.

## RESERVES

A company is not in general bound to allocate certain of its profits to reserves except, as we have seen, on a redemption or purchase of shares out of profits when a capital redemption reserve must be set up. A company may, however, be bound by contract to set aside a certain sum by way of reserve to redeem debentures.

The articles may provide for the directors to set up reserve funds for dividend equalisation or to meet future liabilities. Table A does not give such a power, it being implied that – provided profits and reserves are legally distributable – the shareholders are entitled to them.

## THE TRANSFER AND TRANSMISSION OF SHARES

The coverage of the transfer of shares in this section is confined to the transfer of shares in unlisted companies. The Stock Exchange system for transferring shares listed on that Exchange is not really a suitable vehicle for examination questions and questions on this system seem never to be set. A knowledge of the transfer of unlisted securities will suffice.

## THE TRANSFER OF UNLISTED SHARES

Under s 182, shares are personal property and are transferable subject to any restriction contained in the articles. A company cannot register a transfer of shares or debentures unless a proper instrument of transfer (*see below*), duly stamped, has been delivered to the company (s 183). (The position on purchase of own shares has already been considered.) Following approval of the transfer by the directors, the transfer must be stamped according to the value of the consideration at 50p per £100 or part thereof at an Inland Revenue Stamp Office. Thus an article which provided for the automatic transfer of shares to a director's widow on his death was held invalid (*see Re Greene* [1949] 1 All ER 167). Regulation 24 of Table A gives the directors power to refuse to register the transfer of a share, other than a fully paid share, to a person of whom they do not approve, such as a minor or a person of unsound mind because they can avoid the contract and not pay any calls made, and bankrupts who are obviously insolvent. Regulation 24 also provides that directors may decline to register the transfer of a share, even if fully paid, where the company has a lien on it, e.g. for calls made but not paid (*see* reg 8 of Table A). Special articles of private companies may give the directors the power to refuse to register a transfer of a fully paid share. Under reg 25 and s 183 any power of veto vested in the directors by the articles must be exercised within two months of the lodging of the transfer with the company for registration and the notification to the transferee. If it is not, the court may compel the company to register the transferee as a member (*Re Swaledale Cleaners* [1968] 3 All ER 619).

This rule was affirmed by the High Court in *Re Inverdeck Ltd* [1998] 2 BCLC 242. This later case stresses the need for directors in private companies, as *Inverdeck* was, to observe the relevant corporate formalities in their day-to-day transactions. The power to refuse to register a transfer is a valuable one in that it can prevent persons from acquiring rights in the company which the directors believe are contrary to its interests. However, directors must realise that time is running against them from the moment the application to transfer is received and, unless systems are in place to deal with refusals, the right may be lost in a particular case.

The purchase and sale of shares involves the following separate and distinct legal transactions:

(a) an unconditional contract is agreed between the transferor and the transferee. There is no legal requirement of writing. The transferor then holds the shares as a trustee for the transferee (who has an equitable interest) until registration but he is still a member of the company and retains the right to vote as he chooses;

(b) the transferee pays for the shares. The position remains as in (a) above except that the transferor must now vote as the transferee directs. An unpaid transferor has the right to vote the shares free from any obligation to comply with the transferee's requirements (*JRRT (Investments)* v *Haycraft* [1993] BCLC 401);

(c) the position remains as in (b) above while the transfer is approved by the directors and the transfer is stamped;

(d) the transferee's name is entered on the register of members. At this stage the transferor becomes the member and acquires the legal title to the shares.

The rights of persons to bring an action in court for rectification of the register in order to obtain registration or to enforce equitable rights are considered in Chapter 20.

Finally, s 127 of the Insolvency Act 1986 declares void any transfer of shares after the commencement of winding-up by the court, unless the court orders otherwise.

## Form of transfer

The Stock Transfer Act 1963 introduced a new transfer form called a stock transfer form which is for general use with unlisted shares. The form appears in Sch 1 to the Act. Registrars are required to accept for registration transfers in the form introduced by the Act because it overrides any contrary provision regarding transfer, whether statutory or not. It also overrides any contrary provisions relating to the form of transfer in the articles. The signature of the transferor need not be witnessed and the transferee need not sign the transfer nor need it be in the form of a deed. The Act does not, of course, affect any provision under which the company may refuse to register a person because, for example, the board members do not approve of him. The stock transfer form is not available to transfer partly paid shares or shares in an unlimited company, or a guarantee company. If such companies are encountered reference should be made to the articles for the form of transfer to be used.

## Procedure on transfer of unlisted shares

The shareholder executes (signs) a stock transfer form in favour of the purchaser and hands it to the purchaser, or his agent, together with the share certificate. The purchaser or his agent sends the stock transfer form, along with the certificate, to the company for registration. As we have seen, the transferee need not sign the stock transfer form nor need it be in the form of a deed. The company secretary/registrar deletes the transferor's name from the Register of Members and replaces it with the transferee's name and within two months sends the share certificate made out in the transferee's name to him (s 185). No fee is to be charged for registration where reg 27 of Table A applies.

## Certification of transfers – unlisted shares

The above procedure assumes that on completion of the sale of registered shares the seller delivers his share certificate to the purchaser together with a stock transfer form. This will not happen if he is selling only part of his holding or selling all of his holding but to more than one person, each person purchasing only part of the total holding. In cases such as these the seller will send the share certificate and signed transfer form(s) to the company so that the relevant transfer(s) may be certificated.

The company secretary/registrar or transfer agent will compare the transfer with the register of members and if it appears that the seller is the owner of the shares mentioned in the certificate and that some of those shares are comprised in the transfer the secretary/registrar, or agent, as the case may be, will write in the margin of the transfer a note that the share certificate has been lodged and will sign it on behalf of the company.

The certificated transfer is then returned to the seller, the share certificate being retained by the company or the company's transfer agent. The seller will complete the sale by delivering the certificated transfer to the purchaser who will be safe to accept it as equal to delivery of an uncertificated transfer accompanied by the share certificate. The purchaser will then lodge the transfer with the company or its transfer agent for registration and the company will issue a new share certificate for the shares he has bought and a new certificate showing the seller as the registered holder of the balance of the shares which he retains. He may, of course, not retain any shares if he has sold his whole holding to more than one person, thus bringing into play the certification procedure.

## Liability arising out of certification

This is covered by s 184 and, although a certification is not a warranty by the company that the person transferring the shares has any title to them, it is a representation by the company that documents have been produced to it which show at least a *prima facie* title in the transferor. Where, therefore, the company or its agent fraudulently, or negligently, make a false certification, a purchaser who acts upon it may sue the company for any loss he may have incurred as a result.

For example, if the company certifies a transfer without production of a certificate it may be that the certificate has been used to make a transfer (uncertificated) to another purchaser. If this is the case, two purchasers now exist and both are eligible for entry on the register of members. If the later purchaser achieves registration first he will establish his priority over the certificated transferee who will not then be registered. The company will be liable in damages to the certificated transferee for the loss he suffers. However, if the company registers the certificated transferee and refuses the other purchaser, it will not be liable to the latter because the share certificate does not operate as an estoppel, except at the date of issue which will be some time ago (*see further below*).

## Forged transfers

If a company transfers shares under a forged instrument of transfer, the true owner whose name has been forged as a transferor must be restored to the register, and in so far as this puts the company to expense or loss, it can claim an indemnity from the person presenting the transfer for registration, even though he is quite innocent of the forgery, as *Sheffield Corporation* v *Barclay* [1905] AC 392 decides.

## Estoppel arising from a transfer

This can be best explained by an example. Suppose Jones is the true owner of shares in Boxo Ltd and is on the register of members. His share certificate is stolen by his dishonest clerk, Evans, who forges a transfer in Jones's name to Smith and receives the purchase price from Smith. The company issues a share certificate to Smith. Smith then transfers the shares to McKay and the company issues a share certificate to McKay. Jones then discovers the true position. He must be put back on the register. The company is not liable in estoppel to Smith because the certificate was in the name of the true owner Jones and is not an estoppel except at the date of issue. The company has done nothing wrong. However, it is estopped and liable to compensate McKay because it recognised Smith as the owner during the transfer process and to that extent is involved in the deception. The company may claim an indemnity against Smith who, although innocent of the fraud, warrants that the transfer is good. Smith will have a claim against Evans, as would McKay, but many in his position would rather claim against the company which may have more funds; this is the value of the claim in estoppel.

A company may inform the transferor that a transfer has been received for registration so as to give him a chance to prevent a fraudulent transfer but a transferor is not prejudiced by the fact that he has received notice and he may still deny successfully the validity of the transfer.

### Death of a holder in a joint account

A transfer is not needed to a surviving joint holder or holders on the death of one. It is usual for the company to receive a death certificate certified by the Registrar of Births and Deaths. The necessary alterations in the register of members are made on the basis of these documents and not on the basis of the conventional instrument of transfer. The procedure is a form of transmission of shares which is considered later in this chapter.

## COMPANIES WHOSE ARTICLES RESTRICT TRANSFER

In the case of a company whose articles restrict transfer, a transfer must be submitted to, and approved by, the board and any restriction must be the decision of the directors. In practice, these restrictions are normally found only in the articles of private companies, although a plc which is not listed or quoted on the Stock Exchange could have restrictions on transfer in its articles. Consideration will be given here to the right of pre-emption and the general rules relating to rejection of transfers.

### The right of pre-emption

This means that when a member of the company wishes to sell his shares he must, under a provision in the articles, first offer them to other members of the company before he offers them to outsiders. The price is usually to be calculated by some method laid down in the articles, e.g. at a price fixed by the auditors of the company. In this context it should be noted that the auditor can be sued by the seller of the shares if the valuation is too low because of the auditor's negligence. This is an important claim because the seller will not normally be able to avoid the contract of sale because the contract usually makes the auditor's valuation final and binding on the parties. There are no pre-emption or valuation provisions in Table A. If the other members do not wish to take all the shares, then they may be offered and sold to an outsider (*Ocean Coal Co Ltd* v *Powell Duffryn Steam Coal Co Ltd* [1932] 1 Ch 654).

Most pre-emption clauses state that the member must offer his shares to the other members first so that the offering is mandatory. However, they usually say that the members *may* purchase them. Where this formula is used the members cannot be regarded as contractually bound to take the shares, though the company can obtain an injunction to ensure that the offer is made (*Lyle & Scott Ltd* v *Scott's Trustees* [1959] 2 All ER 661). This decision makes it difficult for a bidder to take over a private company with such a pre-emption clause since the board can ask the court for an injunction requiring any member to offer his shares to the other members rather than to the bidder. Where, more exceptionally, the articles state that the members *must* buy the shares following the offer the members are contractually bound under the relevant article to take them (*see Rayfield* v *Hands* (1958) in Chapter 1).

### Rejection of transfers

Where the articles give the directors power simply to refuse or approve the registration of transfers, as Table A does in reg 24, adding only 'to a person of whom they do not approve', then the power must be exercised in good faith. A refusal to register a transfer may be tested in the courts if it appears to have been merely for a personal reason, such as sex or race or general dislike without a commercial motive. A much stronger rejection article appears in Part II of Table A to the Companies Act 1948, which applies only to private companies governed by that Table A. Article 3 of Part II provides that: 'The directors may in their absolute discretion and without assigning any reason therefor decline to register any transfer of any share whether or not it is a fully paid share.' Where this applies, or where it has been adopted in special articles, Table A to the 1985 Act containing no such provision, then since the directors cannot be required to give reasons the court cannot test them and a transferee can be rejected even for what might be regarded as 'bad faith' reasons – if they were known (*Berry and Stewart* v *Tottenham Hotspur FC* [1935] Ch 718).

## When is a transfer rejected?

Where there is an equality of votes in the board, a transfer cannot be deemed to be rejected but must be accepted (*Re Hackney Pavilion Ltd* [1924] 1 Ch 276). However, it is usual, as in Table A, reg 88, for the chairman to have a casting vote which he can use to decide the issue in favour of rejection or approval. Similarly, a transferee can ask the court to rectify the register so that his name is included on it where one director, by refusing to attend board meetings, and thereby causing the lack of a quorum, is preventing a directors' meeting from being held to consider the registration (*Re Copal Varnish* [1917] 2 Ch 349). In addition, the power of veto must be exercised by the directors within two months of the lodging of the transfer or the court may compel the company to register the transferee, on the grounds that refusal to register must be exercised within a reasonable time, anything longer than two months being *prima facie* an unreasonable time.

Unless the articles otherwise provide, rights of pre-emption and rejection apply only on a transfer of the legal title and do not arise on transmission to a personal representative on death or bankruptcy. Special articles may allow rejection of executors' transfers to themselves as members pending the winding-up of the estate as an alternative to dealing with the shares in a representative capacity, and where this is so they will be unable to vote the deceased's shares. A trustee in bankruptcy in the same situation will at least be able to direct his living debtor how to vote. Rights of pre-emption and rejection do not arise where the shares are still represented by a renounceable letter of allotment (*Re Pool Shipping Ltd* [1920] 1 Ch 251).

## THE TRANSMISSION OF SHARES

This occurs where the rights encompassed in the holding or shares vest in another by operation of law and not by reason of transfer. It occurs in the following cases.

### Death of a shareholder

The shares of the deceased shareholder vest, in terms of the rights they represent, in executors (or administrators if there is no will) who can sell or otherwise dispose of them, e.g. to a beneficiary, without actually being registered, subject to any restrictions on transfer which the articles may contain. Section 187 provides that the company must accept probate of the will, or in the case of administrators, letters of administration, as sufficient evidence of the title of the personal representatives notwithstanding anything in its articles.

Personal representatives can insist on registration as members in respect of the deceased's shares unless the articles otherwise provide. Under Table A, reg 30, the directors have the same power to refuse to register personal representatives as they have to register transfers, provided the shares are not fully paid, i.e. reg 24 applies and they may refuse the transfer on the grounds that the personal representative is a 'person' of whom they do not approve. The company cannot insist that personal representatives be registered as members, but reg 30 of Table A allows them to elect to be registered subject to the above restriction. If they are registered as members, they become personally liable for capital unpaid on the shares with an indemnity from the estate, but they do receive the benefit of being able to vote the shares at general and class meetings and to participate in written resolutions. Table A, reg 31, excludes voting rights unless personal representatives are registered. They receive all the benefits attaching to the shares without registration except voting rights. Where, under the articles, they are refused registration they may now apply to the court for relief, e.g. an order to the company to register them under s 459 on the grounds of unfair prejudice. (*See further* Chapter 20.)

## Mental Health Act patients

Transmission also occurs to a receiver appointed by the Court of Protection to the estate of a person becoming a patient under the Mental Health Act 1983. The authority of the receiver is established by production of the protection order of the court appointing him. The position of the receiver is similar to that of personal representatives.

## Bankruptcy of a shareholder

On the bankruptcy of a member, the right to deal with the shares passes to the trustee in bankruptcy, and he can sell them without actually being registered or he can elect to register subject to any restrictions in the articles. Regulation 30 of Table A allows him to elect to register. He would then be personally liable to pay any calls on the shares subject to a right of indemnity against the estate. When the trustee sells the shares the sale is effected by production to the company of the share certificate together with the Department of Trade and Industry's certificate appointing the trustee and a transfer signed by him. A trustee cannot vote unless he is registered but can direct the bankrupt on the way he must vote (*Morgan* v *Gray* [1953] 1 All ER 213).

A trustee in bankruptcy has a right of disclaimer under which he may disclaim shares as onerous property where there are calls due on them and they would have little value if sold. This power is given by s 315 of the Insolvency Act 1986. Disclaimer is effected by the trustee serving upon the company a notice in writing disclaiming the shares, and he is then not personally liable to pay any calls if registered and the estate of the bankrupt member is no longer liable as such. The company may claim damages, which in the case of shares of little value, which was the reason for the disclaimer, are unlikely to be as much as the calls due but unpaid (*Re Hallett, ex parte National Insurance Co* [1894] WN 156). Shares disclaimed may be reissued as paid up to the extent to which cash has been received on them. However, the company would have to ask the court for an order temporarily vesting the shares in the company so that it could re-issue them. Section 320 of the Insolvency Act 1986 applies. This is because on disclaimer the shares vest in the Crown (Treasury Solicitor) as *bona vacantia* (property without an owner). The situation is one of legal difficulty and doubt and legal advice would have to be sought from a firm specialising in insolvency practice.

## TRUSTEES

The shares, if trust property, are transferred to the trustees by the settlor (in a lifetime trust), or by his personal representatives where the trust is by will. If new trustees or replacement trustees are appointed once the trust has begun, the shares must be transferred to the new trustees by the surviving former trustees in the usual way, i.e. by stock transfer form. There is no transfer by operation of law on the appointment of the new trustee, nor under s 40 of the Trustee Act 1925 where the trustee is appointed by deed.

Section 40 provides for the automatic transfer of property without a transfer or conveyance to include a new trustee where his appointment is by deed. However, the section specifically excludes company shares, which must be transferred into the joint names of the trustees including the new one(s) in the ordinary way.

## GRADED QUESTIONS

### Essay mode

1  Edward owns a small number of shares in Severn Ltd, a private company. He wishes to transfer these shares to a charity but fears that the directors may object.

   For what reasons may the directors refuse to register such a transfer and for how long may they delay their decision?

   *(The Institute of Chartered Accountants in England and Wales)*

2  (a)  What is the procedure for varying the rights attached to a class of shares if the memorandum and articles are silent on the matter? What safeguards are there for a minority of that class?

   (b)  Explain the liability of a person who presents a forged share transfer to the company for registration and is registered accordingly. Can the company ever be liable in this situation?

   *(The Institute of Chartered Secretaries and Administrators)*

3  Sprouts Ltd wishes to change its name to Greenstuff Ltd and trade under the name of Brassica Wholefoods. What steps must be taken to achieve this result?

   *(The Institute of Company Accountants)*

**4** Write notes on TWO of the following:
  (a) The name clause of the memorandum.
  (b) The transfer of shares.
  (c) Variation of class rights.
  (d) Promoters.

*(The Institute of Chartered Secretaries and Administrators)*

### Objective mode

Four alternative answers are given. Select ONE only. Circle the answer which you consider to be correct. Check your answers by referring back to the information given in the chapter and against the answers at the back of the book.

**1** When is it necessary to certify a transfer of shares?
  **A** Where there are pre-emption rights in the articles.
  **B** When a part-holding of shares is being transferred to the transferee(s).
  **C** When shares are being transferred to an existing member.
  **D** On all transfer of unlisted shares.

**2** What is the legal position of a person who buys shares on the faith of a share certificate issued by a company to a transferee on the basis of a forged transfer?

  **A** The person gets an equitable interest in the shares.
  **B** The transfer is valid and the person gets a good title if he has acted in good faith.
  **C** The transfer is void and the person cannot claim against the company.
  **D** The transfer is void but the person has a claim for compensation against the company.

**3** Conwy Ltd has a provision in its articles which allows a transfer of shares to be made orally. This provision is:

  **A** Invalid.
  **B** Valid.
  **C** Voidable.
  **D** Valid if the transfer is to an existing member.

**4** Botham dies and leaves all his shares in Thames Ltd to Gower. Under the articles the shares in Thames 'can only be transferred by the directors'. What must Botham's executor do to pass the shares to Gower?

  **A** Become a member and sign a transfer deed.
  **B** Sign a transfer in the form of a deed.
  **C** Sign a stock transfer form.
  **D** Become a member and sign a stock transfer form once on the register of members.

**5** Maurice has become bankrupt. What is the legal effect of his bankruptcy on his shareholding in Mersey Ltd?

  **A** Maurice retains his title and control of the shares but his trustee can file a stop notice.
  **B** Maurice retains his title but the control of the shares is transmitted to his trustee in bankruptcy.

C  The title to the shares passes to Maurice's trustee in bankruptcy.

D  Maurice retains his title and control of the shares.

6  In which of the following circumstances is Fred not a member of a company?

A  Fred subscribed the memorandum but his name is not as yet on the register of members.

B  Fred has been allotted shares and entered on the register but has not received a letter of allotment.

C  Fred has lodged a transfer with the company as transferee but has not yet been entered on the register of members.

D  Fred has sold all his shares in the company to Bill but Fred's name has not yet been removed from the register of members.

*Answers to questions set in objective mode appear on p 709.*

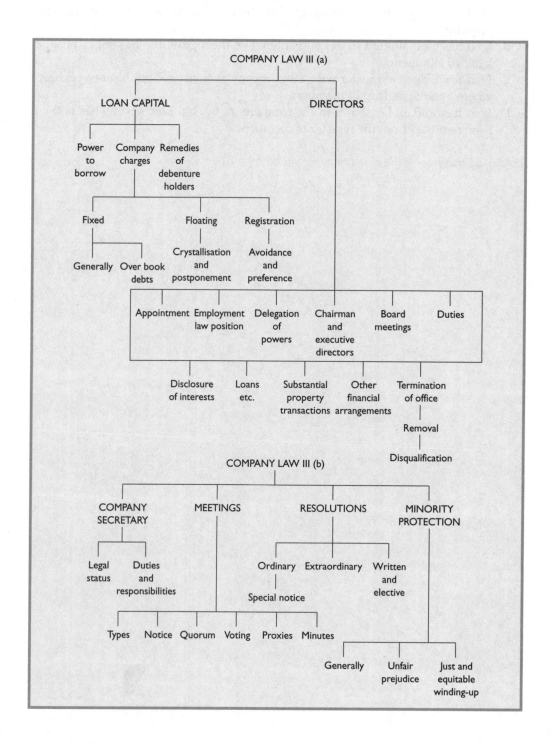

COMPANY LAW III (a)

LOAN CAPITAL

DIRECTORS

Power to borrow

Company charges

Remedies of debenture holders

Fixed

Floating

Registration

Generally

Over book debts

Crystallisation and postponement

Avoidance and preference

Appointment

Employment law position

Delegation of powers

Chairman and executive directors

Board meetings

Duties

Disclosure of interests

Loans etc.

Substantial property transactions

Other financial arrangements

Termination of office

Removal

Disqualification

COMPANY LAW III (b)

COMPANY SECRETARY

MEETINGS

RESOLUTIONS

MINORITY PROTECTION

Legal status

Duties and responsibilities

Ordinary

Extraordinary

Written and elective

Special notice

Types

Notice

Quorum

Voting

Proxies

Minutes

Generally

Unfair prejudice

Just and equitable winding-up

The objectives of this chapter are to consider company borrowing and the use by a company of its assets to secure its borrowing. The chapter then deals with the management of a company in terms of its directors and the secretary and returns, records and registers. It concludes with a consideration of company meetings and resolutions, protection of minority shareholders and a comparison between companies and partnerships.

## POWER TO BORROW

A trading company has an implied power to borrow (*General Auction Estate and Monetary Co v Smith* [1891] 3 Ch 432). Nevertheless, it is usual for an express power to be given in the memorandum. Such a power does not normally impose any limit on the borrowing. A power to borrow, whether express or implied, carries with it, by a further implication of law, a power to give a security for the loan and pay interest on it (*General Auction Estate and Monetary Co v Smith*, above). Again, it is usual for the company's memorandum to give an express power to do these things.

As regards the directors' authority to borrow, Table A, reg 70 gives the board very wide powers of management and under such a regulation (or article) there is no need for a specific power to borrow. Table A places no limit on the amount of money which the directors may borrow so long as they remain within the company's power but, even if the power of the company and the authority of the directors is limited in some way, in view of ss 35 and 35A (*see further* Chapter 18) borrowing beyond any restrictions is not likely to affect a contract of loan with an outsider such as a bank. Nevertheless, the company's constitution should be observed because the CA 1985 still requires this and the directors may be liable to the company for loss caused by exceeding any relevant limit or authority. If the company's constitution makes things difficult, it should be changed (*see further* Chapter 18).

The most usual form of borrowing by companies is by means of what are called debentures, which also give a charge on the company's property. The word 'debenture' has its origin in a Latin word for 'owing'.

It will be appreciated that a person holding a debenture is a creditor and is entitled to interest on the loan (often a bank overdraft facility) whether the company earns profits or not. A private company cannot issue securities including debentures to the public.

## COMPANY CHARGES

### Reform

Reference is made throughout this chapter to provisions of the Companies Act 1989 which contained reforms of the system of registration of company charges. These were not brought into force largely because they removed the conclusive nature of the Registrar's certificate of registration of a charge. Objections to this were made by those in business who rely on the conclusive nature of registration since, if there are any problems relating to incomplete or inaccurate particulars supplied by the company at the time of registration which would render the carge invalid, these are overcome by the conclusive nature of the Registrar's certificate. The matter is still under review, but of all the options it seems likely that the core provisions of existing legislation will be retained with some of the improvements of the 1989 Act and with the conclusive nature of the certificate of registration being retained.

Accordingly, and until matters are made clear, we have retained the provisions of the 1989 Act in this chapter but have made clear that they are not in force and that the provisions of the 1985 Act apply.

### Types of charge

Debentures may be secured by a fixed or a floating charge, or by a combination of both types of charge. The expression 'mortgage debenture' normally means a debenture secured by a fixed charge.

### Fixed (or specific) charge

Such a charge usually takes the form of a legal mortgage over specified assets of the company, e.g. its land and buildings and fixed plant. The mortgage is usually created by a charge by deed expressed to be by way of legal mortgage under s 85(1) of the Law of Property Act 1925. The major disadvantage from the company's point of view is that it cannot dispose of the asset or assets subject to the charge without the consent of the debenture holder. However, there is a major advantage for the directors in a fixed charge because they will almost always have personally guaranteed the company's overdraft, and in an insolvency it is important to them that the bank gets as much as possible from the debenture securing the overdraft so that their liability is extinguished or reduced. In this connection it is worth noting that a fixed charge is not postponed to preferential creditors and other creditors as is a floating charge, and the bank will get more from the security on realisation.

Where the company has no land, buildings or fixed plant, a bank can be asked to take a fixed charge over book debts. (*See below.*)

### Floating charge

This is a charge which is not attached to any particular asset(s) identified when the charge is made. Instead it attaches to the company's assets as they then are, if and when the charge crystallises. The company is in the meantime free to dispose of its assets, and any new assets which the company may acquire are available to the debenture holder should the charge crystallise. Because such a charge does not fix at the time of its creation upon any particular asset, it is equitable by nature, and this is relevant when considering the question of priority of charges when more than one has been created over the assets of the company.

### Fixed charges over book debts

The advantage to the directors, and to the bank as debenture holder, of such a charge has already been considered. However, since a charge over book debts is over after-acquired property, the legal position is not absolutely settled, though it has been held in England that such a charge is valid (*see Siebe Gorman & Co Ltd v Barclays Bank Ltd* [1979] 2 Lloyd's Rep 142) and this decision was affirmed by the Irish Supreme Court in *Re Keenan Bros Ltd* [1985] IR 401, and again by the English Court of Appeal in *Re New Bullas Trading Ltd* [1994] 1 BCLC 485.

There are procedures to be set up by the bank in order to safeguard its position as a fixed charge holder but these are not considered in detail here because they are a matter for the bank's legal advisers and not likely to be examined. However, it is essential to the validity of a fixed charge over book debts that the lender who has taken the charge, often a bank, has *control* over the book debts. The loan arrangements should e.g. require the company to pay the proceeds of its book debts into the company's account with the bank and restrain the company from factoring, discounting, charging or assigning its book or other debts to pay any other person without the bank's consent. Those advising the company can only suggest the fixed charge and point out to the directors its advantage to them in terms of their guarantees to the bank.

## CRYSTALLISATION OF FLOATING CHARGES

A floating charge crystallises:

(a) in the circumstances specified in the debenture. This means that crystallisation can take place by agreement between the parties and the particular debenture must be looked at. However, most usually where the loan is repayable on demand, as in the case of an overdraft, the charge will crystallise automatically when the bank calls in the overdraft which the company cannot pay. The bank may then appoint an administrative receiver. Other circumstances specified include failure of the company to pay interest or the principal sum when due as agreed. These may also result in automatic crystallisation. In some cases the charge may be stipulated to crystallise when the company exceeds a specified borrowing limit;

(b) automatic crystallisation occurs on the appointment of a receiver under a fixed charge or an administrative receiver under a fixed/floating charge, or if the company commences to wind up and on cessation of its business (*Re Woodroffes (Musical Instruments)* [1985] 2 All ER 908).

Once a floating charge crystallises, the assets subject to the charge pass into the eventual control of the receiver and pass out of the control of the company immediately. Any disposition of those assets by the company after the charge crystallises means that the purchaser from the company takes the assets subject to the charge, i.e. the right of the debenture holder to proceed against them to satisfy the debt.

### Notification of crystallisation

Section 410 of the CA 1985 (as inserted by the Companies Act 1989) gives the Secretary of State power to make regulations under which holders of a charge are required to inform the Registrar of Companies of any event which has crystallised a floating charge or of any action taken to enforce a fixed charge. The crystallisation or action will be ineffective unless and until particulars to be prescribed in the Regulations are delivered.

The provision is in the main designed to take care of automatic crystallisation of floating charges as described above. The power to require notice is important to others who may be intending to deal with the company in terms of granting a secured loan or in other ways. Without the system of notice, the register of charges at Companies Registration Office (CRO) will not contain full information about floating or other charges until some time after crystallisation or preliminary action to enforce a fixed charge. Notification is required only if the relevant events are within the knowledge of the owner of the charge. *No Regulations have as yet been made and the above provisions are not in force.*

## POSTPONEMENT OF FLOATING CHARGES

A person who lends money on the security of a fixed charge over the company's property is always entitled to repayment of his loan from the proceeds of sale of the mortgaged property before any other creditor, except a creditor with a prior fixed charge. A person who takes a floating charge is not so secure. There are cases in which his receiver will have to yield priority to other classes of creditors. The detailed law in this area is not considered because it is relevant only in an insolvency and is, therefore, more within the specialist province of the insolvency practitioner. It is not likely to be examined in detail in a general paper on company or business law. However, an outline of the position is given below.

### Preferential creditors

Once a floating charge has crystallised, the owner of the charge, e.g. the bank, is entitled to repayment of the loan out of the assets to which the charge has attached before the company's unsecured creditors. However, there is one statutory exception to this, which is that when a floating charge crystallises the claims which would be preferential in a winding-up rank in front of the debenture holder in respect of realisation of assets under the floating charge. Under s 387 the debenture debt is postponed only to preferential payments accrued at the date of the appointment of an administrative receiver and not to those which accrue subsequently. Sections 40 and 386 together with Sch 6 of the Insolvency Act 1986, apply, and there are no provisions for payment of interest on these debts until payment. Schedule 6 should be referred to if necessary for further detail (and *see also* Chapter 17), but the main preferential debts are as follows:

(a) PAYE and NIC deductions which were made or ought to have been made in the 12 months before the relevant date (i.e. the appointment of the administrative receiver);

(b) value added tax for the six months before the relevant date;

(c) the amount of any car tax for the 12 months before the relevant date;

(d) sums due in respect of general betting duty, gaming licence duty or bingo duty within 12 months before the relevant date;

(e) wages or salaries of employees due within four months before the relevant date, up to a maximum of £800 for each employee. The fees of non-executive directors are not preferential, though executive directors will normally be regarded as employees to the extent of the remuneration paid to them in respect of their duties as executives. A practice has developed of regarding the £800 as a gross sum, thus reducing the amount payable to the relevant preferential creditor. The legislation does not specify net or gross;

(f) all accrued holiday remuneration of employees;

(g) unpaid pension contributions for a maximum of four months before the relevant date.

It should be noted that if a bank has provided funds to pay wages and salaries prior to the receivership that debt becomes preferential under the rule of subrogation.

The justification for the subrogation rule which is contained in Sch 6, para 11 to the Insolvency Act 1986 is that the protection it offers to banks and other lenders may encourage them to advance further money for the payment of wages at a critical time in the debtor company's affairs so as to enable it to continue trading and possibly avoid collapse and a receivership or liquidation.

## Protection of employees

Under Part XII of the Employment Rights Act 1996, an employee who loses his job when his employer becomes insolvent can claim through the National Insurance Fund certain payments which are owed to him rather than relying on the preferential payments procedure. The administrative receiver will normally calculate what is due and obtain authorisation through the Department of Trade and Industry. In so far as any part of this payment is preferential, the rights and remedies of the employee concerned are transferred to the Department of Trade and Industry, which becomes preferential in respect of them. Major debts covered are:

(a) arrears of pay for a period not exceeding eight weeks up to a maximum of £220 per week;

(b) pay in respect of holidays taken and accrued holiday pay up to £220 per week up to a limit of six weeks in the last 12 months of employment;

(c) payments in lieu of notice at a rate not exceeding £220 per week up to the statutory minimum entitlement of a particular employee under the Employment Rights Act 1996 (ERA);

(d) any payment outstanding in regard to an award by an employment tribunal of compensation for unfair dismissal, limited to the amount of the basic award;

(e) reimbursement of the whole or part of any fee or premium paid by an apprentice or articled clerk;

(f) certain unpaid contributions to an occupational or a personal pension scheme.

Here the amount of £220 refers to the employee's gross wage.

There is a provision in s 167 of the ERA for the Department of Trade and Industry to make payments relating to redundancy direct to the employee where the employer is insolvent. The Department will normally claim against the employer, but such a claim is unsecured and does not concern the receiver in terms of preferential payments. There is no qualifying period of employment for claimants on the National Insurance Fund, though, of course, certain periods of employment will have been necessary before an award for unfair dismissal and redundancy would be made.

## Retention of title clauses

These clauses have as their purpose the retention of the seller's ownership in goods supplied until the buyer has paid for them, even though the buyer is given possession of the goods and may resell them or use them in the manufacture of other goods which will be resold.

If the clause is valid and the purchasing company goes into an administrative receivership or liquidation, then the seller may recover the goods which the purchasing company still has in stock, on the basis that the purchaser is a mere *bailee* of the goods and not the owner, the seller being the owner and bailor. This is the position even though the retention clause has not been registered as a charge. These clauses have already been considered (*see* Chapter 11).

## Fixed charges

A fixed charge, whether legal or equitable and whenever created, takes priority over the equitable floating charge on the asset(s) concerned. The only exception is where the floating charge expressly prohibits the creation of charges in priority to the floating charge (called a negative pledge clause) and the person taking the fixed charge knew this to be so. This must be actual knowledge, because registration of the charge at CRO gives only constructive notice of the charge but not its particulars (*see Wilson* v *Kelland* [1910] 2 Ch 306). Section 416 of the CA 1985 (as inserted by the CA 1989) provides that registration of the charge gives constructive notice also of its contents or particulars. This means that the negative pledge clause will be constructively communicated and *Wilson* would be overruled. *Section 416 is not yet in force so at the time of writing Wilson* applies.

There may be an agreement between lenders that a particular floating charge of one shall rank in front of a particular fixed charge of the other. Where this is so, the first ranking floating charge is subject to preferential debts and the second ranking fixed charge is subject to the prior ranking floating charge and the calls of the preferential debts upon it. In such circumstances, the preferential creditors do rank in front of the fixed charge (*see Re Portbase (Clothing) Ltd, Mond* v *Taylor* [1993] 3 All ER 829).

## Other floating charges

If a company is to have power to create a second floating charge over its undertaking ranking before the first, the debenture securing the first charge must so provide. Otherwise, floating charges rank for priority in the order in which they were created.

## Other postponements

Judgment creditors may, in certain circumstances, be able to retain the proceeds of sale of the company's goods taken in execution by bailiffs. Creditors with garnishee orders may be able to abstract funds from the company's bank account and finance companies may be able to recover goods which the company has taken on hire-purchase. Furthermore, a landlord may be able to distrain upon the company's property for unpaid rent in advance of the administrative receiver. However, these are matters of detailed insolvency practice which are not considered further. Examination questions on the postponement of floating charges would be regarded as well answered if the answers dealt with preferential debts, retention of title and the position of other charges, both fixed and floating.

## VALIDITY OF CHARGES

Consideration will now be given to how a charge may be made invalid by failure to register particulars of it, or where it is a floating charge by avoidance under the Insolvency Act 1986 or because the charge is regarded under the same Act as a preference.

## REGISTRATION OF CHARGES

The 1985 Act provides for the registration of certain charges created by companies over their assets. Accordingly, the secured debenture given typically to a bank to secure an overdraft must be registered at CRO. Sections 395 and 396 apply.

### Charges to be registered

These are as follows:

(a) a charge on land or any interest therein belonging to the company and wherever situate, other than a charge on rent payable by another in respect of the land;

(b) a charge on the company's goods where the company is to retain possession of the goods. If the lender takes possession of the goods, as in a pawn or pledge, or takes a document of title to them so that the borrower cannot dispose of them effectively, the charge need not be registered;

(c) charges on the following intangible moveable property of the company:
   (i) goodwill;
   (ii) intellectual property – this covers any patent, trade mark, service mark, registered design, copyright or design right, or any licence under or in respect of any such right;
   (iii) book debts, whether originally owing to the company or assigned to it;
   (iv) uncalled share capital of a company or calls made but not paid;
   (v) charges for securing an issue of debentures;
   (vi) floating charges on the whole or part of the company's property.

It should be noted with regard to (ii) above that the granting of any security (fixed or floating) over a registered trade mark or any right in or under it is itself a registrable transaction (Trade Marks Act 1994, s 25). Until particulars of the charge have been registered at the Trade Marks Registry, the charge is ineffective against a person who acquires a conflicting interest in or under it, e.g. a subsequent chargee in ignorance of it. Registration at the Trade Marks Registry is, therefore, just as important as registering the charge under the CA 1985 at Companies House, which must also be done.

It should be noted that (v) and (vi) above are 'sweep-up' provisions, and (v) above would cover an investment company whose only assets were shares and debentures of other companies. Such a company would have to register a charge over those assets to secure a debenture even though the securities which are its assets are not included specifically under other headings.

So far as (vi) above is concerned, this would cover a floating charge which was not part of the issue of a debenture, and so a charge over mixed goods by means of a retention clause (*see* Chapter 11) would be registrable under this head.

## Registration at Companies House

Section 395 states that it is the duty of the company to deliver particulars of a charge within 21 days of its creation. Section 414 also applies, and in general the date of creation of the charge is when the instrument involved is signed on behalf of the company. The delivery of particulars can be made by 'any person interested in the charge,' such as the lender. The document creating the charge must also be filed, though this will not be necessary if the relevant sections of the CA 1989 come into force. It is an offence for a company and every officer in default to fail to deliver particulars of a charge within the specified time.

The lender, such as a bank, will normally take responsibility for the registration process because of the protection it obtains firstly because the charge is registered and, therefore, not void, and secondly because registration establishes priority since charges registered earlier have priority over those registered later.

At the present time the Registrar will, under s 418, check the particulars and issue a certificate of registration which is (currently) conclusive evidence that the requirements of registration have been satisfied. As we have already seen, the Companies Act 1989 contains provisions under which the conclusive certificate would not be issued, but it is very unlikely that these provisions will ever be brought into force.

## Effect of non-registration

Apart from default fines on the company and its officers in default, failure to deliver particulars within the requisite 21 days will result in the charge being void against a liquidator or an administrator and in consequence the lender is treated as an unsecured creditor. The charge is also void as against other creditors, though in practice only another secured creditor with a prior or, more importantly, subsequent charge could take a legal claim that the charge was void. The charge is not void against the company while it is a going concern and can be enforced, for example, by a sale of the assets charged. Such a sale cannot be set aside in a later liquidation. In addition, when the charge becomes void, i.e. when the time for its registration has expired, all sums including any interest payable become payable immediately on demand.

An unregistered charge is not void in an administrative receivership by the receiver, though individual secured creditors may claim that it is.

## Registration out of time

The court is given power to extend the time allowed for registration but a usual condition is that late registration is to be allowed but 'without prejudice to the rights of any parties acquired prior to the time when the debenture was registered'. This protects those who took and registered charges over the assets of the company while the charge was unregistered. This means that the charge ranks for priority from the date of its late registration. If the relevant sections of the CA 1989 come into force, the power to extend the time for registration will be transferred from the court to the Registrar of Companies.

## Releasing the charge – Companies House

Under s 403 and on application being made to him by the company that the charge has been released or redeemed, the Registrar will enter a memorandum of satisfaction on the register.

If and when the 1989 Act amendments are in force, the new s 403 will additionally provide that if an application is delivered at a time when the debt has not been paid or the charge released, the charge will become void against a liquidator or administrator or a person taking an interest in the property if the relevant event occurs after delivery of the application.

## Releasing the charge – act of parties

A security over property may be released by act of parties. An example is provided by *Western Intelligence Ltd* v *KDO Label Printing Machines Ltd* [1998] BCC 472, where the High Court held that when the goods were transferred with the consent of the bank from a company in financial difficulties to a new company controlled by the same directors, the goods were released from a debenture granted by the original company to the bank.

# COMPANY'S REGISTER

Section 407 provides that every company shall keep at its registered office a register of charges and enter in the register all charges affecting the property of the company. The company must enter in the register a short description of the property charged, the amount of the charge and the names of the persons entitled to the charge, except in the case of securities to bearer.

The company must also keep at its registered office a copy of every instrument creating a charge, whether requiring registration under the Act or not. The documents and register must be kept open to the inspection of members and creditors free of charge and to other persons on payment of a fee.

As regards failure to register a charge in the company's register, there is a default fine on any officer of the company who is in default as well as upon the company itself, but the charge is still valid. In other words, it is only failure to register at CRO which affects the validity of the charge.

The company must keep a register of debenture holders but only if the terms of issue of the debentures require it. The register, if it exists, must be kept at the registered office or the place where it is made up so long as it is within the country in which the company is registered. The register may be inspected free of charge by those who are registered holders of debentures and, in addition, shareholders in the company, and by other persons on payment of a fee. Members, registered holders of debentures and other persons may acquire a copy of the register on payment of a fee. The register of directors' interests must show their debenture holdings also. This register is dealt with more fully later in this chapter.

## AVOIDANCE OF FLOATING CHARGES

Under s 245 of the Insolvency Act 1986, a floating charge created by a company within one year before the commencement of its winding-up or the making of an administration order is void as a security for any debt other than cash paid or goods supplied to the company in consideration of the charge at the time the charge was created or subsequently, with interest, if any, thereon as agreed. The above provisions do not apply if the company was solvent immediately after the creation of the charge. It was held in *Power* v *Sharp Investments Ltd*, *The Times*, 6 June 1993, that a charge was not valid where money was paid *before* the charge was created. It must be at the time of creation or subsequently.

However, if the person in whose favour the charge was created was connected with the company, e.g. a director or shadow director (see later in this chapter), the period is two years, and the charge is void even though the connected person gave consideration at the time or subsequently, and even though the company was solvent immediately after the charge was given.

The purpose of the section is to prevent a company which is unable to pay its debts from, in effect, preferring one of its unsecured creditors to the others by giving him a floating charge on its assets. There is no objection to the creation of a floating charge where the company actually receives funds or goods at the time or afterwards because these may assist it to carry on business, and indeed avoid winding-up or administration. The charge only extends to the value of the funds or goods supplied after it was given and does not secure the existing debt to the unsecured creditor. As regards goods supplied, the charge extends only to the price which could reasonably have been obtained for them in the ordinary course of business at the time when they were supplied. The security would not extend to the whole of the value of goods supplied at an artificially high price.

### Practical points arising

(a) Most importantly, a floating charge is valid as a security for loans made after the date it was created if the lender promised to make such loans (covenanted loans), and even if the lender did not (uncovenanted loans). (*Re Yeovil Glove Co Ltd* (1965), *see below*.) Consequently, advances made to an insolvent company by its bank on an overdraft facility during the year before it is wound up are validly secured in the winding-up (or administration if relevant) by a floating charge given before the advances were made. The debenture creating the charge must expressly cover covenanted and uncovenanted loans, i.e. agreed loans and other loans not agreed at the time.

## Re Yeovil Glove Co Ltd [1965] Ch 148

The company was in liquidation and had an overdraft of £67,000 with the National Provincial Bank Ltd. The overdraft was secured by a floating charge given less than 12 months prior to winding-up at a time when the company was insolvent. The charge was, therefore, void under what is now s 245 of the Insolvency Act 1986. However, the company had paid in some £111,000 and the bank had paid cheques out to the amount of some £110,000. The Court of Appeal *held* that under *Clayton's Case* (1816) 1 Mer 572, under which the earliest payments into an account are set off against the earliest payments out and vice versa, the overdraft, which was not validly secured, had been paid off and the floating charge attached to the money drawn out because the company had received consideration for this. It did not matter that the floating charge did not require the bank to make further advances. It did, however, expressly secure uncovenanted loans.

*Comment:* The Cork Committee said that this case defeated the object of what is now s 245. The Committee thought it should be repealed by statute so that, for the purposes of s 245, payments into the account should be treated as discharging debit items incurred after the creation of the floating charge before those incurred before it. (*See* Cmnd 8558, para 1562.)

(b) The period of one (or two) year(s) from the creation of the floating charge is calculated from the date when the instrument imposing the charge is executed and not from the date of the issue of the debenture which may be later.

(c) If an unsecured creditor makes a new loan to the company on the security of a floating charge on the understanding that the loan will be applied immediately in paying off his existing unsecured debt, the floating charge will normally be invalid unless the company is solvent immediately after the charge is given (*Re Destone Fabrics Ltd* [1941] 1 All ER 545).

(d) Floating charges are invalidated only if the company is wound up or goes into administration, and so if before either of those events it redeems a floating charge which would have been invalid in those situations, the liquidator or administrator cannot require the owner of the charge to repay what he has received (*Re Parkes Garage (Swadlincote) Ltd* [1929] 1 Ch 139). However, if the redemption takes place within six months (two years if the debenture holder is a connected person) before the winding-up or administration, it may be a preference of the debenture holder, in which case the relevant insolvency practitioner can recover the amount paid to the debenture holder under s 239 of the Insolvency Act 1986 (*see below*).

The s 245 avoidance provisions do not apply to fixed charges, but the preference provisions of s 239 do (*see below*).

## PREFERENCE

A liquidator or an administrator may avoid a fixed or floating charge as a preference under s 239 of the Insolvency Act 1986 if:

(a) in giving the charge the company was influenced by a desire to better the position of a creditor or surety. Thus, to give a charge to a lender where the directors had personally guaranteed the loan would be a preference. (*See Re Kushler* [1943] 2 All

ER 22.) However, the giving of a charge to an unsecured creditor about to levy execution on the company's goods may very well not be, because it would be given to preserve the company's assets at market value, bearing in mind that sheriff sales are often at throwaway prices;

(b) the company was insolvent when the charge was given; and

(c) the charge was given within the six months preceding the commencement of the winding-up or administration.

Where the creditor preferred is a connected person, e.g. a director or shadow director, the time period is two years and (a) above is presumed.

In this connection, the High Court decided in *Weisgard* v *Pilkington* [1995] BCC 1108 that a company's transfer by lease of certain of its assets (six flats) to two of its directors before it went into insolvent liquidation – ostensibly in discharge of a debt the company owed them – was a preference to connected persons so that the transfer must be reversed and the flats returned to the company. The directors had not displaced the presumption under s 239 that the transfers constituted a preference to connected persons. The transfers had put the directors in a better position than they would have been in given an insolvent liquidation. This was so even in regard to two of the flats, which were charged to a bank to secure an overdraft, since the charge operated to reduce the directors' liabilities as guarantors of that overdraft.

## REMEDIES OF SECURED DEBENTURE HOLDERS

Where the debentures are secured on the assets of the company the following main remedies are available:

(a) the property charged may be sold or leased;

(b) a receiver may be appointed to take possession of the property.

Where the debenture is secured by a fixed charge, these remedies are available under s 101 of the Law of Property Act 1925. However, since a floating charge may not be covered by s 101 (*see Blaker* v *Herts & Essex Waterworks* (1889) 41 Ch D 399 under earlier similar legislation), the remedies are invariably given in the debenture.

After sale of the assets in a receivership any surplus, after paying off the debenture holders and the cost of realisation and receivers' costs and charges, belongs to the company.

## DIRECTORS

Although the persons who manage a company are usually called directors, it is important to note the provisions of s 741(1) which are that the term 'director', when used in company legislation, is taken to include any person occupying the position of a director regardless of title, for example 'manager' or 'governor' within the company. For some purposes the question of whether or not a person is a director is as much a matter of fact as law and anyone carrying out the functions of a director is included, even a person not actually appointed to the board who may be called a *de facto* director, i.e. a director in fact. Thus s 285 provides that the acts of a director are valid notwithstanding any defect in his appointment and this must of necessity apply to *de facto* directors.

It should also be noted that s 741(2) extends the scope of the above definition by including 'shadow directors'. These are defined as being persons in accordance with whose directions or instructions the directors of the company are accustomed to act. Thus, it is no longer possible for a major shareholder to avoid the liabilities of a director by telling the board how to manage the company without actually being a member of the board. There is, however, an important exception under s 741(2) which is that a person is not to be regarded as a shadow director by reason only that the directors act on advice given by that person in a professional capacity. Professional advisers, such as accountants, are not, therefore, for that reason alone, shadow directors. Whether a person is or is not a shadow director will be a matter of fact to be decided on the circumstances of the case but some indicators are: (a) being a signatory to the company's bank account and/or the attendance at interviews with bank officials; (b) the ordering by the person concerned of goods and/or services for the company; (c) the signing of contracts and/or letters in the capacity of director; (d) attendance at meetings of the board; (e) possession of detailed information about the company. Section 741(3) also exempts a holding company which does not become a shadow director of any of its subsidiaries for the purposes of s 309 (directors' duty to have regard to the interests of employees); s 319 (directors' long-term contracts of employment); ss 320–2 (substantial property transactions involving directors) and ss 330–46 (loans, etc, to directors and connected persons), by reason only that the directors of the subsidiary are accustomed to act in accordance with the holding company's directions or instructions.

The case of *Secretary of State for Trade and Industry* v *Laing* [1996] 2 BCLC 324 strengthens and points up the fact that it is not easy to persuade a court that a person has acted either as a shadow or *de facto* director. It is necessary to present to the court specific evidence of the alleged 'directions' given by the person concerned, plus evidence that they were acted upon by the company to satisfy the test for a shadow director and, for a *de facto* director, that there was a sufficient pattern of activities which could constitute acting as a *de facto* director. Thus in *Laing*, one of the directors had actually signed a contract on behalf of the company, but the court concluded that this was not enough to make him a *de facto* director. The evidence did not establish that he had continued to act as a director for a sufficiently long period of time after that act.

It was held in *Re Sykes* (*Butchers*) *Ltd* [1998] 1 BCLC 110 that a person who denied that he was a director and whose appointment had not been notified to Companies House could nevertheless be disqualified as a *de facto* director following various defaults including a preference in which he paid off a bank overdraft with the company's money to the detriment of other creditors where he had guaranteed the overdraft. He then went on trading with the company in a situation of inevitable insolvency. The court said that it was difficult to lay down one decisive test of whether a person is a *de facto* director. All the relevant facts relating to an involvement in management must be considered.

However, in *Secretary of State for Trade and Industry* v *Tjolle* [1998] 1 BCLC 33 a woman who called herself a director was not regarded as such for the purposes of disqualification because, on the facts of the case, she had no involvement with anything financial and did not form part of the company's real governance.

Under s 744 a director is stated to be an officer of the company and is, therefore, liable for default penalties placed upon a company's officers by company and other legislation.

Different types of directors may exist on a single board. There may be full-time executive directors employed for their expertise under a contract of service, e.g. a finance director. Other non-executive directors may be appointed not to work full time under a contract of service, but to give general advice and business skill and experience to the board or the goodwill attached to their name. They may also carry out a service for the company below board level, as in *Buchan* v *Secretary of State for Employment* [1997] 565 IRLB 2, where Mr Buchan, who was a director of Croydon Scanning Centre Ltd, was also the operator of the scanner and the sales manager.

## APPOINTMENT

Under s 282 a company must have a board of directors numbering at least two in the case of a public company; one will suffice in a private company. However, where a private company has adopted Table A which supports the CA 1985 (*see* SI 1985/805), reg 64 provides that, unless otherwise determined by ordinary (or written) resolution, the number of directors – other than alternate directors (*see below*) – shall not be subject to any maximum but shall not be less than two.

The appointment of the first directors is governed by s 10. This requires that a statement of the first directors of the company together with their signed consents to act shall be filed with the Registrar of Companies with the other incorporation documents. The consenting directors named in the statement are deemed to be appointed from the date of the issue of the company's certificate of incorporation. Subsequent appointments may be made by the members in general meeting in accordance with the provisions of the company's articles. Regulation 78 of Table A requires an ordinary resolution. The appointment of directors at a general meeting of members of a private company need not be voted on individually. A composite (or single) resolution is legally permissible: member approval to this approach is not required as it is in the case of a public company.

The board of directors may make subsequent appointments: (a) to fill casual vacancies which may occur on the resignation, disqualification, removal or death of a director during the period of office; and (b) to appoint additional directors up to the maximum, if any, in the articles. The relevant Table A provision is in reg 79. Persons appointed in these two ways hold office until the next annual general meeting when they come before the members for reappointment under reg 79, and require, under Table A, reg 76, the recommendation of the directors. Regulation 78 gives the members in general meeting a concurrent power to appoint directors to fill casual vacancies and appoint additional directors by ordinary (or written) resolution: should there be a conflict between the persons appointed by the directors and those appointed by the members, the members' choice prevails.

If a person is proposed for election as a director who is neither recommended by the directors nor seeking reappointment after retirement by rotation, the detailed procedures of regs 76 and 77 apply. In essence, they require that before voting on the appointment the members must have received, for example with the notice of the meeting, details of the person to be appointed, which details, if an appointment was made, would have to appear in the company's register of directors and secretaries.

As regards the age of persons appointed as directors, s 293 establishes an upper limit of 70 years. However, this section does not apply to private companies unless they are subsidiaries of public companies and this includes public companies registered in Northern Ireland but not Scotland. Table A does not contain any age provisions but a private company with special articles may have such a provision which may be a lower or higher age than 70.

No general qualifications are required in order to become a company director. However, the Institute of Directors has introduced a professional qualification for directors. The title is 'Chartered Director' and the letters which may be used are 'CDir'. There is an examination and normally a requirement of three years' board experience before obtaining the title. Candidates must be proposed and seconded and will have to undergo an interview. The articles may require directors to take up a certain number of shares as a share qualification to give them a stake in the company. Obviously, Table A does not. The office of director is vacated under s 291 if the shares are not obtained within two months of the appointment and retained thereafter. Special articles may provide for a shorter time. The modern trend is for articles not to require a share qualification for directors since no useful purpose is served by the requirement, the number of shares required as a qualification having been generally small. The requirement also carries a risk that directors will become disqualified and vacate office either because they do not initially acquire sufficient shares or because of an unwitting transfer or during the currency of a takeover bid where they have accepted an offer in respect of their own holdings. If a lack of qualification comes to light it is not enough simply to acquire the necessary number of shares. Having vacated office, the director concerned must also be reappointed, although s 285 provides that the acts of a director or manager are to be valid notwithstanding any defect that may afterwards be discovered in his appointment or qualification. An unqualified person acting as director may under Sch 24 to the CA 1985 be fined for each day he continues to act.

A limited company may be appointed as a director of another limited company. The general principle of company law that sole management should not be put into one pair of hands by the use of corporate directors is preserved by s 283(4) which provides that no company shall have as secretary a corporation, the sole director of which is a sole director of the company, or have as sole director of the company a corporation, the sole director of which is secretary to the company. As regards the use of unanimous written resolutions of members in the making of director appointments, *see* later in this chapter.

Within 14 days of the appointment of a director, a notification form must be sent to the Registrar of Companies giving details of the director's name, address, date of birth and occupation, together with a list of directorships which are currently held and any past directorships held within five years prior to appointment.

## Persons who cannot be appointed

This is to some extent a matter for the articles, which may, for example, provide that a minor or an alien shall not be appointed. Unless there are such express provisions, minors and aliens are not disqualified. Table A does not contain such restrictions. However, the following statutory provisions apply.

### Undischarged bankrupts

Section 11 of the Company Directors Disqualification Act 1986 (CDDA 1986) makes it an offence for an undischarged bankrupt to act as a company director or to be in any way involved in the setting-up or management of a company unless the court which adjudged him bankrupt gives its permission. Under s 12 of the same Act the court may disqualify a person from acting as a director or liquidator or being involved in the setting-up or management of a company if the person concerned has failed to make payments under a County Court administration order. Under such an order the debtor makes regular payments to the court which then distributes the money to scheduled creditors. Even if the court gives leave to act, the company's articles may forbid it. Table A, reg 81(b) provides that a director who becomes bankrupt or makes a composition or arrangement with his creditors generally will vacate office. The article does not prevent an appointment being made, but there is no point in doing so because the person appointed could not act and would immediately vacate office.

### Persons disqualified by court order

Under s 1 of the CDDA 1986 the court may, and in one case must, make an order that the person named therein may not (unless the court gives leave for one or more of the activities) perform any of the following activities during the period specified in the order:

(a) be a director, or liquidator or administrator or a receiver or manager (i.e. an administrative receiver) of a company;
(b) be concerned with or take part in, directly or indirectly, the promotion, formation or management of a company.

The Registrar keeps, under s 18 of the CDDA 1986, a register of all persons against whom disqualification orders are made and they remain on that register for the period for which the order is in force.

The circumstances in which a court may make a disqualification order are set out later in this chapter.

### Articles of association and provisions against sole management

Further disqualifications may be imposed by a company's articles. Table A imposes no disqualifications but does specify circumstances, e.g. bankruptcy, in which directors will vacate office. To avoid the abuse of the general rule against sole management, a person cannot be the company's sole director and its secretary at the same time. This applies to the one-person company since the sole member/director cannot also be the secretary.

## Contractual rights to appoint directors

If a company is governed by Table A then under reg 71 the board may delegate its power to appoint additional directors' to an outsider by power of attorney. This may prove useful when the board wishes, for example, to raise a loan or share capital from persons who are only willing to lend or invest if they can nominate a certain number of directors to the board to protect their interests.

## Alternate directors

The appointment of an alternate director to act in place of a member of the board is useful where that member of the board has many outside commitments which may from time to time result in prolonged absences from the board. Such an appointment can solve problems as to quorum, cheque-signing and so on. There is no statutory authority for a director to appoint an alternate and alternates can only be appointed if the articles provide for it. Table A, reg 65 provides that any director (other than an alternate director) may appoint any other director, or any other person approved by the directors and willing to act, to be an alternate director and may remove from office an alternate director so appointed.

Under reg 66 an alternate is entitled to receive notice of all meetings of the board and of all meetings of committees of directors of which the appointor is a member. The alternate may attend and vote at any such meeting if the appointor is not present in person and will, in general, perform all the functions of the appointor as a director in the appointor's absence. The alternate must comply with any instructions, e.g. as to voting, which may be given to him by the appointor. It is not necessary to give notice of meetings to an alternate who is absent from the United Kingdom. An alternate is not entitled to receive any remuneration from the company for his services as alternate. Thus Table A leaves the matter of remuneration as a private contract between the appointor and the alternate.

Where a director appoints *another member of the board* as his alternate the director/alternate has two votes on a resolution – his own and that of the alternate (reg 88). However, if the appointor would not have been entitled to vote because, for example, of a material interest in the matter before the board, then the alternate's vote cannot be cast (reg 94). An alternate is counted towards the quorum only if the appointor is not present (reg 89). An alternate can sign a unanimous written resolution of the board under reg 93 instead of his appointor. If the appointor signs it the alternate need not do so.

Under reg 67 an alternate ceases to be one if his appointor ceases to be a director. However, if a director retires by rotation or otherwise but is reappointed or deemed to have been reappointed at the meeting at which he retires, any appointment of an alternate made by the director which was in force immediately before the retirement will continue after the reappointment.

Under reg 68 any appointment or removal of an alternate director must be made by notice to the company signed by the director making or revoking the appointment or in any other manner approved by the directors.

Under reg 69, unless otherwise provided in the articles, an alternate is to be deemed for all purposes to be a director and is alone responsible for his own acts and defaults. He is not to be regarded as an agent for the appointor. All the provisions in company legislation relating to directors apply to an alternate. The fact that the office is temporary will not absolve the alternate from the duties and penalties imposed on directors by law. Thus the alternate must, for example, disclose interests in the company's shares and debentures and material contracts. For this reason his particulars should be filed with the Registrar if he is not already a director of the company.

## DIRECTORS AND EMPLOYMENT LAW

Directors may be fee-paid supervisors acting in some ways as trustees for the shareholders, or senior executives or managers who work whole-time as directors of the company and combine this with the giving of a professional service to the company, as in the case of an accountant who takes up an appointment as finance director. Under reg 70 of Table A the directors are empowered to enter into a service contract with an executive director. In addition, the normal procedures relating to the appointment of the executive as a director must be followed.

In particluar, the company's articles must be followed. For example, in *UK Safety Group* v *Heane* [1998] 2 BCLC 208 the main relevant article of UK Safety provided in regard to the appointment of directors to an executive office: 'Any such appointment agreement or arrangement may be made upon such terms as the directors determine and they may remunerate any such director for his services as they think fit'. The managing director of UK Safety appointed a sales and marketing director without reference to the board. The full board was never asked to confirm the appointment, nor did the managing director have general delegated powers to make such appointments. The contract was held to be invalid and the restraints against competing with the company which were in it were unenforceable against the person appointed when he left.

The termination of the contract of service does not of itself terminate the directorship. It is, therefore, advisable for the contract of service of an executive director to provide that the director concerned will resign the directorship on termination of the contract of employment for any reason. That failing, the director would have to be removed under a provision in the articles if any – there is no such provision in Table A – or under s 303. (*See* later in this chapter.)

Removal does not prevent the director concerned from bringing an action for damages for wrongful dismissal. As regards claims for redundancy before employment tribunals, directors who are employed under service contracts will normally have been engaged for a fixed term and may have been required in the contract to waive the right to claim for redundancy. The provisions relating to the exclusion of claims for redundancy may be lawfully contained in a fixed-term contract for at least two years.

Otherwise, an employee/director who is removed before his contractual term expires has a claim before an employment tribunal for unfair dismissal. This may well be a quicker procedure than a court action for wrongful dismissal, though there is a ceiling of £50,000 placed on awards for unfair dismissal.

Employment tribunals also have a jurisdiction to hear claims of wrongful dismissal, but there is a cap of £25,000 on the damages which may be awarded. There is no cap on claims brought in the County Court or the High Court for wrongful dismissal.

Employee directors who have not contracted out may claim a redundancy payment or insolvency payment as a preferential creditor. The fees of an officeholder/director are not so protected. Director employees are also covered by the Sex Discrimination Act 1975, the Race Relations Act 1976, the Equal Pay Act 1970 and the Disability Discrimination Act 1995. The wider definition of 'employer' in the discrimination Acts brings within their scope directors who have contracts for services as where they contract with the company to act as a consultant.

## Directors' contracts of employment

Section 319 deals with the length of directors' service contracts. The section is designed to prevent directors entering into long service contracts with the company so that if the members try to remove them, e.g. under s 303, they may be prevented from doing so because the cost of the compensation would be too great for the company to bear. Removal from office under s 303 or the articles does not affect a director's right to damages for the termination of his separate service contract.

Under s 319 both public and private companies may not incorporate into any agreement a term under which a director's employment with the company is to continue for a period of more than five years if, during that period, the company cannot terminate the contract by notice or the employment can be terminated by notice but only in specified circumstances, unless the members of the company agree by ordinary (or written) resolution. A contract for services is included. Thus the provisions cannot be avoided by directors who enter into long-term consultancy arrangements instead of contracts of employment. The prohibition applies to agreements between a director of a holding company and any of its subsidiaries. Thus the service contract of a director of a holding company who is employed by one of its subsidiaries will require the approval of the shareholders of the holding company (not the subsidiary) if it exceeds five years.

As regards approval by the members, a written memorandum setting out the proposed agreement and incorporating the term regarding length must be available for inspection by the members of the company at the registered office for not less than 15 days ending with the day of the meeting and also at the meeting itself.

The provisions of s 319 do not apply if the agreement continues after five years, but once the five years have passed, it can be determined at the instance of the company by notice. Section 319 contains provisions to prevent avoidance of the long-term contracts rules by the device of entering into a series of agreements. Thus, if after the first year of a five-year contract the director enters into a further five-year contract, approval is required as if the second contract was for nine years. A term in a contract which exceeds five years is void and the contract can be terminated by the company at any time after 'reasonable notice'. Reasonable notice is not defined by the Act, but in *James v Kent & Co Ltd* [1950] 2 All ER 1099 it was held to be an implied term of a company director's contract that three months' notice should be given by the company to terminate it. Any term in the agreement, e.g. salary, which is distinct from the term relating to duration is valid and enforceable. Under s 318 companies must keep copies of all written service agreements and written memoranda of oral service agreements.

## Section 319 and the *Duomatic* principle

In *Wright v Atlas Wright (Europe) Ltd, The Times*, 3 February 1999, the Court of Appeal held that a term in a contract between a company and a director under which the agreement would be for life terminable only by the director and not the company was not void under s 319 because the sole shareholder of the company had consented to it, albeit without a formal meeting, and had known about the agreement for at least the requisite 15-day period. The *Duomatic* principle was applied. This states that the unanimous consent of all the shareholders who have a right to attend and vote at a general meeting of a company can override formal (including statutory) requirements relating to the passing of resolutions at those meetings (*see Re Duomatic* [1969] 1 All ER 161).

## DELEGATION OF POWERS BY DIRECTORS

Under reg 72 of Table A the directors may delegate their powers to a committee or committees of the board consisting of one or more directors and to any managing director or any other director holding any other executive office, such of the directors' powers as they consider desirable to be exercised by such persons.

Regulation 71 allows the directors to appoint any person to be an agent of the company for such purposes and on such conditions as they decide including allowing the agent to delegate all or any of his powers.

## THE CHAIRMAN AND EXECUTIVE DIRECTORS

The special position of the chairman and executive directors is set out below.

### Chairman

Companies are not required by law to appoint a chairman. Since, however, they are bound to hold an annual general meeting of shareholders, unless, in the case of a private company, an elective resolution has been passed dispensing with this requirement, and reg 88 of Table A envisages meetings of the board, there is obviously a need for a chairman to control proceedings at these meetings. A chairman of the company is, therefore, usually appointed. Regulation 91 of Table A gives the board a specific power to appoint one of their number to be chairman of the board and to remove him from that office at any time, and reg 42 states that the chairman of the board shall preside as chairman of general meetings. Provisions are often made in the articles in each case for the chairman's absence, though in practice a deputy chairman is usually appointed to act in the chairman's absence.

The chairman is normally regarded as a non-executive director, even though he may be closely involved with the affairs of the company. Where he is in receipt of fees and is not employed at a salary but is concerned solely with running the board and representing the company as a figurehead, he is properly described as a non-executive director. However, he may not qualify as an 'independent' director where such independence may be required. There is in recent times a tendancy to refer to non-executive directors as 'outside directors' and in many cases the chairman would not truly fit that description.

### Managing director

Before a managing director can be appointed the articles must so provide. Regulation 84 of Table A provides for a member of the board to be appointed to the office of managing director and further states that the managing director is not to be subject to retirement by rotation but that he will cease to be a managing director if he ceases to be a director as where he is removed or becomes disqualified. Regulation 84 also allows the board to fix the managing director's remuneration, while reg 72 allows the board to delegate to the managing director such of their powers as they consider desirable to be exercised by him, subject to a right to review these powers from time to time. This gives the board flexibility to give a managing director a specific portfolio of powers and review the situation from time to time.

## Other executive directors

Under reg 84 of Table A the directors may appoint one or more of their number to any executive office, e.g. finance director, within the company. They may enter into an agreement or arrangement with any director for employment by the company or for the provision of any services outside the scope of the ordinary duties of a director on such terms as the board may decide, remuneration for those services being set by the board as it thinks fit. Appointment as an executive director will come to an end if the director concerned ceases to be a director but a director holding executive office is not subject to retirement by rotation. Under reg 72 the board may delegate to an executive director such of their powers as they consider desirable, subject to the right to review the situation from time to time.

# BOARD MEETINGS

Subject to what has been said above regarding delegation by the board to committees of the board and to executive directors, the powers of the directors must be exercised collectively by passing resolutions at a board meeting. However, reg 93 of Table A provides that a resolution in writing signed by all the directors entitled to notice of a meeting of directors (and directors who are absent from the UK are not under reg 88 entitled to notice) is as valid and effectual as if it had been passed at a meeting of directors and may consist of several documents in the like form each signed by one or more directors. The Regulation applies also to committees of the board and the position of alternate directors in terms of signature of these unanimous written resolutions has already been considered. No previous notice is required of such a resolution and, as the Regulation provides, the signatures need not be on a single document provided the signature is on a document which sets out accurately the terms of the resolution. The date of the passing of a written resolution is the date on which the last director signs. Under reg 88 of Table A a director may, and the secretary shall at the request of a director, summon a board meeting.

## Notice of board meetings

Notice of a board meeting should be given to all the directors. No length of notice is required by law, but it must be reasonable so that all the directors have a chance to attend. It is usual in practice to give seven days' notice. Notice need not be in writing, though it often is and, in addition, sets out the business to be transacted, though this is not a legal requirement. Notice need not be given to a director whose whereabouts are unknown, as where he is travelling or on holiday at an unknown address, and Table A provides that notice need not be sent to a director who is, for the time being, absent from the United Kingdom. The effect of failure to notify all the directors entitled to receive notice is that the proceedings at the meeting will be irregular and, to ensure that this is not so, notice should be sent even to those directors who have indicated that they cannot attend.

## Quorum

It is not necessary for all the directors to attend a board meeting so long as they have received notice of it. However, the necessary number of directors must be present to satisfy the requirements as to quorum. This is fixed by the articles and reg 89 of Table A provides that the quorum shall be fixed by the directors and unless so fixed shall be two. No business can be validly transacted without a quorum. Directors are not usually prevented from entering into contracts with the company but a personal interest is relevant under Table A, reg 94, which provides that a director shall not vote at a meeting of directors or a committee of directors on a resolution concerning a matter in which he has an interest which is material and which conflicts or may conflict with the interests of the company. This rule may be relaxed in certain cases by the articles, and reg 94 does set out cases where the general rule is not to be applied and the director concerned can vote, for example if the resolution relates to a retirement benefits scheme. Regulation 95 provides that a director shall not be counted in the quorum present at the meeting in relation to a resolution on which he is not entitled to vote.

For the purposes of reg 94, an interest of a person who is connected with a director, e.g. a spouse and minor child and others specified in s 346 of the CA 1985 (*see further* later in this chapter), shall be treated as an interest of the director. As we have seen in relation to an alternate director, an interest of his appointor is treated as an interest of the alternate.

Regulation 97 enables a director to vote on the appointment of a fellow director to an office of profit within the company but not upon a similar appointment for himself. The company may by ordinary (or written) resolution under reg 96 suspend or relax to any extent, either generally or in a particular matter, any provision of the articles preventing a director from voting at a meeting of the directors or a committee of the board. There is no reason why the directors should not exercise their votes as shareholders to achieve the ordinary resolution provided they are not attempting to condone their own fraud or justify a wrongful appropriation of the company's property.

## Voting at board meetings

This is dealt with by the articles and commonly they allow each director one vote on each resolution proposed. Regulation 88 of Table A gives the chairman of the meeting a second or casting vote. A majority of one will carry a resolution but an equality of votes means that the resolution is lost, unless the position is resolved by the use of the chairman's casting vote. Although this may be used to ensure that the resolution is passed, it will in some cases be fairer, in view of the clear division of opinion of the board, for the chairman to cast his second vote against the resolution to ensure that it is lost.

## Minutes

Section 382 provides that every company must keep minutes of all proceedings at directors' meetings and where there are managers all proceedings at meetings of managers. The minutes are to be entered in books kept for the purpose. The section goes on to provide that when the minutes are signed by the chairman of the meeting, or by the chairman of the next succeeding meeting (if not the same person), they shall be evidence of the proceedings but not conclusive evidence because express evidence may be heard to prove the minutes wrong. Regulation 100 of Table A provides that the directors must keep minutes in books kept for the purpose of all appointments of officers which they may make and of proceedings at board meetings together with a list of the names of all directors present. The members have no general right to inspect the minutes of directors' meetings (*R* v *Merchant Tailors Co* (1831) 2 B & Ad 115) but the directors have that right. Where the directors have used the unanimous written resolution procedure, this is equivalent to the passing of a resolution at a board meeting and should be entered in the minute book in the same way as a resolution passed at a board meeting.

## DUTIES OF DIRECTORS TO THE COMPANY

As a person involved in the running of a business, a company director must comply with general business legislation in areas such as employment, health and safety at work, consumer protection, pollution, VAT and other taxation. However, the duties of directors are much more onerous than those of sole traders or partners and are an amalgam of non-statutory and statutory roles.

### Non-statutory duties of directors

These duties have been imposed over the years by the judiciary as cases came before them in the courts. Unlike the statutory duties arising, for example, under the CA 1985 with which this chapter is mainly concerned, they are somewhat imprecise and to avoid possible liability under them legal advice may have to be sought. Nevertheless, a short description of them appears below.

#### Fiduciary duties

A director, whether executive or non-executive, owes duties to the company that are in some ways similar to those owed by a trustee to the beneficiaries under the trust. Directors are quasi-trustees or guardians of the company's property and are in a fiduciary position; that is, a position of trust in regard to it, and in terms of the general conduct of the office of director. The two main areas of fiduciary duty are set out below:

(a) *Profits and benefits from office.* A director must account to the company for any personal profit he may make in the course of his dealing with the company's property. He must also account for commissions received from persons who supply goods to the company. In addition, a director who in the course of his employment obtains a contract for himself is liable to account to the company for any profit he makes even if the company might not have got the contract. Accountability arises from the mere fact that a profit is made by the director; it is not a question of loss to the company. (*Industrial Development Consultants* v *Cooley* [1972] 2 All ER 162, where Mr Cooley was held liable to account for the profits on four contracts which he obtained while the managing director of IDC even though it was unlikely on the facts that IDC would have got the contracts.) A director is not accountable for the profits of a competing business which he may be running (*Bell* v *Lever Bros Ltd* [1932] AC 161) unless the articles or his service contract so provide. However, he will be accountable if he uses the company's property in that business or if he uses its trade secrets or induces the company's customers to deal with him. A director is not allowed either during or after service with a company to use for his own purposes confidential information entrusted to him by the company (*Baker* v *Gibbons* [1972] 2 All ER 759). It is, of course, possible for a director's service contract to be so drafted as to debar him from running a competing business allowing the company to seek an injunction if such a business was carried on. It might also justify dismissal for misconduct if the contract was breached.

(b) *Abuse of powers*. The directors' powers must be used for the benefit of the company, that is, for the benefit of the shareholders as a whole, and not for the directors' own benefit. Thus directors have been held to have abused their powers by issuing new shares to themselves or their nominees, for example the company's pension trustees, not because the company needs more capital but merely to defeat a genuine takeover bid made by an outsider (*Hogg* v *Cramphorn* [1966] 3 All ER 420). There is also some statutory protection in this area in that directors require the authority to allot the company's shares and also pre-emption rights are given to existing shareholders unless the shareholders have disapplied them (*see further* Chapter 19).

### Duty of skill and care

In addition to the fiduciary duties, a director also owes a duty of care to the company not to act negligently in managing its affairs. In modern times when the directors of companies are often experts in certain fields, e.g. accounting or law, a good standard of competence is expected of them. Certainly executive directors employed by companies in a professional capacity have to comply with an objective standard of care (*Lister* v *Romford Ice and Cold Storage Co* [1957] 1 All ER 125) (*see further* Chapter 22) and so have non-executive directors who are qualified or experienced in a discipline relevant to business. (*Dorchester Finance Co Ltd* v *Stebbing* [1989] BCLC 498.) Thus they can be liable even if they do their best if that does not equate to a proper professional standard. The position of other non-executive directors has not received a lot of attention in the courts in modern times but in the *Dorchester* case the judge said that all non-executive directors had the same objective standard of care.

Furthermore, the standard for non-qualified or experienced directors is being derived from wrongful trading by directors (*see* later in this chapter). In particular, s 214 of the Insolvency Act 1986 provides for personal liability for directors for such an amount as the court may decide in an insolvent liquidation as a contribution to the company's debts. The section is based on negligence and the standard is objective. The qualified/experienced (or talented) director is judged by the higher standard he ought to have, but other directors are required to reach a level of competence to an objective standard. The court will consider current practice.

Of course, s 214 can only be applied specifically when the company is in insolvent liquidation. But the standard the section requires has been cited in *Norman* v *Theodore Goddard* [1991] BCLC 1028 and *Re D'Jan of London* [1994] 1 BCLC 561 as being an accurate statement of a director's duty at common law that could be applied more widely than in wrongful trading.

As regards the duty of directors not to act negligently so as to injure outsiders, the move towards the incorporation of auditing partnerships with a view to avoiding or limiting claims has increased the relevance of the decision of the court in *Thomas*

*Saunders Partnership* v *Harvey* (1989) 30 Con LR 103 which is now included. The claimants were architects who were retained on a project to refit office premises, one requirement being for raised access flooring. The defendant was a director of a sub-contracting flooring company. He was asked whether the flooring his company offered conformed to the relevant specifications. He confirmed in writing that it did. In fact it did not and the architects were successfully sued by the end-users for £75,000. They sought an indemnity from the defendant, his company having gone into liquidation. Part of the claim was based on negligence and it succeeded even though the written confirmation had been given on behalf of the company. The defendant was a specialist in the field and had assumed a duty of care when making the statement. He was liable in negligence. The judge did not see why the cloak of incorporation should affect liability for individual negligence. The decision has implications for companies whose products or services (e.g. legal or accounting) depend to a considerable extent on the skills and expertise of individual directors.

The High Court has again and more recently decided that a company director can be personally liable for loss caused by the negligent misstatement of his company even though the director dealt through the company and not directly with the person who suffered the loss. (*See Williams* v *Natural Life Health Foods Ltd, The Independent,* 18 January 1996.)

The claimant, W, entered into a franchise agreement with Natural Life to operate a health food franchise based on representations relating to the business experience and expertise of the owner who was also the managing director of Natural Life and who had effective control of the company.

Financial projections were prepared at the direction of the managing director. These showed high initial projected profits but in fact W made a net capital loss of £84,641.

In deciding that the managing director of Natural Life was personally liable for W's loss, Mr Justice Langley found as follows: (1) that the fact that a company director had, as here, effective control of the company did not in itself create personal liability. However, the giving of express directions to the company, as in this case to present financial projections, could give rise to personal responsibility; (2) the representations as to the experience and business expertise of the managing director meant that the financial advice given by Natural Life would be relied on by W and the over-statement in the projections amounted to a breach of a duty of care which the company owed to W; (3) since the business of Natural Life was based upon the managing director's personal expertise, he, too, could be found to have assumed a responsibility to W; (4) since the managing director had expressly directed the preparation of financial projections, he was personally liable to exercise skill and care in the preparation and presentation of the projections; (5) even though W had not dealt directly with the managing director, the latter was nevertheless liable to W for the total net loss suffered.

However, the matter eventually reached the House of Lords (*see Williams* v *Natural Life Health Foods Ltd* [1998] 2 All ER 577) which allowed the managing director's appeal so that he was not liable. Their Lordships said that in order for the MD to be liable, the claimant must show that he could reasonably rely on an assumption of personal responsibility by the MD so that a special relationship was created between the claimant and the MD. The claimant had not established such a relationship. In particular, he did not know the MD and had no significant pre-contractual dealings with him.

Furthermore, there had been no conduct by the MD which would have suggested to the claimant that the MD was accepting personal liability. Nor did the evidence show that the claimant believed he was. Nevertheless, if the special relationship can be established, the court will, in effect, go behind the corporate structure and find liability in those who are effectively in charge of it and regard them as personally liable and not mere agents. In appropriate circumstances this effectively circumvents the commercial advantage of limited liablity, and directors who are owners and effectively controllers of a business, are most at risk. It is a particularly useful approach where the company itself is insolvent.

### Directors' duties and shareholders

As regards loss caused by the directors as a result of breach of fiduciary duty or negligent mismanagement, there would appear to be no duty owed to shareholders individually and, therefore, no claim by individual shareholders in respect of their loss will be entertained. Obviously, their shares could fall in value but the attitude of the courts is that this is not personal loss but merely a reflection of the company's loss. A shareholder's right is that of participating in the company as by attending meetings and so on. These rights are not affected by a fall in the value of the shares.

## RELIEF FROM LIABILITY

A director may be relieved from liability for breach of duty by an ordinary resolution of the members. Thus in *Bamford* v *Bamford* [1969] 1 All ER 969 the directors allotted shares to a company which distributed their products. The object was to fight off a takeover bid and the distributors agreed not to accept it. This was an improper exercise of the directors' powers but the allotment was valid because the members (excluding the distributors' shares) had passed an ordinary resolution ratifying what the directors had done. The directors as members are under no legal obligation not to vote (*North-West Transportation Co Ltd* v *Beatty* (1887) 12 App Cas 589). In addition, although the company's memorandum or articles cannot validly contain a clause exempting directors from liability for breach of duty, s 310 provides that a company may insure its directors against liability to the company (but not liability to outsiders) for breach of duty and indemnify them in terms of the cost of criminal and civil proceedings if these are successfully defended. Regulation 118 of Table A allows the company to indemnify a director in connection with legal proceedings along the lines of s 310. Finally, the court can grant relief under s 727 if it thinks that the director concerned has acted 'honestly and reasonably'.

Furthermore, s 310(3)(a) permits the company to purchase insurance for its directors against liablity to the company for breach of duty (but not against liability to outsiders), and if it does so, it must state the fact in the directors' report prepared under Sch 7 of the 1985 Act. Table A in reg 118 provides for a limited indemnity on the lines of s 310.

# DUTIES OF DIRECTORS TO EMPLOYEES

As we have seen, the directors must exercise their powers 'for the benefit of the company'. In the past this phrase has been given a somewhat restricted meaning, i.e. that the directors must act for the benefit of all the shareholders but not for other persons. However, s 309 states that the matters to which directors of a company are to have regard in the performance of their functions shall include the interests of the company's employees in general as well as the interests of its members. However, the section goes on to provide that this duty is owed by the directors to the company alone and so the employees have no right of redress if they are in disagreement with the decisions of the board. The section appears to be a declaration of good intent and little more. It is unlikely that the company will take action to enforce the duty. However, if directors do acts favourable to the employees in balance with the rights of shareholders, they are not now in breach of duty as they would have been before s 309 became law. The section will clearly become of importance if legislation is ever passed requiring companies to have some worker directors on the board, since their central interest would in many cases be that of the employees.

# DISCLOSURE OF DIRECTORS' INTERESTS

As part of the general theme of directors' duties which involves no conflict of interest, directors are required to make full disclosure of certain of those interests, as set out below.

## Disclosure of interests in securities

There are two aspects of this, as follows:

(a) *Interests held on appointment.* A director must give notice to the company of any interest which he has at the time of his appointment in the shares or debentures of the company. The notice must be in writing and must state that it is made to comply with s 324 – which is the section of the CA 1985 that requires disclosure. 'Interest' is widely defined in Part I of Sch 13 to the CA 1985 and includes cases where the director is not even a member but has an option contract under which he can call for delivery of securities to himself. The director must also notify the company of any interest in securities in the company's subsidiary or holding company or a subsidiary of the company's holding company. If the director knows of the interest when he becomes a director, he must notify it to the company within five days (not including Saturdays, Sundays and bank holidays) starting on the day following his appointment, or within five days of becoming aware of it starting on the day following his becoming aware of the interest. Interests in shares in wholly-owned subsidiaries are excluded but debentures in wholly-owned subsidiaries are not.

(b) *Transactions during the directorship.* A director who alters his holdings must also notify the company of the alteration in writing within five days, stating that the notice fulfils the obligation under s 324. Interests in shares (but not debentures) in wholly-owned subsidiaries need not be notified.

In both (a) and (b) there is no minimum limit on the amount of the interest. Interests of a spouse or minor child are under s 328 treated as interests of the director unless they are themselves directors, in which case they make their own disclosure.

The company must maintain a register of directors' interests and enter in it information received within three days. Further details of this register appear at p 656. Failure to notify within five days makes the director liable to a fine or imprisonment or both. The obligation to notify the interests of spouses and minor children remains with the director. There is no duty upon the company secretary to seek out the information but merely to record it when the director has supplied it.

## Disclosing interests in contracts

Section 317 provides that every director who has an interest whether direct or indirect (as through a connected person) in a contract or proposed contract with the company must disclose his interest either at the board meeting at which the contract is first discussed or if the interest has not arisen at that time then at the first board meeting after the interest arises. In *Guinness* v *Saunders* [1990] 1 All ER 652 the House of Lords decided that disclosure had to be made at a full meeting of the board and not at a meeting of a committee of the board. The section provides for a general notice procedure under which a director may give notice that he is a member of a specified company or a partner in a specified firm and is to be regarded as interested in any contract which may, after the date of the notice, be made with that company or firm. This general notice procedure is not available unless the interest arises only because the director is a member of a company or partner in a firm. Thus, if the interest arises because the director is a director of the other company but not a member of it, disclosure should be made in relation to each transaction as it arises.

A director who fails to make disclosure as required is liable to a fine. In addition, the contract can in appropriate circumstances be regarded as cancelled (or rescinded) but this must be done quickly and preferably before any performance has taken place. The company's articles may waive the right to rescind (Table A does not) or the members by ordinary or unanimous written resolution can do so. There can be no waiver by the board. However, the director concerned can vote in favour of adopting it under the written resolution procedure or at a general meeting and even in the latter case if he controls the voting at the meeting. This is because the director is not in breach of duty in terms of the making of the contract but only in breach of the duty of disclosure. The above disclosures should be made by new directors at the first board meeting in so far as they apply to then existing contracts.

The provisions of s 317 extend to any transaction or arrangement set out in s 330, i.e. loans, quasi-loans and credit to a director or connected persons such as a spouse or minor child of the director. The principle of disclosure also applies whether or not the arrangement is a valid and enforceable contract so that the disclosure provisions cannot be avoided by including in, for example, a loan arrangement a clause to the effect that it is not intended to create legal relations (*see* s 317(5)).

The principles of disclosure are also applied to shadow directors by s 317(8). But the interest of a shadow director must be declared by notice in writing to the directors and not at a meeting of the board. The notice may state a specific interest, and be given before the date of the meeting at which the shadow director would have been required to declare his interest if he had been a director, or a general interest (s 317(8) and (b)).

In *Re Neptune (Vehicle Washing Equipment) Ltd, The Times,* 2 March 1995 the High Court held that even a sole director must declare and record his interest in a contract with the company at a board meeting. The sole director concerned had resolved to pay himself £100,000 as severance pay on the termination of his employment and the shareholders caused the company to recover it on the grounds that he had not disclosed his interest in the contract at a board meeting under the CA 1985, s 317. The court said it was necessary to disclose the contract. The director could have had a meeting on his own or with the company secretary present so that the declaration could be made and recorded in the minutes. Obviously, holding the meeting and recording the contract in the minutes is the important point. It is not necessary, said the court, to declare it aloud.

## Disclosure in accounts

A transaction or arrangement between a company and a director of it or of its holding company or a person connected with such director must be disclosed in the accounts of the company if it is 'material'. Paragraphs 16 and 17 of Sch 6 apply. Whether an interest is material or not is a matter for the board, or a majority of it, excluding the director whose interest it is, to decide.

There are exemptions (in para 25 of Sch 6) from disclosure for material interests of £1,000 or less. Material interests exceeding £5,000 must always be disclosed. Between these two figures it depends upon the net assets of the company. Disclosure is required if the value of the material interest exceeds one per cent of the net assets of the company. Thus a company with net assets of £400,000 would have to disclose a material interest of £4,000 and above. The above thresholds are subject to change by statutory instrument but at the time of writing remain as stated.

# LOANS, QUASI-LOANS AND CREDIT TO DIRECTORS AND CONNECTED PERSONS

This section is concerned with the basic rules relating to loans, quasi-loans and credit to directors of private companies which are either freestanding or members of a group of companies all of which are private companies (referred to as non-relevant companies). Plcs and private companies which are members of a group containing one or more plcs (referred to as relevant companies) are subject to more restrictive rules. The provisions are also extended to connected persons. A description of loans, quasi-loans, credit and connected persons may be useful at this point.

## Loans and quasi-loans

Quasi-loans are widely defined by s 331(3) but basically a quasi-loan occurs when a director or connected person incurs personal expenditure but the company pays the bill, the director or connected person paying the company back later. In a loan situation the company would put the director in funds: he would buy, say, personal goods with the money and then repay the loan. Quasi-loans arise, for example, where the company buys, say, a yearly railway season ticket for a director or a connected person and the director or connected person reimburses the company at a later date. A further example is the use of a company credit card to pay for personal goods, e.g. a video, and the company pays the credit card company and receives reimbursement at a later date.

## Credit

Credit transactions are defined by s 331(7). They include supplying goods under a hire or hire-purchase agreement, leases of land in return for periodical payments and supplying goods or services on the understanding that payment will be deferred. The word 'understanding' implies that the arrangement may be less than a binding agreement. Credit arises, for example, where a furniture company sells furniture to a director or connected person on hire-purchase terms, or the company services a director's personal car in its workshops and payment is deferred, or the company lets a flat to a director for his personal use at a rent.

## Connected persons

A connected person is defined by s 346 as: 'A person is connected with a director of a company if, but only if, he or she is the spouse child or stepchild (under 18 years of age) of that director. Also connected are companies (called associated companies), in which the director or his connected persons have together a one-fifth or more interest in the equity share capital or control the exercise of one-fifth or more of the voting power. Trustees of trusts including discretionary trusts whose beneficiaries include the director or his or her spouse or any child or stepchild (under 18) or any associated company are also connected as is a partner of the director or a partner of the director's connected persons.'

## The prohibitions and exceptions

So far as non-relevant companies are concerned, there are no prohibitions on quasi-loans or credit to directors and their connected persons nor are there any restrictions on loans to connected persons. However, a non-relevant company cannot ignore any such transactions but must keep track of them because s 232 requires that loans, quasi-loans and, with some exceptions, credit in favour of the directors and their connected persons be disclosed in the annual accounts as notes to those accounts. In a relevant company quasi-loans to directors and connected persons taken together are restricted to £5,000 outstanding at any one time and repayment to the company must be made within two months. Credit to a director and any connected person taken together is restricted to £10,000 but there is no particular time for repayment.

## Small loans

All companies, including non-relevant companies, may, under s 334, make a loan to a director of the company or of its holding company, provided that the aggregate amount of the loan does not exceed £5,000. Member approval is not required and the terms of the loan are a matter for the board to decide. These loans are not aggregated with other loans but only with other small loans.

## Loans to assist in duties

A company, including a non-relevant company, may lend money to a director of the company (but not of its holding company) to assist him in the performance of his duties (s 337). Thus, if a director is moved from one part of the country to another, the company may make him a bridging loan and, so far as non-relevant companies are concerned, there is no upper limit to the loan. In a relevant company, a loan to assist a director in his duties is limited to £20,000. However, in both cases certain alternative procedures must be followed, as set out below:

(a) the transaction must be approved by an ordinary resolution of the members at or before the next annual general meeting; or

(b) it must contain a term that, if not so approved, it will be repaid together with any other liability arising under the transaction within six months from the conclusion of that AGM; or

(c) in the case of a private company, the loan is given prior approval by a unanimous written resolution of the members. This will be the only procedure available to a private company which has passed an elective resolution dispensing with the requirement to hold an AGM.

Where approval of the members is given, there must be provided at the meeting, or circulated with the written resolution, information regarding the purpose of the expenditure and the amount of the funds to be provided by the company and its liability under any connected transaction as where, for example, the company is lending only part of the money and is guaranteeing the remainder to be supplied by another source.

## Directors' expenses

The above provisions should not lead to confusion in regard to directors' expenses. Directors are often provided with money to meet expenses to be incurred in the company's business. Expense advances are outside the legislation because it is not intended that they be repaid and the director uses the advance as an agent of the company and for its benefit.

## Moneylending companies

Loans and quasi-loans may be made 'to any person' including directors of the company or its holding company provided the loan is made in the ordinary course of business on ordinary commercial terms (s 338). Thus these companies can do business with their directors and connected persons under the heading of 'any person', provided that the terms reflect the status of the borrower in the same way as they would an outsider. There is no need for member approval and the loan or quasi-loan may be for any purpose, and, in the case of non-relevant companies, there is no maximum amount placed upon the transaction. In a relevant company, the maximum amount which can be lent is £100,000. There is no aggregation with housing loans (*see below*) or small loans.

## Housing loans

Section 338(6) allows moneylending companies to make loans to directors or directors of the holding company on non-commercial terms if the loans are made in the ordinary course of business for the purchase of the director's only or main residence, or for improvements to the director's only or main residence provided similar loans are ordinarily made available by the company to its employees on terms no less favourable. There is a limit of £100,000, in both relevant and non-relevant companies, and there is no aggregation with a general loan or a small loan so the director could be lent in total £205,000 plus a loan to assist in duties as set out above.

## Other arrangements

It should be appreciated that the provisions of the 1985 Act are not confined to direct loans by a non-relevant company to a director or connected person. Under s 330(2) a transaction becomes controlled if the company guarantees a loan made by someone else or gives a security over its assets in respect of the loan. Thus, if a director or connected person borrows from a third-party bank and the company guarantees the loan or provides a security over its assets for it, the loan is controlled by the Act in the same way as if the loan had been made by the company itself.

## Shadow directors

Section 330(5) makes it clear that for the purposes of the provisions relating to loans, quasi-loans and credit, shadow directors are included.

## Loans before appointment

If a loan is made by the company to an outsider and it is still outstanding when the outsider becomes a director, it will not come within the provisions of the 1985 Act though any further advances would, as would also the addition of unpaid interest to the principal sum.

## Disclosure – an outline

Subject to certain exemptions relating to credit, Sch 6 requires disclosure in notes to the accounts of transactions of relevant and non-relevant companies as reviewed above. All loans, quasi-loans and credit provided during the year to directors, shadow directors and their connected persons must be shown in the statutory accounts whether the transaction was lawful or not and irrespective of amount. However, under para 24 of Sch 6, credit transactions need not be disclosed if they have not exceeded in respect of the person(s) concerned £5,000 in the year in question. It should be noted that, although in a plc a director can have credit of up to £10,000, disclosure must be made at £5,000 since it is thought that at that figure it becomes significant enough to disclose.

Under para 22 of Sch 6, the following matters must be included in respect of each person involved:

(a) the principal terms of the transaction;
(b) the name of the person concerned and the nature of his interest in the transaction;
(c) in the case of a loan:
    (i) the amount at the beginning and end of the financial year;
    (ii) the maximum amount during the year;
    (iii) the amount of interest due and not paid (if any);
    (iv) the amount of any provision made for non-payment.

## Auditors' report

Under s 237(4), if the directors do not comply with the above disclosure requirements, the auditors are required to make the disclosures in their report as far as they are reasonably able to do so.

The Companies Act 1985 (Audit Exemption) Regulations 1994 are silent as to the application of this sub-section where the company does not have auditors. Presumably if the company has no auditors there will be no audit report in which to make the disclosure and the provision cannot take effect.

## Consequences of contravention

There are consequences in civil and criminal law as follows.

### Civil remedies

A loan which contravenes the provisions set out above is voidable at the instance of the company but no one else (s 341). In consequence, the company will be able to recover the funds from those into whose hands they have passed and there would appear to be no limit in time for avoiding the transaction. However, there are exceptions, which are as follows:

(a) where it is no longer possible to make restitution, as where the loan has been spent on a cruise;

(b) where the company has been indemnified, e.g. by the borrowing director;

(c) where avoidance of the loan would affect rights which were acquired in good faith and for value and without actual notice by a person other than the person for whom the loan was made. This is the usual protection for third parties and would, for example, cover the shipping company which had provided the cruise referred to at (a) above, so that the loan could not be recovered from such a company.

In addition, whether or not the transaction has been rescinded, the director who is a party to it is liable to account to the company for any gain made from the loan and also to indemnify the company against any loss or damage it has suffered which has not been put right by rescinding the loan. This liability is extended also to any other director who authorised the transaction, though such a person will not be liable if he can show that he did not know the relevant circumstances constituting the contravention at the time the transaction was made.

As an example of the above-mentioned civil remedies, the Court of Appeal held in *Tait Consibee (Oxford) Ltd* v *Tait* [1997] 2 BCLC 349 that a company is entitled under the 1985 Act to demand from a director *immediate* repayment of an illegal loan to a director regardless of any other terms of the contract of loan which may provide differently. The defendant said that it was agreed that the loan made by the company to him, which was not within the terms allowed by the 1985 Act in that it was excessive as to amount, was to be repaid from dividends declared on his shares by the company, and since no dividends had been declared, the loan was not repayable at the relevant time. The court decided that the loan was nevertheless repayable and gave judgment for the company plus interest.

### Criminal penalties

These are set out in s 342 and Sch 24. It is an offence for a director to authorise or permit contravention of the Act. The company is also liable and this should encourage shareholders to take what steps they can to prevent offences. Any other person, e.g. the company secretary, who procures a prohibited transaction is also liable. A successful prosecution will require full knowledge in the defendant.

### Shadow directors

By reason of s 741, shadow directors are included in both the civil and criminal sanctions.

## SUBSTANTIAL PROPERTY TRANSACTIONS

Section 320 places restrictions on substantial property transactions involving directors and their connected persons. By reason of s 741, shadow directors are included. The provisions apply to *all* companies. Thus there are restrictions on any 'arrangement', as the section calls it, under which:

(a) a director of the company or its holding company (but not of any subsidiary company), or any person connected with such a director, is to acquire one or more non-cash assets from the company; or

(b) a company acquires one or more non-cash assets from such a director or connected person *unless* the arrangement is first approved by an ordinary resolution of the members of the company in general meeting, or a unanimous written resolution in the case of a private company, and if the director or connected person is a director of its holding company, or a person connected with such director, by an ordinary resolution or unanimous written resolution of the members of the holding company.

The following matters should be noted when considering such an arrangement.

(a) A non-cash asset means any property or any interest in property except cash (which includes foreign currency) so that leases, patents, copyrights and any other intellectual property would be covered, as would the benefit of book debts (s 739).

(b) Approval of the members is only required if the value of the asset is £2,000 or more and exceeds the lesser of £100,000 or 10 per cent of the company's relevant assets. For this purpose 'relevant assets' means the value of the company's net assets as disclosed in its annual accounts for the last preceding year. If no such accounts have been prepared, 'relevant assets' means the amount of the company's called-up share capital (s 320(2)).

Therefore, if the assets to be transferred exceed £100,000 in value, approval is required, even though the assets involved do not equal 10 per cent of the company's net assets. Conversely, if the value of the assets being transferred is less than £2,000, member approval is not required, even though the assets transferred are more than 10 per cent of the company's net assets.

(c) Approval of the members is not required either where the arrangement is between a company and its wholly-owned subsidiary or between two wholly-owned subsidiaries of the same company (s 321). This facilitates inter-group transactions. However, where there is a minority interest, the government felt that the minority must be safeguarded against the possibility of directors of the holding company transferring assets from one partly-owned subsidiary in which they do not have a personal shareholding to one in which they do and so the exemption relates only to wholly-owned subsidiaries where there is no minority interest requiring protection.

(d) Member approval is not required if the arrangement is entered into by a company which is being wound up unless the winding-up is a members' voluntary winding-up (s 321). If the company is insolvent, which is the case in a compulsory or creditors' voluntary winding-up, the shareholders will have little interest in the disposal of its assets since there will be no surplus assets for distribution. It is, therefore, unnecessary to obtain member approval in a situation where the liquidator plans to sell off some of the company's assets to its directors. The exception does not apply in a members' voluntary winding-up because here the company is of necessity solvent and there will or should be surplus assets for distribution to the members after payment of creditors.

(e) Section 321 makes clear that the prohibition on acquiring non-cash assets of the requisite value does not apply to an arrangement under which a person is to acquire an asset from a company of which he is a member if the arrangement is made with that person in his character as such member. This is to avoid problems which a director might otherwise experience by receiving shares under a rights issue. Section 321 also exempts acquisitions of the company's shares by a director or a connected person on a recognised investment exchange through an independent broker. Thus acquisition of the company's shares on the Stock Exchange through a broker is exempt but this would not apply in a private company where the shares are not listed.

Finally, it should be noted that the 1985 Act refers to 'arrangements' rather than contracts, and this will catch transactions even where they are not to be carried out under legally binding agreements.

## Sales in a liquidation or receivership

In *Demite Ltd* v *Protec Health Ltd* [1998] BCC 638 the High Court ruled that where a company acting by its receiver sells its assets to a director or connected person, the company should obtain member approval of the sale under s 320, otherwise it may be voidable by the company. There is an express exception in regard to companies in liquidation (other than a members' liquidation) but there is no such exemption for companies in receivership.

# OTHER FINANCIAL ARRANGEMENTS WITH DIRECTORS

This section deals with various payments to directors by way of remuneration, pensions and compensation for loss of office.

## Remuneration under the articles – fees

If a director who is not an employee is to receive remuneration by way of fees, the articles must expressly provide for it, and in the absence of such a provision no remuneration is payable even if the members resolve that it shall be (*Re George Newman & Co*

[1895] 1 Ch 674). Table A, reg 82 provides that the remuneration of the directors shall be determined by an ordinary resolution of the members. A written resolution will obviously suffice. Under such an article there must be an authorising resolution by the members. The ability to fix the fees of directors is not within reg 70 (delegation of powers to the board) (*Foster* v *Foster* [1916] 1 Ch 532). However, special articles could allow the directors to fix their own remuneration by a specific provision. Whether a director who vacates office before completing a year in office is entitled to a proportionate part of his remuneration is a matter for the articles. Regulation 82 provides that remuneration shall accrue from day to day and so a proportionate part of remuneration is payable. Section 311 contains a prohibition on tax-free payments to directors.

## Remuneration by way of contract of service

Regulation 84 provides that contracts of service may be made by the board with individual directors. Contracts for services may also be awarded to them under which they provide services to the company as independent contractors. Even under Table A, therefore, the directors have a largely unsupervised freedom to fix their income by using this contractual approach.

Where the power to pay remuneration is expressly set out in the company's articles, as it is in Table A, it would seem that it can be made and is not recoverable from the director even though the company is insolvent. There is no requirement, fraud apart, that directors' remuneration for genuine services rendered to the company be paid only from distributable profits (*Re Halt Garage* (1964) Ltd [1982] 3 All ER 1016.)

## The Greenbury Code of Practice

As regards non-statutory developments, the Greenbury Committee's recommended code of practice requires the setting up of a remuneration committee of non-executive directors only to decide the policy to be adopted on executive directors' remuneration, pension rights and compensation for loss of office and the actual remuneration of each individual director. Admittedly, the code only specifically applies to listed companies and the only sanction is against listed companies since the Stock Exchange has agreed to enforce the Greenbury recommendations through the Listing Rules. But the principles underlying the code apply to all companies. The sanction for non-listed companies is basically bad publicity arising from excessive remuneration for directors, in terms of their relationship with their shareholders rather than the public at large. So far as legislation was concerned, there was no requirement to disclose the actual package being received by directors (but see statutory requirements on disclosure below).

Members do have a right to inspect a copy of a contract of service between a director and the company or its subsidiary. The contract must, under CA 1985, s 318, be available at the register office or principal place of business – not convenient for all shareholders – unless the contract is one that the company can terminate within the next 12 months without compensation. It is also worth nothing again that a director can be given a service contract of up to five years without member approval: this does not assist in the matter of high severance payments when the company terminates the contract before it is due to expire.

The Greenbury code contains a number of provisions to assist disclosure. Importantly the remuneration committee's report is to be attached to the annual report and accounts or incorporated therein. The report will, in particular, disclose full details of the package to be received by each named director, e.g. basic salary, benefits in kind, annual bonus and long-term incentive schemes including share options.

The code does not require that the report be voted upon by the shareholders, but states that the remuneration committee should give annual consideration to whether it should be and minute the conclusions. A vote is required on long-term incentive schemes on the basis that they may lead to a dilution of capital. In addition, the chairman of the committee is to report to the shareholders at the AGM accounting for the relevant decisions on the package disclosed and answering questions on them.

In order to avoid large payments when a director leaves, the code recommends one year or less as the normal notice period in service contracts. It accepts that this may initially at least lead to insecurity, so a two-year period may be acceptable, and even three years for a newly-appointed director with the term reducing after that.

## The Hampel Committee

A further committee on corporate governance under the chairmanship of Sir Ronald Hampel (the Hampel Committee) gave its preliminary report in August 1997. Technically it was set up to review the earlier recommendations of the Cadbury Report on corporate governance for listed companies but took in Greenbury while it was at it. The final Hampel Report was published on 28 January 1998. Hampel states that smaller companies should not enjoy a lighter corporate governance code. The Committee is of the opinion that the principles should be the same for all businesses, especially as shareholders often need more assurance about smaller companies. Beyond that and in terms of directors:

- the Committee generally supports performance-related remuneration but rewards should not be 'excessive';
- the Committee does not recommend that non-executive directors should not participate in share-option schemes, but does consider that the payment of non-executive remuneration by means of shares would compromise their independence;
- there is agreement with Greenbury in that companies should aim to reduce the term of directors' contracts to one year or less;
- directors' service contracts should include detailed provisions regarding early termination rather than relying on directors making claims for damages;
- the Committee endorses the setting up of remuneration committees and is of the view that these should consist solely of independent non-executive directors. The determination of the remuneration of non-executive directors should be delegated to a sub-committee of the full board;
- the Committee suggests a more simplified method of disclosure of individual remuneration packages in the annual report and accounts, combined with a more informative statement about the general principles of the company's report.
- the Committee agrees that shareholder approval should be sought for new long-term incentive plans but not necessarily for the remuneration committee's report.

The government, while welcoming the Hampel Report, seems adverse to the principle of self-regulation in the relevant areas. On 4 March 1998 the government announced the publication of a consultation document entitled *'Modern Company Law for a Competitive Economy'*, which sets out the government's proposals for a major review of company law. It is, therefore, likely that some of the self-regulatory principles stated above will end up on the statute book impacting mainly but not entirely on public companies. The review is some way off since the government has stated that it is a matter for a subsequent Parliament.

## Listed companies

Listed companies are required under a new listing rule to disclose in the annual report and accounts how they have applied the above principles and complied with the detailed provisions of what has become known as the Combined Code, i.e. a combination of Greenbury and Hampel.

## Statutory requirements on disclosure of remuneration

New requirements for the disclosure of directors' remuneration were introduced by the Company Accounts (Disclosure of Directors' Emoluments) Regulations 1997 (SI 1997/570). They apply to all companies listed and unlisted for accounting periods ending on or after 31 March 1997.

The Regulations amend provisions in Part I of Sch 6 to the Companies Act 1985 relating to the disclosure of directors' emoluments or other benefits in the notes to a company's annual accounts in respect of any financial year. They also amend s 246 of the 1985 Act as amended by the Companies Act 1985 (Accounts of Small and Medium-Sized Companies and Minor Accounting Amendments) Regulations 1997 (SI 1997/220). Under the Regulations:

- companies will be required to show aggregate details of directors' remuneration under four headings – emoluments (i.e. basic salary and annual bonuses); gains made on the exercise of share options; gains made under long-term incentive schemes; and company contributions to money purchase pension schemes. Small companies' full accounts can show merely the total of the aggregate amounts;
- where the aggregate remuneration exceeds or is equal to £200,000, companies will be required to show also the figures attributable to the highest paid director and the amount of his accrued retirement benefits if he is a member of a defined benefit pension scheme, i.e. a pension scheme in which the rules specify the benefits to be paid, and the scheme must be financed accordingly;
- companies will no longer be required to show the number of directors whose emoluments fell within each band of £5,000.

Thus for listed companies the Regulations bring the Companies Act into line with Greenbury and the Listing Rules. For unlisted companies they streamline the former disclosure requirements.

### Exceptions for unlisted companies

The above requirements apply to companies listed on the Stock Exchange and on the Alternative Investment Market. Unlisted companies must comply with the requirements with two important exceptions:

- unlisted companies do not have to disclose the amount of gains made when directors exercise share options. They have merely to disclose the number of directors who have exercised their share options;
- unlisted companies do not have to disclose the net value of any assets that comprise shares which would otherwise be disclosed in respect of assets received under long-term incentive schemes. Instead they disclose the number of directors in respect of whose qualifying service shares were received or receivable under long-term incentive schemes.

## Waiver of remuneration

If in, say, difficult times the directors wish to waive all or any of their remuneration, then in order to protect the company from possible claims, for example by personal representatives following the death of a director who had waived, the waiver should be absolute and by irrevocable deed since the company will not normally be able to show that it gave consideration for the waiver. A mere minute of the waiver following a resolution at a board meeting is not enough.

## Expenses

Regulation 83 provides that the directors may be paid all travelling, hotel and other expenses properly incurred by them in attending meetings of the directors, general meetings and class meetings or otherwise in connection with the carrying out of their duties.

## Pensions

The company has implied power to pay pensions to employees only and not to directors unless the articles so provide. Regulation 87 allows the directors to provide benefits, e.g. by means of payment of pensions and insurance, for former directors of the company or its subsidiaries and for their families and dependants. They may also, both during and after a particular director ceases to hold office, contribute to any fund or pay premiums for the purchase or provision of any such benefit.

## Compensation for loss of office

Such compensation can be paid but s 312 provides that the payment must be disclosed to the members and approved by ordinary (or written) resolution. For the purposes of proper disclosure 'members' includes those not entitled to vote, as is usually the case with preference shares unless their dividends are in arrear. Approval is, of course, only by voting members. Unless this procedure is followed, the director concerned holds the money on trust for the company and must repay the sum involved to the company (s 313(2)). A director is also under a duty to disclose compensation for loss of office made in connection with a merger or acquisition of the company. In a merger, disclosure to members and their approval is the same in terms of procedure as required by ss 312 and 313 above. In an acquisition, disclosure and approval concern only those members whose shares are the subject of the offer to acquire (or takeover). Failure to carry out the necessary procedures makes the director concerned liable to a fine and, furthermore, he holds the compensation on trust for those who have sold their shares under the offer and must bear the expense of distributing that sum pro rata. He cannot deduct that expense from the compensation received.

There is a tax exemption in regard to the first £30,000 of these golden handshake payments.

## What is regarded as compensation?

A payment will be treated as compensation for loss of office only if the company is under no legal obligation to pay it. Thus a payment of damages to a director who is dismissed in breach of his service contract or who is removed from office whether settled out of court or by the court does not require disclosure to or approval by the members – nor does a pension (s 316(3)).

In addition, an amount which a director receives under the terms of his service contract on his resignation or removal from office in terms of severance pay is not treated as compensation for loss of office because the company is obliged by the contract to pay it when the resignation or removal takes place and no member approval is required at that time nor when the board makes the service contract (*Taupo Totara Timber Co Ltd* v *Rowe* [1977] 3 All ER 123).

Finally, there are disclosure requirements in terms of notes to the accounts in regard to compensation for loss of office under Sch 6 to the CA 1985, as there are in regard to other payments in the above section. Of particular interest is the Sch 6, para 1(4) requirement to disclose sums paid to a director on accepting office, introduced by the CA 1989. Thus 'Golden Hellos' as well as 'Golden Handshakes' are now covered.

## Contracts with sole member/directors

As we have seen, under s 322B of the CA 1985 (as inserted by SI 1992/1699) a private company limited by shares or guarantee with only one member who is also a director which enters into a contract with that member/director shall ensure that it is in writing or that the terms of the contract are set out in a written memorandum or in the minutes of the first board meeting following the making of the contract. This does not apply to contracts made in the ordinary course of business as where the member/director is a trader and regularly sells goods to the company. Failure to comply means that the company and any officer in default are liable to a fine but the validity of the contract is not affected. Shadow directors are included.

# TERMINATION OF THE OFFICE OF DIRECTOR

The office of director may terminate for a number of reasons. These are set out below.

## Expiration of the period of office

The articles usually provide what the period of office of a director shall be. Table A, reg 73 provides that at the first annual general meeting all the directors shall retire from office and at every subsequent AGM one-third of the directors who are subject to retirement by rotation or if their number is not three or a multiple of three the number nearest to one-third shall retire from office; but if there is only one director who is subject to retirement by rotation he shall retire. Thus reg 73 deals with the position where there is only one director, as the law permits in the case of a private company. It was held in *Re David Moseley & Sons Ltd* [1939] 2 All ER 791, where the court was interpreting an article such as reg 73, that if there are only two directors one must retire each year.

The directors retiring will be those longest in office since their last election. Difficulties may arise in the early years of a company's life as where the first directors were all appointed at the same time. If this is the case those retiring must, under reg 74, be ascertained by agreement among themselves or, that failing, by drawing lots.

Regulation 80 provides that a retiring director shall be eligible for re-election and reg 75 provides that if the office vacated by a director on *retirement by rotation* is not filled the retiring director shall, if he still offers himself for re-election, be deemed to be elected unless the meeting expressly resolves not to fill the vacancy or unless the resolution for the re-election of such director has been put to the meeting and lost.

Regulation 75 does not apply to those coming up for election following the filling by the board of a casual vacancy or the appointment of additional directors. Regulation 80 applies here and unless such persons are actually elected by the members they vacate office at the end of the meeting. There is no automatic deemed election.

Unless the articles deal differently with the question of age, a director who is due to retire by rotation at, for example, the 1997 AGM but reaches the age of 70 in 1996, prior to the AGM in that year, will vacate office at the 1996 AGM and if re-elected will fall to be included in the directors retiring by rotation in 1997. If re-elected this time it will be until the next time he retires by rotation. All appointments would have to be by the special notice procedure (*see below*).

It has already been noted that a person appointed by the directors to fill casual vacancies or as additional directors must stand for re-election at the next AGM and does not count in the one-third retiring but is additional to that number. Furthermore, the managing director and other executive directors do not, under reg 84, retire by rotation and do not count in ascertaining the number of directors one-third of whom must retire.

## Where the AGM has been dispensed with

Private companies may by elective resolution dispense with the holding of the AGM. Where this has been done there is obviously serious effect upon the type of retirement provisions set out in Table A. As regards this situation it is worth noting that the 1985 Act imposes no general requirement to retire by rotation at the AGM or otherwise. It is, therefore, possible to remove all references to the AGM from the articles including those relating to retirement by rotation. This can be done by a special resolution at a general meeting of members or by a unanimous written resolution in private companies. It is essential to do this, otherwise the elective resolution will be ineffective since part of the company's constitution, i.e. the articles, will still require the AGM to be held.

Once the relevant clauses have been removed, there would be no need for the directors to retire at all – probably a welcome bit of deregulation for the smaller private company – bearing in mind that all directors can be removed from office under a provision in the articles if there is one or, in any event, under s 303 where an ordinary resolution at a general meeting of members is required (*see below*). This could be used with particular directors if difficulties in relationships arose and a resignation was not forthcoming. The board has power to call an extraordinary general meeting at any time. As we shall see, the written resolution procedure is not available for removal under s 303.

Alternatively, companies wishing to dispense with the AGM requirement but still wanting retirement by rotation would have to insert an article under which retirement by rotation was triggered in some other way, e.g. by a date, say one-third to retire on 31 March each year. Re-election could then be by written resolution with no requirement for a general meeting of any kind though it should be borne in mind that under s 381B a copy of any intended written resolution must be sent to the company's auditors. However, the resolution is not invalidated if this is not done, though there are criminal sanctions in terms of a fine on directors and the secretary if they knowingly fail to send the resolution to the auditors at or before the time when the resolution is supplied to a member for signature. The auditors receive the resolution as a matter of information only. This is the result of the Deregulation (Resolutions of Private Companies) Order 1996 (SI 1996/1471).

## Removal – under statute

Under s 303 a company may by ordinary resolution remove a director from office before the expiration of the period of office regardless of the way in which he was appointed and notwithstanding anything in the articles or any agreement with him. Special notice *to the company* is required of the intention to move the resolution.

Special notice is defined by s 379 as being notice of the intention to move the resolution which the company receives, normally through its secretary, at least 28 days before the meeting at which it is to be moved. However, if after the date of receiving the notice a meeting is called for a date 28 days or less after the notice has been given, the notice is regarded in law as properly given even though it is not given within the time required (s 379(3)). Basically this provision means that when a member (not necessarily the one who served the special notice) stands to propose the removing resolution the company must have been on notice of his intention to do that for at least 28 days. On receipt of special notice, the company must immediately send a copy to the director concerned (s 304).

The director concerned is allowed to make representations to the members by circulating these with the notice of the meeting at which his removal is to be proposed. Where it is received too late or not sent through the default of the company, the director may require the representations to be read out at the meeting and where this is so he still has a general right to be heard orally and is not confined to a discussion of the material in the statement.

The statement need not be sent out or read at the meeting if the company, or any other person who might be affected, applies to the court and the court finds that the rights given by the above provisions are being used to obtain needless publicity for defamatory matter. The court is given specific power to order the director to pay the company's costs on the application even though the director did not appear before the court when it was heard, in the sense of submitting an oral or written defence (*see* s 304(5)). Presumably the court could also award costs to 'any other person affected' under its general jurisdiction to award costs though there would be difficulty where the director was not before the court in the sense described above. It should be noted that because of the existence of such rights the written resolution procedure already referred to is not available as an alternative to the ordinary resolution required by s 303.

If the director is in fact removed at the meeting, the vacancy so created may be filled at the meeting – provided the special notice procedure has been followed in regard to the person appointed. If the vacancy is not filled at the meeting, it can be filled as a casual vacancy by the board. Any person appointed in place of a director removed under s 303 shall be deemed to hold office for as long as the director who has been removed would have held it and to retire when he would have retired. Under s 303(5) nothing is to deprive a director who is removed of any action he may have for dismissal, as where he has a service contract appointing him for a specified period which has not expired.

### Restrictions on the right to remove a director

At first sight s 303 appears to give any member of a company who is not satisfied with the way in which a director is carrying out his duties the right to ask the members as a whole to consider passing an ordinary resolution in general meeting to remove him. Let us suppose, as would be usual, that John Smith, a member of the company, chooses the AGM for the purpose of removal of a director (or directors). Let us further suppose that he serves special notice on the company secretary in the proper way stating his intention to propose a resolution to remove the director (or directors). Is the board required in law to place the resolution to remove the director (or directors) on the agenda of the AGM and invite the members to vote on it at the AGM? According to the decision of the High Court in *Pedley* v *Inland Waterways Association Ltd* [1977] 1 All ER 209 the answer is no unless, that is, John Smith or members joining with him can satisfy the requirements of s 376 (see later in this chapter). Basically this section provides that members representing not less than one-twentieth of the total voting rights of all the members or 100 or more members holding shares in the company on which has been paid up an average of not less than £100 per member can, by making a written requisition to the company, compel the board in effect to put a particular item of business up at the AGM.

Although the *Pedley* case was concerned with removal at the AGM, the position of the individual member who wishes to remove a director between AGMs also faces difficulty. The board is not required by law to hold an extraordinary general meeting to consider the removal of a director. The members have the right to requisition an EGM, but to do so must comply with s 368 (*see further* later in this chapter). Basically the requisition can be made only by a member or members of the company holding not less than one-tenth of such of the company's paid-up capital as carries voting rights at general meetings of the company.

Thus it would seem that the rights given by s 303 and indeed s 391 (removal of auditors) are much more restricted than might have been thought. In addition, the existence of weighted voting rights may make s 303 ineffective. This can be achieved by a special provision in the articles as in *Bushell* v *Faith* [1969] 1 All ER 1002. The company had adopted Table A as its articles but had inserted a special article 9 which provided that in the event of a resolution being proposed at a general meeting for the removal of a director any shares held by that director should carry not one vote per share, which is the standard Table A provision, but three votes per share. In the *Bushell* case the three members owned 100 shares each and two of them, who were sisters, tried to remove the third, who was their brother, from the board under what is now s 303. The sisters followed the proper special notice procedure and at the meeting cast 200 votes in favour of the brother's removal. He then claimed to cast 300 votes on the matter. The House of Lords eventually decided that special article 9 applied so that the brother was not removed. It should be noted that while Table A does not itself contain weighted voting rights it does allow them by providing in reg 2 that 'any share may be issued with such rights or restrictions as the company may by ordinary resolution determine'.

It is useful, therefore, in, say, a conversion of a partnership to a private company to include weighted voting rights on the lines of *Bushell* in the articles of the company. Expulsion of a general partner from management is in general terms a ground on which he can seek dissolution of the firm in order to recover his capital. Once he becomes a director he can be removed from management under s 303 with no right to recover his capital (the value of his shares) from the members or the company (but *see below*). Weighted voting rights will protect the directors from removal. All the directors must be given the same weighted voting rights and it is vital to ensure that certain of the member/directors cannot, by getting together against one of their number, change the articles to withdraw the weighted voting rights prior to instituting removal procedures. The sisters in *Bushell* could not, as an example, alter the articles having only 200 of the 300 votes in general meeting. A special resolution to change the articles requires a majority of 75 per cent of those present and voting in person or by proxy at a meeting of the company or alternatively, in private companies, a unanimous written resolution.

## Removal – under the articles

The power to remove directors given by the CA 1985 is a useful but somewhat drawn-out procedure and the directors of companies may wish to exercise the power of director removal themselves. A suitable provision in the articles can achieve this so that removal is under the rules of the company's constitution and not under the CA 1985. Such a provision does not appear in Table A and would have to be added. The provision could, for example, provide that a simple majority of the directors be given power to terminate forthwith the directorship of any other director by notice in writing. The power to remove a director in the articles is effective even if the directors who exercise the power have acted with wrong motives, as in *Lee* v *Chou Wen Hsian* [1984] 1 WLR 1202, where a director who was asking for information about the company's dealings and not receiving all the information he wanted asked the secretary to convene a board meeting but was removed by the other directors two days before the meeting under a power in the articles. A removal under s 303 would seem effective in a similar situation.

The fact that the directors have a power of removal would not prevent a member or members with sufficient shareholding from seeking to raise the issue of removal in general meeting under s 303 since this section can be used notwithstanding anything in the articles of the company. However, where the power is given to the board by the articles it will be appreciated that a members' resolution will not be required nor will the director have any rights of representation unless the article gives them – which would defeat the purpose of a quick removal.

## Removal of a director/member – capital recovery

A major problem for a member director who is removed from the board under either s 303 or a provision in the articles is that the person concerned is denied a say in management although his share capital is left in the company. In the smaller family company, for example, it may not be easy to sell the shares outside and the other members may not be prepared, or have the resources, to pay for them. A company may of course purchase its own shares (*see* Chapter 19) but the rest of the board would have to be willing to initiate the necessary procedures. If it is intended to remove a director member from the board, it is advisable to arrange for the purchase of the relevant shares either by the company or by other members at a fair price normally fixed by the auditors since, in the private company with which we are in practice concerned, there is obviously no investment exchange listing or quotation. Failure to do this could lead to legal proceedings by the director to wind the company up in order to recover his capital (*see Ebrahimi* v *Westbourne Galleries* [1972] 2 All ER 492). In more recent times the more versatile remedy of 'unfair prejudice' has been used since this does not involve the winding-up of the company. Section 459 provides that a member (among others) may petition the court on the grounds that the affairs of the company are being, or have been or will be conducted in a manner unfairly prejudicial to the interests of its members generally or some part of its members, including the petitioner himself.

It may be thought that when a director is removed from the board he is prejudiced as a director but not as a member. However, there have been a number of successful petitions by removed directors under s 459 because the courts have consistently held that it was within the 'interest' of a member of a private company that he might legitimately have a place on the board (*see Re A Company (No 00477 of 1986)* [1986] PCC 372). Thus the section is available in removal cases. Among the relief which the court can give is to order the purchase of the removed director's shares at a fair price either by the other members or by the company itself, in which case the court would also authorise a reduction of capital.

## Vacation of office

A director vacates office in the following ways.

(a) Under a provision in the articles. Regulation 81 of Table A provides that the office of director shall be vacated if the director:
   (i) ceases to be a director by reason of any provision of the 1985 Act, e.g. removal under s 303; or becomes prohibited by law from being a director as where he is disqualified by the court; or
   (ii) becomes bankrupt or makes any arrangement or composition with *all* his creditors; or
   (iii) is or may be suffering from mental disorder *and* has either been admitted to hospital for treatment under the Mental Health Act 1983 or the court has made an order for the appointment of a receiver with regard to his property or affairs; or
   (iv) resigns his office by notice to the company. Regulation 81 does not require notice in writing so that oral notice at a board meeting would be effective. Under reg 81 there is no need for the resignation to be accepted by the board:

it is enough for the board to make formal note of it and minute it. Vacation of office will take place when notice is received by the company or at such later time as the notice may specify; or

(v) has, for more than six months, been absent without the permission of the directors from meetings of the directors held during that period *and* the directors resolve that his office shall be vacated. Under Table A one counts from the last meeting attended, not from the first meeting missed. Also, the provisions cover involuntary absence, as where the director is ill.

(b) The matter of vacation of office for failure to obtain a share qualification, if any, and exceeding the age limit of 70 laid down by s 293 (subject to the articles) have already been considered.

(c) A company's articles may modify or add to the circumstances in Table A, e.g. a company may include an automatic removal where a director loses a licence or permission to act from a regulatory body which is essential to his or her duties e.g. where the director concerned is forbidden to act by the Financial Services Authority in regard to the giving of investment advice which is the business of the company.

## The effect of insolvency proceedings

The effect of such proceedings on the directors is given below.

### Liquidation of the company

In a compulsory liquidation, following a petition to the court, or in a members' or creditors' voluntary winding-up, the appointment of a liquidator causes the directors' powers to cease (s 103 of the Insolvency Act 1986). They cannot bind the company with further liabilities and should resign since technically they remain directors. Although the matter is not beyond doubt, it is probable that the liquidator can accept their resignations. Resigning will not free them from any liabilities or obligations which they may have but it will at least mean that after five years following the date of resignation they will not have to include the failed company in their lists of past directorships (*see* later in this chapter).

In a compulsory liquidation the court will normally appoint the Official Receiver as provisional liquidator but, in both a members' and creditors' voluntary winding-up, the liquidation is commenced by resolution of the members and these resolutions can be passed without a liquidator having been appointed. In the interim, until the appointment of a liquidator, the directors' powers do not cease, but they can only exercise them if the court approves by order *except* that they can – under s 114 of the 1986 Act:

(a) ensure compliance with ss 98 and 99 of the 1986 Act in terms of the holding of meetings of creditors and the preparation of a statement of affairs where the winding-up is a creditors' winding-up; and

(b) in both a members' and a creditors' voluntary winding-up, dispose of perishable goods and other items likely to diminish in value unless they are disposed of quickly, and do all such things as may be necessary to protect the assets of the company.

If they exercise any other powers without permission of the court, they commit an offence for which they can be prosecuted before magistrates and fined.

On the appointment of a liquidator in a members' voluntary winding-up, that liquidator or the members of the company in general meeting may agree to the continuance of the directors' powers (s 91 of the 1986 Act). In a creditors' voluntary winding-up, the liquidator, or the liquidation committee, or the creditors if there is no such committee, may agree to the continuance of the directors' powers (s 103 of the 1986 Act) but this would be rare. There are no provisions for the continuance of the directors' powers in a compulsory winding-up.

### Administrative receivership

On the appointment of an administrative receiver, the powers of the directors effectively cease. They are not dismissed, however, though the administrative receiver is entitled to continue the company's business and realise its property without interference by the board (*Gomba Holdings UK Ltd* v *Homan* [1986] 3 All ER 94). There may be rather special situations in which the court will allow the directors to exercise their powers, as where they wish to sue the receiver's appointor, e.g. a bank, where the board believes that the bank's failure to honour an alleged loan commitment to the company has caused its present difficulties, leading to the receiver's appointment (*Newhart Developments Ltd* v *Co-operative Commercial Bank Ltd* [1978] 2 All ER 896, where the court allowed such a claim by the board on behalf of the company).

Under s 235 of the 1986 Act the directors have an obligation to co-operate with an administrative receiver under the penalty of prosecution and a fine if they do not. Continued refusal to co-operate can result in a fine on a daily basis.

### Administrator

Directors' powers are suspended during the administration. They must give way to the administrator and, in addition, the administrator may remove them from office (s 14 of the 1986 Act). However, they are not dismissed merely by the appointment of an administrator and retain some residual powers on the lines of the *Newhart* case. They retain their CA 1985 duties in regard to the keeping of records and the filing of accounts and returns. Companies Registration Office has not in the past required the submission of accounts and returns during an administration but current practice of the CRO should be obtained. The administrator has no statutory obligations in terms of the submission of accounts and returns.

### Notifying changes

The procedure for notifying changes in the directorate will be considered later when dealing with statutory records.

## DISQUALIFICATION AND PERSONAL LIABILITY UNDER STATUTE

This section is based mainly on the provisions of the Company Directors Disqualification Act 1986 (CDDA 1986) and section references are to that Act unless otherwise indicated. Certain sections of the Act contain provisions under which directors may be disqualified from holding office but there is no personal liability for the debts of the company. In other sections there is a power in the court to disqualify and also to impose personal liability for the debts of the company on the director(s) concerned. The following headings and their supporting material reflect this division. Personal liability can also arise under the CA 1985 in regard, for example, to the signing of cheques and orders for goods and, under the Insolvency Act 1986, in connection with what are known as 'Phoenix' companies. These areas of liability are also considered in this section.

Two other general points are worthy of consideration as follows. The High Court decided in *Re Seagull Manufacturing Co (No 2)* [1994] 2 All ER 767 that a disqualification order may be made against a director regardless of his or her nationality and current residence and domicile. Furthermore, the conduct leading to the disqualification need not have occurred within the jurisdiction. In other words, a UK company can be run badly from abroad. The director concerned was a British subject but at all material times was resident and domiciled in the Channel Islands. Nevertheless, he could be disqualified for unfitness (*see below*).

The High Court also decided in *Re Pamstock Ltd* [1994] 1 BCLC 716 that a director who was also the company secretary could be disqualified as much for failure to perform his duties as the secretary as for failure to perform those of a director. There is no power to disqualify a secretary who is not also a director.

It is also worth noting that it is not a defence to an application for a disqualification order that the director concerned was not an active participant in the business of the company. Thus in *Re Park House Properties Ltd* [1997] 2 BCLC 530 the High Court disqualified three directors as unfit by reason of irresponsible trading leading to insolvency, even though they were inactive in the running of the business. The company was run by a husband whose wife, son and daughter were also directors and shareholders, but played no part in the running of the business and did not receive salary or fees. Having disqualified the husband for four years, Neuberger J disqualified the other three directors for two years, in each case, saying that a director has legal duties and could not escape liability by saying that he or she knew nothing about what was going on.

Directors may be disqualified for breach of health and safety law. Disqualification is not confined to situations of breach of general administrative requirements.

## DISQUALIFICATION ONLY

There are five situations to consider. These are set out below.

### Persistent breaches of companies legislation (ss 3 and 5)

The court may disqualify a person from acting as a director for persistently failing to file returns, accounts, or other documents or notices which companies legislation requires to be sent or given to the Registrar of Companies at Companies Registration Office. Thus failure to file a company's annual return, accounts or other documents, e.g. copies of special resolutions, could begin the process of disqualification for 'persistent default'. The Department of Trade and Industry has – in the name of the Secretary of State – the primary responsibility for applying for a disqualification order. It is not necessary for the director concerned to have been convicted of a filing offence. If the

DTI feels that there has been persistent default even though there have been no convictions, it may make application, in general to the High Court, for a disqualification order. However, s 3 provides that persistent default will be conclusively presumed if the director concerned has in fact been convicted of failing to file at least three relevant returns or documents within a five-year period. The convictions can be on the same occasion. If a director is charged on the same day with three or more filing offences and is convicted on three or more, he is available for disqualification if the DTI applies, normally to the Magistrates' Court which made the convictions under the jurisdiction given to it by s 5. The presumption also applies where three or more default orders have been made against the director concerned in a five-year period (or on the same occasion). These default orders are, in effect, compliance orders made under the Companies Act 1985 by the court on the application, for example, of the Registrar. The order requires the directors actually to carry out a requirement placed upon them by the CA 1985 and, for example, s 242 of the CA 1985 allows application to be made for an order requiring defaulting directors to file the company's accounts. There is no minimum period of disqualification but the maximum is five years. It does not involve any personal liability in the director for the company's debts nor is it necessary for the company to be insolvent as it is under some of the heads of disqualification.

## Disqualification for unfitness (ss 6, 7, and 9 and Sch I)

The court *must* disqualify a director (or shadow director) on the application of the Secretary of State through the medium of the DTI, or the Official Receiver if it is satisfied:

(a) that he is, or has been, a director of a company which has at any time been insolvent (while he was a director or subsequently); and
(b) that his conduct as a director of that company (either taken alone or taken together with his conduct as a director of any other company or companies) makes him unfit to be concerned in the management of a company.

Insolvency for this purpose includes the making of an administration order in relation to the company, the appointment of an administrative receiver and liquidations where the company's assets are insufficient to pay its debts and other liabilities including the expenses of winding-up. Winding-up expenses can be substantial so a company may be insolvent for this purpose even though the assets are enough to cover the balance sheet liabilities.

The minimum period of disqualification is two years and the maximum is 15 years. Section 6 is the only disqualification section to carry a minimum period: the court cannot give less if unfitness is proved. As evidence of unfitness the court can take into account a person's conduct as a director of a company even if it is not the insolvent one. Also the word 'subsequently' in the section is in no way limited so that someone who was a director of a company for, say, two months in 1992 could potentially be disqualified if the company became insolvent in 1997.

It was decided in *Secretary of State for Trade and Industry* v *Arif, The Times*, 25 March 1996 that a director who had not been able to act as such for some 2½ years while disqualification proceedings were pending could not set off that period against the disqualification period the court finally decided on.

The application to the court for a disqualification order has to be made within two years of the date when the company became insolvent, though the court may extend the period. The two-year period runs, therefore, from the commencement of insolvent liquidation or the date of an administration order being made by the court or the appointment of an administrative receiver.

The DTI is not bound to make an application to the court unless it appears to be in the public interest and even if an application is made the court is not obliged to make an order unless it is satisfied that the director is unfit.

Schedule 1 to the 1986 Act sets out matters to be taken into account when determining unfitness. The Schedule reflects the experience of the government's insolvency service and the comments and experience of practitioners. It is concerned with the way in which the directors have managed the company and includes matters usually found following incompetent management such as failure to keep accounting records or prepare annual accounts, failure to make annual returns and to keep statutory registers. Schedule 1 is split into two parts: Part 1, which contains among other things the items referred to above and is applicable in all cases and Part II, which contains additional matters applicable where the company is insolvent. This is to take care of disqualification for unfitness after a DTI inspection where the company is not necessarily insolvent so that only Part I reasons for unfitness would be available. Part II contains among other things matters found, or arising, in an insolvency, e.g. failure to submit a statement of affairs to the insolvency practitioner and/or failure to co-operate with him or deliver up to the company's property.

As regards pleas of mitigation by directors in connection with disqualification, the case law would suggest that the following have sometimes been successful:

(a) reliance on professional advice (but see *Re Firedart Ltd below*);
(b) reliance on the professional directors: thus where a board contains, say, a qualified accountant, the others being business amateurs, the court may excuse them while disqualifying the accountant though the court will not in any case excuse sheer incompetence;
(c) the effect on employees may be relevant in the sense that it will be difficult to run the company if the director is disqualified so that jobs may be lost.

There are no provisions in this section relating to personal liability for the debts of the company.

**As regards disqualification under the 'unfairness' head, the Companies Court has stressed, in particular, the relevance of failure to keep proper accounting records when consideration is being given to the disqualification of a director, together with the responsibility for keeping those records where accountants were also involved with the company as the following case illustrates.**

### Re Firedart Ltd, Official Receiver v Fairall [1994] 2 BCLC 340

Mr Alan John Fairall was a director of Firedart whose business was that of an advertising agency. It commenced trading in 1984 and went into insolvent liquidation in 1988. The Official Receiver applied under s 6 of the Company Directors Disqualification Act 1986 (duty of court to disqualify unfit directors of insolvent companies) for Mr Fairall to be disqualified as a director. The main allegations against Mr Fairall were:

- failure to maintain accounting records as required by s 221 of the Companies Act 1985;
- trading while insolvent;
- the receipt of remuneration and benefits in kind which exceeded the level which the company could be expected to bear; and
- improper retention of monies due to the Customs and Excise, the Revenue and DSS.

In disqualifying Mr Fairall for six years, Mrs Justice Arden stated how essential it was for officers of a company to ensure that proper accounting records were maintained. She said:

When directors do not maintain accounting records in accordance with the very specific requirements of s 221 of the Companies Act 1985, they cannot know their company's financial position with accuracy. There is, therefore, a risk that the situation is much worse than they know and that creditors will suffer in consequence. Directors who permit this situation to arise must expect the conclusion to be drawn in an appropriate case that they are in consequence not fit to be concerned in the management of a company.

Also raised was the issue of responsibility for maintenance of accounting records. On this the judge said:

Mr Fairall states that the company's accountants maintained its accounting records from 31 January 1987. The accountants, however, say that they were not responsible for writing up the books prior to August 1987. However that may be, I accept (the) submission on behalf of the Official Receiver that it was Mr Fairall who was responsible for providing information to the accountants to enable the accounting records to be maintained accurately and up to date. I further find that he did not provide all the necessary information and explanations, that there is no excuse for his failure to do so and that therefore he is responsible for the deficiencies in the accounting records even after the firm of accountants had been instructed to carry out the bookkeeping function for the company. According to Terence Anthony Price, Certified Accountant, a partner in or proprietor of Firedart's accountants, the flow of information from Mr Fairall was 'spasmodic' and Mr Fairall was always too busy to provide any necessary explanations. I accept this evidence.

The judge, referring to the tariff set out in *Re Sevenoaks Stationers (Retail) Ltd* [1991] BCLC 325 at 328 decided that in the circumstances the middle bracket of disqualification, i.e. six to ten years, should apply because this was a serious case but did not merit the top bracket, i.e. over 10 years.

It is of interest that the court has once again affirmed that it is the duty of the directors to keep and supply accounting information and that the duty cannot be avoided merely by employing accountants.

*Comment:* The necessity for directors to make use of and understand the company's accounts was also stressed in *Re Continental Assurance Co of London plc* [1996] 28 LS Gaz 29. The High Court disqualified a corporate financier from acting as a director for three years because in his role as a non-executive director he failed to read the company's accounts (which he would clearly have understood) and so did not discover illegal loans made to acquire the company's own shares constituting illegal financial assistance contrary to s 151 of the Companies Act 1985.

### Disqualification after investigation of the company (s 8)

If it appears to the Secretary of State through the medium of the DTI:

(a) from a report made by inspectors under s 437 of the CA 1985 (provision for inspectors to make interim and final reports); or

(b) from information or documents obtained under s 447 (power to require production of documents) or s 448 (regarding entry and search of premises); or

(c) from information or documents obtained under other legislation, such as s 105 of the Financial Services Act 1986 (powers of investigation given to the Financial Services Authority),

that it is in the public interest that a disqualification order should be made against a person who is or has been a director or shadow director of any company (and thus not only the company concerned in the DTI investigations), then the DTI may apply to the court for a disqualification order. The company need not be insolvent. The court is not bound to make an order even if it finds unfitness and Sch 1 applies. There is no minimum period of disqualification. The maximum is 15 years. There are no provisions in s 8 relating to personal liability for the company's debts.

### Disqualification following conviction of an indictable offence (s 2)

The offence must be in connection with the promotion, formation, or management or liquidation of a company or with the receivership or management of a company's property. The power to disqualify would apply to directors but is obviously much wider and applies to 'any person' involved in misconduct in connection with companies which leads to a conviction. Application for a disqualification order may be made by the DTI but others, including past or present members, or creditors of any company involved may do so.

There is no minimum period. The maximum is five years if the conviction is by a Magistrates Court and 15 years if the conviction is in a Crown Court.

There are no provisions relating to personal liability for the company's debts.

### Disqualification following the offence of fraudulent trading (s 4)

The court may make a disqualification order, e.g. on the application of the DTI, if it appears that an offence has been committed by the person concerned under s 458 of the CA 1985 (crime of fraudulent trading) as defined by s 213 of the Insolvency Act 1986 (*see below*). It is not necessary that the person concerned should have been prosecuted to conviction nor is it necessary that the company should be in liquidation as it is if there is to be civil liability for the debts of the company following fraudulent trading. There is no minimum period but the maximum is 15 years. There are no provisions for personal liability if *only the crime* of fraudulent trading is in issue.

### Directors' undertakings not to act

It was held by the High Court in *Re Blackspur Group plc* [1997] 1 WLR 710 that an undertaking by a director not to act as such or in the management of a company was not acceptable to the court except possibly in exceptional circumstances. In *Secretary of State for Trade and Industry* v *Cleland* [1997] 1 BCLC 437 the High Court did grant a stay of disqualification proceedings in return for an undertaking from a director that he would not work as a director in future. There were, however, special circumstances in that the director was 60 years of age and in poor health.

## Disqualification of unfit directors – shorter procedure

Following Practice Notes from the Chancery Division (*see* [1996] 1 All ER 442 and 445) a director can agree the period of disqualification with the DTI and avoid a lengthy trial. The ban will be imposed by court order in summary proceedings provided the judge does not want proceedings to be brought to trial. There is also a plea in the Practice Direction for legislation to allow a ban to be agreed with the DTI and imposed without a court order in appropriate cases, though it is not known whether there will be a government response to this. The Practice Direction recognises that the Chancery Division has been clogged up by a recent increase in DTI applications to ban directors. The new rules will save time in court and cut legal costs. A person expecting a ban will be able to start his punishment more quickly and resume his business career earlier as well as avoiding the cost and stress of a trial.

The government has also stated that it plans to introduce legislation providing a fast-track procedure for disqualification of directors who are found to be unfit to continue as directors. The procedure *will avoid a court hearing* and individuals concerned would have to agree not to serve as directors for a specified period. Such an agreement would have the same effect as a disqualification order made under the 1986 Act.

# DISQUALIFICATION AND PERSONAL LIABILITY

## Disqualification and personal liability from fraudulent and wrongful trading (s 10)

The court may of its own motion disqualify a director who has participated in fraudulent trading under s 213 of the Insolvency Act 1986 (IA 1986) or wrongful trading under s 214 of the same Act. There is no minimum period, the maximum being 15 years.

### Fraudulent trading

The crime of fraudulent trading in s 458 of the CA 1985 is now separated from the personal liability section which is in s 213 of the IA 1986. Criminal liability can arise whether the company is in liquidation or not. Liability for the company's debts arises only if the company is in liquidation. Section 213 provides that if in the course of the winding-up of a company it appears that any business of the company has been carried on with intent to defraud creditors of the company or creditors of any other person or for any fraudulent purpose, the court on the application of the liquidator of the company may declare that any persons who were knowingly parties to the carrying on of the business in the manner above mentioned are to be liable to make such contributions (if any) to the company's assets as the court thinks proper.

Section 213 is available against directors and also against members or others who may participate. Section 214 (*overleaf*) is a more likely jurisdiction as regards actions by liquidators who are trying to swell the assets for payment to creditors against directors.

Directors are potentially liable under s 213 but the need to prove fraud makes it difficult to establish liability. Actions against those who are not directors will have to be brought under s 213 since s 214 is available only against directors and shadow directors. Since only proof of negligence is required under s 214, it would seem that s 214 which sets out the requirements for wrongful trading will clearly become the main section for directors' personal liability in a winding-up and no further consideration is given to s 213 in those circumstances.

### Wrongful trading – generally

The IA 1986, s 214 introduced an important new concept into company law – 'wrongful trading'. The court on the application of the liquidator may find that there has been wrongful trading where:

(a) the company has gone into insolvent liquidation. Under the section this means that its assets are insufficient to pay debts and other liabilities including the expenses of the winding-up; and

(b) at some time before the start of the winding-up the director concerned knew (or ought to have known) that there was no reasonable prospect that the company would avoid going into insolvent liquidation; and

(c) the person concerned was a director of the company at the time.

In cases of wrongful trading the court may declare that the director(s) concerned should make a personal contribution to the company's assets if the liquidator of the company makes an application. The amount of the contribution depends on the facts in each particular case and the court is given a wide discretion. However, the general approach is that the directors' personal contributions should be the amount by which the company's assets have been depleted by their conduct. As we have seen, the court can also make a disqualification order. However, if the court does not make a declaration regarding personal liability, then it cannot make a disqualification order. Directors may have a defence against personal liability for wrongful trading if they can show that they took 'every step' that a reasonably diligent person would have taken to minimise the potential loss to creditors, once they knew (or ought to have known) that the company was unlikely to avoid going into insolvent liquidation. If the directors can establish such a defence, the court cannot make an order against them.

It may be difficult to satisfy the court that a particular director took 'every step' or even most of the steps and the court will have to take a view of conduct in all the circumstances of the case. Taking every step may well involve immediate cessation of trading or if the business can be sold it could mean the appointment of an administrator who will keep the company going until it is sold. Certainly, directors of companies which are in danger of insolvent liquidation should take competent professional advice at the earliest possible opportunity.

### Wrongful trading – abilities of a director

As we have seen, wrongful trading is concerned with liability for negligent mismanagement, not dishonesty, though a dishonest person will, in most if not every case, have been guilty also of negligent mismanagement. The court has to assess what steps a director took (or ought to have taken) when considering whether to apply the relief from liability. The court must take into account the director's conduct by the standard of a reasonably diligent person who has:

(a) *General ability*, i.e. the general knowledge, skill and experience that can reasonably be expected of a person carrying out the same functions as the director. This is the lowest standard allowed. Nevertheless, general incompetence will not be sanctioned. Thus directors may be liable even if they have done their best if their best was not good enough for the office they held. Furthermore, it is no defence for directors to say that in fact they did not carry out any functions such as attending board meetings because they will be judged by the functions of the office with which they have been entrusted.

The general knowledge, skill and experience to be expected of a director of a small company with limited operations will be less than that of the directors of bigger and more sophisticated organisations, although the courts have already decided that there are basic minimum standards to be applied to everyone.

(b) *Actual ability*, i.e. the standard of a reasonably diligent person with the general knowledge, skill and experience that the director actually has. In this case the actual ability of the director will be assessed. This introduces a higher standard for talented and professionally qualified or experienced directors. However, the reverse will not apply and directors with less than average ability will be judged by the general standard even if they are personally below it.

In summary, talented directors are judged by their own standards, while incompetent directors are judged by the standard of reasonably competent directors. The court will consider current standards of business practice.

### Wrongful trading – action by directors

There are several actions which directors can take to avoid disqualification and personal liability if an insolvency were to ensue:

(a) Make sure that the board has up-to-date and adequate financial information. A mitigating factor for the court in deciding whether to disqualify directors or find them personally liable is whether the board has considered regular budgets and whether forecasts were produced carefully even if they turned out to be inaccurate.

(b) Seek professional accounting advice if there are any doubts about the financial position of the company. If things have gone too far, an insolvency practitioner should be asked to give advice on alternative insolvency procedures. If there is still hope for the company, an administration order might be the solution so that ultimately there may be no need for liquidation. The most common applicants for administration orders are directors who hope that the appointment of an administrator may save their companies.

(c) Early warnings from the company's auditors must be heeded. Directors have generally found greater difficulty when asking the court for relief if they have not acted upon warnings from the company's auditors about the financial state of the company.

(d) Any difficulties should be discussed fully at frequent board meetings and the board should try to act unanimously. If one or two directors wish to stop trading but are overruled by the majority who wish to carry on, then the majority may have difficulty later in justifying their decision to continue trading.

(e) The proceedings of board meetings should be minuted properly. Although board minutes are not normally conclusive, they can be good evidence that a board exercised its functions responsibly.

(f) Resignation from the board is not usually an adequate response to a problem within the company because a director must take 'every step' to protect creditors. A director who feels, however, that the rest of the board is unadvisedly but implacably determined to continue trading in spite of insolvency or impending insolvency might usefully write to the board giving his view. If this produces no change and he resigns the court might well accept that resignation was the only course open to him.

However, the High Court has ruled that a director of an insolvent company whose recommendations regarding necessary economies had been disregarded by the controlling directors was not necessarily to be treated as unfit under s 6 of the 1986 Act simply because he failed to resign from the board. He stayed on to try and persuade the controlling directors to cease trading. If he had remained purely to draw his fees or preserve his status, he might have been regarded as unfit, but this was not the case. He was not disqualified. (*See Re a Company No 004803 of 1996, The Times*, 2 December 1996.)

(g) The court is bound to look more favourably on directors who have acted honestly and have not tried to benefit themselves at the expense of creditors. The court is also likely to take into account the willingness of directors to make a financial commitment to the company. The court will also consider relevant personal circumstances, such as matrimonial difficulties or more general factors such as recession.

### Wrongful trading – creditors

If a company becomes insolvent these days then its creditors have a better chance than ever before of gaining access to the private assets of the directors in order to increase the amount which they are likely to receive. At the various creditors' meetings that must be held in insolvent liquidation, creditors can impress upon the liquidator their wish to pursue the recovery of money from the directors personally. Any cash received will be available for distribution to the creditors and improve their position in terms of the dividend which the liquidator can pay.

## Disqualification in other capacities (s 1)

The 1986 Act provides that, when making a disqualification order, the court can disqualify a person not only from acting without leave of the court as a director but also from acting as a liquidator or administrator of a company or from acting as an administrative receiver or from being concerned in any way directly or indirectly in the promotion or formation or management of a company. The legislation could, therefore, bear hard on, say, an accountant director who could be disqualified not only from membership of the board but also from certain of his professional activities.

### Contravention of disqualification orders (s 13)

Those who contravene a disqualification order commit a criminal offence under the 1986 Act which can be punished by a fine and/or imprisonment. The major difficulty facing a disqualified person is that he may fall foul of the provisions relating to the management of a company. Clearly, he should not act as a director or liquidator and so on but management of a company is more vague. A director disqualified for, say, five years may wish to set up a management consultancy practice and may become involved in the management of companies in terms of his work. Case law is not helpful here largely because of its absence. Therefore, the wisest course would be to seek legal advice with a view to an application to the court to give leave to proceed following a ruling that the intended activities do not constitute an offence. In addition, the court may give a disqualified director permission to act as a director during the period of disqualification provided there are safeguards, e.g. the appointment of a qualified accountant as a non-executive director.

### Register of disqualification orders

As we have seen, Companies Registration Office keeps a register of individuals disqualified under provisions contained in s 18 of the CDDA 1986. It is sensible to make a search of the register when a commercial transaction of significance is contemplated and there are doubts about a particular individual involved.

### Leave to act while disqualified

Section 17 of the 1986 Act gives the court power to grant leave to directors to act while disqualified. In *Re Westmid Services Ltd, Secretary of State for Trade and Industry* v *Griffiths* [1998] 2 All ER 124 the Court of Appeal gave guidance as to the exercise of the court's discretion under s 17. This includes:

- the age and state of health of the director;
- the length of time he has been disqualified;
- whether he has admitted the offence;
- his general conduct before and after the offence;
- the periods of disqualification of his co-directors;
- the responsibilities that the disqualified director wishes to take on.

## PERSONAL LIABILITY ONLY

The following areas of the law also provide for situations of personal liability for individuals, including directors.

### Acting while disqualified or bankrupt (s 15)

A person who is disqualified and/or an undischarged bankrupt and who becomes involved in the management of a company is jointly and severally liable with the company and any other person liable for its debts in respect of any debts or other liabilities incurred while he was in management.

In order to prevent disqualified persons and bankrupts from running a company through nominee managers, s 15 provides that any one who acts or is willing to act (without leave of the court) on instructions given by a person whom he knows at the time of acting or being willing to act to be in either or both of the above categories, is also jointly and severally liable for debts and other liabilities of the company incurred while he was acting or willing to act.

## The phoenix syndrome (Insolvency Act 1986, s 216)

The purpose of this section is to prevent a practice under which company directors may contrive to mislead the public by utilising a company name which is the same as, or similar to, one of a failed company, of which they were also directors, to conduct a virtually identical business.

The provisions used to prevent this forbid a person who has been a director or shadow director of the failed company during the 12 months prior to the commencement of its insolvent liquidation from being a director or shadow director of a company with the same or similar name and business to the failed company for five years beginning with the day on which the first company went into liquidation. If persons infringe the above rules, they commit a criminal offence punishable by a fine and/or imprisonment and under s 217 of the IA 1986 are personally liable jointly and severally with the company and other persons who may be liable for its debts and liabilities for the debts and other liabilities of the second company. If they manage through nominees who are aware of the circumstances, the nominees are liable for the company's debts and liabilities in the same way.

The court can give exemption from the above requirements and since a company's name may well be an important asset in its liquidation, the business and the name can be sold by the insolvency practitioner involved and run by a new management. There is no objection to this. It should be noted that in order to prevent evasion of the section a former director of a company which has failed is covered by the relevant provisions of ss 216 and 217 if he carries the business on otherwise than by a company. This would prevent the use, for example, of a partnership to carry on the business under a prohibited name.

## Liability as a signatory (s 349 of the CA 1985)

Section 349 of the CA 1985 provides that any bill of exchange, promissory note, endorsement, cheque or order for money or goods purporting to be signed by or on behalf of the company must state the name of the company in legible characters.

The section further provides that if an officer of the company such as a director signs or authorises to be signed any of the above documents on which the company's name is not so stated he is liable to a fine and is further personally liable to the holder of the bill of exchange, promissory note, cheque or order for money or goods for the amount of it should the company fail to pay. It is the corporate name which is required to be stated so that a director who signs a cheque that contains only the company's business name is liable on it if the company defaults (*Maxform SpA* v *B Mariani & Goodville Ltd* [1981] 2 Lloyd's Rep 54). If a business name is used, the corporate name must also appear as follows: 'Boxo Ltd, Trading As [T/A] Paris Fashions'.

However, it seems that so long as the outsider knows that he is dealing with a company and that the liability of its members is limited, trifling errors in the name will not trigger liability. Thus in *Jenice Ltd* v *Dan* [1993] BCLC 1349 the defendant who was a director of Primekeen Ltd signed a cheque incorrectly printed by the bank in the name of 'Primkeen Ltd'. The company went into liquidation and did not meet the cheque. Nevertheless, Mr Dan was not liable on it. There was no doubt that outsiders would have known that they were dealing with a limited company and no harm had been done. Some judges had in earlier cases interpreted the section strictly and regarded it as requiring that every part of the name be correct. The *Jenice* interpretation seems more sensible.

However, failure to include the word 'limited' or 'Ltd' or 'plc', at the end of the name is always likely to result in personal liability unless in the case of a private company the company is exempt from including that word under s 30 of the 1985 Act. (*See further* Chapter 18.)

# THE COMPANY SECRETARY: RETURNS, RECORDS AND REGISTERS

In this section we deal with the office of company secretary and the relevant duties and responsibilities of this office. It is also convenient to consider here the more important returns, records and registers which a company must send to CRO and keep generally at the registered office.

## Definition and authority of the secretary

The company secretary is the chief administrative officer of the company. The term 'officer' as defined in s 744 includes the secretary. There is also clear and specific recognition that, since s 283 provides that every company must have a secretary, a sole director cannot also be the secretary. A corporation may act as secretary to another company but a company (A) cannot have as its secretary a company (B) if the sole director of company (B) is also the sole director or secretary of company (A). Under s 284 a provision requiring or authorising a thing to be done by or to a director and the secretary is not satisfied by its being done by or to the same person acting both as director and secretary. Section 288 requires the register of directors to include also particulars of the secretary.

A secretary owes fiduciary duties to the company which are similar to those of a director. Thus he must not make secret profits or take secret benefits from his office and if he does he can be made to account for them to the company as a constructive trustee (*see Re Morvah Consols Tin Mining Co. McKay's Case* (1875) 2 Ch D 1).

The criminal law regards him as an organ of the company and a higher managerial agent whose fraudulent conduct can be imputed to the company in order to make it liable along with him, for example, for crimes arising out of fraud and the falsification of documents and returns.

The civil courts now recognise that the secretary in modern times is an important official who enjoys the power to contract on behalf of the company even without authority. This is, however, confined to contracts in the administrative operations of the company including the employment of office staff and the management of the office together with the hiring of transport (*see Panorama Developments (Guildford) Ltd* v *Fidelis Furnishing Fabrics Ltd* [1971] 3 All ER 16).

However, his ostensible (or usual) authority, as it is called, is not unlimited. He cannot without authority borrow money on behalf of the company (*Re Cleadon Trust Ltd* [1939] Ch 286), nor can he without authority commence litigation on the company's behalf (*Daimler Co Ltd* v *Continental Tyre and Rubber Co Ltd* [1916] Act 307). He cannot summon a general meeting without authority from the board (*Re State of Wyoming Syndicate* [1901] 2 Ch 431), nor can he register a transfer without the board's approval (*Chida Mines Ltd* v *Anderson* (1905) 22 TLR 27) nor may he, without board approval, strike a name off the register of members (*Re Indo China Steam Navigation Co* [1917] 2 Ch 100). The duty to register or not or to strike off are powers which are vested in the directors.

## Appointment

The secretary is usually appointed by the board who will fix his term of office and the conditions on which he is to hold office. Regulation 99 of Table A confers such a power on the board together with the power to remove him. The appointment of the first secretary to take effect on incorporation will be ineffective unless his name and consent to act appear on Form 10 with the first directors. The directors of a public company must concern themselves with the qualifications of the appointee. Members of the chartered accountancy bodies and chartered secretaries are eligible as are solicitors and members of the Bar. There are also provisions allowing those with experience who are not so qualified to act. Since these matters are not likely to form an examination question, they are not considered further, but suffice to note that they appear in s 286.

In addition to being an officer of the company, the secretary is also an employee of the company and is regarded as such for the purpose of preferential payments in an insolvency situation (s 175 of and Sch 6 to the IA 1986).

## Removal and resignation

As we have seen, reg 99 allows the board to remove the secretary at any time. There is no special procedure as there is for directors. The secretary may also resign his office at any time and in the case of both removal and resignation notice must be sent to CRO within 14 days of the removal or resignation. It should be borne in mind that although removal and, for that matter, resignation, are simple enough procedures in themselves, there could well be contractual consequences in terms of a claim for dismissal.

## Assistant and deputy secretary: joint secretaries

Statutory recognition of these offices is given by s 283(3), the relevant part of which provides: 'Anything required or authorised to be done by or to the secretary may, if the office is vacant or there is for any other reason no secretary capable of acting, be done by or to any assistant or deputy secretary'. Special articles may delegate the power to appoint assistant or deputy secretaries to the secretary. Otherwise, appointment and removal can be effected by the board in the same way as for the secretary, but there is no need to notify appointment, removal or resignation to CRO.

Companies which have joint secretaries are required by s 290 to give details of them in the register of directors and secretaries and notify CRO of any appointments and changes within 14 days of the occurrence. The resignation of the Secretary must also be notified.

## DUTIES AND RESPONSIBILITIES OF THE SECRETARY

### Specific duties

A company secretary has many duties as an officer of the company but the two major duties which he has in his capacity as secretary are:

(a) completion and signing of the annual return as an alternative to a director (s 363(2)(c));
(b) the signing of the directors' report in the company's annual accounts as an alternative to a director (s 234A (1)).

### Annual return

Under the Companies Act 1985, Part XI, as amended by the Companies Act 1989, a company must file an annual return with the Registrar. It must be made up to a date 12 months after the previous return or, in the case of the first return, 12 months after incorporation. The company may move the date of its annual return by informing the Registrar on Form 363s (the shuttle – *see below*). The new date then governs future annual submissions. The return must be delivered to the Registrar within 28 days of the make-up date.

### *The shuttle concept*

Under the usual system for annual returns the Registrar issues a shuttle document to companies (Form 363s) containing all the information relevant to the annual return which the Registrar already has. The company is merely required to confirm or amend the shuttle document and return it. There is no need to complete a blank form as before. The shuttle document will be sent shortly before the due date for submission.

### *Contents of annual return*

The shuttle document (Form 363s) contains the following matters:

(a) the company's name;
(b) the date of the annual return;
(c) date of next return. The company can put a new date in here and CRO will send the document at the appropriate time *next year*;
(d) the address of the registered office;
(e) principal business activity. All shuttle documents carry Standard Industrial Classification Codes (SIC) for the principal business activity of the company. VAT codes are no longer used (*see* Companies (Principal Business Activities) (Amendment) Regulations 1996 (SI 1996/1105));

(f)  the address where the register of members is kept;

(g)  the place where the register of debenture holders (or duplicate) is kept;

(h)  particulars of the company secretary;

(i)  particulars of directors, which are the same as those contained in the register of directors and secretaries (*see* later in this chapter);

(j)  issued share capital;

(k)  a list of current members and those who have ceased to be members since the last return. If full details have been given on the return for either of the last two years, the company need only give new members since the last return and those ceasing to be members since then, together with those whose holdings of stocks and shares have changed. If there have been no changes, the company's agent ticks the appropriate box;

(l)  a private company which has dispensed with the holding of the annual general meeting and/or the laying of accounts and reports before the company in general meeting by elective resolution must say so in the return.

The return contains a certification section to be signed by the secretary or a director. A filing fee is payable.

### Sanctions if return not made

The company and every officer in default is liable to a fine under Sch 24, and in addition the directors may become disqualified by the court if they persist in failing to file the annual return or other documents. Furthermore, any member or creditor can, under s 713, serve a notice on a defaulting company requiring that company to file an annual return. If it fails to do so within 14 days the member or creditor may make application to the court for a direction that the company shall make the return and the company is liable to pay the applicant's costs.

## Secretary's liability as an officer – returns, records and registers

As we have seen, s 744 includes the company secretary in the definition of 'officer' of the company. The directors are primarily liable if the company does not comply with the law. However, a number of requirements are in practice the primary responsibility of the secretary and where there is default the secretary is almost certain to be responsible along with the directors or even solely where there has been reasonable delegation of a routine task by the board. These requirements are set out below.

## To keep and maintain the company's register of charges and to take safe custody of relevant documents (s 407)

The secretary will also bear in mind the need to allow inspection of the documents and register to members and creditors free and others on payment of a fee (*see further below*). The maximum fees for inspection of copies of entries in registers etc are currently in SI 1991/1998 and are varied by statutory instrument from time to time.

## To keep and maintain a register of members (s 352)

The register must contain the following information:

(a) the names and addresses of the members;
(b) a statement of the shares held by each member, each share being distinguished by its number if it has one;
(c) the amount paid or agreed to be considered as paid up on the shares of each member;
(d) the date on which each person was entered in the register as a member;
(e) the date on which each person ceased to be a member.

Where a company has more than one class of shareholders (or stockholders), the register must show to which class a member belongs and, in the case of a company without a share capital having more than one class of members, the class to which the member belongs. This useful provision enables, for example, members who wish to maintain a campaign against the board to extract for circulation only the names of members holding voting rights.

Failure to keep a register of members makes the company and every officer in default liable to a fine followed by a daily fine for each day during which the default continues. However, the duty to notify changes of address is on the shareholders concerned and the company is not required to trace shareholders where letters are returned or dividend warrants not cashed.

The register may be kept in any form, e.g. in the form of a loose-leaf system, so long as proper precautions are taken to guard against falsification. The 1985 Act allows the use of computers for company records, including the register of members, so long as the records can be reproduced in legible form. A company with more than 50 members must keep an index of its members and if there is any alteration in the register the index must also be altered within 14 days of such alteration. The above provisions do not apply if the register is kept in the form of an index (s 354).

The register and index are to be kept at the registered office of the company but if the register is made up elsewhere then it may be kept at the place where it is made up. The index must be kept with the register. It is necessary to inform the Registrar of the whereabouts of the register and index if it is not kept at the registered office and of any change in that place (ss 353 and 354).

### Statement that company has only one member

Under s 352A (inserted by SI 1992/1699) if the number of members of a private company limited by shares or guarantee falls to one there must, upon the occurrence of that event, be entered in the company's register of members with the name and address of the sole member:

(a) a statement that the company has only one member; and
(b) the date on which the company became a one-member company.

If the membership increases from one to two or more members, an entry must be made on the register of members with the name and address of the person who was formerly the sole member, a statement that the company has ceased to have only one member and the date on which that event occurred. If there is default, the company and every officer in default is liable to a fine and for continued default a daily fine.

### Inspection of the register

The register and index must be kept open for inspection by any member free of charge and by any other person on payment of a fee. The company must make available either to a member or to any other person a copy of any part of the register and may make a charge for this. The company must send the copy within 10 days, commencing on the day after that on which the company received the request. If a company will not allow inspection of its register or give copies of it on request, the company or any director or secretary who is responsible is guilty of an offence and the person wanting inspection and/or a copy can apply to the court for an order that the company shall comply with his request (s 356).

A person inspecting the register has no right himself to take extracts from or make copies of it (*Re Balaghat Co* [1901] 2 KB 665) and the right of inspection terminates on the commencement of winding-up (*Re Kent Coalfields Syndicate* [1898] 1 QB 754). Inspection is then a matter for the insolvency rules and the court.

### Power to close register

Under s 358 a company may, if it gives notice by an advertisement in a newspaper circulating in the district in which its registered office is situated, close the register for any time not exceeding 30 days a year.

### Obsolete entries in the register

A company may remove from the register any entry which relates to a former member where the person concerned has not been a member for at least 20 years.

### Rectification of the register

Although under s 361 the register of members is *prima facie* (and not conclusive) evidence of the matters which the Companies Act requires it to contain, the court has power, under s 359, to rectify the register if application is made to it where:

(a) the name of any person is without sufficient cause entered on or omitted from the register; or
(b) default is made or unnecessary delay takes place in entering on the register the fact that a person has ceased to be a member.

The court may order the company to pay damages to any person aggrieved. Notice of any rectification of the register will be given to the Registrar under the terms of the court's order.

It should also be noted that rectification will be ordered where joint holders wish to split the holding since in general terms the rights attaching to the shares, e.g. voting rights, are vested in the first-named person on the register. (*See Burns* v *Siemens Bros Dynamo Works Ltd* [1919] 1 Ch 225). The company should, therefore, in ordinary circumstances accede to such a request.

### Notice of trusts

Under s 360 no notice of any trust shall be entered on the register of members and Table A, reg 5 carries a similar provision. The rule laid down in s 360 and reg 5 has two branches.

(a) The company is entitled to treat every person whose name appears on the register as the beneficial owner of the shares even though he may in fact hold them in trust for another person. Thus, if the company registers a transfer of shares held by a trustee, it is not liable to the beneficiaries under the trust even though the sale of the shares by the trustee was fraudulent or in breach of the powers given to him in the trust instrument. However, s 360 only protects the company, and where directors register a transfer knowing that it is made in breach of trust or in fraud of some person having rights under the trust they may incur personal liability to the person who suffers loss.

(b) Where persons claim rights in shares under equitable titles, such as a lender who has taken shares under an equitable mortgage by deposit of the share certificate but the borrower is left with the legal title being on the register. Here the company is not made into a trustee of those equitable rights merely because the lender serves notice on the company of his equitable claim. The company will normally issue a new share certificate to a member if he gives an appropriate indemnity to the company and in such a case there could be a further transfer to the detriment of the original lender. The correct way to deal with the problem is for the lender to serve a stop notice on the company under the Rules of Supreme Court. Legal advice and assistance will be required. Nevertheless, in outline, the lender will file with the court an affidavit declaring the nature of his interest in the shares, and this is accompanied by a copy of the notice addressed to the company and signed by the applicant. Copies of the affidavit and the notice are served on the company. Once the stop notice has been served the company cannot register a transfer or pay a dividend – if the notice extends to dividends – without first notifying the lender. However, after the expiration of 14 days (SI 1980/629) from giving notice of the transfer or payment of a dividend the company is bound to make the transfer or pay the dividend unless in the meantime the lender has obtained an injunction from the court prohibiting transfer or payment as the case may be.

It should be noted that, as a practical matter, although the stop notice procedure is the only safe way of protecting an equitable interest it would be unlikely, in practice, that a company would transfer shares to a third party where a lender had himself given notice to the company of his equitable charge.

### Overseas branch register

A company which carries on business in some part of Her Majesty's Dominions as set out in Part 1 of Sch 14 and, in particular, a company which carries on business in some part of Northern Ireland, the Isle of Man or the Channel Islands may under s 362 keep an overseas branch register of members resident in the relevant place. The general purpose is to facilitate the transfer of the shares of those members. The Registrar of Companies must be informed of the situation of the office where the register is kept within 14 days of its opening or of a change or discontinuance.

Copies of all entries on the register must be sent to the company's registered office as soon as possible after they are made and the company must keep a duplicate of the register at the same place as its principal register. Rectification of the register is achieved by application to the appropriate court in the place where the register is kept.

### To keep and maintain the register of directors and secretaries (ss 288–90)

A company must keep at its registered office a register of directors and secretaries and must notify the Registrar of any changes in terms of the persons concerned and their particulars within 14 days of the change. It is important to note that shadow directors are included and that it is necessary to state any other directorships currently held or held within the preceding five years. The object of disclosing past directorships is to enable persons who inspect the register to see whether the directors have been managers of companies which have, for example, failed within the fairly recent past. There are exemptions for both present and past directorships in companies which for the whole five-year period were dormant or within the same wholly-owned group of companies. The register must be open for inspection by any member of the company free and to other persons on payment of the prescribed fee.

### To keep and maintain the register of directors' interests in the company's securities (ss 324, 325, 326, 328 and Sch 13)

Directors and shadow directors are required to notify the company in writing within five days of acquiring or disposing of an interest in shares or debentures of the company or companies in the group. The five days begin on the day following knowledge of the acquisition or disposal. Interests of a spouse or minor child are included as an interest of the director as are interests held behind a nominee. The interests of spouse or minor children are not included if those persons are also directors in which case they will disclose in their own right.

The company must maintain a register of directors' interests and must enter on it information received within three days. The company must tell the Registrar where the register is kept if not at the registered office and of any change in that place. The register is to be open for inspection by members without charge and by others on payment of the prescribed fee. Copies can be obtained on payment, in all cases, of the prescribed fee.

### Other usual duties of the secretary

In summary these are:

(a) *under s 366*: to comply with the requirement to hold an AGM in each year (*see further below*) unless the company has opted out of the requirement by elective resolution;

(b) *under s 382*: to keep minutes of general and board meetings;

(c) *under s 382A*: to record written resolutions. As regards inspection and copies of minutes this is dealt with in s 383, but for practical purposes this is available to members only so far as general meetings are concerned. There is no right of inspection of board minutes except by court order;

(d) *under Sch 7*: involvement in the preparation and dispatch of the Directors' Report and Accounts;

(e) *under s 318*: to keep a copy of each of the directors' service contracts, or a written memorandum thereof, at the registered office or principal place of business or with the register of members. The Registrar must be notified where the copies of service contracts are kept and of changes unless kept at the registered office. Inspection only is free to members; there is no inspection by others. Shadow directors are included;

(f) *under Sch 6*: to be involved in the collation of the interests of directors and shadow directors disclosable in the accounts;

(g) *under s 169*: to deliver to the Registrar details of the purchase by the company of its own shares within 28 days of purchase (*see further* Chapter 19). Also under s 169, to keep a copy of the purchase contract (or memorandum thereof) for 10 years after completion of the share purchases under it. Inspection free of charge must be made available in a private company to members only and in a public company to members and any other person;

(h) *under s 175*: arranging for the publicity in connection with a redemption or purchase of shares from capital and arranging for the inspection by members and creditors of the relevant documents for the required five-week period (*see further* Chapter 19);

(i) it should also be noted that the CA 1985 authorises the company secretary to sign forms prescribed under the Act and which are sent to the Registrar of Companies to inform him of various events within the company, e.g. notice of increase in nominal capital;

(j) an important function of the secretary is in connection with meetings. These matters are considered in the next section.

## MEETINGS AND RESOLUTIONS

### Shareholders' meetings

There are two kinds of company general meeting: the annual general meeting and an extraordinary general meeting.

### Annual general meeting

Section 366 states that an annual general meeting must be held in every calendar year and not more than 15 months after the last one. So if a company held an AGM on 31 March 1998, it must hold the next one in 1999 and on or before 30 June 1999. However, if a company holds its first AGM within 18 months of incorporation it need not hold one in its year of incorporation or the following year. Thus, if a company was incorporated on 1 November 1998, it would have until 30 April 2000 to hold its first AGM. The notice of the meeting must say that it is the AGM. A private company may elect to dispense with the requirement to hold the AGM. However, any member may by giving notice to the company not later than three months before the end of the year in which the AGM should have been held but for the opting out require an AGM to be held in that year. For example, Boxo Ltd holds an AGM in 1999 at which all the members entitled to be present vote and agree to opt out of the AGM requirement. No AGM is held in 2000, but if a member thinks one should be held in 2001, he can achieve this by giving notice to the company not later than 30 September 2001. (Further details of elective resolutions are given *below*.)

### Extraordinary general meetings

All general meetings other than the AGM are extraordinary general meetings. They may be called by the directors at any time.

Section 368 gives holders of not less than one-tenth of the paid-up share capital on which all calls due have been paid the right to requisition an extraordinary general meeting.

It should be noted that s 368 uses the plural expression 'members' throughout, so that the section basically requires two or more members holding the one-tenth share or voting requirement. One member would not suffice, even where he held the one-tenth requirement. This requirement is presumably to ensure that there will be a quorum at the requisitioned meeting.

In fact, the case of *Morgan* v *Morgan Insurance Brokers Ltd* [1993] BCC 145 proceeded on this basis. Briefly, Mr Morgan wanted to requisition an EGM and had 77 per cent of the shares. To mount his requisition, he wanted to transfer one of his shares to his daughter, so that there would be two requisitionists. The other directors blocked the transfer under powers in the articles. Nevertheless, Millett J proceeded on the basis that two requisitionists were required. There are those lawyers who may say that under the Interpretation Act of 1978 the plural includes the singular and vice versa unless there is a contrary intention, and surely there is a contrary intention because, unless there are at least two persons as requisitionists, there may well not be a quorum at the meeting when it is held. Section 371 allows one member to ask the court to call a meeting and says so, but there is no quorum problem here because the court when calling the meeting can fix the quorum even at one if it wishes.

The requisitionists must deposit at the company's registered office a requisition signed by all the requisitionists stating the objects for which they wish a meeting of the company to be held. The directors must then call an EGM and if they have not done so within 21 days after the deposit of the requisition, the requisitionists or any of them representing more than one-half of their total voting rights may themselves call the meeting, so long as they do so within three months of the requisition. The requisitionists can recover reasonable expenses incurred from the company and the company may in turn recover these from the fees or remuneration of the defaulting directors. To ensure that the directors do not call the meeting for a date so far in the future as to frustrate the aims of the minority, s 368(8) provides that the directors are deemed not to have duly called the meeting if they call it for a date more than 28 days after the notice calling it. If they infringe this rule, the requisitionists' power to call the meeting arises. The company's articles cannot deprive the members of the right to requisition a meeting, although they can provide that a smaller number of persons may requisition it, e.g. one-twentieth. An article requiring more than one-tenth would not be effective.

It is important to note that if the requisitionists wish to put resolutions to the meeting, they must be clear and capable of being voted on. It is not enough that they state broad objects. For example, it is not enough for the requisitionists to state in their request for an EGM that the meeting will be asked 'to elect a new board of directors'. Such a resolution would be ineffective in the absence of details as to which persons are to be elected and what is to be the exact size of the new board or which members of the old board are to be removed. Unless resolutions are clear and would be effective if voted on, the directors are not obliged to call the EGM. (*See Rose v McGivern* [1998] 2 BCLC 593.)

## Notice of meetings

This must be given in accordance with the provisions of the articles. Table A requires 21 clear days' notice of the AGM, i.e. excluding the day of service of the notice and the day of the meeting, and the same notice for a meeting to pass a special resolution or appoint a director, and 14 clear days in other cases.

The articles usually provide, as Table A does, that a meeting shall not be invalid because a particular member does not receive notice – unless this is deliberate, as distinct from accidental.

In order to work out the clear days' notice, we also need a provision like the one in Table A which says that notice is deemed (or assumed) to be served so many hours after posting: Table A says 48 hours after posting. Thus, if we post the notice of an extraordinary general meeting on 1 February, it is deemed served on all those entitled to attend on 3 February and the meeting can be held on 18 February at the earliest.

## Short notice

Under s 369 a meeting of a company, if called by a shorter period of notice than that required by the CA 1985 or the company's articles, is regarded as validly called if:

(a) in the case of the AGM *all* members entitled to attend and vote at the meeting agree; and

(b) in the case of any other meeting, it is agreed by a majority in number of the members having the right to attend and vote at the meeting, being a majority together holding not less than 95 per cent in nominal value of the shares giving the right to attend and vote at the meeting; or in the case of a company not having a share capital a majority representing 95 per cent of the total voting rights at the meeting. Private companies may by elective resolution (*see below*) provide that the percentage be reduced from 95 per cent to a figure not less than 90 per cent.

## Quorum at general meetings

No business may be validly done at a general meeting unless a quorum (i.e. minimum number) of members is present when the meeting begins. Table A provides that a quorum must be present throughout the meeting also and that two persons entitled to vote, each being a member or a proxy for a member, shall be a quorum. As we have seen, by reason of s 370A this does not apply to one-member companies.

## Voting

This may be by show of hands in which case, obviously, each member has only one vote regardless of the number of shares or proxies he holds. However, Table A provides that the chairman or two members entitled to vote may demand a poll whereupon each member has one vote per share and proxies can be used. Commonly preference shareholders do not have a right to vote unless their dividend is in arrear.

## Proxies

If the articles so provide, as does Table A, voting on a poll may be by proxy. A proxy is a written authority given by the member to another person to vote for him at a specified meeting. The company may require these authorities to be deposited at the company's office before the meeting. However, under s 372 the articles cannot require them to be deposited more than 48 hours before the meeting and Table A requires 48 hours.

It is worth noting that the acceptance of a faxed proxy is reinforced by the decision of the High Court in *Re a Debtor (No 2021 of 1995), ex parte IRC v the Debtor* [1996] 2 All ER 345 where Laddie J held that a proxy form was signed for the purposes of a creditors' meeting in a proposed voluntary arrangement and under rule 8.2(3) of the Insolvency Rules of 1986 if it bore upon it some distinctive or personal marking which had been placed there by or with the authority of the creditor. When a creditor faxed a proxy form to the chairman of the creditors' meeting he transmitted the contents of the form and the signature applied to it. The receiving fax was instructed by the transmitting creditor to reproduce his signature on the proxy form, which was itself being created at the receiving station. It followed that the received fax was a proxy form signed by the principal. The judge did, however, make it clear that his decision was on the Insolvency Rules and that different considerations may apply to faxed documents in relation to other legislation, but their acceptance is likely.

## Minutes

A company must keep minutes of the proceedings at its general and board meetings. Members have a right to inspect the minutes of general meetings but not those of directors' meetings.

## RESOLUTIONS

There are four main kinds of resolution passed at company meetings as set out below.

(a) *An ordinary resolution*, which may be defined as 'a resolution passed by a majority (over 50 per cent) of persons present and voting in person or by proxy at a general meeting'. Any business may be validly done by this type of resolution unless the articles or the Companies Act provide for a special or extraordinary resolution for that particular business. An example of the use of an ordinary resolution is for the members to give their permission to the directors so that the latter can allot the company's unissued share capital under s 80.

(b) *An extraordinary resolution,* which is one passed by a majority of not less than three-quarters of the members who being entitled to vote do so whether in person or by proxy at a general meeting of which notice has been given specifying the intention to propose the resolution as an extraordinary resolution (s 378(1)). Under s 369, 14 days' notice of the meeting must be given – or seven days' notice in the case of an unlimited company. A company may resolve by extraordinary resolution to wind up if it cannot pay its debts. This will put the company into a creditors' voluntary winding-up.

(c) *A special resolution,* which is one passed by the same majority as is required for an extraordinary resolution at a general meeting of which at least 21 days' notice has been given stating the intention to propose the resolution as a special resolution (s 378(2)).

The distinction between a special and an extraordinary resolution lies, therefore, in the period of notice of the meeting. A special resolution requires 21 days whereas an extraordinary resolution requires only 14. The majorities are the same. It will be appreciated that if an extraordinary resolution is to be proposed at the AGM 21 days' notice must be given, because that is the requirement for the AGM.

A special resolution is required, for example, to alter the objects clause, to change the company's name or the articles or for the company to approve in advance a contract to make an off-market purchase of its shares. Section 380 provides that within 15 days of the passing of an extraordinary resolution or special resolution a copy of the resolution must be sent to the Registrar of Companies. Some ordinary resolutions must be sent to the Registrar but not many; mostly they are not filed. However, an example of one which must be filed is the ordinary resolution to allow the directors to exercise a power of allotment under s 80. The copy sent to the Registrar may be printed or be in any form approved by the Registrar (s 380). He will accept a typewritten copy.

(d) *Ordinary resolutions after special notice.* Section 379 requires that for certain ordinary resolutions, e.g. one removing a director before his period of office has ended, special notice must be given. The requirements of special notice have already been extensively dealt with and nothing more need be said here.

## Members' resolutions at the AGM

Under s 376 members representing not less than one-twentieth of the total voting rights of all the members can by making a written requisition to the company compel the directors:

(a) to give to members who are entitled to receive notice of the next AGM notice of any resolution which may properly be moved and which they intend to move at that meeting; and

(b) to circulate to the members any statement of not more than 1,000 words with respect to the matter referred to in any proposed resolution or the business to be dealt with at the meeting.

The requisition must be made not later than six weeks before the AGM if a resolution is proposed and not less than one week before if no resolution is proposed.

## WRITTEN RESOLUTIONS OF PRIVATE COMPANIES

As part of the deregulation of private companies, the Companies Act 1985, as amended by the Companies Act 1989, provides for written resolutions which can be passed by the members of a private company without the need to call or hold a meeting. The 1985 Act now provides that anything which can be done by a private company by a resolution in general meeting or in a class meeting – as where a class of shareholders is being asked to vary their rights and they are unanimous in wishing to approve the variation (in the absence of unanimity there would have to be a class meeting) – can be done without a meeting, and without any previous notice being required, by a resolution signed by or on behalf of *all* the members of the company who at that date of the resolution were entitled to attend and vote at meetings of the company. The signatures need not be on a single document so that the resolution may, for example, be typed on separate sheets of paper and circulated to the members for signature. The date of the resolution is the date on which it is signed by, or on behalf of, the last member to sign.

There are some cases where the written resolution procedure cannot be used, i.e. the removal of a director or auditor by ordinary resolution after special notice to the company (*see* earlier in this chapter). The ordinary resolution must be passed at a meeting of the company because the director or auditor concerned is allowed to make representations as to why he should not be removed, either in writing with the notice of the meeting, or orally at the meeting.

The company is required to keep a record of written resolutions and the signatures of those members who signed them in a record book which is, in effect, a substitute for what would, in the case of a meeting, be the minutes.

### Involvement of auditors

The Deregulation (Resolutions of Private Companies) Order 1996 (SI 1996/1471) deals with the involvement of the company's auditors (if any) in the written resolution procedure as follows:

- Article 3 repeals the pre-existing provisions of the CA 1985, i.e. ss 381B and 390(2), and substitutes a new section 381B (duty to notify auditors of proposed written resolutions). The new section imposes a duty on the directors and secretary of a company to send the company's auditors (if any) a copy, or otherwise inform them of the contents, of any written resolution proposed under s 381A (written resolutions of private companies) at or before the time that resolution is supplied to a member for signature. Breach of the duty will result in a criminal offence but will not affect the validity of any resolution passed under s 381A.

  As regards the criminal offence it is a defence for the accused to prove:
  - (a) that the circumstances were such that it was not practicable for him to comply with the requirements, or
  - (b) that he believed on reasonable grounds that a copy of the resolution had been sent to the company's auditors or that they had otherwise been informed of its contents.

- Since s 381B is repealed, the auditors have no right to require the company to call a meeting rather than use the written resolution procedure nor need the company wait for seven days to see whether the auditors state whether the resolution does or does not concern them as auditors.

So far as the auditors are concerned, the Regulations operate merely to give them information as to resolutions being passed by the company, bearing in mind that had the company passed the resolution at a general meeting the auditors would have received notice of it and have been entitled to attend and be heard on any part of the business which concerns them as auditors (s 390(1)). If the result of the resolution is that the auditor leaves office, bearing in mind that an auditor cannot be removed before his period of office expires by a written resolution anyway, though he might not be re-appointed at the end of that period by such a resolution, the auditor will be alerted to make a statement under s 394, to be brought to the attention of shareholders if, for example, the circumstances are inimical to their interests.

Finally, Art 4 amends s 381C(1) to make it clear that the statutory written resolution procedure under s 381A may be used notwithstanding any provision in the company's memorandum or articles but does not prevent the use of any power conferred by such a provision instead.

## ELECTIVE RESOLUTIONS OF PRIVATE COMPANIES

Private companies, whether limited or unlimited, are allowed to pass elective resolutions to dispense with the following formalities and requirements:

(a) the holding of the annual general meeting, but any member may require an AGM to be held in any particular year;
(b) the laying of accounts and reports before the company in general meeting, but any member, or the auditors, may require them to be laid in any particular year;
(c) the percentage of shares required to be held by persons agreeing to an extraordinary general meeting being held at short notice may be reduced from 95 per cent to not less than 90 per cent;
(d) the period for which a general meeting may authorise the directors to allot shares may exceed the usual limit of five years;
(e) the requirement to appoint auditors annually.

As we have seen, the resolution required to achieve the opting out is called an elective resolution and it can be passed at a meeting of the company. Such a resolution is not effective unless:

(a) at least 21 days' notice in writing is given of the meeting at which it is to be proposed, the terms of the resolution and the fact that it is an elective resolution being stated; and
(b) the resolution is agreed to at the meeting, in person or by proxy, by all the members entitled to attend and vote at the meeting.

Under the Deregulation (Resolutions of Private Companies) Order 1996 (SI 1996/1471) less than 21 days' notice may be given of a meeting at which an elective resolution is to be proposed, provided that all the members entitled to attend the meeting and vote at it agree to short notice.

An elective resolution may be revoked by an ordinary resolution of the company and an elective resolution ceases to have effect if the company is re-registered as a public company. *A written resolution may be used as an elective resolution.*

## MEETINGS OF SINGLE-MEMBER COMPANIES

The amendments of the law relating to meetings to accommodate the single-member company have already been considered in Chapter 18 but should be revised at this point.

## PROTECTION OF MINORITY INTERESTS

For many years it was difficult, if not impossible, for a minority of members to bring claims on behalf of their company where a wrong resulting in loss had been done to it. The directors could bring the company into court to sue, as could those members who could command more than 50 per cent of the votes in a general meeting. The minority could only in rare circumstances bring what is called a derivative claim on behalf of the company. This was the position at common law as a result of a case called *Foss* v *Harbottle* (1843) 2 Hare 461. It is still the position at common law and lawyers still require a knowledge of the case because it is basically a rule of procedure – how to bring a case into court – but those seeking a background for use in business do not need a knowledge of such things and so we shall now concentrate on the much improved rights given to minorities by statute which have overtaken the *Foss* case.

## MINORITY PROTECTION UNDER STATUTE: GENERALLY

There are a number of sections in the Companies Act 1985 which enable a number of shareholders to defy the majority. For example, under s 5 dissentient holders of 15 per cent of the issued shares can apply for cancellation of an alteration of objects. (*See* Chapter 18.) Furthermore, under s 127 where class rights are varied in pursuance of a clause in the memorandum or articles, or under s 125, dissentient holders of 15 per cent of the issued shares of the class can apply for cancellation of the variation. (*See* Chapter 19.) Furthermore, under s 54, where a public company passes a special resolution to re-register as a private company, holders of not less than 5 per cent in nominal value of the company's issued share capital or any class thereof; or not less than 5 per cent in number of the members of the company, if the company is not limited by shares; or not less than 50 of the company's members may apply to the court to cancel the resolution.

Other examples are the right given by s 157 to 10 per cent in nominal value of the company's issued share capital or any class of it or 10 per cent of the members if the company is not limited by shares, to object to the court where a private company gives financial assistance for the purchase of its own shares (*see further* Chapter 19); and the right given by s 176 to any member who did not consent or vote in favour of the special resolution approving the purchase by a private company of its own shares partly from capital to apply to the court for the cancellation of the resolution (*see further* Chapter 19).

There are also certain minority rights in regard to meetings, i.e. the right given to a 10 per cent minority to require the convening of an extraordinary general meeting (s 368), and the right of a 20 per cent minority to requisition members' resolutions at the AGM (s 376).

As regards investigations, a right is given to a 10 per cent minority to ask the DTI, on the basis of evidence submitted, to order an investigation of the company's affairs or compel an investigation into its ownership.

The rights of a minority to petition the court on the grounds of unfair prejudice or for a winding-up, are considered below.

## STATUTORY PROTECTION AGAINST UNFAIR PREJUDICE

The statutory rights considered above are granted in specific areas for specific purposes, for example, so that a minority can convene an EGM. The rights described under this heading and given by Part XVII of the 1985 Act are more general, being potentially available whenever a minority can show 'unfair prejudice'.

The main provisions of Part XVII are set out below.

### Unfair prejudice

Any member or personal representative, or the Secretary of State as a result of a DTI investigation, may petition the court on the grounds that the affairs of the company are being, or have been, or will be, conducted in a manner unfairly prejudicial to the interests of its members generally, or of some part of its members, including the petitioner himself. The court must, among other things, be satisfied that the petition is well founded.

The provision relating to a petition by personal representatives of a deceased shareholder is important because a major form of abuse in private companies has been the refusal by the board, under powers in the articles, to register the personal representatives of a major deceased shareholder and also to refuse to register the beneficiaries under the will or on intestacy. Although personal representatives have some rights, e.g. to receive dividends, they cannot vote unless they are registered – nor can a beneficiary. The holding is therefore rendered powerless and the motive of the board is often to purchase the holding themselves at an advantageous price.

The provisions apply to conduct past, present or future. In *Re Kenyon Swansea Ltd*, *The Times*, 29 April 1987, the High Court decided that it was sufficient to support a petition that an act had been proposed which if carried out or completed would be prejudicial to the petitioner. The court also decided that it was enough that the affairs of the company had, in the past, been conducted in such a way as to be unfairly prejudicial to the petitioner, even though at the date of the petition the unfairness had been remedied. The court could still make an order to check possible future prejudice.

The use of the word 'conduct' is important since it covers both acts and omissions, e.g. failure to pay proper dividends when profits allow.

Of even greater importance, however, at least in terms of the case law, is the interpretation placed by the courts, in particular by Hoffman J in *Re A Company (No 00477 of 1986)* [1986] PCC 372, on 'interests of its members'. Many of the petitions presented under the unfair prejudice provisions have been in regard to the removal of a director from the board of a private company. The director concerned has been able to establish that the conduct relating to him as a director was also unfairly prejudicial to him as a member because the 'interest' of a member in a private company legitimately includes a place on the board. Some of these cases are set out later in this chapter.

The requirement that the petition be 'well founded' is to ensure that the provisions are not abused or used for a wrongful purpose. An earlier case under different legislation provides a valid illustration. In *Re Bellador Silk Ltd* [1965] 1 All ER 667 a member of the company presented a petition to the court for relief, but mainly as a form of harassment of the board in order to make them pay an alleged debt to one of his companies. The court decided that the petition had a collateral purpose and dismissed it as not a *bona fide* attempt to get relief.

## Relief available

(a) Specific relief. This is as follows:
    (i)   The court may regulate the company's affairs for the future;
    (ii)  The court may restrain the doing of or the continuing of prejudicial acts.
    **The above two heads are illustrated quite validly by the following case decided under earlier legislation.**

### Re H R Harmer Ltd [1958] 3 All ER 689

The company was formed in July 1947 to acquire a business founded by Mr H R Harmer who was born in 1869. The business of the company was stamp auctioneering, and dealing in and valuing stamps. Two of Mr Harmer's sons, Cyril and Bernard Harmer, went into the business on leaving school. The nominal capital of the company was £50,000, and Mr Harmer senior and his wife were between them able to control the general meetings of the company, and could even obtain special and extraordinary resolutions. Mrs Harmer always voted with her husband. The father and his two sons were life directors under the articles, the father being chairman of the board with a casting vote. The sons claimed that their father had repeatedly abused his controlling power in the conduct of the company's affairs so that they were bound to apply for relief. Mr Harmer senior had, they said, always acted as though the right of appointing and dismissing senior staff was vested in him alone, and this right he also extended to the appointment of directors. He also considered that no director should express a contrary view to that expressed by himself, and had generally ignored the views of his sons and the other directors and shareholders. In particular, he had opened a branch of the company in Australia in spite of the protests by the other directors, and the branch had not proved profitable. In addition, he dismissed an old servant and procured the appointment of his own 'yes-men' to the board. He drew unauthorised expenses for himself and his wife and engaged a detective to watch the staff. He also endeavoured to sell off the company's American business which severely damaged its goodwill. Roxburgh J, at first instance, granted relief and the Court of Appeal confirmed the order. Roxburgh J's order provided *inter alia* that the company should contract for the services of Mr Harmer senior as philatelic consultant at a salary of £2,500 per annum; that he should not interfere in the affairs of the company otherwise than in accordance with the valid decisions of the board; and that he be appointed president of the company for life, but that this office should not impose any duties or create any rights or powers to him.

*Comment:* The court's order had the effect of changing the provision in the articles under which Mr Harmer was a director for life with a casting vote. The order also restrained him for the future from interfering with the valid decisions of the board.

(iii) The court may authorise a claim to be brought by the company. This would appear to allow a minority to obtain redress for the company where it had been injured by the wrongful acts of the majority. The claim would not be derivative because the court would authorise the company to commence the action as a claimant. It is the ability of the court to order that a claim be made by the company where it has suffered harm on the petition of even one shareholder which outdates the Rule in *Foss* v *Harbottle*.

(iv) The court may order the purchase of the minority shares at a fair price either by other members or by the company itself, in which case the court would also authorise a reduction of capital. This remedy has been by far the most popular and has largely replaced winding-up under the just and equitable rule – which was formerly the only real way of compelling the majority to return the share capital of the minority (*see further* later in this chapter).

(b) *General relief.* In addition to the above, the court may make such order as it thinks fit for giving relief in respect of the matters complained of. Thus in *Re a Company (No 005287 of 1985)* [1986] 1 WLR 281, the controlling shareholder took all the profits in management fees and was ordered to account for the money to the company and this although at the time of the action he had sold all his shares in the company concerned to his Gibraltar company. Thus a petition can be presented even against a person who has ceased to be a member.

## The Jenkins Committee and unfair prejudice

Part XVII results from recommendations made by the Jenkins Committee on company law reform which reported in 1962. It is of value, therefore, to consider what sort of conduct the Jenkins Committee thought would be 'unfairly prejudicial'. They mentioned the following:

(a) directors appointing themselves to paid posts within the company at excessive rates of remuneration, thus depriving the members of a dividend or an adequate dividend – and indeed it was exactly this sort of scenario which caused the court to find unfair prejudice to a non-director member in *Re Sam Weller* [1989] 3 WLR 923;

(b) directors refusing to register the personal representatives of a deceased member so that, in the absence of a specific provision in the articles, they cannot vote, as part of a scheme to make the personal representatives sell the shares to the directors at an inadequate price;

(c) the issue of shares to directors and others on advantageous terms;

(d) failure of directors to declare dividends on non-cumulative preference shares held by a minority.

Obviously, some of the above matters affect all the shareholders and not merely a minority, e.g. non-payment of dividends. However, the provisions of Part XVII as re-worded by the Companies Act 1989 clearly now include acts affecting the members *generally*.

## Illustrative case law

In *Re a Company (No 00475 of 1982)* [1983] 2 WLR 381, Lord Grantchester QC *held* that no prejudice arose under what is now Part XVII of the 1985 Act simply because the directors of a company refuse to exercise their power to buy the company's shares; nor because they fail to put into effect a scheme which would have entitled the petitioners to sell their shares at a higher price than they might have been able to otherwise; nor because they propose to dissipate the company's liquid resources by investing them in a partly owned subsidiary. Lord Grantchester also said that it would usually be necessary for a member claiming unfair prejudice to show that his shares had been seriously diminished in value. However, in *Re R A Noble (Clothing) Ltd* [1983] BCLC 273 Nourse J said that the jurisdiction under Part XVII was not limited to such a case and that diminution in the value of shares was not essential. In *Re Garage Door Associates* [1984] 1 All ER 434 Mervyn Davies J *held* that a member could present a petition for a winding-up on the just and equitable ground *and* petition for the purchase of his shares under Part XVII. Such a procedure is not an abuse of the process of the court. However, there has more recently been a Practice Direction that the two claims should not be made as a matter of course but only where there is a chance that one or the other will fail.

In *Re Bird Precision Bellows* [1984] 2 WLR 869 and again in *Re London School of Electronics* [1985] 3 WLR 474, Nourse J said that the removal of a member from the board was unfairly prejudicial conduct within what is now Part XVII. He made an order for the purchase of the shares of the petitioners in both cases by the majority shareholders and decided that in valuing the shares there should be no discount in the price because the holdings were minority holdings, unless the minority were in some way to blame for the situation giving rise to the alleged unfair prejudice. However, Nourse J did decide in *Re London School of Electronics*, 1985 (*see above*), that there was no overriding requirement under what is now Part XVII that the petitioner should come to court with clean hands.

In *Re R A Noble (Clothing) Ltd*, 1983 (*see above*), Nourse J decided that a director who had been excluded from management could claim unfair prejudice but not in the particular circumstances of the case because his exclusion was to a large extent due to his own disinterest in the company's affairs so that the other members of the board felt that they had to manage without him.

In *Re a Company (No 008699 of 1985)* [1986] PCC 269, the High Court *held* that it was unfairly prejudicial to minority shareholders where, on a takeover bid for the company, the directors recommended acceptance of a bid by a company in which they had an interest while ignoring a much more favourable alternative offer.

In *Re Mossmain Ltd*, *Financial Times*, 27 June 1986, four persons agreed to form a company. Two of these were husband and wife. Because the husband had a restrictive covenant in a contract of employment which might be infringed if he became a member/director of the company, his shares were held by his wife for the duration of the covenant, he becoming an employee only for the time being. The wife was made a director. Later the husband was dismissed and his wife was removed from the board. Husband and wife petitioned under Part XVII and the court *held* that the husband's name must be struck out of the petition. He did not qualify to petition since he was not a member as Part XVII requires.

Finally, in *Re a Company* [1986] BCLC 362 it was *held* that there was no unfair prejudice where the company made a rights issue to all members pro rata to their shareholding which the petitioner could not afford even though his interest in the company after the issue would be reduced from 25 per cent to 0.125 per cent. The company genuinely needed capital.

# MINORITY PETITION FOR JUST AND EQUITABLE WINDING-UP

The court has a jurisdiction under the Insolvency Act 1986, s 122(1)(g) to wind up a company on the petition of a minority on the ground that it is 'just and equitable' to do so.

This ground is subjected to a flexible interpretation by the courts. In the context of minority rights, however, orders have been made where the managing director who represented the majority shareholder interests in his management of the company refused, for example, to produce accounts or pay dividends (*Loch* v *John Blackwood Ltd* [1924] AC 783) and where, in the case of a small company formed or continued on the basis of a personal relationship involving mutual confidence, and which is in essence a partnership, the person petitioning is excluded from management participation and the circumstances are such as would justify the dissolution of a partnership. This was the approach in *Ebrahimi* v *Westbourne Galleries* [1972] 2 All ER 492. However, since the enactment of the unfair prejudice provisions and following the case of *Re a Company* [1983] 2 All ER 854 other matters have been brought to the fore. These are:

(a) that if the majority make an offer to buy out the shares of the director who has been removed at a fair price, e.g. to be decided on by the company's auditor, the court is not perhaps likely to wind up the company because the ex-director's capital is available by other means. No such offer was made in *Ebrahimi*;

(b) even if no such offer is made, the better approach these days might be by petition under the unfair prejudice provisions. The court can, as we have seen, order the purchase of the ex-director's shares, at a fair price, either by the other members or by the company in reduction of capital.

However, the procedure through just and equitable winding-up is not specifically repealed and there is no rule of law preventing that approach, and indeed it was *held* in *Jesner* v *Jarrad*, *The Times*, 26 October 1992 that a lack of unfair prejudice under s 459 will not prevent the court from winding up a company on the just and equitable ground. In that case a family company was being run in good faith and without prejudice to the claimant who was a family member. Nevertheless, the claimant and his brother and the other members of the family had lost that mutual confidence required in what was really a quasi-partnership, and on the basis of the *Westbourne Galleries* case it was just and equitable that it should be wound up, given the disputes within the family as to how it should be run.

# COMPANIES AND PARTNERSHIPS COMPARED

## General

The following areas should be noted:

(a) a company is a persona at law. A partnership firm is not a persona at law. Thus a company continues to exist despite, for example, the death of any of its members, whereas this event will bring about the dissolution of a partnership;

(b) in a company the shares of the members are freely transferable, whereas no partner can transfer his share without the consent of the other partners, because this would involve the admission of a new partner on which the Partnership Act 1890 requires all partners to agree;

(c) a shareholder is not an agent for the company, but each general partner is an agent of the firm to make contracts which will bind himself and his other partners;

(d) the members of a company have no power to manage its affairs whereas, unless the partnership agreement otherwise provides, all partners have a right to take part in the management of the firm;

(e) the liability of each shareholder may be limited either by shares or by guarantee, but the liability of partners for the debts of the firm is unlimited, except in the case of a limited partner;

(f) the affairs of a registered company are closely controlled by the Companies Act 1985 and it must in general trade within the objects as set out in its memorandum, though where the company has the sole object 'general commercial company' this is not a problem (and *see further* Chapter 18). Partners may enter into any business they please and may make any arrangements they choose regarding the running of the firm, so long, that is, as they stay within the general limits of the law.

## Advantages and disadvantages of incorporation

The *main* advantages put forward by professional advisers for the conversion of a business into a limited company can be summarised as follows:

(a) perpetual succession of the company despite the retirement, bankruptcy, mental disorder or death of members;

(b) liability of members for company's debts is limited to the amount of their respective shareholding;

(c) contractual liability of the company from all contracts in its name;

(d) ownership of property vested in the company is not affected by a change in shareholders;

(e) The company may obtain finance by creating a floating charge with its undertaking or property as security yet may realise assets within that property without the consent of the lenders during the normal course of business until crystallisation occurs. *No other form of business organisation can use such a charge.*

It is generally thought that the above advantages outweigh the suggested disadvantages of incorporation, which are:

(a) public inspection of accounts;

(b) administrative expenses, in terms, for example, of filing fees for documents;

(c) compulsory annual audit, though in certain small companies this can be dispensed with (*see further* Chapter 18).

## GRADED QUESTIONS

### Essay mode

1 'A person who lends on the security of a specific mortgage of a company's property is always entitled to repayment on his loan out of the proceeds of sale of the mortgaged property before any other creditor. A person who takes a floating charge is not in as secure a position.' *Pennington.*

Why is the holder of a floating charge in a less favourable position?

*(The Institute of Chartered Accountants in England and Wales)*

2 'The combined effect of the Insolvency Act 1986 and the Company Directors Disqualification Act 1986 is to give a clear signal to directors that to allow their companies to continue trading and to incur debts at a time when the position is hopeless is both a costly and foolhardy thing to do. In particular, the temptation to use money owed to the Crown to keep their companies afloat must be avoided at all costs.'
Discuss.

*(The Institute of Chartered Secretaries and Administrators)*

3 (a) What members' meetings are held by registered companies?
(b) Name and define the different kinds of resolution which may be passed by such companies in general meeting. In the case of each kind of resolution give one example of business for which such a resolution is necessary.

*(The Institute of Company Accountants)*

4 Explain how the provisions of the Companies Act 1985 attempt to ensure that majority shareholders do not conduct the affairs of a company with complete disregard for the interests of minority shareholders.

*(The Chartered Institute of Management Accountants)*

## Objective mode

Four alternative answers are given. Select ONE only. Circle the answer which you consider to be correct. Check your answers by referring back to the information given in the chapter and against the answers at the back of the book.

1 Thames Ltd is insolvent and is being wound up. The bank has a floating charge over its assets in regard to an overdraft which has not been registered. What is the effect of this?

A The charge is void against the liquidator and the bank proves as an ordinary creditor.
B The debt is void as against the liquidator and the bank will get nothing.
C The charge is voidable by the liquidator if the company was insolvent when the charge was created.
D The charge is void against subsequent secured creditors and the bank loses its priority accordingly.

2 A director can be removed at a general meeting of his company. What kind of resolution is required?

A An ordinary resolution following special notice to the company.
B An ordinary resolution.
C A special resolution following special notice to the company.
D A special resolution.

3 Jones is a director of Shannon Ltd which is a subsidiary of a public company. At what age will Jones have to vacate office and seek re-election at the next annual general meeting?
A no age limit.
B 75.
C 70.
D 65.

4 The court is about to disqualify the directors of Blue Ltd for unfitness. How long may the order last?

   A  A maximum of 15 years with no minimum.
   B  A minimum of two years with a maximum of 15 years.
   C  A minimum of two years with a maximum of five years.
   D  A minimum of five years with a maximum of 15 years.

5 Thames Ltd wishes to pass a special resolution of the members to change the articles. What length of notice is required, and how many of the company's members present and voting in person or by proxy are needed to pass the resolution?

   A  21 days' notice and over 50 per cent.
   B  28 days' notice and over 50 per cent.
   C  21 days' notice and 75 per cent.
   D  28 days' notice and 75 per cent.

6 Which of following can petition the court for relief under Part XVII of the CA 1985?

   A  The company.
   B  Members holding not less than 10 per cent in number of the company's issued shares.
   C  A member of the company.
   D  A creditor of the company.

*Answers to questions set in objective mode appear on p 709.*

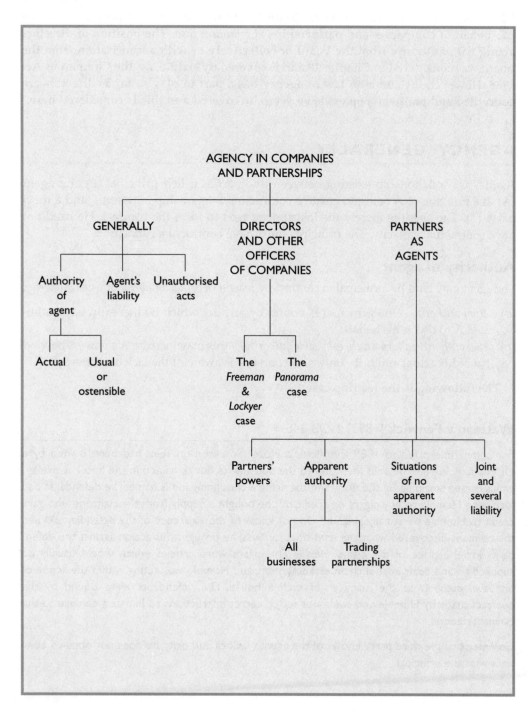

The objectives of this chapter are to deal with the authority of persons to act on behalf of companies and partnerships at *common law*. The position of directors acting with authority from the board or collectively or with authorisation from the board was considered in Chapter 18 and is covered by statute, i.e. the Companies Act 1985. However, the common law of agency has a part to play so far as directors are concerned and partners' powers have yet to be covered and this is considered here.

## AGENCY: GENERALLY

Agency is a relationship existing between two parties called principal (P) and agent (A), the function of A being to create a contractual relationship between P and a third party (T). The agent is merely the instrument used to form the contract. He need not have contractual capacity. The principal must have contractual capacity.

### Authority of agent

The agent may bind his principal in contract by reason of *actual authority* or *usual authority*:

(a) *actual authority* – the principal is bound by any act which he has expressly authorised A to do on his behalf;

(b) *usual authority (alternatively ostensible authority)* – this may increase A's powers beyond that of his actual authority unless, of course, T is aware of the lack of authority.

**The following is the leading case.**

### Watteau v Fenwick [1893] 1 QB 346

For some time prior to 1888 the Victoria Hotel, Stockton-on-Tees, had been owned by a Mr Humble. In 1888 he sold the hotel to the defendants but remained in the hotel as manager, his name remaining on the door and the licence continuing in his name. The defendants had forbidden Humble to buy cigars on credit, but he bought a supply from the claimant who gave credit to Humble personally since he did not know of the existence of the defendants. When the claimant discovered what the true situation was, he brought this action against the defendants for the price of the cigars. *Held* – The cigars were articles which would usually be supplied to and dealt in at such an establishment, and Humble was acting within the scope of his *usual authority* as the manager of such a house. The defendants were bound by the contract made by Humble and could not set up secret instructions to him as a defence to the claimant's action.

*Comment:* If the third party knows of the agent's lack of authority, he does not obtain a contract with the principal.

## Agent's liability

If the agent indicates to the third party that he is contracting as an agent, whether he names his principal or not, the contract is between the principal and the third party and the agent will not normally be liable on it. The agent may be liable, however, in certain circumstances which are set out below.

(a) *Contracts by deed.* Where the agent enters into a deed on behalf of the principal it is the agent who must sue and be sued. Thus, where an accountant entered into an agreement by a deed as liquidator of a company it was *held* that because the agreement was in the form of a deed the defendant accountant was personally liable on it (*Plant Engineers (Sales) v Davies* (1969) 113 SJ 484). In such a case the agent would have a right of indemnity against the principal.

(b) *Third party insistence.* There may be cases where the third party has insisted that the agent also accepts liability before he will make the contract. If the agent has agreed to this he will be liable along with the principal. In other cases the agent may have agreed to be the principal's guarantor.

## Unauthorised acts of the agent

Two situations may arise as follows:

(a) if the agent, although not in fact authorised, acts within his usual (or ostensible) authority, the principal is liable on the contract and the agent is not, though the agent may be liable to the principal for breach of duty (*see Watteau v Fenwick* (1893);

(b) if the act is outside the agent's actual and usual (or ostensible) authority, the principal is not liable, but the agent is liable to the third party for *breach of warranty of authority* and this is so even though the agent acted in good faith believing that he had authority.

The action seems to be based on quasi-contract, for the agent is not liable on the contract as such and cannot be required to carry it out. However, the measure of damages awarded against the agent will include compensation for the loss of the bargain with the principal and damages will be awarded in the same way as if the third party had been suing the principal for breach of contract.

# DIRECTORS AND OTHER OFFICERS OF COMPANIES

We are concerned here to deal with the only aspect of the common law of agency which is relevant in this field, i.e. the effect of usual authority as seen in the *Watteau* case on the *unauthorised* acts of individual directors and other officers of a company. Where a director or other officer of a company has no actual authority or authorisation under s 35 of the CA 1985 to enter into a transaction an outsider may be able to regard the company as bound by it if it is *usual* in the company context for a director or officer to be able to enter into a transaction of the kind in question. Since it is usual to delegate wide powers to a managing director and executive directors, an outsider will normally be protected if he is dealing with a person who is a managing director or another executive director, e.g. sales director, or who has been held out as such by the company.

A managing director would seem to have contractual authority on this basis across the whole of the company's activities. Other executive directors would probably be restricted to contractual authority in their respective spheres. Thus in *Freeman & Lockyer v Buckhurst Park Properties Ltd* [1964] 1 All ER 630 a managing director without express authority of the board, but with their knowledge, employed on behalf of the company a firm of architects and surveyors for the submission of an application for planning permission which involved preparing plans and defining boundaries. It was *held* that the company was liable to pay their fees. The managing director had bound the company by his acts which were within the usual authority of a managing director.

Where, however, the outsider deals with a non-executive director or officer, who has not been authorised under s 35 of the CA 1985, his position is much less secure. An ordinary director and other officers of the company have little usual authority to bind the company.

Once one gets below the director level, the position becomes even more of a problem. There is little, if any, usual authority in the executive of a company to make contracts on its behalf without actual authority, though it would appear that a company secretary has authority to bind the company in contracts relating to day-to-day administration.

Thus in *Panorama Developments* v *Fidelis Furnishing Fabrics* [1971] 3 All ER 16 the secretary of a company ordered cars from a car hire firm representing that they were required to meet the company's customers at London Airport. Instead he used the cars for his own purposes. The company did not pay the bill so the car hire firm claimed from the secretary's company. It was *held* that the company was liable for its secretary had usual authority to make contracts such as the present one which was concerned with the administrative side of the business.

## PARTNERS AS AGENTS

The power of a partner, including a salaried partner, to make himself and his partner liable for transactions which he enters into *on behalf of the firm* (not on his own behalf) is based on the law of agency. Each partner is the agent of his co-partners.

Section 5 of the Partnership Act 1890 makes this clear. It says that every partner is the agent of the firm and of his co-partners for the purpose of the business of the partnership.

### Partners' powers

A partner's authority to enter into transactions on behalf of the firm and his co-partners may be set out under the following headings.

### *Actual authority*

If a partner is asked by his co-partners to buy a new van for the firm's use and makes a contract to purchase one, the firm is bound. Section 6 deals with authorised acts and says that the firm will be liable for the authorised acts of partners and also employees of the firm.

### Apparent authority

If a partner enters into a transaction on behalf of the firm without authority, the person the partner deals with may, if he or she does not know of the lack of authority, hold the firm bound under the provisions of s 5 which gives partners some apparent authority.

However, s 5 says that *the transaction must be connected with the business*. If there is a dispute about this, the court will decide what can be said to be 'connected', regardless of what the partnership agreement may say.

**The following case illustrates the point.**

## Mercantile Credit Co Ltd v Garrod [1962] 3 All ER 1103

Mr Parkin and Mr Garrod had entered into an agreement as partners for the letting of garages and the carrying out of motor repairs, but the agreement expressly excluded the buying and selling of cars. Parkin, without Garrod's knowledge, sold a car to Mercantile for the sum of £700 but the owner of the car had not consented to the sale. The finance company did not, therefore, become owners of the car and wanted its money back. The court *held* that the firm was liable and that Mr Garrod was liable as a partner to repay what the firm owed to Mercantile. The judge dismissed the argument that the transaction did not bind the firm because the agreement excluded the buying and selling of cars. He looked at the matter instead from 'what was apparent to the outside world in general'. Parkin was doing an act of a like kind to the business carried on by persons trading as a garage.

*Comment:* The point of the case is that although the buying and selling of cars was expressly forbidden by the partnership agreement, the firm was bound. This is a correct application of s 8, which provides that internal restrictions on the authority of partners will have effect only if the outsider deals with a partner, but with actual notice of the restrictions. In this case Mercantile had no such knowledge of the restrictions and there is no constructive notice of the contents of partnership agreements.

Also, the transaction must be carried out *in the usual way of business*. In other words, it must be a *normal* transaction for the business. An example can be seen in *Goldberg* v *Jenkins* (1889) 15 VLR 36 where a partner borrowed money on behalf of the firm at 60 per cent interest per annum when money could be borrowed at between 6 per cent and 10 per cent per annum. He had no actual authority to enter into such a transaction and the court *held* that the firm was not bound to accept the loan. The firm did borrow money but it was not usual or normal to borrow at that high rate.

Finally, s 5 says that *the outsider must know or believe that he is dealing with a partner in the firm*. Because of the requirements of the Business Names Act 1985 (*see* Chapter 18) as regards the display of the names of the owners of the firm on various documents and in various places a *dormant partner* is now more likely to be known as a partner to an outsider. So if a dormant partner makes an unauthorised contract in the ordinary course of business in the usual or normal way, the outsider should now be able to say that he knew or believed the dormant partner to be a partner. If he does so say, a dormant partner can enter into an unauthorised transaction which will bind the firm under s 5. If the outsider does not know the dormant partner is a member of the firm, as where the 1985 Act is not being complied with, then the firm will not be bound. A dormant partner would be bound since he made the contract.

677

### Situations of apparent authority as laid down by case law

Section 5 does not say what acts are in the usual course of business. However, the courts have, over the years, and sometimes in cases heard before the 1890 Act was passed codifying the law, decided that there are a number of definite areas in which a partner has apparent authority. These are set out below.

#### All partners in all businesses

Here there is apparent authority to sell the goods (but not the land) of the firm, and to buy goods (but not land) on behalf of the firm, to receive money in payments of debts due to the firm and to give valid receipts. So if A pays a debt due to the firm to B, a partner, who gives A a receipt then fails to put the money into the firm's funds, A is nevertheless discharged from payment of the debt. Partners can also employ workers but once they are taken on they are employees of *all* the partners so that one partner cannot discharge an employee without the consent of the others. Partners also have an insurable interest in the firm's property and can insure it. They may also employ a solicitor to defend the firm if an action is brought against it. The authority of an individual partner to employ a solicitor to bring an action on behalf of the firm seems to be restricted to actions to recover debts owing to the firm.

#### All partners in trading partnerships

Partners in trading firms have powers *which are additional* to those set out above. Thus partners in a firm of grocers have more powers than partners in a professional practice of, for example, law or accountancy. There does not seem to be any good reason for this but it has been confirmed by many cases in court and cannot be ignored.

In *Wheatley* v *Smithers* [1906] 2 KB 321 the judge said in regard to what was meant by the word 'trader': 'One important element in any definition of the term would be that trading implies buying or selling'. This was applied in *Higgins* v *Beauchamp* [1914] 3 KB 1192 where it was decided that a partner in a business running a cinema had no implied power to borrow on behalf of the firm. The partnership agreement did not give power to borrow and because the firm did not trade in the *Wheatley* v *Smithers* sense there was no implied power to borrow. If a firm is engaged in trade, the additional implied powers of the partners are:

(a) to draw, issue, accept, transfer and endorse promissory notes and bills of exchange, including cheques if connected with the business and in the usual way of business. *A partner in a non-trading business only has apparent authority to draw cheques in the firm's name on the firm's bankers.* If the cheque is stopped a payee can sue the firm on it;

(b) to borrow money on the credit of the firm even beyond any limit agreed on by the partners unless this limit is known to the lender. Borrowing includes overdrawing a bank account;

(c) to secure the loan, which means giving the lender a right to sell property belonging to the firm if the loan is not repaid.

## Situations of no apparent authority

No partner, whether in a trading firm or not, has apparent authority in the following situations.

(a) A partner cannot make the firm liable on a deed. He or she needs the authority of the other partners. This authority must be given by deed. In English law an agent who is to make contracts by a deed must be appointed as an agent by a written document stated to be a deed;

(b) A partner cannot give a guarantee, e.g. of another person's debt, on which the firm will be liable;

(c) A partner cannot accept payment of a debt at a discount by, for example, accepting 75p instead of £1, nor can he or she take something for the debt which is not money. A partner cannot, therefore, take shares in a company in payment of a debt owed to the firm;

(d) A partner cannot bind the firm by agreeing to go to arbitration with a dispute. Going to arbitration with a dispute and having it heard by, say, an engineer, if the dispute relates, for example, to the quality of engineering work done under a contract is a sort of compromise of the right to go first to a court of law and have the case heard by a judge. A partner cannot compromise the legal rights of the firm;

(e) As we have seen, a partner has no apparent authority to convey or enter into a contract for the sale of partnership land.

## A partner's liability for debt and breach of contract by the firm

If because of actual or apparent authority, a partner (or for that matter another agent such as an employee) makes the firm liable to pay a debt or carry out a contract, as where goods are ordered and the firm refuses to take delivery, the usual procedure will be to sue the firm in the firm's name. If the court gives the claimant a judgment and the firm does not have sufficient assets to meet it, the partners are liable to pay it from their private assets. Under s 3 of the Civil Liability (Contribution) Act 1978 each partner is liable to pay the amount of the judgment in full. Thus liability is several as well as joint. The partner who has actually paid the debt on behalf of the firm will then have the right to what is called a contribution from co-partners.

Before the 1978 Act contribution was equal. Thus, if A paid a partnership debt of £300, he could ask partners B and C for a contribution of £100 each.

This rule of equal contribution is taken away by s 2 of the 1978 Act which provides that the amount of any contribution which the court may give is to be what it thinks is 'just and equitable' so that it need not in all cases be equal, but most often will be.

The effect of the above rules is that a partner can be required to pay the firm's debts from private assets. From this we can see that only if *all* the partners are unable to pay the firm's debts will the firm be truly insolvent. Under s 9 of the Partnership Act 1890 the estate of a deceased partner is also liable for the debts of the firm which were incurred while the deceased was a partner.

## GRADED QUESTIONS

### Essay mode

1 Exe Limited is a company whose articles of association are in the form of Table A to the Companies Act 1985. No managing director has ever been appointed and the day-to-day business of the company has been conducted by John, the chairman, and Ken, the secretary. The board of directors is aware of the position and has never raised any objection.

   (a) Advise Norman who has entered into contracts with the company through John. It now appears that these contracts are not authorised by the objects clause in the memorandum of association of Exe Limited.

   (b) Advise William who is a taxi driver and is claiming for taxi fares incurred on behalf of the company by Ken. There is a resolution by the board of directors instructing Ken not to order taxis.

*(Institute of Chartered Accountants in England and Wales)*

2 Jim and Alan are partners in a garage. Jim provided the capital and only visits the garage at infrequent intervals. Alan works full time for the firm. It is a term of the partnership agreement that no partner shall incur any debt exceeding £100 without the consent of the other, that oil shall only be purchased from the Ooze Oil Company and that there shall be no trading in second-hand cars. Alan has bought oil to the value of £200 from another company and has bought several second-hand cars on his own account but in the name of the firm

   Advise Jim.

*(Institute of Chartered Accountants in England and Wales)*

### Objective mode

1 The managing director of a company has usual or ostensible authority to bind the company by transactions he enters into on its behalf. Which of the following statements represents the limit of this authority?

   **A** All commercial matters which relate to the running of the business.
   **B** All activities of the company whether commercial or not.
   **C** Such commercial activities as the company may direct in general meeting.
   **D** Such commercial activities as the board may delegate to him.

2 An ordinary director of Grime Ltd who has no responsibility for the acquisition of goods contracts on Grime's behalf (unknown to his fellow directors who are also active in the business) to buy goods from a supplier who has not read Grime's articles nor made enquiries.

   What is Grime's legal position on the contract?

   **A** It is bound by reason of s 35A of the Companies Act 1985.
   **B** It is not bound because an ordinary director has no usual or ostensible authority to bind the company.
   **C** It is bound by reason of case law.
   **D** It is not bound because a company is never bound by the acts of a single director.

3  Maggie has just been appointed managing director of Severn Ltd. What is the nature of her authority to enter into unauthorised contracts on behalf of the company?

   A  Express.
   B  Implied.
   C  Usual (or ostensible).
   D  Apparent.

4  Fred is an ordinary director of Marina Ltd. The board of directors delegates to him the job of purchasing two lorries for the company.
   Ken's authority is known as:

   A  Express actual authority.
   B  Implied authority.
   C  Usual (or ostensible) authority.
   D  Apparent authority.

5  John and Jane are partners. John made a contract with Globe Ltd on behalf of the firm for goods for the firm. There is an unpaid invoice for £3,000 which the firm cannot pay.
   Advise Jane as to her legal position.

   A  John and Jane are each liable to pay the £3,000 and may seek a contribution.
   B  Only John is liable to pay the £3,000.
   C  John can be sued for only £1,500. Globe must sue Jane for the balance.
   D  There is no liability so far as Jane is concerned.

6  Meg and Barney are partners in a pet shop. Barney without discussing the matter with Meg enters into a contract to insure the firm's property. Meg thinks the premium is a little high though in fact it is reasonable. Meg does not wish to go on with the contract.
   What is the legal position?

   A  The firm is bound by the contract.
   B  Only Barney is bound.
   C  Meg and Barney are bound but the firm is not.
   D  The contract of insurance is void because one partner cannot bind the firm and his co-partners without actual authority.

*Answers to questions set in objective mode appear on p 709.*

# 22 NEGLIGENCE – GENERALLY AND THE BUSINESS APPLICATION

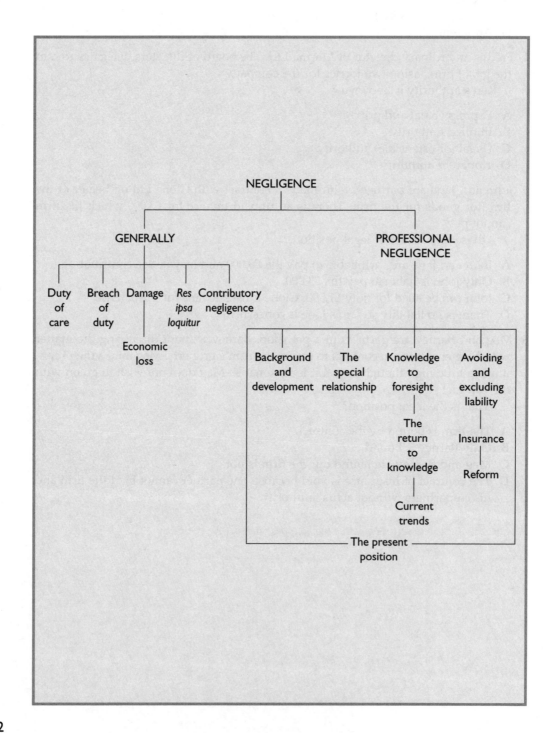

The objectives of this chapter are to explain the legal concept of negligence and to deal in particular with the tort of negligence as it affects business professionals, especially accountants and auditors.

## NEGLIGENCE GENERALLY

In ordinary language, negligence may simply mean not done intentionally, e.g. the negligent publication of a libel. But while negligence may be one factor or ingredient in another tort, it is also a specific and independent tort and with this we are now concerned.

The tort of negligence has three ingredients and to succeed in an action the claimant must show:

(a) the existence of a duty to take care which was owed to him by the defendant;
(b) breach of such duty by the defendant; and
(c) resulting damage to the claimant.

### The duty of care

Whether a duty of care exists or not is a question of law for the judge to decide. Since the decision of the House of Lords in *Donoghue* v *Stevenson* (1932) (*see* Chapter 11), the test has become objective and is based on the foresight of the reasonable man. This derives from Lord Atkin's 'neighbour' test which he formulated in the following words: 'You must take reasonable care to avoid acts or omissions which you can reasonably foresee would be likely to injure your neighbour. Who then is my neighbour? The answer seems to be persons who are so closely and directly affected by my act that I ought reasonably to have them in contemplation as being affected when I am directing my mind to the acts or omissions which are called in question.' As we have seen, the test is objective, not subjective, and the effect of its application is that a person is not liable for every injury which results from his carelessness.

**There must be a duty of care, as the following case illustrates.**

### Hay (or Bourhill) v Young [1943] AC 92

The claimant, a pregnant Edinburgh fishwife, alighted from a tramcar. While she was removing her fish-basket from the tram, Young, a motor cyclist, driving carelessly but unseen by her, passed the tram and collided with a motor car some 15 yards away. Young was killed. The claimant heard the collision, and after Young's body had been removed, she approached the scene of the accident and saw a pool of blood on the road. She suffered a nervous shock and later gave birth to a stillborn child. The House of Lords *held* that her action against Young's personal representative failed, because Young owed no duty of care to persons whom he could not reasonably anticipate would suffer injuries as a result of his conduct on the highway.

*Comment:* Lord Atkin's 'neighbour' test has extended to monetary loss caused by careless misstatements. This has produced a special area of negligence which is referred to as professional negligence. This is considered in detail later in this chapter.

## Breach of the duty

If a duty of care is established as a matter of law, whether or not the defendant was in breach of that duty is a matter of fact. Since juries are not present in negligence cases, this again is a matter to be decided by the judge but on the basis of fact, not law. If the defendant is not in breach of the duty to take care, he will not be liable (*see Daniels* v *White & Sons Ltd* (1938) in Chapter 11).

## Resulting damage to the claimant

It is necessary for the claimant to show that he has suffered some loss since negligence is not actionable *per se* (in itself). Thus I may believe that the man in front of me is driving his car too fast and in that sense negligently, but he would not be liable unless he hit somebody or something and caused damage. Damage would not, of course, be necessary for criminal prosecution for dangerous driving, but it is essential to a civil action. It will have been noted also that damage is not necessary in contract where nominal damages will be awarded even for a technical breach.

## Mere economic loss

The 'neighbour' test of Lord Atkin does not extend to all kinds of damage and, in particular, it should be noted that there is in general no liability where the defendant's act causes mere economic or monetary loss to the claimant unless the economic or monetary loss arises out of or is accompanied by foreseeable physical injury to the claimant or damage to his property. We have already noted, that where the defendant's misstatement, as distinct from his act, causes monetary loss, then this is actionable (*Hedley Byrne* v *Heller & Partners* (1963), in Chapter 5). This is the basis of professional liability which is considered further later in this Chapter.

**An example of parasitical damages appears below.**

### Spartan Steel and Alloys Ltd v Martin & Co Ltd [1972] 3 All ER 557

While digging up a road, the defendants' employees damaged a cable which the defendants knew supplied the claimants' factory. The cable belonged to the local electricity board and the resulting electrical power failure meant that the claimants' factory was deprived of electricity. The temperature of their furnace dropped and so metal that was in melt had to be poured away. Furthermore, while the cable was being repaired the factory received no electricity so it was unable to function for some 14 hours. The Court of Appeal, however, allowed only the claimants' damages for the spoilt metal and the loss of profit on one 'melt'. They refused to allow the claimants to recover their loss of profit which resulted from the factory being unable to function during the period when there was no electricity. Lord Denning MR chose to base his decision on remoteness of damage rather than the absence of any duty of care to avoid causing economic loss. However, he did make it clear that public policy was involved. In the course of his judgment he said:

At bottom I think the question of recovering economic loss is one of policy. Whenever the courts draw a line to mark out the bounds of duty, they do so as a matter of policy so as to limit the responsibility of the defendant. Whenever the courts set bounds to the damages recoverable – saying that they are, or are not, too remote – they do it as a matter of policy so as to limit the liability of the defendant.

### Res ipsa loquitur

Although the burden of proof in negligence normally lies on the claimant, there is a principle known as *res ipsa loquitur* (the thing speaks for itself) and where the principle applies the court is prepared to lighten the claimant's burden. In some cases it is difficult for the claimant to show how much care the defendant has taken and it is a common-sense rule of evidence to allow the claimant to prove the result and not require him to prove any particular act or omission by the defendant. Before the principle can apply, the thing causing the damage must be shown to be under the control of the defendant and the accident which happened must be one which does not normally occur unless negligence is present. On proof of this situation negligence in the defendant will be assumed, and he will be liable unless he can explain the occurrence on grounds other than his negligence. The explanation must, of course, be convincing to the court and it is not enough to offer purely hypothetical explanations. For example, if a tile falls off Y's roof and injures X who is lawfully on the highway below, this would probably be a situation in which *res ipsa loquitur* would apply. But if Y can show that at the time an explosion had occurred nearby and this had probably dislodged the tile and the court is impressed by this explanation of the event, the burden of proof reverts to X.

**Illustrations appear below.**

### Byrne v Boadle (1863) 2 H & C 722

The claimant brought an action in negligence alleging that, as he was walking past the defendant's shop, a barrel of flour fell from a window above the shop and injured him. The defendant was a dealer in flour, but there was no evidence that the defendant or any of his servants were engaged in lowering the barrel of flour at the time. The defendant submitted that there was no evidence of negligence to go to the jury, but it was *held* that the occurrence was of itself evidence of negligence sufficient to entitle the jury to find for the claimant, even in the absence of an explanation by the defendant.

*Comment:* The rule was set in a more modern context in *Ward* v *Tesco Stores Ltd* [1976] 1 All ER 219 where the Court of Appeal ruled that an accident which had occurred due to a spillage of yoghurt on a shop floor put an evidential burden on the defendant shopowner to show that the subsequent accident to the claimant did not occur through any lack of care on the defendant's part. The defendant company was not able to satisfy the burden and the claimant succeeded.

### Pearson v North-Western Gas Board [1968] 2 All ER 669

The claimant's husband was killed by an explosion of gas which also destroyed her house. It appeared from the evidence that a gas main had fractured due to a movement of earth caused by a severe frost. When the weather was very cold the defendants had men standing by ready to deal with reports of gas leaks, but unless they received reports there was no way of predicting or preventing a leak which might lead to an explosion. *Held* – by Rees J – that assuming the principle of *res ipsa loquitur* applied, the defendants had rebutted the presumption of negligence and the claimant's case failed.

## Contributory negligence

Sometimes when an accident occurs both parties have been negligent, and this raises the doctrine of contributory negligence. At common law it was broadly true to say that if the claimant was to blame at all for the accident he would receive no damages. Now, however, under the Law Reform (Contributory Negligence) Act 1945 liability is apportionable between the claimant and defendant. The claim is not defeated but damages may be reduced according to the degree of fault of the claimant.

It should be noted that in *Froom* v *Butcher* [1975] 3 All ER 520 Lord Denning produced an additional definition of contributory negligence so that there are two, namely:

(a) to contribute to the accident, which is the old view of contributory negligence; and
(b) to contribute to the resulting damage, which is a more recent concept in the seat-belt cases.

Furthermore, in *Froom*, Lord Denning laid down a rather precise formula for contributory negligence in regard to seat-belts by saying that if failure to wear a seat-belt would have made no difference, then nothing should be taken off the damages. If it would have prevented the injuries altogether, damages should be reduced by 25 per cent, and if the injuries would have been less severe, the damages should be reduced by 15 per cent, though exemptions would be made, said Lord Denning, for pregnant women and those who were very fat.

Although failure to wear a seat belt may now be a criminal offence in terms of driver and passengers, the courts seem likely to apply the above rules in civil claims for damages and not refuse to give damages altogether on the ground that the injured person was, by not wearing a seat belt, potentially guilty of a criminal offence.

## PROFESSIONAL NEGLIGENCE

In Chapter 11 we considered the scope of a manufacturer's liability for defective products which he puts into circulation and the way in which a consumer can take direct action against a manufacturer in negligence. The law of negligence also applies to the provision of services. In particular, we are concerned with the position of those whose work involves giving professional business advice.

### The background and development

Liability for negligent statements is an important area of the law, and the number of claims continues to increase. Negligent *statements* are now a more potent cause of actions at law than negligent *acts*. This state of affairs has had, and will continue to have, a major influence on the cost of indemnity insurance arrangements.

It was not always so. For example, in *Candler* v *Crane, Christmas & Co* [1951] 2 KB 164 Mr Ogilvie, the owner of a number of companies, was anxious to obtain an investment in them from Mr Candler. The defendants, a firm of accountants, prepared financial statements for Mr Ogilvie, *knowing* that they were to be shown to Mr Candler as a basis for his investment decision. Mr Candler did invest some money but a liquidation followed and he lost it.

He sued the defendants for damages, alleging negligent preparation of the financial statements. It was claimed that the defendants included freehold cottages and leasehold buildings as corporate assets without obtaining ownership evidence.

It was further claimed that the cottages were, in fact, owned by Mr Ogilvie, and that the title deeds were deposited with his bank to secure a personal overdraft. The leasehold buildings, it was alleged, did not belong to the company, but to Mr Ogilvie, and in any case, they had been forfeited, it was said, for non-payment of rent.

To succeed, Mr Candler had first to establish, *as a matter of law*, that the defendants owed him a duty of care. If they had indeed been negligent in the preparation of the accounts, this could then give rise to liability. The majority of the Court of Appeal decided that there was no duty of care in such circumstances, and so the accountants were not liable to Mr Candler, and would not have been, even if it had been proved that the financial statements were prepared negligently. There was no further appeal.

However, Lord Denning dissented from the majority view, being of the opinion that the accountants did owe a duty to Mr Candler, even though he was not a client. In his judgment, he said:

> I think the law would fail to serve the best interests of the community if it should hold that accountants and auditors owe a duty to no one but their client. There is a great difference between the lawyer and the accountant. The lawyer is never called on to express his personal belief in the truth of his client's case, whereas the accountant, who certifies the accounts of his client, is always called on to express his personal opinion whether the accounts exhibit a true and correct view of his client's affairs, and he is required to do this not so much for the satisfaction of his own client, but more for the guidance of shareholders, investors, revenue authorities and others who may have to rely on the accounts in serious matters of business. In my opinion, accountants owe a duty of care not only to their own clients, but also to all those whom they know will rely on their accounts in the transactions for which those accounts are prepared.

However, although Lord Denning was prepared to widen the liability of accountants to encompass a person who was not a client, he does appear to have restricted that liability to persons who it is *known* will rely on the accounts, as the last sentence of the above extract from his judgment clearly reveals. But he was alone in his view of the case, and the expansion of the liability of the accountants (and others) for negligent statements had to wait for more than a decade.

As we have seen in *Hedley Byrne & Co Ltd* v *Heller & Partners* (1963) (*see* Chapter 5), the House of Lords overruled the majority judgment of the Court of Appeal in *Candler*, and approved the dissenting judgment of Lord Denning. The *Hedley Byrne* case, we may remind ourselves, arose from an advertising campaign which Hedley Byrne were to undertake for a company called Easipower. Hedley Byrne went to the company's bankers, Heller, for reference, and later alleged that the reference provided was negligently prepared and gave a false picture of Easipower's financial position, so that Hedley Byrne were unable to recover their fees and expenses in the subsequent liquidation of Easipower.

The House of Lords decided that Heller did owe a duty of care, *even though Hedley Byrne were not customers of the bank*. However, their Lordships were not able to proceed further because Heller had inserted a disclaimer in the reference as follows: 'For your private use and without responsibility on the part of this bank or its officials.' This was adequate to avoid liability even if Heller had been negligent, as was alleged.

The decision in *Hedley Byrne* widened the liability of all professionals (including, of course, accountants), but the House of Lords refrained, as a matter of public policy, from imposing the even wider test of *foresight* formulated by Lord Atkin in *Donoghue* v *Stevenson* (1932) (*see* Chapter 11). That case, as we have seen, related to negligence actions for *physical injury* arising from negligent *acts*, e.g. liability for a negligently manufactured product which causes physical injury to a customer. Liability under that test extended to anyone who might reasonably be foreseen as suffering injury.

### The need for a special relationship – knowledge of victim

Instead the House of Lords decided that in the negligent *statement* cases, there had to be a 'special relationship' between the maker of the statement and the person injured by it. Obviously, this need not be a contractual client relationship. Although their Lordships did not draw up a list of special relationships, comments made by them in their judgments suggested that the duty in regard to a negligent statement would be owed only to those persons whom the maker of the statement knows will rely on it, and not beyond that to those whom he might *foresee* relying on it. Thus the test for negligent statements causing monetary loss (knowledge) was narrower than that for negligent acts causing physical injury (foresight), though, in all honesty, it was difficult to see why liability as such should depend on the nature of the damage.

Indeed, during the decade following *Hedley Byrne* there have been judicial decisions which have suggested that the foresight test propounded in *Donoghue* v *Stevenson* could be appropriate in the negligent statement situation, thus potentially widening liability (*see below*).

### From knowledge to foresight

In *JEB Fasteners Ltd* v *Marks, Bloom & Co* [1981] 3 All ER 289 Mr Justice Woolf was prepared to break out of the strait-jacket of 'special relationship' and go to 'foresight'. In April 1975, the defendants, a firm of accountants, prepared an audited set of accounts for a company called BG Fasteners Ltd for the year ended 31 October 1974. The company's stock, which had been bought for some £11,000, was shown as being worth £23,080, that figure being based on the company's own valuation of the net realisable value of the stock.

The accountants nevertheless described the stock in the accounts as being 'valued at lower of cost and not realisable value'. On the basis of the inflated stock figure, the accounts showed a profit of £11.25. If the stock had been shown at cost, with a discount for possible errors, the accounts would have shown a loss of more than £13,000.

The defendant auditors were aware when they prepared the accounts that the company faced liquidity problems, and was looking for outside financial support from, among other people, the claimants, JEB Fasteners, who manufactured similar products and were anxious to expand their business. The accounts which the defendants had prepared were made available by the directors of BG to the claimants, who, although they had some reservations about the stock valuation, decided that they would take the company over in June 1975 for a nominal amount, because they would in so doing obtain the services of the company's two directors who had considerable experience in the type of manufacturing which the claimants, JEB, carried on.

There were discussions between the claimants and the defendant auditors during the takeover, but the auditors did not inform the claimants that the stock had been put into the accounts at an inflated figure. The merger of the companies was not a financial success, and the claimants brought an action for damages against the defendants.

The claimants alleged that the defendants had prepared the company's accounts negligently, and that they relied on the accounts when buying BG Fasteners, and would not have bought the company had they been aware of its true financial position. It was contended on behalf of JEB that an auditor when preparing a set of accounts owes a duty to all persons whom he ought reasonably to have foreseen would rely on the accounts. The defendant auditors argued that if a duty of care existed, it could only be to persons who had made a specific request for information.

Woolf J decided that the defendant auditors did owe a duty of care to the claimants, but that they were not liable in damages, since their alleged negligence was not the cause of the loss. The overriding reason for the takeover had been to obtain the services of two of BG's directors. On the balance of probabilities, the takeover would have gone ahead even if the accounts had shown the true position.

It was admitted that at the time the accounts in question were audited, Marks, Bloom did not know that they would be relied on by the claimants, or even that any takeover was contemplated.

As regards the foreseeability issue, the judge said:

> As Mr Marks was aware of the financial difficulties of BG Fasteners Ltd, and the fact that they were going to need financial support from outside of some sort, I am satisfied that Mr Marks, whom I can treat as being synonymous with the defendants, ought to have realised the accounts could be relied on until the time that a further audit was carried out by the commercial concerns to whom BG Fasteners were bound to look for financial assistance. When he audited the accounts, Mr Marks would not know precisely who would provide the financial support, or what form the financial support would take, and he certainly had no reason to know that it would be by way of take-over by the [claimants].
>
> However, this was certainly one foreseeable method, and it does not seem to me that it would be right to exclude the duty of care merely because it was not possible to say with precision what machinery would be used to achieve the necessary financial support. Clearly, any form of loan would have been foreseeable, including the raising of money by way of debenture and, while some methods of raising money were more obvious than others, and a take-over was not the most obvious method, it was certainly one method which was within the contemplation of Marks.

The judge went on to decide that the events leading to the take-over of BG were, therefore, foreseeable.

There was an appeal by JEB to the Court of Appeal, which upheld Woolf J's finding that there was a lack of causal connection between JEB's loss and the auditors' alleged negligence. Thus they were not liable.

However, the Court of Appeal went on to say that it was not necessary in order to decide the appeal to determine the scope of an auditor's liability for professional negligence.

## From foresight back to knowledge

**The following two cases show how in recent times the courts have drawn away from the foresight principle to a position of knowledge of user and use.**

### Caparo Industries plc v Dickman and Others [1990] 2 WLR 358

The facts were, briefly, that Caparo, which already held shares in Fidelity plc, eventually acquired the controlling interest in the company. The group later alleged that certain purchases of Fidelity shares and the final bid were made after relying on Fidelity's accounts, which had been prepared by Touche Ross & Co, the second defendants.

The accounts, Caparo alleged, were inaccurate and misleading in that an apparent pre-tax profit of some £1.3m should in fact have been shown as a loss of £400,000. It was also alleged that, if the supposed true facts had been known, Caparo would not have made a bid at the price it did and might not have made a bid at all.

The Court of Appeal decided that while Touche Ross did not have a duty of care towards members of the public in regard to the Fidelity accounts, it did owe a duty of care to Caparo because Caparo was already a shareholder in Fidelity when it made the final purchase of shares and the bid.

The two main judgments in the House of Lords provide an interesting contrast: Lord Bridge concentrates more on the case law and in particular on the dissenting judgment of Lord Denning in *Candler v Crane, Christmas & Co* [1951] 1 All ER 426, where Lord Denning thought that the defendant accountants should have a duty of care to Candler because they had prepared allegedly negligent financial statements on the basis of which they knew Mr Candler might invest in the company concerned; and the judgment of the House of Lords in *Hedley Byrne & Co Ltd v Heller & Partners Ltd* [1963] 2 All ER 575, where a bank supplied an allegedly negligent reference as to the creditworthiness of a company called Easipower, which it knew would be used by Hedley Byrne as a basis for extending credit to the company, which then went into liquidation.

A salient feature of both those cases, said Lord Bridge, was that the defendant giving advice or information was fully aware of the nature of the transaction the claimant was contemplating, knew that the advice or information would be communicated to him, and knew that it was likely that the claimant would rely on that advice or information in deciding whether or not to engage in the transaction in contemplation.

The situation was quite different where the statement was put into more or less general circulation and might foreseeably be relied on by strangers for any one of a variety of different purposes which the maker of the statement had no specific reason to anticipate.

Lord Bridge felt that it was one thing to owe a possibly wider duty of care to avoid causing injury to the person or property of others, but quite another to owe a similar duty to avoid causing others to suffer purely economic loss.

His Lordship concluded that auditors of a public company's accounts owed no duty of care to members of the public at large who relied on the accounts in deciding to buy shares in the company. And as a purchaser of additional shares in reliance on the auditors' report, the shareholder stood in no different position from any other investing member of the public to whom the auditor owed no duty.

Lord Oliver was concerned with establishing the purpose of an audit under the Companies Act 1985. He went on to say that in enacting the statutory provisions Parliament did not have in mind the provision of information for the assistance of purchasers of shares in the market, whether they were already the holders of shares or other securities or people with no previous proprietary interest in the company.

The purpose for which the auditors' certificate was made and published was that of providing those entitled to receive the report with information to enable them to exercise the powers which their respective proprietary rights in the company conferred on them and not for the purposes of individual speculation with a view to profit.

The duty of care was one owed to the shareholders as a body and not to individual shareholders.

**Comment:** (i) It now seems that knowledge as to the user of the statement concerned and, seemingly, also as to the purpose or probable purpose for which it will be used, is required to establish the necessary proximity in these cases where allegedly careless misstatements result in economic loss. It seems unlikely that there will now be any further movement towards foresight of the user and use which had begun to show itself in *JEB Fasteners v Marks, Bloom & Co* [1983] I All ER 583.

(ii) The *Caparo* judgment has angered some in the business world because investors have in a sense lost their right to make investment judgments on the annual audited accounts. This is not really surprising because the annual accounts are in essence stewardship statements – how the directors have conducted the company's business during the year in question. They are by their nature backward-looking and not a suitable vehicle to help speculators to predict a future which is uncertain nor are they intended to be. 'Decision-usefulness' is not the primary purpose of annual accounts.

The accounting statements in *Morgan* (*see below*) went much further.

## Morgan Crucible Co plc v Hill Samuel Bank Ltd and Others,
*Financial Times*, 30 October 1990

The crucial events in the case were as follows. On 6 December 1985, Morgan Crucible (MC) announced a proposed unsolicited offer to acquire the entire share capital of First Castle Electronics plc (FC). When the announcement was made, FC's most recent published financial statements were the reports and audited accounts for the years ended 31 January 1984 and 1985.

On 17 December 1985, MC published a formal offer document which was addressed to FC shareholders. Morgan Grenfell advised MC and Hill Samuel advised FC. The directors of FC, acting on its behalf, sent their shareholders a number of circulars. They were also issued as press releases by Hill Samuel and copies were supplied to MC's advisers.

Two days later, a circular was sent out by the directors of FC, comparing MC's profit record unfavourably with FC's and recommending refusal of the bid. In subsequent circulars reference was made to the published financial statements, and one circular of 31 December 1985 stated that they could be inspected.

An FC circular to its shareholders, issued on 24 January 1986, forecast an increase in profits before tax in the year to 31 January 1986 of 38 per cent. A letter from the auditors, Judkins, was included, saying that the profit forecast had been properly compiled. Included also was a letter from Hill Samuel stating that in its opinion the profit forecast had been prepared after due and careful enquiry.

On 29 January, MC increased its bid; on 31 January, FC's board sent another letter to shareholders recommending acceptance of that increased bid; on 14 February, the bid was declared unconditional; and on 27 February, a further recommendation to accept the bid was sent by FC to its shareholders.

Later, MC alleged that the financial statements (audited and unaudited) issued prior to the bid, the profit forecast of 24 January, and the financial material contained in the circulars and recommendation documents were prepared negligently and were misleading. MC asserted that if the true facts had been known the bid would not have been made or completed. MC issued a writ on 6 May 1987 joining as defendants Hill Samuel, Judkins, and FC's chairman and board. It alleged that the board and the auditors were responsible for circulating the financial statements; that they and Hill Samuel were responsible for the profit forecast; that all of them owed a duty of care to MC as a person who could foreseeably rely on them; that the statements and forecasts were negligently prepared; and that MC relied on them in making and increasing its offer and thereby suffered heavy loss.

In dealing with the allegations and the House of Lords judgment in *Caparo*, Lord Justice Slade said, first, that in *Caparo* all of the representations relied on had been made before an identified bidder had come forward, whereas in this case some of the representations had been made after a bidder had emerged and indeed because a bid had been made. They were clearly made with an identified bidder in mind, i.e. MC. MC had, therefore, applied for leave to amend its statement of claim to representations made after the bid and as part of the takeover battle. This could then distinguish MC's case from the situation in *Caparo*.

The issue before the court was whether MC's allegations as amended disclosed a reasonable cause of action. On the assumption that the allegations were true, was there a duty of care to MC? The judge went on to say, on the assumed facts, that the defendants could have foreseen that MC would or might suffer financial loss if the representations were incorrect; but that foreseeability in itself was not enough for liability to arise – there had to be a sufficient relationship of proximity between the claimant and defendant. In addition, it must be just and reasonable to impose liability on the defendant.

The fatal weakness in the *Caparo* case, the judge said, was that the auditors' statement, i.e. the annual accounts, had not been prepared for the purpose for which the claimant relied on it. It was, therefore, arguable that this case could be distinguished from *Caparo*.

On the assumed facts, the directors of FC, when making the relevant representations, were aware that MC would rely on them for the purpose of deciding to make an increased bid and, indeed, intended that they should. MC did rely on them for that purpose. It was, therefore, arguable that there was a sufficient proximity between the directors of FC and MC to give rise to a duty of care.

For the same reasons, it could be argued that Hill Samuel and Judkins owed MC a duty of care in terms of their representations involving the profit forecast and the audited accounts.

Leave was given to amend the statement of claim. MC's amended case should be permitted to go forward to trial.

*Comment:* So, some reliance can be placed on financial statements and other representations in a takeover after all. If, during the conduct of a contested takeover and after an identified bidder has emerged, the directors and financial advisers of the target company make express representations with a view to influencing the conduct of the bidder, then they owe him a duty of care not to mislead him negligently as was alleged.

## Current trends in liability

A case which appears to widen the liability of auditors beyond statements to mere omissions is *Coulthard* v *Neville Russell, The Times*, 18 December 1997 where the Court of Appeal held that, as a matter of principle, auditors have a duty of care to advise that a transaction which the company and its directors intend to carry out might be a breach of the financial assistance provisions of the Companies Act 1985 (*see also* Chapter 19). The High Court has also ruled that two companies which invested venture capital in a shopfitting company that later went into receivership were entitled to damages from the shopfitters' auditors on the basis of negligent misstatements by the auditors in the company's accounts and in letters sent by the auditors to the investing companies. The auditors owed those companies a duty of care. (*See Yorkshire Enterprise Ltd* v *Robson Rhodes, New Law Online*, 17 June 1998, Transcript Case No 2980610103, approved judgment.) A main problem had been that the provision for bad debts was inadequate. The court was saying, in summary, that had the auditors carried out the audit work thoroughly, they would have found certain bookkeeping errors and would have made a greater and more appropriate provision for bad debts. Thus the auditors were liable in damages. The facts of the case showed that the auditors were aware of the user of their statements and the use to which they would be put.

## Avoiding and excluding liability

The most practical suggestion that can be made in terms of avoiding liability is for an accountant to follow strictly the recommendations of the professional bodies in the field, e.g. the many accounting standards and the more recent Financial Reporting Standards and other published material. If this is done the accountant will at least have the advantage of the judgment of McNair J in *Bolam* v *Friern Hospital Management Committee* [1957] 2 All ER 118. He said in connection with doctors: 'A doctor is not guilty of negligence if he has acted in accordance with a practice accepted as proper by a responsible body of medical men skilled in that particular art . . . merely because there is a body of opinion who would take a contrary view.' The statement is, of course, equally applicable to other professions, including accountants, and was reinforced in the accounting context by the decision in the *Lloyd Cheyham* case (*see* Chapter 19).

The effect of the decision of *Bolitho* v *City and Hackney Health Authority* (1997) is considered in Chapter 19 in connection with company distributions and should be referred to again at this point by way of revision.

As regards ability to exclude liability by notice under s 2(2) of the Unfair Contract Terms Act 1977 (*see* Chapter 6), this will work only if the clause is reasonable. It would seem that there are two factors of major importance in deciding the reasonableness or otherwise of limitations or exclusion of liability for professional negligence and these are: (a) insurance, and (b) the operation of a two-tier service.

As regards insurance, it would seem unreasonable for a professional person to try to exclude totally liability for negligence because that can hardly be regarded as best professional practice. On the other hand, it would probably be reasonable for him to limit his liability to a specified sum. In fact, s 11(4) of the 1977 Act states that if a person seeks to restrict his liability in this way, the court must have regard to the resources which he would expect to be available to him for the purposes of meeting the liability and also how far it was possible for him to cover himself by insurance. It is thought, therefore, that a firm which takes out the maximum insurance cover that is reasonable in the circumstances, being one where the cover is not so great that the effect could be greatly to inflate the fees charged by the firm, then to limit liability to that sum would satisfy the requirement of reasonableness. There is judicial support for this argument in a number of cases, particularly *George Mitchell* v *Finney Lock Seeds* (1983) (*see* Chapter 6).

As regards a two-tier service, a professional person could offer a full service at a full price and a reduced service at a lower price. Again, it would seem that, so long as the user of the service is aware that the two-tier service is available and that he is accepting a reduced service at a reduced price without full liability, then the exclusion clause in a lower-tier service ought to be regarded as reasonable.

It is, of course, worth bearing in mind in all of this that a limitation of liability for professional negligence is much more likely to be regarded as reasonable in a contract with a non-consumer, i.e. a business, than it is in a consumer contract. In fact we have already seen in *Smith* v *Eric S Bush* (1987) (*see* Chapter 5) that a disclaimer used by a professional person in a consumer situation was not effective (but compare *McCullagh* v *Lane Fox* (1995) also in Chapter 5).

It is also worth noting that as regards auditors engaged by a company to carry out a Companies Act audit, s 310 of the Companies Act 1985 makes void any provision in a contract of engagement of the auditors which purports to exclude them from liability for negligence or breach of duty, though the company can now pay the premiums on an insurance policy both for auditors and directors.

## Professional negligence insurance

Professional indemnity policies are available for a whole range of professional persons and experts, e.g. accountants, solicitors, company directors and insurance brokers. These policies carry an excess clause under which the insured bears the first part of the claim up to a fixed amount. The risk covered is variously described but there is now a tendency to cover 'full civil liability' followed by exclusions from cover of things such as libel. The policies usually cover loss caused to a client (i.e. by breach of contract) and to a non-client (i.e. the tort of negligence).

## Reform

The principle of joint and several liability in professional negligence has produced what might be regarded as unfairness, particularly in the audit situation. Suppose that there is a major fraud by an employee of a company which the auditors fail negligently to detect. The person primarily liable to replace the funds fraudulently abstracted is the employee but even if caught the funds may have been used up or impossible to find. Others responsible may be the directors who had not put in place internal controls to prevent fraud. However, the directors will in many cases not have any or much insurance and the best defendant, having the largest pocket, will be the auditors and the loss may well rest with them alone. Obviously, the auditors will have a contribution against other wrongdoers but because of their probable insolvency this will not be of much use.

The Law Commission has looked at this but does not agree that proportionate liability should replace joint and several liability. Under proportionate liability the blame would have to be assessed by the court and the auditors would pay to the company only their share of it. The Law Commission did not feel able to recommend this because the other wrongdoers such as the directors may very well be insolvent so that the company would not be able to recover its money from them.

The Law Commission suggest a number of options as follows:

- a reform of s 310 (*see* Chapter 20) to enable auditors to limit their liability in their contract with the company;
- a review of the Unfair Contract Terms Act 1977 (*see* Chapter 6) to determine whether professional liability can be restricted by an exemption clause. In other words, would such a clause be regarded as 'reasonable';
- to review the possibility that damages awarded against a company's auditors for negligence can be reduced on a finding of contributory negligence by the company's directors. English law does not (so far) provide for this though there are Australian and New Zealand cases which do, but these are only persuasive precedents. To achieve this position in English law, it would be necessary first to impute the directors' negligence to the company, which the antipodean courts were prepared to do. There is a strand of judicial thinking in the UK courts that a company does not always know what its directors are doing, particularly if they are causing it loss. This will have to be overcome. Furthermore, no UK court will lightly hold a person (company) at fault for relying on a statement by a professional adviser who owes him (it) a duty of care.

An additional and likely possibility to assist in the limitation of professional liability is a new form of limited partnership which is considered below.

## New limited liability partnerships

The Department of Trade and Industry has issued a draft Bill and draft Regulations on limited liability partnerships (LLPs). The main proposals are that:

- LLPs would be bodies corporate;
- the members of an LLP would not, in general, have personal liability for its acts or obligations, coupled with the flexibility of the internal organisation of a partnership;
- LLPs would have to file audited accounts and other information;
- they would be subject to insolvency requirements, including liability for wrongful trading broadly similar to those applying to companies;
- for tax purposes an LLP would be treated as a partnership and the members as partners;
- eligibility is currently to be restricted to regulated businesses i.e. those businesses which have a regulator, such as partnerships of accountants and solicitors, which are regulated by their respective professional bodies. In other words, the new form of LLP would not at the moment be intended for a partnership of grocers.

Because the level of litigation that is brought against accountants and lawyers is increasing, incorporation as an LLP is likely to be keenly considered. However, the requirement to file audited accounts at Companies House will bring to an end the financial secrecy which is currently enjoyed by those within the partnership structure and is likely to result in the scrutiny by clients and staff of the level of partnership profits. The requirement of audit will also increase the costs of the firm, since even accountants would have to employ a separate firm of auditors to carry out the audit so that the exercise is seen to be independent and objective.

## The present position regarding duty of care – a summary

As we have seen, the duty of care in regard to negligent misstatements by auditors has been considered in a number of cases since the early 1950s. However, the present position has been the subject of comprehensive analysis by the House of Lords in *Caparo Industries plc* v *Dickman* [1990] 1 All ER 568.

From this decision and two important later ones, the position would appear to be as follows:

(a) auditors do not owe a duty of care to potential investors in the company, e.g. those who rely on the audited accounts when contemplating a takeover bid. The fact that the accounts and auditors' report might foreseeably come into their hands and be relied on is not enough to create a duty of care. In addition, it was decided in *James McNaughton Paper Group* v *Hicks Anderson* [1991] 1 All ER 134 that even if an auditor knew that the audited accounts would be used by a bidder as the basis of a bid, he would not be liable if he reasonably believed and was entitled to assume that the bidder would also seek the advice of his own accountant;

(b) auditors do not owe a duty of care to potential investors even if they already hold shares in the company since, although they are shareholders and auditors are under a statutory duty to report to shareholders, the duty of the auditors is to the shareholders as a whole and not to shareholders as individuals;

(c) even where the auditors are aware of the person or persons who will rely upon the accounts, they are not liable unless they also know what the person or persons concerned will use them for, e.g. as the basis for a takeover;

(d) where there is knowledge of user and use, then in that restricted situation the Court of Appeal *held* in *Morgan Crucible Co plc* v *Hill Samuel Bank Ltd* [1991] 1 All ER 142 that a duty of care would exist in regard to the user. However, even in such a situation the auditor will not be liable if, in the circumstances, he was entitled to assume that the user would also seek the advice of his own accountant and not rely solely on the audited accounts (*see* the *McNaughton* case, *above*). See also *Yorkshire Enterprise Ltd* v *Robson Rhodes* (1998), *above*;

(e) *Coulthard* v *Neville Russell* (1997) would seem to extend liability to mere omissions (*see above*).

## GRADED QUESTIONS

### Essay mode

1 Accountants owe a duty of care to their clients. They may also owe a duty of care in the law of torts to persons who are not their clients.

What is the extent of potential liability of an accountant to a non-client where he gives negligent advice? To what extent can an accountant safeguard against this liability?

*(Association of Chartered Certified Accountants)*

2 John and Joe were on holiday together and had rented a caravan at Nurdsley Bay. The weather was poor and John had been complaining that he could not sleep at night because of the cold. Joe, being a generous sort of person, bought a hot-water bottle from a local shop and gave it to John, refusing to take any payment from John for it. That night the hot-water bottle burst and John was badly scalded. Joe was sleeping on the bunk below and some of the hot water splashed down his face, causing him injury.

Advise John and Joe as to the sort of action, if any, which they may respectively bring and against whom, if anyone, the action will lie.

*(Author's question)*

3 Due to John's carelessness in allowing excessive electric current to develop in his generator, the electricity supply in the locality was cut off for a few hours.

As a result, Joe's factory was at a standstill during this period and he lost £6,000 by way of profits from lost production.

Advise Joe in regard to his rights, if any, against John.

*(Author's question)*

4 Over the last three years George, an accountant, has regularly consulted Arthur, a broker specialising in life assurance, about his investments. George received a large sum of money under his father's will and wished to invest it wisely. He consulted Arthur who advised him to take out a single premium policy with Long Life Ltd. Arthur received an introduction fee from Long Life Ltd and did not charge George for advice. Within six months of the transaction Long Life Ltd went into liquidation because it was in financial difficulties, having been unstable for three years.

Advise George.

Would your advice have been different, and if so in what respect, if it turned out that George had done some accountancy work for Long Life two years ago, and lying forgotten in his files were figures on which George had reached the opinion that Long Life might be in some financial difficulty?

*(Author's question)*

## Objective mode

1 To succeed in an action for negligence the claimant must show:
 (a) the existence of a duty to take _____ which was owed to him by the defendant, and
 (b) _____ of such duty by the defendant
 (c) resulting _____ to the claimant.

2 A, a college lecturer, obtained permission from the principal to use the college library on Sundays for research.

One Sunday he let himself in and locked the main door behind him, proceeding to the library. He left his briefcase near the library door, taking two notebooks he was using into the research section. B, a student who had broken into the premises the previous night because his landlady had thrown him out, walked into the library, fell over the briefcase and fractured his skull. B has no claim against A or his employers. TRUE/FALSE

3   A was carrying out repairs to his front bedroom and left a hammer on the outside sill. Having completed the repair, A slammed the window shut and the hammer fell off the sill striking B who was lawfully upon the pavement below. B is suing A.
    Complete and delete in the following order to produce a correct statement.

> B WILL/WILL NOT carry the full burden of proof in negligence because the principle of _____ DOES NOT/DOES apply.

4   A purchaser of a majority shareholding in Boxo plc has brought an action against the auditors of the company for negligence. The auditors were not aware at the time of the audit that the business was to be acquired. It was, however, in financial difficulties and this was known to the auditors. As regards the duty of care of the auditors which one of the following decisions is the court likely to make? Circle the correct answer.

A The auditor owes a duty of care to his client in contract. The purchaser of the business is not owed a duty since duty in negligence does not extend to economic loss for careless misstatements. The auditor is not liable.

B Liability in negligence for misstatements only extends to a particular person who should have been known to the defendant. In this case there is no such special relationship. The auditor is not liable.

C A duty of care for negligent misstatements extends to those people the defendant should have foreseen as being injured by his negligent acts or omissions. The auditor would be liable if his report was a factor in the decision to purchase.

D The duty of care for false statements is the same as that of a manufacturer. The defendant will be liable to persons who used the accounts on which he reported. The auditor will therefore be liable to the purchaser of the business on the same basis that the manufacturer of the ginger beer was liable to the consumer in *Donoghue* v *Stevenson*. The auditor will be liable.

*Answers to questions set in objective mode appear on p 709.*

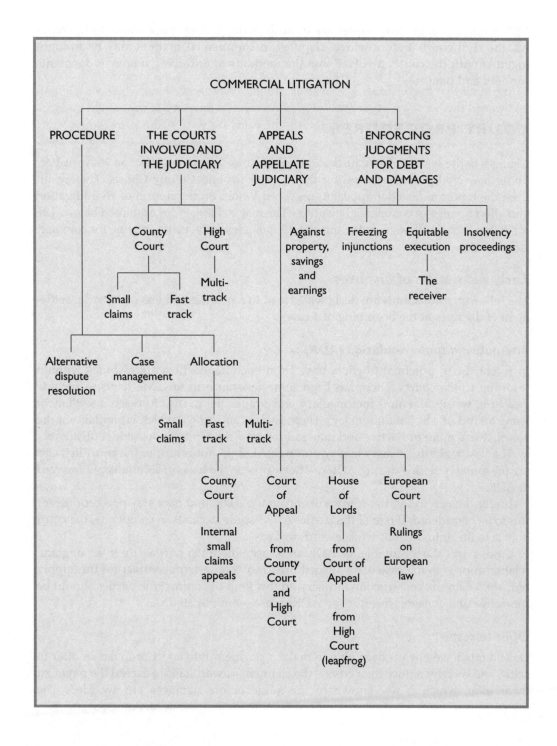

The objectives of this chapter are to outline the general procedures followed in the civil courts before which disputes in commercial matters may be brought together with the courts involved and the methods of enforcing money judgements for debt and damages.

# COURT PROCEDURES

Changes to the system of civil justice in England and Wales took effect on 26 April 1999 under new civil procedure rules for the High Court and County Courts. They result from the report of a senior appeal judge, Lord Woolf, on the reform of civil litigation and affect a range of commercial disputes. The major changes are examined below. The main theme of the changes is the introduction of a less adversarial regime for commercial disputes.

## Early resolution of disputes

The following procedures are designed to lead to a quicker and less adversarial settlement of disputes at the beginning of a case.

### Alternative dispute resolution (ADR)

In recent times, potential litigants have been encouraged to settle disputes without resorting to the courts. There has been some resistance to this. Mechanisms include *mediation*, where a neutral intermediary encourages the parties to reach a settlement using a kind of 'shuttle diplomacy'. There is also *conciliation*, which is similar, but the conciliator is more pro-active and may put forward the terms of possible settlements.

The vast majority of cases that go through ADR do not return to the court list, and are presumably settled during ADR or afterwards on the basis of solutions put forward at ADR.

Under the new rules, the court will encourage ADR, and may stay proceedings for this to be considered. If one of the parties to a dispute declines to co-operate, the court may take this into account when awarding costs.

Cases particularly suitable for ADR are those where the parties are in an ongoing relationship, as in the case of an alleged breach of a long-term contract for the supply of materials in the construction industry. In this kind of contract the parties should be pro-active and consider inserting an ADR clause – but not all do.

### Offer to settle

Defendants have always been able to make a payment into court or make an offer to settle, and thereby reduce their costs if the claimant's award fails to exceed the payment in or offer, which is not known to the judge before damages are awarded. The defendant's rights stay the same, but claimants may now also make offers to settle before or after proceedings are commenced, with similar cost-related benefits, plus the possible award of interest on the claimant's damages if the offer is not accepted.

### Summary judgment

A new summary judgment procedure will be available to the claimant and the defendant, at the court's discretion, to dispense quickly with those issues that have no prospect of success at trial, but which the claimant insists on pursuing.

## Case management by the court

The court, and not, as previously, the opposing parties, will now manage the case. Lawyers' pre-trial delaying tactics – e.g. excessive applications for disclosure of documents that may be difficult to produce and do not illuminate the issues significantly – will end.

### Pre-action protocols

The court's management of the case will be achieved by pre-action protocols, i.e. codes of practice with which the parties must comply and that will ensure effective exchange of information before the proceedings.

In commercial cases, a protocol of major importance will deal with instructing experts, which may often be confined to a joint single expert to deal with technical aspects of the case, if any.

As a result of complying with these protocols, litigation costs will be front-loaded.

### Allocation to track

The court will allocate cases to tracks as follows:

- small claims track – claims of not more than £5,000 will follow a new small claims procedure, normally before a district judge;
- fast track – claims of more than £5,000, and up to £15,000, will follow a set timetable of some 30 weeks from allocation to track. There will be limited powers of disclosure of documents and little oral expert evidence. Fixed costs and a maximum trial length of one day will also apply;
- multi-track – claims over £15,000 will be allocated to the multi-track. Most commercial claims will take this track, which will involve a case management conference – this only applies to multi-track cases. The aim of the conference is to encourage the parties to settle the dispute or to consider ADR. If the case goes to trial, the conference will set a trial date and timetable and review cost estimates, which will no longer be a private matter for each party. The parties are expected to agree to proposals for managing the claim.

### Pre-trial review

A pre-trial review will be necessary in most multi-track cases to ensure that all conference issues have been dealt with. The judge (usually the trial judge) will consider the updated cost estimates, and set a budget and a final programme for the trial, including parameters for its length.

## *Trial*

The trial will be conducted in line with earlier orders given in regard to the case unless, in exceptional cases, the judge orders otherwise.

Civil trial centres in selected cities mainly for multi-track trials have been designated. Claims may start in feeder courts and be transferred to a trial centre after track allocation and case management directions.

## Information technology

The pace at which cases will now move through the system will require rapid systems of document retrieval and storage facilities. There will be automatic cost penalties for failure to comply with timetables. Direct e-mail links with lawyers will be required.

Some large law firms already offer litigation support systems to their clients, though the rules do not expressly require them.

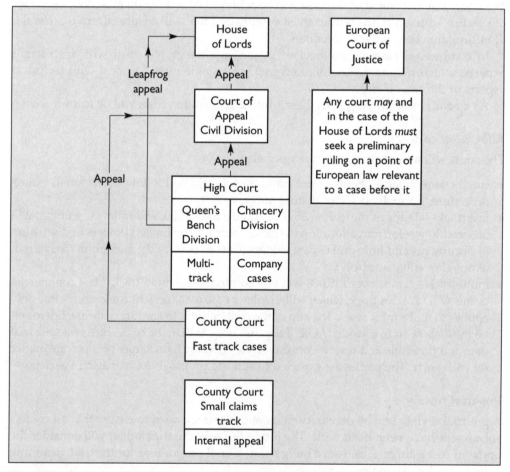

**Fig. 23.1  Commercial litigation – structure of relevant courts**

## COMMENCEMENT OF PROCEEDINGS AND JUDICIARY

### Where the sum(s) in dispute do not exceed £5,000

In such cases, the claim will be made in the County Court and allocated to the small claims track. Parties will not normally wish to have legal representation, though a larger organisation might, since there is a general inability to recover legal costs. The services of a litigation lawyer may, however, be sought for assistance and guidance with small claims matters, including help with drafting the Statement of Case which sets out the basis of the claimant's case.

Small claims will normally be heard by a district judge with appeal in some restricted circumstances, e.g. mistake of law, to the circuit judge who also sits in the County Court as the senior judge. A dispute may be heard by the circuit judge if he or she consents, but then the right of appeal is lost.

### Cases valued as being in excess of £5,000 but not exceeding £15,000

These cases will also be commenced in the County Court and allocated to the fast track. This is designed for cases involving a limited amount of evidence and where the estimated length of the trial is no more than one day. The court will give directions for the conduct of the case and will fix a trial date or a trial window in which the trial is to take place not more than 30 weeks from the date on which the directions were given. There are fixed advocacy costs for lawyers, ranging from £350 to £750. There is, in consequence, a great incentive to settle disputes without going to trial. Where it appears that the trial cannot be completed in one day, e.g. because of basic evidence to be heard, the case will be allocated to the multi-track.

### Where the claim is over £15,000 in value

Such claims will generally be started in the High Court and allocated to the multi-track. The directions here are not standardised as they are in the fast track, e.g. trial in one day. Instead multi-track directions will be made to fit the circumstances of the case.

Multi-track cases are generally heard by High Court judges referred to as, e.g., Mr (or Miss or Mrs) Justice Bloggs (or Bloggs J). Cases may be heard in London or in civil trial centres in the provinces.

Most commercial disputes are heard in the Queen's Bench Division or in a sub-division called the Commercial Court. Company disputes which are rather technical and specialised are head in a sub-division of the Chancery Division called the Companies Court.

Procedure in this latter court is not so much affected by the rules referred to above, though some of the nomenclature has changed. Thus, if you want to see documents held by the other party, you ask for 'disclosure' of them and not as before, 'discovery' of them.

## APPEAL AND APPELLATE JUDICIARY

In *small claims cases*, appeal is internal to the County Court circuit judge, as we have seen.

In *fast-track cases*, appeal is from the County Court to the Court of Appeal Civil Division, though permission is required, e.g. from the Court of Appeal. The judges are called Lord (or Lady) Justices of Appeal (or Bloggs LJ) and three may sit to hear an appeal, though often it may be two or even one, depending on the matter and issues before the court. The court also hears appeals from the Employment Appeal Tribunal. The court may uphold or reverse the decision of the lower court or change the award of damages in terms of amount.

In *multi-track cases*, the first right of appeal is to the Court of Appeal (Civil Division), as above.

## Appeals to the House of Lords

The House of Lords is not only the second chamber of the UK Parliament, but also acts as a final court of appeal, in both civil and criminal matters. The judges are referred to as Lords of Appeal in Ordinary (or Law Lords) who are Life Peers. There are currently no women judges at this level. A minimum of three judges is required to make up a court, but five normally sit to hear an appeal. Decisions are by a majority judgment. This means that one Law Lord reads out or hands down the judgment of the court, which will be in his name. The others merely state their agreement, though if a Law Lord disagrees, the judgment will contain his dissenting judgment and sometimes, while agreeing with the majority judgment, a Law Lord will add some additional points of his own. These also appear after the main judgment.

As regards jurisdiction, the Law Lords hear appeals from the following sources:

- the Court of Appeal with the permission of the Court of Appeal or the House of Lords;
- the High Court under the 'leapfrog' procedure. This form of appeal goes straight to the House of Lords, 'leapfrogging' the Court of Appeal. The trial judge must certify that the case involves a point of law of general public importance relating wholly or mainly to the interpretation of Acts of Parliament, and often concerns matters of taxation. The House of Lords must grant leave to appeal and the parties must consent.

## The European Court of Justice

The European Court sits in Luxembourg and, on joining the European Community (as it then was) in 1973, the UK agreed to accept the rulings of the European Court in matters of European law. The House of Lords continues to be the final court of appeal in purely domestic law, but where a dispute has a European element, as where an Article of the Treaty of Rome might affect the decision, any court or tribunal *may* ask the opinion of the European Court on the point of law in question. A good example is Art 141, which is concerned with equal opportunity and has affected cases involving equal pay, sex discrimination and pensions following rulings from the European Court.

Article 136 of the Treaty of Rome gives this discretion to the courts of member states. However, once a case has reached the final court of appeal of a member state, that court *must* make a reference to the European Court if asked to do so by a party to the case.

In general terms, therefore, the House of Lords has an obligation to make a reference under Art 136. Lower courts may do so, but if they think that the relevant Community law is sufficiently clear to be applied to the case straightaway, they will not make such a referral.

# ENFORCING JUDGMENTS FOR DEBT AND DAMAGES

It may well be that having obtained a judgment from the court in regard to a debt owed, e.g. for goods supplied or damages, such as where the defendant has failed to perform a contract, the defendant is not prepared to pay the relevant sum. How can the claimant get the money which the court has awarded? Some of the more important methods available to judgment creditors, as they are called, are set out below.

## Court orders concerning wages/salary, savings or land

Initially the court can make orders attacking the defendant's goods, his wages or salary, his savings and his land or other property as follows.

### Goods owned by the defendant

The court can order that bailiffs employed by the sheriff's office for the county in which the defendant's goods are located may take them under a court warrant and sell them in order to pay the claimant.

### Wages or salary

The defendant's wages or salary can be attacked by an attachment of earnings order made by the court. Under such an order the defendant's employer is required to deduct a specified sum from the defendant's wages or salary and pay the money into court for the claimant. The court sends the money to the claimant. The main weakness of this procedure is that it is not available against business profits, e.g. of the self-employed.

### Savings

If the defendant has a credit balance on a bank account or, say, a building society account, the claimant may wish to divert the money away from the defendant directly to himself in order to pay the judgment debt. In these circumstances the court may make an order addressed to, e.g. the bank, in regard to defendant's balance. The order is in two parts. The first part forbids the banker from paying any of the money to the defendant. After a period of some seven days the next part of the order is issued by the court requiring the banker to pay the balance in the defendant's account to the claimant unless within that time good cause has been shown why the money should not be paid to the claimant.

### Land or other property such as shares

These may be made the subject of a charging order by the court. Under the charge, the land or shares can be sold by the claimant and he may recover his debt or damages from the proceeds of sale, unless the defendant has paid him, so releasing the charge.

Details of the defendant's finances, essential to ask for the above orders, can be obtained by an order under which the defendant is examined in court in regard to his finances if he will not willingly make these available.

### Freezing injunctions

We have already noted that the court make may an order called a freezing injunction to restrain a party to litigation from moving assets out of the jurisdiction of the court or from dealing with them whether within the jurisdiction or not.

These injunctions are obviously helpful to stop a person from moving assets in a way which will prevent the claimant from exercising his rights to court orders against them to obtain the amount of his judgment. Failure to comply with a freezing order, as by moving assets, makes the defendant in contempt of court, for which he can be fined or imprisoned or both.

## Other measures

### Equitable execution

The court may appoint a receiver where, for example, the defendant owns property. The receiver can take over income such as rent and apply it in order to pay the claimant. The judgment creditor of a person who is a partner can, under s 23 of the Partnership Act 1890, obtain an order charging that partner's interest in the partnership property and profits with payment of the judgment debt. If the judgment creditor feels that he will experience difficulty in getting the firm to pay over, e.g. the profit share of the partner concerned, he can ask for the appointment of a receiver.

The enforcement of a non-money judgment, such as an injunction, is by means of the offence of contempt of court. If a defendant fails to obey an injunction, he is in contempt of court and the court may, if the claimant applies, punish him. It may make, for example, an order for committal under which if the defendant still refuses to comply with the injunction, he may be imprisoned. Alternatively, the court may issue a writ of sequestration. The writ, which is directed by the court to commissioners, usually four in number, commands them to enter the lands and take the rents and profits and seize the goods of the person against whom it is directed. Thus the court can in effect take control of the defendant's property until he has complied with the court's order.

### Bankruptcy or insolvency proceedings

Where the debt exceeds £750, bankruptcy or company insolvency proceedings could be considered. This would at least ensure that an insolvency practitioner (generally an accountant) would be put in charge of the debtor's assets and result in a fair and legal distribution of the assets between creditors as well as effectively preventing the debtor from dealing with them. These procedures are not available to a person who has registered a charging order because by so doing he has made himself a secured creditor and only unsecured creditors can petition for bankruptcy or company winding-up.

# APPENDIX:
# ANSWERS TO QUESTIONS SET IN OBJECTIVE MODE

**Chapter 1** **Justification**

1 (C)   *McManus v Fortescue*
2 (A)   *Dickinson v Dodds*
3 (C)   *Entores v Miles Far East Corp*
4 (B)   *Eaglehill Ltd v J Needham (Builders)*
5 (D)   Unsolicited Goods and Services Act 1971 (as amended)
6 (C)   Rule in *Harvey v Facey*
7 (C)   *G N Railway v Witham*
8 (D)   *Williams v Carwardine* and/or *Carlill's* case

**Chapter 2**

1 (C)   *Re McArdle*
2 (A)   *Dunlop v Selfridge*
3 (D)   *Thomas v Thomas*
4 (D)   Assuming benefit so that *Williams* not *Stilk* applies
5 (C)   *Welby v Drake*
6 (C)   *High Trees* case and/or Sale of Goods Act 1979, s 11(2)
7 (C)   *Balfour v Balfour* and contrast *Merritt v Merritt*
8 (A)   *Balfour v Balfour*

**Chapter 3**

1 (A)   Law of Property Act 1925, ss 52 and 54
2 (A)   Law of Property (Miscellaneous Provisions) Act 1989, s 2(1)
3 (A)   *Del credere* agency: writing not required
4 (C)   *Davies v Beynon-Harris*
5 (D)   Minors Contracts Act 1987, s 3 allows restitution of stock
6 (D)   *Ultra vires* rule does not affect enforceability of contracts by charter corporations
7 (B)   Sales director is authorised and in effect an 'organ' of the company
8 (C)   Purchase of non-necessary goods: contract voidable

**Chapter 4** **Justification**

1 (C)   *Couturier v Hastie: res extincta*
2 (B)   *Raffles v Wichelhaus*
3 (D)   *Lewis v Averay* preferred to *Ingram v Little* (an exceptional case)
4 (D)   *Leaf v International Galleries* and Sale of Goods Act 1979, s 13
5 (B)   *Saunders v Anglia Building Society*: a negligent signature
6 (D)   *Solle v Butcher* and *Grist v Bailey*
7 (D)   *Rose v Pim*
8 (A)   *Wood v Scarth*: the 'sense of the promise'

**Chapter 5**

1 (A)   *See* p 110
2 (B)   *Redgrave v Hurd*
3 (B)   *Gosling v Anderson*
4 (D)   *See* p 123
5 (D)   *Mathew v Bobbins*
6 (B)   *Allcard v Skinner*
7 (D)   As above
8 (D)   As above

**Chapter 6**

1 (C)   A pre-contractual statement
2 (A)   Innominate terms at p 148
3 (D)   *The Moorcock* case and comment
4 (C)   *L'Estrange v Graucob* and Unfair Contract Terms Act 1977
5 (D)   *Hollier v Rambler Motors*
6 (C)   Unfair Contract Terms Act 1977/*Chapleton*
7 (B)   *Bettini v Gye*
8 (C)   *Thompson v LMS Railway*

**Chapter 7**

1 (C)   *See* p 178
2 (C)   *See* p 178
3 (B)   *Home Counties Dairies v Skilton*
4 (C)   *Forster and Sons Ltd v Suggett*
5 (D)   *Wyatt v Kreglinger and Fernau*
6 (A)   *See* p 188
7 (D)   *Esso Petroleum v Harper's Garage*
8 (C)   *See* p 196

**Chapter 8  Justification**

1 (C)  *Hoenig* v *Isaacs*
2 (B)  *Hoenig* v *Isaacs*
3 (D)  *See* p 222
4 (A)  *White & Carter (Councils)* assuming Luxor cannot replace the business and have a 'legitimate interest'
5 (D)  *See* p 215
6 (C)  *Hedley Byrne* v *Heller* covers misstatements as to opinion

**Chapter 9**

1 (A)  *Victoria Laundry* v *Newman Industries*
2 (D)  As above
3 (A)  *Chaplin* v *Hicks*
4 (D)  *Cellulose Acetate Silk* v *Widnes Foundry*
5 (B)  As above
6 (A)  *See* p 162

**Chapter 10**

1 (A)  *See* p 252
2 (C)  *See* p 253
3 (D)  *Beale* v *Taylor*
4 (B)  *See* p 266
5 (D)  *See* p 262
6 (C)  *Household Fire Insurance Co* v *Grant*

**Chapter 11**

1 (B)  *Donoghue* v *Stevenson* and *Grant* v *Australian Knitting Mills Ltd*
2 (B)  Sale of Goods Act 1979, s 18, Rule 2
3 (C)  Sale of Goods Act 1979, s 18, Rule 2
4 (B)  Sale of Goods Act 1979, s 33
5 (C)  Sale of Goods Act 1979, s 6 and/or *Couturier* v *Hastie*
.6 (B)  *Romalpa* case

**Chapter 12**

1 (C)  Original sale was at market price
2 (B)  *See* p 321
3 (B)  *See* p 322
4 (B)  *Pignataro* v *Gilroy*
5 (B)  *See* p 316
6 (B)  *See* p 163
7 (B)  *See* p 336

**Chapter 13  Justification**

1 (A)  *See* p 345
2 (B)  *See* p 351
3 (C)  *Byrne* v *Van Tienhoven*
4 (C)  *Bolton* v *Mahadeva*
5 (B)  *Lewis* v *Averay*
6 (D)  Prefers *Bradbury* v *Morgan* to *Dickinson* v *Dodds*

**Chapter 14**

1 (C)  See p 367 and *Barker* v *Bell*
2 (D)  As above
3 (B)  As above
4 (D)  *See* p 355
5 (A)  *See* p 362
6 (B)  *See* p 359

**Chapter 15**

1 (B)  *See* p 382
2 (B)  *See* p 385
3 (B)  *See* p 401
4 (D)  *See* p 408
5 (C)  *See* p 403
6 (D)  *See* p 415

**Chapter 16**

1  Genuine occupational qualification; *see* p 435
2  False: household exemption
3  False: discriminatory advertisements, p 440
4 (A)  *Johnson* v *Timber Tailors*
5 (C)  The religious cult is not a 'race' and since the same conditions would apply to all workers no other form of discrimination
6 (C)  *Cornelius* v *Manpower Services*

**Chapter 17**

1 (D)  Tom is not working wholly or mainly abroad
2 (B)  No service requirement; dismissal trade union related: automatically unfair
3 (B)  Employer should have considered suitable alternative employment for Barney but is not required to do so for Tomos
4 (A)  Age 37–41 gives four years; 41–45 gives six years: so $10 \times £200 = £2,000$
5  One week's; one month; two years'; two weeks; one week; 12:12 (*see* p 485)
6  £800; four months (*see* p 493)

**Chapter 18 Justification**

| | |
|---|---|
| 1 (D) | No need to file accounts |
| 2 (B) | The *Gilford* case |
| 3 (C) | See p 528 |
| 4 (C) | Resolution requires a three-quarters majority of those present and voting in person or by proxy |
| 5 (C) | *See* CA 1985, s 14 |
| 6 (C) | *See* p 530 |

**Chapter 19**

| | |
|---|---|
| 1 (B) | *See* p 582 |
| 2 (D) | *See* p 583 |
| 3 (A) | *See* p 580 |
| 4 (C) | *See* p 582 and Stock Transfer Act 1963 |
| 5 (B) | *See* p 586 and *Morgan* v *Gray* (1953) |
| 6 (C) | *See* p 581 |

**Chapter 20**

| | |
|---|---|
| 1 (A) | *See* p 598, effect of failure to register a charge |
| 2 (A) | *See* p 632, procedure for removal of a director under s 303 |
| 3 (C) | *See* p 605, restrictions on appointment of directors |
| 4 (B) | *See* p 639, disqualification for unfitness |
| 5 (C) | *See* p 660, majorities required for member resolutions |
| 6 (C) | *See* p 665: unfair prejudice; petitioners |

**Chapter 21 Justification**

| | |
|---|---|
| 1 (A) | *See* p 676 and the *Freeman & Lockyer* case |
| 2 (B) | *See* p 675 usual authority restricted to managing and other executive directors |
| 3 (C) | *See* p 674 |
| 4 (A) | *See* p 676 |
| 5 (A) | Liability is joint and *several, see* p 679 |
| 6 (A) | Apparent authority of partners, *see* p 677 |

**Chapter 22**

| | |
|---|---|
| 1 (a) | Care |
| (b) | Breach *See* p 683 |
| (c) | Damage |
| 2 | True. A had no foresight of the consequences |
| 3 | Will not; *res ipsa loquitur*; does *See Byrne* v *Boadle* |
| 4 (B) | *See Caparo* and related cases at p 696 |

# INDEX